# THE COMPLETE PAYROLL REFERENCE BOOK

## 2020-2021

**Written and compiled by**
Keith Marriott, Kate Upcraft, Cliff Vidgeon and Ian Whyteside
Edited by Ian Whyteside

Published by

the **chartered institute**
of **payroll professionals**

publishing

**An imprint of**
The Chartered Institute of Payroll Professionals
Goldfinger House, 245 Cranmore Boulevard, Shirley, Solihull, B90 4ZL
**t:** 0121 712 1000
**e:** info@cipp.org.uk
**cipp.org.uk**

**ADDITIONAL COPIES**
To purchase additional copies of The Compact Payroll Reference Book, please visit
cipp.org.uk/CPRB

**IMPORTANT NOTE**
Whilst every effort has been made to provide authoritative and accurate information, the
writers and publishers cannot accept liability for any errors or omissions, or any losses arising
from the use of material contained within this book.

**ACKNOWLEDGEMENTS**
The publishers would like to thanks all of those who have assisted in the publication of this
book. With particular thanks to James Bartlett, Nicole Davis and Mike Nicholas.

We would also like to acknowledge the work of JEC Training Ltd who previously published this
book, and from whom CIPP Publishing acquired the publication in 2018. With special
recognition to Janet Cunningham and Cliff Vidgeon for making the book the essential guide
that it is today.

Crown copyright is reproduced with the permission of the Controller of Her Majesty's
Stationery Office and the Queen's Printer for Scotland.

ISBN 978-1-9993639-1

# CONTRIBUTORS BIOGRAPHIES

**Keith Marriott** entered Local Government with Doncaster CBC in October 1958, retiring from Doncaster MBC in June 1995 when he was Chief Payments Officer. He is a founder member of APSA and was the Local Government representative on the Home Office working party which led to the implementation of Statutory Sick Pay (SSP), SMP and SAP. Following his retirement, he has remained active, advising the Police in investigations into local authority member's expense and allowance irregularities in Doncaster and Nationwide. Assisted in the initial development of the Compact Payroll Reference Book. Currently Chair of the Doncaster MBC Elected Members Pay and Expenses Review Panel. His unfulfilled ambition was to be involved in a Home Office investigation into the Payment of Allowances and Expenses of Members of Parliament and The House of Lords.

**Kate Upcraft, AMBCS, mGPA**, is a regular conference speaker, lecturer and writer on legislative issues, including tax and National Insurance, benefits and the whole range of employer compliance responsibilities. She undertakes consultancy work with employers and payroll agents assisting them with topics such as payroll health checks, NMW and auto-enrolment, systems selection and departmental re-engineering. She is the vice chair of the ICAEW Employment Taxes and NI committee and chair of the pan-professional Reward and Employment Engagement Forum. Prior to setting up her own company in 2005, she was the Payroll Legislation Manager at M&S, for whom she worked for 20 years, eleven of them in payroll.

**Ian Whyteside, FMAAT, MCIPP, ATT**, is the tax partner in a thriving accounting practice. He has been actively involved in the payroll profession since March 1979 and is the current editor of the Handbook. Since leaving the public sector in 2001 he has been running his own training, consultancy and education business.

**Cliff Vidgeon BA(Hons), CMA, ACIS, FCIPP** had the idea of an annual reference book for payroll in the mid-1990s. After pondering the idea for a couple of years he contacted his friend Keith Marriott and after a brief chat they set about the task of putting together the first edition of The Compact Payroll Reference Book in 1999. The rest is, as they say, history.

Cliff is currently a Visiting Research Fellow at Aston University. Although his career includes a brief spell as a payroll manager, his main focus has been in pensions' management and human resources. He has been a University Director of Corporate Management and a Director of Human Resources. Cliff is involved in national pension negotiations for the Higher Education Sector and is also a member of the CIPP Board of Directors.

# PREFACE

This reference book has been compiled with a view to providing, in one small volume, as much information as the payroll professional is likely to require in the course of the tax year. It is replete with current and historical tables, rates and data that are presented clearly and concisely.

Every effort has been made to ensure ease and rapidity of reference allowing, at the same time, the maximum amount of information to be contained in a handy-sized book.

No reference has been made in this edition to the temporary measures imposed as part of the country's fight against the COVID-19 virus. Since the book is designed to cover payroll, tax and related matters for the year and that generally these will remain unchanged in principle it was felt to be unnecessary. Some items, such as the deferral of the implementation of "off-payroll working" in the private sector for one year, has been included in the appropriate place.

# ABOUT THE CHARTERED INSTITUTE OF PAYROLL PROFESSIONALS (CIPP)

The CIPP is dedicated to raising the profile of payroll and every year supports over 9,500* people through education or membership benefits such as:

- Guidance and support via the technical Advisory Service helpline
- *Professional in Payroll, Pensions and Reward* magazine providing professional insight on a range of topical issues
- Up to date information through the *News Online* e-newsletter
- *Payroll: need to know; your essential guide to UK payroll legislation and reporting*
- Representation at key consultation forums including:
    - Employment and payroll group
    - Compliance reform
    - Student loans
    - Statutory payments
    - IR35 forum

In addition to membership, the CIPP also hosts legislation and networking events throughout the year and has an extensive industry recognised education programme which ranges from training courses to a level seven qualification.

*Correct at time of publication

# CONTENTS

# CONTENTS

# CONTENTS

# CONTENTS

# CONTENTS

# CONTENTS

# CONTENTS

# CONTENTS

# CONTENTS

Tables within the appendices are reproduced with the permission of Her Majesty's Stationery Office.

# PART 1: DATES, DEFINITIONS AND OBLIGATIONS

## ABBREVIATIONS

| | |
|---|---|
| AAL | Additional Adoption Leave |
| ACT | Advance Corporation Tax |
| ADOC | Actual Date of Childbirth |
| AEO | Attachment of Earnings Order |
| AFR | Advisory Fuel Rate |
| AMAPs | Approved Mileage Allowance Payments (Now MAPs) |
| AML | Additional Maternity Leave |
| APL | Additional Paternity Leave |
| ASPP | Additional Statutory Paternity Pay |
| AUST | Apprentice Upper Secondary Threshold |
| AVC | Additional Voluntary Contribution |
| AWE | Average Weekly Earnings |
| Bacs | Banker's Automated Clearing Service |
| BACSTEL | Banker's Automated Clearing Service Telecommunications |
| BEIS | Department of Business, Energy & Industrial Strategy (was BIS) |
| CAERS | Car Allowances Enhanced Reporting Scheme |
| CAO | Conjoined Arrestment Order |
| CCAEO | Community Charge Attachment of Earnings Order |
| CEP | Contributions Equivalent Premium |
| CGT | Capital Gains Tax |
| CHAPS | Clearing House Automated Payments System |
| CIPD | Chartered Institute of Personnel and Development |
| CIPP | Chartered Institute of Payroll Professionals |
| CIS | Construction Industry Scheme |
| CJEU | Court of Justice of the European Union |
| CMA | Current Maintenance Arrestment |
| COMPS | Contracted-out Money Purchase Scheme |
| COSRS | Contracted-out Salary-Related Scheme |
| CPI | Consumer Prices Index |
| CSL | Collection of Student Loans |
| CTAEO | Council Tax Attachment of Earnings Order |
| CTC | Child Tax Credit |
| DAS | Debt Arrangement Scheme |
| DEA | Direct Earnings Attachment |
| DEO | Deduction from Earnings Order |
| DPTC | Disabled Persons' Tax Credit |
| DWP | Department for Work and Pensions |
| EA | Earnings Arrestment |
| EAT | Employment Appeal Tribunal |
| ECON | Employer's Contracting-out Number |
| ECOS | Employee Car Ownership Scheme |
| EDI | Electronic Data Interchange |
| EEA | European Economic Area |
| EFRBS | Employer-financed Retirement Benefits Scheme |
| EHIC | European Health Insurance Card (replaced forms E111 & E128) |
| EHRC | Equality and Human Rights Commission (formerly EOC) |
| EPS | Employer Payment Summary |
| ERA | Employment Rights Act 1996 |
| ET | Earnings Threshold and Employment Tribunal |
| EYU | Earlier Year Update |
| EWC | Expected Week of Confinement/Childbirth |
| FPCS | Fixed Profit Car Scheme |

| | |
|---|---|
| FPS | Full Payment Submission |
| FSAVC | Freestanding Additional Voluntary Contribution |
| FURBS | Funded Unapproved Retirement Benefit Schemes |
| GAYE | Give As You Earn |
| GDPR | General Data Protection Regulation |
| GMP | Guaranteed Minimum Pension |
| HCI | Home Computing Initiative |
| HMRC | Her Majesty's Revenue and Customs |
| HWS | Health and Work Service |
| ICTA | Income and Corporation Taxes Act (now ITEPA see below) |
| IPA | Income Payment Agreement |
| IPO | Income Payments Order |
| IRAM | Inland Revenue Authorised Mileage rate |
| ISDN | Income Support Deduction Notice |
| ITEPA | Income Tax, Earnings and Pensions Act (2003) |
| KIT | Keeping In Touch Day(s) |
| LEL | Lower Earnings Limit |
| LGPS | Local Government Pension Scheme |
| LPI | Limited Price Indexation |
| MA | Maternity Allowance |
| MAPs | Mileage Allowance Payments (was AMAPs) |
| MIG | Minimum Income Guarantee |
| MPP | Maternity Pay Period |
| NI | National Insurance |
| NIC | National Insurance Contribution(s) |
| NLW | National Living Wage |
| NMW | National Minimum Wage |
| NRA | Normal Retirement Age |
| NVQ | National Vocational Qualification |
| NVR | NINO verification request |
| OAL | Ordinary Adoption Leave |
| O/T | Overtime |
| OML | Ordinary Maternity Leave |
| OMP | Occupational Maternity Pay |
| OpRA | Optional Remuneration Arrangement |
| OSP | Occupational Sick Pay |
| OSPP | Ordinary Statutory Paternity Pay |
| OSPL | Ordinary Statutory Paternity Leave |
| PAYE | Pay As You Earn |
| PENP | Post Employment Notice Pay |
| PGL | Post Graduate Loan |
| PILON | Payment In Lieu of Notice |
| PIW | Period of Incapacity for Work |
| PPF | Pension Protection Fund |
| PPP | Paternity Pay Period |
| PRI | Pregnancy Related Illness |
| PSA | PAYE Settlement Agreement |
| PSS | Pensions Schemes Services (office of HMRC) |
| PTS | Percentage Threshold Scheme |
| PT | Primary Threshold |
| QUALEC | Qualifying Low Emission Car |
| RPI | Retail Prices Index |
| RTI | Real Time Information |
| S2P | State Second Pension |
| SAL | Statutory Adoption Leave |
| SAYE | Save As You Earn |
| SBR | Scottish Basic Rate |
| SCON | Scheme Contracted-out Number |

| | |
|---|---|
| SER | Small Employers' Relief |
| SERPS | State Earnings Related Pension Scheme |
| ShPL | Shared Parental Leave |
| ShPP | Shared Parental Pay |
| SI | Statutory Instrument |
| SIP | Share Incentive Plan |
| SLC | Student Loan Company |
| SLD | Student Loan Deduction |
| SMP | Statutory Maternity Pay |
| SPA | State Pension Age |
| SPL | Statutory Paternity Leave |
| SPP | Statutory Paternity Pay |
| SPTA | Single Person's Tax Allowance |
| SSP | Statutory Sick Pay |
| ST | Secondary Threshold |
| TAS | Taxed Awards Scheme |
| TEC | Training and Enterprise Council |
| TFC | Tax Free Childcare |
| TPR | The Pensions Regulator (formerly OPRA) |
| TURERA | Trade Union Reform and Employment Rights Act 1993 |
| UAP | Upper Accrual Point |
| UEL | Upper Earnings Limit |
| UKBA | UK Border Agency |
| UST | Upper Secondary Threshold for under 21s |
| VAT | Value Added Tax |
| VDEA | Voluntary Deduction from Earnings Order |
| WFTC | Working Families Tax Credit |
| WTC | Working Tax Credit |

## ADOPTION PAY AND LEAVE

Introduced April 2003 to provide a period of time for the adoptive parent and child to bond and adjust to their new surroundings. Adoption leave and potentially pay is available to either parent, if adopting jointly, at the time a child is placed with new parents. The other partner will potentially qualify for Ordinary Statutory Paternity Leave and Pay and have rights under the Shared Parental Leave rules. See Part 4.

## ADVANCES OF PAY

An advance is a payment of net pay made before it is due or can be paid, in legal terms an advance on account of earnings. The gross amount to which the advance relates is treated as pay with the next normal payroll calculation process.

It is important to distinguish a pay advance from a true loan. For example, a sum of money provided to facilitate transfer from weekly to monthly pay, fully recoverable by the employer, is a loan, not an advance and as such is not regarded as earnings. If payments of advances become regular and normal practice - e.g. halfway through each pay period - those might cease to be advances and might then constitute payment for tax and National Insurance purposes.

This is critical for RTI purposes because an advance may become reportable 'on or before the date of payment'. Where this is not possible HMRC allow ad-hoc advances to be reported on the next available FPS (Full Payment Submission).

Some employers avoid any suggestion that advances are becoming too regular by referring to them as loans recoverable next pay day. Employers must ensure the "loan" type advance is fully recovered in all circumstances. Advancing of normal pay in order to avoid or limit tax and NI liability, for example at the start of a tax year when tax/NICs rates are increasing, can be classified as an abnormal pay practice and could be challenged by HMRC.

## AGE EXCEPTION (EXEMPTION) CERTIFICATE CA4140

Until September 2013 a certificate was issued by HMRC to an employed person who had attained State Pension Age, as evidence for the employer that National Insurance deductions should cease. From that date a passport or birth certificate should be used by the employer as evidence. Certificates may still be issued by DWP.

## AGENCY WORKERS

Agency workers work through an agency which finds them work and are often referred to as temps. The end user hiring the worker pays a fee to the agency which in turn pays the worker's wages. Although Agency Workers do not usually have the same employment terms and working conditions as employees, they do have the benefit of many employment rights:

- under the national minimum wage and national living wage legislation
- under the working time regulations (for example to statutory holiday)
- under health and safety regulations and entitlement to earnings-related state benefits.

Agency work requires flexibility in many ways for both worker and end user. The worker may take up and leave an assignment at short notice. End users in turn may terminate the contract with the agency at short notice without liability for unfair dismissal or redundancy pay. However, a contract with the agency may include a specified notice period.

An agency worker's contract is with the agency which must pay the worker whether or not the end user then pays the agency. Where a worker signs a fixed-term contract directly with an end user, different rights apply as this is not agency work so the same employment rights apply as for all other directly recruited employees. The requirement to auto-enrol an agency worker into a qualifying pension scheme rests with the entity who pays the individual and is liable for the secondary NIC.

An agency worker, who is commonly neither an employee of the agency or the end user client, has the right to:

- paid holiday pay and statutory rest breaks
- limits on their working time
- have no unlawful deductions made from their pay
- payment as specified under the national minimum wage legislation
- protection from discrimination under all the Equality Act 2010 (age, race, sex, sexual orientation, disability and religion or belief)
- Statutory Sick Pay (from 27th October 2008).

In addition, agency workers have the same right to be considered for entitlement to Maternity, Adoption or Paternity Pay but not to Maternity, Adoption or Paternity Leave.

The UK government implemented the EU 'Directive on Conditions for Temporary Workers' from 1st October 2011 through the Agency Worker Regulations 2010. These regulations require the agent to pay an agency worker (who may have a full employment contract with the agency or more commonly have a contract for services with the agency that then places them with the end user client):

- the same basic pay plus allowances such as shift allowance, and bonuses that are directly related to the personal performance of the agency worker
- the statutory 4 weeks' holiday - any additional holiday entitlement may be paid at the end of the assignment or rolled up into the hourly rate (rolling up is not permitted for the 4 weeks' statutory pay)
- as a comparable employee of the client after 12 weeks placed at that client. Specifically excluded are the right to contractual benefits such as occupational pensions and sick pay. The continuity of the 12-week period is only blocked by a break of 6 weeks or more excluding any breaks for statutory leave and only if the agency worker begins a substantially different role with the hirer.

The regulations also allow, after 12 weeks placement at the client, those agency workers who are pregnant, have recently given birth or are breastfeeding the right to reasonable paid time off to attend ante-natal appointments and adjustments to working conditions and hours.

In addition, from the start of the assignment the agency worker must have:

- information about vacancies the client has, to give them the same opportunity as other workers to find permanent employment
- equal access to on-site facilities such as child care and transport services.

Employment tribunals have jurisdiction to hear complaints from agency workers.

Agency workers are entitled to lodge a complaint if they consider their rights under the regulations have been breached or that they have suffered a detriment for asserting their rights und,er the regulations. Complaints must be lodged within 3 months from the date of the alleged breach or detriment. A maximum £5,000 fine split between the agency and the end user will be payable if the regulations are flouted.

**PAYE/NICs** - in general terms, standard procedures apply to the agency paying the worker. Even if the worker is engaged under a contract for services the agency will be required to operate PAYE and deduct Class 1 NICs as if the worker was employed by them, however PAYE and NICs do not apply if the worker provides their services as an actor, singer, musician or other entertainer, or as a fashion, photographic or artist's model.

Where there is a liability for NICs it follows that the worker can be entitled to SSP, SMP, SAP, SPP and ShPP. A P45 should be issued to the worker at the earlier of:

* the end of the relationship between the agency and the worker, and
* the end of a period of three months during which the agency makes no relevant payments to the worker.

Some agencies operated a salary sacrifice arrangement in respect of travel and subsistence to the hirer's premises arguing that these are all temporary workplaces so are not normal commuting costs. New regulations in force from January 2011 require that where such sacrifices are in place that the worker is still in receipt of national minimum wage, and from April 2016 the national living wage. If any taxable non-cash benefits or expenses are provided to the worker a P11D or P9D must be completed at the end of the tax year.

Recent case law also shows that such salary sacrifice arrangements which seek to change the tax treatment of travel and subsistence costs do not work for tax purposes and in one case a significant settlement was made with HMRC. In addition, the new rules for tax relief on travel and subsistence introduced on 6 April 2016 specifically exclude salary sacrifice arrangements when determining what tax relief would apply to travel and subsistence costs.

## APPRENTICESHIP FUNDING AND LEVY

From April 2017 a new method of funding apprenticeships came into force, in England alone, and with it a new cost to employers across the whole of the UK, called the Apprenticeship Levy.

In England alone funding is self-managed and drawn by employers from a fund into which they pay their levy and into which an additional 10% is paid by HMRC. Employers select the training provider and approve the sums to be drawn by that provider in relation to that employer's apprentices. Employers have 24 months from the time a levy payment is made into the apprenticeship account to use the funds for apprenticeship training before the unused funds become available for non-levy paying employers.

In Scotland, Northern Ireland and Wales apprenticeship funding remains centrally accessed by training providers, though the money to pay for it will come from the levy itself. Allocation of the funding is based on the employee's address.

The levy is calculated by the employer at a rate of 0.5% of the employer's total national insurable pay each pay period, and on a cumulative basis. Once the levy is established the employer is then permitted to use an allowance of £15,000 a year, also used per pay period, against the levy in order to calculate the amount, if any, to be paid into the apprenticeship account.

Employers within any kind of group structure, which can include public sector bodies, are permitted to use only one allowance for the entire group and this must be split by whatever method the group decides. Unused allowance at the end of the year may be reallocated to other members of the group and this will be useful to groups where the paybill fluctuates.

## ARREARS OF PAY

A payment in arrears is an item of pay paid after it is usually due. More commonly this arises as a result of a retrospective pay award or upgrading, but it can also arise as a result of an error. Arrears are to be included with all other payments as part of gross pay for calculation of PAYE, notwithstanding that the arrears relate to an earlier pay period (or tax year) and that only one amount of free pay can be given in any pay period. For NICs the pay for the earlier period must be calculated separately as if payment had been made at the correct time and then added together rather than NICs being calculated on the total amount in a single pay period. HMRC allows an easement to this strict rule if the employer can prove it is not practicable to do so.

## ARREARS OF PAY FOR CLOSED YEARS

Employers may occasionally be requested by a court or Employment Tribunal to pay arrears of pay for previous (closed) tax years, in respect of equal pay claims or a National Minimum Wage Enforcement Order. Where a few individuals are affected the procedure to be adopted is as follows:

- For tax purposes the arrears are allocated over the relevant years and the extra payment treated as if it had been made in week 53 of that year. (Note HMRC's changed approach to week 53 taxation, see page 137.)
- The tax code that was in force at that time should be used (HMRC can tell you which code was in use if you do not have sufficient records).
- The tax due is paid within thirty days of the payment date to the local Employer Compliance Office quoting 'Employer Amendment Class 6 Settlement' and accompanied by a listing of the names, NINOs and pay and tax for each affected year.
- Each affected employee should be given a letter detailing the pay and tax and advising that if an overpayment of tax has now occurred for that year contact should be made direct with HMRC. No RTI submissions should be sent.
- For NICs the employer should enter the full amount of the arrears paid on the current payroll record at the time of payment and work out the NICs due in the normal way.

For large numbers of employees, employers are required to contact the Compliance Director within the local tax office area (Details of Compliance Directors can be found by telephoning the Employers' helpline on 0300 200 3200).

## ARRESTMENT OF EARNINGS (Scotland)

In Scotland, power to make recovery from earnings for the payment of a civil debt, fine or unpaid Council Tax is made under the Debtors (Scotland) Act 1987 (amended by the Bankruptcy and Diligence Act 2006) and Arrestment rates are up-rated through Diligence Against Earnings Regulations, the latest being the Diligence against Earnings (Variation) (Scotland) Regulations 2018. They must be applied to all new arrestments executed on, or after, 6th April 2013. Employers who choose not to apply the revised regulations to existing arrestments immediately must do so when instructed to do so by a sheriff officer.

Orders may fall into one of three categories:
- Earnings Arrestments (EAs)
- Current Maintenance Arrestments (CMAs)
- Conjoined Arrestment Orders (CAOs) - a combination of two or more EAs or CMAs.

In the case of Earnings Arrestments the court notifies the amount of the debt and the employer applies the deduction to net earnings with reference to a set of prescribed tables. The order comes into force on the day the employer receives it and should be actioned on the next payday.

The Act defines arrestable earnings as wages/salary, fees, commission, pension, SSP (but not a disability pension) but does not include SMP, SAP, OSPP or ASPP. With ASPP having been withdrawn on 6th April 2015 the new ShPP is equally ignored when determining the arrestable earnings.

Arrestable earnings are reduced by the deduction of tax, NICs, child support DEOs, pension contributions (apart from those to stakeholder and Group Personal Pension Plans) including AVCs if they are not freestanding.

On receipt of an EA the employer must:
- make a deduction from the debtor's net earnings every pay day using the supplied tables and pay that deduction over to the arresting creditor (named on the order)
- cease deductions once the debt is fully paid or the debtor leaves that place of employment.

On receipt of a CMA the employer must:
- make a deduction, as specified in the order, from the debtor's earnings every pay-day applying the daily protected earnings figure of £15.12 (from 6th April 2013) before deductions are calculated. (This figure was £13.64 prior to 6th April 2013)
- pay that deduction over to the arresting creditor (named on the order).

## Arrestment Tables (Scotland) Deduction rates from 30th November 1995 to 2nd December 2001

| Weekly Earnings | | | Monthly Earnings | | | Daily Earnings | | |
|---|---|---|---|---|---|---|---|---|
| Over | Up to and incl. | Dedn. | Over | Up to and incl. | Dedn | Over | Up to and incl. | Dedn. |
| £ | £ | £ | £ | £ | £ | £ | £ | £ |
| | 35 | Nil | | 152 | Nil | | 5 | 0.15 |
| 35 | 40 | 1 | 152 | 170 | 5 | 5 | 6 | 0.30 |
| 40 | 45 | 2 | 170 | 185 | 8 | 6 | 7 | 0.45 |
| 45 | 50 | 3 | 185 | 200 | 11 | 7 | 8 | 0.60 |
| 50 | 55 | 4 | 200 | 220 | 14 | 8 | 9 | 1.00 |
| 55 | 60 | 5 | 220 | 240 | 18 | 9 | 10 | 1.20 |
| 60 | 65 | 6 | 240 | 260 | 22 | 10 | 11 | 1.40 |
| 65 | 70 | 7 | 260 | 280 | 26 | 11 | 12 | 1.60 |
| 70 | 75 | 8 | 280 | 300 | 30 | 12 | 13 | 1.80 |
| 75 | 80 | 9 | 300 | 320 | 34 | 13 | 14 | 2.00 |
| 80 | 85 | 10 | 320 | 340 | 38 | 14 | 15 | 2.40 |
| 85 | 90 | 11 | 340 | 360 | 42 | 15 | 17 | 2.70 |
| 90 | 95 | 12 | 360 | 380 | 46 | 17 | 19 | 3.20 |
| 95 | 100 | 13 | 380 | 400 | 50 | 19 | 21 | 3.70 |
| 100 | 110 | 15 | 400 | 440 | 58 | 21 | 23 | 4.30 |
| 110 | 120 | 17 | 440 | 480 | 66 | 23 | 25 | 5.00 |
| 120 | 130 | 19 | 480 | 520 | 74 | 25 | 27 | 6.00 |
| 130 | 140 | 21 | 520 | 560 | 82 | 27 | 30 | 7.00 |
| 140 | 150 | 23 | 560 | 600 | 90 | 30 | 33 | 8.50 |
| 150 | 160 | 26 | 600 | 640 | 98 | 33 | 36 | 10.00 |
| 160 | 170 | 29 | 640 | 680 | 109 | 36 | 39 | 11.50 |
| 170 | 180 | 32 | 720 | 720 | 121 | 39 | 42 | 11.50 |
| 180 | 190 | 35 | 760 | 760 | 133 | 42 | * | 11.50 |
| 190 | 200 | 38 | 800 | 800 | 145 | | | +50% |
| 200 | 220 | 46 | 900 | 900 | 180 | | | |
| 220 | 240 | 54 | 1,000 | 1,100 | 220 | | | |
| 240 | 260 | 63 | 1,100 | 1,200 | 262 | | | |
| 260 | 280 | 73 | 1,200 | 1,300 | 312 | | | |
| 280 | 300 | 83 | 1,300 | 1,300 | 362 | | | |
| 300 | * | 83 +50% | | * | 362 +50% | | | |

* Deductions from earnings which exceed the table maximum to be equal to the sum of the maximum deduction stated plus 50% of earnings above the earnings maximum. The employer may deduct an administration fee of £1 (50p pre-April 2006) per attachment made.

## Arrestment Tables (Scotland) - Deduction rates effective from 3rd December 2001 to 4th April 2006

| Weekly Earnings | | | Monthly Earnings | | | Daily Earnings | | |
|---|---|---|---|---|---|---|---|---|
| Over | Up to and incl. | Dedn. | Over | Up to and incl. | Dedn | Over | Up to and incl. | Dedn. |
| £ | £ | £ | £ | £ | £ | £ | £ | £ |
| | 70 | nil | | 304 | nil | | 10 | |
| 70 | 105 | 3 | 304 | 410 | 13 | 10 | 14 | 0.40 |
| 105 | 115 | 5 | 410 | 460 | 21 | 14 | 17 | 0.80 |
| 115 | 125 | 8 | 460 | 510 | 29 | 17 | 19 | 1.20 |
| 125 | 135 | 11 | 510 | 560 | 38 | 19 | 21 | 1.60 |
| 135 | 150 | 13 | 560 | 610 | 48 | 21 | 24 | 2.70 |

**Arrestment Tables (Scotland) - Deduction rates effective from 3rd December 2001 to 4th April 2006** *continued*

| | | | | | | | | |
|---|---|---|---|---|---|---|---|---|
| 150 | 165 | 16 | 610 | 660 | 59 | 24 | 27 | 3.20 |
| 165 | 180 | 19 | 660 | 710 | 70 | 27 | 30 | 3.70 |
| 180 | 195 | 21 | 710 | 760 | 80 | 30 | 33 | 4.20 |
| 195 | 210 | 24 | 760 | 820 | 91 | 33 | 36 | 4.70 |
| 210 | 225 | 27 | 820 | 880 | 102 | 36 | 40 | 5.20 |
| 225 | 240 | 29 | 880 | 940 | 113 | 40 | 44 | 6.30 |
| 240 | 255 | 32 | 940 | 1,000 | 123 | 44 | 48 | 7.10 |
| 255 | 270 | 35 | 1,000 | 1,070 | 134 | 48 | 53 | 8.40 |
| 270 | 290 | 40 | 1,070 | 1,150 | 155 | 53 | 58 | 9.80 |
| 290 | 310 | 46 | 1,150 | 1,240 | 177 | 58 | 64 | 11.50 |
| 310 | 335 | 51 | 1,240 | 1,340 | 198 | 64 | 70 | 13.50 |
| 335 | 360 | 56 | 1,340 | 1,440 | 220 | 70 | 77 | 16.00 |
| 360 | 385 | 62 | 1,440 | 1,550 | 241 | 77 | 85 | 18.50 |
| 385 | 410 | 70 | 1,550 | 1,660 | 263 | 85 | 94 | 22.50 |
| 410 | 440 | 78 | 1,660 | 1,780 | 292 | 94 | 103 | 26.50 |
| 440 | 470 | 86 | 1,780 | 1,900 | 324 | 103 | 113 | 30.50 |
| 470 | 500 | 94 | 1,900 | 2,020 | 357 | 113 | * | 30.50 |
| 500 | 535 | 102 | 2,020 | 2,140 | 389 | | | +50% |
| 535 | 575 | 123 | 2,140 | 2,400 | 483 | | | |
| 575 | 620 | 145 | 2,400 | 2,660 | 590 | | | |
| 620 | 675 | 169 | 2,660 | 2,930 | 702 | | | |
| 675 | 740 | 196 | 2,930 | 3,205 | 836 | | | |
| 740 | 805 | 223 | 3,205 | 3,485 | 970 | | | |
| 805 | * | 223 +50% | 3,485 | * | 970 +50% | | | |

* Deductions from earnings which exceed the table maximum to be equal to the sum of the maximum deduction stated plus 50% of earnings above the earnings maximum. The employer may deduct an administration fee of £1 (50p pre-April 2006) per attachment made.

**Arrestment Tables (Scotland) - Deduction rates effective from 5th April 2006**

| Weekly Earnings | | | Monthly Earnings | | | Daily Earnings | | |
|---|---|---|---|---|---|---|---|---|
| Over | Up to and incl. | Dedn. | Over | Up to and incl. | Dedn | Over | Up to and incl. | Dedn. |
| £ | £ | £ | £ | £ | £ | £ | £ | £ |
| | 85 | nil | | 370 | nil | | 12 | nil |
| 85 | 125 | 4 | 370 | 490 | 15 | 12 | 16 | 0.50 |
| 125 | 135 | 6 | 490 | 550 | 25 | 16 | 19 | 0.90 |
| 135 | 145 | 9 | 550 | 610 | 34 | 19 | 22 | 1.40 |
| 145 | 160 | 13 | 610 | 670 | 45 | 22 | 25 | 1.90 |
| 160 | 175 | 15 | 670 | 730 | 56 | 25 | 28 | 3.10 |
| 175 | 190 | 19 | 730 | 800 | 69 | 28 | 31 | 3.70 |
| 190 | 210 | 22 | 800 | 870 | 82 | 31 | 35 | 4.30 |
| 210 | 230 | 25 | 870 | 940 | 94 | 35 | 39 | 4.90 |
| 230 | 250 | 28 | 940 | 1,010 | 107 | 39 | 43 | 5.50 |
| 250 | 265 | 32 | 1,010 | 1,090 | 120 | 43 | 47 | 6.10 |
| 265 | 285 | 34 | 1,090 | 1,170 | 133 | 47 | 52 | 7.40 |
| 285 | 300 | 38 | 1,170 | 1,250 | 145 | 52 | 57 | 8.30 |
| 300 | 320 | 41 | 1,250 | 1,340 | 157 | 57 | 62 | 9.90 |
| 320 | 340 | 47 | 1,340 | 1,440 | 182 | 62 | 68 | 11.50 |
| 340 | 365 | 54 | 1,440 | 1,550 | 208 | 68 | 75 | 13.50 |
| 365 | 395 | 60 | 1,550 | 1,660 | 233 | 75 | 82 | 15.90 |
| 395 | 425 | 66 | 1,660 | 1,780 | 259 | 82 | 90 | 18.80 |
| 425 | 455 | 73 | 1,780 | 1,910 | 283 | 90 | 100 | 21.70 |

**Arrestment Tables (Scotland) - Deduction rates effective from 5th April 2006** *continued*

| | | | | | | | | |
|---|---|---|---|---|---|---|---|---|
| 455 | 485 | 82 | 1,910 | 2,040 | 309 | 100 | 110 | 26.40 |
| 485 | 520 | 92 | 2,040 | 2,180 | 343 | 110 | 121 | 31.10 |
| 520 | 555 | 101 | 2,180 | 2,330 | 381 | 121 | 133 | 35.80 |
| 555 | 590 | 110 | 2,330 | 2,490 | 419 | 133 | * | 35.80 |
| 590 | 630 | 120 | 2,490 | 2,680 | 457 | | | +50% |
| 630 | 675 | 145 | 2,680 | 2,900 | 568 | | | |
| 675 | 730 | 170 | 2,900 | 3,150 | 693 | | | |
| 730 | 795 | 199 | 3,150 | 3,450 | 823 | | | |
| 795 | 870 | 230 | 3,450 | 3,800 | 982 | | | |
| 870 | 945 | 262 | 3,800 | 4,100 | 1,140 | | | |
| 945 | * | 262 +50% | 4,100 | * | 1,140 +50% | | | |

*\* Deductions from earnings which exceed the table maximum to be equal to the sum of the maximum deduction stated plus 50% of earnings above the earnings maximum. The employer may deduct an administration fee of £1 (50p pre-April 2006) per attachment made. Employers should note that the effective date of the above table was 5th April 2006, with effect from which date the amount an employer may deduct as an administration fee increased to £1 per attachment made, (the new administration fee also applies to Conjoined Orders and to Debt Arrangement Schemes). Although the rates were effective for the last day of the 2005/06 tax year the Scottish Executive accepted that the rates and fees would come into effect on 6th April 2006 for all new and existing orders for employers using payroll software with in-built court order functionality.*

From 6th April 2010 the Earnings Arrestment tables were simplified as follows:

**Arrestment Tables (Scotland) - Deduction rates effective from 6th April 2010**

**Table A: Deductions from Weekly Earnings**

| Net Earnings | Deduction |
|---|---|
| Not exceeding £95.77 | Nil |
| Exceeding £95.77 but not exceeding £346.15 | £4 or 19% of weekly earnings exceeding £95.77, whichever is the greater |
| Exceeding £346.15 but not exceeding £576.92 | £47.57 plus 23% of weekly earnings exceeding £346.15 |
| Exceeding £576.92 | £100.65 plus 50% of the earnings exceeding £576.92 |

**Table B: Deductions from Monthly Earnings**

| Net Earnings | Deduction |
|---|---|
| Not exceeding £415 | Nil |
| Exceeding £415 but not exceeding £1,500 | £15 or 19% of monthly earnings exceeding £415, whichever is the greater |
| Exceeding £1,500 but not exceeding £2,500 | £206.15 plus 23% of monthly earnings exceeding £1,500 |
| Exceeding £2,500 | £436.15 plus 50% of the earnings exceeding £2,500 |

## Table C: Deductions from Daily Earnings

| Net Earnings | Deduction |
|---|---|
| Not exceeding £13.64 | Nil |
| Exceeding £13.64 but not exceeding £49.32 | £0.50 or 19% of daily earnings exceeding £13.64 whichever is the greater |
| Exceeding £49.32 but not exceeding £82.19 | £6.78 plus 23% of daily earnings exceeding £49.32 |
| Exceeding £82.19 | £14.34 plus 50% of earnings exceeding £82.19 |

## Arrestment Tables (Scotland) - Deduction rates effective from 6th April 2013

## Table A: Deductions from Weekly Earnings

| Net Earnings | Deduction |
|---|---|
| Not exceeding £106.17 | Nil |
| Exceeding £106.17 but not exceeding £383.74 | £4 or 19% of earnings exceeding £106.17, whichever is the greater |
| Exceeding £383.74 but not exceeding £576.92 | £52.74 plus 23% of earnings exceeding £383.74 |
| Exceeding £576.92 | £97.17 plus 50% of earnings exceeding £576.92 |

## Table B: Deductions from Monthly Earnings

| Net Earnings | Deduction |
|---|---|
| Not exceeding £460.06 | Nil |
| Exceeding £460.06 but not exceeding £1,662.88 | £15.00 or 19% of earnings exceeding £460.06, whichever is the greater |
| Exceeding £1,662.88 but not exceeding £2,500.00 | £228.54 plus 23% of earnings exceeding £1,662.88 |
| Exceeding £2,500 | £421.07* plus 50% of earnings exceeding £2,500 |

*might need hard coding as software will calculate £421.08 as the table is in error*

## Table C: Deductions from Daily Earnings

| Net Earnings | Deduction |
|---|---|
| Not exceeding £15.12 | Nil |
| Exceeding £15.12 but not exceeding £49.32 | £0.50 or 19% of daily earnings exceeding £15.12 whichever is the greater |
| Exceeding £54.68 but not exceeding £82.19 | £7.52 plus 23% of daily earnings exceeding £54.68 |
| Exceeding £82.19 | £14.34 plus 50% of earnings exceeding £82.19 |

**Arrestment Tables (Scotland) - Deduction rates effective from 6th April 2016**

**Table A: Deductions from Weekly Earnings**

| Net Earnings | Deduction |
|---|---|
| Not exceeding £113.68 | Nil |
| Exceeding £113.68 but not exceeding £410.90 | £4 or 19% of earnings exceeding £113.68, whichever is the greater |
| Exceeding £410.90 but not exceeding £617.82 | £56.47 plus 23% of earnings exceeding £410.90 |
| Exceeding £617.82 | £104.06 plus 50% of earnings exceeding £617.82 |

**Table B: Deductions from Monthly Earnings**

| Net Earnings | Deduction |
|---|---|
| Not exceeding £494.01 | Nil |
| Exceeding £494.01 but not exceeding £1,785.61 | £15.00 or 19% of earnings exceeding £494.01, whichever is the greater |
| Exceeding £1,785.61 but not exceeding £2,684.51 | £245.40 plus 23% of earnings exceeding £1,785.61 |
| Exceeding £2,684.51 | £452.15 plus 50% of earnings exceeding £2,684.51 |

**Table C: Deductions from Daily Earnings**

| Net Earnings | Deduction |
|---|---|
| Not exceeding £16.24 | Nil |
| Exceeding £16.24 but not exceeding £58.70 | £0.50 or 19% of earnings exceeding £16.24, whichever is the greater |
| Exceeding £58.70 but not exceeding £88.26 | £8.07 plus 23% of earnings exceeding £58.70 |
| Exceeding £88.26 | £14.87 plus 50% of earnings exceeding £88.26 |

There is a minimum amount of £494.01 set for a person's bank account which protects those whose account is being arrested.

**Arrestment Tables (Scotland) - Deduction rates effective from 6th April 2019**

**Table A: Deductions from Weekly Earnings**

| Net Earnings | Deduction |
|---|---|
| Not exceeding £122.28 | Nil |
| Exceeding £122.28 but not exceeding £442.00 | £4.00 or 19% of earnings exceeding £122.28, whichever is the greater |
| Exceeding £442.00 but not exceeding £664.50 | £60.75 plus 23% of earnings exceeding £442.00 |
| Exceeding £664.50 | £111.92 plus 50% of earnings exceeding £664.50 |

## Table B: Deductions from Monthly Earnings

| Net Earnings | Deduction |
|---|---|
| Not exceeding £529.90 | Nil |
| Exceeding £529.90 but not exceeding £1,915.32 | £15.00 or 19% of earnings exceeding £529.90, whichever is the greater |
| Exceeding £1,915.32 but not exceeding £2,879.52 | £263.23 plus 23% of earnings exceeding £1,915.32 |
| Exceeding £2,879.52 | £485.00 plus 50% of earnings exceeding £2,879.52 |

## Table C: Deductions from Daily Earnings

| Net Earnings | Deduction |
|---|---|
| Not exceeding £17.42 | Nil |
| Exceeding £17.42 but not exceeding £62.97 | £0.50 or 19% of earnings exceeding £17.42, whichever is the greater |
| Exceeding £62.97 but not exceeding £94.67 | £8.65 plus 23% of earnings exceeding £62.97 |
| Exceeding £94.67 | £15.95 plus 50% of earnings exceeding £94.67 |

There is a minimum amount of £529.90 set for a person's bank account which protects those whose account is being arrested.

## ASYLUM and IMMIGRATION

Nationals from most of the European Economic Area (EEA), the 28 EU member states plus Norway, Iceland, Liechtenstein and Switzerland, have the automatic right to come to the UK to live and work. There are some restrictions still in place in respect of nationals from Croatia who joined the EU in July 2013 and who may require to hold a worker authorisation certificate. There are no longer any restrictions on Bulgarian and Romanian nationals.

Prior to the 26th November 2008, non-EEA migrant workers, including commonwealth citizens, usually needed a work permit prior to entering the UK. From 27th November 2008 such non-EEA workers have had to apply for permission to enter the UK under the points based system of migration (PBS) and for the most common tiers of entry (2, 4 and 5) employers must be licenced as sponsors prior to recruiting non-EEA nationals. From April 2011 a strict quota of migrants is admitted under each tier each year.

EEA nationals and members of their immediate family can enter and work in the UK without restriction (like British citizens). Employers must however verify any claim to membership of an EEA country, including the UK, before offering employment by inspecting and copying documentary evidence of the individual's nationality and thereby their right to work. Details of documents approved, usually a national passport or national identity card, are contained in 'List A' supplied by the UK Border Agency (UK BA). Note that nationals from EEA countries can no longer use an Identification Card and British citizens a National Identity Card to prove their right to work, these became obsolete on 21st January 2011. Such cards used as proof of right to work prior to that date can still be retained by employers.

### The Asylum and Immigration Act 1996 and The Immigration, Asylum and Nationality Act 2006

The 1996 Act made it unlawful for employers to recruit individuals who did not have permission to work in the UK. The 2006 Act strengthened this principle but does not apply to anyone employed before that date who is subject to the 2004 guidance - see the UK Border Agency website: https://www.gov.uk/government/collections/employers-illegal-working-penalties

The UK Border Agency (UKBA) published a code of practice for employers to accompany the 2006 Act. The code of practice is statutory; it does not impose legal obligations on employers nor is it a statement of law. It can however be used as evidence in legal proceedings. The Code reminds employers of their responsibilities under the act which must be exercised without race discrimination i.e. that all prospective employees have their right to work checked and at the same stage in the recruitment process. A copy of the code, which was updated in August 2017, may be obtained from the UKBA website as above.

From 29 February 2008 new measures were introduced to tackle illegal working including a system of penalties that include:

- a maximum civil penalty per illegal worker of £20,000 for employers who employ illegal migrant workers. This is reduced depending on the number of breaches and also if the employer makes payment within 21 days. Employers can also pay the penalty by instalments up to 24 months and sometimes up to 36 months
- from April 2016, a maximum five years (was two years) prison sentence and/or an unlimited fine for employers who 'knowingly' use illegal migrant labour (a new criminal offence)
- a continuing responsibility for employers of migrant workers with a time-limited immigration status to check their ongoing entitlement to work in the UK on the 12 month anniversary of the first check (on expiry of any time limited leave to remain when the 2013 bill was passed)

Employers have a statutory defence from conviction and/or the above fines where they check and record certain specified documents. The three step procedure for checking the right to work in the UK should ideally be carried out pre-employment as the employer has no defence until it is complete.

Where a potential employee is not permitted to work the employer is entitled to refuse employment. Equally when the employer carries out the repeat check at 12 months (end of leave to remain) on those with limited leave to remain they must end the contract of any individual if they are certain that an individual no longer has the right to work in the UK.

UK BA guidance as above provides details of documents that are acceptable to provide a statutory defence for the employer against prosecution. It was updated in October 2013

- List A - documents which can be used singly or in combination which when checked and copied thereafter provide an employer with defence against prosecution. If an employer can check any of the documents from list A there is no need to ask for further documents contained in list B.
- List B - documents, or combination of documents, which provide a defence but carry a need for post-employment checks. Where the document shows a limited leave to remain, employers must diarise when this is due to expire and check that new permission has been granted or employment must be terminated.

Certain documents are not acceptable as a defence and should not form part of an employer's proof of a person's right to work in the UK:

- a temporary National Insurance Number (NINO) - one beginning with the prefix TN or suffix with the letters E to Z inclusive
- a driving licence issued by the Driver and Vehicle Licensing agency
- a bill issued by a utility company or a financial institution

**Penalties**
Employers found to be using illegal migrant workers will receive a notification of potential liability (NOPL) from UKBA. Evidence provided by/to the visiting immigration officer or team will be considered by the civil penalty compliance team (CPCT) who will then decide whether to issue a notification of liability (NOL) which, since April 2016, carries an unlimited penalty.

Where a notice of liability is issued imposing a civil penalty the employer must, within 28 days:

- pay the civil penalty in full
- submit a request to the CPCT to pay the civil penalty in a series of monthly instalments; or
- submit an objection against the civil penalty to the CPCT; or
- lodge an appeal against the service of the civil penalty to the County Court (England, Wales and Northern Ireland) or the Sheriff Court (Scotland).

**Non-EEA Nationals**
On 27th November 2008 new rules came into force for employing workers from outside the European Economic Area (EEA). The work permit system disappeared and was replaced by the points-based system of migration (PBS). Points are awarded which reflect the migrant's ability, experience, and age and when appropriate, the level of need within the sector in which the migrant intends to work. Non-EEA nationals are required to have a Biometric Residence Permit (BRP) which indicates whether they have the right to work in

the UK and for how long. Where the BRP shows a limited leave to remain, employers must diarise when this is due to expire and check that new permission has been granted or employment must be terminated.

The points-based system consists of five tiers:

- Tier 1 - highly skilled workers e.g. scientists and entrepreneurs who can come to the UK speculatively to look for work
- Tier 2 - skilled workers with a job offer in four categories: skilled workers (general), intra-company transfers, sports people, Ministers of Religion
- Tier 3 - low skilled workers filling specific labour shortages (subject to quota and currently closed)
- Tier 4 - students
- Tier 5 - youth mobility and temporary workers (e.g. musicians coming to play in a concert) primarily here for non-economic reasons such as cultural exchanges. The Youth Mobility Scheme replaces the Working Holidaymaker Scheme

Employers who wish to recruit under tiers 2, 4 or 5 must be licensed as a sponsor and entry is subject to national annual quotas from April 2011. Sponsor licences are valid for four years from either the date of issue or the date that applications start under the relevant tier.

## Sponsors

Sponsors are fully responsible for the actions of any migrant they employ or teach and must ensure that migrants comply with their immigration conditions by keeping individual records and reporting any changes to UK BA e.g. that the individual fails to attend work/study. Employers who fail to comply with their responsibilities may have their licence downgraded or withdrawn.

## Licensed employers

They are given either an A or a B rating and are added to UKBA's published register of sponsors. A category B rating will be given where UKBA believe that the sponsor may be a risk to immigration control or to those employers who do not have robust HR systems in place to meet the sponsor's obligations.

A sponsor must:

- prevent abuse of assessment procedures
- capture patterns of migrant behaviour which cause concern early
- address possible weaknesses in their processes or which cause those patterns, and
- monitor compliance with immigration rules.

For further information contact the employer helpline on 0300 123 4699 or the Business Helpdesk at businesshelpdesk@homeoffice.gsi.gov.uk.

The Immigration Act 2016 introduced new measures to prevent illegal working in the UK and imposed further sanctions against employers who do not comply. Since April 2018 an employer who engages a person who does not have the right to live and work in the UK faces an additional penalty in the loss of the Employment Allowance for a period of one year. (See Part 3: Employment Allowance for more details)

A new code of practice was issued in February 2019 and at the time of writing this does not appear to have been updated.

With the UK having ceased membership of the EU at 23.00 GMT on 31 January 2020, the government and the EU have continued to work on new requirements for UK and EU nationals and the right to free movement and work between the two areas. At the time of writing it is still not known if any agreements in place will be ratified by the UK government and hence it is still possible that the UK will leave without a formal agreement in place. Until this is matter is formally settled we can assume that measures will be put in place to minimise disruption to worker movements and rights to work, however readers are advised to monitor the emerging news and respond accordingly.

# YOUTH MOBILITY SCHEME

The youth mobility scheme is for young people from participating countries and territories who want to come and experience life in the UK. Every year, the UK government allocates a number of places on the scheme for each country and territory. From 27 November 2008 those wishing to enter the UK under this scheme must meet criteria for the Youth Mobility Scheme as a tier 5 worker. Applicants may take up any work and can study as well but the main reason for their stay must not be to study. They must return home at the end of their stay.

Eligibility is based on points attributable to age and having sufficient funds to maintain and accommodate themselves in the UK without recourse to public funds.

## SEASONAL AGRICULTURAL WORKERS SCHEME (SAWS)

A scheme that closed at the end of 2013 that served as a means of bringing in short-term labour to gather the harvest. It was closed when Bulgarian and Romanian nationals had all work restrictions removed from 1 January 2014 so expanding the pool of EEA labour such that SAWS was no longer needed.

## ATTACHMENT OF EARNINGS ORDERS (AEOs)

*(See also Arrestment of Earnings - Scotland)*

There are seventeen types of order that an employer may be asked to operate against earnings, they are commonly referred to by the generic term court, or statutory orders but are enacted under:

- The Attachment of Earnings Act 1971, Debtors (Scotland) Act 1987, and The Magistrates Courts (Northern Ireland) Order 1981
- The Local Government Finance Act 1988 by Local Authorities for the purpose of collecting Council Tax (CTAEOs)
- The Child Support Act 1991, The Child Maintenance and other Payments Act 2008 and the Child Support (Northern Ireland) Order 1991 for the purpose of collecting child maintenance (DEOs).
- The Courts Act 2003 - Schedule 5 Fines Orders
- The Welfare Reform Act 2012 and the Welfare Reform (Northern Ireland) Order 2015 – collection of benefits overpayments
- The Social Security (Overpayment and Recovery) Regulations 2013.

AEOs usually state an amount to be deducted from net attachable earnings, although CTAEOs, Schedule 5 Orders, Scottish Arrestments, DEOs from 2013 and Direct Earnings Attachments (see below) require the employer to calculate the amount deductible using a set of tables or a set formula.

For the purpose of calculating the 'attachable earnings' prior to deduction of an AEO, gross attachable earnings are defined as:

- wages and salary (including overtime, bonuses, fees and commission)
- pension (service pension) and compensation for loss of employment
- statutory sick pay
- holiday pay or other pay advances,

but excluding:

- a disability pension
- statutory maternity, adoption, ordinary/additional paternity pay and shared parental leave payments
- guaranteed minimum pension (as provided by an occupational pension scheme),

and then the following are deducted to calculate attachable earnings:

- PAYE income tax and NI contributions
- some pension or superannuation contributions
- deductions for previously received and higher priority AEOs.

AEOs are classified into two categories, 'priority' or 'non-priority'. For an employer's purpose the type and the date the order is made determines this. In Scotland it is the type and date received that is crucial.

Priority orders are AEOs for fines or maintenance, all child support DEOs and CTAEOs. They are applied by reference to the date of issue, applying the oldest first. After all 'priority' orders are satisfied, non-priority orders, for civil debts (1971 Act orders) are applied. If two orders are made on the same day, then the date and often even the time of receipt is considered. It is the employer's duty to maintain the requisite records in administering AEOs in order to stop deductions on completion of the recovery process.

The employer is responsible for administering the order and paying over the sums deducted to the court or the specified recipient. An administration fee of £1 (50p pre-1st April 1981 in England and Wales and pre-5th April 2006 in Scotland), may also be deducted from the employee for each attachment made.

This fee is only deductible as long as doing so does not reduce wages below that of the NMW/NLW in force at the time. (This is because the administration fee is for the benefit of the employer and hence cannot be taken in these circumstances.) Payments by cheque are to be made payable to HMCS (Her Majesty's Court Service).

## Protected Earnings

Protected Earnings are the amount, which when stated on the order, are the minimum amount below which a person's net earnings may not be reduced. In the case of a priority order, any balance outstanding of the required deduction as a result of applying the protected earnings may be carried forward and added to the potential attachment due for the next pay period. In all other cases the employer may not increase deductions from subsequent earnings to make up any deficit.

Please see Child Support DEOs below for the treatment of arrears in respect of those orders and the later section on determining priority of orders.

## Council Tax Attachment of Earnings Orders (CTAEOs)

These were first introduced on 1st April 1989 in Scotland as part of legislation for the Community Charge and were initially termed CCAEOs. Community Charge was replaced by the Council Tax on 1st April 1993 and orders re-styled as CTAEOs.

They are:
- issued by a local authority, and whilst they must apply to a Magistrates Court for a liability order, the authority are only required to demonstrate that the council tax is due and that it has not been paid. The court has no power of discretion and must, subject to these criteria, issue an order
- served on the employer, who is required to make and remit deductions to the local authority. It is possible for an employer to receive CTAEOs for a single employee from more than one local authority and to be required to deduct more than one CTAEO from one authority at the same time but once a third CTAEO is received it should be returned to the local authority
- to be applied in date order, based on the date the order was made

An employer:
- has 14 days in which to give notice to the local authority if the person named is not employed or has left employment
- may deduct an administration charge of £1 per order in addition to the amount determined by reference to the tables below but not if doing so reduces the pay below the NMW/NLW
- may not deduct a student loan where a CTAEO is in force until it is complete.

### The Community Charges (Administration and Enforcement) regulations 1998 Schedule 4

### Deduction Rates effective from 1st October 1998 to 31st March 2007

| Table A | | Table B | | Table C | | |
|---------|--|---------|--|---------|--|--|
| Weekly Net Earnings | | Monthly Net Earnings | | Daily Net Earnings | | Deduction |
| Exceeding | Not Exceeding | Exceeding | Not Exceeding | Exceeding | Not Exceeding | Rate |
| £ | £ | £ | £ | £ | £ | % |
| 0 | 55 | 0 | 220 | 0 | 8 | Nil |
| 55 | 100 | 220 | 400 | 8 | 15 | 3 |
| 100 | 135 | 400 | 540 | 15 | 20 | 5 |
| 135 | 165 | 540 | 660 | 20 | 24 | 7 |
| 165 | 260 | 660 | 1,040 | 24 | 38 | 12 |
| 260 | 370 | 1,040 | 1,480 | 38 | 53 | 17 |
| 370 | | 1,480 | | 53 | | 50*(17%) |

**The Council Tax and Non-Domestic Rating (Amendment) (England) Regulations 2006 and The Council Tax (Administration and Enforcement) (Amendment) (Wales) Regulations 2007**

**Deduction Rates effective for Council Tax Attachment of Earnings Orders (CTAEOs) made on or after 1st April 2007**

| Table A | | Table B | | Table C | | |
|---|---|---|---|---|---|---|
| Weekly Net Earnings | | Monthly Net Earnings | | Daily Net Earnings | | Deduction |
| Exceeding | Not Exceeding | Exceeding | Not Exceeding | Exceeding | Not Exceeding | Rate |
| £ | £ | £ | £ | £ | £ | % |
| 0 | 75 | 0 | 300 | 0 | 11 | Nil |
| 75 | 135 | 300 | 550 | 11 | 20 | 3 |
| 135 | 185 | 550 | 740 | 20 | 27 | 5 |
| 185 | 225 | 740 | 900 | 27 | 33 | 7 |
| 225 | 355 | 900 | 1,420 | 33 | 52 | 12 |
| 355 | 505 | 1,420 | 2,020 | 52 | 72 | 17 |
| 505 | | 2,020 | | 72 | | 17/50%* |

*For earnings over £505 per week or equivalent, deduction is at 17% for the first £505 and 50% on the excess. From 1st October 1998, local authorities may only operate two CTAEOs per individual at a time.*

**Child Support DEOs**
The Child Maintenance Service (CMS) is part of the Department for Work and Pensions (DWP) and collects child maintenance with recourse to the court system for the raising of Deductions from Earnings Orders (DEOs) where the non-resident parent does not pay maintenance voluntarily. The CMS was to have migrated all CSA orders to the new CMS by 31 December 2017, however following consultation in the summer of 2017 a decision was taken to extend the transition period by 12 months. As a consequence all CSA orders have now terminated unless they had migrated prior to this date. This is despite the Gov.uk website continuing to show that 31 December 2017 was the termination date for all CSA work and enforcement orders.

There is now one type of DEO:
• 2012 orders issued from 10 December 2012 onwards – administered by the CMS.

Pre- and post- March 2003 orders provided the employer with a Normal Deductions Rate (NDR) and a Protected Earnings Rate (PER). DEOs always remain in force until the CMS tells the employer to cease deductions. The date of the order is significant as the treatment of arrears and protected earnings differ. For pre-March 2003 Orders the arrears, protected earnings and deductions were carried forward. For post-March 2003 orders they did not.

On receipt of a CSA DEO the employer had to:
• deduct the amount specified in the order where possible
• pay the amount over to the CSA by the 19th of the following month
• show the deduction on the employee's pay statement
• must inform the CMS within ten days of an employee's date of leaving

The employer was permitted to deduct £1 each time a DEO was actioned even if it reduced the employee's earnings below the PER as long as it did not reduce wages below that of the NMW/NLW which was in force at the time.

Where payments were due to the CSA in Northern Ireland, these had to be sent separately to those due in the rest of the United Kingdom.

## 2012 CMS orders

These indicate a percentage (60% currently) of attachable earnings that is to be treated as the PER. The NDR is shown as a monthly amount to be amended by the employer if the employee is not monthly paid. Once a 2012 order is sent to an employer, reporting changes will kick in for that employer for all DEOs they are operating.

A new online portal is available to employers to report deductions, including

- a reason code on the monthly payment summary that indicates why the deduction has not been as specified as on the order – perhaps due to unpaid leave for example
- the payment schedule must be sent monthly even if the employee's pay frequency is weekly
- a 12-digit employer reference number that begins with a 50 for employers and 51 for agents and a 12-digit employee reference number
- deductions are shown separately for the Child Maintenance Service (CMS) ongoing maintenance, and CSA arrears under the Residual Body Scheme (RBS) (The CSA is classed as the residual body until its functions fully cease in 2018.)
- payslips to show the descriptions:
- 'CMS DEO' for ongoing maintenance and arrears to the CMS
- 'RB DEO' for CSA arrears under the RBS
- All payments to move to BACS or cheque rather than DACT.

## Direct Earnings Attachment

A new court order was introduced on a pilot basis in April 2013 to recover overpaid state benefits where voluntary action has failed. For 2013/14 orders were calculated manually and were incorporated into payroll software from April 2014. Software specifications were issued to over 600 payroll software providers in July 2014. Total court deductions including under a DEA must not exceed 40% of net pay, i.e. protected earnings of 60%, arrears are not carried forward.

Net earnings are defined as after

- tax,
- NICs and
- superannuation contributions.

The following are treated as earnings:

- wages and salary (including overtime, bonuses, fees and commission)
- occupational pensions
- compensation payments
- SSP
- pay in lieu of notice.

The following are not treated as earnings:

- statutory payments – SMP, SAP, OSPP and ShPP
- state pension or benefits
- expenses
- redundancy pay.

Deductions can be either by reference to tables or a fixed deduction. Deductions stop when any notified balance is paid off or the employer is notified to cease deductions. Payment by 19th of the month following the month of deduction is by BACS (or cheque or debit card) and is accompanied by a payment schedule sent with the order; this must be sent even if no deduction is made as earnings are too low.

A £1 admin fee is chargeable as for other 'court orders'. They are non-priority orders so are blocked by a student loan. Local authorities can also issue them to recover overpaid housing benefit and if so the bank details that the payment is paid to are the council's not DWP's as for all other central government DEAs. Originally employers were not required to operate the new orders if they had ten or fewer employees, however this temporary easement only applied if the employer was in this position prior to April 2013, or met some other criteria.

## Table A: deductions from weekly earnings

| Amount of net earnings (net earnings are gross pay, less tax, national insurance and pension contributions) | Deduction from earnings – lower rate | Deduction from earnings – higher rate |
|---|---|---|
| Not exceeding £100 | Nil | 5% |
| Exceeding £100 but not exceeding £160 | 3% | 6% |
| Exceeding £160 but not exceeding £220 | 5% | 10% |
| Exceeding £220 but not exceeding £270 | 7% | 14% |
| Exceeding £270 but not exceeding £375 | 11% | 22% |
| Exceeding £375 but not exceeding £520 | 15% | 30% |
| Exceeding £520 | 20% | 40% |

## Table B: deductions from monthly earnings

| Amount of net earnings (net earnings are gross pay, less tax, national insurance and pension contributions) | Deduction from earnings – lower rate | Deduction from earnings – higher rate |
|---|---|---|
| Not exceeding £430 | Nil | 5% |
| Exceeding £430 but not exceeding £690 | 3% | 6% |
| Exceeding £690 but not exceeding £950 | 5% | 10% |
| Exceeding £950 but not exceeding £1,160 | 7% | 14% |
| Exceeding £1,160 but not exceeding £1,615 | 11% | 22% |
| Exceeding £1,615 but not exceeding £2,240 | 15% | 30% |
| Exceeding £2,240 | 20% | 40% |

## Table C: deductions from daily earnings

| Amount of net earnings (net earnings are gross pay, less tax, national insurance and pension contributions) | Deduction from earnings – lower rate | Deduction from earnings – higher rate |
|---|---|---|
| Not exceeding £15 | Nil | 5% |
| Exceeding £15 but not exceeding £23 | 3% | 6% |
| Exceeding £23 but not exceeding £32 | 5% | 10% |
| Exceeding £32 but not exceeding £39 | 7% | 14% |
| Exceeding £39 but not exceeding £54 | 11% | 22% |
| Exceeding £54 but not exceeding £75 | 15% | 30% |
| Exceeding £75 | 20% | 40% |

Note: in exceptional circumstances DWP may issue a fixed rate deduction notice to replace the formula above. All other criteria will remain unchanged. The latest guide on DEAs, published February 2017 has confirmed the table values remain unchanged.

**Fines Enforcement Scheme**

A pilot scheme, introduced on 5th April 2004, and rolled out nationwide from April 2005, extending the use of Attachment of Earnings Orders (AEOs), to improve the enforcement of fines. Magistrates courts are able to issue Schedule 5 Fines Orders under the Courts Act 2003 that require the employer to use percentage deduction tables in the same way as they do for council tax AEOs. The tables that apply are the pre-1st April 2007 tables even if the order is made after that date.

An order will advise the employer of the total debt owed by the employee and how often deductions are to be made (weekly, monthly), and a table showing the percentage rate to be applied to the employee's earnings

The employer must:
- comply with the order
- write to the Court within 10 days where the person named is not an employee
- write to the Court within 10 days if the employee leaves
- write to the Court within 7 days on learning that a new employee has an existing order, providing details of the employee's earnings.

Orders come into force on the day received by the employer and deductions should begin the next time payment of earnings is made. Failure to comply with an order is an offence subject to a fine.

No fine will apply where the first payday falls within 7 days of the order being received, as it is not reasonable to expect the employer to be able to comply until the next pay day.

The employer may deduct a £1 administration fee for each deduction made, but only if doing so does not reduce wages below that of the NMW/NLW, in force at the time, and must advise the employee about each deduction. A Fines AEO has the power to block the operation of a student loan.

Gross attachable earnings are defined as:
- wages and salary (including overtime, bonuses, fees and commission)
- pension (service pension) and compensation for loss of employment
- statutory sick pay
- holiday pay or other pay advances

but excluding:
- disability pension
- statutory maternity, adoption, paternity and shared parental pay
- guaranteed minimum pension (as provided by an occupational pension scheme).

Deductions can only be made from the attachable earnings after deduction of:
- PAYE (tax and national insurance contributions)
- superannuation or pension contributions (excluding free standing additional voluntary and stakeholder pension contributions).

### Magistrates' Courts Fines AEOs - Fixed Rate Tables from 5th April 2004

| Table A - Deductions from Weekly Earnings | |
|---|---|
| Net earnings | Deduction rate % |
| Not exceeding £55 | 0 |
| Exceeding £55 but not exceeding £100 | 3 |
| Exceeding £100 but not exceeding £135 | 5 |
| Exceeding £135 but not exceeding £165 | 7 |
| Exceeding £165 but not exceeding £260 | 12 |
| Exceeding £260 but not exceeding £370 | 17 |
| Exceeding £370 | 17% in respect of the first £370 and 50% in respect of the remainder |

| Table B - Deductions from Monthly Earnings | |
|---|---|
| Net earnings | Deduction rate % |
| Not exceeding £220 | 0 |
| Exceeding £220 but not exceeding £400 | 3 |
| Exceeding £400 but not exceeding £540 | 5 |
| Exceeding £540 but not exceeding £660 | 7 |
| Exceeding £660 but not exceeding £1040 | 12 |
| Exceeding £1040 but not exceeding £1480 | 17 |
| Exceeding £1480 | 17% in respect of the first £1480 and 50% in respect of the remainder |

| Table C - Deductions from Daily Earnings | |
|---|---|
| Net earnings | Deduction rate % |
| Not exceeding £8 | 0 |
| Exceeding £8 but not exceeding £15 | 3 |
| Exceeding £15 but not exceeding £20 | 5 |
| Exceeding £20 but not exceeding £24 | 7 |
| Exceeding £24 but not exceeding £38 | 12 |
| Exceeding £36 but not exceeding £53 | 17 |
| Exceeding £53 | 17% in respect of the first £53 and 50% in respect of the remainder |

*N.B. For orders made on, or after, 1st April 2007 use tables relating to CTAEOs applicable up to 31st March 2007*

### Income Payment Agreement (IPA)
Introduced on 1st April 2004 an Income Payment Agreement is a legally binding written agreement between a bankrupt and a trustee for a bankrupt (or third party on the bankrupt's behalf) to make regular and specified payments from a bankrupt's income to trustees for a specified period, stated in the agreement, but not exceeding three years. Such an agreement can be extended beyond the date of discharge from bankruptcy but not beyond the three-year limit.

### Income Payments Order (IPO)
An order issued by the courts requiring a bankrupt (or a third party who makes payments to a bankrupt) to make affordable contributions towards their debts from income for a period of up to three years. Orders may be varied by the court on application of either the bankrupt or the trustee. Prior to 1st April 2004 where bankruptcy was discharged prior to the end of the period of the order the order automatically ceased.

### Income Support Deduction Notices (ISDNs)
These notices were, until April 2013, issued by the Department of Work and Pensions and require employers to make deductions from pay to recover overpaid amounts of Income Support paid to the employee immediately following a return to work after a trade dispute.

### Reciprocal Attachment of Maintenance Orders (REMOs)
Countries bound by the Hague Convention - The European Economic Community - have reciprocal arrangements to ensure that Maintenance Orders made by Courts in the United Kingdom are both recognised and enforced in other countries and vice-versa. REMOs are administered under the terms of attachment orders in general. UK employers should be prepared to receive child support orders from overseas courts relating to employees now resident in the UK but who have dependent children abroad. It remains to be seen whether or not such arrangements persist after the UK withdraws from the EU.

## Voluntary Deduction from Earnings Arrangement (VDEA)

A voluntary arrangement introduced as part of the 2006 child support reforms where an employee can ask his employer to make deductions from net pay in respect of child support and forward these to the Child Maintenance Service (CMS). The employer is not obliged to agree to deductions under a VDEA, as the arrangement has no more legal force than any other voluntary net pay deduction. As a result if the employer chooses to place the VDEA last in a list of deductions and in consequence there is insufficient net pay the employer is not obliged to tell the CMS, that is the responsibility of the employee.

## Determining court order priority

Priority is determined by the type of order, and in:
- England, Wales and Northern Ireland by the date on which it was made
- Scotland by the date on which the order is received

**England and Wales** - Attachment of Earnings Orders for civil debts, i.e. non-priority orders, take precedence over each other by the date of issue (Where an employer receives more than one, application may be made to the court for their consolidation).

**Types of Order** - Attachment of Earnings Order (AEO), Child Support Deduction from Earnings Order (DEO), and Council Tax Attachment of Earnings Order (CTAEO).

Order of precedence:
1. AEO for maintenance or a fine, DEO or CTAEO,
2. AEO for civil debt, DEA or student loan

AEOs for maintenance or fines, DEOs and CTAEOs take precedence over each other by date of issue. Student loans block the operation of a DEA.

CTAEOs may be operated with a maximum of two permitted from the same billing authority, a third order received from the same authority should be returned.

Two orders made on the same date should be taken by date of receipt. Where they have been made by the same court, agency or local authority they should be referred back for clarification (it would be wise to request confirmation of the advice in writing).

**Northern Ireland** - AEOs for civil debts take precedence over each other by the date of issue (where an employer receives more than one, application may be made to the court for their consolidation).

**Types of Order** - Attachment of Earnings Order (AEO) or Child Support Deduction from Earnings Order (DEO). Order of precedence:
- AEOs for maintenance and DEOs
- AEOs for civil debts

**Scotland** - Types of Order - Earnings Arrestment (EA), Current Maintenance Arrestment (CMA), Conjoined Arrestment Order (CAO) and Child Support Deduction from Earnings Order (DEO). Scottish EAs should be treated as priority orders and taken in date of receipt order.

Prior to the 1st April 2008, the order of precedence was:
1. Earnings Arrestment
2. Current Maintenance Arrestment.

Where an EA and/or CMA or CAO were in operation and a DEO was received, the DEO has to be applied first and only then the EA and/or CMA or CAO. No more than one Earnings Arrestment or one Current Maintenance Arrestment could be operated at any one time.

A CAO always cancelled an existing EA or CMA. On receiving an EA or CMA whilst currently operating a CAO, it was necessary to notify the creditor of the court that made the CAO in order that the creditor could apply for his debt to be included.

**Order of precedence from 1st April 2008 (Scotland)** - Whilst the effective date is 1st April, employers were given 7 days grace to make changes so in effect the new rules came into effect in the new tax year. Provisions within The Bankruptcy and Diligence (Scotland) Act 2006 changed significantly the prioritising and processing of AEOs in Scotland. The former priority applied to EAs was replaced by a 'sharing' principle. N.B.: Child Support DEOs, being the only UK wide deduction order, take priority over all three types of Scottish order).

Where more than one Attachment Order is received and there are insufficient earnings to permit full recovery, a five step approach is necessary:
- calculate arrestable earnings in the normal manner. Net earnings after tax, NICs, DEO deductions, pension contributions (including AVCs, but not stakeholder or personal pension plan contributions).
- reduce the arrestable earnings by the amount of protected earnings for the CMA
- add together the deductions specified in the CMA and as taken from the tables for the EA
- calculate the deductions for the EA and CMA as a percentage of the total required deduction
- apply the resulting percentages to the amount of arrestable earnings.

The Act also changed the calculation process when applied to holiday pay. Whereas previously advanced holiday pay was added to arrestable earnings for that week and the deduction applied.

Now it is necessary to calculate:
- the required deduction on arrestable earnings excluding holiday pay as above
- the deduction for each week's holiday pay (treating this as the only arrestable earnings for that week, and then
- add together the two or more deduction amounts and apply the total deduction to the pay for the week when advanced holiday pay is included.

Unlike England and Wales, in Scotland monies from EAs and CMAs are sent direct to the creditor and the creditor has a requirement to provide a copy of the EA or CMA to the debtor as does the Court. At the same time the employer must advise the debtor the date and the amount of the first deduction. Once the first deduction has been calculated the employer must tell the creditor (for EAs and CMAs), and the Sheriff Clerk for conjoined orders:
- the debtor's pay frequency
- the date of the first pay day after receipt of the order
- the arrestable earnings and the amount deducted for the CMA and the EA within a conjoined order

A copy of this schedule must also be sent to the debtor and the process must be repeated on the later of the:
- 6th April following receipt of the order, or
- six months after receipt of the order
and, then at the start of each tax year until the order is discharged.

Should the debtor leave employment, the Sheriff Clerk must be notified of the name and address of the employee's new employer. Failing to do so results in an employer being liable to pay the creditor (as a penalty) twice the deduction that might have been taken on the next pay day had the debtor remained in that employment.

# AUTO-ENROLMENT

Since October 2012, employers have been auto-enrolling eligible jobholders (employees aged 22 or over and up to state pension age, earning over the earnings trigger in a pay reference period) into a qualifying pension scheme and applying a minimum level of employer and employee contributions.

Until February 2018 this was a phased implementation. Since October 2017 new employers are immediately responsible for auto enrolling employees. AE is business as usual and all employers must comply with the rules.

Upon being auto enrolled by their employers, employees have the option to:
- opt-out within a one month window that begins when the auto-enrolment notice is provided to the employee, which must be within  six weeks of the auto-enrolment date, and receive a full refund of employee contributions deducted since auto-enrolment (the employer too will receive a full refund)
- opt-in voluntarily after having been notified of that within one month of having been assessed by the employer as being:
  o a non-eligible jobholder:
    ▪ aged 16 to 74 with qualifying earnings more than the lower earnings threshold and at or below the earnings trigger in a pay reference period, or

- ▪ age 16 to 21 or state pension age to 74 with qualifying earnings over the earnings trigger in a pay reference period
- o an entitled worker:
  - ▪ aged 16 to 74, and with qualifying earnings at or below the lower earnings threshold in a pay reference period
- • cease pension membership from the next pay reference period if they miss the opt-out window – no refund need be offered.

Employers can delay assessment for auto-enrolment by up to three months for any, or all, workers. During the period, called postponement, employees can voluntarily opt-in and this overrides the postponement.

The employer must re-enrol all eligible jobholders who are not members of a qualifying pension scheme every three years on the anniversary of their staging date (the date they first became liable to begin auto-enrolling). Re-enrolment can take place three months either side of this anniversary if this is preferable to the employer. Postponement cannot be used during re-enrolment.

Since April 2016 employers have been permitted to exclude certain jobholders under certain controlled circumstances. Jobholders under notice to terminate, have Lifetime Allowance protection for pension savings and who have opted out or otherwise left a compliant scheme in the previous 12 months can be excluded from re-enrolment if the employer wishes.

Following their 2017 review the government published their intention to reduce the auto-enrolment requirement to those aged 18 and above and to remove the Qualifying Earnings Band (QEB) Lower level, currently £6,032 for 2018/19. These changes will not take place until the mid-2020s, subject to parliamentary process.

## COMPANY SHARE OPTION PLAN (CSOP)

A discretionary scheme approved by HMRC, where the company operating the scheme selects individuals it wishes to reward. The terms of a CSOP scheme grant to those selected an option at a fixed future date to purchase shares at today's price.

A maximum value of £30,000 of approved options may be offered per participant, and no participant may own more than 25% of the company. Income tax is not chargeable at the time the option is granted or on any increase in the value of shares, provided:

- • the option is exercised at least 3 years and not more than 10 years after the date granted, or if exercised within 3 years it is done so under a provision within the scheme which allows exercise on cessation due to injury, disability, redundancy or retirement after reaching an age specified within the scheme and exercise is within 6 months of that cessation.

For capital gains tax purposes the cost is normally the price paid for the shares.

## CONSTRUCTION INDUSTRY SCHEME (CIS)

First introduced under the Income and Corporation Taxes Act 1988, significant changes were introduced in the 'New' CIS scheme introduced on 6th April 2007.

The scheme sets out the principles to be applied by a contractor, and certain other businesses, for making set deductions from that part of payment that does not represent costs of materials, when making a payment to a subcontractor under any contract related to construction work carried out in the UK.

Workers in the construction industry are engaged either by:

- • a contractor (a business or other concern paying subcontractors for work)
- • a subcontractor (a business that carries out work for a contractor), or are self-employed.

*N.B. A business may be both a contractor and subcontractor. A construction company or building firm may include government departments or local authorities who are referred to as "deemed contractors".*

### Definition of construction

All construction work (to either a permanent or temporary building structure), carried out in the UK, including offshore work within the 12 mile territorial limit, comes within the terms of the scheme, and includes alteration, construction, decoration, demolition, dismantling, site preparation and repair. Within the official guidance (CIS340) there are many examples to clarify these definitions and contractors are advised to consult this, even if it appears obvious that a particular activity is either included in the scheme or not.

## Definition of contractor
Within the terms of the scheme a business or concern is a 'contractor' if its average annual expenditure on construction work, in the three year period ending with its last accounting date, exceeds £1 million. A business or concern 'deemed' a contractor that has not been trading for the whole of the last three years, also qualifies if construction operations for part of that period exceed £3 million. A 'deemed contractor', will continue to be so until its construction expenditure has been less than £1 million in each of three successive years.

Local managers of decentralised premises, for example schools, may be excluded from the scheme where their construction operations are less than £1,000. Those undertaking their own build or repair operations, for example homeowners, are not covered by CIS.

## Registration
All contractors must and all subcontractors should be registered with HMRC, particularly those subcontractors seeking to be paid gross, and before they can receive payments from a contractor.

Subcontractors can apply to be paid either:
*   gross by the contractor (as tax certificate holders pre 04/2007) or
*   under deduction (as registration card holders pre 04/2007).

New subcontractors when first starting work in the construction industry on a self-employed basis should register under CIS. To register, a subcontractor must contact the HMRC CIS Helpline on 0300 200 3210 and comply with all of the identity and business checks required.

Where a subcontractor fails to register with HMRC, or give relevant information to a contractor, the contractor will be advised, on seeking to 'verify' their payment status with HMRC, that the deduction rate from the labour portion of the invoices is 30% (the highest deduction rate). In order to avoid similar punitive deductions the subcontractor should be encouraged to register with HMRC.

Deductions made by the contractor are set against the subcontractor's overall Corporation tax, income tax and any NIC liabilities. It can be recovered from the subcontractor companies PAYE payments. Subcontractors registered under the pre-April 2007 scheme did not need to register again provided they, or their business, had either a:
*   construction tax certificate - CIS5, CIS5(Partner), CIS6, or
*   permanent registration card, CIS4(P), or temporary registration card CIS4(T) with an expiry date of 04/2007 or later

## Verification
A contractor must first ensure that the relationship with the subcontractor is one of self-employment using the Check Employment Status for Tax service (CEST).

Assuming the service confirms that the subcontractor can be treated as self-employed, it is then necessary to check the registration status for CIS and then whether payment should be made gross or under deduction. A subcontractor is required to supply contractors with name, unique taxpayer reference (UTR) and National Insurance Number (if known). Since April 2017 contractors can only 'verify' online (prior to April 2017 online and by telephone) the status of a subcontractor with HMRC before payment is made.

Exceptions to the verification process are outlined at https://www.gov.uk/what-is-the-construction-industry-scheme. Where a subcontractor is 'verified' as registered by HMRC, the contractor will be instructed to either make payments gross or apply the standard rate of deduction from all payments (20% from 6th April 2007). Where a subcontractor is not 'verified' as being registered by HMRC the contractor will be instructed to make a deduction at the higher rate (30%) from all payments. HMRC may also classify a subcontractor as higher rate if it has concerns about that subcontractors previous relationship with HMRC.

HMRC will supply a 'unique' subcontractor's verification number (which is the same for each subcontractor verified at the same time) indicating that the subcontractor has been verified as matching their records and which is for the contractor's use only.

Where a subcontractor cannot be matched, a unique 'unmatched' number will be supplied. Verification numbers must be noted, as they have to be included on the CIS300 monthly return. Further guidance can be found at the webpage above. N.B. When quoting verification numbers all prefix or suffix letters should be included.

Payment of subcontractors must be made in the manner notified by HMRC:
- gross - to subcontractors registered who have been granted gross payment status by HMRC
- under standard rate (20%) deduction to any other registered subcontractor
- under deduction at the higher rate (30%) to 'unmatched' subcontractors.

To qualify for gross payment, a subcontractor business must fulfil each of the following tests:
- Business test - it must be run in the UK through a bank account
- Turnover test - it must have a construction turnover, excluding cost of materials and VAT, of at least £30,000 each year (or more for partnerships and most companies)
- Compliance test - it must have complied with key statutory obligations.

The 'Turnover test comprises two tests based on 'net' turnover in the 12 months before application. Where the net turnover is insufficient in the 12-month period it may still be possible to pass, for details contact HMRC:
- Standard test - a construction turnover of at least £30,000 in the test period
- Alternative - a subcontractor must have a net turnover of at least £100,000 (£200,000 prior to 6 April 2016) in the test period.

Sole trader subcontractors must pass the Standard test. Partnerships must pass the Standard test in respect of each partner, or the Alternative test. Companies - those wholly owned by companies already having gross status do not have to pass the turnover test. All other companies must pass either test. The Standard test being in respect of each director, and if a close company, for each beneficial shareholder

### Payment statement
A contractor must provide a statement of payment to each subcontractor from whom a deduction has been made (whether at the standard or higher rate). Statements must be issued within 14 days of the end of a tax month and may be issued to cover all payments in a tax month or with each payment. In the case of 'unmatched' subcontractors, the 'unmatched' reference must be entered on each statement in order that tax refunds, where due, can be made at a later date. Subcontractors paid gross do not need to be provided with statements. (The payment statement replaced the CIS25 voucher).

### CIS300 Returns
A contractor must make a monthly online CIS300 return, within 14 days of each tax month end i.e. by 19th of the following month, of all payments paid to subcontractors whether gross or under deduction, giving each subcontractor's name, reference number, payments made, deductions withheld, a declaration that the employment status has been considered for all subcontractors and that those needing to be verified have been.

Nil returns are not required, however a contractor wishing to take advantage of this needs to inform HMRC first. A voluntary nil return can be made, where applicable. Late returns will incur penalties which changed from October 2011 (in many cases they will decrease) and the contractor's own gross status, when acting as a subcontractor may be withdrawn.

### Deductions
Where due, are to be made at the rate set by Treasury Order (see above) from payments made for labour, including travel and subsistence expenses, and should not be made against charges for supply of materials, consumable stores, fuel (except for travelling), plant hire, the cost of manufacture or prefabrication of materials used, VAT unless these have not been identified clearly on the sub-contractors invoice. Payments must reach HMRC as cleared funds monthly by the 22nd of the month following deduction for large employers and those paying electronically, or by 19th of the month in all other cases.

Where a contractor's average monthly deductions are less than £1,500, inclusive of all income tax, NIC and other PAYE liabilities, payments may, by arrangement with HMRC, be remitted quarterly. Where a subcontractor does not comply with some aspects of tax legislation in respect of other taxes, HMRC may remove any gross payment status. The contractor will be notified in writing of the change, which is to be applied to future invoices. Prior to April 2016 the compliance test was significantly more onerous.

## Penalties

Failure to comply with the scheme in any material manner may well lead to the imposition of penalties by HMRC as indicated by the following table:

### CIS Penalties until 30th September 2011

| Offence | Penalty |
|---|---|
| Knowingly or recklessly making a false statement or providing a false document when applying for a certificate | Not exceeding £3,000 |
| Unlawful disposal or possession of CIS documents | |
| Failure to inspect a Registration Card | |
| Failure to notify a change in control in the company | Initial penalty not exceeding £300 |
| Failure to produce records | Daily penalties not exceeding £60 per day |
| Submission of a false declaration or documentation | May incur a fine up to £3,000 |
| Failure to submit the monthly return on time | Automatic penalty of £100 for a return of up to 50 subcontractors, and an additional £100 for each additional 50 subcontractors that should be included |

### CIS Penalties for late returns from 1st October 2011

| Offence | Penalty |
|---|---|
| Failure to submit the monthly return on time | £100 |
| Return still outstanding two months after due date | £200 |
| Return still outstanding six months after due date | the greater of 5% of any deductions shown on the outstanding return or £300 |
| Return still outstanding twelve months after due date | • due to 'deliberate and concealed' actions: 100% of any deductions shown on the return or £3,000.<br>• deliberate but not concealed: the greater of 70% of any deductions shown on the return or £1,500.<br>• in all other cases 5% of any deductions shown on the return or £300 |

## Proposed changes

A further review of CIS in 2017 started the process of migrating CIS to a new platform. Other than this HMRC have updated their list of known CIS software providers. At present CIS is not part of the HMRC making tax digital project.

# DATA PROTECTION

The Data Protection Act 1998 was brought into effect from 1 March 2000, completely replacing The Data Protection Act 1984. The Act requires employers to abide by principles relating to the processing of personal data extending protection to cover most paper records (termed as part of a 'relevant filing system') as well as those that are automatically processed by computer.

The Act introduced eight principles by which employers must abide. They are that data should be:
- processed fairly and lawfully and shall not be processed unless certain conditions are met
- obtained only for specified and lawful purposes
- adequate, relevant and not excessive in relation to the purposes for which it is processed
- accurate and up to date
- kept for no longer than necessary
- processed in accordance with the rights granted under the Act
- kept securely, and
- not transferred outside the EEA without adequate data protection.

Following a written request, the Act gives employees the right to:
- be told whether personal data about them is being processed
- be given a description of the data concerned, the purposes for which it is being processed, and the recipients or classes of recipients to whom it is, or may be, disclosed
- have communicated to them 'in an intelligible form' the personal data concerned, and any information available as to the source of the data,
- be informed in certain circumstances of the logic involved in computer decision making.

Employers must comply with a request from an employee for sight of data held on them within the statutory period, which is currently 40 days.

There are some specific exclusions within the Act in relation to the data that must be disclosed, which include:
- confidential references given by the employer for the purposes of education, training and employment.
- personal data processed for the purposes of management forecasting or planning if disclosure would prejudice the conduct of business
- records of the employer's intentions in regard to negotiations with the employee if disclosure would be likely to prejudice negotiations (e.g. pay increase, severance packages etc.)

Employers are able to charge a fee of £10 for supplying the information to the employee.

The Act provides additional requirements in relation to sensitive data - defined as:
- racial or ethnic origin
- political opinions
- religious or similar beliefs
- membership of trade unions
- sexual orientation
- commission, or alleged commission, of an offence.

Employers can only process sensitive data when:
- an employee gives specific consent, or
- it is necessary for exercising or performing any legal rights or obligations connected with employment.

**Transitional periods**
Prior to 23rd October 2001 manual data subject to processing before 1998, was exempt from the data protection principles and certain other aspects of the Act.
The second transitional period was between 24th October 2001 and 23rd October 2007. During this period eligible data which was held before 24th October 1998 was exempt from the first data protection principle (with some exceptions) and the second, third, fourth and fifth principles.

Hence since 23rd October 2007 all computer and paper records within a 'relevant filing' system i.e. arranged in a structured set of information, specific to the individual and readily accessible are covered.

*N.B. A Code of Practice to assist employers in implementing the 1998 Act was made available. This code is now no longer available as a consequence of the new 2018 Act.*

**The Data Protection Act 2018**
Implemented on 25 May 2018 this has been stated by the Information Commissioner's Office as "the biggest change to data protection law for a generation." In practice it is DPA+ with which employers have to comply. Most of the principles applied by payroll processors from previous legislation remain in place.

One of the main changes for employers is that ICO guidance has been elevated from best practice to legislative status and has led a radical shake up of the terminology and format of DPA guidance.

Each data processor has been required to compile a statement of all the processes carried out by the organisation which have personal data implications with details of how that is being carried out and who is responsible for the different stages of that process. For employers who use third parties to process their payrolls this has involved compiling joint statements regarding the approach and attitude towards data protection and processing of personal and sensitive data.

Subject access and rights have changed substantially in that the 40 day deadline for responding to a subject access request, as required by the DPA 1998, is now one calendar month and the charge of £10 towards disclosure has been abolished.

Data subjects, i.e. employees and increasingly external contractors who find themselves on a payroll, have the right, from 25 May 2018, to rectification of any data they consider to be inaccurate.

Whilst data subjects now have the right to restrict processing and gain the right to be forgotten, it is unlikely that such rights will be an issue for payroll and pensions processing. It has been recommended that as part of their statements regarding compliance with the new act employers ought to set out the limits in respect of such rights, or to announce they will comply with such rights but point out the serious financial implications should an employee attempt to exercise these rights.

The act implements in full the general data protection requirements of the EU.

## DEADLINE DATES for 2020/21

| April 6th | 2020/21 tax year commences |
|---|---|
| April 19th | Final date for tax year 2019/20 returns, i.e. final FPS or EPS* |
| May 19th | A final standard FPS or EPS sent after this date will incur a penalty |
| May 31st | P60s to employees (in current employment at 5th April) |
| July 6th | P11D returns due for 2019/20 |
| July 19th | Class 1A NICs due for 2019/20 |
| Sept. 30th | Self-assessment returns for 2019/20 if HMRC calculating liability |
| Oct. 19th | Final date for settlement of 2019/20 PSA liability - Class 1B NICs |
| Oct. 31st | Final date for paper SA returns for 2019/20 to be sent |
| Jan 31st 2020 | SA returns due for 2019/20 if calculating own liability. |

### Periodical Deadline Dates - Monthly
- **19th:** PAYE 'non-electronic' payments due to HMRC, contributions due to Occupational Pension Scheme and Stakeholder Pension Providers (once staging date for auto-enrolment duties takes place 19th moves to 22nd if paying electronically) and deductions to CSA/CMS in respect of DEOs and DWP for DEAs
- **22nd:** PAYE 'electronic' payments due to HMRC for 'large' employers (those with over 250 employees in PAYE scheme) and voluntary payers from smaller schemes.

*N.B. Where the due date falls on a weekend or bank holiday, payment must be cleared by the previous bank working day.*

*From April 2020 a new YTD FPS has been introduced to replace the Earlier Year Update and to allow for corrections to previous years payroll reporting. An EYU is still needed for corrections to tax years up to and including 2017/2018.

**Quarterly**

Employers and Contractors in the Construction Industry whose average monthly payments in respect of PAYE, NICs, subcontractor deductions and student loans are less than £1,500 may remit their payments quarterly, on the following dates:

### Quarterly return dates

| April 19th or 22nd * | Small employers' payments due - quarter ending 5.4.20 |
|---|---|
| May 3rd | P46 (Car)^ returns due quarter ending 5.4.20 |
| July 19th or 22nd* | Small employers' payments due - quarter ending 5.7.20 |
| August 2nd | P46 (Car) returns due - quarter ending 5.7.20 |
| October 19th or 22nd * | Small employers' payments due - quarter ending 5.10.20 |
| November 2nd | P46 (Car) returns due - quarter ending 5.10.20 |
| January 19th or 22nd * | Small employers' payments due - quarter ending 5.1.21 |
| February 2nd | P46 (Car) returns due - quarter ending 5.1.21 |
| April 19th or 22nd * | Small employers' payments due - quarter ending 5.04.21 |
| May 3rd | P46 (Car) returns due - quarter ending 5.4.21 |

* date dependent on payment method chosen (see above)
^ Employers using voluntary payrolling of company cars will not be required to submit the P46(Car)
See also small business section for calculation of £1,500 threshold. Note that presently it is still not clear if the Apprenticeship levy can legitimately be paid quarterly.

### RTI deadlines

| Full Payment Submission (FPS) | On or before date of payment[1] |
|---|---|
| Employer Payment Summary (EPS) | 20th of the current tax month - 19th of the following tax month |
| Final EPS/FPS | 19th April |
| Earlier Year Update (EYU)[2] | 20th April – 19th May (can be sent after 19th May but risks a penalty) |

[1]The FPS can occasionally be sent in later than the date of payment as long as it is received within three days of that date.
[2]The last EYU will be for 2019/20.

## DEATH of an EMPLOYEE

Following the death of an employee the employer must ensure that all payments due, and outstanding, are correctly calculated and remitted to the appropriate payee.

The employer will immediately require details of the date, time and place of death and, at the earliest opportunity, next of kin, executors or administrators. The first responsibility is to ensure that no further payments are made in the name, or to the account of the deceased employee. Any outstanding payment will normally be paid to either:

- the Executor(s) of the employee's estate if there is a will, or
- the Administrator(s) of the employee's estate if there is no will.

Payments are usually made by cheque to facilitate immediate release of any outstanding pay once a third party's entitlement has been established.

In circumstances where death occurs after payment, but before the end of the pay period, an employer should establish whether or not to recover any part of that payment which relates to the period following death. Technically an overpayment has occurred. Prior to April 2006 this could be resolved by making any balance tax-free paid as an ex-gratia payment but HMRC amended the rules in this regard from that date (see below). Any policy will need to provide a clear guideline about whether it is appropriate to attempt to recover any overpayment.

The following principles should be applied to any payments currently being, or recently, processed:

### Income Tax
Employment ends with the death of the employee so a P45 needs to be issued. All earnings paid after death and within the same tax year, but before a leaving date has been sent to HMRC, are taxed using the deceased's final tax code. The P45 is sent to HMRC only and not sent to the persons executor or representative. A summary of the final pay and tax position should be sent to this person on a standard letter.

Payments made after the submission of a leaving date or in a subsequent tax year are taxed at code 0T on a non-cumulative basis and details recorded on a new payroll record in the name of the deceased employee.

Any tax rebates being withheld due to industrial action (strike) become payable.
If one partner dies where a joint wage or salary is paid to a husband and wife, the following should apply:
- divide wages between them when calculating both PAYE and NICs
- ask HMRC to supply individual tax codes
- prepare separate payroll records for both husband and wife/civil partners

### National Insurance Contributions
NICs are not due on the earnings of an employee who dies before payment is made, irrespective of the period for which the payment is due.

### Statutory Sick Pay
SSP is due up to and including the date of death, subject to all other entitlement conditions being met.

### Statutory Adoption, Maternity, Paternity and Shared Parental Pay
These are payable to the end of the week (usually Saturday) in which death occurred.

### Lump sum payments on death
Where these are paid from a registered pension scheme where no associated pension is payable they are treated as a taxable unauthorised payment which is paid over by the scheme administrator and reported under self-assessment by the deceased's representative. Where a new scheme has been set up since April 2006 to make ex-gratia payments on death this is to be treated as an Employer-Financed Retirement Benefits Scheme (EFRBS) from which all benefits provided are fully taxable under PAYE.

Payments from an EFRBS can only be tax-free where:
- the scheme rules providing for an ex-gratia to be provided in a non-accidental death situation during service were in place before 6th April 2006
- the employee has been charged tax on the employer contributions which funded the lump sum, or
- the payment is in respect of ill-health or disablement or death as a result of an accident whilst the deceased was an employee
- they are benefits under a group life policy or certain prescribed individual life policies.

Tax is due at 55% (35% for deaths prior to 6th April 2011) on payments made to anybody other than an individual. Other lump sums paid on death attract no NICs liability but are in general subject to tax.

### Employee under notice
Where the employee was under notice, for what was held to be unfair dismissal, the date of death becomes the date of dismissal.

### Payment after death
In all cases there will be someone, or a third party, responsible for the collection of all outstanding monies due, and payment of all debts and distribution of any estate, this is usually, but not always, the next of kin. Documentary evidence supporting a representative's rights must be obtained. It is the employer's responsibility to establish the recipient's right to receive the money.

Where the amount of money held is small and there are no complicating issues, documentary evidence such as birth and/or marriage certificate may be sufficient to support the identity of the next of kin. Where the sum payable is more substantial it would be advisable to seek further evidence of legal entitlement, in the form of a grant of representation (see entry under Probate). Each employer should determine reasonable conditions.

It is difficult to establish exactly how much constitutes a "small" estate. The Administration of Estates (Small Payments) Act 1965 originally set a threshold of £100 to indicate a small estate. This was revised to £500 by statutory instrument and then to £5,000 in 1984. In Scotland the definition of a "small" estate is one where the total value of money and property is no greater than £36,000 (was £30,000) but this is for the purpose of administration. Employers need to take this into consideration and make a reasoned and informed decision whether or not to release outstanding wages to someone who appears to be a beneficiary.

## DEATH of a PENSIONER

On receiving notification of the death of a pensioner the pension payer should submit the leaving date to HMRC and apply PAYE to payments after death following submission of a leaving date and made to the deceased's personal representative using code 0T on a non-cumulative basis on the pensioner's payroll record.

Where such payments are made in a later tax year, and after submission of a leaving date, code 0T (non-cumulative) should be applied and details entered on payroll record in the name of the deceased pensioner.

## DEBT ARRANGEMENT SCHEME (DAS) (Scotland)

Debt Arrangement Schemes, which came into force on 30th December 2004, under the Debt Arrangement and Attachment (Scotland) Act 2002, as amended by The Debt Arrangement Scheme (Scotland) Regulations 2011, seek to place debt management before debt enforcement and to reduce the number of Earnings Arrestments being made. A DAS scheme enables an individual to make planned and orderly payment of multiple debts, out of income in excess of that required for basic subsistence, over a period of time and provides for the:

- attachment of articles kept in dwellings in exceptional cases, and
- abolition of the seizure and public auction of household goods and personal property, in order to settle debts, under the authorisation of a Sheriff.

Payment under a programme may be made principally by three methods:

- Payment Mandate to an employer. This is expected to become the most common option
- direct debit or standing order
- smart card, swipe card, smart key or other type of payment card or key.

### Procedure

The employee (debtor) must supply a completed form, Form 3 (DAS(Scotland) Regs 2011, Reg32(1)) to the employer showing the deduction amount. An amount having been agreed with the advisor as 'such an amount that the debtor can afford to pay on each payday'. Employers will be informed when the deductions are to be amended (Form 4) and when the deduction must cease (Form 5).

Employers must send amounts deducted to the Payment Distributor as soon as is reasonably practical, and may deduct a £1 fee for each deduction (as for a Scottish Earnings or Current Maintenance Arrestment (50p prior to 5th April 2006).

There is currently no definition of 'arrestable earnings', simply an instruction to take the set deduction on each payday.

Neither is there any guidance on what to deduct where the employee:

- receives multiple weeks wages at one time
- has insufficient earnings to make the full deduction, or
- is already having deductions under an English court order (Earnings and Current Maintenance Arrestments are recalled when a DAS is set up but the issue around existing English Orders that the Scottish authorities have no power to recall has yet to be resolved).

**Student Loans**
Income related student loans are not included in debts covered by the scheme

# DEFAULT RETIREMENT AGE

The default retirement age of 65 was abolished from 1st October 2011 unless its retention could be objectively justified for a specific employment after that date. No employee may be issued with a default notice of retirement at age 65 after 5th April 2011. Employers will be able to exclude employees from the provision of contractual benefits that are provided on an insured basis e.g. medical insurance if to do so allows premiums to be maintained for other staff at a cost effective level, but not if such benefits are provided as part of pension scheme benefits e.g. life insurance.

# DEPENDANT LEAVE

The right to time off contained in the Employment Rights Act 1996 came into effect on 15th December 1999, via The Maternity and Parental Leave etc. Regulations 1999 (Maternity and Parental Leave etc. Regulations (Northern Ireland 1999) and provides the right for reasonable unpaid leave in family emergencies involving a dependant - parent, wife, husband, child or someone who lives as part of the family and for whom the employee is the main carer.

**Qualification**
This is a "day one" right so no continuous service with the employer is required. Provision for leave applies:

- to help when a dependant falls ill, has been involved in an accident or has been assaulted
- to make longer term care arrangements for a dependant who is ill or injured
- to deal with an unexpected break down in care arrangements for a dependant when a dependant partner gives birth
- to deal with an unexpected disruption or breakdown in care arrangements involving a dependent child during school hours, or on a school trip.

**Contractual provisions**
The employee remains in employment but need not be paid and will not be bound by any contractual terms except terms relating to good faith and confidentiality, which will also bind the employer. On return to work the employee is entitled to return to his or her former job, or a job with the same or better status, terms and conditions as the former without detriment. Seniority and pension rights built up before taking leave are protected during leave.

For redundancy purposes the leave period is treated as a period of normal employment. Where employers fail to agree a scheme with their employees, the model scheme, as defined by BEIS, will automatically apply. An employer's scheme may be more generous than the model scheme. For the model scheme see 'Maternity Leave and Parental Leave'.

# EARNINGS

Earnings are normally defined as total pay less statutory deductions - income tax, national insurance (employee's contribution), student loan repayments and pension fund contributions. Items defined as earnings include:

- wages, salaries, honoraria, earnings, and stipends, overtime, bonuses, commission, and cash allowances, compensation for loss, or reductions in, the work force, Statutory Sick Pay and pensions or annuities in respect of past service.

Some items not defined as earnings include:

- advances of pay - include in gross pay in subsequent pay calculation
- Disablement or Disability Allowance or pension
- expenses reimbursed
- Guaranteed Minimum Pension (or the GMP element of a pension)
- payment for service in the armed forces
- payments by a public department of a foreign country (including Northern Ireland)
- Statutory maternity pay, statutory adoption pay, statutory paternity pay N.B. however these are included in qualifying earnings for auto-enrolment purposes
- State benefits or pensions.

## ELECTRONIC PAYMENT of PAYE

Since tax year 2005/2006, employers with 250 or more employees in a PAYE scheme have been required to pay their monthly remittances to HMRC electronically in full, and on time, or risk incurring a surcharge. From tax year 2010/11, whilst only large employers continued to pay electronically, a requirement was introduced for all PAYE schemes to pay their monthly or quarterly remittances in full and on time or face a surcharge at year end. Surcharge are levied for any remittances that are not paid in full and on time after one un-penalised default.

The surcharge is calculated as follows:
- 1-3 defaults 1% of the total of the defaults
- 4-6 defaults 2% of the total of the defaults
- 7-9 defaults 3% of the total of the defaults
- 10 or more defaults 4% of the total of the defaults, plus
- tax unpaid after 6 months - additional 5% of unpaid tax
- tax unpaid after 12 months - further 5% of unpaid tax.

From tax year 2010/11 schemes had to make an assessment on 31st October each year whether they will be classed as' large' for the following tax year, HMRC ceased to inform them by letter. Monthly remittances are classed as tax, NICs, construction industry and student loan deductions and now includes the apprenticeship levy.

Payments of Class 1A and Class 1B NICs are not included in the requirement to pay electronically but can be paid in this way if the employer chooses. The due date for cleared payments made electronically is the 22nd of the month, or the last working day before the 22nd if this falls at a weekend, public or Bank Holiday.

Any employer can take advantage of this extended date if they choose to pay electronically. Cheque and cash payments still have a due date of 19th of the month.

An employer whose cheque is cleared by 19th of the month will not incur a penalty even though he has not paid electronically.

Approved payment channels are:
- BACS Direct Credit and Direct Debit (introduced January 2009)
- Bank or Building Society Internet or Telephone Banking Service
- Billpay (Debit Card over the Internet, personal cards cannot be used)
- Credit card (introduced January 2009, personal cards cannot be used)
- Faster Payments (introduced December 2011)
- CHAPS and Paymaster
- Bank Giro but only for employers who receive a payment booklet.

Further details on electronic payment can be found on the HMRC website at https://www.gov.uk/pay-paye-tax#3 . From April 2015 the current late payment surcharge was replaced with an automated in-year late payment penalty. In addition, HMRC introduced an on-line appeals process for employers who do not agree with the penalty notice issued.

## EMPLOYMENT EQUALITY (AGE) REGULATIONS 2006

These regulations came into effect on 1st October 2006 and prohibit discrimination in employment and vocational training on grounds of age. Parallel changes were reflected to statutory adoption, maternity, paternity, shared parental and sick pay under amendments to the Social Security & Benefits Act 1992. The introduction of the regulations requires that employers make no:
- reference to age as a condition of employment
- requirement for a person to be 16 or over to be an employee – by redefinition of the term 'employee'
- exclusion from entitlement to SSP for a person over the aged 65 or over, whilst all other qualifying conditions for statutory payments remain (qualifying and entitlement periods).

The regulations also:
- make it a requirement to pay apprentices aged 19 or over, or in their second year of an apprenticeship, the National Minimum Wage (an under 19 rate was introduced from October 2010)

- removed the option to pay the development rate of the NMW to those in receipt of accredited training in their first six months of employment
- removed the upper and lower age limits in respect of statutory redundancy pay and the tapering of entitlement post age 64.

These regulations have now been subsumed into the Equality Act 2010.

## EMPLOYEE SHAREHOLDER STATUS

Introduced in 2013 to increase employees' involvement in the performance of their business, employee shareholders have different employment rights to other employees. The employer offers at least £2,000 (there is no upper limit) worth of shares in their company to those who agree to be an employee shareholder. There is no income tax or national insurance contribution on the first £2,000 worth of employee shareholder shares unless the person already has 25 per cent or more voting rights in the company when they are excluded from this relief.

As a result of accepting employee shareholder status the individual gives up certain employment rights:
- unfair dismissal rights (apart from the automatically unfair reasons, where dismissal is based on discriminatory grounds and in relation to health and safety)
- rights to statutory redundancy pay
- the statutory right to request flexible working except in the 2 week period after a return from parental leave
- the statutory right to request time off to train

In the Autumn Statement of 2016 the government decided to end all tax benefits of an ESS scheme with effect from 1st December 2016, though 2nd December 2016 will apply where relevant independent financial advice was given before the statement. ESS will be abolished completely when legislation is passed to do so.

## SUPPLIER RECOGNITION SCHEME

HMRC replaced its two payroll software standards that accredit payroll software as fit for purpose, with a slimmed down version from 1st October 2011, a revised scheme for 2015 and a further revised scheme from 2017. Systems which satisfy HMRC requirements are simply referred to as being tested and recognised.

## ENTERPRISE MANAGEMENT INCENTIVE

A company that has assets of up to £30 million can offer Enterprise Management Incentives. Employees are given an option to buy shares worth up to £250,000 (£120,000 up to 16th June 2012) without having to pay income tax or national insurance contributions on the difference between what they pay for the shares when they exercise their option and what they are worth at that point. Capital Gains Tax may be due when the shares are sold.

## EQUAL PAY

Article 141 (formerly Article 119) of the Treaty of Rome requires each European Union (EU) member state to maintain and apply the principle that men and women should receive equal pay for like (equal value) work. The Equal Pay Act 1970 came into effect on 29th December 1975. Equal value principles may be applied to completely different types of employment. Assessment follows a comparability study. A subsequent amendment to the Act has established a principle of equality requiring the elimination of pay inequality between male and female employees in respect of any single term of employment, rather than to overall remuneration packages.

The Small Business, Enterprise and Employment Act 2015 required the Secretary of State to enact regulations under the Equality Act 2010 which requires certain employers to report their gender pay gap. (See Section 1: Gender Pay Gap Reporting).

## EU EXIT

Following the enactment of the European Union Referendum Act 2015, which provided for a referendum covering the UK and Gibraltar to be carried out by December 2017, the UK voted, on 23rd June 2016, to leave the EU. The act provided for a non-binding referendum as it was merely designed to test the views of UK citizens towards the EU, however the result, despite being close, was considered to represent a specific desire of the UK to leave.

Legislation is in place which triggered the process by which the UK will leave, under Article 50 of the Treaty on European Union, in March 2017.

Until the new relationships with the rest of the world have been re-negotiated it is difficult to determine how employers will be affected in terms of employment law and taxation, however the UK government has made it clear that all laws in place at the point at which the UK leaves will simply remain as part of UK law.

Most of the tax law which affects UK employers is unlikely to change as it does not originate from any EU directive, the process by which the EU imposes changes upon member states. The exception to this is VAT which is entirely an EU invention and whose rules are largely created by the EU. There was, however, a UK sales tax which existed prior to VAT and therefore it is not likely that the general rules will change by any great degree.

Employment law is almost entirely determined by EU directive and it is understood that such laws will be subject to review post exit and any which are considered to be inconsistent with the new independent UK may be changed.

Although the UK ceased membership of the EU at 23.00 GMT on 31 January 2020 there remains to be agreed various details.

## EXPENSES and BENEFITS

Expenses and benefits of a non-cash nature must be included in annual P11D returns for all Directors and employees, irrespective of their rate of payment. Prior to April 2016 employees whose total annual remuneration, including the value of benefits, was paid at a rate of less than £8,500 had a form P9D completed. Special calculations were needed to determine if an employee was paid at less than £8,500, see HMRC's guidance at -
http://www.hmrc.gov.uk/manuals/eimanual/eim20101.htm

In general terms an employer may reimburse expenses incurred in the performance of duties without attracting liability for tax or NICs (see also Round Sum Allowances) but unless the employer has a dispensation to this effect even business expenses had to be reported on the P11D. Documentary evidence, mostly in the form of receipts, will be required to support the expenditure. In addition, expenditure must be reasonable. On 31st March 2014 HMRC agreed that scanned images of receipts would be accepted as evidence of cost incurred for both expenses purposes and for any reclaim of input VAT.

Where an employer sells an asset below market value to an employee a tax charge also arises on the extent of the benefit of that undervalue. This principle may be applied to all forms of benefit provision. Where a tax liability is determined that employers do not wish to pass onto the employee then a PAYE Settlement Agreement (PSA) should be considered - see separate section. Where a third party wants to provide a benefit a Taxed Awards Scheme (TAS) will be applicable if they do not want to pass the charge onto the employees concerned - see separate section.

In the summer of 2014 the Office for Tax Simplification (OTS) reported on its review of expenses and benefits in kind and HMRC undertook a number of consultation exercises.

Originally OTS had concluded that developments were unlikely to be completed until 2017, however in the 2015 Autumn Statement the government announced the following developments:
- From April 2015 a statutory "trivial benefits" limit of £50 would apply (however, on 24 March 2015 the government announced that it was not, after all going ahead with a statutory trivial benefits limit from April 2015 and would be deferring this to a future date.) The new provisions were in fact implemented on 6 April 2016.
- From April 2016 the £8,500 threshold for P9D was abolished with two notable exceptions, effectively abolishing the P9D
- From April 2016 a simpler test for compliant reimbursed travel and subsistence expenses was introduced, and also
- From April 2016 voluntary payrolling of benefits in kind received statutory backing for benefits in kind, excepting beneficial loans, accommodation, credit tokens and vouchers. These benefits in kind will be added after further consultation.

# FIT NOTES

From 6th April 2010 the Med3 form, commonly known as the sick note, was replaced with a new form known as the Fit Note. On the new form GPs are required to indicate either that the employee is 'unfit for work' or 'fit for some work now'. For the latter category the GP can then indicate what work the employee might undertake if certain adaptations were made to their hours or role. The employer is not bound by these suggestions and if unable to accommodate them, the employee can use the Fit Note as evidence of incapacity for work.

Where an employee comes in to work on reduced hours such a day is not a day of incapacity for SSP purposes, so SSP cannot be paid. Where an employee is working fewer days, for example a Monday to Friday employee is working Monday and Thursday only, then a PIW will not be formed unless there are four days of incapacity. In this example there are not as the phased return to work interrupts the sickness pattern. There will therefore be no SSP entitlement until a PIW is formed.

In 2018 the government agreed to conduct a consultation exercise on modernising the SSP process so that payments can be made during phased return to work and in June 2019 the Secretary for State for Work and Pensions confirmed that the government would carry out major work to improve the way the SSP system works for employees and employers.

# FIXED TERM WORKERS

The EC Fixed Term Workers Directive was adopted by the UK with effect from 1st October 2002 by virtue of the Fixed Term Employees (Prevention of Less Favourable Treatment) Regulations 2002. Fixed term employees:

- have the right to no less favourable treatment than comparable permanent employees, i.e. those not on fixed-term contracts; (unless such treatment can be justified on objective grounds). The comparator can work for the same employer but in a different establishment.
- have the right to receive statutory payments on the same basis as permanent employees (e.g. SSP, medical suspension)
- cannot waive their statutory right to redundancy payments where their fixed term contract is for a period of two or more years
- have the right to receive, and duty to give, one week's notice

Where the overall package or terms is no less favourable, less favourable treatment in individual terms of the contract may be justified.

The use of successive fixed term contracts is limited to a maximum of four years (unless a longer period is objectively justified or varied by workplace or collective agreement). Employees who were already working under a fixed-term contract on 1 October 2002 and who have continued to work under a series of fixed term contracts since then will be treated as having the necessary four years continuity of employment on 1 October 2006. Their contracts become permanent contracts on that date. A fixed term contract ending when a task is completed, or when a specified event does not happen, will be deemed to have ended.

# FLEXIBLE WORKING

From 6th April 2003, parents with children under 6 years of age, or disabled children under age 18, were given the right to request a flexible working pattern with their employer given a duty to consider their applications seriously. From 6th April 2007, the Flexible Working (Eligibility, Complaints and Remedies) (Amendment) Regulations 2006 (there are different regulations and rules for Northern Ireland) extended the right to request flexible working to those employees with a caring responsibility for someone who has a prescribed relationship with the person that they care for.

From 6th April 2009 the right was extended to those with parental responsibility for a child aged under 16 or a disabled child under 18 in receipt of disability living allowance and from 30 June 2014 to all employees with at least 26 weeks service, regardless of whether they have caring responsibilities and the procedure below was replaced with a simple need for the employer to 'act reasonably'.

Until 30 June 2014 the 'relationship' criterion requires the person to be cared for to be:
- married to, or the partner or civil partner of the employee or a near relative*
- neither of the above, but lives at the same address as the employee of the employee
- 18 or over.

*'Near relative' means parents, parents in-law, adult child, adopted adult child, siblings (including sibling in-laws), uncles, aunts, grandparents and step relatives. At the same time the deadline for parents to make a request to work flexibly was reduced from a 14-day deadline to the day before the child's relevant birthday (i.e. six or eighteen).

Employees making such requests must have 26 weeks' service at the date of the request.

In April 2019 a private members bill was introduced to parliament in order to improve the terms of flexible working but failed to complete its passage through parliament.

## Scope of a request
Eligible employees will be able to request:
- a change to their working hours
- a change to their working times
- to work from home.

Flexible working covers such arrangements as annualised hours, compressed hours, flexi-time, home-working, job-sharing, self-rostering, shift-working, staggered hours and term-time working.

## Eligibility
In order to make a request an individual must until 29th June 2014:
- be an employee
- have parental responsibility, this can include foster parents and same sex couples, for a child under 16, or under 18 in the case of a disabled child.
- have worked with their employer continuously for 26 weeks at the date the application is made
- make the application no later the day before the child's 16th birthday or 18th birthday. Prior to the 1st April 2007 the deadline period was 14 days in the case of a disabled child.
- have, or expect to have, responsibility for the child's upbringing
- be making the application to enable them to care for the child
- not be an agency worker
- not be a member of the armed forces
- not have made another application to work flexibly during the past 12 months.

## Procedure
Prior to 30th June 2014, after the employee made a considered application in writing (limited only one application a year), the employer had to, within 28 days, arrange to meet with the employee to discuss the application in depth, and consider how best it might be accommodated.

Within 14 days after the date of the meeting the employer had to either:
- confirm to the employee the agreed new work pattern and start date (not necessarily in writing; or
- provide clear and reasoned applicable business grounds as to why the application cannot be accepted.

Business grounds for refusal may be that the proposal would:
- be too costly, damaging to customer service, product quality or performance
- not fit into planned structural change in the business or impractical as work cannot be relocated
- not be feasible as no additional recruitment could be undertaken or there is insufficient work during employee's preferred working hours

This process was replaced, on 30 June 2014, with a new requirement that the employer should act reasonably when a formal request for flexible working is made.

## Right of appeal
The employee has the right to appeal their employer's decision within 14 days of it being notified to them. A further meeting must then be arranged within 14 days followed by a final decision to be determined within a further 14 days. The employee has the right to be accompanied at each meeting as defined in the Employment Rights Act 1996.

Remedies at a Tribunal may be a maximum of eight weeks' pay plus an additional two weeks' pay where the right to be accompanied has been denied.

An accepted application will result in a permanent change to the employee's terms and conditions of employment.

# GENDER RECOGNITION ACT

Since 4th April 2005 transsexual people have had the right under the Gender Recognition Act to change their recorded gender and in so doing take on the rights and responsibilities of their newly acquired gender. Employers are required to take action on production of a Full Gender Recognition Certificate. Employees who produce an interim Gender Recognition Certificate should be told that no action in respect of PAYE or NICs will be taken until the Full Certificate is issued.

On receipt of a Full Gender Certificate the employer must amend their records to show the acquired gender, the title the employee has chosen and operate PAYE and NICs reflected by the acquired gender e.g. a transsexual female over state pension age should no longer pay NICs from the date on the certificate. Employers are not required to refund/levy any contributions before the date on the certificate, as that is the responsibility of HMRC.

# GRATUITIES, SERVICE CHARGES, TIPS and TRONCS

In principle PAYE must be applied to all payments made by an employer to an employee including tips. A tip or gratuity is a spontaneous payment offered by a customer notwithstanding the method of payment (cash, cheque or debit card). Where tips or gratuities are paid directly to or left for employees voluntarily and without any involvement of the employer or their representative, PAYE does not apply. The employee however has a responsibility to declare such payments to HMRC.

A Service Charge is an amount added to a bill prior to its presentation to a customer. PAYE (Tax and NICs) must be applied by an employer on mandatory service charges irrespective of the distribution process. A service charge added to a bill, clearly defined as optional and at the customer's discretion is recognised as a voluntary service charge.

Where an employer is directly involved in the administration of the payment of tips or gratuities and where there is a contractual entitlement to a share of such payments, the employer is then responsible for administering PAYE on these amounts, including Class 1 NICs.

## Tronc

A Tronc is a French word meaning 'little box". In practice it is a special arrangement for pooling, distributing and administering tips, gratuities or service charges where such payments made to a group of employees are administered by and paid out to employees, by an employee acting as 'Troncmaster' who has responsibility for operating a separate PAYE scheme for all payments made from the Tronc independent of the employer.

Details of the Troncmaster must be notified to HMRC for schemes that come into existence after 6th April 2004 so that a PAYE scheme can be set up in their name. The employer can act as the Troncmaster's payroll agent but the records for each scheme must be kept separate.

The Troncmaster makes deductions on account of tax from the payments out of the Tronc and submits RTI returns in respect of these payments. Even if payments are administered by the Troncmaster (e.g. the headwaiter), the responsibility for ensuring that NICs are calculated, deducted and recorded where due rests with the employer.

The employer must obtain details from the Troncmaster of all payments made and:
- record the amounts and dates of all payments
- include payments in gross pay when calculating NICs if they are due, and
- include all payments on employees' payroll records.

The Troncmaster must record separately the amounts on which NICs both 'are' and 'are not' payable.

If an employer is not satisfied with the administration of the scheme then he would be advised to:
- control the sharing out of payments
- include the formula for sharing out payments in employment contracts.

A single reference in the contract to the participation in a Tronc does not make payments contractual. Where a Troncmaster totally controls the allocation of tips but the employer pays them, then PAYE on them is operated by the Troncmaster. Where the employer has a role in deciding the allocation of the tips, perhaps sets the distribution formula, then PAYE on them must be operated by the employer. Tips given to employees directly by the customer, through a Tronc or paid by an employer through the payroll do not count towards National Minimum Wage. The law was changed to enforce this from October 2009.

In August 2015 BIS issued a call for evidence (a precursor to a full public consultation exercise) on the use of tips and service charges. The consultation was issued in 2016 but transferred to the responsibility of BEIS. In 2019, for a second year running there continued to be no response to the exercise with the gov.uk website continuing to state "We are analysing your feedback".

The Queen's speech at the state opening of parliament on 14 October 2019, however, indicated that one of the major bills to be put to parliament in the current period is the Employment (Allocation of Tips) Bill and hence it is clear that major changes will come into force during 2020.

## HOLIDAYS – STATUTORY ANNUAL ENTITLEMENT

All employees (and workers including agency workers) are entitled to a statutory minimum paid holiday entitlement. Self-employed workers have no such entitlement. Prior to the 1st October 2007, the minimum annual leave entitlement required by the EU Working Time Directive was 20 days, which could include bank and public holidays. At that time entitlement was pro-rated to a five-day working week (6 day workers receiving 24 days). Following consultation the government increased the minimum entitlement to 24 days from the 1st October 2007, at the same time capping the minimum entitlement irrespective of the number of days in the employee's working week.

There are 8 public holidays per year in England and Wales (ten in Northern Ireland, and nine in Scotland). However, The annual holiday entitlement is capped at 28 days (5.6 weeks) throughout the United Kingdom. The public holidays are not an additional right and they may be included in the annual minimum entitlement (8 public holidays + 20 additional days annual leave = 28 days minimum from 1st April 2009).

The necessary amendments are contained in The Working Time (Amendment) Regulations 2007.

### Statutory Annual Minimum Holiday Entitlement

| Date from | Weeks p.a. | Days p.a. |
|---|---|---|
| Pre October 2007 | 4.0 | 20 |
| 01.10.2007 | 4.8 | 24 |
| 01.04.2009 | 5.6 | 28 |

Where a leave year starts on a day other than on the date entitlement changes in the table above, entitlement shall be calculated pro-rata. An online calculator is provided by on the 'GOV' website at https://www.gov.uk/calculate-your-holiday-entitlement.

Since 1st October 2007 employers are no longer required to round up entitlement to the nearest full day in the first year of employment, but may do so on an optional basis if they so desire. However, rounding down is not an option. The amendment regulations leave unchanged the accrual rate for the first year of employment.

Employers may still limit the amount of holiday that can be taken at any point during an employee's first year of employment. Employees are entitled to 1/12th of their annual accrual for each full month worked and the result is rounded up to the nearest full or half day. This does not result in additional entitlement; it is merely an administrative tool to prevent employees from taking holiday before it is earned.

Since October 2007 unused holiday over and above the 20 days may be carried forward into the next holiday year as long as the contract allows. Of course any contractual holiday over and above the 28 days (5.6 weeks) may also be carried forward subject to contractual provisions.

### Holiday Pay - Long-term Sickness

Prior to 6th January 2009 it was generally understood that statutory annual holiday pay did not accrue during periods of long-term sickness. The Working Time Regulations 1998 set the principle that workers who do not use their full statutory entitlement of 4 weeks (20 days) in the current year cannot carry it forward.

In the case of Stringer v HMRC (formally Ainsworth v HMRC), following an appeal to the House of Lords and a referral to the European Court of Justice (ECJ), the ECJ ruled that the four weeks (20 days) statutory minimum holiday entitlement under The Working Time Directive should accrue throughout the duration of sick leave, and may be taken on return to work, carried over, or be paid in full where employment terminates or if there is insufficient time left in the leave year to take the accrued holiday after return from sickness.

This ruling conflicts with the UK's existing Working Time regulations and the UK government has yet to amend the regulations. Public sector employers however are required to abide by the ECJ ruling immediately even though the regulations have not been amended, as ECJ rulings supersede national legislation for public authorities.

A consultation (Modern Workplaces) was published in May 2011 that outlined plans to allow employees to carry forward unused holiday up to the 4 week EU statutory maximum if they have insufficient time to take their entitlement post-sickness before the holiday year ends – entitlement over and above the 4 weeks could be forfeited. Employers may also be able to buy out entitlement over and above the 4 weeks or insist on carry over. BEIS have still not indicated when the proposals will be implemented and the published impact assessments on the proposals merely indicate the likely costs of the preferred option.

In the meantime however they have made a statement on the Gov.uk website - see https://www.gov.uk/taking-sick-leave that indicates payment of SSP can go towards discharging an employer's liability to holiday pay, and equally that SSP need not be paid in addition to holiday pay should the employer choose to make payment of the accrued leave at the end of the holiday year when the employee is still off sick.

Since 2012 there have been a series of ET, EAT and EU employment cases involved in determining the correct method of calculating holiday pay for employees whose pay is made up of non-recurring or intermittent elements of pay.

Once again, by the time of publication the position is by no means final, but that pay must include non-guaranteed overtime (overtime which employers does not have to offer, but when they do the employee is obliged to work) and intrinsically linked payments, such as commissions. This still applies only to the 4 weeks entitlement conferred by the working time directive. In March 2017 the Court of Appeal refused British Gas's application for appeal against the decision made in the Lock case by the EAT. More decisions are awaited from further cases in 2019.

In addition, from April 2020 the reference period for calculating holiday increases to 52 weeks (currently 12 weeks). The Employment Rights (Employment Particulars and Paid Annual Leave) (Amendment) Regulations 2018 have made this change to ensure that seasonal and other similar workers can receive their full entitlement to leave and pay.

In a ruling in the Brazel v Harpur Trust Court of Appeal case, the court ruled that a music teacher who had a zero hours contract and no holiday period work was a "part year" worker and as such her holiday had to be calculated in a different manner to the one normally applied to "term time" workers, where the standard calculation is holiday based on an equivalent of 12.07% of annual hours worked. The teacher's new calculation is a 12 week average of her actual hours worked, which works out as an equivalent of 17.5% of annual pay.

Whilst not being in any way unique, this is nevertheless uncommon; however the ACAS guidance on the calculation requirements has been updated since the court's decision was made.

## INCENTIVE SCHEMES

### Cyclists' breakfasts
An exemption, abolished from 6th April 2013, that allowed employers to provide a breakfast tax and NICs free to employees cycling to work on designated 'cycle to work' days to encourage participation in the scheme.

### Golden Hellos/Carrots/Parachutes
Payments made to an individual as an incentive or inducement to commence employment or leave employment are fully taxable and subject to National Insurance contributions (NICs).

Where paid before commencement of employment they should be included in the first available payroll run following commencement.

**Golden Handcuffs**
Incentive, bonus payments or share issues linked with an agreement tying the employee into a contract of employment of a fixed minimum period, usually a number of years.

**Honoraria**
Payments made to an office holder by the organisation with which that office is held, or paid voluntarily by an employer to an employee who holds an office with a separate organisation (e.g. a company or works sports club) are subject to PAYE (Tax and Class 1 NICs).

**Profit Related Pay (PRP)**
A PRP scheme had to be approved by HMRC, and was then subject to certain tax concessions. Tax relief was calculated for profit periods, which may or may not have been tax years, on the whole of the employees pay up to the lower of 20% of total pay for the period or the table rate. The tax concessions ceased on 1st January 2000.

### Profit Related Pay Earnings Maxima

| Date from | Maximum Limit £ |
|---|---|
| pre 01.04.1989 | 3,000 |
| 01.04.1989 | 4,000 |
| 01.01.1998 | 2,000 |
| 01.01.1999 | 1,000 |
| 01.01.2000 | Nil |

## INDEX LINKED PAY INCREASES

On 10th December 2003 the Government revised the formula for monitoring inflation by transferring the former linkage with the Retail Prices Index (RPI) to the Consumer Prices Index (CPI), previously published as the Harmonised Index of Consumer Prices (HICP). CPI is the measure adopted by the Government for its UK inflation target. In the June 2010 Budget, the Chancellor announced the Government's intention to also use the CPI for the price indexation of benefits, tax credits and public sector pensions from April 2011. The state pension moved to a CPI linked increase from April 2012.

In his budget speech on 11th March 2020 the Chancellor referred to the United Kingdom proposals to address shortcomings in the Retail Price Index. A consultation exercise is underway and measures are not expected to be implemented for some time.

### Monthly Consumer Prices Index

| | 2009 | 2010 | 2011 | 2012 | 2013 | 2014 | 2015 | 2016 | 2017 | 2018 | 2019 |
|---|---|---|---|---|---|---|---|---|---|---|---|
| Jan | 108.7 | 112.4 | 116.9 | 121.1 | 124.4 | 126.7 | 127.1 | 99.5 | 101.8 | 104.5 | 106.3 |
| Feb | 109.6 | 112.9 | 117.8 | 121.8 | 125.2 | 127.4 | 127.4 | 99.8 | 102.4 | 104.9 | 106.8 |
| Mar | 109.8 | 113.5 | 118.1 | 122.2 | 125.6 | 127.7 | 127.7 | 100.2 | 102.7 | 105.1 | 107.0 |
| Apr | 110.1 | 114.2 | 119.3 | 122.9 | 125.9 | 128.1 | 128.0 | 100.2 | 103.2 | 105.5 | 107.6 |
| May | 110.7 | 114.4 | 119.5 | 122.8 | 126.1 | 128.0 | 128.1 | 100.4 | 103.5 | 105.9 | 107.9 |
| Jun | 111.0 | 114.6 | 119.4 | 122.3 | 125.9 | 128.3 | 128.3 | 100.6 | 103.5 | 105.9 | 107.9 |
| Jul | 110.9 | 114.3 | 119.4 | 122.5 | 125.8 | 127.8 | 127.9 | 100.6 | 103.5 | 105.9 | 107.9 |
| Aug | 111.4 | 114.9 | 120.1 | 123.1 | 126.4 | 128.3 | 128.3 | 100.9 | 104.0 | 106.5 | 108.4 |
| Sep | 111.5 | 114.9 | 120.9 | 123.5 | 126.8 | 128.4 | 128.3 | 101.1 | 104.3 | 106.6 | 108.5 |
| Oct | 111.7 | 115.2 | 121.0 | 124.2 | 126.9 | 128.5 | 128.4 | 101.2 | 104.4 | 106.7 | 108.3 |
| Nov | 112.0 | 115.6 | 121.2 | 124.4 | 127.0 | 128.2 | 128.3 | 101.4 | 104.7 | 106.9 | 108.5 |
| Dec | 112.6 | 116.8 | 121.7 | 125.0 | 127.5 | 128.2 | 128.4 | 102.2 | 105.0 | 107.1 | 108.5 |

(The table above now follows the official ONS format after the indices were reset at 100 in 2015 and includes other housing costs)

## Consumer Prices Index: percentage change over 12 months

|      | 2009 | 2010 | 2011 | 2012 | 2013 | 2014 | 2015 | 2016 | 2017 | 2018 | 2019 |
|------|------|------|------|------|------|------|------|------|------|------|------|
| Jan  | 3.0  | 3.0  | 3.8  | 3.6  | 2.7  | 1.9  | 0.4  | 0.3  | 1.8  | 2.7  | 1.8  |
| Feb  | 3.2  | 3.2  | 4.4  | 3.4  | 2.8  | 1.7  | 0.0  | 0.3  | 2.3  | 2.5  | 1.9  |
| Mar  | 2.9  | 2.9  | 4.0  | 3.5  | 2.8  | 1.6  | 0.0  | 0.5  | 2.3  | 2.4  | 1.9  |
| Apr  | 3.0  | 3.0  | 4.5  | 3.0  | 2.4  | 1.8  | -0.1 | 0.3  | 2.7  | 2.3  | 2.1  |
| May  | 2.2  | 2.2  | 4.5  | 2.8  | 2.7  | 1.5  | 0.1  | 0.3  | 2.9  | 2.4  | 2.0  |
| Jun  | 1.8  | 1.8  | 4.2  | 2.4  | 2.9  | 1.9  | 0.0  | 0.5  | 2.6  | 2.4  | 2.0  |
| Jul  | 1.8  | 1.8  | 4.4  | 2.6  | 2.8  | 1.6  | 0.1  | 0.6  | 2.6  | 2.4  | 2.1  |
| Aug  | 1.6  | 1.6  | 4.5  | 2.5  | 2.7  | 1.5  | 0.0  | 0.6  | 2.9  | 2.5  | 1.7  |
| Sep  | 1.1  | 1.1  | 5.2  | 2.2  | 2.2  | 1.2  | -0.1 | 1.0  | 3.0  | 2.3  | 1.7  |
| Oct  | 1.5  | 1.5  | 5.0  | 2.7  | 2.7  | 1.3  | -0.1 | 0.9  | 3.0  | 2.3  | 1.5  |
| Nov  | 1.9  | 1.9  | 4.8  | 2.7  | 2.7  | 1.0  | 0.1  | 1.2  | 3.1  | 2.2  | 1.5  |
| Dec  | 2.9  | 2.9  | 1.2  | 2.7  | 2.7  | 0.5  | 0.2  | 1.6  | 3.0  | 2.1  | 1.3  |

## INDUSTRIAL ACTION

Under common law, an employee earns wages by being ready and willing to do work. It therefore follows that there is no entitlement to pay when an employee is not available due to industrial action/trade dispute (strike). Earnings already due are not affected by subsequent industrial action and should be paid in the normal way. The employer is not obliged to make special arrangements for striking employees to receive payment of wages or salary. Any income tax refunds due to employees must be withheld for as long as they are involved in a trade dispute.

### Strike Pay Calculation

When calculating the amount of deduction that should be made for absence in respect of a strike, employers must, when determining the daily rate of pay, include in the calculation formula payment days classified as a public holiday or annual leave. In the case of Cooper v Isle of Wight College it was determined that deduction should be made using the calculator of 1/260th for each day, not 1/228th (working days).

## INTERNATIONAL STUDENTS

International students who are not nationals of a European Economic Area (EEA) Country may enter the UK to study under Tier 4 of the Points-Based system of Migration introduced in March 2009. The higher education institution must also sponsor them. Whether they are allowed to work whilst in the UK and for how many hours per week will depend on the nature of their leave to remain in the UK and will be shown on their Identity card (also known as a Biometric Residence Permit).

## ITEMISED STATEMENT OF PAY

An employee (see pension payments below) has the right under the Employment Rights Act 1996 (S8), at or before the time of payment, to receive from the employer a written and itemised statement of pay. It is generally accepted that electronic pay statements constitute a written and itemised statement of pay in law. All employers should have, by now, reviewed their electronic statements in the light of the Data Protection Act 2018.

The statement should include:
- the gross amount of wage or salary
- the amounts and details of each fixed and variable deduction
- the net amount of wage or salary due
- the amount of any student loan recovery.

When a net payment is made in multiple and differing ways, details of the amount and pay method in each case should be included. Where an employee has been provided with a detailed schedule of fixed deductions, there is no need for the employer to itemise those elements on every pay statement. Details must however be provided at least once annually, and any changes must be advised.

Since April 2019 the right to an itemised statement to pay has been extended to all "workers". In addition, employers are also now required to include hours of work information on pay statements.

**Pension payments**
Persons in receipt of a pension are not employees in law and hence have no lawful entitlement to an itemised pay statement. It is only necessary to provide initial details of the make-up and amount of any pension payment and notice of any subsequent change or amendment. It is not a legal requirement to provide a regular statement with each payment although it is regarded as good practice to do so. Many pension providers provide statements to support the first and the final annual payment; together with additional statements should there be any significant variation in net pay. This is not affected by the extension to the right to pay statements.

Pension recipients are still entitled to the annual pay and tax statement, the P60, as this is a requirement of tax law rather than employment law.

## JURY SERVICE

An employer is not required to pay an employee for time taken off to complete jury service, other than where provision to do so is included in the employee's terms and conditions of employment. Since 6th April 2005 the Employment Relations Act 2004 makes dismissal for attending jury service automatically unfair.

The court will make payment to jurors for expenses and for loss of earnings (which will require verification by the employer before attendance at court). The court applies a scale rate to such payments as shown below. Many employers limit maximum deductions in line with the official financial loss rates; thereby protecting the level of the employee's net earnings.

Payments for loss of earnings are regarded as loss of net pay; they do not count as earnings, any top-up or deduction of pay made as a result of the juror's allowance is made from/to net pay not gross pay.

New rates for Scottish jurors were introduced from 10th January 2011 under The Jurors' Allowances (Scotland) Regulations 2010, plus for the first time a rate for childcare costs

**Rates of financial loss allowance - Maximum Daily Rates of Financial Loss**
**Justices Courts from 1st May 2000**

|  | Up to 4 hours | | | 4 Hours and above | | |
|---|---|---|---|---|---|---|
|  | 1 – 10 Days | 11 - 200 days | Over 200 days | 1 – 10 Days | 11 - 200 days | Over 200 days |
| Date from | £ | £ | £ | £ | £ | £ |
| 01.05.2000 | 25.34 | 50.68 |  | 50.68 | 101.36 |  |
| 04.06.2001 | 25.85 | 51.68 |  | 51.68 | 103.39 |  |
| 01.04.2002 | 26.32 | 52.64 |  | 52.64 | 105.28 |  |
| 01.04.2003 | 26.85 | 53.69 |  | 53.68 | 107.39 |  |
| 01.04.2004 | 27.60 | 55.19 |  | 55.19 | 110.40 |  |

**Rates of financial loss allowance - Maximum Daily Rates of Financial Loss Justices Courts from 1st May 2000** (continued)

| 01.04.2005 | 28.48 | 56.76 | 100.00 | 56.76 | 113.93 | 200.00 |
|---|---|---|---|---|---|---|
| 01.08.2006 | 29.19 | 58.38 | 102.50 | 58.38 | 116.78 | 205.00 |
| 02.07.2007 | 29.98 | 59.96 | 105.27 | 59.96 | 119.93 | 210.54 |
| 02.06.2008 | 30.64 | 61.28 | 107.59 | 61.28 | 122.57 | 215.17 |
| 01.06.2009 | 31.56 | 63.12 | 110.82 | 63.12 | 126.25 | 221.63 |
| 01.06.2010 | 32.47 | 64.95 | 114.03 | 64.95 | 129.91 | 228.06 |

*N.B.: The Coroners Allowances, Fees and Expenses Regulations 2013 have amended the financial loss allowance for jurors and ordinary witnesses to be the same as for Justices courts.*
*Allowances in Northern Ireland do not provide for any additional allowance for service of over 200 days. Apart from that difference they are the same as the amounts above.*

**Rates of financial loss allowance - Maximum Daily Rates of Financial Loss**

**The Jurors' Allowances (Scotland) Regulations 2010 from 10th January 2011**

| Allowance | Rate |
|---|---|
| Financial loss allowance – first 5 days of service: up to 4 hours | £32.47 |
| Financial loss allowance – first 5 days of service: more than 4 hours | £64.95 |
| Financial loss allowance – 6th to 100th day of service | £129.91 |
| Financial loss allowance – 101st day of service onwards | £230 |
| Adult dependant carer allowance (registered carer) | £6 per hour |
| Adult dependant carer allowance (non-registered carer) | £1 per hour |

**Coroners' Courts – from 1st July 1998**

| | Up to 4 hours | | 4 Hours and above | |
|---|---|---|---|---|
| | First 10 days | Day 11 onwards | First 10 days | Day 11 onwards |
| Date from | £ | £ | £ | £ |
| 01.07.1998 | 26.05 | 52.10 | 52.10 | 104.20 |
| 01.01.2000 | 27.25 | 54.40 | 54.40 | 104.80 |
| 01.01.2004 | 27.60 | 55.19 | 55.19 | 110.40 |
| 01.10.2008 | 32.95 | 65.60 | 65.80 | 131.20 |
| 25.07.2013 | 32.47 | 64.95 | 64.95 | 129.91 |

*Note: The Coroners Allowances, Fees and Expenses Regulations 2013 have amended the financial loss allowance for jurors and ordinary witnesses to be the same as for Justices courts.*

**Magistrates' allowances – from 10th May 2009**

| Date from | Half day | Full day |
|-----------|----------|----------|
| 10.05.2009 | £46.63 | £93.27 |
| 01.05.2010 | £46.63 | £93.27 |

*Note: A self-employed magistrate is entitled to £116.58 for a full day, £58.29 for a half day*

# KEY HISTORICAL DATES

**1451** First taxing of income in Florence

**1680** United Kingdom gold standard introduced - value of guinea linked to gold

**1799** Income tax first introduced as a temporary measure

**1800** First Truck Act gives the right of manual workers to be paid in cash

**1803** Division of Income Tax into five schedules

**1842** Income tax reintroduced (for third time)

**1909** State Pensions commenced in the United Kingdom

**1911** National Health Service introduced on the 5th July

**1912** National Insurance introduced

**1944** Pay As You Earn commences

**1946** Social Security Welfare State instituted

**1948** European Economic Community formed

**1961** Graduated Pension Scheme introduced with earnings-related contributions and benefits

**1965** Corporation Tax & Capital Gains Tax introduced

**1971** Decimal currency introduced on the 15th February

**1975** National Insurance Stamps abolished - end of card exchanges

Graduated Pension Scheme ends

**1978** State Earnings Related Pension Scheme introduced and contracting out for approved pension schemes

**1980** The Association of Payroll and Pensions Administrators (APSA) established

**1983** Statutory Sick Pay introduced

**1984** Data Protection Act becomes law

**1985** Employers' Upper Earnings Limit removed for NICs

The British Payroll Managers Association (BPMA) established

**1986** The Truck Acts repealed with the introduction of the Wages Act

**1987** Statutory Maternity Pay introduced

Payroll Giving introduced

**1988** Tax legislation consolidated by the Income and Corporation Taxes Act

**1989** Community Charge introduced in Scotland

**1990** Community Charge extended to England and Wales

Fixed Profit Car Scheme introduced

Husbands and wives taxed separately

Statutory Sick Pay funding transferred to the Employer

**1992** 20% tax band introduced (within standard rate band)

**1993** Income Tax (Sub Contractors in the Construction Industry) regulations

Income Tax (Employers) Regulations (PAYE regulations)

Trades Union Reform and Employment Rights Act (TURERA)

**1996** Introduction of Self-Assessment

Asylum & Immigration Act and Employment Rights Act become law

**1998** Institute of Payroll and Pensions Management (IPPM) formed

Data Protection Act amended

**1999** The Compact Payroll Reference Book first published

National Minimum Wage Act and Employment Relations Act become law

Working Time Directive adopted

**2000** Metric weights and measures introduced on 1st January by adoption of European directive

Introduction of WFTC & DPTC, Tax Credits to be paid through payroll to replace Family Credit

**2001** Euro currency became legal tender on 1st January in all EU member states except Denmark, Great Britain and Sweden

**2002** Fixed Term Employees (Prevention of less favourable treatment) Regulations introduced

State Second Pension (S2P) replaced the State Earnings Related Pension Scheme (SERPS)

**2003** Statutory Adoption & Statutory Paternity, Pay & Leave introduced

1% Employers' NI charge introduced on earnings above Upper Earnings Limit

Flexible Working Regulations introduced

New Tax Credit regime for payment via employer payrolls

New CSA regime and second type of DEO

**2004** Debt Arrangement schemes introduced

Mandatory Electronic Payment for large employers

**2005** Customs & Excise merger with Inland Revenue to form HM Revenue and Customs (HMRC)

Schedule 5 Fines AEOs introduced

Mandatory online filing of year end returns for large employers

Civil Partnership Act 2004 (in force 5th December 2005)

**2006** Employment Equality (Age) Regulations 2006 (in force 1st October 2006)

Work and Families Act 2006 becomes law - SMP/SAP increased

Mandatory online filing of year end returns for medium as well as large employers

**2007** New Construction Industry Scheme introduced

Additional 4 days annual holiday introduced (1.10.07)

**2008** Statutory Sick Pay Review proposals implemented October

New A4 P45 introduced

**2009** Harmonisation of higher rate Income Tax threshold and NICs UEL

Upper Accrual Point earnings threshold introduced for S2P accrual

In-year online filing for schemes with 50 or more employees

HMRC new penalty regime for incorrect tax returns and new compliance checks

P46 (Pen) and P46(Expat) introduced

Special and General Commissioners replaced by tax tribunals

Tips no longer count as national minimum wage (NMW) pay

Additional 4 days holiday introduced (1.4.09)

**2010** Additional paternity leave and pay becomes law (effective date 3.4.2011)

Transition period begins, raising retirement age of women from 60 to 65

Mandatory online filing of end of year returns for all employers

Additional rate of tax at 50% introduced and personal allowance restricted

In-year surcharge introduced – calculated at year end

Fit note replaces Med3 sickness certificate

Right to request time off for training introduced - 250+ employees

Adult rate of NMW starts at age 21 rather than 22, new apprentice rate

In-year surcharge introduced – calculated at year end

**2011** Electronic P60s permitted (May 2011)

In year online filing for schemes with less than 50 employees

1% increase in employer and employee NICs

Restriction of childcare tax relief to 20%

Agency worker regulations introduced (effective 1.10.11)

Annual allowance for pension tax relief restricted to £50,000 lifetime allowance £1.5m

**2012** NICs exemption for CIS holiday pay schemes removed

Abolition of defined contribution contracting-out

Introduction of auto-enrolment into qualifying workplace pension

Real Time Information provision to HMRC (live pilot commences 11.4.12)

**2013** Unpaid parental leave increase to 18 weeks (8.3.13)

Abolition of luncheon voucher and cyclists' breakfast exemptions

Real Time Information provision to HMRC mandatory for all PAYE schemes (between April and September 2013), P38A, P38(S), P14 and P35 abolished and starter checklist introduced

Direct Earnings attachment introduced

Scottish court order tables amended

**2014** New late in-year late filing penalty for FPS returns (10.14)

Right to request flexible working extend to all employees (30.6.14)

Annual allowance for pension tax relief restricted to £40,000 and lifetime allowance £1.25m

**2015** New shared parental leave and pay rights for babies born on or after 5 April 2015

Abolition of Employer National Insurance Contributions for employees under the age of 21

**2016** Statutory "trivial benefits" threshold of £50 introduced, subject to £300 annual cap for close companies

Introduction of new state pension and abolition of state secondary pensions

Abolition of contracting out for defined benefit pension schemes

Abolition of employers NIC for apprentices under the age of 25

Abolition of the £8,500 threshold for Benefit in Kind reporting

Introduction of a statutory framework for payrolling of benefits in kind

New statutory exemption for employee expenses payments and abolition of the dispensation process

Introduction of a national living wage

Repayment of income contingent student loans commences

Scottish rate of income tax commences

**2017** Implementation of the new Tax Free Childcare Allowance expected early 2017 and notice that existing employer assisted childcare provisions must close for new entrants form April 2018

New rules for benefits in kind to remove tax exemptions for certain BiKs when provided under a salary sacrifice arrangement. Also includes valuing the BiK at the higher of the normal valuation and the sacrifice. Cash for BiK arrangements determined by HMRC as a salary sacrifice arrangement.

Scottish parliament exercises its new powers over taxation and sets a Higher rate threshold lower than the rest of the UK

Apprenticeship levy is implemented

PAYE imposed on fees charged by off payroll workers in the public sector

**2018** Scottish parliament makes sweeping changes to PAYE tax rates and thresholds

Implementation of General Data Protection Regulation

No benefit in kind charges on electric car recharging provided by employers and a new 4% surcharge for some diesel company cars

**2019**  Commitment to a £12,500 personal allowance and £50,000 higher rate threshold brought forward by one year

Euro 6d diesel powered company cars exempt from new 4% surcharge

Welsh income tax becomes a reality with a 10% rate of tax

**2020**  Personal allowance and higher rate threshold frozen. NIC primary threshold rises by over 10% but the secondary (employer's) threshold by less than 2%.
This means the primary and secondary thresholds are different for the first time since 2013.
Electric and part electric company vehicles taxed depending on the number of miles the vehicle can travel on electric only without recharging.
NIC Primary threshold increases by £868 to £9,500, an increase of over 10%.

# MANAGED SERVICE COMPANIES (MSC)

A Managed Service Company is an intermediary company that facilitates workers providing their services to clients. Such companies seek to promote and provide a structure for those workers to reduce tax and NICs liabilities.

From 6th April 2007 all payments received by a worker through an MSC contract are deemed to be employment income whatever form the remuneration may take. From that date all earnings should have been subject to PAYE and in addition, from 6th August 2007 liability extended to Class 1 National Insurance Contributions. Where a MSC is unable to meet its PAYE liability, power exists to transfer the debt to the company's director, the service provider and in certain cases to third parties.

# MATERNITY LEAVE and PAY

### Ordinary Maternity Leave (OML)
A pregnant employee is entitled to 26 weeks' ordinary leave, regardless of service, which can start no earlier than 11 weeks before the baby is born. Significant changes were made to leave and statutory pay rules from April 2007. The Notification Week for leave is 15 weeks before the Expected Week of Childbirth (EWC) - 28 days for SMP.

### Ordinary Maternity Leave Entitlement and Notice periods

| From | Expected Week of Childbirth on or after | Leave Entitlement | Notice Period |
|---|---|---|---|
| Pre April 2000 | | 14 weeks | 21 days |
| April 2000 | 15.12.1999 | 18 weeks | 21 days |
| April 2003 | 06.04.2003 | 26 weeks | Notification Week |

*N.B. A woman is excluded from SSP during the maternity pay period which is deemed a 39 week disqualification period from the first day of entitlement to SMP or Maternity Allowance (MA). If not entitled to SMP or MA the exclusion is only for 18 weeks starting from the earlier of - the first day of absence within 4 weeks of the EWC or the day after the baby is born.*

### Additional Maternity Leave (AML)
All women are entitled to take extended leave commencing at the end of Ordinary Maternity Leave period and continuing for a further 26 weeks (for those with an EWC prior to 1st April 2007 the woman had to have 26 weeks' service at the Notification Week).

## Additional Maternity Leave - Qualification and Entitlement

|  | Earliest Date of Engagement | Service requirement | Entitlement |
|---|---|---|---|
| Pre-April 2000 |  | 2 years | 29 weeks |
| April 2000 | 15.12.1999 | 1 year up to the 11th week before the EWC (61 weeks in total) | calculated from childbirth |
| April 2003 | 24.11.2002 | 26 weeks employment up to the end of the 14th week before the EWC | 26 weeks |
| April 2007 | N/A | No service requirement | 26 weeks |

### Maternity Pay Period (MPP)

For those with an EWC of 1st April 2007 or later the MPP may start on any day of the week and run for up to 39 full weeks. For those with an EWC prior to 1st April 2007 the start date was Sunday for planned leave periods, and on any day for those triggered by early birth i.e. before leave had commenced or triggered by a pregnancy related illness (PRI). For early births or a PRI leave starts on the day after the first day of sickness, or the day after the birth of the baby. The Pregnancy Related Illness trigger is 4 weeks prior to the EWC.

### Evidence

Evidence of pregnancy on form (MAT B1) or equivalent indicates the intention to exercise the right to leave and must be given to the employer no later than during the Notification Week, (the 15th week before the EWC).

The woman must give notice to her employer:

- that she is pregnant
- of her EWC by means of MAT B1, or equivalent
- of the date she wishes to commence leave, in writing if requested.

She may revise the date on which she intends to start maternity leave, as long as she gives 28 days-notice of the new date. If she wishes to return earlier than the 52-week period of leave that she is entitled to she must give 8 weeks' notice. (Prior to 1st April 2007 this was 4 weeks.)

If the baby is born early, before notice has been given, she should notify her employer as soon as reasonably practical, giving the date of the birth.

Within 28 days of notification the employer must respond to the employee in writing informing her of her right to 52 weeks maternity leave and her expected return date. (Prior to April 2003 the employer had to write to the employee, whilst on maternity leave, explaining the implications relating to her return to work).

### Return to work

The employee has a right to return to the same or similar job after Ordinary Maternity Leave. Once she commences Additional Maternity Leave she has the right to return to a job that is 'suitable and appropriate' if her employer chooses not to keep her old job open.

### Penalties

If the required notice (28 days) for the start of Statutory Maternity Pay is not given, the commencement of payment of SMP can be delayed until 28 days after the date that correct notification is provided.

### Contract of Employment - changes for EWCs on, or after, 5th October 2008

Women are entitled to retain the benefit of their normal terms and conditions of employment, except for those relating to remuneration, throughout the period of ordinary and additional maternity leave. In most cases Statutory Maternity Pay or Maternity Allowance will become payable instead of wages. Remuneration means all monetary wages or salary. Therefore the woman is entitled to all her benefits-in-kind e.g. company car, childcare vouchers, contractual and statutory holiday entitlement throughout ordinary and additional maternity leave. With effect for those with an EWC of 1st April 2007 or later, during any paid maternity leave (SMP or contractual) the employer is obliged to pay pension contributions on behalf of the employee based on her pre-leave salary. The employee can choose to continue to pay contributions based on her lower salary. In a final salary scheme benefits must be maintained based on the pre-leave salary.

In March 2016 an Employment Appeals Tribunal case (Peninsula Business Services v Donaldson) determined that where a benefit in kind is provided under a "diverted pay" scheme the benefit is part of the general remuneration and hence had to be suspended during the maternity leave of the complainant, Donaldson. Since this unexpected decision HMRC has continued to advise that BiKs must be maintained during statutory leave and further guidance is awaited.

Prior to 1st April 2007 the employer was only obliged to continue pension contributions to the end of OML as this tied up with the maximum length of the SMP period. The requirements of the Social Security and Benefits Act 1992 are such that from 1st April 2007 employer pension contributions are due until the end of the paid leave period i.e. for up to 13 weeks of the AML until 39 weeks of SMP has been paid or longer if contractual maternity pay is payable.

For those with an EWC of 1st April 2007 or later the woman is entitled to come into work for up to ten days during the maternity pay period with no loss of SMP (see section on Statutory Maternity Pay), these are known as keeping-in-touch (KIT) days.

The employer is entitled to make 'reasonable contact' with the employee whilst she is on leave to discuss details of her return to work without fear that this will lead to a claim of harassment, but making contact does not entitle the employer to end the employee's contract early based on any indication that she may not be returning to work at the end of her leave and simply coming into work for such a discussion is not classed as a KIT day. Women may also extend the 52 week Maternity Leave period by another 4 weeks as unpaid parental leave (See also Dependant Leave and Parental Leave).

## NATIONAL LIVING WAGE (NLW)

Introduced on 1st April 2016, it requires employers to pay to a worker who is over the age of 25 a minimum rate of pay of £8.72 an hour (£8.21 from 1st April 2019). Employers are required to ensure the new rate applies for every day that the worker is 25 or over and not just on the day payment is made.

The NMW will continue to apply to workers who are under 25.

## NATIONAL MINIMUM/LIVING WAGE (NMW/NLW)

Introduced on 1st April 1999, it established a worker's right to be paid not less than a prescribed minimum hourly rate with limited exceptions for certain classes of workers. The rate paid to a worker under the conditions and terms of employment are averaged, over the normal pay frequency, up to a maximum of one month in order to establish that the rate paid for each hour worked is no less than the NMW.

All earnings included in gross pay are to be taken into account including:
- incentive payments
- time spent in travelling during normal working hours
- time spent in training when the employee would normally have been working

Special circumstances to be taken into account:
- earnings at basic rate only are taken into account in cases where enhanced rates are paid, e.g. overtime.
- benefits-in-kind are ignored with the exception of accommodation provision

Excluded classes of employee:
- childminders
- people working and living as part of a family (e.g. au-pairs)

From October 2009 it is illegal to include tips or gratuities in national minimum wage pay however these are paid or calculated. From October 2010 the adult rate of NMW kicked in at age 21 rather than the 22 years of age previously, and a new apprentice minimum wage of £2.50 per hour was introduced.

The apprentice rate applies to those employed apprentices who are under 19, or those that are aged 19 and over but in the first year of their apprenticeship. The NMW does not apply to non-employed apprentices.

From January 2011 agency workers who have agreed a salary sacrifice to fund travel and subsistence to clients must still receive national minimum wage post-sacrifice.

From 1st April 2017 NMW rates will increase alongside the NLW changes.

### National Minimum/Living Wage - Hourly Rates of Pay from 1st April 1999

| | Adult | Adult | Employee | School | Adult | Acc'n | Apprentice |
|---|---|---|---|---|---|---|---|
| | aged 25 & over NLW | aged 22 & over | aged18 to 21(inc) | Leaver Aged 16 to 17 | Development aged 22 and over | Provide d Daily Rate | |
| From date | £ | £ | £ | £ | £ | £ | £ |
| 01.10.2001 | | 4.10 | 3.50 | | 3.50 | | 3.50 |
| 01.10.2002 | | 4.20 | 3.60 | | 3.60 | | 3.60 |
| 01.10.2003 | | 4.50 | 3.80 | | 3.80 | 3.50 | 3.80 |
| 01.10.2004 | | 4.85 | 4.10 | 3.00 | 4.10 | 3.75 | 4.10 |
| 01.10.2005 | | 5.05 | 4.25 | 3.00 | 4.25 | 3.90 | 4.25 |
| 01.10.2006 | | 5.35 | 4.45 | 3.30 | Abolished | 4.15 | Abolished |
| 01.10.2007 | | 5.52 | 4.60 | 3.40 | | 4.30 | |
| 01.10.2008 | | 5.73 | 4.77 | 3.53 | | 4.46 | |
| 01.10.2009 | | 5.80 | 4.83 | 3.57 | | 4.51 | |
| 01.10.2010 | | 5.93^ | 4.92# | 3.64 | | 4.61 | 2.50† |
| 01.10.2011 | | 6.08 | 4.98 | 3.68 | | 4.73 | 2.60† |
| 01.10.2012 | | 6.19 | 4.98 | 3.68 | | 4.82 | 2.65† |
| 01.10.2013 | | 6.31 | 5.03 | 3.72 | | 4.91 | 2.68† |
| 01.10.2014 | | 6.50 | 5.13 | 3.79 | | 5.08 | 2.73† |
| 01.10.2015 | | 6.70* | 5.30 | 3.87 | | 5.35 | 3.30† |
| 01.10.2016 | | 6.95* | 5.55 | 4.00 | | 6.00 | 3.40† |
| 01.04.2017 | 7.50 | 7.05* | 5.60 | 4.05 | | 6.40 | 3.50† |
| 01.04.2018 | 7.83 | 7.38* | 5.90 | 4.20 | | 7.00 | 3.70† |
| 01.04.2019 | 8.21 | 7.70* | 6.15 | 4.35 | | 7.55 | 3.90† |
| 01.04.2020 | 8.72 | 8.20* (21-24) | 6.45 (18-20) | 4.55 | | 8.20 | 4.15† |

^from age 21  *to age 25  # to age 20  †for apprentices under 19/first year of apprenticeship

### Arrears
From 6th April 2009 arrears (in respect of reference periods thereafter) are calculated at current NMW rates where these are higher than during the period the arrears arose (reference Employment Act 2008).

### Enforcement
With effect from 26th May 2015 new penalties accrue where an employer fails to pay the NMW, alongside the new inspection powers available to HMRC since 6th April 2009. HMRC can remove records from an employer's premises for photocopying and will commence a criminal investigation which may result in serious penalties for employers who deliberately fail to pay the NMW.

From 1st April 2016, where an underpayment is found, a 'notice of underpayment' will automatically be issued plus a penalty fee of 200% (was 100%) of the underpayment per worker, subject to a minimum of £100 and maximum of £20,000 per worker. Under amendments to NMW regulations during 2003 a retrospective notice can be served on an employer to make good underpayments of NMW for ex-employees.

**Output (Piece) Workers**

From 1st October 2004 provisions under the regulations relating to output workers, those paid for the piece produced or task performed and not for the time that they work (previously piece workers), and former 'fair estimate' agreements were replaced by a system entitled 'rated output work'. An employer must give workers notice specifying the 'mean hourly output rate'; being the number of hours output work spent in performing subject tasks during a pay reference period.

In order to determine the mean rate, the employer must either:

* conduct a satisfactory test to determine the speed at which every worker produces either a 'subject piece' or 'task of output', or fraction thereof, to determine the average, or mean, speed achieved by all workers producing the piece of work, or
* make a satisfactory estimate of the average speed of performing the piece or task

From 6th April 2005 all workers must be tested in similar working circumstances to those in which actual work will be performed. The number of hours taken by a worker in producing pieces, or performing tasks, during a pay reference period is to be treated as being 120% of the number of hours that a worker working at the mean hourly rate output would have taken to produce or perform the same number of the same type of pieces or tasks.

**NLW/NMW Post 2020**

The government is committed to reviewing the whole structure and effects of statutory rates and consider the future remit of the Low Pay Commission after 2020.

# NEW DEAL SCHEME/THE WORK PROGRAMME

A scheme piloted in April 1997, extended nationwide in April 1998 and funded by the Department for Work and Pensions. In October 2009 a new scheme: 'Flexible new Deal' was launched to replace New Deal which in turn was replaced by The Work Programme in 2011. The scheme provides an in-work subsidy payable to an eligible employee for up to the first 26 weeks of employment, or until such time as employment ceases if earlier. Under the Work programme 'wage incentives' are available for employers across England Scotland and Wales who can offer an 18-24 year old a job through Jobcentre Plus or the Work Programme.

The wage incentive is available if someone is employed for 16 hours or more each week in a job lasting more than 26 weeks. There are two rates:

* for part-time work between 16 and 29 hours a week – £1,137.50
* for full-time work of 30 hours or more a week – £2,275.

This will be paid 26 weeks after the employee starts work. Small businesses with fewer than 50 employees can claim a part payment eight weeks after the employee starts work. Wage incentives are primarily available to private, voluntary and community sectors and social enterprise employers. Central government departments, their executive agencies and Non-Departmental Public Bodies (NDPBs) are excluded from claiming them, however the wider public sector such as NHS trusts, are not. When the young person starts work the Work Programme provider or Jobcentre Plus, will issue a wage incentive claim form with details on how and when to make the claim. The payment is claimed from Jobcentre Plus who validate the claim and make the payment directly into the employer's bank account.

In addition, a new wage incentive scheme is available to employers who recruit a young person from Work Choice in England, Scotland and Wales – a specialist disability employment programme that provides tailored support to help disabled people who have the most complex support needs.

# NON-BANKING PAYDAY

Where a regular pay day falls on a non-banking day and payment is made on the last working day before the normal pay day, the payment shall be treated for PAYE and NIC purposes as though it had been paid on the normal payday. For example a Saturday, Sunday or Bank Holiday (e.g. 6 April 2013 was a Saturday and payment brought forward to 5th April could still be treated as made in the new tax year not taxed as an additional payment in tax year 2012/13).

## NON-CASH VOUCHER

A non-cash voucher is any voucher, or similar document or token capable of being exchanged (either singly or together with any other such vouchers, stamps, documents or tokens, whether immediately or after a time) for money, goods or services (or any combination of two or more of those things) and includes a transport voucher and a cheque voucher.

Care must be taken with some retail vouchers which purport to be exchangeable for goods only but in fact allow the customer to get change in cash if the value of the goods purchased comes to less than the face value of the voucher. For PAYE and NICs purposes this is considered to be a wholly cash voucher.

## NON-CASH BENEFITS

Changes made to the Sex Discrimination Act 1975 and reflected in the Maternity and Parental Leave Regulations (MPLR) were effective from October 2008. They require that non-cash benefits must be provided throughout statutory maternity, paternity and adoption leave. Such benefits include:

- contractual holiday entitlement
- private medical schemes including medical insurance, life assurance, childcare vouchers and gym membership
- company car - where some entitlement for private use of a company car is provided the car should be treated as a benefit and should be retained throughout Ordinary and Additional Maternity leave. The employer may only take the car back where it is provided solely for business purposes. Cash allowances in place of a company car can be withdrawn.
- discretionary annual, Christmas or loyalty bonuses are classified as wages so need not be paid except for bonus payments relating to the compulsory maternity leave period, which is 2 weeks for most workers and 4 weeks for those who work in a factory.

In some cases, should the benefit in kind be provided using a "diverted pay" scheme, usually called salary sacrifice, the employer may have the right to withdraw the benefit during the leave period (Peninsula Business Services v Donaldson (EAT 2016)). Employers need to obtain specialist legal advice before embarking on such a move.

## OFF PAYROLL WORKING

As part of the government's drive to impose equality of taxation between employees and off-payroll workers a new requirement has been imposed for those who make payments to external contractors who are fulfilling contracts. This came into effect from 6 April 2017 within the public sector and from 6 April 2020 for all other sectors.

Since 6th April 2017 all off-payroll workers working within the public sector should be having PAYE and NICs deducted from their fees before the payment is made to them. This is required no matter who is paying the worker, an agency, the worker's own business or the public sector body directly. The new rules will not apply if, taking all the circumstances into consideration, the worker would not have been an employee if taken on directly.

The new PAYE deduction applies to all labour charges and therefore excludes brought in goods and any VAT charged. The invoice submitted by the worker must therefore go through a payroll in order for the necessary deductions to be applied.

The workers will not be permitted to offset any travel and subsistence against their profits for tax purposes, neither will they be able to offset the standard 5% allowance for business costs as permitted under the deemed employment calculation for IR35.

Employer NICs and the new Apprenticeship levy will apply to such payments and must be met by the paying engager.

In December 2017 the government agreed to undertake consultation in 2018 before determining if the new off-payroll working rules will extend to all external contracting. Finance Act 2019 confirms that the new scheme now applies to all external contracting from April 2020, a date which has recently been deferred to April 2021.

# ONLINE FILING

Following the Patrick Carter review commissioned by the Government in 2001, HMRC laid regulations that required all employers (and those running pension only payrolls) to file their End of Year returns online. End of Year Returns were defined as the P35 and accompanying P14s. The phased implementation of the regulations began with the End of Year returns due for the 2004/2005 tax year in May 2005 and was based on the following criteria.

### Online filing - implementation dates

| Tax Year | Scheme size |
|----------|-------------|
| 2004/2005 | 250 or more employees |
| 2005/2006 | 50-249 employees |
| 2009/2010 | Under 50 employees |

## PAYE Schemes

Each PAYE reference is classified as a scheme, not each employer. An employer may have several schemes all of differing sizes with differing deadlines. Small PAYE schemes (those with under 50 payees) were able to qualify for a tax-free incentive payment if they filed that scheme online before they were mandated to do so at the end of tax year 2009/10 (see table below).

Employee counts took place each year to classify schemes. The first was undertaken based on a count on 26th October 2003, and each employer was issued with a statutory notice - The Snapshot Letter - confirming the count, against which there was a right of appeal if the employer believed it to be incorrect. This classified schemes for 2004/2005. The snapshot had to be complete by 30th November prior to the tax year for which it applied.

### Online Filing – Tax-free Incentive Payment Scheme

| End of Year | 2004/5 | 2005/6 | 2006/7 | 2007/8 | 2008/9 | 2009/10 |
|-------------|--------|--------|--------|--------|--------|---------|
| Due by date | 19.05.2005 | 19.05.2006 | 19.05.2007 | 19.05.2008 | 19.05.2009 | |
| Incentive | £ 250 | £ 250 | £ 150 | £ 100 | £ 75 | Abolished |

Online filing means using EDI (Electronic Data Interchange) or the Internet. Use of magnetic media i.e. tapes, cartridges, floppy discs, CD-ROMs is not classified as 'online'. For the last time for 2012/13 employers had to file both online and to HMRC's Quality Standard by 19th May, final returns under RTI will be due by 19th April.

### In-year filing

Employers with 50 or more payees in a PAYE scheme (including pension payrolls) were required to file in-year forms (i.e. P45s and the suite of P46 forms) from 6th April 2009 and schemes with under 50 payees faced the same mandation from 6th April 2011. As at 6th April 2016, there is no requirement to receive forms online from HMRC.

### Future developments

From April 2014 the final groups of specialist PAYE schemes will move on to RTI with only care and support employers and the digitally excluded allowed to file quarterly returns on paper.

# OVERPAYMENTS

There are two key elements to any overpayment of pay: the gross overpayment and the net (gross less statutory and any other deductions). As the element recoverable in law is the net overpayment received by the employee (British Railways Board v Franklin (Court of Appeal 1991)), it is important that all payroll transactions are adjusted (by reversal of the payment process) leaving the net overpayment as the only item of pay remaining outstanding.

Where the overpayment is the result of processing two or more pay periods, a separate recalculation should be made for each pay period involved, and the cumulative values of each element of pay should be reversed.

Where overpayment occurs after a tax year-end (or more than one) the transactions within each tax year should be separately calculated and adjusted. This is to ensure that the cumulative elements within each tax year of tax, national insurance etc. correctly reflect the statutory liabilities due.

### Recovery

Before taking steps to recover the net overpayment outstanding, a decision will have to be made about how it can be done or if the amount should be cleared from the accounts (written off). In all cases it is important that agreement to recover a net overpayment is reached with the employee concerned. Where agreement is not achieved legal advice may be necessary.

Where an employee agrees to repay via salary/wages, written consent should be obtained. When the employee makes repayment whether by deduction from a future payment(s) of salary/wages, or other means, it will be in respect of the net sum outstanding.

Where the amount overpaid is small and/or no change in the statutory liabilities would result were the overpayment recovered gross, it would be administratively acceptable to do so. However, as a general principle all recoveries should be made in the manner outlined above. Adjustments made net will almost always produce a difference in value to that were it to be made gross, as the factors governing the calculation of statutory deductions do not necessarily remain constant throughout successive pay periods.

Whichever method is used, and employers are free to decide on gross or net recovery, the limitations are clear and must be adhered to at all times. The employee must only repay no more than the amount they actually received, the net pay and HM Revenue & Customs will only allow, as a maximum reversal, the amount of PAYE and NICs actually paid across as a consequence of the overpayment.

## PARENTAL BEREAVEMENT LEAVE

Introduced from 6 April 2020 by the Parental Bereavement (Leave and Pay) Act 2018 this new provision gives a right to leave and pay to any employee who suffers the loss of a child. The loss which would give rise to entitlement is defined as a child under the age of 18 or a stillbirth from week 24 onwards.

Many of the qualifying conditions mirror those found in the other statutory payments rights whilst the right to pay and protection are the same as for statutory paternity, shared parental leave.

Further details can be found in Part 4: Statutory Payments.

## PARENTAL LEAVE

The Maternity and Parental Leave Regulations 1999 were introduced on 15th December 1999, provide both mother and father with the right to reasonable leave (unpaid) to look after a child or make arrangements for the child's welfare.

### Qualification

An employee must:
- have at least one year's continuous service with the employer, and
- be the parent (named on the birth certificate) of a child who is under five years of age, or
- have adopted, a child under the age of eighteen. The rights last for five years from the date on which a child is placed for adoption, or until the child's eighteenth birthday, whichever is the sooner, or
- have acquired formal parental responsibility for a child under five years of age. As entitlement is for each child, for twins the entitlement would be two periods of thirteen weeks.

The qualification rule was extended retrospectively on the 10th January 2002 to include those aged up to 5 years born on or after 15th December 1999 and in the case of disabled children leave was extended from 13 to 18 weeks. From 8th March 2013 it was extended to 18 weeks for all children.

## Maximum Entitlement
- 13 weeks' leave for parents of all children who qualify
- 18 weeks' leave for parents of disabled children who qualify.

In addition, the employee:
- remains in employment but need not be paid and will not be bound by any contractual terms except terms relating to good faith and confidentiality, which will bind the employer also
- is, on return to work, entitled to return to his or her former job, or a job with the same or better status, terms and conditions as the former, and pension rights built up before leave was taken are protected.

For redundancy purposes the leave period is treated as a period of continuous employment. Employers are encouraged to offer more than these key elements but must not offer less. Where no alternative policy is agreed the fallback scheme applies.

## Statutory fallback scheme provisions
- leave can only be taken in blocks of a week at a time (parents of disabled children in blocks of less than a week) and
- a maximum of four weeks leave can be taken in each year and
- the employee has to give 21 days' notice of their intention to take leave, and
- the employer has the right to postpone leave for up to 6 months where leave would unduly disrupt business except if it is to be taken immediately after maternity, paternity or adoption leave.

## Notice
A maximum of four weeks leave may be taken in one block and the period of notice must be at least twice the period of leave to be taken. Parents are allowed to take a maximum of 4 weeks Parental Leave immediately following statutory maternity, additional paternity or adoption leave.

## Record Keeping
Employers are not required to keep records of parental leave taken but many choose to do so.

## Shared parental leave
With effect for babies due on or after 5 April 2015/children matched for adoption on or after the same date, 'shared parental leave' was introduced that allows parents to share the care of the child for up to 50 weeks up to the child's first birthday/one year since the placement for adoption.

# PART-TIME WORKERS

The Part-time Workers (Prevention of Less Favourable Treatment) Regulations 2000 were introduced on 1st July 2000 to provide protection for part-time workers in areas of pay, pensions, training and holidays.
The treatment of a part-time worker in these areas must be no less favourable than that of a comparable full-time worker.

A part-time worker must:
- receive the same hourly rate as a comparable full-time worker
- receive the same hourly rate of overtime as a comparable full-time worker, once they have worked more than the normal full-time hours
- not be excluded from training because they work part-time
- have the same annual leave, contractual maternity, parental and dependant leave entitlement on a pro-rata basis as full-time workers
- in a redundancy situation, be treated no less favourably than a full-time equivalent worker
- have the same access to pension schemes, except where justified on objective grounds, as full-time workers, with calculation of benefits on a
- pro-rata basis

Former full-time workers, who return to part-time work after a period of absence, are to be treated no less favourably than they were before becoming part-time.

## PATERNITY LEAVE AND PAY

An eligible employee who is the biological father of a child or the mother's spouse, civil partner or partner is entitled to one or two weeks' ordinary statutory paternity pay and leave. The period within which the ordinary statutory paternity pay period must occur begins on the date of the child's birth and ends 56 days after that date.

The parents of babies due on or after 3rd April 2011 can also be entitled to additional statutory paternity leave and pay of up to 19 weeks if their partner returns to work with between 2 and 19 weeks of unused maternity/adoption pay and leave.

With the introduction of Shared Parental Leave and Pay on 6th April 2015 additional paternity leave and pay was abolished. New regulations extended the right to take ordinary paternity leave and pay to intended parents in a surrogacy situation and approved prospective adopters who look after children as part of a "fostering to adopt" arrangement. Fathers are entitled to take time off to attend up to two ante-natal appointments.

## PAYMENT OF WAGES

The Truck Acts '1831 to 1940' gave manual workers ('Artificers') the right to receive payment in cash. This right was abolished by the Wages Act 1986, which recognised the benefits and security that could be obtained, from automated transfer of pay direct into employees' bank accounts. Where however payment in cash is contained within an employee's contract or terms of employment, any change in those terms must be negotiated and agreed between the parties concerned. The Wages Act has since been subsumed as part of the Employment Rights Act 1999. (The Wages Act also made some provision for the recovery of overpayments).

## PAYE FORMS and RETURNS

### P11 Deductions working sheet
Strictly speaking the way that payroll software records pay and deductions is the computerised version of a paper P11. The form P11 records the individual pay period by pay period details of each employees PAYE income tax, National Insurance Contributions and Statutory Payments. The form, which now includes Student Loan Deductions and other statutory information, or copy should be retained for at least three years after the end of the year to which it relates.

### P11D/P9D - Annual statement of expense and benefit payments
A form P11D (or equivalent) is to be used when reporting expenses and benefits provided to company directors or to employees earning at a rate of £8,500 or more per year. A copy must be provided to each current employee or company director giving details of their individual expenses and benefits. P11Ds are due to HMRC and employees by 6th July annually relating to the previous tax year. The P9D form was used to report a more limited range of employer-provided expense payments or benefits made to an employee earning at a rate of less than £8,500 per year. The last P9D forms applied to the tax year 2015/16 as the threshold for P9D, £8,500 was abolished from 6 April 2016, thereby also abolishing the P9D form. For guidance see https://www.gov.uk/government/publications/paye-end-of-year-expenses-and-benefits-p11d-guide .

Employers using voluntary payrolling of benefits in kind (BiKs) are technically using the full payment submission (FPS) within RTI as a substitute P11D.

### P14 - employee's annual PAYE summary
A P14 was a year-end summary for each individual employee for whom PAYE had been operated, detailing Income Tax, National Insurance Contributions and Statutory Payments. Forms P14 had to accompany the form P35 Employer Annual PAYE return and was submitted to HMRC by 19th May after the tax year to which they related. Under Real Time Information the Full Payment Submission (FPS) sent on or before each payment replaced the annual P14.

### P35 - employer annual PAYE return
The P35 was the Employer Annual PAYE Return of the total PAYE Income Tax deductions, National Insurance Contributions and recovered statutory payments for all employees included on the accompanying P14s. The P35 no longer exists under Real Time Information as FPS submissions are sent each time an employee is

paid. A final FPS or Employer Payment Summary (EPS) closes the scheme down for the year by acting as an employer declaration in the same way that the P35 did.

### P38A - employer supplementary return
Form P38A, abolished from 6th April 2013, was used to report payments made during a tax year to employees for whom no P14 or P38(S) had been completed. The P38A no longer exists under Real Time Information; all employees must have a payroll record even if they are paid under the LEL as long as at least one employee within the PAYE scheme is paid above the LEL.

### P45(1)s - starting in employment
Employers receive P45s from new starters and submit starting details to HMRC via the FPS on or before the first time the employee is paid. All employees from 6th April 2013 must answer the statement A, B or C questions on the starter checklist even if they present a P45. Previous pay and tax figures are entered on the payroll and used to calculate pay and tax due but are not submitted to HMRC. See Real Time Information above for more details on the starter process.  A new 'A4' style P45 was introduced in October 2008 and the 'A5' P45 was then withdrawn as at 6th April 2009. From October 2008 Parts 1a-3 of the 'A4' P45 were able to be printed in black and white on plain paper where employers were filing part 1 online.

### P46 - starting in employment with no P45
A form used to capture new starter information for those not providing a P45 and replaced with the starter checklist from 6th April 2014. If an employee fails to complete the form by the time of the first payment being made the employer must submit the starter declaration via the FPS completing it with a statement C default value allocating code 0T on a non-cumulative basis. Where an employee ticks statement C code BR on a cumulative basis should be used rather than 0T/1. Employers can choose not to ask employees to complete the starter checklist as long as they have an audit trail to prove the individual's personal data. P46 online submission was abolished under RTI the starter data being submitted as part of the Full Payment Submission (FPS). In other words, as with payrolling of BiKs employers are using the FPS as a substitute P45 where required.

From 6th April 2016 the starter declaration, and any employer created equivalent, has enhanced questions regarding student loan deductions in order to deal with the new Plan 2 loan repayments. From 6th April 2019 a new repayment for Post Graduate Loans will commence for employees who took out such loans when they were introduced in the 2016/17 academic year. The starter declaration has been changed again to allow employees to self-declare their liability to make payments whilst some clarifications in respect of the student loan declarations had been made for 6 April 2020.

### P46(Pen)
A form, in use from 6th April 2009 to 5th April 2013 and used to notify HMRC that an ex-employee from the same employer had joined the pension payroll. The P46(Pen) no longer exists under RTI but the same distinction between pensioners staying with the same employer or in receipt of a pension from a pension provider apply and are submitted to HMRC via the FPS.

### P46(Expat)
A form in use from 6th April 2009 to 5th April 2013 which was used when taking on a worker who had been seconded to work in the United Kingdom (UK) and who would be subject to PAYE. The form is no longer submitted under RTI but the same questions must be asked of the secondee to allocate the correct tax code which is then submitted via the FPS.

### P60 - End of Year Certificate
A P60 statement is the document issued to each employee (and to those on pension payrolls from 6th April 1996) employed at 5th April each year, giving details of final pay and tax accumulations for the tax year. It can be provided on paper or electronically (only on paper pre-tax year 2010/11) using the form supplied, or a substitute document approved by HMRC. Prior to 6th April 2003 no duplicate or copy of the initial document could be provided.

## PENALTIES

### Incorrect tax returns
HMRC took a new approach to penalties in respect of return periods beginning on or after 1st April 2008 where the return is due to be filed on or after 1st April 2009. The penalty regime applies to all taxes including PAYE.

Previously a penalty could be levied of up to 100% of the tax understated or over-claimed as a result of negligent or fraudulent conduct. The penalties could then be reduced by up to 20% for disclosure, 40% for co-operation and 40% for seriousness, with a further 10% where disclosure was not prompted by HMRC.

For return periods after 1st April 2008 the new approach commences with:
- the filing of an incorrect tax return where the inaccuracy was careless or deliberate, or
- failure upon receiving an understated tax assessment to notify HMRC within 30 days.

Inaccuracy may be defined in four ways, whether inaccuracy was:
- made despite reasonable care having been taken - no penalty thereby being incurred
- a result of failure to take reasonable care or carelessness
- a deliberate error not concealed
- a deliberate error which was concealed

The maximum penalties that may be imposed are:
- 30% - for careless behaviour
- 70% - for a deliberate but not concealed error
- 100% - for a deliberate and concealed error

Maximum penalties may be reduced where voluntary disclosure has taken place. Such disclosure should include details as to:
- who was involved
- who was aware of the inaccuracy
- for how long the inaccuracy had taken place
- the scale of the inaccuracy.

The quality of the disclosure will also be considered and whether it was prompted in the belief that HMRC had discovered, or might be about to discover, the inaccuracy. Once HMRC have notified an employer of a compliance check of any type a disclosure cannot be classed as unprompted.

### Penalty Percentage Range

| Behaviour | Maximum Penalty | Quality of disclosure range | |
|---|---|---|---|
| | | Prompted | Unprompted |
| Careless | 30% | 15% to 30% | 0% to 30% |
| Deliberate but not concealed | 70% | 35% to 70% | 20% to 70% |
| Deliberate and concealed | 100% | 50% to 100% | 30% to 100% |

No penalties can be levied for errors that occur where reasonable care has been taken. HMRC can agree to suspend a penalty if the employer agrees to certain measures being put in place to prevent recurrence. Where these targets are met to HMRC's satisfaction the penalty can then be cancelled. These penalties will continue under RTI based on the level of accuracy on any Full Payment Submission.

### Late filing of end of year returns
A number of penalties can be levied by HMRC for offences in connection with year-end returns and these also apply to RTI. The penalties were in respect of both the P14 (employee level) and the P35 (employer or PAYE scheme level) returns historically and under RTI the Full Payment Submission and Employer Payment Summary, and they fall into the following categories:
- failing to file online when required to do so;
- failing to file a return at all or by the due deadline.

HMRC may choose to levy more than one penalty - for example, a penalty for failing to file online as well as late filing and inaccuracy penalties.

The due date for the final FPS or EPS for the tax year is 19th April (penalties were only levied from 20th May 2014 for the 2013/14 tax year, and from 20th April for 2014/15 tax year onwards. The penalty is £100 per month per 50 employees, rounded up to the next 50, for the first 12 months. For the returns due on 19th May 2011 Extra Statutory Concession B46, which gave a seven day grace period before penalties could be levied, no longer applied. Interim penalties are sent out in September, January and May if the return is still outstanding.

### Late filing of in-year Full Payment Submission (FPS)
This new penalty was introduced from 6th October 2014 for any FPS received after any date of payment shown within the FPS file for employers with 51 or more employees. Identical penalties for employers with up to 50 employees will be introduced on 6th April 2015.

The late filing penalty will be based on the size of the PAYE scheme. Up to 5th April 2017, no penalty was imposed if the FPS was received up to three days after pay day, however this easement is abolished as of 6th April 2019. One un-penalised default in a 12 month period is permitted. The penalty period for all employers for late filing is one month even if the employees are weekly paid. Late filing penalties will be charged quarterly. An additional tax-geared penalty will apply if the FPS is more than three months late.

| Number of employees | Penalty |
|---|---|
| 1-9 | £100 |
| 10-49 | £200 |
| 50-249 | £300 |
| 250+ | £400 |

No penalty will be levied against a new PAYE scheme if first FPS is within 30 days of first payment to employees.

### Late/underpayment penalty
- A late payment penalty was introduced from 6th April 2015 and is levied automatically where the remittance paid by the employer is less than the value derived from the FPS and any amendments on the EPS. There will be a de-minimis limit of £100 below which a penalty will not be generated. The penalty is based on the current payment surcharge for failing to pay in full and on time as follows:
- 1-3 defaults 1% of the total of the defaults
- 4-6 defaults 2% of the total of the defaults
- 7-9 defaults 3% of the total of the defaults
- 10 or more defaults 4% of the total of the defaults, plus
- tax unpaid after 6 months - additional 5% of unpaid tax
- tax unpaid after 12 months - further 5% of unpaid tax.

### Interest due on late payments from 6th November 1989

| Date from | Rate % | Date from | Rate % | Date from | Rate % |
|---|---|---|---|---|---|
| 06.03.1991 | 11.50 | 31.01.1997 | 8.50 | 06.01.2008 | 7.50 |
| 06.05.1991 | 10.75 | 06.08.1997 | 9.50 | 06.11.2008 | 6.50 |
| 06.07.1991 | 10.00 | 06.01.1999 | 8.50 | 06.12.2008 | 5.50 |
| 06.05.2001 | 7.50 | 06.03.1999 | 7.50 | 06.01.2009 | 4.50 |
| 06.11.2001 | 6.50 | 06.02.2000 | 8.50 | 27.01.2009 | 3.50 |
| 06.10.1991 | 9.25 | 06.05.2001 | 7.50 | 24.03.2009 | 2.50 |
| 06.11.1992 | 7.75 | 06.11.2001 | 6.50 | 29.09.2009 | 3.00 |
| 06.12.1992 | 7.00 | 06.12.2003 | 6.50 | 23.08.2016 | 2.75 |
| 06.03.1993 | 6.25 | 06.09.2004 | 7.50 | 21.11.2017 | 3.00 |
| 06.01.1994 | 5.50 | 06.09.2005 | 6.50 | 21.08.2018 | 3.25 |
| 06.03.1995 | 7.00 | 06.09.2006 | 7.50 | 07.04.2020 | 2.60 |
| 06.02.1996 | 6.25 | 06.08.2007 | 8.50 | | |

*Note: After 6 months of no payment a surcharge of 5% of the total amount outstanding is added plus a further 5% on top of the original penalty and 5% when PAYE has been outstanding for 12 months or more.*

### Recent developments

From 6th April 2014 daily interest has accrued on all unpaid amounts from the due and payable date to the date of payment. Additionally, all penalties are due for payment 30 days following the date of the penalty notice and penalties not paid on time will attract interest.

### Interest due on overpayments from 6th August 1997

| Date from | Rate % | | Date from | Rate % | | Date from | Rate % |
|---|---|---|---|---|---|---|---|
| 06.08.1997 | 4.75 | | 06.08.2003 | 1.50 * | | 06.01.2008 | 3.00 |
| 06.01.1999 | 4.00 | | 06.12.2003 | 2.25 * | | 06.11.2008 | 2.25 |
| 06.03.1999 | 3.00 | | 06.09.2004 | 3.00 * | | 06.12.2008 | 1.50 |
| 06.02.2000 | 4.00 | | 06.09.2005 | 2.25 * | | 06.01.2009 | 0.75 |
| 06.05.2001 | 3.00 * | | 06.09.2006 | 3.00 | | 27.01.2009 | 0.00 |
| 06.11.2001 | 2.25 * | | 06.08.2007 | 4.00 | | 24.09.2009 | 0.50 |

* Rates revised retrospectively on 6th September

## HISTORIC PENALTIES

### Failure to file end of year returns online

### Penalty Charges – failure to file P35/P14s online
### Tax years 2009/10 – 2012/13

| Number of employees for whom P14s should have been filed | 2009/10 £ | 2010/11 – 2012/13 £ |
|---|---|---|
| 1–5 | 0 | 100 |
| 6–49 | 100 | 300 |
| 50–249 | 600 | 600 |
| 250-399 | 900 | 900 |
| 400–499 | 1,200 | 1,200 |
| 500–599 | 1,500 | 1,500 |
| 600–699 | 1,800 | 1,800 |
| 700–799 | 2,100 | 2,100 |
| 800–899 | 2,400 | 2,400 |
| 900-999 | 2,700 | 2,700 |
| 1000 or more | 3,000 | 3,000 |

Failure to file in-year forms online

### Failure to supply in-year forms online from 6th April 2009 – 5th April 2013

| No of items | Penalty 2009/10 and 2010/11 £ | No of items | Penalty 2011/12 and 2012/13 £ |
|---|---|---|---|
| 1 to 5 | Nil | Up to 2 | Nil |
| 6 to 49 | 100 | 3 to 49 | 100 |
| 50 to 149 | 300 | 50 to 149 | 300 |
| 150 to 299 | 600 | 150 to 299 | 600 |
| 250 to 299 | 900 | 250 to 299 | 900 |
| 300 to 399 | 900 | 300 to 399 | 900 |
| 400 to 499 | 1,200 | 400 to 499 | 1,200 |
| 500 to 599 | 1,500 | 500 to 599 | 1,500 |
| 600 to 699 | 1,800 | 600 to 699 | 1,800 |
| 700 to 799 | 2,100 | 700 to 799 | 2,100 |
| 800 to 899 | 2,400 | 800 to 899 | 2,400 |
| 900 to 999 | 2,700 | 900 to 999 | 2,700 |
| 1000 or more | 3,000 | 1000 or more | 3,000 |

Penalties were based on the number of items that were filed on paper in the preceding tax quarter - that is, the periods ending 5 July, 5 October, 5 December and 5 April. Penalties did not begin to be levied until the last quarter of the 2009/10 tax year - that is, January 2010. The count was for each item (that is, P45(1), P45(3), P46, P46(Pen) or P46(Expat)) that was sent on paper, not online, even if some of those items related to the same employee.

## POSTED WORKER

A posted worker is one who, for a limited period, carries out work in the territory of a member state of the EU other than the state in which they normally work. The Posting of Workers Directive that was implemented in the UK on 16th December 1999, requires that where a member state has certain minimum terms and conditions of employment they must be applied to workers on a temporary posting in that state.

A number of UK regulations cover such minimum terms including the Working Time Regulations and the regulations covering protection from discrimination on the grounds of race, sex, sexual orientation and religious belief. The Employment Relations Act 1999 ensured coverage extended to all employees working in the UK even for temporary periods. The Directive does not however prevent workers benefiting from more favourable terms that might apply to similar workers in the state from which they are posted. Workers from non-member countries must not be given more favourable terms and conditions of employment than those applicable to similar workers from Member States.

On 29th May 2018 the EU voted to extend equal pay rights to all posted workers and also to provide better protection against exploitation and fraud. So far the extension appears to have affected construction workers only; however, all member states have until 28th May 2020 to implement the new rules in full.

Further rules on duration were decided upon. Presently there is no word about how this will apply in the UK following its withdrawal from the EU.

## POWER OF ATTORNEY

A person (donor) can delegate authority to another person to act on their behalf in financial and business matters (power of attorney). There is only one type of power that may be granted - lasting, however this can take two forms, health and welfare or property and financial.

A 'lasting power' may be granted by a donor in advance of becoming incapable, enabling the attorney to act after the donor has lost capacity to act independently and this replaced the enduring power of attorney from October 2007, though enduring powers registered prior to October 2007 continue to be operational. A nominated person, or attorney must be over 18 years of age, be mentally capable and not bankrupt. Any number of persons may be appointed, including a bank or a company.

A 'lasting power' must be registered with the Court of Protection before attorneys may act on the donor's behalf and whilst this will always happen when the donor becomes mentally incapable of acting on his or her own behalf, it is advisable to register powers sooner rather than later to account for the time needed between applying and obtain registration. Implementation of the powers, where it is proven they must be exercised, can then occur instantly whereas an unregistered power must be registered before it can be invoked and this may take several weeks, sometimes months. Notice of registration will be given to the donor, certain near relatives and other co-attorneys. A fee is charged for each power to be registered.

Powers, which a donor may delegate to an attorney, include signing of cheques, administering accounts (which includes dealing with an employer and the payroll administrator), share dealing, making reasonable gifts to those related to the donor, and if the health and welfare power is applied for and granted, any decision making in respect of health care. Where more than one attorney is appointed, they may be appointed jointly (they must act together) or severally (they may act individually). In addition, each may be allotted separate areas of responsibility.

## PROBATE

An organisation holding money in a deceased person's name will need to know to whom payment may be made. A specified person will have the responsibility for collecting all monies owed to, paying all debts, and distributing the estate, of a deceased person. Probate is the issuing of a legal document to a person(s) granting that responsibility.

A Grant of Representation, often referred to as probate, is issued by the Probate Registry, which may take one of three types:
* Probate - issued to an executor(s) named in the deceased's will
* Letters of Administration (with will), issued where a will exists with no named executor, or where executors do not wish to deal with the estate.
* Letters of Administration, issued where no will has been made, or where a will is invalid.

A fee will be payable dependant on the size of an estate, and any inheritance tax due against the estate must be paid before a grant of probate can be issued. A grant is not always demanded, some organisations apply conditions that preclude the requirement for a grant of probate, usually where the amount of money held is small and there are no complicating and related issues. The Courts Service issue a useful booklet, PA2, for the guidance of applicants for probate.

## QUALITY STANDARD

A new standard for validating End of Year returns was introduced by HMRC from 6th April 2004 and applied to year end returns (forms P35 and P14) from May 2005 onwards and in-year forms (P45 and the suite of P46 forms) from 6th April 2009 to 5th April 2012. It was replaced by the Enhanced Recognition Scheme from 1st October 2011. The current guidance on the use of recognised software can be found at https://www.gov.uk/payroll-software but contains no recommendations by HMRC.

## QUARTERLY PAYMENT OF PAYE

An employer reasonably assessing that monthly remittances to the HMRC will not exceed the following threshold may choose to pay monies over on a quarterly basis. At April 2017 legislation suggested that the Apprenticeship levy cannot be paid quarterly and this has not been clarified since. It is understood that so few quarterly PAYE payers will be affected that insisting on monthly Apprenticeship levy payment will not occur in practice.

## Quarterly Payment (Monthly PAYE Threshold) from 6th April 1994

| Tax year from | Threshold £ | Tax year from | Threshold £ | Tax year from | Threshold £ |
|---|---|---|---|---|---|
| 06.04.1994 | 400 | 06.04.2002 | 1,500 | 06.04.2010 | 1,500 |
| 06.04.1995 | 600 | 06.04.2003 | 1,500 | 06.04.2011 | 1,500 |
| 06.04.1996 | 600 | 06.04.2004 | 1,500 | 06.04.2012 | 1,500 |
| 06.04.1997 | 600 | 06.04.2005 | 1,500 | 06.04.2013 | 1,500 |
| 06.04.1998 | 600 | 06.04.2006 | 1,500 | 06.04.2014 | 1,500 |
| 06.04.1999 | 1,000 | 06.04.2007 | 1,500 | 06.04.2015 | 1,500 |
| 06.04.2000 | 1,000 | 06.04.2008 | 1,500 | 06.04.2016 | 1,500* |
| 06.04.2001 | 1,000 | 06.04.2009 | 1,500 | *No changes since 2016 | |

# REAL TIME INFORMATION (RTI)

Beginning with a live pilot from April 2012 and with full mandation for virtually all PAYE schemes from September 2013, employers and pension providers have had to send payroll information (a Full Payment Submission (FPS)) to HMRC each time that a payroll is run. Submission channels are as follows:

* Internet via government gateway (this replaced EDI from September 2018)
* EDI – Electronic Data Interchange (decommissioned in September 2018)
* Basic PAYE Tools via HMRC website for small employers with up to 9 employees and without payroll software
* Paper (from April 2014) – for the groups who are exempt from statutory online filing: care and support employers, the digitally excluded and those with a religious objection to the use of computers.

The data supplied is used by HMRC to improve the operation of PAYE by allowing codes to be adjusted in-year and by DWP to drive Universal Credit processes which started in October 2013 and is slowly being rolled-out to all benefit claimants over a long period. To ensure the integrity of payroll data i.e. that a gross to net has been run to accompany a payment, HMRC require:

* that the FPS is received on or before the date of payment (prior to 6th April 2019, within three days of payment), and
* those payees paid by BACS must have a cross reference supplied at employee level on the FPS and on the BACS file that will allow HMRC to match the two entries.

Before the remittance of income tax, NICs and student loan deductions is made each month/quarter, employers may have to send an Employer Payment Summary (EPS) to HMRC. This is necessary if the amount to be paid over differs from the amount HMRC will have derived from the FPS sent for that tax month/quarter, for example where statutory payment compensation or sub-contractor deductions suffered are due to be offset. The EPS for recoveries can be sent simultaneously with the FPS for the same payments (prior to 6th April 2015 this had to be sent between 6th and 19th of the following month) and contain YTD statutory payment figures.

The EPS is also used to inform HMRC that no payments have been made to any payees for the tax month in question. An EPS for 'no payment' can be sent:

* for up to 6 months at a time in advance,
* in-month (from April 2014)
* retrospectively between 6th and 19th for the prior tax month that ended on 5th month.

## New employees

Accurate data capture is vital to allow for matching with HMRC and DWP records. Employers are expected to verify key data: forename, surname, DOB, NINO, gender and address back to an official source (passport, P45 etc) before submitting it to HMRC. A new NINO verification service allows HMRC to supply and verify NINOs electronically to employers after receipt of an FPS.

P45 forms are no longer sent to HMRC as a separate file but are fully incorporated into the FPS. All new employees must complete the new employee statement A, B or C questions even if they present a P45, preferably using the starter checklist at https://www.gov.uk/government/publications/paye-starter-checklist.

This was implemented from April 2014 at which point the P46 was removed. P45s are likely to be abolished in due course.

Even if the P45 has been supplied by the new employer there are circumstances where the new employer will have to change the P45 instructions. Where an in-date P45 is supplied with codes other than BR, 0T or a D Prefix statement B is selected within payroll software and the code from the P45 is used. For P45s with BR, 0T or D Prefix statement C plus the P45 code is used. Where no statement is supplied then option C is used and code 0T/1 allocated. Whilst previous pay and tax are recorded they are not sent to HMRC as they will have been supplied by the previous employer.

### Payroll errors/ad-hoc salary advances
Where a payment to an individual is made outside the payroll cycle to correct an error, the updated YTD figures should be supplied on a supplementary or next main FPS. The remittance to HMRC must not be adjusted until the corrective FPS has been sent.

### Tax codes and student loan notices
These are increasingly being downloaded by employers but continue to be received on paper on the rare occasion that they are necessary. Student loan notices received in respect of an off-payroll worker in the public sector are supposed to be ignored as SLD will not apply to such workers, however many employers have indicated that SL1 instructions will always be honoured.

### Leavers
Leaving dates (the date that contract ends or the date of last payment if that is more than 30 days after the contract end date) are supplied on the FPS and a P45 provided to the payee as now. If HMRC does abolish the P45 form there is every likelihood that a replacement "leaving certificate" will replace it, meaning that in practical terms things will not change, except that there will be no requirement for the certificate to be supplied to the new employer.

### Year End
The provision of a P60 and submission of P11Ds (and P9Ds prior to April 2016) remains unchanged. The scheme must also be 'closed down' for the year by 19th April by submitting a 'final file' declaration. This is done within payroll software on either the last FPS for the tax year or on an EPS if no payments are to be made in month 12. Any YTD corrections to be made after that time must be supplied on an Earlier Year Update file (similar to a P14 adjustment) for employee level corrections and an EPS, for the appropriate tax year, for employer level corrections. Ideally both of these should be received by HMRC by 19th May.

### Generic Notification Service (GNS)
These messages are sent to schemes as an 'early warning' of a potential penalty situation and began to be rolled out late in 2103 but were then suspended as the messages were incorrectly targeted. They were relaunched in 2014. The aim is to be able to provide an electronic warning to the scheme that:
- They have not filed a return at all for the tax month (either a Nil EPs or Nil FPS)
- That have not filed as many returns for the month as HMRC expected
- They have filed an FPS after the date of payment of at least one record in the FPS
- They have not paid their remittance in full and on time
- GNS notices are also being used to advise employers of student loan issues however some doubt remains as to the legal nature of such notices.

### Penalties
Existing PAYE penalties continue for 2014/15 and new ones are introduced as follows:
Existing penalties:
- Incorrect return penalties levied for failure to take reasonable care when submitting any FPS within the tax year. The penalty percentage of between 30% and 70% of the 'potential lost revenue' depends upon the behaviour of the employer that led to the error.
- Late filing at year end (19th May for the last time for 13/14 even though files must be received by 19th April) incurs a penalty of £100 per 50 employees for each month or part-month that the return is outstanding
- The surcharge levied at year end for failing to pay in full and on time after one un-penalised default. The level of the surcharge is as below in the table headed 'late payment penalty'.

New penalties:
- Daily interest for late payment (introduced from April 2014) will be calculated on any outstanding debt and levied when the payment is finally made
- Late filing of FPS in-year (introduced in October 2014 for employers with 51 or more employees and from April 2015 for all other employers):
- if the FPS is filed later than any payment date within an FPS, the return is late. The automated late filing penalty will be based on the size of the PAYE scheme.
- Schemes can dispute their size banding if they are now smaller than the band used.
- Each scheme will be allowed one un-penalised default so that the first filing default every 12 months will not attract a penalty.
- Only one penalty will be levied each tax month (even if the employer defaults more than once in the month as the payroll is run weekly).
- The penalties will be charged quarterly but notified monthly, this will allow the employer to react to the GNS warning and avoid the penalty being levied.
- In-year late payment introduced from April 2015
- The automated late payment penalty will be issued where payment has not been made in full and on time and is based on the current late payment surcharge
- Late filing of FPS penalty from October 2014.

| Number of Employees | Monthly Penalty |
|---|---|
| 1 to 9 | £100 |
| 10 to 49 | £200 |
| 50 to 249 | £300 |
| 250 + | £400 |

| No. of Defaults in the Tax Year | Percentage Penalty |
|---|---|
| 1 to 3 | 1% |
| 4 to 6 | 2% |
| 7 to 9 | 3% |
| 10 + | 4% |

### Viewing liabilities
HMRC introduced a new facility known as both the Business Tax Dashboard or Liabilities and Payments Viewer to allow employers and pension payrolls, but not agents, to see a scheme's liabilities. The viewer is updated with payments made each night Monday to Friday and with FPS and EPS figures twice monthly around 12th and 20th.

This is accessed via PAYE Online using a government gateway password and ID. Any figures shown that cannot be reconciled by the scheme should be referred to the disputed charges team via the Employer Helpline to forestall compliance activity whilst the discrepancy (probably due to a duplicate employment - see 'current issues' below) is investigated. During 2017 a number of developments of the employer dashboard were implemented and this will continue into 2018.

### Specified charge
Where HMRC have not received (or haven't registered as receiving!) an FPS or Nil EPS for a tax month they can legally estimate the payment due based on the last 3 FPSs or 1/12th of the prior year's total liability and can enforce that debt. Where an employer notices a specified charge shown on the viewer and knows a file was sent this is an immediate cause for concern and should be logged with the disputed charges team.

### Current issues
All of the years since RTI was implemented in April 2013 have been a learning curve for HMRC and employers, agents and pension payroll providers. Some areas of concern emerged and some remain unresolved:
- Whilst HMRC's RTI systems appear to be handling 'real world' scenarios much better and improves each year, where taxpayer data has to be amended often, it continues to perform poorly. This continues to be of particular concern around the fundamental activities of starting and ending employment where new employment details are implemented sooner than those of the corresponding leaver.

- A number of routine scenarios such as changes of start or leave date or taxpayer designatory data (such as DOB or marital status) lead HMRC to duplicate the taxpayer's record on receipt of the FPS.

This can have the effect of
- Causing a 0T tax code to be issued to the taxpayer who is perceived to have two employments with the same scheme simultaneously
- Overstating the scheme liabilities as the YTD tax, NICs and student loans from the erroneous record are added in twice

HMRC's new accounting system often then takes these incorrect liability figures and
- outputs them to the Liabilities and Payments Viewer and
- expects payment to be made based on the overstated liability and initiates compliance activity when it's not.

Since 2017 HMRC's use of "dynamic coding" has caused alarming fluctuations in coding for some employees. In many cases the new system appeared to react too quickly to fluctuations in pay and hence applied wholly incorrect tax codes. In some cases employers were unlawfully ignoring code changes in order to prevent financial hardship. For 2019 HMRC promised to make attempts to smooth out the application of new codes and renamed the process "in year triggers". To date this process does not appear to have solved the basic problem and it is expected to continue to cause issues during 2020.

Work continues with HMRC to try to identify and address flaws in the design of the two central systems. Since April 2017 significant improvements have been made. It remains the case, however, that these issues, unchanged since 2018, impact more on the very smallest employers.

## RECORD RETENTION

HMRC advise employers to retain PAYE records for a minimum of three years after the end of the tax year to which they relate in order to comply with the Income Tax (Pay as You Earn) Regulations 2003. This includes details of Statutory Payments (SAP, SMP, SPP and SSP) and student loans. MAT B1 maternity certificates and statutory payment exclusion forms.

The Registered Pension Schemes (Provision of information) Regulations 2006 place similar record retention on sponsoring employers of an occupational pension scheme. For auto-enrolment purposes some records need to be kept for six years to prove compliance.

There are other considerations such as outstanding payments and retrospective pay arrears for which supporting records may need to be retained that precede this period. A more important issue however relates to penalties that could be incurred following an HMRC compliance check if records are not available to mitigate the penalty.

In general terms where an inspection reveals a practice which has resulted in an error (underpayment) in the calculation of PAYE due, the calculation of the total liability may be made on the basis that the error has been perpetuated during the whole of the current year and up to three previous tax years.

All HMRC assessment rules now use this fixed four year period in which penalties can be levied, though in practice HMRC can go back an unlimited period of time if criminal evasion is suspected. Six years is the time limit to enforce a contractual agreement, as prescribed by the Limitation Act 1980.

For example, failure to subject a specific type of payment to PAYE over the period of records inspected, say £1000 underpaid following the examination of two monthly payrolls could result in a penalty calculated thus: £1000 x 6 (One year's liability) x 4 (four year's retrospection) = £24,000.

In order to mitigate such a penalty responsibility rests with the employer to prove otherwise by reference to actual records. For this reason employers may well deem it prudent to retain records for longer than the statutory period of current tax year plus three previous years.

This has become even more important since implementation of the Data Protection Act 2018 in May 2018. Employers must decide what their record retention policy is and which of the variable factors it is going to comply with and then convey that decision to employees as part of its DPA 2018 statement.

Employers will then have to implement strict destruction processes once the time limit decided upon is up.

# SALARY SACRIFICE AND OPTIONAL REMUNERATION

The principle of a salary sacrifice is that an employee forgoes the right to receive part of contractual pay, which may include salary or wages, annual bonus or cash allowance, in return for an agreement that the employer will provide some form of non-cash benefit such as:
- a contribution to an employee's pension scheme
- the provision of childcare vouchers
- an employer-provided bicycle

and that such provision may result in NIC and/or tax savings.

A scheme where a deduction from net pay is used to 'purchase' a benefit will not benefit from NICs and/or tax savings as it will be classed by HMRC as an unsuccessful salary sacrifice, the employee still being able to decide how to apportion the net pay.

Schemes have been termed as "diverted pay" or "optional remuneration" arrangements, however these all are ways of describing salary sacrifice.

Salary sacrifice scheme rules must ensure that:
- potential future salary or bonus is sacrificed before it is treated as received for tax or NICs purposes and that there is an audit trail to support this assertion. (N.B. many employers take a cautious view that an agreement to sacrifice needs to be completed before the pay becomes taxable, which could be deemed to be as early as the 6th of the month in which the wage or salary payment is due
- there is a genuine reconstruction of the contract between employer and employee to reflect a lower cash remuneration, and the provision in return of a non-cash benefit
- the employee's pay is not reduced to a level below the National Minimum or Living Wage and ideally not below the LEL. This requirement is to be discussed as part of the review of the Low Pay Commission's work post 2020 because of the fact that salary sacrifice involves the employee voluntarily giving up pay and is not a deduction for the benefit of the employer.

If the employee is able to give up the benefit at any time resulting in a return to the original 'cash' salary the sacrifice could be both ineffective and chargeable to tax and Class 1 NICs in full. This does not apply to the following benefits where employees may opt-in and out of a sacrifice as often as they wish, or amend the amount so sacrificed as long as this is done before the gross to net is run: All types of employer supported or provided childcare, bicycles and bicycle safety equipment, workplace parking, pension membership (during the statutory opt-out period).

Apart from these benefits changes can be made a maximum of, annually or, when certain 'lifestyle events' occur, e.g. the birth of a child, redundancy of a partner. In essence these should be significant changes that materially affect the employee's personal circumstances that are irregular and could not have been foreseen at the outset (opting-out of a pension scheme within the prescribed "opt-out" period is now included in this definition)

It should be recognised by both parties that other benefits might be affected by the adoption of a salary sacrifice scheme:
- reduced contributory related benefits e.g. Employment and Support Allowance
- earnings-related statutory payments SMP, SSP, SAP, OSPP and ShPP.

Where a portion of salary is sacrificed in exchange for a benefit, the benefit will be treated as a taxable benefit in kind reported on the P11D or within the FPS for payrolled BiKs unless there is an exemption from tax, for example as is the case for a certain amount of childcare vouchers.

Since April 2017 some tax-exempt benefits in kind have lost their exemption if they are obtained using a salary sacrifice arrangement. The main benefits which use salary sacrifice as part of the arrangement, pension funding, pensions advice, childcare provision, cycle to work schemes and ultra-low emissions vehicles will retain their exemption, whether salary sacrifice is used or not, whereas others, such as parking at or near the place of work, will lose their exemption.

Also, since 6th April 2017 the existence of any form of cash for benefit exchange may have the effect of altering the cash equivalent value of a benefit in kind. If the amount of the sacrifice is greater than the charge to tax on the benefit in kind, the benefit in kind will be valued at the higher amount. Cash for benefit arrangements will also be considered to be salary sacrifice arrangements and be affected in the same manner.

Some transitionary arrangements are in place to protect employees who were already tied into a long-term benefit in kind arrangement. This covered all benefits initially until 5th April 2018 but extended to 2021 only for cars, vans, accommodation and school fees. Any amendment to the contract to supply has the effect of ending the transitional arrangement for that employee.

## SETTLEMENT AGREEMENT (compromise agreement pre-July 2013)

A settlement agreement is an arrangement or contract between an employer and an employee for payment of a single sum in full settlement of various outstanding potential claims on termination of employment. The employer will, in making a single payment, seek to ensure that claims cannot be made at a later date through the courts in respect of those items included in the agreement.

Such an agreement may include in the single payment such items as:
- salary or wages not paid in full
- contractual Payment in Lieu of Notice (PILON)
- outstanding issues related to employment rights' legislation
- damages for a breach of contractual terms (period of notice etc.)
- outstanding issues related to discrimination in serving of termination notice.

ACAS provides a template letters and a Code or Practice on their use at
http://www.acas.org.uk/media/pdf/j/8/Acas-Code-of-Practice-on-Settlement-Agreements.pdf

## SHARE OWNERSHIP

### Share Incentive Plan (SIP)
A scheme introduced on 6th April 2000, to encourage employee share ownership. The main features are:
- employers may give employees free shares up to a permitted annual maximum (£3,600 from April 2014, £3000 prior)
- employees may purchase 'partnership' shares out of pre-tax (and NICs) income (including annual bonuses) up to a maximum annual limit (£1,800 from April 2044, £1,500 prior) (or 10% of salary, if less).
- employers may match an award of partnership shares with an annual award of 'matching' shares up to the maximum threshold of 2 free shares per partnership share purchased
- dividends where paid may be reinvested in further shares free of tax, up to certain limits, and must normally be held for a minimum period of three years
- all such shares held for a period of five years are exempt from both income tax, capital gains tax and NICs.

A statutory Corporation Tax deduction for the costs of providing shares is available for accounting periods starting on or after 1st January 2003. Reduced gross pay due to SIP contributions can affect entitlement to earnings related benefits such as SSP.

### Share Ownership Maxima from 6th April 2014

| Date from | Employee | | Employer |
| | Free Share Annual Maxima £ | Partnership Share Annual Maxima £ | Matching Share Annual Maxima £ |
|---|---|---|---|
| 06.04.2014 | 3,600 | 1,800 or 10% of salary | 3,600 |

### Savings Related Share Option Schemes (SAYE)
A scheme where employees have a fixed deduction from pay up to a maximum limit of £500 per month (£250 prior to 6th April 2014) with the option of buying shares at a price fixed (the market value at the time of commencement of the plan or at a discount of no more than 20%), with the accrued savings at the end of the savings period. From April 1996 the savings period is either three or five years. There is no tax or NICs payable

when options under SAYE Scheme are received. However, Capital Gains Tax may be charged where the option is exercised. The employer completes Form 34 at the end of the tax year.

### Sharesave Scheme Interest Rates

| Date from | Bonus Rate x monthly payments | | | Annual Equivalent Rate % | | | Early Leaver |
|---|---|---|---|---|---|---|---|
| | 3 yrs | 5 yrs | 7 yrs | 3 yrs | 5 yrs | 7 yrs | % |
| 01.10.1998 | 2.75 | 7.5 | 13.5 | 4.83 | 4.65 | 4.52 | |
| 01.10.2001 | 2.0 | 6.2 | 11.9 | 3.67 | 3.99 | 4.07 | |
| 01.09.2002 | 1.8 | 5.7 | 11.0 | 3.18 | 3.57 | 3.69 | |
| 27.04.2003 | 1.0 | 3.7 | 7.6 | 1.74 | 2.34 | 2.44 | 1.0 |
| 01.09.2003 | 0.9 | 3.4 | 7.1 | 1.61 | 2.17 | 2.48 | 2.0 |
| 01.09.2005 | 1.4 | 4.4 | 8.4 | 2.49 | 2.79 | 2.91 | 1.5 |
| 01.09.2006 | 1.8 | 5.5 | 10.3 | 3.19 | 3.46 | 3.52 | 2.0 |
| 01.09.2007 | 2.4 | 7.2 | 12.7 | 4.23 | 4.48 | 4.46 | 3.0 |
| 27.12.2008 | 1.5 | 4.8 | 9.3 | 2.67 | 3.04 | 3.20 | 2.0 |
| 17.02.2009 | 0.6 | 2.6 | 5.6 | 1.08 | 1.67 | 1.98 | 0.5 |
| 29.05.2009 | 0.6 | 2.2 | 5.2 | 0.54 | 1.42 | 1.84 | 0.36 |
| 12.09.2010 | 0.0 | 0.9 | 3.2 | 0.0 | 0.59 | 1.15 | 0.0 |
| 27.02.2011 | 0.1 | 1.7 | 4.8 | 0.18 | 1.10 | 1.70 | 0.12 |
| 12.08.2011 | 0.00 | 0.00 | 1.60 | 0.00 | 0.00 | 0.58 | 0.00 |
| 23.09.2011 | 0.00 | 0.90 | 3.50 | 0.00 | 0.59 | 0.25 | 0.00 |
| 01.08.2012 | 0.00 | 0.00 | 0.00 | 0.00 | 0.00 | 0.00 | 0.00 |

Up to £20,000 of shares obtained using either a SIP or SAYE may be transferred into a Stocks and Shares ISA, depending on circumstances and various restrictions and requirements laid down by HMRC.

## SMALL BUSINESS

A 'small employer' as far as HMRC is concerned is one whose total net PAYE is not more than the threshold of £1,500 a month, on average, throughout the tax year, this includes:
- PAYE income tax, plus
- Deductions on account from payments to sub-contractors in CIS plus
- Primary and secondary Class 1 NICs, plus
- Student loan deductions, plus
- Apprenticeship levy*

Less:
- PAYE income tax paid on account to a contractor in the Construction Industry by a sub-contractor that is a limited company
- Amount of SAP, SMP, SPP, ShPP and SSP that the employer is entitled to recover.

*Depending on the corporate structure and the share of the levy allowance it is possible that a small business, despite having a paybill of less than £3m a year, may have to pay the levy.

Employers and contractors in the construction industry, whose average monthly payments in respect of PAYE & NICs are less than £1,500 may remit their payments quarterly on the 22nd July, October, January and April or the 19th if they do not pay electronically (see quarterly payments above).

### Small Employers' Relief (SER) for Statutory Payments
Small Employers for this purpose are defined as those with a total Class 1 NICs of less than £45,000 in the year prior to the year the claim is made. If they qualify, they are entitled to recover 100% of their SMP, SPP,

SAP payments plus compensation for the NICs paid of 3% (103% in total) (104.5% prior to 6th April 2011). To qualify for Small Employers Relief, the total gross employer's plus employees' Class 1 NICs across all PAYE schemes 'in the organisation' for the previous year must be less than the threshold.

| Date from | Threshold £ | | Date from | Threshold £ |
|---|---|---|---|---|
| 06.04.2004 - 05.04.2006 | 40,000 | | 6.04.2007 onwards | 45,000 |

It should be noted that "small employer" has further complications in that different branches of government use different definitions. Examples are "small employer" for pension purposes being five or fewer employees, but the worst example is HMRC who, in addition to the two definitions above, also use fewer than 10 employees as an additional definition of "small employer".

## SOCIAL SECURITY BENEFITS

The National Insurance Fund provides contributory-based benefits against loss of income for the disabled, retired, sick, unemployed and widowed. In addition, it provides some assistance for people with maternity expenses. The National Insurance Fund, established in 1911, is in truth not a fund in the generally understood manner. It is a pay-as-you-go scheme where current contributors fund current beneficiaries.

Whilst the contribution record of an individual may provide the basis for calculating entitlements, the funding of those entitlements will come from contributions made from all current contributors.

This is not an uncommon practice, particularly in the pension field. Some major public sector 'funds' relating to the Health Service, Police and Teachers - are financed on the same principle.

Some benefits previously provided through the Social Security system, have been transferred to employers both in administration and funding. Sickness Benefit was replaced in 1983 by Statutory Sick Pay, which when originally implemented transferred the administration to the employer whilst funding remained with central government.

Similarly, Statutory Maternity Pay replaced Maternity Benefit in 1986. In both cases funding has over the years been gradually transferred to employers (SSP 100%, SMP 8%) with limited exceptions for small employers. Included in this reference book are the basic outlines of the principle payroll related benefits currently available, together with details of some relevant former benefit arrangements. Comprehensive entitlement rights can only be obtained by reference to Jobcentre Plus or HMRC offices.

From October 2013 the following state benefits started their transition to the new Universal Credit (UC): tax credits: housing benefit, incapacity benefit, employment and support allowance and Jobseeker's allowance. UC is designed to flex each month based on real time earnings information sent to HMRC by employers after each payroll run.

## STUDENT LOANS COMPANY (SLC)

Set up in 1990, the SLC is the principal source of funds for undergraduates. It administers the Government's student loan schemes. When taking a loan the learner completes a combined loan application and an agreement form. Each loan is given an individual reference number by the SLC. The agreement is that repayment will be in accordance with government regulations applicable at the time repayments are due.

The Consumer Credit Act does not cover a Student Loan and a formal credit agreement is not required. Repayment is based on the earnings of the borrower. Those of husband, wife, partner or other relatives are not taken into account. Income from disability benefits is also excluded.

Unearned income exceeding the applicable threshold must be declared to HMRC under self-assessment and a separate calculation and repayment will be made. Repayments are calculated as a percentage of income above an agreed annual threshold level.

The interest rate is set each year in advance, effective from 1st September, and is linked to inflation in line with the Retail Prices Index. Additional lump sum repayments may be made by direct agreement with the company.

Complaints are dealt with via the SLC and HMRC's own internal complaints procedures. If these are not resolved they are passed on to the Student Loan Company's Independent Assessor or the Tax Tribunal.

Annual statements are issued to borrowers at the end of August each year until repayment commences at which point an interim statement is issued. Thereafter, the distribution of statements is dependent on the repayment process:

- PAYE - After the end of each tax year, after the SLC have received details from HMRC
- Self-Assessment (SA) - After the end of each tax year, subject to prompt submission of SA returns
- Outside the UK tax system - Shortly after the end of each tax year.

## STUDENT LOANS - COLLECTION

Introduced on 1st April 2000, the scheme passed responsibility to employers for:
deducting student loan repayments from an employee's earnings
- paying deductions recovered to HMRC
- advising the borrower and HMRC of amounts recovered and paid over.

The employer is not responsible for:
- identifying employees who are liable for student loan repayments, except in the case of new employees (this is the responsibility of HMRC)
- responding to enquiries from employees about the loan (this is the responsibility of the Student Loans Company).

HMRC advise the employer of an existing employee against whom deductions are to commence by issuing a Start Notice - SL1. New employees with a continuing loan are identified by the entry 'Y' in the correct student loan (SL) box on form P45 or the appropriate statement on the new employee declaration form. When issuing a form P45 to a leaver it is the employer's responsibility to complete the correct student loan box if a Start Notice has been received even if no deductions have been made.

The employer may cease deductions only when advised by HMRC. This will usually be on receipt of a 'Stop Notice (SL2)'. Exceptionally HMRC may directly request by telephone that deductions cease and in such cases a 'Stop Notice' will be issued in confirmation. Start and stop notices should be implemented on the first reasonably practical pay day after the date of issue shown on the notice.

Under the Repayment of Teachers' Loan Scheme (RTL) (now ended) teachers in certain shortage subjects had their loan written off by DfES for each year they remain teaching that subject. The RTL scheme ran outside the SL1/SL2 process and was controlled by letters exchanged between SLC and the borrower who in turn informed the employer when loan repayments were suspended due to an RTL scheme being in operation. The scheme ended in 2005 but the remaining teachers on the scheme were able to continue to have their loan paid off as the scheme ran until 2015.

Since December 2009 the SLC Student Loan Company has moved borrowers to direct debit for the last 23 months of the predicted loan period to avoid fluctuations of earnings leading to an over-repayment. Employers will simply be issued with an SL2 stop notice in these situations.

From April 2019 SLC put into operation a More Frequent Data Sharing (MFDS) process in order to obtain the necessary information from employers more often and since September 2019 HMRC decided formally to use the GNS process to inform employers of important changes to an employee's deduction. This will only be used when HMRC believes the employer has been sent the required start (SL1) or stop (SL2) notices and then notes that the instruction has not been implemented and requires the employer to implement or cease deductions.

Employers continue to be advised that only the SL1 and SL2 notices can force a change to the payroll as these satisfy statutory requirements. The SL1 satisfies the requirements of section 13–16 of the ERA1996 whereas the GNS notice does not. Employers ought to contact HMRC upon receipt of a GNS notice and check on the position of an appropriate SL1 or SL2 before making any changes, particularly if the instruction is to commence deductions.

In addition, it is intended that from April 2020 payroll records will include an "off-payroll worker" indicator which will be used by HMRC to block SLC notices. Off payroll workers may be subject to PAYE deductions but they are not liable to repay student loans by deductions from payroll.

## Calculation of deduction

Earnings for student loan deduction purposes are those used to calculate Class 1 NICs. No account should be taken of the value of benefits-in-kind or other non-cash payments. Earnings are non-cumulative for the purpose of calculating deductions, i.e. each pay period is treated separately. Where Ni'able earnings in the pay period exceed the earnings threshold, deductions are made with reference to the SL3 tables provided by HMRC https://www.gov.uk/guidance/rates-and-thresholds-for-employers-2018-to-2019 .

Since 6th April 2016 there have been two types of SLD on an employer's payroll: Plan 1 students who are subject to the threshold of £19,390 (£18,935 in 2019/20) and Plan 2 students who are subject to a threshold of £26,575 (£25,725 in 2019/20). The government originally wanted to freeze the thresholds at the 2016/17 level until a review of repayments took place, however from 6th April 2018 both Plan 1 and 2 thresholds rose.

Starting in 2016 the SLC has started processing loans for additional courses which will start being recovered from around 2018/19. So far loans for;
• Taught postgraduate courses,
• PhD/masters research activities,
• Maintenance loans for part-time students and
• Second degrees in STEM subjects,
• have either started, see PGL below, or been discussed. Until full consultation occurs employers won't know whether such loans will be repaid using the current recovery from earnings procedures, nor what type of plan they will be.

In 2017 HMRC announced that on occasion its staff would request a student loan deduction start by telephone. This would only happen in an emergency and HMRC asked that employers adhere to this practice. Most employers are likely to demand an emergency SL1 as evidence before making any such deductions.

From 6th April 2019 one of the new types of study loan, the Post Graduate Loan (PGL) commences repayment. Repayments start at a threshold of £21,000 in earnings per year and carry a repayment rate of 6%.

## Student Loan Earnings Threshold & Repayment Rate (Plan 1)

## From 6th April 2000

| Date from | Annual £ | Monthly £ | Weekly £ | Repayment Rate % |
|---|---|---|---|---|
| 06.04.2000 | 10,000 | 833 | 192 | 9 |
| 06.04.2005 | 15,000 | 1,250 | 288 | 9 |
| 06.04.2012 | 15,795 | 1,316.25 | 303.75 | 9 |
| 06.04.2013 | 16,365 | 1,363.75 | 314.71 | 9 |
| 06.04.2014 | 16,910 | 1,409.16 | 325.19 | 9 |
| 06.04.2015 | 17,335 | 1,444.00 | 333.00 | 9 |
| 06.04.2016 | 17,495 | 1,457.00 | 336.00 | 9 |
| 06.04.2017 | 17,775 | 1,481.25 | 341.00 | 9 |
| 06.04.2018 | 18,330 | 1,527.00 | 352.00 | 9 |
| 06.04.2019 | 18,935 | 1,577.92 | 364.14 | 9 |
| **06.04.2020** | **19,390** | **1,615.83** | **372.88** | **9** |

## Student Loan Earnings Threshold & Repayment Rate (Plan 2)[1]

### From 6th April 2016

[1]Plan 2 is not applicable in Scotland

| Date from | Annual £ | Monthly £ | Weekly £ | Repayment Rate % |
|---|---|---|---|---|
| 06.04.2016 | 21,000 | 1,750.00 | 403.00 | 9 |
| 06.04.2018 | 25,000 | 2,083.00 | 480.00 | 9 |
| 06.04.2019 | 25,725 | 2,143.75 | 494.71 | 9 |
| 06.04.2020 | 26,575 | 2,214.58 | 511.06 | 9 |

## Post Graduate Loan Threshold & Repayment Rate (Plan 2)

### From 6th April 2019

| Date from | Annual £ | Monthly £ | Weekly £ | Repayment Rate % |
|---|---|---|---|---|
| 06.04.2019 | 21,000 | 1,750.00 | 403.85 | 6 |
| 06.04.2020 | 21,000 | 1,750.00 | 403.85 | 6 |

### Priority

Student loan repayment orders are classified as Priority Orders in relation to Attachment of Earnings Orders. When a Council Tax Order CTAEO is received at the same time as a student loan it blocks the repayment of the loan until the order is complete. In Scotland all court orders block the operation of a student loan.

### Returns and remittances

Details of deductions made are to be recorded on Full Payment Submissions and the letter 'Y' entered on form P45 in the appropriate box where termination of employment takes place, whether deductions have been taken or not. Deductions are paid over to HMRC monthly together with the tax and NICs collected during the same period.

### Future developments

In a bid to modernise the repayment system, the government will implement a new online service during 2020. This will allow borrowers to manage their loans more efficiently and provide them with more up to date information on balances.

From April 2021 Scottish graduates will need to be earning £25,000 a year before they start repaying their student loan.

## TIME OFF for TRAINING

From 6th April 2010 employers with more than 250 employees have to allow employees with 26 weeks' service the right to request unpaid time off to undertake training that will provide them with additional business skills.

## TURERA

The Trade Union Reform and Employment Rights Act 1993 introduced major reform of the law governing industrial relations and employment law in a number of areas. Section 15 of the Act established rules governing the deduction of union subscriptions from pay, commonly termed 'check-off'. This section arguably has the most impact on the administration of payroll.

For deductions from pay to be lawful there must be:
- prior written consent from the worker and
- where there is to be an increase in the amount deducted, the employer must give the employee at least one month's advance notice together with a reminder that consent to deductions from pay may be withdrawn at any time.

TURERA includes provisions governing:
- Election and political fund ballots
- Trade union merger ballots
- confidentiality of the independent scrutineers
- repeal of the Secretary of State's power to establish schemes for the funding of trade union ballots
- annual trade union certification returns
- provision of an annual financial statement to all trade union members
- power of investigation into trade union financial affairs
- provision of penalties for criminal offences and disqualification from office
- protection of union members or non-members against acts of discrimination by an employer to either deter employees from, or compel them to, join a trade union
- granting employees the right not to be excluded from union membership
- extension of conduct provisions for which discipline imposed by a trade union is unjustified
- industrial action by postal ballot and notice provisions
- rights of citizens to halt unlawful industrial action which deprives them of goods or services
- maternity leave and absence provisions for all employees regardless of their length of service or hours of work
- rights to written particulars of employment to all those employed for at least 8 hours a week
- right to an itemised statement of pay extended to employees working 8 or more hours per week (subsequently changed by the Employment Rights Act 1996)
- employment protection rights when carrying out duties related to health and safety. Provision for all employees of protection against dismissal for asserting a statutory employment right.

## VALUE ADDED TAX (VAT)

VAT is a tax on the final consumption of certain goods and services in the home market but is collected at every stage of production and distribution. A business should keep a record of its sales and purchases, and the amount of VAT it has charged and can reclaim.

VAT will apply to some aspects of the payroll function, mileage payments and expenses reimbursements, should they be carried out within payroll, however payroll staff need nothing more than a rudimentary knowledge of VAT in respect of record keeping and retention of receipts. All of this can be found in HMRC guidance at https://www.gov.uk/topic/business-tax/vat.

## WEEKLY WORKING HOURS

From 1st April 2009, the calculation of weekly working hours changed as a result of the introduction in the UK of new minimum statutory holiday entitlement in excess of that required by the Working Time Regulations (and the originating EU Directive).
Prior to this date, when calculating the average over a 17-week period, any weeks where a worker took a statutory holiday were included in the total hours (the weeks may not be used to reduce the total and similarly the overall average).

As this principle cannot be extended to the additional 8 days, these days can be used to reduce the average by being re-classified as 'non-working time' in the same manner as contractual leave is now. This may bring difficulties for employers who make regular calculations of working hours in order to ensure adherence to the 48-hour maximum.

## WORKER

A worker as defined for National Minimum and Living Wage regulations is someone:
- working under a contract of employment (an "employee"), or
- under some other form of contract (called a "worker's contract") under which he agrees to perform work personally for someone else but is not self-employed.

A director appointed under the Companies Act 2006 and who assumes the rights and obligations of a director is an office holder and not a "worker" and may or may not be an employee too depending upon whether there is a formal contract of employment.

All persons carrying out work for an organisation are defined as "worker" for various purposes. For automatic enrolment purposes it is important to determine if the person is a worker for the organisation in which case AE will apply or if the person is a worker for someone else in which case the AE requirements fall to that other person.

In some cases, someone subject to the off-payroll working rules, a worker can be an external contractor but their fees, as described upon an invoice for services, must be processed through PAYE in order that statutory deductions can be calculated and accounted for. No other worker rights apply in such cases.

The definition of worker, therefore, can be different for different organisations and for different purposes and it is important for employers to understand the anomalies and apply them accordingly.

## WORKER REGISTRATION SCHEME

The Worker Registration Scheme applied to most nationals of the A8 EU member states from 1st May 2004 to 30th April 2011. The eight nations entering the EU on 1st May 2004, known as the A8 Nations, were - Czech Republic, Estonia, Hungary, Latvia, Lithuania, Poland, Slovakia and Slovenia.

A worker was required to register if intending to work for an employer for more than one month, and, then having worked legally in the UK for 12 months without a break, had full rights of movement and was entitled to receive an EU residence permit in confirmation of their status. Nationals of Cyprus and Malta working in the UK were exempt and they could apply for a residence permit immediately.

In order to meet the requirements of the UKs exit from the EU, a new settled status scheme has been implemented, an application process for which is available on the Gov.uk website. This allows EU workers, including those living and working in the UK under various other schemes to apply to remain in the UK.

## WORKER AUTHORISATION SCHEME

Bulgaria and Romania, known as the A2 Nations, entered the EU On 1st January 2007 and, with specific and limited exceptions, were subject to additional provisions which are restricted to nationals of these two countries alone in respect of working in the UK, as permitted numbers are subject to quota. These restrictions ended on 1st January 2014. When Croatia joined the EU in July 2013 the same restrictions were extended to Croatian nationals who must hold a worker authorisation card.

As with all other matters relating to a worker's right to live and work in the UK, new systems and processes are in place to deal with status after the UK leaves the EU. Some details, however, remain to be determined.

## WORKING TIME REGULATIONS

The Government adopted the European Working Time Directive in 1998. The 1998 Working Time Regulations apply to all workers who are over school leaving age. Enhanced regulations applied to young workers until the 2003 regulations when they were fully incorporated into the WTRs. Prior to 25th October 2001 the regulations only applied to employees who had a contractual relationship for 13 weeks or more with their employers. The objective is to allow flexible working underpinned with minimum standards. Workers will have the recourse to an Employment Tribunal where they are not treated within the principles of the Directive.

### Provisions
- a maximum working week of 48 hours, subject to opt-out rules
- a minimum of 11 hours rest per day
- a break where more than 6 hours continuous working is planned
- restriction on night working
- a minimum of 4 weeks' paid annual leave (3 weeks in 1998) excluding bank holidays from 1st April 2009 (4 weeks including bank holidays prior to that date - see below)
- a minimum rest period of 1 day a week for adults  (2 days for adolescents)

### 48-hour rule
Workers should not work more than 48 hours per week, over a 17-week period, though this may be averaged over a period up to 12 months. Workers have the right to opt-out of this provision by written agreement with the employer or through an elected representative.

The removal of this option has been under debate in the European Parliament for many years but remains a cornerstone of the Uks approach to working time.

**Minimum rest period**
Each worker must have eleven consecutive hours rest in every 24 hours, and where the working day is greater than six hours there must be a break of at least 20 minutes.

**Night workers**
They must average eight hours rest in 24 hours over the averaging period of 17 weeks, although this can be extended with the agreement of the employees affected. All employees have the right to health assessments, and from 6th April 2003, all overtime (previously only guaranteed overtime) is included in the average night working limits.

**Holidays**
Until October 2007 employees were entitled annually to four weeks' (20 days) paid holiday including bank holidays (three weeks up to 1998). In the first year of service entitlement accrues pro-rata, in advance, for each completed month, or part month, of service rounded up to the nearest half day. Annual leave must be taken during the year and cannot be paid in lieu, except on termination of employment. This includes at the end of maternity leave where leave must be taken, it cannot be paid as holiday-in-lieu pay.

From October 2007 entitlement increased to 24 days and then as part of the move to include bank holidays in the total by increasing the entitlement to 28 days from April 2009. The extra 8 days are to be known as 'additional leave' and can be carried over to the following holiday year with the employer's consent. No statutory or additional leave may be bought out except on termination. The requirement to round up to the nearest full or half day was abolished in 2009 except in determining the amount of accrued holiday that is available to take in year one. In Northern Ireland the entitlement will also be to 28 days from April 2009 even though there are ten bank holidays in the province.

**Rolled Up Holiday Pay (RHP)**
An employee is entitled to a minimum of 28 days holiday pay (increased from October 2007 and April 2009 see above) to physically take time away from work. Prior to a ruling in March 2006 in the European Court of Justice (ECJ), officially referred to as the Court of Justice, it was commonplace for those employing casual employees where the nature of their work made it difficult to 'take' holiday, to 'roll up' the value of the holiday pay and add it to basic pay throughout the year. At the time of the ruling BEIS (DTI as it was then) published a statement to the effect that the practice of rolling up could continue whilst contracts were amended, but that employers should be moving to a system that allowed casual employees to 'take' holiday. No employees should any longer be in receipt of RHP although there are no easy alternatives that employers can utilise. Holiday pay is to be treated as 'normal' pay, and holidays accrue during periods of sickness absence (paid or unpaid) and all statutory maternity leave.

Recently it has been agreed that RHP is permissible as long as there is a justifiable reason for it, that employees are fully aware of the practice and know that they are not losing statutory entitlement as a consequence and that it is clearly shown on a statement, usually the pay advice, what is being paid.

**Records**
Must be kept which can show average hours worked, rest breaks and details of holiday paid. A list must be kept of those who have chosen to opt-out of the 48-hour rule.

**Derogations**
Those with unmeasured working time, which includes managing executives and family workers, are only subject to the regulations in respect of paid annual leave. Managers and others who determine their own hours may exceed the 48-hour maximum. Also, specified circumstances where there is a need for continuity of service or there is a surge in activity are accepted as allowing for a derogation from the hours and rest break provisions. This includes security services, hospital services, tourism, and dock workers.

**Holiday pay**
The amount of pay due to an employee who takes annual leave has been the subject of considerable debate and litigation in recent years. This has been caused by the fact that whilst the right to paid annual leave is enshrined in two working time regulation, The Working Time Regulations 2001 and The Working Time

Regulations 2007, the rate of pay applicable when a worker actually takes leave is determined by the their right to a rate of pay which can be found in The Employment Rights Act 1996.

Starting with Macconnachie v Leisure Leagues UK Ltd (2002), UK tribunals and the court of justice of the EU have been asked various questions about how to determine the number of hours applicable for holiday pay and whether this included holiday pay, Bamsey v Albion Engineering and Manufacturing Ltd (2003), and subsequently what the status of a bonus or commission payment is in terms of holiday pay, King v The Sash Window Workshop Ltd (2014).

At the time of publication there are still outstanding questions to be determined by the courts but the position to date continues to be that holiday pay must be determined by the normal working hours of the worker, including any guaranteed overtime and any non-guaranteed overtime.

Guaranteed overtime is defined as a work which an employer includes as part of the contractual terms and conditions of employment. As a consequence the employer is obliged to make the work available, or pay compensation for it, and upon doing so the worker is obliged to carry it out. Failure to do so would, theoretically lead to some form of disciplinary action. Such circumstances leads to the guaranteed overtime period naturally being a part of the normal working hours of the worker.

Non-guaranteed overtime is a period of work which is not enshrined in the workers terms and conditions of employment and hence would normally not be included in working time, however, because the work, when offered, must be performed by the worker the courts have determined that this too must be included in normal working time for the purposes of determining holiday pay.

Casual overtime has remained, technically outside the definition of normal working time for holiday pay purposes, however there is still the question of what happens when such casual overtime becomes so regular that it moves to being non-guaranteed, or even guaranteed by virtue of custom and practice.

The case of ZJR Lock v British Gas Trading Ltd and others (2014), looked into the status of commission payments in relation to holiday pay and concluded that if the workers remuneration includes commission or similar payment then such payment may be required to be included in holiday pay calculations.

This, however, has limited effect generally and it remains to be established exactly how the ruling will affect payments in the future.

During 2016 it emerged that the Lock case determined that some payments would be included in the calculation of holiday pay if they were "intrinsically linked". In addition, there remains some concern about the reference period for averaging variable payments in respect of holiday pay calculations. More answers are awaited from future deliberations and cases.

Employment tribunals in the latter part of 2017 determined that gaps of three months or more will disallow claims of unlawful deduction from pay for underpaid annual leave. This now means that employers liability in such cases is significantly reduced.

Whilst this rule applies generally the Court of Appeal case of Chief Constable of the PSNI v Agnew (and others) has shown that no such limit exists in the equivalent employment rights legislation in Northern Ireland and as a consequence, in NI alone, claims are not blocked by the three month rule.

The Taylor report, "Good Work", has made comment on the referencing period mentioned above and it remains to be seen what changes emerge over the next few years to address the issues raised in the various employment cases.

### Young Workers
From 6th April 2003 regulations were adopted to protect young workers (15 to 18 years of age), in limiting working time to not more than 8 hours a day and 40 hours a week. There are a number of limited exceptions related to particular occupations and circumstances which include workers in:
* hospitals or similar establishments
* cultural, artistic, sporting or advertising activities.

No young worker (adolescent) may work during a 'restricted period' with limited exceptions if the young worker is employed in:
* agriculture

- retail trade
- postal or newspaper deliveries
- hotel, public house, restaurant, bar or similar establishments
- bakeries.

The restricted period being either the period between 10 p.m. and 6 a.m. or, where required to work after 10 p.m., the period between 11p.m. and 7 a.m. Bar and restaurant workers may continue until midnight and from 4 a.m. There is an entitlement to a compensatory rest period where night work restrictions are excluded, and for work under such circumstances to be under adult supervision.

## YEAR END

There are many processes to be followed at the fiscal year end however some which are not part of the statutory return process may easily be overlooked.

### Nics

The records of female employees paying NICs at the married woman's reduced rate (category B) must be examined to ensure that, where no contributions have been made throughout the current year, and none during the preceding year, the contribution category is revised for the forthcoming year to ensure full rate deductions (category A) commence.

The Reduced Rate Certificate should be returned to the employee and a copy, suitably noted, retained for reference. Any NI table letter X entries should be examined to assess if the nil liability is still appropriate. Conversely where category A is set but earnings have been below the Lower Earnings Limit (LEL) £116 a week throughout 2018/19, category X could be inserted instead.

### Tax Codes

Records of employees having tax calculated on a week 1/month 1 basis at the year-end should be examined to ensure that, unless advised to the contrary by HMRC, tax is operated on a cumulative basis in the new tax year. Employers should amend all week 1/month 1 basis codes to cumulative before applying new tax year coding notices, whether manual or automated, which may include week 1/month 1 notifications.

If an employee/pensioner feels their coding for the new-year is incorrect they can ask HMRC to check this using the email enquiry forms to be found at https://www.gov.uk/tax-codes/if-you-think-youve-paid-too-much-tax

### Basic Earnings Assessment

All employees who joined a childcare voucher scheme from 6th April 2011 must have their earnings assessed at the start of each tax year to ensure that only the level of tax relief appropriate to their marginal rate of tax is afforded to them for employer-supported childcare – see https://www.gov.uk/government/publications/employer-supported-childcare

Originally it was thought that the Scottish higher rate threshold would apply to the basic earnings assessment from April 2017 when the Scottish parliament first used its tax raising powers to amend the rates and thresholds applying to taxpayers in Scotland.

However, in March 2017, well in advance of the Scottish parliaments decision to implement sweeping changes to rates and thresholds from April 2018, HMRC issued its own clarification note.

The relief thresholds for 2020/2021 are the same for all taxpayers in the UK and ignore any variations applied by other parts of the UK:

| Assessed income | Relief |
|---|---|
| Less than £50,000 rUK | £55 p.w. /£243 per month for 53 weeks p.a. |
| £50,001 - £150,000 rUK (unless joined scheme before 6.4.2011) | £28 p.w. / £124 per month for 53 weeks p.a. |
| More than £150,000 UK (unless joined scheme before 6.4.2011) | £25 p.w. /£108 per month for 53 weeks p.a. |

**Auto-enrolment qualifying earnings threshold**
Employers should check that their payroll software has the correct qualifying earnings thresholds for the new tax year as these must be input for each pay frequency as supplied by DWP.

### Pay reference period for 2019/2020

|  | Annual | 1 week | Fortnight | 4 weeks | 1 month | 1 quarter | Bi-annual |
|---|---|---|---|---|---|---|---|
| Lower level of qualifying earnings | £6,136 | £118 | £236 | £472 | £512 | £1,534 | £3,072 |
| Earnings trigger for automatic enrolment | £10,000 | £192 | £384 | £768 | £833 | £2,499 | £4,998 |
| Upper level of qualifying earnings | £50,000 | £962 | £1,924 | £3,847 | £4,167 | £12,500 | £25,000 |

### Pay reference period for 2020/2021

|  | Annual | 1 week | Fortnight | 4 weeks | 1 month | 1 quarter | Bi-annual |
|---|---|---|---|---|---|---|---|
| Lower level of qualifying earnings | £6,240 | £120 | £240 | £480 | £520 | £1,540 | £3,080 |
| Earnings trigger for automatic enrolment | £10,000 | £192 | £384 | £768 | £833 | £2,499 | £4,998 |
| Upper level of qualifying earnings | £50,000 | £962 | £1,924 | £3,847 | £4,167 | £12,500 | £25,000 |

# PART 2: TAX

## ANNUAL ALLOWANCES

### Annual allowances 1986/1987 to 2000/2001

| | 1986/87 £ | 1987/88 £ | 1988/89 £ | 1989/90 £ | 1990/91 £ |
|---|---|---|---|---|---|
| Single person | 2,335 | 2,425 | 2,605 | 2,785 | 3,005 |
| Married Man (Couple 1990/91) | 3,655 | 3,795 | 4,095 | 4,375 | 1,720 |
| Wife's earned income (max) | 2,335 | 2,425 | 2,605 | 2,785 | |
| Age Allowance | | Age 65-79 | | Age 65-74 | |
| Single person | 2,850 | 2,960 | 3,180 | 3,400 | 3,670 |
| Married Man (Couple 1990/91) | 4,505 | 4,675 | 5,035 | 5,385 | 2,145 |
| Income Limit | 9,400 | 9,800 | 10,600 | 11,400 | 12,300 |
| | | Age 80+ | | Age 75+ | |
| Single person | | 3,070 | 3,310 | 3,540 | 3,820 |
| Married Man (Couple 1990/91) | | 4,845 | 5,205 | 5,565 | 2,185 |
| Income Limit | | 9,800 | 10,600 | 11,400 | 12,300 |
| Additional Allowances | | | | | |
| Re: Child, claimant or wife ill | 1,320 | 1,370 | 1,490 | 1,590 | 1,720 |
| Blind Person | 360 | 540 | 540 | 540 | 1,080 |
| Widow's Bereavement | 1,320 | 1,370 | 1,490 | 1,590 | 1,720 |
| Emergency Tax Code | 352L | 376L | 404L | 419L | 300L |

| | 1991/92 £ | 1992/93 £ | 1993/94 £ | 1994/95 £ | 1995/96 £ |
|---|---|---|---|---|---|
| Personal Allowances | 3,295 | 3,445 | 3,445 | 3,445 | 3,525 |
| Married Couple | 1,720 | 1,720 | 1,720 | 1,720 | 1,720 |
| Age 65 - 74    Personal | 4,020 | 4,200 | 4,200 | 4,200 | 4,630 |
| Married Couple | 2,355 | 2,465 | 2,465 | 2,665 | 2,995 |
| Income Limit | 13,500 | 14,200 | 14,200 | 14,200 | 14,600 |
| Age 75 or over Personal | 4,180 | 4,370 | 4,370 | 4,370 | 4,800 |
| Married Couple | 2,395 | 2,505 | 2,505 | 2,705 | 3,035 |
| Income Limit | 13,500 | 14,200 | 14,600 | 14,200 | 14,600 |
| Additional Allowances | | | | | |
| Child, claimant or wife ill | 1,720 | 1,720 | 1,720 | 1,720 | 1,720 |
| Blind Person | 1,080 | 1,080 | 1,080 | 1,200 | 1,200 |
| Widow's Bereavement | 1,720 | 1,720 | 1,720 | 1,720 | 1,720 |
| Married Couple's rate restriction | | | | 20% | 15% |
| Emergency Tax Code | 329L | 344L | 344L | 344L | 352L |

| | 1996/97 £ | 1997/98 £ | 1998/99 £ | 1999/00 £ | 2000/01 £ | 2001/02 £ |
|---|---|---|---|---|---|---|
| Personal Allowances | 3,765 | 4,045 | 4,195 | 4,335 | 4,385 | 4,535 |
| Married Couple | 1,790 | 1,830 | 1,900 | 1,970 | | |
| Personal Allowance, age 65 - 74 | 4,910 | 5,220 | 5,410 | 5,720 | 5,790 | 5,590 |
| Personal Allowance, 75 or over | 5,090 | 5,400 | 5,600 | 5,980 | 6,050 | 6,260 |
| Income Limit | 15,200 | 15,600 | 16,200 | 16,800 | 17,000 | 17,600 |
| Married Couple aged 65 - 74 | 3,115 | 3,185 | 3,305 | 5,125 | 5,185 | 5,365 |
| Married Couple aged 75 or over | 3,155 | 3,225 | 3,345 | 5,195 | 5,255 | 5,433 |
| Additional Allowances | | | | | | |
| Re: Child, claimant or wife ill | 1,790 | 1,830 | 1,900 | 1,970 | 2,000 | 2,050 |
| Blind Person | 1,250 | 1,280 | 1,330 | 1,380 | 1,400 | 1,450 |
| Widow's Bereavement | 1,790 | 1,830 | 1,900 | 1,970 | 2,000 | N/A |
| Married Couple's rate restriction | 15% | 15% | 15% | 10% | 10% | 10% |
| Emergency Tax Code | 376L | 404L | 419L | 433L | 438L | 453L |

### Income Tax Annual Allowances 2002/2003 to date

| | 2002/3 £ | 2003/4 £ | 2004/5 £ | 2005/6 £ | 2006/7 £ | 2007/8 £ |
|---|---|---|---|---|---|---|
| Personal Allowances | 4,615 | 4,615 | 4,745 | 4,895 | 5,035 | 5,225 |
| Personal Allowance, age 65 - 74 | 6,100 | 6,610 | 6,830 | 7,090 | 7,280 | 7,550 |
| Personal Allowance, 75 or over | 6,370 | 6,720 | 6,950 | 7,220 | 7,420 | 7,690 |
| Income Limit | 17,900 | 18,300 | 18,900 | 19,500 | 1,660 | 1,730 |
| Married Couple aged 65 - 74 | 5,465 | 5,565 | 5,725 | 5,905 | 6,135 | 6,365 |
| Married Couple aged 75 or over | 5,535 | 5,635 | 5,795 | 5,975 | 6,065 | 6,285 |
| Additional Allowances | | | | | | |
| Re: Child, claimant or wife ill | 2,110 | 2,150 | 2,210 | 2,280 | 20,100 | 20,900 |
| Blind Person's Allowance | 1,480 | 1,510 | 1,560 | 1,610 | 2,350 | 2,440 |
| Married Couple's rate restriction | 10% | 10% | 10% | 10% | 10% | 10% |
| Emergency Tax Code | 461L | 461L | 474L | 489L | 503L | 522L |

| | 2008/9 | | 2009/10 | 2010/11 | 2011/12 | 2012/13 |
|---|---|---|---|---|---|---|
| | 6th April | 7th Sept | | | | |
| | £ | £ | £ | £ | £ | £ |
| Basic Personal Allowance | 5,435 | 6,035 | 6,475 | 6,475 | 7,475 | 8,105 |
| Personal Allowance aged 65 - 74 | 9,030 | | 9,490 | 9,490 | 9,940 | 10,500 |
| Personal Allowance, 75 or over | 9,180 | | 9,640 | 9,640 | 10,090 | 10.660 |
| Blind Person's Allowance | 1,800 | | 1,890 | 1,890 | 1,980 | 2,100 |
| Married Couples Allowance | 6,625 | | 6.965 | 6.965 | 7,295 | 7,705 |
| Married Couple aged 65 - 74 and born before 6th April 1935 | 6,535 | | - | - | - | - |
| Income Limit (Age-related Allowances) | 21,800 | | 22,900 | 22,900 | 24,000 | 25,400 |
| Minimum amount of Married Couples Allowance | 2,540 | | 2,670 | 2,670 | 2,800 | 2,960 |
| Married Couple's Rate Restriction | 10% | | 10% | 10% | 10% | 10% |
| Emergency Tax Code | 543L | 603L | 647L | 647L | 747L | 810L |

| | 2013/14 | 2014/15 | 2015/16 | 2016/17 | 2017/18 | 2018/19 |
|---|---|---|---|---|---|---|
| | £ | £ | £ | £ | £ | £ |
| Basic Personal Allowance - born after 5.4.48 | 9,440 | 10,000 | 10,600 | 11,000 | 11,500 | 11,850 |
| Personal Allowance - born 6.4.38 – 5.4.48 | 10,500 | 10,500 | 10,600 | 11,000 | N/A | N/A |
| Personal Allowance – born before 6.4.38 | 10,660 | 10,660 | 10,660 | 11,000 | N/A | N/A |
| Blind Person's Allowance | 2,160 | 2,230 | 2,290 | 2,290 | 2,320 | 2,320 |
| Married Couples Allowance | 7,915 | 8,165 | 8,355 | 8,355 | 8,445 | 8,445 |
| Minimum amount of Married Couples Allowance | 3,040 | 3,140 | 3,220 | 3,220 | 3,260 | 3,260 |
| Income Limit for personal and **age-related** Allowances to 2016/17 and personal allowance thereafter | 100,000 | 100,000 | 100,000 | 100,000 | 100,000 | 100,000 |
| Married Couple's Rate Restriction | 10% | 10% | 10% | 10% | 10% | 10% |
| Emergency Tax Code | 944L | 1000L | 1060L | 1100L | 1150L | 1185L |
| Marriage allowance and Civil Partnership 10% of Personal Allowance transferrable | | | 1,060 | 1,100 | 1,150 | 1,190 |

| | 2019/20 £ | 2020/21 £ |
|---|---|---|
| Basic Personal Allowance - born after 5.4.48 | 12.500 | **12.500** |
| Blind Person's Allowance | 2,450 | **2,450** |
| Married Couples Allowance | 8,915 | **8,915** |
| Minimum amount of Married Couples Allowance | 3,450 | **3,450** |
| Income limit for MCA | 29,600 | **29,600** |
| Income Limit (personal allowance) | 100,000 | **100,000** |
| Married Couple's Rate Restriction | 10% | **10%** |
| Emergency Tax Code | 1250L | **1250L** |
| Marriage and Civil Partnership Allowance: 10% of Personal Allowance transferrable | 1,250 | **1,250** |

## ALLOWANCES - HISTORICAL NOTES

### April 2000
The Married Couple's Allowance was withdrawn for couples aged under 65, and replaced by Children's Tax Credit on 6th April 2001 (from April 2003 - Child Tax Credit) at which time it ceased to be an allowance. Pensioners previously receiving the Married Couple's Allowance continue to do so whilst they qualify. Widow's Bereavement Allowance, withdrawn on 6th April 2000, was retained for the second year of entitlement for those widowed during 1999/2000.

### 2004/2005
Married Couple's (Civil Partnership) allowance applied to those under age 75 and born before 6th April 1935, and from 5th December 2005 Married Couple's Allowance has been available to Civil Partners and any unused Blind Persons allowance can be transferred to a married or civil partner.

### 2008/2009
The basic personal allowance was revised on the 7th September 2008 with retrospective effect to 6th April 2008.

### April 2010
The basic personal allowance is subject to total income limits of £100,000. Where an individual's income is above £100,000 the allowance will be reduced by £1 for every £2 above the threshold. Income is established via SA returns and the adjustment made to tax codes. Earnings and savings income above £150,000 liable to tax at 50%, to be known as the additional rate. This was delivered through PAYE - new tax tables were provided. Second jobs were not taxed at 50% as code D1 was not re-introduced until April 2011 so arrears accrued.

### April 2013
Earnings and savings income above £150,000 liable to tax at 45%. Age-related-allowances only awarded to those with a date of birth before 5th April 1948.

### April 2015
The age-related allowance for those born between 6th April 1938 and 5th April 1948 has been superseded by the basic personal allowance of £10,600. The age-related allowance for those born before 6th April 1948 remains at £10,660 as it is not subject to inflationary rises. This too is likely to be superseded by any future increases in the personal allowance.

### April 2016
The age-related allowance for those born before 6th April 1948 is now superseded by the standard personal allowance. The marriage allowance rises on 6th April 2016 to 10% of £11,000, £1,100. As a consequence of the personal allowance (PA) rising to £11,000 the loss of PA now occurs at £122,000, a rate of £1 of PA lost per £2 net taxable income over £100,000.

## April 2017

The personal allowance rises to £11,500 bringing with it the marriage allowance to £1,150. Personal allowance is now completely lost when income reaches £123,000. The blind person's addition rises for the first time in two tax years, to an additional £2,320. Employers start to take into consideration a new tax term, rUK, referring to a provision which will not apply to Scotland. Higher rate threshold set at £45,000 for rUK but frozen at £43,000 for Scotland only.

## April 2018

The personal allowance rises to £11,850, taking the Marriage Allowance with it to £1,185. Whilst sweeping changes to the PAYE rates and thresholds are announced by the Scottish parliament, the personal allowance applicable in Scotland must remain at the level set by the UK parliament.

## April 2019

The personal allowance increases to £12,500, a full 12 months earlier than originally announced. This means the marriage allowance is £1,250 from 6th April 2019. Welsh income tax became a reality from 6th April 2019 with the Welsh Assembly agreeing on a standard 10% rate of Welsh income tax and means the headline rates of tax will remain as they are in the area described as rUK.

## April 2020

As expected the personal allowance for the whole of the UK is frozen at £12,500 with all other allowances remaining unchanged. Rates and thresholds for rUK, Scotland and Wales have also remained unchanged. Off payroll working becomes a reality for the private and third sectors bringing with it significant challenges for payroll. The tax-free "working from home" allowance increases from £4 to £6 a week.

# APPROVED MILEAGE ALLOWANCE PAYMENTS (AMAPs)

As a general principle, an employer may reimburse an employee up to the actual value of the cost incurred for the use of their personal car on company business. Such payments are not taxable as long as proof of cost is supplied. However, where mileage allowances are paid in accordance with the Mileage Allowance Payment (MAP) rates (previously AMAPs) provided by HMRC the payment is not taxable and such evidence will not be required.

Prior to 6th April 1990, HMRC took the view that mileage allowances would only be allowable in cases of necessity (where no public service or other travel was available) and they generally accepted mileage rates as published by the AA. On 6th April 1990, HMRC sought to regularise the situation by introducing the Fixed Profit Car Scheme for general use. Where an employee could produce documentary evidence for HMRC that supported the fact that payments received did no more than reimburse the employee for the running costs of the car there was no tax liability - known as the 'Actuals Basis'.

This and all other schemes were replaced in April 2002 by AMAPs and then on 6th April 2016 this was renamed MAPs. These established a tax-exempt mileage rate that employers can pay to employees using their own vehicles for business travel, subject to two main conditions, they must:
- be paid to employees for the use of their own car, van, motor cycle or bicycle for business travel
- not exceed the amount that is equal to the number of business miles multiplied by the appropriate mileage rate.

Mileage allowance payments that employers make to employees for the use of their own cars for business travel will not be subject to NICs provided the rates paid do not exceed the up to 10,000 miles AMAP rates. Amounts paid in excess are to be added to earnings for the purpose of calculating the Class 1 NICs liability. Where an employee has more than one employment with the same employer, or associated employers, the business miles travelled in the employee's own vehicle are to be aggregated.

### Current Approved Mileage Allowance Payment Rates - from 6th April 2002

| Date from | Motor Cars / Vans | | M/Cycles | Bicycles | Passengers |
|---|---|---|---|---|---|
| | Up to 10,000 miles | Over 10,000 miles | | | Per passenger |
| | pence | pence | pence | pence | pence |
| 06.04.2002 | 40 | 25 | 24 | 20 | 5 |
| 06.04.2011 | 45 | 25 | 24 | 20 | 5 |

Where payments do not exceed the MAP rates there is no requirement to report on the year-end return P11D. Where the payment is less than the published MAP rate the employee is entitled to claim an additional tax deduction on the shortfall.

Until about April 2016 HMRC applied a rule which meant that for the passenger addition to be allowed, the passenger, or passengers had to be travelling to the same destination and for the same reason as the driver. A more relaxed approach is now taken.

### MAPs and dispensations

From 6th April 2002 dispensations, or parts of dispensations, relating to payments for travel in an employee's own vehicle ceased to be valid. No new dispensations are being issued. Dispensations cease to be valid from 6th April 2016.

## ADVISORY FUEL RATES

Fuel only rates for company cars were introduced in January 2002. Where an employer reimburses an employee for business travel in their company car, or requires an employee to repay the cost of fuel used for private travel at rates not higher than HMRC Advisory Rates, there will be no taxable profit (i.e. benefit) and no Class 1 NIC liability (rates are also acceptable for VAT purposes).

Rates are reviewed on the 1st January and 1st July (from 2008) unless the price of fuel fluctuates by more than +/- 5%.

A new fuel rate for fully electric vehicles was introduced from 1st June 2018.

### Advisory fuel rates (pence per mile) from 28th January 2002

| Date from | Petrol | | | Diesel | | | LPG | | | Electric |
|---|---|---|---|---|---|---|---|---|---|---|
| | 1400cc or less | 1401-2000cc | Over 2000cc | 1600cc or less | 1601-2000cc | Over 2000cc | 1400cc or less | 1401-2000cc | Over 2000cc | |
| 28.01.2002 | 10 | 12 | 14 | 9 | 12 | | | | | |
| 06.05.2002 | 10 | 12 | 14 | 9 | 12 | | 6 | 7 | 9 | |
| 06.04.2004 | 10 | 12 | 14 | 9 | 12 | | 7 | 8 | 10 | |
| 01.07.2005 | 10 | 12 | 16 | 9 | 13 | | 7 | 8 | 10 | |
| 01.02.2007 | 9 | 11 | 16 | 9 | 12 | | 6 | 7 | 10 | |
| 01.08.2007 | 10 | 13 | 18 | 10 | 13 | | 6 | 8 | 10 | |
| 01.01.2008 | 11 | 13 | 19 | 11 | 14 | | 7 | 8 | 11 | |
| 01.07.2008 | 12 | 15 | 21 | 13 | 17 | | 7 | 9 | 13 | |
| 01.01.2009 | 10 | 12 | 17 | 11 | 14 | | 7 | 9 | 12 | |
| 01.12.2009 | 11 | 14 | 20 | 11 | 14 | | 7 | 8 | 12 | |
| 01.06.2010 | 12 | 15 | 21 | 11 | 16 | | 8 | 10 | 14 | |
| 01.12.2010 | 13 | 15 | 21 | 12 | 15 | | 9 | 10 | 15 | |
| 01.03.2011 | 14 | 16 | 23 | 13 | 16 | | 9 | 12 | 17 | |
| 01.09.2011 | 15 | 18 | 26 | 12 | 15 | 18 | 11 | 12 | 18 | |
| 01.12.2011 | 15 | 18 | 26 | 12 | 15 | 18 | 10 | 12 | 18 | |
| 01.03.2012 | 15 | 18 | 26 | 13 | 15 | 19 | 10 | 12 | 18 | |
| 01.06.2012 | 15 | 18 | 26 | 12 | 15 | 18 | 11 | 13 | 19 | |
| 01.10.2012 | 15 | 18 | 26 | 12 | 15 | 18 | 10 | 13 | 17 | |
| 01.12.2012 | 15 | 18 | 26 | 12 | 15 | 18 | 11 | 13 | 18 | |
| 01.03.2013 | 15 | 18 | 26 | 13 | 15 | 18 | 10 | 12 | 18 | |
| 01.09.2013 | 15 | 18 | 26 | 15 | 15 | 18 | 10 | 11 | 16 | |
| 01.12.2013 | 16 | 14 | 24 | 12 | 14 | 17 | 9 | 11 | 16 | |

**Advisory fuel rates (pence per mile) from 28th January 2002** (continued)

| | | | | | | | | | | |
|---|---|---|---|---|---|---|---|---|---|---|
| 01.03.2014 | 16 | 14 | 24 | 12 | 14 | 17 | 9 | 11 | 17 | |
| 01.06.2014 | 14 | 16 | 24 | 12 | 14 | 17 | 9 | 11 | 16 | |
| 01.09.2014 | 14 | 16 | 24 | 11 | 13 | 17 | 9 | 11 | 16 | |
| 01.12.2014 | 13 | 16 | 23 | 11 | 13 | 16 | 9 | 11 | 16 | |
| 01.03.2015 | 11 | 13 | 20 | 9 | 11 | 14 | 8 | 10 | 14 | |
| 01.06.2015 | 12 | 14 | 21 | 10 | 12 | 14 | 8 | 9 | 14 | |
| 01.09.2015 | 11 | 14 | 21 | 9 | 11 | 13 | 7 | 9 | 14 | |
| 01.12.2015 | 11 | 13 | 20 | 9 | 11 | 13 | 7 | 9 | 13 | |
| 01.03.2016 | 10 | 12 | 19 | 8 | 10 | 11 | 7 | 8 | 13 | |
| 01.06.2016 | 10 | 13 | 20 | 9 | 10 | 12 | 7 | 9 | 13 | |
| 01.09.2016 | 11 | 13 | 20 | 9 | 11 | 13 | 7 | 9 | 13 | |
| 01.12.2016 | 11 | 14 | 21 | 9 | 11 | 13 | 7 | 9 | 13 | |
| 01.03.2017 | 11 | 14 | 22 | 9 | 11 | 13 | 7 | 9 | 14 | |
| 01.06.2017 | 11 | 14 | 21 | 9 | 11 | 13 | 7 | 9 | 14 | |
| 01/09/2017 | 11 | 13 | 21 | 9 | 11 | 12 | 7 | 8 | 13 | |
| 01/12/2017 | 11 | 14 | 21 | 9 | 11 | 13 | 7 | 9 | 14 | |
| 01/03/2018 | 11 | 14 | 22 | 9 | 11 | 13 | 7 | 8 | 13 | Nil |
| 01/06/2018 | 11 | 14 | 22 | 10 | 11 | 13 | 7 | 9 | 14 | 4 |
| 01/09/2018 | 12 | 15 | 22 | 10 | 12 | 13 | 7 | 9 | 13 | 4 |
| 01/12/2018 | 12 | 15 | 22 | 10 | 12 | 14 | 8 | 10 | 15 | 4 |
| 01/03/2019 | 11 | 14 | 21 | 10 | 11 | 13 | 7 | 8 | 13 | 4 |
| 01/06/2019 | 12 | 15 | 22 | 10 | 12 | 14 | 8 | 9 | 14 | 4 |
| 01/09/2019 | 12 | 14 | 21 | 10 | 11 | 14 | 8 | 10 | 14 | 4 |
| 01/12/2019 | 12 | 14 | 21 | 9 | 11 | 14 | 8 | 9 | 14 | 4 |
| 01/03/2020 | 12 | 14 | 20 | 9 | 11 | 13 | 8 | 10 | 14 | 4 |
| **01/06/2020** | **10** | **12** | **17** | **8** | **9** | **12** | **6** | **8** | **11** | **4** |

## ANNUAL and LIFETIME ALLOWANCES

Two controls limit the amount of tax relief available to an employee in respect of pension contributions. Since the 6th April 2014 this is restricted to an annual allowance of £40,000 which is the maximum increase in a fund in a pension input year. Employees attempting to circumvent the restriction by putting additional amounts into their pension fund ahead of tax year 2011/12 were subject to a special annual allowance charge of 20% for higher rate taxpayers or 30% for additional rate taxpayers where they paid more than £20,000 into their fund on an irregular basis (defined as less than quarterly contributions).

In a final salary arrangement the increase in the fund at the start and end of the year is multiplied by a factor of 16. Unused annual allowance for three prior tax years can be used to offset any tax liability. Annual allowance charges of up to £2,000 are coded out automatically by HMRC. Charges above £2,000 can be paid directly or deducted from future benefits by the pension fund and paid to HMRC – this is known as 'scheme pays'.

From 6th April 2016 a tapered reduction in annual allowance applies to anyone with adjusted net taxable income of £150,000 or more. The adjustment will include adding back any pension contributions funded using a salary sacrifice arrangement. The taper will operate at a rate of £1 of the annual allowance for every £2 by which their earnings exceed £150,000. The maximum reduction to the annual allowance will be £30,000. At the same time a one-off annual allowance of £80,000 was applied to the 2015/16 tax year.

The threshold increased to £240,000, adjusted net income, from 6th April 2020 before the annual allowance is affected.

The annual allowance may also be reduced if the contributions to a scheme come from the proceeds of an existing scheme. From 6th April 2017 the annual allowance drops to £4,000 (£10,000 from April 2016) if contributions are made into a scheme that is already paying out an income. The reduction applies in the first full tax year after income is drawn. It can also apply if the scheme is used to make contributions into another scheme.

The lifetime allowance, £1.0731m from April 2020 (£1.055m from April 2019 and previously £1.03m) governs the tax relief available on the total fund value for all pension arrangements. Final salary benefits are valued at 20 x the annual pension in payment or a deferred pension benefit for an employee yet to take their benefits. Funds above the limit can be subject to a charge of up to 55% if drawn as a cash lump sum and 25% if taken as a pension (in addition to the income tax paid on the pension).

Employees had the option to preserve the tax treatment on funds that exceed the lifetime allowance limit at the time the limits changed by applying for fixed protection if their fund already exceeds £1m but is equal to or less than £1.25m, or individual protection if their fund is predicted to exceed £1m in future years. HMRC provides guidance on fixed protection at https://www.gov.uk/tax-on-your-private-pension/lifetime-allowance

## BANK CHARGES

Amounts paid or credited to an employee to meet normal bank charges are subject to PAYE and Class 1 NICs at the time payment is made. However, reimbursement of bank charges arising solely as a result of failure by the employer (for example, crediting bank accounts after the contractually due date of wages or salary) have no liability to tax or NICs either Class 1 or 1A. Such charges are deemed to be compensation resulting from a breach of contract.

Where an Employment Tribunal makes an award for an illegal deduction from wages they can also award compensation for bank charges that arose as a result of the failure to make payment as due, or due to an illegal deduction.

## BENEFICIAL LOANS

An employee with a loan outstanding from an employer during the year will be chargeable to tax on the difference between the interest paid and the official rate of interest as prescribed by the Treasury by Statutory Instrument only if that loan, or total loans, exceed £10,000 (£5,000 till April 2014) at any point in the tax year.

**Actual official interest rate charge on beneficial loans from 6th November 1996**

| Date from | % | Date from | % | Date from | % |
|---|---|---|---|---|---|
| 06.11.1996 | 6.75 | 06.04.2008 | 6.25 | 06.04.2016 | 3.00 |
| 06.08.1997 | 7.25 | 01.03.2009 | 4.75 | 06.04.2017 | 2.50 |
| 06.03.1999 | 6.25 | 06.04.2010 | 4.00 | 06.04.2018 | 2.50 |
| 06.01.2002 | 5.00 | 06.04.2014 | 3.25 | 06.04.2019 | 2.50 |
| 06.04.2007 | 6.25 | 06.04.2015 | 3.00 | 06.04.2020 | 2.25* |

*Subject to necessary Treasury regulations

**Normal Averaging Method** - Introduced in 1995 as an alternative to calculating the benefit strictly in accordance with the prescribed official interest rates. Initially the average interest rate was set in advance by HMRC, but must now be calculated by the employer. The chargeable value is assessed by comparison of the average loan rate (calculated by reference to the periods during which different rates are in force between the start and the end of the tax year) with HMRC's approved rate.

From April 2017, where the loan is made as part of a salary sacrifice, or other remuneration arrangement the Optional Remuneration Arrangement (OpRA) rules apply and the reportable amount is the higher of the interest saved and the cash foregone.

**Annual average interest rate charge on beneficial loans from 2000/2001 to date**

| Date from | % | Date from | % | Date from | % |
|-----------|------|-----------|------|-----------|------|
| 2000/2001 | 6.25 | 2006/2007 | 5.00 | 2015/2016 | 3.00 |
| 2001/2002 | 5.94 | 2007/2008 | 6.25 | 2017/2018 | 2.50 |
| 2002/2003 | 5.00 | 2008/2009 | 6.10 | 2019/2020 | 2.50 |
| 2003/2004 | 5.00 | 2009/2010 | 4.75 | | |
| 2004/2005 | 5.00 | 2010/2011 | 4.00 | | |
| 2005/2006 | 5.00 | 2014/2015 | 3.25 | | |

## BICYCLES AND BICYCLE SAFETY EQUIPMENT

Hired (or loaned) to employees, not sold to them, to cycle to work are exempt from tax (and class 1A NICs) provided:

- the offer of such facilities is open to (though not necessarily used by) all employees, this includes those aged under 18 and those close to national minimum or living wage.
- the cycle is used primarily, no records are required, for 'qualifying' journeys (i.e. home to workplace, workplace to temporary workplace). For guidance this means not less than 50% of the use of the cycle.

Other use of the cycle such as occasional use by members of the employee's family would not disqualify the exemption provided the main use is for 'qualifying' journeys. Where ownership of a bicycle is transferred to an employee after a period of use as a benefit, there is no tax charge as long as the market value at date of transfer is paid by the employee - HMRC provide a matrix of acceptable residual values see http://www.hmrc.gov.uk/manuals/eimanual/EIM21667a.htm.

From April 2017, this exemption from income tax applies even if the bicycle and safety equipment are provided under a salary sacrifice arrangement. The OpRA rules will not apply.

## CANTEEN FACILITIES

Where an employer provides free or subsidised meals, provided the facility is available to all employees, such provision or subsidy is exempt from tax. Where an employer operates more than one site, provided the benefit is available to all employees the exemption applies, and should the facility not be available on all sites the same would apply provided employees could receive the benefit of the service were they to visit a site where the facility is available. From April 2011 the exemption does not apply if the meals are provided as part of a salary sacrifice or flexible benefits scheme.

## CAR ALLOWANCE ENHANCED REPORTING SCHEME (CAERS)

A scheme, replaced in April 2002, which allowed employers to report profit or excess expenditure on mileage allowances paid to employees on an individual basis. The employer had to apply HMRC's authorised car mileage rates (see FPCS) to the full amount of each employee's qualifying business mileage to calculate the amount to be set off against allowances paid.

## CAR FUEL BENEFIT

Where private fuel is provided, or paid for by an employer, for use in a private or company car, a liability for tax is to be charged against the employee. Originally this was based on fuel benefit scale rates determined by the engine capacity of the vehicle. If the employee makes good the cost of all fuel provided for private use, the benefit charge is reduced to zero. HMRC accept reimbursement has taken place if at least the advisory fuel rates are used see page 102. From 6th April 1992 to 5th April 1998 separate rates were set for diesel users and from April 2003 the Car Fuel Scale Charge was renamed the Fuel Benefit Charge and was linked to the vehicle's $CO_2$ emissions.

## Car Fuel Scale Charges - from 1988/1989 to 1991/1992

| Year | 0-1400 ccs £ | 1401-2000 ccs £ | 2001 ccs + £ |
|------|------|------|------|
| 1988/1989 | 480 | 600 | 900 |
| 1989/1990 | 480 | 600 | 900 |
| 1990/1991 | 480 | 600 | 900 |
| 1991/1992 | 480 | 600 | 900 |

## Car Fuel Scale Charges - from 1992/1993 to 2002/2003

| Year | Petrol | | | Diesel | | |
|------|------|------|------|------|------|------|
|  | 0-1400 cc | 1401-2000 cc | 2001+cc | 0-2000cc | 2001+cc | No engine capacity |
|  | £ | £ | £ | £ | £ | £ |
| 1992/1993 | 500 | 630 | 940 | 460 | 590 | |
| 1993/1994 | 600 | 760 | 1,130 | 550 | 710 | |
| 1994/1995 | 640 | 810 | 1,200 | 580 | 750 | 1,200 |
| 1995/1996 | 670 | 850 | 1,260 | 605 | 780 | 1,260 |
| 1996/1997 | 710 | 890 | 1,320 | 640 | 820 | 1,320 |
| 1997/1998 | 800 | 1,010 | 1,490 | 740 | 940 | 1,490 |
| 1998/1999 | 1,010 | 1,280 | 1,890 | 1,280 | 1,890 | 1,890 |
| 1999/2000 | 1,210 | 1,540 | 2,270 | 1,540 | 2,270 | 2,270 |
| 2000/2001 | 1,700 | 2,170 | 3,200 | 2,170 | 3,200 | 3,200 |
| 2001/2002 | 1,930 | 2,460 | 3,620 | 2,460 | 3,620 | 3,620 |
| 2002/2003 | 2,240 | 2,850 | 4,200 | 2,850 | 4,200 | 4,200 |

*N.B.: Before 6th April 1993, where business use exceeded 18,000 miles in the year, the fuel benefit scale rate was halved.*

Car Fuel Benefit Charge - Introduced 6th April 2003 to replace the former scale charge. The charge is linked to the $CO_2$ emissions of the car, with the tax due calculated by multiplying the vehicle's $CO_2$ percentage figure, as set out below in the Company Car Benefit Charge, against a set annual multiplier shown here.

## Car fuel benefit scale charge from 6th April 2005

| Year | Annual multiplier £ | Year | Annual multiplier £ |
|------|------|------|------|
| 2005/06 | 14,400 | 2016/17 | 22,200 |
| 2010/11 | 18,800 | 2017/18 | 22,600 |
| 2013/14 | 20,200 | 2018/19 | 23,400 |
| 2014/15 | 21,700 | 2019/20 | 24,100 |
| 2015/16 | 22,100 | **2020/21** | **24,500** |

Where the employee opts out of free fuel during a tax year, the payment due will be in proportion to that part of the year for which they received free fuel. In addition, the amount of Class 1A NICs will similarly be reduced. Opting back into free fuel later in the year will result in a full year's tax and Class 1A NICs becoming due. Free fuel needs to be fully reimbursed by the employee to the employer in order for no fuel benefit charge to be due.

The new OpRA rules will apply to free fuel in the same manner as they do for the car itself. If the cash foregone, agreed to in order to obtain the car and fuel, is in excess of the combined car and fuel charge to tax then the charge to tax will be the cash foregone.

## CAR PARKING AT WORKPLACE

There is no tax liability in respect of car parking places provided at, or near to an employee's place of work. Where payment for such places is handled via salary sacrifice this is one of the benefits that an employee can opt-in and out of on a regular basis without the sacrifice becoming ineffective.

Since 6th April 2017 car parking at or near the place of work, however provided, has lost its tax exemption if provided under a remuneration arrangement caught by the new OpRA rules.

## CHARITABLE GIVING

Tax relief for gifts to charities in the United Kingdom can be achieved in any of three ways:

- Deed of Covenant - payment of a regular amount for a minimum period of three years. The charity claims the tax paid after the close of the tax year by submitting a return to the HMRC. The tax refund is remitted directly to the charity. The sum paid by the donor is the net value of the donation. This is the value after deduction of tax at the rate paid by the donor
- Gift Aid - introduced October 1990 - making a single cash gift of a minimum net amount with tax relief. See https://www.gov.uk/claim-gift-aid.
- Payroll Giving - deductions made from pay by the employer and passed on to the nominated charity through an agency. The deductions are made before calculation of PAYE thereby giving tax relief at source.

From 6th April 2000 (for a period of four years) payroll giving donations were supplemented by 10% (government funded).

### Payroll Giving - Tax Free Limits 1993/1994 to 1999/2000

| Year | Payroll Giving £ | Gift Aid Minimum Threshold £ | Effective Date |
|---|---|---|---|
| 1993/1994 | 900 | 250 | 16.03.1993 |
| 1994/1995 | 900 | 250 | |
| 1995/1996 | 900 | 250 | |
| 1996/1997 | 1,200 | 250 | |
| 1997/1998 | 1,200 | 250 | |
| 1998/1999 | 1,200 | 250 | |
| 1999/2000 | 1,200 | 250 | |
| 2000/2001 | Thresholds abolished | | |

**Future developments**
From 6th April 2014 the deadline for passing payroll giving deductions to the destination charity is reduced from 60 – 35 days.

## CHILDCARE VOUCHERS & NURSERY PROVISION

Prior to April 2005 unlimited National Insurance relief for both employee and employer was available for the employer provision of childcare vouchers or a workplace nursery. From April 2005 employers were able to pay up to £50 per week (£217 per month), or provide vouchers to the same value, towards childcare costs incurred by an employee, free of tax and NICs. From April 2006 the exempt amount was increased to £55 per week (£243 per month). The scheme must be generally available across an organisation (per PAYE scheme) and to qualify the childcare provided must meet certain standards e.g. The Ofsted registration number is to be held and checked at regular intervals (the standards differ across each country of the United Kingdom).

From April 2007 the registration of childcare changed as a result of the Childcare Act 2006, such that qualifying childcare can be care given by a provider who has voluntarily registered with Ofsted, so increasing the choice employees have as to where employer supported childcare can be utilised.

In contrast to vouchers the provision of a subsidised workplace nursery place attracts complete tax and NI relief as long as the employer 'wholly or partly manages' and 'wholly or partly funds' the provision of care.

To achieve maximum savings at minimum cost for the employer and employee voucher schemes have predominantly been delivered via salary sacrifice, the savings in employer's NICs being used to fund the administrative costs of the voucher scheme. Schemes set up so that vouchers are purchased by the employee as a deduction from net pay and shown as such on the payslip, do not qualify for the exemption as this is not an effective salary sacrifice as the employer is not providing the childcare support, it is being purchased by the employee.

Following a change to the law for women due to have or adopt a baby on, or after, 5th October 2008 childcare support (vouchers or a subsidised nursery place) must continue to be provided by the employer at its cost throughout the full 52 week maternity leave period.

From April 2011 tax relief on childcare support (vouchers or directly contracted care) was restricted to basic rate. For employees who newly join a childcare voucher scheme from 6th April 2011 employers must assess their earnings (contractual wages or salary, including taxable benefits in kind but excluding bonuses and overtime) at the start of the tax year and where those earnings exceed the basic rate limit (the sum of the personal allowance and the basic rate band) the relief will be restricted:

to £28 per week for higher rate taxpayers, and when earnings exceed £150,000, to £25 per week for additional rate taxpayers (£22 per week prior to 6th April 2013)

No recalculation is required if circumstances change mid-year. Employees in receipt of childcare support before 6th April 2011 may continue to receive £55 per week relief regardless of their earnings until they join a childcare scheme at a new employer or have not received vouchers for more than 52 calendar weeks (perhaps as a result of being on maternity leave). Where vouchers over the exempt amount are provided the excess is taxed via the P11D but subject to Class 1 NICs through the payroll for vouchers and Class 1A via the P11D for directly contracted childcare. Workplace nursery tax/NICs relief is still unlimited.

From 6th April 2017, with the introduction of a different higher rate threshold in Scotland employers were originally advised to establish who is a Scottish taxpayer and apply the appropriate threshold when calculating the amount of relief an employee is entitled to. Later, Scottish taxpayers were informed that the restrictions to basic rate relief on childcare vouchers would apply at the rUK threshold of £45,000 (now £50,000) and not the Scottish threshold of £43,000.

This principle has continued to apply since April 2018 when the new Scottish rates and thresholds were implemented.

The provision of childcare vouchers is exempt from the new OpRA rules.

### Transition to Tax Free Childcare
It had been intended that from autumn 2015 no new joiners to a tax advantaged childcare voucher scheme would be permitted and that would allow for the launching of the new childcare support scheme, Tax Free Childcare (TFC) allowance which offers tax relief on up to £10,000 of qualifying childcare per child up to the age of 12.

This is a direct arrangement between the parent and the provider and employers will not be involved unless they wish to provide guidance or add to the online childcare account. This account, held by National Savings, is where parents will deposit cash for the scheme. Tax free childcare accounts were actually implemented from early 2017 and phased in from the youngest child first.

Existing employer provided schemes were due to close to new entrants from April 2018. Following parliamentary debate in March 2018 this was extended to October 2018 and since then employers have not been permitted to admit new employees to old style tax advantaged childcare voucher schemes. It is worth noting that if the employer and the scheme provider allows it there is nothing to stop employees joining a voucher scheme now, however these would not be childcare vouchers carrying any form of tax advantage.

## COMPANY CARS

When an employee is provided with a company car and that car is available for private use, the taxable value of the benefit received from its use was assessed by reference to scale rates published annually by HMRC. There is no requirement for the car to be used for personal purposes, only that it is available. Rates were originally determined by the market value purchase price, age and engine capacity of the vehicle.

### Company Car Benefit Tables

#### Scale rates from 1987/1988 to 1993/1994

| | 1987/88 £ | 1988/89 £ | 1989/90 £ | 1990/91 £ | 1991/92 £ | 1992/93 £ | 1993/94 £ |
|---|---|---|---|---|---|---|---|
| **Table A** Market value | Vehicle under 4 years of age | | | | | | |
| | 19,250 | 19,250 | 19,250 | 19,250 | 19,250 | 19,250 | 19,250 |
| Up to 1400cc | 525 | 1,050 | 1,400 | 1,700 | 2,050 | 2,140 | 2,310 |
| 1401-2000cc | 700 | 1,400 | 1,850 | 2,200 | 2,650 | 2,770 | 2,990 |
| 2001cc + | 1,100 | 2,200 | 2,950 | 3,550 | 4,250 | 4,440 | 4,800 |
| | Vehicle 4 years of age and over | | | | | | |
| Up to 1400cc | 350 | 700 | 950 | 1,150 | 1,400 | 1,460 | 1,580 |
| 1401-2000cc | 470 | 940 | 1,250 | 1,500 | 1,800 | 1,880 | 2,030 |
| 2001cc + | 725 | 1,425 | 1,950 | 2,350 | 2,850 | 2,980 | 3,220 |
| **Table B** Market value | Vehicle under 4 years of age | | | | | | |
| £19251-£29000 | 1,450 | 2,900 | 3,850 | 4,600 | 5,500 | 5,750 | 6,210 |
| £29001+ | 2,300 | 4,600 | 6,150 | 7,400 | 8,900 | 9,300 | 10,040 |
| | Vehicle 4 years of age and over | | | | | | |
| £19251-£29000 | 970 | 1,940 | 2,600 | 3,100 | 3,700 | 3,870 | 4,180 |
| £29001+ | 1,530 | 3,060 | 4,100 | 4,900 | 5,900 | 6,170 | 6,660 |
| **Market Value Table upper limits** | | | | | | | |
| Up to 1400cc | 6,000 | 6,000 | 6,000 | 6,000 | 6,000 | 6,000 | 6,000 |
| 1401cc–2000cc | 8,500 | 8,500 | 8,500 | 8,500 | 8,500 | 8,500 | 8,500 |
| 2000cc + | 19,250 | 19,250 | 19,250 | 19,250 | 19,250 | 19,250 | 19,250 |

### Company car benefit historical notes

From 6th April 1994 to 5th April 2002 the standard car tax benefit charge was based on 35% of the price of the car 'for tax purposes', which could be reduced to take account of:
- the business mileage of the employee
- the age of the car at the end of the tax assessment year
- periods of time when the car was unavailable for use
- any payments made towards the personal use of the car

Where business mileage was lower than 2,500 miles in the year scale rates were increased by 50%. Where business mileage reached 18,000 miles or more in the year, scale rates were reduced by 50%.

The price of the car was usually deemed to be:
- the published price of the car on the day before its first registration, inclusive of VAT, car tax, delivery charges, and

- the list price of any extras,
- minus the total value of any capital contributions made by the employee towards the cost of the car, up to a maximum value of £5,000.

The maximum assessable value was restricted to an upper limit of £80,000, after deduction of any capital contributions.

## Reduced Car Benefit Charge
The full benefit charge was based on 35% of the cost of the car. This could be reduced where the car was used for business purposes. The reduced rates related to the level of business mileage were:

| Business miles p.a. | Tax charge |
|---|---|
| Less than 2500 | 35% full tax charge applied |
| 2500 to 17999 | 25% charge (1/3 reduction pre 6th April 1999) |
| 18000 or more | 15% charge (2/3 reduction pre 6th April 1999) |

The tax charge was reduced by one quarter if the car was 4 years old or more at the end of the tax year. The age was determined from the date of its first registration.

A reduction for unavailability was applicable for any day that fell:
- before the first day the car was made available to the employee, or
- after the last day on which it was available, or
- within a period of 30 days or more during which the car was not available

If the car was not available for a period of less than 30 days, no reduction was applied. During which period there was no additional charge in respect of any replacement car made available, provided it was of a similar type and quality.

## Second car discount
Generally a second car was taxed on 35% of the price of that car each year. Where annual business use exceeded 18000 miles, the charge was reduced to 25%.

## Qualifying Low Emission Cars - QUALECs
From 6th April 2008 - 5th April 2012 a new band was introduced for cars with emission figures of exactly 120 g/km or lower. Cars qualifying under this criterion were called 'Qualifying Low Emission Cars' (QUALECs) and attracted a 10% charge. QUALECs qualified for the diesel supplement however no adjustment for other types of fuel was permitted. Hence the only permitted percentage for this band was 10% for petrol cars and 13% for diesel.

### Qualifying Low Emission Cars (QUALECs) from 6th April 2008 - 5th April 2012

| Year | CO2 g/km | Tax % | Lower Charge Threshold | |
|---|---|---|---|---|
| | | | CO2 g/km | Tax % |
| 2008/2009 | 120 or lower | 10 | 135 | 15 |
| 2009/2010 | 120 or lower | 10 | 135 | 15 |
| 2010/2011 | 120 or lower | 10 | 135 | 15 |
| 2011/2012 | 120 or lower | 10 | 135 | 15 |

## Alternative Fuels
A discount against the benefit charge was applied to environmentally friendly cars (e.g. electric powered) until 5th April 2011. A code entered on the P46(car) form indicated the type of fuel used and this generated the discounted charge. From 6th April 2010 for five years electric cars attract a 0% charge. From 6th April 2011 the alternative fuel discounts were abolished and the CO2 emissions alone dictate the charge. The codes were:

## Alternative fuel adjustment table to 5th April 2011

| Type of fuel or power | P46(Car) Code | % Adjustment |
|---|---|---|
| Petrol | P | Nil |
| Diesel, Euro 4 compliant and registered before 01/01/2006 | L | Nil |
| Diesel, all others | D | + 3% |
| Hybrid, electric and petrol | H | - 3% |
| Bi-fuel, petrol and road fuel gas, with emissions rating for gas, and road fuel gas only | B | - 2% |
| Bi-fuel, petrol and road fuel gas, with emissions rating for petrol | C | Nil |
| Bioethanol, high blend E85 (from 6 April 2008) | G | - 2% |
| Electric Motor | E | - 6% for 2009/10 0% from 2010/11 for 5 years |
| Diesel with emission rating of 120 g/km or less (except those registered before 01.01.2006 and Euro 4 compliant) | - | 13% charge |
| All other cars with emission rating of 120 g/km or less (except electric) | - | 10% charge |
| Ultra-low carbon vehicles cars with emission rating of 75 g/km or less (except electric) | - | 5% charge from 2010/11 |

### Change from 6th April 2011
The list price capping of £80,000 was removed.

### Change from 6th April 2012
The emissions' table was re-drawn as QUALECs were abolished so the table ran from 10% to 35%, 10% being applicable to emission of 100 g/km or less. Electric cars still attract a 0% charge.

### Change from 6th April 2013
The emissions' table was re-drawn again such that to attract the 10% charge the emissions value must be 95 g/km or less.

### Company car benefit 6th April 2002 to date
The tax charge is based on a percentage of the purchase (list) price of the car, that percentage being determined by the car's carbon dioxide ($CO_2$) emissions measured in grams per kilometre (g/km) rounded down to the nearest 5g/km. The charge increases in steps per 5g/km above the minimum level of 7%, with a maximum ceiling of 37%. All diesel cars are subject to a 3% premium in recognition of their higher emission rate although the maximum charge for a diesel car is capped at the same 37% level as applied to petrol engine cars. Until 5th April 2012 that emitted $CO_2$ at, or below a specified level attracted a minimum charge (10% of the car's price - see QUALECs below).

From 6th April 2009 disabled drivers (those with a blue badge) use the list price and C02 emissions of the equivalent manual car if they are required to drive an automatic car.

### Emission details
Vehicles registered from November 2000 have their $CO_2$ emission details recorded on their Vehicle Registration Document (V5). Details for cars first registered from January 1998 are available on the Internet. Those cars first registered after 1st January 1998 for which no approved $CO_2$ emission details are available (imported cars) are assessed on engine size. Those without a cylinder capacity are taxed on 16% of the price where propelled solely by electricity and 37% in other cases.

## Cars with no CO2 emissions' figure from 6th April 2002

| Date from | Tax charge as % of car purchase price | | | | | |
|---|---|---|---|---|---|---|
| | Registered before 1st January 1998 | | | Registered after 1st January 1998 | | |
| | 0 - 1400cc % | 1401 to 2000cc % | Over 2000cc % | 0 - 1400cc % | 1401 to 2000cc % | Over 2000cc % |
| 06.04.2002 | 15 | 22 | 32 | 15 | 25 | 35 |
| 06.04.2015 | 15 | 22 | 32 | 15 | 25 | 37 |
| 06.04.2016 | 16 | 27 | 37 | 16 | 27 | 37 |

### Classic cars
Those 15 or more years old at the end of the tax year, and with a market value of £15000 or more - are taxed on the basis of their market value on the last day of the tax year.

### From 6th April 2014
The emissions' table was re-drawn again such that to attract the new 5% charge the emissions' value had to be 75 g/km or less.

### From 6th April 2015
The zero band (below 75 g/km) was abolished and the lowest charges become:
*   0-50 g/km 5%
*   51-75 g/km 9%
*   76+ g/km: current rates up by 2% from 13% up to 37%

### From 6th April 2016
The 3% diesel supplement which was to be abolished was retained and the rates became:
*   0-50 g/km 7%
*   51-75 g/km 11%
*   76+ g/km: 2015 rates up by 2% from 15% up to 37%

### From 6th April 2017
*   4% points differential between bottom two tiers retained
*   Additional reporting requirements for voluntary payrolling arrangements
*   Company cars made available for private use under a salary sacrifice arrangement are valued at the higher of the normal calculation in the benefit in kind manual and the salary foregone
*   Also applies to any "cash for car" arrangements.

### From 6th April 2018
*   Starting rate for zero emission cars now 13%
*   3% points differential between bottom three tiers
*   Diesel RDE2 compliant cars on same charge rate as petrol
*   Non RDE2 diesel cars now have 4% supplement
*   Highest charge rate of 37% starts at 160g/km for non-RDE2 diesel cars
*   Diesel hybrids not subject to the 3% diesel supplement.

### From 6th April 2019
*   Starting rate for zero emission cars rises to 16%
*   Mixed % points differential for bottom tier
*   Highest charge rate of 37% starts at 145g/km for non-RDE2 diesel cars.

### From 6th April 2020
*   Introduction of two separate tables to replace the existing single table
*   Zero emission cars first registered on or after 6th April 2020 to pay no company car tax under a temporary measure.
*   A new set of rates for low emission and hybrid cars linked to the number of miles which can be driven on zero emissions.

## Company Car Benefit Charge Scale from 2010/2011

### Emissions in grams per kilometre

| 2010-2011 | 2011-2012 | 2012-2013 | 2013-2014 | Charge % | 2014-2015 | Charge % | 2015-2016 Emissions | Charge % |
|---|---|---|---|---|---|---|---|---|
| | | | 0 Electric | 0 | | | 0-50 | 5 |
| | | | 1-75 | 5 | | | 51-75 | 9 |
| | | Less than 100 | 76-94 | 10 | 0 | 0 | 76-94 | 13 |
| | | 100 | 95-99 | 11 | 1 to 75 | 5 | 95-99 | 14 |
| | | 105 | 100-104 | 12 | 76-94 | 11 | 100-104 | 15 |
| | | 110 | 105-109 | 13 | 95-99 | 12 | 105-109 | 16 |
| | | 115 | 110-114 | 14 | 100-104 | 13 | 110-114 | 17 |
| 130 | 125 | 120 | 115-119 | 15 | 105-109 | 14 | 115-119 | 18 |
| 135 | 130 | 125 | 120-124 | 16 | 110-114 | 15 | 120-124 | 19 |
| 140 | 135 | 130 | 125-129 | 17 | 115-119 | 16 | 125-129 | 20 |
| 145 | 140 | 135 | 130-134 | 18 | 120-124 | 17 | 130-134 | 21 |
| 150 | 145 | 140 | 135-139 | 19 | 125-129 | 18 | 135-139 | 22 |
| 155 | 150 | 145 | 140-144 | 20 | 130-134 | 19 | 140-144 | 23 |
| 160 | 155 | 150 | 145-149 | 21 | 135-139 | 20 | 145-149 | 24 |
| 165 | 160 | 155 | 150-154 | 22 | 140-144 | 21 | 150-154 | 25 |
| 170 | 165 | 160 | 155-159 | 23 | 145-149 | 22 | 155-159 | 26 |
| 175 | 170 | 165 | 160-164 | 24 | 150-154 | 23 | 160-164 | 27 |
| 180 | 175 | 170 | 165-169 | 25 | 155-159 | 24 | 165-169 | 28 |
| 185 | 180 | 175 | 170-174 | 26 | 160-164 | 25 | 170-174 | 29 |
| 190 | 185 | 180 | 175-179 | 27 | 165-169 | 26 | 175-179 | 30 |
| 195 | 190 | 185 | 180-184 | 28 | 170-174 | 27 | 180-184 | 31 |
| 200 | 195 | 190 | 185-189 | 29 | 175-179 | 28 | 185-189 | 32 |
| 205 | 200 | 195 | 190-194 | 30 | 180-184 | 29 | 190-194 | 33 |
| 210 | 205 | 200 | 195-199 | 31 | 185-189 | 30 | 195-199 | 34 |
| 215 | 210 | 205 | 200-204 | 32 | 190-194 | 31 | 200-204 | 35 |
| 220 | 215 | 210 | 205-209 | 33 * | 195-199 | 32 | 205-209 | 36 |
| 225 | 220 | 215 | 210-214 | 34 * | 200-204 | 33 | 210 + | 37 |
| 230 | 225 | 220 | 215 + | 35 * | 205-209 | 34 | | |
| | | | | | 210+ | 35 | | |

## Company Car Benefit Charge Scale from 2010/2011 (continued)

| Vehicle CO2 g/km | 2016–2017: Charge % Petrol | Diesel | 2017-2018: Charge % Petrol | Diesel | 2018-2019: Charge% Petrol and RDE2 Diesel | Diesel Non DRE2 | 2019-2020: Charge% Petrol and RDE2 Diesel | Diesel Non RDE2 |
|---|---|---|---|---|---|---|---|---|
| 0-50 | 7 | 10 | 9 | 12 | 13 | 17 | 16 | 20 |
| 51-75 | 11 | 13 | 13 | 16 | 16 | 20 | 19 | 23 |
| 76-94 | 15 | 18 | 17 | 20 | 19 | 23 | 22 | 26 |
| 95-99 | 16 | 19 | 18 | 21 | 20 | 24 | 23 | 29 |
| 100-104 | 17 | 20 | 19 | 22 | 21 | 25 | 24 | 28 |
| 105-109 | 18 | 21 | 20 | 23 | 22 | 26 | 25 | 29 |
| 110-114 | 19 | 22 | 21 | 24 | 23 | 27 | 26 | 30 |
| 115-119 | 20 | 23 | 22 | 25 | 24 | 28 | 27 | 31 |
| 120-124 | 21 | 24 | 23 | 26 | 25 | 29 | 28 | 32 |
| 125-129 | 22 | 25 | 24 | 27 | 26 | 30 | 29 | 33 |
| 130-134 | 23 | 26 | 25 | 28 | 27 | 31 | 30 | 34 |
| 135-139 | 24 | 27 | 26 | 29 | 28 | 32 | 31 | 35 |
| 140-144 | 25 | 28 | 27 | 30 | 29 | 33 | 32 | 36 |
| 145-149 | 26 | 29 | 28 | 31 | 30 | 34 | 33 | 37 |
| 150-154 | 27 | 30 | 29 | 32 | 31 | 35 | 34 | 37 |
| 155-159 | 28 | 31 | 30 | 33 | 32 | 36 | 35 | 37 |
| 160-164 | 29 | 32 | 31 | 34 | 33 | 37 | 36 | 37 |
| 165-169 | 30 | 33 | 32 | 35 | 34 | 37 | 37 | 37 |
| 170-174 | 31 | 34 | 33 | 36 | 35 | 37 | 37 | 37 |
| 175-179 | 32 | 35 | 34 | 37 | 36 | 37 | 37 | 37 |
| 180-184 | 33 | 36 | 35 | 37 | 37 | 37 | 37 | 37 |
| 185-189 | 34 | 37 | 36 | 37 | 37 | 37 | 37 | 37 |
| 190-194 | 35 | 37 | 37 | 37 | 37 | 37 | 37 | 37 |
| 195-199 | 36 | 37 | 37 | 37 | 37 | 37 | 37 | 37 |
| 200 + | 37 | 37 | 37 | 37 | 37 | 37 | 37 | 37 |

N.B. The figures up to 2015/16 are for petrol only, for vehicles which
run solely on diesel do not meet the Euro IV standard or were registered from 1st January 2006 a supplement
of 3% is applied until further notice.

*supplement reduced to i) 2%, ii) 1%, iii) nil.

From 2016/17 the figures are for both petrol and diesel cars
Starting from 2018/19 diesel cars which comply with the RDE2 (Real Driving Emissions) rules are treated as
petrol for the purposes of company car BiKs.
Hybrid diesel cars are not subject to any supplement, they are treated as petrol hybrids.

## Company Car Benefit Charge Scale from 2020/2021

| | Car benefit charge 2020/21 Percentage charge to tax | | | Car benefit charge 2020/21 Electric cars registered on or after 6 April 2020^ Percentage charge to tax | | | |
|---|---|---|---|---|---|---|---|
| Vehicle CO2 g/km | Electric vehicle range* | Petrol Electric RDE2 Diesel | Diesel Non DRE2 | Vehicle CO2 g/km | Electric vehicle range* | Petrol Electric RDE2 Diesel | Diesel Non DRE2 |
| 0g/Km | | 0 | | 0g/Km | | 0 | |
| 1-50g/Km | 130+ | 2 | | 1-50g/Km | 130+ | 0 | |
| 1-50g/Km | 70-129 | 5 | | 1-50g/Km | 70-129 | 3 | |
| 1-50g/Km | 40-69 | 8 | | 1-50g/Km | 40-69 | 6 | |
| 1-50g/Km | 30-39 | 12 | | 1-50g/Km | 30-39 | 10 | |
| 1-50g/Km | <30 | 14 | | 1-50g/Km | <30 | 12 | |
| 51-54g/Km | | 15 | | 51-54g/Km | | 13 | |
| 55-59g/Km | | 16 | | 55-59g/Km | | 14 | |
| 60-64g/Km | | 17 | | 60-64g/Km | | 15 | |
| 65-69g/Km | | 18 | | 65-69g/Km | | 16 | |
| 70-74g/Km | | 19 | | 70-74g/Km | | 17 | |
| 75g/Km | | 20 | | 75-79g/Km | | 18 | 22 |
| 76-94g/Km | | 20 | 24 | | | | |
| Each additional 5g/Km | Plus | 1 | 1 | | | 1 | 1 |
| Maximum charge in all cases | | 37 | 37 | | | 37 | 37 |

*This refers to the maximum number of miles travelled on a single charge.
^Only electric vehicles registered on or after 6 April 2020 will benefit from this range of charge.
Diesel hybrid cars are exempt from the 4% surcharge.
Lower Charge Thresholds from 6th April 2002 – 5th April 2008

| Year | CO2 g/km | Tax % | Year | CO2 g/km | Tax % |
|---|---|---|---|---|---|
| 2002/2003 | 165 | 15 | 2005/2006 | 140 | 15 |
| 2003/2004 | 155 | 15 | 2006/2007 | 140 | 15 |
| 2004/2005 | 145 | 15 | 2007/2008 | 140 | 15 |

## COMPANY VANS

Since 6th April 1993, where vans have been made available for the private use of employees - including travel to or from work - a basic scale charge has been assessed on a personal basis.

Reductions may be applied if the employee contributes towards the cost of private use, or where the van is not available for the full year. If private use is available on a shared basis, the benefit of all vans shared are added and the total is divided by the number of employees to whom they are available, subject to a maximum rate at the level equivalent to that for the use of a single van.

## Scale rates – 6th April 1993 – 5th April 2005

- £500 basic charge
- £350 where the vehicle is four years old or more at the end of the tax year

Prior to 6th April 2005, a chargeable benefit generally occurred where a van was available for use. It was not necessary to establish whether, or to what extent, actual 'personal' use took place. A nil rate applied where private use was insignificant in quantity and quality.

## Company van benefit from 6th April 2005

From 6th April 2005 employees have no tax liability where, only:

- work journeys are undertaken, or
- work journeys and travelling between home and work take place, and also where private use is insignificant

## Company van benefit from 6th April 2007

From 6th April 2007 the discount for older vans was removed, the scale charge for unrestricted private use increased to £3,000 and where an employer provides free or subsidised fuel for private mileage an additional fuel charge.

### Company van and fuel benefit charge from 6th April 2010

| Date from | Van benefit charge | Fuel benefit charge |
|---|---|---|
| 6th April 2010 | £3,000 | £550 |
| 6th April 2013 | £3,000 | £564 |
| 6th April 2014 | £3,090 | £581 |
| 6th April 2015 | £3,150 | £594 |
| 6th April 2016 | £3,170 | £598 |
| 6th April 2017 | £3,230 | £610 |
| 6th April 2018 | £3,350 | £633 |
| 6th April 2019 | £3,430 | £655 |
| **6th April 2020** | **£3,490** | **£666** |

### Company van zero emission reduction from 6th April 2015

| Date from | Reduction for zero emission |
|---|---|
| 6th April 2015 | 80% |
| 6th April 2016 | 80% |
| 6th April 2017 | 80% |
| 6th April 2018 | 60% |
| 6th April 2019 | 10% |
| 6th April 2020 | Zero |

From 6th April 2010 there was a nil rate charge for zero emission vans. From 6th April 2015 this was intended to be withdrawn over a six year period so that by 2020/2021 all vans would carry an identical charge. This was deferred and currently the reduction remains at 80%.

## DISPENSATIONS

A dispensation was a written authorisation from HMRC to ignore ('dispense with') P11D and P9D reporting of certain benefits and expenses that HMRC considers would not create a tax liability for the employee even if those benefits and expenses were reported. Dispensations could be revoked by HMRC at any time and potentially retrospectively where it is felt that the employer has failed to comply with the terms of the dispensation, or did not declare to HMRC all the necessary information when the dispensation was granted. In addition, penalties, including retrospective penalties, may still be imposed where a serious breach of the dispensation has occurred. To be valid, a dispensation had to be agreed between an employer and the employer's PAYE compliance officer.

The terms of every dispensation had to be regularly examined by the employer to ensure that any expenses paid gross still complied with the agreement. For example, a dispensation for a specific expense payable at a stated fixed rate became invalid when the reimbursed value of that expense changed. It could never be assumed that current practice was covered by dispensation. For example, from 6th April 2002 all, or parts, of dispensations, relating to payments for travel in an employee's own vehicle ceased to be valid.

The need for dispensations was replaced on 6th April 2016 by a new statutory exemption for expenses reimbursed. Employers still need clear policies and processes with robust verification procedures in order to use the new exemption.

## ELECTRIC VEHICLE CHARGING SCHEME

From April 2018 employees will not incur a benefit in kind charge to tax on the cost to the employer of electricity used to charge an electric vehicle. This will apply whether the car is a company car or personally owned vehicle. Whether or not the car is used for employer business will also not have an effect on the tax relief.

## EMPLOYEE CAR OWNERSHIP SCHEME (ECOS)

An ECOS scheme, or similarly named arrangement, is designed to provide employees with a benefit similar to that of a company car in such a way as to avoid a Company Car Benefit charge. To avoid a car benefit one of the conditions that defines a company car must not apply.

A scheme may be designed by an employer, by a company within the same group as the employer, or by a specialist third party, whereby employees buy cars from a specified (often single) source and within a specified financing period.

The definition of when a company car benefit arises with conditions identified (i) to (viii) is when -
(i)      a car
(ii)     is made available,
(iii)    to an employee (including a Director),
(iv)     (or to a member of their family or household),
(v)      without any transfer of the property in it,
(vi)     by reason of the employment,
(vii)    is available for private use (it does not have to be used), and
(viii)   the benefit of the car does not constitute earnings from the employment by any other provision.

The two key factors in deciding whether the provision of the car through an ECOS avoids the provision of a Company Car Benefit charge is whether:
- availability is by reason of employment (clearly in a scheme set up by the employer this principle cannot be avoided), and
- ownership of the car passed direct to the employee at the outset (without any transfer of the property in it)

If ownership passes to the employee direct from the supplier then this condition is met and there can be no car benefit as this is not a company car but a car belonging to the employee.

In addition, the employee must not be in excluded employment i.e. is not:
- In lower paid employment (earning at a rate of less than £8,500 p.a.)
- A director in lower paid employment with no interest in the company and is either:
- A full-time working director or
- The company is non-profit making or established for charitable purposes only.

ECOS schemes may also be called - ECO; ECOPs; or ECPs (Employees' Car Plan).

# ENTERTAINMENT

## Corporate
The provision of business entertainment at sporting or other public functions often including the use of private or corporate hospitality boxes or tents is a benefit-in-kind. HMRC will rarely allow employees to make a claim for tax relief for such taxable expenses - see http://www.hmrc.gov.uk/manuals/eimanual/eim21729.htm.

## Working Lunches
It is very hard for entertaining (and that includes working lunches) that simply involves meeting with colleagues to satisfy HMRC's rules on the expense being 'wholly, exclusively and necessarily incurred in the performance of the employee's duties', which are enshrined in section 336 of ITEPA. Just because it is felt to be good for morale to have contact with other employees it carries with it an element of socialising, and so cannot meet the 'exclusively' part of the test.

There are only two circumstances where HMRC accepts that the reimbursement of such expenses is not a taxable benefit, which are:
* entertainment in the course of negotiating the renewal or alteration of a service contract, or
* entertainment on the occasion of a 'briefing visit' when local staff have to stay late in order to meet a senior head office visitor, such as a director.

# EXEMPT MINOR BENEFITS
A limited number of minor benefits are excluded from liability for tax, some of which are subject to an annual threshold. An employee may, subject to the stated maximum annual threshold, receive tax-free:
* a long service award subject to a maximum value for each year of service, that the award marks at least 20 years' service and that no other long service award has been made to the employee within the previous 10 years
* a gift from a third party (not contractual) that is not cash or a non-cash voucher
* a payment towards any additional costs incurred (without supporting evidence) whilst working at home as long as this is regular and within the published levels
* the cash equivalent of the benefit of providing pension information and advice in a year of assessment provided it is available to all employees
* an annual function provided by the employer subject to a maximum expenditure per head (not just counting employees attending) per annum. As this is an exemption not an allowance if the cost per head exceeds £150 the whole amount is taxable.

See also Trivial Benefits below.

### Exempt Minor Benefits – Annual Thresholds

| Date from | Long service Award | 3rd Party gift (to value of) | Pension advice (to value of) | Cyclists' breakfast* No. p.a. | Additional expenses for Homeworkers -per week | Annual events (per head) |
|---|---|---|---|---|---|---|
| | £20 | £150 | - | - | - | £75 |
| 06.04.1999 | | | | 6 | - | |
| 06.04.2003 | | £250 | | no limit | £2 | £150 |
| 13.06.2003 | £50 | | | | | |
| 06.04.2005 | | | £150 | | | |
| 06.04.2008 | | | | | £3 | |
| 06.04.2012 | | | | | £4 | |
| 06.04.2013 | | | | Abolished* | | |
| 06.04.2017 | | | £500 | | | |
| 06.04.2020 | | | | | £6 | |

* abolished from April 2013

*N.B. There is also no tax charge where employees use recreational facilities or receive free or subsidised meals on the premises of another employer, where the benefit is provided by that employer on the same basis for their own employees. The recreational facilities must not be open to the public to qualify. The OpRA rules apply which means that if the facility is provided under a salary sacrifice arrangement there will be a tax charge equating to the higher of the cost of the provision and the cash foregone.*

### Tax reliefs available on other benefits

- pension contributions (tax relief but not NICs relief given and relief restricted to £50,000 p.a. from April 2011 and £40,000 p.a. from April 2014 – see annual and lifetime allowance above)
- childcare vouchers up to £55 per week/£243 per month (restricted from April 2011 see vouchers below)
- car parking at or near place of employment from 6th April 1988 (including cycles and motor cycles from April 1999) (See car parking at place of work above)
- the purchase of a bicycle previously loaned by the employer and mainly used for home to work travel (from 6th April 2005) (see bicycle and bicycle safety equipment above).

## EXTRA STATUTORY CONCESSIONS (ESCs)

A number of minor benefits are excluded from liability for tax. Such exclusions have no statutory authority and are allowed as a concession to avoid unnecessary administration. HMRC publish a listing of current of ESCs – see https://www.gov.uk/government/collections/extra-statutory-concessions

## FIXED PROFIT CAR SCHEME (FPCS)

A scheme replaced in April 2002 by the Approved Mileage Allowance Payments (AMAPs) scheme, whereby rates published by HMRC were accepted as the threshold at which any excess payment would be regarded as a taxable profit.

The scheme was a voluntary agreement to the extent that employees maintained the right to provide documentary evidence to support tax-free payment at higher rates where they so desired. An advantage of the FPCS scheme was that the employee was not required to maintain detailed records and receipts of costs incurred to support their tax returns.

### FPCS Authorised Mileage Rates from 6th April 1992 to 5th April 2002

| Year | First 4000 business miles | | | | Mileage in excess of 4000 miles | | | |
|---|---|---|---|---|---|---|---|---|
| | Up to 1000cc | 1001 to 1500cc | 1501 to 2000cc | Over 2000cc | Up to 1000cc | 1001 to 1500cc | 1501 to 2000cc | Over 2000cc |
| | p | p | p | p | p | p | p | p |
| 1992/1993 | 25 | 30 | 38 | 51 | 14 | 17 | 21 | 27 |
| 1993/1994 | 26 | 32 | 40 | 54 | 15 | 18 | 22 | 30 |
| 1994/1995 | 27 | 33 | 41 | 56 | 15 | 19 | 23 | 31 |
| 1995/1996 | 27 | 34 | 43 | 60 | 15 | 19 | 23 | 32 |
| 1996/1997 | 27 | 34 | 43 | 61 | 16 | 19 | 23 | 33 |
| 1997/1998 | 28 | 35 | 45 | 63 | 17 | 20 | 25 | 36 |
| 1998/1999 | 28 | 35 | 45 | 63 | 17 | 20 | 25 | 36 |
| 1999/2000 | 28 | 35 | 45 | 63 | 17 | 20 | 25 | 36 |
| 2000/2001 | 28 | 35 | 45 | 63 | 17 | 20 | 25 | 36 |
| 2001/2002 | 40 | 40 | 45 | 63 | 25 | 25 | 25 | 36 |

| Using the average rate for more than one vehicle | | | | | | |
|---|---|---|---|---|---|---|
| Year | Business miles | | | | Business miles | |
| | Up to 4000 | Over 4000 | | | Up to 4000 | Over 4000 |
| | p | p | | | p | p |
| 1992/1993 | 34 | 19 | | 1997/1998 | 40 | 22.5 |
| 1993/1994 | 36 | 20 | | 1998/1999 | 40 | 22.5 |
| 1994/1995 | 37 | 21 | | 1999/2000 | 40 | 22.5 |
| 1995/1996 | 38.5 | 21 | | 2000/2001 | 40 | 22.5 |
| 1996/1997 | 38.5 | 21 | | 2001/2002 | 42.5 | 25 |

N.B. A separately negotiated scale of authorised mileage rates NHS/FPCS' negotiated through the Whitley Council and approved by HMRC, was applied in the Health Service.

## HEALTH INSURANCE and ASSISTANCE

Where an employer contributes to a Medical Insurance scheme under which an employee, and or members of the employee's family, is a beneficiary, the employee is chargeable for tax in respect of cost to the employer less any amount made good by the employee. Where the employer makes a single contribution on behalf of a number of employees the amount chargeable per employee shall be calculated on a pro-rata basis.

The employer is liable for Class 1A national insurance contributions on the cost incurred, less any amount made good by the employee.

There is also a tax charge on the cost incurred of any medical treatment over and above the cost of the insurance premiums. This includes any excess charge paid before the insurance company takes on the liability.

Since April 2017 and the application of the new OpRA rules, if health insurance and treatment is provided under a salary sacrifice scheme, the charge to tax is the higher of the cost to the employer, less amounts made good, and the cash foregone.

No tax charge applies in the case of any cover specifically arranged to cover the employee during overseas business journeys. This will include cover for a spouse or civil partner if the spouse or civil partner has specific business duties in relation to the journey.

There is, since 1st January 2015, an exemption of £500 towards a necessary medical intervention under the new "Fit for Work" scheme. There are certain restrictions to observe. See further details in "Health Screening" below.

From 6th April 2020 the government has extended the scope of services covered by the exemption. It now includes cognitive therapy treatment in appropriate cases.

## HEALTH SCREENING

The provision of periodic medical checks/screening for employees should not be considered as a taxable benefit; however, where such checks are provided to family members who are not employees the cost of such checks would qualify as a chargeable benefit.
Health screening is an assessment to identify employees who might be at risk of ill-health. A medical check-up is a physical examination by a health professional to determine the employee's state of health.

With effect from 14th August 2007, new regulations from HMRC established that where an employer provides up to one health screening, and/or medical check-up per year for an employee, the cost is exempt from tax provided such health screening or medical check-up is available to all employees, or to all employees identified in previous screening as needing a check-up. This provision replaced former guidance under trivial benefit provisions.

Representations were made by employers, pointing out that many schemes now found themselves subject to a tax charge where none had existed before. Representatives pointed out that in many cases providing check-ups less frequently than annually and restricting such check-ups was necessary for certain employments, such as airline pilots and public service vehicle drivers.

HMRC agreed and by concession restored the original treatment for the whole of the 2007/2008 and 2008/2009 tax years. From 6th April 2009 HMRC finally formalised this concession such that the benefit is not taxable regardless of which employees are entitled to receive the benefit or how often.

### Use of Visual Display Units (VDUs)

In cases where an employee is required to use a VDU as part of his or her normal duties, no chargeable benefit arises on:

- an eyesight test and
- cost of spectacles or contact lenses required solely for VDU use.

Where a test is required under the Display Screen Equipment Regulations and specialist glasses/equipment are available generally to all employees, it should be noted that the cost of spectacles or contact lenses required for general use, including VDU use, which do not require a special prescription for VDU use will be treated as a taxable benefit.

From 1st January 2015 the introduction of the Health and Work Service (HWS) permits employers who use the service or whose own occupational health team recommend a 'medical intervention' that would assist an employee's earlier return into the workplace from sickness absence can provide this with no taxable or Class 1A NICs charge up to a value of £500 per employee per year. This could cover, for example, physiotherapy costs that prior to the introduction of the HWS would be deemed a taxable benefit.

## HOME COMPUTING INITIATIVE (HCI)

From 6th April 1999 - 5th April 2006 a £500 annual tax exemption existed to enable companies to loan computers to their employees with a view to purchasing the computer from the employer at the end of the loan period. From April 2005, provided the employee paid the full market value at the time of transfer, no further tax charge applied. Most schemes ceased in April 2009 once those on loan at 5th April 2006 had been purchased.

## MARORS (Mileage Allowance Relief Optional Reporting Scheme)

Where mileage allowances are paid at rates less than the statutory rates, employees may be entitled to claim tax relief on the difference between the allowances paid and the allowances that would have been paid had the statutory rates (see MAPs above) been applied. The claim is made via the employee's self-assessment return or on Form P87 if they do not receive a self-assessment return.

Whilst there is no statutory duty requiring an employer to report such amounts, the 'negative' amounts, which represent the difference between the amount that could have been paid free of tax under the statutory mileage scheme and the lesser amount paid by the employer, may be reported by employers using the alternative and voluntary MARORS scheme.

N.B. The authorised reporting scheme (MAPs) must not be used to report on P11Ds allowances that are paid at a rate less than the statutory rate. Whilst use of the MARORS reporting scheme is voluntary, some consider it to be a good and prudent employment practice to advise employees of their entitlement to receive tax relief, and to consider the use of the MARORS scheme.

To enter the scheme, the employer should contact HMRC.

Alternatively HMRC will accept an employer provided claim for relief under section 336 of ITEPA2003 if it is submitted with the P11D returns.

## PAYE SETTLEMENT AGREEMENTS (PSA)

These were introduced on 6th April 1996 to replace informal arrangements called Annual Voluntary Settlements. PSAs provide a statutory basis for the settlement of tax liability on certain expenses or benefits-in-kind provided by employers.

They are voluntary agreements made between an employer and HMRC whereby the employer agrees to meet an employee's tax liability. Expenses and benefits covered by a PSA must not be included on P11D, P9D or self-assessment returns and the employer does not need to account for tax or Class 1 NICs.

The tax liability is calculated using 'grossed up' principles based on the tax rates of the employees covered by the PSA.

Items, which may be covered by a PSA, are:
- minor items
- payments or benefits made irregularly
- payments or benefits on which it is either difficult or impractical to apply PAYE.

Items upon which it may prove difficult to apply PAYE may, for example, arise where a benefit is shared amongst a number of employees and it would prove difficult to apportion the value of benefits between the individual employees, or where to deduct tax from the benefit would significantly reduce the way the benefit is perceived by the employee.

PAYE Settlement Agreements cannot be used for major benefits, i.e.:
- provision of a company car
- beneficial loans
- round sum allowances (see above).

Applications for a PSA are made, in writing, to HMRC, identifying the items of expense or benefit to be included in the agreement. Payment of tax, and from 6th April 1999 Class 1B NICs, due under a PSA is payable as a lump sum not later than the 22nd October after the end of the tax year. Class 1B NICs are due on the value of the benefit plus the tax calculated as part of the PSA.

Where items in the PSA would normally be subject to Class 1 (e.g. vouchers) then the Class 1 charge is also added in to the settlement, as is the Class 1A where any is due on items included. A PSA must be agreed by 6th July following the tax year to which it relates. For the third party provision of benefits to employees see Taxed Awards Schemes below.

From 6th April 2016 employers must provide separate PSA computations for all Scottish taxpayers.

Since 6th April 2017 some relaxations in the process mean that employers no longer have to agree PSAs in advance. A new digital service was to be introduced in April 2018 but this has been delayed indefinitely. New guidance has been published.

From April 2019 employers had to implement the Welsh taxation process for PAYE. Currently the Welsh rate of income tax remains the same as for rUK and hence no requirement to produce a separate PSA for Welsh taxpayers. When this position changes and there is a different set of income tax rates for Welsh taxpayers then new arrangements will be needed for PSAs.

## PENSIONS ADVICE

With effect from 6th April 2017 a new exemption from tax and reporting was introduced. This exempts costs of up to £500 incurred by the employer in providing pensions advice to an employee.

This replaced the previous threshold of £150 introduced on 14th December 2004 which suffered from a restriction regarding general financial advice for the employee and was a threshold and not an exemption. Since Financial Conduct Authority (FCA) rules require financial advisers to compile a whole of life financial summary and ensure pensions guidance does not conflict with the employee's general financial situation the original exemption was very rarely used by employers.

The new exemption is more flexible in that as long as the two conditions are met, one, that it is available to all employees generally and two, circumstances relating to age and ill-health, the first £500 of costs incurred in the provision is exempt. The new exemption will also apply as long as additional financial advice is limited to that required to satisfy FCA rules.

## PROFESSIONAL FEES AND SUBSCRIPTIONS

Professional Fees and Subscriptions paid to a Professional Body or Learned Society are exempt from tax provided the membership is necessary or required for the job and the Society or Body is approved by HMRC. A full list of approved societies (List 3) is available on the HMRC website at https://www.gov.uk/government/publications/professional-bodies-approved-for-tax-relief-list-3, and is updated from time to time.

## RELOCATION

Relocation packages are usually made available to assist employees in moving home under one of three circumstances to:

- take up new employment with a new employer
- take up new employment with a current employer
- continue current employment at a new location.

In general terms where relocation is required for job purposes, the first £8,000 of qualifying expenditure in any package is tax-exempt subject to certain conditions:

- the existing home is not within reasonable daily travelling distance of the new workplace
- the new home is within reasonable daily travelling distance of the new workplace.

In practice the assistance is provided in order to allow the employee to move closer to the normal place of work, however it is possible for the employee to move further away from the normal place of work and still qualify for tax-exempt assistance. To qualify the arrangement has to satisfy the two conditions above.

To qualify for tax exemption the expenses must, with limited exceptions, be incurred (or benefits received) before the end of the tax year following the tax year in which the new job commenced, although there are limited circumstances where this rule can be relaxed e.g. children on examination courses, difficulty in selling the former home. It is not a requirement that the former home be disposed of, however the new home must become the sole or main residence of the employee and his or her family.

Allowable expenses and benefits include the cost of disposing of the existing home:

- legal fees and services
- advertising, estate agent and auctioneer's fees and services
- disconnection of services to existing property (electricity, gas, water and telephone)
- costs incurred in redeeming loans raised to purchase existing home
- cost in redeeming loans secured on the existing home
- insurance, maintenance, rent and security provision of existing property left empty prior to sale.

Travel and subsistence:

- family visits to new location and when the actual move takes place
- own travel and accommodation where required to commute until transfer of home is completed
- temporary accommodation where former home left before occupation of new home takes place
- accommodation and travel for child (under 19) required to stay at former, or to move to new, location in advance to maintain continuity of education.

Costs in acquiring new home:

- legal fees and services including Stamp Duty and Land Registry fees
- loan arrangement costs
- surveys and valuations
- costs in connecting services.

Cost of moving possessions:

- packing and unpacking, insurance in transit
- removal and refitting of domestic appliances, temporary storage.

Replacement of domestic goods:

- carpets, curtains and cookers disposed of, less the value of any sale made, provided they are unsuitable for installation in the new home. It should be noted that this condition requires the disposal of old goods. Relocation packages are not available for the fitting out of a second home.

Interest payments on bridging loans:
- provided the loan is used solely for the redemption of the loan on the former home or to purchase the new home
- to the extent that the loan does not exceed the market value of the former home at the time of the purchase of the new.

Certain expenses and benefits are excluded, e.g.:
- mortgage or housing subsidy where moving to a higher cost area
- interest payments on the former home mortgage
- mail re-direction
- council tax bills for the former home
- purchase of children's school uniforms
- compensation for lost benefits such as unused season tickets
- compensation for any loss on the sale of the former home.

From 6th April 1998 relocation packages, to the extent that they exceed £8,000, are subject to NICs in alignment with tax. Further advice is available on the HMRC website at https://www.gov.uk/expenses-and-benefits-relocation.

## ROUND SUM ALLOWANCES AND SCALE RATES

Where an employer makes payment by fixed rate allowance for an item of expense, such allowances are normally subject to tax and NICs (unless previously agreed with HMRC as part of a dispensation).

Where a round sum allowance is less than actual expenditure (verified by receipts) it is the employee's responsibility to claim any additional tax relief via their self-assessment return or using Form P87, which would be reflected in a subsequent year's coding allowance. HMRC officers will not only seek to establish that actual expenditure has been incurred, but also that such expenditure was reasonable.

Scale rates are different to round sum allowances as they are intended to do no more than reimburse an employee but without the need for receipts. From February 2008 HMRC agreed that scale rates for travel and subsistence could be agreed to be paid as part of an employer's dispensation (i.e. paid without any taxable benefit occurring or reporting being required) as long as a sampling exercise had been carried out to demonstrate no profit had been received by the employee.

HMRC subsequently introduced benchmark scale rates from April 2009 that can be used without any prior sampling. Benchmark rates for foreign travel are available from the HMRC website (previously the Foreign and Commonwealth office) – see https://www.gov.uk/government/publications/scale-rate-expenses-payments-employee-travelling-outside-the-uk .

As part of the benefit in kind changes which were implemented on 6th April 2016 a change to the established method of approving scale rates was introduced. HMRC has retained its list of benchmark rates but has scaled down its approval of bespoke rates. Employers can retain bespoke rates but this will apply only from 6th April for a maximum of five years.

As soon as an existing bespoke rate comes up for renewal HMRC will expect the employer's re-application to include consideration of the current benchmark rates. Failure to reapply will render the bespoke rate invalid and a corresponding benchmark rate will become applicable. Employers no longer have to submit extensive sampling data in order to prove a bespoke rate is required.

From April 2018 employers will not be required to retain documents where reimbursement by established and agreed scale rates is used.

## SCOTTISH INCOME TAX

### Scottish variable rate (SVR) and SRIT (Scottish Rate of Income Tax)
Legislation to create the Scottish Parliament, The Scotland Bill 1998, included provision for variation to the United Kingdom standard rate of taxation by a factor of +/- 3% (in 0.5% steps) know as Scottish Variable Rate (SVR). This was repealed by the Scotland Act 2012 and that provides from 2016/17 that the Scottish

parliament (regardless of the result of the independence referendum) can deduct 10% from the UK rate of tax and add the SRIT (Scottish Rate of Income Tax).

Qualification for deduction at the SRIT will be based on location rather than citizenship. Where 50% of the year or more is spent in Scotland, the rate will apply - 50% being assessed on the number of days (part of a day constituting a full day for this purpose) spent in Scotland. The rate will be applicable to earnings wherever payroll is administered throughout the United Kingdom.

HMRC has:
* separately notified all Scottish taxpayers and is allocating S prefix codes
* issued notification forms P2 to Scottish employees and P6 to employers
* provided employers affected with clearly identifiable SRIT Tax Tables.

The code prefix S will enable HMRC to identify deductions at the variable rate for allocation purposes from employers' FPS returns. The Westminster government will continue to set initial rates, thresholds and allowances.

From 6th April 2016 the Scottish parliament elected to replace a 10% reduction in the basic rates of tax in rUK with a new 10% Scottish Rate of Income Tax.

From 6th April 2017 the Scottish parliament elected to retain the 10% SRIT, for a second year, however it determined not to adopt the increase in the higher rate threshold to £45,000 as implemented in rUK. In Scotland the threshold was frozen at £43,000.

From 6th April 2018, however, the Scottish parliament has implemented extensive changes to both the rates and thresholds for income tax to apply to Scottish taxpayers only. The full table of rates and thresholds to be processed by employers and HMRC is:

| Year | Rate % | Income band* £ | Year | Rate % | Income band* £ |
|------|--------|----------------|------|--------|----------------|
| 2018/19 | 19 | 1– 2,000 | 2019/20 | 19 | 1– 2,049 |
| | 20 | 2,001 – 12,150 | | 20 | 2,050 – 12,444 |
| | 21 | 12,151 – 31,580 | | 21 | 12,445 – 30,930 |
| | 41 | 31,581 – 150,000 | | 41 | 30,930 – 150,000 |
| | 46 | > 150,000 | | 46 | > 150,000 |
| | HR | £43,430 | | | £43,430 |

*After allowing for the full personal allowance as set by the UK parliament

| Year | Rate % | Income band* £ |
|------|--------|----------------|
| 2020/21 | 19 | 1– 2,085 |
| | 20 | 2,086 – 12,658 |
| | 21 | 12,659 – 30,930 |
| | 41 | 30,931 – 150,000 |
| | 46 | > 150,000 |
| | HR | £43,430 |

*After allowing for the full personal allowance as set by the UK parliament

The codes used changed from April 2018 in order to identify the different rates to use: Scottish basic rate referred to as SBR, the Scottish intermediate rate of 21% is SD0, Scottish higher rate is SD1, and the Scottish additional rate is SD2. There is no code for the Scottish starter rate.

## SELF-ASSESSMENT (SA)

Introduced 6th April 1996 (1996/1997 being the first year of assessment) and extended to include Corporation Tax for accounting periods ending on or after the 1st July 1999. Before the introduction of Self-Assessment, HMRC issued an assessment, per appropriate schedule, to the taxpayer. The responsibility for appeal against HMRC's assessment rested with the taxpayer.

Under Self-Assessment, the responsibility for completing and submitting an assessment transferred to the taxpayer together with the option to calculate their liability.

Payment of the assessed liability is often remitted by the taxpayer in two equal instalments with a final balancing payment or refund dealt with when the return is submitted. The introduction of Self-Assessment also saw changes in the requirement for employers to provide year-end information to the employee.

For 1996/97 and subsequent years, employers have been required to calculate and supply HMRC and employees with details of the cash value of all benefits-in-kind and expenses using the P11D. From 6th April 1996, a revised four-part form P45 was introduced. The additional part 1a is now supplied to the employee for retention and use in completing their Self-Assessment return.

### Timetable
For Self-assessment new and revised year-end return deadlines were introduced:
- a P60 to be provided to all employees in employment as at 5th April, by 31st May of the year following the end of the tax year, with penalties for failing to do so. From tax year 2010/11 it may be provided electronically.
- a P11D to be returned to HMRC by 6th July, following the end of the tax year, and a copy to be given to the tax payer.
- returns for occupational pension recipients in receipt of benefits-in-kind that are taxable were introduced for the 2007/8 tax year onwards to the same timetable as P11D returns, but with no corresponding notification for the pensioner although it is good practice to do so. The return is made by listing to HMRC containing all the recipients' details, as P11Ds can only be submitted for employees

Generally taxpayers whose tax liabilities are dealt with by PAYE will not be required to submit self-assessment tax returns. For many there has been a requirement to do so, even though no tax liability accrues as a result of compiling and submitting a return.

HMRC has for many years been deselecting such taxpayers and assisted that process with thresholds for declaring and paying tax on investment income and dividends.

In 2017 HMRC started to implement "Simple self-assessment", whereby a PAYE taxpayer can upload details of minor additional income to the personal tax account and have the liability dealt with in that manner.

## SELF-EMPLOYED STATUS

The failure of engagers to correctly assess a person's PAYE status has regularly proved to be a costly oversight for an engager. This often happens when the engager concentrates on employment status when the current tests are designed to test for PAYE liability instead. The advantage for an employer of using the services of a self-employed person is obvious. However, avoidance of both secondary (employer's) Class 1 National Insurance Contributions and the removal of the need to undertake administration of PAYE at source can be attractive as well.

There are seven key issues that must be addressed when considering the relationship that exists between the parties:
- the existence of a formal contract - for a person to be employed a contract of service must exist; this may be written, oral or implied
- self-employment requires a contract for services. Where the true relationship is one of master and servant the contract is clearly one of service see Massey v Crown Life Insurance Company at https://www.gov.uk/hmrc-internal-manuals/employment-status-manual
- exclusivity - the self-employed are not restricted to providing services to a single engager. They should be able not only to perform the tasks required but be able to appoint a substitute
- mutual obligation - an employer is obliged to provide work for an employee and the employee is required to undertake such work but no such obligation will exist in a contract for services except that specified in a schedule of work

- control - determination of where and by whom work is done is one of the key issues in determining the status of self-employment. An employer has the power to select employees, to pay remuneration, to control the method and time of work and has the right of dismissal
- financial risk - an individual truly self-employed must be clearly seen to be taking the financial risk. The following questions are relevant - Does the individual provide or own his or her own equipment? Does the individual stand to suffer losses as well as profit, dependent upon his or her performance?
- method of payment - the self-employed will normally receive a fixed sum for performing a specific task. They may also be subject to penalties in the event of full or partial failure to complete work to time or to standard. Provision of hours of work, rates of pay, place of work, will almost certainly indicate that a status of employment exists. Should any doubt exist, advice should be sought from HMRC (in writing).

During 2005 HMRC launched an internet based Employment Status Indicator (ESI) tool to assist employers in making correct status decisions. The focus on status increased significantly with the advent of the new CIS scheme in April 2007 and the need to make a declaration on each CIS300 monthly return that the status of all subcontractors included on the return has been checked.

For guidance on status see https://www.gov.uk/employment-status . Ever since the requirement to identify workers for auto-enrolment in October 2012 the need to accurately determine the true status of a worker has become more important. A worker for the purposes of automatic enrolment has a much wider definition than that applicable to an employee. For more information see Part 1, Off Payroll Working.

## IR35 - (Personal Service Company Legislation)
IR35 is the number of a press release issued by HMRC that introduced new legislation which came into effect on 6th April 2000. This outlined the treatment of payments for income tax and National Insurance purposes where an individual provides a personal service through an intermediary. In this respect a service company is an intermediary through which a worker provides a service to an employer whilst seeking to retain self-employment status.

The worker is often remunerated by payment of dividends from the service company and the end user pays the service company for the service provided. Under the provisions of IR35, a worker 'is deemed to be employed' where the engagement is for a period of one month or more, and the contract requires the worker to work:

- where the client requests
- for an agreed number of hours per week
- at an agreed rate of pay

And where the worker must:

- keep a time sheet checked by the client
- be subject to the direction of the client
- is unable to perform work for anyone else, and
- must not sub-contract their work to anyone else.

An individual working for an employer under such terms would be treated as employed (and not self-employed) for tax and NIC purposes only, and this distinction establishes that a worker under such circumstance would have an employer with responsibility for administering a full PAYE scheme.

From 6th April 2016 HMRC moved to restrict tax relief for the self-employed by removing travel and subsistence relief where the engager has the right to apply too great a level of supervision, direction and control (SDC). Whilst no definition was given for what too great a level of SDC meant it is clear that only those contractors who truly trade their specialist skills would retain their relief.

From 6th April 2017 self-employed workers who perform services personally for a public sector body have had PAYE applied to their invoices. A new self-employed test was introduced (see https://www.gov.uk/guidance/check-employment-status-for-tax ) (CEST) in order that public sector bodies could determine quickly which tax regime to apply to particular worker. Whilst this has been a difficult regime to apply to the self-employed, HMRC have since determined that the change has had such positive results that they indicated a wish to extend the off-payroll working rules to all external contracting.

In the budget of Autumn 2017, the start point for the finance act of 2018, the Chancellor of the Exchequer indicated that the government intended to take a more cautious approach and a full consultation exercise will take place first and a decision taken on private sector contracting later in 2018 with a view to making any legislative changes for April 2019.

Budget 2018, for the Finance Act 2019, confirmed that off payroll working would extend to the private sector, but be delayed until April 2020 to give both sides time to prepare. A full consultation exercise was launched on 5th March 2019.

From 6th April 2021 (delayed by 12 months) medium and large private sector businesses, when they engage a worker who works through an intermediary, are responsible for determining the income tax and NIC status of any payments made for work done. As with the public sector, the engager must make an individual determination of the status of the contract based on the normal rules for determination. Following several, high profile, status cases during 2019 HMRC has been revising the status determination tool, CEST. Following a determination the worker has the right to lodge an appeal against a determination they disagree with and an appeals process has to be in place to deal with it. HMRC can be asked to provide a ruling if the worker disagrees with the appeal decision and further appeals can be made to the courts.

A number of businesses have already made a corporate decision not to engage any external workers and to provide direct employment instead. It is not known if self-employed workers have any appeal against this decision as it is not a formal determination using the CEST process. In addition it is not known if all such engagers will be providing a full employment contract or if they will use the "Limb B worker" category which requires the payment of tax and NIC under PAYE but does not require them to provide any employment rights or benefits.

## STATUTORY RESIDENCE TEST (SRT)

The SRT came into force on 6th April 2013. It put beyond doubt an individual's tax residency position following the protracted case of Robert Gaines-Cooper. He has consistently argued that since he left Britain for the Seychelles in 1976, he has obeyed the rule that gives non-resident status and tax benefits to anyone who spends less than 90 days a year in the country.

However, High Court and Appeal Court judges ruled he had not made a "clean break", citing a family house in Henley-on-Thames, a UK-based collection of classic Rolls-Royces and trips to Ascot.

From 6th April 2013 there will be three strands to the SRT:
- Conclusive non-residence
- Conclusive residence
- Other connection facts and day-counting
- Conclusive UK non-residence: if one of these tests is met:
- Resident in the UK for one or more of 3 previous tax years and will spend fewer than 16 days in the UK in current tax year, or
- Not resident in UK for any of last 3 tax years and will spend fewer than 46 days in UK in current tax year
- In current tax year leaves UK to take up full-time post overseas
- Dies in current tax year having spent less than 46 days in UK
- Conclusive residence: if one of these tests met
- At least 183 days in UK in tax year
- 91 days with a UK home and no overseas home
- Working full-time in UK during current tax year
- Dies in current tax year subject to conditions, one of which is to have been UK resident during last three years.

Other connection facts and day-counting
- Number of days in UK plus 'connection with UK':
- UK-resident family
- Substantive UK employment or self-employment
- Available accommodation in UK
- 91 days in UK in at least one of the previous two tax years

There will no longer be a concept of ordinary residence. For many individuals their tax status will not change but going forward for many people it will be much clearer what their status is, although as ever there will be some grey areas where individuals fall into two camps.

Extra Statutory Concessions A11 and A78, that allow tax years to be split, became obsolete from April 2013 when Schedule 45, FA2013 replaced them. Overseas Workday Relief (OWR) excludes earnings for overseas work from UK tax for non-UK domiciled individuals who are resident in the UK for less than three years provided the earnings are not remitted to the UK. Individuals claiming OWR under the old rules for 2012/13 will continue to use these old rules rather than adopt the new ones which came into force from April 2013.

From April 2017 the concept of permanent "non-domiciled" status ended and was replaced with a new test to establish whether a taxpayer is liable to UK taxes or not. Where a person has been resident in the UK for 15 years out of the previous 20 they will be considered domiciled in the UK for tax purposes.

## STUDENT EMPLOYMENT

Until the 6th April 2013 the PAYE treatment of students undertaking short-term work during vacations was different in some respects from that of other employees provided certain conditions applied. Employers who did not wish to operate the tax exemption as they felt it too burdensome could simply subject students to the normal P45/P46 process.

### Tax
There was no liability (even where the student's pay in a pay period exceeded the Earnings Threshold) provided the required declaration was completed and signed.

### NICs
There is still no liability, for either employee or employer, if the payment is made before the student reaches the age of 16 years; after age 16 NICs is deducted in the normal way. From 1st October 2006 SSP has been payable to under 16s so NI'able pay must not be used to assess SSP entitlement.

### Hours of work
Employment of students is subject to restrictions relating to the number of hours and/or days worked; for children of school age, the type of work undertaken is regulated locally by individual local authority bylaws – see
https://www.gov.uk/government/uploads/system/uploads/attachment_data/file/193326/Child_employment09.pdf.

### Foreign students
Foreign national students may well be given permission to enter the UK to study but may have restrictions placed on their ability to take paid work, employers should check carefully the terms shown on their Biometric Residence Permit.

## STUDENT TAX EXEMPTION SCHEME - P38(S)

The scheme, which was abolished on the 5th April 2013 allowed the employer to make payment exempt of tax, was initially introduced with the P38(S) as both the student's statement of status and as a year-end process document. P38(S) forms are now simply retained for inspection, if required, by HMRC. The scheme was based on the presumption that the student's earnings for working outside term time would not generally attract a tax liability and the P38(S) exemption avoided post year end refunding of tax by HMRC which might otherwise occur. The P38(S) exemption does not apply to NICs, which must be collected where, in any earnings period earnings exceed the LEL regardless of whether the pay period falls within term time and if the employee is aged 16 or over.

## TAXED AWARDS SCHEME (TAS)

A Taxed Awards Scheme (TAS) is an agreement between HMRC and an incentive award provider (i.e. a third party not the direct employer) for payment of the tax liability on the grossed up value of non-cash benefits provided to someone else's employees. The provider is required to maintain tax records for other people's employees included in the scheme.

From 6th April 2001 either a Class 1 or a Class 1A NICs liability arises in respect of all third party benefits payable by the supplier even if he chooses to pass the tax charge back to the employees rather than enter into a TAS - to assess which charge arises see HMRC's A-Z of benefits at: https://www.gov.uk/expenses-and-benefits-a-to-z .

The supplier must tax third party awards made in cash and their direct employer must deduct Class 1 NICs from the employee. Cash vouchers given by third parties are taxed and subject to Class 1 NICs through the direct employer's payroll. Awards of non-cash vouchers, unless they are exempt e.g. childcare vouchers, are subject to Class 1 NICs if the direct employer has any involvement in arranging the awards. There is a full list of exempt non-cash vouchers in the *CWG2 Employer further guide to PAYE and NICs* https://www.gov.uk/government/publications/cwg2-further-guide-to-paye-and-national-insurance-contributions

At the end of each tax year each higher rate tax-paying recipient of an award must be provided with a form P433 certificate showing the details of the award and the tax paid. The scheme provider must submit end of year returns P35(TAS) and P440 within 90 days of the end of the tax year. The tax is paid over by 19 July (22 July if paying electronically which is not mandatory), after the tax year to which it relates. HMRC provides the supplier with a special payslip for this purpose in the End of Year pack. If payments are late, HMRC may withdraw the TAS.

Increasingly HMRC are proposing that TAS providers use the PSA process to account for income tax and NIC as this avoids the need for detailed tax records for other employers' employees.

## TAX - AN EARLY HISTORY

On 3rd December 1798, William Pitt (The Younger) placed before Parliament a Bill for the introduction of Income Tax. The rising cost of the Napoleonic Wars and the trebling of existing taxes in 1797 (Triple Taxation) prompted the introduction of a temporary Incomes Tax. The bill was made Law on 9th January 1799 and repealed in May 1802.

In 1842 Robert Peel reintroduced the principle, and notwithstanding plans for its abolition by William Gladstone in 1874, it has continued as a temporary tax thereafter. Even today failure to approve the annual Finance Bill by the 1st August in any year would indeed see the demise of Income Tax. Such a measure would no doubt itself prove 'temporary!' On its introduction in 1799, incomes below £60 per year were exempt, for those between £60 and £200 a graduated scale from 1/20 to 1/10 applied, and on incomes above £200 the rate was 1/10 (10%).

## TAX CODES

The tax code is a means of amending the annual amount of tax-free pay (earnings which an employee may receive before income tax becomes due and deductible). In addition to the code, a prefix or suffix letter will be linked to that code. In certain cases letters may take the place of a code. The annual personal allowance is directly related to the code. The tax code denotes the annual value of the personal allowances/adjustment by omitting the unit element, e.g. Annual allowance £12,500, code = 1250. By reversing the process, the value of the annual personal allowance may be determined (within minimal limits) by multiplying the code by a factor of 10 and adding 9 e.g. code 1250 personal allowance value for payroll purposes = £12,509 (1250 x 10 + 9). Individuals are notified of their code via a form P2. Taxpayers who think their code is wrong should inform HMRC by email at https://www.gov.uk/tax-codes. Scottish taxpayers have a "S" prefix code.

## TAX CODE PREFIX AND SUFFIX LETTERS

The suffix letter is used annually - if required - as a means of adjusting employees' codes en-bloc when the Government increases, or decreases, the value of annual personal allowances. Form P9X, issued annually by HMRC, advises employers of the changes to be actioned. Where a code must be individually assessed by HMRC (T prefix codes) a P9 is issued before the start of the relevant tax year. If further changes are made as a result of a late Budget, to take effect normally in tax week 7 or 11 depending upon the date of the Budget, a P7X form is issued which acts as the authority to amend codes en-masse and further P6(B) forms are issued where individual codes need to be amended.

Most PAYE schemes now download all coding notices as part of the payroll process and this has become more prevalent since the implementation of RTI in April 2013.

### Prefix Letters and Suffix Letters

| | |
|------|-------------------------------------------------------------------------------|
| **D** | Tax is to be deducted at the higher/additional rate on all earnings. D0 = 40%, D1 = 45% |
| **SD** | Scottish taxpayers only, SD0 = 21%, SD1 = 41% and SD2 = 46% |
| **K** | Employee with additional taxable pay, rather than free pay, which indicates that tax is to be collected on both earnings/benefits in that employment plus earnings or income from another source. |
| **SK** | A Scottish taxpayer with additional taxable pay instead of tax free pay. |
| **L** | Basic personal allowance |

| M | A spouse or civil partner receiving the Marriage Allowance from April 2015 |
|---|---|
| N | A spouse or civil partner giving up the Marriage Allowance from April 2015 |
| S | Introduced from 6th April 2016 this prefix indicates the person is a Scottish taxpayer. S125L etc. |
| T | Suffix codes, the employer may only adjust the value of the code following individual notification from HMRC. Codes of 0T are issued i.e. no free pay is permitted but the employee will pay tax at 20%, 40% and 45%. |

### All Letter Codes

| BR | Tax deductible on all earnings at basic rate, currently 20% - no free pay |
|---|---|
| D0 | Tax deductible on all earnings at higher rate, currently 40% - no free pay |
| D1 | Tax deductible on all earnings at additional rate, currently 45% - no free pay) code introduced from April 2011 |
| NT | This indicates the employee is not subject to tax in that employment e.g. expatriates. A new statutory resident test was introduced from 6.4.13 that dictates the use of this code |
| SD0 | Scottish taxpayer, tax deductible on all earnings at the intermediate rate, currently 21% - no free pay |
| SD1 | Scottish taxpayer, tax deductible on all earnings at the higher rate, currently 41% - no free pay |
| SD2 | Scottish taxpayer, tax deductible on all earnings at the at the additional rate, currently 46% - no free pay |

### Suffix Letters withdrawn

| A | Basic allowance plus half the children's tax credit, subject to tax at basic rate |
|---|---|
| J | Basic allowance plus married couple's allowance or additional personal allowance, taxable income enters higher rate band (2001/2002 only) |
| H | Higher - basic personal allowance plus children's tax credit, subject to tax at basic rate |
| P | Age-related single person's allowance, person aged between 65 and 74 - abolished completely from April 2015 |
| V | Elderly - basic personal allowance for person aged between 65 and 74 years plus married couple's allowance, subject to tax at basic rate |
| Y | Higher age-related single person's allowance - age 75 and over - abolished for those reaching 65 on or after 06.04.2013 |

*N.B. A, & J were discontinued at 6th April 1999; H at 6th April 2003 and V at 6th April 2009 as those to whom the suffix applied would be aged 75 by 5th April 2010.*

The codes used to deal with the changes to rates and thresholds for Scottish taxpayers from April 2018 in order to identify the different rates to use, will be known as SBR for the Scottish basic rate, the Scottish intermediate rate of 21% is SD0, Scottish higher rate is SD1 and the Scottish additional rate is SD2. There is no code for the Scottish starter rate.

## TAX CALCULATIONS

Cumulation is the normal method for operating a tax code when the 'free pay', taxable pay and tax paid are each accumulated from the beginning of the tax year up to and including the current pay period. The cumulative totals are used for each calculation of tax deductible. With the exception of the first week/month in the tax year it may be said that the tax deducted in any pay period is a balance of tax outstanding for the year to date rather than the tax due solely on that pay period.

### Week 53

* Where a 53rd pay week occurs at the end of a tax year, tax is to be assessed on pay in that pay period without reference to the current cumulative pay or tax details - 'on a week 1/month 1 basis'. As this will lead to an underpayment of tax, as in effect too much free pay has been taken into account, employees in self-assessment will receive an underpayment notice after a week 53 has been processed. Since 2014 HMRC has been making efforts to recover underpayments from all taxpayers and not just those who submit self-assessment tax returns.
* Where free pay at Week 52 exceeds total pay for the year, no tax is to be deducted at week 53.
* Where free pay at Week 52 is less than total pay for the year, the tax tables to be used are: Weekly Pay - week 1, Fortnightly Pay - week 2, Four Weekly Pay - week 4

**Pay after employee has left employment**
- there is no specific rule about issuing a P45 but employers are required to issue " as soon as is reasonably practicably."
- where a P45 has not been issued, tables for the week in which the pay day falls should be used - pay and tax to be included in the P45 entries
- where a P45 has been issued, tax should be deducted at basic rate, BR, on all taxable pay (no free pay allowance) until 5th April 2011 and using code 0T non-cumulatively from 6th April 2011 onwards. Employers must not issue an amended or additional P45 and must provide the employee with confirmation of the payment even if this is just a payslip and include the amount in the next available Full Payment Submission marking this as a payment after leaving and including the payment in the YTD figures.

**Holiday pay - paid in advance**
Where an employee receives payment of holiday pay in advance, calculation should be made with reference to the employee's tax code, either
- cumulative - calculate PAYE tax due using the last week in which no pay is received, or the last day of the tax year if this is earlier, or
- week 1/month 1 - divide the holiday pay equally between each week/month making separate calculations for each week, then deducting the total amount of tax due by adding together these calculations.

Where an employee is leaving employment after the holiday PAYE should be calculated by using the tax week/month in which actual payment is made.
If the holiday overlaps into the next tax year, and the holiday pay is being paid in week 52 and there would normally be:
- 52 pay days in the tax year, all holiday pay paid in week 52 must be subject to PAYE in week 52, or
- 53 pay days in the tax year, and the holiday pay paid in week 52 includes the pay which would normally be paid in week 53, the amount that relates to week 53 should be subject to PAYE as a week 53 payment. The remainder should be regarded as a week 52 payment

## TAX - FREE PAY

The amount of money an employee or pensioner will be allowed to receive in a tax year before becoming eligible for payment of income tax. To ensure that deductions are evenly operated throughout the year, the annual allowance is apportioned throughout the pay periods and is applied to each weekly, monthly or other period of payment. Tables A - Free Pay Adjustment Tables are a ready reckoner provided for this purpose by HMRC. The tables have not changed since 1993 and can be found at https://www.gov.uk/government/publications/tables-a-pay-adjustment-tables .

## TAX RATES AND BANDINGS

### Rates and Bandings from 1986/1987 to 2007/2008

|  | Basic rate | | Higher rate | |
|  | % | to £ | % | over £ |
|---|---|---|---|---|
| 1986/1987 | 29 | | | |
| 1987/1988 | 27 | | | |
| 1988/1989 | 25 | 19,300 | 40 | 19,300 |
| 1989/1990 | 25 | 20,700 | 40 | 20,700 |
| 1990/1991 | 25 | 20,700 | 40 | 20,700 |
| 1991/1992 | 25 | 23,700 | 40 | 23,700 |

## Rates and Bandings from 1986/1987 to 2007/2008 continued

|  | Lower rate | | Basic rate | | | Higher rate | |
|---|---|---|---|---|---|---|---|
|  | % | up-to £ | % | from £ | to £ | % | over £ |
| 1992/1993 | 20 | 2,000 | 25 | 2,001 | 23,700 | 40 | 23,700 |
| 1993/1994 | 20 | 2,500 | 25 | 2,501 | 23,700 | 40 | 23,700 |
| 1994/1995 | 20 | 3,000 | 25 | 3,001 | 23,700 | 40 | 23,700 |
| 1995/1996 | 20 | 3,200 | 24 | 3,201 | 24,300 | 40 | 24,300 |
| 1996/1997 | 20 | 3,900 | 24 | 3,901 | 25,500 | 40 | 25,500 |
| 1997/1998 | 20 | 4,100 | 23 | 4,101 | 26,100 | 40 | 26,100 |
| 1998/1999 | 20 | 4,300 | 23 | 4,301 | 27,100 | 40 | 27,100 |
| 1999/2000 | 10 | 1,500 | 23 | 1,501 | 28,000 | 40 | 28,000 |
| 2000/2001 | 10 | 1,520 | 22 | 1,521 | 28,400 | 40 | 28,400 |
| 2001/2002 | 10 | 1,880 | 22 | 1,881 | 29,400 | 40 | 29,400 |
| 2002/2003 | 10 | 1,920 | 22 | 1,921 | 29,900 | 40 | 29,900 |
| 2003/2004 | 10 | 1,960 | 22 | 1,961 | 30,500 | 40 | 30,500 |
| 2004/2005 | 10 | 2,020 | 22 | 2,021 | 31,400 | 40 | 31,400 |
| 2005/2006 | 10 | 2,090 | 22 | 2,090 | 32,400 | 40 | 32,400 |
| 2006/2007 | 10 | 2,150 | 22 | 2,151 | 33,300 | 40 | 33,300 |
| 2007/2008 | 10 | 2,230 | 22 | 2,231 | 34,600 | 40 | 34,600 |

## Rates and Bandings from 2008/2009

|  | Basic rate[1] | | Higher rate | | Additional rate | |
|---|---|---|---|---|---|---|
|  | % | up-to £ | % | over £ | % | over £ |
| 2008/2009 | 20 | 36,000 | 40 | 36,000 |  |  |
| 7.9.2008 | 20 | 34,800 | 40 | 34,800 |  |  |
| 2009/2010 | 20 | 37,400 | 40 | 37,400 |  |  |
| 2010/2011 | 20 | 37,400 | 40 | 37,400 | 50 | 150,000 |
| 2011/2012 | 20 | 35,000 | 40 | 35,000 | 50 | 150,000 |
| 2012/2013 | 20 | 34,370 | 40 | 34,370 | 50 | 150,000 |
| 2013/2014 | 20 | 32,010 | 40 | 32,010 | 45 | 150,000 |
| 2014/15 | 20 | 31,865 | 40 | 31,865 | 45 | 150,000 |
| 2015/16 | 20 | 31,785 | 40 | 31,785 | 45 | 150,000 |
| 2016/17 EW | 20 | 32,000 | 40 | 32,000 | 45 | 150,000 |
| 2016/17 S | 10 | 32,000 | 30 | 32,000 | 35 | 150,000 |
| 2016/17 SRIT | 10 | 32,000 | 10 | 32,000 | 10 | 150,000 |
| 2017/18 rUK | 20 | 45,000 | 40 | 45,000 | 45 | 150,000 |
| 2017/18 S | 10 | 43,000 | 30 | 43,000 | 35 | 150,000 |
| 2017/18 SRIT | 10 | 43,000 | 10 | 43,000 | 10 | 150,000 |
| 2018/19 rUK | 20 | 46,350 | 40 | 46,350 | 45 | 150,000 |
| 2019/20 rUK | 20 | 50,000 | 40 | 50,000 | 45 | 150,000 |
| 2020/21 | 20 | 50,000 | 40 | 50,000 | 45 | 150,000 |

[1]This includes the taxpayers personal allowance, currently £12,500

*N.B. The Scottish rates and thresholds can be found now under the section entitled "Scottish Income Tax".*

*N.B.*
- *7th September 2008 the higher rate threshold was revised with retrospective effect to offset the increased basic personal allowance introduced at that time. These steps were taken to restore (in part) the unforeseen effects on certain tax payers following the abolition of the 10% (lower rate) tax band on the 6th April 2008. The September change was not intended to benefit those paying tax at the higher rate hence the amendment to the threshold. This principle, of making changes to the personal allowance benefit only those on the basic rate of income tax, was brought back in 2011/12 and has continued since.*
- *In 2013/14 the increase in the personal allowance was only partly clawed back in a reduced basic rate threshold.*
- *In April 2015 almost all of the personal allowance was applied to all taxpayers.*
- *In April 2016 the Scottish Rate of Income Tax of 10% was applied splitting the total tax liability in Scotland into two rates.*
- *From April 2017 the Scottish rate of income tax remained at 10% but the higher rate threshold was frozen at £43,000.*
- *From April 2018 all Scottish rates and thresholds form part of a unique table to cover the extensive changes made.*

## LOWER RATE BAND (formerly Lower Rate Relief)

From 6th April 1994 to 5th April 2008, the basic rate tables (Table B) as issued by HMRC provided for calculation at basic rate only.

As the lower rate band was dealt with as a banding within the basic rate band, in order to adjust the over-deduction of tax that would otherwise occur, 'Table B Subtraction Tables' were therefore provided for use in conjunction with Table B. An adjustment was required to make allowance for earnings within the lower rate band at the differential between the lower and basic rates.

### Lower Rate Band Historical Chart from 1999 to 2008

| Tax Year | Basic Rate % | Lower Rate % | Lower Rate Band Limit £ | Annual SRR £ |
|----------|--------------|--------------|-------------------------|--------------|
| 1999/2000 | 23 | 10 | 1,500 | 195.00 |
| 2000/2001 | 22 | 10 | 1,520 | 182.40 |
| 2001/2002 | 22 | 10 | 1,880 | 225.60 |

### Lower Rate Band Historical Chart from 1999 to 2008 (continued)

| | | | | |
|----------|--------------|--------------|-------------------------|--------------|
| 2002/2003 | 22 | 10 | 1,920 | 230.40 |
| 2003/2004 | 22 | 10 | 1,960 | 235.20 |
| 2004/2005 | 22 | 10 | 2,020 | 242.40 |
| 2005/2006 | 22 | 10 | 2,090 | 250.80 |
| 2006/2007 | 22 | 10 | 2,150 | 258.00 |
| 2007/2008 | 22 | 10 | 2,230 | 267.60 |

The annual lower rate band allowance (2007/2008) was calculated as follows –

| | |
|---|---|
| Basic Rate 22% | Lower Rate 10% |
| Lower Rate Band Limit | £2,230 |
| Annual Lower Rate Band | £2,230 x 12% = £267.60 |

From the 6th April 2008 Taxable Pay Tables B to D were re-branded to reflect the removal of the 10% band.

## TAX AVOIDANCE SCHEMES

New rules were introduced on 1st August 2004 in an effort to filter out the increasingly elaborate schemes that were being created to assist employers in reducing tax, and particularly employers' NI contributions. Each scheme promoter is allotted a scheme reference number (SRN) on notification to HMRC.

Each employer using the scheme must be given the SRN by the promoter and must complete a form AAG1 for each tax year for which the scheme is expected to provide a tax advantage. The first report must be made by 19th May of the year when the scheme was first used, and by the 19th May for each subsequent year. For further help see https://www.gov.uk/dealing-with-hmrc/tax-avoidance.

## TAXIS - LATE NIGHT

The provision of a taxi paid for by an employer for a work to home journey is in general terms a taxable benefit. However, an exemption applies where all the following conditions are met:
- the employee is required to work later than usual and at least until 9 pm
- that the occurrence of the late night working is irregular – e.g. not part of any scheduled working pattern, i.e. annually.
- that by the time their work finishes public transport has ceased or it would be unreasonable (see below) to expect the employee to use public transport.

It is the responsibility of the employer to maintain adequate records to show that provision meets these requirements. HMRC will not accept that an exemption may apply solely on the grounds that the employee:
- has to travel home in the dark
- has a long working day and as a result is tired
- has a heavy briefcase, laptop computer, etc to take home
- travels by public transport to an unmanned station.

Where a journey includes more than one form of public transport, the cessation of any one of those portions of the journey would justify the unreasonableness.

Provision shall not exceed 60 occasions per annum, which does not imply that the first 60 such journeys per year are exempt, rather that the number of qualifying journeys shall not exceed 60 in total per year. For compliance purposes the importance of record keeping cannot be underestimated.

In 2016 HMRC indicated that because of continued abuse of the concession they are mindful to withdraw it. No date has been given for this at time of publication.

## TELEPHONES - HOME

Where the employee is the subscriber named in the telephone directory, the employee must meet the full cost of the rental and private calls. A chargeable benefit will otherwise accrue. Where the employer is the subscriber, in general terms there is no chargeable benefit if private use is insignificant. When private use is significant, the employee must meet the cost of private calls, and a proportion of the rental otherwise there is a chargeable benefit. See also mobile phones below.

## TELEPHONES - MOBILE

Prior to 6th April 1999 a scale charge of £200 per year, or part of a year, was assessable to tax for the provision of a mobile phone. Where the employee had no private calls, or the cost was made good including a proportion of the capital cost and standing charges, no assessable benefit accrued.

From 6th April 2006 the provision of one mobile phone* for private use by the employer to an employee (not the employee's family or household member) including the payment of the line rental and cost of calls by the employer is   tax-free. Payments made to employees for the business use of their own mobile phone are taxable. It follows then that a mobile phone provided for business use is not taxable either.

If the employer provides more than one mobile phone to an employee solely for business use, and private use is not significant, the second phone is not taxable. If only one mobile phone is provided for both business and private use it will be exempt. If two mobile phones are provided for mixed business and private use, one will be exempt and the other will represent a benefit.

It is up to the employee and employer to decide which one will be exempt and which one will be chargeable.

*The definition of mobile phone was tightened from April 2006 to exclude Smartphones and other Personal Digital Assistants (PDAs) but relaxed from 6th April 2012 to reclassify Smartphones as mobile phones and any class 1A paid by the employer or tax by the employee between 2006-2011 was refunded, but only to those employers who applied for the refund.

Prior to 6th April 2006 the exemptions were allowed in respect of personal use by the employee or family members, and there was no limit on the number of mobile phones per employee.

From 6th April 2017 the exemption for one mobile phone is lost if the phone is provided under a salary sacrifice arrangement. In addition, if salary sacrifice applies then the reportable benefit in kind is the higher of the cost to the employer and the cash foregone.

## TERMINATION SETTLEMENTS

Lump sum payments made on termination or loss of office/change of duties, provided they are not normal earnings and are not separately taxable under any other tax provisions, are free of tax subject to a maximum limit of £30,000. All qualifying payments and benefits in kind (e.g. car) should be aggregated for the purpose of assessing any liability. Implications following the Finance Act 1998:

- the use of the term 'termination settlement' rather than 'termination payment' indicates that both cash and non-cash benefits are to be treated equally. The cash equivalent of non-cash benefits e.g. car, loan or use of assets, must be taken into account
- employers only need to report termination settlements inclusive of all non-cash benefits where the sum total exceeds the taxable threshold
- assessment for tax is made in the year that payment is made (previously assessment was made in the year of termination) and at rates applicable to the year of payment. This may require the carry forward of any 'unused' part of the exemption limit from one tax year into a subsequent tax year, as it is directly related to the termination and is not an annual allowance, cash is taxed first followed by benefits in any year
- where a termination settlement is known at the initial stage, provided there is no significant subsequent variation (deemed to be an increase exceeding £10,000), the employer must report any settlement which exceeds the threshold by 6th July at the latest following the year of termination.
- It is possible that payments as part of a termination agreement may be made from more than one source (e.g. redundancy lump sum from an employer and enhanced retirement lump sum benefit from an occupational pension scheme). In such cases all payments and benefits are to be aggregated when assessing the tax liability.

All payments included as part of a termination package within these provisions will need to meet, to HMRC's satisfaction, the criteria that they are being paid solely as compensation for loss of office and are not remuneration for services provided in the course of employment or office. Where this is the case there is no £30,000 exemption and the package will be liable to tax and national insurance contributions in full as earnings.

### PILONS (Payments in Lieu of Notice)

In general terms (and except where on its own, or in combination with other termination payments, it exceeds £30,000) a payment in lieu of notice does not attract income tax or NICs. However, where such a payment can be shown to result from contractual terms or conditions of employment, including potentially custom and practice, such payments should be assessed for tax/NICs liability. A PILON occurs where an employer ends the contract of employment without fulfilling the statutory and contractual notice provisions, and in recognition makes a lump sum payment by way of compensation in place of the normal contractual/statutory payments that would otherwise be due. For HMRC's latest position on termination payments see their Employment Income Manual at http://www.hmrc.gov.uk/manuals/eimanual/EIM12977.htm

From 6th April 2018 all PILON payments are to be included in the £30,000 exemption figure for terminations and must be treated as liable to both income tax and NICs to the extent that the amount is a Post-Employment Notice Period (PENP) sum.

This is calculated as BP x D/P − T, where BP is the Basic pay in the last pay period before the trigger date (the relevant date which triggers the requirement for the calculation), D is the number of Days in the PENP, P is the number of days in the Pay period and T is the Total value of the payments or benefits received in connection with the termination, excluding compensation for holidays not taken or any bonuses.

Any sum which is calculated as a PENP is treated as normal pay for tax and NIC purposes and any remainder will be used against the £30,000 exemption for termination payments.

From 6th April 2019 further changes were implemented:
- Payments in excess of the £30,000 exemption to attract employer's NICs
- All PILONs to be treated as earnings, attracting income tax and NICs in full.

## TRAVEL AND SUBSISTENCE

Travel by an employee between two workplaces that he or she must attend to carry out the duties of the same employment is classed as business travel. Business travel expenses are generally exempt from PAYE liability.

Allowable expenses may include:
- public transport costs
- hotel accommodation
- meals
- tolls, congestion charges, parking fees
- business phone calls, fax or photocopying expenses

but may not include anything not directly related to the business such as private phone calls or newspapers except when covered by the exemptions for incidental expenses - see Incidental Overnight Expenses below.

Travel between the workplaces of two different employments is not business travel with one exception - where a person is an employee of more than one company in the same group of companies, travel between the workplaces of each employment is business travel - see http://www.hmrc.gov.uk/manuals/eimanual/EIM32035.htm.

Travel between home and a temporary workplace is not normal commuting as long as:
- the employee is likely to spend less than 40 per cent of his or her working time at that particular workplace, or
- it is not a regular occurrence, or
- the duration of the attachment to the temporary workplace is no more than 24 months.

Where business travel conditions are not met, the workplace is regarded by HMRC as a permanent workplace. Travel between the new workplace and home will then be classed as ordinary commuting, and so cannot be reimbursed without a tax and NICs charge arising. The change from business travel to ordinary commuting occurs as soon as it is **known** that the temporary workplace travelling will exceed 24 months, not when the 24 months expires.

### Incidental Overnight Expenses
An employer may reimburse, tax-free, incidental expenses (e.g. private phone calls or newspapers) incurred to the maximum value of £5 per night (£10 outside the UK) when the employee is on company business. Where the payment exceeds the limit the whole payment is taxable (not just the excess). Where the employer requires that an employee pay back any excess over the limit the payment should be deemed as not exceeding the limit.

Where such expenses cover a continuous period in excess of one night away, the £5 exemption for each night is applied on a cumulative basis to the total payments throughout the period. This 'averaging' principle must be applied to an unbroken period of consecutive nights in its entirety. An entire continuous stay cannot be broken up into separate claim periods in an attempt to meet this principle.

*N.B. Business expenses which meet the above criteria incur neither Class 1 or Class 1A NIC, nor PAYE liability and need not be entered on P11D or P9D returns.*

## TRIVIAL BENEFITS

Section 203(1) of the Income Tax (Earnings and Pensions) Act (ITEPA) 2003 permits benefits to be exempt from tax if their cash equivalent value is so trivial that it is not worth reporting and charging to tax. There are no set rules for determining whether a gift might be classified as trivial.

Cash benefits, benefits with a monetary value and non-cash vouchers, however small in amount, cannot be classified as trivial. Trivial benefits will often be of a consumable or perishable nature and common sense must be applied. Current HMRC guidance on trivial benefits can be found at https://www.gov.uk/expenses-and-benefits-trivial-benefits .

HMRC guidance for example quotes such items as:
- tea, coffee or water provided at the workplace;
- a small gift in recognition of an event such as the birth of a baby or marriage, but not as a thank you for a service provided, or
- a seasonal gift such as a turkey, bottle of wine or box of chocolates
- seasonal flu jabs
- the repair of employer-provided bicycles up to £20 in value.

Where a gift is in excess of the above examples (a crate of wine as opposed to a single bottle at Christmas) it will be necessary to consider content and cost, in determining  whether the benefit is trivial or not. Such items cannot be included in a PAYE Settlement Agreement, but if HMRC agrees that they are 'trivial', they will confirm this by letter.

Finance Act 2015 was to contain a new statutory exemption for trivial benefits to apply on and after 6 April 2015. The proposed new limit was £50 and ostensibly replaced the unofficial £25 limit currently in use as a guide to triviality. A number of conditions were to be implemented in order to prevent employers providing a series of benefits in kind and exempting them as trivial and these were to be detailed in the 2015 finance act. This was not enacted as expected.

From 6th April 2016 the new statutory exemption for trivial benefits was applied, removing from tax charge most benefits in kind where the value on each occasion is £50 or less and it is not being provided under a salary sacrifice arrangement.

There is no limit to the number of occasions a trivial benefit is provided unless it is a close company (a micro business with five or fewer shareholders, or members) and the benefit is provided to one of the members or to a member of that person's family. In such cases there is an annual cap of six occasions and £300.

Cash and cash vouchers and any benefit in kind provided by way of a salary sacrifice arrangement are not included in the new exemption, neither are benefits provided for services performed in the course of employment.

## VOLUNTEER DRIVERS

Tax is not payable on mileage or other allowances paid to volunteer drivers except where the allowances received exceed the expenses incurred. Tax in such cases will be due at the employee's lowest marginal rate. As volunteer driving is not gainful employment there is no liability for either Class 2 or Class 4 NICs.

### Volunteer Driver Mileage Rates from 6th April 1998

| Engine Capacity | Annual Mileage | |
| Cc | On first 4000 miles | On each mile over 4000 miles |
| --- | --- | --- |
| Up to 1000 | 28 p | 17 p |
| 1001-1500 | 35 p | 20 p |
| 1501-2000 | 45 p | 25 p |
| Over 2000 | 63 p | 36 p |

### Volunteer Driver Mileage Rates from 6th April 2002

| Date from | Annual Threshold | Rate per mile Up to threshold | Rate per mile Above threshold | Passengers Per passenger |
|---|---|---|---|---|
| | Miles | p per mile | p per mile | p per mile |
| 6.4.2002 | 10,000 | 40 | 25 | - |
| 6.4.2011 | 10,000 | 45 | 25 | 5 |

However as some organisations pay a flat rate allowance per mile irrespective of the total annual mileage, and some costs do not increase, the following table may be used in such cases to determine whether or not a profit has accrued to the user (upon which tax will be due).

| Annual Mileage | Allowance per mile | Annual Mileage | Allowance per mile |
|---|---|---|---|
| Up to 10,000 | 40p | 14,000 – 16,000 | 34p |
| 10,000 – 12,000 | 37p | 16,000 – 18,000 | 33p |
| 12,000 – 14,000 | 35p | 18,000 – 20,000 | 32p |

## VOUCHERS

Vouchers are liable to tax and NICs, however their treatment depends on the nature of the voucher.

### Cash Vouchers
Where these are redeemable or exchangeable for cash, either in whole or part - the taxable value is that for which the voucher can be exchanged not, it should be noted, the cost incurred in providing the voucher if this is less.

### Non-cash Vouchers
These are defined as any voucher, stamp, similar document, or token capable of being exchanged for money, goods or services for example, retail gift vouchers or a flight ticket). The taxable value is that incurred in providing the voucher (discounted cost) and this value should be reported on forms P9D or P11D. Unusually in the case of childcare vouchers which are classed as non-cash vouchers, this is relaxed and the costs of the service/administration charge from the voucher provider, if borne by the employer, may be paid with no liability to tax or NICs as long as no more than the exempt amounts. The service/administration charge does not form part of the exempt amount but can be paid by the employer tax/NICs free in addition to the exempt amount for the vouchers themselves.

Prior to April 1999 non-cash vouchers were not subject to NICs, but some exceptions remain:
- vouchers exchangeable for sports/recreational activities
- vouchers provided to recognise long service (minimum 20 years' service, maximum. value £50 per year)
- vouchers awarded under tax-free suggestion schemes
- transport vouchers for severely disabled staff
- vouchers (tickets) exchangeable for meals in canteen facilities where meals are provided for staff generally.

Non-cash vouchers which allow the user to obtain "change" for the unused portion of the voucher are treated as cash vouchers for the purposes of taxation.

For non-cash vouchers provided by third parties see Taxed Awards Schemes above. Special rules apply where non-cash vouchers are used to obtain the following - stocks and shares, gold bullion, futures, commodities or fine wines, and specialist advice should be sought.

## WELSH INCOME TAX

From April 2019 the Welsh Assembly takes on the authority to vary the rates and thresholds for income tax for Welsh taxpayers. HMRC will undertake the collection of all specific taxes for Wales.

The first Welsh rate of income tax has been set at 10% and means that for the first year the headline rate of tax used in payroll will remain at the rUK rates laid down.

The Welsh assembly budget press release of 26 February 2020 confirmed the retention of the 10% Welsh rate of income tax and hence the rUK rates remain in force for Wales for the 2020/21 tax year. There is, however, a commitment to have a supplementary budget following the rUK one to deal with any additional matters.

## WORKS BUSES & PUBLIC BUS SUBSIDIES

Employees may travel from home to work income tax and NICs free on an employer provided bus with 9 or more seats. This exemption came into effect on the 6th April 2002, and extends that introduced in the 1999 Finance Act which related to buses with a seating capacity of 12 passenger seats or more.

Normally, if an employer pays for, or subsidises, home to work travel for employees, the amount of the benefit is liable to tax and NICs (see also late night taxis above).

Where an employer subsidises a public bus service the exemption from income tax only applies on a specific bus route for qualifying journeys (i.e. to/from work and between sites) so providing a general bus pass that can be used across a geographic area as many employers have done is not within the exemption.

# PART 3: NATIONAL INSURANCE

## INTRODUCTION

National Insurance was introduced in 1911 as a means of funding a National Social Security Scheme. Although there is a general reference to the National Insurance Fund there is in fact no fund as such; the proceeds are used within the government's annual budgets to finance the current year's welfare expenditure, on a 'pay as you' go basis. The qualifying conditions for the basic state pension establish a clear link between the NI contributions paid by an individual and the benefit entitlement of that individual, usually referred to as 'the contributory principle'.

It may however be argued that in recent years this principle has been eroded with the introduction of certain classes of NI contribution, notably Class 1A, where contributions paid in respect of an individual do not count against the individual's contribution record for benefit purposes. National Insurance is administered by HMRC's National Insurance Contributions and Employer Office (prior to 1.4.1999 - The Contributions Agency). All contributors are allocated a unique contribution record reference - their National Insurance Number comprising two letters, six numbers and a final letter. National Insurance numbers are issued to individuals as they attain the age 16.

## NATIONAL INSURANCE CONTRIBUTION CLASSES

National Insurance is assessed within five categories or 'classes'.

### Class 1
Earnings related contributions, assessed against paid employment (not pensions). Both employee (primary) and employer (secondary) contributions make up payments that are usually remitted to HMRC under PAYE arrangements. Primary contributions are not due after state pension age however the employer pays secondary contributions. Contributions are determined as a percentage of earnings within limits set annually.

### Class 1A
Employer only contributions originally assessed on the taxable value of company cars or any fuel provided by an employer for private use. Extended from April 2000 to include most taxable benefits-in-kind.

### Class 1B
Introduced on 6th April 1999, contributions are chargeable as a lump sum on expenses, payments and benefits-in-kind taxed under a PAYE Settlement Agreement (PSA) - see Part 2.

### Class 2
Flat-rate contributions paid by the self-employed. This was originally collected directly by HMRC via a direct debit arrangement. From April 2014 collection was switched to self-assessment.

### Class 3
Flat-rate voluntary contributions of a fixed amount to either protect, make up a deficit, or to enhance benefit entitlement.

### Class 3A
A one-off addition which applied from 12th October 2015 until 5th April 2017 and allowed those who were due to reach state retirement age before 6th April 2016 to top up their contributions and achieve a larger state retirement pension than they would otherwise have done.

### Class 4
Self-employed contributions, paid at a percentage rate on profits between lower and upper limits.

Classes 1, 2 and 3 count towards an employee's contribution record. The definition of an employed earner in relation to National Insurance classification is critical, and includes:

*   employees under a contract of service, and
*   persons in elected office (company directors, local authority elected members, MPs and Ministers of religion)

In cases of doubt about the contractual status of an employee, advice should be sought from HMRC's National Insurance Contributions and Employer Office.

### Future developments

The government intends to abolish the Class 2 NIC and its voluntary equivalent and may extend the scope of Class 4 to make such contributions count towards contributory benefits. This was included in the 2017 finance act but withdrawn almost immediately afterwards following widespread criticism. There is still an intention to make significant changes to self-employed NICs so that both the contribution rate and access to benefits is equal to that enjoyed by employed earners.

## NATIONAL INSURANCE – HISTORICAL NOTES

### From April 1976 to March 1978

When earnings reached the Lower Earnings Limit (LEL) the employee paid contributions as a percentage of all earnings up to the Upper Earnings Limit (UEL).

### From April 1977 to 1st October 1984

Secondary contributions included a National Insurance Surcharge as part of general tax revenue.

### From April 1978

From April the contribution rate was dependent on whether the employee was contracted-out of the State Earnings Related Pension Scheme (SERPS), now S2P. Employees and employers who were contracted-out paid lower primary and secondary contributions on earnings between the LEL and the UEL (the NI Rebate). The contribution rate on earnings up to the LEL was payable at the not contracted-out rate in all cases.

### From October 1985

From October a sliding scale of contributions was introduced. Employers' contributions on earnings above the UEL were payable at not contracted-out rates. This principle applied to both contracted-out and not contracted-out employment. Contracted-out rebates applied solely on earnings between the LEL and the UEL.

### From October 1989

From October, employee's contributions were restructured. A contribution rate of 2% on earnings up to the LEL was introduced. Earnings between the LEL and the UEL attracted the appropriate contracted-out or not contracted-out rate.

### From April 1999

New principles were introduced aimed at removing anomalies in levels of contribution that occurred previously when earnings moved from one banding to another. A small increase in earnings could result in a relatively large increase in contributions and a reduction in net earnings. No employees' (primary) contributions became due until earnings reached the LEL. Where earnings exceeded this threshold contributions became due solely on those earnings in excess of the LEL and up to the UEL. No secondary or employer's contributions became due until earnings reached a new (secondary) threshold equal in value to the Single Person's Tax Allowance (SPTA). Where earnings exceeded this threshold, secondary contributions became due on all earnings in excess of the SPTA.

### From April 2000

A further Earnings Threshold (ET) was introduced at which employee's primary contributions commence rather than the LEL. Earnings at the Lower Earnings Limit (LEL) up to and including the Earnings Threshold are treated as earnings on which NICs have actually been paid, even though they haven't, in order to protect contributory benefits. The contracted-out rebate is still due on the earnings in the banding between the LEL and the ET even though no contributions have actually been paid. This could result in a rebate for both employee and employer, generally shown on payslips as 'NI Rebate', rather than the employee contribution being netted off.

### From April 2001

The Employee's (Primary) and Employer's (Secondary) thresholds aligned as the Earnings Threshold (ET), and linked to income tax personal allowance, but are still two distinct thresholds.

**From April 2002**
The contracted-out rebate was due as the employee was now contracted-out of S2P, the replacement for SERPS.

**From April 2003**
The employee and employer contributions increased by 1%, the 1% addition to employee contributions extended to earnings above the Upper Earnings Limit (an increase from zero% to 1%). Employees in deferred employment holding a CA2700 pay only 1% on all earnings above the Earnings Threshold in the second employment. The NI rebate (see below) now netted off even when the result is a 'negative' contribution and therefore does not appear as a separate entry on payslips.

**From September 2008**
With the introduction of a mid-year increase to the tax thresholds to deliver compensation for low-paid employees for the removal of the 20% tax band, the tax and NICs thresholds (both primary and secondary) were split apart for the first time since 2001.

**From April 2009**
The Upper Accrual Point (UAP) was introduced as the ceiling for state pension accrual. From 6th April 2009 employers and employees with occupational pension schemes are only entitled to contracted-out rebates on earnings between the Lower Earnings Level (LEL) and the UAP, NICs being due on earnings between the UAP and UEL at not contracted-out rates.

All employers were required to record and report 4 bands of earnings within their payroll software and on their 2009/2010 annual returns until such time as the option to contract out was abolished for members of defined contribution pension schemes (April 2012). The rebates for defined benefit schemes will be abolished too in April 2016 when the single tier state pension is introduced. The Upper Earnings Limit (UEL) was harmonised with the higher rate tax threshold.

**From 22nd June 2010 to 5 September 2013**
Regional NICs holiday introduced in certain geographic areas for new
businesses, allowing for savings of £5,000 of employer NICs for each of first ten recruited employees into the business.

**From April 2011**
Class 1 and Class 4 main rates increased by 1.0% to 12.00% and 9.00% respectively. The Class 1 employers' rate was increased by 1.0% to 13.8%. Class 1A and 1B increased by 1.0% to 13.8%. The additional rate of Class 1 and Class 4 over the UEL/UPL for employees increased by 1.0% to 2.0%. The employee's earnings threshold for NICs (primary threshold) increased to £139 p.a. to protect low earners from the increase. The employer's (secondary NICs' threshold) was set at £136 and was no longer aligned with the earnings threshold for tax - three thresholds across tax and NICs existed.

**From April 2012**
Contracted-out rebates removed for DC schemes. Contracted-out rebates for DB schemes reduced by 0.5% for both employers and employees to 3.4% for employers and 1.4% for employees.

**From April 2015**
Employers NICs were abolished up to an Upper Secondary Threshold, for all employees who were under 21 at the point of payment.

**From April 2016**
Contracted-out rebates removed for DB pension schemes. Upper Accrual Point becomes redundant and removed. Employers NICs abolished, up to an Apprentice Upper Secondary Threshold, for all apprentice employees who are under 25 at the point of payment.

**From April 2017**
Limits and thresholds increase after two tax years and primary and secondary thresholds aligned following representation by the Office for Tax Simplification.

**From April 2020**
After another period of identical primary and secondary thresholds 2020 sees a significant divergence between the two values. The primary (employee) threshold rises £17 to £183 a week whilst the secondary (employer)

threshold rises by just £3 to £169 a week. In addition the upper earnings thresholds and limit remains unchanged at £962 a week which significantly reduces the 12% contributions band.
The Employment Allowance rises to £4,000 but is restricted to employers with a total NIC bill of less than £100,000.

## NATIONAL INSURANCE CLASS 1 EARNINGS LIMITS

The tables on the following pages show the basic Not Contracted-out rates. Contracted-out rates are obtained by applying the rebates shown at the bottom of each page. The rebate is the difference between the Not Contracted-out and Contracted-out rates. Contracted out rebates were abolished, firstly on 6th April 2012 for contracted out defined contribution pensions schemes and then finally on 6th April 2016 for defined benefit schemes.

### Class 1 National Insurance Earnings Limits

#### From 1992/93

| Year | Lower Earnings Limit | | | Upper Earnings Limit | | |
|---|---|---|---|---|---|---|
| | Weekly £ | Monthly £ | Annual £ | Weekly £ | Monthly £ | Annual £ |
| 1992/1993 | 54 | 234 | 2,808 | 405 | 1,755 | 21,060 |
| 1993/1994 | 56 | 243 | 2,912 | 420 | 1,820 | 21,840 |
| 1994/1995 | 57 | 247 | 2,964 | 430 | 1,864 | 22,360 |
| 1995/1996 | 58 | 252 | 3,016 | 440 | 1,907 | 22,880 |
| 1996/1997 | 61 | 265 | 3,172 | 455 | 1,972 | 23,660 |
| 1997/1998 | 62 | 269 | 3,224 | 465 | 2,015 | 24,180 |
| 1998/1999 | 64 | 278 | 3,328 | 485 | 2,102 | 25,220 |
| 1999/2000 | 66 | 286 | 3,432 | 500 | 2,167 | 26,000 |
| 2000/2001 | 67 | 291 | 3,484 | 535 | 2,319 | 27,820 |
| 2001/2002 | 72 | 312 | 3,744 | 575 | 2,492 | 29,900 |
| 2002/2003 | 75 | 325 | 3,900 | 585 | 2,535 | 30,420 |
| 2003/2004 | 77 | 334 | 4,004 | 595 | 2,579 | 30,940 |
| 2004/2005 | 79 | 343 | 4,108 | 610 | 2,644 | 31,720 |
| 2005/2006 | 82 | 356 | 4,264 | 630 | 2,730 | 32,760 |
| 2006/2007 | 84 | 364 | 4,368 | 645 | 2,795 | 33,540 |
| 2007/2008 | 87 | 377 | 4,524 | 670 | 2,905 | 34,840 |
| 2008/2009 | 90 | 390 | 4,680 | 770 | 3,337 | 40,040 |
| 2009/2010 | 95 | 412 | 4,940 | 844 | 3,656 | 43,875 |
| 2010/2011 | 97 | 421 | 5,044 | 844 | 3,656 | 43,875 |
| 2011/2012 | 102 | 442 | 5,304 | 817 | 3,540 | 42,475 |
| 2012/2013 | 107 | 464 | 5,564 | 817 | 3,540 | 42,475 |
| 2013/2014 | 109 | 473 | 5,668 | 797 | 3,454 | 41,450 |
| 2014/2015 | 111 | 481 | 5,772 | 805 | 3,489 | 41,865 |
| 2015/2016 | 112 | 486 | 5,824 | 815 | 3,532 | 42,385 |
| 2016/2017 | 112 | 486 | 5,824 | 827 | 3,583 | 43,000 |
| 2017/2018 | 113 | 490 | 5,876 | 866 | 3,750 | 45,000 |
| 2018/2019 | 116 | 503 | 6,032 | 892 | 3,863 | 46,350 |
| 2019/2020 | 118 | 512 | 6,136 | 962 | 4,167 | 50,000 |
| 2020/2021 | 120 | 520 | 6,240 | 962 | 4,167 | 50,000 |

## CLASS 1 NATIONAL INSURANCE EARNINGS THRESHOLDS

A NIC Earnings Threshold (the Secondary Threshold) was introduced on 1st April 1999 at which level employer's contributions commence. It was set at the same amount as the annual Single Person's Tax Allowance.

Primary and Secondary thresholds were unified and aligned with Personal Tax Allowance on 6th April 2001, but still exist as two separate thresholds. In September 2008 this linkage was broken.

For 2014/2015 employers finally had identical primary and secondary thresholds to deal with, however from 6 April 2015 the two rates were different once again. Alignment was achieved again from 6th April 2017 but from 6th April 2020 they are different again, this time significantly different.

### Earnings Thresholds from 6th April 2001

| Year | Employee's Earnings Threshold | | | Employer's Earnings Threshold | | |
|------|--------|---------|--------|--------|---------|--------|
| | Weekly £ | Monthly £ | Annual £ | Weekly £ | Monthly £ | Annual £ |
| 2001/2002 | 87 | 378 | 4,535 | 87 | 378 | 4,535 |
| 2002/2003 | 89 | 385 | 4,615 | 89 | 385 | 4,615 |
| 2003/2004 | 89 | 385 | 4,615 | 89 | 385 | 4,615 |
| 2004/2005 | 91 | 395 | 4,745 | 91 | 395 | 4,745 |
| 2005/2006 | 94 | 408 | 4,895 | 94 | 408 | 4,895 |
| 2006/2007 | 97 | 420 | 5,035 | 97 | 420 | 5,035 |
| 2007/2008 | 100 | 435 | 5,225 | 100 | 435 | 5,225 |
| 2008/2009 | 105 | 453 | 5,435 | 105 | 453 | 5,435 |
| 2009/2010 | 110 | 476 | 5,715 | 110 | 476 | 5,715 |
| 2010/2011 | 110 | 476 | 5,715 | 110 | 476 | 5,715 |
| 2011/2012 | 139 | 602 | 7,225 | 136 | 589 | 7,072 |
| 2012/2013 | 146 | 634 | 7,605 | 144 | 624 | 7,488 |
| 2013/2014 | 149 | 646 | 7,755 | 148 | 641 | 7,696 |
| 2014/2015 | 153 | 663 | 7,956 | 153 | 663 | 7,956 |
| 2015/2016 | 155 | 672 | 8,060 | 156 | 676 | 8,112 |
| 2016/2017 | 155 | 672 | 8,060 | 156 | 676 | 8,112 |
| 2017/2018 | 157 | 680 | 8,164 | 157 | 680 | 8,164 |
| 2018/2019 | 162 | 702 | 8,424 | 162 | 702 | 8,424 |
| 2019/2020 | 166 | 719 | 8,632 | 166 | 719 | 8,632 |
| 2020/2021 | 183 | 792 | 9,500 | 169 | 732 | 8,788 |

## CLASS 1 NATIONAL INSURANCE CONTRIBUTION RATES

### Not contracted-out employment rates - 6th April 1986 to 5th October 1988

| Date from | Earnings | Employee | | Employer |
|-----------|----------|----------|---------|----------|
| | £ per week | Standard | Reduced | |
| 6 April 1986 | Under £38.00 (LEL) | 0% | 0% | 0% |
| | £38.00 to £59.99 | 5.00% | 3.85% | 5.00% |
| | £60.00 to £94.99 | 7.00% | 3.85% | 7.00% |
| | £95.00 to £285.00 | 9.00% | 3.85% | 9.00% |
| | Over £285 (UEL) | (£25.65pw) | (£10.97pw) | 10.45% |

## Not contracted-out employment rates - 6th April 1986 to 5th October 1988 (continued)

| 6 April 1987 | Under £39.00 (LEL) | 0% | 0% | 0% |
|---|---|---|---|---|
| | £39.00 to £64.99 | 5.00% | 3.85% | 5.00% |
| | £65.00 to £99.99 | 7.00% | 3.85% | 7.00% |
| | £100.00 to £295.00 | 9.00% | 3.85% | 9.00% |
| | Over £295 (UEL) | (£26.55 pw) | (£11.36 pw) | 10.45% |
| 6 April 1988 | Under £41.00 (LEL) | 0% | 0% | 0% |
| | £41.00 to £69.99 | 5.00% | 3.85% | 5.00% |
| | £70.00 to £104.99 | 7.00% | 3.85% | 7.00% |
| | £105.00 to £305.00 | 9.00% | 3.85% | 9.00% |
| | Over £305 (UEL) | (£27.45 pw) | (£11.74 pw) | 10.45% |

## Not contracted-out employment rates - 6th October 1989 to 5th April 1992

| Date from | Earnings | Employee | | | Employer |
|---|---|---|---|---|---|
| | | Standard A | Reduced B | Age exempt C | on all Earnings A, B & C |
| | £ per week | | | | |
| 6 October 1989 | First £43.00 (to LEL) | 2.00% | 3.85% | Nil | |
| | £43.00 to £74.99 | 9.00% | 3.85% | Nil | 5.00% |
| | £75.00 to £114.99 | 9.00% | 3.85% | Nil | 7.00% |
| | £115.00 to £164.99 | 9.00% | 3.85% | Nil | 9.00% |
| | £165.00 to £325.00 | 9.00% | 3.85% | Nil | 10.45% |
| | Over £325 (UEL) | Nil | Nil | Nil | 10.45% |
| 6 April 1990 | First £46.00 (to LEL) | 2.00% | 3.85% | Nil | |
| | £46.00 to £79.99 | 9.00% | 3.85% | Nil | 5.00% |
| | £80.00 to £124.99 | 9.00% | 3.85% | Nil | 7.00% |
| | £125.00 to £174.99 | 9.00% | 3.85% | Nil | 9.00% |
| | £175.00 to £350.00 | 9.00% | 3.85% | Nil | 10.45% |
| | Over £350 (UEL) | Nil | Nil | Nil | 10.45% |
| 6 April 1991 | First £52.00 (to LEL) | 2.00% | 0% | Nil | 0% |
| | £52.00 to £84.99 | 9.00% | 3.85% | Nil | 4.60% |
| | £85.00 to £129.99 | 9.00% | 3.85% | Nil | 6.60% |
| | £130.00 to £184.99 | 9.00% | 3.85% | Nil | 8.60% |
| | £185.00 to £390.00 | 9.00% | 3.85% | Nil | 10.40% |
| | Over £390 (UEL) | Nil | Nil | Nil | 10.40% |

### Contracted-out employment rebates 1986 - 1989

| | Employee | Employer |
|---|---|---|
| 6th April 1986 to 5th April 1988 | 2.15% | 4.10% |
| 6th April 1988 to 5th April 1991 | 2.00% | 3.80% |

applicable to earnings between the LEL and UEL.

**Not contracted-out employment rates - 6th April 1992 to 5th April 1994**

| Date from | Earnings £ per week | Employee | | | Employer |
|---|---|---|---|---|---|
| | | Standard A | Reduced B | Age Exempt C | on all earnings A, B & C |
| 6 April 1992 | First £54.00 (LEL) | 2.00% | 0% | Nil | 0% |
| | £54.00 to £89.99 | 9.00% | 3.85% | Nil | 4.60% |
| | £90.00 to £134.99 | 9.00% | 3.85% | Nil | 6.60% |
| | £135.00 to £189.99 | 9.00% | 3.85% | Nil | 8.60% |
| | £190.00 to £405.00 | 9.00% | 3.85% | Nil | 10.40% |
| | Over £405 (UEL) | Nil | Nil | Nil | 10.40% |
| 6 April 1993 | First £56.00 (to LEL) | 2.00% | 3.85% | Nil | |
| | £56.00 to £94.99 | 9.00% | 3.85% | Nil | 4.60% |
| | £95.00 to £139.99 | 9.00% | 3.85% | Nil | 6.60% |
| | £140.00 to £194.99 | 9.00% | 3.85% | Nil | 8.60% |
| | £195.00 to £420.00 | 9.00% | 3.85% | Nil | 10.40% |
| | Over £420 (UEL) | Nil | Nil I | Nil | 10.40% |

**Not contracted-out employment rates - 6th April 1994 to 5th April 1998**

| 6 April 1994 | First £57.00 (to LEL) | 2.00% | 3.85% | Nil | |
|---|---|---|---|---|---|
| | £57.00 to £99.99 | 10.00% | 3.85% | Nil | 3.60% |
| | £100.00 to £144.99 | 10.00% | 3.85% | Nil | 5.60% |
| | £145.00 to £199.00 | 10.00% | 3.85% | Nil | 7.60% |
| | £200.00 to £430.00 | 10.00% | 3.85% | Nil | 10.20% |
| | Over £430 (UEL) | Nil | Nil | Nil | 10.20% |
| 6 April 1995 | First £58.00 (to LEL) | 2.00% | 0% | Nil | 0% |
| | £58.00 to £104.99 | 10.00% | 3.85% | Nil | 3.00% |
| | £105.00 to £149.99 | 10.00% | 3.85% | Nil | 5.00% |
| | £150.00 to £204.99 | 10.00% | 3.85% | Nil | 7.00% |
| | £205.00 to £440.00 | 10.00% | 3.85% | Nil | 10.20% |
| | Over £440.00 (UEL) | Nil | Nil | Nil | 10.20% |
| 6 April 1996 | First £61.00 (to LEL) | 2.00% | 0% | Nil | 0% |
| | £61.00 to £109.99 | 10.00% | 3.85% | Nil | 3.00% |
| | £110.00 to £154.99 | 10.00% | 3.85% | Nil | 5.00% |
| | £155.00 to £209.99 | 10.00% | 3.85% | Nil | 7.00% |
| | £210.00 to £455.00 | 10.00% | 3.85% | Nil | 10.20% |
| | Over £455 (UEL) | Nil | Nil | Nil | 10.20% |

### Not contracted-out employment rates - 6th April 1994 to 5th April 1998 (continued)

| 6 April 1997 | First £62.00 (to LEL) | 2.00% | 3.85% | Nil | |
| | £62.00 to £109.99 | 10.00% | 3.85% | Nil | 3.00% |
| | £110.00 to £154.99 | 10.00% | 3.85% | Nil | 5.00% |
| | £155.00 to £209.99 | 10.00% | 3.85% | Nil | 7.00% |
| | £210.00 to £465.00 | 10.00% | 3.85% | Nil | 10.00% |
| | Over £465.00 (UEL) | Nil | Nil | Nil | 10.00% |

### Contracted-out employment rebates 1992 – 1997

| | Employee | Employer | |
|---|---|---|---|
| 6th April 1992 to 5th April 1993 | 2.00% | 3.80% | |
| 6th April 1993 to 5th April 1995 | 1.80 % | 3.00% | |
| 6th April 1995 to 5th April 1997 | 1.80 % | 3.00 % | |
| | | COMPS | COSRS |
| 6th April 1997 to 5th April 1998 | 1.6 % | 1.5 % | 3.0 % |

### Not contracted-out employment rates - 6th April 1998 to 5th April 2000

| Date from | Earnings £ per week | Employee | | | Employer |
| | | Standard A | Reduced B | Age Exempt C | on all Earnings A, B & C |
|---|---|---|---|---|---|
| 6 April 1998 | First £64.00 (to LEL) | 2.00% | 3.85% | Nil | |
| | £64.00 to £109.99 | 10.00% | 3.85% | Nil | 3.00% |
| | £110.00 to £154.99 | 10.00% | 3.85% | Nil | 5.00% |
| | £155.00 to £209.99 | 10.00% | 3.85% | Nil | 7.00% |
| | £210.00 to £485.00 | 10.00% | 3.85% | Nil | 10.00% |
| | Over £485 (UEL) | Nil | Nil | Nil | 10.00% |
| 6 April 1999 | First £66.00 (to LEL) | Nil | Nil | Nil | Nil |
| | £66.01 to £83.00 (ST) | 10.00% | 3.85% | Nil | Nil |
| | £83.01 to £500 | 10.00% | 3.85% | Nil | 12.20% |
| | Over £500 (UEL) | Nil | Nil | Nil | 12.20% |

### Not contracted-out employment rates - 6th April 2000 to 5th April 2005

| 6 April 2000 | First £67 (to LEL) | Nil | Nil | Nil | Nil |
|---|---|---|---|---|---|
| | £67.00 to £76.00 (PT) | 0% | 0% | Nil | Nil |
| | £76.01 to £84.00 (ST) | 10.00% | 3.85% | Nil | Nil |
| | £84.01 to £535 | 10.00% | 3.85% | Nil | 12.20% |
| | Over £535 (UEL) | Nil | Nil | Nil | 12.20% |
| 6 April 2001 | First £72.00 (LEL) | Nil | Nil | Nil | Nil |
| | £72.01 to £87.00 | 0% | 0% | Nil | 0% |
| | £87.01 to £575 | 10.00% | 3.85% | Nil | 11.90% |

| | | | | | |
|---|---|---|---|---|---|
| | Over £575 | Nil | Nil | Nil | 11.90% |
| 6 April 2002 | First £75.00 (LEL) | Nil | Nil | Nil | Nil |
| | £75.01 to £89.00 | 0% | 0% | Nil | 0% |
| | £89.01 to £585.00 | 10.00% | 3.85% | Nil | 11.80% |
| | Over £585 (UEL) | Nil | Nil | Nil | 11.80% |
| 6 April 2003 | First £77.00 (LEL) | Nil | Nil | Nil | Nil |
| | £77.01 to £89.00 | 0% | 0% | Nil | 0% |
| | £89.01 to £595.00 | 11.00% | 4.85% | Nil | 12.80% |
| | Over £595 (UEL) | 1.00% | 1.00% | Nil | 12.80% |
| 6 April 2004 | First £79.00 (LEL) | Nil | Nil | Nil | Nil |
| | £79.01 to £91.00 | 0% | 0% | Nil | 0% |
| | £91.01 to £610.00 | 11.00% | 4.85% | Nil | 12.80% |
| | Over £610 (UEL) | 1.00% | 1.00% | Nil | 12.80% |

### Contracted-out employment rebates 1998 – 2004

| | Employee | Employer | |
|---|---|---|---|
| | | COMPS | COSRS |
| 6th April 1998 to 5th April 1999 | 1.6 % | 1.5 % | 3.0 % |
| 6th April 1999 to 5th April 2000 | 1.6 % | 0.6 % | 3.0 % |
| 6th April 2001 to 5th April 2002 | 1.6 % | 1.0 % | 3.5 % |
| 6th April 2002 to 5th April 2004 | 1.6 % | 1.0 % | 3.5 % |

### Not contracted-out employment rates - 6th April 2005 to 5th April 2008

| Date from | Earnings £ per week | Employee | | | Employer |
|---|---|---|---|---|---|
| | | Standard A | Reduced B | Age Exempt C | on all Earnings A, B & C |
| 6 April 2005 | First £82.00 (LEL) | Nil | Nil | Nil | Nil |
| | £82.01 to £94.00 | 0% | 0% | Nil | 0% |
| | £94.01 to £630.00 | 11.00% | 4.85% | Nil | 12.80% |
| | Over £630 (UEL) | 1.00% | 1.00% | Nil | 12.80% |
| 6 April 2006 | First £84.00 (to LEL) | Nil | Nil | Nil | Nil |
| | £84.01 to £97.00 | 0% | 0% | Nil | 0% |
| | £97.01 to £645.00 | 11.00% | 4.85 | Nil | 12.80% |
| | Over £645 (UEL) | 1.00% | 1.00% | Nil | 12.80% |
| 6 April 2007 | First £87.00 (LEL) | Nil | Nil | Nil | Nil |
| | £87.01 to £100.00 | 0% | 0% | Nil | 0% |
| | £100.01 to £670.00 | 11% | 4.85% | Nil | 12.80% |
| | Over £670 (UEL) | 1.00% | 1.00% | Nil | 12.80% |

## Not contracted-out employment rates - 6th April 2008 to 5th April 2011

| | | | | | |
|---|---|---|---|---|---|
| 6 April 2008 | First £90.00 (LEL) | Nil | Nil | Nil | Nil |
| | £90.01 to £105.00 | 0% | 0% | Nil | 0% |
| | £105.01 to £770.00 | 11% | 4.85% | Nil | 12.80% |
| | Over £770 (UEL) | 1.00% | 1.00% | Nil | 12.80% |
| 6 April 2009 | First £95.00 (LEL) | Nil | Nil | Nil | Nil |
| | £95.01 to £110.00 | 0% | 0% | Nil | 0% |
| | £110.01 to £770.00 (UAP) | 11% | 4.85% | Nil | 12.80% |
| | £770.01 to £844 | 11% | 4.85% | Nil | 12.80% |
| | Over £884 (UEL) | 1.00% | 1.00% | Nil | 12.80% |
| 6 April 2010 | First £97.00 (LEL) | Nil | Nil | Nil | Nil |
| | £97.01 to £110.00 | 0% | 0% | Nil | Nil |
| | £110.01 to £770.00 (UAP) | 11% | 4.85% | Nil | 12.80% |
| | £770.01 to £844 | 11% | 4.85% | Nil | 12.80% |
| | Over £884 (UEL) | 1.00% | 1.00% | Nil | 12.80% |

From 6th April 2011 the employer and employee thresholds were split as follows

## Not contracted-out employment rates - 6th April 2011 – 5th April 2012

| Date from | Earnings £ per week | Employee | | | |
|---|---|---|---|---|---|
| | | Standard A | Reduced B | Age Exempt C | Deferred J |
| 6 April 2011 | First £102.00 (LEL) | Nil | Nil | Nil | Nil |
| | £102.01 to £139.00 | 0% | 0% | Nil | 0% |
| | £139.01 to £770.00 (UAP) | 12.00% | 5.85% | Nil | 2% |
| | £770.01 to £817.00 | 12.00% | 5.85% | Nil | 2% |
| | Over £817 (UEL) | 2.00% | 2.00% | Nil | 2% |
| 6 April 2011 | First £102.00 (LEL) | Nil | Nil | Nil | Nil |
| | £102.01 to £136.00 | 0% | 0% | Nil | 0% |
| | £136.01 to £770.00 | 13.8% | 13.8% | Nil | 13.8% |
| | £770.01 - £817.00 | 13.8% | 13.8% | Nil | 13.8% |
| | Over £817 (UEL) | 13.8% | 13.8% | Nil | 13.8% |

## Not contracted-out employment rates - 6th April 2012 – 5th April 2013

| Date from | Earnings £ per week | Employee | | | |
|---|---|---|---|---|---|
| | | Standard A | Reduced B | Age Exempt C | Deferred J |
| 6 April 2012 | First £107.00 (LEL) | Nil | Nil | Nil | Nil |
| | £107.01 to £146.00 | 0% | 0% | Nil | 0% |
| | £146.01 to £770.00 (UAP) | 12.00% | 5.85% | Nil | 2% |

| | £770.01 to £817.00 | 12.00% | 5.85% | Nil | 2% |
|---|---|---|---|---|---|
| | Over £817 (UEL) | 2.00% | 2.00% | Nil | 2% |
| 6 April 2012 | First £107.00 (LEL) | Nil | Nil | Nil | Nil |
| | £107.01 to £144.00 | 0% | 0% | Nil | 0% |
| | £144.01 to £770.00 | 13.8% | 13.8% | 13.8% | 13.8% |
| | £770.01 - £817.00 | 13.8% | 13.8% | 13.8% | 13.8% |
| | Over £817 (UEL) | 13.8% | 13.8% | 13.8% | 13.8% |

### Not contracted-out employment rates - 6th April 2013 – 5th April 2015

| Date from | Earnings £ per week | Employee | | | |
|---|---|---|---|---|---|
| | | Standard A | Reduced B | Age Exempt C | Deferred J |
| 6 April 2013 | First £109.00 (LEL) | Nil | Nil | Nil | Nil |
| | £109.01 to £149.00 | 0% | 0% | Nil | 0% |
| | £149.01 to £770.00 (UAP) | 12.00% | 5.85% | Nil | 2% |
| | £770.01 to £797.00 | 12.00% | 5.85% | Nil | 2% |
| | Over £797 (UEL) | 2.00% | 2.00% | Nil | 2% |
| 6 April 2013 | First £109.00 (LEL) | Nil | Nil | Nil | Nil |
| | £109.01 to £148.00 | 0% | 0% | Nil | 0% |
| | £148.01 to £770.00 | 13.8% | 13.8% | Nil | 13.8% |
| | £770.01 - £797.00 | 13.8% | 13.8% | Nil | 13.8% |
| | Over £797 (UEL) | 13.8% | 13.8% | Nil | 13.8% |
| 6 April 2014 | First £111.00 (LEL) | Nil | Nil | Nil | Nil |
| | £111.01 to £153.00 | 0% | 0% | Nil | 0% |
| | £153.01 to £770.00 | 13.8% | 13.8% | Nil | 13.8% |
| | £770.01 - £805.00 | 13.8% | 13.8% | Nil | 13.8% |
| | Over £805 (UEL) | 13.8% | 13.8% | Nil | 13.8% |

### Not contracted-out employment rates - 6th April 2015 – 5th April 2016

| Date from | Earnings £ per week | Employee | | | | |
|---|---|---|---|---|---|---|
| | | Standard A | Under 21 M | Reduced B | Age Exempt C | Deferred J & Z |
| 6 April 2015 | First £112.00 (LEL) | Nil | Nil | Nil | Nil | Nil |
| | £112.01 to £155.00 | 0% | 0% | 0% | Nil | 0% |
| | £155.01 to £770.00 | 12.00% | 12.00% | 5.85% | Nil | 2% |
| | £770.01 - £815.00 | 12.00% | 12.00% | 5.85% | Nil | 2% |
| | Over £815 (UEL) | 2% | 2% | 2% | Nil | 2% |

| 6 April 2015 | First £112.00 (LEL) | Nil | Nil | Nil | Nil | Nil |
|---|---|---|---|---|---|---|
| | £112.01 to £155.00 | 0% | 0% | 0% | 0% | 0% |
| | £155.01 to £770.00 | 13.8% | 0% | 13.8% | 13.8% | 13.8% |
| | £770.01 - £815.00 | 13.8% | 0% | 13.8% | 13.8% | 13.8% |
| | Over £815 (UEL) | 13.8% | 13.8% | 13.8% | 13.8% | 13.8% |

## Not contracted-out employment rates - 6th April 2016 – 5th April 2017

| Date from | Earnings £ per week | Standard A | Under 21 M | Under 25 App H | Reduced B | Age Exempt C | Deferred J & Z |
|---|---|---|---|---|---|---|---|
| 6 April 2016 | First £112.00 (LEL) | Nil | Nil | Nil | Nil | Nil | Nil |
| | £112.01 to £155.00 | 0% | 0% | 0% | 0% | Nil | 0% |
| | £155.01 - £827.00 | 12.00% | 12.00% | 12.00% | 5.85% | Nil | 2% |
| | Over £827 (UEL) | 2% | 2% | 2% | 2% | Nil | 2% |
| 6 April 2016 | First £112.00 (LEL) | Nil | Nil | Nil | Nil | Nil | Nil |
| | £112.01 to £155.00 | 0% | 0% | 0% | 0% | 0% | 0% |
| | £155.01 - £827.00 | 13.8% | 0% | 0% | 13.8% | 13.8% | 13.8% |
| | Over £827 (UEL) | 13.8% | 13.8% | 13.8% | 13.8% | 13.8% | 13.8% |

## Not contracted-out employment rates - 6th April 2017 – 5th April 2018

| Date from | Earnings £ per week | Standard A | Under 21 M | Under 25 App H | Reduced B | Age Exempt C | Deferred J & Z |
|---|---|---|---|---|---|---|---|
| 6 April 2017 | First £113.00 (LEL) | Nil | Nil | Nil | Nil | Nil | Nil |
| | £113.01 to £157.00 | 0% | 0% | 0% | 0% | Nil | 0% |
| | £157.01 - £866.00 | 12.00% | 12.00% | 12.00% | 5.85% | Nil | 2% |
| | Over £866 (UEL) | 2% | 2% | 2% | 2% | Nil | 2% |
| 6 April 2017 | First £113.00 (LEL) | Nil | Nil | Nil | Nil | Nil | Nil |
| | £113.01 to £157.00 | 0% | 0% | 0% | 0% | 0% | 0% |
| | £157.01 - £866.00 | 13.8% | 0% | 0% | 13.8% | 13.8% | 13.8% |
| | Over £866 (UEL/UST/AUST) | 13.8% | 13.8% | 13.8% | 13.8% | 13.8% | 13.8% |

## 6th April 2018 – 5th April 2019

| Date from | Earnings £ per week | | Employee | | | | | |
|---|---|---|---|---|---|---|---|---|
| | | Standard A | Under 21 M | Under 25 App H | Reduced B | Age Exempt C | Deferred J & Z |
| 6 April 2018 | First £116.00 (LEL) | Nil | Nil | Nil | Nil | Nil | Nil |
| | £116.01 to £162.00 | 0% | 0% | 0% | 0% | Nil | 0% |
| | £162.01 - £892.00 | 12.00% | 12.00% | 12.00% | 5.85% | Nil | 2% |
| | Over £892 (UEL) | 2% | 2% | 2% | 2% | Nil | 2% |
| 6 April 2018 | First £116.00 (LEL) | Nil | Nil | Nil | Nil | Nil | Nil |
| | £116.01 to £162.00 | 0% | 0% | 0% | 0% | 0% | 0% |
| | £162.01 - £892.00 | 13.8% | 0% | 0% | 13.8% | 13.8% | 13.8% |
| | Over £892 (UEL/UST/AUST) | 13.8% | 13.8% | 13.8% | 13.8% | 13.8% | 13.8% |

## 6th April 2019 – 5th April 2020

| Date from | Earnings £ per week | | Employee | | | | | |
|---|---|---|---|---|---|---|---|---|
| | | Standard A | Under 21 M | Under 25 App H | Reduced B | Age Exempt C | Deferred J & Z |
| 6 April 2019 | First £118.00 (LEL) | Nil | Nil | Nil | Nil | Nil | Nil |
| | £118.01 to £166.00 | 0% | 0% | 0% | 0% | Nil | 0% |
| | £166.01 - £962.00 | 12.00% | 12.00% | 12.00% | 5.85% | Nil | 2% |
| | Over £962 (UEL) | 2% | 2% | 2% | 2% | Nil | 2% |
| 6 April 2019 | First £118.00 (LEL) | Nil | Nil | Nil | Nil | Nil | Nil |
| | £118.01 to £166.00 | 0% | 0% | 0% | 0% | 0% | 0% |
| | £166.01 - £962.00 | 13.8% | 0% | 0% | 13.8% | 13.8% | 13.8% |
| | Over £962 (UEL/UST/AUST) | 13.8% | 13.8% | 13.8% | 13.8% | 13.8% | 13.8% |

## 6th April 2020 – 5th April 2021

| Date from | Earnings £ per week | | Employee | | | | | |
|---|---|---|---|---|---|---|---|---|
| | | Standard A | Under 21 M | Under 25 App H | Reduced B | Age Exempt C | Deferred J & Z |
| 6 April 2020 | First £120.00 (LEL) | Nil | Nil | Nil | Nil | Nil | Nil |
| | £120.01 to £183.00 | 0% | 0% | 0% | 0% | Nil | 0% |
| | £183.01 - £962.00 | 12.00% | 12.00% | 12.00% | 5.85% | Nil | 2% |
| | Over £962 (UEL) | 2% | 2% | 2% | 2% | Nil | 2% |

| | | | | | | | |
|---|---|---|---|---|---|---|---|
| 6 April 2020 | First £120.00 (LEL) | Nil | Nil | Nil | Nil | Nil | Nil |
| | £120.01 to £169.00 | 0% | 0% | 0% | 0% | 0% | 0% |
| | £169.01 - £962.00 | 13.8% | 0% | 0% | 13.8% | 13.8% | 13.8% |
| | Over £962 (UEL/UST/AUST) | 13.8% | 13.8% | 13.8% | 13.8% | 13.8% | 13.8% |

### Contracted-out employment rebates 2005 - 2016

| | Employee | Employer | |
|---|---|---|---|
| | | COMPS | COSRS |
| 6th April 2005 to 5th April 2006 | 1.6 % | 1.0 % | 3.5 % |
| 6th April 2007 to 5th April 2012 | 1.6 % | 1.4 % | 3.7 % |
| 6th April 2012 – 5th April 2016 | 1.4% (COSR) | Nil | 3.4% |
| 6th April 2016 onwards | Nil | Nil | Nil |

## NIC REBATES

As a result of the rebates above a negative or minus employer's rate was created on earnings between the Lower Earnings Limit (LEL) and the Earnings Threshold (ET). In cases where an employee's rebate exceeds the contribution due, the balance remaining was available to offset against the employer's wider NICs liability.

From 6th April 2003 NIC rebates have been offset against NICs due on forms P11 and P14. The NICs rebate is no longer shown separately on statutory forms and need not be shown on payslips as it was previously. It is now the net NICs contributions after deduction of rebate that is shown.

For employees earning above the Earnings Threshold (ET) this can result in a negative NICs contribution that is shown with a letter 'R' on all returns. From 6th April 2009 rebates apply only to earnings between the Lower Earnings limit (LEL) and the Upper Accrual Point (UAP). Previously rebates applied on earnings between the LEL and the Upper Earnings Limit (UEL).

From 6th April 2012 rebates were abolished for contracted-out (COMP) DC schemes and were reduced for DB (COSR) schemes by 0.5%, to 3.4% for employers and 1.4% for employees. From April 2016 rebates for DB schemes were abolished to coincide with the introduction of the new single tier state pension.

## CLASS 1 and 2 AGE EXCEPTION CERTIFICATE CA4140/CF384

Liability for payment of Class 1 or Class 2 National Insurance Contributions ceases at State Pension Age (SPA) which is progressively increasing from April 2010 - see Part 4). At SPA employees are moved on to category letter C (prior to April 2016 was C not contracted out regardless of their pension scheme status), an employer-only charge. For the self-employed liability for Class 4 contributions, which is an annual charge, continues to the end of the tax year during which SPA is attained.

Until September 2013 an employee staying in employment after attaining SPA could apply for a certificate from HMRC as evidence for their employer(s) that deductions should cease. Now either a birth certificate or passport must be used for the same purpose, a letter from HMRC to the employer is only provided where a passport or birth certificate is not available. Supporting letters may be obtained by application to:
HMRC National Insurance Contributions Employer Office,
Evening Work Centre,
Benton Park View,
Newcastle upon Tyne, NE98 1ZZ.

Employers relying on passports and birth certificates should consult the calculator at https://www.gov.uk/calculate-state-pension for the correct age at which to cease employee NICs deductions. DWP may still issue an Age Exception Certificate.

## AGGREGATION OF EARNINGS

Employees with two or more jobs generally fall within one of three categories and the calculation of NICs must be carried out accordingly:

1. Employment with, and separately paid by different employers:
   - each employer must calculate NICs in the normal way, ignoring the payments received in the other job(s).
   - however where employers are in business 'in association' with each other, earnings must be added together from each job and NICs calculated on the total, except where not reasonably practicable to do so.
   - Carrying on business in association will apply where:
   - respective businesses serve a common purpose, and
   - such things as accommodation, personnel, equipment or customers are shared to a significant degree
2. Single payment of earnings for separate jobs with separate employers:
   - the calculation will depend on whether the employers are, or are not, in business in association with one another:
   - **If they are:** NICs are due from the employer who pays the employee
   - **If they are not:** NICs are paid by each employer on their share of the payment.
3. Employment in two or more jobs with the same employer:
   - The general rule is that all earnings must be added together for the calculation of NICs. However, where earnings from each job are separately calculated and it is 'not reasonably practicable' to do so, it may not be necessary to do so. Employers would be unwise to adopt a policy of separation of earnings as a means to reduce NICs liabilities, as it will be necessary for the employer to establish that to do so is not practicable. Any such decision may be reviewed by HMRC. There is no definitive HMRC definition of 'not reasonably practicable'. Resolution will generally be determined by case law. Further information on the issue may be obtained from the National Insurance Manual (accessed via the Gov website), or the employer's tax office.

Prior to April 2016, calculations had to be made using contracted out earnings first. Since the abolition of contracting out this is no longer necessary. When working out NICs where earnings from separate jobs are added together and NICs are not due at contracted-out rate in all jobs, NICs should be calculated on the total earnings using the shortest earnings period.

*N.B. Aggregation applies only to NICs, never to income tax!*

## CLASS 1 NICs - RECOVERY OF UNDERPAID CONTRIBUTIONS

Provision for recovering underpaid contributions is restricted. Prior to 6th April 2004 an employer could recover underpaid contributions from later earnings periods within the same tax year, subject to a maximum additional deduction in any earnings period not greater than a sum equal to the amount of normal primary contributions due in that period, (the double deduction principle).

From 6th April 2004 where an under deduction has been made by the employer acting 'in good faith' recovery can made from any payment of earnings in the current and the next tax year subject to the double deduction principle.

## CLASS 1A NATIONAL INSURANCE

Class 1A contributions, introduced 6th April 1991, are levied on the employer (not employees) and were initially charged only on car and fuel benefits at the standard rate of employers' NIC. Class 1A was extended from 6th April 2000 (first payments due July 2001) to most taxable benefits-in-kind except those:
- where Class 1 NICs are due, or
- covered by a dispensation, or
- included in a PAYE Settlement Agreement (PSA)

- provided for employees earning at a rate of less than £8,500 a year, or
- otherwise not required to be reported via a P11D return

Other limited exemptions:
- exempt minor benefits (see under tax)
- small amounts of private use of items provided by employer for employee's work e.g. computer
- qualifying beneficial loans
- subsidised canteen meals available generally to employees (extra-statutory concession A74) including light refreshment
- employer provided childcare support (see page 96)

### Class 1A Contribution Rates from 6th April 1992

| Date from | Class 1A % | Date from | Class 1A % | Date from | Class 1A % |
|---|---|---|---|---|---|
| 06.04.1992 | 10.4 | 06.04.2001 | 11.9 | 06.04.2010 | 12.8 |
| 06.04.1993 | 10.4 | 06.04.2002 | 11.8 | 06.04.2011 | 12.8 |
| 06.04.1994 | 10.2 | 06.04.2003 | 12.8 | 06.04.2012 | 13.8 |
| 06.04.1995 | 10.2 | 06.04.2004 | 12.8 | 06.04.2013 | 13.8 |
| 06.04.1996 | 10.2 | 06.04.2005 | 12.8 | 06.04.2014 | 13.8 |
| 06.04.1997 | 10.0 | 06.04.2006 | 12.8 | 06.04.2015 | 13.8 |
| 06.04.1998 | 10.0 | 06.04.2007 | 12.8 | 06.04.2016 | 13.8* |
| 06.04.1999 | 12.2 | 06.04.2008 | 12.8 | | |
| 06.04.2000 | 12.2 | 06.04.2009 | 12.8 | | |

*N.B.: no change to the Class 1A rate is expected before 2021.*

### Class 1A Fuel scale charges from 6th April 1991 to 5th April 2003

| Date from | Petrol Engine Cars | | | Diesel Engine Cars | | Cars with no engine Capacity |
|---|---|---|---|---|---|---|
| | 1400cc or less £ | 1401cc - 2000cc £ | Over 2000cc £ | 2000cc or less £ | Over 2000cc £ | £ |
| 06.04.1991 | 480 | 600 | 900 | - | - | |
| 06.04.1992 | 500 | 630 | 940 | 460 | 590 | |
| 06.04.1993 | 600 | 760 | 1,130 | 550 | 710 | |
| 06.04.1994 | 640 | 810 | 1,200 | 580 | 750 | 1,200 |
| 06.04.1995 | 670 | 850 | 1,260 | 605 | 780 | 1,260 |
| 06.04.1996 | 710 | 890 | 1,320 | 640 | 820 | 1,320 |
| 06.04.1997 | 800 | 1,010 | 1,490 | 740 | 940 | 1,490 |
| 06.04.1998 | 1,010 | 1,280 | 1,890 | 1,280 | 1,890 | 1,890 |
| 06.04.1999 | 1,210 | 1,540 | 2,270 | 1,540 | 2,270 | 2,270 |
| 06.04.2000 | 1,700 | 2,170 | 3,200 | 2,170 | 3,200 | 3,200 |
| 06.04.2001 | 1,930 | 2,460 | 3,620 | 2,460 | 3,620 | 3,620 |
| 06.04.2002 | 2,240 | 2,850 | 4,200 | 2,850 | 4,200 | 4,200 |

Before 6th April 1993, the fuel scale charge was reduced by 50% for employees travelling 18,000 or more business miles per year.

## CLASS 1B NATIONAL INSURANCE

Introduced on 6th April 1999, Class 1B contributions are chargeable as a lump sum on expenses, payments and benefits-in-kind taxed under a PAYE Settlement Agreement (PSA). Under such an agreement the tax liability is met by the employer as a lump sum settlement following agreement with HMRC. In a similar manner National Insurance Contributions are payable in a single lump sum assessable against the value of all items covered by the PSA, which would otherwise attract a Class 1 or Class 1A liability plus Class 1B NICs contributions levied on the grossed up tax payable by the employer under the PSA.

### Class 1B Contribution Rates - from 6th April 2002

| Date from | Rate % | Date from | Rate % | Date from | Rate % |
|---|---|---|---|---|---|
| 06.04.2002 | 11.8 | 06.04.2007 | 12.8 | 06.04.2012 | 13.8 |
| 06.04.2003 | 12.8 | 06.04.2008 | 12.8 | 06.04.2013 | 13.8 |
| 06.04.2004 | 12.8 | 06.04.2009 | 12.8 | 06.04.2014 | 13.8 |
| 06.04.2005 | 12.8 | 06.04.2010 | 12.8 | 06.04.2015 | 13.8 |
| 06.04.2006 | 12.8 | 06.04.2011 | 13.8 | 06.04.2016 | 13.8* |

*N.B.: No change to the Class 1B rate is expected before 2021.*

## CLASS 2 NATIONAL INSURANCE

A fixed weekly contribution rate payable by the self-employed except where earnings are below the exemption limit (small earnings threshold). Payment allows the contributor to claim certain social security benefits (subject to other conditions) including State Retirement Pension. Exemption based on low earnings must be claimed by the 31st January after the tax year-end in question.

### Class 2 Self-employed Contributions from 12th April 1987

| Date from | Standard £ | Share Fishermen £ p.w | Volunteer Development Worker £ p.w | Exemption Limit £ |
|---|---|---|---|---|
| 12.04.1987 | 3.85 | 6.55 | 6.55 | 2,125 |
| 10.04.1988 | 4.05 | 6.55 | 6.55 | 2,250 |
| 09.04.1989 | 4.25 | 5.80 | 4.30 | 2,350 |
| 08.04.1990 | 4.55 | 6.15 | 3.22 | 2,600 |
| 07.04.1991 | 5.15 | 6.20 | 3.43 | 2,900 |
| 12.04.1992 | 5.35 | 7.00 | 3.56 | 3,030 |
| 11.04.1993 | 5.55 | 7.75 | 3.70 | 3,140 |
| 10.04.1994 | 5.65 | 7.75 | 3.19 | 3,200 |
| 10.04.1994 | 5.65 | 7.75 | 3.19 | 3,200 |
| 09.04.1995 | 5.75 | 7.30 | 2.90 | 3,260 |
| 07.04.1996 | 6.05 | 7.20 | 3.05 | 3,430 |
| 06.04.1997 | 6.15 | 6.80 | 3.10 | 3,480 |
| 08.04.1998 | 6.35 | 7.00 | 3.20 | 3,590 |
| 06.04.1999 | 6.55 | 7.20 | 3.30 | 3,770 |
| 06.04.2000 | 2.00 | 2.65 | 3.35 | 3,825 |
| 06.04.2001 | 2.00 | 2.65 | 3.60 | 3,955 |
| 06.04.2002 | 2.00 | 2.65 | 3.75 | 4,025 |
| 06.04.2003 | 2.00 | 2.65 | 3.85 | 4,095 |

**Class 2 Self-employed Contributions from 12th April 1987** (continued)

| | | | |
|---|---|---|---|
| 06.04.2004 | 2.05 | 2.70 | 3.95 | 4,215 |
| 06.04.2005 | 2.10 | 2.75 | 4.10 | 4,345 |
| 06.04.2006 | 2.10 | 2.75 | 4.20 | 4,465 |
| 06.04.2007 | 2.20 | 2.85 | 4.35 | 4,635 |
| 06.04.2008 | 2.30 | 2.95 | 4.50 | 4,825 |
| 06.04.2009 | 2.40 | 3.05 | 4.75 | 5,075 |
| 06.04.2010 | 2.40 | 3.05 | 4.85 | 5,075 |
| 06.04.2011 | 2.50 | 3.15 | 5.10 | 5,315 |
| 06.04.2012 | 2.65 | 3.30 | 5.35 | 5,595 |
| 06.04.2013 | 2.70 | 3.35 | 5.45 | 5,725 |
| 06.04.2014 | 2.75 | 3.40 | 5.55 | 5,885 |
| 06.04.2015 | 2.80 | 3.45 | 5.60 | 5,965 |
| 06.04.2016 | 2.80 | 3.45 | 5.60 | 5,965 |
| 06.04.2017 | 2.85 | 3.50 | 5.65 | 6,025 |
| 06.04.2018 | 2.95 | 3.60 | 5.80 | 6,205 |
| 06.04.2019 | 3.00 | 3.65 | 5.90 | 6,365 |
| **06.04.2020** | **3.05** | | | **6,475** |

*N.B. Class 2 NIC is collected as part of the self-assessment return process from 6th April 2016.*

In the Spring budget 2017, Finance Act 2017, the government announced it would abolish Class 2 from April 2018 and replace it with a revised Class 4 process. In the Autumn budget for Finance Act 2018 this was delayed until April 2019 with a promise of consultation during 2018. At the time of publication this matter is still to be decided.

## CLASS 3 NATIONAL INSURANCE

Class 3 contributions are payable on a voluntary basis in order to maintain a contribution record and thereby protect, or maximise, state pension and other social security benefit entitlements. This may be advisable following receipt of a Deficiency Notice (notification of a shortfall of contributions), sent annually each autumn to both employees and the self-employed, which indicated if the previous tax year was not a qualifying year for state pension purposes.

**Class 3 voluntary contributions from 7th April 1993**

| Date from | £ | Date from | £ | Date from | £ |
|---|---|---|---|---|---|
| 07.04.1993 | 5.45 | 06.04.2003 | 6.95 | 06.04.2013 | 13.55 |
| 12.04.1994 | 5.45 | 06.04.2004 | 7.15 | 06.04.2014 | 13.90 |
| 11.04.1995 | 5.65 | 06.04.2005 | 7.35 | 06.04.2015 | 14.10 |
| 09.04.1996 | 5.95 | 06.04.2006 | 7.55 | 06.04.2016 | 14.10 |
| 07.04.1997 | 6.05 | 06.04.2007 | 7.80 | 06.04.2017 | 14.25 |
| 07.04.1998 | 6.25 | 06.04.2008 | 8.10 | 06.04.2018 | 14.65 |
| 08.04.1999 | 6.45 | 06.04.2009 | 12.05 | 06.04.2019 | 15.00 |
| 06.04.2000 | 6.55 | 06.04.2010 | 12.05 | **06.04.2020** | **15.30** |
| 06.04.2001 | 6.75 | 06.04.2011 | 12.60 | | |
| 06.04.2002 | 6.75 | 06.04.2012 | 13.25 | | |

# CLASS 4 NATIONAL INSURANCE (for self-employed earners)

### Percentage contribution rates from 6th June 1986 to 5th April 2003

| Date from | Lower profits Limit £ | Rate between Limits % | Upper Profits Limit £ | Date from | Lower Profits Limit £ | Rate between limits % | Upper Profits Limit £ |
|---|---|---|---|---|---|---|---|
| 06.06.1986 | 4,450 | 6.30 | 14,820 | 09.04.1995 | 6,640 | 7.30 | 22,880 |
| 12.04.1987 | 4,590 | 6.30 | 15,340 | 07.04.1996 | 6,860 | 6.00 | 23,660 |
| 10.04.1988 | 4,750 | 6.30 | 15,860 | 07.04.1997 | 7,010 | 6.00 | 24,180 |
| 09.04.1989 | 5,050 | 6.30 | 16,900 | 08.04.1998 | 7,310 | 6.00 | 25,220 |
| 08.04.1990 | 5,450 | 6.30 | 18,200 | 06.04.1999 | 7,530 | 6.00 | 26,000 |
| 07.04.1991 | 5,900 | 6.30 | 20,280 | 06.04.2000 | 4,385 | 7.00 | 27,820 |
| 12.04.1992 | 6,120 | 6.30 | 21,060 | 06.04.2001 | 4,535 | 7.00 | 29,900 |
| 11.04.1993 | 6,340 | 6.30 | 21,840 | 06.04.2002 | 4,615 | 7.00 | 30,420 |
| 10.04.1994 | 6,490 | 7.30 | 22,360 | | | | |

### Percentage contribution rates from 6th April 2004

| Date from | Lower Profits Limit £ | Rate Between Limits % | Upper Profits Limit £ | Rate above Upper Limit * % |
|---|---|---|---|---|
| 06.04.2004 | 4,745 | 8.00 | 31,720 | 1.00 |
| 06.04.2005 | 4,895 | 8.00 | 32,760 | 1.00 |
| 06.04.2006 | 5,035 | 8.00 | 33,540 | 1.00 |
| 06.04.2007 | 5,225 | 8.00 | 34,840 | 1.00 |
| 06.04.2008 | 5,435 | 8.00 | 40,040 | 1.00 |
| 06.04.2009 | 5,715 | 8.00 | 43,875 | 1.00 |
| 06.04.2010 | 5,715 | 8.00 | 43,875 | 1.00 |
| 06.04.2011 | 7,225 | 9.00 | 42,475 | 2.00 |
| 06.04.2012 | 7,605 | 9.00 | 42,475 | 2.00 |
| 06.04.2013 | 7,755 | 9.00 | 41,450 | 2.00 |
| 06.04.2014 | 7,956 | 9.00 | 41,865 | 2.00 |
| 06.04.2015 | 8,060 | 9.00 | 42,385 | 2.00 |
| 06.04.2016 | 8,060 | 9.00 | 43,000 | 2.00 |
| 06.04.2017 | 8,164 | 9.00 | 45,000 | 2.00 |
| 06.04.2018 | 8,424 | 9.00 | 46,350 | 2.00 |
| 06.04.2019 | 8,632 | 9.00 | 50,000 | 2.00 |
| **06.04.2020** | **9,500** | **9.00** | **50,000** | **2.00** |

From 6th April 2003 a contribution has been payable on all earnings above the upper limit in line with employed earners' Class 1 Contributions. N.B. tax relief is allowable on 50% of contributions paid. Budget 2017 produced an announcement that the rate for Class 4 NIC would increase to 10%, however this was reversed, almost immediately. Consultation is promised in 2018 with the intention to abolish Class 2 NICs and implement a revised Class 4 scheme for April 2019.

In September 2018 the government announced that the planned abolition of Class 2 NICs and the implementation of a revised Class 4 NICs scheme would not proceed, however following emergency measures introduced in March to June 2020 the government confirmed that they would move quickly to evening up the contribution rates and benefit access for all contributors.

## COMPANY CARS, VANS AND FUEL

Class 1A National Insurance Contributions are payable by the employer, there is no employee liability, on the benefit received by an employee for the private use of, and the provision of fuel for private use in, a company provided car. Contributions are due on the value of the benefit of:

- cars made available to most directors and employees (prior to April 2016 it was only employees with £8,500 pay and benefits p.a.), members of the employees families, dependants, servants and their guests, even if they do not avail themselves of the private use.
- fuel provided for private use
- vans and private fuel, where the van is made available for private use

Class 1A is not charged on:

- privately owned cars, and fuel made available for use in privately owned cars
- company cars used exclusively for business
- pooled cars
- fuel provided for company cars solely for business use or where the proportion of any fuel used privately is fully made good by the employee

Assessment of liability:

**Car** - the charge is based upon the $CO_2$ emissions and the list price of the car in question, minus allowable capital contributions and contributions for private use. For five years from 6th April 2010 no charge arose on electric cars. Where fuel is provided for private use and is not fully reimbursed, the fuel scale charge is calculated by applying the same percentage as for calculating the car benefit to the fixed charge of **£24,500** (£24,100 2019/20, £23,400 2018/19, £22,600 2017/18, £22,200 2016/17, £22,100 2015/16, £21,700 2014/15, £21,100 2013/14, £20,200 2012/13, £18,800 2010/2012, £16,900 2009/10 and £14,400 pre-6.4.2008).

**Vans** - a fixed scale rate for unlimited private use of **£3,490** (£3,430 2019/20, £3,350 2018/19, £3,230 2017/18, £3,170 2016/17, £3,150 2015/16, £3,090 2014/15 and £3,000 prior to this) is due plus a fuel charge for the provision of free private fuel of **£666** (£655 2019/20, £633 2018/19, £610 2017/18, £598 2016/17, £594 2015/16, £581 2014/15, £564 2013/14 and £550 pre 2013).

### Historical Note

Prior to 6th April 2002 the car benefit was determined by:

- the price of the car immediately prior to registration, plus
- the price of certain accessories provided either at registration or later, including fitting costs

The price of the car was inclusive of custom duty, VAT and car tax, and it did not include vehicle excise duty.

Benefit reductions:

- annual business mileage
- less than 2,500 miles - full 35% charge
- 2,500 to 17,999 miles - 25% charge
- 18,000 or more miles - 15% charge
- unavailability - proportionate to the period during which the car was unavailable, expressed as a daily fraction of 365.
- age of car - after adjustment for business mileage, a reduction of one third where the car was four or more years old at the end of the tax year in which it was made available

## COMPANY DIRECTORS

A company director is a person who holds the post of, or acts as, a director of a company within the terms, yet not necessarily the conditions, of the Companies Act 2006 (sections 250 and 251). In this capacity a company director is classed as an office holder and is liable for Class 1 NICs provided the earnings are chargeable to income tax.

Section 251 refers to a "Shadow director" as being defined as a director for the purposes of the companies act. A shadow director is a person who is not a company director but who advises the board and whose advice and guidance is habitually acted upon by the board of directors. For the purposes of NICs a shadow director is treated in the same manner as a director.

Contributions are normally (see below for alternative approach) assessed on an annual, or pro-rata annual, earnings period. A calculation should be made each time a payment of earnings is made, deducting payments already made during the tax year, to arrive at the balance due. All earnings are to be included, including fees and bonuses. When assessing liability, annual earnings limits and rate bands, or their pro-rata equivalents, should be used.

It is common for directors to hold several directorships all attracting fees. In such cases contributions are paid in the main employment and the director can be granted deferment in the other employments, thereby only paying NICs at the 1% rate introduced in April 2003 and increased to 2% from April 2011. In order to operate deferment the employer so affected must hold a copy of the director's Deferment Certificate, CA2700, granted by HMRC. (See also Deferred Contributions).

From 6th April 1999 HMRC has operated alternative arrangements for the assessment and payment of NICs for company directors. The earnings period for a director remains annual; however, subject to the following qualifying conditions payment of NICs may be made on account where:
- the director agrees
- the director normally receives earnings in a regular pattern and these earnings are above the LEL in each pay period.

*N.B. Care must be taken when applying the alternative arrangement that, where a director commences or terminates employment during the tax year, earnings and contributions are re-assessed on the annual earnings basis.*

The business must have a notional ledger account into which payments of monies due to the director (net salary/fees/bonuses/dividends etc) are accounted for. If at any time the account becomes overdrawn, i.e. the director owes money to the business, NICs become due on the overdrawn amount.

Where the director has more than one job with the same company, or with companies working in association, all earnings must be aggregated before calculating liability, and the exact percentage method of calculation applied.

For further information see HMRC's *Helpbook CA44 National Insurance for Company Directors.*

## CONTRACTING-OUT

Until 5th April 2016 where an employee was a contributor to an occupational or private pension scheme, which provides minimum pension benefits, or a GMP (Guaranteed Minimum Pension) at least as good as that which is provided by the state second pension (S2P) the scheme members were permitted to be contracted-out of S2P. In acknowledgement of the provision of an occupational pension providing additional benefits and not reliant on S2P the employer/employee pay lower NICs contributions - see NICs rebate above.

Contracted-out National Insurance contributions were payable at a reduced level on assessable earnings above the LEL up to the UAP (prior to 6th April 2009 to the UEL). When S2P was abolished on 6th April 2016, the last contracting-out ceased to exist.

### Age-related Rebates
Over the period 6 April 1993 to 5 April 1997 an extra 1% rebate, in addition to the normal rebate, applied to those aged over 30. This was replaced by age-related rebates that apply to all defined contribution pension schemes and Appropriate Personal Pension schemes. The rebates were paid into an individual's pension account. Rebates for tax years 2002/2003 onwards were split into three categories of earnings (lower, middle and higher) in accordance with the actual bands for the State Second Pension. The table below shows the rates related to the higher earnings band. It had to be multiplied by 2 in the lower, and by 0.5 for the middle band. Age-related rebates were abolished from 6th April 2012.

### Contracting-out Rebate
The rate at which the contributions are reduced was known as the contracting-out rebate. On the advice of the Government Actuary, the Secretary of State for Social Security set the value of the rebate usually, but not always, at five-year intervals. Contracting-out rebates were abolished for COMP schemes from 6th April 2012 and reduced by 0.5% for COSR schemes from 6th April 2012 - 5th April 2016. These were then abolished for COSR schemes from 6th April 2016.

## Contracting-out Rebate from 1981/1982

| Years | Employee | Employer | Years | Employee | | Employer COMPS | Employer COSRS |
|-------|----------|----------|-------|----------|---|-------|-------|
| 1983/84 to 1987/88 | 2.15% | 4.10% | 2002/03 to 2006/07 | 1.60% | | 1.00% | 3.50% |
| 1988/89 to 1992/93 | 2.00% | 3.80% | 2007/08 onwards | 1.60% | | 1.40% | 3.70% |
| 1993/94 to 1996/97 | 1.80% | 3.00% | 2012/13 to 2015/16 | COMP | COSR | Nil | 3.4% |
| 1997/98 to 1998/99 | 1.60% | 1.5% | | Nil | 1.4% | | |

## Appropriate Personal Pension Schemes (APPS)

### Age-related payments from 1997/1998 to 2006/2007

| Age | 1997/1998 | 1998/1999 | 1999/2000 | 2000/2001 | 2001/2002 | 2002/2003 | 2003/2004 | 2004/2005 | 2005/2006 | 2006/2007 |
|-----|-----------|-----------|-----------|-----------|-----------|-----------|-----------|-----------|-----------|-----------|
| 15 | 3.4 | 3.4 | 3.8 | 3.8 | 3.8 | 4.2 | 4.2 | 4.2 | 4.2 | 4.2 |
| 16 | 3.4 | 3.4 | 3.8 | 3.8 | 3.8 | 4.2 | 4.2 | 4.2 | 4.2 | 4.2 |
| 17 | 3.5 | 3.5 | 3.9 | 3.9 | 3.9 | 4.2 | 4.2 | 4.2 | 4.2 | 4.2 |
| 18 | 3.5 | 3.5 | 3.9 | 3.9 | 3.9 | 4.3 | 4.3 | 4.3 | 4.3 | 4.3 |
| 19 | 3.6 | 3.6 | 4.0 | 4.0 | 4.0 | 4.3 | 4.3 | 4.3 | 4.3 | 4.3 |
| 20 | 3.6 | 3.6 | 4.0 | 4.0 | 4.0 | 4.4 | 4.4 | 4.4 | 4.4 | 4.4 |
| 21 | 3.7 | 3.7 | 4.1 | 4.1 | 4.1 | 4.4 | 4.4 | 4.4 | 4.4 | 4.4 |
| 22 | 3.7 | 3.7 | 4.1 | 4.1 | 4.1 | 4.5 | 4.5 | 4.5 | 4.5 | 4.5 |
| 23 | 3.8 | 3.8 | 4.2 | 4.2 | 4.2 | 4.5 | 4.5 | 4.5 | 4.5 | 4.5 |
| 24 | 3.8 | 3.8 | 4.2 | 4.2 | 4.2 | 4.5 | 4.5 | 4.5 | 4.5 | 4.5 |
| 25 | 3.9 | 3.9 | 4.3 | 4.3 | 4.3 | 4.6 | 4.6 | 4.6 | 4.6 | 4.6 |
| 26 | 3.9 | 3.9 | 4.3 | 4.3 | 4.3 | 4.6 | 4.6 | 4.6 | 4.6 | 4.6 |
| 27 | 4.0 | 4.0 | 4.4 | 4.4 | 4.4 | 4.7 | 4.7 | 4.7 | 4.7 | 4.7 |
| 28 | 4.0 | 4.0 | 4.4 | 4.4 | 4.4 | 4.7 | 4.7 | 4.7 | 4.7 | 4.7 |
| 29 | 4.1 | 4.1 | 4.5 | 4.5 | 4.5 | 4.8 | 4.8 | 4.8 | 4.8 | 4.8 |
| 30 | 4.2 | 4.2 | 4.5 | 4.5 | 4.5 | 4.8 | 4.8 | 4.8 | 4.8 | 4.8 |
| 31 | 4.2 | 4.2 | 4.6 | 4.6 | 4.6 | 4.9 | 4.9 | 4.9 | 4.9 | 4.9 |
| 32 | 4.3 | 4.3 | 4.6 | 4.6 | 4.6 | 4.9 | 4.9 | 4.9 | 4.9 | 4.9 |
| 33 | 4.3 | 4.3 | 4.7 | 4.7 | 4.7 | 5.0 | 5.0 | 5.0 | 5.0 | 5.0 |
| 34 | 4.4 | 4.4 | 4.7 | 4.7 | 4.7 | 5.0 | 5.0 | 5.0 | 5.0 | 5.0 |
| 35 | 4.5 | 4.4 | 4.8 | 4.8 | 4.8 | 5.0 | 5.0 | 5.1 | 5.1 | 5.1 |
| 36 | 4.7 | 4.6 | 4.8 | 4.8 | 4.8 | 5.1 | 5.1 | 5.1 | 5.1 | 5.1 |
| 37 | 4.9 | 4.8 | 5.0 | 4.9 | 4.9 | 5.1 | 5.1 | 5.1 | 5.2 | 5.2 |
| 38 | 5.0 | 4.9 | 5.1 | 5.0 | 4.9 | 5.2 | 5.2 | 5.2 | 5.2 | 5.2 |
| 39 | 5.2 | 5.1 | 5.3 | 5.2 | 5.1 | 5.2 | 5.2 | 5.2 | 5.2 | 5.3 |
| 40 | 5.4 | 5.3 | 5.5 | 5.4 | 5.3 | 5.4 | 5.3 | 5.3 | 5.3 | 5.3 |
| 41 | 5.6 | 5.5 | 5.7 | 5.5 | 5.4 | 5.6 | 5.5 | 5.3 | 5.3 | 5.4 |
| 42 | 6.0 | 5.7 | 5.9 | 5.7 | 5.6 | 5.7 | 5.6 | 5.5 | 5.4 | 5.4 |
| 43 | 6.7 | 6.1 | 6.1 | 5.9 | 5.8 | 5.9 | 5.8 | 5.7 | 5.6 | 5.5 |

## Age-related payments from 1997/1998 to 2006/2007 (continued)

| 44 | 7.4 | 6.8 | 6.5 | 6.1 | 6.0 | 6.1 | 16.0 | 5.9 | 5.7 | 5.6 |
| 45 | 8.2 | 7.5 | 7.1 | 6.6 | 6.2 | 6.3 | 6.2 | 6.0 | 5.9 | 5.8 |
| 46 | 9.0 | 8.3 | 7.9 | 7.2 | 6.6 | 6.5 | 6.4 | 6.2 | 6.1 | 6.0 |
| 47 | 9.0 | 9.0 | 8.7 | 8.0 | 7.3 | 7.0 | 6.6 | 6.4 | 6.3 | 6.2 |
| 48 | 9.0 | 9.0 | 9.0 | 8.8 | 8.1 | 7.8 | 7.1 | 6.6 | 6.5 | 6.4 |
| 49 | 9.0 | 9.0 | 9.0 | 9.0 | 8.9 | 8.8 | 7.9 | 7.2 | 6.7 | 6.6 |
| 50 | 9.0 | 9.0 | 9.0 | 9.0 | 9.0 | 9.9 | 8.9 | 8.0 | 7.3 | 6.8 |
| 51 | 9.0 | 9.0 | 9.0 | 9.0 | 9.0 | 10.5 | 10.0 | 9.0 | 8.0 | 7.3 |
| 52 | 9.0 | 9.0 | 9.0 | 9.0 | 9.0 | 10.5 | 10.5 | 10.1 | 9.0 | 8.1 |
| 53 | 9.0 | 9.0 | 9.0 | 9.0 | 9.0 | 10.5 | 10.5 | 10.5 | 10.2 | 9.1 |
| 54 | 9.0 | 9.0 | 9.0 | 9.0 | 9.0 | 10.5 | 10.5 | 10.5 | 10.5 | 10.3 |
| 55 | 9.0 | 9.0 | 9.0 | 9.0 | 9.0 | 10.5 | 10.5 | 10.5 | 10.5 | 10.5 |
| 56 | 9.0 | 9.0 | 9.0 | 9.0 | 9.0 | 10.5 | 10.5 | 10.5 | 10.5 | 10.5 |
| 57 | 9.0 | 9.0 | 9.0 | 9.0 | 9.0 | 10.5 | 10.5 | 10.5 | 10.5 | 10.5 |
| 58 | 9.0 | 9.0 | 9.0 | 9.0 | 9.0 | 10.5 | 10.5 | 10.5 | 10.5 | 10.5 |
| 59 | 9.0 | 9.0 | 9.0 | 9.0 | 9.0 | 10.5 | 10.5 | 10.5 | 10.5 | 10.5 |
| 60 | 9.0 | 9.0 | 9.0 | 9.0 | 9.0 | 10.5 | 10.5 | 10.5 | 10.5 | 10.5 |
| 61 | 9.0 | 9.0 | 9.0 | 9.0 | 9.0 | 10.5 | 10.5 | 10.5 | 10.5 | 10.5 |
| 62 | 9.0 | 9.0 | 9.0 | 9.0 | 9.0 | 10.5 | 10.5 | 10.5 | 10.5 | 10.5 |
| 63 | 9.0 | 9.0 | 9.0 | 9.0 | 9.0 | 10.5 | 10.5 | 10.5 | 10.5 | 10.5 |

## Appropriate Personal Pension Schemes (APPS)

### Age-related payments from 2007/2008 to 2009/2010

| Age | 2007/2008 | | | 2008/2009 | | | 2009/2010 | | |
|---|---|---|---|---|---|---|---|---|---|
| | to LET | LET-UET | UET + | to LET | LET-UET | UET + | to LET | LET-UET | UET + |
| 15 | 9.4 | 2.35 | 4.7 | 9.4 | 2.35 | 4.7 | 9.4 | 2.35 | 4.7 |
| 16 | 9.4 | 2.35 | 4.7 | 9.4 | 2.35 | 4.7 | 9.4 | 2.35 | 4.7 |
| 17 | 9.6 | 2.40 | 4.8 | 9.6 | 2.40 | 4.8 | 9.6 | 2.40 | 4.8 |
| 18 | 9.8 | 2.45 | 4.9 | 9.8 | 2.45 | 4.9 | 9.8 | 2.45 | 4.9 |
| 19 | 9.8 | 2.45 | 4.9 | 9.8 | 2.45 | 4.9 | 9.8 | 2.45 | 4.9 |
| 20 | 10.0 | 2.50 | 5.0 | 10.0 | 2.50 | 5.0 | 10.0 | 2.50 | 5.0 |
| 21 | 10.2 | 2.55 | 5.1 | 10.2 | 2.55 | 5.1 | 10.2 | 2.55 | 5.1 |
| 22 | 10.4 | 2.60 | 5.2 | 10.4 | 2.60 | 5.2 | 10.4 | 2.60 | 5.2 |
| 23 | 10.4 | 2.60 | 5.2 | 10.4 | 2.60 | 5.2 | 10.4 | 2.60 | 5.2 |
| 24 | 10.6 | 2.65 | 5.3 | 10.6 | 2.65 | 5.3 | 10.6 | 2.65 | 5.3 |
| 25 | 10.8 | 2.70 | 5.4 | 10.8 | 2.70 | 5.4 | 10.8 | 2.70 | 5.4 |
| 26 | 11.0 | 2.75 | 5.5 | 11.0 | 2.75 | 5.5 | 11.0 | 2.75 | 5.5 |
| 27 | 11.0 | 2.75 | 5.5 | 11.0 | 2.75 | 5.5 | 11.2 | 2.80 | 5.6 |
| 28 | 11.2 | 2.80 | 5.6 | 11.2 | 2.80 | 5.6 | 11.2 | 2.80 | 5.6 |
| 29 | 11.4 | 2.85 | 5.7 | 11.4 | 2.85 | 5.7 | 11.4 | 2.85 | 5.7 |

## Age-related payments from 2007/2008 to 2009/2010 (continued)

| | | | | | | | | | |
|---|---|---|---|---|---|---|---|---|---|
| 30 | 11.6 | 2.90 | 5.8 | 11.6 | 2.90 | 5.8 | 11.6 | 2.90 | 5.8 |
| 31 | 11.8 | 2.95 | 5.9 | 11.8 | 2.95 | 5.9 | 11.8 | 2.95 | 5.9 |
| 32 | 12.0 | 3.00 | 6.0 | 12.0 | 3.00 | 6.0 | 12.0 | 3.00 | 6.0 |
| 33 | 12.0 | 3.00 | 6.0 | 12.0 | 3.00 | 6.0 | 12.0 | 3.00 | 6.0 |
| 34 | 12.2 | 3.05 | 6.1 | 12.2 | 3.05 | 6.1 | 12.2 | 3.05 | 6.1 |
| 35 | 12.6 | 3.15 | 6.3 | 12.6 | 3.15 | 6.3 | 12.6 | 3.15 | 6.3 |
| 36 | 12.8 | 3.20 | 6.4 | 12.8 | 3.20 | 6.4 | 12.8 | 3.20 | 6.4 |
| 37 | 13.0 | 3.25 | 6.5 | 13.2 | 3.30 | 6.6 | 13.2 | 3.30 | 6.6 |
| 38 | 13.4 | 3.35 | 6.7 | 13.4 | 3.35 | 6.7 | 13.4 | 3.35 | 6.7 |
| 39 | 13.6 | 3.40 | 6.8 | 13.6 | 3.40 | 6.8 | 13.6 | 3.40 | 6.8 |
| 40 | 14.0 | 3.50 | 7.0 | 14.0 | 3.50 | 7.0 | 14.0 | 3.50 | 7.0 |
| 41 | 14.2 | 3.55 | 7.1 | 14.2 | 3.55 | 7.1 | 14.2 | 3.55 | 7.1 |
| 42 | 14.4 | 3.60 | 7.2 | 14.4 | 3.60 | 7.2 | 14.4 | 3.60 | 7.2 |
| 43 | 14.8 | 3.70 | 7.4 | 14.8 | 3.70 | 7.4 | 14.8 | 3.70 | 7.4 |
| 44 | 14.8 | 3.70 | 7.4 | 14.8 | 3.70 | 7.4 | 14.8 | 3.70 | 7.4 |
| 45 | 14.8 | 3.70 | 7.4 | 14.8 | 3.70 | 7.4 | 14.8 | 3.70 | 7.4 |
| 46 | 14.8 | 3.70 | 7.4 | 14.8 | 3.70 | 7.4 | 14.8 | 3.70 | 7.4 |
| 47 | 14.8 | 3.70 | 7.4 | 14.8 | 3.70 | 7.4 | 14.8 | 3.70 | 7.4 |
| 48 | 14.8 | 3.70 | 7.4 | 14.8 | 3.70 | 7.4 | 14.8 | 3.70 | 7.4 |
| 49 | 14.8 | 3.70 | 7.4 | 14.8 | 3.70 | 7.4 | 14.8 | 3.70 | 7.4 |
| 50 | 14.8 | 3.70 | 7.4 | 14.8 | 3.70 | 7.4 | 14.8 | 3.70 | 7.4 |
| 51 | 14.8 | 3.70 | 7.4 | 14.8 | 3.70 | 7.4 | 14.8 | 3.70 | 7.4 |
| 52 | 14.8 | 3.70 | 7.4 | 14.8 | 3.70 | 7.4 | 14.8 | 3.70 | 7.4 |
| 53 | 14.8 | 3.70 | 7.4 | 14.8 | 3.70 | 7.4 | 14.8 | 3.70 | 7.4 |
| 54 | 14.8 | 3.70 | 7.4 | 14.8 | 3.70 | 7.4 | 14.8 | 3.70 | 7.4 |
| 55 | 14.8 | 3.70 | 7.4 | 14.8 | 3.70 | 7.4 | 14.8 | 3.70 | 7.4 |
| 56 | 14.8 | 3.70 | 7.4 | 14.8 | 3.70 | 7.4 | 14.8 | 3.70 | 7.4 |
| 57 | 14.8 | 3.70 | 7.4 | 14.8 | 3.70 | 7.4 | 14.8 | 3.70 | 7.4 |
| 58 | 14.8 | 3.70 | 7.4 | 14.8 | 3.70 | 7.4 | 14.8 | 3.70 | 7.4 |
| 59 | 14.8 | 3.70 | 7.4 | 14.8 | 3.70 | 7.4 | 14.8 | 3.70 | 7.4 |
| 60 | 14.8 | 3.70 | 7.4 | 14.8 | 3.70 | 7.4 | 14.8 | 3.70 | 7.4 |
| 61 | 14.8 | 3.70 | 7.4 | 14.8 | 3.70 | 7.4 | 14.8 | 3.70 | 7.4 |
| 62 | 14.8 | 3.70 | 7.4 | 14.8 | 3.70 | 7.4 | 14.8 | 3.70 | 7.4 |
| 63 | 14.8 | 3.70 | 7.4 | 14.8 | 3.70 | 7.4 | 14.8 | 3.70 | 7.4 |

## Appropriate Personal Pension Schemes (APPS)

## Age-related payments from 2010/2011 to 2011/2012

| Age | 2010/2011 | | | 2011/2012 | | |
|---|---|---|---|---|---|---|
| | to LET | LET-UET | UET + | to LET | LET-UET | UET + |
| 15 | 9.4 | 2.35 | 4.7 | 9.4 | 2.35 | 4.7 |
| 16 | 9.4 | 2.35 | 4.7 | 9.4 | 2.35 | 4.7 |
| 17 | 9.6 | 2.40 | 4.8 | 9.6 | 2.40 | 4.8 |
| 18 | 9.8 | 2.45 | 4.9 | 9.8 | 2.45 | 4.9 |
| 19 | 9.8 | 2.45 | 4.9 | 10.0 | 2.50 | 5.0 |
| 20 | 10.0 | 2.50 | 5.0 | 10.0 | 2.50 | 5.0 |
| 21 | 10.2 | 2.55 | 5.1 | 10.2 | 2.55 | 5.1 |
| 22 | 10.4 | 2.60 | 5.2 | 10.4 | 2.60 | 5.2 |
| 23 | 10.4 | 2.60 | 5.2 | 10.4 | 2.60 | 5.2 |
| 24 | 10.6 | 2.65 | 5.3 | 10.6 | 2.65 | 5.3 |
| 25 | 10.8 | 2.70 | 5.4 | 10.8 | 2.70 | 5.4 |
| 26 | 11.0 | 2.75 | 5.5 | 11.0 | 2.75 | 5.5 |
| 27 | 11.2 | 2.80 | 5.6 | 11.2 | 2.80 | 5.6 |
| 28 | 11.2 | 2.80 | 5.6 | 11.2 | 2.80 | 5.6 |
| 29 | 11.4 | 2.85 | 5.7 | 11.4 | 2.85 | 5.7 |
| 30 | 11.6 | 2.90 | 5.8 | 11.6 | 2.90 | 5.8 |
| 31 | 11.8 | 2.95 | 5.9 | 11.8 | 2.95 | 5.9 |
| 32 | 12.0 | 3.00 | 6.0 | 12.0 | 3.00 | 6.0 |
| 33 | 12.2 | 3.05 | 6.1 | 12.2 | 3.05 | 6.1 |
| 34 | 12.2 | 3.05 | 6.1 | 12.2 | 3.05 | 6.1 |
| 35 | 12.6 | 3.15 | 6.3 | 12.6 | 3.15 | 6.3 |
| 36 | 12.8 | 3.20 | 6.4 | 12.8 | 3.20 | 6.4 |
| 37 | 13.2 | 3.30 | 6.6 | 13.2 | 3.30 | 6.6 |
| 38 | 13.4 | 3.35 | 6.7 | 13.4 | 3.35 | 6.7 |
| 39 | 13.6 | 3.40 | 6.8 | 13.8 | 3.45 | 6.9 |
| 40 | 14.0 | 3.50 | 7.0 | 14.0 | 3.50 | 7.0 |
| 41 | 14.2 | 3.55 | 7.1 | 14.2 | 3.55 | 7.1 |
| 42 | 14.6 | 3.65 | 7.3 | 14.6 | 3.65 | 7.3 |
| 43 | 14.8 | 3.70 | 7.4 | 14.8 | 3.70 | 7.4 |
| 44 | 14.8 | 3.70 | 7.4 | 14.8 | 3.70 | 7.4 |
| 45 | 14.8 | 3.70 | 7.4 | 14.8 | 3.70 | 7.4 |
| 46 | 14.8 | 3.70 | 7.4 | 14.8 | 3.70 | 7.4 |
| 47 | 14.8 | 3.70 | 7.4 | 14.8 | 3.70 | 7.4 |
| 48 | 14.8 | 3.70 | 7.4 | 14.8 | 3.70 | 7.4 |
| 49 | 14.8 | 3.70 | 7.4 | 14.8 | 3.70 | 7.4 |
| 50 | 14.8 | 3.70 | 7.4 | 14.8 | 3.70 | 7.4 |
| 51 | 14.8 | 3.70 | 7.4 | 14.8 | 3.70 | 7.4 |
| 52 | 14.8 | 3.70 | 7.4 | 14.8 | 3.70 | 7.4 |
| 53 | 14.8 | 3.70 | 7.4 | 14.8 | 3.70 | 7.4 |
| 54 | 14.8 | 3.70 | 7.4 | 14.8 | 3.70 | 7.4 |
| 55 | 14.8 | 3.70 | 7.4 | 14.8 | 3.70 | 7.4 |
| 56 | 14.8 | 3.70 | 7.4 | 14.8 | 3.70 | 7.4 |
| 57 | 14.8 | 3.70 | 7.4 | 14.8 | 3.70 | 7.4 |

| 58 | 14.8 | 3.70 | 7.4 | 14.8 | 3.70 | 7.4 |
| 59 | 14.8 | 3.70 | 7.4 | 14.8 | 3.70 | 7.4 |
| 60 | 14.8 | 3.70 | 7.4 | 14.8 | 3.70 | 7.4 |
| 61 | 14.8 | 3.70 | 7.4 | 14.8 | 3.70 | 7.4 |
| 62 | 14.8 | 3.70 | 7.4 | 14.8 | 3.70 | 7.4 |
| 63 | 14.8 | 3.70 | 7.4 | 14.8 | 3.70 | 7.4 |

### Contracted Out Money Purchase Schemes (COMPS)

### Age-related payments from 1997/1998 to 2006/2007

| Age | 1997 /1998 | 1998/ 1999 | 1999/ 2000 | 2000/ 2001 | 2001/ 2002 | 2002/ 2003 | 2003/ 2004 | 2004/ 2005 | 2005/ 2006 | 2006/ 2007 |
|---|---|---|---|---|---|---|---|---|---|---|
| 15 | 3.1 | 3.1 | 2.2 | 2.2 | 2.2 | 2.6 | 2.6 | 2.6 | 2.6 | 2.6 |
| 16 | 3.2 | 3.2 | 2.2 | 2.2 | 2.2 | 2.6 | 2.6 | 2.6 | 2.6 | 2.6 |
| 17 | 3.2 | 3.2 | 2.3 | 2.3 | 2.3 | 2.7 | 2.7 | 2.7 | 2.7 | 2.7 |
| 18 | 3.3 | 3.3 | 2.3 | 2.3 | 2.3 | 2.7 | 2.7 | 2.7 | 2.7 | 2.7 |
| 19 | 3.3 | 3.3 | 2.3 | 2.4 | 2.4 | 2.8 | 2.8 | 2.8 | 2.8 | 2.8 |
| 20 | 3.4 | 3.4 | 2.4 | 2.4 | 2.4 | 2.8 | 2.8 | 2.8 | 2.8 | 2.8 |
| 21 | 3.4 | 3.4 | 2.5 | 2.5 | 2.5 | 2.9 | 2.9 | 2.9 | 2.9 | 2.9 |
| 22 | 3.5 | 3.5 | 2.5 | 2.5 | 2.5 | 2.9 | 2.9 | 2.9 | 2.9 | 2.9 |
| 23 | 3.5 | 3.5 | 2.6 | 2.6 | 2.6 | 3.0 | 3.0 | 3.0 | 3.0 | 3.0 |
| 24 | 3.6 | 3.6 | 2.6 | 2.6 | 2.6 | 3.1 | 3.1 | 3.1 | 3.1 | 3.1 |
| 25 | 3.6 | 3.7 | 2.7 | 2.7 | 2.7 | 3.1 | 3.1 | 3.1 | 3.1 | 3.1 |
| 26 | 3.7 | 3.7 | 2.7 | 2.7 | 2.7 | 3.2 | 3.2 | 3.2 | 3.2 | 3.2 |
| 27 | 3.8 | 3.8 | 2.8 | 2.8 | 2.8 | 3.2 | 3.2 | 3.2 | 3.2 | 3.2 |
| 28 | 3.8 | 3.8 | 2.9 | 2.9 | 2.9 | 3.3 | 3.3 | 3.3 | 3.3 | 3.3 |
| 29 | 3.9 | 3.9 | 2.9 | 2.9 | 2.9 | 3.4 | 3.4 | 3.4 | 3.4 | 3.4 |
| 30 | 3.9 | 3.9 | 3.0 | 3.0 | 3.0 | 3.4 | 3.4 | 3.4 | 3.4 | 3.4 |
| 31 | 4.0 | 4.0 | 3.0 | 3.0 | 3.0 | 3.6 | 3.6 | 3.6 | 3.6 | 3.6 |
| 32 | 4.0 | 4.0 | 3.1 | 3.1 | 3.1 | 3.6 | 3.6 | 3.6 | 3.6 | 3.6 |
| 33 | 4.2 | 4.1 | 3.2 | 3.2 | 3.2 | 3.7 | 3.7 | 3.7 | 3.7 | 3.7 |
| 34 | 4.2 | 4.2 | 3.2 | 3.2 | 3.3 | 3.8 | 3.8 | 3.8 | 3.8 | 3.8 |
| 35 | 4.3 | 4.2 | 3.3 | 3.3 | 3.3 | 3.8 | 3.8 | 3.8 | 3.8 | 3.8 |
| 36 | 4.5 | 4.4 | 3.4 | 3.4 | 3.4 | 3.9 | 3.9 | 3.9 | 3.9 | 3.9 |
| 37 | 4.6 | 4.5 | 3.5 | 3.5 | 3.5 | 4.0 | 4.0 | 4.0 | 4.0 | 4.0 |
| 38 | 4.8 | 4.7 | 3.7 | 3.6 | 3.5 | 4.1 | 4.1 | 4.1 | 4.1 | 4.1 |
| 39 | 5.0 | 4.9 | 3.8 | 3.8 | 3.7 | 4.1 | 4.1 | 4.1 | 4.1 | 4.1 |
| 40 | 5.2 | 5.1 | 4.0 | 3.9 | 3.9 | 4.3 | 4.2 | 4.2 | 4.2 | 4.2 |
| 41 | 5.4 | 5.3 | 4.2 | 4.1 | 4.0 | 4.4 | 4.4 | 4.3 | 4.3 | 4.3 |
| 42 | 5.8 | 5.5 | 4.4 | 4.3 | 4.2 | 4.6 | 4.5 | 4.4 | 4.4 | 4.4 |
| 43 | 6.4 | 5.9 | 4.6 | 4.5 | 4.4 | 4.8 | 4.7 | 4.6 | 4.5 | 4.4 |
| 44 | 7.2 | 6.5 | 5.0 | 4.7 | 4.6 | 5.0 | 4.9 | 4.8 | 4.7 | 4.6 |
| 45 | 8.0 | 7.3 | 5.6 | 5.1 | 4.8 | 5.3 | 5.1 | 5.0 | 4.9 | 4.8 |

| 46 | 8.9 | 8.1 | 6.3 | 5.7 | 5.2 | 5.5 | 5.4 | 5.3 | 5.1 | 5.0 |
|----|-----|-----|-----|-----|-----|------|------|------|------|------|
| 47 | 9.0 | 9.0 | 7.1 | 6.4 | 5.8 | 6.0 | 5.6 | 5.5 | 5.4 | 5.3 |
| 48 | 9.0 | 9.0 | 8.0 | 7.2 | 6.6 | 6.8 | 6.1 | 5.7 | 5.6 | 5.5 |
| 49 | 9.0 | 9.0 | 8.8 | 8.2 | 7.4 | 7.8 | 6.9 | 6.2 | 5.8 | 5.7 |
| 50 | 9.0 | 9.0 | 9.0 | 9.0 | 8.4 | 9.0 | 7.9 | 7.1 | 6.4 | 5.9 |
| 51 | 9.0 | 9.0 | 9.0 | 9.0 | 9.0 | 10.3 | 9.1 | 8.1 | 7.2 | 6.5 |
| 52 | 9.0 | 9.0 | 9.0 | 9.0 | 9.0 | 10.5 | 10.5 | 9.3 | 8.2 | 7.4 |
| 53 | 9.0 | 9.0 | 9.0 | 9.0 | 9.0 | 10.5 | 10.5 | 10.5 | 9.5 | 8.4 |
| 54 | 9.0 | 9.0 | 9.0 | 9.0 | 9.0 | 10.5 | 10.5 | 10.5 | 10.5 | 9.7 |
| 55 | 9.0 | 9.0 | 9.0 | 9.0 | 9.0 | 10.5 | 10.5 | 10.5 | 10.5 | 10.5 |
| 56 | 9.0 | 9.0 | 9.0 | 9.0 | 9.0 | 10.5 | 10.5 | 10.5 | 10.5 | 10.5 |
| 57 | 9.0 | 9.0 | 9.0 | 9.0 | 9.0 | 10.5 | 10.5 | 10.5 | 10.5 | 10.5 |
| 58 | 9.0 | 9.0 | 9.0 | 9.0 | 9.0 | 10.5 | 10.5 | 10.5 | 10.5 | 10.5 |
| 59 | 9.0 | 9.0 | 9.0 | 9.0 | 9.0 | 10.5 | 10.5 | 10.5 | 10.5 | 10.5 |
| 60 | 9.0 | 9.0 | 9.0 | 9.0 | 9.0 | 10.5 | 10.5 | 10.5 | 10.5 | 10.5 |
| 61 | 9.0 | 9.0 | 9.0 | 9.0 | 9.0 | 10.5 | 10.5 | 10.5 | 10.5 | 10.5 |
| 62 | 9.0 | 9.0 | 9.0 | 9.0 | 9.0 | 10.5 | 10.5 | 10.5 | 10.5 | 10.5 |
| 63 | 9.0 | 9.0 | 9.0 | 9.0 | 9.0 | 10.5 | 10.5 | 10.5 | 10.5 | 10.5 |

## Contracted Out Money Purchase Schemes (COMPS)

### Age-related payments from 2007/2008 to 2011/2012

| Age | 2007/2008 | 2008/2009 | 2009/2010 | 2010/2011 | 2011/2012 |
|-----|-----------|-----------|-----------|-----------|-----------|
| 15 | 3.0 | 3.0 | 3.0 | 3.0 | 3.0 |
| 16 | 3.0 | 3.0 | 3.0 | 3.0 | 3.0 |
| 17 | 3.1 | 3.1 | 3.1 | 3.1 | 3.1 |
| 18 | 3.2 | 3.2 | 3.2 | 3.2 | 3.2 |
| 19 | 3.3 | 3.3 | 3.3 | 3.3 | 3.3 |
| 20 | 3.4 | 3.4 | 3.4 | 3.4 | 3.4 |
| 21 | 3.4 | 3.4 | 3.4 | 3.4 | 3.4 |
| 22 | 3.5 | 3.5 | 3.5 | 3.5 | 3.5 |
| 23 | 3.6 | 3.6 | 3.6 | 3.6 | 3.6 |
| 24 | 3.7 | 3.7 | 3.7 | 3.7 | 3.7 |
| 25 | 3.8 | 3.8 | 3.8 | 3.8 | 3.8 |
| 26 | 3.9 | 3.9 | 3.9 | 3.9 | 3.9 |
| 27 | 4.0 | 4.0 | 4.0 | 4.0 | 4.0 |
| 28 | 4.1 | 4.1 | 4.1 | 4.1 | 4.1 |
| 29 | 4.1 | 4.2 | 4.2 | 4.2 | 4.2 |
| 30 | 4.2 | 4.3 | 4.3 | 4.3 | 4.3 |

| | | | | | |
|---|---|---|---|---|---|
| 31 | 4.3 | 4.4 | 4.4 | 4.4 | 4.4 |
| 32 | 4.5 | 4.5 | 4.5 | 4.5 | 4.5 |
| 33 | 4.6 | 4.6 | 4.6 | 4.6 | 4.6 |
| 34 | 4.7 | 4.7 | 4.7 | 4.7 | 4.7 |
| 35 | 4.8 | 4.8 | 4.8 | 4.8 | 4.8 |
| 36 | 5.0 | 5.0 | 5.0 | 5.0 | 5.0 |
| 37 | 5.1 | 5.1 | 5.1 | 5.1 | 5.2 |
| 38 | 5.3 | 5.3 | 5.3 | 5.3 | 5.3 |
| 39 | 5.5 | 5.5 | 5.5 | 5.5 | 5.5 |
| 40 | 5.6 | 5.6 | 5.6 | 5.6 | 5.6 |
| 41 | 5.8 | 5.8 | 5.8 | 5.8 | 5.8 |
| 42 | 5.9 | 5.9 | 6.0 | 6.0 | 6.0 |
| 43 | 6.1 | 6.1 | 6.1 | 6.1 | 6.1 |
| 44 | 6.3 | 6.3 | 6.3 | 6.3 | 6.3 |
| 45 | 6.6 | 6.4 | 6.4 | 6.5 | 6.5 |
| 46 | 6.9 | 6.7 | 6.6 | 6.6 | 6.6 |
| 47 | 7.2 | 7.1 | 6.9 | 6.8 | 6.8 |
| 48 | 7.4 | 7.4 | 7.2 | 7.1 | 7.0 |
| 49 | 7.4 | 7.4 | 7.4 | 7.4 | 7.3 |
| 50 | 7.4 | 7.4 | 7.4 | 7.4 | 7.4 |
| 51 | 7.4 | 7.4 | 7.4 | 7.4 | 7.4 |
| 52 | 7.4 | 7.4 | 7.4 | 7.4 | 7.4 |
| 53 | 7.4 | 7.4 | 7.4 | 7.4 | 7.4 |
| 54 | 7.4 | 7.4 | 7.4 | 7.4 | 7.4 |
| 55 | 7.4 | 7.4 | 7.4 | 7.4 | 7.4 |
| 56 | 7.4 | 7.4 | 7.4 | 7.4 | 7.4 |
| 57 | 7.4 | 7.4 | 7.4 | 7.4 | 7.4 |
| 58 | 7.4 | 7.4 | 7.4 | 7.4 | 7.4 |
| 59 | 7.4 | 7.4 | 7.4 | 7.4 | 7.4 |
| 60 | 7.4 | 7.4 | 7.4 | 7.4 | 7.4 |
| 61 | 7.4 | 7.4 | 7.4 | 7.4 | 7.4 |
| 62 | 7.4 | 7.4 | 7.4 | 7.4 | 7.4 |
| 63 | 7.4 | 7.4 | 7.4 | 7.4 | 7.4 |

# CONTRIBUTION TABLE LETTERS

### Current categories

**A**   Standard Rate
**B**   Married Woman's/Widow's reduced rate not-contracted out
**C**   Age Exempt, employer only contribution (employee at or over state pension age)
**G**   New employee only contribution category for apprentice mariners under the age of 25, introduced 6th April 2016
**H**   New employee only contribution category for apprentices under the age of 25, introduced on 6th April 2016
**J**   Non-Mariner deferment
**M**   Standard rate, under 21 years of age
**Q**   Mariner Deferment
**X**   No NICs liability - under minimum age (16)
**Z**   Deferment, under 21 years of age

### Abolished NIC categories

**D**   Standard Rate COSRS (Contracted Out Salary Related Schemes) and abolished 6th April 2016
**E**   Reduced Rate COSRS (contracted-out reduced rate) and abolished 6th April 2016
**F**   Standard Rate COMPS (Contracted Out Money Purchase Schemes) or COMP (Stakeholder Pension SHP) abolished 6th April 2012
**G**   Reduced Rate COMPS (Married woman's/widow's reduced rate) abolished 6th April 2012
**H**   Mariner Standard Rate - Contracted Out and abolished 6th April 2016
**I**   Standard rate COSRS, under 21 years of age and abolished 6th April 2016
**K**   Deferment, COSRS, under 21 years of age and abolished on 6th April 2016
**L**   (Non-Mariner) Contracted-out salary related deferment and abolished on 6th April 2016
**N**   Mariner Contracted-out - ocean going employment and abolished on 6th April 2016
**O**   Mariner Exempt - Contracted-out and abolished on 6th April 2016
**P**   NIC Holiday Rebate Claimed (to 05.04.1999) removed 2005/06
**S**   Exempt Employee COMPS (with certificate CA2700) abolished 6th April 2012
**V**   Mariner Contracted Out Money Purchase deferment and abolished on 6th April 2016

From April 2003, following the introduction of employee contributions on earnings above the upper earnings limit, age exempt table letter C may now only be used where the contributor is above state pension age.

## DEFERRED CONTRIBUTIONS

Employees with more than one job, who expect to pay maximum annual Class 1 contributions in one of their jobs, may apply for a deferment of their NIC liability for the other job(s) to the end of the current tax year. The employer should only operate deferment after receipt of a current form CA2700 from the employee.

From 6 April 2003 the exemption does not apply to any contributions liable on earnings above the Earnings Threshold in any of the second or additional jobs where NICs are due at 2% (1% prior to 6th April 2011) on all such earnings in any secondary or subsequent job.

## DEFICIENCY NOTICE

A statement issued by HMRC National Insurance Contributions and Employer Office advising the employed, and self-employed, that National Insurance Contributions credited in a specific year will be insufficient for that year to count as a qualifying year for state pension provision. It was announced in January 2007 that any individuals who had paid voluntary contributions from the 25th May 2006 to 27th July 2007 in the belief that these were needed to make up a NICs deficiency that subsequently turned out not to be needed (the state pension age and the qualifying NICs years were reduced from April 2010) could have such contributions refunded. Contributions made before or after those dates, which is when the proposals on state pension reform were announced and subsequently received Royal Assent may not be refunded. For topping-up shortage years see https://www.gov.uk/voluntary-national-insurance-contributions/deadlines

## EMPLOYEES SECONDED ABROAD - NICs

As it may be difficult for employers to complete the reporting and payment of NIC liability within normal filing and deadline dates, the PAYE scheme may apply to defer reporting and payment of secondary NIC contributions.

Prior to 5th April 2006 it was possible, subject to HMRC agreement to defer reporting and payment to 31st January following the end of the relevant tax year. From April 2006 employers have been required to include on the relevant year end return the best estimate of earnings by the 19th May (final FPS by 19th April under RTI) following the year end and submit any excess of the best estimate figures on a NIC Settlement Return by 31st March following the year end. Where the estimate proves to be in excess the employer may claim a refund. This arrangement applies where an employee is:
- seconded abroad
- non-resident and not liable to tax
- paid UK earnings in excess of the annual Upper Earnings Limit and receives part of their earnings from a payroll abroad

## EMPLOYMENT ALLOWANCE

Introduced from 6 April 2014 onwards, up to **£4,000** (£3,000 prior to 6th April 2020 and £2,000 prior to 6th April 2016) of Class 1 employer NICs per tax year does not need to be paid over to HMRC. Eligibility for Employment Allowance is complex but in essence it is available to:
- employers, and
- charities including community amateur sports clubs

It is not available to:
- public sector employers such as local authorities, central government departments, prisons, NHS trusts, GP practices, state schools (independent schools and universities are usually charities so qualify)
- businesses where there is only one person on the PAYE scheme and that person is a director/shareholder of the business. This will also apply if the second person on the payroll is earning at a rate less than the earnings threshold.

Only one PAYE scheme may claim if the entity operates more than one scheme and the employer must choose the scheme it wishes to claim against, using the Employer Payment Summary (EPS) to set a marker to that effect which will remain in force for the tax year in question and subsequent years unless it is set to 'No'. A claim for a different scheme can be made only at the start of a tax year.

The employer may take the allowance as soon as they have a Class 1 Employer NIC liability up to £4,000 (£3,000 prior to 6th April 2020, £2,000 prior to 6th April 2016). It can be claimed in instalments if that suits the cash flow of the scheme. HMRC will record the amount claimed.

Employers who are convicted of using workers who do not have the right to live and work in the UK may, from April 2018, lose their Employment Allowance for a period of one year.

From April 2020 eligibility for the Employment Allowance is restricted to employers whose total Class 1 secondary (employers) NIC liability was less than £100,000 in the previous tax year. In addition to this, also from April 2020, employers are required to declare that the addition of the allowance to any other amounts of state aid does not exceed the relevant EU de minimus state aid threshold.

This was originally going to be a requirement for payroll returns, the EPS process, however it has since been agreed that this is not feasible.

## EMPLOYMENT OF VETERANS

From 6th April 2021 employers will be exempt from the secondary NIC, employers, when they employee a forces veteran. More details are expected in advance of implementation but this is expected to be for the first year of the veteran's employment.

## HOLIDAY PAY IN ADVANCE

For NICs purposes:
- Divide the payment into its separate weekly/monthly components and calculate NICs for each week/month separately, or
- Calculate NICs on the whole sum by dividing the payment by the number of weeks/months covered. This method may be used for employees whose pay intervals are multiples of a week but not where the exact percentage method for calculating NICs is used; neither may it be applied to monthly pay calculations.

For tax treatment see part 2.

## HOLIDAY PAY SCHEMES/HOLIDAY PAY STAMP FUND

Historically in some industries, principally in the building sector, an employer contributed to a holiday fund by the purchase of stamps through a holiday scheme.

The current employer, when paying the employee holiday pay and operating PAYE in the normal manner, reclaimed the payment from the scheme by cashing in the stamps. This allowed workers with transient employments to receive holiday pay without the cost burden falling upon the current employer. From the early 1960s holiday payments treated in this manner have been exempt from NICs.

The exemption was withdrawn on 30th October 2007 for all businesses outside those deemed to be construction operations for whom the scheme was withdrawn on 30th October 2012. The effect of the withdrawal was to bring such payments into Class 1 NICs liability. The exemption was withdrawn because non-construction businesses had taken advantage of the loose wording of the legislation and had set up schemes in order to make huge savings on employer NICs on the payment of holiday pay.

## HOLIDAY CREDIT SCHEME

In a 'holiday credit' scheme, an employer sets aside money each pay day to pay the employee in a lump sum when taking a holiday. Where an employee has the right to the money at any time then liability for NICs is at the time the credit is laid aside and is deemed to have been 'paid'. Where the employee has no entitlement to the money until holiday is taken then NICs will be due at that time.

## MAXIMUM ANNUAL CONTRIBUTION THRESHOLD

An employed earner's total NICs contributions in any year are subject to an annual 'maxima'. Prior to 6th April 2003 it was the equivalent of the weekly table "A" x 53. From April 2003, in addition to the 'maxima' shown in the table, an additional 1% must be added on the sum of:
- the total earnings between the Earnings Threshold (ET) and the Upper Earnings Limit (UEL) from each employment, less
- the difference between the weekly Earnings Threshold (ET) threshold and the weekly Upper Earnings Limit (UEL) x 53

HMRC has the responsibility for refunding 'excess' contributions. From April 2009 the introduction of the Upper Accrual Point (UAP) changed the calculation to account for the fact that standard rate NICs is paid between the UAP and UEL in contracted-out employment. From April 2011 the percentage above the UEL increased to 2%.

## NATIONAL INSURANCE NUMBER

The Department for Work and Pensions (DWP) issue a National Insurance Number (NINO) for each potential contributor to the National Insurance Fund. HMRC's National Insurance Contributions and Employer Office notifies individuals of their NINO. Numbers are notified by the DWP to all individuals on attaining the age of 16 years and to adults and contributors who have not previously been allocated a NINO (e.g. newly arrived foreign nationals).

The prime purpose of the NINO is to identify and record contributions whether deducted from pay by employers, or paid directly by an individual (usually when   self-employed). The numbers must be submitted on annual tax and contribution returns (P14s), and should be used in all correspondence with HMRC. Being unique to each individual, the NINO is often used by employers and various bodies for identification purposes, principally HMRC, Department for Work and Pensions and employers. It forms a prime record in the prevention of the employment of illegal immigrants.

It is therefore important that the NINO recorded against an employee's payroll record is accurate and available as soon as possible to enable matching for Real Time Information.

Under RTI a NINO verification Request (NVR) will check the format and 'ownership' of NINOs for all employees when they are first aligned and for new starters submitted on the FPS. HMRC will notify employers electronically if NINOs should be amended or do not 'belong' to the employee concerned. Employers may also have functionality in their software to generate ad-hoc NVRs to check legacy records. From 6th April 2017 HMRC will be using an updated NVR process which will apply to the FPS, and EAS.

## Applying for a NINO through Jobcentre Plus

This process applies to:
- adults who were not issued with a number automatically at aged 15 plus, and
- children who have not been part of a Child Benefit claim as otherwise they automatically get a NINO allocated at aged 15, plus
- people coming in to the UK from abroad
- In order to get a NINO, the applicant must be either:
- working, about to start work or actively seeking employment, or
- making a claim to benefit, or
- be entitled to and wish to pay voluntary Class 3 NICs
- be referred by the student loan company
- and must attend an "Evidence of Identity interview" at a local Jobcentre Plus office where they must be able to prove that they are who they say they are and that they satisfy the criteria for needing a NINO. Children under 20 do not have to attend for an interview as they should have automatically been allocated a NINO.

The Jobcentre Plus interviewing officer will usually complete security form CA5400 Application for a NINO on behalf of the applicant who will then sign the form (applicants may complete the form themselves if they wish). The form is countersigned within DWP and passed to a DWP Central Control Unit (CCU) together with copies of supporting identity documents for allocation of a NINO on DCI (DWP's Departmental Central Index). The papers are then referred to HMRC NICO NI Registration section to create a full NI account on NPS (the National Insurance and PAYE Service) and to arrange the issue of a NINO. This process is supported throughout by a series of robust security checks.

Special arrangements may apply to individuals:
- going to, coming from or living abroad
- from the Isle of Man
- from the Channel Islands

Between January and April 2006 DWP rolled out a new process for the allocation of numbers to individuals newly arrived in this country. The NINO contact centre can be telephoned on 0845 600 0643 and will direct them to one of 14 interview 'hubs' across the country who allocate the applicant an appointment via an electronic appointment system. For those with large numbers of affected individuals or in remote areas a visiting service is available.

## Format
Each NINO has the format of two alpha characters followed by six numeric digits and a final alpha character, e.g. YZ987654A. The prefix letters are an approved alphabetical combination - see below. The final alpha character must be one of the following, A B C or D, but if this is missing any of these can be used.

## Temporary NI Number (TNs)
Comprised of the DOB plus gender e.g. 130463F. From 2004/2005-2012/13 a permanent NINO had to be provided on P14 year-end returns. Where this was not possible, the NINO field was left blank and the gender and date of birth were be provided in the appropriate fields.

The former option of providing a temporary number where no NINO has been obtained was no longer acceptable. For P11D returns the use of TNs is permitted but if more than 5% are submitted online, P11D returns will be rejected. Under RTI if there is no NINO it is mandatory to firstly leave the NINO field blank or fill it with zero's, then to ensure both date of birth and gender fields are completed and to report 2 lines of the employee's address to assist HMRC in finding the record.

## Historical notes

The letters A, B, C and D are historical and were used in the days when contributions were paid by the purchase of National Insurance Stamps from a Post Office, which were affixed to an individual employee's record card. 'Given your cards', the term sometimes referred to on termination of employment stems from this process. Prior to 1975, National Insurance cards were exchanged annually, there being SPAce for 52 weekly or 12 monthly stamps on each card. The cards due for exchange at each quarter end were identified by the NINO suffix as follows:

- A - Jan to Mar
- B - Apr to Jun
- C - July to Aug
- D - Sep to Dec

Following the abolition of the card system in 1975, the suffix letters have been retained and have no special significance but must not be omitted from returns. It is therefore unimportant whether A, B C, or D is inserted as long as one of the four letters is used.

## PRIVATE CAR DRIVERS (MAPS & NICs)

The arrangements for dealing with NICs on motor expenses paid to employees who use their own cars for business purposes changed on 6th April 2002 with the introduction of a statutory scheme. These rules also apply to employees who use their own van, motor cycle or bicycle.

The amount to be disregarded from NICs is calculated by reference to the Mileage Allowance Payment (MAP), previously AMAPs, rates for tax purposes (see part 2). Amounts paid in excess of the MAP rates are to be added to any other earnings in the period in which motoring expenses are paid and Class 1 NICs calculated on the total earnings.

For privately owned cars and vans the MAP rate (see part 2) to be applied is that for the first 10,000 business miles irrespective of the number of miles travelled. All business miles travelled must be used in the calculation whether or not the employee is reimbursed for all business mileage.

The rules for paying the passenger rate and determining what constitutes business travel are those applied for tax purposes. These rules apply to all motoring expenses including:

- mileage allowances based on a set rate per mile
- lump sum business car use allowances
- payments for fuel purchased for business use.

## REDUCED RATE NI CONTRIBUTIONS

Up to 11th May 1977, married women or widows could elect to pay NICs contributions at a reduced rate. This principle assumed that their contributory benefits would be protected by their husband's contributions. Reduced rate contributions were maintained to 'purchase' specific and limited benefits - Industrial Injury and Maternity Benefits. In confirmation of her election a Certificate of Election (CA4139 or CF383 or CF 380A, often called a reduced rate card) was issued to the woman, which must be held by her employer if reduced rate contributions are applied.

From 11th May 1977, women with current Certificates of Election were entitled to continue making contributions at the reduced rate. However, that right automatically ceases under certain circumstances:

- marriage ended, other than by the death of the husband
- re-marriage
- earnings fall below the LEL for two successive years from 5th April 1978 (i.e. no NICs contributions deemed to be made in two successive years)

Employers must have an annual process to check the validity of all reduced rate certificates to ensure the employee's status continues to meet the above criteria, as the employer may be liable for any shortfall. Where an employee has been self-employed and paying NICs during the two years when no NICs from employment was due her right to reduced rate is retained.

## UPPER ACCRUAL POINT (UAP)

Introduced on the 6th April 2009 the UAP sets the upper limit for National Insurance contracted-out contribution rebates and is in addition to, not a replacement of, the Upper Earnings Limit (UEL). Up to the 5th April 2009 the UEL (which continues to be the upper earnings limit for standard rate contributions) was the upper earnings limit for both contributions and contracted-out rebates. From April 2009 employers and employees with occupational pension schemes contracted out of the State Second Pension (S2P) are only entitled to contracted-out rebates between the Lower Earnings Limit (LEL) and the UAP.

All employers, including those who do not have occupational pension schemes, are required to record earnings between the Primary Threshold and UAP as well as those between the UAP and UEL.

This continued until 5th April 2012, the date at which the option to contract out was abolished for members of defined contribution schemes, as they may have had employees in pension schemes into which HMRC make minimum payments which were also limited to the UAP from 6th April 2009.

The additional earnings details will be required because only those earnings up to the UAP were used to calculate S2P rights. S2P rights earned up to 5th April 2016 have been retained now that S2P, the UAP and contracting-out for DB schemes has been abolished.

## VOUCHERS

Are normally liable for tax and NICs, however their treatment depends on the nature of the voucher. For further details see part 2.

# PART 4: STATUTORY PAYMENTS

## ADOPTION - STATUTORY ADOPTION PAY (SAP) AND LEAVE

Adoptive parents are entitled to 52 weeks' leave of which 39 may be paid if they have 26 weeks service as at their matching date for adoption. The first 26 weeks are classed as ordinary adoption leave and the second 26 additional adoption leave. The right to return to work is the same as for maternity leave (see Part 1). The 39 week adoption pay period is paid in the same way as maternity pay, the first 6 weeks due at 90% of average weekly earnings with the balance paid at the standard rate in force for that tax year. Prior to 6th April 2015 all adoption pay was paid at the standard rate. N.B. Where changes are referred to as effective in April they apply to employees due to adopt on or after the first Sunday in April of that year.

### Qualification for leave
In order to qualify for leave the employee must be:
- the adopter (or joint adopter)
- married to the adopter themselves or
- living with the adopter in an 'enduring family relationship' or
- in a same sex/unmarried couple relationship with the adopter (from April 2004)

### Qualification for pay
In order to qualify for pay the employee must:
- have worked for the employer for not less than 26 weeks at the point of being matched with a child (the 'matching date'). In effect this becomes the 'Notification Week' for an adoption case and
- have Average Weekly Earnings of at least the Lower Earnings Limit over the eight weeks preceding the matching date

### Entitlement
Is to a maximum of one year's adoption leave. Prior to 6th April 2015 the adopter needed 26 weeks' service at the matching date. There are two types of adoption leave the first 26 weeks are classed as Ordinary leave and the second 26 weeks as Additional leave. Additional leave runs immediately from the end of Ordinary leave. Statutory Adoption Pay (SAP) is payable at 90% of average weekly earnings for the first 6 weeks followed by the lower of 90% of average weekly earnings and the standard rate (see table below) for 33 weeks (increased from 39 weeks at the standard rate only and 26 weeks at the standard rate only with effect from 1st April 2007)

Ordinary and Additional Adoption Leave can be taken in conjunction with up to 4 weeks' unpaid Parental Leave. Couples that adopt can choose which of them takes the adoption leave (Until 2004 this applied only to married couples). The other partner may qualify for Ordinary Statutory Paternity Leave and Pay (OSPL and OSPP) (and Additional Statutory Paternity Leave and Pay (OSPP/ASPP) prior to April 2016) so a female adopter can be in receipt of paternity pay and leave. The compulsory leave requirements applicable in the case of the mother and a new born child do not apply, i.e. that the mother may not work for 2 weeks (4 if in a factory) following the birth of a child.

For matching dates on, or after, 3rd April 2011 and up to and including 4th April 2015 adoptive parents are able to transfer between two and 26 weeks adoption leave and up to 19 weeks' pay to a partner - see Additional paternity leave and pay. Since April 2015 Shared Parental Leave rights apply and APL no longer exists.

### Daily Rates
From April 2007 employers may align payment of SAP with their normal payment cycle i.e. to pay for calendar months rather than in blocks of four or five weeks dependent upon the number of Saturdays in the month. In order to enable this to take place, calculations may be made using daily rates.

The legislation only permits the daily rate to be calculated by dividing the weekly rate by seven, so the daily rate option cannot be used where there is a payment of occupational adoption pay to be offset against the SAP and this is not calculated on a seven-day basis.

The daily rate for 2020/21 is £21.60 (2019/20 £21.24, 2018/19 £20.74). Legislation will continue to refer to weekly rates and the employer must ensure that only full weeks are paid where due, even if these straddle two pay periods.

## Exceptions

Adoption Leave does not apply to step family adoptions or adoptions by foster carers where there is already an established relationship (see future developments below). It can however be granted in cases where a foster placement takes place as a precursor to adoption e.g. where a court case is ongoing but a foster placement is needed in the interim with the same family due to adopt the child when the court process is complete.

## Keeping In Touch (KIT) Days

Introduced in April 2007. An employee is entitled to come into work for up to a maximum of 10 days' work during the adoption leave period without losing Statutory Adoption Pay (originally during the payment period).

The ten days are part of the 52 week adoption leave period and do not extend it. KIT days are intended to help employees to keep in touch with their workplace and ease their transition back into work, e.g. to allow for training. Any such work must be agreed both by the employee and the employer.

Where an employee returns to work with at least a week's equivalent of unused KIT days, and before the expiry of the 52 weeks leave period, the employer may continue to pay and recover SAP on the basis that the employee is utilising her KIT day entitlement even though she has returned to work.

## Statutory Adoption Pay

### Table of Weekly Rates and Reclaim from 6th April 2003

| From | Earnings Threshold £ | Weekly Rate (the lesser of either:-) | | Reclaim Large Employer Reclaim % | Small Employer Reclaim % | Threshold £ |
| | | Flat Rate £ | Earnings % | | | |
|------|------|------|------|------|------|------|
| 06.04.2003 | 77.00 | 100.00 | 90 | 92 | 104.5 | 40,000 |
| 04.04.2004 | 79.00 | 102.80 | 90 | 92 | 104.5 | 45,000 |
| 03.04.2005 | 82.00 | 106.00 | 90 | 92 | 104.5 | 45,000 |
| 02.04.2006 | 84.00 | 108.85 | 90 | 92 | 104.5 | 45,000 |
| 01.04.2007 | 87.00 | 112.75 | 90 | 92 | 104.5 | 45,000 |
| 06.04.2008 | 90.00 | 117.18 | 90 | 92 | 104.5 | 45,000 |
| 05.04.2009 | 95.00 | 123.06 | 90 | 92 | 104.5 | 45,000 |
| 04.04.2010 | 97.00 | 124.88 | 90 | 92 | 104.5 | 45,000 |
| 03.04.2011 | 102.00 | 128.73 | 90 | 92 | 103 | 45,000 |
| 01.04.2012 | 107.00 | 135.45 | 90 | 92 | 103 | 45,000 |
| 07.04.2013 | 109.00 | 136.78 | 90 | 92 | 103 | 45,000 |
| 06.04.2014 | 111.00 | 138.18 | 90 | 92 | 103 | 45,000 |
| 05.04.2015 | 112.00 | 139.58 | 90 | 92 | 103 | 45,000 |
| 03.04.2016 | 112.00 | 139.58 | 90 | 92 | 103 | 45,000 |
| 02.04.2017 | 113.00 | 140.98 | 90 | 92 | 103 | 45,000 |
| 01.04.2018 | 116.00 | 145.18 | 90 | 92 | 103 | 45,000 |
| 07.04.2019 | 118.00 | 148.68 | 90 | 92 | 103 | 45,000 |
| **05.04.2020** | **120.00** | **151.20** | **90** | **92** | **103** | **45,000** |

## Notice

The employee must give:
- 28 days' notice of the start date for SAP, and
- notice of intent to take leave within 7 days of the matching certificate having been issued

The matching certificate must be retained for HMRC inspection as evidence to justify the 92% (or 103%) reclaim of Statutory Adoption Pay. If the employee intends to return to work before the end of their adoption leave period, or vary their start date, they must give 56 days (28 prior to April 2007) notice to the employer of their date of return.

## Notification
The employee must notify the employer when they have been approved for adoption and of the indicative placement date they have been given by the adoption agency. The placement date is the best estimate of when the adoption leave might start, and will be notified in writing by the agency for forwarding to the employer within 7 days. This date is the best estimate and is no guarantee that a placement will actually be made on that date.

## Exclusions
Statutory Adoption Pay is payable for a maximum of 8 weeks after the death of an adoptive child, or the unexpected termination of a placement for other reasons. If the employee falls sick during paternity or adoption leave SAP/SPP/ShPP ceases and SSP becomes payable if the employee qualifies.

Entitlement to either SAP or SPP/ShPP ceases if the employee is taken into custody; in such cases HMRC take over responsibility for payment on release.

## Payment
SAP is administered by the employer (in the same manner as SMP and:
- is subject to average weekly earnings reaching the Lower Earnings Limit (LEL) for the eight-week period prior to the matching date. It is treated as earnings and is subject to PAYE income tax and NICs. Other lawful deductions applicable to pay may be applied, but not court orders of any type
- can be paid in a lump sum subject to the agreement of both parties
- is not payable for any week in which any work is performed for the employer paying the SAP once the employee has taken their entitlement of ten KIT days
- is still made where the employee has qualified but leaves employment after placement as long as they do not take another job with an employer who did not employ them at the matching week

## Advanced funding
Where employers have insufficient tax, NICs, student loan and Construction Industry Scheme deductions to fund the payment of SAP, they can apply to HMRC for advance funding at https://www.gov.uk/recover-statutory-payments/if-you-cant-afford-to-make-payments

## Rates at the start of a tax year
The 2004/5 tax year saw a change to the way new rates 'kicked in' as a result of the new statutory payments regime that came into force in April 2003. There are now several scenarios where a statutory payment week can straddle the old and new tax years, this relates to:
- a week of Statutory Paternity Pay (for 'fathers' or adoptive partners)
- a week of Statutory Adoption Pay
- a week of SMP as a result of an early birth or pregnancy related illness.

For 2020/21, where any SAP, SMP, SPP or ShPP week begins on, or after, 5th April, the new rate is payable from the start of that week.

## Guidance
The HMRC Helpbooks E16 'Employer Helpbook for Statutory Adoption Pay' and E19 'Employer Helpbook for Statutory Paternity Pay' were abolished from 6th April 2014. Guidance can now be found at https://www.gov.uk/adoption-pay-leave. The table below indicates the appropriate dates for 2019/20.

## Statutory Adoption Pay and Leave Tables 2020/21

| Matching week | | Latest start date for employment |
|---|---|---|
| Sunday | Saturday | Saturday |
| 05/04/2020 | 11/04/2020 | 19/10/2019 |
| 12/04/2020 | 18/04/2020 | 26/10/2019 |
| 19/04/2020 | 25/04/2020 | 02/11/2019 |
| 26/04/2020 | 02/05/2020 | 09/11/2019 |
| 03/05/2020 | 09/05/2020 | 16/11/2019 |
| 10/05/2020 | 16/05/2020 | 23/11/2019 |
| 17/05/2020 | 23/05/2020 | 30/11/2019 |
| 24/05/2020 | 30/05/2020 | 07/12/2019 |
| 31/05/2020 | 06/06/2020 | 14/12/2019 |
| 07/06/2020 | 13/06/2020 | 21/12/2019 |
| 14/06/2020 | 20/06/2020 | 28/12/2019 |
| 21/06/2020 | 27/06/2020 | 04/01/2020 |
| 28/06/2020 | 04/07/2020 | 11/01/2020 |
| 05/07/2020 | 11/07/2020 | 18/01/2020 |
| 12/07/2020 | 18/07/2020 | 25/01/2020 |
| 19/07/2020 | 25/07/2020 | 01/02/2020 |
| 26/07/2020 | 01/08/2020 | 08/02/2020 |
| 02/08/2020 | 08/08/2020 | 15/02/2020 |
| 09/08/2020 | 15/08/2020 | 22/02/2020 |
| 16/08/2020 | 22/08/2020 | 29/02/2020 |
| 23/08/2020 | 29/08/2020 | 07/03/2020 |
| 30/08/2020 | 05/09/2020 | 14/03/2020 |
| 06/09/2020 | 12/09/2020 | 21/03/2020 |
| 13/09/2020 | 19/09/2020 | 28/03/2020 |
| 20/09/2020 | 26/09/2020 | 04/04/2020 |
| 27/09/2020 | 03/10/2020 | 11/04/2020 |
| 04/10/2020 | 10/10/2020 | 18/04/2020 |
| 11/10/2020 | 17/10/2020 | 25/04/2020 |
| 18/10/2020 | 24/10/2020 | 02/05/2020 |
| 25/10/2020 | 31/10/2020 | 09/05/2020 |
| 01/11/2020 | 07/11/2020 | 16/05/2020 |
| 08/11/2020 | 14/11/2020 | 23/05/2020 |
| 15/11/2020 | 21/11/2020 | 30/05/2020 |
| 22/11/2020 | 28/11/2020 | 06/06/2020 |
| 29/11/2020 | 05/12/2020 | 13/06/2020 |
| 06/12/2020 | 12/12/2020 | 20/06/2020 |
| 13/12/2020 | 19/12/2020 | 27/06/2020 |
| 20/12/2020 | 26/12/2020 | 04/07/2020 |
| 27/12/2020 | 02/01/2021 | 11/07/2020 |
| 03/01/2021 | 09/01/2021 | 18/07/2020 |

| | | |
|---|---|---|
| 10/01/2021 | 16/01/2021 | 25/07/2020 |
| 17/01/2021 | 23/01/2021 | 01/08/2020 |
| 24/01/2021 | 30/01/2021 | 08/08/2020 |
| 31/01/2021 | 06/02/2021 | 15/08/2020 |
| 07/02/2021 | 13/02/2021 | 22/08/2020 |
| 14/02/2021 | 20/02/2021 | 29/08/2020 |
| 21/02/2021 | 27/02/2021 | 05/09/2020 |
| 28/02/2021 | 06/03/2021 | 12/09/2020 |
| 07/03/2021 | 13/03/2021 | 19/09/2020 |
| 14/03/2021 | 20/03/2021 | 26/09/2020 |
| 21/03/2021 | 27/03/2021 | 03/10/2020 |
| 28/03/2021 | 03/04/2021 | 10/10/2020 |
| 04/04/2021 | 10/04/2021 | 17/10/2020 |
| 11/04/2021 | 17/04/2021 | 24/10/2020 |
| 18/04/2021 | 24/04/2021 | 31/10/2020 |
| 25/04/2021 | 01/05/2021 | 07/11/2020 |
| 02/05/2021 | 08/05/2021 | 14/11/2020 |
| 09/05/2021 | 15/05/2021 | 21/11/2020 |
| 16/05/2021 | 22/05/2021 | 29/11/2020 |
| 23/05/2021 | 29/05/2021 | 05/12/2020 |
| 30/05/2021 | 05/06/2021 | 12/12/2020 |

## Penalties

For refusal or repeated failure to:

- pay SAP to an employee who has entitlement
- produce or keep required SAP records

A fine not exceeding £3000 will be levied in respect of each offence. For failure to produce records, documents or to provide information the maximum penalty is £300. For fraud or negligence in respect of incorrect statements, records, documents and payments of SAP a further fine of up to £40 per day may be applied for continuance of the failure.

## Employment rights

Adoptive parents should not experience any detriment for exercising their right to take adoption leave. Following a period of:

- Ordinary Adoption Leave (OAL), i.e. the first 26 weeks, parents are guaranteed the right to return to the same job on terms and conditions no less favourable than those which would have applied had they not been absent (unless a redundancy has arisen)
- Additional Adoption Leave, the employee only has a right to a 'suitable and appropriate' job on return to work.

Joint adopters have the right to change their minds about who takes the Adoption Leave only if there is a significant change in circumstances:

- unexpected long-term sick leave of the nominated parent resulting in their being physically incapable of looking after the child
- a change in the earning power of the other adoptive parent that would make it more economically viable for the nominated parent to work instead

Other circumstances to note:

- with effect from expected dates of placement of 5th October 2008 or later contractual non-cash benefits e.g. annual leave, company cars, childcare vouchers must be provided for the whole adoption leave period – up to 52 weeks. Prior to this date the provision of contractual non-cash benefits could cease at the end of the 26-week ordinary adoption leave period

- Following the Peninsula case in January 2016 there are circumstances where an employer can stop providing childcare vouchers during the period of leave. Employers are advised to take specialist advice before embarking on a decision like this.
- Employees who do not qualify for SAP must be issued with an SAP1. Unlike maternity situations there is no state benefit fall back for adoption.

## STATUTORY MATERNITY PAY (SMP)

### Historical notes
SMP was introduced in 1987 when the administration and payment of State Maternity Benefit was transferred from the then Department of Health and Social Security to employers and payment moved from a means-tested benefit to a flat rate allowance.

**April 1987** – Three-quarter and half rates abolished.

**November 1984** – Additional child dependency allowance abolished.

**April 2000** – Earnings threshold introduced and scheme extended to pregnant women whose earnings reached the qualifying threshold. Standard Rate replaced former Higher Rate.

**August 2000** – Scheme extended to those not earning enough to pay NICs.

**April 2001** – Lower Rate removed .

**April 2003** – Payment period extended from 18 to 26 weeks and a new framework for maternity pay and leave introduced in line with provisions for adoption and paternity leave introduced at the same time under the Employment Act 2002. Notification arrangements were harmonised to a single date, the Notification Week, being the 15th week before the expected week of childbirth (EWC). Previously there were two different qualification requirements for SMP and leave:
26 weeks' service, before the 15th week before the EWC
leave – one year's continuous service, before the 11th week before the EWC.

**October 2006** – The Employment Equality (Age) Regulations 2006, removed the minimum age of 16 years as a condition of employment, and therefore as a condition of entitlement to MA/SMP.

**April 2007** – The Work and Families Act 2006, extended the payment period from 26 to 39 weeks and introduced Keeping-in-Touch days for those with an Expected Week of Childbirth of 1st April 2007 or later Any day start dates and daily rate calculations were introduced as an option for employers to align the payment of SMP to normal pay practices and the start of leave.

**April 2010** – New regulations in force to allow couples to transfer the second 26 weeks of leave from the mother/adoptive parent. A maximum of 19 weeks can be paid as additional paternity pay. The regulations are effective for expected dates of childbirth/matching dates of 3rd April 2011 or later.

### Qualification and entitlement comparator chart

### Pre- April 2003, April 2003 and April 2007 reviews

| Pre April 2003 | | | | |
|---|---|---|---|---|
| Qualification | 26 weeks employment up to the 15th week before the EWC | Qualified regardless of length of employment | 26 weeks employment in the 66 weeks before the baby is due with average earnings in 13 of those weeks of at least £30 | 1 years' service up to the 11th week before the EWC |

| Entitlement | 18 weeks | 18 weeks (paid if entitled to SMP) | 18 weeks | 29 weeks (unpaid) calculated from childbirth |
|---|---|---|---|---|
| **From April 2003 – March 2007** | | | | |
| Qualification | 26 weeks employment up to the 15th week before the EWC | Qualified regardless of length of employment | 26 weeks employment in the 66 weeks before the baby is due | 26 weeks employment up to the 14th week before the Expected Week of Childbirth |
| | 26 weeks | 26 weeks (paid if entitled to SMP) | 26 weeks | 26 weeks (unpaid) |
| **From April 2007** | | | | |
| Qualification | 39 weeks | 26 weeks (paid if entitled to SMP) | 39 weeks | 26 weeks (first 13 paid if entitled to SMP. No qualifying service required) |
| **From 3rd April 2011** | | | | |
| Mothers can transfer between 2 and 26 weeks of maternity leave to their partner, formed of a maximum of 19 weeks of SMP and 7 weeks unpaid leave as additional statutory paternity leave and pay | | | | |
| **From 5th April 2015** | | | | |
| Additional statutory paternity leave and pay abolished but mothers can curtail their SML early and transfer the balance of their entitlement to a new shared parental leave arrangement. | | | | |
| **From 1st February 2016** | | | | |
| New rules introduced to all part weeks of service achieved at any time up to and including the QW to be rounded up to a complete week. This means the employee can qualify if her service is in excess of 25 weeks at any time during the QW. | | | | |

## SMP Entitlement and qualification from April 2007

- A maximum of 39 weeks SMP, paid 6 weeks @ 90% of Average Weekly Earnings (AWE) and 33 weeks at 90% of earnings (or the current flat rate for SMP), whichever is the lower
- 26 weeks' Ordinary Maternity Leave and 26 weeks' Additional Maternity Leave (AML), to run directly from the end of the Ordinary Maternity Leave period, and to be available to all women
- 26 weeks' service qualification period at the 15th week before the EWC for SMP
- 4 weeks' notice to start SMP and 4 weeks' sickness trigger for Pregnancy Related Illnesses which automatically starts the maternity pay period.

## Keeping-In-Touch (KIT) Days

These were introduced April 2007 and allow for a woman to do up to a maximum of 10 days work or engage in up to 10 days of contact during her Maternity Leave Period without bringing her leave to an end, or losing any Statutory Maternity Pay or Maternity Allowance. KIT days are intended to help women to keep in touch with their workplace and ease their transition back into work, e.g. to allow for training.

Any such work must be agreed both by the woman and the employer. Where an employee returns to work with at least a week's equivalent of unused KIT days and before exhausting her full 52 week entitlement to leave or receiving 39 weeks' SMP, the employer may continue to pay and recover SMP on the basis that the employee is utilising her KIT day entitlement. Where any work is performed in a week in excess of ten days, that week of SMP is lost.

## Qualification for pay

In order to qualify for SMP, an employee must satisfy all the following conditions. She must:

- have been continuously employed for at least 26 weeks continuing into the 15th week before the baby is due. The 15th week being known as the 'Notification Week' (Any part week during the 26 week period is rounded up)
- have Average Weekly Earnings (AWE) in the eight weeks before the Notification Week of not less than the Lower Earnings Limit (LEL)
- still be pregnant at the 11th week before the week the baby is due, or have had the baby by that time
- provide medical evidence of the date her baby is due, at the Notification Week in the form of a MAT B1 or other equivalent evidence (see below)
- have stopped working for her employer (wholly or partly because of pregnancy)
- give notice of the date her Maternity Pay Period is due to start at least 28 days (21 days prior to April 2003). Where this is not practical, notice must be given as soon as reasonably practical.

*N.B. where all the above conditions are met the employee qualifies for receipt of SMP, even if she does not intend to return to work after the baby is born.*

Once she has qualified, should she leave, SMP is due regardless of her reason for leaving until she takes another job with an employer who did not employ her at the notification week.

## Evidence of Pregnancy

The employee must provide medical evidence of the date the baby is due; normally by submission of a form MAT B1. Payment of SMP must not commence until the medical evidence has been received. An employer may accept certificates issued from the 20th week before the EWC (period increased from 14 to 20 weeks on 28th September 2001).

An employer should not accept medical evidence issued more than 20 weeks before the week the baby is expected. The date of issue is the date it was signed by the doctor or midwife.

Employers may not be able to obtain an original copy of the MATB1. In circumstances where other employers are involved in determining a woman's entitlement to SMP an employer may have to accept a copy of the MATB1.

## Calculation of Average Weekly Earnings (AWE)

The 'relevant period' for the calculation of Average Weekly Earnings (AWE) is that between:

- the last normal payday before the end of the Notification Week, i.e. before the Saturday of the 15th week, and
- the last normal payday falling at least eight weeks before the pay-day at (a) above,

The normal payday is that specified in the contract, or the day usually paid where there is no contract or the contract does not specify a payday.

**Weekly paid employees**: add together all earnings in the relevant period and divide the total by the number of weeks covered by the payments. Earnings are any gross payments treated as earnings for NICs purposes.

**Monthly paid employees**: add together the gross earnings in the relevant period and divide by the number of months covered by the payments (where not a whole number of months, to the nearest whole number) multiply the result by 12 and divide by 52. In both cases do not round down to ensure the employee can qualify if possible

Where the baby is born before, or during, the Notification Week, the period over which the average earnings are calculated is the eight weeks ending with the last payday in the week in which the baby was born. In August 2017 HMRC revised the guidance on this matter.

In addition, to the usual rules, employers are required to assume the 26 weeks continuous employment criterion has been achieved if she would have achieved it if it were not for the early birth. The relevant period is worked out using the birth date and not the QW.

In September 2017 further clarification was published regarding some forms of employment and how they affected earnings calculations, primarily to cater for the position directors often find themselves in.

This guidance can be found at https://www.gov.uk/guidance/statutory-maternity-pay-how-different-employment-types-affect-what-you-pay#directors but essentially it splits calculations between incorporations prior to 1 October 2009 and those incorporated afterwards.

The new guidance confirms that if a director receives regular fees by way of salary then this salary is the earnings for the purposes of the AWE assessment.

Any payments voted by the board, which are classified as earnings, are assessed at the time the vote occurs, however any drawings taken in anticipation of a board vote on payment will not be included in the AWE assessment unless the vote occurs during the averaging period.

## Backdated Pay Rises - the effect of a pay rise on SMP

Two employment law cases affect the calculation of SMP where a pay rise has, or will occur. The Gillespie case requires SMP to be recalculated as a result of a pay rise backdated into the relevant period. The Alabaster case led to a change of regulations from 6th April 2005 as follows.

Where the effective date of a pay rise:
- falls within the period starting with the beginning of the relevant period and ending with the end of either Ordinary or Additional Maternity leave, or
- before the start of the relevant period, but the earnings calculated at the time SMP was calculated, but had not been adjusted,

the Average Weekly Earnings (AWE) must be recalculated to include the pay rise as though it was effective from the beginning of the set period and any additional SMP that results must be paid (although of course any payment of OMP can go towards discharging this liability). This could be for a maximum 17-month period and routines must be in place to capture this information.

Where a pay rise is awarded which, on recalculation, results in increased earnings that create an entitlement to SMP where none existed previously:
- work out 90% of the Average Weekly Earnings
- deduct the standard rate of SMP and pay any difference for six weeks.

If however 90% of AWE is less than standard rate no payment falls due (as the employee will have received sufficient MA), except where no entitlement to Maternity Allowance (MA) existed, in which case the employee needs to produce a letter to this effect from Jobcentre Plus before the employer can pay the 39 weeks SMP that is due. Where an employee has received less than the standard rate of MA, Jobcentre Plus will provide a letter to that effect so the employer can pay the additional SMP due.

The employee must benefit from a pay rise even if she does not intend to return to work after maternity leave has ended. Where a pay award is made following termination of employment, and the pay rise is backdated into the time of employment, her record should be checked to verify her entitlement. In cases where more than one pay rise has been awarded during the period, separate calculations will be necessary. In cases where pay adjustments to correct previous payments have taken place, gross earnings will be those that have taken adjustments into account.

Employers are not expected to recalculate SMP retrospectively for pay rises falling before April 2005, however when an employee so requests it, a recalculation must be performed going back three years from the date of the request and up to six years if the employee has the requisite data (e.g. payslips) to facilitate a recalculation. Employees, with aggregated earnings for NICs - can choose to have all earnings added together for calculation of Average Weekly Earnings for SMP.

*N.B. Even if additional SMP is calculated as being due, any payment of Occupational Maternity Pay (OMP) can be offset against this, so you may only have to produce a payslip and accounting change to show additional SMP offset by a reduction in OMP. The OMP scheme however will determine whether this is the case, or whether additional OMP is due to be paid as well.*

## Maternity Pay Period (MPP)

Once an employee has qualified, SMP is payable for up to 39 weeks (even where the employee does not intend to return to work after the birth of the baby), unless the employee goes to work for an employer who did not employ her at the Notification Week. This is called the Maternity Pay Period (MPP) and it may commence at any time from the start of the 11th week before the Expected Week of Confinement (EWC). The starting date is usually mutually agreed between employee and employer, but the final decision rests with the employee.

Where the baby is born before the MPP is due to commence, the MPP will be the period of 39 weeks beginning from the day after the actual date of birth (ADOB).

From April 2007 the employee may choose to start her Maternity Pay Period on any day of the week. Leavers who leave after qualification at the 15th week but before the 11th week will start their MPP on the Sunday of the 11th week, or if leaving after the 11th week, the MPP begins on the day after the last day she worked for the employer.

Where the employee is absent with a Pregnancy Related Illness within the four-week period starting on the Sunday of the 4th week before the week the baby is due, the MPP and OML begin on the day after the first complete day of absence from work.

### Payment rates
There are two weekly rates of payment:
- an earnings related rate of 90% of the employee's Average Weekly Earnings (see above) payable for the first six weeks of the Maternity Pay Period
- 33 weeks at 90% of Average Weekly Earnings or the current flat rate, whichever is the lower

**Table of SMP weeks' payable, earnings thresholds, rates, rebates, and recovery from 1987/1988 to date**

| Year | SMP Weeks Payable | Earnings Threshold £ | Earnings Related Rate % | Standard rate £ | Rebate % | Rebate/ Reclaim % | Small Employer's Relief threshold (SER)[1] £ |
|---|---|---|---|---|---|---|---|
| 1987/1988 | 18 | 39.00 | 90 | 32.85 | 100 | Nil | |
| 1988/1989 | 18 | 41.00 | 90 | 34.25 | 100 | 7.0 | |
| 1989/1990 | 18 | 43.00 | 90 | 36.25 | 100 | 7.5 | |
| 1990/1991 | 18 | 46.00 | 90 | 39.25 | 100 | 7.0 | |
| 1991/1992 | 18 | 52.00 | 90 | 44.50 | 100 | 4.5 | |
| 1992/1993 | 18 | 54.00 | 90 | 46.30 | 100 | 4.5 | |
| 1993/1994 | 18 | 56.00 | 90 | 47.95 | 100 | 4.5 | |
| 1994/1995 | 18 | 57.00 | 90 | 48.80 | 92 | 104.0[2] | 20,000 |
| 1995/1996 | 18 | 58.00 | 90 | 52.50 | 92 | 105.0 | 20,000 |
| 1996/1997 | 18 | 61.00 | 90 | 54.55 | 92 | 105.5 | 20,000 |
| 1997/1998 | 18 | 62.00 | 90 | 55.70 | 92 | 106.5 | 20,000 |
| 1998/1999 | 18 | 64.00 | 90 | 57.70 | 92 | 107.0 | 20,000 |
| 1999/2000 | 18 | 66.00 | 90 | 59.55 | 92 | 105.0 | 20,000 |
| 2000/2001 | 18 | 67.00 | 90 | 60.20 | 92 | 105.0 | 20,000 |
| 2001/2002 | 18 | 72.00 | 90 | 62.20 | 92 | 105.0 | 20,000 |
| 2002/2003 | 18 | 75.00 | 90 | 75.00 | 92 | 104.5 | 40,000 |
| 2003/2004 | 26 | 77.00 | 90 | 100.00 | 92 | 104.5 | 40,000 |
| 2004/2005 | 26 | 79.00 | 90 | 102.80 | 92 | 104.5 | 45,000 |
| 2005/2006 | 26 | 82.00 | 90 | 106.00 | 92 | 104.5 | 45,000 |
| 2006/2007 | 26 | 84.00 | 90 | 108.85 | 92 | 104.5 | 45,000 |
| 2007/2008 | 39 | 87.00 | 90 | 112.75 | 92 | 104.5 | 45,000 |

| | | | | | | | |
|---|---|---|---|---|---|---|---|
| 2008/2009 | 39 | 90.00 | 90 | 117.18 | 92 | 104.5 | 45,000 |
| 2009/2010 | 39 | 95.00 | 90 | 123.06 | 92 | 104.5 | 45,000 |
| 2010/2011 | 39 | 97.00 | 90 | 124.88 | 92 | 104.5 | 45,000 |
| 2011/2012 | 39 | 102.00 | 90 | 128.73 | 92 | 103 | 45,000 |
| 2012/2013 | 39 | 107.00 | 90 | 135.45 | 92 | 103 | 45,000 |
| 2013/2014 | 39 | 109.00 | 90 | 136.78 | 92 | 103 | 45,000 |
| 2014/2015 | 39 | 111.00 | 90 | 138.18 | 92 | 103 | 45,000 |
| 2015/2016 | 39 | 112.00 | 90 | 139.58 | 92 | 103 | 45,000 |
| 2016/2017 | 39 | 112.00 | 90 | 139.58 | 92 | 103 | 45,000 |
| 2017/2018 | 39 | 113.00 | 90 | 140.98 | 92 | 103 | 45,000 |
| 2018/2019 | 39 | 116.00 | 90 | 145.18 | 92 | 103 | 45,000 |
| 2019/2020 | 39 | 118.00 | 90 | 148.68 | 92 | 103 | 45,000 |
| **2020/2021** | **39** | **120.00** | **90** | **151.20** | **92** | **103** | **45,000** |

[1] From 1987 to 1994 Compensation, from 1994 Small Employer's Relief

*N.B. the Lower Rate for those entering the scheme in 1994/1995 under the revised rules was £52.50 p.w.*

[2] From 1994 the Small Employers Relief is worked out as 100% recovery of the statutory payment made, plus an additional percentage, currently 3% to compensate the employer for any additional employers NIC paid.

### Payment of Statutory Maternity Pay
Payment will normally be at the time that earnings are paid for the same period. SMP is treated as earnings and is subject to PAYE, Other lawful deductions applicable to pay may be applied to SMP e.g. pension contributions, but not any type of Attachment of Earnings.

An employer may treat an employee's wages or any occupational maternity or sickness payments as payments towards SMP if payment of:
- wages continues for any week in which SMP is due, or
- occupational maternity or sick pay is due for the same week as SMP

Some employer's conditions of service, particularly in the public sector, may provide for payment of SMP in addition to contractual maternity pay, subject to the gross payment not being in excess of normal full pay.

Employees who do not qualify for SMP from their employer may be entitled to Maternity Allowance, payable by the Department of Work and Pensions (DWP). Employees who are not entitled to SMP must be issued with a completed form SMP1 by their employer. Any maternity certificate provided (usually the MAT B1) must be returned.

### Daily Rates
From April 2007 employers may align payment of SMP with their normal payment cycle, in order to enable this to take place calculations may be made using daily rates. The daily rate for 2020/21 is £21.60.

The correct method of alignment is to pay full weeks for the number of SMP weeks she is entitled to and to adjust the part weeks accordingly at each end of the month. This can be a complex calculation and for this reason many employers keep to the standard payment based on the number of SMP weeks start days in the month.

### Rates at the start of a tax year
The 2004/5 tax year saw a change to the way new rates 'kicked in' as a result of the new statutory payments regime that came into force in April 2003. There are now several scenarios where a statutory payment week can straddle the old and new tax years, this relates to:
- a week of Statutory Paternity Pay (for 'fathers' or adoptive partners)
- a week of Statutory Adoption Pay
- a week of SMP as a result of an early birth or pregnancy related illness

## Multiple employment

An employee who satisfies the qualifying rules with more than one employer can receive SMP from each, and choose a different Maternity Pay Period with each. Where an employee works under two distinct contracts with the same employer, and National Insurance Contributions are paid separately for each contract, SMP liability may arise separately under each contract. Where earnings from each employment are aggregated for NICs, there is only one SMP liability.

## Stillbirths

Even if the baby survives for only an instant it is deemed a live birth. If the baby is stillborn before the 24th week of pregnancy SMP is not payable. In such a case it should be determined whether SSP is due as an alternative. If the baby is stillborn after the 24th week of pregnancy, the employee should be treated as if a live birth had taken place and SMP is to be paid.

## Disqualifying Period from SSP

The 39 week period which spans the week during which the baby is expected to be born is known as the disqualifying period. It starts from the beginning of the week the employee is entitled to either Statutory Maternity Pay from the employer, or Maternity Allowance from the Department for Work and Pensions.

During this period an employee is not entitled to Statutory Sick Pay. Should they return to work and then fall sick within this period i.e. up to 39 weeks they revert back to SMP; however, as the maternity leave period has been brought to an end the leave must be classed as unpaid contractual leave. For those employees entitled to neither SMP nor Maternity Allowance the disqualification period is only 18 weeks.

## Recovery of SMP paid

A percentage of SMP paid may be recovered from the monthly remittance of tax and NICs. For current and previous year's recovery rates see table above.

## Advanced funding

Where employers have insufficient tax, NICs, student loan and Construction Industry Scheme deductions to fund the payment of SMP, they can apply to HMRC for advance funding using the e-mail facility available from the HMRC website at https://www.gov.uk/recover-statutory-payments/if-you-cant-afford-to-make-payments .

## Penalties

For refusal or repeated failure to:
- pay SMP to an employee who has entitlement
- produce or keep required SMP records.

A fine not exceeding £3000 will be levied in respect of each offence. For failure to produce records, documents or to provide information the maximum penalty is £300. For fraud or negligence in respect of incorrect statements, records, documents and payments of SMP a further fine of up to £40 per day may be applied for continuance of the failure.

## Records

The employer must:
- keep any medical evidence provided by employees to whom SMP is paid - usually form MAT B1
- keep a copy of any medical evidence where the original has been returned to the employee
- keep a record of the dates of maternity absence notified by employees
- keep a record of any weeks in the Maternity Pay Period for which SMP was not paid, together with reasons
- record SMP payments on the employee's payroll record
- show the total SMP payments on employee's end of year returns (P14)
- show on the P35 employer's annual return the amount of SMP recovered and NICs compensation recovered where applicable.

## SMP Forms

| MAT B1 - Maternity Certificate | Can be issued from the 20th week before the EWC (prior to 28th September 2001 the 14th week before the EWC) |
|---|---|
| SMP1* | Must be completed and sent to an employee if employed or treated as employed in the qualifying week and is not entitled to SMP, or entitlement ceases |
| SMP2 Record Sheet | A form designed and supplied by HMRC, optionally available to assist small businesses in the operation of SMP |

*In October 2019 HMRC provided a new version of the SMP1 which allows for the majority of the information to be completed on screen. A signature is still required and the form must still be printed off.*

### Guidance
HMRC's helpbook E15: 'Employer helpbook for Statutory Maternity Pay' was abolished from 6th April 2014. See https://www.gov.uk/maternity-pay-leave for guidance. The table below indicates the appropriate dates for 2017/18.

### Statutory Maternity Pay and Leave Tables 2020/21

| Week baby due | | Qualifying week | | Latest start date for employment | Start of 11th week before the week the baby is due | Start of 4th week before the week baby is due |
|---|---|---|---|---|---|---|
| Sunday | Saturday | Sunday | Saturday | Saturday | | |
| 05/04/2020 | 11/04/2020 | 22/12/2019 | 28/12/2019 | 06/07/2019 | 19/01/2020 | 08/03/2020 |
| 12/04/2020 | 18/04/2020 | 29/12/2019 | 04/01/2020 | 13/07/2019 | 26/01/2020 | 15/03/2020 |
| 19/04/2020 | 25/04/2020 | 05/01/2020 | 11/01/2020 | 20/07/2019 | 02/02/2020 | 22/03/2020 |
| 26/04/2020 | 02/05/2020 | 12/01/2020 | 18/01/2020 | 27/07/2019 | 09/02/2020 | 29/03/2020 |
| 03/05/2020 | 09/05/2020 | 19/01/2020 | 25/01/2020 | 03/08/2019 | 16/02/2020 | 05/04/2020 |
| 10/05/2020 | 16/05/2020 | 26/01/2020 | 01/02/2020 | 10/08/2019 | 23/02/2020 | 12/04/2020 |
| 17/05/2020 | 23/05/2020 | 02/02/2020 | 08/02/2020 | 17/08/2019 | 01/03/2020 | 19/04/2020 |
| 24/05/2020 | 30/05/2020 | 09/02/2020 | 15/02/2020 | 24/08/2019 | 08/03/2020 | 26/04/2020 |
| 31/05/2020 | 06/06/2020 | 16/02/2020 | 22/02/2020 | 31/08/2019 | 15/03/2020 | 03/05/2020 |
| 07/06/2020 | 13/06/2020 | 23/02/2020 | 29/02/2020 | 07/09/2019 | 22/03/2020 | 10/05/2020 |
| 14/06/2020 | 20/06/2020 | 01/03/2020 | 07/03/2020 | 14/09/2019 | 29/03/2020 | 17/05/2020 |
| 21/06/2020 | 27/06/2020 | 08/03/2020 | 14/03/2020 | 21/09/2019 | 05/04/2020 | 24/05/2020 |
| 28/06/2020 | 04/07/2020 | 15/03/2020 | 21/03/2020 | 28/09/2019 | 12/04/2020 | 31/05/2020 |
| 05/07/2020 | 11/07/2020 | 22/03/2020 | 28/03/2020 | 05/10/2019 | 19/04/2020 | 07/06/2020 |
| 12/07/2020 | 18/07/2020 | 29/03/2020 | 04/04/2020 | 12/10/2019 | 26/04/2020 | 14/06/2020 |
| 19/07/2020 | 25/07/2020 | 05/04/2020 | 11/04/2020 | 19/10/2019 | 03/05/2020 | 21/06/2020 |
| 26/07/2020 | 01/08/2020 | 12/04/2020 | 18/04/2020 | 26/10/2019 | 10/05/2020 | 28/06/2020 |
| 02/08/2020 | 08/08/2020 | 19/04/2020 | 25/04/2020 | 02/11/2019 | 17/05/2020 | 05/07/2020 |
| 09/08/2020 | 15/08/2020 | 26/04/2020 | 02/05/2020 | 09/11/2019 | 24/05/2020 | 12/07/2020 |

| | | | | | | |
|---|---|---|---|---|---|---|
| 16/08/2020 | 22/08/2020 | 03/05/2020 | 09/05/2020 | 16/11/2019 | 31/05/2020 | 19/07/2020 |
| 23/08/2020 | 29/08/2020 | 10/05/2020 | 16/05/2020 | 23/11/2019 | 07/06/2020 | 26/07/2020 |
| 30/08/2020 | 05/09/2020 | 17/05/2020 | 23/05/2020 | 30/11/2019 | 14/06/2020 | 02/08/2020 |
| 06/09/2020 | 12/09/2020 | 24/05/2020 | 30/05/2020 | 07/12/2019 | 21/06/2020 | 09/08/2020 |
| 13/09/2020 | 19/09/2020 | 31/05/2020 | 06/06/2020 | 14/12/2019 | 28/06/2020 | 16/08/2020 |
| 20/09/2020 | 26/09/2020 | 07/06/2020 | 13/06/2020 | 21/12/2019 | 05/07/2020 | 23/08/2020 |
| 27/09/2020 | 03/10/2020 | 14/06/2020 | 20/06/2020 | 28/12/2019 | 12/07/2020 | 30/08/2020 |
| 04/10/2020 | 10/10/2020 | 21/06/2020 | 27/06/2020 | 04/01/2020 | 19/07/2020 | 06/09/2020 |
| 11/10/2020 | 17/10/2020 | 28/06/2020 | 04/07/2020 | 11/01/2020 | 26/07/2020 | 13/09/2020 |
| 18/10/2020 | 24/10/2020 | 05/07/2020 | 11/07/2020 | 18/01/2020 | 02/08/2020 | 20/09/2020 |
| 25/10/2020 | 31/10/2020 | 12/07/2020 | 18/07/2020 | 25/01/2020 | 09/08/2020 | 27/09/2020 |
| 01/11/2020 | 07/11/2020 | 19/07/2020 | 25/07/2020 | 01/02/2020 | 16/08/2020 | 04/10/2020 |
| 08/11/2020 | 14/11/2020 | 26/07/2020 | 01/08/2020 | 08/02/2020 | 23/08/2020 | 11/10/2020 |
| 15/11/2020 | 21/11/2020 | 02/08/2020 | 08/08/2020 | 15/02/2020 | 30/08/2020 | 18/10/2020 |
| 22/11/2020 | 28/11/2020 | 09/08/2020 | 15/08/2020 | 22/02/2020 | 06/09/2020 | 25/10/2020 |
| 29/11/2020 | 05/12/2020 | 16/08/2020 | 22/08/2020 | 29/02/2020 | 13/09/2020 | 01/11/2020 |
| 06/12/2020 | 12/12/2020 | 23/08/2020 | 29/08/2020 | 07/03/2020 | 20/09/2020 | 08/11/2020 |
| 13/12/2020 | 19/12/2020 | 30/08/2020 | 05/09/2020 | 14/03/2020 | 27/09/2020 | 15/11/2020 |
| 20/12/2020 | 26/12/2020 | 06/09/2020 | 12/09/2020 | 21/03/2020 | 04/10/2020 | 22/11/2020 |
| 27/12/2020 | 02/01/2021 | 13/09/2020 | 19/09/2020 | 28/03/2020 | 11/10/2020 | 29/11/2020 |
| 03/01/2021 | 09/01/2021 | 20/09/2020 | 26/09/2020 | 04/04/2020 | 18/10/2020 | 06/12/2020 |
| 10/01/2021 | 16/01/2021 | 27/09/2020 | 03/10/2020 | 11/04/2020 | 25/10/2020 | 13/12/2020 |
| 17/01/2021 | 23/01/2021 | 04/10/2020 | 10/10/2020 | 18/04/2020 | 01/11/2020 | 20/12/2020 |

## Statutory Maternity Pay and Leave Tables 2020/21

| | | | | | | |
|---|---|---|---|---|---|---|
| 24/01/2021 | 30/01/2021 | 11/10/2020 | 17/10/2020 | 25/04/2020 | 08/11/2020 | 27/12/2020 |
| 31/01/2021 | 06/02/2021 | 18/10/2020 | 24/10/2020 | 02/05/2020 | 15/11/2020 | 03/01/2021 |
| 07/02/2021 | 13/02/2021 | 25/10/2020 | 31/10/2020 | 09/05/2020 | 22/11/2020 | 10/01/2021 |
| 14/02/2021 | 20/02/2021 | 01/11/2020 | 07/11/2020 | 16/05/2020 | 29/11/2020 | 17/01/2021 |
| 21/02/2021 | 27/02/2021 | 08/11/2020 | 14/11/2020 | 23/05/2020 | 06/12/2020 | 24/01/2021 |
| 28/02/2021 | 06/03/2021 | 15/11/2020 | 21/11/2020 | 30/05/2020 | 13/12/2020 | 31/01/2021 |
| 07/03/2021 | 13/03/2021 | 22/11/2020 | 28/11/2020 | 06/06/2020 | 20/12/2020 | 07/02/2021 |
| 14/03/2021 | 20/03/2021 | 29/11/2020 | 05/12/2020 | 13/06/2020 | 27/12/2020 | 14/02/2021 |
| 21/03/2021 | 27/03/2021 | 06/12/2020 | 12/12/2020 | 20/06/2020 | 03/01/2021 | 21/02/2021 |
| 28/03/2021 | 03/04/2021 | 13/12/2020 | 19/12/2020 | 27/06/2020 | 10/01/2021 | 28/02/2021 |

| | | | | | | |
|---|---|---|---|---|---|---|
| 04/04/2021 | 10/04/2021 | 20/12/2020 | 26/12/2020 | 04/07/2020 | 17/01/2021 | 07/03/2021 |
| 11/04/2021 | 17/04/2021 | 27/12/2020 | 02/01/2021 | 11/07/2020 | 24/01/2021 | 14/03/2021 |
| 18/04/2021 | 24/04/2021 | 03/01/2021 | 09/01/2021 | 18/07/2020 | 31/01/2021 | 21/03/2021 |
| 25/04/2021 | 01/05/2021 | 10/01/2021 | 16/01/2021 | 25/07/2020 | 07/02/2021 | 28/03/2021 |
| 02/05/2021 | 08/05/2021 | 17/01/2021 | 23/01/2021 | 01/08/2020 | 14/02/2021 | 04/04/2021 |
| 09/05/2021 | 15/05/2021 | 24/01/2021 | 30/01/2021 | 08/08/2020 | 21/02/2021 | 11/04/2021 |
| 16/05/2021 | 22/05/2021 | 31/01/2021 | 06/02/2021 | 15/08/2020 | 28/02/2021 | 18/04/2021 |
| 23/05/2021 | 29/05/2021 | 07/02/2021 | 13/02/2021 | 22/08/2020 | 07/03/2021 | 25/04/2021 |
| 30/05/2021 | 05/06/2021 | 14/02/2021 | 20/02/2021 | 29/08/2020 | 14/03/2021 | 02/05/2021 |

## STATUTORY MATERNITY LEAVE

All female employees who are pregnant have a statutory right to up to 26 weeks' Ordinary Maternity Leave (OML), and a further 26 weeks of Additional Maternity Leave (AML) regardless of length of service, hours of work or earnings. Prior to 15th December 2002 (babies expected on or after 30th April 2003) the maximum was 18 weeks. Between April 2003 and Expected Weeks of Childbirth (EWCs) of 31st March 2007 or earlier there was a 26 week service qualification for entitlement to Additional Maternity Leave.

**Return to work**
If the employee wishes to return before the end of her 52nd week of leave she is required to give a minimum of eight weeks (56 days) notice of her date of return to work when plans change (28 days prior to April 2007).

## SHARED PARENTAL LEAVE

All employees have a right to shared parental leave since 5th April 2015. After the compulsory 2 or 4 weeks maternity leave the remaining up to 48 or 50 weeks of leave with up to 37 week's pay can be shared between both parents. There is no longer and right to take additional statutory paternity pay and leave.

Parents are able to take shared parental leave simultaneously and have breaks between their periods of leave as long as all of the leave has been taken by the day of the child's first birthday or 52 weeks from the date of the adoption.

Other key rules:
- 6 weeks after birth is the deadline for the 'mother' to change her mind completely about handing over her some or all of her leave and pay to 'father'
- the employer can refuse to accept more than three notifications of shared leave plans which must be self-certified by the parents to their respective employers with at least eight weeks' notice. Each leave plan proposing more than one period of leave for each parent can be accepted, refused, or re-negotiated (plans for one period of leave per parent must be accepted by the respective employers
- 10 KIT days still apply during maternity leave
- up to 20 working, or SPLIT days for each parent can be taken during shared leave
- both parents have the right to return to their old job after any period of leave that adds up in total to 26 weeks or less (even if it isn't in one block). Where more than 26 weeks is taken it will be the right to return to a job that is suitable and appropriate
- fathers have the statutory right to unpaid time off to attend 2 ante-natal appointments
- there is no change to SMP qualification or the various start dates for maternity leave
- there is no service requirement for fathers to receive paid parental leave so new employees are entitled to leave immediately
- self-employed Dads are entitled to Universal Credit to allow them to take shared parental leave.

## THE EU PREGNANT WORKERS' DIRECTIVE - REFORM

The European Commission has also published proposals to improve paid maternity leave under the Pregnant Workers' Directive. It continues to be proposed that:

- the fully paid maternity leave period be extended from 14 to 18 weeks (although the UK does not meet this it appears that capping full pay at the level of SSP indicates the UK scheme will comply)
- that the compulsory maternity leave period be extended from four to six weeks for those working in a factory
- that the woman's former job must be held open for the full period of her leave i.e. up to 52 weeks. This would mean that ordinary and additional maternity leave would be abolished and it would simply be a 52 week leave period
- that women would not be restricted to going on leave only 11 weeks before the EWC.

These proposals received a second formal reading in December 2015, however there is still no agreement from the member states at present and at the point of publication the proposals continue to be under review.

## MATERNITY ALLOWANCE

Introduced on 5th July 1948, Maternity Allowance (MA) is a contributory and non-taxable benefit available to a woman who has worked and paid full National Insurance Contributions in the relevant period. The relevant period is the 66 weeks up to and including the week before the week the baby is due.

The average earnings are worked out using earnings from any 13 weeks in the relevant period. As long as the average earnings per week exceed the earnings threshold (£30) MA is payable, hence few women do not qualify.

It is payable for 39 weeks (26 weeks for those with an Expected Week of Childbirth prior to 1st April 2007), commencing at the earliest 11 weeks before the baby is due. It is paid at the same standard rate as SMP - see table below.

From 6th April 1987 many women who work for an employer and who pay Class 1 National Insurance Contributions are entitled to Statutory Maternity Pay. But, where an employed woman is unable to claim Statutory Maternity pay (e.g. low earnings in the relevant period) Maternity Allowance is available.

Women who are self-employed at the 15th week before the baby is due get the standard rate of Maternity Allowance.

**Maternity Allowance rates - from 23rd November 1981 to 11th April 1994**

| Date from | Lower Rate £ | Adult Dependant £ | Date from | Lower Rate £ | Adult Dependant £ |
|---|---|---|---|---|---|
| 23.11.1981 | 22.50 | 13.90 | 11.04.1988 | 31.30 | 19.40 |
| 22.11.1982 | 25.00 | 15.45 | 10.04.1989 | 33.20 | 20.55 |
| 21.11.1983 | 25.95 | 16.00 | 09.04.1990 | 35.70 | 22.10 |
| 26.11.1984 | 27.25 | 16.80 | 08.04.1991 | 40.60 | 24 .50 |
| 25.11.1985 | 29.15 | 18.00 | 06.04.1992 | 42.50 | 25.50 |
| 28.07.1986 | 29.45 | 18.20 | 12.04.1993 | 43.75 | 26.40 |
| 06.04.1987 | 30.05 | 18.60 | 11.04.1994 | 44.55 | 26.90 |

**Maternity Allowance rates - from 16th October 1994**

| Date from | Lower Rate £ | Standard Rate £ | Earnings Threshold £ | Adult Dependant £ |
|---|---|---|---|---|
| 16.10.1994 | 44.55 | 52.50 | | 26.90 |
| 10.04.1995 | 45.55 | 52.50 | | 27.50 |
| 08.04.1996 | 47.35 | 54.55 | | 28.55 |
| 07.04.1997 | 48.35 | 55.70 | | 29.15 |
| 06.04.1998 | 50.10 | 57.70 | | 30.20 |
| 12.04.1999 | 51.70 | 59.55 | | 31.15 |
| 10.04.2000 | 52.55 | 60.20 | 30.00 | 31.50 |
| 09.04.2001 | | 62.20 | 30.00 | 32.55 |
| 08.04.2002 | | 75.00 | 30.00 | 33.10 |
| 07.04.2003 | | 100.00 | 30.00 | 33.65 |
| 12.04.2004 | | 102.80 | 30.00 | 34.60 |
| 11.04.2005 | | 106.00 | 30.00 | 35.65 |
| 10.04.2006 | | 108.85 | 30.00 | 36.60 |
| 09.04.2007 | | 112.75 | 30.00 | 37.90 |
| 07.04.2008 | | 117.18 | 30.00 | 39.40 |
| 06.04.2009 | | 123.06 | 30.00 | 41.35 |
| 12.04.2010 | | 124.88 | 30.00 | 41.35 |
| 11.04.2011 | | 128.73 | 30.00 | 42.65 |
| 09.04.2012 | | 135.45 | 30.00 | 44.85 |
| 08.04.2013 | | 136.78 | 30.00 | 45.85 |
| 07.04.2014 | | 138.18 | 30.00 | 47.10 |
| 06.04.2015 | | 139.58 | 30.00 | 47.58 |
| 03.04.2016 | | 139.58 | 30.00 | 47.58* |
| 02.04.2017 | | 140.98 | 30.00 | N/A |
| 01.04.2018 | | 145.18 | 30.00 | N/A |
| 07/04/2019 | | 148.68 | 30.00 | N/A |
| **05/04/2020** | | **151.20** | **30.00** | **N/A** |

*Not confirmed

## Keeping In Touch (KIT) Days

A woman is entitled to perform up to a maximum of 10 days' work during her Maternity Allowance Period (MAP) without losing any Maternity Allowance (MA). KIT days are intended to help women to keep in touch with their workplace and ease their transition back into work, e.g. to allow for training. Any such work must be agreed both by the woman and the employer. Where a woman comes into work for more than ten days during her MAP she is responsible for telling DWP so that her MA can be reduced by one week for each day worked in an MA week.

# MATERNITY GRANT

A contributory benefit lump sum based on either the woman's own, or her husband's, contributory NICs record. Payable initially, to women who gave birth before 4th July 1982, towards initial expenditure. From 5th July 1982 to 5th April 1987 the grant was available as a non-contributory benefit subject to a test of presence in Great Britain.

From April 1987 the payment is subject to need and comes from the Social Fund. The Maternity Grant became officially known as The Sure Start Maternity Grant in 1999, and was available at the applicable rate for each child expected, born, adopted or the subject of a parental order on, or after, the date shown in the table below.

From babies due, adopted or born on, or after 11 April 2011 the £500 grant is only available if there are no other children in the household under the age of 16 or a dependent child is under age 20 when she has a first baby.

The grant is payable to those in receipt of specific state benefits:
- Income Support
- income-based Jobseeker's Allowance
- income-related Employment and Support Allowance
- Pension Credit
- Child Tax Credit at a rate higher than the family element
- Working Tax Credit where a disability or severe disability element is included in the award, or
- Universal Credit.

The grant is not means-tested and may be claimed at any time from the 29th week of pregnancy until the child is three months old. If adopting a baby the grant must be claimed within three months of adoption, and the baby should be no more than 12 months old. Where a parental order has been granted the claim must be made within three months of the date of the parental order

### Sure Start Maternity Grant rates from 6th April 1987

| Date from | Lump Sum £ | Date from | Lump Sum £ |
|---|---|---|---|
| 06.04.1987 | 80 | 11.06.1999 | 200 |
| 11.04.1988 | 85 | 03.12.2000 | 300 |
| 09.04.1990 | 100 | 08.04.2002 onwards | 500 |

**Health in pregnancy grant**
Introduced in April 2009 as a grant of £190 which was non means-tested and available to all women who were in receipt of medical advice at the 25th week of pregnancy. It was abolished from 1st January 2011.

## PARENTAL BEREAVEMENT - STATUTORY PARENTAL BEREAVEMENT LEAVE (SPBL) AND PAY (SPBP)

Introduced on th April 2020 to provide parents who lose a child or suffer a stillbirth with a day-one employment right to take two weeks off work. Eligible parents will also be entitled to two weeks' statutory pay.

**Definition**
This captures a broad range of "parents", including adoptive parents, parents of a child born to a surrogate, parents who are fostering to adopt as well as individuals who have been caring for the child in their own home, continuously for a period of four weeks ending with the date of death, with responsibility for the child's care during that period.

**Qualification**
In order to qualify for statutory parental bereavement leave the employee has to:
- have a parental relationship to the deceased child within the broad definition above
- supply evidence to the employer in the form of a death certificate where it is practicable to do so
- have suffered a stillbirth from the 24th week of pregnancy
- be employed by the employer.

**Notice**
The employee will not need to provide written notice of their intention to take leave. The amount of notice required in order to take the leave will depend on whether the employee intends to take leave within the first eight weeks following the death (Period A), or later (Period B).

- For leave taken in Period A, the employee will need to notify their employer before they would be due to start work on the first day of absence.
- For leave taken in Period B, the employee will need to provide notice at least one week prior to the start of the leave period.

## Entitlement
There is an entitlement to two weeks' leave which may be taken as a single block or as two separate weeks.

## Parental bereavement leave
PBL should be taken:
- as two weeks either as a single block or as two separate weeks
- within 56 weeks of the date of the date of death.

## Statutory Parental Bereavement Pay (SPBP)
To qualify for SPBP the employee must in addition to the above conditions have Average Weekly Earnings (AWE) in the eight weeks before the date if death at, or above, the Lower Earnings Limit (LEL) for National Insurance (£120 p.w. for 2020/21).

## Employment rights
During leave the employee is entitled to:
- the provision of all contractual non-cash benefits e.g. a company car, childcare vouchers
- protection from detriment for asserting the right to take leave
- return to the same job on the same terms and conditions at the end of leave.

## Administration of SPBP
Like other statutory payments, SPBP is administered by the employer, is treated as earnings and is subject to PAYE income tax and NICs. Other lawful deductions applicable to pay may be applied to SPBP but not any type of Attachment of Earnings Order (AEO).

## Small Employers' Relief (SER) for Statutory Payments
To qualify for Small Employers' Relief (SER), the total gross employers' Class 1 NICs for the previous year must be less than the threshold shown. The qualifying year is the last complete tax year before the partner's Qualifying/Matching Week. Small Employers are entitled to recover 100% of their statutory payments (excluding SSP), plus 3% as compensation for NICs paid, for all payments made from 6th April 2011 onwards (4.5% prior to 6th April 2011).

## Rates at the start of a tax year
Generally new statutory payment rates apply on the first Sunday in April. For the 2020/21 tax year this is 5th April 2020. This will not affect 2020/21 as the new entitlement does come into effect until 6th April, however any new rates for 2021/22 will come into effect from 4th April 2021.

## Statutory Parental Bereavement Pay Forms
At the time of writing the detailed guidance on the new right was yet to be published, however it is expected that the forms accompanying the provision will be similar in type and purpose to those available for other statutory rights.

## Advanced funding
Employers who have insufficient tax, NICs and student loan repayments to fund payment of SPBP may make a request for advanced funding to HMRC. This is done via https://www.gov.uk/recover-statutory-payments on the gov.uk website.

## Penalties
For refusal or repeated failure to:
- pay SPBP to an employee who has entitlement
- produce or keep required SPBP records
it is expected that fines identical to those for the other statutory leave and payment entitlements will apply.

This will mean a fine not exceeding £300 for SPBP will be levied in respect of each offence. For failure to produce records, documents or to provide information the maximum penalty is £300. For fraud or negligence in respect of incorrect statements, records, documents and payments of SPBP a further fine of up to £40 per day is expected to be applied for continuance of the failure.

## Guidance

An HMRC Helpbook for statutory parental bereavement leave and pay is expected to be produced in time for the new tax year. At the time of writing this guidance is not available and readers should consult HMRC at https://www.gov.uk/paternity-pay-leave to obtain the guidance when it becomes available.

# PATERNITY- STATUTORY PATERNITY LEAVE (SPL) AND PAY (SPP)

Introduced on 6th April 2003 to provide birth or adoptive fathers with the choice, and opportunity to spend more time with, and support their partner in adapting to the responsibilities and pressures of raising a new born child. From 5th December 2005 civil partners have also been entitled to receive SPP/SPL. From 6th April 2010 new regulations came into force that allow couples to transfer unused maternity/adoption pay and leave to the other party in the relationship. From 6th April 2015, however, the introduction of shared parental leave (ShPL & P) this right of transfer ceased.

The regulations came into force for expected dates of childbirth/matching dates for adoption on, or after, 3rd April 2011. Until 5th April 2015, as a result of the introduction of additional statutory paternity leave (APSL) and additional statutory paternity pay (ASPP), the one or two weeks of leave and pay taken around the birth was renamed ordinary statutory paternity leave (OSPL) and ordinary statutory paternity pay (OSPP).

## Qualification

In order to qualify for statutory paternity leave, both ordinary and additional, the employee had to:

- have a relationship - biological father, married to the mother, live with mother or adopter in an 'enduring family relationship' and be able to make a 'declaration of family commitment on form SC7 for births and SC8 for adoptions'
- supply evidence to the employer in the form of a completed self-certificate SC3 for birth parents or SC4 for adoptive parents for ordinary leave.
- have worked with the employer for not less than 26 weeks before the Qualifying or Matching Week (based on partner's Expected week of Childbirth (EWC) and stayed with the same employer to the Actual Date Of Childbirth (ADOC) see tables below.

In addition:

- for additional leave only and only up to the introduction of shared parental leave: the mother must have qualified for SMP, SAP or Maternity Allowance and returned to work* with at least 2 weeks' unused leave i.e. no later than at the end of week 50
- for additional pay only: the mother must have qualified for SMP, SAP or Maternity Allowance and returned to work* with at least 2 weeks' unused statutory pay weeks i.e. no later than at the end of week 37

*returned to work simply means bringing the statutory pay and leave period to an end so that unused weeks can be assessed, the employee can be on holiday or on parental leave so need not be physically have returned to work

*N.B. The Employment Equality (Age) Regulations 2006, which came into effect on the 1st October 2006 amended the definition of an employee by removing the minimum and maximum age restrictions of 16 and 65 years respectively, thereby extending the entitlement to Statutory Paternity Pay.*

## Notice

The employee had to give 28 days' notice before commencement of ordinary leave, and 28 days' notice to change the date given on form SC3 for ordinary leave. For additional leave the employee had to give eight weeks' notice to the employer on forms SC7 or SC8 and six weeks' notice to change or cancel additional leave dates.

## Entitlement

This was a maximum of one or two weeks' consecutive ordinary paternity leave around the time of birth, plus a minimum of two and a maximum of 26 weeks' additional leave of which a maximum of 19 could have been paid if the mother returned to work at the end of the 20th week of SMP.

## Notification Week

The employee had to notify the employer of the intention to take ordinary paternity leave by the 15th week before the child's expected week of birth and eight weeks before he wishes to take additional leave. The employer was required to confirm entitlement to additional leave within 28 days of notice being received.

### Ordinary paternity leave
- had to be taken as one or two consecutive complete weeks
- had to be completed within 56 days of the actual date of confinement (ADOC) or first day of the Expected Week, of Childbirth (EWC), whichever is the later
- when notified the intention to take the leave at the date of the child's birth, it had to be so taken, whether the child is born early or late
- from 5th April 2015 any period of Statutory Paternity Leave has to be completed before the mother or main adopter curtails their maternity of adoption leave in favour of Shared Parental Leave.

### Additional paternity leave (until April 2015 only)
- could not be taken before the child was 20 weeks old, or 20 weeks since the date of placement - unless the mother or adoptive parent dies, see below
- had to be completed by the date of the child's first birthday, or it is one year since the date of placement
- was abolished with effect from 5th April 2015 and replaced by the right to Shared Parental Leave.

### Statutory Paternity Pay (SPP)
To qualify for SPP the employee must in addition to the above conditions have Average Weekly Earnings (AWE) in the eight weeks before the partner's Qualifying/Matching week at, or above, the Lower Earnings Limit (LEL) for National Insurance (£120 p.w. for 2020/21).

### Additional Statutory Paternity Pay (ASPP) (to April 2015 only)
To qualify for ASPP the employee had to have qualified for OSPP and remained in the same employment. A reduction in earnings cannot lead to a loss of entitlement. If AWE were high enough for OSPP, no recalculation is performed. If the employee did not take OSPP the employer had to perform an AWE calculation based on the eight weeks before the partner's Qualifying/Matching week to check that average earnings were at, or above, the Lower Earnings Limit (LEL) for National Insurance - £112 p.w. for 2016/17.

The rate for ASPP was not been increased for 5th April 2015 in line with ASPL being abolished at that date.

### Keeping in touch (KIT) days
Employees were entitled to take up to ten KIT days during additional paternity leave with no loss of ASPP, regardless of the length of leave taken, in order to come into work or to undertake training. This entitlement has also ended with the abolition of ASPP.

### Employment rights
During ordinary leave the employee is entitled to:
- the provision of all contractual non-cash benefits e.g. a company car, childcare vouchers
- protection from detriment for asserting the right to take leave
- return to the same job on the same terms and conditions at the end of leave
- to take up to four weeks parental leave at the end of the statutory leave period
- to more than one amount of OSPP if employed by two or more employers at the Qualifying/Matching Week
- having two or more jobs, may take leave from one whilst remaining at work in another, without jeopardising payment in the former provided they are employed by both at the Qualifying/Matching Week

### Administration of OSPP/ASPP
Like other statutory payments, ASPP was administered by the employer, was treated as earnings and is subject to PAYE income tax and NICs. Other lawful deductions applicable to pay may be applied to OSPP and ASPP but not any type of Attachment of Earnings Order (AEO). Small Employers' Relief (SER) is available to an employer who pays, or is liable to pay total employers and employees gross Class 1 NICs of the prescribed amount (threshold) or less, in the qualifying tax year.

Employers were permitted to align payment of OSPP/ASPP with their normal payment cycle to pay for weeks as they fall within monthly or weekly pay periods i.e. with odd days at the beginning or end of the pay period.

In order to enable this to take place calculations were made using daily rates. The legislation only permits the daily rate to be calculated by dividing the weekly rate by seven, so the daily rate option cannot be used where there is a payment of occupational paternity pay to be offset against the SPP and this is not calculated on a seven day basis. Legislation will continue to refer to weekly rates and the employer must ensure that only full weeks are paid where due even if these straddle two pay periods. The daily rate for SPP for 2020/21 is £21.60. No daily rate is necessary for ASPP since its abolition on 5th April 2015.

## Table of weekly Statutory Paternity Pay rates from 25th November 2002

| Paternity Pay Period | Earnings Threshold | Weekly Rate (the lower of) | | Employers Reclaim | Small Employers Relief | |
|---|---|---|---|---|---|---|
| | | Std. rate | Earnings | | Reclaim | Threshold |
| From | £ | £ | % | % | % | £ |
| 25.11.2002 | 75 | 75.00 | - | 92 | 104.5 | 40,000 |
| 06.04.2003 | 77 | 100.00 | 90 | 92 | 104.5 | 40,000 |
| 04.04.2004 | 79 | 102.80 | 90 | 92 | 104.5 | 45,000 |
| 03.04.2005 | 82 | 106.00 | 90 | 92 | 104.5 | 45,000 |
| 02.04.2006 | 84 | 108.85 | 90 | 92 | 104.5 | 45,000 |
| 01.04.2007 | 87 | 112.75 | 90 | 92 | 104.5 | 45,000 |
| 06.04.2008 | 90 | 117.18 | 90 | 92 | 104.5 | 45,000 |
| 05.04.2009 | 95 | 123.06 | 90 | 92 | 104.5 | 45,000 |
| 04.04.2010 | 97 | 124.88 | 90 | 92 | 104.5 | 45,000 |
| 03.04.2011 | 102 | 128.73 | 90 | 92 | 103 | 45,000 |
| 01.04.2012 | 107 | 135.45 | 90 | 92 | 103 | 45,000 |
| 07.04.2013 | 109 | 136.78 | 90 | 92 | 103 | 45,000 |
| 06.04.2014 | 111 | 138.18 | 90 | 92 | 103 | 45,000 |
| 05.04.2015 | 112 | 139.58 | 90 | 92 | 103 | 45,000 |
| 03.04.2016 | 112 | 139.58 | 90 | 92 | 103 | 45,000 |
| 02.04.2017 | 113 | 140.98 | 90 | 92 | 103 | 45,000 |
| 01.04.2018 | 116 | 145.18 | 90 | 92 | 103 | 45,000 |
| 07.04.2019 | 118 | 148.68 | 90 | 92 | 103 | 45,000 |
| **05.04.2020** | **120** | **151.20** | **90** | **92** | **103** | **45,000** |

### Small Employers' Relief (SER) for Statutory Payments

To qualify for Small Employers' Relief (SER), the total gross employers' Class 1 NICs for the previous year must be less than the threshold shown. The qualifying year is the last complete tax year before the partner's Qualifying/Matching Week. Small Employers are entitled to recover 100% of their statutory payments, plus 3% as compensation for NICs paid, for all payments made from 6th April 2011 onwards (4.5% prior to 6th April 2011).

### Rates at the start of a tax year

The 2004/5 tax year saw a change to the way new rates 'kicked in' as a result of the new statutory payments regime that came into force in April 2003. There are now several scenarios where a statutory payment week can straddle the old and new tax years, this relates to:

- a week of Statutory Paternity Pay (for 'fathers' or adoptive partners)
- a week of Statutory Adoption Pay
- a week of SMP as a result of an early birth or pregnancy related illness

For 2017/2018, where any of these begins on, or after, 2nd April, the NEW rate is payable. Employers are required to manage the split week.

### Self-certification

The declaration of family commitment and mother's entitlement is to be taken at face value once the SC3/SC4 or SC7/SC8 is received. The original forms must be retained as proof for reclaim and may be inspected by HMRC in the same way as a MAT B1. Where fraudulent claims are discovered by HMRC the employer will not be asked to repay SPP.

## Statutory Paternity Pay Forms

| SPP2 Statutory Paternity Pay Record Sheet | A form designed and supplied by HMRC on Basic PAYE Tools optionally available to assist small businesses in the operation of SMP |
|---|---|
| SPP1 exclusion form (ASPP1 applied to 4th April 2015 only) | Must be completed and sent to an employee if not entitled to OSPP or ASPP or entitlement ceases |
| SC3/SC4 | Self-certification forms used to apply for OSPP and leave |
| SC7/SC8/SC9 and SC10 to 4th April 2015 only | Self-certification forms used to apply for ASPP and leave |
| ASPP3 check sheet (to 4th April 2015 only) | Employer check sheet for Additional Statutory Paternity Pay and additional paternity leave |

## Advanced funding

Employers who have insufficient tax, NICs and student loan repayments to fund payment of SPP may make a request for advanced funding to HMRC. This is done via https://www.gov.uk/recover-statutory-payments on the gov.uk website.

## Penalties

For refusal or repeated failure to:

- pay SPP to an employee who has entitlement
- produce or keep required SPP and up to 4th April 2015 ASPP records (now superseded by the standard retention of records rules)
- A fine not exceeding £300 for SPP will be levied in respect of each offence. For failure to produce records, documents or to provide information the maximum penalty is £300. For fraud or negligence in respect of incorrect statements, records, documents and payments of SPP a further fine of up to £40 per day may be applied for continuance of the failure.

## Guidance

The HMRC E19 Helpbook for statutory paternity pay was abolished from 6th April 2013. Guidance can now be found at https://www.gov.uk/paternity-pay-leave . The table below indicates the appropriate dates for 2018/19.

### Statutory Paternity Pay and Leave Table 2020/21

| Week baby due | | Qualifying week | | Latest start date for employment (Birth) | Latest start date for employment (Adoption) |
|---|---|---|---|---|---|
| Sunday | Saturday | Sunday | Saturday | Saturday | Saturday |
| 29/03/2020 | 04/04/2020 | 15/12/2019 | 21/12/2019 | 29/06/2019 | 12/10/2019 |
| 05/04/2020 | 11/04/2020 | 22/12/2019 | 28/12/2019 | 06/07/2019 | 19/10/2019 |
| 12/04/2020 | 18/04/2020 | 29/12/2019 | 04/01/2020 | 13/07/2019 | 26/10/2019 |
| 19/04/2020 | 25/04/2020 | 05/01/2020 | 11/01/2020 | 20/07/2019 | 02/11/2019 |
| 26/04/2020 | 02/05/2020 | 12/01/2020 | 18/01/2020 | 27/07/2019 | 09/11/2019 |
| 03/05/2020 | 09/05/2020 | 19/01/2020 | 25/01/2020 | 03/08/2019 | 16/11/2019 |
| 10/05/2020 | 16/05/2020 | 26/01/2020 | 01/02/2020 | 10/08/2019 | 23/11/2019 |
| 17/05/2020 | 23/05/2020 | 02/02/2020 | 08/02/2020 | 17/08/2019 | 30/11/2019 |
| 24/05/2020 | 30/05/2020 | 09/02/2020 | 15/02/2020 | 24/08/2019 | 07/12/2019 |

PART 4: STATUTORY PAYMENTS

| | | | | | |
|---|---|---|---|---|---|
| 31/05/2020 | 06/06/2020 | 16/02/2020 | 22/02/2020 | 31/08/2019 | 14/12/2019 |
| 07/06/2020 | 13/06/2020 | 23/02/2020 | 29/02/2020 | 07/09/2019 | 21/12/2019 |
| 14/06/2020 | 20/06/2020 | 01/03/2020 | 07/03/2020 | 14/09/2019 | 28/12/2019 |
| 21/06/2020 | 27/06/2020 | 08/03/2020 | 14/03/2020 | 21/09/2019 | 04/01/2020 |
| 28/06/2020 | 04/07/2020 | 15/03/2020 | 21/03/2020 | 28/09/2019 | 11/01/2020 |
| 05/07/2020 | 11/07/2020 | 22/03/2020 | 29/03/2020 | 05/10/2019 | 18/01/2020 |
| 12/07/2020 | 18/07/2020 | 29/03/2020 | 04/04/2020 | 12/10/2019 | 25/01/2020 |
| 19/07/2020 | 25/07/2020 | 05/04/2020 | 11/04/2020 | 19/10/2019 | 01/02/2020 |
| 26/07/2020 | 01/08/2020 | 12/04/2020 | 18/04/2020 | 26/10/2019 | 08/02/2020 |
| 02/08/2020 | 08/08/2020 | 19/04/2020 | 25/04/2020 | 02/11/2019 | 15/02/2020 |
| 09/08/2020 | 15/08/2020 | 26/04/2020 | 02/05/2020 | 09/11/2019 | 22/02/2020 |
| 16/08/2020 | 22/08/2020 | 03/05/2020 | 09/05/2020 | 16/11/2019 | 29/02/2020 |
| 23/08/2020 | 29/08/2020 | 10/05/2020 | 16/05/2020 | 23/11/2019 | 07/03/2020 |
| 30/08/2020 | 05/09/2020 | 17/05/2020 | 23/05/2020 | 30/11/2019 | 14/03/2020 |
| 06/09/2020 | 12/09/2020 | 24/05/2020 | 30/05/2020 | 07/12/2019 | 21/03/2020 |
| 13/09/2020 | 19/09/2020 | 31/05/2020 | 06/06/2020 | 14/12/2019 | 28/03/2020 |
| 20/09/2020 | 26/09/2020 | 07/06/2020 | 13/06/2020 | 21/12/2019 | 04/04/2020 |
| 27/09/2020 | 03/10/2020 | 14/06/2020 | 20/06/2020 | 28/12/2019 | 11/04/2020 |
| 04/10/2020 | 10/10/2020 | 21/06/2020 | 27/06/2020 | 04/01/2020 | 18/04/2020 |
| 11/10/2020 | 17/10/2020 | 28/06/2020 | 04/07/2020 | 11/01/2020 | 25/04/2020 |
| 18/10/2020 | 24/10/2020 | 05/07/2020 | 11/07/2020 | 18/01/2020 | 02/05/2020 |
| 25/10/2020 | 31/10/2020 | 12/07/2020 | 18/07/2020 | 25/01/2020 | 09/05/2020 |
| 01/11/2020 | 07/11/2020 | 19/07/2020 | 25/07/2020 | 01/02/2020 | 16/05/2020 |
| 08/11/2020 | 14/11/2020 | 26/07/2020 | 01/08/2020 | 08/02/2020 | 23/05/2020 |
| 15/11/2020 | 21/11/2020 | 02/08/2020 | 08/08/2020 | 15/02/2020 | 30/05/2020 |
| 22/11/2020 | 29/11/2020 | 09/08/2020 | 15/08/2020 | 22/02/2020 | 06/06/2020 |
| 29/11/2020 | 05/12/2020 | 16/08/2020 | 22/08/2020 | 29/02/2020 | 13/06/2020 |
| 06/12/2020 | 12/12/2020 | 23/08/2020 | 29/08/2020 | 07/03/2020 | 20/06/2020 |
| 13/12/2020 | 19/12/2020 | 30/08/2020 | 05/09/2020 | 14/03/2020 | 27/06/2020 |
| 20/12/2020 | 26/12/2020 | 06/09/2020 | 12/09/2020 | 21/03/2020 | 04/07/2020 |
| 27/12/2020 | 02/01/2021 | 13/09/2020 | 19/09/2020 | 28/03/2020 | 11/07/2020 |

| | | | | | |
|---|---|---|---|---|---|
| 03/01/2021 | 09/01/2021 | 20/09/2020 | 26/09/2020 | 04/04/2020 | 18/07/2020 |
| 10/01/2021 | 16/01/2021 | 27/09/2020 | 03/10/2020 | 11/04/2020 | 25/07/2020 |
| 17/01/2021 | 23/01/2021 | 04/10/2020 | 10/10/2020 | 18/04/2020 | 01/08/2020 |
| 24/01/2021 | 30/01/2021 | 11/10/2020 | 17/10/2020 | 25/04/2020 | 08/08/2020 |
| 31/01/2021 | 06/02/2021 | 18/10/2020 | 24/10/2020 | 02/05/2020 | 15/08/2020 |
| 07/02/2021 | 13/02/2021 | 25/10/2020 | 31/10/2020 | 09/05/2020 | 22/08/2020 |
| 14/02/2021 | 20/02/2021 | 01/11/2020 | 07/11/2020 | 16/05/2020 | 29/08/2020 |
| 21/02/2021 | 27/02/2021 | 08/11/2020 | 14/11/2020 | 23/05/2020 | 05/09/2020 |
| 28/02/2021 | 06/03/2021 | 15/11/2020 | 21/11/2020 | 30/05/2020 | 12/09/2020 |
| 07/03/2021 | 13/03/2021 | 22/11/2020 | 28/11/2020 | 06/06/2020 | 19/09/2020 |
| 14/03/2021 | 20/03/2021 | 29/11/2020 | 05/12/2020 | 13/06/2020 | 26/09/2020 |
| 21/03/2021 | 27/03/2021 | 06/12/2020 | 12/12/2020 | 20/06/2020 | 03/10/2020 |
| 28/03/2021 | 03/04/2021 | 13/12/2020 | 19/12/2020 | 27/06/2020 | 10/10/2020 |
| 04/04/2021 | 10/04/2021 | 20/12/2020 | 26/12/2020 | 04/07/2020 | 17/10/2020 |
| 11/04/2021 | 17/04/2021 | 27/12/2020 | 02/01/2021 | 11/07/2020 | 24/10/2020 |
| 18/04/2021 | 24/04/2021 | 03/01/2021 | 09/01/2021 | 18/07/2020 | 31/10/2020 |
| 25/04/2021 | 01/05/2021 | 10/01/2021 | 16/01/2021 | 25/07/2020 | 07/11/2020 |
| 02/05/2021 | 08/05/2021 | 17/01/2021 | 23/01/2021 | 01/08/2020 | 14/11/2020 |
| 09/05/2021 | 15/05/2021 | 24/01/2021 | 30/01/2021 | 08/08/2020 | 21/11/2020 |
| 16/05/2021 | 22/05/2021 | 31/01/2021 | 06/02/2021 | 15/08/2020 | 28/11/2020 |

## REDUNDANCY - PAYMENT IN LIEU OF NOTICE (PILON)

A payment in lieu of notice (PILON) is due where an employer terminates the employee's contract without giving due notice as required by either the contract or the employee's statutory minimum rights. The employee becomes entitled to receive a payment in lieu of that which would have been due had the full period of notice been served.

PILON can be compensation for breach of the contractual right to notice. If the contract or any other company documentation is silent on the option to make a payment in lieu of notice then such payments may not be subject to NICs or tax but see http://www.hmrc.gov.uk/manuals/eimanual/EIM12977.htm for HMRC's latest position on PILONs and CWG2 'Employer Further Guide to PAYE & NICs'.

Where the option of a PILON is, or is deemed to be a contractual entitlement then the payment will attract income tax and NIC liability. (See also - Termination Payments in Part 2). Contractual entitlement may be established by either:
- reference to written conditions of employment, or other documentation or
- the employer's custom and practice in previous terminations.

From 6th April 2018 all PILON payments are treated as earnings for income tax and NICs irrespective of the circumstances. This ends all speculation concerning contractual and non-contractual treatment.

Employers are required to work out the Post Employment Notice Payment (PENP) using a formula laid down by HMRC. Any PENP is subject to income tax and NICs in the normal manner and any sum outside this can be covered by the £30,000 exemption.

## REDUNDANCY - STATUTORY PAYMENTS

Statutory Redundancy Pay was introduced in 1965 and is a lump sum payment payable when an employee's job is lost as a result of redundancy. The legislative source is now the Employment Rights Act 1996.

In general, a Statutory Redundancy Payment is due when an employee is dismissed (rather than having resigned) due to redundancy. For redundancy to exist, whether compulsory or voluntary, a job must disappear. This may be as a result of an employer closing down, a reduction in the workforce or a decision to reduce 'or remove entirely' particular employees (but note that a redundancy does not exist where an employee is directly replaced). Where employees have elected to retire in the context of projected redundancies, this might be construed as resignation or termination by mutual consent. In these circumstances the employee may not be entitled to receive redundancy pay (Court of Appeal, Birch and Humber v University of Liverpool (1985)). There are also limited but specific employment exclusions e.g. share fishermen, merchant seamen, and employees of the Crown.

### Qualification
The current provisions are based on the amendments to the scheme made from 1st October 2006 to accommodate the Age Equality Regulations.

Employees are entitled to statutory redundancy pay if they have been working in Great Britain and have completed at least two years' service. There is no lower age limit (age 18 prior to 1st October 2006). There is no upper age limit (prior to April 1994 the maximum age of entitlement for women was 60 and prior to 1st October 2006 the upper age limit for entitlement was 65, with entitlement tapering off after age 64).

### Service
Calculation of entitlement is directly related to the employee's period of continuous service with that employer, (reckonable service). Length of service is counted backwards from the "relevant date". In cases where the employer gives less notice than the employee is entitled, the "relevant date" is the date at the end of the employee's proper notice entitlement.

Absences caused by adoption, pregnancy, paternity leave, sickness or temporary shortage of work will generally count towards continuous service. Periods lost through industrial disputes do not count (but they do not break continuous service).

### Calculating Redundancy Pay
The number of years' service is calculated in whole (completed) years and entitlement is calculated for each completed year within age groupings

| | |
|---|---|
| age 17 to 22 | ½ week's pay |
| age 22 to 41 | 1 week's pay |
| age 41 upwards | 1½ week's pay. |

Statutory Redundancy Pay is not subject to tax deduction provided that when added to any contractual redundancy or other termination payments the whole amount does not exceed £30,000. It is paid free of employee NICs regardless of the total amount.

From 6th April 2019 employers NICs are due on all redundancy amounts above the threshold of £30,000.

### A Week's Pay
- Redundancy Pay is based on the rate of pay that is in force under an employee's terms and conditions at the 'relevant date'. The 'relevant' or 'calculation date' is usually the date on which minimum notice is required by law. In cases where no notice is given, the calculation date is the last day of employment. Pay awards agreed but not applied will count at the re-graded rate; pay awards pending but not agreed will not count. The rate of pay will include all contractual payments, but overtime earnings are not usually included unless overtime is guaranteed so is contractual.
- Where earnings change from week to week as a result of piecework or a productivity bonus, a week's pay is determined by multiplying the number of hours normally worked in a week by the average hourly earnings over the 12 weeks prior to the 'calculation date'.

- If normal working hours vary due to shift arrangements, and earnings vary, the average hourly earnings are multiplied by the average weekly hours over the 12 weeks prior to the 'calculation date'.
- If there are no fixed working hours, a week's pay is the average weekly earnings for the 12 weeks prior to the 'calculation date'
- There is a limit on the week's pay that is taken into account. The limit is reviewed annually - normally in February but a one off increase was applied in October 2009.

### "Week's Pay" statutory maximum for redundancy calculations from 1990/1991

| Year * | £ | Date from * | £ |
|---|---|---|---|
| 1990/1991 | 184 | 01.02.2006 | 290 |
| 1991/1992 | 198 | 01.02.2007 | 310 |
| 1992/1993 | 205 | 01.02.2008 | 330 |
| 1993/1994 | 205 | 01.02.2009 | 350 |
| 1994/1995 | 205 | 01.02.2010 | 380 |
| 1995/1996 | 210 | 01.10.2011 | 400 |
| 1996/1997 | 210 | 01.02.2012 | 430 |
| 1997/1998 | 210 | 01.02.2013 | 450 |
| 1998/1999 | 220 | 01.02.2014 | 464 |
| 1999/2000 | 220 | 06.04.2015 | 475 |
| 2000/2001 | 230 | 06.04.2016 | 479 |
| 2001/2002 | 240 | 06.04.2017 | 489 |
| 01.02.2002 | 250 | 06.04.2018 | 508 |
| 01.02.2003 | 260 | 06.04.2019 | 525 |
| 01.02.2004 | 270 | **06.04.2020** | **538** |
| 01.02.2005 | 280 | | |

* With effect from 1st February 2002, then 1st February annually, from 6th April 2014 it will be from 6th April.

## REDUNDANCY READY RECKONER

The following table gives the number of weeks' redundancy pay up to the statutory maximum in accordance with the employee's age and years of completed service.

### Redundancy ready reckoner in force to 30th September 2006

| Age yrs | 2 | 3 | 4 | 5 | 6 | 7 | 8 | 9 | 10 | 11 | 12 | 13 | 14 | 15 | 16 | 17 | 18 | 19 | 20 |
|---|---|---|---|---|---|---|---|---|---|---|---|---|---|---|---|---|---|---|---|
| 20 | 1 | 1 | 1 | 1 | | | | | | | | | | | | | | | |
| 21 | 1 | 1½ | 1½ | 1½ | 1½ | | | | | | | | | | | | | | |
| 22 | 1 | 1½ | 2 | 2 | 2 | 2 | | | | | | | | | | | | | |
| 23 | 1½ | 2 | 2½ | 3 | 3 | 3 | 3 | | | | | | | | | | | | |
| 24 | 2 | 2½ | 3 | 3½ | 4 | 4 | 4 | 4 | | | | | | | | | | | |
| 25 | 2 | 3 | 3½ | 4 | 4½ | 5 | 5 | 5 | 5 | | | | | | | | | | |
| 26 | 2 | 3 | 4 | 4½ | 5 | 5½ | 6 | 6 | 6 | 6 | | | | | | | | | |
| 27 | 2 | 3 | 4 | 5 | 5½ | 6 | 6½ | 7 | 7 | 7 | 7 | | | | | | | | |
| 28 | 2 | 3 | 4 | 5 | 6 | 6½ | 7 | 7½ | 8 | 8 | 8 | 8 | | | | | | | |
| 29 | 2 | 3 | 4 | 5 | 6 | 7 | 7½ | 8 | 8½ | 9 | 9 | 9 | 9 | | | | | | |
| 30 | 2 | 3 | 4 | 5 | 6 | 7 | 8 | 8½ | 9 | 9½ | 10 | 10 | 10 | 10 | | | | | |
| 31 | 2 | 3 | 4 | 5 | 6 | 7 | 8 | 9 | 9½ | 10 | 10½ | 11 | 11 | 11 | 11 | | | | |
| 32 | 2 | 3 | 4 | 5 | 6 | 7 | 8 | 9 | 10 | 10½ | 11 | 11½ | 12 | 12 | 12 | 12 | | | |
| 33 | 2 | 3 | 4 | 5 | 6 | 7 | 8 | 9 | 10 | 11 | 11½ | 12 | 12½ | 13 | 13 | 13 | 13 | | |
| 34 | 2 | 3 | 4 | 5 | 6 | 7 | 8 | 9 | 10 | 11 | 12 | 12½ | 13 | 13½ | 14 | 14 | 14 | 14 | |
| 35 | 2 | 3 | 4 | 5 | 6 | 7 | 8 | 9 | 10 | 11 | 12 | 13 | 13½ | 14 | 14½ | 15 | 15 | 15 | 15 |
| 36 | 2 | 3 | 4 | 5 | 6 | 7 | 8 | 9 | 10 | 11 | 12 | 13 | 14 | 14½ | 15 | 15½ | 16 | 16 | 16 |
| 37 | 2 | 3 | 4 | 5 | 6 | 7 | 8 | 9 | 10 | 11 | 12 | 13 | 14 | 15 | 15½ | 16 | 16½ | 17 | 17 |
| 38 | 2 | 3 | 4 | 5 | 6 | 7 | 8 | 9 | 10 | 11 | 12 | 13 | 14 | 15 | 16 | 16½ | 17 | 17½ | 18 |
| 39 | 2 | 3 | 4 | 5 | 6 | 7 | 8 | 9 | 10 | 11 | 12 | 13 | 14 | 15 | 16 | 17 | 17½ | 18 | 18½ |
| 40 | 2 | 3 | 4 | 5 | 6 | 7 | 8 | 9 | 10 | 11 | 12 | 13 | 14 | 15 | 16 | 17 | 18 | 18½ | 19 |
| 41 | 2 | 3 | 4 | 5 | 6 | 7 | 8 | 9 | 10 | 11 | 12 | 13 | 14 | 15 | 16 | 17 | 18 | 19 | 19½ |
| 42 | 2½ | 3½ | 4½ | 5½ | 6½ | 7½ | 8½ | 9½ | 10½ | 11½ | 12½ | 13½ | 14½ | 15½ | 16½ | 17½ | 18½ | 19½ | 20½ |
| 43 | 3 | 4 | 5 | 6 | 7 | 8 | 9 | 10 | 11 | 12 | 13 | 14 | 15 | 16 | 17 | 18 | 19 | 20 | 21 |
| 44 | 3 | 4½ | 5½ | 6½ | 7½ | 8½ | 9½ | 10½ | 11½ | 12½ | 13½ | 14½ | 15½ | 16½ | 17½ | 18½ | 19½ | 20½ | 21½ |
| 45 | 3 | 4½ | 6 | 7 | 8 | 9 | 10 | 11 | 12 | 13 | 14 | 15 | 16 | 17 | 18 | 19 | 20 | 21 | 22 |
| 46 | 3 | 4½ | 6 | 7½ | 8½ | 9½ | 10½ | 11½ | 12½ | 13½ | 14½ | 15½ | 16½ | 17½ | 18½ | 19½ | 20½ | 21½ | 22½ |
| 47 | 3 | 4½ | 6 | 7½ | 9 | 10 | 11 | 12 | 13 | 14 | 15 | 16 | 17 | 18 | 19 | 20 | 21 | 22 | 23 |
| 48 | 3 | 4½ | 6 | 7½ | 9 | 10½ | 11½ | 12½ | 13½ | 14½ | 15½ | 16½ | 17½ | 18½ | 19½ | 20½ | 21½ | 22½ | 23½ |
| 49 | 3 | 4½ | 6 | 7½ | 9 | 10½ | 12 | 13 | 14 | 15 | 16 | 17 | 18 | 19 | 20 | 21 | 22 | 23 | 24 |
| 50 | 3 | 4½ | 6 | 7½ | 9 | 10½ | 12 | 13½ | 14½ | 15½ | 16½ | 17½ | 18½ | 19½ | 20½ | 21½ | 22½ | 23½ | 24½ |
| 51 | 3 | 4½ | 6 | 7½ | 9 | 10½ | 12 | 13½ | 15 | 16 | 17 | 18 | 19 | 20 | 21 | 22 | 23 | 24 | 25 |
| 52 | 3 | 4½ | 6 | 7½ | 9 | 10½ | 12 | 13½ | 15 | 16½ | 17½ | 18½ | 19½ | 20½ | 21½ | 22½ | 23½ | 24½ | 25½ |
| 53 | 3 | 4½ | 6 | 7½ | 9 | 10½ | 12 | 13½ | 15 | 16½ | 18 | 19 | 20 | 21 | 22 | 23 | 24 | 25 | 26 |
| 54 | 3 | 4½ | 6 | 7½ | 9 | 10½ | 12 | 13½ | 15 | 16½ | 18 | 19½ | 20½ | 21½ | 22½ | 23½ | 24½ | 25½ | 26½ |
| 55 | 3 | 4½ | 6 | 7½ | 9 | 10½ | 12 | 13½ | 15 | 16½ | 18 | 19½ | 21 | 22 | 23 | 24 | 25 | 26 | 27 |
| 56 | 3 | 4½ | 6 | 7½ | 9 | 10½ | 12 | 13½ | 15 | 16½ | 18 | 19½ | 21 | 22½ | 23½ | 24½ | 25½ | 26½ | 27½ |
| 57 | 3 | 4½ | 6 | 7½ | 9 | 10½ | 12 | 13½ | 15 | 16½ | 18 | 19½ | 21 | 22½ | 24 | 25 | 26 | 27 | 28 |
| 58 | 3 | 4½ | 6 | 7½ | 9 | 10½ | 12 | 13½ | 15 | 16½ | 18 | 19½ | 21 | 22½ | 24 | 25½ | 26½ | 27½ | 28½ |
| 59 | 3 | 4½ | 6 | 7½ | 9 | 10½ | 12 | 13½ | 15 | 16½ | 18 | 19½ | 21 | 22½ | 24 | 25½ | 27 | 28 | 29 |
| 60 | 3 | 4½ | 6 | 7½ | 9 | 10½ | 12 | 13½ | 15 | 16½ | 18 | 19½ | 21 | 22½ | 24 | 25½ | 27 | 28½ | 29½ |
| 61 | 3 | 4½ | 6 | 7½ | 9 | 10½ | 12 | 13½ | 15 | 16½ | 18 | 19½ | 21 | 22½ | 24 | 25½ | 27 | 28½ | 30 |
| 62 | 3 | 4½ | 6 | 7½ | 9 | 10½ | 12 | 13½ | 15 | 16½ | 18 | 19½ | 21 | 22½ | 24 | 25½ | 27 | 28½ | 30 |
| 63 | 3 | 4½ | 6 | 7½ | 9 | 10½ | 12 | 13½ | 15 | 16½ | 18 | 19½ | 21 | 22½ | 24 | 25½ | 27 | 28½ | 30 |
| 64 | 3 | 4½ | 6 | 7½ | 9 | 10½ | 12 | 13½ | 15 | 16½ | 18 | 19½ | 21 | 22½ | 24 | 25½ | 27 | 28½ | 30 |

## Redundancy ready reckoner in force from 1st October 2006

The table was amended with the introduction of the Employment Equality (Age) Regulations in October 2006

| Age Yrs | Service (years) 2 | 3 | 4 | 5 | 6 | 7 | 8 | 9 | 10 | 11 | 12 | 13 | 14 | 15 | 16 | 17 | 18 | 18 | 20 |
|---|---|---|---|---|---|---|---|---|---|---|---|---|---|---|---|---|---|---|---|
| 17 | 1 | | | | | | | | | | | | | | | | | | |
| 18 | 1 | 1½ | | | | | | | | | | | | | | | | | |
| 19 | 1 | 1½ | 2 | | | | | | | | | | | | | | | | |
| 20 | 1 | 1½ | 2 | 2½ | | | | | | | | | | | | | | | |
| 21 | 1 | 1½ | 2 | 2½ | 3 | | | | | | | | | | | | | | |
| 22 | 1 | 1½ | 2 | 2½ | 3 | 3½ | | | | | | | | | | | | | |
| 23 | 1½ | 2 | 2½ | 3 | 3½ | 4 | 4½ | | | | | | | | | | | | |
| 24 | 2 | 2½ | 3 | 3½ | 4 | 4½ | 5 | 5½ | | | | | | | | | | | |
| 25 | 2 | 3 | 3½ | 4 | 4½ | 5 | 5½ | 6 | 6½ | | | | | | | | | | |
| 26 | 2 | 3 | 4 | 4½ | 5 | 5½ | 6 | 6½ | 7 | 7½ | | | | | | | | | |
| 27 | 2 | 3 | 4 | 5 | 5½ | 6 | 6½ | 7 | 7½ | 8 | 8½ | | | | | | | | |
| 28 | 2 | 3 | 4 | 5 | 6 | 6½ | 7 | 7½ | 8 | 8½ | 9 | 9½ | | | | | | | |
| 29 | 2 | 3 | 4 | 5 | 6 | 7 | 7½ | 8 | 8½ | 9 | 9½ | 10 | 10½ | | | | | | |
| 30 | 2 | 3 | 4 | 5 | 6 | 7 | 8 | 8½ | 9 | 9½ | 10 | 10½ | 11 | 11½ | | | | | |
| 31 | 2 | 3 | 4 | 5 | 6 | 7 | 8 | 9 | 9½ | 10 | 10½ | 11 | 11½ | 12 | 12½ | | | | |
| 32 | 2 | 3 | 4 | 5 | 6 | 7 | 8 | 9 | 10 | 10½ | 11 | 11½ | 12 | 12½ | 13 | 13½ | | | |
| 33 | 2 | 3 | 4 | 5 | 6 | 7 | 8 | 9 | 10 | 11 | 11½ | 12 | 12½ | 13 | 13½ | 14 | 14½ | | |
| 34 | 2 | 3 | 4 | 5 | 6 | 7 | 8 | 9 | 20 | 11 | 12 | 12½ | 13 | 13½ | 14 | 14½ | 15 | 15½ | |
| 35 | 2 | 3 | 4 | 5 | 6 | 7 | 8 | 9 | 10 | 11 | 12 | 13 | 13½ | 14 | 14½ | 15 | 15½ | 16 | 16½ |
| 36 | 2 | 3 | 4 | 5 | 6 | 7 | 8 | 9 | 10 | 11 | 12 | 13 | 14 | 14½ | 15 | 15½ | 16 | 16½ | 17 |
| 37 | 2 | 3 | 4 | 5 | 6 | 7 | 8 | 9 | 10 | 11 | 12 | 13 | 14 | 15 | 15½ | 16 | 16½ | 17 | 17½ |
| 38 | 2 | 3 | 4 | 5 | 6 | 7 | 8 | 9 | 10 | 11 | 12 | 13 | 14 | 15 | 16 | 16½ | 17 | 17½ | 18 |
| 39 | 2 | 3 | 4 | 5 | 6 | 7 | 8 | 9 | 10 | 11 | 12 | 13 | 14 | 15 | 16 | 17 | 17½ | 18 | 18½ |
| 40 | 2 | 3 | 4 | 5 | 6 | 7 | 8 | 9 | 10 | 11 | 12 | 13 | 14 | 15 | 16 | 17 | 18 | 18½ | 19 |
| 41 | 2 | 3 | 4 | 5 | 6 | 7 | 8 | 9 | 10 | 11 | 12 | 13 | 14 | 15 | 16 | 17 | 18 | 19 | 19½ |
| 42 | 2½ | 3½ | 4½ | 5½ | 6½ | 7½ | 8½ | 9½ | 10½ | 11½ | 12½ | 13½ | 14½ | 15½ | 16½ | 17½ | 18½ | 19½ | 20½ |
| 43 | 3 | 4 | 5 | 6 | 7 | 8 | 9 | 10 | 11 | 12 | 13 | 14 | 15 | 16 | 17 | 18 | 19 | 20 | 21 |
| 44 | 3 | 4½ | 5½ | 6½ | 7½ | 8½ | 9½ | 10½ | 11½ | 12½ | 13½ | 14½ | 15½ | 16½ | 17½ | 18½ | 19½ | 20½ | 21½ |
| 45 | 3 | 4½ | 6 | 7 | 8 | 9 | 10 | 11 | 12 | 13 | 14 | 15 | 16 | 17 | 18 | 19 | 20 | 21 | 22 |
| 46 | 3 | 4½ | 6 | 7½ | 8½ | 9½ | 10½ | 11½ | 12½ | 13½ | 14½ | 15½ | 16½ | 17½ | 18½ | 19½ | 20½ | 21½ | 22½ |
| 47 | 3 | 4½ | 6 | 7½ | 9 | 10 | 11 | 12 | 13 | 14 | 15 | 16 | 17 | 18 | 19 | 20 | 21 | 22 | 23 |
| 48 | 3 | 4½ | 6 | 7½ | 9 | 10½ | 11½ | 12½ | 13½ | 14½ | 15½ | 16½ | 17½ | 18½ | 19½ | 20½ | 21½ | 22½ | 23½ |
| 49 | 3 | 4½ | 6 | 7½ | 9 | 10½ | 12 | 13 | 14 | 15 | 16 | 17 | 18 | 19 | 20 | 21 | 22 | 23 | 24 |
| 50 | 3 | 4½ | 6 | 7½ | 9 | 10½ | 12 | 13½ | 14½ | 15½ | 16½ | 17½ | 18½ | 19½ | 20½ | 21½ | 22½ | 23½ | 24½ |
| 51 | 3 | 4½ | 6 | 7½ | 9 | 10½ | 12 | 13½ | 15 | 16 | 17 | 18 | 19 | 20 | 21 | 22 | 23 | 24 | 25 |
| 52 | 3 | 4½ | 6 | 7½ | 9 | 10½ | 12 | 13½ | 15 | 16½ | 17½ | 18½ | 19½ | 20½ | 21½ | 22½ | 23½ | 24½ | 25½ |
| 53 | 3 | 4½ | 6 | 7½ | 9 | 10½ | 12 | 13½ | 15 | 16½ | 18 | 19 | 20 | 21 | 22 | 23 | 24 | 25 | 26 |
| 54 | 3 | 4½ | 6 | 7½ | 9 | 10½ | 12 | 13½ | 15 | 16½ | 18 | 19½ | 20½ | 21½ | 22½ | 23½ | 24½ | 25½ | 26½ |
| 55 | 3 | 4½ | 6 | 7½ | 9 | 10½ | 12 | 13½ | 15 | 16½ | 18 | 19½ | 21 | 22 | 23 | 24 | 25 | 26 | 27 |
| 56 | 3 | 4½ | 6 | 7½ | 9 | 10½ | 12 | 13½ | 15 | 16½ | 18 | 19½ | 21 | 22½ | 23½ | 24½ | 25½ | 26½ | 27½ |
| 57 | 3 | 4½ | 6 | 7½ | 9 | 10½ | 12 | 13½ | 15 | 16½ | 18 | 19½ | 21 | 22½ | 24 | 25 | 26 | 27 | 28 |
| 58 | 3 | 4½ | 6 | 7½ | 9 | 10½ | 12 | 13½ | 15 | 16½ | 18 | 19½ | 21 | 22½ | 24 | 25½ | 26½ | 27½ | 28½ |
| 59 | 3 | 4½ | 6 | 7½ | 9 | 10½ | 12 | 13½ | 15 | 16½ | 18 | 19½ | 21 | 22½ | 24 | 25½ | 27 | 28 | 29 |
| 60 | 3 | 4½ | 6 | 7½ | 9 | 10½ | 12 | 13½ | 15 | 16½ | 18 | 19½ | 21 | 22½ | 24 | 25½ | 27 | 28½ | 29½ |
| 61 | 3 | 4½ | 6 | 7½ | 9 | 10½ | 12 | 13½ | 15 | 16½ | 18 | 19½ | 21 | 22½ | 24 | 25½ | 27 | 28½ | 30 |
| | 2 | 3 | 4 | 5 | 6 | 7 | 8 | 9 | 10 | 11 | 12 | 13 | 14 | 15 | 16 | 17 | 18 | 19 | 20 |

The table starts at age 17, as it is possible for a 17 year old to have 2 years' service. Compulsory school leaving age can be 153/4 or 154/5 where a child is 16 before 1st September. For all employees age 61 and over, payment remains the same as for age 61.

## STATUTORY LIMITS ON COMPENSATION PAYMENTS

Employment Protection Legislation makes provision to limit both minimum and maximum amounts of compensatory payments that may be awarded by Employment Tribunals, and other amounts paid under employment legislation provisions. The Secretary of State for Employment is required to update the limits as set out under the various Acts of Parliament on an annual basis.

Acts of Parliament applicable to compensatory payments are as follows:
* Employment Protection (Consolidation) Act 1978
* Trades Union & Labour Relations Act 1992
* Trades Union Reform & Employment Rights Act 1993 (TURERA)
* Employment Rights Act 1996 (ERA)

Minimum payments are to be applied to the following:
* basic compensation award for unfair dismissal
* awards to an individual excluded, or expelled, from a trade union

Maximum limits apply to the following payments:
* compensatory awards for unfair dismissal
* in respect of a debt to which part xii of the ERA 1996 applies and is referable to a period of time
* a week's pay to be used in the calculation of either a basic or additional award of compensation for unfair dismissal or redundancy payments

The annual cycle of increases is determined by the Consumer Prices Index (CPI).

### Limits on compensation payments

| Minimum Limits | | | | Trades Union |
|---|---|---|---|---|
| Date from | Unfair Dismissal Basic | Trade Union Exclusion | Unfair Dismissal 1996 Act | Activities Unlawful Inducement |
| | £ | £ | £ | £ |
| 01.02.2004 | 3,600 | 5,900 | 3,600 | |
| 01.02.2005 | 3,800 | 6,100 | 3,800 | 2,500 |
| 01.02.2006 | 4,000 | 6,300 | 4,000 | 2,600 |
| 01.02.2007 | 4,200 | 6,600 | 4,200 | 2,700 |
| 01.02.2008 | 4,400 | 6,900 | 4,400 | 2,900 |
| 01.02.2009 | 4,700 | 7,300 | 4,700 | 3,100 |
| 01.02.2010 | 4,700 | 7,300 | 4,700 | 3,100 |
| 01.02.2011 | 5,000 | 7,600 | 5,000 | 3,300 |
| 01.02.2012 | 5,300 | 8,100 | 5,300 | 3,500 |
| 01.02.2013 | 5,500 | 8,400 | 5,500 | 3,600 |
| 06.04.2014 | 5,676 | 8,669 | 5,676 | 3,715 |
| 06.05.2015 | 5,807 | 8,868 | 5,807 | 3,800 |
| 06.04.2016 | 5,853 | 8,939 | 5,853 | 3,830 |
| 06.04.2017 | 5,970 | 9,118 | 5,970 | 3,907 |
| 06.04.2018 | 6,203 | 9,474 | 6,203 | 4,059 |
| 06.04.2019 | 6,408 | 9,787 | 6,408 | 4,193 |
| **06.04.2020** | **6,562** | **10,022** | **6,562** | **4,294** |

**Maximum Limits**

| Date from | Daily Guarantee Payment £ | Unfair Dismissal (30 weeks) £ | Unfair Dismissal Compensatory Award £ | Weekly Debt Payment £ | A Weeks Pay £ |
|---|---|---|---|---|---|
| 01.02.2002 | 17.00 | 7,500 | 52,600 | 250 | 250 |
| 01.02.2003 | 17.30 | 7,800 | 53,500 | 260 | 260 |
| 01.02.2004 | 17.80 | 8,100 | 55,000 | 270 | 270 |
| 01.02.2005 | 18.40 | 8,400 | 56,800 | 280 | 280 |
| 01.02.2006 | 18.90 | 8,700 | 58,400 | 290 | 290 |
| 01.02.2007 | 19.60 | 9,300 | 60,600 | 310 | 310 |
| 01.02.2008 | 20.40 | 9,900 | 63,000 | 330 | 330 |
| 01.02.2009 | 21.50 | 10,500 | 66,200 | 350 | 350 |
| 01.02.2010 | 21.20 | 11,400 | 65,300 | 380 | 380* |
| 01.02.2011 | 22.20 | 12,000 | 68,400 | 400 | 400 |
| 01.02.2012 | 23.50 | 12,900 | 73,200 | 430 | 430 |
| 01.02.2013 | 24.20 | 13,500 | from 29.7.13 the lower of £74,200 and 52 times the claimant's weekly pay | 450 | 450 |
| 06.04.2014 | 25.00 | 13,900 | The lower of £76,574 and 52 times the claimant's weekly pay | 464 | 464 |
| 06.04.2015 | 26.00 | 14,250 | The lower of £78,335 and 52 times the claimant's weekly pay | 475 | 475 |
| 06.04.2016 | 26.00 | 14,370 | The lower of £78,962 and 52 times the claimant's weekly pay | 479 | 479 |
| 06.04.2017 | 27.00 | 14,670 | The lower of £80,541 and 52 times the claimant's weekly pay | 489 | 489 |
| 06.04.2018 | 28.00 | 15,240 | The lower of £83,862 and 52 times the claimant's weekly pay | 508 | 508 |
| 06.04.2019 | 29.00 | 15,750 | The lower of £86,444 and 52 times the claimant's weekly pay | 525 | 525 |
| 06.04.2020 | 30.00 | 16,140 | The lower of £88,519 and 52 times the claimant's weekly pay | 538 | 538 |

*uplifted as a one off increase from 1st October 2009 and unchanged in February 2010

## STATUTORY SICK PAY (SSP)

Introduced in 1983 when the administration and payment of State Sickness Benefit was transferred from the then Department of Health and Social Security to employers. In the process payment moved from a means-tested benefit to a flat rate allowance. Initially paid for a maximum period of eight weeks, it was extended to 28 weeks from 6th April 1986. Statutory Sick Pay is a minimum sick pay entitlement for all employees whose earnings attract, or would attract, Class 1 National Insurance Contributions.

## Qualification

To qualify for SSP an employee must:

- be incapable of work for a period of at least four or more consecutive calendar days. Such a period is called a Period of Incapacity for Work (PIW). All days of incapacity count towards these days including weekends, holidays and any other day on which the employee would not normally be expected to work. If the employee performs any work on a day this cannot be counted as a day of incapacity for work so SSP is not payable
- in the 8-week period up to and including the last pay day before the PIW, have Average Weekly Earnings (AWE) not less than the Lower Earnings Limit (LEL) for NICs which is £116 p.w. for 2018/19.

## Disqualification

Employees do not qualify where on the first day of the Period of Incapacity for Work (PIW):

- their PIW links with a recent claim for state sickness benefit (either Incapacity Benefit or Employment and Support Allowance) in such cases a linking letter ESA220, ESA220A, ESA220B or ESA220C will have been received by the employee and allow the employer not to pay SSP until the date shown on the letter, and for the employee to revert back to the higher rate of Employment and Support Allowance (ESA) they were in receipt of previously. It is therefore advisable for employers to ask all new starters or those returning from sickness if they have a linking letter. If the letter has been mislaid the employee can request a copy from Jobcentre Plus
- they have received 28 weeks' SSP in a linked PIW. periods of SSP with a previous employer no longer count towards the maximum entitlement to SSP. Therefore employers are no longer required to take into account whether a new employee received SSP from a former employer if falling sick within the first 8 weeks of starting their new job. As a result the SSP1(L) form has been discontinued
- their Average Weekly Earnings (AWE) are below the Lower Earnings Limit (LEL) of £116 p.w. for 2018/19
- a female employee is within the disqualifying period related to her pregnancy. There is a 39 week period during which SMP or Maternity allowance is payable when SSP is not paid, unless the woman is not entitled to either SMP or Maternity Allowance (MA) in such cases the disqualification period is 18 week.
- they are away from work because of a trade dispute
- they are in legal custody (at any time on the first day of the PIW)
- they have not undertaken any work for the employer
- they are outside the European Economic Area and are not liable to pay Class 1 National Insurance Contributions, or would not be liable even if earnings were high enough.

Where the employee is not entitled to SSP, the employer must, provided the employee has been sick for four or more days in a row, i.e. have formed a PIW, complete a form SSP1 or approved equivalent, to enable the employee to claim Employment and Support Allowance.

The form SSP1 must be supplied to the employee no later than:

- seven days after notification that the employee's sickness would last at least four days, or
- the first pay day in the tax month following the one in which the reason for issuing the form SSP1 arose (where payroll arrangements are such that it is impractical to issue it within seven days).

NHS Trust employees who:

- previously worked under a single contract for a Health Authority at more than one Hospital, and
- as a direct result of the transfer of their employment to separate Trusts, subsequently have two or more separate contracts of employment may elect to have the contracts treated as one for the purpose of determining SSP entitlement.

The amount of information required in part C of the SSP1 was reduced from 27th October 2008 following the introduction of Employment and Support Allowance (ESA) - see section below. An employer is no longer required to either keep records of, or supply information about, the first day of sickness, qualifying days, days normally worked nor days and length of time SSP has been paid. A version of the form for use specifically for employees based in Northern Ireland can be obtained from https://www.nidirect.gov.uk/publications/statutory-sick-pay-and-employees-claim-benefit-ssp1 .

## Earlier disqualification rules

Employees who were outside the European Economic Area on the first day of a PIW starting prior to 6th April 1996 were not entitled to SSP. Employees with a contract of service for a specified period of three months or less, with separate contracts with the same employer separated by 56 days or less if added together, were disqualified prior to 1st October 2002.

Prior to the 1st October 2006 entitlement was restricted to those aged 16 or over and under 65 (as a limitation of the definition of an employed earner). However, where an employee became 65 during a PIW, entitlement to SSP continued until the end of that PIW. With the adoption of the Employment Equality (Age) Regulations 2006, age limits were removed.

### Agency workers and SSP
Following a ruling against HMRC in the Thorn Baker case the government amended the Fixed Term Employees (Prevention of less favourable treatment) Regulations 2002 from 27th October 2008 such that agency workers on short term contracts of less than 13 weeks now have an entitlement to SSP.

### Entitlement
SSP is payable at a standard rate when Average Weekly Earnings in the eight weeks prior to the start of the PIW (see below) are equal to or above the Lower Earnings Limit (LEL) of £120 p.w. for 2020/21 (£118 for 2019/2020), subject to the other qualifying conditions being met. The rate of SSP normally changes each year on the 6th April, see table below for current and past rates.

### Notification
The employee is required to notify the employer that they are sick. Notification is the starting point for entitlement. For this purpose notification in writing must be treated as made on the day posted.

The employer cannot insist that the employee notifies sickness:
- in person
- earlier than the first qualifying day in a spell of sickness
- more frequently than once a week during the period of sickness
- on a special form
- on a medical certificate
- If the employee fails to follow the notification process SSP can be denied.

### Linking Periods of Incapacity for Work (PIWs)
Any two PIWs separated by eight weeks (56 days) or less are treated as one

### Waiting Days
SSP is not payable for the first three qualifying days in a PIW, which are known as 'waiting' days. The only days for which SSP can be paid or count as waiting days are Qualifying Days. They are usually those days on which employees are required, by contract, to be available for work. Other periods may be used subject to agreement between the employer and employees. For example, all 7 days of the week or a 5-day standard working week. Where no qualifying day is specified HMRC will deem it to be a Wednesday.

Note: As an emergency measure, in response to the COVID-19 virus the Prime Minister, in an announcement on 4th March 2020, the three waiting days before SSP can be paid will be waived for anyone absent from work as a result of self-isolating in accordance with medical guidance. At the time of writing the government and the NHS has pledged to bring forward a temporary "fit-note" to provide some measure of evidence to support the claim for self-isolation.

### Interaction with Paternity and Adoption Pay
From 6th April 2003 when Statutory Adoption Pay and Statutory Paternity Pay were introduced, an employee in receipt of SSP must be 'fit for work' before either of these payments commence. OSPP, ShPP and SAP is not payable for any week in which SSP is due.

### Calculation of Average Weekly Earnings
Average Weekly Earnings are assessed during the 'relevant period', which for weekly paid employees is normally the eight week period up to and including the last pay day before the start of the PIW. To establish the average, earnings in the relevant eight-week period are added together and divided by eight.

Where the employee is normally paid monthly, the gross earnings in the relevant period (normally two months pay) are divided by total by the number of months covered by the payments. The result is multiplied by 12 and divided by 52.

Where the 'relevant period, is less than eight weeks (e.g. a new starter), the employee's normal weekly earnings should be averaged over the period in respect of which they have actually been paid.

Where employment is part-time, earnings should be calculated on a pro-rata basis (e.g. employee contracted to work two days a week, works for and receives two weeks and one day's pay before commencement of sickness, the earnings represent 2½ week's earnings). This amends previous guidance and was introduced with retrospective effect from 6th April 1999.

## End of entitlement
This usually occurs because the incapacity for work ends and the employee returns to work (or a Fit note (see part 1) has expired). In addition, the employer does not have to pay SSP for any day after the:
- employee's contract of service ends
- employee has received 28 weeks SSP in a PIW
- employee's linked PIW has run for three years
- employee's disqualifying period related to pregnancy begins
- employee is taken into legal custody
- employee goes outside the EEA and there is no liability for Class 1 NICs
- employee dies

*N.B. each time an employee begins a new PIW that does not link with an earlier PIW the maximum liability for SSP is 28 times the weekly rate. The linking period for a PIW is 56 days (see 'Linking' above).*

In March 2017 the government announced it wanted to consult on flexible SSP arrangements, to be managed by employers, as part of flexible fitness to work proposals.

Consultation is on-going but the intention is still to implement a more flexible application of SSP at some point in the near future.

## Leaver's statements
A form SSP1(L), leaver's statement, was issued at the request of the employee and, where SSP was payable for at least one week in the eight weeks before the termination of employment. It was withdrawn from 27th October 2008.

## Opting-out of SSP
Employers can choose to opt-out of SSP as long as their contractual pay is equal to, or more than, SSP. This can be done without applying to HMRC and the opt-out can apply to some or all employees, but sufficient records must still be available to issue an SSP1 if required and to prove SSP compliance to HMRC.

## Guidance
HMRC's E14 Employer helpbook for Statutory Sick Pay was abolished on 6th April 2013. Guidance can now be found at https://www.gov.uk/statutory-sick-pay .

## Records
It is a statutory requirement that a record is maintained of dates of sickness lasting at least four calendar days in a row (PIWs) reported by employees, and of all payments of SSP made during a PIW.

## Recovery of SSP
SSP may be only recovered under the Percentage Threshold Scheme (PTS) until 5th April 2014 when the scheme was abolished. In order to recover SSP an employer must:
- establish the total (employee's and employer's) gross Class 1 NIC liability for the tax month and deduct any contracted-out NI rebate, 'across all PAYE records'
- multiply by 13%, rounding down fractions of a penny
- establish the total SSP payments in that month.

Where the amount at (c) is more than the amount at (b) the difference may be recovered from the monthly PAYE remittance and is shown on the Employer Payment Summary (EPS). Recoveries for SSP paid up until 5th April 2014 and paid after that date are made via an SP32 Form https://www.gov.uk/government/publications/statutory-payments-and-national-insurance-contributions-late-claim-sp32 or on a 2013/14 EPS.

The Chancellor in his 2020 budget pledged to reimburse the 14 days SSP to employers where it has been paid out for self-isolation. This measure will only be available to employers with up to 250 employees.

## Statutory Sick Pay Forms

| SC2 | Self-certification form optionally for use by employees |
|---|---|
| SSP1 | notification of exclusion from SSP. A form SSP1 (amended 27th October 2008 see above) must be completed by an employer and given to an employee who is sick and is either not entitled to Statutory Sick Pay, or entitlement to SSP has ended |
| SSP1(L) | Withdrawn from 27th October 2008, previously Issued on request to employees who had received SSP in the eight weeks prior to terminating their employment. In earlier years the issue of this form was mandatory. |
| SSP2 | A form available for small employers to assist in the recording and operation of SSP |
| Linking letters ESA220A, ESA220B, and ESA220C | Supplied to people who have recently claimed Employment and Support Allowance (ESA) |

## Penalties

For refusal or repeated failure to:
- pay SSP to an employee who has entitlement
- produce or keep required SSP records.
- 

A fine not exceeding £3000 will be levied in respect of each offence. For failure to produce records, documents or to provide information the maximum penalty is £300. For fraud or negligence in respect of incorrect statements, records, documents and payments of SSP a further fine of up to £40 per day may be applied for continuance of the failure. In addition, using false documents to recover SSP under the PTS (see below), a fine not exceeding £5000 or a term of imprisonment not exceeding three months, or both

## Percentage Threshold Scheme (PTS)

From 6th April 1995 – 5th April 2014 compensation was available to all employers where the SSP paid in a tax month exceeded 13% of the total NIC liability for that month. Only the excess was reclaimable by deduction from the Class 1 NICs payable. The recovery was abolished on 6th April 2014 and the savings transferred to the new "Fit for Work" service.

## Statutory Sick Pay - week's payable, rebates & compensation from 1983/1984

| Year | Week's Payable | Rebate % | Comp'n % | Notes |
|---|---|---|---|---|
| 1983/1984 | 8 | 100 | Zero | |
| 1984/1985 | 8 | 100 | Zero | |
| 1985/1986 | 8 | 100 | 9 | Compensation added |
| 1986/1987 | 28 | 100 | 9 | |
| 1987/1988 | 28 | 100 | 7 | |
| 1988/1989 | 28 | 100 | 7 | |
| 1989/1990 | 28 | 100 | 7.5 | |
| 1990/1991 | 28 | 100 | 7 | |
| 1991/1992 | 28 | 80 | Zero | Compensation removed |
| 1992/1993 | 28 | 80 | Zero | |
| 1993/1994 | 28 | 80 | Zero | |
| 1994/1995 onwards | 28 | Zero | Zero | 100% cost to employers |

### SSP - table of weekly earnings bandings and rates payable from 1983/1984

| Year | Earnings | | SSP lower rate | Earnings | | SSP middle rate | Earnings | SSP higher rate |
|------|------|----|------|------|----|------|------|------|
| | from | To | | From | To | | from | |
| | £ | £ | £ | £ | £ | £ | £ | £ |
| 1983/1984 | 32.50 | 48.49 | 27.50 | 48.50 | 64.99 | 33.75 | 65.00 | 40.25 |
| 1984/1985 | 34.00 | 50.49 | 28.55 | 50.50 | 67.99 | 35.45 | 68.00 | 42.25 |
| 1985/1986 | 35.50 | 52.99 | 30.00 | 53.00 | 70.99 | 37.20 | 71.00 | 44.35 |
| 1986/1987 | 38.00 | 55.49 | 31.60 | 55.50 | 74.49 | 39.20 | 74.50 | 46.75 |

### SSP - table of weekly earnings bandings and rates payable from 1987/1988 to 1994/1995

| Year | Earnings from | to | SSP Rate | Earnings over | SSP Rate |
|------|------|----|------|------|------|
| | £ | £ | £ | £ | £ |
| 1987/1988 | 39.00 | 76.49 | 32.85 | 76.50 | 47.20 |
| 1988/1989 | 41.00 | 79.49 | 34.25 | 79.50 | 49.20 |
| 1989/1990 | 43.00 | 83.99 | 36.25 | 84.00 | 52.10 |
| 1990/1991 | 46.00 | 114.99 | 39.25 | 115.00 | 52.50 |
| 1991/1992 | 52.00 | 184.99 | 43.50 | 185.00 | 52.50 |
| 1992/1993 | 54.00 | 189.99 | 45.30 | 190.00 | 52.00 |
| 1993/1994 | 56.00 | 194.99 | 46.95 | 195.00 | 52.50 |
| 1994/1995 | 57.00 | 199.99 | 47.80 | 200.00 | 52.50 |

### SSP - table of weekly earnings bandings and rates payable from 1996/1997

| Year | Earnings From | SSP rate | Year | Earnings from | SSP Rate |
|------|------|------|------|------|------|
| | £ | £ | | £ | £ |
| 1996/1997 | 61.00 | 54.55 | 2009/2010 | 95.00 | 79.15 |
| 1997/1998 | 62.00 | 55.70 | 2010/2011 | 97.00 | 79.15 |
| 1998/1999 | 64.00 | 57.70 | 2011/2012 | 102.00 | 81.60 |
| 1999/2000 | 66.00 | 59.55 | 2012/2013 | 107.00 | 85.85 |
| 2000/2001 | 67.00 | 60.20 | 2013/2014 | 109.00 | 86.70 |
| 2001/2002 | 72.00 | 62.20 | 2014/2015 | 111.00 | 87.55 |
| 2002/2003 | 75.00 | 63.25 | 2015/2016 | 112.00 | 88.45 |
| 2003/2004 | 77.00 | 64.35 | 2016/2017 | 112.00 | 88.45 |
| 2004/2005 | 79.00 | 66.15 | 2017/2018 | 113.00 | 89.35 |
| 2005/2006 | 82.00 | 68.20 | 2018/2019 | 116.00 | 92.05 |
| 2006/2007 | 84.00 | 70.05 | 2019/2020 | 118.00 | 94.25 |
| 2007/2008 | 87.00 | 72.55 | **2020/2021** | **120.00** | **95.85** |
| 2008/2009 | 90.00 | 75.40 | | | |

**Statutory Sick Pay daily rates table 2020/21 effective 6th April 2020**

| Unrounded daily rates* | No. of QDs in week | Number of days to pay | | | | | | |
|---|---|---|---|---|---|---|---|---|
| | | 1 | 2 | 3 | 4 | 5 | 6 | 7 |
| £ 13.6928 | 7 | £ 13.70 | £ 27.39 | £ 41.80 | £ 54.78 | £ 68.47 | £ 82.16 | £ 95.85 |
| £ 15.9750 | 6 | £ 15.98 | £ 31.95 | £ 47.93 | £ 63.90 | £ 79.88 | £ 95.85 | |
| £ 19.1700 | 5 | £ 19.17 | £ 38.34 | £ 57.51 | £ 76.68 | £ 95.85 | | |
| £ 23.9625 | 4 | £ 23.97 | £ 47.93 | £ 71.89 | £ 95.85 | | | |
| £ 31.9500 | 3 | £ 31.95 | £ 63.90 | £ 95.85 | | | | |
| £ 47.9250 | 2 | £ 47.93 | £ 95.85 | | | | | |
| £ 95.8500 | 1 | £ 95.85 | | | | | | |

* Unrounded daily rates are shown for employers with computerised payroll systems.

## Advanced funding

Until 5th April 2014 employers who had insufficient tax, NICs and student loan repayments to fund payment of SSP could make a request for advanced funding to HMRC. This facility is no longer available.

### Tables for linking Periods of Incapacity for Work (PIWs) for SSP

#### 2020/21

| April 2020 | | May 2020 | | June 2020 | | July 2020 | |
|---|---|---|---|---|---|---|---|
| First Day of PIW | Previous PIW links if on or after | First Day of PIW | Previous PIW links if on or after | First Day of PIW | Previous PIW links if on or after | First Day of PIW | Previous PIW links if on or after |
| 6 | 09/02/2020 | 1 | 05/03/2020 | 1 | 05/04/2020 | 1 | 05/05/2020 |
| 7 | 10/02/2020 | 2 | 06/03/2020 | 2 | 06/04/2020 | 2 | 06/05/2020 |
| 8 | 11/02/2020 | 3 | 07/03/2020 | 3 | 07/04/2020 | 3 | 07/05/2020 |
| 9 | 12/02/2020 | 4 | 08/03/2020 | 4 | 08/04/2020 | 4 | 08/05/2020 |
| 10 | 13/02/2020 | 5 | 09/03/2020 | 5 | 09/04/2020 | 5 | 09/05/2020 |
| 11 | 14/02/2020 | 6 | 10/03/2020 | 6 | 10/04/2020 | 6 | 10/05/2020 |
| 12 | 15/02/2020 | 7 | 11/03/2020 | 7 | 11/04/2020 | 7 | 11/05/2020 |
| 13 | 16/02/2020 | 8 | 12/03/2020 | 8 | 12/04/2020 | 8 | 12/05/2020 |
| 14 | 17/02/2020 | 9 | 13/03/2020 | 9 | 13/04/2020 | 9 | 13/05/2020 |
| 15 | 18/02/2020 | 10 | 14/03/2020 | 10 | 14/04/2020 | 10 | 14/05/2020 |
| 16 | 19/02/2020 | 11 | 15/03/2020 | 11 | 15/04/2020 | 11 | 15/05/2020 |
| 17 | 20/02/2020 | 12 | 16/03/2020 | 12 | 16/04/2020 | 12 | 16/05/2020 |
| 18 | 21/02/2020 | 13 | 17/03/2020 | 13 | 17/04/2020 | 13 | 17/05/2020 |
| 19 | 22/02/2020 | 14 | 18/03/2020 | 14 | 18/04/2020 | 14 | 18/05/2020 |
| 20 | 23/02/2020 | 15 | 19/03/2020 | 15 | 19/04/2020 | 15 | 19/05/2020 |
| 21 | 24/02/2020 | 16 | 20/03/2020 | 16 | 20/04/2020 | 16 | 20/05/2020 |
| 22 | 25/02/2020 | 17 | 21/03/2020 | 17 | 21/04/2020 | 17 | 21/05/2020 |
| 23 | 26/02/2020 | 18 | 22/03/2020 | 18 | 22/04/2020 | 18 | 22/05/2020 |
| 24 | 27/02/2020 | 19 | 23/03/2020 | 19 | 23/04/2020 | 19 | 23/05/2020 |
| 25 | 28/02/2020 | 20 | 24/03/2020 | 20 | 24/04/2020 | 20 | 24/05/2020 |
| 26 | 29/02/2020 | 21 | 25/03/2020 | 21 | 25/04/2020 | 21 | 25/05/2020 |
| 27 | 01/03/2020 | 22 | 26/03/2020 | 22 | 26/04/2020 | 22 | 26/05/2020 |

| | | | | | | | |
|---|---|---|---|---|---|---|---|
| 28 | 02/03/2020 | 23 | 27/03/2020 | 23 | 27/04/2020 | 23 | 27/05/2020 |
| 29 | 03/03/2020 | 24 | 28/03/2020 | 24 | 28/04/2020 | 24 | 28/05/2020 |
| 30 | 04/03/2020 | 25 | 29/03/2020 | 25 | 29/04/2020 | 25 | 29/05/2020 |
| | | 26 | 30/03/2020 | 26 | 30/04/2020 | 26 | 30/05/2020 |
| | | 27 | 31/03/2020 | 27 | 01/05/2020 | 27 | 31/05/2020 |
| | | 28 | 01/04/2020 | 28 | 02/05/2020 | 28 | 01/06/2020 |
| | | 29 | 02/04/2020 | 29 | 03/05/2020 | 29 | 02/06/2020 |
| | | 30 | 03/04/2020 | 30 | 04/05/2020 | 30 | 03/06/2020 |
| | | 31 | 04/04/2020 | | | 31 | 04/06/2020 |

## Tables for linking Periods of Incapacity for Work (PIWs) for SSP

### 2020/21

| August 2020 | | September 2020 | | October 2020 | | November 2020 | |
|---|---|---|---|---|---|---|---|
| First Day of PIW | Previous PIW links if on or after | First Day of PIW | Previous PIW links if on or after | First Day of PIW | Previous PIW links if on or after | First Day of PIW | Previous PIW links if on or after |
| 1 | 05/06/2020 | 1 | 06/07/2020 | 1 | 05/08/2020 | 1 | 05/09/2020 |
| 2 | 06/06/2020 | 2 | 07/07/2020 | 2 | 06/08/2020 | 2 | 06/09/2020 |
| 3 | 07/06/2020 | 3 | 08/07/2020 | 3 | 07/08/2020 | 3 | 07/09/2020 |
| 4 | 08/06/2020 | 4 | 09/07/2020 | 4 | 08/08/2020 | 4 | 08/09/2020 |
| 5 | 09/06/2020 | 5 | 10/07/2020 | 5 | 09/08/2020 | 5 | 09/09/2020 |
| 6 | 10/06/2020 | 6 | 11/07/2020 | 6 | 10/08/2020 | 6 | 10/09/2020 |
| 7 | 11/06/2020 | 7 | 12/07/2020 | 7 | 11/08/2020 | 7 | 11/09/2020 |
| 8 | 12/06/2020 | 8 | 13/07/2020 | 8 | 12/08/2020 | 8 | 12/09/2020 |
| 9 | 13/06/2020 | 9 | 14/07/2020 | 9 | 13/08/2020 | 9 | 13/09/2020 |
| 10 | 14/06/2020 | 10 | 15/07/2020 | 10 | 14/08/2020 | 10 | 14/09/2020 |
| 11 | 15/06/2020 | 11 | 16/07/2020 | 11 | 15/08/2020 | 11 | 15/09/2020 |
| 12 | 16/06/2020 | 12 | 17/07/2020 | 12 | 16/08/2020 | 12 | 16/09/2020 |
| 13 | 17/06/2020 | 13 | 18/07/2020 | 13 | 17/08/2020 | 13 | 17/09/2020 |
| 14 | 18/06/2020 | 14 | 19/07/2020 | 14 | 18/08/2020 | 14 | 18/09/2020 |
| 15 | 19/06/2020 | 15 | 20/07/2020 | 15 | 19/08/2020 | 15 | 19/09/2020 |
| 16 | 20/06/2020 | 16 | 21/07/2020 | 16 | 20/08/2020 | 16 | 20/09/2020 |
| 17 | 21/06/2020 | 17 | 22/07/2020 | 17 | 21/08/2020 | 17 | 21/09/2020 |
| 18 | 22/06/2020 | 18 | 23/07/2020 | 18 | 22/08/2020 | 18 | 22/09/2020 |
| 19 | 23/06/2020 | 19 | 24/07/2020 | 19 | 23/08/2020 | 19 | 23/09/2020 |
| 20 | 24/06/2020 | 20 | 25/07/2020 | 20 | 24/08/2020 | 20 | 24/09/2020 |
| 21 | 25/06/2020 | 21 | 26/07/2020 | 21 | 25/08/2020 | 21 | 25/09/2020 |
| 22 | 26/06/2020 | 22 | 27/07/2020 | 22 | 26/08/2020 | 22 | 26/09/2020 |
| 23 | 27/06/2020 | 23 | 28/07/2020 | 23 | 27/08/2020 | 23 | 27/09/2020 |
| 24 | 28/06/2020 | 24 | 29/07/2020 | 24 | 28/08/2020 | 24 | 28/09/2020 |
| 25 | 29/06/2020 | 25 | 30/07/2020 | 25 | 29/08/2020 | 25 | 29/09/2020 |
| 26 | 30/06/2020 | 26 | 31/07/2020 | 26 | 30/08/2020 | 26 | 30/09/2020 |
| 27 | 01/07/2020 | 27 | 01/08/2020 | 27 | 31/08/2020 | 27 | 01/10/2020 |
| 28 | 02/07/2020 | 28 | 02/08/2020 | 28 | 01/09/2020 | 28 | 02/10/2020 |

| 29 | 03/07/2020 | 29 | 03/08/2020 | 29 | 02/09/2020 | 29 | 03/10/2020 |
| 30 | 04/07/2020 | 30 | 04/08/2020 | 30 | 03/09/2020 | 30 | 04/10/2020 |
| 31 | 05/07/2020 | | | 31 | 04/09/2020 | | |

## Tables for linking Periods of Incapacity for Work (PIWs) for SSP

### 2020/21

| December 2020 | | January 2021 | | February 2021 | | March/April 2021 | |
|---|---|---|---|---|---|---|---|
| First Day of PIW | Previous PIW links if on or after | First Day of PIW | Previous PIW links if on or after | First Day of PIW | Previous PIW links if on or after | First Day of PIW | Previous PIW links if on or after |
| 1 | 05/10/2020 | 1 | 05/11/2020 | 1 | 06/12/2020 | 1 | 03/01/2021 |
| 2 | 06/10/2020 | 2 | 06/11/2020 | 2 | 07/12/2020 | 2 | 04/01/2021 |
| 3 | 07/10/2020 | 3 | 07/11/2020 | 3 | 08/12/2020 | 3 | 05/01/2021 |
| 4 | 08/10/2020 | 4 | 08/11/2020 | 4 | 09/12/2020 | 4 | 06/01/2021 |
| 5 | 09/10/2020 | 5 | 09/11/2020 | 5 | 10/12/2020 | 5 | 07/01/2021 |
| 6 | 10/10/2020 | 6 | 10/11/2020 | 6 | 11/12/2020 | 6 | 08/01/2021 |
| 7 | 11/10/2020 | 7 | 11/11/2020 | 7 | 12/12/2020 | 7 | 09/01/2021 |
| 8 | 12/10/2020 | 8 | 12/11/2020 | 8 | 13/12/2020 | 8 | 10/01/2021 |
| 9 | 13/10/2020 | 9 | 13/11/2020 | 9 | 14/12/2020 | 9 | 11/01/2021 |
| 10 | 14/10/2020 | 10 | 14/11/2020 | 10 | 15/12/2020 | 10 | 12/01/2021 |
| 11 | 15/10/2020 | 11 | 15/11/2020 | 11 | 16/12/2020 | 11 | 13/01/2021 |
| 12 | 16/10/2020 | 12 | 16/11/2020 | 12 | 17/12/2020 | 12 | 14/01/2021 |
| 13 | 17/10/2020 | 13 | 17/11/2020 | 13 | 18/12/2020 | 13 | 15/01/2021 |
| 14 | 18/10/2020 | 14 | 18/11/2020 | 14 | 19/12/2020 | 14 | 16/01/2021 |
| 15 | 19/10/2020 | 15 | 19/11/2020 | 15 | 20/12/2020 | 15 | 17/01/2021 |
| 16 | 20/10/2020 | 16 | 20/11/2019 | 16 | 21/12/2020 | 16 | 18/01/2021 |
| 17 | 21/10/2020 | 17 | 21/11/2019 | 17 | 22/12/2020 | 17 | 19/01/2021 |
| 18 | 22/10/2020 | 18 | 22/11/2019 | 18 | 23/12/2020 | 18 | 20/01/2021 |
| 19 | 23/10/2020 | 19 | 23/11/2019 | 19 | 24/12/2020 | 19 | 21/01/2021 |
| 20 | 24/10/2020 | 20 | 24/11/2019 | 20 | 25/12/2020 | 20 | 22/01/2021 |
| 21 | 25/10/2020 | 21 | 25/11/2019 | 21 | 26/12/2020 | 21 | 23/01/2021 |
| 22 | 26/10/2020 | 22 | 26/11/2019 | 22 | 27/12/2020 | 22 | 24/01/2021 |
| 23 | 27/10/2020 | 23 | 27/11/2019 | 23 | 28/12/2020 | 23 | 25/01/2021 |
| 24 | 28/10/2020 | 24 | 28/11/2019 | 24 | 29/12/2020 | 24 | 26/01/2021 |
| 25 | 29/10/2020 | 25 | 29/11/2019 | 25 | 30/12/2020 | 25 | 27/01/2021 |
| 26 | 30/10/2020 | 26 | 30/11/2020 | 26 | 31/12/2020 | 26 | 28/01/2021 |
| 27 | 31/10/2020 | 27 | 01/12/2020 | 27 | 01/01/2021 | 27 | 29/01/2021 |
| 28 | 01/11/2020 | 28 | 02/12/2020 | 28 | 02/01/2021 | 28 | 30/01/2021 |
| 29 | 02/11/2020 | 29 | 03/12/2020 | | | 29 | 31/01/2021 |
| 30 | 03/11/2020 | 30 | 04/12/2020 | | | 30 | 01/02/2021 |
| 31 | 04/11/2020 | 31 | 05/12/2020 | | | 31 | 02/02/2021 |
| | | | | | | 1 | 03/02/2021 |
| | | | | | | 2 | 04/02/2021 |
| | | | | | | 3 | 05/02/2021 |
| | | | | | | 4 | 06/02/2021 |
| | | | | | | 5 | 07/02/2021 |

## MEDICAL ABBREVIATIONS

(Commonly used on Fit Notes)

| | |
|---|---|
| BP^ | hypertension |
| CAT | coronary artery thrombosis |
| CHD | coronary heart disease |
| COAD | chronic obstructive airways disease |
| COPD | chronic obstructive pulmonary disease |
| CVA | cerebrovascular accident |
| D&C | dilation and curettage |
| DS | disseminated (multiple) sclerosis |
| DU | duodenal ulcer |
| DVT | deep vein thrombosis |
| D&V | diarrhoea and vomiting |
| FB | foreign body |
| GU | gastric ulcer |
| IDK(J) | internal derangement of the knee (joint) |
| IHD | ischaemic heart disease |
| LIH | left inguinal hernia |
| LVF | left ventricular failure |
| MI | myocardial infarction |
| MS | multiple sclerosis |
| NAD | no abnormality detected |
| NYD | not yet diagnosed |
| OA | osteoarthritis |
| PE | pulmonary embolism |
| PID | prolapsed intervertebral disc |
| PUO | pyrexia of unknown origin |
| RIH | right inguinal hernia |
| RSI | repetitive strain injury |
| SOB | shortness of breath |
| TIA | transient ischaemic attack |
| URTI | upper respiratory tract infection |
| UTI | urinary tract infection |
| VVs | varicose veins |

# STATUTORY PAYMENTS – STATE BENEFITS

## BEREAVEMENT ALLOWANCE

Formerly part of Widow's Benefit, a means-tested, non-contributory and non-taxable benefit, extended from 9th April 2001 to both men and women. Payable to a spouse under pension age when widowed.

There are three benefits:

- a tax-free lump sum bereavement payment
- a parent's allowance for those with children under 16 (or under 19 if in     full-time, sixth form education). Part of this allowance will be ignored in calculating claims for certain other benefits, and
- a flat-rate bereavement allowance payable for 12 months, for those aged 45 or over without dependent children

Claims should be made within 3 months of the date of death, using form BB1.

*N.B. For deaths occurring before 11th April 1988 the Bereavement Allowance was age-related and was payable on a sliding scale.*

### Bereavement Allowance from 7th April 2003

| Date from | Bereavement Payment Lump sum | Widowed Parent's Allowance | Bereavement Allowance Full rate | Bereavement support payment* Standard Lump sum | Monthly | Higher Lump sum | Monthly |
|---|---|---|---|---|---|---|---|
| | £ | £ | £ | £ | £ | £ | £ |
| 07.04.2003 | 2,000 | 77.45 | 77.45 | | | | |
| 12.04.2004 | 2,000 | 79.60 | 79.60 | | | | |
| 11.04.2005 | 2,000 | 82.05 | 82.05 | | | | |
| 10.04.2006 | 2,000 | 84.25 | 84.25 | | | | |
| 09.04.2007 | 2,000 | 87.30 | 87.30 | | | | |
| 07.04.2008 | 2,000 | 90.70 | 90.70 | | | | |
| 06.04.2009 | 2,000 | 95.25 | 95.25 | | | | |
| 12.04.2010 | 2,000 | 97.65 | 97.65 | | | | |
| 11.04.2011 | 2,000 | 100.70 | 100.70 | | | | |
| 09.04.2012 | 2,000 | 105.95 | 105.95 | | | | |
| 08.04.2013 | 2,000 | 108.30 | 108.30 | | | | |
| 07.04.2014 | 2,000 | 111.20 | 111.20 | | | | |
| 06.04.2015 | 2,000 | 112.55 | 112.55 | | | | |
| 06.04.2016 | 2,000 | 112.55 | 112.55 | | | | |
| 06.04.2017 | 2,000 | 113.70 | 113.70 | | | | |
| 06.04.2018 | 2,500.00 | 117.10 | 117.10 | 2,500.00 | 100.00 | 3,500.00 | 350.00 |
| 06.04.2019 | 2,500.00 | 119.90 | 119.90 | 2,500.00 | 100.00 | 3,500.00 | 350.00 |
| **06.04.2020** | **2,500.00** | **121.95** | **121.95** | **2,500.00** | **100.00** | **3,500.00** | **350.00** |

*For deaths occurring on or after 6th April 2017

## CHILD BENEFIT and GUARDIANS' ALLOWANCE

Child Benefit is a non-contributory, non-taxable and non means-tested benefit, which replaced Family Allowance from 5th April 1977 bringing all children into the scheme.

It is normally payable for children:

- up to the age of 16 years.
- aged under 19 and studying full-time up to A level, AVCE or equivalent.
- aged 16 or 17 who have left school recently and has registered for work or training with the Careers or Connexions Service (in Northern Ireland the Training and Employment Agency).

A higher rate for the eldest or only child, known as Child Benefit (Lone Parent) is payable to certain people who are bringing up children on their own. The rate incorporated the former One-Parent Benefit that was introduced in 1977 (replacing the Child Benefit increase paid from April 1976).

Guardians' Allowance was introduced on 5th July 1948. A non-contributory, non-taxable and non means-tested benefit. Payable in addition to Child Benefit to someone bringing up a child, or children, and whose parents have died.

*N.B. From April 1997, One-parent Benefit was incorporated into the main Lone Parent benefit. From 7th January 2013 the "High Earner Child Benefit Charge" was introduced. This is a tax charge of 1% for every £100 of income over £50,000 and becomes equal to child benefit for a single child when income reaches £60,000. Parents and carers are given the choice of either voluntarily giving up child benefit or paying the charge.*

### Child Benefit and Guardians' Allowance from 6th April 1998

| Date From | First Child £ | Other Children £ | Lone Parent £ | Guardians' Allowance £ |
|---|---|---|---|---|
| 06.04.1998 | 11.45 | 9.30 | 17.10 | 11.30 |
| 12.04.1999 | 14.40 | 9.60 | 17.10 | 11.35 |
| 10.04.2000 | 15.00 | 10.00 | 17.55 | 11.35 |
| 09.04.2001 | 15.50 | 10.35 | 17.55 | 11.35 |
| 08.04.2002 | 15.75 | 10.55 | 17.55 | 11.35 |
| 07.04.2003 | 16.05 | 10.75 | 17.55 | 11.55 |
| 12.04.2004 | 16.50 | 11.05 | 17.55 | 11.85 |
| 11.04.2005 | 17.00 | 11.40 | 17.55 | 12.20 |
| 10.04.2006 | 17.45 | 11.70 | 17.55 | 12.50 |
| 09.04.2007 | 18.10 | 12.20 | abolished | 12.95 |
| 07.04.2008 | 18.80 | 12.55 | | 13.45 |
| 05.01.2009 | 20.00 | 13.20 | | |
| 06.04.2009 | | | | 14.10 |
| 12.04.2010 | 20.30 | 13.40 | | 14.30 |
| 11.04.2011 | 20.30 | 13.40 | | 14.75 |
| 09.04.2012 | 20.30 | 13.40 | | 15.55 |
| 08.04.2013 | 20.30 | 13.40 | | 15.90 |
| 07.04.2014 | 20.50 | 13.55 | | 16.35 |
| 06.04.2015 | 20.70 | 13.67 | | 16.55 |
| 06.04.2016 | 20.70 | 13.70 | | 16.55 |
| 06.04.2017 | 20.70 | 13.70 | | 16.70 |
| 06.04.2018 | 20.70 | 13.70 | | 17.20 |
| 06.04.2019 | 20.70 | 13.70 | | 17.20 |
| **06.04.2020** | **21.05** | **13.95** | | **17.90** |

# DISABILITY LIVING ALLOWANCE (DLA)

Introduced on 6th April 1992 to replace extended Attendance Allowance and Mobility Allowance and gradually replaced by Personal Independence Payments from 8th April 2013, Disability Living Allowance was a non-contributory, non-taxable and non means-tested benefit available for people who became disabled before age 65. It comprised two parts:

- a care component for those who needed help with personal care
- a mobility component for those who needed help in getting about (not available for those under age 3 (age 5 pre 9th April 2001)).

Personal Independence Payment has two components:
- daily living
- mobility.

These are assessed on a points system based on how much the health condition or disability affects daily living or mobility. The condition/disability needs to have existed for three months at the point of claim and to be likely to exist for a further nine months. This time dependency does not apply to those with a terminal illness.

### Disability Living Allowance – Care and Mobility – From 6th April 1998

| Date from | Care Component | | | Mobility Component | |
|---|---|---|---|---|---|
| | Higher £ | Middle £ | Lower £ | Higher £ | Lower £ |
| 06.04.1998 | 51.30 | 34.10 | 13.60 | 35.85 | 13.60 |
| 12.04.1999 | 52.95 | 35.40 | 14.05 | 37.00 | 14.05 |
| 10.04.2000 | 53.55 | 35.80 | 14.20 | 37.40 | 14.20 |
| 08.04.2002 | 56.25 | 37.65 | 14.90 | 39.30 | 14.90 |
| 07.04.2003 | 57.20 | 38.30 | 15.15 | 39.95 | 15.15 |
| 12.04.2004 | 58.80 | 39.35 | 15.55 | 41.05 | 15.55 |
| 11.04.2005 | 60.60 | 40.55 | 16.05 | 42.30 | 16.05 |
| 10.04.2006 | 62.25 | 41.65 | 16.50 | 43.45 | 16.50 |
| 09.04.2007 | 64.50 | 43.15 | 17.10 | 45.00 | 17.10 |
| 07.04.2008 | 67.00 | 44.85 | 17.75 | 46.75 | 17.75 |
| 06.04.2009 | 70.35 | 47.10 | 18.65 | 49.10 | 18.65 |
| 12.04.2010 | 71.40 | 47.80 | 18.95 | 49.85 | 18.95 |
| 11.04.2011 | 73.60 | 49.30 | 19.55 | 51.40 | 19.55 |
| 09.04.2012 | 77.45 | 51.85 | 20.55 | 54.05 | 20.55 |
| 08.04.2013* | 79.15 | 53.00 | 21.00 | 55.25 | 21.00 |
| 07.04.2014 | 81.30 | 54.45 | 21.55 | 56.75 | 21.55 |
| 06.04.2015 | 82.30 | 55.10 | 21.80 | 57.45 | 21.80 |
| 06.04.2016 | 82.30 | 55.10 | 21.80 | 57.45 | 21.80 |
| 06.04.2017 | 83.10 | 55.65 | 22.00 | 58.00 | 22.00 |
| 06.04.2018 | 85.60 | 57.30 | 22.65 | 59.75 | 22.65 |
| 06.04.2019 | 87.65 | 58.70 | 23.20 | 61.20 | 23.20 |
| **06.04.2020** | **89.15** | **59.70** | **23.60** | **62.25** | **23.60** |

*between 8.4.13 and April 2015 transition to Personal Independence Payment

## DISABILITY WORKING ALLOWANCE

Introduced on 1st April 1992 and replaced on 5th October 1999 by Disabled Persons Tax Credit (see under part 1 Tax), the Disability Working Allowance was a non-contributory, non-taxable and non means-tested benefit for disabled people who were in low paid work. The claimant had to be aged 16 or over and work, on average, over 16 hours per week. In addition, they had to have a disability or illness which disadvantaged them in getting a job and:

- receive Disability Living Allowance, or Attendance Allowance, or Constant Attendance Allowance with either War Disablement Pension or Industrial Injuries Disablement Benefit, or a Monthly Supplement with War Disablement Pension; or
- have an invalid three wheeler vehicle from the DWP; or
- have been receiving, within the last 56, days short term Incapacity Benefit at the higher rate, long-term Incapacity Benefit, or Severe Disablement Allowance; or
- have been receiving, within the last 56 days, a disability or higher pensioner premium with Income Support, Housing Benefit or Council Tax Benefit.

Entitlement was dependant on the claimant's income, capital and family type. The first £3000 of capital was ignored. Between £3000 and £16000, benefit was reduced by £1 per week for each £250 or part over £3000. Capital over £16000 disqualified entitlement. In addition, certain other welfare benefits were available where savings were no more than £6000.

## EMPLOYMENT AND SUPPORT ALLOWANCE (ESA)

Introduced on 27th October 2008 for those incapable of work. ESA replaced Incapacity Benefit and Income Support by 2013. The scheme provides access to specially trained personal advisors, employment training and management support.

To qualify for the allowance the claimant must be:
- over age 16 and under State Pension Age, and
- unemployed, or
- self employed, or
- working for an employer but unable to get Statutory Sick Pay, or
- having received Statutory Sick Pay that has now stopped.

ESA is applied in two phases, an assessment and a main phase. It will not be paid for the first three days of the claim (waiting days) and will continue under the assessment phase whilst a decision regarding work capability is assessed (a Work Capability Assessment).

The main phase commences from week 14 where illness or disability limits ability to work.

Claimant allowances are categorised in three groupings:

**Assessment Phase** - payable for the first thirteen weeks of the claim period for those eligible, having sick notes and either having paid sufficient National Insurance Contributions or passing a means test similar to that previously used for claimants of Incapacity Benefit.

**The Work Capability Assessment** - comprises a physical and mental health test that is both more demanding and replaces the former Incapacity Benefit. Personal Capability Assessment. Exemptions from the tests may be permitted for terminally ill claimants, some pregnant women and those receiving chemotherapy.

**Work-Related Activity Phase** - payable after thirteen weeks (as an additional allowance), subject to the claimant progressing through the assessment stage.

To qualify claimants will have to attend work-focused interviews and submit an action plan detailing planned progress towards moving into work. Failure to do so will result in reduced benefit entitlement.

During this phase a personal advisor will help and advise with a claimant's:
- job goals
- skills, strengths and abilities
- steps towards finding suitable work, and
- ideas, problems and work related issues.

Refusal to attend either work-focused interviews or to participate fully in interviews may affect entitlement to the allowance.

Support Group - higher allowances available for the most severely disabled claimants who will not have to do anything in return for the increased benefits unlike those in the Work Related Activity Group.

### Employment and Support Allowance maxima from 27th October 2008

| Date from | Personal allowance – single person | | | | Main Phase supplement | |
|---|---|---|---|---|---|---|
| | Assessment Phase | | | | | |
| | Under 25 yrs | 25 yrs or over | lone parent Under 18 | 18 or over | work related activity | support |
| | £ | £ | £ | £ | £ | £ |
| 01.04.2009 | 50.95 | 64.30 | 50.95 | 64.30 | 25.50 | 30.85 |
| 12.04.2010 | 51.85 | 65.45 | 51.85 | 65.45 | 25.95 | 31.40 |
| 11.04.2011 | 53.45 | 67.50 | 53.45 | 67.50 | 26.75 | 32.35 |
| 09.04.2012 | 56.25 | 71.00 | 56.25 | 71.00 | 28.15 | 34.05 |
| 09.04.2013 | 56.80 | 71.70 | 56.80 | 71.70 | 28.45 | 34.80 |
| 07.04.2014 | 57.35 | 72.40 | 57.35 | 72.40 | 28.75 | 35.75 |
| 06.04.2015 | 57.90 | 73.10 | 57.90 | 73.10 | 29.05 | 36.20 |
| 06.04.2016 | 57.90 | 73.10 | 57.90 | 73.10 | 29.05 | 36.20 |
| 06.04.2017 | 57.90 | 73.10 | 57.90 | 73.10 | 29.05 | 36.55 |
| 06.04.2018 | 57.90 | 73.10 | 57.90 | 73.10 | 29.05 | 37.65 |
| **06.04.2019** | **57.90** | **73.10** | **57.90** | **73.10** | **29.05** | **38.55** |

| Date from | Personal allowance – couple | | | | one or both over 18 | Carer Premium |
|---|---|---|---|---|---|---|
| | both under 18 | | | | | |
| | assessment phase | | main phase | | | |
| | no child * | with child | no child ** | premium | | |
| | £ | £ | £ | £ | £ | £ |
| 01.04.2009 | 50.95 | 76.90 | 64.30 | 100.95 | 100.95 | 29.50 |
| 12.04.2010 | 51.85 | 78.30 | 65.45 | 102.75 | 102.75 | 30.05 |
| 11.04.2011 | 53.45 | 80.75 | 67.50 | 105.95 | 105.95 | 31.00 |
| 09.04.2012 | 56.25 | 84.95 | 71.00 | 111.45 | 111.45 | 32.60 |
| 09.04.2013 | 56.80 | 85.80 | 71.70 | 112.55 | 112.55 | 33.30 |
| 07.04.2014 | 57.35 | 86.65 | 72.40 | 113.70 | 113.70 | 34.20 |
| 06.04.2015 | 57.90 | 87.50 | 73.10 | 114.85 | 114.85 | 34.60 |
| 06.04.2016 | 57.90 | 87.50 | 73.10 | 114.85 | 114.85 | 34.60 |
| 06.04.2017 | 57.90 | 87.50 | 73.10 | 114.85 | 114.85 | 34.95 |
| 06.04.2018 | 57.90 | 87.50 | 73.10 | 114.85 | 114.85 | 36.00 |
| 06.04.2019 | 57.90 | 87.50 | 73.10 | 114.85 | 114.85 | 36.85 |
| **06.04.2020** | **58.90** | **89.00** | **74.35** | **116.80** | **116.80** | **37.50** |

| * | Rate payable where claimant under 25 and partner under 18 |
|---|---|
| ** | Rate payable where claimant 25 or over and partner under 18 |
| ** | Rate payable where claimant in main phase and partner under 18 |

| Component – Weekly Rates | | |
|---|---|---|
| Date from | Work-related Activity £ | Support Group £ |
| 01.04.2009 | 25.50 | 30.85 |
| 12.04.2010 | 25.95 | 31.40 |
| 11.04.2011 | 26.75 | 32.35 |
| 09.04.2012 | 28.15 | 34.05 |
| 09.04.2013 | 28.45 | 34.80 |
| 07.04.2014 | 28.75 | 35.75 |
| 06.04.2015 | 29.05 | 36.20 |
| 06.04.2016 | 29.05 | 36.20 |
| 06.04.2017 | 29.05 | 36.55 |
| 06.04.2018 | 29.05 | 37.65 |
| 06.04.2019 | 29.05 | 38.55 |
| **06.04.2020** | **29.55** | **39.20** |

### Employment and Support Allowance Earnings Thresholds from April 2009

| Date from | Carer Allowance £ | Permitted work earnings Higher £ | Permitted work earnings Lower £ | Maternity Allowance £ | Industrial Injury Unemployment supplement £ pa |
|---|---|---|---|---|---|
| 01.04.2009 | 95.00 | 92.00 | 20.00 | 41.35 | 4,784.00 |
| 12.04.2010 | 95.00 | 93.00 | 20.00 | 41.35 | 4,836.00 |
| 11.04.2011 | 100.00 | 95.00 | 20.00 | 42.65 | 4,940.00 |
| 09.04.2012 | 100.00 | 97.50 | 20.00 | 44.85 | 5,070.00 |
| 09.04.2013 | 100.00 | 99.50 | 20.00 | 45.85 | 5,174.00 |
| 07.04.2014 | 102.00 | 101.00 | 20.00 | 47.10 | 5,252.00 |
| 06.04.2015 | 110.00 | 104.00 | 20.00 | 47.65 | 5,408.00 |
| 06.04.2016 | 110.00 | 115.50 | 20.00 | 47.65 | 6,006.00 |
| 06.04.2017 | 116.00 | 120.00 | 20.00 | 48.15 | 6,240.00 |
| 06.04.2018 | 120.00 | 125.50 | 20.00 | 49.60 | 6,526.00 |
| 06.04.2019 | 123.00 | 131.50 | 20.00 | 50.80 | 6,838.00 |
| **06.04.2020** | **128.00** | **TBC** | **20.00** | **51.65** | **TBC** |

In addition, to the above allowances, a number of premium payments may apply for enhanced disability, severe disability, carer and pensioner cases.

Linking provision - there are set of linking letters supplied to claimants coming off ESA and returning to work that reduce an employer's requirement to pay SSP until the date shown on the form. ESA has a 12-week linking period which will be indicated by the provision of an ESA220, ESA220A or ESA220C. If an employee says that they have lost their linking letter they can ask Jobcentre plus to provide a copy so that you can reduce your liability to SSP. Always ask new employees who fall sick within their first two years at work or those returning to work after sickness if they have a linking letter.

# FAMILY CREDIT

Introduced on 1st April 1988 and replaced on 5th October 1999 by Working Family Tax Credits. Family Credit was a weekly, non-contributory, means-tested and tax-free benefit for people who were responsible for bringing up at least one child under the age of 16 (age 19 in full-time education up to A level or equivalent). The claimant had to be working for 16 hours or more a week.

Entitlement was dependent on the number and ages of the children, weekly net earnings, savings and other income.

The benefit was paid for a period of 26 weeks at a fixed rate irrespective of changes in circumstances.

## Family Credit rates from April 1996 to March 2000

| April | Adult Credit £ | 30 hour Credit £ | Applicable Amount £ | Child Credit age bandings | | | |
|---|---|---|---|---|---|---|---|
| | | | | Under 11 £ | 11 - 15 £ | 16 - 17 £ | 18 £ |
| 1996 | 46.45 | 10.30 | 75.20 | 11.75 | 19.45 | 24.15 | 33.80 |
| 1997 | 47.65 | 10.55 | 77.15 | 12.05 | 19.95 | 24.80 | 34.70 |
| 1998 | 48.80 | 10.80 | 79.00 | 12.35 | 20.45 | 25.40 | 35.55 |
| 1999 | 49.80 | 11.05 | 80.65 | 15.15 | 20.90 | 25.95 (Over 15) | |

Child credits were applicable from birth, and from September following the 11th and 16th birthdays.

In addition, to Family Credit, certain other benefits entitlements accrued:
- free NHS prescriptions, dental treatment and sight tests
- NHS vouchers to help towards the cost of glasses
- refund of travel costs to and from hospital for NHS treatment
- free NHS wigs and fabric supports
- dried milk for babies under a year old at reduced rates

# INCAPACITY BENEFIT (IB)

Introduced on 13th April 1995 and replaced in 2008, Incapacity Benefit replaced Sickness Benefit and Invalidity Benefit. It is a contributory, taxable and semi means-tested benefit, available to people assessed as being incapable of work. For the first 28 weeks of incapacity, people will be assessed on the 'own occupation' test. After 28 weeks of incapacity, or from the start of the claim for people who did not previously have a job, incapacity is based on an 'all work' test. There are certain exemptions from the 'all work' test.

## Short Term Incapacity from 12th April 1999

| Date from | Under Pension Age | | | Over Pension Age | | | Return To Work Credit |
|---|---|---|---|---|---|---|---|
| | Lower Rate £ | Higher Rate £ | Adult Dependent £ | Lower Rate £ | Higher Rate £ | Dependent Adult £ | £ |
| 12.04.1999 | 50.35 | 59.55 | 31.15 | 64.05 | 66.75 | 38.40 | |
| 10.04.2000 | 50.90 | 60.20 | 31.50 | 64.75 | 67.50 | 38.80 | |
| 09.04.2001 | 52.60 | 62.90 | 32.55 | 66.90 | 69.75 | 40.10 | |
| 08.04.2002 | 53.50 | 63.25 | 33.10 | 68.05 | 70.95 | 40.80 | |
| 07.04.2003 | 54.40 | 64.35 | 33.65 | 69.20 | 72.15 | 41.50 | |
| 12.04.2004 | 55.90 | 66.15 | 34.60 | 71.15 | 74.15 | 42.65 | 40.00 |
| 11.04.2005 | 57.65 | 68.20 | 35.65 | 73.35 | 76.45 | 43.95 | 40.00 |
| 10.04.2006 | 59.20 | 70.05 | 36.60 | 75.35 | 78.50 | 45.15 | 40.00 |

| | | | | | | | |
|---|---|---|---|---|---|---|---|
| 09.04.2007 | 61.35 | 72.55 | 37.90 | 78.05 | 81.35 | 46.80 | 40.00 |
| 07.04.2008 | 63.75 | 75.40 | 39.40 | 81.10 | 84.50 | 48.65 | 40.00 |
| 06.04.2009 | 67.75 | 80.15 | 41.35 | 86.20 | 89.80 | 51.10 | 40.00 |
| 12.04.2010 | 68.95 | 81.60 | 41.35 | 87.75 | 91.40 | 51.10 | 40.00 |
| 11.04.2011 | 71.10 | 84.15 | 42.65 | 90.45 | 94.25 | 52.70 | 40.00 |
| 09.04.2012 | 74.80 | 88.55 | 44.85 | 95.15 | 99.15 | 55.45 | 40.00 |
| 09.04.2013 | 76.45 | 90.50 | 45.85 | 97.25 | 101.35 | 56.65 | 40.00 |
| 07.04.2014 | 78.50 | 92.95 | 47.10 | 99.90 | 104.10 | 58.20 | |
| 06.04.2015 | 79.45 | 94.05 | 47.65 | 101.10 | 105.35 | 58.90 | |
| 06.04.2016 | 79.45 | 94.05 | 47.65 | 101.10 | 105.35 | 58.90 | |
| 06.04.2017 | 80.25 | 95.00 | 48.15 | 102.10 | 106.40 | 59.50 | |
| 06.04.2018 | 82.65 | 97.85 | 49.60 | 105.15 | 109.60 | 61.30 | |
| 06.04.2019 | 84.65 | 100.20 | 50.80 | 107.65 | 112.25 | 62.75 | |
| **06.04.2020** | **86.10** | **101.90** | **51.65** | **109.50** | **114.15** | **63.80** | |

## Long-term Incapacity from 6th April 1998

| Date from | Under Pension Age | | Age Addition | |
|---|---|---|---|---|
| | Standard | Dependant adult | Higher | Lower |
| | £ | £ | £ | £ |
| 06.04.1998 | 64.70 | 38.70 | 13.60 | 6.80 |
| 12.04.1999 | 66.75 | 39.95 | 14.05 | 7.05 |
| 10.04.2000 | 67.50 | 40.40 | 14.20 | 7.10 |
| 09.04.2001 | 69.75 | 41.75 | 14.65 | 7.35 |
| 08.04.2002 | 70.95 | 42.45 | 14.90 | 7.45 |
| 07.04.2003 | 72.15 | 43.15 | 15.15 | 7.60 |
| 12.04.2004 | 74.15 | 47.65 | 15.55 | 7.80 |
| 11.04.2005 | 76.45 | 49.15 | 16.05 | 8.05 |
| 10.04.2006 | 78.50 | 50.50 | 16.50 | 8.25 |
| 09.04.2007 | 81.35 | 52.30 | 17.10 | 8.55 |
| 07.04.2008 | 84.50 | 54.35 | 17.75 | 8.90 |
| 06.04.2009 | 89.80 | 57.05 | 15.65 | 6.55 |
| 12.04.2010 | 91.40 | 57.05 | 15.00 | 5.80 |
| 11.04.2011 | 94.25 | 58.80 | 13.80 | 5.60 |
| 09.04.2012 | 99.15 | 61.85 | 11.70 | 5.90 |
| 09.04.2013 | 101.35 | 63.20 | 10.70 | 6.00 |
| 07.04.2014 | 104.10 | 64.90 | 11.00 | 6.15 |
| 06.04.2015 | 105.35 | 65.70 | 11.15 | 6.20 |
| 06.04.2016 | 105.35 | 65.70 | 11.15 | 6.20 |
| 06.04.2017 | 106.40 | 66.35 | 11.25 | 6.25 |
| 06.04.2018 | 109.60 | 68.35 | 11.60 | 6.45 |
| 06.04.2019 | 112.25 | 70.00 | 11.90 | 6.60 |
| **06.04.2020** | **114.15** | **TBC** | **12.10** | **6.70** |

# INCOME SUPPORT

Introduced on 11th April 1988 as a non-contributory, taxable and means-tested benefit and replaced from October 1996 by Jobseeker's Allowance for unemployed people. It is now generally only available to pensioners, lone parents, disabled people and (from April 2004) 19 year olds completing an approved training course. Income Support is available to those who are:

- in Great Britain
- aged 16 or over
- not working 16 or more hours per week
- have less money coming in than the established minimum to live on.

### Rates of Jobseeker's Allowance from 7th April 1997

| Date from | Single Person | | 18 to 24 | 25 yrs or over | Lone Parent | | 18 yrs or over |
|---|---|---|---|---|---|---|---|
| | Under 25 rate | | | | Under 18 rate | | |
| | Usual | Higher | | | Usual | Higher | |
| | £ | £ | £ | £ | £ | £ | £ |
| 07.04.1997 | 29.60 | 38.90 | 38.90 | 49.15 | 29.60 | 38.90 | 49.15 |
| 06.04.1998 | 30.30 | 39.85 | 39.85 | 50.35 | 30.30 | 39.85 | 50.35 |
| 12.04.1999 | 30.95 | 40.70 | 40.70 | 51.40 | 30.95 | 40.70 | 51.40 |
| 10.04.2000 | 31.45 | 41.35 | 41.35 | 52.20 | 31.45 | 41.35 | 52.20 |
| 09.04.2001 | 31.95 | 42.00 | 42.00 | 53.05 | 31.95 | 42.00 | 53.05 |
| 08.04.2002 | 32.50 | 42.70 | 42.70 | 53.95 | 32.50 | 42.70 | 53.95 |
| 07.04.2003 | 32.90 | 43.25 | 43.25 | 54.65 | 32.90 | 43.25 | 54.65 |
| 12.04.2004 | 33.50 | 44.05 | 44.05 | 55.65 | 33.50 | 44.05 | 55.65 |
| 11.04.2005 | 33.85 | 44.50 | 44.50 | 56.20 | 33.85 | 44.50 | 56.20 |
| 10.04.2006 | 34.60 | 45.50 | 45.50 | 57.45 | 34.60 | 45.50 | 57.45 |
| 09.04.2007 | 35.65 | 46.85 | 46.85 | 59.15 | 35.65 | 46.85 | 59.15 |
| 07.04.2008 | 47.95 | 47.95 | 60.50 | 47.95 | 60.50 | | |
| 06.04.2009 | 50.95 | | 50.95 | 64.30 | 50.95 | | 64.30 |
| | Under 25 | | | | | | |
| 12.04.2010 | 51.85 | | | 65.45 | 51.85 | | 65.45 |
| 11.04.2011 | 53.45 | | | 67.50 | 53.45 | | 67.50 |
| 09.04.2012 | 56.25 | | | 71.00 | 56.25 | | 71.00 |
| 09.04.2013 | 56.80 | | | 71.70 | 56.80 | | 71.70 |
| 07.04.2014 | 57.35 | | | 72.40 | 57.35 | | 72.40 |
| 06.04.2015 | 57.90 | | | 73.10 | 57.90 | | 73.10 |
| 06.04.2016 | 57.90 | | | 73.10 | 57.90 | | 73.10 |
| 06.04.2017 | 57.90 | | | 73.10 | 57.90 | | 73.10 |
| 06.04.2018 | 57.90 | | | 73.10 | 57.90 | | 73.10 |
| 06.04.2019 | 57.90 | | | 73.10 | 57.90 | | 73.10 |
| **06.04.2020** | **58.90** | | | **74.35** | **58.90** | | **74.35** |

## Family, Lone Parent and Pensioner Premium

### From 8th April 1996

| Date from | Premium £ | Date from | Premium £ |
|---|---|---|---|
| 08.04.1996 | 5.20 | 06.04.2009 | 17.30 |
| 07.04.1997 | 15.75 | 12.04.2010 | 17.40 |
| 06.04.1998 | 15.75 | 11.04.2011 | 17.40 |
| 12.04.1999 | 15.75 | 09.04.2012 | 17.40 |
| 10.04.2000 | 15.90 | 09.04.2013 | 17.40 |
| 09.04.2001 | 15.90 | 07.04.2014 | 17.45 |
| 08.04.2002 | 15.90 | 06.04.2015 | 17.45 |
| 07.04.2003 | 15.90 | 06.04.2016 | 17.45 |
| 12.04.2004 | 15.95 | 06.04.2017 | 17.45 |
| 11.04.2005 | 16.10 | 06.04.2018 | 17.45 |
| 10.04.2006 | 16.25 | 06.04.2019 | 17.45 |
| 09.04.2007 | 16.43 | **06.04.2020** | **17.60** |
| 07.04.2008 | 16.75 | | |

## Non-Dependant Deductions - From 8th April 1996

| | Below | Gross Income and Deductions Band widths | | | | |
|---|---|---|---|---|---|---|
| 08.04.1996 | £76 | £76-114 | £114-150 | £150 plus | | |
| | 6.00 | 12.00 | 16.00 | 32.00 | | |
| 07.04.1997 | £78 | £78–116 | £116–152 | £152–200 | £200-250 | £250 plus |
| | 7.00 | 13.00 | 17.00 | 33.00 | 36.00 | 39.00 |
| 06.04.1998 | 7.00 | 16.00 | 22.00 | 36.00 | 41.00 | 45.00 |
| 12.04.1999 | £80 | £80–118 | £118–155 | £155–204 | £204-255 | £255 plus |
| | 7.20 | 16.50 | 22.65 | 37.10 | 42.25 | 46.35 |
| 10.04.2000 | £81 | £81-118 | £118-155 | £155-204 | £204-255 | £255 plus |
| | 7.40 | 17.00 | 23.35 | 38.20 | 43.50 | 47.75 |
| 09.04.2001 | £84 | £84-125 | £125-163 | £163-215 | £215-269 | £269 plus |
| | 7.40 | 17.00 | 23.35 | 38.20 | 43.50 | 47.75 |
| 08.04.2002 | £88 | £88-131 | £131-170 | £170-225 | £225-281 | £281 plus |
| | 7.40 | 17.00 | 23.35 | 38.20 | 43.50 | 47.75 |
| 07.04.2003 | £92 | £92-137 | £137-£177 | £177-£235 | £235-293 | £293 plus |
| | 7.40 | 17.00 | 23.35 | 38.20 | 43.50 | 47.75 |
| 12.04.2004 | £97 | £97-144 | £144-186 | £186-247 | £247-308 | £308 plus |
| | 7.40 | 17.00 | 23.35 | 38.20 | 43.50 | 47.75 |
| 11.04.2005 | £101 | £101-150 | £150-194 | £194-258 | £258-521 | £522 plus |
| | 7.40 | 17.00 | 23.35 | 38.20 | 43.50 | 47.75 |

## Non-Dependant Deductions - From 8th April 1996 continued

| 10.04.2006 | £106 | £106-157 | £157-204 | £204-271 | £271-338 | £338 plus |
|---|---|---|---|---|---|---|
|  | 7.40 | 17.00 | 23.35 | 38.20 | 43.50 | 47.75 |
| 09.04.2007 | £111 | £111-165 | £165-214 | £214-283 | £283-353 | £353 plus |
|  | 7.40 | 17.00 | 23.35 | 38.20 | 43.50 | 47.75 |
| 07.04.2008 | £116 | £116-172 | £172-223 | £223-296 | £296-369 | £369 plus |
|  | 7.40 | 17.00 | 23.35 | 38.20 | 43.50 | 47.75 |
| 06.04.2009 | £120 | £120-178 | £178-231 | £231-306 | £306-382 | £382 plus |
|  | 7.40 | 17.00 | 23.35 | 38.20 | 43.50 | 47.75 |
| 12.04.2010 | £120 | £120-178 | £178-231 | £231-306 | £306-382 | £382 plus |
|  | 7.40 | 17.00 | 23.35 | 38.20 | 43.50 | 47.75 |
| 11.04.2011 | £122 | £120-179 | £180-233 | £234-309 | £310-386 | £387 plus |
|  | 9.40 | 21.55 | 29.60 | 48.45 | 55.20 | 60.60 |
| 09.04.2012 | £124 | £124-182 | £183-237 | £238-315 | £316-393 | £394 plus |
|  | 11.45 | 26.25 | 36.10 | 59.05 | 67.25 | 73.85 |
| 09.04.2013 | £124 | £124-182 | £183-237 | £238-315 | £316-393 | £394 plus |
|  | 13.60 | 31.25 | 42.90 | 70.20 | 79.95 | 87.75 |
| 07.04.2014 | £128 | £124-187 | £188-244 | £245-325 | £326-393 | £406 plus |
|  | 14.15 | 32.45 | 44.55 | 72.95 | 83.05 | 91.15 |
| 06.04.2015 | £129 | £129-189 | £189-246 | £246-328 | £328-408 | £408 plus |
|  | 14.55 | 33.40 | 45.85 | 75.05 | 85.45 | 93.80 |
| 06.04.2016 | £133 | 133-194.99 | 195-252.99 | 253-337.99 | 338-419.99 | £420 plus |
|  | 14.65 | 33.65 | 46.20 | 75.60 | 86.10 | 94.50 |
| 06.04.2017 | £136 | 136–199.99 | 200-258.99 | 259-345.99 | 346-429.99 | £430 plus |
|  | £14.80 | £34.00 | £46.65 | £76.35 | £86.95 | £95.45 |
| 06.04.2018 | £139 | 139-203.99 | 204-264.99 | 265-353.99 | 354-438.99 | £439 plus |
|  | £15.25 | £35 | £48.05 | £78.65 | £89.55 | £98.30 |
| 06.04.2019 | £143 | 143-208.99 | 209-271.99 | 272-362.99 | 363-450.99 | £451 plus |
|  | £15.60 | £35.85 | £49.20 | £80.55 | £91.70 | £100.65 |
| 06.04.2020 | < £149 | £149 - £216.99 | £217 - £282.99 | £283– £376.99 | £377- £468.99 | £469 + |
|  | £15.85 | £36.45 | £50.05 | £81.90 | £93.25 | £102.35 |

## INCOME SUPPORT – MINIMUM INCOME GUARANTEE (MIG)

Introduced in April 1999 and replaced in October 2003 by Pension Credit, it was payable to pensioners (aged 60 or over) through Income Support giving a guaranteed minimum earnings level. Benefit was reduced by £1 per week for every £250 of savings between the lower and upper capital limits.

| Date from | Minimum Earnings Level | | Capital Limits | |
| | Single | Couples | Lower | Upper |
| | £ | £ | £ | £ |
|---|---|---|---|---|
| 12.04.1999 | 75.00 | 116.60 | 3,000 | 8,000 |
| 10.04.2000 | 78.45 | 121.95 | 3,000 | 8,000 |
| 09.04.2001 | 92.15 | 140.55 | 6,000 | 12,000 |
| 08.04.2002 | 98.18 | 149.80 | 6,000 | 12,000 |
| 07.04.2003 | 102.10 | 155.80 | 6,000 | 12,000 |

## INDUSTRIAL INJURY DEATH BENEFIT

Introduced on 5th July 1948, Industrial Injury Death Benefit is a non-contributory, taxable and non means-tested benefit paid to parents, certain dependant relatives and a woman looking after children of the deceased after a person died from either industrial accident or disease. Prior to 11th April 1988 it could be paid as a pension, allowance or lump sum.

For the first 26 weeks a widow would be paid at the higher rate, followed by a permanent pension dependant on age and circumstances. Some widowers also received a weekly pension.

The benefit cannot be awarded for deaths that occurred after 11th April 1988, widows now receive National Insurance Widows Benefit instead. The widower's rate is the same as the higher rate but there is no lower rate applicable.

### Industrial Injury Death Benefit – Widows Pension from 10th April 1996

| Date from | Higher Rate | Lower Rate | Date from | Higher Rate | Lower Rate |
| | £ | £ | | £ | £ |
|---|---|---|---|---|---|
| 10.04.1996 | 61.15 | 18.35 | 06.04.2009 | 95.25 | 28.58 |
| 09.04.1997 | 62.45 | 18.74 | 12.04.2010 | 97.65 | 29.30 |
| 06.04.1998 | 64.70 | 19.41 | 11.04.2011 | 102.15 | 30.65 |
| 12.04.1999 | 66.75 | 20.03 | 09.04.2012 | 107.45 | 32.24 |
| 10.04.2000 | 67.50 | 20.25 | 09.04.2013 | 110.15 | 33.05 |
| 09.04.2001 | 72.50 | 21.25 | 07.04.2014 | 113.10 | 33.93 |
| 09.04.2002 | 75.50 | 22.65 | 06.04.2015 | 115.95 | 34.79 |
| 08.04.2003 | 77.45 | 23.24 | 06.04.2016 | 119.30 | 35.79 |
| 12.04.2004 | 79.60 | 23.89 | 06.04.2017 | 122.30 | 36.69 |
| 11.04.2005 | 82.05 | 24.62 | 06.04.2018 | 125.95 | 37.79 |
| 10.04.2006 | 84.25 | 25.28 | 06.04.2019 | 129.20 | 38.76 |
| 09.04.2007 | 87.30 | 26.27 | **06.04.2020** | **134.25** | **40.28** |
| 07.04.2008 | 90.70 | 27.21 | | | |

## INDUSTRIAL INJURIES DISABLEMENT BENEFIT

Introduced on 5th July 1948, a non-contributory, non-taxable and non means-tested benefit for those who are disabled because of an industrial accident or industrial disease.

The benefit is not payable until 90 days after the date of the accident, or the date the recipient started to suffer from the prescribed disease (excluding Sundays.) The degree of disability is expressed as a percentage and is established by medical assessment.

## Industrial Injuries Disablement Benefit

### Premium Rate tables for people aged 18 and over from 7th April 1997

| Date from | Percentage degree of disablement | | | | |
| --- | --- | --- | --- | --- | --- |
| | 100% | 90% | 80% | 70% | 60% |
| | £ | £ | £ | £ | £ |
| 07.04.1997 | 101.10 | 90.99 | 80.88 | 70.77 | 60.66 |
| 06.04.1998 | 104.70 | 94.23 | 83.76 | 73.29 | 62.82 |
| 12.04.1999 | 108.10 | 97.29 | 86.48 | 75.67 | 64.86 |
| 10.04.2000 | 109.30 | 98.37 | 87.44 | 76.51 | 65.58 |
| 09.04.2001 | 112.90 | 101.61 | 90.32 | 79.03 | 67.76 |
| 08.04.2002 | 114.80 | 103.32 | 91.84 | 80.36 | 68.88 |
| 07.04.2003 | 116.80 | 105.12 | 93.44 | 81.76 | 70.08 |
| 12.04.2004 | 120.10 | 108.09 | 96.08 | 84.07 | 72.06 |
| 11.04.2005 | 123.80 | 111.42 | 99.04 | 86.66 | 74.28 |
| 10.04.2006 | 127.10 | 114.39 | 101.68 | 88.97 | 76.26 |
| 09.04.2007 | 131.70 | 118.53 | 105.36 | 92.19 | 79.02 |
| 07.04.2008 | 136.80 | 123.12 | 109.44 | 95.76 | 82.08 |
| 06.04.2009 | 143.60 | 129.24 | 114.88 | 100.52 | 86.16 |
| 12.04.2010 | 145.80 | 131.22 | 116.64 | 102.06 | 87.48 |
| 11.04.2011 | 150.30 | 135.27 | 120.24 | 105.21 | 90.18 |
| 09.04.2012 | 158.10 | 142.29 | 126.48 | 110.67 | 94.86 |
| 09.04.2013 | 161.60 | 145.44 | 129.28 | 113.12 | 96.96 |
| 07.04.2014 | 166.00 | 149.40 | 132.80 | 116.20 | 99.60 |
| 06.04.2015 | 168.00 | 151.20 | 134.40 | 117.60 | 100.80 |
| 06.04.2016 | 168.00 | 151.20 | 134.40 | 117.60 | 100.80 |
| 06.04.2017 | 169.70 | 152.73 | 135.76 | 118.79 | 101.82 |
| 06.04.2018 | 174.80 | 157.32 | 139.84 | 122.36 | 104.88 |
| 06.04.2019 | 179.00 | 161.10 | 143.20 | 125.30 | 107.40 |
| **06.04.2020** | **182.00** | **163.80** | **145.60** | **127.40** | **109.20** |

| | Percentage degree of disablement | | | | |
| --- | --- | --- | --- | --- | --- |
| Date from | 50% | 40% | 30% | 20% | 10% |
| | £ | £ | £ | £ | £ |
| 10.04.1996 | 49.50 | 39.60 | 29.70 | 19.80 | 9.90 |
| 07.04.1997 | 50.55 | 40.44 | 30.33 | 20.22 | 10.11 |
| 06.04.1998 | 52.35 | 41.88 | 31.41 | 20.94 | 10.47 |
| 12.04.1999 | 54.05 | 43.24 | 32.43 | 21.62 | 10.81 |
| 10.04.2000 | 54.65 | 43.72 | 32.79 | 21.86 | 10.93 |
| 09.04.2001 | 56.45 | 45.16 | 33.87 | 22.58 | 11.29 |
| 08.04.2002 | 57.40 | 45.92 | 34.44 | 22.96 | 11.46 |

| | | | | | |
|---|---|---|---|---|---|
| 07.04.2003 | 58.40 | 46.72 | 35.04 | 23.36 | 11.68 |
| 12.04.2004 | 60.05 | 48.04 | 36.03 | 24.02 | 12.01 |
| 11.04.2005 | 61.90 | 49.52 | 37.14 | 24.76 | 12.38 |
| 10.04.2006 | 63.55 | 50.84 | 38.13 | 25.42 | 12.71 |
| 09.04.2007 | 65.95 | 52.68 | 39.51 | 26.34 | 13.17 |
| 07.04.2008 | 68.40 | 54.72 | 41.04 | 27.36 | 13.68 |
| 06.04.2009 | 71.80 | 57.44 | 43.08 | 28.72 | 14.36 |
| 12.04.2010 | 72.90 | 58.32 | 43.74 | 29.16 | abolished |
| 11.04.2011 | 75.15 | 60.12 | 45.09 | 30.06 | |
| 09.04.2012 | 79.05 | 63.24 | 47.43 | 31.62 | |
| Industrial Injuries Disablement Benefit - continued | | | | | |
| 09.04.2013 | 80.80 | 64.64 | 48.48 | 32.32 | |
| 07.04.2014 | 83.00 | 66.40 | 49.80 | 33.20 | |
| 06.04.2015 | 84.00 | 67.20 | 50.40 | 33.60 | |
| 06.04.2016 | 84.00 | 67.20 | 50.40 | 33.60 | |
| 06.04.2017 | 84.85 | 67.88 | 50.91 | 33.94 | |
| 06.04.2018 | 87.40 | 69.92 | 52.44 | 34.96 | |
| 06.04.2019 | 89.50 | 71.60 | 53.70 | 35.80 | |
| **06.04.2020** | **91.00** | **72.80** | **54.60** | **36.40** | |

## INDUSTRIAL INJURIES DISABLEMENT SUPPLEMENTS

**Unemployability Supplement** (UB Sup), available prior to 8th April 1987 for those who could not work as a result of their disability and would be unlikely to work again.

**Exceptionally Severe Disablement Allowance** (ESDA) was available to a person entitled to Constant Attendance Allowance (CAA) at one of the two higher rates. They must be likely to need the same amount of care permanently

**Constant Attendance Allowance** (CAA) can be paid to a person receiving Industrial

**Injuries Disablement Allowance** (IIDA) Benefit at 100% rate where constant care and attention is required as a result of the industrial injury or disease

**Reduced Earnings Allowance** (REA) for cases where an individual cannot return to their normal job, or one that pays as much. Those who receive REA of £2 per week or more, and are not regularly employed, on attaining retirement age may receive a Retirement Allowance in place of REA and at 25% of their rate of REA subject to a specified maximum.

### Industrial Injury Disablement Supplement Rates

### From 12th April 1995

| Date from | UB Supplement Base Rate £ | ESDA £ | Constant Attendance Allowance | | | Reduced Earnings Allowance £ |
|---|---|---|---|---|---|---|
| | | | Exceptional rate 'max' £ | Intermediate rate £ | Normal max £ | |
| 12.04.1995 | 58.85 | 38.20 | 76.40 | 57.30 | 38.20 | 38.12 |
| 10.04.1996 | 61.15 | 39.70 | 79.40 | 59.55 | 39.70 | 39.60 |

| | | | | | | |
|---|---|---|---|---|---|---|
| 07.04.1997 | 62.45 | 40.50 | 81.00 | 60.75 | 40.50 | 40.44 |
| 06.04.1998 | 64.70 | 42.00 | 84.00 | 63.00 | 42.00 | 41.88 |
| 12.04.1999 | 66.75 | 43.30 | 86.60 | 64.95 | 43.30 | 43.24 |
| 10.04.2000 | 67.50 | 43.80 | 87.60 | 65.70 | 43.80 | 43.72 |
| 09.04.2001 | 69.75 | 45.20 | 90.40 | 67.80 | 45.20 | 45.16 |
| 08.04.2002 | 70.95 | 46.00 | 92.00 | 69.00 | 46.00 | 45.92 |
| 07.04.2003 | 72.15 | 46.80 | 93.60 | 70.20 | 46.80 | 46.72 |
| 12.04.2004 | 74.15 | 48.10 | 96.20 | 72.15 | 48.10 | 48.00 |
| 11.04.2005 | 76.45 | 49.60 | 99.20 | 74.40 | 49.60 | 49.50 |
| 10.04.2006 | 78.50 | 50.90 | 101.80 | 76.35 | 50.90 | 50.90 |
| 09.04.2007 | 81.35 | 52.70 | 105.40 | 79.10 | 52.70 | 52.70 |
| 07.04.2008 | 84.50 | 54.80 | 109.60 | 82.20 | 54.80 | 54.72 |
| 06.04.2009 | 88.75 | 57.50 | 115.00 | 86.25 | 57.50 | 57.44 |
| 12.04.2010 | 90.10 | 58.40 | 116.80 | 87.60 | 58.40 | 58.32 |
| 11.04.2011 | 92.90 | 60.20 | 120.40 | 90.30 | 60.20 | 60.12 |
| 09.04.2012 | 97.75 | 63.30 | 126.60 | 94.95 | 63.30 | 63.24 |
| 09.04.2013 | 99.90 | 64.70 | 129.40 | 97.05 | 64.70 | 64.64 |
| 07.04.2014 | 102.60 | 66.40 | 132.80 | 99.60 | 66.40 | 66.40 |
| 06.04.2015 | 103.85 | 67.20 | 134.40 | 100.80 | 67.20 | 67.20 |
| 06.04.2016 | 103.85 | 67.20 | 134.40 | 100.80 | 67.20 | 67.20 |
| 06.04.2017 | 104.90 | 67.88 | 135.80 | 101.85 | 67.90 | 67.88 |
| 06.04.2018 | 108.05 | 69.92 | 139.80 | 104.85 | 69.90 | 69.92 |
| 06.04.2019 | 110.65 | 71.60 | 143.20 | 107.40 | 71.60 | 71.60 |
| **06.04.2020** | **112.55** | **72.80** | **145.60** | **109.20** | **72.80** | **72.80** |

*N.B. Constant Attendance Allowance - part-time workers receive benefit at 50% of the normal maximum rate.*

## PENSION CREDIT

The credit was introduced on 6th October 2003 and consists of two elements:
- A Credit Guarantee (income guarantee) - of a minimum income below which no pensioner's income need fall, and
- A Savings Credit (reward) - for those who save for retirement

### Qualification
To qualify the claimant must be resident in Great Britain, have attained the qualifying age, and either:
- a) To qualify for Guarantee Credit:
    - have attained the minimum qualifying age for women to receive the basic state retirement pension (currently 60 years)
    - have no income; or
    - income which does not exceed the minimum guarantee
- b) b) To qualify for Savings Credit:
- c) have attained the age of 65; or
- d) be a member of a married couple or unmarried couple where the other member has attained that age; and
- e) have qualifying income in excess of the savings credit threshold.

In the case of couples Pension Credit may only be claimed by one (not both), and the income of both shall, subject to prescribed conditions, be treated as if it is that of the claimant.

### Weekly Guarantee Credit from April 2004

| Date from | Standard Minimum Guarantee | | Disablement Additional Amount | | Additional Amount (Carers) |
| --- | --- | --- | --- | --- | --- |
| | Single £ | Couple £ | Single £ | Couple £ | £ |
| 12.04.2004 | 105.45 | 160.95 | 44.15 | 88.30 | 25.55 |
| 11.04.2005 | 109.45 | 167.05 | 45.50 | 91.00 | 25.80 |
| 10.04.2006 | 114.05 | 174.05 | 46.75 | 93.50 | 26.35 |
| 09.04.2007 | 119.05 | 181.70 | 48.45 | 96.90 | 27.15 |
| 07.04.2008 | 124.05 | 189.35 | 50.35 | 100.70 | 27.75 |
| 06.04.2009 | 130.00 | 198.45 | 52.85 | 105.70 | 29.50 |
| 12.04.2010 | 132.60 | 202.40 | 53.65 | 107.30 | 30.05 |
| 11.04.2011 | 137.35 | 209.70 | 55.30 | 110.60 | 31.00 |
| 09.04.2012 | 142.70 | 217.90 | 58.20 | 116.40 | 32.60 |
| 09.04.2013 | 145.40 | 222.05 | 59.50 | 119.00 | 33.30 |
| 07.04.2014 | 148.35 | 226.50 | 61.10 | 122.20 | 34.20 |
| 06.04.2015 | 151.20 | 230.85 | 61.85 | 123.70 | 34.60 |
| 06.04.2016 | 155.60 | 237.55 | 61.85 | 123.70 | 34.60 |
| 06.04.2017 | 159.35 | 243.25 | 62.45 | 124.90 | 34.95 |
| 06.04.2018 | 163.00 | 248.80 | 64.30 | 128.60 | 36.00 |
| 06.04.2019 | 167.25 | 255.25 | 65.85 | 131.70 | 36.85 |
| **06.04.2020** | **173.75** | **265.20** | **66.95** | **133.90** | **37.50** |

'Disablement additional amount' will only be paid where the claimant is severely disabled.

Additional amount (Carers) will be payable where the claimant is, or is the member of a couple the other member of which is, entitled to an allowance for caring for another person, and from 6th April 2003 Carers Allowance, formerly Invalid Care Allowance.

Where the claimant is entitled to a savings credit, the amount of the savings credit shall be the amount by which amount A exceeds amount B where -
A is the smaller of:
- the maximum savings credit (MSC); and
- a prescribed percentage of the amount by which the claimant's qualifying income exceeds the savings credit threshold; and
B is:
- a prescribed percentage of the amount (if any) by which the claimant's income exceeds the appropriate minimum guarantee (AMG); or
- if there is no such excess, nil

## Weekly Savings Credit Thresholds from October 2003

| Date from | Savings Credit Threshold | | Prescribed Percentage | | Savings Threshold | |
|---|---|---|---|---|---|---|
| | Single | Couple | A (MSC.) | B (AMG) | Basic | Residual Care |
| | £ | £ | % | % | £ | £ |
| 06.10.2003 | 77.45 | 123.80 | 60 | 40 | 6,000 | 10,000 |
| 12.04.2004 | 79.60 | 127.25 | 60 | 40 | 6,000 | 10,000 |
| 11.04.2005 | 82.05 | 131.20 | 60 | 40 | 6,000 | 10,000 |
| 10.04.2006 | 84.25 | 134.75 | 60 | 40 | 6,000 | 10,000 |
| 09.04.2007 | 87.30 | 139.60 | 60 | 40 | 6,000 | 10,000 |
| 07.04.2008 | 91.20 | 145.80 | 60 | 40 | 6,000 | 10,000 |
| 06.04.2009 | 96.00 | 153.40 | 60 | 40 | 6,000 | 10,000 |
| 12.04.2010 | 98.40 | 157.25 | 60 | 40 | 10,000 | 10,000 |
| 11.04.2011 | 103.15 | 164.55 | 60 | 40 | 10,000 | 10,000 |
| 09.04.2012 | 111.80 | 178.35 | 60 | 40 | 10,000 | 10,000 |
| 06.04.2013 | 115.30 | 183.90 | 60 | 40 | 10,000 | 10,000 |
| 07.04.2014 | 120.35 | 192.00 | 60 | 40 | 10,000 | 10,000 |
| 06.04.2015 | 126.50 | 201.80 | 60 | 40 | 10,000 | 10,000 |
| 06.04.2016 | 133.82 | 212.97 | 60 | 40 | 10,000 | 10,000 |
| 06.04.2017 | 137.35 | 218.42 | 60 | 40 | 10,000 | 10,000 |
| 06.04.2018 | 140.67 | 223.82 | 60 | 40 | 10,000 | 10,000 |
| 06.04.2019 | 144.38 | 229.67 | 60 | 40 | 10,000 | 10,000 |
| **06.04.2020** | **150.47** | **239.17** | **60** | **40** | **10,000** | **10,000** |

## Maximum Weekly Savings Credit from 12th April 2004

| Date from | Single £ | Couple £ | Date from | Single £ | Couple £ |
|---|---|---|---|---|---|
| 12.04.2004 | 15.51 | 20.22 | 09.04.2013 | 18.06 | 22.89 |
| 11.04.2005 | 16.44 | 21.51 | 07.04.2014 | 16.80 | 20.70 |
| 10.04.2006 | 17.88 | 23.58 | 06.04.2015 | 14.82 | 17.43 |
| 09.04.2007 | 19.05 | 25.26 | 06.04.2016 | 13.07 | 14.74 |
| 07.04.2008 | 19.71 | 26.13 | 06.04.2017 | 13.20 | 14.90 |
| 06.04.2009 | 20.40 | 27.03 | 06.04.2018 | 13.40 | 14.99 |
| 12.04.2010 | 20.52 | 27.09 | 06.04.2019 | 13.73 | 15.35 |
| 11.04.2011 | 20.52 | 27.09 | **06.04.2020** | **13.97** | **15.62** |
| 09.04.2012 | 18.54 | 23.73 | | | |

Entitlement once calculated will normally, and following any re-assessment, run for a period of 5 years during which there will be no requirement to report changes in income other than significant life events or changes in the composition of the pensioner's household. A claimant may request an interim re-assessment where there is a decrease in their personal retirement provision.

## SICKNESS BENEFIT

Replaced by Incapacity Benefit from 13th April 1995. Earlier additional benefits:
- earnings related supplement payable with standard benefit to June 1982
- child dependency addition to November 1984
- three quarter and half rates payable to October 1986

### Sickness Benefit Rates from 27th November 1980 to 6th April 1998

| Date from | Standard £ | Adult Dependant £ | Date from | Standard £ | Adult Dependant £ |
|---|---|---|---|---|---|
| 27.11.1980 | 20.65 | 12.75 | 13.04.1989 | 33.20 | 20.55 |
| 26.11.1981 | 22.50 | 13.90 | 12.04.1990 | 35.70 | 22.10 |
| 25.11.1982 | 25.00 | 15.45 | 11.04.1991 | 39.60 | 24.50 |
| 24.11.1983 | 25.95 | 16.00 | 09.04.1992 | 41.20 | 25.50 |
| 29.11.1984 | 27.25 | 16.80 | 15.04.1993 | 42.70 | 26.40 |
| 28.11.1985 | 29.15 | 18.00 | 14.04.1994 | 43.45 | 26.90 |
| 31.07.1986 | 29.45 | 18.20 | 13.04.1995 | 44.40 | 27.50 |
| 09.04.1987 | 30.05 | 18.60 | 11.04.1996 | 46.15 | 28.55 |
| 14.04.1988 | 31.30 | 19.40 | 07.04.1997 | 47.10 | 29.15 |

The rates shown above for 1996/97 and 1997/98 are transitional rates.

## SOCIAL FUND

Introduced on 6th April 1987, the fund is made up of regulated and discretionary payments.

**Budgeting Loans** (from April 1988). Interest-free loans to meet intermittent expenses, are available for those receiving Income Support or income based Jobseeker's Allowance for at least 26 weeks.

**Cold Weather Payments** (from November 1988). Payments of £8.50 per week are made when the average temperature is recorded, or forecast to be, zero° centigrade or below over any 7 consecutive days. Paid to those on Income Support or Jobseekers' Allowance, who have a pensioner or disability premium, or a child under the age of five years.

**Community Care Grant** (from April 1988). Available to those on Income Support or income based Jobseeker's Allowance who have special circumstances.

**Crisis Loans** (from April 1988). Interest free loans available in an emergency or as a consequence of a disaster, for people with no alternative financial means of avoiding serious damage or risk to their health or safety.

## STATE PENSION

A contributory, taxable and non-means tested benefit, introduced on 1st January 1909. Until April 2016 there were two categories of contributory pension, and two of non-contributory retirement pension.

### Contributory Pension
- category A which is dependent on a person's own contributory record
- category B which is dependent on contributions paid by a spouse

Conditions for payment are that:
- the person has reached State Pension Age, and
- contributions conditions are satisfied.

Where the conditions are met a flat rate basic pension is payable at the standard rate. Where conditions are only partly met, the basic pension is reduced.

## Non-Contributory Pension

- category C - people over state pension age on 5th July 1948, thereby excluded from the National Insurance Scheme
- category D - for people who either - attain age 80, or satisfy certain residence qualifications but fail to qualify for a Category A or B pension, or would receive less than the non-contributory rate.

A married woman can receive a category A pension where the conditions are met on her own contribution record, otherwise a category B pension may be payable on her husband's contribution record, when she has reached State Pension Age. She can also claim a category B pension if her own would be less than that payable as a result of her husband's contribution record.

An additional earnings-related element (S2P) was, for any one reaching state pension age before April 2016, also payable based on earnings between the Lower Earnings Threshold (LET) and Upper Earnings Limit (UEL) for National Insurance contributions in tax years from April 1978 up to 5th April 2009 - only up to the Upper Accrual Point from 6th April 2009. The final relevant year is the last complete tax year before a person attains state pension age. Entitlement to S2P is given up where an employee is a member of a contracted-out pension scheme.

Prior to 6th April 1997, Contracted-Out Salary Related Schemes (COSRS) provided a Guaranteed Minimum Pension (GMP) worth about the same or greater than the additional pension payable under the state scheme. Contracted-Out Money Purchase Schemes (COMPS) and Personal Pensions have no guaranteed minimum but there is similarly no S2P entitlement.

From 6th April 1997 the links with SERPS - see below (now S2P) were broken and there is no longer a requirement for COSRS to pay a GMP. A new quality test for such schemes was introduced and no S2P is payable, but rights earned before that date are protected.

From 6th April 2016 S2P was abolished and the new single tier state pension was introduced and paid to those retiring from that date. This is subject to the recipient not being in contracted-out employment at any time in their contributory record.

A graduated retirement benefit is payable to those who paid into the Graduated Pension scheme which ceased on 5th April 1975. Entitlement is based on each unit of Graduated Pension paid (for details see Retirement Pension - Graduated Retirement Benefit below).

## Basic State Retirement Pension

### Weekly Rates from 23rd November 1981

| Date from | Contributory Pension | | Non-Contributory Pension | |
|---|---|---|---|---|
| | On own contribution record | On husband's cont'n record (Cat A) | On own cont'n record (Cat B) | On husband's cont'n record (Cat C) |
| | £ | £ | £ | £ |
| 23.11.1981 | 29.60 | 17.75 | 17.75 | 10.65 |
| 22.11.1982 | 32.85 | 19.70 | 19.70 | 11.80 |
| 21.11.1983 | 34.05 | 20.45 | 20.45 | 12.25 |
| 26.11.1984 | 35.80 | 21.50 | 21.50 | 12.85 |
| 25.11.1985 | 38.30 | 23.00 | 23.00 | 13.75 |
| 28.07.1986 | 38.70 | 23.25 | 23.25 | 13.90 |
| 06.04.1987 | 39.50 | 23.75 | 23.75 | 14.20 |
| 11.04.1988 | 41.15 | 24.75 | 24.75 | 14.80 |
| 10.04.1989 | 43.60 | 26.20 | 26.20 | 15.65 |
| 09.04.1990 | 46.90 | 28.20 | 28.20 | 16.85 |
| 08.04.1991 | 52.00 | 31.25 | 31.25 | 18.70 |

| | | | | |
|---|---|---|---|---|
| 06.04.1992 | 54.15 | 32.55 | 32.55 | 19.45 |
| 12.04.1993 | 56.10 | 33.70 | 33.70 | 20.15 |
| 11.04.1994 | 57.60 | 34.50 | 34.50 | 20.65 |
| 10.04.1995 | 58.85 | 35.25 | 35.25 | 21.10 |
| 08.04.1996 | 61.15 | 36.60 | 36.60 | 21.90 |
| 07.04.1997 | 62.45 | 37.35 | 37.25 | 22.35 |
| 06.04.1998 | 64.70 | 38.70 | 38.70 | 23.15 |
| 12.04.1999 | 66.75 | 39.95 | 39.95 | 23.90 |
| 10.04.2000 | 67.50 | 40.40 | 40.40 | 24.15 |
| 09.04.2001 | 72.50 | 43.40 | 43.40 | 24.95 |
| 08.04.2002 | 75.50 | 45.20 | 45.20 | 27.00 |
| 07.04.2003 | 77.45 | 46.35 | 46.35 | 27.70 |
| 12.04.2004 | 79.60 | 47.65 | 47.65 | 28.50 |
| 11.04.2005 | 82.05 | 49.15 | 49.15 | 29.40 |
| 10.04.2006 | 84.25 | 50.50 | 50.50 | 30.20 |
| 09.04.2007 | 87.30 | 52.30 | 52.30 | 31.30 |
| 07.04.2008 | 90.70 | 54.35 | 54.45 | 32.50 |
| 06.04.2009 | 95.25 | 57.05 | 57.05 | 34.15 |
| 12.04.2010 | 97.65 | 58.50 | 58.50 | 58.50 |
| 11.04.2011 | 102.15 | 61.20 | 61.20 | 61.20 |
| 09.04.2012 | 107.45 | 64.40 | 64.40 | 64.40 |
| 09.04.2013 | 110.15 | 66.00 | 66.00 | 66.00 |
| 07.04.2014 | 113.10 | 67.80 | 67.80 | 67.80 |
| 06.04.2015 | 115.95 | 69.50 | 69.50 | 69.50 |
| 06.04.2016 | 119.30 | 71.50 | 71.50 | 71.50 |
| 06.04.2017 | 122.30 | 73.30 | 73.30 | 73.30 |
| 06.04.2018 | 125.95 | 75.50 | 75.50 | 75.50 |
| 06.04.2019 | 129.20 | 77.45 | 77.45 | 77.45 |
| **06.04.2020** | **134.25** | **80.45** | **80.45** | **80.45** |

All pensioners aged over 80 years receive an addition of 25p per week paid with the State Retirement Pension. Whilst most benefit rates are unchanged as at 6th April 2016, the state pension has been increased as part of the governments "triple lock" policy. As at the date of publication the advisory committee on pensions and benefits had advised that the "triple lock" policy was unsustainable. The government will consult on changes to this.

### State pension - calculation and qualification
The amount of state pension received is dependent on the number of years' contributions that have been paid subject to an annual minimum 'qualifying' threshold. It is not, as often perceived, based on the total value of contributions paid over time. From 6th April 2020 individuals retiring will receive a single tier state pension of £175.20 per week (was £168.60 from 6th April 2019, £164.35 from 6th April 2018, £159.55 from 6th April 2017 and £155.65 per week from 6th April 2016) (see below).

Entitlement to the current full state pension is subject to a minimum of 35 years (39 for women or 44 for men prior to April 2010) 'qualifying years' contributions. A qualifying year being a tax year during which earnings were not less than 52 times the NICs Lower Earnings Limit (LEL) - £116 a week for 2018/19.

In certain circumstances National Insurance credits, which count towards a contribution record, are added to protect a contributor's entitlement:

- when in receipt of certain benefits e.g. Jobseeker's Allowance, Statutory Maternity Pay, Statutory Sick Pay, Maternity Allowance, Working Tax Credit.
- for each tax year between the age of 60 to 65.

Married women may be entitled to receive state pension based on their husband's contribution record - see Category B above. For women the full benefit will also be dependent on age (see State Pension Equalisation below).

## State pension - deferment

From April 2005 the Government introduced the option to take a deferred state pension as a taxable lump sum instead of a higher weekly pension. By deferring the pension by at least a year a lump sum will be payable and interest will become payable on the deferred pension at Bank of England base rate +2%. The Pension Act 2004 brought forward the previously announced change to the late retirement increase from 1/7% to 1/5% for each week by which an individual defers the receipt of the State Pension. The maximum deferral period of five years was abolished and the minimum period of deferral was reduced from seven to five weeks. From 6th April 2006 a person deferring state pension may claim an additional 1% of their weekly pension for every 5 weeks of deferment or a one-off lump sum provided deferment is for at least 12 consecutive months.

### Bank of England Base Rate from 8th September 1999

| Date from | Rate % | Date from | Rate % | Date from | Rate % |
|-----------|--------|-----------|--------|-----------|--------|
| 08.09.1999 | 5.25 | 06.11.2003 | 3.75 | 10.04.2008 | 5.00 |
| 04.11.1999 | 5.50 | 05.02.2004 | 4.00 | 08.10.2008 | 4.50 |
| 13.01.2000 | 5.75 | 06.05.2004 | 4.25 | 06.11.2008 | 3.00 |
| 10.02.2000 | 6.00 | 10.06.2004 | 4.50 | 04.12.2008 | 2.00 |
| 08.02.2001 | 5.75 | 05.08.2004 | 4.75 | 08.01.2009 | 1.50 |
| 04.04.2001 | 5.50 | 04.08.2005 | 4.50 | 05.02.2009 | 1.00 |
| 08.05.2001 | 5.25 | 03.08.2006 | 4.75 | 05.03.2009 | 0.50 |
| 02.08.2001 | 5.00 | 09.11.2006 | 5.00 | 04.08.2016 | 0.25 |
| 18.09.2001 | 4.75 | 11.01.2007 | 5.25 | 02.11.2017 | 0.50 |
| 04.10.2001 | 4.50 | 10.05.2007 | 5.50 | 02.08.2018 | 0.75 |
| 08.11.2001 | 4.00 | 05.07.2007 | 5.75 | **11.03.2020** | 0.25 |
| 06.02.2003 | 3.75 | 06.12.2007 | 5.50 | | |
| 10.07.2003 | 3.50 | 07.02.2008 | 5.25 | | |

## State pension - deficiency notice

A statement issued by HMRC eighteen months after the end of the relevant tax year advising contributors to the State Pension that National Insurance Contributions credited in a specific year will be insufficient to guarantee maximum future provision. Future benefit may be improved by payment of additional voluntary Class 3 (or from 2015 Class 3a) National Insurance Contributions – see Part 3.

Prior to 1998 Deficiency Notices were issued at the end of each financial year informing contributors where contributions credited throughout the year were not sufficient to make that year count towards the Basic State Pension, and to advise whether voluntary contributions would be appropriate. Notices were not issued between 1996/1997 and 2001/2002 and rules have been relaxed to enable contributors to redress any deficiency. From 2005/2006 onwards the annual production of notices recommenced.

## State pension equalisation

State pension ages have been unequal since 1940. Until April 2010 women had the right to claim pensions at age 60 whereas men had to wait until age 65. The Pensions Act 1995 made provision for equalising the age at which pension entitlements fall due for both men and women on reaching age 65 by the year 2020 (now accelerated to December 2018) and 66 by April 2020. This was due to the requirement for progressive implementation of equal treatment in social security matters (EU Directive 79/7) and schemes (EU Directive 86/378).

## State pension age

| By 6th December 2018 | State pension age increasing to 65 for women |
|---|---|
| From 6th December 2018 - 6th October 2020 | State pension age increasing to 66 |
| 6th April 2026 – 6th April 2028 (in Pension Act 2013) | State pension age increasing to 67 |
| 6th April 2044 – 6th April 2046 | State pension age increasing to 68 |

These dates are subject to frequent revision, the latest one proposes that the increase of SPA to 68 should now occur between 6th April 2037 and 6th April 2039.

### State pension forecast
The Department for Work and Pensions (DWP) will, on application, provide a state retirement pension forecast in one of two formats, provided the applicant is more than four months away from state pension retirement age. Application can be made by completion of form BR19.
- Combined Pension Forecast (CPF) - A forecast of an individual's State Pension and information in respect of their occupational or private pension issued by their employer or pension provider,
- Automatic State Pension Forecast (APF) - issued from May 2003, at regular intervals, to all of working age who do not have access to a CPF through their employer or pension provider.

A forecast statement will provide the following details-

Basic Pension:
- the amount already earned at today's values:
- the amount to expect on earnings to date and earnings which might be earned to the date of retirement
- It will advise if there is any way in which the Basic Pension entitlement might be improved, and

Additional Pension: an additional element, which may comprise:
- An additional element which may comprise
- State Earnings Related Pension (SERPS) - dependent upon earnings since 1978
- State Second Pension - which replaced SERPS in April 2002
- Graduated Retirement Benefit - dependent upon NI contributions paid between 1961 and 1975.

Widowed or divorced contributor - contributions of a former spouse may provide a better pension entitlement, and in such cases the forecast will give details.

Form BR19 should be completed and forwarded to:
Newcastle Pension Centre, Futures Group
The Pension Service 9,
Mail Handling Site A,
Wolverhampton, WV98 1LU.

A full record of NI contributions and the state pension forecast is now part of the digital personal tax account (PTA). All taxpayers have a new PTA whilst some 14m are regular users of the account.

### State pension - Graduated Retirement Benefit (GRB)
Introduced in April 1961 to provide an additional benefit to the basic state pension. Contributions were based on income to a maximum threshold (1961 @ £15 to 1975 @ £62) the scheme closed in April 1975. Contributions purchased 'units' at the rate of £7.50 (men) and £9 (women). The maximum number of units per contributor being, 86 (men) and 77 (women). In the case of contracted-out employees, 48 units and 40 units respectively. The benefit is calculated in addition to, and paid together with, the basic state pension at a fixed weekly rate per unit, and rates are up-lifted annually. Widows and Widowers (whose partner deceased after 5th April 1979), receive half their partner's pension on the death of the contributory partner. The annual % increase is also applied to increases for deferred retirement.

## Graduated Retirement Benefit

Weekly rate per unit from 8th April 1997

| Date From | GRB Pence per unit | Annual increase % | Date from | GRB pence per unit | Annual increase% |
|---|---|---|---|---|---|
| 07.04.1997 | 8.11 | 2.1 | 12.04.2004 | 9.63 | 2.8 |
| 06.04.1998 | 8.40 | 3.6 | 12.04.2010 | 11.53 | 0.0 |
| 12.04.1999 | 8.67 | 3.2 | 11.04.2011 | 11.89 | 3.1 |
| 10.04.2000 | 8.77 | 1.1 | 09.04.2012 | 12.51 | 5.2 |
| 09.04.2001 | 9.06 | 3.3 | 09.04.2013 | 12.79 | 3.5 |
| 08.04.2002 | 9.21 | 1.7 | 07.04.2014 | 13.14 | 2.7 |
| 07.04.2003 | 9.37 | 1.7 | 06.04.2015 | 13.30 | 1.2 |
| 12.04.2004 | 9.63 | 2.8 | 06.04.2016 | 13.30 | 0.0 |
| 11.04.2005 | 9.93 | 3.1 | 06.04.2017 | 13.43 | 1.0 |
| 10.04.2006 | 9.93 | 2.7 | 06.04.2018 | 13.83 | 1.0 |
| 09.04.2007 | 10.57 | 3.6 | 06.04.2019 | 14.16 | 2.4 |
| 07.04.2008 | 10.98 | 3.9 | **06.04.2020** | **14.40** | **1.7** |
| 06.04.2009 | 11.53 | 3.0 | | | |

## STATE EARNINGS RELATED PENSION SCHEME (SERPS)

SERPS was that part of the State Pension Scheme that related to earnings between the National Insurance Lower and Upper Earnings Limits. The Scheme commenced in 1978 with the intention that employees could accrue a maximum of 25% of 'revalued relevant earnings'. The Social Security Act 1986 reduced this to a maximum of 20% introduced over a transitional period from 1999/2000. The State Second Pension Scheme (S2P) replaced SERPS on The 6th April 2002. Employers with pension schemes, which met certain conditions, were able to contract scheme members out of SERPS (S2P).

With effect from 6th October 2002, Widows and Widowers entitled to SERPS based on a deceased partner's contributions will have their entitlement reduced to a maximum level of 50%. The reduction will apply in full to those who reach pension age on or after 6th October 2010 and will be introduced in stages linked to the contributor's date of birth. The reduction is to be applied in respect of the spouse who dies first. The age of the surviving spouse is not relevant and the rule is to be applied equally to men and women.

### SERPS Widows' and Widowers' rebate

| Date of birth of contributor | | SERPS entitlement |
|---|---|---|
| Men born | Women born | |
| prior to 06.10.1937 | prior to 06.10.1942 | 100% |
| 06.10.1937 to 05.10.1939 | 06.10.1942 to 05.10.1944 | 90% |
| 06.10.1939 to 05.10.1941 | 06.10.1944 to 05.10.1946 | 80% |
| 06.10.1941 to 05.10.1943 | 06.10.1946 to 05.10.1948 | 70% |
| 06.10.1943 to 05.10.1945 | 06.10.1948 to 05.10.1950 | 60% |
| 06.10.1945 onwards | 06.10.1950 onwards | 50% |

## STATE SECOND PENSION (S2P)

S2P replaced SERPS in April 2002 and will no longer be payable to anyone whose state retirement occurs on or after 6th April 2016.

## State Second Pension Bandings from April 2002

| Tax year | Band 1 | Band 2 | Band 3 |
|----------|--------|--------|--------|
| 2002-2003 | up to £10,800 | £10,801 - £24,600 | £24,601 - £30,420 |
| 2003-2004 | up to £11,200 | £11,201 - £25,600 | £25,601 - £30,940 |
| 2004-2005 | up to £11,600 | £11,601 - £26,600 | £26,601 - £31,720 |
| 2005-2006 | up to £12,100 | £12,101 - £27,800 | £27,801 - £32,760 |
| 2006-2007 | up to £12,500 | £12,501 - £28,800 | £28,801 - £33,540 |
| 2007-2008 | up to £13,000 | £13,001 - £30,000 | £30,001 - £34,840 |
| 2008-2009 | up to £13,500 | £13,501 - £31,100 | £31,101 - £40,040 |
| 2009-2010 | up to £13,900 | £13,901 - £31,800 | £31,801 - £43,875 |
| 2010-2011 | up to £14,100 | £14,101 - £40,040 | abolished |
| 2011-2012 | up to £14,100 | £14,101 - £40.040 | |
| 2012-2013 | Up to £14,700 | £14,701 - £40.040 | |
| 2013-2014 | Up to £15,000 | £15,001 - £40,040 | |
| 2014-2015 | Up to £15,100 | £15,101 - £40,040 | |
| 2015-2016 | Up to £15,300 | £15,301 - £40,040 | |

Low Earnings Threshold - the amount by reference to which the three surplus earnings bands, are determined for the purpose of calculating the state second pension (the additional pension), within the state retirement pension.

## Low Earnings Threshold from 6th April 2004

| Date from | £ | Date from | £ |
|-----------|---|-----------|---|
| 06.04.2004 | 11,600 | 06.04.2010 | 14,100 |
| 06.04.2005 | 12,100 | 06.04.2011 | 14,400 |
| 06.04.2006 | 12,500 | 06.04.2012 | 14,700 |
| 06.04.2007 | 13,000 | 06.04.2013 | 15,000 |
| 06.04.2008 | 13,500 | 07.04.2014 | 15,100 |
| 06.04.2009 | 13,900 | 06.04.2015 | 15,300 |

## STATE PENSION – SINGLE TIER

The New State Pension was introduced for those reaching state pension age after 6th April 2016. This means:
- Women born on or after 6.4.53, and
- Men born on or after 6.4.51

Pensions in payment as at 6th April 2016 will not change and those starting work from this date will only ever have the new pension entitlement. Everyone retiring on or after 6th April 2016 will go through a revaluation exercise before 6th April 2016 to convert existing NICs records. Anyone can check their record as long as they are more than 4 months away from SPA by requesting a state pension forecast at: https://www.gov.uk/check-state-pension .

Those with contracted-out service will get less than the new state pension amount of £175.20 (£168.60 from 6th April 2019, £164.35 from 6th April 2018, £159.55 from 6th April 2017, £155.65 from 6th April 2016), reflecting the contracted-out service, those with SERPS and/or S2P entitlements will get more.

The new state pension will depend on an individual's contribution only. This will affect not only UK residents but will also ensure that people living overseas who have not paid into the UK social security system cannot claim a state pension based on the national insurance contributions of their spouse. Transitional arrangements will allow those reaching state pension age from 6th April 2016 to protect their entitlement to a pension based on their spouse's record up to the start date of the new pension in April 2016 (for example women paying reduced rate national insurance).

A DWP Factsheet to explain the changes is available at:
https://www.gov.uk/government/publications/state-pension-fact-sheets .

## TAX CREDITS

The introduction of Tax Credits on 6th April 2001 was an extension of the transference of responsibility for the administration of a statutory benefit from central Government to employers first adopted with the introduction of Statutory Sick Pay (SSP) in 1983. Tax Credits were not an amount of income receivable without payment of tax (unlike personal tax allowances) instead they were a payment made as an addition to gross pay.

Entitlement took the form of a working tax credit, if applicable including a childcare element and, again if applicable, the child tax credit. Both were subject to income limits which, when reached, reduced the amounts payable.

From April 2001 to March 2006 payment was made by the employer on a gross basis without application of statutory deductions and irrespective of any other pay entitlement. From April 2006 the payment of Tax Credits has been wholly administered and paid by HMRC.

From April 2017 no further rates have been published in line with the migration of all tax credit recipients to the new Universal credit entitlement (see below).

## WELFARE REFORM - THE FUTURE OF STATE BENEFITS

The Welfare Reform Act 2012 received Royal Assent on 8th March 2012. It provides for the introduction of a new all-encompassing benefit called Universal Credit. Universal Credit (UC) start to be paid to new claimants in October 2013, with migration from the existing benefits system over the next four years.

UC is a single household payment which merges Income Support, income-based Job Seeker's Allowance, income-related Employment and Support Allowance, Housing Benefit, Child Tax Credit and Working Tax Credit into one payment, controlled by DWP. Personal Independence Payments (PIP) will also replace the current Disability Living Allowance (DLA).

The DWP will calculate a household's entitlement to the UC by reference to personal and earnings information that is provided to them by HMRC through Real Time Information (RTI) - see Part 1.

N.B.: the section on statutory payments is not designed to be a comprehensive guide on the benefit system. Only key statutory payments are reproduced here. A full set of benefits can be found at: https://www.gov.uk/government/publications/proposed-benefit-and-pension-rates-2019-to-2020 .

# APPENDIX 1

## USEFUL ADDRESSES, HELPLINES, and WEBSITES

| **Advisory Conciliation and Arbitration Service (ACAS)** | |
|---|---|
| Helpline | 0300 123 1100 |
| Text Relay service | 18001 0300 123 1100 |
| Website | http://www.acas.org.uk |

| **UK Visas and Immigration** | |
|---|---|
| Employers' and sponsors' helpline | 0300 123 4699 |
| Website | https://www.gov.uk/sponsor-management-system |

| **BACS** | |
|---|---|
| 2 Thomas More Square, London, E1W 1YN | |
| Telephone | 0370 165 0018 |
| Website | http://www.bacs.co.uk |

| **Chartered Institute of Payroll Professionals (CIPP)** | |
|---|---|
| Goldfinger House, 245 Cranmore Boulevard, Shirley, Solihull, West Midlands, B90 4ZL | |
| Tel | 0121 712 1000 |
| Fax | 0121 712 1001 |
| Website | http://www.cipp.org.uk/ |

| **Child Maintenance Service** | |
|---|---|
| Tel | 0800 232 1961 |
| CSA Employer Helpline | 08001712248 |
| Website | http://www.cmoptions.org/ |

| **Data Protection (Information Commissioner)** | |
|---|---|
| Tel | 0303 123 1113 |
| Scotland | 0303 123 1115 |
| Wales | 03304146421 |
| Northern Ireland | 0303 123 1114 |
| Website | https://ico.org.uk/ |

| **Department for Business, Energy, & Industrial Strategy (BEIS)** | |
|---|---|
| Website | https://www.gov.uk/government/organisations/department-for-business-innovation-skills |

| **Working Time Regulations** | |
|---|---|
| Website | www.gov.uk/rest-breaks-work |

| Department for Work and Pensions (DWP) | |
| --- | --- |
| Website | https://www.gov.uk/government/organisations/department-for-work-pensions |
| Leaflets | https://www.gov.uk/government/collections/dwp-leaflets-and-how-to-order-them |

| Health and Safety Executive | |
| --- | --- |
| Tel (major injuries only) | 0345 300 9923 |
| Website | http://www.hse.gov.uk/ |

| HM Revenue and Customs (HMRC) | |
| --- | --- |
| Website | https://www.gov.uk/government/organisations/hm-revenue-customs |

# ACCOUNTING AND PAYMENTS SERVICE

| Accounting and Payments Service Cumbernauld | |
| --- | --- |
| HMRC Accounts Office, Bradford, BD98 1YY | |
| Tel | 0300 200 3401 |

| Accounting and Payments Service Shipley | |
| --- | --- |
| HMRC Accounts Office, Bradford, BD98 1GG | |
| Tel | 0300 200 3401 |
| Apprenticeship levy advice | 0300 200 3200 |

| Complaint adjudication | |
| --- | --- |
| Where a complaint against is not settled a final appeal may be made to the Adjudicator | |
| The Adjudicator's Office, PO Box 10280, Nottingham, NG2 9PF | |
| Tel | 0300 057 1111 |
| Fax | 0300 059 4513 |
| Website | http://www.adjudicatorsoffice.gov.uk |

| Employers: Stationery and forms ordering | |
| --- | --- |
| Tel | 0300 123 1074 |
| Textphone | 18001 0300 123 1074 |
| Website | https://www.gov.uk/government/organisations/hm-revenue-customs/contact/employer-stationery-and-forms-ordering |

| Employer Helpline | |
| --- | --- |
| Tel | 0300 200 3200 |
| Textphone | 0300 200 3212 |

| Incentive Awards - Taxed Award Schemes | |
| --- | --- |
| Incentive Award Unit, National Insurance Contributions and Employer Office, HM Revenue & Customs, BX9 1BX | |
| Tel | 0300 200 3200 |

| National Insurance | |
| --- | --- |
| Tel | 0300 200 3500 |
| Textphone | 0300 200 3519 |

# PENSIONS

| HMRC – Pension Schemes Service | |
|---|---|
| Tel | 0300 123 1079 |

| Pension Tracing Service | |
|---|---|
| The Pensions Service 9, Mail Handling Site A, Wolverhampton, WV98 1LU | |
| Tel | 0800 731 0193 |
| Textphone | 0800 731 0176 |
| Website | https://www.gov.uk/find-pension-contact-details |

| Share Schemes | |
|---|---|
| Website | https://www.gov.uk/business-tax/employment-related-securities |

| Tax Credits | |
|---|---|
| Helpline | 0345 300 3900 |
| Textphone | 0345 300 3909 |
| Website | https://www.gov.uk/browse/benefits/tax-credits |

| Welsh speakers' contact centre | |
|---|---|
| Helpline | 0300 200 1900 |

| Low Pay Commission | |
|---|---|
| Tel | 020 7211 8119 |
| Website | https://www.gov.uk/government/organisations/low-pay-commission |

| Office for National Statistics | |
|---|---|
| Tel | 0845 601 3034 |
| Webiste | http://www.ons.gov.uk/ |

# HELPLINES

| CIS | |
|---|---|
| Tel | 0300 200 3210 (8.00-8.00 mon-fri: 8.00-4.00 Sat) |
| Textphone | 0300 200 3219 |

| Employment Rights ACAS - helpline | |
|---|---|
| Tel | 0300 123 1100 |

| CIPP Advisory Service helpline (members only) | |
|---|---|
| Tel | 0121 712 1099 (9:00-5 mon-thurs: 9-4:30 fri |

| Payroll Giving – HMRC charities helpline | |
|---|---|
| Tel | 0300 123 1073 |

| The Pensions Regulator (auto-enrolment helpline) | |
|---|---|
| Tel | 0345 600 1011 |

| **Pensions Service** | |
|---|---|
| Pension claims | 0800 731 7898 |
| Textphone | 0800 731 7339 |
| Online help | 0345 604 3349 |
| Textphone | 0345 604 3412 |
| Change in circumstances | 0800 731 0469 |
| Textphone | 0345 606 0285 |

| **Pension Tracing Service** | |
|---|---|
| Tel | 0800 731 0193 (Mon – Fri 8.00 – 6.00) |
| Textphone | 0800 731 0176 |

| **PAYE tax and NICs** | |
|---|---|
| Centre for Non-Residents* | 0300 322 7657 |
| Child Tax Credit | 0345 300 3900 (8.00-8.00 daily) |
| Employers' Order line | 0300 123 1074 (8.00-6.00 mon-fri) |
| Textphone | 18001 0300 123 1074 |

| **Employers' helpline** | |
|---|---|
| Established employers | 0300 200 3200 |
| New employer 'up to 3 years' | 0300 200 3211 |

| **Foreign nationals helpline** *(tax queries for those seconded to the UK)* | | |
|---|---|---|
| Tel | 0161 261 3398 | |
| IR35 Advice line | 0300 123 2326 | ir35@hmrc.gov.uk |
| NI Deficiencies | 0300 200 3500 | (8.30-5.00 mon-fri) |
| NI Registration help line *(for those aged under 16 who are just qualifying for a NINO)* | 0300 200 3500) | (8.30-5.00 mon-fri |
| Online Services help desk | 0300 200 3600 | (8.00-8.00 daily/8.00-4.00 sat) |
| Self-Assessment | 0300 200 3310 | (8.00-8.00 daily/8.00-4.00 sat) |
| Self-Employed | 0300 200 3300 | (8.00-8.00 daily/8.00-4.00 sat) |
| Student loan enquiries | 0300 100 0611 | (8.00-8.00 daily/9.00-4.00 Sat |
| Wales | 0300 100 0370 | |
| Overpayments | 0300 100 0628 | (8.00-8.00 M-T/5.30 Fr/9.00-1.00 Sat) |
| Tax Credits | 0345 300 3900 | (8.00-8.00 daily/8.00-4.00 sat) |
| Tax Evasion hotline | 0800 788 887 | (8.00-8.00 daily/8.00-4.00 sat) |
| Universal credit helpline | 0345 600 0723 | |
| Textphone | 0345 600 0743 | |
| Value Added Tax (VAT) | 0300 200 3700 | (8.00-6.00 mon-fri) |
| Welsh Language | 0300 200 1900 | (8.30-5.00 mon-fri) |

# APPENDIX 2

## STUDENT LOAN DEDUCTIONS

### Plan 1 loan repayment

| Date | Annual threshold | Weekly threshold | Monthly threshold | Repayment rate |
|------|------------------|------------------|-------------------|----------------|
| 06.04.2016 | £17,495 | £336 | £1,457 | 9%* |
| 06.04.2017 | £17,775 | £341 | £1,481 | 9%* |
| 06.04.2018 | £18,330 | £352 | £1,527 | 9%* |
| 06.04.2019 06.04.2020 | £18,935 £19,390 | £365 £372.88 | £1,578 £1,615.83 | 9%* 9%* |

*Repayment is rounded down to the lower exact whole pounds.*

### Plan 2 loan repayment

| Date | Annual threshold | Weekly threshold | Monthly threshold | Repayment rate |
|------|------------------|------------------|-------------------|----------------|
| 06.04.2016 | £21,000 | £403 | £1,750 | 9%* |
| 06.04.2017 | £21,000 | £403 | £1,750 | 9%* |
| 06.04.2018 | £25,000 | £480 | £2,083 | 9%* |
| 06.04.2019 06.04.2020 | £25,725 £26,575 | £495 £511.05 | £2,144 £2,214.58 | 9%* 9%* |

*Repayment is rounded down to the lower exact whole pounds.*

### Post Graduate loan repayment

| Date | Annual threshold | Weekly threshold | Monthly threshold | Repayment rate |
|------|------------------|------------------|-------------------|----------------|
| 06.04.2019 | £21,000 | £404 | £1,750 | 6%* |
| 06.04.2020 | £21,000 | £403.84 | £1,750 | 6%* |

*Repayment is rounded down to the lower exact whole pounds.*

These tables should only be used to manually calculate Student or Postgraduate Loan deductions when you cannot or do not use either of the following:

- commercial payroll software
- HMRC Basic PAYE tools

You can download HMRC Basic PAYE tools.

If you're doing a manual calculation use the weekly or monthly tables below for existing employees for whom you've received either form SL1 'Student Loan Start Notice' or form PGL1 'Postgraduate Loan Start Notice' and for new employees who have:

- told you they are repaying an Income Contingent student loan and either the relevant plan or loan type, or both
- given you a form P45 with a 'Y' entry in box 5 'Student Loan deductions to continue'
- completed a starter declaration and ticked the student loan box indicating either the relevant plan or loan type, or both

Before you can use these tables, you must work out the correct figure of employee earnings on which Student or Postgraduate Loan deductions are due. The figure to use is the same gross pay amount that you would use to calculate your employer's secondary Class 1 National Insurance contributions.

## 2. How to use these tables

Go to the table which corresponds to your employee's loan or plan type. Look up the amount of weekly or monthly earnings in the left hand column to find the corresponding deduction in the right hand column. If the exact amount of earnings is not shown, look for the nearest figure below and use the amount of deduction shown for that range of earnings.

If you need help using these tables phone the Employer Helpline.

## 3. Earnings for week or month exceed highest amount of earnings shown in the tables

For borrowers repaying on Student Loan Plan 1 - if earnings in the week or month exceed the highest amount of earnings shown in the tables you'll need to deduct the 'pay period threshold' from total earnings in the week or month. Do this by deducting:

- £372.88 from weekly earnings for weekly paid employees
- £1,615.83 from monthly earnings for monthly paid employees

Multiply the result (the excess) by 9% (0.09), round down this figure to the nearest whole pound.

For borrowers repaying on Student Loan Plan 2 - if earnings in the week or month exceed the highest amount of earnings shown in the tables you'll need to deduct the 'pay period threshold' from total earnings in the week or month. Do this by deducting:

- £511.05 from weekly earnings for weekly paid employees

- £2,214.58 from monthly earnings for monthly paid employees

Multiply the result (the excess) by 9% (0.09), round down this figure to the nearest whole pound.

For borrowers repaying a Postgraduate Loan - if earnings in the week or month exceed the highest amount of earnings shown in the tables you'll need to deduct the 'pay period threshold' from total earnings in the week or month. Do this by deducting:

- £403.84 from weekly earnings for weekly paid employees
- £1,750.00 from monthly earnings for monthly paid employees

Multiply the result (the excess) by 6% (0.06), round down this figure to the nearest whole pound.

Record the amount of Student or Postgraduate Loan deduction on the employee's payroll record. Only employers exempt from filing payroll information online will not have to use payroll software to do this.

## 3.1 Example weekly paid employee on Student Loan Plan 1

| For weekly earnings of £420 | The £4.00 Student Loan deduction is calculated as follows: |
| --- | --- |
| Deduct the 'pay period threshold' of £372.88 from the weekly earnings of £420 | The excess is £47.12 |
| Multiply £47.12 by 0.09 | £4.24 |
| Round down £4.24 to the nearest £ | £4.00 |

## 3.2 Example monthly paid employee on PGL

| For monthly earnings of £2083 | The £19.00 PGL deduction is calculated as follows: |
| --- | --- |
| Deduct the 'pay period threshold' of £1750 from the monthly earnings of £2083 | The excess is £333 |
| Multiply £333 by 0.06 | £19.98 |
| Round down £19.98 to the nearest £ | £19.00 |

# 4. Pay periods other than weekly or monthly

The pay period for Student and Postgraduate Loan deductions is always exactly the same as the earnings period for National Insurance contributions.

For earnings periods of less than 7 days use a pay period of 1 week.

If the pay period is a multiple of a week or a month:

1. Divide the earnings into equal weekly or monthly amounts to get an average weekly or monthly amount.

2. Find the amount of Student or Postgraduate Loan deduction due for the average weekly or monthly amount.
3. Multiply the amount of Student or Postgraduate Loan deduction by the number of weeks or months in the pay period.
4. Record the result of step 3 on the employee's payroll records at the appropriate week or month.

If, exceptionally, the earnings period for National Insurance contributions is longer than a week, but not a multiple of a week or month:

1. Work out the number of days in the pay period.
2. Multiply the number of days by £19,390 for Student Loan Plan 1 or £26,575 for Student Loan Plan 2 or £21,000 for Postgraduate Loans and then divide the result by the number of days in the year to give you the pay period threshold. Round down the resulting figure to the nearest penny.
3. Deduct the 'pay period threshold' from the total earnings in the pay period.
4. Multiply the result of step 3 (the excess) by 9% (0.09) for Student Loan Plans 1 and 2 or by 6% (0.06) for Postgraduate Loans.
5. Round down the resulting figure to the nearest whole pound.
6. Record the amount of Student or Postgraduate Loan deduction on the employee's payroll records at the appropriate week or month.

## 4.1 Example for employee on Student Loan Plan 1

| Employee receives earnings of £1,448 for a pay period consisting of 25 days | The amount of Student Loan deduction of £10 is calculated as follows: |
|---|---|
| Number of days in pay period | 25 |
| Pay period threshold | 25 × £19,390 ÷ 365 = £1,328.08 after rounding |
| Deduct pay period threshold from earnings | £1,448 - £1,328.08 = £119.92 |
| Excess £119.92 | Multiply excess by 0.09 = £10.79 |
| Round down to nearest £ | £10 |

## 4.2 Example for employee on PGL

| Employee receives earnings of £1,998 for a pay period consisting of 25 days | The amount of PGL deduction of £33 is calculated as follows: |
|---|---|
| Number of days in pay period | 25 |
| Pay period threshold | 25 × £21,000 ÷ 365 = £1,438.35 after rounding |
| Deduct pay period threshold from earnings | £1,998 - £1,438.35 = £559.65 |
| Excess £559.65 | Multiply excess by 0.06 = £33.57 |

3/26

| Employee receives earnings of £1,998 for a pay period consisting of 25 days | The amount of PGL deduction of £33 is calculated as follows: |
| --- | --- |
| Round down to nearest £ | £33 |

## 5. Student Loan Plan 1 weekly table

| Earnings in week £ | Student Loan Deduction £ | Earnings in week £ | Student Loan Deduction £ |
| --- | --- | --- | --- |
| 1 - 383 | 0 | 807 - 817 | 39 |
| 384 - 395 | 1 | 818 - 828 | 40 |
| 396 - 406 | 2 | 829 - 839 | 41 |
| 407 - 417 | 3 | 840 - 820 | 42 |
| 418 - 428 | 4 | 851 - 861 | 43 |
| 429 - 439 | 5 | 862 - 872 | 44 |
| 440 - 450 | 6 | 873 - 883 | 45 |
| 451 - 461 | 7 | 884 - 895 | 46 |
| 462 - 472 | 8 | 896 - 906 | 47 |
| 473 - 483 | 9 | 907 - 917 | 48 |
| 484 - 495 | 10 | 918 - 928 | 49 |
| 496 - 506 | 11 | 929 - 939 | 50 |
| 507 - 517 | 12 | 940 - 950 | 51 |
| 518 - 528 | 13 | 951 - 961 | 52 |
| 529 - 539 | 14 | 962 - 972 | 53 |
| 540 - 550 | 15 | 973 - 983 | 54 |
| 551 - 561 | 16 | 984 - 995 | 55 |
| 562 - 572 | 17 | 996 - 1006 | 56 |
| 573 - 583 | 18 | 1007 - 1017 | 57 |
| 584 - 595 | 19 | 1018 - 1028 | 58 |
| 596 - 606 | 20 | 1029 - 1039 | 59 |
| 607 - 617 | 21 | 1040 - 1050 | 60 |

| Earnings in week £ | Student Loan Deduction £ | Earnings in week £ | Student Loan Deduction £ |
|---|---|---|---|
| 618 - 628 | 22 | 1051 - 1061 | 61 |
| 629 - 639 | 23 | 1062 - 1072 | 62 |
| 640 - 650 | 24 | 1073 - 1083 | 63 |
| 651 - 661 | 25 | 1084 - 1095 | 64 |
| 662 - 672 | 26 | 1096 - 1106 | 65 |
| 673 - 683 | 27 | 1107 - 1117 | 66 |
| 684 - 695 | 28 | 1118 - 1128 | 67 |
| 696 - 706 | 29 | 1129 - 1139 | 68 |
| 707 - 717 | 30 | 1140 - 1150 | 69 |
| 718 - 728 | 31 | 1151 - 1161 | 70 |
| 729 - 739 | 32 | 1162 - 1172 | 71 |
| 740 - 750 | 33 | 1173 - 1183 | 72 |
| 751 - 761 | 34 | 1184 - 1195 | 73 |
| 762 - 772 | 35 | 1196 - 1206 | 74 |
| 773 - 783 | 36 | 1207 - 1217 | 75 |
| 784 - 795 | 37 | 1218 - 1228 | 76 |
| 796 - 806 | 38 | 1229 - 1239 | 77 |

## 6. Student Loan Plan 1 monthly table

| Earnings in month £ | Student Loan Deduction £ | Earnings in month £ | Student Loan Deduction £ | Earnings in month £ | Student Loan Deduction £ | Earnings in month £ | Student Loan Deduction £ |
|---|---|---|---|---|---|---|---|
| 1 - 1626 | 0 | 2583 - 2593 | 87 | 3550 - 3560 | 174 | 4516 - 4526 | 261 |
| 1627 - 1638 | 1 | 2594 - 2604 | 88 | 3561 - 3571 | 175 | 4527 - 4538 | 262 |
| 1639 - 1649 | 2 | 2605 - 2615 | 89 | 3572 - 3582 | 176 | 4539 - 4549 | 263 |

| Earnings in month £ | Student Loan Deduction £ | Earnings in month £ | Student Loan Deduction £ | Earnings in month £ | Student Loan Deduction £ | Earnings in month £ | Student Loan Deduction £ |
|---|---|---|---|---|---|---|---|
| 1650 - 1660 | 3 | 2616 - 2626 | 90 | 3583 - 3593 | 177 | 4550 - 4560 | 264 |
| 1661 - 1671 | 4 | 2627 - 2638 | 91 | 3594 - 3604 | 178 | 4561 - 4571 | 265 |
| 1672 - 1682 | 5 | 2639 - 2649 | 92 | 3605 - 3615 | 179 | 4572 - 4582 | 266 |
| 1683 - 1693 | 6 | 2650 - 2660 | 93 | 3616 - 3626 | 180 | 4583 - 4593 | 267 |
| 1694 - 1704 | 7 | 2661 - 2671 | 94 | 3627 - 3638 | 181 | 4594 - 4604 | 268 |
| 1705 - 1715 | 8 | 2672 - 2682 | 95 | 3639 - 3649 | 182 | 4605 - 4615 | 269 |
| 1716 - 1726 | 9 | 2683 - 2693 | 96 | 3650 - 3660 | 183 | 4616 - 4626 | 270 |
| 1727 - 1738 | 10 | 2694 - 2704 | 97 | 3661 - 3671 | 184 | 4627 - 4638 | 271 |
| 1739 - 1749 | 11 | 2705 - 2715 | 98 | 3672 - 3682 | 185 | 4639 - 4649 | 272 |
| 1750 - 1760 | 12 | 2716 - 2726 | 99 | 3683 - 3693 | 186 | 4650 - 4660 | 273 |
| 1761 - 1771 | 13 | 2727 - 2738 | 100 | 3694 - 3704 | 187 | 4661 - 4671 | 274 |
| 1772 - 1782 | 14 | 2739 - 2749 | 101 | 3705 - 3715 | 188 | 4672 - 4682 | 275 |
| 1783 - 1793 | 15 | 2750 - 2760 | 102 | 3716 - 3726 | 189 | 4683 - 4693 | 276 |
| 1794 - 1804 | 16 | 2761 - 2771 | 103 | 3727 - 3738 | 190 | 4694 - 4704 | 277 |
| 1805 - 1815 | 17 | 2772 - 2782 | 104 | 3739 - 3749 | 191 | 4705 - 4715 | 278 |
| 1816 - 1826 | 18 | 2783 - 2793 | 105 | 3750 - 3760 | 192 | 4716 - 4726 | 279 |

| Earnings in month £ | Student Loan Deduction £ | Earnings in month £ | Student Loan Deduction £ | Earnings in month £ | Student Loan Deduction £ | Earnings in month £ | Student Loan Deduction £ |
|---|---|---|---|---|---|---|---|
| 1827 - 1838 | 19 | 2794 - 2804 | 106 | 3761 - 3771 | 193 | 4727 - 4738 | 280 |
| 1839 - 1849 | 20 | 2805 - 2815 | 107 | 3772 - 3782 | 194 | 4739 - 4749 | 281 |
| 1850 - 1860 | 21 | 2816 - 2826 | 108 | 3783 - 3793 | 195 | 4750 - 4760 | 282 |
| 1861 - 1871 | 22 | 2827 - 2838 | 109 | 3794 - 3804 | 196 | 4761 - 4771 | 283 |
| 1872 - 1882 | 23 | 2839 - 2849 | 110 | 3805 - 3815 | 197 | 4772 - 4782 | 284 |
| 1883 - 1893 | 24 | 2850 - 2860 | 111 | 3816 - 3826 | 198 | 4783 - 4793 | 285 |
| 1894 - 1904 | 25 | 2861 - 2871 | 112 | 3827 - 3838 | 199 | 4794 - 4804 | 286 |
| 1905 - 1915 | 26 | 2872 - 2882 | 113 | 3839 - 3849 | 200 | 4805 - 4815 | 287 |
| 1916 - 1926 | 27 | 2883 - 2893 | 114 | 3850 - 3860 | 201 | 4816 - 4826 | 288 |
| 1927 - 1938 | 28 | 2894 - 2904 | 115 | 3861 - 3871 | 202 | 4827 - 4838 | 289 |
| 1939 - 1949 | 29 | 2905 - 2915 | 116 | 3872 - 3882 | 203 | 4839 - 4849 | 290 |
| 1950 - 1960 | 30 | 2916 - 2926 | 117 | 3883 - 3893 | 204 | 4850 - 4860 | 291 |
| 1961 - 1971 | 31 | 2927 - 2938 | 118 | 3894 - 3904 | 205 | 4861 - 4871 | 292 |
| 1972 - 1982 | 32 | 2939 - 2949 | 119 | 3905 - 3915 | 206 | 4872 - 4882 | 293 |
| 1983 - 1993 | 33 | 2950 - 2960 | 120 | 3916 - 3926 | 207 | 4883 - 4893 | 294 |
| 1994 - 2004 | 34 | 2961 - 2971 | 121 | 3927 - 3938 | 208 | 4894 - 4904 | 295 |

| Earnings in month £ | Student Loan Deduction £ | Earnings in month £ | Student Loan Deduction £ | Earnings in month £ | Student Loan Deduction £ | Earnings in month £ | Student Loan Deduction £ |
|---|---|---|---|---|---|---|---|
| 2005 - 2015 | 35 | 2972 - 2982 | 122 | 3939 - 3949 | 209 | 4905 - 4915 | 296 |
| 2016 - 2026 | 36 | 2983 - 2993 | 123 | 3950 - 3960 | 210 | 4916 - 4926 | 297 |
| 2027 - 2038 | 37 | 2994 - 3004 | 124 | 3961 - 3971 | 211 | 4927 - 4938 | 298 |
| 2039 - 2049 | 38 | 3005 - 3015 | 125 | 3972 - 3982 | 212 | 4939 - 4949 | 299 |
| 2050 - 2060 | 39 | 3016 - 3026 | 126 | 3983 - 3993 | 213 | 4950 - 4960 | 300 |
| 2061 - 2071 | 40 | 3027 - 3038 | 127 | 3994 - 4004 | 214 | 4961 - 4971 | 301 |
| 2072 - 2082 | 41 | 3039 - 3049 | 128 | 4005 - 4015 | 215 | 4971 - 4982 | 302 |
| 2083 - 2093 | 42 | 3050 - 3060 | 129 | 4016 - 4026 | 216 | 4983 - 4993 | 303 |
| 2094 - 2104 | 43 | 3061 - 3071 | 130 | 4027 - 4038 | 217 | 4994 - 5004 | 304 |
| 2105 - 2115 | 44 | 3072 - 3082 | 131 | 4039 - 4049 | 218 | 5005 - 5015 | 305 |
| 2116 - 2126 | 45 | 3083 - 3093 | 132 | 4050 - 4060 | 219 | 5016 - 5026 | 306 |
| 2127 - 2138 | 46 | 3094 - 3104 | 133 | 4061 - 4071 | 220 | 5027 - 5038 | 307 |
| 2139 - 2149 | 47 | 3105 - 3115 | 134 | 4072 - 4082 | 221 | 5039 - 5049 | 308 |
| 2150 - 2160 | 48 | 3116 - 3126 | 135 | 4083 - 4093 | 222 | 5050 - 5060 | 309 |
| 2161 - 2171 | 49 | 3127 - 3138 | 136 | 4094 - 4104 | 223 | 5061 - 5071 | 310 |
| 2172 - 2182 | 50 | 3139 - 3149 | 137 | 4105 - 4115 | 224 | 5072 - 5082 | 311 |

8/26

259

| Earnings in month £ | Student Loan Deduction £ | Earnings in month £ | Student Loan Deduction £ | Earnings in month £ | Student Loan Deduction £ | Earnings in month £ | Student Loan Deduction £ |
|---|---|---|---|---|---|---|---|
| 2183 - 2193 | 51 | 3150 - 3160 | 138 | 4116 - 4126 | 225 | 5083 - 5093 | 312 |
| 2194 - 2204 | 52 | 3161 - 3171 | 139 | 4127 - 4138 | 226 | 5094 - 5104 | 313 |
| 2205 - 2215 | 53 | 3172 - 3182 | 140 | 4139 - 4149 | 227 | 5105 - 5115 | 314 |
| 2216 - 2226 | 54 | 3183 - 3193 | 141 | 4150 - 4160 | 228 | 5116 - 5126 | 315 |
| 2227 - 2238 | 55 | 3194 - 3204 | 142 | 4161 - 4171 | 229 | 5127 - 5138 | 316 |
| 2239 - 2249 | 56 | 3205 - 3215 | 143 | 4172 - 4182 | 230 | 5139 - 5149 | 317 |
| 2250 - 2260 | 57 | 3216 - 3226 | 144 | 4183 - 4193 | 231 | 5150 - 5160 | 318 |
| 2261 - 2271 | 58 | 3227 - 3238 | 145 | 4194 - 4204 | 232 | 5172 - 5182 | 320 |
| 2272 - 2282 | 59 | 3239 - 3249 | 146 | 4216 - 4226 | 234 | 5183 - 5193 | 321 |
| 2283 - 2293 | 60 | 3261 - 3271 | 148 | 4227 - 4238 | 235 | 5194 - 5204 | 322 |
| 2305 - 2315 | 62 | 3272 - 3282 | 149 | 4239 - 4249 | 236 | 5205 - 5215 | 323 |
| 2316 - 2326 | 63 | 3283 - 3293 | 150 | 4250 - 4260 | 237 | 5216 - 5226 | 324 |
| 2327 - 2338 | 64 | 3294 - 3304 | 151 | 4261 - 4271 | 238 | 5227 - 5238 | 325 |
| 2339 - 2349 | 65 | 3305 - 3315 | 152 | 4272 - 4282 | 239 | 5239 - 5249 | 326 |
| 2350 - 2360 | 66 | 3316 - 3326 | 153 | 4283 - 4293 | 240 | 5250 - 5260 | 327 |
| 2361 - 2371 | 67 | 3327 - 3338 | 154 | 4294 - 4304 | 241 | 5261 - 5271 | 328 |

| Earnings in month £ | Student Loan Deduction £ | Earnings in month £ | Student Loan Deduction £ | Earnings in month £ | Student Loan Deduction £ | Earnings in month £ | Student Loan Deduction £ |
|---|---|---|---|---|---|---|---|
| 2372 - 2382 | 68 | 3339 - 3349 | 155 | 4305 - 4215 | 242 | 5272 - 5282 | 329 |
| 2383 - 2393 | 69 | 3350 - 3360 | 156 | 4316 - 4326 | 243 | 5283 - 5293 | 330 |
| 2394 - 2404 | 70 | 3361 - 3371 | 157 | 4327 - 4338 | 244 | 5294 - 5304 | 331 |
| 2405 - 2415 | 71 | 3372 - 3382 | 158 | 4339 - 4349 | 245 | 5305 - 5315 | 332 |
| 2416 - 2426 | 72 | 3383 - 3393 | 159 | 4350 - 4360 | 246 | 5316 - 5326 | 333 |
| 2427 - 2438 | 73 | 3394 - 3404 | 160 | 4361 - 4371 | 247 | 5327 - 5338 | 334 |
| 2439 - 2449 | 74 | 3405 - 3415 | 161 | 4372 - 4382 | 248 | 5339 - 4349 | 335 |
| 2450 - 2460 | 75 | 3416 - 3426 | 162 | 4383 - 4393 | 249 | 5350 - 5360 | 336 |
| 2461 - 2471 | 76 | 3427 - 3438 | 163 | 4394 - 4404 | 250 | 5351 - 5371 | 337 |
| 2472 - 2482 | 77 | 3439 - 3449 | 164 | 4405 - 4415 | 251 | | |
| 2483 - 2493 | 78 | 3450 - 3460 | 165 | 4416 - 4426 | 252 | | |
| 2494 - 2504 | 79 | 3461 - 3471 | 166 | 4427 - 4438 | 253 | | |
| 2505 - 2515 | 80 | 3472 - 3482 | 167 | 4439 - 4449 | 254 | | |
| 2516 - 2526 | 81 | 3483 - 3493 | 168 | 4450 - 4460 | 255 | | |
| 2527 - 2538 | 82 | 3494 - 3504 | 169 | 4461 - 4471 | 256 | | |
| 2539 - 2549 | 83 | 3505 - 3515 | 170 | 4472 - 4482 | 257 | | |

| Earnings in month £ | Student Loan Deduction £ | Earnings in month £ | Student Loan Deduction £ | Earnings in month £ | Student Loan Deduction £ | Earnings in month £ | Student Loan Deduction £ |
|---|---|---|---|---|---|---|---|
| 2550 - 2560 | 84 | 3516 - 3526 | 171 | 4483 - 4493 | 258 | | |
| 2561 - 2571 | 85 | 3527 - 3538 | 172 | 4494 - 4504 | 259 | | |
| 2572 - 2582 | 86 | 3539 - 3549 | 173 | 4505 - 4515 | 260 | | |

## 7. Student Loan Plan 2 weekly table

| Earnings in week £ | Student Loan Deduction £ | Earnings in week £ | Student Loan Deduction £ |
|---|---|---|---|
| 1 - 522 | 0 | 945 - 955 | 39 |
| 523 - 533 | 1 | 956 - 966 | 40 |
| 534 - 544 | 2 | 967 - 977 | 41 |
| 545 - 555 | 3 | 978 - 988 | 42 |
| 556 - 566 | 4 | 989 - 999 | 43 |
| 567 - 577 | 5 | 1000 - 1011 | 44 |
| 578 - 588 | 6 | 1012 - 1022 | 45 |
| 589 - 599 | 7 | 1023 - 1033 | 46 |
| 600 - 611 | 8 | 1034 - 1044 | 47 |
| 612 - 622 | 9 | 1045 - 1055 | 48 |
| 623 - 633 | 10 | 1056 - 1066 | 49 |
| 634 - 644 | 11 | 1067 - 1077 | 50 |
| 645 - 655 | 12 | 1078 - 1088 | 51 |
| 656 - 666 | 13 | 1089 - 1099 | 52 |
| 667 - 677 | 14 | 1100 - 1111 | 53 |
| 678 - 688 | 15 | 1112 - 1122 | 54 |
| 689 - 699 | 16 | 1123 - 1133 | 55 |

| Earnings in week £ | Student Loan Deduction £ | Earnings in week £ | Student Loan Deduction £ |
|---|---|---|---|
| 700 - 711 | 17 | 1134 - 1144 | 56 |
| 712 - 722 | 18 | 1145 - 1155 | 57 |
| 723 - 733 | 19 | 1156 - 1166 | 58 |
| 734 - 744 | 20 | 1167 - 1177 | 59 |
| 745 - 755 | 21 | 1178 - 1188 | 60 |
| 756 - 766 | 22 | 1189 - 1199 | 61 |
| 767 - 777 | 23 | 1200 - 1211 | 62 |
| 778 - 788 | 24 | 1212 - 1222 | 63 |
| 789 - 799 | 25 | 1223 - 1233 | 64 |
| 800 - 811 | 26 | 1234 - 1244 | 65 |
| 812 - 822 | 27 | 1245 - 1255 | 66 |
| 823 - 833 | 28 | 1256 - 1266 | 67 |
| 834 - 844 | 29 | 1267 - 1277 | 68 |
| 845 - 855 | 30 | 1278 - 1288 | 69 |
| 856 - 866 | 31 | 1289 - 1299 | 70 |
| 867 - 877 | 32 | 1300 - 1311 | 71 |
| 878 - 888 | 33 | 1312 - 1322 | 72 |
| 889 - 899 | 34 | 1323 - 1333 | 73 |
| 900 - 911 | 35 | 1334 - 1344 | 74 |
| 912 - 922 | 36 | 1345 - 1355 | 75 |
| 923 - 933 | 37 | 1356 - 1366 | 76 |
| 934 - 944 | 38 | 1367 - 1377 | 77 |

## 8. Student Loan Plan 2 monthly table

12/26

| Earnings in month £ | Student Loan Deduction £ | Earnings in month £ | Student Loan Deduction £ | Earnings in month £ | Student Loan Deduction £ | Earnings in month £ | Student Loan Deduction £ |
|---|---|---|---|---|---|---|---|
| 1 - 2225 | 0 | 3171 - 3181 | 86 | 4126 - 4136 | 172 | 5082 - 5092 | 258 |
| 2226 - 2236 | 1 | 3182 - 3192 | 87 | 4137 - 4147 | 173 | 5093 - 5103 | 259 |
| 2237 - 2247 | 2 | 3193 - 3203 | 88 | 4148 - 4159 | 174 | 5104 - 5114 | 260 |
| 2248 - 2259 | 3 | 3204 - 3214 | 89 | 4160 - 4170 | 175 | 5115 - 5125 | 261 |
| 2260 - 2270 | 4 | 3215 - 3225 | 90 | 4171 - 4181 | 176 | 5126 - 5136 | 262 |
| 2271 - 2281 | 5 | 3226 - 3236 | 91 | 4182 - 4192 | 177 | 5137 - 5147 | 263 |
| 2282 - 2292 | 6 | 3237 - 3247 | 92 | 4193 - 4203 | 178 | 5148 - 5159 | 264 |
| 2293 - 2303 | 7 | 3248 - 3259 | 93 | 4204 - 4214 | 179 | 5160 - 5170 | 265 |
| 2304 - 2314 | 8 | 3260 - 3270 | 94 | 4215 - 4225 | 180 | 5171 - 5181 | 266 |
| 2315 - 2325 | 9 | 3271 - 3281 | 95 | 4226 - 4236 | 181 | 5182 - 5192 | 267 |
| 2326 - 2336 | 10 | 3282 - 3292 | 96 | 4236 - 4247 | 182 | 5193 - 5203 | 268 |
| 2337 - 2347 | 11 | 3293 - 3303 | 97 | 4248 - 4259 | 183 | 5204 - 5214 | 269 |
| 2348 - 2359 | 12 | 3304 - 3314 | 98 | 4260 - 4270 | 184 | 5215 - 5225 | 270 |
| 2360 - 2370 | 13 | 3315 - 3325 | 99 | 4271 - 4281 | 185 | 5226 - 5236 | 271 |
| 2371 - 2381 | 14 | 3326 - 3336 | 100 | 4282 - 4292 | 186 | 5237 - 5247 | 272 |
| 2382 - 2392 | 15 | 3337 - 3347 | 101 | 4293 - 4303 | 187 | 5248 - 5259 | 273 |

13/26

| Earnings in month £ | Student Loan Deduction £ | Earnings in month £ | Student Loan Deduction £ | Earnings in month £ | Student Loan Deduction £ | Earnings in month £ | Student Loan Deduction £ |
|---|---|---|---|---|---|---|---|
| 2393 - 2403 | 16 | 3348 - 3359 | 102 | 4304 - 4314 | 188 | 5260 - 5270 | 274 |
| 2404 - 2414 | 17 | 3360 - 3370 | 103 | 4315 - 4325 | 189 | 5271 - 5281 | 275 |
| 2415 - 2425 | 18 | 3371 - 3381 | 104 | 4326 - 4336 | 190 | 5282 - 5292 | 276 |
| 2426 - 2436 | 19 | 3382 - 3392 | 105 | 4337 - 4347 | 191 | 5293 - 5303 | 277 |
| 2437 - 2447 | 20 | 3393 - 3403 | 106 | 4348 - 4359 | 192 | 5304 - 5314 | 278 |
| 2448 - 2459 | 21 | 3404 - 3414 | 107 | 4360 - 4370 | 193 | 5315 - 5325 | 279 |
| 2460 - 2470 | 22 | 3415 - 3425 | 108 | 4371 - 4381 | 194 | 5326 - 5336 | 280 |
| 2471 - 2481 | 23 | 3426 - 3436 | 109 | 4382 - 4392 | 195 | 5337 - 5347 | 281 |
| 2482 - 2492 | 24 | 3437 - 3447 | 110 | 4393 - 4403 | 196 | 5348 - 5359 | 282 |
| 2493 - 2503 | 25 | 3448 - 3459 | 111 | 4404 - 4414 | 197 | 5360 - 5370 | 283 |
| 2504 - 2514 | 26 | 3460 - 3470 | 112 | 4415 - 4425 | 198 | 5371 - 5381 | 284 |
| 2515 - 2525 | 27 | 3471 - 3481 | 113 | 4426 - 4436 | 199 | 5382 - 5392 | 285 |
| 2526 - 2536 | 28 | 3482 - 3492 | 114 | 4437 - 4447 | 200 | 5393 - 5403 | 286 |
| 2537 - 2547 | 29 | 3493 - 3503 | 115 | 4448 - 4459 | 201 | 5404 - 5414 | 287 |
| 2548 - 2559 | 30 | 3504 - 3514 | 116 | 4460 - 4470 | 202 | 5415 - 5425 | 288 |
| 2560 - 2570 | 31 | 3515 - 3525 | 117 | 4471 - 4481 | 203 | 5426 - 5436 | 289 |

APPENDIX 2: STUDENT LOAN DEDUCTIONS

| Earnings in month £ | Student Loan Deduction £ | Earnings in month £ | Student Loan Deduction £ | Earnings in month £ | Student Loan Deduction £ | Earnings in month £ | Student Loan Deduction £ |
|---|---|---|---|---|---|---|---|
| 2571 - 2581 | 32 | 3526 - 3536 | 118 | 4482 - 4492 | 204 | 5437 - 5447 | 290 |
| 2582 - 2592 | 33 | 3537 - 3547 | 119 | 4493 - 4503 | 205 | 5448 - 5459 | 291 |
| 2593 - 2603 | 34 | 3548 - 3559 | 120 | 4504 - 4514 | 206 | 5460 - 5470 | 292 |
| 2604 - 2614 | 35 | 3560 - 3570 | 121 | 4515 - 4525 | 207 | 5471 - 5481 | 293 |
| 2615 - 2625 | 36 | 3571 - 3581 | 122 | 4526 - 4536 | 208 | 5482 - 5492 | 294 |
| 2626 - 2636 | 37 | 3582 - 3592 | 123 | 4537 - 4547 | 209 | 5493 - 5503 | 295 |
| 2637 - 2647 | 38 | 3593 - 3603 | 124 | 4548 - 4559 | 210 | 5504 - 5514 | 296 |
| 2648 - 2659 | 39 | 3604 - 3614 | 125 | 4560 - 4570 | 211 | 5515 - 5525 | 297 |
| 2660 - 2670 | 40 | 3615 - 3625 | 126 | 4571 - 4581 | 212 | 5526 - 5536 | 298 |
| 2671 - 2681 | 41 | 3626 - 3636 | 127 | 4582 - 4592 | 213 | 5537 - 5547 | 299 |
| 2682 - 2692 | 42 | 3637 - 3647 | 128 | 4593 - 4603 | 214 | 5548 - 5559 | 300 |
| 2693 - 2703 | 43 | 3648 - 3659 | 129 | 4604 - 4614 | 215 | 5560 - 5570 | 301 |
| 2704 - 2714 | 44 | 3660 - 3670 | 130 | 4615 - 4625 | 216 | 5571 - 5581 | 302 |
| 2715 - 2725 | 45 | 3671 - 3681 | 131 | 4626 - 4636 | 217 | 5582 - 5592 | 303 |
| 2726 - 2736 | 46 | 3682 - 3692 | 132 | 4637 - 4647 | 218 | 5593 - 5603 | 304 |
| 2737 - 2747 | 47 | 3693 - 3703 | 133 | 4648 - 4659 | 219 | 5604 - 5614 | 305 |

| Earnings in month £ | Student Loan Deduction £ | Earnings in month £ | Student Loan Deduction £ | Earnings in month £ | Student Loan Deduction £ | Earnings in month £ | Student Loan Deduction £ |
|---|---|---|---|---|---|---|---|
| 2748 - 2759 | 48 | 3704 - 3714 | 134 | 4660 - 4670 | 220 | 5615 - 5625 | 306 |
| 2760 - 2770 | 49 | 3715 - 3725 | 135 | 4671 - 4681 | 221 | 5626 - 5636 | 307 |
| 2771 - 2781 | 50 | 3726 - 3736 | 136 | 4682 - 4692 | 222 | 5637 - 5647 | 308 |
| 2782 - 2792 | 51 | 3737 - 3747 | 137 | 4693 - 4703 | 223 | 5648 - 5659 | 309 |
| 2793 - 2803 | 52 | 3748 - 3759 | 138 | 4704 - 4714 | 224 | 5660 - 5670 | 310 |
| 2804 - 2814 | 53 | 3760 - 3770 | 139 | 4715 - 4725 | 225 | 5671 - 5681 | 311 |
| 2815 - 2825 | 54 | 3771 - 3781 | 140 | 4726 - 4736 | 226 | 5682 - 5692 | 312 |
| 2826 - 2836 | 55 | 3782 - 3792 | 141 | 4737 - 4747 | 227 | 5704 - 5714 | 314 |
| 2837 - 2847 | 56 | 3793 - 3803 | 142 | 4748 - 4759 | 228 | 5715 - 5725 | 315 |
| 2848 - 2859 | 57 | 3804 - 3814 | 143 | 4760 - 4770 | 229 | 5726 - 5736 | 316 |
| 2860 - 2870 | 58 | 3815 - 3825 | 144 | 4771 - 4781 | 230 | 5737 - 5747 | 317 |
| 2871 - 2881 | 59 | 3826 - 3836 | 145 | 4782 - 4792 | 231 | 5748 - 5759 | 318 |
| 2882 - 2892 | 60 | 3837 - 3847 | 146 | 4793 - 4803 | 232 | 5760 - 5770 | 319 |
| 2893 - 2903 | 61 | 3848 - 3859 | 147 | 4804 - 4814 | 233 | 5771 - 5781 | 320 |
| 2904 - 2914 | 62 | 3860 - 3870 | 148 | 4815 - 4825 | 234 | 5782 - 5792 | 321 |
| 2915 - 2925 | 63 | 3871 - 3881 | 149 | 4826 - 4836 | 235 | 5793 - 5803 | 322 |

| Earnings in month £ | Student Loan Deduction £ | Earnings in month £ | Student Loan Deduction £ | Earnings in month £ | Student Loan Deduction £ | Earnings in month £ | Student Loan Deduction £ |
|---|---|---|---|---|---|---|---|
| 2926 - 2936 | 64 | 3882 - 3892 | 150 | 4837 - 4847 | 236 | 5804 - 5814 | 323 |
| 2937 - 2947 | 65 | 3893 - 3903 | 151 | 4848 - 4859 | 237 | 5815 - 5825 | 324 |
| 2948 - 2959 | 66 | 3904 - 3914 | 152 | 4860 - 4870 | 238 | 5826 - 5836 | 325 |
| 2960 - 2970 | 67 | 3915 - 3925 | 153 | 4871 - 4881 | 239 | 5837 - 5847 | 326 |
| 2971 - 2981 | 68 | 3926 - 3936 | 154 | 4882 - 4892 | 240 | 5848 - 5859 | 327 |
| 2982 - 2992 | 69 | 3937 - 3947 | 155 | 4893 - 4903 | 241 | 5860 - 5870 | 328 |
| 2993 - 3003 | 70 | 3948 - 3959 | 156 | 4904 - 4914 | 242 | 5871 - 5881 | 329 |
| 3004 - 3014 | 71 | 3960 - 3970 | 157 | 4915 - 4925 | 243 | 5882 - 5892 | 330 |
| 3015 - 3025 | 72 | 3971 - 3981 | 158 | 4926 - 4936 | 244 | 5893 - 5903 | 331 |
| 3026 - 3036 | 73 | 3982 - 3992 | 159 | 4937 - 4947 | 245 | 5904 - 5914 | 332 |
| 3037 - 3047 | 74 | 3993 - 4003 | 160 | 4948 - 4959 | 246 | 5915 - 5925 | 333 |
| 3048 - 3059 | 75 | 4004 - 4014 | 161 | 4960 - 4970 | 247 | 5926 - 5936 | 334 |
| 3060 - 3070 | 76 | 4015 - 4025 | 162 | 4971 - 4981 | 248 | 5937 - 5947 | 335 |
| 3071 - 3081 | 77 | 4026 - 4036 | 163 | 4982 - 4992 | 249 | 5948 - 5959 | 336 |
| 3082 - 3092 | 78 | 4037 - 4047 | 164 | 4993 - 5003 | 250 | 5960 - 5970 | 337 |
| 3093 - 3103 | 79 | 4048 - 4059 | 165 | 5004 - 5014 | 251 | | |

| Earnings in month £ | Student Loan Deduction £ | Earnings in month £ | Student Loan Deduction £ | Earnings in month £ | Student Loan Deduction £ | Earnings in month £ | Student Loan Deduction £ |
|---|---|---|---|---|---|---|---|
| 3104 - 3114 | 80 | 4060 - 4070 | 166 | 5015 - 5025 | 252 | | |
| 3115 - 3125 | 81 | 4071 - 4081 | 167 | 5026 - 5036 | 253 | | |
| 3126 - 3136 | 82 | 4082 - 4092 | 168 | 5037 - 5047 | 254 | | |
| 3137 - 3147 | 83 | 4093 - 4103 | 169 | 5048 - 5059 | 255 | | |
| 3148 - 3159 | 84 | 4104 - 4114 | 170 | 5060 - 5070 | 256 | | |
| 3160 - 3170 | 85 | 4115 - 4125 | 171 | 5071 - 5081 | 257 | | |

## 9. Postgraduate Loan weekly table

| Earnings in week £ | Student Loan Deduction £ | Earnings in week £ | Student Loan Deduction £ |
|---|---|---|---|
| 1 - 420 | 0 | 1054 - 1070 | 39 |
| 421 - 437 | 1 | 1071 - 1087 | 40 |
| 438 - 453 | 2 | 1088 - 1103 | 41 |
| 454 - 470 | 3 | 1104 - 1120 | 42 |
| 471 - 487 | 4 | 1121 - 1137 | 43 |
| 488 - 503 | 5 | 1138 - 1153 | 44 |
| 504 - 520 | 6 | 1154 - 1170 | 45 |
| 521 - 537 | 7 | 1171 - 1187 | 46 |
| 538 - 553 | 8 | 1188 - 1203 | 47 |
| 554 - 570 | 9 | 1204 - 1220 | 48 |
| 571 - 587 | 10 | 1221 - 1237 | 49 |
| 588 - 603 | 11 | 1238 - 1253 | 50 |
| 604 - 620 | 12 | 1254 - 1270 | 51 |

18/26

# APPENDIX 2: STUDENT LOAN DEDUCTIONS

| Earnings in week £ | Student Loan Deduction £ | Earnings in week £ | Student Loan Deduction £ |
|---|---|---|---|
| 621 - 637 | 13 | 1271 - 1287 | 52 |
| 638 - 653 | 14 | 1288 - 1303 | 53 |
| 654 - 670 | 15 | 1304 - 1320 | 54 |
| 671 - 687 | 16 | 1321 - 1337 | 55 |
| 688 - 703 | 17 | 1338 - 1353 | 56 |
| 704 - 720 | 18 | 1354 - 1370 | 57 |
| 721 - 737 | 19 | 1371 - 1387 | 58 |
| 738 - 753 | 20 | 1388 - 1403 | 59 |
| 754 - 770 | 21 | 1404 - 1420 | 60 |
| 771 - 787 | 22 | 1421 - 1437 | 61 |
| 788 - 803 | 23 | 1438 - 1453 | 62 |
| 804 - 820 | 24 | 1454 - 1470 | 63 |
| 821 - 837 | 25 | 1471 - 1487 | 64 |
| 838 - 853 | 26 | 1488 - 1503 | 65 |
| 854 - 870 | 27 | 1504 - 1520 | 66 |
| 871 - 887 | 28 | 1521 - 1537 | 67 |
| 888 - 903 | 29 | 1538 - 1553 | 68 |
| 904 - 920 | 30 | 1554 - 1570 | 69 |
| 921 - 937 | 31 | 1571 - 1587 | 70 |
| 938 - 953 | 32 | 1588 - 1603 | 71 |
| 954 - 970 | 33 | 1604 - 1620 | 72 |
| 971 - 987 | 34 | 1621 - 1637 | 73 |
| 988 - 1003 | 35 | 1638 - 1653 | 74 |
| 1004 - 1020 | 36 | 1654 - 1670 | 75 |
| 1021 - 1037 | 37 | 1671 - 1687 | 76 |
| 1038 - 1053 | 38 | 1688 - 1703 | 77 |

## 10. Postgraduate Loan monthly table

| Earnings in month £ | Student Loan Deduction £ | Earnings in month £ | Student Loan Deduction £ |
|---|---|---|---|
| 1 - 1766 | 0 | 4567 - 4583 | 169 |
| 1767 - 1783 | 1 | 4584 - 4599 | 170 |
| 1784 - 1799 | 2 | 4600 - 4616 | 171 |
| 1800 - 1816 | 3 | 4617 - 4633 | 172 |
| 1817 - 1833 | 4 | 4634 - 4649 | 173 |
| 1834 - 1849 | 5 | 4650 - 4666 | 174 |
| 1850 - 1866 | 6 | 4667 - 4683 | 175 |
| 1867 - 1883 | 7 | 4684 - 4699 | 176 |
| 1884 - 1899 | 8 | 4700 - 4716 | 177 |
| 1900 - 1916 | 9 | 4717 - 4733 | 178 |
| 1917 - 1933 | 10 | 4734 - 4749 | 179 |
| 1934 - 1949 | 11 | 4750 - 4766 | 180 |
| 1950 - 1966 | 12 | 4767 - 4783 | 181 |
| 1967 - 1983 | 13 | 4784 - 4799 | 182 |
| 1984 - 1999 | 14 | 4800 - 4816 | 183 |
| 2000 - 2016 | 15 | 4817 - 4833 | 184 |
| 2017 - 2033 | 16 | 4834 - 4849 | 185 |
| 2034 - 2049 | 17 | 4850 - 4866 | 186 |
| 2050 - 2066 | 18 | 4867 - 4883 | 187 |
| 2067 - 2083 | 19 | 4884 - 4899 | 188 |
| 2084 - 2099 | 20 | 4900 - 4916 | 189 |
| 2100 - 2116 | 21 | 4917 - 4933 | 190 |
| 2117 - 2133 | 22 | 4934 - 4949 | 191 |
| 2134 - 2149 | 23 | 4950 - 4966 | 192 |
| 2150 - 2166 | 24 | 4967 - 4983 | 193 |

| Earnings in month £ | Student Loan Deduction £ | Earnings in month £ | Student Loan Deduction £ |
|---|---|---|---|
| 2167 - 2183 | 25 | 4984 - 4999 | 194 |
| 2184 - 2199 | 26 | 5000 - 5016 | 195 |
| 2200 - 2216 | 27 | 5017 - 5033 | 196 |
| 2217 - 2233 | 28 | 5034 - 5049 | 197 |
| 2234 - 2249 | 29 | 5050 - 5066 | 198 |
| 2250 - 2266 | 30 | 5067 - 5083 | 199 |
| 2267 - 2283 | 31 | 5084 - 5099 | 200 |
| 2284 - 2299 | 32 | 5100 - 5116 | 201 |
| 2300 - 2316 | 33 | 5117 - 5133 | 202 |
| 2317 - 2333 | 34 | 5134 - 5149 | 203 |
| 2334 - 2349 | 35 | 5150 - 5166 | 204 |
| 2350 - 2366 | 36 | 5167 - 5183 | 205 |
| 2367 - 2383 | 37 | 5184 - 5199 | 206 |
| 2384 - 2399 | 38 | 5200 - 5216 | 207 |
| 2400 - 2416 | 39 | 5217 - 5233 | 208 |
| 2417 - 2433 | 40 | 5234 - 5249 | 209 |
| 2434 - 2449 | 41 | 5250 - 5266 | 210 |
| 2450 - 2466 | 42 | 5267 - 5283 | 211 |
| 2467 - 2483 | 43 | 5284 - 5299 | 212 |
| 2484 - 2499 | 44 | 5300 - 5316 | 213 |
| 2500 - 2516 | 45 | 5317 - 5333 | 214 |
| 2517 - 2533 | 46 | 5334 - 5349 | 215 |
| 2534 - 2549 | 47 | 5350 - 5366 | 216 |
| 2550 - 2566 | 48 | 5367 - 5383 | 217 |
| 2567 - 2583 | 49 | 5384 - 5399 | 218 |
| 2584 - 2599 | 50 | 5400 - 5416 | 219 |
| 2600 - 2616 | 51 | 5417 - 5433 | 220 |

| Earnings in month £ | Student Loan Deduction £ | Earnings in month £ | Student Loan Deduction £ |
|---|---|---|---|
| 2617 - 2633 | 52 | 5434 - 5449 | 221 |
| 2634 - 2649 | 53 | 5450 - 5466 | 222 |
| 2650 - 2666 | 54 | 5467 - 5483 | 223 |
| 2667 - 2683 | 55 | 5484 - 5499 | 224 |
| 2684 - 2699 | 56 | 5500 - 5516 | 225 |
| 2700 - 2716 | 57 | 5517 - 5533 | 226 |
| 2717 - 2733 | 58 | 5534 - 5549 | 227 |
| 2734 - 2749 | 59 | 5550 - 5566 | 228 |
| 2750 - 2766 | 60 | 5567 - 5583 | 229 |
| 2767 - 2783 | 61 | 5584 - 5599 | 230 |
| 2784 - 2799 | 62 | 5600 - 5616 | 231 |
| 2800 - 2816 | 63 | 5617 - 5633 | 232 |
| 2817 - 2833 | 64 | 5634 - 5649 | 233 |
| 2834 - 2849 | 65 | 5650 - 5666 | 234 |
| 2850 - 2866 | 66 | 5667 - 5683 | 235 |
| 2867 - 2883 | 67 | 5684 - 5699 | 236 |
| 2884 - 2899 | 68 | 5700 - 5716 | 237 |
| 2900 - 2916 | 69 | 5717 - 5733 | 238 |
| 2917 - 2933 | 70 | 5734 - 5749 | 239 |
| 2934 - 2949 | 71 | 5750 - 5766 | 240 |
| 2950 - 2966 | 72 | 5767 - 5783 | 241 |
| 2967 - 2983 | 73 | 5784 - 5799 | 242 |
| 2984 - 2999 | 74 | 5800 - 5816 | 243 |
| 3000 - 3016 | 75 | 5817 - 5833 | 244 |
| 3017 - 3033 | 76 | 5834 - 5849 | 245 |
| 3034 - 3049 | 77 | 5850 - 5866 | 246 |
| 3050 - 3066 | 78 | 5867 - 5883 | 247 |

| Earnings in month £ | Student Loan Deduction £ | Earnings in month £ | Student Loan Deduction £ |
|---|---|---|---|
| 3067 - 3083 | 79 | 5884 - 5899 | 248 |
| 3084 - 3099 | 80 | 5900 - 5916 | 249 |
| 3100 - 3116 | 81 | 5917 - 5933 | 250 |
| 3117 - 3133 | 82 | 5934 - 5949 | 251 |
| 3134 - 3149 | 83 | 5950 - 5966 | 252 |
| 3150 - 3166 | 84 | 5967 - 5983 | 253 |
| 3167 - 3183 | 85 | 5984 - 5999 | 254 |
| 3184 - 3199 | 86 | 6000 - 6016 | 255 |
| 3200 - 3216 | 87 | 6017 - 6033 | 256 |
| 3217 - 3233 | 88 | 6034 - 6049 | 257 |
| 3234 - 3249 | 89 | 6050 - 6066 | 258 |
| 3250 - 3266 | 90 | 6067 - 6083 | 259 |
| 3267 - 3283 | 91 | 6084 - 6099 | 260 |
| 3284 - 3299 | 92 | 6100 - 6116 | 261 |
| 3300 - 3316 | 93 | 6117 - 6133 | 262 |
| 3317 - 3333 | 94 | 6134 - 6149 | 263 |
| 3334 - 3349 | 95 | 6150 - 6166 | 264 |
| 3350 - 3366 | 96 | 6167 - 6183 | 265 |
| 3367 - 3383 | 97 | 6184 - 6199 | 266 |
| 3384 - 3399 | 98 | 6200 - 6216 | 267 |
| 3400 - 3416 | 99 | 6217 - 6233 | 268 |
| 3417 - 3433 | 100 | 6234 - 6249 | 269 |
| 3434 - 3449 | 101 | 6250 - 6266 | 270 |
| 3450 - 3466 | 102 | 6267 - 6283 | 271 |
| 3467 - 3483 | 103 | 6284 - 6299 | 272 |
| 3484 - 3499 | 104 | 6300 - 6316 | 273 |
| 3500 - 3516 | 105 | 6317 - 6333 | 274 |

| Earnings in month £ | Student Loan Deduction £ | Earnings in month £ | Student Loan Deduction £ |
|---|---|---|---|
| 3517 - 3533 | 106 | 6334 - 6349 | 275 |
| 3534 - 3549 | 107 | 6350 - 6366 | 276 |
| 3550 - 3566 | 108 | 6367 - 6383 | 277 |
| 3567 - 3583 | 109 | 6384 - 6399 | 278 |
| 3584 - 3599 | 110 | 6400 - 6416 | 279 |
| 3600 - 3616 | 111 | 6417 - 6433 | 280 |
| 3617 - 3633 | 112 | 6434 - 6449 | 281 |
| 3634 - 3649 | 113 | 6450 - 6466 | 282 |
| 3650 - 3666 | 114 | 6467 - 6483 | 283 |
| 3667 - 3683 | 115 | 6484 - 6499 | 284 |
| 3684 - 3699 | 116 | 6500 - 6516 | 285 |
| 3700 - 3716 | 117 | 6517 - 6533 | 286 |
| 3717 - 3733 | 118 | 6534 - 6549 | 287 |
| 3734 - 3749 | 119 | 6550 - 6566 | 288 |
| 3750 - 3766 | 120 | 6567 - 6583 | 289 |
| 3767 - 3783 | 121 | 6584 - 6599 | 290 |
| 3784 - 3799 | 122 | 6600 - 6616 | 291 |
| 3800 - 3816 | 123 | 6617 - 6633 | 292 |
| 3817 - 3833 | 124 | 6634 - 6649 | 293 |
| 3834 - 3849 | 125 | 6650 - 6666 | 294 |
| 3850 - 3866 | 126 | 6667 - 6683 | 295 |
| 3867 - 3883 | 127 | 6684 - 6699 | 296 |
| 3884 - 3899 | 128 | 6700 - 6716 | 297 |
| 3900 - 3916 | 129 | 6717 - 6733 | 298 |
| 3917 - 3933 | 130 | 6734 - 6749 | 299 |
| 3934 - 3949 | 131 | 6750 - 6766 | 300 |
| 3950 - 3966 | 132 | 6767 - 6783 | 301 |

| Earnings in month £ | Student Loan Deduction £ | Earnings in month £ | Student Loan Deduction £ |
|---|---|---|---|
| 3967 - 3983 | 133 | 6784 - 6799 | 302 |
| 3984 - 3999 | 134 | 6800 - 6816 | 303 |
| 4000 - 4016 | 135 | 6817 - 6833 | 304 |
| 4017 - 4033 | 136 | 6834 - 6849 | 305 |
| 4034 - 4049 | 137 | 6850 - 6866 | 306 |
| 4050 - 4066 | 138 | 6867 - 6883 | 307 |
| 4067 - 4083 | 139 | 6884 - 6899 | 308 |
| 4084 - 4099 | 140 | 6900 - 6916 | 309 |
| 4100 - 4116 | 141 | 6917 - 6933 | 310 |
| 4117 - 4133 | 142 | 6934 - 6949 | 311 |
| 4134 - 4149 | 143 | 6950 - 6966 | 312 |
| 4150 - 4166 | 144 | 6967 - 6983 | 313 |
| 4167 - 4183 | 145 | 6984 - 6999 | 314 |
| 4184 - 4199 | 146 | 7000 - 7016 | 315 |
| 4200 - 4216 | 147 | 7017 - 7033 | 316 |
| 4217 - 4233 | 148 | 7034 - 7049 | 317 |
| 4234 - 4249 | 149 | 7050 - 7066 | 318 |
| 4250 - 4266 | 150 | 7067 - 7083 | 319 |
| 4267 - 4283 | 151 | 7084 - 7099 | 320 |
| 4284 - 4299 | 152 | 7100 - 7116 | 321 |
| 4300 - 4316 | 153 | 7117 - 7133 | 322 |
| 4317 - 4333 | 154 | 7134 - 7149 | 323 |
| 4334 - 4349 | 155 | 7150 - 7166 | 324 |
| 4350 - 4366 | 156 | 7167 - 7183 | 325 |
| 4367 - 4383 | 157 | 7184 - 7199 | 326 |
| 4384 - 4399 | 158 | 7200 - 7216 | 327 |
| 4400 - 4416 | 159 | 7217 - 7233 | 328 |

| Earnings in month £ | Student Loan Deduction £ | Earnings in month £ | Student Loan Deduction £ |
|---|---|---|---|
| 4417 - 4433 | 160 | 7234 - 7249 | 329 |
| 4434 - 4449 | 161 | 7250 - 7266 | 330 |
| 4450 - 4466 | 162 | 7267 - 7283 | 331 |
| 4467 - 4483 | 163 | 7284 - 7299 | 332 |
| 4484 - 4499 | 164 | 7300 - 7316 | 333 |
| 4500 - 4516 | 165 | 7317 - 7333 | 334 |
| 4517 - 4533 | 166 | 7334 - 7349 | 335 |
| 4534 - 4549 | 167 | 7350 - 7366 | 336 |
| 4550 - 4566 | 168 | 7367 - 7383 | 337 |

# APPENDIX 2: STUDENT LOAN DEDUCTIONS

## Weekly table for standard rate NICs for use from 6 April 2020 to 5 April 2021

**Table letter A**

Use this table for employees who are aged 21 or over and under State Pension age **or** employees who are on Approved Apprenticeship scheme and over the age of 25.

Do not use this table for:

- any tax year other than 2020 to 2021
- employees who are under the age of 21 (go to Table letter M)
- employees who are on an Approved Apprenticeship scheme and under the age of 25 (go to Table letter H)
- married women or widows who have the right to pay reduced rate employee's NICs (go to Table letter B in booklet CA41)
- employees who are State Pension age or over (go to Table letter C in booklet CA41)
- employees who are aged 21 or over, for whom you hold form CA2700 (go to Table letter J)
- employees who are under the age of 21, for whom you hold form CA2700 (go to Table letter Z)

**Completing form RT11, 'Deductions working sheet' or substitute**

1 Enter 'A' in the NICs Category Letter column on form RT11.

2 Copy the figures in columns 1a – 1e of the table to columns 1a – 1e on the line next to the tax week in which the employee is paid, on form RT11.

If the employee's total earnings fall between the LEL and the UEL/UST/AUST and the exact gross pay is not shown in the table, use the next smaller figure shown. If the employee's total earnings exceed the UEL/UST/AUST, go to page 163.

The figures in the left-hand column of each table show steps between the LEL and the UEL/UST/AUST. The NICs liability for each step, with the exception of the LEL, ST, PT, UEL and UST/AUST, is worked out at the mid-point of the steps so you and your employee may pay slightly more or less than if you used the exact percentage method.

| Employee's earnings up to and including the UEL | Earnings at the LEL (where earnings are equal to or exceed the LEL) | Earnings above the LEL, up to and including the PT | Earnings above the PT, up to and including the UEL | Employer's NICs due on all earnings above the ST | Employee's NICs due on all earnings above the PT | Total of employee's and employer's NICs (for information only) |
|---|---|---|---|---|---|---|
| | 1a | 1b | 1c | 1d | 1e | |
| £ | £ | £ p | £ p | £ p | £ p | £ p |
| £119.99 | No NICs liability, make no entries on form RT11 | | | | | |
| 120 | 120 | 0.00 | 0.00 | 0.00 | 0.00 | 0.00 |
| 121 | 120 | 1.00 | 0.00 | 0.00 | 0.00 | 0.00 |
| 122 | 120 | 2.00 | 0.00 | 0.00 | 0.00 | 0.00 |
| 123 | 120 | 3.00 | 0.00 | 0.00 | 0.00 | 0.00 |
| 124 | 120 | 4.00 | 0.00 | 0.00 | 0.00 | 0.00 |
| 125 | 120 | 5.00 | 0.00 | 0.00 | 0.00 | 0.00 |
| 126 | 120 | 6.00 | 0.00 | 0.00 | 0.00 | 0.00 |
| 127 | 120 | 7.00 | 0.00 | 0.00 | 0.00 | 0.00 |
| 128 | 120 | 8.00 | 0.00 | 0.00 | 0.00 | 0.00 |
| 129 | 120 | 9.00 | 0.00 | 0.00 | 0.00 | 0.00 |
| 130 | 120 | 10.00 | 0.00 | 0.00 | 0.00 | 0.00 |
| 131 | 120 | 11.00 | 0.00 | 0.00 | 0.00 | 0.00 |
| 132 | 120 | 12.00 | 0.00 | 0.00 | 0.00 | 0.00 |
| 133 | 120 | 13.00 | 0.00 | 0.00 | 0.00 | 0.00 |
| 134 | 120 | 14.00 | 0.00 | 0.00 | 0.00 | 0.00 |
| 135 | 120 | 15.00 | 0.00 | 0.00 | 0.00 | 0.00 |
| 136 | 120 | 16.00 | 0.00 | 0.00 | 0.00 | 0.00 |
| 137 | 120 | 17.00 | 0.00 | 0.00 | 0.00 | 0.00 |
| 138 | 120 | 18.00 | 0.00 | 0.00 | 0.00 | 0.00 |
| 139 | 120 | 19.00 | 0.00 | 0.00 | 0.00 | 0.00 |
| 140 | 120 | 20.00 | 0.00 | 0.00 | 0.00 | 0.00 |
| 141 | 120 | 21.00 | 0.00 | 0.00 | 0.00 | 0.00 |
| 142 | 120 | 22.00 | 0.00 | 0.00 | 0.00 | 0.00 |
| 143 | 120 | 23.00 | 0.00 | 0.00 | 0.00 | 0.00 |
| 144 | 120 | 24.00 | 0.00 | 0.00 | 0.00 | 0.00 |

**Weekly table**

**Table letter A**

| Employee's earnings up to and including the UEL | Earnings at the LEL (where earnings are equal to or exceed the LEL) | Earnings above the LEL, up to and including the PT | Earnings above the PT and including the UEL | Employer's NICs due on all earnings above the ST | Employee's NICs due on all earnings above the PT | Total of employee's and employer's NICs (for information only) |
|---|---|---|---|---|---|---|
| | 1a | 1b | 1c | 1d | 1e | |
| £ | £ | £ p | £ p | £ p | £ p | £ p |
| 145 | 120 | 25.00 | 0.00 | 0.00 | 0.00 | 0.00 |
| 146 | 120 | 26.00 | 0.00 | 0.00 | 0.00 | 0.00 |
| 147 | 120 | 27.00 | 0.00 | 0.00 | 0.00 | 0.00 |
| 148 | 120 | 28.00 | 0.00 | 0.00 | 0.00 | 0.00 |
| 149 | 120 | 29.00 | 0.00 | 0.00 | 0.00 | 0.00 |
| 150 | 120 | 30.00 | 0.00 | 0.00 | 0.00 | 0.00 |
| 151 | 120 | 31.00 | 0.00 | 0.00 | 0.00 | 0.00 |
| 152 | 120 | 32.00 | 0.00 | 0.00 | 0.00 | 0.00 |
| 153 | 120 | 33.00 | 0.00 | 0.00 | 0.00 | 0.00 |
| 154 | 120 | 34.00 | 0.00 | 0.00 | 0.00 | 0.00 |
| 155 | 120 | 35.00 | 0.00 | 0.00 | 0.00 | 0.00 |
| 156 | 120 | 36.00 | 0.00 | 0.00 | 0.00 | 0.00 |
| 157 | 120 | 37.00 | 0.00 | 0.00 | 0.00 | 0.00 |
| 158 | 120 | 38.00 | 0.00 | 0.00 | 0.00 | 0.00 |
| 159 | 120 | 39.00 | 0.00 | 0.00 | 0.00 | 0.00 |
| 160 | 120 | 40.00 | 0.00 | 0.00 | 0.00 | 0.00 |
| 161 | 120 | 41.00 | 0.00 | 0.00 | 0.00 | 0.00 |
| 162 | 120 | 42.00 | 0.00 | 0.00 | 0.00 | 0.00 |
| 163 | 120 | 43.00 | 0.00 | 0.00 | 0.00 | 0.00 |
| 164 | 120 | 44.00 | 0.00 | 0.00 | 0.00 | 0.00 |
| 165 | 120 | 45.00 | 0.00 | 0.00 | 0.00 | 0.00 |
| 166 | 120 | 46.00 | 0.00 | 0.00 | 0.00 | 0.00 |
| 167 | 120 | 47.00 | 0.00 | 0.00 | 0.00 | 0.00 |
| 168 | 120 | 48.00 | 0.00 | 0.00 | 0.00 | 0.00 |
| 169 | 120 | 49.00 | 0.00 | 0.00 | 0.00 | 0.00 |
| 170 | 120 | 50.00 | 0.00 | 0.21 | 0.00 | 0.21 |
| 171 | 120 | 51.00 | 0.00 | 0.34 | 0.00 | 0.34 |
| 172 | 120 | 52.00 | 0.00 | 0.48 | 0.00 | 0.48 |
| 173 | 120 | 53.00 | 0.00 | 0.62 | 0.00 | 0.62 |
| 174 | 120 | 54.00 | 0.00 | 0.76 | 0.00 | 0.76 |
| 175 | 120 | 55.00 | 0.00 | 0.90 | 0.00 | 0.90 |
| 176 | 120 | 56.00 | 0.00 | 1.03 | 0.00 | 1.03 |
| 177 | 120 | 57.00 | 0.00 | 1.17 | 0.00 | 1.17 |
| 178 | 120 | 58.00 | 0.00 | 1.31 | 0.00 | 1.31 |
| 179 | 120 | 59.00 | 0.00 | 1.45 | 0.00 | 1.45 |
| 180 | 120 | 60.00 | 0.00 | 1.59 | 0.00 | 1.59 |
| 181 | 120 | 61.00 | 0.00 | 1.72 | 0.00 | 1.72 |
| 182 | 120 | 62.00 | 0.00 | 1.86 | 0.00 | 1.86 |
| 183 | 120 | 63.00 | 0.00 | 1.93 | 0.00 | 1.93 |
| 184 | 120 | 63.00 | 1.00 | 2.14 | 0.18 | 2.32 |
| 185 | 120 | 63.00 | 2.00 | 2.27 | 0.30 | 2.57 |
| 186 | 120 | 63.00 | 3.00 | 2.41 | 0.42 | 2.83 |
| 187 | 120 | 63.00 | 4.00 | 2.55 | 0.54 | 3.09 |
| 188 | 120 | 63.00 | 5.00 | 2.69 | 0.66 | 3.35 |
| 189 | 120 | 63.00 | 6.00 | 2.83 | 0.78 | 3.61 |
| 190 | 120 | 63.00 | 7.00 | 2.96 | 0.90 | 3.86 |
| 191 | 120 | 63.00 | 8.00 | 3.10 | 1.02 | 4.12 |
| 192 | 120 | 63.00 | 9.00 | 3.24 | 1.14 | 4.38 |
| 193 | 120 | 63.00 | 10.00 | 3.38 | 1.26 | 4.64 |
| 194 | 120 | 63.00 | 11.00 | 3.52 | 1.38 | 4.90 |
| 195 | 120 | 63.00 | 12.00 | 3.65 | 1.50 | 5.15 |
| 196 | 120 | 63.00 | 13.00 | 3.79 | 1.62 | 5.41 |
| 197 | 120 | 63.00 | 14.00 | 3.93 | 1.74 | 5.67 |
| 198 | 120 | 63.00 | 15.00 | 4.07 | 1.86 | 5.93 |
| 199 | 120 | 63.00 | 16.00 | 4.21 | 1.98 | 6.19 |

## Table letter A

**Weekly table**

| Employee's earnings up to and including the UEL | Earnings at the LEL (where earnings are equal to or exceed the LEL) 1a | Earnings above the LEL, up to and including the PT 1b | Earnings above the PT, up to and including the UEL 1c | Employer's NICs due on all earnings above the ST 1d | Employee's NICs due on all earnings above the PT 1e | Total of employee's and employer's NICs (for information only) |
|---|---|---|---|---|---|---|
| £ | £ | £ p | £ p | £ p | £ p | £ p |
| 200 | 120 | 63.00 | 17.00 | 4.34 | 2.10 | 6.44 |
| 201 | 120 | 63.00 | 18.00 | 4.48 | 2.22 | 6.70 |
| 202 | 120 | 63.00 | 19.00 | 4.62 | 2.34 | 6.96 |
| 203 | 120 | 63.00 | 20.00 | 4.76 | 2.46 | 7.22 |
| 204 | 120 | 63.00 | 21.00 | 4.90 | 2.58 | 7.48 |
| 205 | 120 | 63.00 | 22.00 | 5.03 | 2.70 | 7.73 |
| 206 | 120 | 63.00 | 23.00 | 5.17 | 2.82 | 7.99 |
| 207 | 120 | 63.00 | 24.00 | 5.31 | 2.94 | 8.25 |
| 208 | 120 | 63.00 | 25.00 | 5.45 | 3.06 | 8.51 |
| 209 | 120 | 63.00 | 26.00 | 5.59 | 3.18 | 8.77 |
| 210 | 120 | 63.00 | 27.00 | 5.72 | 3.30 | 9.02 |
| 211 | 120 | 63.00 | 28.00 | 5.86 | 3.42 | 9.28 |
| 212 | 120 | 63.00 | 29.00 | 6.00 | 3.54 | 9.54 |
| 213 | 120 | 63.00 | 30.00 | 6.14 | 3.66 | 9.80 |
| 214 | 120 | 63.00 | 31.00 | 6.28 | 3.78 | 10.06 |
| 215 | 120 | 63.00 | 32.00 | 6.41 | 3.90 | 10.31 |
| 216 | 120 | 63.00 | 33.00 | 6.55 | 4.02 | 10.57 |
| 217 | 120 | 63.00 | 34.00 | 6.69 | 4.14 | 10.83 |
| 218 | 120 | 63.00 | 35.00 | 6.83 | 4.26 | 11.09 |
| 219 | 120 | 63.00 | 36.00 | 6.97 | 4.38 | 11.35 |
| 220 | 120 | 63.00 | 37.00 | 7.10 | 4.50 | 11.60 |
| 221 | 120 | 63.00 | 38.00 | 7.24 | 4.62 | 11.86 |
| 222 | 120 | 63.00 | 39.00 | 7.38 | 4.74 | 12.12 |
| 223 | 120 | 63.00 | 40.00 | 7.52 | 4.86 | 12.38 |
| 224 | 120 | 63.00 | 41.00 | 7.66 | 4.98 | 12.64 |
| 225 | 120 | 63.00 | 42.00 | 7.79 | 5.10 | 12.89 |
| 226 | 120 | 63.00 | 43.00 | 7.93 | 5.22 | 13.15 |
| 227 | 120 | 63.00 | 44.00 | 8.07 | 5.34 | 13.41 |
| 228 | 120 | 63.00 | 45.00 | 8.21 | 5.46 | 13.67 |
| 229 | 120 | 63.00 | 46.00 | 8.35 | 5.58 | 13.93 |
| 230 | 120 | 63.00 | 47.00 | 8.48 | 5.70 | 14.18 |
| 231 | 120 | 63.00 | 48.00 | 8.62 | 5.82 | 14.44 |
| 232 | 120 | 63.00 | 49.00 | 8.76 | 5.94 | 14.70 |
| 233 | 120 | 63.00 | 50.00 | 8.90 | 6.06 | 14.96 |
| 234 | 120 | 63.00 | 51.00 | 9.04 | 6.18 | 15.22 |
| 235 | 120 | 63.00 | 52.00 | 9.17 | 6.30 | 15.47 |
| 236 | 120 | 63.00 | 53.00 | 9.31 | 6.42 | 15.73 |
| 237 | 120 | 63.00 | 54.00 | 9.45 | 6.54 | 15.99 |
| 238 | 120 | 63.00 | 55.00 | 9.59 | 6.66 | 16.25 |
| 239 | 120 | 63.00 | 56.00 | 9.73 | 6.78 | 16.51 |
| 240 | 120 | 63.00 | 57.00 | 9.86 | 6.90 | 16.76 |
| 241 | 120 | 63.00 | 58.00 | 10.00 | 7.02 | 17.02 |
| 242 | 120 | 63.00 | 59.00 | 10.14 | 7.14 | 17.28 |
| 243 | 120 | 63.00 | 60.00 | 10.28 | 7.26 | 17.54 |
| 244 | 120 | 63.00 | 61.00 | 10.42 | 7.38 | 17.80 |
| 245 | 120 | 63.00 | 62.00 | 10.55 | 7.50 | 18.05 |
| 246 | 120 | 63.00 | 63.00 | 10.69 | 7.62 | 18.31 |
| 247 | 120 | 63.00 | 64.00 | 10.83 | 7.74 | 18.57 |
| 248 | 120 | 63.00 | 65.00 | 10.97 | 7.86 | 18.83 |
| 249 | 120 | 63.00 | 66.00 | 11.11 | 7.98 | 19.09 |
| 250 | 120 | 63.00 | 67.00 | 11.24 | 8.10 | 19.34 |
| 251 | 120 | 63.00 | 68.00 | 11.38 | 8.22 | 19.60 |
| 252 | 120 | 63.00 | 69.00 | 11.52 | 8.34 | 19.86 |
| 253 | 120 | 63.00 | 70.00 | 11.66 | 8.46 | 20.12 |
| 254 | 120 | 63.00 | 71.00 | 11.80 | 8.58 | 20.38 |

## Weekly table

**Table letter A**

| Employee's earnings up to and including the UEL | Earnings at the LEL (where earnings are equal to or exceed the LEL) | Earnings above the LEL, up to and including the PT | Earnings above the PT, up to and including the UEL | Employer's NICs due on all earnings above the ST | Employee's NICs due on all earnings above the PT | Total of employee's and employer's NICs (for information only) |
|---|---|---|---|---|---|---|
| | 1a | 1b | 1c | 1d | 1e | |
| £ | £ | £ p | £ p | £ p | £ p | £ p |
| 255 | 120 | 63.00 | 72.00 | 11.93 | 8.70 | 20.63 |
| 256 | 120 | 63.00 | 73.00 | 12.07 | 8.82 | 20.89 |
| 257 | 120 | 63.00 | 74.00 | 12.21 | 8.94 | 21.15 |
| 258 | 120 | 63.00 | 75.00 | 12.35 | 9.06 | 21.41 |
| 259 | 120 | 63.00 | 76.00 | 12.49 | 9.18 | 21.67 |
| 260 | 120 | 63.00 | 77.00 | 12.62 | 9.30 | 21.92 |
| 261 | 120 | 63.00 | 78.00 | 12.76 | 9.42 | 22.18 |
| 262 | 120 | 63.00 | 79.00 | 12.90 | 9.54 | 22.44 |
| 263 | 120 | 63.00 | 80.00 | 13.04 | 9.66 | 22.70 |
| 264 | 120 | 63.00 | 81.00 | 13.18 | 9.78 | 22.96 |
| 265 | 120 | 63.00 | 82.00 | 13.31 | 9.90 | 23.21 |
| 266 | 120 | 63.00 | 83.00 | 13.45 | 10.02 | 23.47 |
| 267 | 120 | 63.00 | 84.00 | 13.59 | 10.14 | 23.73 |
| 268 | 120 | 63.00 | 85.00 | 13.73 | 10.26 | 23.99 |
| 269 | 120 | 63.00 | 86.00 | 13.87 | 10.38 | 24.25 |
| 270 | 120 | 63.00 | 87.00 | 14.00 | 10.50 | 24.50 |
| 271 | 120 | 63.00 | 88.00 | 14.14 | 10.62 | 24.76 |
| 272 | 120 | 63.00 | 89.00 | 14.28 | 10.74 | 25.02 |
| 273 | 120 | 63.00 | 90.00 | 14.42 | 10.86 | 25.28 |
| 274 | 120 | 63.00 | 91.00 | 14.56 | 10.98 | 25.54 |
| 275 | 120 | 63.00 | 92.00 | 14.69 | 11.10 | 25.79 |
| 276 | 120 | 63.00 | 93.00 | 14.83 | 11.22 | 26.05 |
| 277 | 120 | 63.00 | 94.00 | 14.97 | 11.34 | 26.31 |
| 278 | 120 | 63.00 | 95.00 | 15.11 | 11.46 | 26.57 |
| 279 | 120 | 63.00 | 96.00 | 15.25 | 11.58 | 26.83 |
| 280 | 120 | 63.00 | 97.00 | 15.38 | 11.70 | 27.08 |
| 281 | 120 | 63.00 | 98.00 | 15.52 | 11.82 | 27.34 |
| 282 | 120 | 63.00 | 99.00 | 15.66 | 11.94 | 27.60 |
| 283 | 120 | 63.00 | 100.00 | 15.80 | 12.06 | 27.86 |
| 284 | 120 | 63.00 | 101.00 | 15.94 | 12.18 | 28.12 |
| 285 | 120 | 63.00 | 102.00 | 16.07 | 12.30 | 28.37 |
| 286 | 120 | 63.00 | 103.00 | 16.21 | 12.42 | 28.63 |
| 287 | 120 | 63.00 | 104.00 | 16.35 | 12.54 | 28.89 |
| 288 | 120 | 63.00 | 105.00 | 16.49 | 12.66 | 29.15 |
| 289 | 120 | 63.00 | 106.00 | 16.63 | 12.78 | 29.41 |
| 290 | 120 | 63.00 | 107.00 | 16.76 | 12.90 | 29.66 |
| 291 | 120 | 63.00 | 108.00 | 16.90 | 13.02 | 29.92 |
| 292 | 120 | 63.00 | 109.00 | 17.04 | 13.14 | 30.18 |
| 293 | 120 | 63.00 | 110.00 | 17.18 | 13.26 | 30.44 |
| 294 | 120 | 63.00 | 111.00 | 17.32 | 13.38 | 30.70 |
| 295 | 120 | 63.00 | 112.00 | 17.45 | 13.50 | 30.95 |
| 296 | 120 | 63.00 | 113.00 | 17.59 | 13.62 | 31.21 |
| 297 | 120 | 63.00 | 114.00 | 17.73 | 13.74 | 31.47 |
| 298 | 120 | 63.00 | 115.00 | 17.87 | 13.86 | 31.73 |
| 299 | 120 | 63.00 | 116.00 | 18.01 | 13.98 | 31.99 |
| 300 | 120 | 63.00 | 117.00 | 18.14 | 14.10 | 32.24 |
| 301 | 120 | 63.00 | 118.00 | 18.28 | 14.22 | 32.50 |
| 302 | 120 | 63.00 | 119.00 | 18.42 | 14.34 | 32.76 |
| 303 | 120 | 63.00 | 120.00 | 18.56 | 14.46 | 33.02 |
| 304 | 120 | 63.00 | 121.00 | 18.70 | 14.58 | 33.28 |
| 305 | 120 | 63.00 | 122.00 | 18.83 | 14.70 | 33.53 |
| 306 | 120 | 63.00 | 123.00 | 18.97 | 14.82 | 33.79 |
| 307 | 120 | 63.00 | 124.00 | 19.11 | 14.94 | 34.05 |
| 308 | 120 | 63.00 | 125.00 | 19.25 | 15.06 | 34.31 |
| 309 | 120 | 63.00 | 126.00 | 19.39 | 15.18 | 34.57 |

## Table letter A

**Weekly table**

| Employee's earnings up to and including the UEL | Earnings at the LEL (where earnings are equal to or exceed the LEL) | Earnings above the LEL, up to and including the PT | Earnings above the PT, up to and including the UEL | Employer's NICs due on all earnings above the ST | Employee's NICs due on all earnings above the PT | Total of employee's and employer's NICs (for information only) |
|---|---|---|---|---|---|---|
| | | 1a | 1b | 1c | 1d | 1e |
| £ | £ | £ p | £ p | £ p | £ p | £ p |
| 310 | 120 | 63.00 | 127.00 | 19.52 | 15.30 | 34.82 |
| 311 | 120 | 63.00 | 128.00 | 19.66 | 15.42 | 35.08 |
| 312 | 120 | 63.00 | 129.00 | 19.80 | 15.54 | 35.34 |
| 313 | 120 | 63.00 | 130.00 | 19.94 | 15.66 | 35.60 |
| 314 | 120 | 63.00 | 131.00 | 20.08 | 15.78 | 35.86 |
| 315 | 120 | 63.00 | 132.00 | 20.21 | 15.90 | 36.11 |
| 316 | 120 | 63.00 | 133.00 | 20.35 | 16.02 | 36.37 |
| 317 | 120 | 63.00 | 134.00 | 20.49 | 16.14 | 36.63 |
| 318 | 120 | 63.00 | 135.00 | 20.63 | 16.26 | 36.89 |
| 319 | 120 | 63.00 | 136.00 | 20.77 | 16.38 | 37.15 |
| 320 | 120 | 63.00 | 137.00 | 20.90 | 16.50 | 37.40 |
| 321 | 120 | 63.00 | 138.00 | 21.04 | 16.62 | 37.66 |
| 322 | 120 | 63.00 | 139.00 | 21.18 | 16.74 | 37.92 |
| 323 | 120 | 63.00 | 140.00 | 21.32 | 16.86 | 38.18 |
| 324 | 120 | 63.00 | 141.00 | 21.46 | 16.98 | 38.44 |
| 325 | 120 | 63.00 | 142.00 | 21.59 | 17.10 | 38.69 |
| 326 | 120 | 63.00 | 143.00 | 21.73 | 17.22 | 38.95 |
| 327 | 120 | 63.00 | 144.00 | 21.87 | 17.34 | 39.21 |
| 328 | 120 | 63.00 | 145.00 | 22.01 | 17.46 | 39.47 |
| 329 | 120 | 63.00 | 146.00 | 22.15 | 17.58 | 39.73 |
| 330 | 120 | 63.00 | 147.00 | 22.28 | 17.70 | 39.98 |
| 331 | 120 | 63.00 | 148.00 | 22.42 | 17.82 | 40.24 |
| 332 | 120 | 63.00 | 149.00 | 22.56 | 17.94 | 40.50 |
| 333 | 120 | 63.00 | 150.00 | 22.70 | 18.06 | 40.76 |
| 334 | 120 | 63.00 | 151.00 | 22.84 | 18.18 | 41.02 |
| 335 | 120 | 63.00 | 152.00 | 22.97 | 18.30 | 41.27 |
| 336 | 120 | 63.00 | 153.00 | 23.11 | 18.42 | 41.53 |
| 337 | 120 | 63.00 | 154.00 | 23.25 | 18.54 | 41.79 |
| 338 | 120 | 63.00 | 155.00 | 23.39 | 18.66 | 42.05 |
| 339 | 120 | 63.00 | 156.00 | 23.53 | 18.78 | 42.31 |
| 340 | 120 | 63.00 | 157.00 | 23.66 | 18.90 | 42.56 |
| 341 | 120 | 63.00 | 158.00 | 23.80 | 19.02 | 42.82 |
| 342 | 120 | 63.00 | 159.00 | 23.94 | 19.14 | 43.08 |
| 343 | 120 | 63.00 | 160.00 | 24.08 | 19.26 | 43.34 |
| 344 | 120 | 63.00 | 161.00 | 24.22 | 19.38 | 43.60 |
| 345 | 120 | 63.00 | 162.00 | 24.35 | 19.50 | 43.85 |
| 346 | 120 | 63.00 | 163.00 | 24.49 | 19.62 | 44.11 |
| 347 | 120 | 63.00 | 164.00 | 24.63 | 19.74 | 44.37 |
| 348 | 120 | 63.00 | 165.00 | 24.77 | 19.86 | 44.63 |
| 349 | 120 | 63.00 | 166.00 | 24.91 | 19.98 | 44.89 |
| 350 | 120 | 63.00 | 167.00 | 25.04 | 20.10 | 45.14 |
| 351 | 120 | 63.00 | 168.00 | 25.18 | 20.22 | 45.40 |
| 352 | 120 | 63.00 | 169.00 | 25.32 | 20.34 | 45.66 |
| 353 | 120 | 63.00 | 170.00 | 25.46 | 20.46 | 45.92 |
| 354 | 120 | 63.00 | 171.00 | 25.60 | 20.58 | 46.18 |
| 355 | 120 | 63.00 | 172.00 | 25.73 | 20.70 | 46.43 |
| 356 | 120 | 63.00 | 173.00 | 25.87 | 20.82 | 46.69 |
| 357 | 120 | 63.00 | 174.00 | 26.01 | 20.94 | 46.95 |
| 358 | 120 | 63.00 | 175.00 | 26.15 | 21.06 | 47.21 |
| 359 | 120 | 63.00 | 176.00 | 26.29 | 21.18 | 47.47 |
| 360 | 120 | 63.00 | 177.00 | 26.42 | 21.30 | 47.72 |
| 361 | 120 | 63.00 | 178.00 | 26.56 | 21.42 | 47.98 |
| 362 | 120 | 63.00 | 179.00 | 26.70 | 21.54 | 48.24 |
| 363 | 120 | 63.00 | 180.00 | 26.84 | 21.66 | 48.50 |
| 364 | 120 | 63.00 | 181.00 | 26.98 | 21.78 | 48.76 |

**Weekly table**

**Table letter A**

| Employee's earnings up to and including the UEL £ | Earnings at the LEL (where earnings are equal to or exceed the LEL) 1a £ | Earnings above the LEL, up to and including the PT 1b £ p | Earnings above the PT, up to and including the UEL 1c £ p | Employer's NICs due on all earnings above the ST 1d £ p | Employee's NICs due on all earnings above the PT 1e £ p | Total of employee's and employer's NICs (for information only) £ p |
|---|---|---|---|---|---|---|
| 365 | 120 | 63.00 | 182.00 | 27.11 | 21.90 | 49.01 |
| 366 | 120 | 63.00 | 183.00 | 27.25 | 22.02 | 49.27 |
| 367 | 120 | 63.00 | 184.00 | 27.39 | 22.14 | 49.53 |
| 368 | 120 | 63.00 | 185.00 | 27.53 | 22.26 | 49.79 |
| 369 | 120 | 63.00 | 186.00 | 27.67 | 22.38 | 50.05 |
| 370 | 120 | 63.00 | 187.00 | 27.80 | 22.50 | 50.30 |
| 371 | 120 | 63.00 | 188.00 | 27.94 | 22.62 | 50.56 |
| 372 | 120 | 63.00 | 189.00 | 28.08 | 22.74 | 50.82 |
| 373 | 120 | 63.00 | 190.00 | 28.22 | 22.86 | 51.08 |
| 374 | 120 | 63.00 | 191.00 | 28.36 | 22.98 | 51.34 |
| 375 | 120 | 63.00 | 192.00 | 28.49 | 23.10 | 51.59 |
| 376 | 120 | 63.00 | 193.00 | 28.63 | 23.22 | 51.85 |
| 377 | 120 | 63.00 | 194.00 | 28.77 | 23.34 | 52.11 |
| 378 | 120 | 63.00 | 195.00 | 28.91 | 23.46 | 52.37 |
| 379 | 120 | 63.00 | 196.00 | 29.05 | 23.58 | 52.63 |
| 380 | 120 | 63.00 | 197.00 | 29.18 | 23.70 | 52.88 |
| 381 | 120 | 63.00 | 198.00 | 29.32 | 23.82 | 53.14 |
| 382 | 120 | 63.00 | 199.00 | 29.46 | 23.94 | 53.40 |
| 383 | 120 | 63.00 | 200.00 | 29.60 | 24.06 | 53.66 |
| 384 | 120 | 63.00 | 201.00 | 29.74 | 24.18 | 53.92 |
| 385 | 120 | 63.00 | 202.00 | 29.87 | 24.30 | 54.17 |
| 386 | 120 | 63.00 | 203.00 | 30.01 | 24.42 | 54.43 |
| 387 | 120 | 63.00 | 204.00 | 30.15 | 24.54 | 54.69 |
| 388 | 120 | 63.00 | 205.00 | 30.29 | 24.66 | 54.95 |
| 389 | 120 | 63.00 | 206.00 | 30.43 | 24.78 | 55.21 |
| 390 | 120 | 63.00 | 207.00 | 30.56 | 24.90 | 55.46 |
| 391 | 120 | 63.00 | 208.00 | 30.70 | 25.02 | 55.72 |
| 392 | 120 | 63.00 | 209.00 | 30.84 | 25.14 | 55.98 |
| 393 | 120 | 63.00 | 210.00 | 30.98 | 25.26 | 56.24 |
| 394 | 120 | 63.00 | 211.00 | 31.12 | 25.38 | 56.50 |
| 395 | 120 | 63.00 | 212.00 | 31.25 | 25.50 | 56.75 |
| 396 | 120 | 63.00 | 213.00 | 31.39 | 25.62 | 57.01 |
| 397 | 120 | 63.00 | 214.00 | 31.53 | 25.74 | 57.27 |
| 398 | 120 | 63.00 | 215.00 | 31.67 | 25.86 | 57.53 |
| 399 | 120 | 63.00 | 216.00 | 31.81 | 25.98 | 57.79 |
| 400 | 120 | 63.00 | 217.00 | 31.94 | 26.10 | 58.04 |
| 401 | 120 | 63.00 | 218.00 | 32.08 | 26.22 | 58.30 |
| 402 | 120 | 63.00 | 219.00 | 32.22 | 26.34 | 58.56 |
| 403 | 120 | 63.00 | 220.00 | 32.36 | 26.46 | 58.82 |
| 404 | 120 | 63.00 | 221.00 | 32.50 | 26.58 | 59.08 |
| 405 | 120 | 63.00 | 222.00 | 32.63 | 26.70 | 59.33 |
| 406 | 120 | 63.00 | 223.00 | 32.77 | 26.82 | 59.59 |
| 407 | 120 | 63.00 | 224.00 | 32.91 | 26.94 | 59.85 |
| 408 | 120 | 63.00 | 225.00 | 33.05 | 27.06 | 60.11 |
| 409 | 120 | 63.00 | 226.00 | 33.19 | 27.18 | 60.37 |
| 410 | 120 | 63.00 | 227.00 | 33.32 | 27.30 | 60.62 |
| 411 | 120 | 63.00 | 228.00 | 33.46 | 27.42 | 60.88 |
| 412 | 120 | 63.00 | 229.00 | 33.60 | 27.54 | 61.14 |
| 413 | 120 | 63.00 | 230.00 | 33.74 | 27.66 | 61.40 |
| 414 | 120 | 63.00 | 231.00 | 33.88 | 27.78 | 61.66 |
| 415 | 120 | 63.00 | 232.00 | 34.01 | 27.90 | 61.91 |
| 416 | 120 | 63.00 | 233.00 | 34.15 | 28.02 | 62.17 |
| 417 | 120 | 63.00 | 234.00 | 34.29 | 28.14 | 62.43 |
| 418 | 120 | 63.00 | 235.00 | 34.43 | 28.26 | 62.69 |
| 419 | 120 | 63.00 | 236.00 | 34.57 | 28.38 | 62.95 |

## Table letter A

**Weekly table**

| Employee's earnings up to and including the UEL | Earnings at the LEL (where earnings are equal to or exceed the LEL) | Earnings above the LEL, up to and including the PT | Earnings above the PT, up to and including the UEL | Employer's NICs due on all earnings above the ST | Employee's NICs due on all earnings above the PT | Total of employee's and employer's NICs (for information only) |
|---|---|---|---|---|---|---|
| | 1a | 1b | 1c | 1d | 1e | |
| £ | £ | £ p | £ p | £ p | £ p | £ p |
| 420 | 120 | 63.00 | 237.00 | 34.70 | 28.50 | 63.20 |
| 421 | 120 | 63.00 | 238.00 | 34.84 | 28.62 | 63.46 |
| 422 | 120 | 63.00 | 239.00 | 34.98 | 28.74 | 63.72 |
| 423 | 120 | 63.00 | 240.00 | 35.12 | 28.86 | 63.98 |
| 424 | 120 | 63.00 | 241.00 | 35.26 | 28.98 | 64.24 |
| 425 | 120 | 63.00 | 242.00 | 35.39 | 29.10 | 64.49 |
| 426 | 120 | 63.00 | 243.00 | 35.53 | 29.22 | 64.75 |
| 427 | 120 | 63.00 | 244.00 | 35.67 | 29.34 | 65.01 |
| 428 | 120 | 63.00 | 245.00 | 35.81 | 29.46 | 65.27 |
| 429 | 120 | 63.00 | 246.00 | 35.95 | 29.58 | 65.53 |
| 430 | 120 | 63.00 | 247.00 | 36.08 | 29.70 | 65.78 |
| 431 | 120 | 63.00 | 248.00 | 36.22 | 29.82 | 66.04 |
| 432 | 120 | 63.00 | 249.00 | 36.36 | 29.94 | 66.30 |
| 433 | 120 | 63.00 | 250.00 | 36.50 | 30.06 | 66.56 |
| 434 | 120 | 63.00 | 251.00 | 36.64 | 30.18 | 66.82 |
| 435 | 120 | 63.00 | 252.00 | 36.77 | 30.30 | 67.07 |
| 436 | 120 | 63.00 | 253.00 | 36.91 | 30.42 | 67.33 |
| 437 | 120 | 63.00 | 254.00 | 37.05 | 30.54 | 67.59 |
| 438 | 120 | 63.00 | 255.00 | 37.19 | 30.66 | 67.85 |
| 439 | 120 | 63.00 | 256.00 | 37.33 | 30.78 | 68.11 |
| 440 | 120 | 63.00 | 257.00 | 37.46 | 30.90 | 68.36 |
| 441 | 120 | 63.00 | 258.00 | 37.60 | 31.02 | 68.62 |
| 442 | 120 | 63.00 | 259.00 | 37.74 | 31.14 | 68.88 |
| 443 | 120 | 63.00 | 260.00 | 37.88 | 31.26 | 69.14 |
| 444 | 120 | 63.00 | 261.00 | 38.02 | 31.38 | 69.40 |
| 445 | 120 | 63.00 | 262.00 | 38.15 | 31.50 | 69.65 |
| 446 | 120 | 63.00 | 263.00 | 38.29 | 31.62 | 69.91 |
| 447 | 120 | 63.00 | 264.00 | 38.43 | 31.74 | 70.17 |
| 448 | 120 | 63.00 | 265.00 | 38.57 | 31.86 | 70.43 |
| 449 | 120 | 63.00 | 266.00 | 38.71 | 31.98 | 70.69 |
| 450 | 120 | 63.00 | 267.00 | 38.84 | 32.10 | 70.94 |
| 451 | 120 | 63.00 | 268.00 | 38.98 | 32.22 | 71.20 |
| 452 | 120 | 63.00 | 269.00 | 39.12 | 32.34 | 71.46 |
| 453 | 120 | 63.00 | 270.00 | 39.26 | 32.46 | 71.72 |
| 454 | 120 | 63.00 | 271.00 | 39.40 | 32.58 | 71.98 |
| 455 | 120 | 63.00 | 272.00 | 39.53 | 32.70 | 72.23 |
| 456 | 120 | 63.00 | 273.00 | 39.67 | 32.82 | 72.49 |
| 457 | 120 | 63.00 | 274.00 | 39.81 | 32.94 | 72.75 |
| 458 | 120 | 63.00 | 275.00 | 39.95 | 33.06 | 73.01 |
| 459 | 120 | 63.00 | 276.00 | 40.09 | 33.18 | 73.27 |
| 460 | 120 | 63.00 | 277.00 | 40.22 | 33.30 | 73.52 |
| 461 | 120 | 63.00 | 278.00 | 40.36 | 33.42 | 73.78 |
| 462 | 120 | 63.00 | 279.00 | 40.50 | 33.54 | 74.04 |
| 463 | 120 | 63.00 | 280.00 | 40.64 | 33.66 | 74.30 |
| 464 | 120 | 63.00 | 281.00 | 40.78 | 33.78 | 74.56 |
| 465 | 120 | 63.00 | 282.00 | 40.91 | 33.90 | 74.81 |
| 466 | 120 | 63.00 | 283.00 | 41.05 | 34.02 | 75.07 |
| 467 | 120 | 63.00 | 284.00 | 41.19 | 34.14 | 75.33 |
| 468 | 120 | 63.00 | 285.00 | 41.33 | 34.26 | 75.59 |
| 469 | 120 | 63.00 | 286.00 | 41.47 | 34.38 | 75.85 |
| 470 | 120 | 63.00 | 287.00 | 41.60 | 34.50 | 76.10 |
| 471 | 120 | 63.00 | 288.00 | 41.74 | 34.62 | 76.36 |
| 472 | 120 | 63.00 | 289.00 | 41.88 | 34.74 | 76.62 |
| 473 | 120 | 63.00 | 290.00 | 42.02 | 34.86 | 76.88 |
| 474 | 120 | 63.00 | 291.00 | 42.16 | 34.98 | 77.14 |

# Weekly table

**Table letter A**

| Employee's earnings up to and including the UEL | Earnings at the LEL (where earnings are equal to or exceed the LEL) 1a | Earnings above the LEL, up to and including the PT 1b | Earnings above the PT, up to and including the UEL 1c | Employer's NICs due on all earnings above the ST 1d | Employee's NICs due on all earnings above the PT 1e | Total of employee's and employer's NICs (for information only) |
|---|---|---|---|---|---|---|
| £ | £ | £ p | £ p | £ p | £ p | £ p |
| 475 | 120 | 63.00 | 292.00 | 42.29 | 35.10 | 77.39 |
| 476 | 120 | 63.00 | 293.00 | 42.43 | 35.22 | 77.65 |
| 477 | 120 | 63.00 | 294.00 | 42.57 | 35.34 | 77.91 |
| 478 | 120 | 63.00 | 295.00 | 42.71 | 35.46 | 78.17 |
| 479 | 120 | 63.00 | 296.00 | 42.85 | 35.58 | 78.43 |
| 480 | 120 | 63.00 | 297.00 | 42.98 | 35.70 | 78.68 |
| 481 | 120 | 63.00 | 298.00 | 43.12 | 35.82 | 78.94 |
| 482 | 120 | 63.00 | 299.00 | 43.26 | 35.94 | 79.20 |
| 483 | 120 | 63.00 | 300.00 | 43.40 | 36.06 | 79.46 |
| 484 | 120 | 63.00 | 301.00 | 43.54 | 36.18 | 79.72 |
| 485 | 120 | 63.00 | 302.00 | 43.67 | 36.30 | 79.97 |
| 486 | 120 | 63.00 | 303.00 | 43.81 | 36.42 | 80.23 |
| 487 | 120 | 63.00 | 304.00 | 43.95 | 36.54 | 80.49 |
| 488 | 120 | 63.00 | 305.00 | 44.09 | 36.66 | 80.75 |
| 489 | 120 | 63.00 | 306.00 | 44.23 | 36.78 | 81.01 |
| 490 | 120 | 63.00 | 307.00 | 44.36 | 36.90 | 81.26 |
| 491 | 120 | 63.00 | 308.00 | 44.50 | 37.02 | 81.52 |
| 492 | 120 | 63.00 | 309.00 | 44.64 | 37.14 | 81.78 |
| 493 | 120 | 63.00 | 310.00 | 44.78 | 37.26 | 82.04 |
| 494 | 120 | 63.00 | 311.00 | 44.92 | 37.38 | 82.30 |
| 495 | 120 | 63.00 | 312.00 | 45.05 | 37.50 | 82.55 |
| 496 | 120 | 63.00 | 313.00 | 45.19 | 37.62 | 82.81 |
| 497 | 120 | 63.00 | 314.00 | 45.33 | 37.74 | 83.07 |
| 498 | 120 | 63.00 | 315.00 | 45.47 | 37.86 | 83.33 |
| 499 | 120 | 63.00 | 316.00 | 45.61 | 37.98 | 83.59 |
| 500 | 120 | 63.00 | 317.00 | 45.74 | 38.10 | 83.84 |
| 501 | 120 | 63.00 | 318.00 | 45.88 | 38.22 | 84.10 |
| 502 | 120 | 63.00 | 319.00 | 46.02 | 38.34 | 84.36 |
| 503 | 120 | 63.00 | 320.00 | 46.16 | 38.46 | 84.62 |
| 504 | 120 | 63.00 | 321.00 | 46.30 | 38.58 | 84.88 |
| 505 | 120 | 63.00 | 322.00 | 46.43 | 38.70 | 85.13 |
| 506 | 120 | 63.00 | 323.00 | 46.57 | 38.82 | 85.39 |
| 507 | 120 | 63.00 | 324.00 | 46.71 | 38.94 | 85.65 |
| 508 | 120 | 63.00 | 325.00 | 46.85 | 39.06 | 85.91 |
| 509 | 120 | 63.00 | 326.00 | 46.99 | 39.18 | 86.17 |
| 510 | 120 | 63.00 | 327.00 | 47.12 | 39.30 | 86.42 |
| 511 | 120 | 63.00 | 328.00 | 47.26 | 39.42 | 86.68 |
| 512 | 120 | 63.00 | 329.00 | 47.40 | 39.54 | 86.94 |
| 513 | 120 | 63.00 | 330.00 | 47.54 | 39.66 | 87.20 |
| 514 | 120 | 63.00 | 331.00 | 47.68 | 39.78 | 87.46 |
| 515 | 120 | 63.00 | 332.00 | 47.81 | 39.90 | 87.71 |
| 516 | 120 | 63.00 | 333.00 | 47.95 | 40.02 | 87.97 |
| 517 | 120 | 63.00 | 334.00 | 48.09 | 40.14 | 88.23 |
| 518 | 120 | 63.00 | 335.00 | 48.23 | 40.26 | 88.49 |
| 519 | 120 | 63.00 | 336.00 | 48.37 | 40.38 | 88.75 |
| 520 | 120 | 63.00 | 337.00 | 48.50 | 40.50 | 89.00 |
| 521 | 120 | 63.00 | 338.00 | 48.64 | 40.62 | 89.26 |
| 522 | 120 | 63.00 | 339.00 | 48.78 | 40.74 | 89.52 |
| 523 | 120 | 63.00 | 340.00 | 48.92 | 40.86 | 89.78 |
| 524 | 120 | 63.00 | 341.00 | 49.06 | 40.98 | 90.04 |
| 525 | 120 | 63.00 | 342.00 | 49.19 | 41.10 | 90.29 |
| 526 | 120 | 63.00 | 343.00 | 49.33 | 41.22 | 90.55 |
| 527 | 120 | 63.00 | 344.00 | 49.47 | 41.34 | 90.81 |
| 528 | 120 | 63.00 | 345.00 | 49.61 | 41.46 | 91.07 |
| 529 | 120 | 63.00 | 346.00 | 49.75 | 41.58 | 91.33 |

# Table letter A

**Weekly table**

| Employee's earnings up to and including the UEL | Earnings at the LEL (where earnings are equal to or exceed the LEL) 1a | Earnings above the LEL, up to and including the PT 1b | Earnings above the PT, up to and including the UEL 1c | Employer's NICs due on all earnings above the ST 1d | Employee's NICs due on all earnings above the PT 1e | Total of employee's and employer's NICs (for information only) |
|---|---|---|---|---|---|---|
| £ | £ | £ p | £ p | £ p | £ p | £ p |
| 530 | 120 | 63.00 | 347.00 | 49.88 | 41.70 | 91.58 |
| 531 | 120 | 63.00 | 348.00 | 50.02 | 41.82 | 91.84 |
| 532 | 120 | 63.00 | 349.00 | 50.16 | 41.94 | 92.10 |
| 533 | 120 | 63.00 | 350.00 | 50.30 | 42.06 | 92.36 |
| 534 | 120 | 63.00 | 351.00 | 50.44 | 42.18 | 92.62 |
| 535 | 120 | 63.00 | 352.00 | 50.57 | 42.30 | 92.87 |
| 536 | 120 | 63.00 | 353.00 | 50.71 | 42.42 | 93.13 |
| 537 | 120 | 63.00 | 354.00 | 50.85 | 42.54 | 93.39 |
| 538 | 120 | 63.00 | 355.00 | 50.99 | 42.66 | 93.65 |
| 539 | 120 | 63.00 | 356.00 | 51.13 | 42.78 | 93.91 |
| 540 | 120 | 63.00 | 357.00 | 51.26 | 42.90 | 94.16 |
| 541 | 120 | 63.00 | 358.00 | 51.40 | 43.02 | 94.42 |
| 542 | 120 | 63.00 | 359.00 | 51.54 | 43.14 | 94.68 |
| 543 | 120 | 63.00 | 360.00 | 51.68 | 43.26 | 94.94 |
| 544 | 120 | 63.00 | 361.00 | 51.82 | 43.38 | 95.20 |
| 545 | 120 | 63.00 | 362.00 | 51.95 | 43.50 | 95.45 |
| 546 | 120 | 63.00 | 363.00 | 52.09 | 43.62 | 95.71 |
| 547 | 120 | 63.00 | 364.00 | 52.23 | 43.74 | 95.97 |
| 548 | 120 | 63.00 | 365.00 | 52.37 | 43.86 | 96.23 |
| 549 | 120 | 63.00 | 366.00 | 52.51 | 43.98 | 96.49 |
| 550 | 120 | 63.00 | 367.00 | 52.64 | 44.10 | 96.74 |
| 551 | 120 | 63.00 | 368.00 | 52.78 | 44.22 | 97.00 |
| 552 | 120 | 63.00 | 369.00 | 52.92 | 44.34 | 97.26 |
| 553 | 120 | 63.00 | 370.00 | 53.06 | 44.46 | 97.52 |
| 554 | 120 | 63.00 | 371.00 | 53.20 | 44.58 | 97.78 |
| 555 | 120 | 63.00 | 372.00 | 53.33 | 44.70 | 98.03 |
| 556 | 120 | 63.00 | 373.00 | 53.47 | 44.82 | 98.29 |
| 557 | 120 | 63.00 | 374.00 | 53.61 | 44.94 | 98.55 |
| 558 | 120 | 63.00 | 375.00 | 53.75 | 45.06 | 98.81 |
| 559 | 120 | 63.00 | 376.00 | 53.89 | 45.18 | 99.07 |
| 560 | 120 | 63.00 | 377.00 | 54.02 | 45.30 | 99.32 |
| 561 | 120 | 63.00 | 378.00 | 54.16 | 45.42 | 99.58 |
| 562 | 120 | 63.00 | 379.00 | 54.30 | 45.54 | 99.84 |
| 563 | 120 | 63.00 | 380.00 | 54.44 | 45.66 | 100.10 |
| 564 | 120 | 63.00 | 381.00 | 54.58 | 45.78 | 100.36 |
| 565 | 120 | 63.00 | 382.00 | 54.71 | 45.90 | 100.61 |
| 566 | 120 | 63.00 | 383.00 | 54.85 | 46.02 | 100.87 |
| 567 | 120 | 63.00 | 384.00 | 54.99 | 46.14 | 101.13 |
| 568 | 120 | 63.00 | 385.00 | 55.13 | 46.26 | 101.39 |
| 569 | 120 | 63.00 | 386.00 | 55.27 | 46.38 | 101.65 |
| 570 | 120 | 63.00 | 387.00 | 55.40 | 46.50 | 101.90 |
| 571 | 120 | 63.00 | 388.00 | 55.54 | 46.62 | 102.16 |
| 572 | 120 | 63.00 | 389.00 | 55.68 | 46.74 | 102.42 |
| 573 | 120 | 63.00 | 390.00 | 55.82 | 46.86 | 102.68 |
| 574 | 120 | 63.00 | 391.00 | 55.96 | 46.98 | 102.94 |
| 575 | 120 | 63.00 | 392.00 | 56.09 | 47.10 | 103.19 |
| 576 | 120 | 63.00 | 393.00 | 56.23 | 47.22 | 103.45 |
| 577 | 120 | 63.00 | 394.00 | 56.37 | 47.34 | 103.71 |
| 578 | 120 | 63.00 | 395.00 | 56.51 | 47.46 | 103.97 |
| 579 | 120 | 63.00 | 396.00 | 56.65 | 47.58 | 104.23 |
| 580 | 120 | 63.00 | 397.00 | 56.78 | 47.70 | 104.48 |
| 581 | 120 | 63.00 | 398.00 | 56.92 | 47.82 | 104.74 |
| 582 | 120 | 63.00 | 399.00 | 57.06 | 47.94 | 105.00 |
| 583 | 120 | 63.00 | 400.00 | 57.20 | 48.06 | 105.26 |
| 584 | 120 | 63.00 | 401.00 | 57.34 | 48.18 | 105.52 |

**Weekly table**

**Table letter A**

| Employee's earnings up to and including the UEL | Earnings at the LEL (where earnings are equal to or exceed the LEL) 1a | Earnings above the LEL, up to and including the PT 1b | Earnings above the PT, up to and including the UEL 1c | Employer's NICs due on all earnings above the ST 1d | Employee's NICs due on all earnings above the PT 1e | Total of employee's and employer's NICs (for information only) |
|---|---|---|---|---|---|---|
| £ | £ | £ p | £ p | £ p | £ p | £ p |
| 585 | 120 | 63.00 | 402.00 | 57.47 | 48.30 | 105.77 |
| 586 | 120 | 63.00 | 403.00 | 57.61 | 48.42 | 106.03 |
| 587 | 120 | 63.00 | 404.00 | 57.75 | 48.54 | 106.29 |
| 588 | 120 | 63.00 | 405.00 | 57.89 | 48.66 | 106.55 |
| 589 | 120 | 63.00 | 406.00 | 58.03 | 48.78 | 106.81 |
| 590 | 120 | 63.00 | 407.00 | 58.16 | 48.90 | 107.06 |
| 591 | 120 | 63.00 | 408.00 | 58.30 | 49.02 | 107.32 |
| 592 | 120 | 63.00 | 409.00 | 58.44 | 49.14 | 107.58 |
| 593 | 120 | 63.00 | 410.00 | 58.58 | 49.26 | 107.84 |
| 594 | 120 | 63.00 | 411.00 | 58.72 | 49.38 | 108.10 |
| 595 | 120 | 63.00 | 412.00 | 58.85 | 49.50 | 108.35 |
| 596 | 120 | 63.00 | 413.00 | 58.99 | 49.62 | 108.61 |
| 597 | 120 | 63.00 | 414.00 | 59.13 | 49.74 | 108.87 |
| 598 | 120 | 63.00 | 415.00 | 59.27 | 49.86 | 109.13 |
| 599 | 120 | 63.00 | 416.00 | 59.41 | 49.98 | 109.39 |
| 600 | 120 | 63.00 | 417.00 | 59.54 | 50.10 | 109.64 |
| 601 | 120 | 63.00 | 418.00 | 59.68 | 50.22 | 109.90 |
| 602 | 120 | 63.00 | 419.00 | 59.82 | 50.34 | 110.16 |
| 603 | 120 | 63.00 | 420.00 | 59.96 | 50.46 | 110.42 |
| 604 | 120 | 63.00 | 421.00 | 60.10 | 50.58 | 110.68 |
| 605 | 120 | 63.00 | 422.00 | 60.23 | 50.70 | 110.93 |
| 606 | 120 | 63.00 | 423.00 | 60.37 | 50.82 | 111.19 |
| 607 | 120 | 63.00 | 424.00 | 60.51 | 50.94 | 111.45 |
| 608 | 120 | 63.00 | 425.00 | 60.65 | 51.06 | 111.71 |
| 609 | 120 | 63.00 | 426.00 | 60.79 | 51.18 | 111.97 |
| 610 | 120 | 63.00 | 427.00 | 60.92 | 51.30 | 112.22 |
| 611 | 120 | 63.00 | 428.00 | 61.06 | 51.42 | 112.48 |
| 612 | 120 | 63.00 | 429.00 | 61.20 | 51.54 | 112.74 |
| 613 | 120 | 63.00 | 430.00 | 61.34 | 51.66 | 113.00 |
| 614 | 120 | 63.00 | 431.00 | 61.48 | 51.78 | 113.26 |
| 615 | 120 | 63.00 | 432.00 | 61.61 | 51.90 | 113.51 |
| 616 | 120 | 63.00 | 433.00 | 61.75 | 52.02 | 113.77 |
| 617 | 120 | 63.00 | 434.00 | 61.89 | 52.14 | 114.03 |
| 618 | 120 | 63.00 | 435.00 | 62.03 | 52.26 | 114.29 |
| 619 | 120 | 63.00 | 436.00 | 62.17 | 52.38 | 114.55 |
| 620 | 120 | 63.00 | 437.00 | 62.30 | 52.50 | 114.80 |
| 621 | 120 | 63.00 | 438.00 | 62.44 | 52.62 | 115.06 |
| 622 | 120 | 63.00 | 439.00 | 62.58 | 52.74 | 115.32 |
| 623 | 120 | 63.00 | 440.00 | 62.72 | 52.86 | 115.58 |
| 624 | 120 | 63.00 | 441.00 | 62.86 | 52.98 | 115.84 |
| 625 | 120 | 63.00 | 442.00 | 62.99 | 53.10 | 116.09 |
| 626 | 120 | 63.00 | 443.00 | 63.13 | 53.22 | 116.35 |
| 627 | 120 | 63.00 | 444.00 | 63.27 | 53.34 | 116.61 |
| 628 | 120 | 63.00 | 445.00 | 63.41 | 53.46 | 116.87 |
| 629 | 120 | 63.00 | 446.00 | 63.55 | 53.58 | 117.13 |
| 630 | 120 | 63.00 | 447.00 | 63.68 | 53.70 | 117.38 |
| 631 | 120 | 63.00 | 448.00 | 63.82 | 53.82 | 117.64 |
| 632 | 120 | 63.00 | 449.00 | 63.96 | 53.94 | 117.90 |
| 633 | 120 | 63.00 | 450.00 | 64.10 | 54.06 | 118.16 |
| 634 | 120 | 63.00 | 451.00 | 64.24 | 54.18 | 118.42 |
| 635 | 120 | 63.00 | 452.00 | 64.37 | 54.30 | 118.67 |
| 636 | 120 | 63.00 | 453.00 | 64.51 | 54.42 | 118.93 |
| 637 | 120 | 63.00 | 454.00 | 64.65 | 54.54 | 119.19 |
| 638 | 120 | 63.00 | 455.00 | 64.79 | 54.66 | 119.45 |
| 639 | 120 | 63.00 | 456.00 | 64.93 | 54.78 | 119.71 |

## Table letter A

**Weekly table**

| Employee's earnings up to and including the UEL | Earnings at the LEL (where earnings are equal to or exceed the LEL) | Earnings above the LEL, up to and including the PT | Earnings above the PT, up to and including the UEL | Employer's NICs due on all earnings above the ST | Employee's NICs due on all earnings above the PT | Total of employee's and employer's NICs (for information only) |
|---|---|---|---|---|---|---|
| | 1a | 1b | 1c | 1d | 1e | |
| £ | £ | £ p | £ p | £ p | £ p | £ p |
| 640 | 120 | 63.00 | 457.00 | 65.06 | 54.90 | 119.96 |
| 641 | 120 | 63.00 | 458.00 | 65.20 | 55.02 | 120.22 |
| 642 | 120 | 63.00 | 459.00 | 65.34 | 55.14 | 120.48 |
| 643 | 120 | 63.00 | 460.00 | 65.48 | 55.26 | 120.74 |
| 644 | 120 | 63.00 | 461.00 | 65.62 | 55.38 | 121.00 |
| 645 | 120 | 63.00 | 462.00 | 65.75 | 55.50 | 121.25 |
| 646 | 120 | 63.00 | 463.00 | 65.89 | 55.62 | 121.51 |
| 647 | 120 | 63.00 | 464.00 | 66.03 | 55.74 | 121.77 |
| 648 | 120 | 63.00 | 465.00 | 66.17 | 55.86 | 122.03 |
| 649 | 120 | 63.00 | 466.00 | 66.31 | 55.98 | 122.29 |
| 650 | 120 | 63.00 | 467.00 | 66.44 | 56.10 | 122.54 |
| 651 | 120 | 63.00 | 468.00 | 66.58 | 56.22 | 122.80 |
| 652 | 120 | 63.00 | 469.00 | 66.72 | 56.34 | 123.06 |
| 653 | 120 | 63.00 | 470.00 | 66.86 | 56.46 | 123.32 |
| 654 | 120 | 63.00 | 471.00 | 67.00 | 56.58 | 123.58 |
| 655 | 120 | 63.00 | 472.00 | 67.13 | 56.70 | 123.83 |
| 656 | 120 | 63.00 | 473.00 | 67.27 | 56.82 | 124.09 |
| 657 | 120 | 63.00 | 474.00 | 67.41 | 56.94 | 124.35 |
| 658 | 120 | 63.00 | 475.00 | 67.55 | 57.06 | 124.61 |
| 659 | 120 | 63.00 | 476.00 | 67.69 | 57.18 | 124.87 |
| 660 | 120 | 63.00 | 477.00 | 67.82 | 57.30 | 125.12 |
| 661 | 120 | 63.00 | 478.00 | 67.96 | 57.42 | 125.38 |
| 662 | 120 | 63.00 | 479.00 | 68.10 | 57.54 | 125.64 |
| 663 | 120 | 63.00 | 480.00 | 68.24 | 57.66 | 125.90 |
| 664 | 120 | 63.00 | 481.00 | 68.38 | 57.78 | 126.16 |
| 665 | 120 | 63.00 | 482.00 | 68.51 | 57.90 | 126.41 |
| 666 | 120 | 63.00 | 483.00 | 68.65 | 58.02 | 126.67 |
| 667 | 120 | 63.00 | 484.00 | 68.79 | 58.14 | 126.93 |
| 668 | 120 | 63.00 | 485.00 | 68.93 | 58.26 | 127.19 |
| 669 | 120 | 63.00 | 486.00 | 69.07 | 58.38 | 127.45 |
| 670 | 120 | 63.00 | 487.00 | 69.20 | 58.50 | 127.70 |
| 671 | 120 | 63.00 | 488.00 | 69.34 | 58.62 | 127.96 |
| 672 | 120 | 63.00 | 489.00 | 69.48 | 58.74 | 128.22 |
| 673 | 120 | 63.00 | 490.00 | 69.62 | 58.86 | 128.48 |
| 674 | 120 | 63.00 | 491.00 | 69.76 | 58.98 | 128.74 |
| 675 | 120 | 63.00 | 492.00 | 69.89 | 59.10 | 128.99 |
| 676 | 120 | 63.00 | 493.00 | 70.03 | 59.22 | 129.25 |
| 677 | 120 | 63.00 | 494.00 | 70.17 | 59.34 | 129.51 |
| 678 | 120 | 63.00 | 495.00 | 70.31 | 59.46 | 129.77 |
| 679 | 120 | 63.00 | 496.00 | 70.45 | 59.58 | 130.03 |
| 680 | 120 | 63.00 | 497.00 | 70.58 | 59.70 | 130.28 |
| 681 | 120 | 63.00 | 498.00 | 70.72 | 59.82 | 130.54 |
| 682 | 120 | 63.00 | 499.00 | 70.86 | 59.94 | 130.80 |
| 683 | 120 | 63.00 | 500.00 | 71.00 | 60.06 | 131.06 |
| 684 | 120 | 63.00 | 501.00 | 71.14 | 60.18 | 131.32 |
| 685 | 120 | 63.00 | 502.00 | 71.27 | 60.30 | 131.57 |
| 686 | 120 | 63.00 | 503.00 | 71.41 | 60.42 | 131.83 |
| 687 | 120 | 63.00 | 504.00 | 71.55 | 60.54 | 132.09 |
| 688 | 120 | 63.00 | 505.00 | 71.69 | 60.66 | 132.35 |
| 689 | 120 | 63.00 | 506.00 | 71.83 | 60.78 | 132.61 |
| 690 | 120 | 63.00 | 507.00 | 71.96 | 60.90 | 132.86 |
| 691 | 120 | 63.00 | 508.00 | 72.10 | 61.02 | 133.12 |
| 692 | 120 | 63.00 | 509.00 | 72.24 | 61.14 | 133.38 |
| 693 | 120 | 63.00 | 510.00 | 72.38 | 61.26 | 133.64 |
| 694 | 120 | 63.00 | 511.00 | 72.52 | 61.38 | 133.90 |

**Weekly table**

**Table letter A**

| Employee's earnings up to and including the UEL | Earnings at the LEL (where earnings are equal to or exceed the LEL) 1a | Earnings above the LEL, up to and including the PT 1b | Earnings above the PT, up to and including the UEL 1c | Employer's NICs due on all earnings above the ST 1d | Employee's NICs due on all earnings above the PT 1e | Total of employee's and employer's NICs (for information only) |
|---|---|---|---|---|---|---|
| £ | £ | £ p | £ p | £ p | £ p | £ p |
| 695 | 120 | 63.00 | 512.00 | 72.65 | 61.50 | 134.15 |
| 696 | 120 | 63.00 | 513.00 | 72.79 | 61.62 | 134.41 |
| 697 | 120 | 63.00 | 514.00 | 72.93 | 61.74 | 134.67 |
| 698 | 120 | 63.00 | 515.00 | 73.07 | 61.86 | 134.93 |
| 699 | 120 | 63.00 | 516.00 | 73.21 | 61.98 | 135.19 |
| 700 | 120 | 63.00 | 517.00 | 73.34 | 62.10 | 135.44 |
| 701 | 120 | 63.00 | 518.00 | 73.48 | 62.22 | 135.70 |
| 702 | 120 | 63.00 | 519.00 | 73.62 | 62.34 | 135.96 |
| 703 | 120 | 63.00 | 520.00 | 73.76 | 62.46 | 136.22 |
| 704 | 120 | 63.00 | 521.00 | 73.90 | 62.58 | 136.48 |
| 705 | 120 | 63.00 | 522.00 | 74.03 | 62.70 | 136.73 |
| 706 | 120 | 63.00 | 523.00 | 74.17 | 62.82 | 136.99 |
| 707 | 120 | 63.00 | 524.00 | 74.31 | 62.94 | 137.25 |
| 708 | 120 | 63.00 | 525.00 | 74.45 | 63.06 | 137.51 |
| 709 | 120 | 63.00 | 526.00 | 74.59 | 63.18 | 137.77 |
| 710 | 120 | 63.00 | 527.00 | 74.72 | 63.30 | 138.02 |
| 711 | 120 | 63.00 | 528.00 | 74.86 | 63.42 | 138.28 |
| 712 | 120 | 63.00 | 529.00 | 75.00 | 63.54 | 138.54 |
| 713 | 120 | 63.00 | 530.00 | 75.14 | 63.66 | 138.80 |
| 714 | 120 | 63.00 | 531.00 | 75.28 | 63.78 | 139.06 |
| 715 | 120 | 63.00 | 532.00 | 75.41 | 63.90 | 139.31 |
| 716 | 120 | 63.00 | 533.00 | 75.55 | 64.02 | 139.57 |
| 717 | 120 | 63.00 | 534.00 | 75.69 | 64.14 | 139.83 |
| 718 | 120 | 63.00 | 535.00 | 75.83 | 64.26 | 140.09 |
| 719 | 120 | 63.00 | 536.00 | 75.97 | 64.38 | 140.35 |
| 720 | 120 | 63.00 | 537.00 | 76.10 | 64.50 | 140.60 |
| 721 | 120 | 63.00 | 538.00 | 76.24 | 64.62 | 140.86 |
| 722 | 120 | 63.00 | 539.00 | 76.38 | 64.74 | 141.12 |
| 723 | 120 | 63.00 | 540.00 | 76.52 | 64.86 | 141.38 |
| 724 | 120 | 63.00 | 541.00 | 76.66 | 64.98 | 141.64 |
| 725 | 120 | 63.00 | 542.00 | 76.79 | 65.10 | 141.89 |
| 726 | 120 | 63.00 | 543.00 | 76.93 | 65.22 | 142.15 |
| 727 | 120 | 63.00 | 544.00 | 77.07 | 65.34 | 142.41 |
| 728 | 120 | 63.00 | 545.00 | 77.21 | 65.46 | 142.67 |
| 729 | 120 | 63.00 | 546.00 | 77.35 | 65.58 | 142.93 |
| 730 | 120 | 63.00 | 547.00 | 77.48 | 65.70 | 143.18 |
| 731 | 120 | 63.00 | 548.00 | 77.62 | 65.82 | 143.44 |
| 732 | 120 | 63.00 | 549.00 | 77.76 | 65.94 | 143.70 |
| 733 | 120 | 63.00 | 550.00 | 77.90 | 66.06 | 143.96 |
| 734 | 120 | 63.00 | 551.00 | 78.04 | 66.18 | 144.22 |
| 735 | 120 | 63.00 | 552.00 | 78.17 | 66.30 | 144.47 |
| 736 | 120 | 63.00 | 553.00 | 78.31 | 66.42 | 144.73 |
| 737 | 120 | 63.00 | 554.00 | 78.45 | 66.54 | 144.99 |
| 738 | 120 | 63.00 | 555.00 | 78.59 | 66.66 | 145.25 |
| 739 | 120 | 63.00 | 556.00 | 78.73 | 66.78 | 145.51 |
| 740 | 120 | 63.00 | 557.00 | 78.86 | 66.90 | 145.76 |
| 741 | 120 | 63.00 | 558.00 | 79.00 | 67.02 | 146.02 |
| 742 | 120 | 63.00 | 559.00 | 79.14 | 67.14 | 146.28 |
| 743 | 120 | 63.00 | 560.00 | 79.28 | 67.26 | 146.54 |
| 744 | 120 | 63.00 | 561.00 | 79.42 | 67.38 | 146.80 |
| 745 | 120 | 63.00 | 562.00 | 79.55 | 67.50 | 147.05 |
| 746 | 120 | 63.00 | 563.00 | 79.69 | 67.62 | 147.31 |
| 747 | 120 | 63.00 | 564.00 | 79.83 | 67.74 | 147.57 |
| 748 | 120 | 63.00 | 565.00 | 79.97 | 67.86 | 147.83 |
| 749 | 120 | 63.00 | 566.00 | 80.11 | 67.98 | 148.09 |

## Table letter A                                                                          Weekly table

| Employee's earnings up to and including the UEL | Earnings at the LEL (where earnings are equal to or exceed the LEL) | Earnings above the LEL, up to and including the PT | Earnings above the PT, up to and including the UEL | Employer's NICs due on all earnings above the ST | Employee's NICs due on all earnings above the PT | Total of employee's and employer's NICs (for information only) |
|---|---|---|---|---|---|---|
| | 1a | 1b | 1c | 1d | 1e | |
| £ | £ | £ p | £ p | £ p | £ p | £ p |
| 750 | 120 | 63.00 | 567.00 | 80.24 | 68.10 | 148.34 |
| 751 | 120 | 63.00 | 568.00 | 80.38 | 68.22 | 148.60 |
| 752 | 120 | 63.00 | 569.00 | 80.52 | 68.34 | 148.86 |
| 753 | 120 | 63.00 | 570.00 | 80.66 | 68.46 | 149.12 |
| 754 | 120 | 63.00 | 571.00 | 80.80 | 68.58 | 149.38 |
| 755 | 120 | 63.00 | 572.00 | 80.93 | 68.70 | 149.63 |
| 756 | 120 | 63.00 | 573.00 | 81.07 | 68.82 | 149.89 |
| 757 | 120 | 63.00 | 574.00 | 81.21 | 68.94 | 150.15 |
| 758 | 120 | 63.00 | 575.00 | 81.35 | 69.06 | 150.41 |
| 759 | 120 | 63.00 | 576.00 | 81.49 | 69.18 | 150.67 |
| 760 | 120 | 63.00 | 577.00 | 81.62 | 69.30 | 150.92 |
| 761 | 120 | 63.00 | 578.00 | 81.76 | 69.42 | 151.18 |
| 762 | 120 | 63.00 | 579.00 | 81.90 | 69.54 | 151.44 |
| 763 | 120 | 63.00 | 580.00 | 82.04 | 69.66 | 151.70 |
| 764 | 120 | 63.00 | 581.00 | 82.18 | 69.78 | 151.96 |
| 765 | 120 | 63.00 | 582.00 | 82.31 | 69.90 | 152.21 |
| 766 | 120 | 63.00 | 583.00 | 82.45 | 70.02 | 152.47 |
| 767 | 120 | 63.00 | 584.00 | 82.59 | 70.14 | 152.73 |
| 768 | 120 | 63.00 | 585.00 | 82.73 | 70.26 | 152.99 |
| 769 | 120 | 63.00 | 586.00 | 82.87 | 70.38 | 153.25 |
| 770 | 120 | 63.00 | 587.00 | 83.00 | 70.50 | 153.50 |
| 771 | 120 | 63.00 | 588.00 | 83.14 | 70.62 | 153.76 |
| 772 | 120 | 63.00 | 589.00 | 83.28 | 70.74 | 154.02 |
| 773 | 120 | 63.00 | 590.00 | 83.42 | 70.86 | 154.28 |
| 774 | 120 | 63.00 | 591.00 | 83.56 | 70.98 | 154.54 |
| 775 | 120 | 63.00 | 592.00 | 83.69 | 71.10 | 154.79 |
| 776 | 120 | 63.00 | 593.00 | 83.83 | 71.22 | 155.05 |
| 777 | 120 | 63.00 | 594.00 | 83.97 | 71.34 | 155.31 |
| 778 | 120 | 63.00 | 595.00 | 84.11 | 71.46 | 155.57 |
| 779 | 120 | 63.00 | 596.00 | 84.25 | 71.58 | 155.83 |
| 780 | 120 | 63.00 | 597.00 | 84.38 | 71.70 | 156.08 |
| 781 | 120 | 63.00 | 598.00 | 84.52 | 71.82 | 156.34 |
| 782 | 120 | 63.00 | 599.00 | 84.66 | 71.94 | 156.60 |
| 783 | 120 | 63.00 | 600.00 | 84.80 | 72.06 | 156.86 |
| 784 | 120 | 63.00 | 601.00 | 84.94 | 72.18 | 157.12 |
| 785 | 120 | 63.00 | 602.00 | 85.07 | 72.30 | 157.37 |
| 786 | 120 | 63.00 | 603.00 | 85.21 | 72.42 | 157.63 |
| 787 | 120 | 63.00 | 604.00 | 85.35 | 72.54 | 157.89 |
| 788 | 120 | 63.00 | 605.00 | 85.49 | 72.66 | 158.15 |
| 789 | 120 | 63.00 | 606.00 | 85.63 | 72.78 | 158.41 |
| 790 | 120 | 63.00 | 607.00 | 85.76 | 72.90 | 158.66 |
| 791 | 120 | 63.00 | 608.00 | 85.90 | 73.02 | 158.92 |
| 792 | 120 | 63.00 | 609.00 | 86.04 | 73.14 | 159.18 |
| 793 | 120 | 63.00 | 610.00 | 86.18 | 73.26 | 159.44 |
| 794 | 120 | 63.00 | 611.00 | 86.32 | 73.38 | 159.70 |
| 795 | 120 | 63.00 | 612.00 | 86.45 | 73.50 | 159.95 |
| 796 | 120 | 63.00 | 613.00 | 86.59 | 73.62 | 160.21 |
| 797 | 120 | 63.00 | 614.00 | 86.73 | 73.74 | 160.47 |
| 798 | 120 | 63.00 | 615.00 | 86.87 | 73.86 | 160.73 |
| 799 | 120 | 63.00 | 616.00 | 87.01 | 73.98 | 160.99 |
| 800 | 120 | 63.00 | 617.00 | 87.14 | 74.10 | 161.24 |
| 801 | 120 | 63.00 | 618.00 | 87.28 | 74.22 | 161.50 |
| 802 | 120 | 63.00 | 619.00 | 87.42 | 74.34 | 161.76 |
| 803 | 120 | 63.00 | 620.00 | 87.56 | 74.46 | 162.02 |
| 804 | 120 | 63.00 | 621.00 | 87.70 | 74.58 | 162.28 |

**Weekly table**

**Table letter A**

| Employee's earnings up to and including the UEL | Earnings at the LEL (where earnings are equal to or exceed the LEL) 1a | Earnings above the LEL, up to and including the PT 1b | Earnings above the PT, up to and including the UEL 1c | Employer's NICs due on all earnings above the ST 1d | Employee's NICs due on all earnings above the PT 1e | Total of employee's and employer's NICs (for information only) |
|---|---|---|---|---|---|---|
| £ | £ | £ p | £ p | £ p | £ p | £ p |
| 805 | 120 | 63.00 | 622.00 | 87.83 | 74.70 | 162.53 |
| 806 | 120 | 63.00 | 623.00 | 87.97 | 74.82 | 162.79 |
| 807 | 120 | 63.00 | 624.00 | 88.11 | 74.94 | 163.05 |
| 808 | 120 | 63.00 | 625.00 | 88.25 | 75.06 | 163.31 |
| 809 | 120 | 63.00 | 626.00 | 88.39 | 75.18 | 163.57 |
| 810 | 120 | 63.00 | 627.00 | 88.52 | 75.30 | 163.82 |
| 811 | 120 | 63.00 | 628.00 | 88.66 | 75.42 | 164.08 |
| 812 | 120 | 63.00 | 629.00 | 88.80 | 75.54 | 164.34 |
| 813 | 120 | 63.00 | 630.00 | 88.94 | 75.66 | 164.60 |
| 814 | 120 | 63.00 | 631.00 | 89.08 | 75.78 | 164.86 |
| 815 | 120 | 63.00 | 632.00 | 89.21 | 75.90 | 165.11 |
| 816 | 120 | 63.00 | 633.00 | 89.35 | 76.02 | 165.37 |
| 817 | 120 | 63.00 | 634.00 | 89.49 | 76.14 | 165.63 |
| 818 | 120 | 63.00 | 635.00 | 89.63 | 76.26 | 165.89 |
| 819 | 120 | 63.00 | 636.00 | 89.77 | 76.38 | 166.15 |
| 820 | 120 | 63.00 | 637.00 | 89.90 | 76.50 | 166.40 |
| 821 | 120 | 63.00 | 638.00 | 90.04 | 76.62 | 166.66 |
| 822 | 120 | 63.00 | 639.00 | 90.18 | 76.74 | 166.92 |
| 823 | 120 | 63.00 | 640.00 | 90.32 | 76.86 | 167.18 |
| 824 | 120 | 63.00 | 641.00 | 90.46 | 76.98 | 167.44 |
| 825 | 120 | 63.00 | 642.00 | 90.59 | 77.10 | 167.69 |
| 826 | 120 | 63.00 | 643.00 | 90.73 | 77.22 | 167.95 |
| 827 | 120 | 63.00 | 644.00 | 90.87 | 77.34 | 168.21 |
| 828 | 120 | 63.00 | 645.00 | 91.01 | 77.46 | 168.47 |
| 829 | 120 | 63.00 | 646.00 | 91.15 | 77.58 | 168.73 |
| 830 | 120 | 63.00 | 647.00 | 91.28 | 77.70 | 168.98 |
| 831 | 120 | 63.00 | 648.00 | 91.42 | 77.82 | 169.24 |
| 832 | 120 | 63.00 | 649.00 | 91.56 | 77.94 | 169.50 |
| 833 | 120 | 63.00 | 650.00 | 91.70 | 78.06 | 169.76 |
| 834 | 120 | 63.00 | 651.00 | 91.84 | 78.18 | 170.02 |
| 835 | 120 | 63.00 | 652.00 | 91.97 | 78.30 | 170.27 |
| 836 | 120 | 63.00 | 653.00 | 92.11 | 78.42 | 170.53 |
| 837 | 120 | 63.00 | 654.00 | 92.25 | 78.54 | 170.79 |
| 838 | 120 | 63.00 | 655.00 | 92.39 | 78.66 | 171.05 |
| 839 | 120 | 63.00 | 656.00 | 92.53 | 78.78 | 171.31 |
| 840 | 120 | 63.00 | 657.00 | 92.66 | 78.90 | 171.56 |
| 841 | 120 | 63.00 | 658.00 | 92.80 | 79.02 | 171.82 |
| 842 | 120 | 63.00 | 659.00 | 92.94 | 79.14 | 172.08 |
| 843 | 120 | 63.00 | 660.00 | 93.08 | 79.26 | 172.34 |
| 844 | 120 | 63.00 | 661.00 | 93.22 | 79.38 | 172.60 |
| 845 | 120 | 63.00 | 662.00 | 93.35 | 79.50 | 172.85 |
| 846 | 120 | 63.00 | 663.00 | 93.49 | 79.62 | 173.11 |
| 847 | 120 | 63.00 | 664.00 | 93.63 | 79.74 | 173.37 |
| 848 | 120 | 63.00 | 665.00 | 93.77 | 79.86 | 173.63 |
| 849 | 120 | 63.00 | 666.00 | 93.91 | 79.98 | 173.89 |
| 850 | 120 | 63.00 | 667.00 | 94.04 | 80.10 | 174.14 |
| 851 | 120 | 63.00 | 668.00 | 94.18 | 80.22 | 174.40 |
| 852 | 120 | 63.00 | 669.00 | 94.32 | 80.34 | 174.66 |
| 853 | 120 | 63.00 | 670.00 | 94.46 | 80.46 | 174.92 |
| 854 | 120 | 63.00 | 671.00 | 94.60 | 80.58 | 175.18 |
| 855 | 120 | 63.00 | 672.00 | 94.73 | 80.70 | 175.43 |
| 856 | 120 | 63.00 | 673.00 | 94.87 | 80.82 | 175.69 |
| 857 | 120 | 63.00 | 674.00 | 95.01 | 80.94 | 175.95 |
| 858 | 120 | 63.00 | 675.00 | 95.15 | 81.06 | 176.21 |
| 859 | 120 | 63.00 | 676.00 | 95.29 | 81.18 | 176.47 |

**Table letter A**  **Weekly table**

| Employee's earnings up to and including the UEL | Earnings at the LEL (where earnings are equal to or exceed the LEL) | Earnings above the LEL, up to and including the PT | Earnings above the PT, up to and including the UEL | Employer's NICs due on all earnings above the ST | Employee's NICs due on all earnings above the PT | Total of employee's and employer's NICs (for information only) |
|---|---|---|---|---|---|---|
| | 1a | 1b | 1c | 1d | 1e | |
| £ | £ | £ p | £ p | £ p | £ p | £ p |
| 860 | 120 | 63.00 | 677.00 | 95.42 | 81.30 | 176.72 |
| 861 | 120 | 63.00 | 678.00 | 95.56 | 81.42 | 176.98 |
| 862 | 120 | 63.00 | 679.00 | 95.70 | 81.54 | 177.24 |
| 863 | 120 | 63.00 | 680.00 | 95.84 | 81.66 | 177.50 |
| 864 | 120 | 63.00 | 681.00 | 95.98 | 81.78 | 177.76 |
| 865 | 120 | 63.00 | 682.00 | 96.11 | 81.90 | 178.01 |
| 866 | 120 | 63.00 | 683.00 | 96.25 | 82.02 | 178.27 |
| 867 | 120 | 63.00 | 684.00 | 96.39 | 82.14 | 178.53 |
| 868 | 120 | 63.00 | 685.00 | 96.53 | 82.26 | 178.79 |
| 869 | 120 | 63.00 | 686.00 | 96.67 | 82.38 | 179.05 |
| 870 | 120 | 63.00 | 687.00 | 96.80 | 82.50 | 179.30 |
| 871 | 120 | 63.00 | 688.00 | 96.94 | 82.62 | 179.56 |
| 872 | 120 | 63.00 | 689.00 | 97.08 | 82.74 | 179.82 |
| 873 | 120 | 63.00 | 690.00 | 97.22 | 82.86 | 180.08 |
| 874 | 120 | 63.00 | 691.00 | 97.36 | 82.98 | 180.34 |
| 875 | 120 | 63.00 | 692.00 | 97.49 | 83.10 | 180.59 |
| 876 | 120 | 63.00 | 693.00 | 97.63 | 83.22 | 180.85 |
| 877 | 120 | 63.00 | 694.00 | 97.77 | 83.34 | 181.11 |
| 878 | 120 | 63.00 | 695.00 | 97.91 | 83.46 | 181.37 |
| 879 | 120 | 63.00 | 696.00 | 98.05 | 83.58 | 181.63 |
| 880 | 120 | 63.00 | 697.00 | 98.18 | 83.70 | 181.88 |
| 881 | 120 | 63.00 | 698.00 | 98.32 | 83.82 | 182.14 |
| 882 | 120 | 63.00 | 699.00 | 98.46 | 83.94 | 182.40 |
| 883 | 120 | 63.00 | 700.00 | 98.60 | 84.06 | 182.66 |
| 884 | 120 | 63.00 | 701.00 | 98.74 | 84.18 | 182.92 |
| 885 | 120 | 63.00 | 702.00 | 98.87 | 84.30 | 183.17 |
| 886 | 120 | 63.00 | 703.00 | 99.01 | 84.42 | 183.43 |
| 887 | 120 | 63.00 | 704.00 | 99.15 | 84.54 | 183.69 |
| 888 | 120 | 63.00 | 705.00 | 99.29 | 84.66 | 183.95 |
| 889 | 120 | 63.00 | 706.00 | 99.43 | 84.78 | 184.21 |
| 890 | 120 | 63.00 | 707.00 | 99.56 | 84.90 | 184.46 |
| 891 | 120 | 63.00 | 708.00 | 99.70 | 85.02 | 184.72 |
| 892 | 120 | 63.00 | 709.00 | 99.84 | 85.14 | 184.98 |
| 893 | 120 | 63.00 | 710.00 | 99.98 | 85.26 | 185.24 |
| 894 | 120 | 63.00 | 711.00 | 100.12 | 85.38 | 185.50 |
| 895 | 120 | 63.00 | 712.00 | 100.25 | 85.50 | 185.75 |
| 896 | 120 | 63.00 | 713.00 | 100.39 | 85.62 | 186.01 |
| 897 | 120 | 63.00 | 714.00 | 100.53 | 85.74 | 186.27 |
| 898 | 120 | 63.00 | 715.00 | 100.67 | 85.86 | 186.53 |
| 899 | 120 | 63.00 | 716.00 | 100.81 | 85.98 | 186.79 |
| 900 | 120 | 63.00 | 717.00 | 100.94 | 86.10 | 187.04 |
| 901 | 120 | 63.00 | 718.00 | 101.08 | 86.22 | 187.30 |
| 902 | 120 | 63.00 | 719.00 | 101.22 | 86.34 | 187.56 |
| 903 | 120 | 63.00 | 720.00 | 101.36 | 86.46 | 187.82 |
| 904 | 120 | 63.00 | 721.00 | 101.50 | 86.58 | 188.08 |
| 905 | 120 | 63.00 | 722.00 | 101.63 | 86.70 | 188.33 |
| 906 | 120 | 63.00 | 723.00 | 101.77 | 86.82 | 188.59 |
| 907 | 120 | 63.00 | 724.00 | 101.91 | 86.94 | 188.85 |
| 908 | 120 | 63.00 | 725.00 | 102.05 | 87.06 | 189.11 |
| 909 | 120 | 63.00 | 726.00 | 102.19 | 87.18 | 189.37 |
| 910 | 120 | 63.00 | 727.00 | 102.32 | 87.30 | 189.62 |
| 911 | 120 | 63.00 | 728.00 | 102.46 | 87.42 | 189.88 |
| 912 | 120 | 63.00 | 729.00 | 102.60 | 87.54 | 190.14 |
| 913 | 120 | 63.00 | 730.00 | 102.74 | 87.66 | 190.40 |
| 914 | 120 | 63.00 | 731.00 | 102.88 | 87.78 | 190.66 |

**Weekly table**                                                                 **Table letter A**

| Employee's earnings up to and including the UEL | Earnings at the LEL (where earnings are equal to or exceed the LEL) | Earnings above the LEL, up to and including the PT | Earnings above the PT, up to and including the UEL | Employer's NICs due on all earnings above the ST | Employee's NICs due on all earnings above the PT | Total of employee's and employer's NICs (for information only) |
|---|---|---|---|---|---|---|
| | 1a | 1b | 1c | 1d | 1e | |
| £ | £ | £ p | £ p | £ p | £ p | £ p |
| 915 | 120 | 63.00 | 732.00 | 103.01 | 87.90 | 190.91 |
| 916 | 120 | 63.00 | 733.00 | 103.15 | 88.02 | 191.17 |
| 917 | 120 | 63.00 | 734.00 | 103.29 | 88.14 | 191.43 |
| 918 | 120 | 63.00 | 735.00 | 103.43 | 88.26 | 191.69 |
| 919 | 120 | 63.00 | 736.00 | 103.57 | 88.38 | 191.95 |
| 920 | 120 | 63.00 | 737.00 | 103.70 | 88.50 | 192.20 |
| 921 | 120 | 63.00 | 738.00 | 103.84 | 88.62 | 192.46 |
| 922 | 120 | 63.00 | 739.00 | 103.98 | 88.74 | 192.72 |
| 923 | 120 | 63.00 | 740.00 | 104.12 | 88.86 | 192.98 |
| 924 | 120 | 63.00 | 741.00 | 104.26 | 88.98 | 193.24 |
| 925 | 120 | 63.00 | 742.00 | 104.39 | 89.10 | 193.49 |
| 926 | 120 | 63.00 | 743.00 | 104.53 | 89.22 | 193.75 |
| 927 | 120 | 63.00 | 744.00 | 104.67 | 89.34 | 194.01 |
| 928 | 120 | 63.00 | 745.00 | 104.81 | 89.46 | 194.27 |
| 929 | 120 | 63.00 | 746.00 | 104.95 | 89.58 | 194.53 |
| 930 | 120 | 63.00 | 747.00 | 105.08 | 89.70 | 194.78 |
| 931 | 120 | 63.00 | 748.00 | 105.22 | 89.82 | 195.04 |
| 932 | 120 | 63.00 | 749.00 | 105.36 | 89.94 | 195.30 |
| 933 | 120 | 63.00 | 750.00 | 105.50 | 90.06 | 195.56 |
| 934 | 120 | 63.00 | 751.00 | 105.64 | 90.18 | 195.82 |
| 935 | 120 | 63.00 | 752.00 | 105.77 | 90.30 | 196.07 |
| 936 | 120 | 63.00 | 753.00 | 105.91 | 90.42 | 196.33 |
| 937 | 120 | 63.00 | 754.00 | 106.05 | 90.54 | 196.59 |
| 938 | 120 | 63.00 | 755.00 | 106.19 | 90.66 | 196.85 |
| 939 | 120 | 63.00 | 756.00 | 106.33 | 90.78 | 197.11 |
| 940 | 120 | 63.00 | 757.00 | 106.46 | 90.90 | 197.36 |
| 941 | 120 | 63.00 | 758.00 | 106.60 | 91.02 | 197.62 |
| 942 | 120 | 63.00 | 759.00 | 106.74 | 91.14 | 197.88 |
| 943 | 120 | 63.00 | 760.00 | 106.88 | 91.26 | 198.14 |
| 944 | 120 | 63.00 | 761.00 | 107.02 | 91.38 | 198.40 |
| 945 | 120 | 63.00 | 762.00 | 107.15 | 91.50 | 198.65 |
| 946 | 120 | 63.00 | 763.00 | 107.29 | 91.62 | 198.91 |
| 947 | 120 | 63.00 | 764.00 | 107.43 | 91.74 | 199.17 |
| 948 | 120 | 63.00 | 765.00 | 107.57 | 91.86 | 199.43 |
| 949 | 120 | 63.00 | 766.00 | 107.71 | 91.98 | 199.69 |
| 950 | 120 | 63.00 | 767.00 | 107.84 | 92.10 | 199.94 |
| 951 | 120 | 63.00 | 768.00 | 107.98 | 92.22 | 200.20 |
| 952 | 120 | 63.00 | 769.00 | 108.12 | 92.34 | 200.46 |
| 953 | 120 | 63.00 | 770.00 | 108.26 | 92.46 | 200.72 |
| 954 | 120 | 63.00 | 771.00 | 108.40 | 92.58 | 200.98 |
| 955 | 120 | 63.00 | 772.00 | 108.53 | 92.70 | 201.23 |
| 956 | 120 | 63.00 | 773.00 | 108.67 | 92.82 | 201.49 |
| 957 | 120 | 63.00 | 774.00 | 108.81 | 92.94 | 201.75 |
| 958 | 120 | 63.00 | 775.00 | 108.95 | 93.06 | 202.01 |
| 959 | 120 | 63.00 | 776.00 | 109.09 | 93.18 | 202.27 |
| 960 | 120 | 63.00 | 777.00 | 109.22 | 93.30 | 202.52 |
| 961 | 120 | 63.00 | 778.00 | 109.36 | 93.42 | 202.78 |
| 962 | 120 | 63.00 | 779.00 | 109.43 | 93.48 | 202.91 |

If the employee's gross pay is over £962, go to page 178.

## Monthly table for standard rate NICs for use from 6 April 2020 to 5 April 2021

**Table letter A**

Use this table for employees who are aged 21 or over and under State Pension age **or** employees who are on an Approved Apprenticeship scheme and over the age of 25.

Do not use this table for:

- any tax year other than 2020 to 2021
- employees who are under the age of 21 (go to Table letter M)
- employees who are on an Approved Apprenticeship scheme and under the age of 25 (go to Table letter H)
- married women or widows who have the right to pay reduced rate employee's NICs (go to Table letter B in booklet CA41)
- employees who are State Pension age or over (go to Table letter C in booklet CA41)
- employees who are aged 21 or over, for whom you hold form CA2700 (go to Table letter J)
- employees who are under the age of 21, for whom you hold form CA2700 (go to Table letter Z)

**Completing form RT11, 'Deductions working sheet' or substitute**

1 Enter 'A' in the NICs Category Letter column on form RT11.

2 Copy the figures in columns 1a – 1e of the table to columns 1a – 1e on the line next to the tax month in which the employee is paid, on form RT11.

If the employee's total earnings fall between the LEL and the UEL/UST/AUST and the exact gross pay is not shown in the table, use the next smaller figure shown. If the employee's total earnings exceed the UEL/UST/AUST go to page 163.

The figures in the left-hand column of each table show steps between the LEL and the UEL/UST/AUST. The NICs liability for each step, with the exception of the LEL, ST, PT, UEL and UST/AUST, is worked out at the mid-point of the steps so you and your employee may pay slightly more or less than if you used the exact percentage method.

| Employee's earnings up to and including the UEL | Earnings at the LEL (where earnings are equal to or exceed the LEL) | Earnings above the LEL, up to and including the PT | Earnings above the PT, up to and including the UEL | Employer's NICs due on all earnings above the ST | Employee's NICs due on all earnings above the PT | Total of employee's and employer's NICs (for information only) |
|---|---|---|---|---|---|---|
| 1a | 1b | 1c | 1d | 1e | | |
| £ | £ | £ p | £ p | £ p | £ p | £ p |
| Up to and including £519.99 | No NICs liability, make no entries on form RT11 | | | | | |
| 520 | 520 | 0.00 | 0.00 | 0.00 | 0.00 | 0.00 |
| 524 | 520 | 4.00 | 0.00 | 0.00 | 0.00 | 0.00 |
| 528 | 520 | 8.00 | 0.00 | 0.00 | 0.00 | 0.00 |
| 532 | 520 | 12.00 | 0.00 | 0.00 | 0.00 | 0.00 |
| 536 | 520 | 16.00 | 0.00 | 0.00 | 0.00 | 0.00 |
| 540 | 520 | 20.00 | 0.00 | 0.00 | 0.00 | 0.00 |
| 544 | 520 | 24.00 | 0.00 | 0.00 | 0.00 | 0.00 |
| 548 | 520 | 28.00 | 0.00 | 0.00 | 0.00 | 0.00 |
| 552 | 520 | 32.00 | 0.00 | 0.00 | 0.00 | 0.00 |
| 556 | 520 | 36.00 | 0.00 | 0.00 | 0.00 | 0.00 |
| 560 | 520 | 40.00 | 0.00 | 0.00 | 0.00 | 0.00 |
| 564 | 520 | 44.00 | 0.00 | 0.00 | 0.00 | 0.00 |
| 568 | 520 | 48.00 | 0.00 | 0.00 | 0.00 | 0.00 |
| 572 | 520 | 52.00 | 0.00 | 0.00 | 0.00 | 0.00 |
| 576 | 520 | 56.00 | 0.00 | 0.00 | 0.00 | 0.00 |
| 580 | 520 | 60.00 | 0.00 | 0.00 | 0.00 | 0.00 |
| 584 | 520 | 64.00 | 0.00 | 0.00 | 0.00 | 0.00 |
| 588 | 520 | 68.00 | 0.00 | 0.00 | 0.00 | 0.00 |
| 592 | 520 | 72.00 | 0.00 | 0.00 | 0.00 | 0.00 |
| 596 | 520 | 76.00 | 0.00 | 0.00 | 0.00 | 0.00 |
| 600 | 520 | 80.00 | 0.00 | 0.00 | 0.00 | 0.00 |
| 604 | 520 | 84.00 | 0.00 | 0.00 | 0.00 | 0.00 |
| 608 | 520 | 88.00 | 0.00 | 0.00 | 0.00 | 0.00 |
| 612 | 520 | 92.00 | 0.00 | 0.00 | 0.00 | 0.00 |
| 616 | 520 | 96.00 | 0.00 | 0.00 | 0.00 | 0.00 |

## Monthly table
**Table letter A**

| Employee's earnings up to and including the UEL | Earnings at the LEL (where earnings are equal to or exceed the LEL) 1a | Earnings above the LEL, up to and including the PT 1b | Earnings above the PT, up to and including the UEL 1c | Employer's NICs due on all earnings above the ST 1d | Employee's NICs due on all earnings above the PT 1e | Total of employee's and employer's NICs (for information only) |
|---|---|---|---|---|---|---|
| £ | £ | £ p | £ p | £ p | £ p | £ p |
| 620 | 520 | 100.00 | 0.00 | 0.00 | 0.00 | 0.00 |
| 624 | 520 | 104.00 | 0.00 | 0.00 | 0.00 | 0.00 |
| 628 | 520 | 108.00 | 0.00 | 0.00 | 0.00 | 0.00 |
| 632 | 520 | 112.00 | 0.00 | 0.00 | 0.00 | 0.00 |
| 636 | 520 | 116.00 | 0.00 | 0.00 | 0.00 | 0.00 |
| 640 | 520 | 120.00 | 0.00 | 0.00 | 0.00 | 0.00 |
| 644 | 520 | 124.00 | 0.00 | 0.00 | 0.00 | 0.00 |
| 648 | 520 | 128.00 | 0.00 | 0.00 | 0.00 | 0.00 |
| 652 | 520 | 132.00 | 0.00 | 0.00 | 0.00 | 0.00 |
| 656 | 520 | 136.00 | 0.00 | 0.00 | 0.00 | 0.00 |
| 660 | 520 | 140.00 | 0.00 | 0.00 | 0.00 | 0.00 |
| 664 | 520 | 144.00 | 0.00 | 0.00 | 0.00 | 0.00 |
| 668 | 520 | 148.00 | 0.00 | 0.00 | 0.00 | 0.00 |
| 672 | 520 | 152.00 | 0.00 | 0.00 | 0.00 | 0.00 |
| 676 | 520 | 156.00 | 0.00 | 0.00 | 0.00 | 0.00 |
| 680 | 520 | 160.00 | 0.00 | 0.00 | 0.00 | 0.00 |
| 684 | 520 | 164.00 | 0.00 | 0.00 | 0.00 | 0.00 |
| 688 | 520 | 168.00 | 0.00 | 0.00 | 0.00 | 0.00 |
| 692 | 520 | 172.00 | 0.00 | 0.00 | 0.00 | 0.00 |
| 696 | 520 | 176.00 | 0.00 | 0.00 | 0.00 | 0.00 |
| 700 | 520 | 180.00 | 0.00 | 0.00 | 0.00 | 0.00 |
| 704 | 520 | 184.00 | 0.00 | 0.00 | 0.00 | 0.00 |
| 708 | 520 | 188.00 | 0.00 | 0.00 | 0.00 | 0.00 |
| 712 | 520 | 192.00 | 0.00 | 0.00 | 0.00 | 0.00 |
| 716 | 520 | 196.00 | 0.00 | 0.00 | 0.00 | 0.00 |
| 720 | 520 | 200.00 | 0.00 | 0.00 | 0.00 | 0.00 |
| 724 | 520 | 204.00 | 0.00 | 0.00 | 0.00 | 0.00 |
| 728 | 520 | 208.00 | 0.00 | 0.00 | 0.00 | 0.00 |
| 732 | 520 | 212.00 | 0.00 | 0.00 | 0.00 | 0.00 |
| 736 | 520 | 216.00 | 0.00 | 0.83 | 0.00 | 0.83 |
| 740 | 520 | 220.00 | 0.00 | 1.38 | 0.00 | 1.38 |
| 744 | 520 | 224.00 | 0.00 | 1.93 | 0.00 | 1.93 |
| 748 | 520 | 228.00 | 0.00 | 2.48 | 0.00 | 2.48 |
| 752 | 520 | 232.00 | 0.00 | 3.04 | 0.00 | 3.04 |
| 756 | 520 | 236.00 | 0.00 | 3.59 | 0.00 | 3.59 |
| 760 | 520 | 240.00 | 0.00 | 4.14 | 0.00 | 4.14 |
| 764 | 520 | 244.00 | 0.00 | 4.69 | 0.00 | 4.69 |
| 768 | 520 | 248.00 | 0.00 | 5.24 | 0.00 | 5.24 |
| 772 | 520 | 252.00 | 0.00 | 5.80 | 0.00 | 5.80 |
| 776 | 520 | 256.00 | 0.00 | 6.35 | 0.00 | 6.35 |
| 780 | 520 | 260.00 | 0.00 | 6.90 | 0.00 | 6.90 |
| 784 | 520 | 264.00 | 0.00 | 7.45 | 0.00 | 7.45 |
| 788 | 520 | 268.00 | 0.00 | 8.00 | 0.00 | 8.00 |
| 792 | 520 | 272.00 | 0.00 | 8.28 | 0.00 | 8.28 |
| 796 | 520 | 272.00 | 4.00 | 9.11 | 0.72 | 9.83 |
| 800 | 520 | 272.00 | 8.00 | 9.66 | 1.20 | 10.86 |
| 804 | 520 | 272.00 | 12.00 | 10.21 | 1.68 | 11.89 |
| 808 | 520 | 272.00 | 16.00 | 10.76 | 2.16 | 12.92 |
| 812 | 520 | 272.00 | 20.00 | 11.32 | 2.64 | 13.96 |
| 816 | 520 | 272.00 | 24.00 | 11.87 | 3.12 | 14.99 |
| 820 | 520 | 272.00 | 28.00 | 12.42 | 3.60 | 16.02 |
| 824 | 520 | 272.00 | 32.00 | 12.97 | 4.08 | 17.05 |
| 828 | 520 | 272.00 | 36.00 | 13.52 | 4.56 | 18.08 |
| 832 | 520 | 272.00 | 40.00 | 14.08 | 5.04 | 19.12 |
| 836 | 520 | 272.00 | 44.00 | 14.63 | 5.52 | 20.15 |

## Table letter A

**Monthly table**

| Employee's earnings up to and including the UEL | Earnings at the LEL (where earnings are equal to or exceed the LEL) 1a | Earnings above the LEL, up to and including the PT 1b | Earnings above the PT, up to and including the UEL 1c | Employer's NICs due on all earnings above the ST 1d | Employee's NICs due on all earnings above the PT 1e | Total of employee's and employer's NICs (for information only) |
|---|---|---|---|---|---|---|
| £ | £ | £ p | £ p | £ p | £ p | £ p |
| 840 | 520 | 272.00 | 48.00 | 15.18 | 6.00 | 21.18 |
| 844 | 520 | 272.00 | 52.00 | 15.73 | 6.48 | 22.21 |
| 848 | 520 | 272.00 | 56.00 | 16.28 | 6.96 | 23.24 |
| 852 | 520 | 272.00 | 60.00 | 16.84 | 7.44 | 24.28 |
| 856 | 520 | 272.00 | 64.00 | 17.39 | 7.92 | 25.31 |
| 860 | 520 | 272.00 | 68.00 | 17.94 | 8.40 | 26.34 |
| 864 | 520 | 272.00 | 72.00 | 18.49 | 8.88 | 27.37 |
| 868 | 520 | 272.00 | 76.00 | 19.04 | 9.36 | 28.40 |
| 872 | 520 | 272.00 | 80.00 | 19.60 | 9.84 | 29.44 |
| 876 | 520 | 272.00 | 84.00 | 20.15 | 10.32 | 30.47 |
| 880 | 520 | 272.00 | 88.00 | 20.70 | 10.80 | 31.50 |
| 884 | 520 | 272.00 | 92.00 | 21.25 | 11.28 | 32.53 |
| 888 | 520 | 272.00 | 96.00 | 21.80 | 11.76 | 33.56 |
| 892 | 520 | 272.00 | 100.00 | 22.36 | 12.24 | 34.60 |
| 896 | 520 | 272.00 | 104.00 | 22.91 | 12.72 | 35.63 |
| 900 | 520 | 272.00 | 108.00 | 23.46 | 13.20 | 36.66 |
| 904 | 520 | 272.00 | 112.00 | 24.01 | 13.68 | 37.69 |
| 908 | 520 | 272.00 | 116.00 | 24.56 | 14.16 | 38.72 |
| 912 | 520 | 272.00 | 120.00 | 25.12 | 14.64 | 39.76 |
| 916 | 520 | 272.00 | 124.00 | 25.67 | 15.12 | 40.79 |
| 920 | 520 | 272.00 | 128.00 | 26.22 | 15.60 | 41.82 |
| 924 | 520 | 272.00 | 132.00 | 26.77 | 16.08 | 42.85 |
| 928 | 520 | 272.00 | 136.00 | 27.32 | 16.56 | 43.88 |
| 932 | 520 | 272.00 | 140.00 | 27.88 | 17.04 | 44.92 |
| 936 | 520 | 272.00 | 144.00 | 28.43 | 17.52 | 45.95 |
| 940 | 520 | 272.00 | 148.00 | 28.98 | 18.00 | 46.98 |
| 944 | 520 | 272.00 | 152.00 | 29.53 | 18.48 | 48.01 |
| 948 | 520 | 272.00 | 156.00 | 30.08 | 18.96 | 49.04 |
| 952 | 520 | 272.00 | 160.00 | 30.64 | 19.44 | 50.08 |
| 956 | 520 | 272.00 | 164.00 | 31.19 | 19.92 | 51.11 |
| 960 | 520 | 272.00 | 168.00 | 31.74 | 20.40 | 52.14 |
| 964 | 520 | 272.00 | 172.00 | 32.29 | 20.88 | 53.17 |
| 968 | 520 | 272.00 | 176.00 | 32.84 | 21.36 | 54.20 |
| 972 | 520 | 272.00 | 180.00 | 33.40 | 21.84 | 55.24 |
| 976 | 520 | 272.00 | 184.00 | 33.95 | 22.32 | 56.27 |
| 980 | 520 | 272.00 | 188.00 | 34.50 | 22.80 | 57.30 |
| 984 | 520 | 272.00 | 192.00 | 35.05 | 23.28 | 58.33 |
| 988 | 520 | 272.00 | 196.00 | 35.60 | 23.76 | 59.36 |
| 992 | 520 | 272.00 | 200.00 | 36.16 | 24.24 | 60.40 |
| 996 | 520 | 272.00 | 204.00 | 36.71 | 24.72 | 61.43 |
| 1000 | 520 | 272.00 | 208.00 | 37.26 | 25.20 | 62.46 |
| 1004 | 520 | 272.00 | 212.00 | 37.81 | 25.68 | 63.49 |
| 1008 | 520 | 272.00 | 216.00 | 38.36 | 26.16 | 64.52 |
| 1012 | 520 | 272.00 | 220.00 | 38.92 | 26.64 | 65.56 |
| 1016 | 520 | 272.00 | 224.00 | 39.47 | 27.12 | 66.59 |
| 1020 | 520 | 272.00 | 228.00 | 40.02 | 27.60 | 67.62 |
| 1024 | 520 | 272.00 | 232.00 | 40.57 | 28.08 | 68.65 |
| 1028 | 520 | 272.00 | 236.00 | 41.12 | 28.56 | 69.68 |
| 1032 | 520 | 272.00 | 240.00 | 41.68 | 29.04 | 70.72 |
| 1036 | 520 | 272.00 | 244.00 | 42.23 | 29.52 | 71.75 |
| 1040 | 520 | 272.00 | 248.00 | 42.78 | 30.00 | 72.78 |
| 1044 | 520 | 272.00 | 252.00 | 43.33 | 30.48 | 73.81 |
| 1048 | 520 | 272.00 | 256.00 | 43.88 | 30.96 | 74.84 |
| 1052 | 520 | 272.00 | 260.00 | 44.44 | 31.44 | 75.88 |
| 1056 | 520 | 272.00 | 264.00 | 44.99 | 31.92 | 76.91 |

## Monthly table

**Table letter A**

| Employee's earnings up to and including the UEL | Earnings at the LEL (where earnings are equal to or exceed the LEL) | Earnings above the LEL, up to and including the PT | Earnings above the PT, up to and including the UEL | Employer's NICs due on all earnings above the ST | Employee's NICs due on all earnings above the PT | Total of employee's and employer's NICs (for information only) |
|---|---|---|---|---|---|---|
| | | 1a | 1b | 1c | 1d | 1e |
| £ | £ | £ p | £ p | £ p | £ p | £ p |
| 1060 | 520 | 272.00 | 268.00 | 45.54 | 32.40 | 77.94 |
| 1064 | 520 | 272.00 | 272.00 | 46.09 | 32.88 | 78.97 |
| 1068 | 520 | 272.00 | 276.00 | 46.64 | 33.36 | 80.00 |
| 1072 | 520 | 272.00 | 280.00 | 47.20 | 33.84 | 81.04 |
| 1076 | 520 | 272.00 | 284.00 | 47.75 | 34.32 | 82.07 |
| 1080 | 520 | 272.00 | 288.00 | 48.30 | 34.80 | 83.10 |
| 1084 | 520 | 272.00 | 292.00 | 48.85 | 35.28 | 84.13 |
| 1088 | 520 | 272.00 | 296.00 | 49.40 | 35.76 | 85.16 |
| 1092 | 520 | 272.00 | 300.00 | 49.96 | 36.24 | 86.20 |
| 1096 | 520 | 272.00 | 304.00 | 50.51 | 36.72 | 87.23 |
| 1100 | 520 | 272.00 | 308.00 | 51.06 | 37.20 | 88.26 |
| 1104 | 520 | 272.00 | 312.00 | 51.61 | 37.68 | 89.29 |
| 1108 | 520 | 272.00 | 316.00 | 52.16 | 38.16 | 90.32 |
| 1112 | 520 | 272.00 | 320.00 | 52.72 | 38.64 | 91.36 |
| 1116 | 520 | 272.00 | 324.00 | 53.27 | 39.12 | 92.39 |
| 1120 | 520 | 272.00 | 328.00 | 53.82 | 39.60 | 93.42 |
| 1124 | 520 | 272.00 | 332.00 | 54.37 | 40.08 | 94.45 |
| 1128 | 520 | 272.00 | 336.00 | 54.92 | 40.56 | 95.48 |
| 1132 | 520 | 272.00 | 340.00 | 55.48 | 41.04 | 96.52 |
| 1136 | 520 | 272.00 | 344.00 | 56.03 | 41.52 | 97.55 |
| 1140 | 520 | 272.00 | 348.00 | 56.58 | 42.00 | 98.58 |
| 1144 | 520 | 272.00 | 352.00 | 57.13 | 42.48 | 99.61 |
| 1148 | 520 | 272.00 | 356.00 | 57.68 | 42.96 | 100.64 |
| 1152 | 520 | 272.00 | 360.00 | 58.24 | 43.44 | 101.68 |
| 1156 | 520 | 272.00 | 364.00 | 58.79 | 43.92 | 102.71 |
| 1160 | 520 | 272.00 | 368.00 | 59.34 | 44.40 | 103.74 |
| 1164 | 520 | 272.00 | 372.00 | 59.89 | 44.88 | 104.77 |
| 1168 | 520 | 272.00 | 376.00 | 60.44 | 45.36 | 105.80 |
| 1172 | 520 | 272.00 | 380.00 | 61.00 | 45.84 | 106.84 |
| 1176 | 520 | 272.00 | 384.00 | 61.55 | 46.32 | 107.87 |
| 1180 | 520 | 272.00 | 388.00 | 62.10 | 46.80 | 108.90 |
| 1184 | 520 | 272.00 | 392.00 | 62.65 | 47.28 | 109.93 |
| 1188 | 520 | 272.00 | 396.00 | 63.20 | 47.76 | 110.96 |
| 1192 | 520 | 272.00 | 400.00 | 63.76 | 48.24 | 112.00 |
| 1196 | 520 | 272.00 | 404.00 | 64.31 | 48.72 | 113.03 |
| 1200 | 520 | 272.00 | 408.00 | 64.86 | 49.20 | 114.06 |
| 1204 | 520 | 272.00 | 412.00 | 65.41 | 49.68 | 115.09 |
| 1208 | 520 | 272.00 | 416.00 | 65.96 | 50.16 | 116.12 |
| 1212 | 520 | 272.00 | 420.00 | 66.52 | 50.64 | 117.16 |
| 1216 | 520 | 272.00 | 424.00 | 67.07 | 51.12 | 118.19 |
| 1220 | 520 | 272.00 | 428.00 | 67.62 | 51.60 | 119.22 |
| 1224 | 520 | 272.00 | 432.00 | 68.17 | 52.08 | 120.25 |
| 1228 | 520 | 272.00 | 436.00 | 68.72 | 52.56 | 121.28 |
| 1232 | 520 | 272.00 | 440.00 | 69.28 | 53.04 | 122.32 |
| 1236 | 520 | 272.00 | 444.00 | 69.83 | 53.52 | 123.35 |
| 1240 | 520 | 272.00 | 448.00 | 70.38 | 54.00 | 124.38 |
| 1244 | 520 | 272.00 | 452.00 | 70.93 | 54.48 | 125.41 |
| 1248 | 520 | 272.00 | 456.00 | 71.48 | 54.96 | 126.44 |
| 1252 | 520 | 272.00 | 460.00 | 72.04 | 55.44 | 127.48 |
| 1256 | 520 | 272.00 | 464.00 | 72.59 | 55.92 | 128.51 |
| 1260 | 520 | 272.00 | 468.00 | 73.14 | 56.40 | 129.54 |
| 1264 | 520 | 272.00 | 472.00 | 73.69 | 56.88 | 130.57 |
| 1268 | 520 | 272.00 | 476.00 | 74.24 | 57.36 | 131.60 |
| 1272 | 520 | 272.00 | 480.00 | 74.80 | 57.84 | 132.64 |
| 1276 | 520 | 272.00 | 484.00 | 75.35 | 58.32 | 133.67 |

## Table letter A                                                                 Monthly table

| Employee's earnings up to and including the UEL | Earnings at the LEL (where earnings are equal to or exceed the LEL) | Earnings above the LEL, up to and including the PT | Earnings above the PT, up to and including the UEL | Employer's NICs due on all earnings above the ST | Employee's NICs due on all earnings above the PT | Total of employee's and employer's NICs (for information only) |
|---|---|---|---|---|---|---|
| | | 1a | 1b | 1c | 1d | 1e |
| £ | £ | £ p | £ p | £ p | £ p | £ p |
| 1280 | 520 | 272.00 | 488.00 | 75.90 | 58.80 | 134.70 |
| 1284 | 520 | 272.00 | 492.00 | 76.45 | 59.28 | 135.73 |
| 1288 | 520 | 272.00 | 496.00 | 77.00 | 59.76 | 136.76 |
| 1292 | 520 | 272.00 | 500.00 | 77.56 | 60.24 | 137.80 |
| 1296 | 520 | 272.00 | 504.00 | 78.11 | 60.72 | 138.83 |
| 1300 | 520 | 272.00 | 508.00 | 78.66 | 61.20 | 139.86 |
| 1304 | 520 | 272.00 | 512.00 | 79.21 | 61.68 | 140.89 |
| 1308 | 520 | 272.00 | 516.00 | 79.76 | 62.16 | 141.92 |
| 1312 | 520 | 272.00 | 520.00 | 80.32 | 62.64 | 142.96 |
| 1316 | 520 | 272.00 | 524.00 | 80.87 | 63.12 | 143.99 |
| 1320 | 520 | 272.00 | 528.00 | 81.42 | 63.60 | 145.02 |
| 1324 | 520 | 272.00 | 532.00 | 81.97 | 64.08 | 146.05 |
| 1328 | 520 | 272.00 | 536.00 | 82.52 | 64.56 | 147.08 |
| 1332 | 520 | 272.00 | 540.00 | 83.08 | 65.04 | 148.12 |
| 1336 | 520 | 272.00 | 544.00 | 83.63 | 65.52 | 149.15 |
| 1340 | 520 | 272.00 | 548.00 | 84.18 | 66.00 | 150.18 |
| 1344 | 520 | 272.00 | 552.00 | 84.73 | 66.48 | 151.21 |
| 1348 | 520 | 272.00 | 556.00 | 85.28 | 66.96 | 152.24 |
| 1352 | 520 | 272.00 | 560.00 | 85.84 | 67.44 | 153.28 |
| 1356 | 520 | 272.00 | 564.00 | 86.39 | 67.92 | 154.31 |
| 1360 | 520 | 272.00 | 568.00 | 86.94 | 68.40 | 155.34 |
| 1364 | 520 | 272.00 | 572.00 | 87.49 | 68.88 | 156.37 |
| 1368 | 520 | 272.00 | 576.00 | 88.04 | 69.36 | 157.40 |
| 1372 | 520 | 272.00 | 580.00 | 88.60 | 69.84 | 158.44 |
| 1376 | 520 | 272.00 | 584.00 | 89.15 | 70.32 | 159.47 |
| 1380 | 520 | 272.00 | 588.00 | 89.70 | 70.80 | 160.50 |
| 1384 | 520 | 272.00 | 592.00 | 90.25 | 71.28 | 161.53 |
| 1388 | 520 | 272.00 | 596.00 | 90.80 | 71.76 | 162.56 |
| 1392 | 520 | 272.00 | 600.00 | 91.36 | 72.24 | 163.60 |
| 1396 | 520 | 272.00 | 604.00 | 91.91 | 72.72 | 164.63 |
| 1400 | 520 | 272.00 | 608.00 | 92.46 | 73.20 | 165.66 |
| 1404 | 520 | 272.00 | 612.00 | 93.01 | 73.68 | 166.69 |
| 1408 | 520 | 272.00 | 616.00 | 93.56 | 74.16 | 167.72 |
| 1412 | 520 | 272.00 | 620.00 | 94.12 | 74.64 | 168.76 |
| 1416 | 520 | 272.00 | 624.00 | 94.67 | 75.12 | 169.79 |
| 1420 | 520 | 272.00 | 628.00 | 95.22 | 75.60 | 170.82 |
| 1424 | 520 | 272.00 | 632.00 | 95.77 | 76.08 | 171.85 |
| 1428 | 520 | 272.00 | 636.00 | 96.32 | 76.56 | 172.88 |
| 1432 | 520 | 272.00 | 640.00 | 96.88 | 77.04 | 173.92 |
| 1436 | 520 | 272.00 | 644.00 | 97.43 | 77.52 | 174.95 |
| 1440 | 520 | 272.00 | 648.00 | 97.98 | 78.00 | 175.98 |
| 1444 | 520 | 272.00 | 652.00 | 98.53 | 78.48 | 177.01 |
| 1448 | 520 | 272.00 | 656.00 | 99.08 | 78.96 | 178.04 |
| 1452 | 520 | 272.00 | 660.00 | 99.64 | 79.44 | 179.08 |
| 1456 | 520 | 272.00 | 664.00 | 100.19 | 79.92 | 180.11 |
| 1460 | 520 | 272.00 | 668.00 | 100.74 | 80.40 | 181.14 |
| 1464 | 520 | 272.00 | 672.00 | 101.29 | 80.88 | 182.17 |
| 1468 | 520 | 272.00 | 676.00 | 101.84 | 81.36 | 183.20 |
| 1472 | 520 | 272.00 | 680.00 | 102.40 | 81.84 | 184.24 |
| 1476 | 520 | 272.00 | 684.00 | 102.95 | 82.32 | 185.27 |
| 1480 | 520 | 272.00 | 688.00 | 103.50 | 82.80 | 186.30 |
| 1484 | 520 | 272.00 | 692.00 | 104.05 | 83.28 | 187.33 |
| 1488 | 520 | 272.00 | 696.00 | 104.60 | 83.76 | 188.36 |
| 1492 | 520 | 272.00 | 700.00 | 105.16 | 84.24 | 189.40 |
| 1496 | 520 | 272.00 | 704.00 | 105.71 | 84.72 | 190.43 |

## Monthly table

Table letter A

| Employee's earnings up to and including the UEL | Earnings at the LEL (where earnings are equal to or exceed the LEL) | Earnings above the LEL, up to and including the PT | Earnings above the PT, up to and including the UEL | Employer's NICs due on all earnings above the ST | Employee's NICs due on all earnings above the PT | Total of employee's and employer's NICs (for information only) |
|---|---|---|---|---|---|---|
| | | 1a | 1b | 1c | 1d | 1e |
| £ | £ | £ p | £ p | £ p | £ p | £ p |
| 1500 | 520 | 272.00 | 708.00 | 106.26 | 85.20 | 191.46 |
| 1504 | 520 | 272.00 | 712.00 | 106.81 | 85.68 | 192.49 |
| 1508 | 520 | 272.00 | 716.00 | 107.36 | 86.16 | 193.52 |
| 1512 | 520 | 272.00 | 720.00 | 107.92 | 86.64 | 194.56 |
| 1516 | 520 | 272.00 | 724.00 | 108.47 | 87.12 | 195.59 |
| 1520 | 520 | 272.00 | 728.00 | 109.02 | 87.60 | 196.62 |
| 1524 | 520 | 272.00 | 732.00 | 109.57 | 88.08 | 197.65 |
| 1528 | 520 | 272.00 | 736.00 | 110.12 | 88.56 | 198.68 |
| 1532 | 520 | 272.00 | 740.00 | 110.68 | 89.04 | 199.72 |
| 1536 | 520 | 272.00 | 744.00 | 111.23 | 89.52 | 200.75 |
| 1540 | 520 | 272.00 | 748.00 | 111.78 | 90.00 | 201.78 |
| 1544 | 520 | 272.00 | 752.00 | 112.33 | 90.48 | 202.81 |
| 1548 | 520 | 272.00 | 756.00 | 112.88 | 90.96 | 203.84 |
| 1552 | 520 | 272.00 | 760.00 | 113.44 | 91.44 | 204.88 |
| 1556 | 520 | 272.00 | 764.00 | 113.99 | 91.92 | 205.91 |
| 1560 | 520 | 272.00 | 768.00 | 114.54 | 92.40 | 206.94 |
| 1564 | 520 | 272.00 | 772.00 | 115.09 | 92.88 | 207.97 |
| 1568 | 520 | 272.00 | 776.00 | 115.64 | 93.36 | 209.00 |
| 1572 | 520 | 272.00 | 780.00 | 116.20 | 93.84 | 210.04 |
| 1576 | 520 | 272.00 | 784.00 | 116.75 | 94.32 | 211.07 |
| 1580 | 520 | 272.00 | 788.00 | 117.30 | 94.80 | 212.10 |
| 1584 | 520 | 272.00 | 792.00 | 117.85 | 95.28 | 213.13 |
| 1588 | 520 | 272.00 | 796.00 | 118.40 | 95.76 | 214.16 |
| 1592 | 520 | 272.00 | 800.00 | 118.96 | 96.24 | 215.20 |
| 1596 | 520 | 272.00 | 804.00 | 119.51 | 96.72 | 216.23 |
| 1600 | 520 | 272.00 | 808.00 | 120.06 | 97.20 | 217.26 |
| 1604 | 520 | 272.00 | 812.00 | 120.61 | 97.68 | 218.29 |
| 1608 | 520 | 272.00 | 816.00 | 121.16 | 98.16 | 219.32 |
| 1612 | 520 | 272.00 | 820.00 | 121.72 | 98.64 | 220.36 |
| 1616 | 520 | 272.00 | 824.00 | 122.27 | 99.12 | 221.39 |
| 1620 | 520 | 272.00 | 828.00 | 122.82 | 99.60 | 222.42 |
| 1624 | 520 | 272.00 | 832.00 | 123.37 | 100.08 | 223.45 |
| 1628 | 520 | 272.00 | 836.00 | 123.92 | 100.56 | 224.48 |
| 1632 | 520 | 272.00 | 840.00 | 124.48 | 101.04 | 225.52 |
| 1636 | 520 | 272.00 | 844.00 | 125.03 | 101.52 | 226.55 |
| 1640 | 520 | 272.00 | 848.00 | 125.58 | 102.00 | 227.58 |
| 1644 | 520 | 272.00 | 852.00 | 126.13 | 102.48 | 228.61 |
| 1648 | 520 | 272.00 | 856.00 | 126.68 | 102.96 | 229.64 |
| 1652 | 520 | 272.00 | 860.00 | 127.24 | 103.44 | 230.68 |
| 1656 | 520 | 272.00 | 864.00 | 127.79 | 103.92 | 231.71 |
| 1660 | 520 | 272.00 | 868.00 | 128.34 | 104.40 | 232.74 |
| 1664 | 520 | 272.00 | 872.00 | 128.89 | 104.88 | 233.77 |
| 1668 | 520 | 272.00 | 876.00 | 129.44 | 105.36 | 234.80 |
| 1672 | 520 | 272.00 | 880.00 | 130.00 | 105.84 | 235.84 |
| 1676 | 520 | 272.00 | 884.00 | 130.55 | 106.32 | 236.87 |
| 1680 | 520 | 272.00 | 888.00 | 131.10 | 106.80 | 237.90 |
| 1684 | 520 | 272.00 | 892.00 | 131.65 | 107.28 | 238.93 |
| 1688 | 520 | 272.00 | 896.00 | 132.20 | 107.76 | 239.96 |
| 1692 | 520 | 272.00 | 900.00 | 132.76 | 108.24 | 241.00 |
| 1696 | 520 | 272.00 | 904.00 | 133.31 | 108.72 | 242.03 |
| 1700 | 520 | 272.00 | 908.00 | 133.86 | 109.20 | 243.06 |
| 1704 | 520 | 272.00 | 912.00 | 134.41 | 109.68 | 244.09 |
| 1708 | 520 | 272.00 | 916.00 | 134.96 | 110.16 | 245.12 |
| 1712 | 520 | 272.00 | 920.00 | 135.52 | 110.64 | 246.16 |
| 1716 | 520 | 272.00 | 924.00 | 136.07 | 111.12 | 247.19 |

## Table letter A

## Monthly table

| Employee's earnings up to and including the UEL | Earnings at the LEL (where earnings are equal to or exceed the LEL) | Earnings above the LEL, up to and including the PT | Earnings above the PT, up to and including the UEL | Employer's NICs due on all earnings above the ST | Employee's NICs due on all earnings above the PT | Total of employee's and employer's NICs (for information only) |
|---|---|---|---|---|---|---|
| | 1a | 1b | 1c | 1d | 1e | |
| £ | £ | £ p | £ p | £ p | £ p | £ p |
| 1720 | 520 | 272.00 | 928.00 | 136.62 | 111.60 | 248.22 |
| 1724 | 520 | 272.00 | 932.00 | 137.17 | 112.08 | 249.25 |
| 1728 | 520 | 272.00 | 936.00 | 137.72 | 112.56 | 250.28 |
| 1732 | 520 | 272.00 | 940.00 | 138.28 | 113.04 | 251.32 |
| 1736 | 520 | 272.00 | 944.00 | 138.83 | 113.52 | 252.35 |
| 1740 | 520 | 272.00 | 948.00 | 139.38 | 114.00 | 253.38 |
| 1744 | 520 | 272.00 | 952.00 | 139.93 | 114.48 | 254.41 |
| 1748 | 520 | 272.00 | 956.00 | 140.48 | 114.96 | 255.44 |
| 1752 | 520 | 272.00 | 960.00 | 141.04 | 115.44 | 256.48 |
| 1756 | 520 | 272.00 | 964.00 | 141.59 | 115.92 | 257.51 |
| 1760 | 520 | 272.00 | 968.00 | 142.14 | 116.40 | 258.54 |
| 1764 | 520 | 272.00 | 972.00 | 142.69 | 116.88 | 259.57 |
| 1768 | 520 | 272.00 | 976.00 | 143.24 | 117.36 | 260.60 |
| 1772 | 520 | 272.00 | 980.00 | 143.80 | 117.84 | 261.64 |
| 1776 | 520 | 272.00 | 984.00 | 144.35 | 118.32 | 262.67 |
| 1780 | 520 | 272.00 | 988.00 | 144.90 | 118.80 | 263.70 |
| 1784 | 520 | 272.00 | 992.00 | 145.45 | 119.28 | 264.73 |
| 1788 | 520 | 272.00 | 996.00 | 146.00 | 119.76 | 265.76 |
| 1792 | 520 | 272.00 | 1000.00 | 146.56 | 120.24 | 266.80 |
| 1796 | 520 | 272.00 | 1004.00 | 147.11 | 120.72 | 267.83 |
| 1800 | 520 | 272.00 | 1008.00 | 147.66 | 121.20 | 268.86 |
| 1804 | 520 | 272.00 | 1012.00 | 148.21 | 121.68 | 269.89 |
| 1808 | 520 | 272.00 | 1016.00 | 148.76 | 122.16 | 270.92 |
| 1812 | 520 | 272.00 | 1020.00 | 149.32 | 122.64 | 271.96 |
| 1816 | 520 | 272.00 | 1024.00 | 149.87 | 123.12 | 272.99 |
| 1820 | 520 | 272.00 | 1028.00 | 150.42 | 123.60 | 274.02 |
| 1824 | 520 | 272.00 | 1032.00 | 150.97 | 124.08 | 275.05 |
| 1828 | 520 | 272.00 | 1036.00 | 151.52 | 124.56 | 276.08 |
| 1832 | 520 | 272.00 | 1040.00 | 152.08 | 125.04 | 277.12 |
| 1836 | 520 | 272.00 | 1044.00 | 152.63 | 125.52 | 278.15 |
| 1840 | 520 | 272.00 | 1048.00 | 153.18 | 126.00 | 279.18 |
| 1844 | 520 | 272.00 | 1052.00 | 153.73 | 126.48 | 280.21 |
| 1848 | 520 | 272.00 | 1056.00 | 154.28 | 126.96 | 281.24 |
| 1852 | 520 | 272.00 | 1060.00 | 154.84 | 127.44 | 282.28 |
| 1856 | 520 | 272.00 | 1064.00 | 155.39 | 127.92 | 283.31 |
| 1860 | 520 | 272.00 | 1068.00 | 155.94 | 128.40 | 284.34 |
| 1864 | 520 | 272.00 | 1072.00 | 156.49 | 128.88 | 285.37 |
| 1868 | 520 | 272.00 | 1076.00 | 157.04 | 129.36 | 286.40 |
| 1872 | 520 | 272.00 | 1080.00 | 157.60 | 129.84 | 287.44 |
| 1876 | 520 | 272.00 | 1084.00 | 158.15 | 130.32 | 288.47 |
| 1880 | 520 | 272.00 | 1088.00 | 158.70 | 130.80 | 289.50 |
| 1884 | 520 | 272.00 | 1092.00 | 159.25 | 131.28 | 290.53 |
| 1888 | 520 | 272.00 | 1096.00 | 159.80 | 131.76 | 291.56 |
| 1892 | 520 | 272.00 | 1100.00 | 160.36 | 132.24 | 292.60 |
| 1896 | 520 | 272.00 | 1104.00 | 160.91 | 132.72 | 293.63 |
| 1900 | 520 | 272.00 | 1108.00 | 161.46 | 133.20 | 294.66 |
| 1904 | 520 | 272.00 | 1112.00 | 162.01 | 133.68 | 295.69 |
| 1908 | 520 | 272.00 | 1116.00 | 162.56 | 134.16 | 296.72 |
| 1912 | 520 | 272.00 | 1120.00 | 163.12 | 134.64 | 297.76 |
| 1916 | 520 | 272.00 | 1124.00 | 163.67 | 135.12 | 298.79 |
| 1920 | 520 | 272.00 | 1128.00 | 164.22 | 135.60 | 299.82 |
| 1924 | 520 | 272.00 | 1132.00 | 164.77 | 136.08 | 300.85 |
| 1928 | 520 | 272.00 | 1136.00 | 165.32 | 136.56 | 301.88 |
| 1932 | 520 | 272.00 | 1140.00 | 165.88 | 137.04 | 302.92 |
| 1936 | 520 | 272.00 | 1144.00 | 166.43 | 137.52 | 303.95 |

**Monthly table**                                                                                           **Table letter A**

| Employee's earnings up to and including the UEL | Earnings at the LEL (where earnings are equal to or exceed the LEL) | Earnings above the LEL, up to and including the PT | Earnings above the PT, up to and including the UEL | Employer's NICs due on all earnings above the ST | Employee's NICs due on all earnings above the PT | Total of employee's and employer's NICs (for information only) |
|---|---|---|---|---|---|---|
| | | 1a | 1b | 1c | 1d | 1e |
| £ | £ | £ p | £ p | £ p | £ p | £ p |
| 1940 | 520 | 272.00 | 1148.00 | 166.98 | 138.00 | 304.98 |
| 1944 | 520 | 272.00 | 1152.00 | 167.53 | 138.48 | 306.01 |
| 1948 | 520 | 272.00 | 1156.00 | 168.08 | 138.96 | 307.04 |
| 1952 | 520 | 272.00 | 1160.00 | 168.64 | 139.44 | 308.08 |
| 1956 | 520 | 272.00 | 1164.00 | 169.19 | 139.92 | 309.11 |
| 1960 | 520 | 272.00 | 1168.00 | 169.74 | 140.40 | 310.14 |
| 1964 | 520 | 272.00 | 1172.00 | 170.29 | 140.88 | 311.17 |
| 1968 | 520 | 272.00 | 1176.00 | 170.84 | 141.36 | 312.20 |
| 1972 | 520 | 272.00 | 1180.00 | 171.40 | 141.84 | 313.24 |
| 1976 | 520 | 272.00 | 1184.00 | 171.95 | 142.32 | 314.27 |
| 1980 | 520 | 272.00 | 1188.00 | 172.50 | 142.80 | 315.30 |
| 1984 | 520 | 272.00 | 1192.00 | 173.05 | 143.28 | 316.33 |
| 1988 | 520 | 272.00 | 1196.00 | 173.60 | 143.76 | 317.36 |
| 1992 | 520 | 272.00 | 1200.00 | 174.16 | 144.24 | 318.40 |
| 1996 | 520 | 272.00 | 1204.00 | 174.71 | 144.72 | 319.43 |
| 2000 | 520 | 272.00 | 1208.00 | 175.26 | 145.20 | 320.46 |
| 2004 | 520 | 272.00 | 1212.00 | 175.81 | 145.68 | 321.49 |
| 2008 | 520 | 272.00 | 1216.00 | 176.36 | 146.16 | 322.52 |
| 2012 | 520 | 272.00 | 1220.00 | 176.92 | 146.64 | 323.56 |
| 2016 | 520 | 272.00 | 1224.00 | 177.47 | 147.12 | 324.59 |
| 2020 | 520 | 272.00 | 1228.00 | 178.02 | 147.60 | 325.62 |
| 2024 | 520 | 272.00 | 1232.00 | 178.57 | 148.08 | 326.65 |
| 2028 | 520 | 272.00 | 1236.00 | 179.12 | 148.56 | 327.68 |
| 2032 | 520 | 272.00 | 1240.00 | 179.68 | 149.04 | 328.72 |
| 2036 | 520 | 272.00 | 1244.00 | 180.23 | 149.52 | 329.75 |
| 2040 | 520 | 272.00 | 1248.00 | 180.78 | 150.00 | 330.78 |
| 2044 | 520 | 272.00 | 1252.00 | 181.33 | 150.48 | 331.81 |
| 2048 | 520 | 272.00 | 1256.00 | 181.88 | 150.96 | 332.84 |
| 2052 | 520 | 272.00 | 1260.00 | 182.44 | 151.44 | 333.88 |
| 2056 | 520 | 272.00 | 1264.00 | 182.99 | 151.92 | 334.91 |
| 2060 | 520 | 272.00 | 1268.00 | 183.54 | 152.40 | 335.94 |
| 2064 | 520 | 272.00 | 1272.00 | 184.09 | 152.88 | 336.97 |
| 2068 | 520 | 272.00 | 1276.00 | 184.64 | 153.36 | 338.00 |
| 2072 | 520 | 272.00 | 1280.00 | 185.20 | 153.84 | 339.04 |
| 2076 | 520 | 272.00 | 1284.00 | 185.75 | 154.32 | 340.07 |
| 2080 | 520 | 272.00 | 1288.00 | 186.30 | 154.80 | 341.10 |
| 2084 | 520 | 272.00 | 1292.00 | 186.85 | 155.28 | 342.13 |
| 2088 | 520 | 272.00 | 1296.00 | 187.40 | 155.76 | 343.16 |
| 2092 | 520 | 272.00 | 1300.00 | 187.96 | 156.24 | 344.20 |
| 2096 | 520 | 272.00 | 1304.00 | 188.51 | 156.72 | 345.23 |
| 2100 | 520 | 272.00 | 1308.00 | 189.06 | 157.20 | 346.26 |
| 2104 | 520 | 272.00 | 1312.00 | 189.61 | 157.68 | 347.29 |
| 2108 | 520 | 272.00 | 1316.00 | 190.16 | 158.16 | 348.32 |
| 2112 | 520 | 272.00 | 1320.00 | 190.72 | 158.64 | 349.36 |
| 2116 | 520 | 272.00 | 1324.00 | 191.27 | 159.12 | 350.39 |
| 2120 | 520 | 272.00 | 1328.00 | 191.82 | 159.60 | 351.42 |
| 2124 | 520 | 272.00 | 1332.00 | 192.37 | 160.08 | 352.45 |
| 2128 | 520 | 272.00 | 1336.00 | 192.92 | 160.56 | 353.48 |
| 2132 | 520 | 272.00 | 1340.00 | 193.48 | 161.04 | 354.52 |
| 2136 | 520 | 272.00 | 1344.00 | 194.03 | 161.52 | 355.55 |
| 2140 | 520 | 272.00 | 1348.00 | 194.58 | 162.00 | 356.58 |
| 2144 | 520 | 272.00 | 1352.00 | 195.13 | 162.48 | 357.61 |
| 2148 | 520 | 272.00 | 1356.00 | 195.68 | 162.96 | 358.64 |
| 2152 | 520 | 272.00 | 1360.00 | 196.24 | 163.44 | 359.68 |
| 2156 | 520 | 272.00 | 1364.00 | 196.79 | 163.92 | 360.71 |

## Table letter A

## Monthly table

| Employee's earnings up to and including the UEL | Earnings at the LEL (where earnings are equal to or exceed the LEL) 1a | Earnings above the LEL, up to and including the PT 1b | Earnings above the PT, up to and including the UEL 1c | Employer's NICs due on all earnings above the ST 1d | Employee's NICs due on all earnings above the PT 1e | Total of employee's and employer's NICs (for information only) |
|---|---|---|---|---|---|---|
| £ | £ | £ p | £ p | £ p | £ p | £ p |
| 2160 | 520 | 272.00 | 1368.00 | 197.34 | 164.40 | 361.74 |
| 2164 | 520 | 272.00 | 1372.00 | 197.89 | 164.88 | 362.77 |
| 2168 | 520 | 272.00 | 1376.00 | 198.44 | 165.36 | 363.80 |
| 2172 | 520 | 272.00 | 1380.00 | 199.00 | 165.84 | 364.84 |
| 2176 | 520 | 272.00 | 1384.00 | 199.55 | 166.32 | 365.87 |
| 2180 | 520 | 272.00 | 1388.00 | 200.10 | 166.80 | 366.90 |
| 2184 | 520 | 272.00 | 1392.00 | 200.65 | 167.28 | 367.93 |
| 2188 | 520 | 272.00 | 1396.00 | 201.20 | 167.76 | 368.96 |
| 2192 | 520 | 272.00 | 1400.00 | 201.76 | 168.24 | 370.00 |
| 2196 | 520 | 272.00 | 1404.00 | 202.31 | 168.72 | 371.03 |
| 2200 | 520 | 272.00 | 1408.00 | 202.86 | 169.20 | 372.06 |
| 2204 | 520 | 272.00 | 1412.00 | 203.41 | 169.68 | 373.09 |
| 2208 | 520 | 272.00 | 1416.00 | 203.96 | 170.16 | 374.12 |
| 2212 | 520 | 272.00 | 1420.00 | 204.52 | 170.64 | 375.16 |
| 2216 | 520 | 272.00 | 1424.00 | 205.07 | 171.12 | 376.19 |
| 2220 | 520 | 272.00 | 1428.00 | 205.62 | 171.60 | 377.22 |
| 2224 | 520 | 272.00 | 1432.00 | 206.17 | 172.08 | 378.25 |
| 2228 | 520 | 272.00 | 1436.00 | 206.72 | 172.56 | 379.28 |
| 2232 | 520 | 272.00 | 1440.00 | 207.28 | 173.04 | 380.32 |
| 2236 | 520 | 272.00 | 1444.00 | 207.83 | 173.52 | 381.35 |
| 2240 | 520 | 272.00 | 1448.00 | 208.38 | 174.00 | 382.38 |
| 2244 | 520 | 272.00 | 1452.00 | 208.93 | 174.48 | 383.41 |
| 2248 | 520 | 272.00 | 1456.00 | 209.48 | 174.96 | 384.44 |
| 2252 | 520 | 272.00 | 1460.00 | 210.04 | 175.44 | 385.48 |
| 2256 | 520 | 272.00 | 1464.00 | 210.59 | 175.92 | 386.51 |
| 2260 | 520 | 272.00 | 1468.00 | 211.14 | 176.40 | 387.54 |
| 2264 | 520 | 272.00 | 1472.00 | 211.69 | 176.88 | 388.57 |
| 2268 | 520 | 272.00 | 1476.00 | 212.24 | 177.36 | 389.60 |
| 2272 | 520 | 272.00 | 1480.00 | 212.80 | 177.84 | 390.64 |
| 2276 | 520 | 272.00 | 1484.00 | 213.35 | 178.32 | 391.67 |
| 2280 | 520 | 272.00 | 1488.00 | 213.90 | 178.80 | 392.70 |
| 2284 | 520 | 272.00 | 1492.00 | 214.45 | 179.28 | 393.73 |
| 2288 | 520 | 272.00 | 1496.00 | 215.00 | 179.76 | 394.76 |
| 2292 | 520 | 272.00 | 1500.00 | 215.56 | 180.24 | 395.80 |
| 2296 | 520 | 272.00 | 1504.00 | 216.11 | 180.72 | 396.83 |
| 2300 | 520 | 272.00 | 1508.00 | 216.66 | 181.20 | 397.86 |
| 2304 | 520 | 272.00 | 1512.00 | 217.21 | 181.68 | 398.89 |
| 2308 | 520 | 272.00 | 1516.00 | 217.76 | 182.16 | 399.92 |
| 2312 | 520 | 272.00 | 1520.00 | 218.32 | 182.64 | 400.96 |
| 2316 | 520 | 272.00 | 1524.00 | 218.87 | 183.12 | 401.99 |
| 2320 | 520 | 272.00 | 1528.00 | 219.42 | 183.60 | 403.02 |
| 2324 | 520 | 272.00 | 1532.00 | 219.97 | 184.08 | 404.05 |
| 2328 | 520 | 272.00 | 1536.00 | 220.52 | 184.56 | 405.08 |
| 2332 | 520 | 272.00 | 1540.00 | 221.08 | 185.04 | 406.12 |
| 2336 | 520 | 272.00 | 1544.00 | 221.63 | 185.52 | 407.15 |
| 2340 | 520 | 272.00 | 1548.00 | 222.18 | 186.00 | 408.18 |
| 2344 | 520 | 272.00 | 1552.00 | 222.73 | 186.48 | 409.21 |
| 2348 | 520 | 272.00 | 1556.00 | 223.28 | 186.96 | 410.24 |
| 2352 | 520 | 272.00 | 1560.00 | 223.84 | 187.44 | 411.28 |
| 2356 | 520 | 272.00 | 1564.00 | 224.39 | 187.92 | 412.31 |
| 2360 | 520 | 272.00 | 1568.00 | 224.94 | 188.40 | 413.34 |
| 2364 | 520 | 272.00 | 1572.00 | 225.49 | 188.88 | 414.37 |
| 2368 | 520 | 272.00 | 1576.00 | 226.04 | 189.36 | 415.40 |
| 2372 | 520 | 272.00 | 1580.00 | 226.60 | 189.84 | 416.44 |
| 2376 | 520 | 272.00 | 1584.00 | 227.15 | 190.32 | 417.47 |

**Monthly table**                                                                         **Table letter A**

| Employee's earnings up to and including the UEL | Earnings at the LEL (where earnings are equal to or exceed the LEL) 1a | Earnings above the LEL, up to and including the PT 1b | Earnings above the PT, up to and including the UEL 1c | Employer's NICs due on all earnings above the ST 1d | Employee's NICs due on all earnings above the PT 1e | Total of employee's and employer's NICs (for information only) |
|---|---|---|---|---|---|---|
| £ | £ | £ p | £ p | £ p | £ p | £ p |
| 2380 | 520 | 272.00 | 1588.00 | 227.70 | 190.80 | 418.50 |
| 2384 | 520 | 272.00 | 1592.00 | 228.25 | 191.28 | 419.53 |
| 2388 | 520 | 272.00 | 1596.00 | 228.80 | 191.76 | 420.56 |
| 2392 | 520 | 272.00 | 1600.00 | 229.36 | 192.24 | 421.60 |
| 2396 | 520 | 272.00 | 1604.00 | 229.91 | 192.72 | 422.63 |
| 2400 | 520 | 272.00 | 1608.00 | 230.46 | 193.20 | 423.66 |
| 2404 | 520 | 272.00 | 1612.00 | 231.01 | 193.68 | 424.69 |
| 2408 | 520 | 272.00 | 1616.00 | 231.56 | 194.16 | 425.72 |
| 2412 | 520 | 272.00 | 1620.00 | 232.12 | 194.64 | 426.76 |
| 2416 | 520 | 272.00 | 1624.00 | 232.67 | 195.12 | 427.79 |
| 2420 | 520 | 272.00 | 1628.00 | 233.22 | 195.60 | 428.82 |
| 2424 | 520 | 272.00 | 1632.00 | 233.77 | 196.08 | 429.85 |
| 2428 | 520 | 272.00 | 1636.00 | 234.32 | 196.56 | 430.88 |
| 2432 | 520 | 272.00 | 1640.00 | 234.88 | 197.04 | 431.92 |
| 2436 | 520 | 272.00 | 1644.00 | 235.43 | 197.52 | 432.95 |
| 2440 | 520 | 272.00 | 1648.00 | 235.98 | 198.00 | 433.98 |
| 2444 | 520 | 272.00 | 1652.00 | 236.53 | 198.48 | 435.01 |
| 2448 | 520 | 272.00 | 1656.00 | 237.08 | 198.96 | 436.04 |
| 2452 | 520 | 272.00 | 1660.00 | 237.64 | 199.44 | 437.08 |
| 2456 | 520 | 272.00 | 1664.00 | 238.19 | 199.92 | 438.11 |
| 2460 | 520 | 272.00 | 1668.00 | 238.74 | 200.40 | 439.14 |
| 2464 | 520 | 272.00 | 1672.00 | 239.29 | 200.88 | 440.17 |
| 2468 | 520 | 272.00 | 1676.00 | 239.84 | 201.36 | 441.20 |
| 2472 | 520 | 272.00 | 1680.00 | 240.40 | 201.84 | 442.24 |
| 2476 | 520 | 272.00 | 1684.00 | 240.95 | 202.32 | 443.27 |
| 2480 | 520 | 272.00 | 1688.00 | 241.50 | 202.80 | 444.30 |
| 2484 | 520 | 272.00 | 1692.00 | 242.05 | 203.28 | 445.33 |
| 2488 | 520 | 272.00 | 1696.00 | 242.60 | 203.76 | 446.36 |
| 2492 | 520 | 272.00 | 1700.00 | 243.16 | 204.24 | 447.40 |
| 2496 | 520 | 272.00 | 1704.00 | 243.71 | 204.72 | 448.43 |
| 2500 | 520 | 272.00 | 1708.00 | 244.26 | 205.20 | 449.46 |
| 2504 | 520 | 272.00 | 1712.00 | 244.81 | 205.68 | 450.49 |
| 2508 | 520 | 272.00 | 1716.00 | 245.36 | 206.16 | 451.52 |
| 2512 | 520 | 272.00 | 1720.00 | 245.92 | 206.64 | 452.56 |
| 2516 | 520 | 272.00 | 1724.00 | 246.47 | 207.12 | 453.59 |
| 2520 | 520 | 272.00 | 1728.00 | 247.02 | 207.60 | 454.62 |
| 2524 | 520 | 272.00 | 1732.00 | 247.57 | 208.08 | 455.65 |
| 2528 | 520 | 272.00 | 1736.00 | 248.12 | 208.56 | 456.68 |
| 2532 | 520 | 272.00 | 1740.00 | 248.68 | 209.04 | 457.72 |
| 2536 | 520 | 272.00 | 1744.00 | 249.23 | 209.52 | 458.75 |
| 2540 | 520 | 272.00 | 1748.00 | 249.78 | 210.00 | 459.78 |
| 2544 | 520 | 272.00 | 1752.00 | 250.33 | 210.48 | 460.81 |
| 2548 | 520 | 272.00 | 1756.00 | 250.88 | 210.96 | 461.84 |
| 2552 | 520 | 272.00 | 1760.00 | 251.44 | 211.44 | 462.88 |
| 2556 | 520 | 272.00 | 1764.00 | 251.99 | 211.92 | 463.91 |
| 2560 | 520 | 272.00 | 1768.00 | 252.54 | 212.40 | 464.94 |
| 2564 | 520 | 272.00 | 1772.00 | 253.09 | 212.88 | 465.97 |
| 2568 | 520 | 272.00 | 1776.00 | 253.64 | 213.36 | 467.00 |
| 2572 | 520 | 272.00 | 1780.00 | 254.20 | 213.84 | 468.04 |
| 2576 | 520 | 272.00 | 1784.00 | 254.75 | 214.32 | 469.07 |
| 2580 | 520 | 272.00 | 1788.00 | 255.30 | 214.80 | 470.10 |
| 2584 | 520 | 272.00 | 1792.00 | 255.85 | 215.28 | 471.13 |
| 2588 | 520 | 272.00 | 1796.00 | 256.40 | 215.76 | 472.16 |
| 2592 | 520 | 272.00 | 1800.00 | 256.96 | 216.24 | 473.20 |
| 2596 | 520 | 272.00 | 1804.00 | 257.51 | 216.72 | 474.23 |

## Table letter A

**Monthly table**

| Employee's earnings up to and including the UEL | Earnings at the LEL (where earnings are equal to or exceed the LEL) 1a | Earnings above the LEL, up to and including the PT 1b | Earnings above the PT, up to and including the UEL 1c | Employer's NICs due on all earnings above the ST 1d | Employee's NICs due on all earnings above the PT 1e | Total of employee's and employer's NICs (for information only) |
|---|---|---|---|---|---|---|
| £ | £ | £ p | £ p | £ p | £ p | £ p |
| 2600 | 520 | 272.00 | 1808.00 | 258.06 | 217.20 | 475.26 |
| 2604 | 520 | 272.00 | 1812.00 | 258.61 | 217.68 | 476.29 |
| 2608 | 520 | 272.00 | 1816.00 | 259.16 | 218.16 | 477.32 |
| 2612 | 520 | 272.00 | 1820.00 | 259.72 | 218.64 | 478.36 |
| 2616 | 520 | 272.00 | 1824.00 | 260.27 | 219.12 | 479.39 |
| 2620 | 520 | 272.00 | 1828.00 | 260.82 | 219.60 | 480.42 |
| 2624 | 520 | 272.00 | 1832.00 | 261.37 | 220.08 | 481.45 |
| 2628 | 520 | 272.00 | 1836.00 | 261.92 | 220.56 | 482.48 |
| 2632 | 520 | 272.00 | 1840.00 | 262.48 | 221.04 | 483.52 |
| 2636 | 520 | 272.00 | 1844.00 | 263.03 | 221.52 | 484.55 |
| 2640 | 520 | 272.00 | 1848.00 | 263.58 | 222.00 | 485.58 |
| 2644 | 520 | 272.00 | 1852.00 | 264.13 | 222.48 | 486.61 |
| 2648 | 520 | 272.00 | 1856.00 | 264.68 | 222.96 | 487.64 |
| 2652 | 520 | 272.00 | 1860.00 | 265.24 | 223.44 | 488.68 |
| 2656 | 520 | 272.00 | 1864.00 | 265.79 | 223.92 | 489.71 |
| 2660 | 520 | 272.00 | 1868.00 | 266.34 | 224.40 | 490.74 |
| 2664 | 520 | 272.00 | 1872.00 | 266.89 | 224.88 | 491.77 |
| 2668 | 520 | 272.00 | 1876.00 | 267.44 | 225.36 | 492.80 |
| 2672 | 520 | 272.00 | 1880.00 | 268.00 | 225.84 | 493.84 |
| 2676 | 520 | 272.00 | 1884.00 | 268.55 | 226.32 | 494.87 |
| 2680 | 520 | 272.00 | 1888.00 | 269.10 | 226.80 | 495.90 |
| 2684 | 520 | 272.00 | 1892.00 | 269.65 | 227.28 | 496.93 |
| 2688 | 520 | 272.00 | 1896.00 | 270.20 | 227.76 | 497.96 |
| 2692 | 520 | 272.00 | 1900.00 | 270.76 | 228.24 | 499.00 |
| 2696 | 520 | 272.00 | 1904.00 | 271.31 | 228.72 | 500.03 |
| 2700 | 520 | 272.00 | 1908.00 | 271.86 | 229.20 | 501.06 |
| 2704 | 520 | 272.00 | 1912.00 | 272.41 | 229.68 | 502.09 |
| 2708 | 520 | 272.00 | 1916.00 | 272.96 | 230.16 | 503.12 |
| 2712 | 520 | 272.00 | 1920.00 | 273.52 | 230.64 | 504.16 |
| 2716 | 520 | 272.00 | 1924.00 | 274.07 | 231.12 | 505.19 |
| 2720 | 520 | 272.00 | 1928.00 | 274.62 | 231.60 | 506.22 |
| 2724 | 520 | 272.00 | 1932.00 | 275.17 | 232.08 | 507.25 |
| 2728 | 520 | 272.00 | 1936.00 | 275.72 | 232.56 | 508.28 |
| 2732 | 520 | 272.00 | 1940.00 | 276.28 | 233.04 | 509.32 |
| 2736 | 520 | 272.00 | 1944.00 | 276.83 | 233.52 | 510.35 |
| 2740 | 520 | 272.00 | 1948.00 | 277.38 | 234.00 | 511.38 |
| 2744 | 520 | 272.00 | 1952.00 | 277.93 | 234.48 | 512.41 |
| 2748 | 520 | 272.00 | 1956.00 | 278.48 | 234.96 | 513.44 |
| 2752 | 520 | 272.00 | 1960.00 | 279.04 | 235.44 | 514.48 |
| 2756 | 520 | 272.00 | 1964.00 | 279.59 | 235.92 | 515.51 |
| 2760 | 520 | 272.00 | 1968.00 | 280.14 | 236.40 | 516.54 |
| 2764 | 520 | 272.00 | 1972.00 | 280.69 | 236.88 | 517.57 |
| 2768 | 520 | 272.00 | 1976.00 | 281.24 | 237.36 | 518.60 |
| 2772 | 520 | 272.00 | 1980.00 | 281.80 | 237.84 | 519.64 |
| 2776 | 520 | 272.00 | 1984.00 | 282.35 | 238.32 | 520.67 |
| 2780 | 520 | 272.00 | 1988.00 | 282.90 | 238.80 | 521.70 |
| 2784 | 520 | 272.00 | 1992.00 | 283.45 | 239.28 | 522.73 |
| 2788 | 520 | 272.00 | 1996.00 | 284.00 | 239.76 | 523.76 |
| 2792 | 520 | 272.00 | 2000.00 | 284.56 | 240.24 | 524.80 |
| 2796 | 520 | 272.00 | 2004.00 | 285.11 | 240.72 | 525.83 |
| 2800 | 520 | 272.00 | 2008.00 | 285.66 | 241.20 | 526.86 |
| 2804 | 520 | 272.00 | 2012.00 | 286.21 | 241.68 | 527.89 |
| 2808 | 520 | 272.00 | 2016.00 | 286.76 | 242.16 | 528.92 |
| 2812 | 520 | 272.00 | 2020.00 | 287.32 | 242.64 | 529.96 |
| 2816 | 520 | 272.00 | 2024.00 | 287.87 | 243.12 | 530.99 |

## Monthly table                                                                 Table letter A

| Employee's earnings up to and including the UEL | Earnings at the LEL (where earnings are equal to or exceed the LEL) 1a | Earnings above the LEL, up to and including the PT 1b | Earnings above the PT, up to and including the UEL 1c | Employer's NICs due on all earnings above the ST 1d | Employee's NICs due on all earnings above the PT 1e | Total of employee's and employer's NICs (for information only) |
|---|---|---|---|---|---|---|
| £ | £ | £ p | £ p | £ p | £ p | £ p |
| 2820 | 520 | 272.00 | 2028.00 | 288.42 | 243.60 | 532.02 |
| 2824 | 520 | 272.00 | 2032.00 | 288.97 | 244.08 | 533.05 |
| 2828 | 520 | 272.00 | 2036.00 | 289.52 | 244.56 | 534.08 |
| 2832 | 520 | 272.00 | 2040.00 | 290.08 | 245.04 | 535.12 |
| 2836 | 520 | 272.00 | 2044.00 | 290.63 | 245.52 | 536.15 |
| 2840 | 520 | 272.00 | 2048.00 | 291.18 | 246.00 | 537.18 |
| 2844 | 520 | 272.00 | 2052.00 | 291.73 | 246.48 | 538.21 |
| 2848 | 520 | 272.00 | 2056.00 | 292.28 | 246.96 | 539.24 |
| 2852 | 520 | 272.00 | 2060.00 | 292.84 | 247.44 | 540.28 |
| 2856 | 520 | 272.00 | 2064.00 | 293.39 | 247.92 | 541.31 |
| 2860 | 520 | 272.00 | 2068.00 | 293.94 | 248.40 | 542.34 |
| 2864 | 520 | 272.00 | 2072.00 | 294.49 | 248.88 | 543.37 |
| 2868 | 520 | 272.00 | 2076.00 | 295.04 | 249.36 | 544.40 |
| 2872 | 520 | 272.00 | 2080.00 | 295.60 | 249.84 | 545.44 |
| 2876 | 520 | 272.00 | 2084.00 | 296.15 | 250.32 | 546.47 |
| 2880 | 520 | 272.00 | 2088.00 | 296.70 | 250.80 | 547.50 |
| 2884 | 520 | 272.00 | 2092.00 | 297.25 | 251.28 | 548.53 |
| 2888 | 520 | 272.00 | 2096.00 | 297.80 | 251.76 | 549.56 |
| 2892 | 520 | 272.00 | 2100.00 | 298.36 | 252.24 | 550.60 |
| 2896 | 520 | 272.00 | 2104.00 | 298.91 | 252.72 | 551.63 |
| 2900 | 520 | 272.00 | 2108.00 | 299.46 | 253.20 | 552.66 |
| 2904 | 520 | 272.00 | 2112.00 | 300.01 | 253.68 | 553.69 |
| 2908 | 520 | 272.00 | 2116.00 | 300.56 | 254.16 | 554.72 |
| 2912 | 520 | 272.00 | 2120.00 | 301.12 | 254.64 | 555.76 |
| 2916 | 520 | 272.00 | 2124.00 | 301.67 | 255.12 | 556.79 |
| 2920 | 520 | 272.00 | 2128.00 | 302.22 | 255.60 | 557.82 |
| 2924 | 520 | 272.00 | 2132.00 | 302.77 | 256.08 | 558.85 |
| 2928 | 520 | 272.00 | 2136.00 | 303.32 | 256.56 | 559.88 |
| 2932 | 520 | 272.00 | 2140.00 | 303.88 | 257.04 | 560.92 |
| 2936 | 520 | 272.00 | 2144.00 | 304.43 | 257.52 | 561.95 |
| 2940 | 520 | 272.00 | 2148.00 | 304.98 | 258.00 | 562.98 |
| 2944 | 520 | 272.00 | 2152.00 | 305.53 | 258.48 | 564.01 |
| 2948 | 520 | 272.00 | 2156.00 | 306.08 | 258.96 | 565.04 |
| 2952 | 520 | 272.00 | 2160.00 | 306.64 | 259.44 | 566.08 |
| 2956 | 520 | 272.00 | 2164.00 | 307.19 | 259.92 | 567.11 |
| 2960 | 520 | 272.00 | 2168.00 | 307.74 | 260.40 | 568.14 |
| 2964 | 520 | 272.00 | 2172.00 | 308.29 | 260.88 | 569.17 |
| 2968 | 520 | 272.00 | 2176.00 | 308.84 | 261.36 | 570.20 |
| 2972 | 520 | 272.00 | 2180.00 | 309.40 | 261.84 | 571.24 |
| 2976 | 520 | 272.00 | 2184.00 | 309.95 | 262.32 | 572.27 |
| 2980 | 520 | 272.00 | 2188.00 | 310.50 | 262.80 | 573.30 |
| 2984 | 520 | 272.00 | 2192.00 | 311.05 | 263.28 | 574.33 |
| 2988 | 520 | 272.00 | 2196.00 | 311.60 | 263.76 | 575.36 |
| 2992 | 520 | 272.00 | 2200.00 | 312.16 | 264.24 | 576.40 |
| 2996 | 520 | 272.00 | 2204.00 | 312.71 | 264.72 | 577.43 |
| 3000 | 520 | 272.00 | 2208.00 | 313.26 | 265.20 | 578.46 |
| 3004 | 520 | 272.00 | 2212.00 | 313.81 | 265.68 | 579.49 |
| 3008 | 520 | 272.00 | 2216.00 | 314.36 | 266.16 | 580.52 |
| 3012 | 520 | 272.00 | 2220.00 | 314.92 | 266.64 | 581.56 |
| 3016 | 520 | 272.00 | 2224.00 | 315.47 | 267.12 | 582.59 |
| 3020 | 520 | 272.00 | 2228.00 | 316.02 | 267.60 | 583.62 |
| 3024 | 520 | 272.00 | 2232.00 | 316.57 | 268.08 | 584.65 |
| 3028 | 520 | 272.00 | 2236.00 | 317.12 | 268.56 | 585.68 |
| 3032 | 520 | 272.00 | 2240.00 | 317.68 | 269.04 | 586.72 |
| 3036 | 520 | 272.00 | 2244.00 | 318.23 | 269.52 | 587.75 |

## Table letter A

## Monthly table

| Employee's earnings up to and including the UEL | Earnings at the LEL (where earnings are equal to or exceed the LEL) 1a | Earnings above the LEL, up to and including the PT 1b | Earnings above the PT, up to and including the UEL 1c | Employer's NICs due on all earnings above the ST 1d | Employee's NICs due on all earnings above the PT 1e | Total of employee's and employer's NICs (for information only) |
|---|---|---|---|---|---|---|
| £ | £ | £ p | £ p | £ p | £ p | £ p |
| 3040 | 520 | 272.00 | 2248.00 | 318.78 | 270.00 | 588.78 |
| 3044 | 520 | 272.00 | 2252.00 | 319.33 | 270.48 | 589.81 |
| 3048 | 520 | 272.00 | 2256.00 | 319.88 | 270.96 | 590.84 |
| 3052 | 520 | 272.00 | 2260.00 | 320.44 | 271.44 | 591.88 |
| 3056 | 520 | 272.00 | 2264.00 | 320.99 | 271.92 | 592.91 |
| 3060 | 520 | 272.00 | 2268.00 | 321.54 | 272.40 | 593.94 |
| 3064 | 520 | 272.00 | 2272.00 | 322.09 | 272.88 | 594.97 |
| 3068 | 520 | 272.00 | 2276.00 | 322.64 | 273.36 | 596.00 |
| 3072 | 520 | 272.00 | 2280.00 | 323.20 | 273.84 | 597.04 |
| 3076 | 520 | 272.00 | 2284.00 | 323.75 | 274.32 | 598.07 |
| 3080 | 520 | 272.00 | 2288.00 | 324.30 | 274.80 | 599.10 |
| 3084 | 520 | 272.00 | 2292.00 | 324.85 | 275.28 | 600.13 |
| 3088 | 520 | 272.00 | 2296.00 | 325.40 | 275.76 | 601.16 |
| 3092 | 520 | 272.00 | 2300.00 | 325.96 | 276.24 | 602.20 |
| 3096 | 520 | 272.00 | 2304.00 | 326.51 | 276.72 | 603.23 |
| 3100 | 520 | 272.00 | 2308.00 | 327.06 | 277.20 | 604.26 |
| 3104 | 520 | 272.00 | 2312.00 | 327.61 | 277.68 | 605.29 |
| 3108 | 520 | 272.00 | 2316.00 | 328.16 | 278.16 | 606.32 |
| 3112 | 520 | 272.00 | 2320.00 | 328.72 | 278.64 | 607.36 |
| 3116 | 520 | 272.00 | 2324.00 | 329.27 | 279.12 | 608.39 |
| 3120 | 520 | 272.00 | 2328.00 | 329.82 | 279.60 | 609.42 |
| 3124 | 520 | 272.00 | 2332.00 | 330.37 | 280.08 | 610.45 |
| 3128 | 520 | 272.00 | 2336.00 | 330.92 | 280.56 | 611.48 |
| 3132 | 520 | 272.00 | 2340.00 | 331.48 | 281.04 | 612.52 |
| 3136 | 520 | 272.00 | 2344.00 | 332.03 | 281.52 | 613.55 |
| 3140 | 520 | 272.00 | 2348.00 | 332.58 | 282.00 | 614.58 |
| 3144 | 520 | 272.00 | 2352.00 | 333.13 | 282.48 | 615.61 |
| 3148 | 520 | 272.00 | 2356.00 | 333.68 | 282.96 | 616.64 |
| 3152 | 520 | 272.00 | 2360.00 | 334.24 | 283.44 | 617.68 |
| 3156 | 520 | 272.00 | 2364.00 | 334.79 | 283.92 | 618.71 |
| 3160 | 520 | 272.00 | 2368.00 | 335.34 | 284.40 | 619.74 |
| 3164 | 520 | 272.00 | 2372.00 | 335.89 | 284.88 | 620.77 |
| 3168 | 520 | 272.00 | 2376.00 | 336.44 | 285.36 | 621.80 |
| 3172 | 520 | 272.00 | 2380.00 | 337.00 | 285.84 | 622.84 |
| 3176 | 520 | 272.00 | 2384.00 | 337.55 | 286.32 | 623.87 |
| 3180 | 520 | 272.00 | 2388.00 | 338.10 | 286.80 | 624.90 |
| 3184 | 520 | 272.00 | 2392.00 | 338.65 | 287.28 | 625.93 |
| 3188 | 520 | 272.00 | 2396.00 | 339.20 | 287.76 | 626.96 |
| 3192 | 520 | 272.00 | 2400.00 | 339.76 | 288.24 | 628.00 |
| 3196 | 520 | 272.00 | 2404.00 | 340.31 | 288.72 | 629.03 |
| 3200 | 520 | 272.00 | 2408.00 | 340.86 | 289.20 | 630.06 |
| 3204 | 520 | 272.00 | 2412.00 | 341.41 | 289.68 | 631.09 |
| 3208 | 520 | 272.00 | 2416.00 | 341.96 | 290.16 | 632.12 |
| 3212 | 520 | 272.00 | 2420.00 | 342.52 | 290.64 | 633.16 |
| 3216 | 520 | 272.00 | 2424.00 | 343.07 | 291.12 | 634.19 |
| 3220 | 520 | 272.00 | 2428.00 | 343.62 | 291.60 | 635.22 |
| 3224 | 520 | 272.00 | 2432.00 | 344.17 | 292.08 | 636.25 |
| 3228 | 520 | 272.00 | 2436.00 | 344.72 | 292.56 | 637.28 |
| 3232 | 520 | 272.00 | 2440.00 | 345.28 | 293.04 | 638.32 |
| 3236 | 520 | 272.00 | 2444.00 | 345.83 | 293.52 | 639.35 |
| 3240 | 520 | 272.00 | 2448.00 | 346.38 | 294.00 | 640.38 |
| 3244 | 520 | 272.00 | 2452.00 | 346.93 | 294.48 | 641.41 |
| 3248 | 520 | 272.00 | 2456.00 | 347.48 | 294.96 | 642.44 |
| 3252 | 520 | 272.00 | 2460.00 | 348.04 | 295.44 | 643.48 |
| 3256 | 520 | 272.00 | 2464.00 | 348.59 | 295.92 | 644.51 |

## Monthly table

**Table letter A**

| Employee's earnings up to and including the UEL | Earnings at the LEL (where earnings are equal to or exceed the LEL) | Earnings above the LEL, up to and including the PT | Earnings above the PT, up to and including the UEL | Employer's NICs due on all earnings above the ST | Employee's NICs due on all earnings above the PT | Total of employee's and employer's NICs (for information only) |
|---|---|---|---|---|---|---|
| | 1a | 1b | 1c | 1d | 1e | |
| £ | £ | £ p | £ p | £ p | £ p | £ p |
| 3260 | 520 | 272.00 | 2468.00 | 349.14 | 296.40 | 645.54 |
| 3264 | 520 | 272.00 | 2472.00 | 349.69 | 296.88 | 646.57 |
| 3268 | 520 | 272.00 | 2476.00 | 350.24 | 297.36 | 647.60 |
| 3272 | 520 | 272.00 | 2480.00 | 350.80 | 297.84 | 648.64 |
| 3276 | 520 | 272.00 | 2484.00 | 351.35 | 298.32 | 649.67 |
| 3280 | 520 | 272.00 | 2488.00 | 351.90 | 298.80 | 650.70 |
| 3284 | 520 | 272.00 | 2492.00 | 352.45 | 299.28 | 651.73 |
| 3288 | 520 | 272.00 | 2496.00 | 353.00 | 299.76 | 652.76 |
| 3292 | 520 | 272.00 | 2500.00 | 353.56 | 300.24 | 653.80 |
| 3296 | 520 | 272.00 | 2504.00 | 354.11 | 300.72 | 654.83 |
| 3300 | 520 | 272.00 | 2508.00 | 354.66 | 301.20 | 655.86 |
| 3304 | 520 | 272.00 | 2512.00 | 355.21 | 301.68 | 656.89 |
| 3308 | 520 | 272.00 | 2516.00 | 355.76 | 302.16 | 657.92 |
| 3312 | 520 | 272.00 | 2520.00 | 356.32 | 302.64 | 658.96 |
| 3316 | 520 | 272.00 | 2524.00 | 356.87 | 303.12 | 659.99 |
| 3320 | 520 | 272.00 | 2528.00 | 357.42 | 303.60 | 661.02 |
| 3324 | 520 | 272.00 | 2532.00 | 357.97 | 304.08 | 662.05 |
| 3328 | 520 | 272.00 | 2536.00 | 358.52 | 304.56 | 663.08 |
| 3332 | 520 | 272.00 | 2540.00 | 359.08 | 305.04 | 664.12 |
| 3336 | 520 | 272.00 | 2544.00 | 359.63 | 305.52 | 665.15 |
| 3340 | 520 | 272.00 | 2548.00 | 360.18 | 306.00 | 666.18 |
| 3344 | 520 | 272.00 | 2552.00 | 360.73 | 306.48 | 667.21 |
| 3348 | 520 | 272.00 | 2556.00 | 361.28 | 306.96 | 668.24 |
| 3352 | 520 | 272.00 | 2560.00 | 361.84 | 307.44 | 669.28 |
| 3356 | 520 | 272.00 | 2564.00 | 362.39 | 307.92 | 670.31 |
| 3360 | 520 | 272.00 | 2568.00 | 362.94 | 308.40 | 671.34 |
| 3364 | 520 | 272.00 | 2572.00 | 363.49 | 308.88 | 672.37 |
| 3368 | 520 | 272.00 | 2576.00 | 364.04 | 309.36 | 673.40 |
| 3372 | 520 | 272.00 | 2580.00 | 364.60 | 309.84 | 674.44 |
| 3376 | 520 | 272.00 | 2584.00 | 365.15 | 310.32 | 675.47 |
| 3380 | 520 | 272.00 | 2588.00 | 365.70 | 310.80 | 676.50 |
| 3384 | 520 | 272.00 | 2592.00 | 366.25 | 311.28 | 677.53 |
| 3388 | 520 | 272.00 | 2596.00 | 366.80 | 311.76 | 678.56 |
| 3392 | 520 | 272.00 | 2600.00 | 367.36 | 312.24 | 679.60 |
| 3396 | 520 | 272.00 | 2604.00 | 367.91 | 312.72 | 680.63 |
| 3400 | 520 | 272.00 | 2608.00 | 368.46 | 313.20 | 681.66 |
| 3404 | 520 | 272.00 | 2612.00 | 369.01 | 313.68 | 682.69 |
| 3408 | 520 | 272.00 | 2616.00 | 369.56 | 314.16 | 683.72 |
| 3412 | 520 | 272.00 | 2620.00 | 370.12 | 314.64 | 684.76 |
| 3416 | 520 | 272.00 | 2624.00 | 370.67 | 315.12 | 685.79 |
| 3420 | 520 | 272.00 | 2628.00 | 371.22 | 315.60 | 686.82 |
| 3424 | 520 | 272.00 | 2632.00 | 371.77 | 316.08 | 687.85 |
| 3428 | 520 | 272.00 | 2636.00 | 372.32 | 316.56 | 688.88 |
| 3432 | 520 | 272.00 | 2640.00 | 372.88 | 317.04 | 689.92 |
| 3436 | 520 | 272.00 | 2644.00 | 373.43 | 317.52 | 690.95 |
| 3440 | 520 | 272.00 | 2648.00 | 373.98 | 318.00 | 691.98 |
| 3444 | 520 | 272.00 | 2652.00 | 374.53 | 318.48 | 693.01 |
| 3448 | 520 | 272.00 | 2656.00 | 375.08 | 318.96 | 694.04 |
| 3452 | 520 | 272.00 | 2660.00 | 375.64 | 319.44 | 695.08 |
| 3456 | 520 | 272.00 | 2664.00 | 376.19 | 319.92 | 696.11 |
| 3460 | 520 | 272.00 | 2668.00 | 376.74 | 320.40 | 697.14 |
| 3464 | 520 | 272.00 | 2672.00 | 377.29 | 320.88 | 698.17 |
| 3468 | 520 | 272.00 | 2676.00 | 377.84 | 321.36 | 699.20 |
| 3472 | 520 | 272.00 | 2680.00 | 378.40 | 321.84 | 700.24 |
| 3476 | 520 | 272.00 | 2684.00 | 378.95 | 322.32 | 701.27 |

# Table letter A

**Monthly table**

| Employee's earnings up to and including the UEL | Earnings at the LEL (where earnings are equal to or exceed the LEL) 1a | Earnings above the LEL, up to and including the PT 1b | Earnings above the PT, up to and including the UEL 1c | Employer's NICs due on all earnings above the ST 1d | Employee's NICs due on all earnings above the PT 1e | Total of employee's and employer's NICs (for information only) |
|---|---|---|---|---|---|---|
| £ | £ | £ p | £ p | £ p | £ p | £ p |
| 3480 | 520 | 272.00 | 2688.00 | 379.50 | 322.80 | 702.30 |
| 3484 | 520 | 272.00 | 2692.00 | 380.05 | 323.28 | 703.33 |
| 3488 | 520 | 272.00 | 2696.00 | 380.60 | 323.76 | 704.36 |
| 3492 | 520 | 272.00 | 2700.00 | 381.16 | 324.24 | 705.40 |
| 3496 | 520 | 272.00 | 2704.00 | 381.71 | 324.72 | 706.43 |
| 3500 | 520 | 272.00 | 2708.00 | 382.26 | 325.20 | 707.46 |
| 3504 | 520 | 272.00 | 2712.00 | 382.81 | 325.68 | 708.49 |
| 3508 | 520 | 272.00 | 2716.00 | 383.36 | 326.16 | 709.52 |
| 3512 | 520 | 272.00 | 2720.00 | 383.92 | 326.64 | 710.56 |
| 3516 | 520 | 272.00 | 2724.00 | 384.47 | 327.12 | 711.59 |
| 3520 | 520 | 272.00 | 2728.00 | 385.02 | 327.60 | 712.62 |
| 3524 | 520 | 272.00 | 2732.00 | 385.57 | 328.08 | 713.65 |
| 3528 | 520 | 272.00 | 2736.00 | 386.12 | 328.56 | 714.68 |
| 3532 | 520 | 272.00 | 2740.00 | 386.68 | 329.04 | 715.72 |
| 3536 | 520 | 272.00 | 2744.00 | 387.23 | 329.52 | 716.75 |
| 3540 | 520 | 272.00 | 2748.00 | 387.78 | 330.00 | 717.78 |
| 3544 | 520 | 272.00 | 2752.00 | 388.33 | 330.48 | 718.81 |
| 3548 | 520 | 272.00 | 2756.00 | 388.88 | 330.96 | 719.84 |
| 3552 | 520 | 272.00 | 2760.00 | 389.44 | 331.44 | 720.88 |
| 3556 | 520 | 272.00 | 2764.00 | 389.99 | 331.92 | 721.91 |
| 3560 | 520 | 272.00 | 2768.00 | 390.54 | 332.40 | 722.94 |
| 3564 | 520 | 272.00 | 2772.00 | 391.09 | 332.88 | 723.97 |
| 3568 | 520 | 272.00 | 2776.00 | 391.64 | 333.36 | 725.00 |
| 3572 | 520 | 272.00 | 2780.00 | 392.20 | 333.84 | 726.04 |
| 3576 | 520 | 272.00 | 2784.00 | 392.75 | 334.32 | 727.07 |
| 3580 | 520 | 272.00 | 2788.00 | 393.30 | 334.80 | 728.10 |
| 3584 | 520 | 272.00 | 2792.00 | 393.85 | 335.28 | 729.13 |
| 3588 | 520 | 272.00 | 2796.00 | 394.40 | 335.76 | 730.16 |
| 3592 | 520 | 272.00 | 2800.00 | 394.96 | 336.24 | 731.20 |
| 3596 | 520 | 272.00 | 2804.00 | 395.51 | 336.72 | 732.23 |
| 3600 | 520 | 272.00 | 2808.00 | 396.06 | 337.20 | 733.26 |
| 3604 | 520 | 272.00 | 2812.00 | 396.61 | 337.68 | 734.29 |
| 3608 | 520 | 272.00 | 2816.00 | 397.16 | 338.16 | 735.32 |
| 3612 | 520 | 272.00 | 2820.00 | 397.72 | 338.64 | 736.36 |
| 3616 | 520 | 272.00 | 2824.00 | 398.27 | 339.12 | 737.39 |
| 3620 | 520 | 272.00 | 2828.00 | 398.82 | 339.60 | 738.42 |
| 3624 | 520 | 272.00 | 2832.00 | 399.37 | 340.08 | 739.45 |
| 3628 | 520 | 272.00 | 2836.00 | 399.92 | 340.56 | 740.48 |
| 3632 | 520 | 272.00 | 2840.00 | 400.48 | 341.04 | 741.52 |
| 3636 | 520 | 272.00 | 2844.00 | 401.03 | 341.52 | 742.55 |
| 3640 | 520 | 272.00 | 2848.00 | 401.58 | 342.00 | 743.58 |
| 3644 | 520 | 272.00 | 2852.00 | 402.13 | 342.48 | 744.61 |
| 3648 | 520 | 272.00 | 2856.00 | 402.68 | 342.96 | 745.64 |
| 3652 | 520 | 272.00 | 2860.00 | 403.24 | 343.44 | 746.68 |
| 3656 | 520 | 272.00 | 2864.00 | 403.79 | 343.92 | 747.71 |
| 3660 | 520 | 272.00 | 2868.00 | 404.34 | 344.40 | 748.74 |
| 3664 | 520 | 272.00 | 2872.00 | 404.89 | 344.88 | 749.77 |
| 3668 | 520 | 272.00 | 2876.00 | 405.44 | 345.36 | 750.80 |
| 3672 | 520 | 272.00 | 2880.00 | 406.00 | 345.84 | 751.84 |
| 3676 | 520 | 272.00 | 2884.00 | 406.55 | 346.32 | 752.87 |
| 3680 | 520 | 272.00 | 2888.00 | 407.10 | 346.80 | 753.90 |
| 3684 | 520 | 272.00 | 2892.00 | 407.65 | 347.28 | 754.93 |
| 3688 | 520 | 272.00 | 2896.00 | 408.20 | 347.76 | 755.96 |
| 3692 | 520 | 272.00 | 2900.00 | 408.76 | 348.24 | 757.00 |
| 3696 | 520 | 272.00 | 2904.00 | 409.31 | 348.72 | 758.03 |

**Monthly table**

**Table letter A**

| Employee's earnings up to and including the UEL | Earnings at the LEL (where earnings are equal to or exceed the LEL) | Earnings above the LEL, up to and including the PT | Earnings above the PT, up to and including the UEL | Employer's NICs due on all earnings above the ST | Employee's NICs due on all earnings above the PT | Total of employee's and employer's NICs (for information only) |
|---|---|---|---|---|---|---|
| | | 1a | 1b | 1c | 1d | 1e |
| £ | £ | £ p | £ p | £ p | £ p | £ p |
| 3700 | 520 | 272.00 | 2908.00 | 409.86 | 349.20 | 759.06 |
| 3704 | 520 | 272.00 | 2912.00 | 410.41 | 349.68 | 760.09 |
| 3708 | 520 | 272.00 | 2916.00 | 410.96 | 350.16 | 761.12 |
| 3712 | 520 | 272.00 | 2920.00 | 411.52 | 350.64 | 762.16 |
| 3716 | 520 | 272.00 | 2924.00 | 412.07 | 351.12 | 763.19 |
| 3720 | 520 | 272.00 | 2928.00 | 412.62 | 351.60 | 764.22 |
| 3724 | 520 | 272.00 | 2932.00 | 413.17 | 352.08 | 765.25 |
| 3728 | 520 | 272.00 | 2936.00 | 413.72 | 352.56 | 766.28 |
| 3732 | 520 | 272.00 | 2940.00 | 414.28 | 353.04 | 767.32 |
| 3736 | 520 | 272.00 | 2944.00 | 414.83 | 353.52 | 768.35 |
| 3740 | 520 | 272.00 | 2948.00 | 415.38 | 354.00 | 769.38 |
| 3744 | 520 | 272.00 | 2952.00 | 415.93 | 354.48 | 770.41 |
| 3748 | 520 | 272.00 | 2956.00 | 416.48 | 354.96 | 771.44 |
| 3752 | 520 | 272.00 | 2960.00 | 417.04 | 355.44 | 772.48 |
| 3756 | 520 | 272.00 | 2964.00 | 417.59 | 355.92 | 773.51 |
| 3760 | 520 | 272.00 | 2968.00 | 418.14 | 356.40 | 774.54 |
| 3764 | 520 | 272.00 | 2972.00 | 418.69 | 356.88 | 775.57 |
| 3768 | 520 | 272.00 | 2976.00 | 419.24 | 357.36 | 776.60 |
| 3772 | 520 | 272.00 | 2980.00 | 419.80 | 357.84 | 777.64 |
| 3776 | 520 | 272.00 | 2984.00 | 420.35 | 358.32 | 778.67 |
| 3780 | 520 | 272.00 | 2988.00 | 420.90 | 358.80 | 779.70 |
| 3784 | 520 | 272.00 | 2992.00 | 421.45 | 359.28 | 780.73 |
| 3788 | 520 | 272.00 | 2996.00 | 422.00 | 359.76 | 781.76 |
| 3792 | 520 | 272.00 | 3000.00 | 422.56 | 360.24 | 782.80 |
| 3796 | 520 | 272.00 | 3004.00 | 423.11 | 360.72 | 783.83 |
| 3800 | 520 | 272.00 | 3008.00 | 423.66 | 361.20 | 784.86 |
| 3804 | 520 | 272.00 | 3012.00 | 424.21 | 361.68 | 785.89 |
| 3808 | 520 | 272.00 | 3016.00 | 424.76 | 362.16 | 786.92 |
| 3812 | 520 | 272.00 | 3020.00 | 425.32 | 362.64 | 787.96 |
| 3816 | 520 | 272.00 | 3024.00 | 425.87 | 363.12 | 788.99 |
| 3820 | 520 | 272.00 | 3028.00 | 426.42 | 363.60 | 790.02 |
| 3824 | 520 | 272.00 | 3032.00 | 426.97 | 364.08 | 791.05 |
| 3828 | 520 | 272.00 | 3036.00 | 427.52 | 364.56 | 792.08 |
| 3832 | 520 | 272.00 | 3040.00 | 428.08 | 365.04 | 793.12 |
| 3836 | 520 | 272.00 | 3044.00 | 428.63 | 365.52 | 794.15 |
| 3840 | 520 | 272.00 | 3048.00 | 429.18 | 366.00 | 795.18 |
| 3844 | 520 | 272.00 | 3052.00 | 429.73 | 366.48 | 796.21 |
| 3848 | 520 | 272.00 | 3056.00 | 430.28 | 366.96 | 797.24 |
| 3852 | 520 | 272.00 | 3060.00 | 430.84 | 367.44 | 798.28 |
| 3856 | 520 | 272.00 | 3064.00 | 431.39 | 367.92 | 799.31 |
| 3860 | 520 | 272.00 | 3068.00 | 431.94 | 368.40 | 800.34 |
| 3864 | 520 | 272.00 | 3072.00 | 432.49 | 368.88 | 801.37 |
| 3868 | 520 | 272.00 | 3076.00 | 433.04 | 369.36 | 802.40 |
| 3872 | 520 | 272.00 | 3080.00 | 433.60 | 369.84 | 803.44 |
| 3876 | 520 | 272.00 | 3084.00 | 434.15 | 370.32 | 804.47 |
| 3880 | 520 | 272.00 | 3088.00 | 434.70 | 370.80 | 805.50 |
| 3884 | 520 | 272.00 | 3092.00 | 435.25 | 371.28 | 806.53 |
| 3888 | 520 | 272.00 | 3096.00 | 435.80 | 371.76 | 807.56 |
| 3892 | 520 | 272.00 | 3100.00 | 436.36 | 372.24 | 808.60 |
| 3896 | 520 | 272.00 | 3104.00 | 436.91 | 372.72 | 809.63 |
| 3900 | 520 | 272.00 | 3108.00 | 437.46 | 373.20 | 810.66 |
| 3904 | 520 | 272.00 | 3112.00 | 438.01 | 373.68 | 811.69 |
| 3908 | 520 | 272.00 | 3116.00 | 438.56 | 374.16 | 812.72 |
| 3912 | 520 | 272.00 | 3120.00 | 439.12 | 374.64 | 813.76 |
| 3916 | 520 | 272.00 | 3124.00 | 439.67 | 375.12 | 814.79 |

## Table letter A

**Monthly table**

| Employee's earnings up to and including the UEL | Earnings at the LEL (where earnings are equal to or exceed the LEL) | Earnings above the LEL, up to and including the PT | Earnings above the PT, up to and including the UEL | Employer's NICs due on all earnings above the ST | Employee's NICs due on all earnings above the PT | Total of employee's and employer's NICs (for information only) |
|---|---|---|---|---|---|---|
| | | 1a | 1b | 1c | 1d | 1e |
| £ | £ | £ p | £ p | £ p | £ p | £ p |
| 3920 | 520 | 272.00 | 3128.00 | 440.22 | 375.60 | 815.82 |
| 3924 | 520 | 272.00 | 3132.00 | 440.77 | 376.08 | 816.85 |
| 3928 | 520 | 272.00 | 3136.00 | 441.32 | 376.56 | 817.88 |
| 3932 | 520 | 272.00 | 3140.00 | 441.88 | 377.04 | 818.92 |
| 3936 | 520 | 272.00 | 3144.00 | 442.43 | 377.52 | 819.95 |
| 3940 | 520 | 272.00 | 3148.00 | 442.98 | 378.00 | 820.98 |
| 3944 | 520 | 272.00 | 3152.00 | 443.53 | 378.48 | 822.01 |
| 3948 | 520 | 272.00 | 3156.00 | 444.08 | 378.96 | 823.04 |
| 3952 | 520 | 272.00 | 3160.00 | 444.64 | 379.44 | 824.08 |
| 3956 | 520 | 272.00 | 3164.00 | 445.19 | 379.92 | 825.11 |
| 3960 | 520 | 272.00 | 3168.00 | 445.74 | 380.40 | 826.14 |
| 3964 | 520 | 272.00 | 3172.00 | 446.29 | 380.88 | 827.17 |
| 3968 | 520 | 272.00 | 3176.00 | 446.84 | 381.36 | 828.20 |
| 3972 | 520 | 272.00 | 3180.00 | 447.40 | 381.84 | 829.24 |
| 3976 | 520 | 272.00 | 3184.00 | 447.95 | 382.32 | 830.27 |
| 3980 | 520 | 272.00 | 3188.00 | 448.50 | 382.80 | 831.30 |
| 3984 | 520 | 272.00 | 3192.00 | 449.05 | 383.28 | 832.33 |
| 3988 | 520 | 272.00 | 3196.00 | 449.60 | 383.76 | 833.36 |
| 3992 | 520 | 272.00 | 3200.00 | 450.16 | 384.24 | 834.40 |
| 3996 | 520 | 272.00 | 3204.00 | 450.71 | 384.72 | 835.43 |
| 4000 | 520 | 272.00 | 3208.00 | 451.26 | 385.20 | 836.46 |
| 4004 | 520 | 272.00 | 3212.00 | 451.81 | 385.68 | 837.49 |
| 4008 | 520 | 272.00 | 3216.00 | 452.36 | 386.16 | 838.52 |
| 4012 | 520 | 272.00 | 3220.00 | 452.92 | 386.64 | 839.56 |
| 4016 | 520 | 272.00 | 3224.00 | 453.47 | 387.12 | 840.59 |
| 4020 | 520 | 272.00 | 3228.00 | 454.02 | 387.60 | 841.62 |
| 4024 | 520 | 272.00 | 3232.00 | 454.57 | 388.08 | 842.65 |
| 4028 | 520 | 272.00 | 3236.00 | 455.12 | 388.56 | 843.68 |
| 4032 | 520 | 272.00 | 3240.00 | 455.68 | 389.04 | 844.72 |
| 4036 | 520 | 272.00 | 3244.00 | 456.23 | 389.52 | 845.75 |
| 4040 | 520 | 272.00 | 3248.00 | 456.78 | 390.00 | 846.78 |
| 4044 | 520 | 272.00 | 3252.00 | 457.33 | 390.48 | 847.81 |
| 4048 | 520 | 272.00 | 3256.00 | 457.88 | 390.96 | 848.84 |
| 4052 | 520 | 272.00 | 3260.00 | 458.44 | 391.44 | 849.88 |
| 4056 | 520 | 272.00 | 3264.00 | 458.99 | 391.92 | 850.91 |
| 4060 | 520 | 272.00 | 3268.00 | 459.54 | 392.40 | 851.94 |
| 4064 | 520 | 272.00 | 3272.00 | 460.09 | 392.88 | 852.97 |
| 4068 | 520 | 272.00 | 3276.00 | 460.64 | 393.36 | 854.00 |
| 4072 | 520 | 272.00 | 3280.00 | 461.20 | 393.84 | 855.04 |
| 4076 | 520 | 272.00 | 3284.00 | 461.75 | 394.32 | 856.07 |
| 4080 | 520 | 272.00 | 3288.00 | 462.30 | 394.80 | 857.10 |
| 4084 | 520 | 272.00 | 3292.00 | 462.85 | 395.28 | 858.13 |
| 4088 | 520 | 272.00 | 3296.00 | 463.40 | 395.76 | 859.16 |
| 4092 | 520 | 272.00 | 3300.00 | 463.96 | 396.24 | 860.20 |
| 4096 | 520 | 272.00 | 3304.00 | 464.51 | 396.72 | 861.23 |
| 4100 | 520 | 272.00 | 3308.00 | 465.06 | 397.20 | 862.26 |
| 4104 | 520 | 272.00 | 3312.00 | 465.61 | 397.68 | 863.29 |
| 4108 | 520 | 272.00 | 3316.00 | 466.16 | 398.16 | 864.32 |
| 4112 | 520 | 272.00 | 3320.00 | 466.72 | 398.64 | 865.36 |
| 4116 | 520 | 272.00 | 3324.00 | 467.27 | 399.12 | 866.39 |
| 4120 | 520 | 272.00 | 3328.00 | 467.82 | 399.60 | 867.42 |
| 4124 | 520 | 272.00 | 3332.00 | 468.37 | 400.08 | 868.45 |
| 4128 | 520 | 272.00 | 3336.00 | 468.92 | 400.56 | 869.48 |
| 4132 | 520 | 272.00 | 3340.00 | 469.48 | 401.04 | 870.52 |
| 4136 | 520 | 272.00 | 3344.00 | 470.03 | 401.52 | 871.55 |

**Monthly table**                                                                 **Table letter A**

| Employee's earnings up to and including the UEL | Earnings at the LEL (where earnings are equal to or exceed the LEL) 1a | Earnings above the LEL, up to and including the PT 1b | Earnings above the PT, up to and including the UEL 1c | Employer's NICs due on all earnings above the ST 1d | Employee's NICs due on all earnings above the PT 1e | Total of employee's and employer's NICs (for information only) |
|---|---|---|---|---|---|---|
| £ | £ | £ p | £ p | £ p | £ p | £ p |
| 4140 | 520 | 272.00 | 3348.00 | 470.58 | 402.00 | 872.58 |
| 4144 | 520 | 272.00 | 3352.00 | 471.13 | 402.48 | 873.61 |
| 4148 | 520 | 272.00 | 3356.00 | 471.68 | 402.96 | 874.64 |
| 4152 | 520 | 272.00 | 3360.00 | 472.24 | 403.44 | 875.68 |
| 4156 | 520 | 272.00 | 3364.00 | 472.79 | 403.92 | 876.71 |
| 4160 | 520 | 272.00 | 3368.00 | 473.34 | 404.40 | 877.74 |
| 4164 | 520 | 272.00 | 3372.00 | 473.82 | 404.82 | 878.64 |
| 4167 | 520 | 272.00 | 3375.00 | 474.03 | 405.00 | 879.03 |

If the employee's gross pay is over £4,167, go to page 178.

# Weekly table for standard rate NICs for use from 6 April 2020 to 5 April 2021

**Table letter H**

Use this table for employees who are apprentices on an Approved Apprenticeship scheme and under the age of 25.

Do not use this table for:

- any tax year other than 2020 to 2021
- employees who are under the age of 21 unless they are on an Approved Apprenticeship scheme (go to Table letter M)
- married women or widows who have the right to pay reduced rate employee's NICs (go to Table letter B in booklet CA41)
- employees who are State Pension age or over (go to Table letter C in booklet CA41)
- employees who are aged 21 or over, for whom you hold form CA2700 (go to Table letter J)
- employees who are under the age of 21, for whom you hold form CA2700 (go to Table letter Z)

**Completing form RT11, 'Deductions working sheet' or substitute**

1 Enter 'H' in the NICs Category Letter column on form RT11.

2 Copy the figures in columns 1a – 1e of the table to columns 1a – 1e on the line next to the tax week in which the employee is paid, on form RT11.

If the employee's total earnings fall between the LEL and the UEL/UST/AUST and the exact gross pay is not shown in the table, use the next smaller figure shown. If the employee's total earnings exceed the UEL/UST/AUST, go to page 163.

The figures in the left-hand column of each table show steps between the LEL and the UEL/UST/AUST. The NICs liability for each step, with the exception of the LEL, ST, PT, UEL, UST and AUST, is worked out at the mid-point of the steps so you and your employee may pay slightly more or less than if you used the exact percentage method.

| Employee's earnings up to and including the UEL | Earnings at the LEL (where earnings are equal to or exceed the LEL) | Earnings above the LEL, up to and including the PT | Earnings above the PT, up to and including the UEL | Employer's NICs due on all earnings above the ST | Employee's NICs due on all earnings above the PT | Total of employee's and employer's NICs (for information only) |
|---|---|---|---|---|---|---|
| | 1a | 1b | 1c | 1d | 1e | |
| £ | £ | £ p | £ p | £ p | £ p | £ p |
| Up to and including £119.99 | No NICs liability, make no entries on form RT11 | | | | | |
| 120 | 120 | 0.00 | 0.00 | 0.00 | 0.00 | 0.00 |
| 121 | 120 | 1.00 | 0.00 | 0.00 | 0.00 | 0.00 |
| 122 | 120 | 2.00 | 0.00 | 0.00 | 0.00 | 0.00 |
| 123 | 120 | 3.00 | 0.00 | 0.00 | 0.00 | 0.00 |
| 124 | 120 | 4.00 | 0.00 | 0.00 | 0.00 | 0.00 |
| 125 | 120 | 5.00 | 0.00 | 0.00 | 0.00 | 0.00 |
| 126 | 120 | 6.00 | 0.00 | 0.00 | 0.00 | 0.00 |
| 127 | 120 | 7.00 | 0.00 | 0.00 | 0.00 | 0.00 |
| 128 | 120 | 8.00 | 0.00 | 0.00 | 0.00 | 0.00 |
| 129 | 120 | 9.00 | 0.00 | 0.00 | 0.00 | 0.00 |
| 130 | 120 | 10.00 | 0.00 | 0.00 | 0.00 | 0.00 |
| 131 | 120 | 11.00 | 0.00 | 0.00 | 0.00 | 0.00 |
| 132 | 120 | 12.00 | 0.00 | 0.00 | 0.00 | 0.00 |
| 133 | 120 | 13.00 | 0.00 | 0.00 | 0.00 | 0.00 |
| 134 | 120 | 14.00 | 0.00 | 0.00 | 0.00 | 0.00 |
| 135 | 120 | 15.00 | 0.00 | 0.00 | 0.00 | 0.00 |
| 136 | 120 | 16.00 | 0.00 | 0.00 | 0.00 | 0.00 |
| 137 | 120 | 17.00 | 0.00 | 0.00 | 0.00 | 0.00 |
| 138 | 120 | 18.00 | 0.00 | 0.00 | 0.00 | 0.00 |
| 139 | 120 | 19.00 | 0.00 | 0.00 | 0.00 | 0.00 |
| 140 | 120 | 20.00 | 0.00 | 0.00 | 0.00 | 0.00 |
| 141 | 120 | 21.00 | 0.00 | 0.00 | 0.00 | 0.00 |
| 142 | 120 | 22.00 | 0.00 | 0.00 | 0.00 | 0.00 |
| 143 | 120 | 23.00 | 0.00 | 0.00 | 0.00 | 0.00 |
| 144 | 120 | 24.00 | 0.00 | 0.00 | 0.00 | 0.00 |

Page 42

**Weekly table**

**Table letter H**

| Employee's earnings up to and including the UEL | Earnings at the LEL (where earnings are equal to or exceed the LEL) 1a | Earnings above the LEL, up to and including the PT 1b | Earnings above the PT, up to and including the UEL 1c | Employer's NICs due on all earnings above the ST 1d | Employee's NICs due on all earnings above the PT 1e | Total of employee's and employer's NICs (for information only) |
|---|---|---|---|---|---|---|
| £ | £ | £ p | £ p | £ p | £ p | £ p |
| 145 | 120 | 25.00 | 0.00 | 0.00 | 0.00 | 0.00 |
| 146 | 120 | 26.00 | 0.00 | 0.00 | 0.00 | 0.00 |
| 147 | 120 | 27.00 | 0.00 | 0.00 | 0.00 | 0.00 |
| 148 | 120 | 28.00 | 0.00 | 0.00 | 0.00 | 0.00 |
| 149 | 120 | 29.00 | 0.00 | 0.00 | 0.00 | 0.00 |
| 150 | 120 | 30.00 | 0.00 | 0.00 | 0.00 | 0.00 |
| 151 | 120 | 31.00 | 0.00 | 0.00 | 0.00 | 0.00 |
| 152 | 120 | 32.00 | 0.00 | 0.00 | 0.00 | 0.00 |
| 153 | 120 | 33.00 | 0.00 | 0.00 | 0.00 | 0.00 |
| 154 | 120 | 34.00 | 0.00 | 0.00 | 0.00 | 0.00 |
| 155 | 120 | 35.00 | 0.00 | 0.00 | 0.00 | 0.00 |
| 156 | 120 | 36.00 | 0.00 | 0.00 | 0.00 | 0.00 |
| 157 | 120 | 37.00 | 0.00 | 0.00 | 0.00 | 0.00 |
| 158 | 120 | 38.00 | 0.00 | 0.00 | 0.00 | 0.00 |
| 159 | 120 | 39.00 | 0.00 | 0.00 | 0.00 | 0.00 |
| 160 | 120 | 40.00 | 0.00 | 0.00 | 0.00 | 0.00 |
| 161 | 120 | 41.00 | 0.00 | 0.00 | 0.00 | 0.00 |
| 162 | 120 | 42.00 | 0.00 | 0.00 | 0.00 | 0.00 |
| 163 | 120 | 43.00 | 0.00 | 0.00 | 0.00 | 0.00 |
| 164 | 120 | 44.00 | 0.00 | 0.00 | 0.00 | 0.00 |
| 165 | 120 | 45.00 | 0.00 | 0.00 | 0.00 | 0.00 |
| 166 | 120 | 46.00 | 0.00 | 0.00 | 0.00 | 0.00 |
| 167 | 120 | 47.00 | 0.00 | 0.00 | 0.00 | 0.00 |
| 168 | 120 | 48.00 | 0.00 | 0.00 | 0.00 | 0.00 |
| 169 | 120 | 49.00 | 0.00 | 0.00 | 0.00 | 0.00 |
| 170 | 120 | 50.00 | 0.00 | 0.00 | 0.00 | 0.00 |
| 171 | 120 | 51.00 | 0.00 | 0.00 | 0.00 | 0.00 |
| 172 | 120 | 52.00 | 0.00 | 0.00 | 0.00 | 0.00 |
| 173 | 120 | 53.00 | 0.00 | 0.00 | 0.00 | 0.00 |
| 174 | 120 | 54.00 | 0.00 | 0.00 | 0.00 | 0.00 |
| 175 | 120 | 55.00 | 0.00 | 0.00 | 0.00 | 0.00 |
| 176 | 120 | 56.00 | 0.00 | 0.00 | 0.00 | 0.00 |
| 177 | 120 | 57.00 | 0.00 | 0.00 | 0.00 | 0.00 |
| 178 | 120 | 58.00 | 0.00 | 0.00 | 0.00 | 0.00 |
| 179 | 120 | 59.00 | 0.00 | 0.00 | 0.00 | 0.00 |
| 180 | 120 | 60.00 | 0.00 | 0.00 | 0.00 | 0.00 |
| 181 | 120 | 61.00 | 0.00 | 0.00 | 0.00 | 0.00 |
| 182 | 120 | 62.00 | 0.00 | 0.00 | 0.00 | 0.00 |
| 183 | 120 | 63.00 | 0.00 | 0.00 | 0.00 | 0.00 |
| 184 | 120 | 63.00 | 1.00 | 0.00 | 0.18 | 0.18 |
| 185 | 120 | 63.00 | 2.00 | 0.00 | 0.30 | 0.30 |
| 186 | 120 | 63.00 | 3.00 | 0.00 | 0.42 | 0.42 |
| 187 | 120 | 63.00 | 4.00 | 0.00 | 0.54 | 0.54 |
| 188 | 120 | 63.00 | 5.00 | 0.00 | 0.66 | 0.66 |
| 189 | 120 | 63.00 | 6.00 | 0.00 | 0.78 | 0.78 |
| 190 | 120 | 63.00 | 7.00 | 0.00 | 0.90 | 0.90 |
| 191 | 120 | 63.00 | 8.00 | 0.00 | 1.02 | 1.02 |
| 192 | 120 | 63.00 | 9.00 | 0.00 | 1.14 | 1.14 |
| 193 | 120 | 63.00 | 10.00 | 0.00 | 1.26 | 1.26 |
| 194 | 120 | 63.00 | 11.00 | 0.00 | 1.38 | 1.38 |
| 195 | 120 | 63.00 | 12.00 | 0.00 | 1.50 | 1.50 |
| 196 | 120 | 63.00 | 13.00 | 0.00 | 1.62 | 1.62 |
| 197 | 120 | 63.00 | 14.00 | 0.00 | 1.74 | 1.74 |
| 198 | 120 | 63.00 | 15.00 | 0.00 | 1.86 | 1.86 |
| 199 | 120 | 63.00 | 16.00 | 0.00 | 1.98 | 1.98 |

## Table letter H

**Weekly table**

| Employee's earnings up to and including the UEL | Earnings at the LEL (where earnings are equal to or exceed the LEL) 1a | Earnings above the LEL, up to and including the PT 1b | Earnings above the PT, up to and including the UEL 1c | Employer's NICs due on all earnings above the ST 1d | Employee's NICs due on all earnings above the PT 1e | Total of employee's and employer's NICs (for information only) |
|---|---|---|---|---|---|---|
| £ | £ | £ p | £ p | £ p | £ p | £ p |
| 200 | 120 | 63.00 | 17.00 | 0.00 | 2.10 | 2.10 |
| 201 | 120 | 63.00 | 18.00 | 0.00 | 2.22 | 2.22 |
| 202 | 120 | 63.00 | 19.00 | 0.00 | 2.34 | 2.34 |
| 203 | 120 | 63.00 | 20.00 | 0.00 | 2.46 | 2.46 |
| 204 | 120 | 63.00 | 21.00 | 0.00 | 2.58 | 2.58 |
| 205 | 120 | 63.00 | 22.00 | 0.00 | 2.70 | 2.70 |
| 206 | 120 | 63.00 | 23.00 | 0.00 | 2.82 | 2.82 |
| 207 | 120 | 63.00 | 24.00 | 0.00 | 2.94 | 2.94 |
| 208 | 120 | 63.00 | 25.00 | 0.00 | 3.06 | 3.06 |
| 209 | 120 | 63.00 | 26.00 | 0.00 | 3.18 | 3.18 |
| 210 | 120 | 63.00 | 27.00 | 0.00 | 3.30 | 3.30 |
| 211 | 120 | 63.00 | 28.00 | 0.00 | 3.42 | 3.42 |
| 212 | 120 | 63.00 | 29.00 | 0.00 | 3.54 | 3.54 |
| 213 | 120 | 63.00 | 30.00 | 0.00 | 3.66 | 3.66 |
| 214 | 120 | 63.00 | 31.00 | 0.00 | 3.78 | 3.78 |
| 215 | 120 | 63.00 | 32.00 | 0.00 | 3.90 | 3.90 |
| 216 | 120 | 63.00 | 33.00 | 0.00 | 4.02 | 4.02 |
| 217 | 120 | 63.00 | 34.00 | 0.00 | 4.14 | 4.14 |
| 218 | 120 | 63.00 | 35.00 | 0.00 | 4.26 | 4.26 |
| 219 | 120 | 63.00 | 36.00 | 0.00 | 4.38 | 4.38 |
| 220 | 120 | 63.00 | 37.00 | 0.00 | 4.50 | 4.50 |
| 221 | 120 | 63.00 | 38.00 | 0.00 | 4.62 | 4.62 |
| 222 | 120 | 63.00 | 39.00 | 0.00 | 4.74 | 4.74 |
| 223 | 120 | 63.00 | 40.00 | 0.00 | 4.86 | 4.86 |
| 224 | 120 | 63.00 | 41.00 | 0.00 | 4.98 | 4.98 |
| 225 | 120 | 63.00 | 42.00 | 0.00 | 5.10 | 5.10 |
| 226 | 120 | 63.00 | 43.00 | 0.00 | 5.22 | 5.22 |
| 227 | 120 | 63.00 | 44.00 | 0.00 | 5.34 | 5.34 |
| 228 | 120 | 63.00 | 45.00 | 0.00 | 5.46 | 5.46 |
| 229 | 120 | 63.00 | 46.00 | 0.00 | 5.58 | 5.58 |
| 230 | 120 | 63.00 | 47.00 | 0.00 | 5.70 | 5.70 |
| 231 | 120 | 63.00 | 48.00 | 0.00 | 5.82 | 5.82 |
| 232 | 120 | 63.00 | 49.00 | 0.00 | 5.94 | 5.94 |
| 233 | 120 | 63.00 | 50.00 | 0.00 | 6.06 | 6.06 |
| 234 | 120 | 63.00 | 51.00 | 0.00 | 6.18 | 6.18 |
| 235 | 120 | 63.00 | 52.00 | 0.00 | 6.30 | 6.30 |
| 236 | 120 | 63.00 | 53.00 | 0.00 | 6.42 | 6.42 |
| 237 | 120 | 63.00 | 54.00 | 0.00 | 6.54 | 6.54 |
| 238 | 120 | 63.00 | 55.00 | 0.00 | 6.66 | 6.66 |
| 239 | 120 | 63.00 | 56.00 | 0.00 | 6.78 | 6.78 |
| 240 | 120 | 63.00 | 57.00 | 0.00 | 6.90 | 6.90 |
| 241 | 120 | 63.00 | 58.00 | 0.00 | 7.02 | 7.02 |
| 242 | 120 | 63.00 | 59.00 | 0.00 | 7.14 | 7.14 |
| 243 | 120 | 63.00 | 60.00 | 0.00 | 7.26 | 7.26 |
| 244 | 120 | 63.00 | 61.00 | 0.00 | 7.38 | 7.38 |
| 245 | 120 | 63.00 | 62.00 | 0.00 | 7.50 | 7.50 |
| 246 | 120 | 63.00 | 63.00 | 0.00 | 7.62 | 7.62 |
| 247 | 120 | 63.00 | 64.00 | 0.00 | 7.74 | 7.74 |
| 248 | 120 | 63.00 | 65.00 | 0.00 | 7.86 | 7.86 |
| 249 | 120 | 63.00 | 66.00 | 0.00 | 7.98 | 7.98 |
| 250 | 120 | 63.00 | 67.00 | 0.00 | 8.10 | 8.10 |
| 251 | 120 | 63.00 | 68.00 | 0.00 | 8.22 | 8.22 |
| 252 | 120 | 63.00 | 69.00 | 0.00 | 8.34 | 8.34 |
| 253 | 120 | 63.00 | 70.00 | 0.00 | 8.46 | 8.46 |
| 254 | 120 | 63.00 | 71.00 | 0.00 | 8.58 | 8.58 |

# Weekly table

Table letter H

| Employee's earnings up to and including the UEL | Earnings at the LEL (where earnings are equal to or exceed the LEL) 1a | Earnings above the LEL, up to and including the PT 1b | Earnings above the PT, up to and including the UEL 1c | Employer's NICs due on all earnings above the ST 1d | Employee's NICs due on all earnings above the PT 1e | Total of employee's and employer's NICs (for information only) |
|---|---|---|---|---|---|---|
| £ | £ | £ p | £ p | £ p | £ p | £ p |
| 255 | 120 | 63.00 | 72.00 | 0.00 | 8.70 | 8.70 |
| 256 | 120 | 63.00 | 73.00 | 0.00 | 8.82 | 8.82 |
| 257 | 120 | 63.00 | 74.00 | 0.00 | 8.94 | 8.94 |
| 258 | 120 | 63.00 | 75.00 | 0.00 | 9.06 | 9.06 |
| 259 | 120 | 63.00 | 76.00 | 0.00 | 9.18 | 9.18 |
| 260 | 120 | 63.00 | 77.00 | 0.00 | 9.30 | 9.30 |
| 261 | 120 | 63.00 | 78.00 | 0.00 | 9.42 | 9.42 |
| 262 | 120 | 63.00 | 79.00 | 0.00 | 9.54 | 9.54 |
| 263 | 120 | 63.00 | 80.00 | 0.00 | 9.66 | 9.66 |
| 264 | 120 | 63.00 | 81.00 | 0.00 | 9.78 | 9.78 |
| 265 | 120 | 63.00 | 82.00 | 0.00 | 9.90 | 9.90 |
| 266 | 120 | 63.00 | 83.00 | 0.00 | 10.02 | 10.02 |
| 267 | 120 | 63.00 | 84.00 | 0.00 | 10.14 | 10.14 |
| 268 | 120 | 63.00 | 85.00 | 0.00 | 10.26 | 10.26 |
| 269 | 120 | 63.00 | 86.00 | 0.00 | 10.38 | 10.38 |
| 270 | 120 | 63.00 | 87.00 | 0.00 | 10.50 | 10.50 |
| 271 | 120 | 63.00 | 88.00 | 0.00 | 10.62 | 10.62 |
| 272 | 120 | 63.00 | 89.00 | 0.00 | 10.74 | 10.74 |
| 273 | 120 | 63.00 | 90.00 | 0.00 | 10.86 | 10.86 |
| 274 | 120 | 63.00 | 91.00 | 0.00 | 10.98 | 10.98 |
| 275 | 120 | 63.00 | 92.00 | 0.00 | 11.10 | 11.10 |
| 276 | 120 | 63.00 | 93.00 | 0.00 | 11.22 | 11.22 |
| 277 | 120 | 63.00 | 94.00 | 0.00 | 11.34 | 11.34 |
| 278 | 120 | 63.00 | 95.00 | 0.00 | 11.46 | 11.46 |
| 279 | 120 | 63.00 | 96.00 | 0.00 | 11.58 | 11.58 |
| 280 | 120 | 63.00 | 97.00 | 0.00 | 11.70 | 11.70 |
| 281 | 120 | 63.00 | 98.00 | 0.00 | 11.82 | 11.82 |
| 282 | 120 | 63.00 | 99.00 | 0.00 | 11.94 | 11.94 |
| 283 | 120 | 63.00 | 100.00 | 0.00 | 12.06 | 12.06 |
| 284 | 120 | 63.00 | 101.00 | 0.00 | 12.18 | 12.18 |
| 285 | 120 | 63.00 | 102.00 | 0.00 | 12.30 | 12.30 |
| 286 | 120 | 63.00 | 103.00 | 0.00 | 12.42 | 12.42 |
| 287 | 120 | 63.00 | 104.00 | 0.00 | 12.54 | 12.54 |
| 288 | 120 | 63.00 | 105.00 | 0.00 | 12.66 | 12.66 |
| 289 | 120 | 63.00 | 106.00 | 0.00 | 12.78 | 12.78 |
| 290 | 120 | 63.00 | 107.00 | 0.00 | 12.90 | 12.90 |
| 291 | 120 | 63.00 | 108.00 | 0.00 | 13.02 | 13.02 |
| 292 | 120 | 63.00 | 109.00 | 0.00 | 13.14 | 13.14 |
| 293 | 120 | 63.00 | 110.00 | 0.00 | 13.26 | 13.26 |
| 294 | 120 | 63.00 | 111.00 | 0.00 | 13.38 | 13.38 |
| 295 | 120 | 63.00 | 112.00 | 0.00 | 13.50 | 13.50 |
| 296 | 120 | 63.00 | 113.00 | 0.00 | 13.62 | 13.62 |
| 297 | 120 | 63.00 | 114.00 | 0.00 | 13.74 | 13.74 |
| 298 | 120 | 63.00 | 115.00 | 0.00 | 13.86 | 13.86 |
| 299 | 120 | 63.00 | 116.00 | 0.00 | 13.98 | 13.98 |
| 300 | 120 | 63.00 | 117.00 | 0.00 | 14.10 | 14.10 |
| 301 | 120 | 63.00 | 118.00 | 0.00 | 14.22 | 14.22 |
| 302 | 120 | 63.00 | 119.00 | 0.00 | 14.34 | 14.34 |
| 303 | 120 | 63.00 | 120.00 | 0.00 | 14.46 | 14.46 |
| 304 | 120 | 63.00 | 121.00 | 0.00 | 14.58 | 14.58 |
| 305 | 120 | 63.00 | 122.00 | 0.00 | 14.70 | 14.70 |
| 306 | 120 | 63.00 | 123.00 | 0.00 | 14.82 | 14.82 |
| 307 | 120 | 63.00 | 124.00 | 0.00 | 14.94 | 14.94 |
| 308 | 120 | 63.00 | 125.00 | 0.00 | 15.06 | 15.06 |
| 309 | 120 | 63.00 | 126.00 | 0.00 | 15.18 | 15.18 |

## Table letter H

**Weekly table**

| Employee's earnings up to and including the UEL | Earnings at the LEL (where earnings are equal to or exceed the LEL) | Earnings above the LEL, up to and including the PT | Earnings above the PT, up to and including the UEL | Employer's NICs due on all earnings above the ST | Employee's NICs due on all earnings above the PT | Total of employee's and employer's NICs (for information only) |
|---|---|---|---|---|---|---|
| | 1a | 1b | 1c | 1d | 1e | |
| £ | £ | £ p | £ p | £ p | £ p | £ p |
| 310 | 120 | 63.00 | 127.00 | 0.00 | 15.30 | 15.30 |
| 311 | 120 | 63.00 | 128.00 | 0.00 | 15.42 | 15.42 |
| 312 | 120 | 63.00 | 129.00 | 0.00 | 15.54 | 15.54 |
| 313 | 120 | 63.00 | 130.00 | 0.00 | 15.66 | 15.66 |
| 314 | 120 | 63.00 | 131.00 | 0.00 | 15.78 | 15.78 |
| 315 | 120 | 63.00 | 132.00 | 0.00 | 15.90 | 15.90 |
| 316 | 120 | 63.00 | 133.00 | 0.00 | 16.02 | 16.02 |
| 317 | 120 | 63.00 | 134.00 | 0.00 | 16.14 | 16.14 |
| 318 | 120 | 63.00 | 135.00 | 0.00 | 16.26 | 16.26 |
| 319 | 120 | 63.00 | 136.00 | 0.00 | 16.38 | 16.38 |
| 320 | 120 | 63.00 | 137.00 | 0.00 | 16.50 | 16.50 |
| 321 | 120 | 63.00 | 138.00 | 0.00 | 16.62 | 16.62 |
| 322 | 120 | 63.00 | 139.00 | 0.00 | 16.74 | 16.74 |
| 323 | 120 | 63.00 | 140.00 | 0.00 | 16.86 | 16.86 |
| 324 | 120 | 63.00 | 141.00 | 0.00 | 16.98 | 16.98 |
| 325 | 120 | 63.00 | 142.00 | 0.00 | 17.10 | 17.10 |
| 326 | 120 | 63.00 | 143.00 | 0.00 | 17.22 | 17.22 |
| 327 | 120 | 63.00 | 144.00 | 0.00 | 17.34 | 17.34 |
| 328 | 120 | 63.00 | 145.00 | 0.00 | 17.46 | 17.46 |
| 329 | 120 | 63.00 | 146.00 | 0.00 | 17.58 | 17.58 |
| 330 | 120 | 63.00 | 147.00 | 0.00 | 17.70 | 17.70 |
| 331 | 120 | 63.00 | 148.00 | 0.00 | 17.82 | 17.82 |
| 332 | 120 | 63.00 | 149.00 | 0.00 | 17.94 | 17.94 |
| 333 | 120 | 63.00 | 150.00 | 0.00 | 18.06 | 18.06 |
| 334 | 120 | 63.00 | 151.00 | 0.00 | 18.18 | 18.18 |
| 335 | 120 | 63.00 | 152.00 | 0.00 | 18.30 | 18.30 |
| 336 | 120 | 63.00 | 153.00 | 0.00 | 18.42 | 18.42 |
| 337 | 120 | 63.00 | 154.00 | 0.00 | 18.54 | 18.54 |
| 338 | 120 | 63.00 | 155.00 | 0.00 | 18.66 | 18.66 |
| 339 | 120 | 63.00 | 156.00 | 0.00 | 18.78 | 18.78 |
| 340 | 120 | 63.00 | 157.00 | 0.00 | 18.90 | 18.90 |
| 341 | 120 | 63.00 | 158.00 | 0.00 | 19.02 | 19.02 |
| 342 | 120 | 63.00 | 159.00 | 0.00 | 19.14 | 19.14 |
| 343 | 120 | 63.00 | 160.00 | 0.00 | 19.26 | 19.26 |
| 344 | 120 | 63.00 | 161.00 | 0.00 | 19.38 | 19.38 |
| 345 | 120 | 63.00 | 162.00 | 0.00 | 19.50 | 19.50 |
| 346 | 120 | 63.00 | 163.00 | 0.00 | 19.62 | 19.62 |
| 347 | 120 | 63.00 | 164.00 | 0.00 | 19.74 | 19.74 |
| 348 | 120 | 63.00 | 165.00 | 0.00 | 19.86 | 19.86 |
| 349 | 120 | 63.00 | 166.00 | 0.00 | 19.98 | 19.98 |
| 350 | 120 | 63.00 | 167.00 | 0.00 | 20.10 | 20.10 |
| 351 | 120 | 63.00 | 168.00 | 0.00 | 20.22 | 20.22 |
| 352 | 120 | 63.00 | 169.00 | 0.00 | 20.34 | 20.34 |
| 353 | 120 | 63.00 | 170.00 | 0.00 | 20.46 | 20.46 |
| 354 | 120 | 63.00 | 171.00 | 0.00 | 20.58 | 20.58 |
| 355 | 120 | 63.00 | 172.00 | 0.00 | 20.70 | 20.70 |
| 356 | 120 | 63.00 | 173.00 | 0.00 | 20.82 | 20.82 |
| 357 | 120 | 63.00 | 174.00 | 0.00 | 20.94 | 20.94 |
| 358 | 120 | 63.00 | 175.00 | 0.00 | 21.06 | 21.06 |
| 359 | 120 | 63.00 | 176.00 | 0.00 | 21.18 | 21.18 |
| 360 | 120 | 63.00 | 177.00 | 0.00 | 21.30 | 21.30 |
| 361 | 120 | 63.00 | 178.00 | 0.00 | 21.42 | 21.42 |
| 362 | 120 | 63.00 | 179.00 | 0.00 | 21.54 | 21.54 |
| 363 | 120 | 63.00 | 180.00 | 0.00 | 21.66 | 21.66 |
| 364 | 120 | 63.00 | 181.00 | 0.00 | 21.78 | 21.78 |

**Weekly table**  Table letter H

| Employee's earnings up to and including the UEL | Earnings at the LEL (where earnings are equal to or exceed the LEL) | Earnings above the LEL, up to and including the PT | Earnings above the PT, up to and including the UEL | Employer's NICs due on all earnings above the ST | Employee's NICs due on all earnings above the PT | Total of employee's and employer's NICs (for information only) |
|---|---|---|---|---|---|---|
| | | 1a | 1b | 1c | 1d | 1e |
| £ | £ | £ p | £ p | £ p | £ p | £ p |
| 365 | 120 | 63.00 | 182.00 | 0.00 | 21.90 | 21.90 |
| 366 | 120 | 63.00 | 183.00 | 0.00 | 22.02 | 22.02 |
| 367 | 120 | 63.00 | 184.00 | 0.00 | 22.14 | 22.14 |
| 368 | 120 | 63.00 | 185.00 | 0.00 | 22.26 | 22.26 |
| 369 | 120 | 63.00 | 186.00 | 0.00 | 22.38 | 22.38 |
| 370 | 120 | 63.00 | 187.00 | 0.00 | 22.50 | 22.50 |
| 371 | 120 | 63.00 | 188.00 | 0.00 | 22.62 | 22.62 |
| 372 | 120 | 63.00 | 189.00 | 0.00 | 22.74 | 22.74 |
| 373 | 120 | 63.00 | 190.00 | 0.00 | 22.86 | 22.86 |
| 374 | 120 | 63.00 | 191.00 | 0.00 | 22.98 | 22.98 |
| 375 | 120 | 63.00 | 192.00 | 0.00 | 23.10 | 23.10 |
| 376 | 120 | 63.00 | 193.00 | 0.00 | 23.22 | 23.22 |
| 377 | 120 | 63.00 | 194.00 | 0.00 | 23.34 | 23.34 |
| 378 | 120 | 63.00 | 195.00 | 0.00 | 23.46 | 23.46 |
| 379 | 120 | 63.00 | 196.00 | 0.00 | 23.58 | 23.58 |
| 380 | 120 | 63.00 | 197.00 | 0.00 | 23.70 | 23.70 |
| 381 | 120 | 63.00 | 198.00 | 0.00 | 23.82 | 23.82 |
| 382 | 120 | 63.00 | 199.00 | 0.00 | 23.94 | 23.94 |
| 383 | 120 | 63.00 | 200.00 | 0.00 | 24.06 | 24.06 |
| 384 | 120 | 63.00 | 201.00 | 0.00 | 24.18 | 24.18 |
| 385 | 120 | 63.00 | 202.00 | 0.00 | 24.30 | 24.30 |
| 386 | 120 | 63.00 | 203.00 | 0.00 | 24.42 | 24.42 |
| 387 | 120 | 63.00 | 204.00 | 0.00 | 24.54 | 24.54 |
| 388 | 120 | 63.00 | 205.00 | 0.00 | 24.66 | 24.66 |
| 389 | 120 | 63.00 | 206.00 | 0.00 | 24.78 | 24.78 |
| 390 | 120 | 63.00 | 207.00 | 0.00 | 24.90 | 24.90 |
| 391 | 120 | 63.00 | 208.00 | 0.00 | 25.02 | 25.02 |
| 392 | 120 | 63.00 | 209.00 | 0.00 | 25.14 | 25.14 |
| 393 | 120 | 63.00 | 210.00 | 0.00 | 25.26 | 25.26 |
| 394 | 120 | 63.00 | 211.00 | 0.00 | 25.38 | 25.38 |
| 395 | 120 | 63.00 | 212.00 | 0.00 | 25.50 | 25.50 |
| 396 | 120 | 63.00 | 213.00 | 0.00 | 25.62 | 25.62 |
| 397 | 120 | 63.00 | 214.00 | 0.00 | 25.74 | 25.74 |
| 398 | 120 | 63.00 | 215.00 | 0.00 | 25.86 | 25.86 |
| 399 | 120 | 63.00 | 216.00 | 0.00 | 25.98 | 25.98 |
| 400 | 120 | 63.00 | 217.00 | 0.00 | 26.10 | 26.10 |
| 401 | 120 | 63.00 | 218.00 | 0.00 | 26.22 | 26.22 |
| 402 | 120 | 63.00 | 219.00 | 0.00 | 26.34 | 26.34 |
| 403 | 120 | 63.00 | 220.00 | 0.00 | 26.46 | 26.46 |
| 404 | 120 | 63.00 | 221.00 | 0.00 | 26.58 | 26.58 |
| 405 | 120 | 63.00 | 222.00 | 0.00 | 26.70 | 26.70 |
| 406 | 120 | 63.00 | 223.00 | 0.00 | 26.82 | 26.82 |
| 407 | 120 | 63.00 | 224.00 | 0.00 | 26.94 | 26.94 |
| 408 | 120 | 63.00 | 225.00 | 0.00 | 27.06 | 27.06 |
| 409 | 120 | 63.00 | 226.00 | 0.00 | 27.18 | 27.18 |
| 410 | 120 | 63.00 | 227.00 | 0.00 | 27.30 | 27.30 |
| 411 | 120 | 63.00 | 228.00 | 0.00 | 27.42 | 27.42 |
| 412 | 120 | 63.00 | 229.00 | 0.00 | 27.54 | 27.54 |
| 413 | 120 | 63.00 | 230.00 | 0.00 | 27.66 | 27.66 |
| 414 | 120 | 63.00 | 231.00 | 0.00 | 27.78 | 27.78 |
| 415 | 120 | 63.00 | 232.00 | 0.00 | 27.90 | 27.90 |
| 416 | 120 | 63.00 | 233.00 | 0.00 | 28.02 | 28.02 |
| 417 | 120 | 63.00 | 234.00 | 0.00 | 28.14 | 28.14 |
| 418 | 120 | 63.00 | 235.00 | 0.00 | 28.26 | 28.26 |
| 419 | 120 | 63.00 | 236.00 | 0.00 | 28.38 | 28.38 |

## Table letter H

**Weekly table**

| Employee's earnings up to and including the UEL | Earnings at the LEL (where earnings are equal to or exceed the LEL) | Earnings above the LEL, up to and including the PT | Earnings above the PT, up to and including the UEL | Employer's NICs due on all earnings above the ST | Employee's NICs due on all earnings above the PT | Total of employee's and employer's NICs (for information only) |
|---|---|---|---|---|---|---|
| | 1a | 1b | 1c | 1d | 1e | |
| £ | £ | £ p | £ p | £ p | £ p | £ p |
| 420 | 120 | 63.00 | 237.00 | 0.00 | 28.50 | 28.50 |
| 421 | 120 | 63.00 | 238.00 | 0.00 | 28.62 | 28.62 |
| 422 | 120 | 63.00 | 239.00 | 0.00 | 28.74 | 28.74 |
| 423 | 120 | 63.00 | 240.00 | 0.00 | 28.86 | 28.86 |
| 424 | 120 | 63.00 | 241.00 | 0.00 | 28.98 | 28.98 |
| 425 | 120 | 63.00 | 242.00 | 0.00 | 29.10 | 29.10 |
| 426 | 120 | 63.00 | 243.00 | 0.00 | 29.22 | 29.22 |
| 427 | 120 | 63.00 | 244.00 | 0.00 | 29.34 | 29.34 |
| 428 | 120 | 63.00 | 245.00 | 0.00 | 29.46 | 29.46 |
| 429 | 120 | 63.00 | 246.00 | 0.00 | 29.58 | 29.58 |
| 430 | 120 | 63.00 | 247.00 | 0.00 | 29.70 | 29.70 |
| 431 | 120 | 63.00 | 248.00 | 0.00 | 29.82 | 29.82 |
| 432 | 120 | 63.00 | 249.00 | 0.00 | 29.94 | 29.94 |
| 433 | 120 | 63.00 | 250.00 | 0.00 | 30.06 | 30.06 |
| 434 | 120 | 63.00 | 251.00 | 0.00 | 30.18 | 30.18 |
| 435 | 120 | 63.00 | 252.00 | 0.00 | 30.30 | 30.30 |
| 436 | 120 | 63.00 | 253.00 | 0.00 | 30.42 | 30.42 |
| 437 | 120 | 63.00 | 254.00 | 0.00 | 30.54 | 30.54 |
| 438 | 120 | 63.00 | 255.00 | 0.00 | 30.66 | 30.66 |
| 439 | 120 | 63.00 | 256.00 | 0.00 | 30.78 | 30.78 |
| 440 | 120 | 63.00 | 257.00 | 0.00 | 30.90 | 30.90 |
| 441 | 120 | 63.00 | 258.00 | 0.00 | 31.02 | 31.02 |
| 442 | 120 | 63.00 | 259.00 | 0.00 | 31.14 | 31.14 |
| 443 | 120 | 63.00 | 260.00 | 0.00 | 31.26 | 31.26 |
| 444 | 120 | 63.00 | 261.00 | 0.00 | 31.38 | 31.38 |
| 445 | 120 | 63.00 | 262.00 | 0.00 | 31.50 | 31.50 |
| 446 | 120 | 63.00 | 263.00 | 0.00 | 31.62 | 31.62 |
| 447 | 120 | 63.00 | 264.00 | 0.00 | 31.74 | 31.74 |
| 448 | 120 | 63.00 | 265.00 | 0.00 | 31.86 | 31.86 |
| 449 | 120 | 63.00 | 266.00 | 0.00 | 31.98 | 31.98 |
| 450 | 120 | 63.00 | 267.00 | 0.00 | 32.10 | 32.10 |
| 451 | 120 | 63.00 | 268.00 | 0.00 | 32.22 | 32.22 |
| 452 | 120 | 63.00 | 269.00 | 0.00 | 32.34 | 32.34 |
| 453 | 120 | 63.00 | 270.00 | 0.00 | 32.46 | 32.46 |
| 454 | 120 | 63.00 | 271.00 | 0.00 | 32.58 | 32.58 |
| 455 | 120 | 63.00 | 272.00 | 0.00 | 32.70 | 32.70 |
| 456 | 120 | 63.00 | 273.00 | 0.00 | 32.82 | 32.82 |
| 457 | 120 | 63.00 | 274.00 | 0.00 | 32.94 | 32.94 |
| 458 | 120 | 63.00 | 275.00 | 0.00 | 33.06 | 33.06 |
| 459 | 120 | 63.00 | 276.00 | 0.00 | 33.18 | 33.18 |
| 460 | 120 | 63.00 | 277.00 | 0.00 | 33.30 | 33.30 |
| 461 | 120 | 63.00 | 278.00 | 0.00 | 33.42 | 33.42 |
| 462 | 120 | 63.00 | 279.00 | 0.00 | 33.54 | 33.54 |
| 463 | 120 | 63.00 | 280.00 | 0.00 | 33.66 | 33.66 |
| 464 | 120 | 63.00 | 281.00 | 0.00 | 33.78 | 33.78 |
| 465 | 120 | 63.00 | 282.00 | 0.00 | 33.90 | 33.90 |
| 466 | 120 | 63.00 | 283.00 | 0.00 | 34.02 | 34.02 |
| 467 | 120 | 63.00 | 284.00 | 0.00 | 34.14 | 34.14 |
| 468 | 120 | 63.00 | 285.00 | 0.00 | 34.26 | 34.26 |
| 469 | 120 | 63.00 | 286.00 | 0.00 | 34.38 | 34.38 |
| 470 | 120 | 63.00 | 287.00 | 0.00 | 34.50 | 34.50 |
| 471 | 120 | 63.00 | 288.00 | 0.00 | 34.62 | 34.62 |
| 472 | 120 | 63.00 | 289.00 | 0.00 | 34.74 | 34.74 |
| 473 | 120 | 63.00 | 290.00 | 0.00 | 34.86 | 34.86 |
| 474 | 120 | 63.00 | 291.00 | 0.00 | 34.98 | 34.98 |

**Weekly table**  **Table letter H**

| Employee's earnings up to and including the UEL | Earnings at the LEL (where earnings are equal to or exceed the LEL) 1a | Earnings above the LEL, up to and including the PT 1b | Earnings above the PT, up to and including the UEL 1c | Employer's NICs due on all earnings above the ST 1d | Employee's NICs due on all earnings above the PT 1e | Total of employee's and employer's NICs (for information only) |
|---|---|---|---|---|---|---|
| £ | £ | £ p | £ p | £ p | £ p | £ p |
| 475 | 120 | 63.00 | 292.00 | 0.00 | 35.10 | 35.10 |
| 476 | 120 | 63.00 | 293.00 | 0.00 | 35.22 | 35.22 |
| 477 | 120 | 63.00 | 294.00 | 0.00 | 35.34 | 35.34 |
| 478 | 120 | 63.00 | 295.00 | 0.00 | 35.46 | 35.46 |
| 479 | 120 | 63.00 | 296.00 | 0.00 | 35.58 | 35.58 |
| 480 | 120 | 63.00 | 297.00 | 0.00 | 35.70 | 35.70 |
| 481 | 120 | 63.00 | 298.00 | 0.00 | 35.82 | 35.82 |
| 482 | 120 | 63.00 | 299.00 | 0.00 | 35.94 | 35.94 |
| 483 | 120 | 63.00 | 300.00 | 0.00 | 36.06 | 36.06 |
| 484 | 120 | 63.00 | 301.00 | 0.00 | 36.18 | 36.18 |
| 485 | 120 | 63.00 | 302.00 | 0.00 | 36.30 | 36.30 |
| 486 | 120 | 63.00 | 303.00 | 0.00 | 36.42 | 36.42 |
| 487 | 120 | 63.00 | 304.00 | 0.00 | 36.54 | 36.54 |
| 488 | 120 | 63.00 | 305.00 | 0.00 | 36.66 | 36.66 |
| 489 | 120 | 63.00 | 306.00 | 0.00 | 36.78 | 36.78 |
| 490 | 120 | 63.00 | 307.00 | 0.00 | 36.90 | 36.90 |
| 491 | 120 | 63.00 | 308.00 | 0.00 | 37.02 | 37.02 |
| 492 | 120 | 63.00 | 309.00 | 0.00 | 37.14 | 37.14 |
| 493 | 120 | 63.00 | 310.00 | 0.00 | 37.26 | 37.26 |
| 494 | 120 | 63.00 | 311.00 | 0.00 | 37.38 | 37.38 |
| 495 | 120 | 63.00 | 312.00 | 0.00 | 37.50 | 37.50 |
| 496 | 120 | 63.00 | 313.00 | 0.00 | 37.62 | 37.62 |
| 497 | 120 | 63.00 | 314.00 | 0.00 | 37.74 | 37.74 |
| 498 | 120 | 63.00 | 315.00 | 0.00 | 37.86 | 37.86 |
| 499 | 120 | 63.00 | 316.00 | 0.00 | 37.98 | 37.98 |
| 500 | 120 | 63.00 | 317.00 | 0.00 | 38.10 | 38.10 |
| 501 | 120 | 63.00 | 318.00 | 0.00 | 38.22 | 38.22 |
| 502 | 120 | 63.00 | 319.00 | 0.00 | 38.34 | 38.34 |
| 503 | 120 | 63.00 | 320.00 | 0.00 | 38.46 | 38.46 |
| 504 | 120 | 63.00 | 321.00 | 0.00 | 38.58 | 38.58 |
| 505 | 120 | 63.00 | 322.00 | 0.00 | 38.70 | 38.70 |
| 506 | 120 | 63.00 | 323.00 | 0.00 | 38.82 | 38.82 |
| 507 | 120 | 63.00 | 324.00 | 0.00 | 38.94 | 38.94 |
| 508 | 120 | 63.00 | 325.00 | 0.00 | 39.06 | 39.06 |
| 509 | 120 | 63.00 | 326.00 | 0.00 | 39.18 | 39.18 |
| 510 | 120 | 63.00 | 327.00 | 0.00 | 39.30 | 39.30 |
| 511 | 120 | 63.00 | 328.00 | 0.00 | 39.42 | 39.42 |
| 512 | 120 | 63.00 | 329.00 | 0.00 | 39.54 | 39.54 |
| 513 | 120 | 63.00 | 330.00 | 0.00 | 39.66 | 39.66 |
| 514 | 120 | 63.00 | 331.00 | 0.00 | 39.78 | 39.78 |
| 515 | 120 | 63.00 | 332.00 | 0.00 | 39.90 | 39.90 |
| 516 | 120 | 63.00 | 333.00 | 0.00 | 40.02 | 40.02 |
| 517 | 120 | 63.00 | 334.00 | 0.00 | 40.14 | 40.14 |
| 518 | 120 | 63.00 | 335.00 | 0.00 | 40.26 | 40.26 |
| 519 | 120 | 63.00 | 336.00 | 0.00 | 40.38 | 40.38 |
| 520 | 120 | 63.00 | 337.00 | 0.00 | 40.50 | 40.50 |
| 521 | 120 | 63.00 | 338.00 | 0.00 | 40.62 | 40.62 |
| 522 | 120 | 63.00 | 339.00 | 0.00 | 40.74 | 40.74 |
| 523 | 120 | 63.00 | 340.00 | 0.00 | 40.86 | 40.86 |
| 524 | 120 | 63.00 | 341.00 | 0.00 | 40.98 | 40.98 |
| 525 | 120 | 63.00 | 342.00 | 0.00 | 41.10 | 41.10 |
| 526 | 120 | 63.00 | 343.00 | 0.00 | 41.22 | 41.22 |
| 527 | 120 | 63.00 | 344.00 | 0.00 | 41.34 | 41.34 |
| 528 | 120 | 63.00 | 345.00 | 0.00 | 41.46 | 41.46 |
| 529 | 120 | 63.00 | 346.00 | 0.00 | 41.58 | 41.58 |

## Table letter H

**Weekly table**

| Employee's earnings up to and including the UEL | Earnings at the LEL (where earnings are equal to or exceed the LEL) | Earnings above the LEL, up to and including the PT | Earnings above the PT, up to and including the UEL | Employer's NICs due on all earnings above the ST | Employee's NICs due on all earnings above the PT | Total of employee's and employer's NICs (for information only) |
|---|---|---|---|---|---|---|
| | 1a | 1b | 1c | 1d | 1e | |
| £ | £ | £ p | £ p | £ p | £ p | £ p |
| 530 | 120 | 63.00 | 347.00 | 0.00 | 41.70 | 41.70 |
| 531 | 120 | 63.00 | 348.00 | 0.00 | 41.82 | 41.82 |
| 532 | 120 | 63.00 | 349.00 | 0.00 | 41.94 | 41.94 |
| 533 | 120 | 63.00 | 350.00 | 0.00 | 42.06 | 42.06 |
| 534 | 120 | 63.00 | 351.00 | 0.00 | 42.18 | 42.18 |
| 535 | 120 | 63.00 | 352.00 | 0.00 | 42.30 | 42.30 |
| 536 | 120 | 63.00 | 353.00 | 0.00 | 42.42 | 42.42 |
| 537 | 120 | 63.00 | 354.00 | 0.00 | 42.54 | 42.54 |
| 538 | 120 | 63.00 | 355.00 | 0.00 | 42.66 | 42.66 |
| 539 | 120 | 63.00 | 356.00 | 0.00 | 42.78 | 42.78 |
| 540 | 120 | 63.00 | 357.00 | 0.00 | 42.90 | 42.90 |
| 541 | 120 | 63.00 | 358.00 | 0.00 | 43.02 | 43.02 |
| 542 | 120 | 63.00 | 359.00 | 0.00 | 43.14 | 43.14 |
| 543 | 120 | 63.00 | 360.00 | 0.00 | 43.26 | 43.26 |
| 544 | 120 | 63.00 | 361.00 | 0.00 | 43.38 | 43.38 |
| 545 | 120 | 63.00 | 362.00 | 0.00 | 43.50 | 43.50 |
| 546 | 120 | 63.00 | 363.00 | 0.00 | 43.62 | 43.62 |
| 547 | 120 | 63.00 | 364.00 | 0.00 | 43.74 | 43.74 |
| 548 | 120 | 63.00 | 365.00 | 0.00 | 43.86 | 43.86 |
| 549 | 120 | 63.00 | 366.00 | 0.00 | 43.98 | 43.98 |
| 550 | 120 | 63.00 | 367.00 | 0.00 | 44.10 | 44.10 |
| 551 | 120 | 63.00 | 368.00 | 0.00 | 44.22 | 44.22 |
| 552 | 120 | 63.00 | 369.00 | 0.00 | 44.34 | 44.34 |
| 553 | 120 | 63.00 | 370.00 | 0.00 | 44.46 | 44.46 |
| 554 | 120 | 63.00 | 371.00 | 0.00 | 44.58 | 44.58 |
| 555 | 120 | 63.00 | 372.00 | 0.00 | 44.70 | 44.70 |
| 556 | 120 | 63.00 | 373.00 | 0.00 | 44.82 | 44.82 |
| 557 | 120 | 63.00 | 374.00 | 0.00 | 44.94 | 44.94 |
| 558 | 120 | 63.00 | 375.00 | 0.00 | 45.06 | 45.06 |
| 559 | 120 | 63.00 | 376.00 | 0.00 | 45.18 | 45.18 |
| 560 | 120 | 63.00 | 377.00 | 0.00 | 45.30 | 45.30 |
| 561 | 120 | 63.00 | 378.00 | 0.00 | 45.42 | 45.42 |
| 562 | 120 | 63.00 | 379.00 | 0.00 | 45.54 | 45.54 |
| 563 | 120 | 63.00 | 380.00 | 0.00 | 45.66 | 45.66 |
| 564 | 120 | 63.00 | 381.00 | 0.00 | 45.78 | 45.78 |
| 565 | 120 | 63.00 | 382.00 | 0.00 | 45.90 | 45.90 |
| 566 | 120 | 63.00 | 383.00 | 0.00 | 46.02 | 46.02 |
| 567 | 120 | 63.00 | 384.00 | 0.00 | 46.14 | 46.14 |
| 568 | 120 | 63.00 | 385.00 | 0.00 | 46.26 | 46.26 |
| 569 | 120 | 63.00 | 386.00 | 0.00 | 46.38 | 46.38 |
| 570 | 120 | 63.00 | 387.00 | 0.00 | 46.50 | 46.50 |
| 571 | 120 | 63.00 | 388.00 | 0.00 | 46.62 | 46.62 |
| 572 | 120 | 63.00 | 389.00 | 0.00 | 46.74 | 46.74 |
| 573 | 120 | 63.00 | 390.00 | 0.00 | 46.86 | 46.86 |
| 574 | 120 | 63.00 | 391.00 | 0.00 | 46.98 | 46.98 |
| 575 | 120 | 63.00 | 392.00 | 0.00 | 47.10 | 47.10 |
| 576 | 120 | 63.00 | 393.00 | 0.00 | 47.22 | 47.22 |
| 577 | 120 | 63.00 | 394.00 | 0.00 | 47.34 | 47.34 |
| 578 | 120 | 63.00 | 395.00 | 0.00 | 47.46 | 47.46 |
| 579 | 120 | 63.00 | 396.00 | 0.00 | 47.58 | 47.58 |
| 580 | 120 | 63.00 | 397.00 | 0.00 | 47.70 | 47.70 |
| 581 | 120 | 63.00 | 398.00 | 0.00 | 47.82 | 47.82 |
| 582 | 120 | 63.00 | 399.00 | 0.00 | 47.94 | 47.94 |
| 583 | 120 | 63.00 | 400.00 | 0.00 | 48.06 | 48.06 |
| 584 | 120 | 63.00 | 401.00 | 0.00 | 48.18 | 48.18 |

## Weekly table

**Table letter H**

| Employee's earnings up to and including the UEL | Earnings at the LEL (where earnings are equal to or exceed the LEL) 1a | Earnings above the LEL, up to and including the PT 1b | Earnings above the PT, up to and including the UEL 1c | Employer's NICs due on all earnings above the ST 1d | Employee's NICs due on all earnings above the PT 1e | Total of employee's and employer's NICs (for information only) |
|---|---|---|---|---|---|---|
| £ | £ | £ p | £ p | £ p | £ p | £ p |
| 585 | 120 | 63.00 | 402.00 | 0.00 | 48.30 | 48.30 |
| 586 | 120 | 63.00 | 403.00 | 0.00 | 48.42 | 48.42 |
| 587 | 120 | 63.00 | 404.00 | 0.00 | 48.54 | 48.54 |
| 588 | 120 | 63.00 | 405.00 | 0.00 | 48.66 | 48.66 |
| 589 | 120 | 63.00 | 406.00 | 0.00 | 48.78 | 48.78 |
| 590 | 120 | 63.00 | 407.00 | 0.00 | 48.90 | 48.90 |
| 591 | 120 | 63.00 | 408.00 | 0.00 | 49.02 | 49.02 |
| 592 | 120 | 63.00 | 409.00 | 0.00 | 49.14 | 49.14 |
| 593 | 120 | 63.00 | 410.00 | 0.00 | 49.26 | 49.26 |
| 594 | 120 | 63.00 | 411.00 | 0.00 | 49.38 | 49.38 |
| 595 | 120 | 63.00 | 412.00 | 0.00 | 49.50 | 49.50 |
| 596 | 120 | 63.00 | 413.00 | 0.00 | 49.62 | 49.62 |
| 597 | 120 | 63.00 | 414.00 | 0.00 | 49.74 | 49.74 |
| 598 | 120 | 63.00 | 415.00 | 0.00 | 49.86 | 49.86 |
| 599 | 120 | 63.00 | 416.00 | 0.00 | 49.98 | 49.98 |
| 600 | 120 | 63.00 | 417.00 | 0.00 | 50.10 | 50.10 |
| 601 | 120 | 63.00 | 418.00 | 0.00 | 50.22 | 50.22 |
| 602 | 120 | 63.00 | 419.00 | 0.00 | 50.34 | 50.34 |
| 603 | 120 | 63.00 | 420.00 | 0.00 | 50.46 | 50.46 |
| 604 | 120 | 63.00 | 421.00 | 0.00 | 50.58 | 50.58 |
| 605 | 120 | 63.00 | 422.00 | 0.00 | 50.70 | 50.70 |
| 606 | 120 | 63.00 | 423.00 | 0.00 | 50.82 | 50.82 |
| 607 | 120 | 63.00 | 424.00 | 0.00 | 50.94 | 50.94 |
| 608 | 120 | 63.00 | 425.00 | 0.00 | 51.06 | 51.06 |
| 609 | 120 | 63.00 | 426.00 | 0.00 | 51.18 | 51.18 |
| 610 | 120 | 63.00 | 427.00 | 0.00 | 51.30 | 51.30 |
| 611 | 120 | 63.00 | 428.00 | 0.00 | 51.42 | 51.42 |
| 612 | 120 | 63.00 | 429.00 | 0.00 | 51.54 | 51.54 |
| 613 | 120 | 63.00 | 430.00 | 0.00 | 51.66 | 51.66 |
| 614 | 120 | 63.00 | 431.00 | 0.00 | 51.78 | 51.78 |
| 615 | 120 | 63.00 | 432.00 | 0.00 | 51.90 | 51.90 |
| 616 | 120 | 63.00 | 433.00 | 0.00 | 52.02 | 52.02 |
| 617 | 120 | 63.00 | 434.00 | 0.00 | 52.14 | 52.14 |
| 618 | 120 | 63.00 | 435.00 | 0.00 | 52.26 | 52.26 |
| 619 | 120 | 63.00 | 436.00 | 0.00 | 52.38 | 52.38 |
| 620 | 120 | 63.00 | 437.00 | 0.00 | 52.50 | 52.50 |
| 621 | 120 | 63.00 | 438.00 | 0.00 | 52.62 | 52.62 |
| 622 | 120 | 63.00 | 439.00 | 0.00 | 52.74 | 52.74 |
| 623 | 120 | 63.00 | 440.00 | 0.00 | 52.86 | 52.86 |
| 624 | 120 | 63.00 | 441.00 | 0.00 | 52.98 | 52.98 |
| 625 | 120 | 63.00 | 442.00 | 0.00 | 53.10 | 53.10 |
| 626 | 120 | 63.00 | 443.00 | 0.00 | 53.22 | 53.22 |
| 627 | 120 | 63.00 | 444.00 | 0.00 | 53.34 | 53.34 |
| 628 | 120 | 63.00 | 445.00 | 0.00 | 53.46 | 53.46 |
| 629 | 120 | 63.00 | 446.00 | 0.00 | 53.58 | 53.58 |
| 630 | 120 | 63.00 | 447.00 | 0.00 | 53.70 | 53.70 |
| 631 | 120 | 63.00 | 448.00 | 0.00 | 53.82 | 53.82 |
| 632 | 120 | 63.00 | 449.00 | 0.00 | 53.94 | 53.94 |
| 633 | 120 | 63.00 | 450.00 | 0.00 | 54.06 | 54.06 |
| 634 | 120 | 63.00 | 451.00 | 0.00 | 54.18 | 54.18 |
| 635 | 120 | 63.00 | 452.00 | 0.00 | 54.30 | 54.30 |
| 636 | 120 | 63.00 | 453.00 | 0.00 | 54.42 | 54.42 |
| 637 | 120 | 63.00 | 454.00 | 0.00 | 54.54 | 54.54 |
| 638 | 120 | 63.00 | 455.00 | 0.00 | 54.66 | 54.66 |
| 639 | 120 | 63.00 | 456.00 | 0.00 | 54.78 | 54.78 |

## Table letter H

**Weekly table**

| Employee's earnings up to and including the UEL | Earnings at the LEL (where earnings are equal to or exceed the LEL) | Earnings above the LEL, up to and including the PT | Earnings above the PT, up to and including the UEL | Employer's NICs due on all earnings above the ST | Employee's NICs due on all earnings above the PT | Total of employee's and employer's NICs (for information only) |
|---|---|---|---|---|---|---|
| | 1a | 1b | 1c | 1d | 1e | |
| £ | £ | £ p | £ p | £ p | £ p | £ p |
| 640 | 120 | 63.00 | 457.00 | 0.00 | 54.90 | 54.90 |
| 641 | 120 | 63.00 | 458.00 | 0.00 | 55.02 | 55.02 |
| 642 | 120 | 63.00 | 459.00 | 0.00 | 55.14 | 55.14 |
| 643 | 120 | 63.00 | 460.00 | 0.00 | 55.26 | 55.26 |
| 644 | 120 | 63.00 | 461.00 | 0.00 | 55.38 | 55.38 |
| 645 | 120 | 63.00 | 462.00 | 0.00 | 55.50 | 55.50 |
| 646 | 120 | 63.00 | 463.00 | 0.00 | 55.62 | 55.62 |
| 647 | 120 | 63.00 | 464.00 | 0.00 | 55.74 | 55.74 |
| 648 | 120 | 63.00 | 465.00 | 0.00 | 55.86 | 55.86 |
| 649 | 120 | 63.00 | 466.00 | 0.00 | 55.98 | 55.98 |
| 650 | 120 | 63.00 | 467.00 | 0.00 | 56.10 | 56.10 |
| 651 | 120 | 63.00 | 468.00 | 0.00 | 56.22 | 56.22 |
| 652 | 120 | 63.00 | 469.00 | 0.00 | 56.34 | 56.34 |
| 653 | 120 | 63.00 | 470.00 | 0.00 | 56.46 | 56.46 |
| 654 | 120 | 63.00 | 471.00 | 0.00 | 56.58 | 56.58 |
| 655 | 120 | 63.00 | 472.00 | 0.00 | 56.70 | 56.70 |
| 656 | 120 | 63.00 | 473.00 | 0.00 | 56.82 | 56.82 |
| 657 | 120 | 63.00 | 474.00 | 0.00 | 56.94 | 56.94 |
| 658 | 120 | 63.00 | 475.00 | 0.00 | 57.06 | 57.06 |
| 659 | 120 | 63.00 | 476.00 | 0.00 | 57.18 | 57.18 |
| 660 | 120 | 63.00 | 477.00 | 0.00 | 57.30 | 57.30 |
| 661 | 120 | 63.00 | 478.00 | 0.00 | 57.42 | 57.42 |
| 662 | 120 | 63.00 | 479.00 | 0.00 | 57.54 | 57.54 |
| 663 | 120 | 63.00 | 480.00 | 0.00 | 57.66 | 57.66 |
| 664 | 120 | 63.00 | 481.00 | 0.00 | 57.78 | 57.78 |
| 665 | 120 | 63.00 | 482.00 | 0.00 | 57.90 | 57.90 |
| 666 | 120 | 63.00 | 483.00 | 0.00 | 58.02 | 58.02 |
| 667 | 120 | 63.00 | 484.00 | 0.00 | 58.14 | 58.14 |
| 668 | 120 | 63.00 | 485.00 | 0.00 | 58.26 | 58.26 |
| 669 | 120 | 63.00 | 486.00 | 0.00 | 58.38 | 58.38 |
| 670 | 120 | 63.00 | 487.00 | 0.00 | 58.50 | 58.50 |
| 671 | 120 | 63.00 | 488.00 | 0.00 | 58.62 | 58.62 |
| 672 | 120 | 63.00 | 489.00 | 0.00 | 58.74 | 58.74 |
| 673 | 120 | 63.00 | 490.00 | 0.00 | 58.86 | 58.86 |
| 674 | 120 | 63.00 | 491.00 | 0.00 | 58.98 | 58.98 |
| 675 | 120 | 63.00 | 492.00 | 0.00 | 59.10 | 59.10 |
| 676 | 120 | 63.00 | 493.00 | 0.00 | 59.22 | 59.22 |
| 677 | 120 | 63.00 | 494.00 | 0.00 | 59.34 | 59.34 |
| 678 | 120 | 63.00 | 495.00 | 0.00 | 59.46 | 59.46 |
| 679 | 120 | 63.00 | 496.00 | 0.00 | 59.58 | 59.58 |
| 680 | 120 | 63.00 | 497.00 | 0.00 | 59.70 | 59.70 |
| 681 | 120 | 63.00 | 498.00 | 0.00 | 59.82 | 59.82 |
| 682 | 120 | 63.00 | 499.00 | 0.00 | 59.94 | 59.94 |
| 683 | 120 | 63.00 | 500.00 | 0.00 | 60.06 | 60.06 |
| 684 | 120 | 63.00 | 501.00 | 0.00 | 60.18 | 60.18 |
| 685 | 120 | 63.00 | 502.00 | 0.00 | 60.30 | 60.30 |
| 686 | 120 | 63.00 | 503.00 | 0.00 | 60.42 | 60.42 |
| 687 | 120 | 63.00 | 504.00 | 0.00 | 60.54 | 60.54 |
| 688 | 120 | 63.00 | 505.00 | 0.00 | 60.66 | 60.66 |
| 689 | 120 | 63.00 | 506.00 | 0.00 | 60.78 | 60.78 |
| 690 | 120 | 63.00 | 507.00 | 0.00 | 60.90 | 60.90 |
| 691 | 120 | 63.00 | 508.00 | 0.00 | 61.02 | 61.02 |
| 692 | 120 | 63.00 | 509.00 | 0.00 | 61.14 | 61.14 |
| 693 | 120 | 63.00 | 510.00 | 0.00 | 61.26 | 61.26 |
| 694 | 120 | 63.00 | 511.00 | 0.00 | 61.38 | 61.38 |

**Weekly table**

**Table letter H**

| Employee's earnings up to and including the UEL £ | Earnings at the LEL (where earnings are equal to or exceed the LEL) 1a £ | Earnings above the LEL, up to and including the PT 1b £ p | Earnings above the PT, up to and including the UEL 1c £ p | Employer's NICs due on all earnings above the ST 1d £ p | Employee's NICs due on all earnings above the PT 1e £ p | Total of employee's and employer's NICs (for information only) £ p |
|---|---|---|---|---|---|---|
| 695 | 120 | 63.00 | 512.00 | 0.00 | 61.50 | 61.50 |
| 696 | 120 | 63.00 | 513.00 | 0.00 | 61.62 | 61.62 |
| 697 | 120 | 63.00 | 514.00 | 0.00 | 61.74 | 61.74 |
| 698 | 120 | 63.00 | 515.00 | 0.00 | 61.86 | 61.86 |
| 699 | 120 | 63.00 | 516.00 | 0.00 | 61.98 | 61.98 |
| 700 | 120 | 63.00 | 517.00 | 0.00 | 62.10 | 62.10 |
| 701 | 120 | 63.00 | 518.00 | 0.00 | 62.22 | 62.22 |
| 702 | 120 | 63.00 | 519.00 | 0.00 | 62.34 | 62.34 |
| 703 | 120 | 63.00 | 520.00 | 0.00 | 62.46 | 62.46 |
| 704 | 120 | 63.00 | 521.00 | 0.00 | 62.58 | 62.58 |
| 705 | 120 | 63.00 | 522.00 | 0.00 | 62.70 | 62.70 |
| 706 | 120 | 63.00 | 523.00 | 0.00 | 62.82 | 62.82 |
| 707 | 120 | 63.00 | 524.00 | 0.00 | 62.94 | 62.94 |
| 708 | 120 | 63.00 | 525.00 | 0.00 | 63.06 | 63.06 |
| 709 | 120 | 63.00 | 526.00 | 0.00 | 63.18 | 63.18 |
| 710 | 120 | 63.00 | 527.00 | 0.00 | 63.30 | 63.30 |
| 711 | 120 | 63.00 | 528.00 | 0.00 | 63.42 | 63.42 |
| 712 | 120 | 63.00 | 529.00 | 0.00 | 63.54 | 63.54 |
| 713 | 120 | 63.00 | 530.00 | 0.00 | 63.66 | 63.66 |
| 714 | 120 | 63.00 | 531.00 | 0.00 | 63.78 | 63.78 |
| 715 | 120 | 63.00 | 532.00 | 0.00 | 63.90 | 63.90 |
| 716 | 120 | 63.00 | 533.00 | 0.00 | 64.02 | 64.02 |
| 717 | 120 | 63.00 | 534.00 | 0.00 | 64.14 | 64.14 |
| 718 | 120 | 63.00 | 535.00 | 0.00 | 64.26 | 64.26 |
| 719 | 120 | 63.00 | 536.00 | 0.00 | 64.38 | 64.38 |
| 720 | 120 | 63.00 | 537.00 | 0.00 | 64.50 | 64.50 |
| 721 | 120 | 63.00 | 538.00 | 0.00 | 64.62 | 64.62 |
| 722 | 120 | 63.00 | 539.00 | 0.00 | 64.74 | 64.74 |
| 723 | 120 | 63.00 | 540.00 | 0.00 | 64.86 | 64.86 |
| 724 | 120 | 63.00 | 541.00 | 0.00 | 64.98 | 64.98 |
| 725 | 120 | 63.00 | 542.00 | 0.00 | 65.10 | 65.10 |
| 726 | 120 | 63.00 | 543.00 | 0.00 | 65.22 | 65.22 |
| 727 | 120 | 63.00 | 544.00 | 0.00 | 65.34 | 65.34 |
| 728 | 120 | 63.00 | 545.00 | 0.00 | 65.46 | 65.46 |
| 729 | 120 | 63.00 | 546.00 | 0.00 | 65.58 | 65.58 |
| 730 | 120 | 63.00 | 547.00 | 0.00 | 65.70 | 65.70 |
| 731 | 120 | 63.00 | 548.00 | 0.00 | 65.82 | 65.82 |
| 732 | 120 | 63.00 | 549.00 | 0.00 | 65.94 | 65.94 |
| 733 | 120 | 63.00 | 550.00 | 0.00 | 66.06 | 66.06 |
| 734 | 120 | 63.00 | 551.00 | 0.00 | 66.18 | 66.18 |
| 735 | 120 | 63.00 | 552.00 | 0.00 | 66.30 | 66.30 |
| 736 | 120 | 63.00 | 553.00 | 0.00 | 66.42 | 66.42 |
| 737 | 120 | 63.00 | 554.00 | 0.00 | 66.54 | 66.54 |
| 738 | 120 | 63.00 | 555.00 | 0.00 | 66.66 | 66.66 |
| 739 | 120 | 63.00 | 556.00 | 0.00 | 66.78 | 66.78 |
| 740 | 120 | 63.00 | 557.00 | 0.00 | 66.90 | 66.90 |
| 741 | 120 | 63.00 | 558.00 | 0.00 | 67.02 | 67.02 |
| 742 | 120 | 63.00 | 559.00 | 0.00 | 67.14 | 67.14 |
| 743 | 120 | 63.00 | 560.00 | 0.00 | 67.26 | 67.26 |
| 744 | 120 | 63.00 | 561.00 | 0.00 | 67.38 | 67.38 |
| 745 | 120 | 63.00 | 562.00 | 0.00 | 67.50 | 67.50 |
| 746 | 120 | 63.00 | 563.00 | 0.00 | 67.62 | 67.62 |
| 747 | 120 | 63.00 | 564.00 | 0.00 | 67.74 | 67.74 |
| 748 | 120 | 63.00 | 565.00 | 0.00 | 67.86 | 67.86 |
| 749 | 120 | 63.00 | 566.00 | 0.00 | 67.98 | 67.98 |

## Table letter H

**Weekly table**

| Employee's earnings up to and including the UEL | Earnings at the LEL (where earnings are equal to or exceed the LEL) 1a | Earnings above the LEL, up to and including the PT 1b | Earnings above the PT, up to and including the UEL 1c | Employer's NICs due on all earnings above the ST 1d | Employee's NICs due on all earnings above the PT 1e | Total of employee's and employer's NICs (for information only) |
|---|---|---|---|---|---|---|
| £ | £ | £ p | £ p | £ p | £ p | £ p |
| 750 | 120 | 63.00 | 567.00 | 0.00 | 68.10 | 68.10 |
| 751 | 120 | 63.00 | 568.00 | 0.00 | 68.22 | 68.22 |
| 752 | 120 | 63.00 | 569.00 | 0.00 | 68.34 | 68.34 |
| 753 | 120 | 63.00 | 570.00 | 0.00 | 68.46 | 68.46 |
| 754 | 120 | 63.00 | 571.00 | 0.00 | 68.58 | 68.58 |
| 755 | 120 | 63.00 | 572.00 | 0.00 | 68.70 | 68.70 |
| 756 | 120 | 63.00 | 573.00 | 0.00 | 68.82 | 68.82 |
| 757 | 120 | 63.00 | 574.00 | 0.00 | 68.94 | 68.94 |
| 758 | 120 | 63.00 | 575.00 | 0.00 | 69.06 | 69.06 |
| 759 | 120 | 63.00 | 576.00 | 0.00 | 69.18 | 69.18 |
| 760 | 120 | 63.00 | 577.00 | 0.00 | 69.30 | 69.30 |
| 761 | 120 | 63.00 | 578.00 | 0.00 | 69.42 | 69.42 |
| 762 | 120 | 63.00 | 579.00 | 0.00 | 69.54 | 69.54 |
| 763 | 120 | 63.00 | 580.00 | 0.00 | 69.66 | 69.66 |
| 764 | 120 | 63.00 | 581.00 | 0.00 | 69.78 | 69.78 |
| 765 | 120 | 63.00 | 582.00 | 0.00 | 69.90 | 69.90 |
| 766 | 120 | 63.00 | 583.00 | 0.00 | 70.02 | 70.02 |
| 767 | 120 | 63.00 | 584.00 | 0.00 | 70.14 | 70.14 |
| 768 | 120 | 63.00 | 585.00 | 0.00 | 70.26 | 70.26 |
| 769 | 120 | 63.00 | 586.00 | 0.00 | 70.38 | 70.38 |
| 770 | 120 | 63.00 | 587.00 | 0.00 | 70.50 | 70.50 |
| 771 | 120 | 63.00 | 588.00 | 0.00 | 70.62 | 70.62 |
| 772 | 120 | 63.00 | 589.00 | 0.00 | 70.74 | 70.74 |
| 773 | 120 | 63.00 | 590.00 | 0.00 | 70.86 | 70.86 |
| 774 | 120 | 63.00 | 591.00 | 0.00 | 70.98 | 70.98 |
| 775 | 120 | 63.00 | 592.00 | 0.00 | 71.10 | 71.10 |
| 776 | 120 | 63.00 | 593.00 | 0.00 | 71.22 | 71.22 |
| 777 | 120 | 63.00 | 594.00 | 0.00 | 71.34 | 71.34 |
| 778 | 120 | 63.00 | 595.00 | 0.00 | 71.46 | 71.46 |
| 779 | 120 | 63.00 | 596.00 | 0.00 | 71.58 | 71.58 |
| 780 | 120 | 63.00 | 597.00 | 0.00 | 71.70 | 71.70 |
| 781 | 120 | 63.00 | 598.00 | 0.00 | 71.82 | 71.82 |
| 782 | 120 | 63.00 | 599.00 | 0.00 | 71.94 | 71.94 |
| 783 | 120 | 63.00 | 600.00 | 0.00 | 72.06 | 72.06 |
| 784 | 120 | 63.00 | 601.00 | 0.00 | 72.18 | 72.18 |
| 785 | 120 | 63.00 | 602.00 | 0.00 | 72.30 | 72.30 |
| 786 | 120 | 63.00 | 603.00 | 0.00 | 72.42 | 72.42 |
| 787 | 120 | 63.00 | 604.00 | 0.00 | 72.54 | 72.54 |
| 788 | 120 | 63.00 | 605.00 | 0.00 | 72.66 | 72.66 |
| 789 | 120 | 63.00 | 606.00 | 0.00 | 72.78 | 72.78 |
| 790 | 120 | 63.00 | 607.00 | 0.00 | 72.90 | 72.90 |
| 791 | 120 | 63.00 | 608.00 | 0.00 | 73.02 | 73.02 |
| 792 | 120 | 63.00 | 609.00 | 0.00 | 73.14 | 73.14 |
| 793 | 120 | 63.00 | 610.00 | 0.00 | 73.26 | 73.26 |
| 794 | 120 | 63.00 | 611.00 | 0.00 | 73.38 | 73.38 |
| 795 | 120 | 63.00 | 612.00 | 0.00 | 73.50 | 73.50 |
| 796 | 120 | 63.00 | 613.00 | 0.00 | 73.62 | 73.62 |
| 797 | 120 | 63.00 | 614.00 | 0.00 | 73.74 | 73.74 |
| 798 | 120 | 63.00 | 615.00 | 0.00 | 73.86 | 73.86 |
| 799 | 120 | 63.00 | 616.00 | 0.00 | 73.98 | 73.98 |
| 800 | 120 | 63.00 | 617.00 | 0.00 | 74.10 | 74.10 |
| 801 | 120 | 63.00 | 618.00 | 0.00 | 74.22 | 74.22 |
| 802 | 120 | 63.00 | 619.00 | 0.00 | 74.34 | 74.34 |
| 803 | 120 | 63.00 | 620.00 | 0.00 | 74.46 | 74.46 |
| 804 | 120 | 63.00 | 621.00 | 0.00 | 74.58 | 74.58 |

**Table letter H**  **Weekly table**

| Employee's earnings up to and including the UEL | Earnings at the LEL (where earnings are equal to or exceed the LEL) 1a | Earnings above the LEL, up to and including the PT 1b | Earnings above the PT, up to and including the UEL 1c | Employer's NICs due on all earnings above the ST 1d | Employee's NICs due on all earnings above the PT 1e | Total of employee's and employer's NICs (for information only) |
|---|---|---|---|---|---|---|
| £ | £ | £ p | £ p | £ p | £ p | £ p |
| 805 | 120 | 63.00 | 622.00 | 0.00 | 74.70 | 74.70 |
| 806 | 120 | 63.00 | 623.00 | 0.00 | 74.82 | 74.82 |
| 807 | 120 | 63.00 | 624.00 | 0.00 | 74.94 | 74.94 |
| 808 | 120 | 63.00 | 625.00 | 0.00 | 75.06 | 75.06 |
| 809 | 120 | 63.00 | 626.00 | 0.00 | 75.18 | 75.18 |
| 810 | 120 | 63.00 | 627.00 | 0.00 | 75.30 | 75.30 |
| 811 | 120 | 63.00 | 628.00 | 0.00 | 75.42 | 75.42 |
| 812 | 120 | 63.00 | 629.00 | 0.00 | 75.54 | 75.54 |
| 813 | 120 | 63.00 | 630.00 | 0.00 | 75.66 | 75.66 |
| 814 | 120 | 63.00 | 631.00 | 0.00 | 75.78 | 75.78 |
| 815 | 120 | 63.00 | 632.00 | 0.00 | 75.90 | 75.90 |
| 816 | 120 | 63.00 | 633.00 | 0.00 | 76.02 | 76.02 |
| 817 | 120 | 63.00 | 634.00 | 0.00 | 76.14 | 76.14 |
| 818 | 120 | 63.00 | 635.00 | 0.00 | 76.26 | 76.26 |
| 819 | 120 | 63.00 | 636.00 | 0.00 | 76.38 | 76.38 |
| 820 | 120 | 63.00 | 637.00 | 0.00 | 76.50 | 76.50 |
| 821 | 120 | 63.00 | 638.00 | 0.00 | 76.62 | 76.62 |
| 822 | 120 | 63.00 | 639.00 | 0.00 | 76.74 | 76.74 |
| 823 | 120 | 63.00 | 640.00 | 0.00 | 76.86 | 76.86 |
| 824 | 120 | 63.00 | 641.00 | 0.00 | 76.98 | 76.98 |
| 825 | 120 | 63.00 | 642.00 | 0.00 | 77.10 | 77.10 |
| 826 | 120 | 63.00 | 643.00 | 0.00 | 77.22 | 77.22 |
| 827 | 120 | 63.00 | 644.00 | 0.00 | 77.34 | 77.34 |
| 828 | 120 | 63.00 | 645.00 | 0.00 | 77.46 | 77.46 |
| 829 | 120 | 63.00 | 646.00 | 0.00 | 77.58 | 77.58 |
| 830 | 120 | 63.00 | 647.00 | 0.00 | 77.70 | 77.70 |
| 831 | 120 | 63.00 | 648.00 | 0.00 | 77.82 | 77.82 |
| 832 | 120 | 63.00 | 649.00 | 0.00 | 77.94 | 77.94 |
| 833 | 120 | 63.00 | 650.00 | 0.00 | 78.06 | 78.06 |
| 834 | 120 | 63.00 | 651.00 | 0.00 | 78.18 | 78.18 |
| 835 | 120 | 63.00 | 652.00 | 0.00 | 78.30 | 78.30 |
| 836 | 120 | 63.00 | 653.00 | 0.00 | 78.42 | 78.42 |
| 837 | 120 | 63.00 | 654.00 | 0.00 | 78.54 | 78.54 |
| 838 | 120 | 63.00 | 655.00 | 0.00 | 78.66 | 78.66 |
| 839 | 120 | 63.00 | 656.00 | 0.00 | 78.78 | 78.78 |
| 840 | 120 | 63.00 | 657.00 | 0.00 | 78.90 | 78.90 |
| 841 | 120 | 63.00 | 658.00 | 0.00 | 79.02 | 79.02 |
| 842 | 120 | 63.00 | 659.00 | 0.00 | 79.14 | 79.14 |
| 843 | 120 | 63.00 | 660.00 | 0.00 | 79.26 | 79.26 |
| 844 | 120 | 63.00 | 661.00 | 0.00 | 79.38 | 79.38 |
| 845 | 120 | 63.00 | 662.00 | 0.00 | 79.50 | 79.50 |
| 846 | 120 | 63.00 | 663.00 | 0.00 | 79.62 | 79.62 |
| 847 | 120 | 63.00 | 664.00 | 0.00 | 79.74 | 79.74 |
| 848 | 120 | 63.00 | 665.00 | 0.00 | 79.86 | 79.86 |
| 849 | 120 | 63.00 | 666.00 | 0.00 | 79.98 | 79.98 |
| 850 | 120 | 63.00 | 667.00 | 0.00 | 80.10 | 80.10 |
| 851 | 120 | 63.00 | 668.00 | 0.00 | 80.22 | 80.22 |
| 852 | 120 | 63.00 | 669.00 | 0.00 | 80.34 | 80.34 |
| 853 | 120 | 63.00 | 670.00 | 0.00 | 80.46 | 80.46 |
| 854 | 120 | 63.00 | 671.00 | 0.00 | 80.58 | 80.58 |
| 855 | 120 | 63.00 | 672.00 | 0.00 | 80.70 | 80.70 |
| 856 | 120 | 63.00 | 673.00 | 0.00 | 80.82 | 80.82 |
| 857 | 120 | 63.00 | 674.00 | 0.00 | 80.94 | 80.94 |
| 858 | 120 | 63.00 | 675.00 | 0.00 | 81.06 | 81.06 |
| 859 | 120 | 63.00 | 676.00 | 0.00 | 81.18 | 81.18 |

## Weekly table

**Table letter H**

| Employee's earnings up to and including the UEL | Earnings at the LEL (where earnings are equal to or exceed the LEL) | Earnings above the LEL, up to and including the PT | Earnings above the PT, up to and including the UEL | Employer's NICs due on all earnings above the ST | Employee's NICs due on all earnings above the PT | Total of employee's and employer's NICs (for information only) |
|---|---|---|---|---|---|---|
| | | 1a | 1b | 1c | 1d | 1e |
| £ | £ | £ p | £ p | £ p | £ p | £ p |
| 860 | 120 | 63.00 | 677.00 | 0.00 | 81.30 | 81.30 |
| 861 | 120 | 63.00 | 678.00 | 0.00 | 81.42 | 81.42 |
| 862 | 120 | 63.00 | 679.00 | 0.00 | 81.54 | 81.54 |
| 863 | 120 | 63.00 | 680.00 | 0.00 | 81.66 | 81.66 |
| 864 | 120 | 63.00 | 681.00 | 0.00 | 81.78 | 81.78 |
| 865 | 120 | 63.00 | 682.00 | 0.00 | 81.90 | 81.90 |
| 866 | 120 | 63.00 | 683.00 | 0.00 | 82.02 | 82.02 |
| 867 | 120 | 63.00 | 684.00 | 0.00 | 82.14 | 82.14 |
| 868 | 120 | 63.00 | 685.00 | 0.00 | 82.26 | 82.26 |
| 869 | 120 | 63.00 | 686.00 | 0.00 | 82.38 | 82.38 |
| 870 | 120 | 63.00 | 687.00 | 0.00 | 82.50 | 82.50 |
| 871 | 120 | 63.00 | 688.00 | 0.00 | 82.62 | 82.62 |
| 872 | 120 | 63.00 | 689.00 | 0.00 | 82.74 | 82.74 |
| 873 | 120 | 63.00 | 690.00 | 0.00 | 82.86 | 82.86 |
| 874 | 120 | 63.00 | 691.00 | 0.00 | 82.98 | 82.98 |
| 875 | 120 | 63.00 | 692.00 | 0.00 | 83.10 | 83.10 |
| 876 | 120 | 63.00 | 693.00 | 0.00 | 83.22 | 83.22 |
| 877 | 120 | 63.00 | 694.00 | 0.00 | 83.34 | 83.34 |
| 878 | 120 | 63.00 | 695.00 | 0.00 | 83.46 | 83.46 |
| 879 | 120 | 63.00 | 696.00 | 0.00 | 83.58 | 83.58 |
| 880 | 120 | 63.00 | 697.00 | 0.00 | 83.70 | 83.70 |
| 881 | 120 | 63.00 | 698.00 | 0.00 | 83.82 | 83.82 |
| 882 | 120 | 63.00 | 699.00 | 0.00 | 83.94 | 83.94 |
| 883 | 120 | 63.00 | 700.00 | 0.00 | 84.06 | 84.06 |
| 884 | 120 | 63.00 | 701.00 | 0.00 | 84.18 | 84.18 |
| 885 | 120 | 63.00 | 702.00 | 0.00 | 84.30 | 84.30 |
| 886 | 120 | 63.00 | 703.00 | 0.00 | 84.42 | 84.42 |
| 887 | 120 | 63.00 | 704.00 | 0.00 | 84.54 | 84.54 |
| 888 | 120 | 63.00 | 705.00 | 0.00 | 84.66 | 84.66 |
| 889 | 120 | 63.00 | 706.00 | 0.00 | 84.78 | 84.78 |
| 890 | 120 | 63.00 | 707.00 | 0.00 | 84.90 | 84.90 |
| 891 | 120 | 63.00 | 708.00 | 0.00 | 85.02 | 85.02 |
| 892 | 120 | 63.00 | 709.00 | 0.00 | 85.14 | 85.14 |
| 893 | 120 | 63.00 | 710.00 | 0.00 | 85.26 | 85.26 |
| 894 | 120 | 63.00 | 711.00 | 0.00 | 85.38 | 85.38 |
| 895 | 120 | 63.00 | 712.00 | 0.00 | 85.50 | 85.50 |
| 896 | 120 | 63.00 | 713.00 | 0.00 | 85.62 | 85.62 |
| 897 | 120 | 63.00 | 714.00 | 0.00 | 85.74 | 85.74 |
| 898 | 120 | 63.00 | 715.00 | 0.00 | 85.86 | 85.86 |
| 899 | 120 | 63.00 | 716.00 | 0.00 | 85.98 | 85.98 |
| 900 | 120 | 63.00 | 717.00 | 0.00 | 86.10 | 86.10 |
| 901 | 120 | 63.00 | 718.00 | 0.00 | 86.22 | 86.22 |
| 902 | 120 | 63.00 | 719.00 | 0.00 | 86.34 | 86.34 |
| 903 | 120 | 63.00 | 720.00 | 0.00 | 86.46 | 86.46 |
| 904 | 120 | 63.00 | 721.00 | 0.00 | 86.58 | 86.58 |
| 905 | 120 | 63.00 | 722.00 | 0.00 | 86.70 | 86.70 |
| 906 | 120 | 63.00 | 723.00 | 0.00 | 86.82 | 86.82 |
| 907 | 120 | 63.00 | 724.00 | 0.00 | 86.94 | 86.94 |
| 908 | 120 | 63.00 | 725.00 | 0.00 | 87.06 | 87.06 |
| 909 | 120 | 63.00 | 726.00 | 0.00 | 87.18 | 87.18 |
| 910 | 120 | 63.00 | 727.00 | 0.00 | 87.30 | 87.30 |
| 911 | 120 | 63.00 | 728.00 | 0.00 | 87.42 | 87.42 |
| 912 | 120 | 63.00 | 729.00 | 0.00 | 87.54 | 87.54 |
| 913 | 120 | 63.00 | 730.00 | 0.00 | 87.66 | 87.66 |
| 914 | 120 | 63.00 | 731.00 | 0.00 | 87.78 | 87.78 |

**Weekly table**

**Table letter H**

| Employee's earnings up to and including the UEL | Earnings at the LEL (where earnings are equal to or exceed the LEL) | Earnings above the LEL, up to and including the PT | Earnings above the PT, up to and including the UEL | Employer's NICs due on all earnings above the ST | Employee's NICs due on all earnings above the PT | Total of employee's and employer's NICs (for information only) |
|---|---|---|---|---|---|---|
| | 1a | 1b | 1c | 1d | 1e | |
| £ | £ | £ p | £ p | £ p | £ p | £ p |
| 915 | 120 | 63.00 | 732.00 | 0.00 | 87.90 | 87.90 |
| 916 | 120 | 63.00 | 733.00 | 0.00 | 88.02 | 88.02 |
| 917 | 120 | 63.00 | 734.00 | 0.00 | 88.14 | 88.14 |
| 918 | 120 | 63.00 | 735.00 | 0.00 | 88.26 | 88.26 |
| 919 | 120 | 63.00 | 736.00 | 0.00 | 88.38 | 88.38 |
| 920 | 120 | 63.00 | 737.00 | 0.00 | 88.50 | 88.50 |
| 921 | 120 | 63.00 | 738.00 | 0.00 | 88.62 | 88.62 |
| 922 | 120 | 63.00 | 739.00 | 0.00 | 88.74 | 88.74 |
| 923 | 120 | 63.00 | 740.00 | 0.00 | 88.86 | 88.86 |
| 924 | 120 | 63.00 | 741.00 | 0.00 | 88.98 | 88.98 |
| 925 | 120 | 63.00 | 742.00 | 0.00 | 89.10 | 89.10 |
| 926 | 120 | 63.00 | 743.00 | 0.00 | 89.22 | 89.22 |
| 927 | 120 | 63.00 | 744.00 | 0.00 | 89.34 | 89.34 |
| 928 | 120 | 63.00 | 745.00 | 0.00 | 89.46 | 89.46 |
| 929 | 120 | 63.00 | 746.00 | 0.00 | 89.58 | 89.58 |
| 930 | 120 | 63.00 | 747.00 | 0.00 | 89.70 | 89.70 |
| 931 | 120 | 63.00 | 748.00 | 0.00 | 89.82 | 89.82 |
| 932 | 120 | 63.00 | 749.00 | 0.00 | 89.94 | 89.94 |
| 933 | 120 | 63.00 | 750.00 | 0.00 | 90.06 | 90.06 |
| 934 | 120 | 63.00 | 751.00 | 0.00 | 90.18 | 90.18 |
| 935 | 120 | 63.00 | 752.00 | 0.00 | 90.30 | 90.30 |
| 936 | 120 | 63.00 | 753.00 | 0.00 | 90.42 | 90.42 |
| 937 | 120 | 63.00 | 754.00 | 0.00 | 90.54 | 90.54 |
| 938 | 120 | 63.00 | 755.00 | 0.00 | 90.66 | 90.66 |
| 939 | 120 | 63.00 | 756.00 | 0.00 | 90.78 | 90.78 |
| 940 | 120 | 63.00 | 757.00 | 0.00 | 90.90 | 90.90 |
| 941 | 120 | 63.00 | 758.00 | 0.00 | 91.02 | 91.02 |
| 942 | 120 | 63.00 | 759.00 | 0.00 | 91.14 | 91.14 |
| 943 | 120 | 63.00 | 760.00 | 0.00 | 91.26 | 91.26 |
| 944 | 120 | 63.00 | 761.00 | 0.00 | 91.38 | 91.38 |
| 945 | 120 | 63.00 | 762.00 | 0.00 | 91.50 | 91.50 |
| 946 | 120 | 63.00 | 763.00 | 0.00 | 91.62 | 91.62 |
| 947 | 120 | 63.00 | 764.00 | 0.00 | 91.74 | 91.74 |
| 948 | 120 | 63.00 | 765.00 | 0.00 | 91.86 | 91.86 |
| 949 | 120 | 63.00 | 766.00 | 0.00 | 91.98 | 91.98 |
| 950 | 120 | 63.00 | 767.00 | 0.00 | 92.10 | 92.10 |
| 951 | 120 | 63.00 | 768.00 | 0.00 | 92.22 | 92.22 |
| 952 | 120 | 63.00 | 769.00 | 0.00 | 92.34 | 92.34 |
| 953 | 120 | 63.00 | 770.00 | 0.00 | 92.46 | 92.46 |
| 954 | 120 | 63.00 | 771.00 | 0.00 | 92.58 | 92.58 |
| 955 | 120 | 63.00 | 772.00 | 0.00 | 92.70 | 92.70 |
| 956 | 120 | 63.00 | 773.00 | 0.00 | 92.82 | 92.82 |
| 957 | 120 | 63.00 | 774.00 | 0.00 | 92.94 | 92.94 |
| 958 | 120 | 63.00 | 775.00 | 0.00 | 93.06 | 93.06 |
| 959 | 120 | 63.00 | 776.00 | 0.00 | 93.18 | 93.18 |
| 960 | 120 | 63.00 | 777.00 | 0.00 | 93.30 | 93.30 |
| 961 | 120 | 63.00 | 778.00 | 0.00 | 93.42 | 93.42 |
| 962 | 120 | 63.00 | 779.00 | 0.00 | 93.48 | 93.48 |

If the employee's gross pay is over £962, go to page 178.

# Monthly table for standard rate NICs for use from 6 April 2020 to 5 April 2021

**Table letter H**

Use this table for employees who are apprentices on an Approved Apprenticeship scheme and aged under 25.

Do not use this table for:

- any tax year other than 2020 to 2021
- employees who are under the age of 21 unless they are on an Approved Apprenticeship scheme (go to Table letter M)
- married women or widows who have the right to pay reduced rate employee's NICs (go to Table letter B in booklet CA41)
- employees who are State Pension age or over (go to Table letter C in booklet CA41)
- employees who are aged 21 or over, for whom you hold form CA2700 (go to Table letter J)
- employees who are under the age of 21, for whom you hold form CA2700 (go to Table letter Z)

**Completing form RT11, 'Deductions working sheet' or substitute**

1 Enter 'H' in the NICs Category Letter column on form RT11.

2 Copy the figures in columns 1a – 1e of the table to columns 1a – 1e on the line next to the tax month in which the employee is paid, on form RT11.

If the employee's total earnings fall between the LEL and the UEL/UST/AUST and the exact gross pay is not shown in the table, use the next smaller figure shown. If the employee's total earnings exceed the UEL/UST/AUST, go to page 163.

The figures in the left-hand column of each table show steps between the LEL and the UEL/UST/AUST. The NICs liability for each step, with the exception of the LEL, ST, PT, UEL and UST and AUST, is worked out at the mid-point of the steps so you and your employee may pay slightly more or less than if you used the exact percentage method.

| Employee's earnings up to and including the UEL | Earnings at the LEL (where earnings are equal to or exceed the LEL) | Earnings above the LEL, up to and including the PT | Earnings above the PT, up to and including the UEL | Employer's NICs due on all earnings above the ST | Employee's NICs due on all earnings above the PT | Total of employee's and employer's NICs (for information only) |
|---|---|---|---|---|---|---|
| | 1a | 1b | 1c | 1d | 1e | |
| £ | £ | £ p | £ p | £ p | £ p | £ p |
| Up to and including £519.99 | No NICs liability, make no entries on form RT11 | | | | | |
| 520 | 520 | 0.00 | 0.00 | 0.00 | 0.00 | 0.00 |
| 524 | 520 | 4.00 | 0.00 | 0.00 | 0.00 | 0.00 |
| 528 | 520 | 8.00 | 0.00 | 0.00 | 0.00 | 0.00 |
| 532 | 520 | 12.00 | 0.00 | 0.00 | 0.00 | 0.00 |
| 536 | 520 | 16.00 | 0.00 | 0.00 | 0.00 | 0.00 |
| 540 | 520 | 20.00 | 0.00 | 0.00 | 0.00 | 0.00 |
| 544 | 520 | 24.00 | 0.00 | 0.00 | 0.00 | 0.00 |
| 548 | 520 | 28.00 | 0.00 | 0.00 | 0.00 | 0.00 |
| 552 | 520 | 32.00 | 0.00 | 0.00 | 0.00 | 0.00 |
| 556 | 520 | 36.00 | 0.00 | 0.00 | 0.00 | 0.00 |
| 560 | 520 | 40.00 | 0.00 | 0.00 | 0.00 | 0.00 |
| 564 | 520 | 44.00 | 0.00 | 0.00 | 0.00 | 0.00 |
| 568 | 520 | 48.00 | 0.00 | 0.00 | 0.00 | 0.00 |
| 572 | 520 | 52.00 | 0.00 | 0.00 | 0.00 | 0.00 |
| 576 | 520 | 56.00 | 0.00 | 0.00 | 0.00 | 0.00 |
| 580 | 520 | 60.00 | 0.00 | 0.00 | 0.00 | 0.00 |
| 584 | 520 | 64.00 | 0.00 | 0.00 | 0.00 | 0.00 |
| 588 | 520 | 68.00 | 0.00 | 0.00 | 0.00 | 0.00 |
| 592 | 520 | 72.00 | 0.00 | 0.00 | 0.00 | 0.00 |
| 596 | 520 | 76.00 | 0.00 | 0.00 | 0.00 | 0.00 |
| 600 | 520 | 80.00 | 0.00 | 0.00 | 0.00 | 0.00 |
| 604 | 520 | 84.00 | 0.00 | 0.00 | 0.00 | 0.00 |
| 608 | 520 | 88.00 | 0.00 | 0.00 | 0.00 | 0.00 |
| 612 | 520 | 92.00 | 0.00 | 0.00 | 0.00 | 0.00 |
| 616 | 520 | 96.00 | 0.00 | 0.00 | 0.00 | 0.00 |

Page 58

**Monthly table**                                                                     **Table letter H**

| Employee's earnings up to and including the UEL | Earnings at the LEL (where earnings are equal to or exceed the LEL) | Earnings above the LEL, up to and including the PT | Earnings above the PT, up to and including the UEL | Employer's NICs due on all earnings above the ST | Employee's NICs due on all earnings above the PT | Total of employee's and employer's NICs (for information only) |
|---|---|---|---|---|---|---|
|  |  | 1a | 1b | 1c | 1d | 1e |
| £ | £ | £ p | £ p | £ p | £ p | £ p |
| 620 | 520 | 100.00 | 0.00 | 0.00 | 0.00 | 0.00 |
| 624 | 520 | 104.00 | 0.00 | 0.00 | 0.00 | 0.00 |
| 628 | 520 | 108.00 | 0.00 | 0.00 | 0.00 | 0.00 |
| 632 | 520 | 112.00 | 0.00 | 0.00 | 0.00 | 0.00 |
| 636 | 520 | 116.00 | 0.00 | 0.00 | 0.00 | 0.00 |
| 640 | 520 | 120.00 | 0.00 | 0.00 | 0.00 | 0.00 |
| 644 | 520 | 124.00 | 0.00 | 0.00 | 0.00 | 0.00 |
| 648 | 520 | 128.00 | 0.00 | 0.00 | 0.00 | 0.00 |
| 652 | 520 | 132.00 | 0.00 | 0.00 | 0.00 | 0.00 |
| 656 | 520 | 136.00 | 0.00 | 0.00 | 0.00 | 0.00 |
| 660 | 520 | 140.00 | 0.00 | 0.00 | 0.00 | 0.00 |
| 664 | 520 | 144.00 | 0.00 | 0.00 | 0.00 | 0.00 |
| 668 | 520 | 148.00 | 0.00 | 0.00 | 0.00 | 0.00 |
| 672 | 520 | 152.00 | 0.00 | 0.00 | 0.00 | 0.00 |
| 676 | 520 | 156.00 | 0.00 | 0.00 | 0.00 | 0.00 |
| 680 | 520 | 160.00 | 0.00 | 0.00 | 0.00 | 0.00 |
| 684 | 520 | 164.00 | 0.00 | 0.00 | 0.00 | 0.00 |
| 688 | 520 | 168.00 | 0.00 | 0.00 | 0.00 | 0.00 |
| 692 | 520 | 172.00 | 0.00 | 0.00 | 0.00 | 0.00 |
| 696 | 520 | 176.00 | 0.00 | 0.00 | 0.00 | 0.00 |
| 700 | 520 | 180.00 | 0.00 | 0.00 | 0.00 | 0.00 |
| 704 | 520 | 184.00 | 0.00 | 0.00 | 0.00 | 0.00 |
| 708 | 520 | 188.00 | 0.00 | 0.00 | 0.00 | 0.00 |
| 712 | 520 | 192.00 | 0.00 | 0.00 | 0.00 | 0.00 |
| 716 | 520 | 196.00 | 0.00 | 0.00 | 0.00 | 0.00 |
| 720 | 520 | 200.00 | 0.00 | 0.00 | 0.00 | 0.00 |
| 724 | 520 | 204.00 | 0.00 | 0.00 | 0.00 | 0.00 |
| 728 | 520 | 208.00 | 0.00 | 0.00 | 0.00 | 0.00 |
| 732 | 520 | 212.00 | 0.00 | 0.00 | 0.00 | 0.00 |
| 736 | 520 | 216.00 | 0.00 | 0.00 | 0.00 | 0.00 |
| 740 | 520 | 220.00 | 0.00 | 0.00 | 0.00 | 0.00 |
| 744 | 520 | 224.00 | 0.00 | 0.00 | 0.00 | 0.00 |
| 748 | 520 | 228.00 | 0.00 | 0.00 | 0.00 | 0.00 |
| 752 | 520 | 232.00 | 0.00 | 0.00 | 0.00 | 0.00 |
| 756 | 520 | 236.00 | 0.00 | 0.00 | 0.00 | 0.00 |
| 760 | 520 | 240.00 | 0.00 | 0.00 | 0.00 | 0.00 |
| 764 | 520 | 244.00 | 0.00 | 0.00 | 0.00 | 0.00 |
| 768 | 520 | 248.00 | 0.00 | 0.00 | 0.00 | 0.00 |
| 772 | 520 | 252.00 | 0.00 | 0.00 | 0.00 | 0.00 |
| 776 | 520 | 256.00 | 0.00 | 0.00 | 0.00 | 0.00 |
| 780 | 520 | 260.00 | 0.00 | 0.00 | 0.00 | 0.00 |
| 784 | 520 | 264.00 | 0.00 | 0.00 | 0.00 | 0.00 |
| 788 | 520 | 268.00 | 0.00 | 0.00 | 0.00 | 0.00 |
| 792 | 520 | 272.00 | 0.00 | 0.00 | 0.00 | 0.00 |
| 796 | 520 | 272.00 | 4.00 | 0.00 | 0.72 | 0.72 |
| 800 | 520 | 272.00 | 8.00 | 0.00 | 1.20 | 1.20 |
| 804 | 520 | 272.00 | 12.00 | 0.00 | 1.68 | 1.68 |
| 808 | 520 | 272.00 | 16.00 | 0.00 | 2.16 | 2.16 |
| 812 | 520 | 272.00 | 20.00 | 0.00 | 2.64 | 2.64 |
| 816 | 520 | 272.00 | 24.00 | 0.00 | 3.12 | 3.12 |
| 820 | 520 | 272.00 | 28.00 | 0.00 | 3.60 | 3.60 |
| 824 | 520 | 272.00 | 32.00 | 0.00 | 4.08 | 4.08 |
| 828 | 520 | 272.00 | 36.00 | 0.00 | 4.56 | 4.56 |
| 832 | 520 | 272.00 | 40.00 | 0.00 | 5.04 | 5.04 |
| 836 | 520 | 272.00 | 44.00 | 0.00 | 5.52 | 5.52 |

# Table letter H

## Monthly table

| Employee's earnings up to and including the UEL | Earnings at the LEL (where earnings are equal to or exceed the LEL) | Earnings above the LEL, up to and including the PT | Earnings above the PT, up to and including the UEL | Employer's NICs due on all earnings above the ST | Employee's NICs due on all earnings above the PT | Total of employee's and employer's NICs (for information only) |
|---|---|---|---|---|---|---|
| | 1a | 1b | 1c | 1d | 1e | |
| £ | £ | £ p | £ p | £ p | £ p | £ p |
| 840 | 520 | 272.00 | 48.00 | 0.00 | 6.00 | 6.00 |
| 844 | 520 | 272.00 | 52.00 | 0.00 | 6.48 | 6.48 |
| 848 | 520 | 272.00 | 56.00 | 0.00 | 6.96 | 6.96 |
| 852 | 520 | 272.00 | 60.00 | 0.00 | 7.44 | 7.44 |
| 856 | 520 | 272.00 | 64.00 | 0.00 | 7.92 | 7.92 |
| 860 | 520 | 272.00 | 68.00 | 0.00 | 8.40 | 8.40 |
| 864 | 520 | 272.00 | 72.00 | 0.00 | 8.88 | 8.88 |
| 868 | 520 | 272.00 | 76.00 | 0.00 | 9.36 | 9.36 |
| 872 | 520 | 272.00 | 80.00 | 0.00 | 9.84 | 9.84 |
| 876 | 520 | 272.00 | 84.00 | 0.00 | 10.32 | 10.32 |
| 880 | 520 | 272.00 | 88.00 | 0.00 | 10.80 | 10.80 |
| 884 | 520 | 272.00 | 92.00 | 0.00 | 11.28 | 11.28 |
| 888 | 520 | 272.00 | 96.00 | 0.00 | 11.76 | 11.76 |
| 892 | 520 | 272.00 | 100.00 | 0.00 | 12.24 | 12.24 |
| 896 | 520 | 272.00 | 104.00 | 0.00 | 12.72 | 12.72 |
| 900 | 520 | 272.00 | 108.00 | 0.00 | 13.20 | 13.20 |
| 904 | 520 | 272.00 | 112.00 | 0.00 | 13.68 | 13.68 |
| 908 | 520 | 272.00 | 116.00 | 0.00 | 14.16 | 14.16 |
| 912 | 520 | 272.00 | 120.00 | 0.00 | 14.64 | 14.64 |
| 916 | 520 | 272.00 | 124.00 | 0.00 | 15.12 | 15.12 |
| 920 | 520 | 272.00 | 128.00 | 0.00 | 15.60 | 15.60 |
| 924 | 520 | 272.00 | 132.00 | 0.00 | 16.08 | 16.08 |
| 928 | 520 | 272.00 | 136.00 | 0.00 | 16.56 | 16.56 |
| 932 | 520 | 272.00 | 140.00 | 0.00 | 17.04 | 17.04 |
| 936 | 520 | 272.00 | 144.00 | 0.00 | 17.52 | 17.52 |
| 940 | 520 | 272.00 | 148.00 | 0.00 | 18.00 | 18.00 |
| 944 | 520 | 272.00 | 152.00 | 0.00 | 18.48 | 18.48 |
| 948 | 520 | 272.00 | 156.00 | 0.00 | 18.96 | 18.96 |
| 952 | 520 | 272.00 | 160.00 | 0.00 | 19.44 | 19.44 |
| 956 | 520 | 272.00 | 164.00 | 0.00 | 19.92 | 19.92 |
| 960 | 520 | 272.00 | 168.00 | 0.00 | 20.40 | 20.40 |
| 964 | 520 | 272.00 | 172.00 | 0.00 | 20.88 | 20.88 |
| 968 | 520 | 272.00 | 176.00 | 0.00 | 21.36 | 21.36 |
| 972 | 520 | 272.00 | 180.00 | 0.00 | 21.84 | 21.84 |
| 976 | 520 | 272.00 | 184.00 | 0.00 | 22.32 | 22.32 |
| 980 | 520 | 272.00 | 188.00 | 0.00 | 22.80 | 22.80 |
| 984 | 520 | 272.00 | 192.00 | 0.00 | 23.28 | 23.28 |
| 988 | 520 | 272.00 | 196.00 | 0.00 | 23.76 | 23.76 |
| 992 | 520 | 272.00 | 200.00 | 0.00 | 24.24 | 24.24 |
| 996 | 520 | 272.00 | 204.00 | 0.00 | 24.72 | 24.72 |
| 1000 | 520 | 272.00 | 208.00 | 0.00 | 25.20 | 25.20 |
| 1004 | 520 | 272.00 | 212.00 | 0.00 | 25.68 | 25.68 |
| 1008 | 520 | 272.00 | 216.00 | 0.00 | 26.16 | 26.16 |
| 1012 | 520 | 272.00 | 220.00 | 0.00 | 26.64 | 26.64 |
| 1016 | 520 | 272.00 | 224.00 | 0.00 | 27.12 | 27.12 |
| 1020 | 520 | 272.00 | 228.00 | 0.00 | 27.60 | 27.60 |
| 1024 | 520 | 272.00 | 232.00 | 0.00 | 28.08 | 28.08 |
| 1028 | 520 | 272.00 | 236.00 | 0.00 | 28.56 | 28.56 |
| 1032 | 520 | 272.00 | 240.00 | 0.00 | 29.04 | 29.04 |
| 1036 | 520 | 272.00 | 244.00 | 0.00 | 29.52 | 29.52 |
| 1040 | 520 | 272.00 | 248.00 | 0.00 | 30.00 | 30.00 |
| 1044 | 520 | 272.00 | 252.00 | 0.00 | 30.48 | 30.48 |
| 1048 | 520 | 272.00 | 256.00 | 0.00 | 30.96 | 30.96 |
| 1052 | 520 | 272.00 | 260.00 | 0.00 | 31.44 | 31.44 |
| 1056 | 520 | 272.00 | 264.00 | 0.00 | 31.92 | 31.92 |

**Monthly table**                                                                              **Table letter H**

| Employee's earnings up to and including the UEL | Earnings at the LEL (where earnings are equal to or exceed the LEL) | Earnings above the LEL, up to and including the PT | Earnings above the PT, up to and including the UEL | Employer's NICs due on all earnings above the ST | Employee's NICs due on all earnings above the PT | Total of employee's and employer's NICs (for information only) |
|---|---|---|---|---|---|---|
| | **1a** | **1b** | **1c** | **1d** | **1e** | |
| **£** | **£** | **£ p** | **£ p** | **£ p** | **£ p** | **£ p** |
| 1060 | 520 | 272.00 | 268.00 | 0.00 | 32.40 | 32.40 |
| 1064 | 520 | 272.00 | 272.00 | 0.00 | 32.88 | 32.88 |
| 1068 | 520 | 272.00 | 276.00 | 0.00 | 33.36 | 33.36 |
| 1072 | 520 | 272.00 | 280.00 | 0.00 | 33.84 | 33.84 |
| 1076 | 520 | 272.00 | 284.00 | 0.00 | 34.32 | 34.32 |
| 1080 | 520 | 272.00 | 288.00 | 0.00 | 34.80 | 34.80 |
| 1084 | 520 | 272.00 | 292.00 | 0.00 | 35.28 | 35.28 |
| 1088 | 520 | 272.00 | 296.00 | 0.00 | 35.76 | 35.76 |
| 1092 | 520 | 272.00 | 300.00 | 0.00 | 36.24 | 36.24 |
| 1096 | 520 | 272.00 | 304.00 | 0.00 | 36.72 | 36.72 |
| 1100 | 520 | 272.00 | 308.00 | 0.00 | 37.20 | 37.20 |
| 1104 | 520 | 272.00 | 312.00 | 0.00 | 37.68 | 37.68 |
| 1108 | 520 | 272.00 | 316.00 | 0.00 | 38.16 | 38.16 |
| 1112 | 520 | 272.00 | 320.00 | 0.00 | 38.64 | 38.64 |
| 1116 | 520 | 272.00 | 324.00 | 0.00 | 39.12 | 39.12 |
| 1120 | 520 | 272.00 | 328.00 | 0.00 | 39.60 | 39.60 |
| 1124 | 520 | 272.00 | 332.00 | 0.00 | 40.08 | 40.08 |
| 1128 | 520 | 272.00 | 336.00 | 0.00 | 40.56 | 40.56 |
| 1132 | 520 | 272.00 | 340.00 | 0.00 | 41.04 | 41.04 |
| 1136 | 520 | 272.00 | 344.00 | 0.00 | 41.52 | 41.52 |
| 1140 | 520 | 272.00 | 348.00 | 0.00 | 42.00 | 42.00 |
| 1144 | 520 | 272.00 | 352.00 | 0.00 | 42.48 | 42.48 |
| 1148 | 520 | 272.00 | 356.00 | 0.00 | 42.96 | 42.96 |
| 1152 | 520 | 272.00 | 360.00 | 0.00 | 43.44 | 43.44 |
| 1156 | 520 | 272.00 | 364.00 | 0.00 | 43.92 | 43.92 |
| 1160 | 520 | 272.00 | 368.00 | 0.00 | 44.40 | 44.40 |
| 1164 | 520 | 272.00 | 372.00 | 0.00 | 44.88 | 44.88 |
| 1168 | 520 | 272.00 | 376.00 | 0.00 | 45.36 | 45.36 |
| 1172 | 520 | 272.00 | 380.00 | 0.00 | 45.84 | 45.84 |
| 1176 | 520 | 272.00 | 384.00 | 0.00 | 46.32 | 46.32 |
| 1180 | 520 | 272.00 | 388.00 | 0.00 | 46.80 | 46.80 |
| 1184 | 520 | 272.00 | 392.00 | 0.00 | 47.28 | 47.28 |
| 1188 | 520 | 272.00 | 396.00 | 0.00 | 47.76 | 47.76 |
| 1192 | 520 | 272.00 | 400.00 | 0.00 | 48.24 | 48.24 |
| 1196 | 520 | 272.00 | 404.00 | 0.00 | 48.72 | 48.72 |
| 1200 | 520 | 272.00 | 408.00 | 0.00 | 49.20 | 49.20 |
| 1204 | 520 | 272.00 | 412.00 | 0.00 | 49.68 | 49.68 |
| 1208 | 520 | 272.00 | 416.00 | 0.00 | 50.16 | 50.16 |
| 1212 | 520 | 272.00 | 420.00 | 0.00 | 50.64 | 50.64 |
| 1216 | 520 | 272.00 | 424.00 | 0.00 | 51.12 | 51.12 |
| 1220 | 520 | 272.00 | 428.00 | 0.00 | 51.60 | 51.60 |
| 1224 | 520 | 272.00 | 432.00 | 0.00 | 52.08 | 52.08 |
| 1228 | 520 | 272.00 | 436.00 | 0.00 | 52.56 | 52.56 |
| 1232 | 520 | 272.00 | 440.00 | 0.00 | 53.04 | 53.04 |
| 1236 | 520 | 272.00 | 444.00 | 0.00 | 53.52 | 53.52 |
| 1240 | 520 | 272.00 | 448.00 | 0.00 | 54.00 | 54.00 |
| 1244 | 520 | 272.00 | 452.00 | 0.00 | 54.48 | 54.48 |
| 1248 | 520 | 272.00 | 456.00 | 0.00 | 54.96 | 54.96 |
| 1252 | 520 | 272.00 | 460.00 | 0.00 | 55.44 | 55.44 |
| 1256 | 520 | 272.00 | 464.00 | 0.00 | 55.92 | 55.92 |
| 1260 | 520 | 272.00 | 468.00 | 0.00 | 56.40 | 56.40 |
| 1264 | 520 | 272.00 | 472.00 | 0.00 | 56.88 | 56.88 |
| 1268 | 520 | 272.00 | 476.00 | 0.00 | 57.36 | 57.36 |
| 1272 | 520 | 272.00 | 480.00 | 0.00 | 57.84 | 57.84 |
| 1276 | 520 | 272.00 | 484.00 | 0.00 | 58.32 | 58.32 |

# Table letter H

## Monthly table

| Employee's earnings up to and including the UEL | Earnings at the LEL (where earnings are equal to or exceed the LEL) | Earnings above the LEL, up to and including the PT | Earnings above the PT, up to and including the UEL | Employer's NICs due on all earnings above the ST | Employee's NICs due on all earnings above the PT | Total of employee's and employer's NICs (for information only) |
|---|---|---|---|---|---|---|
| | 1a | 1b | 1c | 1d | 1e | |
| £ | £ | £ p | £ p | £ p | £ p | £ p |
| 1280 | 520 | 272.00 | 488.00 | 0.00 | 58.80 | 58.80 |
| 1284 | 520 | 272.00 | 492.00 | 0.00 | 59.28 | 59.28 |
| 1288 | 520 | 272.00 | 496.00 | 0.00 | 59.76 | 59.76 |
| 1292 | 520 | 272.00 | 500.00 | 0.00 | 60.24 | 60.24 |
| 1296 | 520 | 272.00 | 504.00 | 0.00 | 60.72 | 60.72 |
| 1300 | 520 | 272.00 | 508.00 | 0.00 | 61.20 | 61.20 |
| 1304 | 520 | 272.00 | 512.00 | 0.00 | 61.68 | 61.68 |
| 1308 | 520 | 272.00 | 516.00 | 0.00 | 62.16 | 62.16 |
| 1312 | 520 | 272.00 | 520.00 | 0.00 | 62.64 | 62.64 |
| 1316 | 520 | 272.00 | 524.00 | 0.00 | 63.12 | 63.12 |
| 1320 | 520 | 272.00 | 528.00 | 0.00 | 63.60 | 63.60 |
| 1324 | 520 | 272.00 | 532.00 | 0.00 | 64.08 | 64.08 |
| 1328 | 520 | 272.00 | 536.00 | 0.00 | 64.56 | 64.56 |
| 1332 | 520 | 272.00 | 540.00 | 0.00 | 65.04 | 65.04 |
| 1336 | 520 | 272.00 | 544.00 | 0.00 | 65.52 | 65.52 |
| 1340 | 520 | 272.00 | 548.00 | 0.00 | 66.00 | 66.00 |
| 1344 | 520 | 272.00 | 552.00 | 0.00 | 66.48 | 66.48 |
| 1348 | 520 | 272.00 | 556.00 | 0.00 | 66.96 | 66.96 |
| 1352 | 520 | 272.00 | 560.00 | 0.00 | 67.44 | 67.44 |
| 1356 | 520 | 272.00 | 564.00 | 0.00 | 67.92 | 67.92 |
| 1360 | 520 | 272.00 | 568.00 | 0.00 | 68.40 | 68.40 |
| 1364 | 520 | 272.00 | 572.00 | 0.00 | 68.88 | 68.88 |
| 1368 | 520 | 272.00 | 576.00 | 0.00 | 69.36 | 69.36 |
| 1372 | 520 | 272.00 | 580.00 | 0.00 | 69.84 | 69.84 |
| 1376 | 520 | 272.00 | 584.00 | 0.00 | 70.32 | 70.32 |
| 1380 | 520 | 272.00 | 588.00 | 0.00 | 70.80 | 70.80 |
| 1384 | 520 | 272.00 | 592.00 | 0.00 | 71.28 | 71.28 |
| 1388 | 520 | 272.00 | 596.00 | 0.00 | 71.76 | 71.76 |
| 1392 | 520 | 272.00 | 600.00 | 0.00 | 72.24 | 72.24 |
| 1396 | 520 | 272.00 | 604.00 | 0.00 | 72.72 | 72.72 |
| 1400 | 520 | 272.00 | 608.00 | 0.00 | 73.20 | 73.20 |
| 1404 | 520 | 272.00 | 612.00 | 0.00 | 73.68 | 73.68 |
| 1408 | 520 | 272.00 | 616.00 | 0.00 | 74.16 | 74.16 |
| 1412 | 520 | 272.00 | 620.00 | 0.00 | 74.64 | 74.64 |
| 1416 | 520 | 272.00 | 624.00 | 0.00 | 75.12 | 75.12 |
| 1420 | 520 | 272.00 | 628.00 | 0.00 | 75.60 | 75.60 |
| 1424 | 520 | 272.00 | 632.00 | 0.00 | 76.08 | 76.08 |
| 1428 | 520 | 272.00 | 636.00 | 0.00 | 76.56 | 76.56 |
| 1432 | 520 | 272.00 | 640.00 | 0.00 | 77.04 | 77.04 |
| 1436 | 520 | 272.00 | 644.00 | 0.00 | 77.52 | 77.52 |
| 1440 | 520 | 272.00 | 648.00 | 0.00 | 78.00 | 78.00 |
| 1444 | 520 | 272.00 | 652.00 | 0.00 | 78.48 | 78.48 |
| 1448 | 520 | 272.00 | 656.00 | 0.00 | 78.96 | 78.96 |
| 1452 | 520 | 272.00 | 660.00 | 0.00 | 79.44 | 79.44 |
| 1456 | 520 | 272.00 | 664.00 | 0.00 | 79.92 | 79.92 |
| 1460 | 520 | 272.00 | 668.00 | 0.00 | 80.40 | 80.40 |
| 1464 | 520 | 272.00 | 672.00 | 0.00 | 80.88 | 80.88 |
| 1468 | 520 | 272.00 | 676.00 | 0.00 | 81.36 | 81.36 |
| 1472 | 520 | 272.00 | 680.00 | 0.00 | 81.84 | 81.84 |
| 1476 | 520 | 272.00 | 684.00 | 0.00 | 82.32 | 82.32 |
| 1480 | 520 | 272.00 | 688.00 | 0.00 | 82.80 | 82.80 |
| 1484 | 520 | 272.00 | 692.00 | 0.00 | 83.28 | 83.28 |
| 1488 | 520 | 272.00 | 696.00 | 0.00 | 83.76 | 83.76 |
| 1492 | 520 | 272.00 | 700.00 | 0.00 | 84.24 | 84.24 |
| 1496 | 520 | 272.00 | 704.00 | 0.00 | 84.72 | 84.72 |

**Monthly table**

**Table letter H**

| Employee's earnings up to and including the UEL | Earnings at the LEL (where earnings are equal to or exceed the LEL) 1a | Earnings above the LEL, up to and including the PT 1b | Earnings above the PT, up to and including the UEL 1c | Employer's NICs due on all earnings above the ST 1d | Employee's NICs due on all earnings above the PT 1e | Total of employee's and employer's NICs (for information only) |
|---|---|---|---|---|---|---|
| £ | £ | £ p | £ p | £ p | £ p | £ p |
| 1500 | 520 | 272.00 | 708.00 | 0.00 | 85.20 | 85.20 |
| 1504 | 520 | 272.00 | 712.00 | 0.00 | 85.68 | 85.68 |
| 1508 | 520 | 272.00 | 716.00 | 0.00 | 86.16 | 86.16 |
| 1512 | 520 | 272.00 | 720.00 | 0.00 | 86.64 | 86.64 |
| 1516 | 520 | 272.00 | 724.00 | 0.00 | 87.12 | 87.12 |
| 1520 | 520 | 272.00 | 728.00 | 0.00 | 87.60 | 87.60 |
| 1524 | 520 | 272.00 | 732.00 | 0.00 | 88.08 | 88.08 |
| 1528 | 520 | 272.00 | 736.00 | 0.00 | 88.56 | 88.56 |
| 1532 | 520 | 272.00 | 740.00 | 0.00 | 89.04 | 89.04 |
| 1536 | 520 | 272.00 | 744.00 | 0.00 | 89.52 | 89.52 |
| 1540 | 520 | 272.00 | 748.00 | 0.00 | 90.00 | 90.00 |
| 1544 | 520 | 272.00 | 752.00 | 0.00 | 90.48 | 90.48 |
| 1548 | 520 | 272.00 | 756.00 | 0.00 | 90.96 | 90.96 |
| 1552 | 520 | 272.00 | 760.00 | 0.00 | 91.44 | 91.44 |
| 1556 | 520 | 272.00 | 764.00 | 0.00 | 91.92 | 91.92 |
| 1560 | 520 | 272.00 | 768.00 | 0.00 | 92.40 | 92.40 |
| 1564 | 520 | 272.00 | 772.00 | 0.00 | 92.88 | 92.88 |
| 1568 | 520 | 272.00 | 776.00 | 0.00 | 93.36 | 93.36 |
| 1572 | 520 | 272.00 | 780.00 | 0.00 | 93.84 | 93.84 |
| 1576 | 520 | 272.00 | 784.00 | 0.00 | 94.32 | 94.32 |
| 1580 | 520 | 272.00 | 788.00 | 0.00 | 94.80 | 94.80 |
| 1584 | 520 | 272.00 | 792.00 | 0.00 | 95.28 | 95.28 |
| 1588 | 520 | 272.00 | 796.00 | 0.00 | 95.76 | 95.76 |
| 1592 | 520 | 272.00 | 800.00 | 0.00 | 96.24 | 96.24 |
| 1596 | 520 | 272.00 | 804.00 | 0.00 | 96.72 | 96.72 |
| 1600 | 520 | 272.00 | 808.00 | 0.00 | 97.20 | 97.20 |
| 1604 | 520 | 272.00 | 812.00 | 0.00 | 97.68 | 97.68 |
| 1608 | 520 | 272.00 | 816.00 | 0.00 | 98.16 | 98.16 |
| 1612 | 520 | 272.00 | 820.00 | 0.00 | 98.64 | 98.64 |
| 1616 | 520 | 272.00 | 824.00 | 0.00 | 99.12 | 99.12 |
| 1620 | 520 | 272.00 | 828.00 | 0.00 | 99.60 | 99.60 |
| 1624 | 520 | 272.00 | 832.00 | 0.00 | 100.08 | 100.08 |
| 1628 | 520 | 272.00 | 836.00 | 0.00 | 100.56 | 100.56 |
| 1632 | 520 | 272.00 | 840.00 | 0.00 | 101.04 | 101.04 |
| 1636 | 520 | 272.00 | 844.00 | 0.00 | 101.52 | 101.52 |
| 1640 | 520 | 272.00 | 848.00 | 0.00 | 102.00 | 102.00 |
| 1644 | 520 | 272.00 | 852.00 | 0.00 | 102.48 | 102.48 |
| 1648 | 520 | 272.00 | 856.00 | 0.00 | 102.96 | 102.96 |
| 1652 | 520 | 272.00 | 860.00 | 0.00 | 103.44 | 103.44 |
| 1656 | 520 | 272.00 | 864.00 | 0.00 | 103.92 | 103.92 |
| 1660 | 520 | 272.00 | 868.00 | 0.00 | 104.40 | 104.40 |
| 1664 | 520 | 272.00 | 872.00 | 0.00 | 104.88 | 104.88 |
| 1668 | 520 | 272.00 | 876.00 | 0.00 | 105.36 | 105.36 |
| 1672 | 520 | 272.00 | 880.00 | 0.00 | 105.84 | 105.84 |
| 1676 | 520 | 272.00 | 884.00 | 0.00 | 106.32 | 106.32 |
| 1680 | 520 | 272.00 | 888.00 | 0.00 | 106.80 | 106.80 |
| 1684 | 520 | 272.00 | 892.00 | 0.00 | 107.28 | 107.28 |
| 1688 | 520 | 272.00 | 896.00 | 0.00 | 107.76 | 107.76 |
| 1692 | 520 | 272.00 | 900.00 | 0.00 | 108.24 | 108.24 |
| 1696 | 520 | 272.00 | 904.00 | 0.00 | 108.72 | 108.72 |
| 1700 | 520 | 272.00 | 908.00 | 0.00 | 109.20 | 109.20 |
| 1704 | 520 | 272.00 | 912.00 | 0.00 | 109.68 | 109.68 |
| 1708 | 520 | 272.00 | 916.00 | 0.00 | 110.16 | 110.16 |
| 1712 | 520 | 272.00 | 920.00 | 0.00 | 110.64 | 110.64 |
| 1716 | 520 | 272.00 | 924.00 | 0.00 | 111.12 | 111.12 |

# Table letter H

**Monthly table**

| Employee's earnings up to and including the UEL £ | Earnings at the LEL (where earnings are equal to or exceed the LEL) 1a £ | Earnings above the LEL, up to and including the PT 1b £ p | Earnings above the PT, up to and including the UEL 1c £ p | Employer's NICs due on all earnings above the ST 1d £ p | Employee's NICs due on all earnings above the PT 1e £ p | Total of employee's and employer's NICs (for information only) £ p |
|---|---|---|---|---|---|---|
| 1720 | 520 | 272.00 | 928.00 | 0.00 | 111.60 | 111.60 |
| 1724 | 520 | 272.00 | 932.00 | 0.00 | 112.08 | 112.08 |
| 1728 | 520 | 272.00 | 936.00 | 0.00 | 112.56 | 112.56 |
| 1732 | 520 | 272.00 | 940.00 | 0.00 | 113.04 | 113.04 |
| 1736 | 520 | 272.00 | 944.00 | 0.00 | 113.52 | 113.52 |
| 1740 | 520 | 272.00 | 948.00 | 0.00 | 114.00 | 114.00 |
| 1744 | 520 | 272.00 | 952.00 | 0.00 | 114.48 | 114.48 |
| 1748 | 520 | 272.00 | 956.00 | 0.00 | 114.96 | 114.96 |
| 1752 | 520 | 272.00 | 960.00 | 0.00 | 115.44 | 115.44 |
| 1756 | 520 | 272.00 | 964.00 | 0.00 | 115.92 | 115.92 |
| 1760 | 520 | 272.00 | 968.00 | 0.00 | 116.40 | 116.40 |
| 1764 | 520 | 272.00 | 972.00 | 0.00 | 116.88 | 116.88 |
| 1768 | 520 | 272.00 | 976.00 | 0.00 | 117.36 | 117.36 |
| 1772 | 520 | 272.00 | 980.00 | 0.00 | 117.84 | 117.84 |
| 1776 | 520 | 272.00 | 984.00 | 0.00 | 118.32 | 118.32 |
| 1780 | 520 | 272.00 | 988.00 | 0.00 | 118.80 | 118.80 |
| 1784 | 520 | 272.00 | 992.00 | 0.00 | 119.28 | 119.28 |
| 1788 | 520 | 272.00 | 996.00 | 0.00 | 119.76 | 119.76 |
| 1792 | 520 | 272.00 | 1000.00 | 0.00 | 120.24 | 120.24 |
| 1796 | 520 | 272.00 | 1004.00 | 0.00 | 120.72 | 120.72 |
| 1800 | 520 | 272.00 | 1008.00 | 0.00 | 121.20 | 121.20 |
| 1804 | 520 | 272.00 | 1012.00 | 0.00 | 121.68 | 121.68 |
| 1808 | 520 | 272.00 | 1016.00 | 0.00 | 122.16 | 122.16 |
| 1812 | 520 | 272.00 | 1020.00 | 0.00 | 122.64 | 122.64 |
| 1816 | 520 | 272.00 | 1024.00 | 0.00 | 123.12 | 123.12 |
| 1820 | 520 | 272.00 | 1028.00 | 0.00 | 123.60 | 123.60 |
| 1824 | 520 | 272.00 | 1032.00 | 0.00 | 124.08 | 124.08 |
| 1828 | 520 | 272.00 | 1036.00 | 0.00 | 124.56 | 124.56 |
| 1832 | 520 | 272.00 | 1040.00 | 0.00 | 125.04 | 125.04 |
| 1836 | 520 | 272.00 | 1044.00 | 0.00 | 125.52 | 125.52 |
| 1840 | 520 | 272.00 | 1048.00 | 0.00 | 126.00 | 126.00 |
| 1844 | 520 | 272.00 | 1052.00 | 0.00 | 126.48 | 126.48 |
| 1848 | 520 | 272.00 | 1056.00 | 0.00 | 126.96 | 126.96 |
| 1852 | 520 | 272.00 | 1060.00 | 0.00 | 127.44 | 127.44 |
| 1856 | 520 | 272.00 | 1064.00 | 0.00 | 127.92 | 127.92 |
| 1860 | 520 | 272.00 | 1068.00 | 0.00 | 128.40 | 128.40 |
| 1864 | 520 | 272.00 | 1072.00 | 0.00 | 128.88 | 128.88 |
| 1868 | 520 | 272.00 | 1076.00 | 0.00 | 129.36 | 129.36 |
| 1872 | 520 | 272.00 | 1080.00 | 0.00 | 129.84 | 129.84 |
| 1876 | 520 | 272.00 | 1084.00 | 0.00 | 130.32 | 130.32 |
| 1880 | 520 | 272.00 | 1088.00 | 0.00 | 130.80 | 130.80 |
| 1884 | 520 | 272.00 | 1092.00 | 0.00 | 131.28 | 131.28 |
| 1888 | 520 | 272.00 | 1096.00 | 0.00 | 131.76 | 131.76 |
| 1892 | 520 | 272.00 | 1100.00 | 0.00 | 132.24 | 132.24 |
| 1896 | 520 | 272.00 | 1104.00 | 0.00 | 132.72 | 132.72 |
| 1900 | 520 | 272.00 | 1108.00 | 0.00 | 133.20 | 133.20 |
| 1904 | 520 | 272.00 | 1112.00 | 0.00 | 133.68 | 133.68 |
| 1908 | 520 | 272.00 | 1116.00 | 0.00 | 134.16 | 134.16 |
| 1912 | 520 | 272.00 | 1120.00 | 0.00 | 134.64 | 134.64 |
| 1916 | 520 | 272.00 | 1124.00 | 0.00 | 135.12 | 135.12 |
| 1920 | 520 | 272.00 | 1128.00 | 0.00 | 135.60 | 135.60 |
| 1924 | 520 | 272.00 | 1132.00 | 0.00 | 136.08 | 136.08 |
| 1928 | 520 | 272.00 | 1136.00 | 0.00 | 136.56 | 136.56 |
| 1932 | 520 | 272.00 | 1140.00 | 0.00 | 137.04 | 137.04 |
| 1936 | 520 | 272.00 | 1144.00 | 0.00 | 137.52 | 137.52 |

**Monthly table**

| Employee's earnings up to and including the UEL | Earnings at the LEL (where earnings are equal to or exceed the LEL) 1a | Earnings above the LEL, up to and including the PT 1b | Earnings above the PT, up to and including the UEL 1c | Employer's NICs due on all earnings above the ST 1d | Employee's NICs due on all earnings above the PT 1e | Total of employee's and employer's NICs (for information only) |
|---|---|---|---|---|---|---|
| £ | £ | £ p | £ p | £ p | £ p | £ p |
| 1940 | 520 | 272.00 | 1148.00 | 0.00 | 138.00 | 138.00 |
| 1944 | 520 | 272.00 | 1152.00 | 0.00 | 138.48 | 138.48 |
| 1948 | 520 | 272.00 | 1156.00 | 0.00 | 138.96 | 138.96 |
| 1952 | 520 | 272.00 | 1160.00 | 0.00 | 139.44 | 139.44 |
| 1956 | 520 | 272.00 | 1164.00 | 0.00 | 139.92 | 139.92 |
| 1960 | 520 | 272.00 | 1168.00 | 0.00 | 140.40 | 140.40 |
| 1964 | 520 | 272.00 | 1172.00 | 0.00 | 140.88 | 140.88 |
| 1968 | 520 | 272.00 | 1176.00 | 0.00 | 141.36 | 141.36 |
| 1972 | 520 | 272.00 | 1180.00 | 0.00 | 141.84 | 141.84 |
| 1976 | 520 | 272.00 | 1184.00 | 0.00 | 142.32 | 142.32 |
| 1980 | 520 | 272.00 | 1188.00 | 0.00 | 142.80 | 142.80 |
| 1984 | 520 | 272.00 | 1192.00 | 0.00 | 143.28 | 143.28 |
| 1988 | 520 | 272.00 | 1196.00 | 0.00 | 143.76 | 143.76 |
| 1992 | 520 | 272.00 | 1200.00 | 0.00 | 144.24 | 144.24 |
| 1996 | 520 | 272.00 | 1204.00 | 0.00 | 144.72 | 144.72 |
| 2000 | 520 | 272.00 | 1208.00 | 0.00 | 145.20 | 145.20 |
| 2004 | 520 | 272.00 | 1212.00 | 0.00 | 145.68 | 145.68 |
| 2008 | 520 | 272.00 | 1216.00 | 0.00 | 146.16 | 146.16 |
| 2012 | 520 | 272.00 | 1220.00 | 0.00 | 146.64 | 146.64 |
| 2016 | 520 | 272.00 | 1224.00 | 0.00 | 147.12 | 147.12 |
| 2020 | 520 | 272.00 | 1228.00 | 0.00 | 147.60 | 147.60 |
| 2024 | 520 | 272.00 | 1232.00 | 0.00 | 148.08 | 148.08 |
| 2028 | 520 | 272.00 | 1236.00 | 0.00 | 148.56 | 148.56 |
| 2032 | 520 | 272.00 | 1240.00 | 0.00 | 149.04 | 149.04 |
| 2036 | 520 | 272.00 | 1244.00 | 0.00 | 149.52 | 149.52 |
| 2040 | 520 | 272.00 | 1248.00 | 0.00 | 150.00 | 150.00 |
| 2044 | 520 | 272.00 | 1252.00 | 0.00 | 150.48 | 150.48 |
| 2048 | 520 | 272.00 | 1256.00 | 0.00 | 150.96 | 150.96 |
| 2052 | 520 | 272.00 | 1260.00 | 0.00 | 151.44 | 151.44 |
| 2056 | 520 | 272.00 | 1264.00 | 0.00 | 151.92 | 151.92 |
| 2060 | 520 | 272.00 | 1268.00 | 0.00 | 152.40 | 152.40 |
| 2064 | 520 | 272.00 | 1272.00 | 0.00 | 152.88 | 152.88 |
| 2068 | 520 | 272.00 | 1276.00 | 0.00 | 153.36 | 153.36 |
| 2072 | 520 | 272.00 | 1280.00 | 0.00 | 153.84 | 153.84 |
| 2076 | 520 | 272.00 | 1284.00 | 0.00 | 154.32 | 154.32 |
| 2080 | 520 | 272.00 | 1288.00 | 0.00 | 154.80 | 154.80 |
| 2084 | 520 | 272.00 | 1292.00 | 0.00 | 155.28 | 155.28 |
| 2088 | 520 | 272.00 | 1296.00 | 0.00 | 155.76 | 155.76 |
| 2092 | 520 | 272.00 | 1300.00 | 0.00 | 156.24 | 156.24 |
| 2096 | 520 | 272.00 | 1304.00 | 0.00 | 156.72 | 156.72 |
| 2100 | 520 | 272.00 | 1308.00 | 0.00 | 157.20 | 157.20 |
| 2104 | 520 | 272.00 | 1312.00 | 0.00 | 157.68 | 157.68 |
| 2108 | 520 | 272.00 | 1316.00 | 0.00 | 158.16 | 158.16 |
| 2112 | 520 | 272.00 | 1320.00 | 0.00 | 158.64 | 158.64 |
| 2116 | 520 | 272.00 | 1324.00 | 0.00 | 159.12 | 159.12 |
| 2120 | 520 | 272.00 | 1328.00 | 0.00 | 159.60 | 159.60 |
| 2124 | 520 | 272.00 | 1332.00 | 0.00 | 160.08 | 160.08 |
| 2128 | 520 | 272.00 | 1336.00 | 0.00 | 160.56 | 160.56 |
| 2132 | 520 | 272.00 | 1340.00 | 0.00 | 161.04 | 161.04 |
| 2136 | 520 | 272.00 | 1344.00 | 0.00 | 161.52 | 161.52 |
| 2140 | 520 | 272.00 | 1348.00 | 0.00 | 162.00 | 162.00 |
| 2144 | 520 | 272.00 | 1352.00 | 0.00 | 162.48 | 162.48 |
| 2148 | 520 | 272.00 | 1356.00 | 0.00 | 162.96 | 162.96 |
| 2152 | 520 | 272.00 | 1360.00 | 0.00 | 163.44 | 163.44 |
| 2156 | 520 | 272.00 | 1364.00 | 0.00 | 163.92 | 163.92 |

## Table letter H

**Monthly table**

| Employee's earnings up to and including the UEL | Earnings at the LEL (where earnings are equal to or exceed the LEL) 1a | Earnings above the LEL, up to and including the PT 1b | Earnings above the PT, up to and including the UEL 1c | Employer's NICs due on all earnings above the ST 1d | Employee's NICs due on all earnings above the PT 1e | Total of employee's and employer's NICs (for information only) |
|---|---|---|---|---|---|---|
| £ | £ | £ p | £ p | £ p | £ p | £ p |
| 2160 | 520 | 272.00 | 1368.00 | 0.00 | 164.40 | 164.40 |
| 2164 | 520 | 272.00 | 1372.00 | 0.00 | 164.88 | 164.88 |
| 2168 | 520 | 272.00 | 1376.00 | 0.00 | 165.36 | 165.36 |
| 2172 | 520 | 272.00 | 1380.00 | 0.00 | 165.84 | 165.84 |
| 2176 | 520 | 272.00 | 1384.00 | 0.00 | 166.32 | 166.32 |
| 2180 | 520 | 272.00 | 1388.00 | 0.00 | 166.80 | 166.80 |
| 2184 | 520 | 272.00 | 1392.00 | 0.00 | 167.28 | 167.28 |
| 2188 | 520 | 272.00 | 1396.00 | 0.00 | 167.76 | 167.76 |
| 2192 | 520 | 272.00 | 1400.00 | 0.00 | 168.24 | 168.24 |
| 2196 | 520 | 272.00 | 1404.00 | 0.00 | 168.72 | 168.72 |
| 2200 | 520 | 272.00 | 1408.00 | 0.00 | 169.20 | 169.20 |
| 2204 | 520 | 272.00 | 1412.00 | 0.00 | 169.68 | 169.68 |
| 2208 | 520 | 272.00 | 1416.00 | 0.00 | 170.16 | 170.16 |
| 2212 | 520 | 272.00 | 1420.00 | 0.00 | 170.64 | 170.64 |
| 2216 | 520 | 272.00 | 1424.00 | 0.00 | 171.12 | 171.12 |
| 2220 | 520 | 272.00 | 1428.00 | 0.00 | 171.60 | 171.60 |
| 2224 | 520 | 272.00 | 1432.00 | 0.00 | 172.08 | 172.08 |
| 2228 | 520 | 272.00 | 1436.00 | 0.00 | 172.56 | 172.56 |
| 2232 | 520 | 272.00 | 1440.00 | 0.00 | 173.04 | 173.04 |
| 2236 | 520 | 272.00 | 1444.00 | 0.00 | 173.52 | 173.52 |
| 2240 | 520 | 272.00 | 1448.00 | 0.00 | 174.00 | 174.00 |
| 2244 | 520 | 272.00 | 1452.00 | 0.00 | 174.48 | 174.48 |
| 2248 | 520 | 272.00 | 1456.00 | 0.00 | 174.96 | 174.96 |
| 2252 | 520 | 272.00 | 1460.00 | 0.00 | 175.44 | 175.44 |
| 2256 | 520 | 272.00 | 1464.00 | 0.00 | 175.92 | 175.92 |
| 2260 | 520 | 272.00 | 1468.00 | 0.00 | 176.40 | 176.40 |
| 2264 | 520 | 272.00 | 1472.00 | 0.00 | 176.88 | 176.88 |
| 2268 | 520 | 272.00 | 1476.00 | 0.00 | 177.36 | 177.36 |
| 2272 | 520 | 272.00 | 1480.00 | 0.00 | 177.84 | 177.84 |
| 2276 | 520 | 272.00 | 1484.00 | 0.00 | 178.32 | 178.32 |
| 2280 | 520 | 272.00 | 1488.00 | 0.00 | 178.80 | 178.80 |
| 2284 | 520 | 272.00 | 1492.00 | 0.00 | 179.28 | 179.28 |
| 2288 | 520 | 272.00 | 1496.00 | 0.00 | 179.76 | 179.76 |
| 2292 | 520 | 272.00 | 1500.00 | 0.00 | 180.24 | 180.24 |
| 2296 | 520 | 272.00 | 1504.00 | 0.00 | 180.72 | 180.72 |
| 2300 | 520 | 272.00 | 1508.00 | 0.00 | 181.20 | 181.20 |
| 2304 | 520 | 272.00 | 1512.00 | 0.00 | 181.68 | 181.68 |
| 2308 | 520 | 272.00 | 1516.00 | 0.00 | 182.16 | 182.16 |
| 2312 | 520 | 272.00 | 1520.00 | 0.00 | 182.64 | 182.64 |
| 2316 | 520 | 272.00 | 1524.00 | 0.00 | 183.12 | 183.12 |
| 2320 | 520 | 272.00 | 1528.00 | 0.00 | 183.60 | 183.60 |
| 2324 | 520 | 272.00 | 1532.00 | 0.00 | 184.08 | 184.08 |
| 2328 | 520 | 272.00 | 1536.00 | 0.00 | 184.56 | 184.56 |
| 2332 | 520 | 272.00 | 1540.00 | 0.00 | 185.04 | 185.04 |
| 2336 | 520 | 272.00 | 1544.00 | 0.00 | 185.52 | 185.52 |
| 2340 | 520 | 272.00 | 1548.00 | 0.00 | 186.00 | 186.00 |
| 2344 | 520 | 272.00 | 1552.00 | 0.00 | 186.48 | 186.48 |
| 2348 | 520 | 272.00 | 1556.00 | 0.00 | 186.96 | 186.96 |
| 2352 | 520 | 272.00 | 1560.00 | 0.00 | 187.44 | 187.44 |
| 2356 | 520 | 272.00 | 1564.00 | 0.00 | 187.92 | 187.92 |
| 2360 | 520 | 272.00 | 1568.00 | 0.00 | 188.40 | 188.40 |
| 2364 | 520 | 272.00 | 1572.00 | 0.00 | 188.88 | 188.88 |
| 2368 | 520 | 272.00 | 1576.00 | 0.00 | 189.36 | 189.36 |
| 2372 | 520 | 272.00 | 1580.00 | 0.00 | 189.84 | 189.84 |
| 2376 | 520 | 272.00 | 1584.00 | 0.00 | 190.32 | 190.32 |

**Monthly table**                                                                    **Table letter H**

| Employee's earnings up to and including the UEL | Earnings at the LEL (where earnings are equal to or exceed the LEL) | Earnings above the LEL, up to and including the PT | Earnings above the PT, up to and including the UEL | Employer's NICs due on all earnings above the ST | Employee's NICs due on all earnings above the PT | Total of employee's and employer's NICs (for information only) |
|---|---|---|---|---|---|---|
| | | 1a | 1b | 1c | 1d | 1e |
| £ | £ | £ p | £ p | £ p | £ p | £ p |
| 2380 | 520 | 272.00 | 1588.00 | 0.00 | 190.80 | 190.80 |
| 2384 | 520 | 272.00 | 1592.00 | 0.00 | 191.28 | 191.28 |
| 2388 | 520 | 272.00 | 1596.00 | 0.00 | 191.76 | 191.76 |
| 2392 | 520 | 272.00 | 1600.00 | 0.00 | 192.24 | 192.24 |
| 2396 | 520 | 272.00 | 1604.00 | 0.00 | 192.72 | 192.72 |
| 2400 | 520 | 272.00 | 1608.00 | 0.00 | 193.20 | 193.20 |
| 2404 | 520 | 272.00 | 1612.00 | 0.00 | 193.68 | 193.68 |
| 2408 | 520 | 272.00 | 1616.00 | 0.00 | 194.16 | 194.16 |
| 2412 | 520 | 272.00 | 1620.00 | 0.00 | 194.64 | 194.64 |
| 2416 | 520 | 272.00 | 1624.00 | 0.00 | 195.12 | 195.12 |
| 2420 | 520 | 272.00 | 1628.00 | 0.00 | 195.60 | 195.60 |
| 2424 | 520 | 272.00 | 1632.00 | 0.00 | 196.08 | 196.08 |
| 2428 | 520 | 272.00 | 1636.00 | 0.00 | 196.56 | 196.56 |
| 2432 | 520 | 272.00 | 1640.00 | 0.00 | 197.04 | 197.04 |
| 2436 | 520 | 272.00 | 1644.00 | 0.00 | 197.52 | 197.52 |
| 2440 | 520 | 272.00 | 1648.00 | 0.00 | 198.00 | 198.00 |
| 2444 | 520 | 272.00 | 1652.00 | 0.00 | 198.48 | 198.48 |
| 2448 | 520 | 272.00 | 1656.00 | 0.00 | 198.96 | 198.96 |
| 2452 | 520 | 272.00 | 1660.00 | 0.00 | 199.44 | 199.44 |
| 2456 | 520 | 272.00 | 1664.00 | 0.00 | 199.92 | 199.92 |
| 2460 | 520 | 272.00 | 1668.00 | 0.00 | 200.40 | 200.40 |
| 2464 | 520 | 272.00 | 1672.00 | 0.00 | 200.88 | 200.88 |
| 2468 | 520 | 272.00 | 1676.00 | 0.00 | 201.36 | 201.36 |
| 2472 | 520 | 272.00 | 1680.00 | 0.00 | 201.84 | 201.84 |
| 2476 | 520 | 272.00 | 1684.00 | 0.00 | 202.32 | 202.32 |
| 2480 | 520 | 272.00 | 1688.00 | 0.00 | 202.80 | 202.80 |
| 2484 | 520 | 272.00 | 1692.00 | 0.00 | 203.28 | 203.28 |
| 2488 | 520 | 272.00 | 1696.00 | 0.00 | 203.76 | 203.76 |
| 2492 | 520 | 272.00 | 1700.00 | 0.00 | 204.24 | 204.24 |
| 2496 | 520 | 272.00 | 1704.00 | 0.00 | 204.72 | 204.72 |
| 2500 | 520 | 272.00 | 1708.00 | 0.00 | 205.20 | 205.20 |
| 2504 | 520 | 272.00 | 1712.00 | 0.00 | 205.68 | 205.68 |
| 2508 | 520 | 272.00 | 1716.00 | 0.00 | 206.16 | 206.16 |
| 2512 | 520 | 272.00 | 1720.00 | 0.00 | 206.64 | 206.64 |
| 2516 | 520 | 272.00 | 1724.00 | 0.00 | 207.12 | 207.12 |
| 2520 | 520 | 272.00 | 1728.00 | 0.00 | 207.60 | 207.60 |
| 2524 | 520 | 272.00 | 1732.00 | 0.00 | 208.08 | 208.08 |
| 2528 | 520 | 272.00 | 1736.00 | 0.00 | 208.56 | 208.56 |
| 2532 | 520 | 272.00 | 1740.00 | 0.00 | 209.04 | 209.04 |
| 2536 | 520 | 272.00 | 1744.00 | 0.00 | 209.52 | 209.52 |
| 2540 | 520 | 272.00 | 1748.00 | 0.00 | 210.00 | 210.00 |
| 2544 | 520 | 272.00 | 1752.00 | 0.00 | 210.48 | 210.48 |
| 2548 | 520 | 272.00 | 1756.00 | 0.00 | 210.96 | 210.96 |
| 2552 | 520 | 272.00 | 1760.00 | 0.00 | 211.44 | 211.44 |
| 2556 | 520 | 272.00 | 1764.00 | 0.00 | 211.92 | 211.92 |
| 2560 | 520 | 272.00 | 1768.00 | 0.00 | 212.40 | 212.40 |
| 2564 | 520 | 272.00 | 1772.00 | 0.00 | 212.88 | 212.88 |
| 2568 | 520 | 272.00 | 1776.00 | 0.00 | 213.36 | 213.36 |
| 2572 | 520 | 272.00 | 1780.00 | 0.00 | 213.84 | 213.84 |
| 2576 | 520 | 272.00 | 1784.00 | 0.00 | 214.32 | 214.32 |
| 2580 | 520 | 272.00 | 1788.00 | 0.00 | 214.80 | 214.80 |
| 2584 | 520 | 272.00 | 1792.00 | 0.00 | 215.28 | 215.28 |
| 2588 | 520 | 272.00 | 1796.00 | 0.00 | 215.76 | 215.76 |
| 2592 | 520 | 272.00 | 1800.00 | 0.00 | 216.24 | 216.24 |
| 2596 | 520 | 272.00 | 1804.00 | 0.00 | 216.72 | 216.72 |

## Table letter H

**Monthly table**

| Employee's earnings up to and including the UEL | Earnings at the LEL (where earnings are equal to or exceed the LEL) | Earnings above the LEL, up to and including the PT | Earnings above the PT, up to and including the UEL | Employer's NICs due on all earnings above the ST | Employee's NICs due on all earnings above the PT | Total of employee's and employer's NICs (for information only) |
|---|---|---|---|---|---|---|
| | 1a | 1b | 1c | 1d | 1e | |
| £ | £ | £ p | £ p | £ p | £ p | £ p |
| 2600 | 520 | 272.00 | 1808.00 | 0.00 | 217.20 | 217.20 |
| 2604 | 520 | 272.00 | 1812.00 | 0.00 | 217.68 | 217.68 |
| 2608 | 520 | 272.00 | 1816.00 | 0.00 | 218.16 | 218.16 |
| 2612 | 520 | 272.00 | 1820.00 | 0.00 | 218.64 | 218.64 |
| 2616 | 520 | 272.00 | 1824.00 | 0.00 | 219.12 | 219.12 |
| 2620 | 520 | 272.00 | 1828.00 | 0.00 | 219.60 | 219.60 |
| 2624 | 520 | 272.00 | 1832.00 | 0.00 | 220.08 | 220.08 |
| 2628 | 520 | 272.00 | 1836.00 | 0.00 | 220.56 | 220.56 |
| 2632 | 520 | 272.00 | 1840.00 | 0.00 | 221.04 | 221.04 |
| 2636 | 520 | 272.00 | 1844.00 | 0.00 | 221.52 | 221.52 |
| 2640 | 520 | 272.00 | 1848.00 | 0.00 | 222.00 | 222.00 |
| 2644 | 520 | 272.00 | 1852.00 | 0.00 | 222.48 | 222.48 |
| 2648 | 520 | 272.00 | 1856.00 | 0.00 | 222.96 | 222.96 |
| 2652 | 520 | 272.00 | 1860.00 | 0.00 | 223.44 | 223.44 |
| 2656 | 520 | 272.00 | 1864.00 | 0.00 | 223.92 | 223.92 |
| 2660 | 520 | 272.00 | 1868.00 | 0.00 | 224.40 | 224.40 |
| 2664 | 520 | 272.00 | 1872.00 | 0.00 | 224.88 | 224.88 |
| 2668 | 520 | 272.00 | 1876.00 | 0.00 | 225.36 | 225.36 |
| 2672 | 520 | 272.00 | 1880.00 | 0.00 | 225.84 | 225.84 |
| 2676 | 520 | 272.00 | 1884.00 | 0.00 | 226.32 | 226.32 |
| 2680 | 520 | 272.00 | 1888.00 | 0.00 | 226.80 | 226.80 |
| 2684 | 520 | 272.00 | 1892.00 | 0.00 | 227.28 | 227.28 |
| 2688 | 520 | 272.00 | 1896.00 | 0.00 | 227.76 | 227.76 |
| 2692 | 520 | 272.00 | 1900.00 | 0.00 | 228.24 | 228.24 |
| 2696 | 520 | 272.00 | 1904.00 | 0.00 | 228.72 | 228.72 |
| 2700 | 520 | 272.00 | 1908.00 | 0.00 | 229.20 | 229.20 |
| 2704 | 520 | 272.00 | 1912.00 | 0.00 | 229.68 | 229.68 |
| 2708 | 520 | 272.00 | 1916.00 | 0.00 | 230.16 | 230.16 |
| 2712 | 520 | 272.00 | 1920.00 | 0.00 | 230.64 | 230.64 |
| 2716 | 520 | 272.00 | 1924.00 | 0.00 | 231.12 | 231.12 |
| 2720 | 520 | 272.00 | 1928.00 | 0.00 | 231.60 | 231.60 |
| 2724 | 520 | 272.00 | 1932.00 | 0.00 | 232.08 | 232.08 |
| 2728 | 520 | 272.00 | 1936.00 | 0.00 | 232.56 | 232.56 |
| 2732 | 520 | 272.00 | 1940.00 | 0.00 | 233.04 | 233.04 |
| 2736 | 520 | 272.00 | 1944.00 | 0.00 | 233.52 | 233.52 |
| 2740 | 520 | 272.00 | 1948.00 | 0.00 | 234.00 | 234.00 |
| 2744 | 520 | 272.00 | 1952.00 | 0.00 | 234.48 | 234.48 |
| 2748 | 520 | 272.00 | 1956.00 | 0.00 | 234.96 | 234.96 |
| 2752 | 520 | 272.00 | 1960.00 | 0.00 | 235.44 | 235.44 |
| 2756 | 520 | 272.00 | 1964.00 | 0.00 | 235.92 | 235.92 |
| 2760 | 520 | 272.00 | 1968.00 | 0.00 | 236.40 | 236.40 |
| 2764 | 520 | 272.00 | 1972.00 | 0.00 | 236.88 | 236.88 |
| 2768 | 520 | 272.00 | 1976.00 | 0.00 | 237.36 | 237.36 |
| 2772 | 520 | 272.00 | 1980.00 | 0.00 | 237.84 | 237.84 |
| 2776 | 520 | 272.00 | 1984.00 | 0.00 | 238.32 | 238.32 |
| 2780 | 520 | 272.00 | 1988.00 | 0.00 | 238.80 | 238.80 |
| 2784 | 520 | 272.00 | 1992.00 | 0.00 | 239.28 | 239.28 |
| 2788 | 520 | 272.00 | 1996.00 | 0.00 | 239.76 | 239.76 |
| 2792 | 520 | 272.00 | 2000.00 | 0.00 | 240.24 | 240.24 |
| 2796 | 520 | 272.00 | 2004.00 | 0.00 | 240.72 | 240.72 |
| 2800 | 520 | 272.00 | 2008.00 | 0.00 | 241.20 | 241.20 |
| 2804 | 520 | 272.00 | 2012.00 | 0.00 | 241.68 | 241.68 |
| 2808 | 520 | 272.00 | 2016.00 | 0.00 | 242.16 | 242.16 |
| 2812 | 520 | 272.00 | 2020.00 | 0.00 | 242.64 | 242.64 |
| 2816 | 520 | 272.00 | 2024.00 | 0.00 | 243.12 | 243.12 |

## Monthly table

**Table letter H**

| Employee's earnings up to and including the UEL | Earnings at the LEL (where earnings are equal to or exceed the LEL) 1a | Earnings above the LEL, up to and including the PT 1b | Earnings above the PT, up to and including the UEL 1c | Employer's NICs due on all earnings above the ST 1d | Employee's NICs due on all earnings above the PT 1e | Total of employee's and employer's NICs (for information only) |
|---|---|---|---|---|---|---|
| £ | £ | £ p | £ p | £ p | £ p | £ p |
| 2820 | 520 | 272.00 | 2028.00 | 0.00 | 243.60 | 243.60 |
| 2824 | 520 | 272.00 | 2032.00 | 0.00 | 244.08 | 244.08 |
| 2828 | 520 | 272.00 | 2036.00 | 0.00 | 244.56 | 244.56 |
| 2832 | 520 | 272.00 | 2040.00 | 0.00 | 245.04 | 245.04 |
| 2836 | 520 | 272.00 | 2044.00 | 0.00 | 245.52 | 245.52 |
| 2840 | 520 | 272.00 | 2048.00 | 0.00 | 246.00 | 246.00 |
| 2844 | 520 | 272.00 | 2052.00 | 0.00 | 246.48 | 246.48 |
| 2848 | 520 | 272.00 | 2056.00 | 0.00 | 246.96 | 246.96 |
| 2852 | 520 | 272.00 | 2060.00 | 0.00 | 247.44 | 247.44 |
| 2856 | 520 | 272.00 | 2064.00 | 0.00 | 247.92 | 247.92 |
| 2860 | 520 | 272.00 | 2068.00 | 0.00 | 248.40 | 248.40 |
| 2864 | 520 | 272.00 | 2072.00 | 0.00 | 248.88 | 248.88 |
| 2868 | 520 | 272.00 | 2076.00 | 0.00 | 249.36 | 249.36 |
| 2872 | 520 | 272.00 | 2080.00 | 0.00 | 249.84 | 249.84 |
| 2876 | 520 | 272.00 | 2084.00 | 0.00 | 250.32 | 250.32 |
| 2880 | 520 | 272.00 | 2088.00 | 0.00 | 250.80 | 250.80 |
| 2884 | 520 | 272.00 | 2092.00 | 0.00 | 251.28 | 251.28 |
| 2888 | 520 | 272.00 | 2096.00 | 0.00 | 251.76 | 251.76 |
| 2892 | 520 | 272.00 | 2100.00 | 0.00 | 252.24 | 252.24 |
| 2896 | 520 | 272.00 | 2104.00 | 0.00 | 252.72 | 252.72 |
| 2900 | 520 | 272.00 | 2108.00 | 0.00 | 253.20 | 253.20 |
| 2904 | 520 | 272.00 | 2112.00 | 0.00 | 253.68 | 253.68 |
| 2908 | 520 | 272.00 | 2116.00 | 0.00 | 254.16 | 254.16 |
| 2912 | 520 | 272.00 | 2120.00 | 0.00 | 254.64 | 254.64 |
| 2916 | 520 | 272.00 | 2124.00 | 0.00 | 255.12 | 255.12 |
| 2920 | 520 | 272.00 | 2128.00 | 0.00 | 255.60 | 255.60 |
| 2924 | 520 | 272.00 | 2132.00 | 0.00 | 256.08 | 256.08 |
| 2928 | 520 | 272.00 | 2136.00 | 0.00 | 256.56 | 256.56 |
| 2932 | 520 | 272.00 | 2140.00 | 0.00 | 257.04 | 257.04 |
| 2936 | 520 | 272.00 | 2144.00 | 0.00 | 257.52 | 257.52 |
| 2940 | 520 | 272.00 | 2148.00 | 0.00 | 258.00 | 258.00 |
| 2944 | 520 | 272.00 | 2152.00 | 0.00 | 258.48 | 258.48 |
| 2948 | 520 | 272.00 | 2156.00 | 0.00 | 258.96 | 258.96 |
| 2952 | 520 | 272.00 | 2160.00 | 0.00 | 259.44 | 259.44 |
| 2956 | 520 | 272.00 | 2164.00 | 0.00 | 259.92 | 259.92 |
| 2960 | 520 | 272.00 | 2168.00 | 0.00 | 260.40 | 260.40 |
| 2964 | 520 | 272.00 | 2172.00 | 0.00 | 260.88 | 260.88 |
| 2968 | 520 | 272.00 | 2176.00 | 0.00 | 261.36 | 261.36 |
| 2972 | 520 | 272.00 | 2180.00 | 0.00 | 261.84 | 261.84 |
| 2976 | 520 | 272.00 | 2184.00 | 0.00 | 262.32 | 262.32 |
| 2980 | 520 | 272.00 | 2188.00 | 0.00 | 262.80 | 262.80 |
| 2984 | 520 | 272.00 | 2192.00 | 0.00 | 263.28 | 263.28 |
| 2988 | 520 | 272.00 | 2196.00 | 0.00 | 263.76 | 263.76 |
| 2992 | 520 | 272.00 | 2200.00 | 0.00 | 264.24 | 264.24 |
| 2996 | 520 | 272.00 | 2204.00 | 0.00 | 264.72 | 264.72 |
| 3000 | 520 | 272.00 | 2208.00 | 0.00 | 265.20 | 265.20 |
| 3004 | 520 | 272.00 | 2212.00 | 0.00 | 265.68 | 265.68 |
| 3008 | 520 | 272.00 | 2216.00 | 0.00 | 266.16 | 266.16 |
| 3012 | 520 | 272.00 | 2220.00 | 0.00 | 266.64 | 266.64 |
| 3016 | 520 | 272.00 | 2224.00 | 0.00 | 267.12 | 267.12 |
| 3020 | 520 | 272.00 | 2228.00 | 0.00 | 267.60 | 267.60 |
| 3024 | 520 | 272.00 | 2232.00 | 0.00 | 268.08 | 268.08 |
| 3028 | 520 | 272.00 | 2236.00 | 0.00 | 268.56 | 268.56 |
| 3032 | 520 | 272.00 | 2240.00 | 0.00 | 269.04 | 269.04 |
| 3036 | 520 | 272.00 | 2244.00 | 0.00 | 269.52 | 269.52 |

## Table letter H

**Monthly table**

| Employee's earnings up to and including the UEL | Earnings at the LEL (where earnings are equal to or exceed the LEL) | Earnings above the LEL, up to and including the PT | Earnings above the PT, up to and including the UEL | Employer's NICs due on all earnings above the ST | Employee's NICs due on all earnings above the PT | Total of employee's and employer's NICs (for information only) |
|---|---|---|---|---|---|---|
| | | 1a | 1b | 1c | 1d | 1e |
| £ | £ | £ p | £ p | £ p | £ p | £ p |
| 3040 | 520 | 272.00 | 2248.00 | 0.00 | 270.00 | 270.00 |
| 3044 | 520 | 272.00 | 2252.00 | 0.00 | 270.48 | 270.48 |
| 3048 | 520 | 272.00 | 2256.00 | 0.00 | 270.96 | 270.96 |
| 3052 | 520 | 272.00 | 2260.00 | 0.00 | 271.44 | 271.44 |
| 3056 | 520 | 272.00 | 2264.00 | 0.00 | 271.92 | 271.92 |
| 3060 | 520 | 272.00 | 2268.00 | 0.00 | 272.40 | 272.40 |
| 3064 | 520 | 272.00 | 2272.00 | 0.00 | 272.88 | 272.88 |
| 3068 | 520 | 272.00 | 2276.00 | 0.00 | 273.36 | 273.36 |
| 3072 | 520 | 272.00 | 2280.00 | 0.00 | 273.84 | 273.84 |
| 3076 | 520 | 272.00 | 2284.00 | 0.00 | 274.32 | 274.32 |
| 3080 | 520 | 272.00 | 2288.00 | 0.00 | 274.80 | 274.80 |
| 3084 | 520 | 272.00 | 2292.00 | 0.00 | 275.28 | 275.28 |
| 3088 | 520 | 272.00 | 2296.00 | 0.00 | 275.76 | 275.76 |
| 3092 | 520 | 272.00 | 2300.00 | 0.00 | 276.24 | 276.24 |
| 3096 | 520 | 272.00 | 2304.00 | 0.00 | 276.72 | 276.72 |
| 3100 | 520 | 272.00 | 2308.00 | 0.00 | 277.20 | 277.20 |
| 3104 | 520 | 272.00 | 2312.00 | 0.00 | 277.68 | 277.68 |
| 3108 | 520 | 272.00 | 2316.00 | 0.00 | 278.16 | 278.16 |
| 3112 | 520 | 272.00 | 2320.00 | 0.00 | 278.64 | 278.64 |
| 3116 | 520 | 272.00 | 2324.00 | 0.00 | 279.12 | 279.12 |
| 3120 | 520 | 272.00 | 2328.00 | 0.00 | 279.60 | 279.60 |
| 3124 | 520 | 272.00 | 2332.00 | 0.00 | 280.08 | 280.08 |
| 3128 | 520 | 272.00 | 2336.00 | 0.00 | 280.56 | 280.56 |
| 3132 | 520 | 272.00 | 2340.00 | 0.00 | 281.04 | 281.04 |
| 3136 | 520 | 272.00 | 2344.00 | 0.00 | 281.52 | 281.52 |
| 3140 | 520 | 272.00 | 2348.00 | 0.00 | 282.00 | 282.00 |
| 3144 | 520 | 272.00 | 2352.00 | 0.00 | 282.48 | 282.48 |
| 3148 | 520 | 272.00 | 2356.00 | 0.00 | 282.96 | 282.96 |
| 3152 | 520 | 272.00 | 2360.00 | 0.00 | 283.44 | 283.44 |
| 3156 | 520 | 272.00 | 2364.00 | 0.00 | 283.92 | 283.92 |
| 3160 | 520 | 272.00 | 2368.00 | 0.00 | 284.40 | 284.40 |
| 3164 | 520 | 272.00 | 2372.00 | 0.00 | 284.88 | 284.88 |
| 3168 | 520 | 272.00 | 2376.00 | 0.00 | 285.36 | 285.36 |
| 3172 | 520 | 272.00 | 2380.00 | 0.00 | 285.84 | 285.84 |
| 3176 | 520 | 272.00 | 2384.00 | 0.00 | 286.32 | 286.32 |
| 3180 | 520 | 272.00 | 2388.00 | 0.00 | 286.80 | 286.80 |
| 3184 | 520 | 272.00 | 2392.00 | 0.00 | 287.28 | 287.28 |
| 3188 | 520 | 272.00 | 2396.00 | 0.00 | 287.76 | 287.76 |
| 3192 | 520 | 272.00 | 2400.00 | 0.00 | 288.24 | 288.24 |
| 3196 | 520 | 272.00 | 2404.00 | 0.00 | 288.72 | 288.72 |
| 3200 | 520 | 272.00 | 2408.00 | 0.00 | 289.20 | 289.20 |
| 3204 | 520 | 272.00 | 2412.00 | 0.00 | 289.68 | 289.68 |
| 3208 | 520 | 272.00 | 2416.00 | 0.00 | 290.16 | 290.16 |
| 3212 | 520 | 272.00 | 2420.00 | 0.00 | 290.64 | 290.64 |
| 3216 | 520 | 272.00 | 2424.00 | 0.00 | 291.12 | 291.12 |
| 3220 | 520 | 272.00 | 2428.00 | 0.00 | 291.60 | 291.60 |
| 3224 | 520 | 272.00 | 2432.00 | 0.00 | 292.08 | 292.08 |
| 3228 | 520 | 272.00 | 2436.00 | 0.00 | 292.56 | 292.56 |
| 3232 | 520 | 272.00 | 2440.00 | 0.00 | 293.04 | 293.04 |
| 3236 | 520 | 272.00 | 2444.00 | 0.00 | 293.52 | 293.52 |
| 3240 | 520 | 272.00 | 2448.00 | 0.00 | 294.00 | 294.00 |
| 3244 | 520 | 272.00 | 2452.00 | 0.00 | 294.48 | 294.48 |
| 3248 | 520 | 272.00 | 2456.00 | 0.00 | 294.96 | 294.96 |
| 3252 | 520 | 272.00 | 2460.00 | 0.00 | 295.44 | 295.44 |
| 3256 | 520 | 272.00 | 2464.00 | 0.00 | 295.92 | 295.92 |

**Monthly table**

**Table letter H**

| Employee's earnings up to and including the UEL | Earnings at the LEL (where earnings are equal to or exceed the LEL) | Earnings above the LEL, up to and including the PT | Earnings above the PT, up to and including the UEL | Employer's NICs due on all earnings above the ST | Employee's NICs due on all earnings above the PT | Total of employee's and employer's NICs (for information only) |
|---|---|---|---|---|---|---|
| | | 1a | 1b | 1c | 1d | 1e |
| £ | £ | £ p | £ p | £ p | £ p | £ p |
| 3260 | 520 | 272.00 | 2468.00 | 0.00 | 296.40 | 296.40 |
| 3264 | 520 | 272.00 | 2472.00 | 0.00 | 296.88 | 296.88 |
| 3268 | 520 | 272.00 | 2476.00 | 0.00 | 297.36 | 297.36 |
| 3272 | 520 | 272.00 | 2480.00 | 0.00 | 297.84 | 297.84 |
| 3276 | 520 | 272.00 | 2484.00 | 0.00 | 298.32 | 298.32 |
| 3280 | 520 | 272.00 | 2488.00 | 0.00 | 298.80 | 298.80 |
| 3284 | 520 | 272.00 | 2492.00 | 0.00 | 299.28 | 299.28 |
| 3288 | 520 | 272.00 | 2496.00 | 0.00 | 299.76 | 299.76 |
| 3292 | 520 | 272.00 | 2500.00 | 0.00 | 300.24 | 300.24 |
| 3296 | 520 | 272.00 | 2504.00 | 0.00 | 300.72 | 300.72 |
| 3300 | 520 | 272.00 | 2508.00 | 0.00 | 301.20 | 301.20 |
| 3304 | 520 | 272.00 | 2512.00 | 0.00 | 301.68 | 301.68 |
| 3308 | 520 | 272.00 | 2516.00 | 0.00 | 302.16 | 302.16 |
| 3312 | 520 | 272.00 | 2520.00 | 0.00 | 302.64 | 302.64 |
| 3316 | 520 | 272.00 | 2524.00 | 0.00 | 303.12 | 303.12 |
| 3320 | 520 | 272.00 | 2528.00 | 0.00 | 303.60 | 303.60 |
| 3324 | 520 | 272.00 | 2532.00 | 0.00 | 304.08 | 304.08 |
| 3328 | 520 | 272.00 | 2536.00 | 0.00 | 304.56 | 304.56 |
| 3332 | 520 | 272.00 | 2540.00 | 0.00 | 305.04 | 305.04 |
| 3336 | 520 | 272.00 | 2544.00 | 0.00 | 305.52 | 305.52 |
| 3340 | 520 | 272.00 | 2548.00 | 0.00 | 306.00 | 306.00 |
| 3344 | 520 | 272.00 | 2552.00 | 0.00 | 306.48 | 306.48 |
| 3348 | 520 | 272.00 | 2556.00 | 0.00 | 306.96 | 306.96 |
| 3352 | 520 | 272.00 | 2560.00 | 0.00 | 307.44 | 307.44 |
| 3356 | 520 | 272.00 | 2564.00 | 0.00 | 307.92 | 307.92 |
| 3360 | 520 | 272.00 | 2568.00 | 0.00 | 308.40 | 308.40 |
| 3364 | 520 | 272.00 | 2572.00 | 0.00 | 308.88 | 308.88 |
| 3368 | 520 | 272.00 | 2576.00 | 0.00 | 309.36 | 309.36 |
| 3372 | 520 | 272.00 | 2580.00 | 0.00 | 309.84 | 309.84 |
| 3376 | 520 | 272.00 | 2584.00 | 0.00 | 310.32 | 310.32 |
| 3380 | 520 | 272.00 | 2588.00 | 0.00 | 310.80 | 310.80 |
| 3384 | 520 | 272.00 | 2592.00 | 0.00 | 311.28 | 311.28 |
| 3388 | 520 | 272.00 | 2596.00 | 0.00 | 311.76 | 311.76 |
| 3392 | 520 | 272.00 | 2600.00 | 0.00 | 312.24 | 312.24 |
| 3396 | 520 | 272.00 | 2604.00 | 0.00 | 312.72 | 312.72 |
| 3400 | 520 | 272.00 | 2608.00 | 0.00 | 313.20 | 313.20 |
| 3404 | 520 | 272.00 | 2612.00 | 0.00 | 313.68 | 313.68 |
| 3408 | 520 | 272.00 | 2616.00 | 0.00 | 314.16 | 314.16 |
| 3412 | 520 | 272.00 | 2620.00 | 0.00 | 314.64 | 314.64 |
| 3416 | 520 | 272.00 | 2624.00 | 0.00 | 315.12 | 315.12 |
| 3420 | 520 | 272.00 | 2628.00 | 0.00 | 315.60 | 315.60 |
| 3424 | 520 | 272.00 | 2632.00 | 0.00 | 316.08 | 316.08 |
| 3428 | 520 | 272.00 | 2636.00 | 0.00 | 316.56 | 316.56 |
| 3432 | 520 | 272.00 | 2640.00 | 0.00 | 317.04 | 317.04 |
| 3436 | 520 | 272.00 | 2644.00 | 0.00 | 317.52 | 317.52 |
| 3440 | 520 | 272.00 | 2648.00 | 0.00 | 318.00 | 318.00 |
| 3444 | 520 | 272.00 | 2652.00 | 0.00 | 318.48 | 318.48 |
| 3448 | 520 | 272.00 | 2656.00 | 0.00 | 318.96 | 318.96 |
| 3452 | 520 | 272.00 | 2660.00 | 0.00 | 319.44 | 319.44 |
| 3456 | 520 | 272.00 | 2664.00 | 0.00 | 319.92 | 319.92 |
| 3460 | 520 | 272.00 | 2668.00 | 0.00 | 320.40 | 320.40 |
| 3464 | 520 | 272.00 | 2672.00 | 0.00 | 320.88 | 320.88 |
| 3468 | 520 | 272.00 | 2676.00 | 0.00 | 321.36 | 321.36 |
| 3472 | 520 | 272.00 | 2680.00 | 0.00 | 321.84 | 321.84 |
| 3476 | 520 | 272.00 | 2684.00 | 0.00 | 322.32 | 322.32 |

# Monthly table

**Table letter H**

| Employee's earnings up to and including the UEL | Earnings at the LEL (where earnings are equal to or exceed the LEL) 1a | Earnings above the LEL, up to and including the PT 1b | Earnings above the PT, up to and including the UEL 1c | Employer's NICs due on all earnings above the ST 1d | Employee's NICs due on all earnings above the PT 1e | Total of employee's and employer's NICs (for information only) |
|---|---|---|---|---|---|---|
| £ | £ | £ p | £ p | £ p | £ p | £ p |
| 3480 | 520 | 272.00 | 2688.00 | 0.00 | 322.80 | 322.80 |
| 3484 | 520 | 272.00 | 2692.00 | 0.00 | 323.28 | 323.28 |
| 3488 | 520 | 272.00 | 2696.00 | 0.00 | 323.76 | 323.76 |
| 3492 | 520 | 272.00 | 2700.00 | 0.00 | 324.24 | 324.24 |
| 3496 | 520 | 272.00 | 2704.00 | 0.00 | 324.72 | 324.72 |
| 3500 | 520 | 272.00 | 2708.00 | 0.00 | 325.20 | 325.20 |
| 3504 | 520 | 272.00 | 2712.00 | 0.00 | 325.68 | 325.68 |
| 3508 | 520 | 272.00 | 2716.00 | 0.00 | 326.16 | 326.16 |
| 3512 | 520 | 272.00 | 2720.00 | 0.00 | 326.64 | 326.64 |
| 3516 | 520 | 272.00 | 2724.00 | 0.00 | 327.12 | 327.12 |
| 3520 | 520 | 272.00 | 2728.00 | 0.00 | 327.60 | 327.60 |
| 3524 | 520 | 272.00 | 2732.00 | 0.00 | 328.08 | 328.08 |
| 3528 | 520 | 272.00 | 2736.00 | 0.00 | 328.56 | 328.56 |
| 3532 | 520 | 272.00 | 2740.00 | 0.00 | 329.04 | 329.04 |
| 3536 | 520 | 272.00 | 2744.00 | 0.00 | 329.52 | 329.52 |
| 3540 | 520 | 272.00 | 2748.00 | 0.00 | 330.00 | 330.00 |
| 3544 | 520 | 272.00 | 2752.00 | 0.00 | 330.48 | 330.48 |
| 3548 | 520 | 272.00 | 2756.00 | 0.00 | 330.96 | 330.96 |
| 3552 | 520 | 272.00 | 2760.00 | 0.00 | 331.44 | 331.44 |
| 3556 | 520 | 272.00 | 2764.00 | 0.00 | 331.92 | 331.92 |
| 3560 | 520 | 272.00 | 2768.00 | 0.00 | 332.40 | 332.40 |
| 3564 | 520 | 272.00 | 2772.00 | 0.00 | 332.88 | 332.88 |
| 3568 | 520 | 272.00 | 2776.00 | 0.00 | 333.36 | 333.36 |
| 3572 | 520 | 272.00 | 2780.00 | 0.00 | 333.84 | 333.84 |
| 3576 | 520 | 272.00 | 2784.00 | 0.00 | 334.32 | 334.32 |
| 3580 | 520 | 272.00 | 2788.00 | 0.00 | 334.80 | 334.80 |
| 3584 | 520 | 272.00 | 2792.00 | 0.00 | 335.28 | 335.28 |
| 3588 | 520 | 272.00 | 2796.00 | 0.00 | 335.76 | 335.76 |
| 3592 | 520 | 272.00 | 2800.00 | 0.00 | 336.24 | 336.24 |
| 3596 | 520 | 272.00 | 2804.00 | 0.00 | 336.72 | 336.72 |
| 3600 | 520 | 272.00 | 2808.00 | 0.00 | 337.20 | 337.20 |
| 3604 | 520 | 272.00 | 2812.00 | 0.00 | 337.68 | 337.68 |
| 3608 | 520 | 272.00 | 2816.00 | 0.00 | 338.16 | 338.16 |
| 3612 | 520 | 272.00 | 2820.00 | 0.00 | 338.64 | 338.64 |
| 3616 | 520 | 272.00 | 2824.00 | 0.00 | 339.12 | 339.12 |
| 3620 | 520 | 272.00 | 2828.00 | 0.00 | 339.60 | 339.60 |
| 3624 | 520 | 272.00 | 2832.00 | 0.00 | 340.08 | 340.08 |
| 3628 | 520 | 272.00 | 2836.00 | 0.00 | 340.56 | 340.56 |
| 3632 | 520 | 272.00 | 2840.00 | 0.00 | 341.04 | 341.04 |
| 3636 | 520 | 272.00 | 2844.00 | 0.00 | 341.52 | 341.52 |
| 3640 | 520 | 272.00 | 2848.00 | 0.00 | 342.00 | 342.00 |
| 3644 | 520 | 272.00 | 2852.00 | 0.00 | 342.48 | 342.48 |
| 3648 | 520 | 272.00 | 2856.00 | 0.00 | 342.96 | 342.96 |
| 3652 | 520 | 272.00 | 2860.00 | 0.00 | 343.44 | 343.44 |
| 3656 | 520 | 272.00 | 2864.00 | 0.00 | 343.92 | 343.92 |
| 3660 | 520 | 272.00 | 2868.00 | 0.00 | 344.40 | 344.40 |
| 3664 | 520 | 272.00 | 2872.00 | 0.00 | 344.88 | 344.88 |
| 3668 | 520 | 272.00 | 2876.00 | 0.00 | 345.36 | 345.36 |
| 3672 | 520 | 272.00 | 2880.00 | 0.00 | 345.84 | 345.84 |
| 3676 | 520 | 272.00 | 2884.00 | 0.00 | 346.32 | 346.32 |
| 3680 | 520 | 272.00 | 2888.00 | 0.00 | 346.80 | 346.80 |
| 3684 | 520 | 272.00 | 2892.00 | 0.00 | 347.28 | 347.28 |
| 3688 | 520 | 272.00 | 2896.00 | 0.00 | 347.76 | 347.76 |
| 3692 | 520 | 272.00 | 2900.00 | 0.00 | 348.24 | 348.24 |
| 3696 | 520 | 272.00 | 2904.00 | 0.00 | 348.72 | 348.72 |

**Monthly table**  Table letter H

| Employee's earnings up to and including the UEL | Earnings at the LEL (where earnings are equal to or exceed the LEL) 1a | Earnings above the LEL, up to and including the PT 1b | Earnings above the PT, up to and including the UEL 1c | Employer's NICs due on all earnings above the ST 1d | Employee's NICs due on all earnings above the PT 1e | Total of employee's and employer's NICs (for information only) |
|---|---|---|---|---|---|---|
| £ | £ | £ p | £ p | £ p | £ p | £ p |
| 3700 | 520 | 272.00 | 2908.00 | 0.00 | 349.20 | 349.20 |
| 3704 | 520 | 272.00 | 2912.00 | 0.00 | 349.68 | 349.68 |
| 3708 | 520 | 272.00 | 2916.00 | 0.00 | 350.16 | 350.16 |
| 3712 | 520 | 272.00 | 2920.00 | 0.00 | 350.64 | 350.64 |
| 3716 | 520 | 272.00 | 2924.00 | 0.00 | 351.12 | 351.12 |
| 3720 | 520 | 272.00 | 2928.00 | 0.00 | 351.60 | 351.60 |
| 3724 | 520 | 272.00 | 2932.00 | 0.00 | 352.08 | 352.08 |
| 3728 | 520 | 272.00 | 2936.00 | 0.00 | 352.56 | 352.56 |
| 3732 | 520 | 272.00 | 2940.00 | 0.00 | 353.04 | 353.04 |
| 3736 | 520 | 272.00 | 2944.00 | 0.00 | 353.52 | 353.52 |
| 3740 | 520 | 272.00 | 2948.00 | 0.00 | 354.00 | 354.00 |
| 3744 | 520 | 272.00 | 2952.00 | 0.00 | 354.48 | 354.48 |
| 3748 | 520 | 272.00 | 2956.00 | 0.00 | 354.96 | 354.96 |
| 3752 | 520 | 272.00 | 2960.00 | 0.00 | 355.44 | 355.44 |
| 3756 | 520 | 272.00 | 2964.00 | 0.00 | 355.92 | 355.92 |
| 3760 | 520 | 272.00 | 2968.00 | 0.00 | 356.40 | 356.40 |
| 3764 | 520 | 272.00 | 2972.00 | 0.00 | 356.88 | 356.88 |
| 3768 | 520 | 272.00 | 2976.00 | 0.00 | 357.36 | 357.36 |
| 3772 | 520 | 272.00 | 2980.00 | 0.00 | 357.84 | 357.84 |
| 3776 | 520 | 272.00 | 2984.00 | 0.00 | 358.32 | 358.32 |
| 3780 | 520 | 272.00 | 2988.00 | 0.00 | 358.80 | 358.80 |
| 3784 | 520 | 272.00 | 2992.00 | 0.00 | 359.28 | 359.28 |
| 3788 | 520 | 272.00 | 2996.00 | 0.00 | 359.76 | 359.76 |
| 3792 | 520 | 272.00 | 3000.00 | 0.00 | 360.24 | 360.24 |
| 3796 | 520 | 272.00 | 3004.00 | 0.00 | 360.72 | 360.72 |
| 3800 | 520 | 272.00 | 3008.00 | 0.00 | 361.20 | 361.20 |
| 3804 | 520 | 272.00 | 3012.00 | 0.00 | 361.68 | 361.68 |
| 3808 | 520 | 272.00 | 3016.00 | 0.00 | 362.16 | 362.16 |
| 3812 | 520 | 272.00 | 3020.00 | 0.00 | 362.64 | 362.64 |
| 3816 | 520 | 272.00 | 3024.00 | 0.00 | 363.12 | 363.12 |
| 3820 | 520 | 272.00 | 3028.00 | 0.00 | 363.60 | 363.60 |
| 3824 | 520 | 272.00 | 3032.00 | 0.00 | 364.08 | 364.08 |
| 3828 | 520 | 272.00 | 3036.00 | 0.00 | 364.56 | 364.56 |
| 3832 | 520 | 272.00 | 3040.00 | 0.00 | 365.04 | 365.04 |
| 3836 | 520 | 272.00 | 3044.00 | 0.00 | 365.52 | 365.52 |
| 3840 | 520 | 272.00 | 3048.00 | 0.00 | 366.00 | 366.00 |
| 3844 | 520 | 272.00 | 3052.00 | 0.00 | 366.48 | 366.48 |
| 3848 | 520 | 272.00 | 3056.00 | 0.00 | 366.96 | 366.96 |
| 3852 | 520 | 272.00 | 3060.00 | 0.00 | 367.44 | 367.44 |
| 3856 | 520 | 272.00 | 3064.00 | 0.00 | 367.92 | 367.92 |
| 3860 | 520 | 272.00 | 3068.00 | 0.00 | 368.40 | 368.40 |
| 3864 | 520 | 272.00 | 3072.00 | 0.00 | 368.88 | 368.88 |
| 3868 | 520 | 272.00 | 3076.00 | 0.00 | 369.36 | 369.36 |
| 3872 | 520 | 272.00 | 3080.00 | 0.00 | 369.84 | 369.84 |
| 3876 | 520 | 272.00 | 3084.00 | 0.00 | 370.32 | 370.32 |
| 3880 | 520 | 272.00 | 3088.00 | 0.00 | 370.80 | 370.80 |
| 3884 | 520 | 272.00 | 3092.00 | 0.00 | 371.28 | 371.28 |
| 3888 | 520 | 272.00 | 3096.00 | 0.00 | 371.76 | 371.76 |
| 3892 | 520 | 272.00 | 3100.00 | 0.00 | 372.24 | 372.24 |
| 3896 | 520 | 272.00 | 3104.00 | 0.00 | 372.72 | 372.72 |
| 3900 | 520 | 272.00 | 3108.00 | 0.00 | 373.20 | 373.20 |
| 3904 | 520 | 272.00 | 3112.00 | 0.00 | 373.68 | 373.68 |
| 3908 | 520 | 272.00 | 3116.00 | 0.00 | 374.16 | 374.16 |
| 3912 | 520 | 272.00 | 3120.00 | 0.00 | 374.64 | 374.64 |
| 3916 | 520 | 272.00 | 3124.00 | 0.00 | 375.12 | 375.12 |

## Table letter H

**Monthly table**

| Employee's earnings up to and including the UEL | Earnings at the LEL (where earnings are equal to or exceed the LEL) 1a | Earnings above the LEL, up to and including the PT 1b | Earnings above the PT, up to and including the UEL 1c | Employer's NICs due on all earnings above the ST 1d | Employee's NICs due on all earnings above the PT 1e | Total of employee's and employer's NICs (for information only) |
|---|---|---|---|---|---|---|
| £ | £ | £ p | £ p | £ p | £ p | £ p |
| 3920 | 520 | 272.00 | 3128.00 | 0.00 | 375.60 | 375.60 |
| 3924 | 520 | 272.00 | 3132.00 | 0.00 | 376.08 | 376.08 |
| 3928 | 520 | 272.00 | 3136.00 | 0.00 | 376.56 | 376.56 |
| 3932 | 520 | 272.00 | 3140.00 | 0.00 | 377.04 | 377.04 |
| 3936 | 520 | 272.00 | 3144.00 | 0.00 | 377.52 | 377.52 |
| 3940 | 520 | 272.00 | 3148.00 | 0.00 | 378.00 | 378.00 |
| 3944 | 520 | 272.00 | 3152.00 | 0.00 | 378.48 | 378.48 |
| 3948 | 520 | 272.00 | 3156.00 | 0.00 | 378.96 | 378.96 |
| 3952 | 520 | 272.00 | 3160.00 | 0.00 | 379.44 | 379.44 |
| 3956 | 520 | 272.00 | 3164.00 | 0.00 | 379.92 | 379.92 |
| 3960 | 520 | 272.00 | 3168.00 | 0.00 | 380.40 | 380.40 |
| 3964 | 520 | 272.00 | 3172.00 | 0.00 | 380.88 | 380.88 |
| 3968 | 520 | 272.00 | 3176.00 | 0.00 | 381.36 | 381.36 |
| 3972 | 520 | 272.00 | 3180.00 | 0.00 | 381.84 | 381.84 |
| 3976 | 520 | 272.00 | 3184.00 | 0.00 | 382.32 | 382.32 |
| 3980 | 520 | 272.00 | 3188.00 | 0.00 | 382.80 | 382.80 |
| 3984 | 520 | 272.00 | 3192.00 | 0.00 | 383.28 | 383.28 |
| 3988 | 520 | 272.00 | 3196.00 | 0.00 | 383.76 | 383.76 |
| 3992 | 520 | 272.00 | 3200.00 | 0.00 | 384.24 | 384.24 |
| 3996 | 520 | 272.00 | 3204.00 | 0.00 | 384.72 | 384.72 |
| 4000 | 520 | 272.00 | 3208.00 | 0.00 | 385.20 | 385.20 |
| 4004 | 520 | 272.00 | 3212.00 | 0.00 | 385.68 | 385.68 |
| 4008 | 520 | 272.00 | 3216.00 | 0.00 | 386.16 | 386.16 |
| 4012 | 520 | 272.00 | 3220.00 | 0.00 | 386.64 | 386.64 |
| 4016 | 520 | 272.00 | 3224.00 | 0.00 | 387.12 | 387.12 |
| 4020 | 520 | 272.00 | 3228.00 | 0.00 | 387.60 | 387.60 |
| 4024 | 520 | 272.00 | 3232.00 | 0.00 | 388.08 | 388.08 |
| 4028 | 520 | 272.00 | 3236.00 | 0.00 | 388.56 | 388.56 |
| 4032 | 520 | 272.00 | 3240.00 | 0.00 | 389.04 | 389.04 |
| 4036 | 520 | 272.00 | 3244.00 | 0.00 | 389.52 | 389.52 |
| 4040 | 520 | 272.00 | 3248.00 | 0.00 | 390.00 | 390.00 |
| 4044 | 520 | 272.00 | 3252.00 | 0.00 | 390.48 | 390.48 |
| 4048 | 520 | 272.00 | 3256.00 | 0.00 | 390.96 | 390.96 |
| 4052 | 520 | 272.00 | 3260.00 | 0.00 | 391.44 | 391.44 |
| 4056 | 520 | 272.00 | 3264.00 | 0.00 | 391.92 | 391.92 |
| 4060 | 520 | 272.00 | 3268.00 | 0.00 | 392.40 | 392.40 |
| 4064 | 520 | 272.00 | 3272.00 | 0.00 | 392.88 | 392.88 |
| 4068 | 520 | 272.00 | 3276.00 | 0.00 | 393.36 | 393.36 |
| 4072 | 520 | 272.00 | 3280.00 | 0.00 | 393.84 | 393.84 |
| 4076 | 520 | 272.00 | 3284.00 | 0.00 | 394.32 | 394.32 |
| 4080 | 520 | 272.00 | 3288.00 | 0.00 | 394.80 | 394.80 |
| 4084 | 520 | 272.00 | 3292.00 | 0.00 | 395.28 | 395.28 |
| 4088 | 520 | 272.00 | 3296.00 | 0.00 | 395.76 | 395.76 |
| 4092 | 520 | 272.00 | 3300.00 | 0.00 | 396.24 | 396.24 |
| 4096 | 520 | 272.00 | 3304.00 | 0.00 | 396.72 | 396.72 |
| 4100 | 520 | 272.00 | 3308.00 | 0.00 | 397.20 | 397.20 |
| 4104 | 520 | 272.00 | 3312.00 | 0.00 | 397.68 | 397.68 |
| 4108 | 520 | 272.00 | 3316.00 | 0.00 | 398.16 | 398.16 |
| 4112 | 520 | 272.00 | 3320.00 | 0.00 | 398.64 | 398.64 |
| 4116 | 520 | 272.00 | 3324.00 | 0.00 | 399.12 | 399.12 |
| 4120 | 520 | 272.00 | 3328.00 | 0.00 | 399.60 | 399.60 |
| 4124 | 520 | 272.00 | 3332.00 | 0.00 | 400.08 | 400.08 |
| 4128 | 520 | 272.00 | 3336.00 | 0.00 | 400.56 | 400.56 |
| 4132 | 520 | 272.00 | 3340.00 | 0.00 | 401.04 | 401.04 |
| 4136 | 520 | 272.00 | 3344.00 | 0.00 | 401.52 | 401.52 |

## Monthly table

**Table letter H**

| Employee's earnings up to and including the UEL | Earnings at the LEL (where earnings are equal to or exceed the LEL) | Earnings above the LEL, up to and including the PT | Earnings above the PT, up to and including the UEL | Employer's NICs due on all earnings above the ST | Employee's NICs due on all earnings above the PT | Total of employee's and employer's NICs (for information only) |
|---|---|---|---|---|---|---|
| | 1a | 1b | 1c | 1d | 1e | |
| £ | £ | £ p | £ p | £ p | £ p | £ p |
| 4140 | 520 | 272.00 | 3348.00 | 0.00 | 402.00 | 402.00 |
| 4144 | 520 | 272.00 | 3352.00 | 0.00 | 402.48 | 402.48 |
| 4148 | 520 | 272.00 | 3356.00 | 0.00 | 402.96 | 402.96 |
| 4152 | 520 | 272.00 | 3360.00 | 0.00 | 403.44 | 403.44 |
| 4156 | 520 | 272.00 | 3364.00 | 0.00 | 403.92 | 403.92 |
| 4160 | 520 | 272.00 | 3368.00 | 0.00 | 404.40 | 404.40 |
| 4164 | 520 | 272.00 | 3372.00 | 0.00 | 404.82 | 404.82 |
| 4167 | 520 | 272.00 | 3375.00 | 0.00 | 405.00 | 405.00 |

If the employee's gross pay is over £4,167, go to page 178.

# Weekly table for NICs where employee has deferment for use from 6 April 2020 to 5 April 2021

**Table letter J**

Use this table for employees who are aged 21 or over, for whom you hold form CA2700.

Do not use this table for:

- any tax year other than 2020 to 2021
- employees who are under the age of 21, for whom you hold form CA2700 (go to Table letter Z)
- employees who are State Pension age or over (go to Table letter C in booklet CA41)

**Completing form RT11, 'Deductions working sheet' or substitute**

1 Enter 'J' in the NICs Category Letter column on form RT11.

2 Copy the figures in columns 1a – 1e of the table to columns 1a – 1e on the line next to the tax week in which the employee is paid, on form RT11.

If the employee's total earnings fall between the LEL and the UEL/UST/AUST and the exact gross pay is not shown in the table, use the next smaller figure shown. If the employee's total earnings exceed the UEL/UST/AUST, go to page 163.

The figures in the left-hand column of each table show steps between the LEL and the UEL/UST/AUST. The NICs liability for each step, with the exception of the LEL, ST, PT, UEL, UST and AUST is worked out at the mid-point of the steps so you and your employee may pay slightly more or less than if you used the exact percentage method.

| Employee's earnings up to and including the UEL | Earnings at the LEL (where earnings are equal to or exceed the LEL) | Earnings above the LEL, up to and including the PT | Earnings above the PT, up to and including the UEL | Employer's NICs due on all earnings above the ST | Employee's NICs due on all earnings above the PT | Total of employee's and employer's NICs (for information only) |
|---|---|---|---|---|---|---|
| | | 1a | 1b | 1c | 1d | 1e |
| £ | £ | £ p | £ p | £ p | £ p | £ p |
| Up to and including £119.99 | | No NICs liability, make no entry on form RT11 | | | | |
| 120 | 120 | 0.00 | 0.00 | 0.00 | 0.00 | 0.00 |
| 121 | 120 | 1.00 | 0.00 | 0.00 | 0.00 | 0.00 |
| 122 | 120 | 2.00 | 0.00 | 0.00 | 0.00 | 0.00 |
| 123 | 120 | 3.00 | 0.00 | 0.00 | 0.00 | 0.00 |
| 124 | 120 | 4.00 | 0.00 | 0.00 | 0.00 | 0.00 |
| 125 | 120 | 5.00 | 0.00 | 0.00 | 0.00 | 0.00 |
| 126 | 120 | 6.00 | 0.00 | 0.00 | 0.00 | 0.00 |
| 127 | 120 | 7.00 | 0.00 | 0.00 | 0.00 | 0.00 |
| 128 | 120 | 8.00 | 0.00 | 0.00 | 0.00 | 0.00 |
| 129 | 120 | 9.00 | 0.00 | 0.00 | 0.00 | 0.00 |
| 130 | 120 | 10.00 | 0.00 | 0.00 | 0.00 | 0.00 |
| 131 | 120 | 11.00 | 0.00 | 0.00 | 0.00 | 0.00 |
| 132 | 120 | 12.00 | 0.00 | 0.00 | 0.00 | 0.00 |
| 133 | 120 | 13.00 | 0.00 | 0.00 | 0.00 | 0.00 |
| 134 | 120 | 14.00 | 0.00 | 0.00 | 0.00 | 0.00 |
| 135 | 120 | 15.00 | 0.00 | 0.00 | 0.00 | 0.00 |
| 136 | 120 | 16.00 | 0.00 | 0.00 | 0.00 | 0.00 |
| 137 | 120 | 17.00 | 0.00 | 0.00 | 0.00 | 0.00 |
| 138 | 120 | 18.00 | 0.00 | 0.00 | 0.00 | 0.00 |
| 139 | 120 | 19.00 | 0.00 | 0.00 | 0.00 | 0.00 |
| 140 | 120 | 20.00 | 0.00 | 0.00 | 0.00 | 0.00 |
| 141 | 120 | 21.00 | 0.00 | 0.00 | 0.00 | 0.00 |
| 142 | 120 | 22.00 | 0.00 | 0.00 | 0.00 | 0.00 |
| 143 | 120 | 23.00 | 0.00 | 0.00 | 0.00 | 0.00 |
| 144 | 120 | 24.00 | 0.00 | 0.00 | 0.00 | 0.00 |

## Weekly table

**Table letter J**

| Employee's earnings up to and including the UEL | Earnings at the LEL (where earnings are equal to or exceed the LEL) | Earnings above the LEL, up to and including the PT | Earnings above the PT, up to and including the UEL | Employer's NICs due on all earnings above the ST | Employee's NICs due on all earnings above the PT | Total of employee's and employer's NICs (for information only) |
|---|---|---|---|---|---|---|
| | 1a | 1b | 1c | 1d | 1e | |
| £ | £ | £ p | £ p | £ p | £ p | £ p |
| 145 | 120 | 25.00 | 0.00 | 0.00 | 0.00 | 0.00 |
| 146 | 120 | 26.00 | 0.00 | 0.00 | 0.00 | 0.00 |
| 147 | 120 | 27.00 | 0.00 | 0.00 | 0.00 | 0.00 |
| 148 | 120 | 28.00 | 0.00 | 0.00 | 0.00 | 0.00 |
| 149 | 120 | 29.00 | 0.00 | 0.00 | 0.00 | 0.00 |
| 150 | 120 | 30.00 | 0.00 | 0.00 | 0.00 | 0.00 |
| 151 | 120 | 31.00 | 0.00 | 0.00 | 0.00 | 0.00 |
| 152 | 120 | 32.00 | 0.00 | 0.00 | 0.00 | 0.00 |
| 153 | 120 | 33.00 | 0.00 | 0.00 | 0.00 | 0.00 |
| 154 | 120 | 34.00 | 0.00 | 0.00 | 0.00 | 0.00 |
| 155 | 120 | 35.00 | 0.00 | 0.00 | 0.00 | 0.00 |
| 156 | 120 | 36.00 | 0.00 | 0.00 | 0.00 | 0.00 |
| 157 | 120 | 37.00 | 0.00 | 0.00 | 0.00 | 0.00 |
| 158 | 120 | 38.00 | 0.00 | 0.00 | 0.00 | 0.00 |
| 159 | 120 | 39.00 | 0.00 | 0.00 | 0.00 | 0.00 |
| 160 | 120 | 40.00 | 0.00 | 0.00 | 0.00 | 0.00 |
| 161 | 120 | 41.00 | 0.00 | 0.00 | 0.00 | 0.00 |
| 162 | 120 | 42.00 | 0.00 | 0.00 | 0.00 | 0.00 |
| 163 | 120 | 43.00 | 0.00 | 0.00 | 0.00 | 0.00 |
| 164 | 120 | 44.00 | 0.00 | 0.00 | 0.00 | 0.00 |
| 165 | 120 | 45.00 | 0.00 | 0.00 | 0.00 | 0.00 |
| 166 | 120 | 46.00 | 0.00 | 0.00 | 0.00 | 0.00 |
| 167 | 120 | 47.00 | 0.00 | 0.00 | 0.00 | 0.00 |
| 168 | 120 | 48.00 | 0.00 | 0.00 | 0.00 | 0.00 |
| 169 | 120 | 49.00 | 0.00 | 0.00 | 0.00 | 0.00 |
| 170 | 120 | 50.00 | 0.00 | 0.21 | 0.00 | 0.21 |
| 171 | 120 | 51.00 | 0.00 | 0.34 | 0.00 | 0.34 |
| 172 | 120 | 52.00 | 0.00 | 0.48 | 0.00 | 0.48 |
| 173 | 120 | 53.00 | 0.00 | 0.62 | 0.00 | 0.62 |
| 174 | 120 | 54.00 | 0.00 | 0.76 | 0.00 | 0.76 |
| 175 | 120 | 55.00 | 0.00 | 0.90 | 0.00 | 0.90 |
| 176 | 120 | 56.00 | 0.00 | 1.03 | 0.00 | 1.03 |
| 177 | 120 | 57.00 | 0.00 | 1.17 | 0.00 | 1.17 |
| 178 | 120 | 58.00 | 0.00 | 1.31 | 0.00 | 1.31 |
| 179 | 120 | 59.00 | 0.00 | 1.45 | 0.00 | 1.45 |
| 180 | 120 | 60.00 | 0.00 | 1.59 | 0.00 | 1.59 |
| 181 | 120 | 61.00 | 0.00 | 1.72 | 0.00 | 1.72 |
| 182 | 120 | 62.00 | 0.00 | 1.86 | 0.00 | 1.86 |
| 183 | 120 | 63.00 | 0.00 | 1.93 | 0.00 | 1.93 |
| 184 | 120 | 63.00 | 1.00 | 2.14 | 0.03 | 2.17 |
| 185 | 120 | 63.00 | 2.00 | 2.27 | 0.05 | 2.32 |
| 186 | 120 | 63.00 | 3.00 | 2.41 | 0.07 | 2.48 |
| 187 | 120 | 63.00 | 4.00 | 2.55 | 0.09 | 2.64 |
| 188 | 120 | 63.00 | 5.00 | 2.69 | 0.11 | 2.80 |
| 189 | 120 | 63.00 | 6.00 | 2.83 | 0.13 | 2.96 |
| 190 | 120 | 63.00 | 7.00 | 2.96 | 0.15 | 3.11 |
| 191 | 120 | 63.00 | 8.00 | 3.10 | 0.17 | 3.27 |
| 192 | 120 | 63.00 | 9.00 | 3.24 | 0.19 | 3.43 |
| 193 | 120 | 63.00 | 10.00 | 3.38 | 0.21 | 3.59 |
| 194 | 120 | 63.00 | 11.00 | 3.52 | 0.23 | 3.75 |
| 195 | 120 | 63.00 | 12.00 | 3.65 | 0.25 | 3.90 |
| 196 | 120 | 63.00 | 13.00 | 3.79 | 0.27 | 4.06 |
| 197 | 120 | 63.00 | 14.00 | 3.93 | 0.29 | 4.22 |
| 198 | 120 | 63.00 | 15.00 | 4.07 | 0.31 | 4.38 |
| 199 | 120 | 63.00 | 16.00 | 4.21 | 0.33 | 4.54 |

# Table letter J

**Weekly table**

| Employee's earnings up to and including the UEL | Earnings at the LEL (where earnings are equal to or exceed the LEL) | Earnings above the LEL, up to and including the PT | Earnings above the PT, up to and including the UEL | Employer's NICs due on all earnings above the ST | Employee's NICs due on all earnings above the PT | Total of employee's and employer's NICs (for information only) |
|---|---|---|---|---|---|---|
| | 1a | 1b | 1c | 1d | 1e | |
| £ | £ | £ p | £ p | £ p | £ p | £ p |
| 200 | 120 | 63.00 | 17.00 | 4.34 | 0.35 | 4.69 |
| 201 | 120 | 63.00 | 18.00 | 4.48 | 0.37 | 4.85 |
| 202 | 120 | 63.00 | 19.00 | 4.62 | 0.39 | 5.01 |
| 203 | 120 | 63.00 | 20.00 | 4.76 | 0.41 | 5.17 |
| 204 | 120 | 63.00 | 21.00 | 4.90 | 0.43 | 5.33 |
| 205 | 120 | 63.00 | 22.00 | 5.03 | 0.45 | 5.48 |
| 206 | 120 | 63.00 | 23.00 | 5.17 | 0.47 | 5.64 |
| 207 | 120 | 63.00 | 24.00 | 5.31 | 0.49 | 5.80 |
| 208 | 120 | 63.00 | 25.00 | 5.45 | 0.51 | 5.96 |
| 209 | 120 | 63.00 | 26.00 | 5.59 | 0.53 | 6.12 |
| 210 | 120 | 63.00 | 27.00 | 5.72 | 0.55 | 6.27 |
| 211 | 120 | 63.00 | 28.00 | 5.86 | 0.57 | 6.43 |
| 212 | 120 | 63.00 | 29.00 | 6.00 | 0.59 | 6.59 |
| 213 | 120 | 63.00 | 30.00 | 6.14 | 0.61 | 6.75 |
| 214 | 120 | 63.00 | 31.00 | 6.28 | 0.63 | 6.91 |
| 215 | 120 | 63.00 | 32.00 | 6.41 | 0.65 | 7.06 |
| 216 | 120 | 63.00 | 33.00 | 6.55 | 0.67 | 7.22 |
| 217 | 120 | 63.00 | 34.00 | 6.69 | 0.69 | 7.38 |
| 218 | 120 | 63.00 | 35.00 | 6.83 | 0.71 | 7.54 |
| 219 | 120 | 63.00 | 36.00 | 6.97 | 0.73 | 7.70 |
| 220 | 120 | 63.00 | 37.00 | 7.10 | 0.75 | 7.85 |
| 221 | 120 | 63.00 | 38.00 | 7.24 | 0.77 | 8.01 |
| 222 | 120 | 63.00 | 39.00 | 7.38 | 0.79 | 8.17 |
| 223 | 120 | 63.00 | 40.00 | 7.52 | 0.81 | 8.33 |
| 224 | 120 | 63.00 | 41.00 | 7.66 | 0.83 | 8.49 |
| 225 | 120 | 63.00 | 42.00 | 7.79 | 0.85 | 8.64 |
| 226 | 120 | 63.00 | 43.00 | 7.93 | 0.87 | 8.80 |
| 227 | 120 | 63.00 | 44.00 | 8.07 | 0.89 | 8.96 |
| 228 | 120 | 63.00 | 45.00 | 8.21 | 0.91 | 9.12 |
| 229 | 120 | 63.00 | 46.00 | 8.35 | 0.93 | 9.28 |
| 230 | 120 | 63.00 | 47.00 | 8.48 | 0.95 | 9.43 |
| 231 | 120 | 63.00 | 48.00 | 8.62 | 0.97 | 9.59 |
| 232 | 120 | 63.00 | 49.00 | 8.76 | 0.99 | 9.75 |
| 233 | 120 | 63.00 | 50.00 | 8.90 | 1.01 | 9.91 |
| 234 | 120 | 63.00 | 51.00 | 9.04 | 1.03 | 10.07 |
| 235 | 120 | 63.00 | 52.00 | 9.17 | 1.05 | 10.22 |
| 236 | 120 | 63.00 | 53.00 | 9.31 | 1.07 | 10.38 |
| 237 | 120 | 63.00 | 54.00 | 9.45 | 1.09 | 10.54 |
| 238 | 120 | 63.00 | 55.00 | 9.59 | 1.11 | 10.70 |
| 239 | 120 | 63.00 | 56.00 | 9.73 | 1.13 | 10.86 |
| 240 | 120 | 63.00 | 57.00 | 9.86 | 1.15 | 11.01 |
| 241 | 120 | 63.00 | 58.00 | 10.00 | 1.17 | 11.17 |
| 242 | 120 | 63.00 | 59.00 | 10.14 | 1.19 | 11.33 |
| 243 | 120 | 63.00 | 60.00 | 10.28 | 1.21 | 11.49 |
| 244 | 120 | 63.00 | 61.00 | 10.42 | 1.23 | 11.65 |
| 245 | 120 | 63.00 | 62.00 | 10.55 | 1.25 | 11.80 |
| 246 | 120 | 63.00 | 63.00 | 10.69 | 1.27 | 11.96 |
| 247 | 120 | 63.00 | 64.00 | 10.83 | 1.29 | 12.12 |
| 248 | 120 | 63.00 | 65.00 | 10.97 | 1.31 | 12.28 |
| 249 | 120 | 63.00 | 66.00 | 11.11 | 1.33 | 12.44 |
| 250 | 120 | 63.00 | 67.00 | 11.24 | 1.35 | 12.59 |
| 251 | 120 | 63.00 | 68.00 | 11.38 | 1.37 | 12.75 |
| 252 | 120 | 63.00 | 69.00 | 11.52 | 1.39 | 12.91 |
| 253 | 120 | 63.00 | 70.00 | 11.66 | 1.41 | 13.07 |
| 254 | 120 | 63.00 | 71.00 | 11.80 | 1.43 | 13.23 |

**Weekly table**

Table letter J

| Employee's earnings up to and including the UEL | Earnings at the LEL (where earnings are equal to or exceed the LEL) | Earnings above the LEL, up to and including the PT | Earnings above the PT, up to and including the UEL | Employer's NICs due on all earnings above the ST | Employee's NICs due on all earnings above the PT | Total of employee's and employer's NICs (for information only) |
|---|---|---|---|---|---|---|
| | | 1a | 1b | 1c | 1d | 1e |
| £ | £ | £ p | £ p | £ p | £ p | £ p |
| 255 | 120 | 63.00 | 72.00 | 11.93 | 1.45 | 13.38 |
| 256 | 120 | 63.00 | 73.00 | 12.07 | 1.47 | 13.54 |
| 257 | 120 | 63.00 | 74.00 | 12.21 | 1.49 | 13.70 |
| 258 | 120 | 63.00 | 75.00 | 12.35 | 1.51 | 13.86 |
| 259 | 120 | 63.00 | 76.00 | 12.49 | 1.53 | 14.02 |
| 260 | 120 | 63.00 | 77.00 | 12.62 | 1.55 | 14.17 |
| 261 | 120 | 63.00 | 78.00 | 12.76 | 1.57 | 14.33 |
| 262 | 120 | 63.00 | 79.00 | 12.90 | 1.59 | 14.49 |
| 263 | 120 | 63.00 | 80.00 | 13.04 | 1.61 | 14.65 |
| 264 | 120 | 63.00 | 81.00 | 13.18 | 1.63 | 14.81 |
| 265 | 120 | 63.00 | 82.00 | 13.31 | 1.65 | 14.96 |
| 266 | 120 | 63.00 | 83.00 | 13.45 | 1.67 | 15.12 |
| 267 | 120 | 63.00 | 84.00 | 13.59 | 1.69 | 15.28 |
| 268 | 120 | 63.00 | 85.00 | 13.73 | 1.71 | 15.44 |
| 269 | 120 | 63.00 | 86.00 | 13.87 | 1.73 | 15.60 |
| 270 | 120 | 63.00 | 87.00 | 14.00 | 1.75 | 15.75 |
| 271 | 120 | 63.00 | 88.00 | 14.14 | 1.77 | 15.91 |
| 272 | 120 | 63.00 | 89.00 | 14.28 | 1.79 | 16.07 |
| 273 | 120 | 63.00 | 90.00 | 14.42 | 1.81 | 16.23 |
| 274 | 120 | 63.00 | 91.00 | 14.56 | 1.83 | 16.39 |
| 275 | 120 | 63.00 | 92.00 | 14.69 | 1.85 | 16.54 |
| 276 | 120 | 63.00 | 93.00 | 14.83 | 1.87 | 16.70 |
| 277 | 120 | 63.00 | 94.00 | 14.97 | 1.89 | 16.86 |
| 278 | 120 | 63.00 | 95.00 | 15.11 | 1.91 | 17.02 |
| 279 | 120 | 63.00 | 96.00 | 15.25 | 1.93 | 17.18 |
| 280 | 120 | 63.00 | 97.00 | 15.38 | 1.95 | 17.33 |
| 281 | 120 | 63.00 | 98.00 | 15.52 | 1.97 | 17.49 |
| 282 | 120 | 63.00 | 99.00 | 15.66 | 1.99 | 17.65 |
| 283 | 120 | 63.00 | 100.00 | 15.80 | 2.01 | 17.81 |
| 284 | 120 | 63.00 | 101.00 | 15.94 | 2.03 | 17.97 |
| 285 | 120 | 63.00 | 102.00 | 16.07 | 2.05 | 18.12 |
| 286 | 120 | 63.00 | 103.00 | 16.21 | 2.07 | 18.28 |
| 287 | 120 | 63.00 | 104.00 | 16.35 | 2.09 | 18.44 |
| 288 | 120 | 63.00 | 105.00 | 16.49 | 2.11 | 18.60 |
| 289 | 120 | 63.00 | 106.00 | 16.63 | 2.13 | 18.76 |
| 290 | 120 | 63.00 | 107.00 | 16.76 | 2.15 | 18.91 |
| 291 | 120 | 63.00 | 108.00 | 16.90 | 2.17 | 19.07 |
| 292 | 120 | 63.00 | 109.00 | 17.04 | 2.19 | 19.23 |
| 293 | 120 | 63.00 | 110.00 | 17.18 | 2.21 | 19.39 |
| 294 | 120 | 63.00 | 111.00 | 17.32 | 2.23 | 19.55 |
| 295 | 120 | 63.00 | 112.00 | 17.45 | 2.25 | 19.70 |
| 296 | 120 | 63.00 | 113.00 | 17.59 | 2.27 | 19.86 |
| 297 | 120 | 63.00 | 114.00 | 17.73 | 2.29 | 20.02 |
| 298 | 120 | 63.00 | 115.00 | 17.87 | 2.31 | 20.18 |
| 299 | 120 | 63.00 | 116.00 | 18.01 | 2.33 | 20.34 |
| 300 | 120 | 63.00 | 117.00 | 18.14 | 2.35 | 20.49 |
| 301 | 120 | 63.00 | 118.00 | 18.28 | 2.37 | 20.65 |
| 302 | 120 | 63.00 | 119.00 | 18.42 | 2.39 | 20.81 |
| 303 | 120 | 63.00 | 120.00 | 18.56 | 2.41 | 20.97 |
| 304 | 120 | 63.00 | 121.00 | 18.70 | 2.43 | 21.13 |
| 305 | 120 | 63.00 | 122.00 | 18.83 | 2.45 | 21.28 |
| 306 | 120 | 63.00 | 123.00 | 18.97 | 2.47 | 21.44 |
| 307 | 120 | 63.00 | 124.00 | 19.11 | 2.49 | 21.60 |
| 308 | 120 | 63.00 | 125.00 | 19.25 | 2.51 | 21.76 |
| 309 | 120 | 63.00 | 126.00 | 19.39 | 2.53 | 21.92 |

## Table letter J

**Weekly table**

| Employee's earnings up to and including the UEL | Earnings at the LEL (where earnings are equal to or exceed the LEL) 1a | Earnings above the LEL, up to and including the PT 1b | Earnings above the PT, up to and including the UEL 1c | Employer's NICs due on all earnings above the ST 1d | Employee's NICs due on all earnings above the PT 1e | Total of employee's and employer's NICs (for information only) |
|---|---|---|---|---|---|---|
| £ | £ | £ p | £ p | £ p | £ p | £ p |
| 310 | 120 | 63.00 | 127.00 | 19.52 | 2.55 | 22.07 |
| 311 | 120 | 63.00 | 128.00 | 19.66 | 2.57 | 22.23 |
| 312 | 120 | 63.00 | 129.00 | 19.80 | 2.59 | 22.39 |
| 313 | 120 | 63.00 | 130.00 | 19.94 | 2.61 | 22.55 |
| 314 | 120 | 63.00 | 131.00 | 20.08 | 2.63 | 22.71 |
| 315 | 120 | 63.00 | 132.00 | 20.21 | 2.65 | 22.86 |
| 316 | 120 | 63.00 | 133.00 | 20.35 | 2.67 | 23.02 |
| 317 | 120 | 63.00 | 134.00 | 20.49 | 2.69 | 23.18 |
| 318 | 120 | 63.00 | 135.00 | 20.63 | 2.71 | 23.34 |
| 319 | 120 | 63.00 | 136.00 | 20.77 | 2.73 | 23.50 |
| 320 | 120 | 63.00 | 137.00 | 20.90 | 2.75 | 23.65 |
| 321 | 120 | 63.00 | 138.00 | 21.04 | 2.77 | 23.81 |
| 322 | 120 | 63.00 | 139.00 | 21.18 | 2.79 | 23.97 |
| 323 | 120 | 63.00 | 140.00 | 21.32 | 2.81 | 24.13 |
| 324 | 120 | 63.00 | 141.00 | 21.46 | 2.83 | 24.29 |
| 325 | 120 | 63.00 | 142.00 | 21.59 | 2.85 | 24.44 |
| 326 | 120 | 63.00 | 143.00 | 21.73 | 2.87 | 24.60 |
| 327 | 120 | 63.00 | 144.00 | 21.87 | 2.89 | 24.76 |
| 328 | 120 | 63.00 | 145.00 | 22.01 | 2.91 | 24.92 |
| 329 | 120 | 63.00 | 146.00 | 22.15 | 2.93 | 25.08 |
| 330 | 120 | 63.00 | 147.00 | 22.28 | 2.95 | 25.23 |
| 331 | 120 | 63.00 | 148.00 | 22.42 | 2.97 | 25.39 |
| 332 | 120 | 63.00 | 149.00 | 22.56 | 2.99 | 25.55 |
| 333 | 120 | 63.00 | 150.00 | 22.70 | 3.01 | 25.71 |
| 334 | 120 | 63.00 | 151.00 | 22.84 | 3.03 | 25.87 |
| 335 | 120 | 63.00 | 152.00 | 22.97 | 3.05 | 26.02 |
| 336 | 120 | 63.00 | 153.00 | 23.11 | 3.07 | 26.18 |
| 337 | 120 | 63.00 | 154.00 | 23.25 | 3.09 | 26.34 |
| 338 | 120 | 63.00 | 155.00 | 23.39 | 3.11 | 26.50 |
| 339 | 120 | 63.00 | 156.00 | 23.53 | 3.13 | 26.66 |
| 340 | 120 | 63.00 | 157.00 | 23.66 | 3.15 | 26.81 |
| 341 | 120 | 63.00 | 158.00 | 23.80 | 3.17 | 26.97 |
| 342 | 120 | 63.00 | 159.00 | 23.94 | 3.19 | 27.13 |
| 343 | 120 | 63.00 | 160.00 | 24.08 | 3.21 | 27.29 |
| 344 | 120 | 63.00 | 161.00 | 24.22 | 3.23 | 27.45 |
| 345 | 120 | 63.00 | 162.00 | 24.35 | 3.25 | 27.60 |
| 346 | 120 | 63.00 | 163.00 | 24.49 | 3.27 | 27.76 |
| 347 | 120 | 63.00 | 164.00 | 24.63 | 3.29 | 27.92 |
| 348 | 120 | 63.00 | 165.00 | 24.77 | 3.31 | 28.08 |
| 349 | 120 | 63.00 | 166.00 | 24.91 | 3.33 | 28.24 |
| 350 | 120 | 63.00 | 167.00 | 25.04 | 3.35 | 28.39 |
| 351 | 120 | 63.00 | 168.00 | 25.18 | 3.37 | 28.55 |
| 352 | 120 | 63.00 | 169.00 | 25.32 | 3.39 | 28.71 |
| 353 | 120 | 63.00 | 170.00 | 25.46 | 3.41 | 28.87 |
| 354 | 120 | 63.00 | 171.00 | 25.60 | 3.43 | 29.03 |
| 355 | 120 | 63.00 | 172.00 | 25.73 | 3.45 | 29.18 |
| 356 | 120 | 63.00 | 173.00 | 25.87 | 3.47 | 29.34 |
| 357 | 120 | 63.00 | 174.00 | 26.01 | 3.49 | 29.50 |
| 358 | 120 | 63.00 | 175.00 | 26.15 | 3.51 | 29.66 |
| 359 | 120 | 63.00 | 176.00 | 26.29 | 3.53 | 29.82 |
| 360 | 120 | 63.00 | 177.00 | 26.42 | 3.55 | 29.97 |
| 361 | 120 | 63.00 | 178.00 | 26.56 | 3.57 | 30.13 |
| 362 | 120 | 63.00 | 179.00 | 26.70 | 3.59 | 30.29 |
| 363 | 120 | 63.00 | 180.00 | 26.84 | 3.61 | 30.45 |
| 364 | 120 | 63.00 | 181.00 | 26.98 | 3.63 | 30.61 |

## Weekly table

**Table letter J**

| Employee's earnings up to and including the UEL | Earnings at the LEL (where earnings are equal to or exceed the LEL) 1a | Earnings above the LEL, up to and including the PT 1b | Earnings above the PT, up to and including the UEL 1c | Employer's NICs due on all earnings above the ST 1d | Employee's NICs due on all earnings above the PT 1e | Total of employee's and employer's NICs (for information only) |
|---|---|---|---|---|---|---|
| £ | £ | £ p | £ p | £ p | £ p | £ p |
| 365 | 120 | 63.00 | 182.00 | 27.11 | 3.65 | 30.76 |
| 366 | 120 | 63.00 | 183.00 | 27.25 | 3.67 | 30.92 |
| 367 | 120 | 63.00 | 184.00 | 27.39 | 3.69 | 31.08 |
| 368 | 120 | 63.00 | 185.00 | 27.53 | 3.71 | 31.24 |
| 369 | 120 | 63.00 | 186.00 | 27.67 | 3.73 | 31.40 |
| 370 | 120 | 63.00 | 187.00 | 27.80 | 3.75 | 31.55 |
| 371 | 120 | 63.00 | 188.00 | 27.94 | 3.77 | 31.71 |
| 372 | 120 | 63.00 | 189.00 | 28.08 | 3.79 | 31.87 |
| 373 | 120 | 63.00 | 190.00 | 28.22 | 3.81 | 32.03 |
| 374 | 120 | 63.00 | 191.00 | 28.36 | 3.83 | 32.19 |
| 375 | 120 | 63.00 | 192.00 | 28.49 | 3.85 | 32.34 |
| 376 | 120 | 63.00 | 193.00 | 28.63 | 3.87 | 32.50 |
| 377 | 120 | 63.00 | 194.00 | 28.77 | 3.89 | 32.66 |
| 378 | 120 | 63.00 | 195.00 | 28.91 | 3.91 | 32.82 |
| 379 | 120 | 63.00 | 196.00 | 29.05 | 3.93 | 32.98 |
| 380 | 120 | 63.00 | 197.00 | 29.18 | 3.95 | 33.13 |
| 381 | 120 | 63.00 | 198.00 | 29.32 | 3.97 | 33.29 |
| 382 | 120 | 63.00 | 199.00 | 29.46 | 3.99 | 33.45 |
| 383 | 120 | 63.00 | 200.00 | 29.60 | 4.01 | 33.61 |
| 384 | 120 | 63.00 | 201.00 | 29.74 | 4.03 | 33.77 |
| 385 | 120 | 63.00 | 202.00 | 29.87 | 4.05 | 33.92 |
| 386 | 120 | 63.00 | 203.00 | 30.01 | 4.07 | 34.08 |
| 387 | 120 | 63.00 | 204.00 | 30.15 | 4.09 | 34.24 |
| 388 | 120 | 63.00 | 205.00 | 30.29 | 4.11 | 34.40 |
| 389 | 120 | 63.00 | 206.00 | 30.43 | 4.13 | 34.56 |
| 390 | 120 | 63.00 | 207.00 | 30.56 | 4.15 | 34.71 |
| 391 | 120 | 63.00 | 208.00 | 30.70 | 4.17 | 34.87 |
| 392 | 120 | 63.00 | 209.00 | 30.84 | 4.19 | 35.03 |
| 393 | 120 | 63.00 | 210.00 | 30.98 | 4.21 | 35.19 |
| 394 | 120 | 63.00 | 211.00 | 31.12 | 4.23 | 35.35 |
| 395 | 120 | 63.00 | 212.00 | 31.25 | 4.25 | 35.50 |
| 396 | 120 | 63.00 | 213.00 | 31.39 | 4.27 | 35.66 |
| 397 | 120 | 63.00 | 214.00 | 31.53 | 4.29 | 35.82 |
| 398 | 120 | 63.00 | 215.00 | 31.67 | 4.31 | 35.98 |
| 399 | 120 | 63.00 | 216.00 | 31.81 | 4.33 | 36.14 |
| 400 | 120 | 63.00 | 217.00 | 31.94 | 4.35 | 36.29 |
| 401 | 120 | 63.00 | 218.00 | 32.08 | 4.37 | 36.45 |
| 402 | 120 | 63.00 | 219.00 | 32.22 | 4.39 | 36.61 |
| 403 | 120 | 63.00 | 220.00 | 32.36 | 4.41 | 36.77 |
| 404 | 120 | 63.00 | 221.00 | 32.50 | 4.43 | 36.93 |
| 405 | 120 | 63.00 | 222.00 | 32.63 | 4.45 | 37.08 |
| 406 | 120 | 63.00 | 223.00 | 32.77 | 4.47 | 37.24 |
| 407 | 120 | 63.00 | 224.00 | 32.91 | 4.49 | 37.40 |
| 408 | 120 | 63.00 | 225.00 | 33.05 | 4.51 | 37.56 |
| 409 | 120 | 63.00 | 226.00 | 33.19 | 4.53 | 37.72 |
| 410 | 120 | 63.00 | 227.00 | 33.32 | 4.55 | 37.87 |
| 411 | 120 | 63.00 | 228.00 | 33.46 | 4.57 | 38.03 |
| 412 | 120 | 63.00 | 229.00 | 33.60 | 4.59 | 38.19 |
| 413 | 120 | 63.00 | 230.00 | 33.74 | 4.61 | 38.35 |
| 414 | 120 | 63.00 | 231.00 | 33.88 | 4.63 | 38.51 |
| 415 | 120 | 63.00 | 232.00 | 34.01 | 4.65 | 38.66 |
| 416 | 120 | 63.00 | 233.00 | 34.15 | 4.67 | 38.82 |
| 417 | 120 | 63.00 | 234.00 | 34.29 | 4.69 | 38.98 |
| 418 | 120 | 63.00 | 235.00 | 34.43 | 4.71 | 39.14 |
| 419 | 120 | 63.00 | 236.00 | 34.57 | 4.73 | 39.30 |

## Table letter J

**Weekly table**

| Employee's earnings up to and including the UEL | Earnings at the LEL (where earnings are equal to or exceed the LEL) | Earnings above the LEL, up to and including the PT | Earnings above the PT, up to and including the UEL | Employer's NICs due on all earnings above the ST | Employee's NICs due on all earnings above the PT | Total of employee's and employer's NICs (for information only) |
|---|---|---|---|---|---|---|
| | 1a | 1b | 1c | 1d | 1e | |
| £ | £ | £ p | £ p | £ p | £ p | £ p |
| 420 | 120 | 63.00 | 237.00 | 34.70 | 4.75 | 39.45 |
| 421 | 120 | 63.00 | 238.00 | 34.84 | 4.77 | 39.61 |
| 422 | 120 | 63.00 | 239.00 | 34.98 | 4.79 | 39.77 |
| 423 | 120 | 63.00 | 240.00 | 35.12 | 4.81 | 39.93 |
| 424 | 120 | 63.00 | 241.00 | 35.26 | 4.83 | 40.09 |
| 425 | 120 | 63.00 | 242.00 | 35.39 | 4.85 | 40.24 |
| 426 | 120 | 63.00 | 243.00 | 35.53 | 4.87 | 40.40 |
| 427 | 120 | 63.00 | 244.00 | 35.67 | 4.89 | 40.56 |
| 428 | 120 | 63.00 | 245.00 | 35.81 | 4.91 | 40.72 |
| 429 | 120 | 63.00 | 246.00 | 35.95 | 4.93 | 40.88 |
| 430 | 120 | 63.00 | 247.00 | 36.08 | 4.95 | 41.03 |
| 431 | 120 | 63.00 | 248.00 | 36.22 | 4.97 | 41.19 |
| 432 | 120 | 63.00 | 249.00 | 36.36 | 4.99 | 41.35 |
| 433 | 120 | 63.00 | 250.00 | 36.50 | 5.01 | 41.51 |
| 434 | 120 | 63.00 | 251.00 | 36.64 | 5.03 | 41.67 |
| 435 | 120 | 63.00 | 252.00 | 36.77 | 5.05 | 41.82 |
| 436 | 120 | 63.00 | 253.00 | 36.91 | 5.07 | 41.98 |
| 437 | 120 | 63.00 | 254.00 | 37.05 | 5.09 | 42.14 |
| 438 | 120 | 63.00 | 255.00 | 37.19 | 5.11 | 42.30 |
| 439 | 120 | 63.00 | 256.00 | 37.33 | 5.13 | 42.46 |
| 440 | 120 | 63.00 | 257.00 | 37.46 | 5.15 | 42.61 |
| 441 | 120 | 63.00 | 258.00 | 37.60 | 5.17 | 42.77 |
| 442 | 120 | 63.00 | 259.00 | 37.74 | 5.19 | 42.93 |
| 443 | 120 | 63.00 | 260.00 | 37.88 | 5.21 | 43.09 |
| 444 | 120 | 63.00 | 261.00 | 38.02 | 5.23 | 43.25 |
| 445 | 120 | 63.00 | 262.00 | 38.15 | 5.25 | 43.40 |
| 446 | 120 | 63.00 | 263.00 | 38.29 | 5.27 | 43.56 |
| 447 | 120 | 63.00 | 264.00 | 38.43 | 5.29 | 43.72 |
| 448 | 120 | 63.00 | 265.00 | 38.57 | 5.31 | 43.88 |
| 449 | 120 | 63.00 | 266.00 | 38.71 | 5.33 | 44.04 |
| 450 | 120 | 63.00 | 267.00 | 38.84 | 5.35 | 44.19 |
| 451 | 120 | 63.00 | 268.00 | 38.98 | 5.37 | 44.35 |
| 452 | 120 | 63.00 | 269.00 | 39.12 | 5.39 | 44.51 |
| 453 | 120 | 63.00 | 270.00 | 39.26 | 5.41 | 44.67 |
| 454 | 120 | 63.00 | 271.00 | 39.40 | 5.43 | 44.83 |
| 455 | 120 | 63.00 | 272.00 | 39.53 | 5.45 | 44.98 |
| 456 | 120 | 63.00 | 273.00 | 39.67 | 5.47 | 45.14 |
| 457 | 120 | 63.00 | 274.00 | 39.81 | 5.49 | 45.30 |
| 458 | 120 | 63.00 | 275.00 | 39.95 | 5.51 | 45.46 |
| 459 | 120 | 63.00 | 276.00 | 40.09 | 5.53 | 45.62 |
| 460 | 120 | 63.00 | 277.00 | 40.22 | 5.55 | 45.77 |
| 461 | 120 | 63.00 | 278.00 | 40.36 | 5.57 | 45.93 |
| 462 | 120 | 63.00 | 279.00 | 40.50 | 5.59 | 46.09 |
| 463 | 120 | 63.00 | 280.00 | 40.64 | 5.61 | 46.25 |
| 464 | 120 | 63.00 | 281.00 | 40.78 | 5.63 | 46.41 |
| 465 | 120 | 63.00 | 282.00 | 40.91 | 5.65 | 46.56 |
| 466 | 120 | 63.00 | 283.00 | 41.05 | 5.67 | 46.72 |
| 467 | 120 | 63.00 | 284.00 | 41.19 | 5.69 | 46.88 |
| 468 | 120 | 63.00 | 285.00 | 41.33 | 5.71 | 47.04 |
| 469 | 120 | 63.00 | 286.00 | 41.47 | 5.73 | 47.20 |
| 470 | 120 | 63.00 | 287.00 | 41.60 | 5.75 | 47.35 |
| 471 | 120 | 63.00 | 288.00 | 41.74 | 5.77 | 47.51 |
| 472 | 120 | 63.00 | 289.00 | 41.88 | 5.79 | 47.67 |
| 473 | 120 | 63.00 | 290.00 | 42.02 | 5.81 | 47.83 |
| 474 | 120 | 63.00 | 291.00 | 42.16 | 5.83 | 47.99 |

**Weekly table**　　　　　　　　　　　　　　　　　　　　　　　　　　**Table letter J**

| Employee's earnings up to and including the UEL | Earnings at the LEL (where earnings are equal to or exceed the LEL) 1a | Earnings above the LEL, up to and including the PT 1b | Earnings above the PT, up to and including the UEL 1c | Employer's NICs due on all earnings above the ST 1d | Employee's NICs due on all earnings above the PT 1e | Total of employee's and employer's NICs (for information only) |
|---|---|---|---|---|---|---|
| £ | £ | £ p | £ p | £ p | £ p | £ p |
| 475 | 120 | 63.00 | 292.00 | 42.29 | 5.85 | 48.14 |
| 476 | 120 | 63.00 | 293.00 | 42.43 | 5.87 | 48.30 |
| 477 | 120 | 63.00 | 294.00 | 42.57 | 5.89 | 48.46 |
| 478 | 120 | 63.00 | 295.00 | 42.71 | 5.91 | 48.62 |
| 479 | 120 | 63.00 | 296.00 | 42.85 | 5.93 | 48.78 |
| 480 | 120 | 63.00 | 297.00 | 42.98 | 5.95 | 48.93 |
| 481 | 120 | 63.00 | 298.00 | 43.12 | 5.97 | 49.09 |
| 482 | 120 | 63.00 | 299.00 | 43.26 | 5.99 | 49.25 |
| 483 | 120 | 63.00 | 300.00 | 43.40 | 6.01 | 49.41 |
| 484 | 120 | 63.00 | 301.00 | 43.54 | 6.03 | 49.57 |
| 485 | 120 | 63.00 | 302.00 | 43.67 | 6.05 | 49.72 |
| 486 | 120 | 63.00 | 303.00 | 43.81 | 6.07 | 49.88 |
| 487 | 120 | 63.00 | 304.00 | 43.95 | 6.09 | 50.04 |
| 488 | 120 | 63.00 | 305.00 | 44.09 | 6.11 | 50.20 |
| 489 | 120 | 63.00 | 306.00 | 44.23 | 6.13 | 50.36 |
| 490 | 120 | 63.00 | 307.00 | 44.36 | 6.15 | 50.51 |
| 491 | 120 | 63.00 | 308.00 | 44.50 | 6.17 | 50.67 |
| 492 | 120 | 63.00 | 309.00 | 44.64 | 6.19 | 50.83 |
| 493 | 120 | 63.00 | 310.00 | 44.78 | 6.21 | 50.99 |
| 494 | 120 | 63.00 | 311.00 | 44.92 | 6.23 | 51.15 |
| 495 | 120 | 63.00 | 312.00 | 45.05 | 6.25 | 51.30 |
| 496 | 120 | 63.00 | 313.00 | 45.19 | 6.27 | 51.46 |
| 497 | 120 | 63.00 | 314.00 | 45.33 | 6.29 | 51.62 |
| 498 | 120 | 63.00 | 315.00 | 45.47 | 6.31 | 51.78 |
| 499 | 120 | 63.00 | 316.00 | 45.61 | 6.33 | 51.94 |
| 500 | 120 | 63.00 | 317.00 | 45.74 | 6.35 | 52.09 |
| 501 | 120 | 63.00 | 318.00 | 45.88 | 6.37 | 52.25 |
| 502 | 120 | 63.00 | 319.00 | 46.02 | 6.39 | 52.41 |
| 503 | 120 | 63.00 | 320.00 | 46.16 | 6.41 | 52.57 |
| 504 | 120 | 63.00 | 321.00 | 46.30 | 6.43 | 52.73 |
| 505 | 120 | 63.00 | 322.00 | 46.43 | 6.45 | 52.88 |
| 506 | 120 | 63.00 | 323.00 | 46.57 | 6.47 | 53.04 |
| 507 | 120 | 63.00 | 324.00 | 46.71 | 6.49 | 53.20 |
| 508 | 120 | 63.00 | 325.00 | 46.85 | 6.51 | 53.36 |
| 509 | 120 | 63.00 | 326.00 | 46.99 | 6.53 | 53.52 |
| 510 | 120 | 63.00 | 327.00 | 47.12 | 6.55 | 53.67 |
| 511 | 120 | 63.00 | 328.00 | 47.26 | 6.57 | 53.83 |
| 512 | 120 | 63.00 | 329.00 | 47.40 | 6.59 | 53.99 |
| 513 | 120 | 63.00 | 330.00 | 47.54 | 6.61 | 54.15 |
| 514 | 120 | 63.00 | 331.00 | 47.68 | 6.63 | 54.31 |
| 515 | 120 | 63.00 | 332.00 | 47.81 | 6.65 | 54.46 |
| 516 | 120 | 63.00 | 333.00 | 47.95 | 6.67 | 54.62 |
| 517 | 120 | 63.00 | 334.00 | 48.09 | 6.69 | 54.78 |
| 518 | 120 | 63.00 | 335.00 | 48.23 | 6.71 | 54.94 |
| 519 | 120 | 63.00 | 336.00 | 48.37 | 6.73 | 55.10 |
| 520 | 120 | 63.00 | 337.00 | 48.50 | 6.75 | 55.25 |
| 521 | 120 | 63.00 | 338.00 | 48.64 | 6.77 | 55.41 |
| 522 | 120 | 63.00 | 339.00 | 48.78 | 6.79 | 55.57 |
| 523 | 120 | 63.00 | 340.00 | 48.92 | 6.81 | 55.73 |
| 524 | 120 | 63.00 | 341.00 | 49.06 | 6.83 | 55.89 |
| 525 | 120 | 63.00 | 342.00 | 49.19 | 6.85 | 56.04 |
| 526 | 120 | 63.00 | 343.00 | 49.33 | 6.87 | 56.20 |
| 527 | 120 | 63.00 | 344.00 | 49.47 | 6.89 | 56.36 |
| 528 | 120 | 63.00 | 345.00 | 49.61 | 6.91 | 56.52 |
| 529 | 120 | 63.00 | 346.00 | 49.75 | 6.93 | 56.68 |

## Table letter J

**Weekly table**

| Employee's earnings up to and including the UEL | Earnings at the LEL (where earnings are equal to or exceed the LEL) | Earnings above the LEL, up to and including the PT | Earnings above the PT, up to and including the UEL | Employer's NICs due on all earnings above the ST | Employee's NICs due on all earnings above the PT | Total of employee's and employer's NICs (for information only) |
|---|---|---|---|---|---|---|
| | 1a | 1b | 1c | 1d | 1e | |
| £ | £ | £ p | £ p | £ p | £ p | £ p |
| 530 | 120 | 63.00 | 347.00 | 49.88 | 6.95 | 56.83 |
| 531 | 120 | 63.00 | 348.00 | 50.02 | 6.97 | 56.99 |
| 532 | 120 | 63.00 | 349.00 | 50.16 | 6.99 | 57.15 |
| 533 | 120 | 63.00 | 350.00 | 50.30 | 7.01 | 57.31 |
| 534 | 120 | 63.00 | 351.00 | 50.44 | 7.03 | 57.47 |
| 535 | 120 | 63.00 | 352.00 | 50.57 | 7.05 | 57.62 |
| 536 | 120 | 63.00 | 353.00 | 50.71 | 7.07 | 57.78 |
| 537 | 120 | 63.00 | 354.00 | 50.85 | 7.09 | 57.94 |
| 538 | 120 | 63.00 | 355.00 | 50.99 | 7.11 | 58.10 |
| 539 | 120 | 63.00 | 356.00 | 51.13 | 7.13 | 58.26 |
| 540 | 120 | 63.00 | 357.00 | 51.26 | 7.15 | 58.41 |
| 541 | 120 | 63.00 | 358.00 | 51.40 | 7.17 | 58.57 |
| 542 | 120 | 63.00 | 359.00 | 51.54 | 7.19 | 58.73 |
| 543 | 120 | 63.00 | 360.00 | 51.68 | 7.21 | 58.89 |
| 544 | 120 | 63.00 | 361.00 | 51.82 | 7.23 | 59.05 |
| 545 | 120 | 63.00 | 362.00 | 51.95 | 7.25 | 59.20 |
| 546 | 120 | 63.00 | 363.00 | 52.09 | 7.27 | 59.36 |
| 547 | 120 | 63.00 | 364.00 | 52.23 | 7.29 | 59.52 |
| 548 | 120 | 63.00 | 365.00 | 52.37 | 7.31 | 59.68 |
| 549 | 120 | 63.00 | 366.00 | 52.51 | 7.33 | 59.84 |
| 550 | 120 | 63.00 | 367.00 | 52.64 | 7.35 | 59.99 |
| 551 | 120 | 63.00 | 368.00 | 52.78 | 7.37 | 60.15 |
| 552 | 120 | 63.00 | 369.00 | 52.92 | 7.39 | 60.31 |
| 553 | 120 | 63.00 | 370.00 | 53.06 | 7.41 | 60.47 |
| 554 | 120 | 63.00 | 371.00 | 53.20 | 7.43 | 60.63 |
| 555 | 120 | 63.00 | 372.00 | 53.33 | 7.45 | 60.78 |
| 556 | 120 | 63.00 | 373.00 | 53.47 | 7.47 | 60.94 |
| 557 | 120 | 63.00 | 374.00 | 53.61 | 7.49 | 61.10 |
| 558 | 120 | 63.00 | 375.00 | 53.75 | 7.51 | 61.26 |
| 559 | 120 | 63.00 | 376.00 | 53.89 | 7.53 | 61.42 |
| 560 | 120 | 63.00 | 377.00 | 54.02 | 7.55 | 61.57 |
| 561 | 120 | 63.00 | 378.00 | 54.16 | 7.57 | 61.73 |
| 562 | 120 | 63.00 | 379.00 | 54.30 | 7.59 | 61.89 |
| 563 | 120 | 63.00 | 380.00 | 54.44 | 7.61 | 62.05 |
| 564 | 120 | 63.00 | 381.00 | 54.58 | 7.63 | 62.21 |
| 565 | 120 | 63.00 | 382.00 | 54.71 | 7.65 | 62.36 |
| 566 | 120 | 63.00 | 383.00 | 54.85 | 7.67 | 62.52 |
| 567 | 120 | 63.00 | 384.00 | 54.99 | 7.69 | 62.68 |
| 568 | 120 | 63.00 | 385.00 | 55.13 | 7.71 | 62.84 |
| 569 | 120 | 63.00 | 386.00 | 55.27 | 7.73 | 63.00 |
| 570 | 120 | 63.00 | 387.00 | 55.40 | 7.75 | 63.15 |
| 571 | 120 | 63.00 | 388.00 | 55.54 | 7.77 | 63.31 |
| 572 | 120 | 63.00 | 389.00 | 55.68 | 7.79 | 63.47 |
| 573 | 120 | 63.00 | 390.00 | 55.82 | 7.81 | 63.63 |
| 574 | 120 | 63.00 | 391.00 | 55.96 | 7.83 | 63.79 |
| 575 | 120 | 63.00 | 392.00 | 56.09 | 7.85 | 63.94 |
| 576 | 120 | 63.00 | 393.00 | 56.23 | 7.87 | 64.10 |
| 577 | 120 | 63.00 | 394.00 | 56.37 | 7.89 | 64.26 |
| 578 | 120 | 63.00 | 395.00 | 56.51 | 7.91 | 64.42 |
| 579 | 120 | 63.00 | 396.00 | 56.65 | 7.93 | 64.58 |
| 580 | 120 | 63.00 | 397.00 | 56.78 | 7.95 | 64.73 |
| 581 | 120 | 63.00 | 398.00 | 56.92 | 7.97 | 64.89 |
| 582 | 120 | 63.00 | 399.00 | 57.06 | 7.99 | 65.05 |
| 583 | 120 | 63.00 | 400.00 | 57.20 | 8.01 | 65.21 |
| 584 | 120 | 63.00 | 401.00 | 57.34 | 8.03 | 65.37 |

**Weekly table**

**Table letter J**

| Employee's earnings up to and including the UEL | Earnings at the LEL (where earnings are equal to or exceed the LEL) | Earnings above the LEL, up to and including the PT | Earnings above the PT, up to and including the UEL | Employer's NICs due on all earnings above the ST | Employee's NICs due on all earnings above the PT | Total of employee's and employer's NICs (for information only) |
|---|---|---|---|---|---|---|
| | | 1a | 1b | 1c | 1d | 1e |
| £ | £ | £ p | £ p | £ p | £ p | £ p |
| 585 | 120 | 63.00 | 402.00 | 57.47 | 8.05 | 65.52 |
| 586 | 120 | 63.00 | 403.00 | 57.61 | 8.07 | 65.68 |
| 587 | 120 | 63.00 | 404.00 | 57.75 | 8.09 | 65.84 |
| 588 | 120 | 63.00 | 405.00 | 57.89 | 8.11 | 66.00 |
| 589 | 120 | 63.00 | 406.00 | 58.03 | 8.13 | 66.16 |
| 590 | 120 | 63.00 | 407.00 | 58.16 | 8.15 | 66.31 |
| 591 | 120 | 63.00 | 408.00 | 58.30 | 8.17 | 66.47 |
| 592 | 120 | 63.00 | 409.00 | 58.44 | 8.19 | 66.63 |
| 593 | 120 | 63.00 | 410.00 | 58.58 | 8.21 | 66.79 |
| 594 | 120 | 63.00 | 411.00 | 58.72 | 8.23 | 66.95 |
| 595 | 120 | 63.00 | 412.00 | 58.85 | 8.25 | 67.10 |
| 596 | 120 | 63.00 | 413.00 | 58.99 | 8.27 | 67.26 |
| 597 | 120 | 63.00 | 414.00 | 59.13 | 8.29 | 67.42 |
| 598 | 120 | 63.00 | 415.00 | 59.27 | 8.31 | 67.58 |
| 599 | 120 | 63.00 | 416.00 | 59.41 | 8.33 | 67.74 |
| 600 | 120 | 63.00 | 417.00 | 59.54 | 8.35 | 67.89 |
| 601 | 120 | 63.00 | 418.00 | 59.68 | 8.37 | 68.05 |
| 602 | 120 | 63.00 | 419.00 | 59.82 | 8.39 | 68.21 |
| 603 | 120 | 63.00 | 420.00 | 59.96 | 8.41 | 68.37 |
| 604 | 120 | 63.00 | 421.00 | 60.10 | 8.43 | 68.53 |
| 605 | 120 | 63.00 | 422.00 | 60.23 | 8.45 | 68.68 |
| 606 | 120 | 63.00 | 423.00 | 60.37 | 8.47 | 68.84 |
| 607 | 120 | 63.00 | 424.00 | 60.51 | 8.49 | 69.00 |
| 608 | 120 | 63.00 | 425.00 | 60.65 | 8.51 | 69.16 |
| 609 | 120 | 63.00 | 426.00 | 60.79 | 8.53 | 69.32 |
| 610 | 120 | 63.00 | 427.00 | 60.92 | 8.55 | 69.47 |
| 611 | 120 | 63.00 | 428.00 | 61.06 | 8.57 | 69.63 |
| 612 | 120 | 63.00 | 429.00 | 61.20 | 8.59 | 69.79 |
| 613 | 120 | 63.00 | 430.00 | 61.34 | 8.61 | 69.95 |
| 614 | 120 | 63.00 | 431.00 | 61.48 | 8.63 | 70.11 |
| 615 | 120 | 63.00 | 432.00 | 61.61 | 8.65 | 70.26 |
| 616 | 120 | 63.00 | 433.00 | 61.75 | 8.67 | 70.42 |
| 617 | 120 | 63.00 | 434.00 | 61.89 | 8.69 | 70.58 |
| 618 | 120 | 63.00 | 435.00 | 62.03 | 8.71 | 70.74 |
| 619 | 120 | 63.00 | 436.00 | 62.17 | 8.73 | 70.90 |
| 620 | 120 | 63.00 | 437.00 | 62.30 | 8.75 | 71.05 |
| 621 | 120 | 63.00 | 438.00 | 62.44 | 8.77 | 71.21 |
| 622 | 120 | 63.00 | 439.00 | 62.58 | 8.79 | 71.37 |
| 623 | 120 | 63.00 | 440.00 | 62.72 | 8.81 | 71.53 |
| 624 | 120 | 63.00 | 441.00 | 62.86 | 8.83 | 71.69 |
| 625 | 120 | 63.00 | 442.00 | 62.99 | 8.85 | 71.84 |
| 626 | 120 | 63.00 | 443.00 | 63.13 | 8.87 | 72.00 |
| 627 | 120 | 63.00 | 444.00 | 63.27 | 8.89 | 72.16 |
| 628 | 120 | 63.00 | 445.00 | 63.41 | 8.91 | 72.32 |
| 629 | 120 | 63.00 | 446.00 | 63.55 | 8.93 | 72.48 |
| 630 | 120 | 63.00 | 447.00 | 63.68 | 8.95 | 72.63 |
| 631 | 120 | 63.00 | 448.00 | 63.82 | 8.97 | 72.79 |
| 632 | 120 | 63.00 | 449.00 | 63.96 | 8.99 | 72.95 |
| 633 | 120 | 63.00 | 450.00 | 64.10 | 9.01 | 73.11 |
| 634 | 120 | 63.00 | 451.00 | 64.24 | 9.03 | 73.27 |
| 635 | 120 | 63.00 | 452.00 | 64.37 | 9.05 | 73.42 |
| 636 | 120 | 63.00 | 453.00 | 64.51 | 9.07 | 73.58 |
| 637 | 120 | 63.00 | 454.00 | 64.65 | 9.09 | 73.74 |
| 638 | 120 | 63.00 | 455.00 | 64.79 | 9.11 | 73.90 |
| 639 | 120 | 63.00 | 456.00 | 64.93 | 9.13 | 74.06 |

## Table letter J

## Weekly table

| Employee's earnings up to and including the UEL | Earnings at the LEL (where earnings are equal to or exceed the LEL) 1a | Earnings above the LEL, up to and including the PT 1b | Earnings above the PT, up to and including the UEL 1c | Employer's NICs due on all earnings above the ST 1d | Employee's NICs due on all earnings above the PT 1e | Total of employee's and employer's NICs (for information only) |
|---|---|---|---|---|---|---|
| £ | £ | £ p | £ p | £ p | £ p | £ p |
| 640 | 120 | 63.00 | 457.00 | 65.06 | 9.15 | 74.21 |
| 641 | 120 | 63.00 | 458.00 | 65.20 | 9.17 | 74.37 |
| 642 | 120 | 63.00 | 459.00 | 65.34 | 9.19 | 74.53 |
| 643 | 120 | 63.00 | 460.00 | 65.48 | 9.21 | 74.69 |
| 644 | 120 | 63.00 | 461.00 | 65.62 | 9.23 | 74.85 |
| 645 | 120 | 63.00 | 462.00 | 65.75 | 9.25 | 75.00 |
| 646 | 120 | 63.00 | 463.00 | 65.89 | 9.27 | 75.16 |
| 647 | 120 | 63.00 | 464.00 | 66.03 | 9.29 | 75.32 |
| 648 | 120 | 63.00 | 465.00 | 66.17 | 9.31 | 75.48 |
| 649 | 120 | 63.00 | 466.00 | 66.31 | 9.33 | 75.64 |
| 650 | 120 | 63.00 | 467.00 | 66.44 | 9.35 | 75.79 |
| 651 | 120 | 63.00 | 468.00 | 66.58 | 9.37 | 75.95 |
| 652 | 120 | 63.00 | 469.00 | 66.72 | 9.39 | 76.11 |
| 653 | 120 | 63.00 | 470.00 | 66.86 | 9.41 | 76.27 |
| 654 | 120 | 63.00 | 471.00 | 67.00 | 9.43 | 76.43 |
| 655 | 120 | 63.00 | 472.00 | 67.13 | 9.45 | 76.58 |
| 656 | 120 | 63.00 | 473.00 | 67.27 | 9.47 | 76.74 |
| 657 | 120 | 63.00 | 474.00 | 67.41 | 9.49 | 76.90 |
| 658 | 120 | 63.00 | 475.00 | 67.55 | 9.51 | 77.06 |
| 659 | 120 | 63.00 | 476.00 | 67.69 | 9.53 | 77.22 |
| 660 | 120 | 63.00 | 477.00 | 67.82 | 9.55 | 77.37 |
| 661 | 120 | 63.00 | 478.00 | 67.96 | 9.57 | 77.53 |
| 662 | 120 | 63.00 | 479.00 | 68.10 | 9.59 | 77.69 |
| 663 | 120 | 63.00 | 480.00 | 68.24 | 9.61 | 77.85 |
| 664 | 120 | 63.00 | 481.00 | 68.38 | 9.63 | 78.01 |
| 665 | 120 | 63.00 | 482.00 | 68.51 | 9.65 | 78.16 |
| 666 | 120 | 63.00 | 483.00 | 68.65 | 9.67 | 78.32 |
| 667 | 120 | 63.00 | 484.00 | 68.79 | 9.69 | 78.48 |
| 668 | 120 | 63.00 | 485.00 | 68.93 | 9.71 | 78.64 |
| 669 | 120 | 63.00 | 486.00 | 69.07 | 9.73 | 78.80 |
| 670 | 120 | 63.00 | 487.00 | 69.20 | 9.75 | 78.95 |
| 671 | 120 | 63.00 | 488.00 | 69.34 | 9.77 | 79.11 |
| 672 | 120 | 63.00 | 489.00 | 69.48 | 9.79 | 79.27 |
| 673 | 120 | 63.00 | 490.00 | 69.62 | 9.81 | 79.43 |
| 674 | 120 | 63.00 | 491.00 | 69.76 | 9.83 | 79.59 |
| 675 | 120 | 63.00 | 492.00 | 69.89 | 9.85 | 79.74 |
| 676 | 120 | 63.00 | 493.00 | 70.03 | 9.87 | 79.90 |
| 677 | 120 | 63.00 | 494.00 | 70.17 | 9.89 | 80.06 |
| 678 | 120 | 63.00 | 495.00 | 70.31 | 9.91 | 80.22 |
| 679 | 120 | 63.00 | 496.00 | 70.45 | 9.93 | 80.38 |
| 680 | 120 | 63.00 | 497.00 | 70.58 | 9.95 | 80.53 |
| 681 | 120 | 63.00 | 498.00 | 70.72 | 9.97 | 80.69 |
| 682 | 120 | 63.00 | 499.00 | 70.86 | 9.99 | 80.85 |
| 683 | 120 | 63.00 | 500.00 | 71.00 | 10.01 | 81.01 |
| 684 | 120 | 63.00 | 501.00 | 71.14 | 10.03 | 81.17 |
| 685 | 120 | 63.00 | 502.00 | 71.27 | 10.05 | 81.32 |
| 686 | 120 | 63.00 | 503.00 | 71.41 | 10.07 | 81.48 |
| 687 | 120 | 63.00 | 504.00 | 71.55 | 10.09 | 81.64 |
| 688 | 120 | 63.00 | 505.00 | 71.69 | 10.11 | 81.80 |
| 689 | 120 | 63.00 | 506.00 | 71.83 | 10.13 | 81.96 |
| 690 | 120 | 63.00 | 507.00 | 71.96 | 10.15 | 82.11 |
| 691 | 120 | 63.00 | 508.00 | 72.10 | 10.17 | 82.27 |
| 692 | 120 | 63.00 | 509.00 | 72.24 | 10.19 | 82.43 |
| 693 | 120 | 63.00 | 510.00 | 72.38 | 10.21 | 82.59 |
| 694 | 120 | 63.00 | 511.00 | 72.52 | 10.23 | 82.75 |

**Weekly table**

**Table letter J**

| Employee's earnings up to and including the UEL | Earnings at the LEL (where earnings are equal to or exceed the LEL) 1a | Earnings above the LEL, up to and including the PT 1b | Earnings above the PT, up to and including the UEL 1c | Employer's NICs due on all earnings above the ST 1d | Employee's NICs due on all earnings above the PT 1e | Total of employee's and employer's NICs (for information only) |
|---|---|---|---|---|---|---|
| £ | £ | £ p | £ p | £ p | £ p | £ p |
| 695 | 120 | 63.00 | 512.00 | 72.65 | 10.25 | 82.90 |
| 696 | 120 | 63.00 | 513.00 | 72.79 | 10.27 | 83.06 |
| 697 | 120 | 63.00 | 514.00 | 72.93 | 10.29 | 83.22 |
| 698 | 120 | 63.00 | 515.00 | 73.07 | 10.31 | 83.38 |
| 699 | 120 | 63.00 | 516.00 | 73.21 | 10.33 | 83.54 |
| 700 | 120 | 63.00 | 517.00 | 73.34 | 10.35 | 83.69 |
| 701 | 120 | 63.00 | 518.00 | 73.48 | 10.37 | 83.85 |
| 702 | 120 | 63.00 | 519.00 | 73.62 | 10.39 | 84.01 |
| 703 | 120 | 63.00 | 520.00 | 73.76 | 10.41 | 84.17 |
| 704 | 120 | 63.00 | 521.00 | 73.90 | 10.43 | 84.33 |
| 705 | 120 | 63.00 | 522.00 | 74.03 | 10.45 | 84.48 |
| 706 | 120 | 63.00 | 523.00 | 74.17 | 10.47 | 84.64 |
| 707 | 120 | 63.00 | 524.00 | 74.31 | 10.49 | 84.80 |
| 708 | 120 | 63.00 | 525.00 | 74.45 | 10.51 | 84.96 |
| 709 | 120 | 63.00 | 526.00 | 74.59 | 10.53 | 85.12 |
| 710 | 120 | 63.00 | 527.00 | 74.72 | 10.55 | 85.27 |
| 711 | 120 | 63.00 | 528.00 | 74.86 | 10.57 | 85.43 |
| 712 | 120 | 63.00 | 529.00 | 75.00 | 10.59 | 85.59 |
| 713 | 120 | 63.00 | 530.00 | 75.14 | 10.61 | 85.75 |
| 714 | 120 | 63.00 | 531.00 | 75.28 | 10.63 | 85.91 |
| 715 | 120 | 63.00 | 532.00 | 75.41 | 10.65 | 86.06 |
| 716 | 120 | 63.00 | 533.00 | 75.55 | 10.67 | 86.22 |
| 717 | 120 | 63.00 | 534.00 | 75.69 | 10.69 | 86.38 |
| 718 | 120 | 63.00 | 535.00 | 75.83 | 10.71 | 86.54 |
| 719 | 120 | 63.00 | 536.00 | 75.97 | 10.73 | 86.70 |
| 720 | 120 | 63.00 | 537.00 | 76.10 | 10.75 | 86.85 |
| 721 | 120 | 63.00 | 538.00 | 76.24 | 10.77 | 87.01 |
| 722 | 120 | 63.00 | 539.00 | 76.38 | 10.79 | 87.17 |
| 723 | 120 | 63.00 | 540.00 | 76.52 | 10.81 | 87.33 |
| 724 | 120 | 63.00 | 541.00 | 76.66 | 10.83 | 87.49 |
| 725 | 120 | 63.00 | 542.00 | 76.79 | 10.85 | 87.64 |
| 726 | 120 | 63.00 | 543.00 | 76.93 | 10.87 | 87.80 |
| 727 | 120 | 63.00 | 544.00 | 77.07 | 10.89 | 87.96 |
| 728 | 120 | 63.00 | 545.00 | 77.21 | 10.91 | 88.12 |
| 729 | 120 | 63.00 | 546.00 | 77.35 | 10.93 | 88.28 |
| 730 | 120 | 63.00 | 547.00 | 77.48 | 10.95 | 88.43 |
| 731 | 120 | 63.00 | 548.00 | 77.62 | 10.97 | 88.59 |
| 732 | 120 | 63.00 | 549.00 | 77.76 | 10.99 | 88.75 |
| 733 | 120 | 63.00 | 550.00 | 77.90 | 11.01 | 88.91 |
| 734 | 120 | 63.00 | 551.00 | 78.04 | 11.03 | 89.07 |
| 735 | 120 | 63.00 | 552.00 | 78.17 | 11.05 | 89.22 |
| 736 | 120 | 63.00 | 553.00 | 78.31 | 11.07 | 89.38 |
| 737 | 120 | 63.00 | 554.00 | 78.45 | 11.09 | 89.54 |
| 738 | 120 | 63.00 | 555.00 | 78.59 | 11.11 | 89.70 |
| 739 | 120 | 63.00 | 556.00 | 78.73 | 11.13 | 89.86 |
| 740 | 120 | 63.00 | 557.00 | 78.86 | 11.15 | 90.01 |
| 741 | 120 | 63.00 | 558.00 | 79.00 | 11.17 | 90.17 |
| 742 | 120 | 63.00 | 559.00 | 79.14 | 11.19 | 90.33 |
| 743 | 120 | 63.00 | 560.00 | 79.28 | 11.21 | 90.49 |
| 744 | 120 | 63.00 | 561.00 | 79.42 | 11.23 | 90.65 |
| 745 | 120 | 63.00 | 562.00 | 79.55 | 11.25 | 90.80 |
| 746 | 120 | 63.00 | 563.00 | 79.69 | 11.27 | 90.96 |
| 747 | 120 | 63.00 | 564.00 | 79.83 | 11.29 | 91.12 |
| 748 | 120 | 63.00 | 565.00 | 79.97 | 11.31 | 91.28 |
| 749 | 120 | 63.00 | 566.00 | 80.11 | 11.33 | 91.44 |

# Table letter J

## Weekly table

| Employee's earnings up to and including the UEL | Earnings at the LEL (where earnings are equal to or exceed the LEL) 1a | Earnings above the LEL, up to and including the PT 1b | Earnings above the PT, up to and including the UEL 1c | Employer's NICs due on all earnings above the ST 1d | Employee's NICs due on all earnings above the PT 1e | Total of employee's and employer's NICs (for information only) |
|---|---|---|---|---|---|---|
| £ | £ | £ p | £ p | £ p | £ p | £ p |
| 750 | 120 | 63.00 | 567.00 | 80.24 | 11.35 | 91.59 |
| 751 | 120 | 63.00 | 568.00 | 80.38 | 11.37 | 91.75 |
| 752 | 120 | 63.00 | 569.00 | 80.52 | 11.39 | 91.91 |
| 753 | 120 | 63.00 | 570.00 | 80.66 | 11.41 | 92.07 |
| 754 | 120 | 63.00 | 571.00 | 80.80 | 11.43 | 92.23 |
| 755 | 120 | 63.00 | 572.00 | 80.93 | 11.45 | 92.38 |
| 756 | 120 | 63.00 | 573.00 | 81.07 | 11.47 | 92.54 |
| 757 | 120 | 63.00 | 574.00 | 81.21 | 11.49 | 92.70 |
| 758 | 120 | 63.00 | 575.00 | 81.35 | 11.51 | 92.86 |
| 759 | 120 | 63.00 | 576.00 | 81.49 | 11.53 | 93.02 |
| 760 | 120 | 63.00 | 577.00 | 81.62 | 11.55 | 93.17 |
| 761 | 120 | 63.00 | 578.00 | 81.76 | 11.57 | 93.33 |
| 762 | 120 | 63.00 | 579.00 | 81.90 | 11.59 | 93.49 |
| 763 | 120 | 63.00 | 580.00 | 82.04 | 11.61 | 93.65 |
| 764 | 120 | 63.00 | 581.00 | 82.18 | 11.63 | 93.81 |
| 765 | 120 | 63.00 | 582.00 | 82.31 | 11.65 | 93.96 |
| 766 | 120 | 63.00 | 583.00 | 82.45 | 11.67 | 94.12 |
| 767 | 120 | 63.00 | 584.00 | 82.59 | 11.69 | 94.28 |
| 768 | 120 | 63.00 | 585.00 | 82.73 | 11.71 | 94.44 |
| 769 | 120 | 63.00 | 586.00 | 82.87 | 11.73 | 94.60 |
| 770 | 120 | 63.00 | 587.00 | 83.00 | 11.75 | 94.75 |
| 771 | 120 | 63.00 | 588.00 | 83.14 | 11.77 | 94.91 |
| 772 | 120 | 63.00 | 589.00 | 83.28 | 11.79 | 95.07 |
| 773 | 120 | 63.00 | 590.00 | 83.42 | 11.81 | 95.23 |
| 774 | 120 | 63.00 | 591.00 | 83.56 | 11.83 | 95.39 |
| 775 | 120 | 63.00 | 592.00 | 83.69 | 11.85 | 95.54 |
| 776 | 120 | 63.00 | 593.00 | 83.83 | 11.87 | 95.70 |
| 777 | 120 | 63.00 | 594.00 | 83.97 | 11.89 | 95.86 |
| 778 | 120 | 63.00 | 595.00 | 84.11 | 11.91 | 96.02 |
| 779 | 120 | 63.00 | 596.00 | 84.25 | 11.93 | 96.18 |
| 780 | 120 | 63.00 | 597.00 | 84.38 | 11.95 | 96.33 |
| 781 | 120 | 63.00 | 598.00 | 84.52 | 11.97 | 96.49 |
| 782 | 120 | 63.00 | 599.00 | 84.66 | 11.99 | 96.65 |
| 783 | 120 | 63.00 | 600.00 | 84.80 | 12.01 | 96.81 |
| 784 | 120 | 63.00 | 601.00 | 84.94 | 12.03 | 96.97 |
| 785 | 120 | 63.00 | 602.00 | 85.07 | 12.05 | 97.12 |
| 786 | 120 | 63.00 | 603.00 | 85.21 | 12.07 | 97.28 |
| 787 | 120 | 63.00 | 604.00 | 85.35 | 12.09 | 97.44 |
| 788 | 120 | 63.00 | 605.00 | 85.49 | 12.11 | 97.60 |
| 789 | 120 | 63.00 | 606.00 | 85.63 | 12.13 | 97.76 |
| 790 | 120 | 63.00 | 607.00 | 85.76 | 12.15 | 97.91 |
| 791 | 120 | 63.00 | 608.00 | 85.90 | 12.17 | 98.07 |
| 792 | 120 | 63.00 | 609.00 | 86.04 | 12.19 | 98.23 |
| 793 | 120 | 63.00 | 610.00 | 86.18 | 12.21 | 98.39 |
| 794 | 120 | 63.00 | 611.00 | 86.32 | 12.23 | 98.55 |
| 795 | 120 | 63.00 | 612.00 | 86.45 | 12.25 | 98.70 |
| 796 | 120 | 63.00 | 613.00 | 86.59 | 12.27 | 98.86 |
| 797 | 120 | 63.00 | 614.00 | 86.73 | 12.29 | 99.02 |
| 798 | 120 | 63.00 | 615.00 | 86.87 | 12.31 | 99.18 |
| 799 | 120 | 63.00 | 616.00 | 87.01 | 12.33 | 99.34 |
| 800 | 120 | 63.00 | 617.00 | 87.14 | 12.35 | 99.49 |
| 801 | 120 | 63.00 | 618.00 | 87.28 | 12.37 | 99.65 |
| 802 | 120 | 63.00 | 619.00 | 87.42 | 12.39 | 99.81 |
| 803 | 120 | 63.00 | 620.00 | 87.56 | 12.41 | 99.97 |
| 804 | 120 | 63.00 | 621.00 | 87.70 | 12.43 | 100.13 |

**Weekly table**  Table letter J

| Employee's earnings up to and including the UEL | Earnings at the LEL (where earnings are equal to or exceed the LEL) | Earnings above the LEL, up to and including the PT | Earnings above the PT, up to and including the UEL | Employer's NICs due on all earnings above the ST | Employee's NICs due on all earnings above the PT | Total of employee's and employer's NICs (for information only) |
|---|---|---|---|---|---|---|
| | | 1a | 1b | 1c | 1d | 1e |
| £ | £ | £ p | £ p | £ p | £ p | £ p |
| 805 | 120 | 63.00 | 622.00 | 87.83 | 12.45 | 100.28 |
| 806 | 120 | 63.00 | 623.00 | 87.97 | 12.47 | 100.44 |
| 807 | 120 | 63.00 | 624.00 | 88.11 | 12.49 | 100.60 |
| 808 | 120 | 63.00 | 625.00 | 88.25 | 12.51 | 100.76 |
| 809 | 120 | 63.00 | 626.00 | 88.39 | 12.53 | 100.92 |
| 810 | 120 | 63.00 | 627.00 | 88.52 | 12.55 | 101.07 |
| 811 | 120 | 63.00 | 628.00 | 88.66 | 12.57 | 101.23 |
| 812 | 120 | 63.00 | 629.00 | 88.80 | 12.59 | 101.39 |
| 813 | 120 | 63.00 | 630.00 | 88.94 | 12.61 | 101.55 |
| 814 | 120 | 63.00 | 631.00 | 89.08 | 12.63 | 101.71 |
| 815 | 120 | 63.00 | 632.00 | 89.21 | 12.65 | 101.86 |
| 816 | 120 | 63.00 | 633.00 | 89.35 | 12.67 | 102.02 |
| 817 | 120 | 63.00 | 634.00 | 89.49 | 12.69 | 102.18 |
| 818 | 120 | 63.00 | 635.00 | 89.63 | 12.71 | 102.34 |
| 819 | 120 | 63.00 | 636.00 | 89.77 | 12.73 | 102.50 |
| 820 | 120 | 63.00 | 637.00 | 89.90 | 12.75 | 102.65 |
| 821 | 120 | 63.00 | 638.00 | 90.04 | 12.77 | 102.81 |
| 822 | 120 | 63.00 | 639.00 | 90.18 | 12.79 | 102.97 |
| 823 | 120 | 63.00 | 640.00 | 90.32 | 12.81 | 103.13 |
| 824 | 120 | 63.00 | 641.00 | 90.46 | 12.83 | 103.29 |
| 825 | 120 | 63.00 | 642.00 | 90.59 | 12.85 | 103.44 |
| 826 | 120 | 63.00 | 643.00 | 90.73 | 12.87 | 103.60 |
| 827 | 120 | 63.00 | 644.00 | 90.87 | 12.89 | 103.76 |
| 828 | 120 | 63.00 | 645.00 | 91.01 | 12.91 | 103.92 |
| 829 | 120 | 63.00 | 646.00 | 91.15 | 12.93 | 104.08 |
| 830 | 120 | 63.00 | 647.00 | 91.28 | 12.95 | 104.23 |
| 831 | 120 | 63.00 | 648.00 | 91.42 | 12.97 | 104.39 |
| 832 | 120 | 63.00 | 649.00 | 91.56 | 12.99 | 104.55 |
| 833 | 120 | 63.00 | 650.00 | 91.70 | 13.01 | 104.71 |
| 834 | 120 | 63.00 | 651.00 | 91.84 | 13.03 | 104.87 |
| 835 | 120 | 63.00 | 652.00 | 91.97 | 13.05 | 105.02 |
| 836 | 120 | 63.00 | 653.00 | 92.11 | 13.07 | 105.18 |
| 837 | 120 | 63.00 | 654.00 | 92.25 | 13.09 | 105.34 |
| 838 | 120 | 63.00 | 655.00 | 92.39 | 13.11 | 105.50 |
| 839 | 120 | 63.00 | 656.00 | 92.53 | 13.13 | 105.66 |
| 840 | 120 | 63.00 | 657.00 | 92.66 | 13.15 | 105.81 |
| 841 | 120 | 63.00 | 658.00 | 92.80 | 13.17 | 105.97 |
| 842 | 120 | 63.00 | 659.00 | 92.94 | 13.19 | 106.13 |
| 843 | 120 | 63.00 | 660.00 | 93.08 | 13.21 | 106.29 |
| 844 | 120 | 63.00 | 661.00 | 93.22 | 13.23 | 106.45 |
| 845 | 120 | 63.00 | 662.00 | 93.35 | 13.25 | 106.60 |
| 846 | 120 | 63.00 | 663.00 | 93.49 | 13.27 | 106.76 |
| 847 | 120 | 63.00 | 664.00 | 93.63 | 13.29 | 106.92 |
| 848 | 120 | 63.00 | 665.00 | 93.77 | 13.31 | 107.08 |
| 849 | 120 | 63.00 | 666.00 | 93.91 | 13.33 | 107.24 |
| 850 | 120 | 63.00 | 667.00 | 94.04 | 13.35 | 107.39 |
| 851 | 120 | 63.00 | 668.00 | 94.18 | 13.37 | 107.55 |
| 852 | 120 | 63.00 | 669.00 | 94.32 | 13.39 | 107.71 |
| 853 | 120 | 63.00 | 670.00 | 94.46 | 13.41 | 107.87 |
| 854 | 120 | 63.00 | 671.00 | 94.60 | 13.43 | 108.03 |
| 855 | 120 | 63.00 | 672.00 | 94.73 | 13.45 | 108.18 |
| 856 | 120 | 63.00 | 673.00 | 94.87 | 13.47 | 108.34 |
| 857 | 120 | 63.00 | 674.00 | 95.01 | 13.49 | 108.50 |
| 858 | 120 | 63.00 | 675.00 | 95.15 | 13.51 | 108.66 |
| 859 | 120 | 63.00 | 676.00 | 95.29 | 13.53 | 108.82 |

Page 89

## Table letter J

**Weekly table**

| Employee's earnings up to and including the UEL | Earnings at the LEL (where earnings are equal to or exceed the LEL) 1a | Earnings above the LEL, up to and including the PT 1b | Earnings above the PT, up to and including the UEL 1c | Employer's NICs due on all earnings above the ST 1d | Employee's NICs due on all earnings above the PT 1e | Total of employee's and employer's NICs (for information only) |
|---|---|---|---|---|---|---|
| £ | £ | £ p | £ p | £ p | £ p | £ p |
| 860 | 120 | 63.00 | 677.00 | 95.42 | 13.55 | 108.97 |
| 861 | 120 | 63.00 | 678.00 | 95.56 | 13.57 | 109.13 |
| 862 | 120 | 63.00 | 679.00 | 95.70 | 13.59 | 109.29 |
| 863 | 120 | 63.00 | 680.00 | 95.84 | 13.61 | 109.45 |
| 864 | 120 | 63.00 | 681.00 | 95.98 | 13.63 | 109.61 |
| 865 | 120 | 63.00 | 682.00 | 96.11 | 13.65 | 109.76 |
| 866 | 120 | 63.00 | 683.00 | 96.25 | 13.67 | 109.92 |
| 867 | 120 | 63.00 | 684.00 | 96.39 | 13.69 | 110.08 |
| 868 | 120 | 63.00 | 685.00 | 96.53 | 13.71 | 110.24 |
| 869 | 120 | 63.00 | 686.00 | 96.67 | 13.73 | 110.40 |
| 870 | 120 | 63.00 | 687.00 | 96.80 | 13.75 | 110.55 |
| 871 | 120 | 63.00 | 688.00 | 96.94 | 13.77 | 110.71 |
| 872 | 120 | 63.00 | 689.00 | 97.08 | 13.79 | 110.87 |
| 873 | 120 | 63.00 | 690.00 | 97.22 | 13.81 | 111.03 |
| 874 | 120 | 63.00 | 691.00 | 97.36 | 13.83 | 111.19 |
| 875 | 120 | 63.00 | 692.00 | 97.49 | 13.85 | 111.34 |
| 876 | 120 | 63.00 | 693.00 | 97.63 | 13.87 | 111.50 |
| 877 | 120 | 63.00 | 694.00 | 97.77 | 13.89 | 111.66 |
| 878 | 120 | 63.00 | 695.00 | 97.91 | 13.91 | 111.82 |
| 879 | 120 | 63.00 | 696.00 | 98.05 | 13.93 | 111.98 |
| 880 | 120 | 63.00 | 697.00 | 98.18 | 13.95 | 112.13 |
| 881 | 120 | 63.00 | 698.00 | 98.32 | 13.97 | 112.29 |
| 882 | 120 | 63.00 | 699.00 | 98.46 | 13.99 | 112.45 |
| 883 | 120 | 63.00 | 700.00 | 98.60 | 14.01 | 112.61 |
| 884 | 120 | 63.00 | 701.00 | 98.74 | 14.03 | 112.77 |
| 885 | 120 | 63.00 | 702.00 | 98.87 | 14.05 | 112.92 |
| 886 | 120 | 63.00 | 703.00 | 99.01 | 14.07 | 113.08 |
| 887 | 120 | 63.00 | 704.00 | 99.15 | 14.09 | 113.24 |
| 888 | 120 | 63.00 | 705.00 | 99.29 | 14.11 | 113.40 |
| 889 | 120 | 63.00 | 706.00 | 99.43 | 14.13 | 113.56 |
| 890 | 120 | 63.00 | 707.00 | 99.56 | 14.15 | 113.71 |
| 891 | 120 | 63.00 | 708.00 | 99.70 | 14.17 | 113.87 |
| 892 | 120 | 63.00 | 709.00 | 99.84 | 14.19 | 114.03 |
| 893 | 120 | 63.00 | 710.00 | 99.98 | 14.21 | 114.19 |
| 894 | 120 | 63.00 | 711.00 | 100.12 | 14.23 | 114.35 |
| 895 | 120 | 63.00 | 712.00 | 100.25 | 14.25 | 114.50 |
| 896 | 120 | 63.00 | 713.00 | 100.39 | 14.27 | 114.66 |
| 897 | 120 | 63.00 | 714.00 | 100.53 | 14.29 | 114.82 |
| 898 | 120 | 63.00 | 715.00 | 100.67 | 14.31 | 114.98 |
| 899 | 120 | 63.00 | 716.00 | 100.81 | 14.33 | 115.14 |
| 900 | 120 | 63.00 | 717.00 | 100.94 | 14.35 | 115.29 |
| 901 | 120 | 63.00 | 718.00 | 101.08 | 14.37 | 115.45 |
| 902 | 120 | 63.00 | 719.00 | 101.22 | 14.39 | 115.61 |
| 903 | 120 | 63.00 | 720.00 | 101.36 | 14.41 | 115.77 |
| 904 | 120 | 63.00 | 721.00 | 101.50 | 14.43 | 115.93 |
| 905 | 120 | 63.00 | 722.00 | 101.63 | 14.45 | 116.08 |
| 906 | 120 | 63.00 | 723.00 | 101.77 | 14.47 | 116.24 |
| 907 | 120 | 63.00 | 724.00 | 101.91 | 14.49 | 116.40 |
| 908 | 120 | 63.00 | 725.00 | 102.05 | 14.51 | 116.56 |
| 909 | 120 | 63.00 | 726.00 | 102.19 | 14.53 | 116.72 |
| 910 | 120 | 63.00 | 727.00 | 102.32 | 14.55 | 116.87 |
| 911 | 120 | 63.00 | 728.00 | 102.46 | 14.57 | 117.03 |
| 912 | 120 | 63.00 | 729.00 | 102.60 | 14.59 | 117.19 |
| 913 | 120 | 63.00 | 730.00 | 102.74 | 14.61 | 117.35 |
| 914 | 120 | 63.00 | 731.00 | 102.88 | 14.63 | 117.51 |

**Weekly table**              **Table letter J**

| Employee's earnings up to and including the UEL | Earnings at the LEL (where earnings are equal to or exceed the LEL) | Earnings above the LEL, up to and including the PT | Earnings above the PT, up to and including the UEL | Employer's NICs due on all earnings above the ST | Employee's NICs due on all earnings above the PT | Total of employee's and employer's NICs (for information only) |
|---|---|---|---|---|---|---|
| | | 1a | 1b | 1c | 1d | 1e |
| £ | £ | £ p | £ p | £ p | £ p | £ p |
| 915 | 120 | 63.00 | 732.00 | 103.01 | 14.65 | 117.66 |
| 916 | 120 | 63.00 | 733.00 | 103.15 | 14.67 | 117.82 |
| 917 | 120 | 63.00 | 734.00 | 103.29 | 14.69 | 117.98 |
| 918 | 120 | 63.00 | 735.00 | 103.43 | 14.71 | 118.14 |
| 919 | 120 | 63.00 | 736.00 | 103.57 | 14.73 | 118.30 |
| 920 | 120 | 63.00 | 737.00 | 103.70 | 14.75 | 118.45 |
| 921 | 120 | 63.00 | 738.00 | 103.84 | 14.77 | 118.61 |
| 922 | 120 | 63.00 | 739.00 | 103.98 | 14.79 | 118.77 |
| 923 | 120 | 63.00 | 740.00 | 104.12 | 14.81 | 118.93 |
| 924 | 120 | 63.00 | 741.00 | 104.26 | 14.83 | 119.09 |
| 925 | 120 | 63.00 | 742.00 | 104.39 | 14.85 | 119.24 |
| 926 | 120 | 63.00 | 743.00 | 104.53 | 14.87 | 119.40 |
| 927 | 120 | 63.00 | 744.00 | 104.67 | 14.89 | 119.56 |
| 928 | 120 | 63.00 | 745.00 | 104.81 | 14.91 | 119.72 |
| 929 | 120 | 63.00 | 746.00 | 104.95 | 14.93 | 119.88 |
| 930 | 120 | 63.00 | 747.00 | 105.08 | 14.95 | 120.03 |
| 931 | 120 | 63.00 | 748.00 | 105.22 | 14.97 | 120.19 |
| 932 | 120 | 63.00 | 749.00 | 105.36 | 14.99 | 120.35 |
| 933 | 120 | 63.00 | 750.00 | 105.50 | 15.01 | 120.51 |
| 934 | 120 | 63.00 | 751.00 | 105.64 | 15.03 | 120.67 |
| 935 | 120 | 63.00 | 752.00 | 105.77 | 15.05 | 120.82 |
| 936 | 120 | 63.00 | 753.00 | 105.91 | 15.07 | 120.98 |
| 937 | 120 | 63.00 | 754.00 | 106.05 | 15.09 | 121.14 |
| 938 | 120 | 63.00 | 755.00 | 106.19 | 15.11 | 121.30 |
| 939 | 120 | 63.00 | 756.00 | 106.33 | 15.13 | 121.46 |
| 940 | 120 | 63.00 | 757.00 | 106.46 | 15.15 | 121.61 |
| 941 | 120 | 63.00 | 758.00 | 106.60 | 15.17 | 121.77 |
| 942 | 120 | 63.00 | 759.00 | 106.74 | 15.19 | 121.93 |
| 943 | 120 | 63.00 | 760.00 | 106.88 | 15.21 | 122.09 |
| 944 | 120 | 63.00 | 761.00 | 107.02 | 15.23 | 122.25 |
| 945 | 120 | 63.00 | 762.00 | 107.15 | 15.25 | 122.40 |
| 946 | 120 | 63.00 | 763.00 | 107.29 | 15.27 | 122.56 |
| 947 | 120 | 63.00 | 764.00 | 107.43 | 15.29 | 122.72 |
| 948 | 120 | 63.00 | 765.00 | 107.57 | 15.31 | 122.88 |
| 949 | 120 | 63.00 | 766.00 | 107.71 | 15.33 | 123.04 |
| 950 | 120 | 63.00 | 767.00 | 107.84 | 15.35 | 123.19 |
| 951 | 120 | 63.00 | 768.00 | 107.98 | 15.37 | 123.35 |
| 952 | 120 | 63.00 | 769.00 | 108.12 | 15.39 | 123.51 |
| 953 | 120 | 63.00 | 770.00 | 108.26 | 15.41 | 123.67 |
| 954 | 120 | 63.00 | 771.00 | 108.40 | 15.43 | 123.83 |
| 955 | 120 | 63.00 | 772.00 | 108.53 | 15.45 | 123.98 |
| 956 | 120 | 63.00 | 773.00 | 108.67 | 15.47 | 124.14 |
| 957 | 120 | 63.00 | 774.00 | 108.81 | 15.49 | 124.30 |
| 958 | 120 | 63.00 | 775.00 | 108.95 | 15.51 | 124.46 |
| 959 | 120 | 63.00 | 776.00 | 109.09 | 15.53 | 124.62 |
| 960 | 120 | 63.00 | 777.00 | 109.22 | 15.55 | 124.77 |
| 961 | 120 | 63.00 | 778.00 | 109.36 | 15.57 | 124.93 |
| 962 | 120 | 63.00 | 779.00 | 109.43 | 15.58 | 125.01 |

If the employee's gross pay is over £962, go to page 178.

## Monthly table for NICs where employee has deferment for use from 6 April 2020 to 5 April 2021

**Table letter J**

Use this table for employees who are aged 21 or over, for whom you hold form CA2700.

Do not use this table for:

- any tax year other than 2020 to 2021
- employees who are under the age of 21, for whom you hold form CA2700 (go to Table letter Z)
- employees who are State Pension age or over (go to Table letter C in booklet CA41)

**Completing form RT11, 'Deductions working sheet' or substitute**

1  Enter 'J' in the NICs Category Letter column on form RT11.

2  Copy the figures in columns 1a – 1e of the table to columns 1a – 1e on the line next to the tax month in which the employee is paid, on form RT11.

If the employee's total earnings fall between the LEL and the UEL/UST/AUST and the exact gross pay is not shown in the table, use the next smaller figure shown. If the employee's total earnings exceed the UEL/UST/AUST, go to page 163.

The figures in the left-hand column of each table show steps between the LEL and the UEL/UST/AUST. The NICs liability for each step, with the exception of the LEL, ST, PT, UEL, UST and AUST, is worked out at the mid-point of the steps so you and your employee may pay slightly more or less than if you used the exact percentage method.

| Employee's earnings up to and including the UEL | Earnings at the LEL (where earnings are equal to or exceed the LEL) | Earnings above the LEL, up to and including the PT | Earnings above the PT, up to and including the UEL | Employer's NICs due on all earnings above the ST | Employee's NICs due on all earnings above the PT | Total of employee's and employer's NICs (for information only) |
|---|---|---|---|---|---|---|
| | 1a | 1b | 1c | 1d | 1e | |
| £ | £ | £ p | £ p | £ p | £ p | £ p |
| Up to and including £519.99 | No NICs liability, make no entries on form RT11 | | | | | |
| 520 | 520 | 0.00 | 0.00 | 0.00 | 0.00 | 0.00 |
| 524 | 520 | 4.00 | 0.00 | 0.00 | 0.00 | 0.00 |
| 528 | 520 | 8.00 | 0.00 | 0.00 | 0.00 | 0.00 |
| 532 | 520 | 12.00 | 0.00 | 0.00 | 0.00 | 0.00 |
| 536 | 520 | 16.00 | 0.00 | 0.00 | 0.00 | 0.00 |
| 540 | 520 | 20.00 | 0.00 | 0.00 | 0.00 | 0.00 |
| 544 | 520 | 24.00 | 0.00 | 0.00 | 0.00 | 0.00 |
| 548 | 520 | 28.00 | 0.00 | 0.00 | 0.00 | 0.00 |
| 552 | 520 | 32.00 | 0.00 | 0.00 | 0.00 | 0.00 |
| 556 | 520 | 36.00 | 0.00 | 0.00 | 0.00 | 0.00 |
| 560 | 520 | 40.00 | 0.00 | 0.00 | 0.00 | 0.00 |
| 564 | 520 | 44.00 | 0.00 | 0.00 | 0.00 | 0.00 |
| 568 | 520 | 48.00 | 0.00 | 0.00 | 0.00 | 0.00 |
| 572 | 520 | 52.00 | 0.00 | 0.00 | 0.00 | 0.00 |
| 576 | 520 | 56.00 | 0.00 | 0.00 | 0.00 | 0.00 |
| 580 | 520 | 60.00 | 0.00 | 0.00 | 0.00 | 0.00 |
| 584 | 520 | 64.00 | 0.00 | 0.00 | 0.00 | 0.00 |
| 588 | 520 | 68.00 | 0.00 | 0.00 | 0.00 | 0.00 |
| 592 | 520 | 72.00 | 0.00 | 0.00 | 0.00 | 0.00 |
| 596 | 520 | 76.00 | 0.00 | 0.00 | 0.00 | 0.00 |
| 600 | 520 | 80.00 | 0.00 | 0.00 | 0.00 | 0.00 |
| 604 | 520 | 84.00 | 0.00 | 0.00 | 0.00 | 0.00 |
| 608 | 520 | 88.00 | 0.00 | 0.00 | 0.00 | 0.00 |
| 612 | 520 | 92.00 | 0.00 | 0.00 | 0.00 | 0.00 |
| 616 | 520 | 96.00 | 0.00 | 0.00 | 0.00 | 0.00 |

## Monthly table                                                      Table letter J

| Employee's earnings up to and including the UEL | Earnings at the LEL (where earnings are equal to or exceed the LEL) 1a | Earnings above the LEL, up to and including the PT 1b | Earnings above the PT, up to and including the UEL 1c | Employer's NICs due on all earnings above the ST 1d | Employee's NICs due on all earnings above the PT 1e | Total of employee's and employer's NICs (for information only) |
|---|---|---|---|---|---|---|
| £ | £ | £ p | £ p | £ p | £ p | £ p |
| 620 | 520 | 100.00 | 0.00 | 0.00 | 0.00 | 0.00 |
| 624 | 520 | 104.00 | 0.00 | 0.00 | 0.00 | 0.00 |
| 628 | 520 | 108.00 | 0.00 | 0.00 | 0.00 | 0.00 |
| 632 | 520 | 112.00 | 0.00 | 0.00 | 0.00 | 0.00 |
| 636 | 520 | 116.00 | 0.00 | 0.00 | 0.00 | 0.00 |
| 640 | 520 | 120.00 | 0.00 | 0.00 | 0.00 | 0.00 |
| 644 | 520 | 124.00 | 0.00 | 0.00 | 0.00 | 0.00 |
| 648 | 520 | 128.00 | 0.00 | 0.00 | 0.00 | 0.00 |
| 652 | 520 | 132.00 | 0.00 | 0.00 | 0.00 | 0.00 |
| 656 | 520 | 136.00 | 0.00 | 0.00 | 0.00 | 0.00 |
| 660 | 520 | 140.00 | 0.00 | 0.00 | 0.00 | 0.00 |
| 664 | 520 | 144.00 | 0.00 | 0.00 | 0.00 | 0.00 |
| 668 | 520 | 148.00 | 0.00 | 0.00 | 0.00 | 0.00 |
| 672 | 520 | 152.00 | 0.00 | 0.00 | 0.00 | 0.00 |
| 676 | 520 | 156.00 | 0.00 | 0.00 | 0.00 | 0.00 |
| 680 | 520 | 160.00 | 0.00 | 0.00 | 0.00 | 0.00 |
| 684 | 520 | 164.00 | 0.00 | 0.00 | 0.00 | 0.00 |
| 688 | 520 | 168.00 | 0.00 | 0.00 | 0.00 | 0.00 |
| 692 | 520 | 172.00 | 0.00 | 0.00 | 0.00 | 0.00 |
| 696 | 520 | 176.00 | 0.00 | 0.00 | 0.00 | 0.00 |
| 700 | 520 | 180.00 | 0.00 | 0.00 | 0.00 | 0.00 |
| 704 | 520 | 184.00 | 0.00 | 0.00 | 0.00 | 0.00 |
| 708 | 520 | 188.00 | 0.00 | 0.00 | 0.00 | 0.00 |
| 712 | 520 | 192.00 | 0.00 | 0.00 | 0.00 | 0.00 |
| 716 | 520 | 196.00 | 0.00 | 0.00 | 0.00 | 0.00 |
| 720 | 520 | 200.00 | 0.00 | 0.00 | 0.00 | 0.00 |
| 724 | 520 | 204.00 | 0.00 | 0.00 | 0.00 | 0.00 |
| 728 | 520 | 208.00 | 0.00 | 0.00 | 0.00 | 0.00 |
| 732 | 520 | 212.00 | 0.00 | 0.00 | 0.00 | 0.00 |
| 736 | 520 | 216.00 | 0.00 | 0.83 | 0.00 | 0.83 |
| 740 | 520 | 220.00 | 0.00 | 1.38 | 0.00 | 1.38 |
| 744 | 520 | 224.00 | 0.00 | 1.93 | 0.00 | 1.93 |
| 748 | 520 | 228.00 | 0.00 | 2.48 | 0.00 | 2.48 |
| 752 | 520 | 232.00 | 0.00 | 3.04 | 0.00 | 3.04 |
| 756 | 520 | 236.00 | 0.00 | 3.59 | 0.00 | 3.59 |
| 760 | 520 | 240.00 | 0.00 | 4.14 | 0.00 | 4.14 |
| 764 | 520 | 244.00 | 0.00 | 4.69 | 0.00 | 4.69 |
| 768 | 520 | 248.00 | 0.00 | 5.24 | 0.00 | 5.24 |
| 772 | 520 | 252.00 | 0.00 | 5.80 | 0.00 | 5.80 |
| 776 | 520 | 256.00 | 0.00 | 6.35 | 0.00 | 6.35 |
| 780 | 520 | 260.00 | 0.00 | 6.90 | 0.00 | 6.90 |
| 784 | 520 | 264.00 | 0.00 | 7.45 | 0.00 | 7.45 |
| 788 | 520 | 268.00 | 0.00 | 8.00 | 0.00 | 8.00 |
| 792 | 520 | 272.00 | 0.00 | 8.28 | 0.00 | 8.28 |
| 796 | 520 | 272.00 | 4.00 | 9.11 | 0.12 | 9.23 |
| 800 | 520 | 272.00 | 8.00 | 9.66 | 0.20 | 9.86 |
| 804 | 520 | 272.00 | 12.00 | 10.21 | 0.28 | 10.49 |
| 808 | 520 | 272.00 | 16.00 | 10.76 | 0.36 | 11.12 |
| 812 | 520 | 272.00 | 20.00 | 11.32 | 0.44 | 11.76 |
| 816 | 520 | 272.00 | 24.00 | 11.87 | 0.52 | 12.39 |
| 820 | 520 | 272.00 | 28.00 | 12.42 | 0.60 | 13.02 |
| 824 | 520 | 272.00 | 32.00 | 12.97 | 0.68 | 13.65 |
| 828 | 520 | 272.00 | 36.00 | 13.52 | 0.76 | 14.28 |
| 832 | 520 | 272.00 | 40.00 | 14.08 | 0.84 | 14.92 |
| 836 | 520 | 272.00 | 44.00 | 14.63 | 0.92 | 15.55 |

## Table letter J
**Monthly table**

| Employee's earnings up to and including the UEL | Earnings at the LEL (where earnings are equal to or exceed the LEL) | Earnings above the LEL, up to and including the PT | Earnings above the PT, up to and including the UEL | Employer's NICs due on all earnings above the ST | Employee's NICs due on all earnings above the PT | Total of employee's and employer's NICs (for information only) |
|---|---|---|---|---|---|---|
| | 1a | 1b | 1c | 1d | 1e | |
| £ | £ | £ p | £ p | £ p | £ p | £ p |
| 840 | 520 | 272.00 | 48.00 | 15.18 | 1.00 | 16.18 |
| 844 | 520 | 272.00 | 52.00 | 15.73 | 1.08 | 16.81 |
| 848 | 520 | 272.00 | 56.00 | 16.28 | 1.16 | 17.44 |
| 852 | 520 | 272.00 | 60.00 | 16.84 | 1.24 | 18.08 |
| 856 | 520 | 272.00 | 64.00 | 17.39 | 1.32 | 18.71 |
| 860 | 520 | 272.00 | 68.00 | 17.94 | 1.40 | 19.34 |
| 864 | 520 | 272.00 | 72.00 | 18.49 | 1.48 | 19.97 |
| 868 | 520 | 272.00 | 76.00 | 19.04 | 1.56 | 20.60 |
| 872 | 520 | 272.00 | 80.00 | 19.60 | 1.64 | 21.24 |
| 876 | 520 | 272.00 | 84.00 | 20.15 | 1.72 | 21.87 |
| 880 | 520 | 272.00 | 88.00 | 20.70 | 1.80 | 22.50 |
| 884 | 520 | 272.00 | 92.00 | 21.25 | 1.88 | 23.13 |
| 888 | 520 | 272.00 | 96.00 | 21.80 | 1.96 | 23.76 |
| 892 | 520 | 272.00 | 100.00 | 22.36 | 2.04 | 24.40 |
| 896 | 520 | 272.00 | 104.00 | 22.91 | 2.12 | 25.03 |
| 900 | 520 | 272.00 | 108.00 | 23.46 | 2.20 | 25.66 |
| 904 | 520 | 272.00 | 112.00 | 24.01 | 2.28 | 26.29 |
| 908 | 520 | 272.00 | 116.00 | 24.56 | 2.36 | 26.92 |
| 912 | 520 | 272.00 | 120.00 | 25.12 | 2.44 | 27.56 |
| 916 | 520 | 272.00 | 124.00 | 25.67 | 2.52 | 28.19 |
| 920 | 520 | 272.00 | 128.00 | 26.22 | 2.60 | 28.82 |
| 924 | 520 | 272.00 | 132.00 | 26.77 | 2.68 | 29.45 |
| 928 | 520 | 272.00 | 136.00 | 27.32 | 2.76 | 30.08 |
| 932 | 520 | 272.00 | 140.00 | 27.88 | 2.84 | 30.72 |
| 936 | 520 | 272.00 | 144.00 | 28.43 | 2.92 | 31.35 |
| 940 | 520 | 272.00 | 148.00 | 28.98 | 3.00 | 31.98 |
| 944 | 520 | 272.00 | 152.00 | 29.53 | 3.08 | 32.61 |
| 948 | 520 | 272.00 | 156.00 | 30.08 | 3.16 | 33.24 |
| 952 | 520 | 272.00 | 160.00 | 30.64 | 3.24 | 33.88 |
| 956 | 520 | 272.00 | 164.00 | 31.19 | 3.32 | 34.51 |
| 960 | 520 | 272.00 | 168.00 | 31.74 | 3.40 | 35.14 |
| 964 | 520 | 272.00 | 172.00 | 32.29 | 3.48 | 35.77 |
| 968 | 520 | 272.00 | 176.00 | 32.84 | 3.56 | 36.40 |
| 972 | 520 | 272.00 | 180.00 | 33.40 | 3.64 | 37.04 |
| 976 | 520 | 272.00 | 184.00 | 33.95 | 3.72 | 37.67 |
| 980 | 520 | 272.00 | 188.00 | 34.50 | 3.80 | 38.30 |
| 984 | 520 | 272.00 | 192.00 | 35.05 | 3.88 | 38.93 |
| 988 | 520 | 272.00 | 196.00 | 35.60 | 3.96 | 39.56 |
| 992 | 520 | 272.00 | 200.00 | 36.16 | 4.04 | 40.20 |
| 996 | 520 | 272.00 | 204.00 | 36.71 | 4.12 | 40.83 |
| 1000 | 520 | 272.00 | 208.00 | 37.26 | 4.20 | 41.46 |
| 1004 | 520 | 272.00 | 212.00 | 37.81 | 4.28 | 42.09 |
| 1008 | 520 | 272.00 | 216.00 | 38.36 | 4.36 | 42.72 |
| 1012 | 520 | 272.00 | 220.00 | 38.92 | 4.44 | 43.36 |
| 1016 | 520 | 272.00 | 224.00 | 39.47 | 4.52 | 43.99 |
| 1020 | 520 | 272.00 | 228.00 | 40.02 | 4.60 | 44.62 |
| 1024 | 520 | 272.00 | 232.00 | 40.57 | 4.68 | 45.25 |
| 1028 | 520 | 272.00 | 236.00 | 41.12 | 4.76 | 45.88 |
| 1032 | 520 | 272.00 | 240.00 | 41.68 | 4.84 | 46.52 |
| 1036 | 520 | 272.00 | 244.00 | 42.23 | 4.92 | 47.15 |
| 1040 | 520 | 272.00 | 248.00 | 42.78 | 5.00 | 47.78 |
| 1044 | 520 | 272.00 | 252.00 | 43.33 | 5.08 | 48.41 |
| 1048 | 520 | 272.00 | 256.00 | 43.88 | 5.16 | 49.04 |
| 1052 | 520 | 272.00 | 260.00 | 44.44 | 5.24 | 49.68 |
| 1056 | 520 | 272.00 | 264.00 | 44.99 | 5.32 | 50.31 |

## Monthly table

Table letter J

| Employee's earnings up to and including the UEL | Earnings at the LEL (where earnings are equal to or exceed the LEL) | Earnings above the LEL, up to and including the PT | Earnings above the PT, up to and including the UEL | Employer's NICs due on all earnings above the ST | Employee's NICs due on all earnings above the PT | Total of employee's and employer's NICs (for information only) |
|---|---|---|---|---|---|---|
| | | 1a | 1b | 1c | 1d | 1e |
| £ | £ | £ p | £ p | £ p | £ p | £ p |
| 1060 | 520 | 272.00 | 268.00 | 45.54 | 5.40 | 50.94 |
| 1064 | 520 | 272.00 | 272.00 | 46.09 | 5.48 | 51.57 |
| 1068 | 520 | 272.00 | 276.00 | 46.64 | 5.56 | 52.20 |
| 1072 | 520 | 272.00 | 280.00 | 47.20 | 5.64 | 52.84 |
| 1076 | 520 | 272.00 | 284.00 | 47.75 | 5.72 | 53.47 |
| 1080 | 520 | 272.00 | 288.00 | 48.30 | 5.80 | 54.10 |
| 1084 | 520 | 272.00 | 292.00 | 48.85 | 5.88 | 54.73 |
| 1088 | 520 | 272.00 | 296.00 | 49.40 | 5.96 | 55.36 |
| 1092 | 520 | 272.00 | 300.00 | 49.96 | 6.04 | 56.00 |
| 1096 | 520 | 272.00 | 304.00 | 50.51 | 6.12 | 56.63 |
| 1100 | 520 | 272.00 | 308.00 | 51.06 | 6.20 | 57.26 |
| 1104 | 520 | 272.00 | 312.00 | 51.61 | 6.28 | 57.89 |
| 1108 | 520 | 272.00 | 316.00 | 52.16 | 6.36 | 58.52 |
| 1112 | 520 | 272.00 | 320.00 | 52.72 | 6.44 | 59.16 |
| 1116 | 520 | 272.00 | 324.00 | 53.27 | 6.52 | 59.79 |
| 1120 | 520 | 272.00 | 328.00 | 53.82 | 6.60 | 60.42 |
| 1124 | 520 | 272.00 | 332.00 | 54.37 | 6.68 | 61.05 |
| 1128 | 520 | 272.00 | 336.00 | 54.92 | 6.76 | 61.68 |
| 1132 | 520 | 272.00 | 340.00 | 55.48 | 6.84 | 62.32 |
| 1136 | 520 | 272.00 | 344.00 | 56.03 | 6.92 | 62.95 |
| 1140 | 520 | 272.00 | 348.00 | 56.58 | 7.00 | 63.58 |
| 1144 | 520 | 272.00 | 352.00 | 57.13 | 7.08 | 64.21 |
| 1148 | 520 | 272.00 | 356.00 | 57.68 | 7.16 | 64.84 |
| 1152 | 520 | 272.00 | 360.00 | 58.24 | 7.24 | 65.48 |
| 1156 | 520 | 272.00 | 364.00 | 58.79 | 7.32 | 66.11 |
| 1160 | 520 | 272.00 | 368.00 | 59.34 | 7.40 | 66.74 |
| 1164 | 520 | 272.00 | 372.00 | 59.89 | 7.48 | 67.37 |
| 1168 | 520 | 272.00 | 376.00 | 60.44 | 7.56 | 68.00 |
| 1172 | 520 | 272.00 | 380.00 | 61.00 | 7.64 | 68.64 |
| 1176 | 520 | 272.00 | 384.00 | 61.55 | 7.72 | 69.27 |
| 1180 | 520 | 272.00 | 388.00 | 62.10 | 7.80 | 69.90 |
| 1184 | 520 | 272.00 | 392.00 | 62.65 | 7.88 | 70.53 |
| 1188 | 520 | 272.00 | 396.00 | 63.20 | 7.96 | 71.16 |
| 1192 | 520 | 272.00 | 400.00 | 63.76 | 8.04 | 71.80 |
| 1196 | 520 | 272.00 | 404.00 | 64.31 | 8.12 | 72.43 |
| 1200 | 520 | 272.00 | 408.00 | 64.86 | 8.20 | 73.06 |
| 1204 | 520 | 272.00 | 412.00 | 65.41 | 8.28 | 73.69 |
| 1208 | 520 | 272.00 | 416.00 | 65.96 | 8.36 | 74.32 |
| 1212 | 520 | 272.00 | 420.00 | 66.52 | 8.44 | 74.96 |
| 1216 | 520 | 272.00 | 424.00 | 67.07 | 8.52 | 75.59 |
| 1220 | 520 | 272.00 | 428.00 | 67.62 | 8.60 | 76.22 |
| 1224 | 520 | 272.00 | 432.00 | 68.17 | 8.68 | 76.85 |
| 1228 | 520 | 272.00 | 436.00 | 68.72 | 8.76 | 77.48 |
| 1232 | 520 | 272.00 | 440.00 | 69.28 | 8.84 | 78.12 |
| 1236 | 520 | 272.00 | 444.00 | 69.83 | 8.92 | 78.75 |
| 1240 | 520 | 272.00 | 448.00 | 70.38 | 9.00 | 79.38 |
| 1244 | 520 | 272.00 | 452.00 | 70.93 | 9.08 | 80.01 |
| 1248 | 520 | 272.00 | 456.00 | 71.48 | 9.16 | 80.64 |
| 1252 | 520 | 272.00 | 460.00 | 72.04 | 9.24 | 81.28 |
| 1256 | 520 | 272.00 | 464.00 | 72.59 | 9.32 | 81.91 |
| 1260 | 520 | 272.00 | 468.00 | 73.14 | 9.40 | 82.54 |
| 1264 | 520 | 272.00 | 472.00 | 73.69 | 9.48 | 83.17 |
| 1268 | 520 | 272.00 | 476.00 | 74.24 | 9.56 | 83.80 |
| 1272 | 520 | 272.00 | 480.00 | 74.80 | 9.64 | 84.44 |
| 1276 | 520 | 272.00 | 484.00 | 75.35 | 9.72 | 85.07 |

## Table letter J

**Monthly table**

| Employee's earnings up to and including the UEL | Earnings at the LEL (where earnings are equal to or exceed the LEL) | Earnings above the LEL, up to and including the PT | Earnings above the PT, up to and including the UEL | Employer's NICs due on all earnings above the ST | Employee's NICs due on all earnings above the PT | Total of employee's and employer's NICs (for information only) |
|---|---|---|---|---|---|---|
| | 1a | 1b | 1c | 1d | 1e | |
| £ | £ | £ p | £ p | £ p | £ p | £ p |
| 1280 | 520 | 272.00 | 488.00 | 75.90 | 9.80 | 85.70 |
| 1284 | 520 | 272.00 | 492.00 | 76.45 | 9.88 | 86.33 |
| 1288 | 520 | 272.00 | 496.00 | 77.00 | 9.96 | 86.96 |
| 1292 | 520 | 272.00 | 500.00 | 77.56 | 10.04 | 87.60 |
| 1296 | 520 | 272.00 | 504.00 | 78.11 | 10.12 | 88.23 |
| 1300 | 520 | 272.00 | 508.00 | 78.66 | 10.20 | 88.86 |
| 1304 | 520 | 272.00 | 512.00 | 79.21 | 10.28 | 89.49 |
| 1308 | 520 | 272.00 | 516.00 | 79.76 | 10.36 | 90.12 |
| 1312 | 520 | 272.00 | 520.00 | 80.32 | 10.44 | 90.76 |
| 1316 | 520 | 272.00 | 524.00 | 80.87 | 10.52 | 91.39 |
| 1320 | 520 | 272.00 | 528.00 | 81.42 | 10.60 | 92.02 |
| 1324 | 520 | 272.00 | 532.00 | 81.97 | 10.68 | 92.65 |
| 1328 | 520 | 272.00 | 536.00 | 82.52 | 10.76 | 93.28 |
| 1332 | 520 | 272.00 | 540.00 | 83.08 | 10.84 | 93.92 |
| 1336 | 520 | 272.00 | 544.00 | 83.63 | 10.92 | 94.55 |
| 1340 | 520 | 272.00 | 548.00 | 84.18 | 11.00 | 95.18 |
| 1344 | 520 | 272.00 | 552.00 | 84.73 | 11.08 | 95.81 |
| 1348 | 520 | 272.00 | 556.00 | 85.28 | 11.16 | 96.44 |
| 1352 | 520 | 272.00 | 560.00 | 85.84 | 11.24 | 97.08 |
| 1356 | 520 | 272.00 | 564.00 | 86.39 | 11.32 | 97.71 |
| 1360 | 520 | 272.00 | 568.00 | 86.94 | 11.40 | 98.34 |
| 1364 | 520 | 272.00 | 572.00 | 87.49 | 11.48 | 98.97 |
| 1368 | 520 | 272.00 | 576.00 | 88.04 | 11.56 | 99.60 |
| 1372 | 520 | 272.00 | 580.00 | 88.60 | 11.64 | 100.24 |
| 1376 | 520 | 272.00 | 584.00 | 89.15 | 11.72 | 100.87 |
| 1380 | 520 | 272.00 | 588.00 | 89.70 | 11.80 | 101.50 |
| 1384 | 520 | 272.00 | 592.00 | 90.25 | 11.88 | 102.13 |
| 1388 | 520 | 272.00 | 596.00 | 90.80 | 11.96 | 102.76 |
| 1392 | 520 | 272.00 | 600.00 | 91.36 | 12.04 | 103.40 |
| 1396 | 520 | 272.00 | 604.00 | 91.91 | 12.12 | 104.03 |
| 1400 | 520 | 272.00 | 608.00 | 92.46 | 12.20 | 104.66 |
| 1404 | 520 | 272.00 | 612.00 | 93.01 | 12.28 | 105.29 |
| 1408 | 520 | 272.00 | 616.00 | 93.56 | 12.36 | 105.92 |
| 1412 | 520 | 272.00 | 620.00 | 94.12 | 12.44 | 106.56 |
| 1416 | 520 | 272.00 | 624.00 | 94.67 | 12.52 | 107.19 |
| 1420 | 520 | 272.00 | 628.00 | 95.22 | 12.60 | 107.82 |
| 1424 | 520 | 272.00 | 632.00 | 95.77 | 12.68 | 108.45 |
| 1428 | 520 | 272.00 | 636.00 | 96.32 | 12.76 | 109.08 |
| 1432 | 520 | 272.00 | 640.00 | 96.88 | 12.84 | 109.72 |
| 1436 | 520 | 272.00 | 644.00 | 97.43 | 12.92 | 110.35 |
| 1440 | 520 | 272.00 | 648.00 | 97.98 | 13.00 | 110.98 |
| 1444 | 520 | 272.00 | 652.00 | 98.53 | 13.08 | 111.61 |
| 1448 | 520 | 272.00 | 656.00 | 99.08 | 13.16 | 112.24 |
| 1452 | 520 | 272.00 | 660.00 | 99.64 | 13.24 | 112.88 |
| 1456 | 520 | 272.00 | 664.00 | 100.19 | 13.32 | 113.51 |
| 1460 | 520 | 272.00 | 668.00 | 100.74 | 13.40 | 114.14 |
| 1464 | 520 | 272.00 | 672.00 | 101.29 | 13.48 | 114.77 |
| 1468 | 520 | 272.00 | 676.00 | 101.84 | 13.56 | 115.40 |
| 1472 | 520 | 272.00 | 680.00 | 102.40 | 13.64 | 116.04 |
| 1476 | 520 | 272.00 | 684.00 | 102.95 | 13.72 | 116.67 |
| 1480 | 520 | 272.00 | 688.00 | 103.50 | 13.80 | 117.30 |
| 1484 | 520 | 272.00 | 692.00 | 104.05 | 13.88 | 117.93 |
| 1488 | 520 | 272.00 | 696.00 | 104.60 | 13.96 | 118.56 |
| 1492 | 520 | 272.00 | 700.00 | 105.16 | 14.04 | 119.20 |
| 1496 | 520 | 272.00 | 704.00 | 105.71 | 14.12 | 119.83 |

## Monthly table

**Table letter J**

| Employee's earnings up to and including the UEL | Earnings at the LEL (where earnings are equal to or exceed the LEL) 1a | Earnings above the LEL, up to and including the PT 1b | Earnings above the PT, up to and including the UEL 1c | Employer's NICs due on all earnings above the ST 1d | Employee's NICs due on all earnings above the PT 1e | Total of employee's and employer's NICs (for information only) |
|---|---|---|---|---|---|---|
| £ | £ | £ p | £ p | £ p | £ p | £ p |
| 1500 | 520 | 272.00 | 708.00 | 106.26 | 14.20 | 120.46 |
| 1504 | 520 | 272.00 | 712.00 | 106.81 | 14.28 | 121.09 |
| 1508 | 520 | 272.00 | 716.00 | 107.36 | 14.36 | 121.72 |
| 1512 | 520 | 272.00 | 720.00 | 107.92 | 14.44 | 122.36 |
| 1516 | 520 | 272.00 | 724.00 | 108.47 | 14.52 | 122.99 |
| 1520 | 520 | 272.00 | 728.00 | 109.02 | 14.60 | 123.62 |
| 1524 | 520 | 272.00 | 732.00 | 109.57 | 14.68 | 124.25 |
| 1528 | 520 | 272.00 | 736.00 | 110.12 | 14.76 | 124.88 |
| 1532 | 520 | 272.00 | 740.00 | 110.68 | 14.84 | 125.52 |
| 1536 | 520 | 272.00 | 744.00 | 111.23 | 14.92 | 126.15 |
| 1540 | 520 | 272.00 | 748.00 | 111.78 | 15.00 | 126.78 |
| 1544 | 520 | 272.00 | 752.00 | 112.33 | 15.08 | 127.41 |
| 1548 | 520 | 272.00 | 756.00 | 112.88 | 15.16 | 128.04 |
| 1552 | 520 | 272.00 | 760.00 | 113.44 | 15.24 | 128.68 |
| 1556 | 520 | 272.00 | 764.00 | 113.99 | 15.32 | 129.31 |
| 1560 | 520 | 272.00 | 768.00 | 114.54 | 15.40 | 129.94 |
| 1564 | 520 | 272.00 | 772.00 | 115.09 | 15.48 | 130.57 |
| 1568 | 520 | 272.00 | 776.00 | 115.64 | 15.56 | 131.20 |
| 1572 | 520 | 272.00 | 780.00 | 116.20 | 15.64 | 131.84 |
| 1576 | 520 | 272.00 | 784.00 | 116.75 | 15.72 | 132.47 |
| 1580 | 520 | 272.00 | 788.00 | 117.30 | 15.80 | 133.10 |
| 1584 | 520 | 272.00 | 792.00 | 117.85 | 15.88 | 133.73 |
| 1588 | 520 | 272.00 | 796.00 | 118.40 | 15.96 | 134.36 |
| 1592 | 520 | 272.00 | 800.00 | 118.96 | 16.04 | 135.00 |
| 1596 | 520 | 272.00 | 804.00 | 119.51 | 16.12 | 135.63 |
| 1600 | 520 | 272.00 | 808.00 | 120.06 | 16.20 | 136.26 |
| 1604 | 520 | 272.00 | 812.00 | 120.61 | 16.28 | 136.89 |
| 1608 | 520 | 272.00 | 816.00 | 121.16 | 16.36 | 137.52 |
| 1612 | 520 | 272.00 | 820.00 | 121.72 | 16.44 | 138.16 |
| 1616 | 520 | 272.00 | 824.00 | 122.27 | 16.52 | 138.79 |
| 1620 | 520 | 272.00 | 828.00 | 122.82 | 16.60 | 139.42 |
| 1624 | 520 | 272.00 | 832.00 | 123.37 | 16.68 | 140.05 |
| 1628 | 520 | 272.00 | 836.00 | 123.92 | 16.76 | 140.68 |
| 1632 | 520 | 272.00 | 840.00 | 124.48 | 16.84 | 141.32 |
| 1636 | 520 | 272.00 | 844.00 | 125.03 | 16.92 | 141.95 |
| 1640 | 520 | 272.00 | 848.00 | 125.58 | 17.00 | 142.58 |
| 1644 | 520 | 272.00 | 852.00 | 126.13 | 17.08 | 143.21 |
| 1648 | 520 | 272.00 | 856.00 | 126.68 | 17.16 | 143.84 |
| 1652 | 520 | 272.00 | 860.00 | 127.24 | 17.24 | 144.48 |
| 1656 | 520 | 272.00 | 864.00 | 127.79 | 17.32 | 145.11 |
| 1660 | 520 | 272.00 | 868.00 | 128.34 | 17.40 | 145.74 |
| 1664 | 520 | 272.00 | 872.00 | 128.89 | 17.48 | 146.37 |
| 1668 | 520 | 272.00 | 876.00 | 129.44 | 17.56 | 147.00 |
| 1672 | 520 | 272.00 | 880.00 | 130.00 | 17.64 | 147.64 |
| 1676 | 520 | 272.00 | 884.00 | 130.55 | 17.72 | 148.27 |
| 1680 | 520 | 272.00 | 888.00 | 131.10 | 17.80 | 148.90 |
| 1684 | 520 | 272.00 | 892.00 | 131.65 | 17.88 | 149.53 |
| 1688 | 520 | 272.00 | 896.00 | 132.20 | 17.96 | 150.16 |
| 1692 | 520 | 272.00 | 900.00 | 132.76 | 18.04 | 150.80 |
| 1696 | 520 | 272.00 | 904.00 | 133.31 | 18.12 | 151.43 |
| 1700 | 520 | 272.00 | 908.00 | 133.86 | 18.20 | 152.06 |
| 1704 | 520 | 272.00 | 912.00 | 134.41 | 18.28 | 152.69 |
| 1708 | 520 | 272.00 | 916.00 | 134.96 | 18.36 | 153.32 |
| 1712 | 520 | 272.00 | 920.00 | 135.52 | 18.44 | 153.96 |
| 1716 | 520 | 272.00 | 924.00 | 136.07 | 18.52 | 154.59 |

# Table letter J

**Monthly table**

| Employee's earnings up to and including the UEL | Earnings at the LEL (where earnings are equal to or exceed the LEL) | Earnings above the LEL, up to and including the PT | Earnings above the PT, up to and including the UEL | Employer's NICs due on all earnings above the ST | Employee's NICs due on all earnings above the PT | Total of employee's and employer's NICs (for information only) |
|---|---|---|---|---|---|---|
| | 1a | 1b | 1c | 1d | 1e | |
| £ | £ | £ p | £ p | £ p | £ p | £ p |
| 1720 | 520 | 272.00 | 928.00 | 136.62 | 18.60 | 155.22 |
| 1724 | 520 | 272.00 | 932.00 | 137.17 | 18.68 | 155.85 |
| 1728 | 520 | 272.00 | 936.00 | 137.72 | 18.76 | 156.48 |
| 1732 | 520 | 272.00 | 940.00 | 138.28 | 18.84 | 157.12 |
| 1736 | 520 | 272.00 | 944.00 | 138.83 | 18.92 | 157.75 |
| 1740 | 520 | 272.00 | 948.00 | 139.38 | 19.00 | 158.38 |
| 1744 | 520 | 272.00 | 952.00 | 139.93 | 19.08 | 159.01 |
| 1748 | 520 | 272.00 | 956.00 | 140.48 | 19.16 | 159.64 |
| 1752 | 520 | 272.00 | 960.00 | 141.04 | 19.24 | 160.28 |
| 1756 | 520 | 272.00 | 964.00 | 141.59 | 19.32 | 160.91 |
| 1760 | 520 | 272.00 | 968.00 | 142.14 | 19.40 | 161.54 |
| 1764 | 520 | 272.00 | 972.00 | 142.69 | 19.48 | 162.17 |
| 1768 | 520 | 272.00 | 976.00 | 143.24 | 19.56 | 162.80 |
| 1772 | 520 | 272.00 | 980.00 | 143.80 | 19.64 | 163.44 |
| 1776 | 520 | 272.00 | 984.00 | 144.35 | 19.72 | 164.07 |
| 1780 | 520 | 272.00 | 988.00 | 144.90 | 19.80 | 164.70 |
| 1784 | 520 | 272.00 | 992.00 | 145.45 | 19.88 | 165.33 |
| 1788 | 520 | 272.00 | 996.00 | 146.00 | 19.96 | 165.96 |
| 1792 | 520 | 272.00 | 1000.00 | 146.56 | 20.04 | 166.60 |
| 1796 | 520 | 272.00 | 1004.00 | 147.11 | 20.12 | 167.23 |
| 1800 | 520 | 272.00 | 1008.00 | 147.66 | 20.20 | 167.86 |
| 1804 | 520 | 272.00 | 1012.00 | 148.21 | 20.28 | 168.49 |
| 1808 | 520 | 272.00 | 1016.00 | 148.76 | 20.36 | 169.12 |
| 1812 | 520 | 272.00 | 1020.00 | 149.32 | 20.44 | 169.76 |
| 1816 | 520 | 272.00 | 1024.00 | 149.87 | 20.52 | 170.39 |
| 1820 | 520 | 272.00 | 1028.00 | 150.42 | 20.60 | 171.02 |
| 1824 | 520 | 272.00 | 1032.00 | 150.97 | 20.68 | 171.65 |
| 1828 | 520 | 272.00 | 1036.00 | 151.52 | 20.76 | 172.28 |
| 1832 | 520 | 272.00 | 1040.00 | 152.08 | 20.84 | 172.92 |
| 1836 | 520 | 272.00 | 1044.00 | 152.63 | 20.92 | 173.55 |
| 1840 | 520 | 272.00 | 1048.00 | 153.18 | 21.00 | 174.18 |
| 1844 | 520 | 272.00 | 1052.00 | 153.73 | 21.08 | 174.81 |
| 1848 | 520 | 272.00 | 1056.00 | 154.28 | 21.16 | 175.44 |
| 1852 | 520 | 272.00 | 1060.00 | 154.84 | 21.24 | 176.08 |
| 1856 | 520 | 272.00 | 1064.00 | 155.39 | 21.32 | 176.71 |
| 1860 | 520 | 272.00 | 1068.00 | 155.94 | 21.40 | 177.34 |
| 1864 | 520 | 272.00 | 1072.00 | 156.49 | 21.48 | 177.97 |
| 1868 | 520 | 272.00 | 1076.00 | 157.04 | 21.56 | 178.60 |
| 1872 | 520 | 272.00 | 1080.00 | 157.60 | 21.64 | 179.24 |
| 1876 | 520 | 272.00 | 1084.00 | 158.15 | 21.72 | 179.87 |
| 1880 | 520 | 272.00 | 1088.00 | 158.70 | 21.80 | 180.50 |
| 1884 | 520 | 272.00 | 1092.00 | 159.25 | 21.88 | 181.13 |
| 1888 | 520 | 272.00 | 1096.00 | 159.80 | 21.96 | 181.76 |
| 1892 | 520 | 272.00 | 1100.00 | 160.36 | 22.04 | 182.40 |
| 1896 | 520 | 272.00 | 1104.00 | 160.91 | 22.12 | 183.03 |
| 1900 | 520 | 272.00 | 1108.00 | 161.46 | 22.20 | 183.66 |
| 1904 | 520 | 272.00 | 1112.00 | 162.01 | 22.28 | 184.29 |
| 1908 | 520 | 272.00 | 1116.00 | 162.56 | 22.36 | 184.92 |
| 1912 | 520 | 272.00 | 1120.00 | 163.12 | 22.44 | 185.56 |
| 1916 | 520 | 272.00 | 1124.00 | 163.67 | 22.52 | 186.19 |
| 1920 | 520 | 272.00 | 1128.00 | 164.22 | 22.60 | 186.82 |
| 1924 | 520 | 272.00 | 1132.00 | 164.77 | 22.68 | 187.45 |
| 1928 | 520 | 272.00 | 1136.00 | 165.32 | 22.76 | 188.08 |
| 1932 | 520 | 272.00 | 1140.00 | 165.88 | 22.84 | 188.72 |
| 1936 | 520 | 272.00 | 1144.00 | 166.43 | 22.92 | 189.35 |

**Monthly table**

**Table letter J**

| Employee's earnings up to and including the UEL | Earnings at the LEL (where earnings are equal to or exceed the LEL) 1a | Earnings above the LEL, up to and including the PT 1b | Earnings above the PT, up to and including the UEL 1c | Employer's NICs due on all earnings above the ST 1d | Employee's NICs due on all earnings above the PT 1e | Total of employee's and employer's NICs (for information only) |
|---|---|---|---|---|---|---|
| £ | £ | £ p | £ p | £ p | £ p | £ p |
| 1940 | 520 | 272.00 | 1148.00 | 166.98 | 23.00 | 189.98 |
| 1944 | 520 | 272.00 | 1152.00 | 167.53 | 23.08 | 190.61 |
| 1948 | 520 | 272.00 | 1156.00 | 168.08 | 23.16 | 191.24 |
| 1952 | 520 | 272.00 | 1160.00 | 168.64 | 23.24 | 191.88 |
| 1956 | 520 | 272.00 | 1164.00 | 169.19 | 23.32 | 192.51 |
| 1960 | 520 | 272.00 | 1168.00 | 169.74 | 23.40 | 193.14 |
| 1964 | 520 | 272.00 | 1172.00 | 170.29 | 23.48 | 193.77 |
| 1968 | 520 | 272.00 | 1176.00 | 170.84 | 23.56 | 194.40 |
| 1972 | 520 | 272.00 | 1180.00 | 171.40 | 23.64 | 195.04 |
| 1976 | 520 | 272.00 | 1184.00 | 171.95 | 23.72 | 195.67 |
| 1980 | 520 | 272.00 | 1188.00 | 172.50 | 23.80 | 196.30 |
| 1984 | 520 | 272.00 | 1192.00 | 173.05 | 23.88 | 196.93 |
| 1988 | 520 | 272.00 | 1196.00 | 173.60 | 23.96 | 197.56 |
| 1992 | 520 | 272.00 | 1200.00 | 174.16 | 24.04 | 198.20 |
| 1996 | 520 | 272.00 | 1204.00 | 174.71 | 24.12 | 198.83 |
| 2000 | 520 | 272.00 | 1208.00 | 175.26 | 24.20 | 199.46 |
| 2004 | 520 | 272.00 | 1212.00 | 175.81 | 24.28 | 200.09 |
| 2008 | 520 | 272.00 | 1216.00 | 176.36 | 24.36 | 200.72 |
| 2012 | 520 | 272.00 | 1220.00 | 176.92 | 24.44 | 201.36 |
| 2016 | 520 | 272.00 | 1224.00 | 177.47 | 24.52 | 201.99 |
| 2020 | 520 | 272.00 | 1228.00 | 178.02 | 24.60 | 202.62 |
| 2024 | 520 | 272.00 | 1232.00 | 178.57 | 24.68 | 203.25 |
| 2028 | 520 | 272.00 | 1236.00 | 179.12 | 24.76 | 203.88 |
| 2032 | 520 | 272.00 | 1240.00 | 179.68 | 24.84 | 204.52 |
| 2036 | 520 | 272.00 | 1244.00 | 180.23 | 24.92 | 205.15 |
| 2040 | 520 | 272.00 | 1248.00 | 180.78 | 25.00 | 205.78 |
| 2044 | 520 | 272.00 | 1252.00 | 181.33 | 25.08 | 206.41 |
| 2048 | 520 | 272.00 | 1256.00 | 181.88 | 25.16 | 207.04 |
| 2052 | 520 | 272.00 | 1260.00 | 182.44 | 25.24 | 207.68 |
| 2056 | 520 | 272.00 | 1264.00 | 182.99 | 25.32 | 208.31 |
| 2060 | 520 | 272.00 | 1268.00 | 183.54 | 25.40 | 208.94 |
| 2064 | 520 | 272.00 | 1272.00 | 184.09 | 25.48 | 209.57 |
| 2068 | 520 | 272.00 | 1276.00 | 184.64 | 25.56 | 210.20 |
| 2072 | 520 | 272.00 | 1280.00 | 185.20 | 25.64 | 210.84 |
| 2076 | 520 | 272.00 | 1284.00 | 185.75 | 25.72 | 211.47 |
| 2080 | 520 | 272.00 | 1288.00 | 186.30 | 25.80 | 212.10 |
| 2084 | 520 | 272.00 | 1292.00 | 186.85 | 25.88 | 212.73 |
| 2088 | 520 | 272.00 | 1296.00 | 187.40 | 25.96 | 213.36 |
| 2092 | 520 | 272.00 | 1300.00 | 187.96 | 26.04 | 214.00 |
| 2096 | 520 | 272.00 | 1304.00 | 188.51 | 26.12 | 214.63 |
| 2100 | 520 | 272.00 | 1308.00 | 189.06 | 26.20 | 215.26 |
| 2104 | 520 | 272.00 | 1312.00 | 189.61 | 26.28 | 215.89 |
| 2108 | 520 | 272.00 | 1316.00 | 190.16 | 26.36 | 216.52 |
| 2112 | 520 | 272.00 | 1320.00 | 190.72 | 26.44 | 217.16 |
| 2116 | 520 | 272.00 | 1324.00 | 191.27 | 26.52 | 217.79 |
| 2120 | 520 | 272.00 | 1328.00 | 191.82 | 26.60 | 218.42 |
| 2124 | 520 | 272.00 | 1332.00 | 192.37 | 26.68 | 219.05 |
| 2128 | 520 | 272.00 | 1336.00 | 192.92 | 26.76 | 219.68 |
| 2132 | 520 | 272.00 | 1340.00 | 193.48 | 26.84 | 220.32 |
| 2136 | 520 | 272.00 | 1344.00 | 194.03 | 26.92 | 220.95 |
| 2140 | 520 | 272.00 | 1348.00 | 194.58 | 27.00 | 221.58 |
| 2144 | 520 | 272.00 | 1352.00 | 195.13 | 27.08 | 222.21 |
| 2148 | 520 | 272.00 | 1356.00 | 195.68 | 27.16 | 222.84 |
| 2152 | 520 | 272.00 | 1360.00 | 196.24 | 27.24 | 223.48 |
| 2156 | 520 | 272.00 | 1364.00 | 196.79 | 27.32 | 224.11 |

**Table letter J**  **Monthly table**

| Employee's earnings up to and including the UEL | Earnings at the LEL (where earnings are equal to or exceed the LEL) 1a | Earnings above the LEL, up to and including the PT 1b | Earnings above the PT, up to and including the UEL 1c | Employer's NICs due on all earnings above the ST 1d | Employee's NICs due on all earnings above the PT 1e | Total of employee's and employer's NICs (for information only) |
|---|---|---|---|---|---|---|
| £ | £ | £ p | £ p | £ p | £ p | £ p |
| 2160 | 520 | 272.00 | 1368.00 | 197.34 | 27.40 | 224.74 |
| 2164 | 520 | 272.00 | 1372.00 | 197.89 | 27.48 | 225.37 |
| 2168 | 520 | 272.00 | 1376.00 | 198.44 | 27.56 | 226.00 |
| 2172 | 520 | 272.00 | 1380.00 | 199.00 | 27.64 | 226.64 |
| 2176 | 520 | 272.00 | 1384.00 | 199.55 | 27.72 | 227.27 |
| 2180 | 520 | 272.00 | 1388.00 | 200.10 | 27.80 | 227.90 |
| 2184 | 520 | 272.00 | 1392.00 | 200.65 | 27.88 | 228.53 |
| 2188 | 520 | 272.00 | 1396.00 | 201.20 | 27.96 | 229.16 |
| 2192 | 520 | 272.00 | 1400.00 | 201.76 | 28.04 | 229.80 |
| 2196 | 520 | 272.00 | 1404.00 | 202.31 | 28.12 | 230.43 |
| 2200 | 520 | 272.00 | 1408.00 | 202.86 | 28.20 | 231.06 |
| 2204 | 520 | 272.00 | 1412.00 | 203.41 | 28.28 | 231.69 |
| 2208 | 520 | 272.00 | 1416.00 | 203.96 | 28.36 | 232.32 |
| 2212 | 520 | 272.00 | 1420.00 | 204.52 | 28.44 | 232.96 |
| 2216 | 520 | 272.00 | 1424.00 | 205.07 | 28.52 | 233.59 |
| 2220 | 520 | 272.00 | 1428.00 | 205.62 | 28.60 | 234.22 |
| 2224 | 520 | 272.00 | 1432.00 | 206.17 | 28.68 | 234.85 |
| 2228 | 520 | 272.00 | 1436.00 | 206.72 | 28.76 | 235.48 |
| 2232 | 520 | 272.00 | 1440.00 | 207.28 | 28.84 | 236.12 |
| 2236 | 520 | 272.00 | 1444.00 | 207.83 | 28.92 | 236.75 |
| 2240 | 520 | 272.00 | 1448.00 | 208.38 | 29.00 | 237.38 |
| 2244 | 520 | 272.00 | 1452.00 | 208.93 | 29.08 | 238.01 |
| 2248 | 520 | 272.00 | 1456.00 | 209.48 | 29.16 | 238.64 |
| 2252 | 520 | 272.00 | 1460.00 | 210.04 | 29.24 | 239.28 |
| 2256 | 520 | 272.00 | 1464.00 | 210.59 | 29.32 | 239.91 |
| 2260 | 520 | 272.00 | 1468.00 | 211.14 | 29.40 | 240.54 |
| 2264 | 520 | 272.00 | 1472.00 | 211.69 | 29.48 | 241.17 |
| 2268 | 520 | 272.00 | 1476.00 | 212.24 | 29.56 | 241.80 |
| 2272 | 520 | 272.00 | 1480.00 | 212.80 | 29.64 | 242.44 |
| 2276 | 520 | 272.00 | 1484.00 | 213.35 | 29.72 | 243.07 |
| 2280 | 520 | 272.00 | 1488.00 | 213.90 | 29.80 | 243.70 |
| 2284 | 520 | 272.00 | 1492.00 | 214.45 | 29.88 | 244.33 |
| 2288 | 520 | 272.00 | 1496.00 | 215.00 | 29.96 | 244.96 |
| 2292 | 520 | 272.00 | 1500.00 | 215.56 | 30.04 | 245.60 |
| 2296 | 520 | 272.00 | 1504.00 | 216.11 | 30.12 | 246.23 |
| 2300 | 520 | 272.00 | 1508.00 | 216.66 | 30.20 | 246.86 |
| 2304 | 520 | 272.00 | 1512.00 | 217.21 | 30.28 | 247.49 |
| 2308 | 520 | 272.00 | 1516.00 | 217.76 | 30.36 | 248.12 |
| 2312 | 520 | 272.00 | 1520.00 | 218.32 | 30.44 | 248.76 |
| 2316 | 520 | 272.00 | 1524.00 | 218.87 | 30.52 | 249.39 |
| 2320 | 520 | 272.00 | 1528.00 | 219.42 | 30.60 | 250.02 |
| 2324 | 520 | 272.00 | 1532.00 | 219.97 | 30.68 | 250.65 |
| 2328 | 520 | 272.00 | 1536.00 | 220.52 | 30.76 | 251.28 |
| 2332 | 520 | 272.00 | 1540.00 | 221.08 | 30.84 | 251.92 |
| 2336 | 520 | 272.00 | 1544.00 | 221.63 | 30.92 | 252.55 |
| 2340 | 520 | 272.00 | 1548.00 | 222.18 | 31.00 | 253.18 |
| 2344 | 520 | 272.00 | 1552.00 | 222.73 | 31.08 | 253.81 |
| 2348 | 520 | 272.00 | 1556.00 | 223.28 | 31.16 | 254.44 |
| 2352 | 520 | 272.00 | 1560.00 | 223.84 | 31.24 | 255.08 |
| 2356 | 520 | 272.00 | 1564.00 | 224.39 | 31.32 | 255.71 |
| 2360 | 520 | 272.00 | 1568.00 | 224.94 | 31.40 | 256.34 |
| 2364 | 520 | 272.00 | 1572.00 | 225.49 | 31.48 | 256.97 |
| 2368 | 520 | 272.00 | 1576.00 | 226.04 | 31.56 | 257.60 |
| 2372 | 520 | 272.00 | 1580.00 | 226.60 | 31.64 | 258.24 |
| 2376 | 520 | 272.00 | 1584.00 | 227.15 | 31.72 | 258.87 |

**Monthly table**                                                                 **Table letter J**

| Employee's earnings up to and including the UEL | Earnings at the LEL (where earnings are equal to or exceed the LEL) | Earnings above the LEL, up to and including the PT | Earnings above the PT, up to and including the UEL | Employer's NICs due on all earnings above the ST | Employee's NICs due on all earnings above the PT | Total of employee's and employer's NICs (for information only) |
|---|---|---|---|---|---|---|
| | | 1a | 1b | 1c | 1d | 1e |
| £ | £ | £ p | £ p | £ p | £ p | £ p |
| 2380 | 520 | 272.00 | 1588.00 | 227.70 | 31.80 | 259.50 |
| 2384 | 520 | 272.00 | 1592.00 | 228.25 | 31.88 | 260.13 |
| 2388 | 520 | 272.00 | 1596.00 | 228.80 | 31.96 | 260.76 |
| 2392 | 520 | 272.00 | 1600.00 | 229.36 | 32.04 | 261.40 |
| 2396 | 520 | 272.00 | 1604.00 | 229.91 | 32.12 | 262.03 |
| 2400 | 520 | 272.00 | 1608.00 | 230.46 | 32.20 | 262.66 |
| 2404 | 520 | 272.00 | 1612.00 | 231.01 | 32.28 | 263.29 |
| 2408 | 520 | 272.00 | 1616.00 | 231.56 | 32.36 | 263.92 |
| 2412 | 520 | 272.00 | 1620.00 | 232.12 | 32.44 | 264.56 |
| 2416 | 520 | 272.00 | 1624.00 | 232.67 | 32.52 | 265.19 |
| 2420 | 520 | 272.00 | 1628.00 | 233.22 | 32.60 | 265.82 |
| 2424 | 520 | 272.00 | 1632.00 | 233.77 | 32.68 | 266.45 |
| 2428 | 520 | 272.00 | 1636.00 | 234.32 | 32.76 | 267.08 |
| 2432 | 520 | 272.00 | 1640.00 | 234.88 | 32.84 | 267.72 |
| 2436 | 520 | 272.00 | 1644.00 | 235.43 | 32.92 | 268.35 |
| 2440 | 520 | 272.00 | 1648.00 | 235.98 | 33.00 | 268.98 |
| 2444 | 520 | 272.00 | 1652.00 | 236.53 | 33.08 | 269.61 |
| 2448 | 520 | 272.00 | 1656.00 | 237.08 | 33.16 | 270.24 |
| 2452 | 520 | 272.00 | 1660.00 | 237.64 | 33.24 | 270.88 |
| 2456 | 520 | 272.00 | 1664.00 | 238.19 | 33.32 | 271.51 |
| 2460 | 520 | 272.00 | 1668.00 | 238.74 | 33.40 | 272.14 |
| 2464 | 520 | 272.00 | 1672.00 | 239.29 | 33.48 | 272.77 |
| 2468 | 520 | 272.00 | 1676.00 | 239.84 | 33.56 | 273.40 |
| 2472 | 520 | 272.00 | 1680.00 | 240.40 | 33.64 | 274.04 |
| 2476 | 520 | 272.00 | 1684.00 | 240.95 | 33.72 | 274.67 |
| 2480 | 520 | 272.00 | 1688.00 | 241.50 | 33.80 | 275.30 |
| 2484 | 520 | 272.00 | 1692.00 | 242.05 | 33.88 | 275.93 |
| 2488 | 520 | 272.00 | 1696.00 | 242.60 | 33.96 | 276.56 |
| 2492 | 520 | 272.00 | 1700.00 | 243.16 | 34.04 | 277.20 |
| 2496 | 520 | 272.00 | 1704.00 | 243.71 | 34.12 | 277.83 |
| 2500 | 520 | 272.00 | 1708.00 | 244.26 | 34.20 | 278.46 |
| 2504 | 520 | 272.00 | 1712.00 | 244.81 | 34.28 | 279.09 |
| 2508 | 520 | 272.00 | 1716.00 | 245.36 | 34.36 | 279.72 |
| 2512 | 520 | 272.00 | 1720.00 | 245.92 | 34.44 | 280.36 |
| 2516 | 520 | 272.00 | 1724.00 | 246.47 | 34.52 | 280.99 |
| 2520 | 520 | 272.00 | 1728.00 | 247.02 | 34.60 | 281.62 |
| 2524 | 520 | 272.00 | 1732.00 | 247.57 | 34.68 | 282.25 |
| 2528 | 520 | 272.00 | 1736.00 | 248.12 | 34.76 | 282.88 |
| 2532 | 520 | 272.00 | 1740.00 | 248.68 | 34.84 | 283.52 |
| 2536 | 520 | 272.00 | 1744.00 | 249.23 | 34.92 | 284.15 |
| 2540 | 520 | 272.00 | 1748.00 | 249.78 | 35.00 | 284.78 |
| 2544 | 520 | 272.00 | 1752.00 | 250.33 | 35.08 | 285.41 |
| 2548 | 520 | 272.00 | 1756.00 | 250.88 | 35.16 | 286.04 |
| 2552 | 520 | 272.00 | 1760.00 | 251.44 | 35.24 | 286.68 |
| 2556 | 520 | 272.00 | 1764.00 | 251.99 | 35.32 | 287.31 |
| 2560 | 520 | 272.00 | 1768.00 | 252.54 | 35.40 | 287.94 |
| 2564 | 520 | 272.00 | 1772.00 | 253.09 | 35.48 | 288.57 |
| 2568 | 520 | 272.00 | 1776.00 | 253.64 | 35.56 | 289.20 |
| 2572 | 520 | 272.00 | 1780.00 | 254.20 | 35.64 | 289.84 |
| 2576 | 520 | 272.00 | 1784.00 | 254.75 | 35.72 | 290.47 |
| 2580 | 520 | 272.00 | 1788.00 | 255.30 | 35.80 | 291.10 |
| 2584 | 520 | 272.00 | 1792.00 | 255.85 | 35.88 | 291.73 |
| 2588 | 520 | 272.00 | 1796.00 | 256.40 | 35.96 | 292.36 |
| 2592 | 520 | 272.00 | 1800.00 | 256.96 | 36.04 | 293.00 |
| 2596 | 520 | 272.00 | 1804.00 | 257.51 | 36.12 | 293.63 |

# Table letter J

**Monthly table**

| Employee's earnings up to and including the UEL | Earnings at the LEL (where earnings are equal to or exceed the LEL) 1a | Earnings above the LEL, up to and including the PT 1b | Earnings above the PT, up to and including the UEL 1c | Employer's NICs due on all earnings above the ST 1d | Employee's NICs due on all earnings above the PT 1e | Total of employee's and employer's NICs (for information only) |
|---|---|---|---|---|---|---|
| £ | £ | £ p | £ p | £ p | £ p | £ p |
| 2600 | 520 | 272.00 | 1808.00 | 258.06 | 36.20 | 294.26 |
| 2604 | 520 | 272.00 | 1812.00 | 258.61 | 36.28 | 294.89 |
| 2608 | 520 | 272.00 | 1816.00 | 259.16 | 36.36 | 295.52 |
| 2612 | 520 | 272.00 | 1820.00 | 259.72 | 36.44 | 296.16 |
| 2616 | 520 | 272.00 | 1824.00 | 260.27 | 36.52 | 296.79 |
| 2620 | 520 | 272.00 | 1828.00 | 260.82 | 36.60 | 297.42 |
| 2624 | 520 | 272.00 | 1832.00 | 261.37 | 36.68 | 298.05 |
| 2628 | 520 | 272.00 | 1836.00 | 261.92 | 36.76 | 298.68 |
| 2632 | 520 | 272.00 | 1840.00 | 262.48 | 36.84 | 299.32 |
| 2636 | 520 | 272.00 | 1844.00 | 263.03 | 36.92 | 299.95 |
| 2640 | 520 | 272.00 | 1848.00 | 263.58 | 37.00 | 300.58 |
| 2644 | 520 | 272.00 | 1852.00 | 264.13 | 37.08 | 301.21 |
| 2648 | 520 | 272.00 | 1856.00 | 264.68 | 37.16 | 301.84 |
| 2652 | 520 | 272.00 | 1860.00 | 265.24 | 37.24 | 302.48 |
| 2656 | 520 | 272.00 | 1864.00 | 265.79 | 37.32 | 303.11 |
| 2660 | 520 | 272.00 | 1868.00 | 266.34 | 37.40 | 303.74 |
| 2664 | 520 | 272.00 | 1872.00 | 266.89 | 37.48 | 304.37 |
| 2668 | 520 | 272.00 | 1876.00 | 267.44 | 37.56 | 305.00 |
| 2672 | 520 | 272.00 | 1880.00 | 268.00 | 37.64 | 305.64 |
| 2676 | 520 | 272.00 | 1884.00 | 268.55 | 37.72 | 306.27 |
| 2680 | 520 | 272.00 | 1888.00 | 269.10 | 37.80 | 306.90 |
| 2684 | 520 | 272.00 | 1892.00 | 269.65 | 37.88 | 307.53 |
| 2688 | 520 | 272.00 | 1896.00 | 270.20 | 37.96 | 308.16 |
| 2692 | 520 | 272.00 | 1900.00 | 270.76 | 38.04 | 308.80 |
| 2696 | 520 | 272.00 | 1904.00 | 271.31 | 38.12 | 309.43 |
| 2700 | 520 | 272.00 | 1908.00 | 271.86 | 38.20 | 310.06 |
| 2704 | 520 | 272.00 | 1912.00 | 272.41 | 38.28 | 310.69 |
| 2708 | 520 | 272.00 | 1916.00 | 272.96 | 38.36 | 311.32 |
| 2712 | 520 | 272.00 | 1920.00 | 273.52 | 38.44 | 311.96 |
| 2716 | 520 | 272.00 | 1924.00 | 274.07 | 38.52 | 312.59 |
| 2720 | 520 | 272.00 | 1928.00 | 274.62 | 38.60 | 313.22 |
| 2724 | 520 | 272.00 | 1932.00 | 275.17 | 38.68 | 313.85 |
| 2728 | 520 | 272.00 | 1936.00 | 275.72 | 38.76 | 314.48 |
| 2732 | 520 | 272.00 | 1940.00 | 276.28 | 38.84 | 315.12 |
| 2736 | 520 | 272.00 | 1944.00 | 276.83 | 38.92 | 315.75 |
| 2740 | 520 | 272.00 | 1948.00 | 277.38 | 39.00 | 316.38 |
| 2744 | 520 | 272.00 | 1952.00 | 277.93 | 39.08 | 317.01 |
| 2748 | 520 | 272.00 | 1956.00 | 278.48 | 39.16 | 317.64 |
| 2752 | 520 | 272.00 | 1960.00 | 279.04 | 39.24 | 318.28 |
| 2756 | 520 | 272.00 | 1964.00 | 279.59 | 39.32 | 318.91 |
| 2760 | 520 | 272.00 | 1968.00 | 280.14 | 39.40 | 319.54 |
| 2764 | 520 | 272.00 | 1972.00 | 280.69 | 39.48 | 320.17 |
| 2768 | 520 | 272.00 | 1976.00 | 281.24 | 39.56 | 320.80 |
| 2772 | 520 | 272.00 | 1980.00 | 281.80 | 39.64 | 321.44 |
| 2776 | 520 | 272.00 | 1984.00 | 282.35 | 39.72 | 322.07 |
| 2780 | 520 | 272.00 | 1988.00 | 282.90 | 39.80 | 322.70 |
| 2784 | 520 | 272.00 | 1992.00 | 283.45 | 39.88 | 323.33 |
| 2788 | 520 | 272.00 | 1996.00 | 284.00 | 39.96 | 323.96 |
| 2792 | 520 | 272.00 | 2000.00 | 284.56 | 40.04 | 324.60 |
| 2796 | 520 | 272.00 | 2004.00 | 285.11 | 40.12 | 325.23 |
| 2800 | 520 | 272.00 | 2008.00 | 285.66 | 40.20 | 325.86 |
| 2804 | 520 | 272.00 | 2012.00 | 286.21 | 40.28 | 326.49 |
| 2808 | 520 | 272.00 | 2016.00 | 286.76 | 40.36 | 327.12 |
| 2812 | 520 | 272.00 | 2020.00 | 287.32 | 40.44 | 327.76 |
| 2816 | 520 | 272.00 | 2024.00 | 287.87 | 40.52 | 328.39 |

## Monthly table

**Table letter J**

| Employee's earnings up to and including the UEL | Earnings at the LEL (where earnings are equal to or exceed the LEL) | Earnings above the LEL, up to and including the PT | Earnings above the PT, up to and including the UEL | Employer's NICs due on all earnings above the ST | Employee's NICs due on all earnings above the PT | Total of employee's and employer's NICs (for information only) |
|---|---|---|---|---|---|---|
| | | 1a | 1b | 1c | 1d | 1e |
| £ | £ | £ p | £ p | £ p | £ p | £ p |
| 2820 | 520 | 272.00 | 2028.00 | 288.42 | 40.60 | 329.02 |
| 2824 | 520 | 272.00 | 2032.00 | 288.97 | 40.68 | 329.65 |
| 2828 | 520 | 272.00 | 2036.00 | 289.52 | 40.76 | 330.28 |
| 2832 | 520 | 272.00 | 2040.00 | 290.08 | 40.84 | 330.92 |
| 2836 | 520 | 272.00 | 2044.00 | 290.63 | 40.92 | 331.55 |
| 2840 | 520 | 272.00 | 2048.00 | 291.18 | 41.00 | 332.18 |
| 2844 | 520 | 272.00 | 2052.00 | 291.73 | 41.08 | 332.81 |
| 2848 | 520 | 272.00 | 2056.00 | 292.28 | 41.16 | 333.44 |
| 2852 | 520 | 272.00 | 2060.00 | 292.84 | 41.24 | 334.08 |
| 2856 | 520 | 272.00 | 2064.00 | 293.39 | 41.32 | 334.71 |
| 2860 | 520 | 272.00 | 2068.00 | 293.94 | 41.40 | 335.34 |
| 2864 | 520 | 272.00 | 2072.00 | 294.49 | 41.48 | 335.97 |
| 2868 | 520 | 272.00 | 2076.00 | 295.04 | 41.56 | 336.60 |
| 2872 | 520 | 272.00 | 2080.00 | 295.60 | 41.64 | 337.24 |
| 2876 | 520 | 272.00 | 2084.00 | 296.15 | 41.72 | 337.87 |
| 2880 | 520 | 272.00 | 2088.00 | 296.70 | 41.80 | 338.50 |
| 2884 | 520 | 272.00 | 2092.00 | 297.25 | 41.88 | 339.13 |
| 2888 | 520 | 272.00 | 2096.00 | 297.80 | 41.96 | 339.76 |
| 2892 | 520 | 272.00 | 2100.00 | 298.36 | 42.04 | 340.40 |
| 2896 | 520 | 272.00 | 2104.00 | 298.91 | 42.12 | 341.03 |
| 2900 | 520 | 272.00 | 2108.00 | 299.46 | 42.20 | 341.66 |
| 2904 | 520 | 272.00 | 2112.00 | 300.01 | 42.28 | 342.29 |
| 2908 | 520 | 272.00 | 2116.00 | 300.56 | 42.36 | 342.92 |
| 2912 | 520 | 272.00 | 2120.00 | 301.12 | 42.44 | 343.56 |
| 2916 | 520 | 272.00 | 2124.00 | 301.67 | 42.52 | 344.19 |
| 2920 | 520 | 272.00 | 2128.00 | 302.22 | 42.60 | 344.82 |
| 2924 | 520 | 272.00 | 2132.00 | 302.77 | 42.68 | 345.45 |
| 2928 | 520 | 272.00 | 2136.00 | 303.32 | 42.76 | 346.08 |
| 2932 | 520 | 272.00 | 2140.00 | 303.88 | 42.84 | 346.72 |
| 2936 | 520 | 272.00 | 2144.00 | 304.43 | 42.92 | 347.35 |
| 2940 | 520 | 272.00 | 2148.00 | 304.98 | 43.00 | 347.98 |
| 2944 | 520 | 272.00 | 2152.00 | 305.53 | 43.08 | 348.61 |
| 2948 | 520 | 272.00 | 2156.00 | 306.08 | 43.16 | 349.24 |
| 2952 | 520 | 272.00 | 2160.00 | 306.64 | 43.24 | 349.88 |
| 2956 | 520 | 272.00 | 2164.00 | 307.19 | 43.32 | 350.51 |
| 2960 | 520 | 272.00 | 2168.00 | 307.74 | 43.40 | 351.14 |
| 2964 | 520 | 272.00 | 2172.00 | 308.29 | 43.48 | 351.77 |
| 2968 | 520 | 272.00 | 2176.00 | 308.84 | 43.56 | 352.40 |
| 2972 | 520 | 272.00 | 2180.00 | 309.40 | 43.64 | 353.04 |
| 2976 | 520 | 272.00 | 2184.00 | 309.95 | 43.72 | 353.67 |
| 2980 | 520 | 272.00 | 2188.00 | 310.50 | 43.80 | 354.30 |
| 2984 | 520 | 272.00 | 2192.00 | 311.05 | 43.88 | 354.93 |
| 2988 | 520 | 272.00 | 2196.00 | 311.60 | 43.96 | 355.56 |
| 2992 | 520 | 272.00 | 2200.00 | 312.16 | 44.04 | 356.20 |
| 2996 | 520 | 272.00 | 2204.00 | 312.71 | 44.12 | 356.83 |
| 3000 | 520 | 272.00 | 2208.00 | 313.26 | 44.20 | 357.46 |
| 3004 | 520 | 272.00 | 2212.00 | 313.81 | 44.28 | 358.09 |
| 3008 | 520 | 272.00 | 2216.00 | 314.36 | 44.36 | 358.72 |
| 3012 | 520 | 272.00 | 2220.00 | 314.92 | 44.44 | 359.36 |
| 3016 | 520 | 272.00 | 2224.00 | 315.47 | 44.52 | 359.99 |
| 3020 | 520 | 272.00 | 2228.00 | 316.02 | 44.60 | 360.62 |
| 3024 | 520 | 272.00 | 2232.00 | 316.57 | 44.68 | 361.25 |
| 3028 | 520 | 272.00 | 2236.00 | 317.12 | 44.76 | 361.88 |
| 3032 | 520 | 272.00 | 2240.00 | 317.68 | 44.84 | 362.52 |
| 3036 | 520 | 272.00 | 2244.00 | 318.23 | 44.92 | 363.15 |

## Table letter J

**Monthly table**

| Employee's earnings up to and including the UEL | Earnings at the LEL (where earnings are equal to or exceed the LEL) 1a | Earnings above the LEL, up to and including the PT 1b | Earnings above the PT, up to and including the UEL 1c | Employer's NICs due on all earnings above the ST 1d | Employee's NICs due on all earnings above the PT 1e | Total of employee's and employer's NICs (for information only) |
|---|---|---|---|---|---|---|
| £ | £ | £ p | £ p | £ p | £ p | £ p |
| 3040 | 520 | 272.00 | 2248.00 | 318.78 | 45.00 | 363.78 |
| 3044 | 520 | 272.00 | 2252.00 | 319.33 | 45.08 | 364.41 |
| 3048 | 520 | 272.00 | 2256.00 | 319.88 | 45.16 | 365.04 |
| 3052 | 520 | 272.00 | 2260.00 | 320.44 | 45.24 | 365.68 |
| 3056 | 520 | 272.00 | 2264.00 | 320.99 | 45.32 | 366.31 |
| 3060 | 520 | 272.00 | 2268.00 | 321.54 | 45.40 | 366.94 |
| 3064 | 520 | 272.00 | 2272.00 | 322.09 | 45.48 | 367.57 |
| 3068 | 520 | 272.00 | 2276.00 | 322.64 | 45.56 | 368.20 |
| 3072 | 520 | 272.00 | 2280.00 | 323.20 | 45.64 | 368.84 |
| 3076 | 520 | 272.00 | 2284.00 | 323.75 | 45.72 | 369.47 |
| 3080 | 520 | 272.00 | 2288.00 | 324.30 | 45.80 | 370.10 |
| 3084 | 520 | 272.00 | 2292.00 | 324.85 | 45.88 | 370.73 |
| 3088 | 520 | 272.00 | 2296.00 | 325.40 | 45.96 | 371.36 |
| 3092 | 520 | 272.00 | 2300.00 | 325.96 | 46.04 | 372.00 |
| 3096 | 520 | 272.00 | 2304.00 | 326.51 | 46.12 | 372.63 |
| 3100 | 520 | 272.00 | 2308.00 | 327.06 | 46.20 | 373.26 |
| 3104 | 520 | 272.00 | 2312.00 | 327.61 | 46.28 | 373.89 |
| 3108 | 520 | 272.00 | 2316.00 | 328.16 | 46.36 | 374.52 |
| 3112 | 520 | 272.00 | 2320.00 | 328.72 | 46.44 | 375.16 |
| 3116 | 520 | 272.00 | 2324.00 | 329.27 | 46.52 | 375.79 |
| 3120 | 520 | 272.00 | 2328.00 | 329.82 | 46.60 | 376.42 |
| 3124 | 520 | 272.00 | 2332.00 | 330.37 | 46.68 | 377.05 |
| 3128 | 520 | 272.00 | 2336.00 | 330.92 | 46.76 | 377.68 |
| 3132 | 520 | 272.00 | 2340.00 | 331.48 | 46.84 | 378.32 |
| 3136 | 520 | 272.00 | 2344.00 | 332.03 | 46.92 | 378.95 |
| 3140 | 520 | 272.00 | 2348.00 | 332.58 | 47.00 | 379.58 |
| 3144 | 520 | 272.00 | 2352.00 | 333.13 | 47.08 | 380.21 |
| 3148 | 520 | 272.00 | 2356.00 | 333.68 | 47.16 | 380.84 |
| 3152 | 520 | 272.00 | 2360.00 | 334.24 | 47.24 | 381.48 |
| 3156 | 520 | 272.00 | 2364.00 | 334.79 | 47.32 | 382.11 |
| 3160 | 520 | 272.00 | 2368.00 | 335.34 | 47.40 | 382.74 |
| 3164 | 520 | 272.00 | 2372.00 | 335.89 | 47.48 | 383.37 |
| 3168 | 520 | 272.00 | 2376.00 | 336.44 | 47.56 | 384.00 |
| 3172 | 520 | 272.00 | 2380.00 | 337.00 | 47.64 | 384.64 |
| 3176 | 520 | 272.00 | 2384.00 | 337.55 | 47.72 | 385.27 |
| 3180 | 520 | 272.00 | 2388.00 | 338.10 | 47.80 | 385.90 |
| 3184 | 520 | 272.00 | 2392.00 | 338.65 | 47.88 | 386.53 |
| 3188 | 520 | 272.00 | 2396.00 | 339.20 | 47.96 | 387.16 |
| 3192 | 520 | 272.00 | 2400.00 | 339.76 | 48.04 | 387.80 |
| 3196 | 520 | 272.00 | 2404.00 | 340.31 | 48.12 | 388.43 |
| 3200 | 520 | 272.00 | 2408.00 | 340.86 | 48.20 | 389.06 |
| 3204 | 520 | 272.00 | 2412.00 | 341.41 | 48.28 | 389.69 |
| 3208 | 520 | 272.00 | 2416.00 | 341.96 | 48.36 | 390.32 |
| 3212 | 520 | 272.00 | 2420.00 | 342.52 | 48.44 | 390.96 |
| 3216 | 520 | 272.00 | 2424.00 | 343.07 | 48.52 | 391.59 |
| 3220 | 520 | 272.00 | 2428.00 | 343.62 | 48.60 | 392.22 |
| 3224 | 520 | 272.00 | 2432.00 | 344.17 | 48.68 | 392.85 |
| 3228 | 520 | 272.00 | 2436.00 | 344.72 | 48.76 | 393.48 |
| 3232 | 520 | 272.00 | 2440.00 | 345.28 | 48.84 | 394.12 |
| 3236 | 520 | 272.00 | 2444.00 | 345.83 | 48.92 | 394.75 |
| 3240 | 520 | 272.00 | 2448.00 | 346.38 | 49.00 | 395.38 |
| 3244 | 520 | 272.00 | 2452.00 | 346.93 | 49.08 | 396.01 |
| 3248 | 520 | 272.00 | 2456.00 | 347.48 | 49.16 | 396.64 |
| 3252 | 520 | 272.00 | 2460.00 | 348.04 | 49.24 | 397.28 |
| 3256 | 520 | 272.00 | 2464.00 | 348.59 | 49.32 | 397.91 |

**Monthly table**

| Employee's earnings up to and including the UEL | Earnings at the LEL (where earnings are equal to or exceed the LEL) | Earnings above the LEL, up to and including the PT | Earnings above the PT, up to and including the UEL | Employer's NICs due on all earnings above the ST | Employee's NICs due on all earnings above the PT | Total of employee's and employer's NICs (for information only) |
|---|---|---|---|---|---|---|
| | | 1a | 1b | 1c | 1d | 1e |
| £ | £ | £ p | £ p | £ p | £ p | £ p |
| 3260 | 520 | 272.00 | 2468.00 | 349.14 | 49.40 | 398.54 |
| 3264 | 520 | 272.00 | 2472.00 | 349.69 | 49.48 | 399.17 |
| 3268 | 520 | 272.00 | 2476.00 | 350.24 | 49.56 | 399.80 |
| 3272 | 520 | 272.00 | 2480.00 | 350.80 | 49.64 | 400.44 |
| 3276 | 520 | 272.00 | 2484.00 | 351.35 | 49.72 | 401.07 |
| 3280 | 520 | 272.00 | 2488.00 | 351.90 | 49.80 | 401.70 |
| 3284 | 520 | 272.00 | 2492.00 | 352.45 | 49.88 | 402.33 |
| 3288 | 520 | 272.00 | 2496.00 | 353.00 | 49.96 | 402.96 |
| 3292 | 520 | 272.00 | 2500.00 | 353.56 | 50.04 | 403.60 |
| 3296 | 520 | 272.00 | 2504.00 | 354.11 | 50.12 | 404.23 |
| 3300 | 520 | 272.00 | 2508.00 | 354.66 | 50.20 | 404.86 |
| 3304 | 520 | 272.00 | 2512.00 | 355.21 | 50.28 | 405.49 |
| 3308 | 520 | 272.00 | 2516.00 | 355.76 | 50.36 | 406.12 |
| 3312 | 520 | 272.00 | 2520.00 | 356.32 | 50.44 | 406.76 |
| 3316 | 520 | 272.00 | 2524.00 | 356.87 | 50.52 | 407.39 |
| 3320 | 520 | 272.00 | 2528.00 | 357.42 | 50.60 | 408.02 |
| 3324 | 520 | 272.00 | 2532.00 | 357.97 | 50.68 | 408.65 |
| 3328 | 520 | 272.00 | 2536.00 | 358.52 | 50.76 | 409.28 |
| 3332 | 520 | 272.00 | 2540.00 | 359.08 | 50.84 | 409.92 |
| 3336 | 520 | 272.00 | 2544.00 | 359.63 | 50.92 | 410.55 |
| 3340 | 520 | 272.00 | 2548.00 | 360.18 | 51.00 | 411.18 |
| 3344 | 520 | 272.00 | 2552.00 | 360.73 | 51.08 | 411.81 |
| 3348 | 520 | 272.00 | 2556.00 | 361.28 | 51.16 | 412.44 |
| 3352 | 520 | 272.00 | 2560.00 | 361.84 | 51.24 | 413.08 |
| 3356 | 520 | 272.00 | 2564.00 | 362.39 | 51.32 | 413.71 |
| 3360 | 520 | 272.00 | 2568.00 | 362.94 | 51.40 | 414.34 |
| 3364 | 520 | 272.00 | 2572.00 | 363.49 | 51.48 | 414.97 |
| 3368 | 520 | 272.00 | 2576.00 | 364.04 | 51.56 | 415.60 |
| 3372 | 520 | 272.00 | 2580.00 | 364.60 | 51.64 | 416.24 |
| 3376 | 520 | 272.00 | 2584.00 | 365.15 | 51.72 | 416.87 |
| 3380 | 520 | 272.00 | 2588.00 | 365.70 | 51.80 | 417.50 |
| 3384 | 520 | 272.00 | 2592.00 | 366.25 | 51.88 | 418.13 |
| 3388 | 520 | 272.00 | 2596.00 | 366.80 | 51.96 | 418.76 |
| 3392 | 520 | 272.00 | 2600.00 | 367.36 | 52.04 | 419.40 |
| 3396 | 520 | 272.00 | 2604.00 | 367.91 | 52.12 | 420.03 |
| 3400 | 520 | 272.00 | 2608.00 | 368.46 | 52.20 | 420.66 |
| 3404 | 520 | 272.00 | 2612.00 | 369.01 | 52.28 | 421.29 |
| 3408 | 520 | 272.00 | 2616.00 | 369.56 | 52.36 | 421.92 |
| 3412 | 520 | 272.00 | 2620.00 | 370.12 | 52.44 | 422.56 |
| 3416 | 520 | 272.00 | 2624.00 | 370.67 | 52.52 | 423.19 |
| 3420 | 520 | 272.00 | 2628.00 | 371.22 | 52.60 | 423.82 |
| 3424 | 520 | 272.00 | 2632.00 | 371.77 | 52.68 | 424.45 |
| 3428 | 520 | 272.00 | 2636.00 | 372.32 | 52.76 | 425.08 |
| 3432 | 520 | 272.00 | 2640.00 | 372.88 | 52.84 | 425.72 |
| 3436 | 520 | 272.00 | 2644.00 | 373.43 | 52.92 | 426.35 |
| 3440 | 520 | 272.00 | 2648.00 | 373.98 | 53.00 | 426.98 |
| 3444 | 520 | 272.00 | 2652.00 | 374.53 | 53.08 | 427.61 |
| 3448 | 520 | 272.00 | 2656.00 | 375.08 | 53.16 | 428.24 |
| 3452 | 520 | 272.00 | 2660.00 | 375.64 | 53.24 | 428.88 |
| 3456 | 520 | 272.00 | 2664.00 | 376.19 | 53.32 | 429.51 |
| 3460 | 520 | 272.00 | 2668.00 | 376.74 | 53.40 | 430.14 |
| 3464 | 520 | 272.00 | 2672.00 | 377.29 | 53.48 | 430.77 |
| 3468 | 520 | 272.00 | 2676.00 | 377.84 | 53.56 | 431.40 |
| 3472 | 520 | 272.00 | 2680.00 | 378.40 | 53.64 | 432.04 |
| 3476 | 520 | 272.00 | 2684.00 | 378.95 | 53.72 | 432.67 |

**Monthly table**

**Table letter J**

| Employee's earnings up to and including the UEL | Earnings at the LEL (where earnings are equal to or exceed the LEL) | Earnings above the LEL, up to and including the PT | Earnings above the PT, up to and including the UEL | Employer's NICs due on all earnings above the ST | Employee's NICs due on all earnings above the PT | Total of employee's and employer's NICs (for information only) |
|---|---|---|---|---|---|---|
| | | 1a | 1b | 1c | 1d | 1e |
| £ | £ | £ p | £ p | £ p | £ p | £ p |
| 3480 | 520 | 272.00 | 2688.00 | 379.50 | 53.80 | 433.30 |
| 3484 | 520 | 272.00 | 2692.00 | 380.05 | 53.88 | 433.93 |
| 3488 | 520 | 272.00 | 2696.00 | 380.60 | 53.96 | 434.56 |
| 3492 | 520 | 272.00 | 2700.00 | 381.16 | 54.04 | 435.20 |
| 3496 | 520 | 272.00 | 2704.00 | 381.71 | 54.12 | 435.83 |
| 3500 | 520 | 272.00 | 2708.00 | 382.26 | 54.20 | 436.46 |
| 3504 | 520 | 272.00 | 2712.00 | 382.81 | 54.28 | 437.09 |
| 3508 | 520 | 272.00 | 2716.00 | 383.36 | 54.36 | 437.72 |
| 3512 | 520 | 272.00 | 2720.00 | 383.92 | 54.44 | 438.36 |
| 3516 | 520 | 272.00 | 2724.00 | 384.47 | 54.52 | 438.99 |
| 3520 | 520 | 272.00 | 2728.00 | 385.02 | 54.60 | 439.62 |
| 3524 | 520 | 272.00 | 2732.00 | 385.57 | 54.68 | 440.25 |
| 3528 | 520 | 272.00 | 2736.00 | 386.12 | 54.76 | 440.88 |
| 3532 | 520 | 272.00 | 2740.00 | 386.68 | 54.84 | 441.52 |
| 3536 | 520 | 272.00 | 2744.00 | 387.23 | 54.92 | 442.15 |
| 3540 | 520 | 272.00 | 2748.00 | 387.78 | 55.00 | 442.78 |
| 3544 | 520 | 272.00 | 2752.00 | 388.33 | 55.08 | 443.41 |
| 3548 | 520 | 272.00 | 2756.00 | 388.88 | 55.16 | 444.04 |
| 3552 | 520 | 272.00 | 2760.00 | 389.44 | 55.24 | 444.68 |
| 3556 | 520 | 272.00 | 2764.00 | 389.99 | 55.32 | 445.31 |
| 3560 | 520 | 272.00 | 2768.00 | 390.54 | 55.40 | 445.94 |
| 3564 | 520 | 272.00 | 2772.00 | 391.09 | 55.48 | 446.57 |
| 3568 | 520 | 272.00 | 2776.00 | 391.64 | 55.56 | 447.20 |
| 3572 | 520 | 272.00 | 2780.00 | 392.20 | 55.64 | 447.84 |
| 3576 | 520 | 272.00 | 2784.00 | 392.75 | 55.72 | 448.47 |
| 3580 | 520 | 272.00 | 2788.00 | 393.30 | 55.80 | 449.10 |
| 3584 | 520 | 272.00 | 2792.00 | 393.85 | 55.88 | 449.73 |
| 3588 | 520 | 272.00 | 2796.00 | 394.40 | 55.96 | 450.36 |
| 3592 | 520 | 272.00 | 2800.00 | 394.96 | 56.04 | 451.00 |
| 3596 | 520 | 272.00 | 2804.00 | 395.51 | 56.12 | 451.63 |
| 3600 | 520 | 272.00 | 2808.00 | 396.06 | 56.20 | 452.26 |
| 3604 | 520 | 272.00 | 2812.00 | 396.61 | 56.28 | 452.89 |
| 3608 | 520 | 272.00 | 2816.00 | 397.16 | 56.36 | 453.52 |
| 3612 | 520 | 272.00 | 2820.00 | 397.72 | 56.44 | 454.16 |
| 3616 | 520 | 272.00 | 2824.00 | 398.27 | 56.52 | 454.79 |
| 3620 | 520 | 272.00 | 2828.00 | 398.82 | 56.60 | 455.42 |
| 3624 | 520 | 272.00 | 2832.00 | 399.37 | 56.68 | 456.05 |
| 3628 | 520 | 272.00 | 2836.00 | 399.92 | 56.76 | 456.68 |
| 3632 | 520 | 272.00 | 2840.00 | 400.48 | 56.84 | 457.32 |
| 3636 | 520 | 272.00 | 2844.00 | 401.03 | 56.92 | 457.95 |
| 3640 | 520 | 272.00 | 2848.00 | 401.58 | 57.00 | 458.58 |
| 3644 | 520 | 272.00 | 2852.00 | 402.13 | 57.08 | 459.21 |
| 3648 | 520 | 272.00 | 2856.00 | 402.68 | 57.16 | 459.84 |
| 3652 | 520 | 272.00 | 2860.00 | 403.24 | 57.24 | 460.48 |
| 3656 | 520 | 272.00 | 2864.00 | 403.79 | 57.32 | 461.11 |
| 3660 | 520 | 272.00 | 2868.00 | 404.34 | 57.40 | 461.74 |
| 3664 | 520 | 272.00 | 2872.00 | 404.89 | 57.48 | 462.37 |
| 3668 | 520 | 272.00 | 2876.00 | 405.44 | 57.56 | 463.00 |
| 3672 | 520 | 272.00 | 2880.00 | 406.00 | 57.64 | 463.64 |
| 3676 | 520 | 272.00 | 2884.00 | 406.55 | 57.72 | 464.27 |
| 3680 | 520 | 272.00 | 2888.00 | 407.10 | 57.80 | 464.90 |
| 3684 | 520 | 272.00 | 2892.00 | 407.65 | 57.88 | 465.53 |
| 3688 | 520 | 272.00 | 2896.00 | 408.20 | 57.96 | 466.16 |
| 3692 | 520 | 272.00 | 2900.00 | 408.76 | 58.04 | 466.80 |
| 3696 | 520 | 272.00 | 2904.00 | 409.31 | 58.12 | 467.43 |

**Table letter J**  **Monthly table**

| Employee's earnings up to and including the UEL | Earnings at the LEL (where earnings are equal to or exceed the LEL) 1a | Earnings above the LEL, up to and including the PT 1b | Earnings above the PT, up to and including the UEL 1c | Employer's NICs due on all earnings above the ST 1d | Employee's NICs due on all earnings above the PT 1e | Total of employee's and employer's NICs (for information only) |
|---|---|---|---|---|---|---|
| £ | £ | £ p | £ p | £ p | £ p | £ p |
| 3700 | 520 | 272.00 | 2908.00 | 409.86 | 58.20 | 468.06 |
| 3704 | 520 | 272.00 | 2912.00 | 410.41 | 58.28 | 468.69 |
| 3708 | 520 | 272.00 | 2916.00 | 410.96 | 58.36 | 469.32 |
| 3712 | 520 | 272.00 | 2920.00 | 411.52 | 58.44 | 469.96 |
| 3716 | 520 | 272.00 | 2924.00 | 412.07 | 58.52 | 470.59 |
| 3720 | 520 | 272.00 | 2928.00 | 412.62 | 58.60 | 471.22 |
| 3724 | 520 | 272.00 | 2932.00 | 413.17 | 58.68 | 471.85 |
| 3728 | 520 | 272.00 | 2936.00 | 413.72 | 58.76 | 472.48 |
| 3732 | 520 | 272.00 | 2940.00 | 414.28 | 58.84 | 473.12 |
| 3736 | 520 | 272.00 | 2944.00 | 414.83 | 58.92 | 473.75 |
| 3740 | 520 | 272.00 | 2948.00 | 415.38 | 59.00 | 474.38 |
| 3744 | 520 | 272.00 | 2952.00 | 415.93 | 59.08 | 475.01 |
| 3748 | 520 | 272.00 | 2956.00 | 416.48 | 59.16 | 475.64 |
| 3752 | 520 | 272.00 | 2960.00 | 417.04 | 59.24 | 476.28 |
| 3756 | 520 | 272.00 | 2964.00 | 417.59 | 59.32 | 476.91 |
| 3760 | 520 | 272.00 | 2968.00 | 418.14 | 59.40 | 477.54 |
| 3764 | 520 | 272.00 | 2972.00 | 418.69 | 59.48 | 478.17 |
| 3768 | 520 | 272.00 | 2976.00 | 419.24 | 59.56 | 478.80 |
| 3772 | 520 | 272.00 | 2980.00 | 419.80 | 59.64 | 479.44 |
| 3776 | 520 | 272.00 | 2984.00 | 420.35 | 59.72 | 480.07 |
| 3780 | 520 | 272.00 | 2988.00 | 420.90 | 59.80 | 480.70 |
| 3784 | 520 | 272.00 | 2992.00 | 421.45 | 59.88 | 481.33 |
| 3788 | 520 | 272.00 | 2996.00 | 422.00 | 59.96 | 481.96 |
| 3792 | 520 | 272.00 | 3000.00 | 422.56 | 60.04 | 482.60 |
| 3796 | 520 | 272.00 | 3004.00 | 423.11 | 60.12 | 483.23 |
| 3800 | 520 | 272.00 | 3008.00 | 423.66 | 60.20 | 483.86 |
| 3804 | 520 | 272.00 | 3012.00 | 424.21 | 60.28 | 484.49 |
| 3808 | 520 | 272.00 | 3016.00 | 424.76 | 60.36 | 485.12 |
| 3812 | 520 | 272.00 | 3020.00 | 425.32 | 60.44 | 485.76 |
| 3816 | 520 | 272.00 | 3024.00 | 425.87 | 60.52 | 486.39 |
| 3820 | 520 | 272.00 | 3028.00 | 426.42 | 60.60 | 487.02 |
| 3824 | 520 | 272.00 | 3032.00 | 426.97 | 60.68 | 487.65 |
| 3828 | 520 | 272.00 | 3036.00 | 427.52 | 60.76 | 488.28 |
| 3832 | 520 | 272.00 | 3040.00 | 428.08 | 60.84 | 488.92 |
| 3836 | 520 | 272.00 | 3044.00 | 428.63 | 60.92 | 489.55 |
| 3840 | 520 | 272.00 | 3048.00 | 429.18 | 61.00 | 490.18 |
| 3844 | 520 | 272.00 | 3052.00 | 429.73 | 61.08 | 490.81 |
| 3848 | 520 | 272.00 | 3056.00 | 430.28 | 61.16 | 491.44 |
| 3852 | 520 | 272.00 | 3060.00 | 430.84 | 61.24 | 492.08 |
| 3856 | 520 | 272.00 | 3064.00 | 431.39 | 61.32 | 492.71 |
| 3860 | 520 | 272.00 | 3068.00 | 431.94 | 61.40 | 493.34 |
| 3864 | 520 | 272.00 | 3072.00 | 432.49 | 61.48 | 493.97 |
| 3868 | 520 | 272.00 | 3076.00 | 433.04 | 61.56 | 494.60 |
| 3872 | 520 | 272.00 | 3080.00 | 433.60 | 61.64 | 495.24 |
| 3876 | 520 | 272.00 | 3084.00 | 434.15 | 61.72 | 495.87 |
| 3880 | 520 | 272.00 | 3088.00 | 434.70 | 61.80 | 496.50 |
| 3884 | 520 | 272.00 | 3092.00 | 435.25 | 61.88 | 497.13 |
| 3888 | 520 | 272.00 | 3096.00 | 435.80 | 61.96 | 497.76 |
| 3892 | 520 | 272.00 | 3100.00 | 436.36 | 62.04 | 498.40 |
| 3896 | 520 | 272.00 | 3104.00 | 436.91 | 62.12 | 499.03 |
| 3900 | 520 | 272.00 | 3108.00 | 437.46 | 62.20 | 499.66 |
| 3904 | 520 | 272.00 | 3112.00 | 438.01 | 62.28 | 500.29 |
| 3908 | 520 | 272.00 | 3116.00 | 438.56 | 62.36 | 500.92 |
| 3912 | 520 | 272.00 | 3120.00 | 439.12 | 62.44 | 501.56 |
| 3916 | 520 | 272.00 | 3124.00 | 439.67 | 62.52 | 502.19 |

Page 107

## Table letter J

**Monthly table**

| Employee's earnings up to and including the UEL | Earnings at the LEL (where earnings are equal to or exceed the LEL) 1a | Earnings above the LEL, up to and including the PT 1b | Earnings above the PT, up to and including the UEL 1c | Employer's NICs due on all earnings above the ST 1d | Employee's NICs due on all earnings above the PT 1e | Total of employee's and employer's NICs (for information only) |
|---|---|---|---|---|---|---|
| £ | £ | £ p | £ p | £ p | £ p | £ p |
| 3920 | 520 | 272.00 | 3128.00 | 440.22 | 62.60 | 502.82 |
| 3924 | 520 | 272.00 | 3132.00 | 440.77 | 62.68 | 503.45 |
| 3928 | 520 | 272.00 | 3136.00 | 441.32 | 62.76 | 504.08 |
| 3932 | 520 | 272.00 | 3140.00 | 441.88 | 62.84 | 504.72 |
| 3936 | 520 | 272.00 | 3144.00 | 442.43 | 62.92 | 505.35 |
| 3940 | 520 | 272.00 | 3148.00 | 442.98 | 63.00 | 505.98 |
| 3944 | 520 | 272.00 | 3152.00 | 443.53 | 63.08 | 506.61 |
| 3948 | 520 | 272.00 | 3156.00 | 444.08 | 63.16 | 507.24 |
| 3952 | 520 | 272.00 | 3160.00 | 444.64 | 63.24 | 507.88 |
| 3956 | 520 | 272.00 | 3164.00 | 445.19 | 63.32 | 508.51 |
| 3960 | 520 | 272.00 | 3168.00 | 445.74 | 63.40 | 509.14 |
| 3964 | 520 | 272.00 | 3172.00 | 446.29 | 63.48 | 509.77 |
| 3968 | 520 | 272.00 | 3176.00 | 446.84 | 63.56 | 510.40 |
| 3972 | 520 | 272.00 | 3180.00 | 447.40 | 63.64 | 511.04 |
| 3976 | 520 | 272.00 | 3184.00 | 447.95 | 63.72 | 511.67 |
| 3980 | 520 | 272.00 | 3188.00 | 448.50 | 63.80 | 512.30 |
| 3984 | 520 | 272.00 | 3192.00 | 449.05 | 63.88 | 512.93 |
| 3988 | 520 | 272.00 | 3196.00 | 449.60 | 63.96 | 513.56 |
| 3992 | 520 | 272.00 | 3200.00 | 450.16 | 64.04 | 514.20 |
| 3996 | 520 | 272.00 | 3204.00 | 450.71 | 64.12 | 514.83 |
| 4000 | 520 | 272.00 | 3208.00 | 451.26 | 64.20 | 515.46 |
| 4004 | 520 | 272.00 | 3212.00 | 451.81 | 64.28 | 516.09 |
| 4008 | 520 | 272.00 | 3216.00 | 452.36 | 64.36 | 516.72 |
| 4012 | 520 | 272.00 | 3220.00 | 452.92 | 64.44 | 517.36 |
| 4016 | 520 | 272.00 | 3224.00 | 453.47 | 64.52 | 517.99 |
| 4020 | 520 | 272.00 | 3228.00 | 454.02 | 64.60 | 518.62 |
| 4024 | 520 | 272.00 | 3232.00 | 454.57 | 64.68 | 519.25 |
| 4028 | 520 | 272.00 | 3236.00 | 455.12 | 64.76 | 519.88 |
| 4032 | 520 | 272.00 | 3240.00 | 455.68 | 64.84 | 520.52 |
| 4036 | 520 | 272.00 | 3244.00 | 456.23 | 64.92 | 521.15 |
| 4040 | 520 | 272.00 | 3248.00 | 456.78 | 65.00 | 521.78 |
| 4044 | 520 | 272.00 | 3252.00 | 457.33 | 65.08 | 522.41 |
| 4048 | 520 | 272.00 | 3256.00 | 457.88 | 65.16 | 523.04 |
| 4052 | 520 | 272.00 | 3260.00 | 458.44 | 65.24 | 523.68 |
| 4056 | 520 | 272.00 | 3264.00 | 458.99 | 65.32 | 524.31 |
| 4060 | 520 | 272.00 | 3268.00 | 459.54 | 65.40 | 524.94 |
| 4064 | 520 | 272.00 | 3272.00 | 460.09 | 65.48 | 525.57 |
| 4068 | 520 | 272.00 | 3276.00 | 460.64 | 65.56 | 526.20 |
| 4072 | 520 | 272.00 | 3280.00 | 461.20 | 65.64 | 526.84 |
| 4076 | 520 | 272.00 | 3284.00 | 461.75 | 65.72 | 527.47 |
| 4080 | 520 | 272.00 | 3288.00 | 462.30 | 65.80 | 528.10 |
| 4084 | 520 | 272.00 | 3292.00 | 462.85 | 65.88 | 528.73 |
| 4088 | 520 | 272.00 | 3296.00 | 463.40 | 65.96 | 529.36 |
| 4092 | 520 | 272.00 | 3300.00 | 463.96 | 66.04 | 530.00 |
| 4096 | 520 | 272.00 | 3304.00 | 464.51 | 66.12 | 530.63 |
| 4100 | 520 | 272.00 | 3308.00 | 465.06 | 66.20 | 531.26 |
| 4104 | 520 | 272.00 | 3312.00 | 465.61 | 66.28 | 531.89 |
| 4108 | 520 | 272.00 | 3316.00 | 466.16 | 66.36 | 532.52 |
| 4112 | 520 | 272.00 | 3320.00 | 466.72 | 66.44 | 533.16 |
| 4116 | 520 | 272.00 | 3324.00 | 467.27 | 66.52 | 533.79 |
| 4120 | 520 | 272.00 | 3328.00 | 467.82 | 66.60 | 534.42 |
| 4124 | 520 | 272.00 | 3332.00 | 468.37 | 66.68 | 535.05 |
| 4128 | 520 | 272.00 | 3336.00 | 468.92 | 66.76 | 535.68 |
| 4132 | 520 | 272.00 | 3340.00 | 469.48 | 66.84 | 536.32 |
| 4136 | 520 | 272.00 | 3344.00 | 470.03 | 66.92 | 536.95 |

**Monthly table** **Table letter J**

| Employee's earnings up to and including the UEL | Earnings at the LEL (where earnings are equal to or exceed the LEL) 1a | Earnings above the LEL, up to and including the PT 1b | Earnings above the PT, up to and including the UEL 1c | Employer's NICs due on all earnings above the ST 1d | Employee's NICs due on all earnings above the PT 1e | Total of employee's and employer's NICs (for information only) |
|---|---|---|---|---|---|---|
| £ | £ | £  p | £  p | £  p | £  p | £  p |
| 4140 | 520 | 272.00 | 3348.00 | 470.58 | 67.00 | 537.58 |
| 4144 | 520 | 272.00 | 3352.00 | 471.13 | 67.08 | 538.21 |
| 4148 | 520 | 272.00 | 3356.00 | 471.68 | 67.16 | 538.84 |
| 4152 | 520 | 272.00 | 3360.00 | 472.24 | 67.24 | 539.48 |
| 4156 | 520 | 272.00 | 3364.00 | 472.79 | 67.32 | 540.11 |
| 4160 | 520 | 272.00 | 3368.00 | 473.34 | 67.40 | 540.74 |
| 4164 | 520 | 272.00 | 3372.00 | 473.82 | 67.47 | 541.29 |
| 4167 | 520 | 272.00 | 3375.00 | 474.03 | 67.50 | 541.53 |

If the employee's gross pay over £4,167, go to page 178.

## Weekly table for standard rate NICs for use from 6 April 2020 to 5 April 2021

**Table letter M**

Use this table for employees who are under the age of 21.

Do not use this table for:

- any tax year other than 2020 to 2021
- employees who are aged 21 or over and under State Pension age. (go to Table letter A)
- married women or widows who have the right to pay reduced rate employee's NICs (go to Table letter B in booklet CA41)
- employees who are State Pension age or over (go to Table letter C in booklet CA41)
- employees on an Approved Apprenticeship scheme under the age of 25 (go to Table letter H)
- employees who are aged 21 or over, for whom you hold form CA2700 (go to Table letter J)
- employees who are under the age of 21, for whom you hold form CA2700 (go to Table letter Z)

### Completing form RT11, 'Deductions working sheet' or substitute

1. Enter 'M' in the NICs Category Letter column on form RT11.
2. Copy the figures in columns 1a – 1e of the table to columns 1a – 1e on the line next to the tax week in which the employee is paid, on form RT11.

If the employee's total earnings fall between the LEL and the UEL/UST/AUST and the exact gross pay is not shown in the table, use the next smaller figure shown. If the employee's total earnings exceed the UEL/UST/AUST, go to page 163.

The figures in the left-hand column of each table show steps between the LEL and the UEL/UST/AUST. The NICs liability for each step, with the exception of the LEL, ST, PT, UEL, UST and AUST is worked out at the mid-point of the steps so you and your employee may pay slightly more or less than if you used the exact percentage method.

| Employee's earnings up to and including the UEL | Earnings at the LEL (where earnings are equal to or exceed the LEL) | Earnings above the LEL, up to and including the PT | Earnings above the PT, up to and including the UEL | Employer's NICs due on all earnings above the ST | Employee's NICs due on all earnings above the PT | Total of employee's and employer's NICs (for information only) |
|---|---|---|---|---|---|---|
| | 1a | 1b | 1c | 1d | 1e | |
| £ | £ | £ p | £ p | £ p | £ p | £ p |
| Up to and including £119.99 | No NICs liability, make no entries on form RT11 | | | | | |
| 120 | 120 | 0.00 | 0.00 | 0.00 | 0.00 | 0.00 |
| 121 | 120 | 1.00 | 0.00 | 0.00 | 0.00 | 0.00 |
| 122 | 120 | 2.00 | 0.00 | 0.00 | 0.00 | 0.00 |
| 123 | 120 | 3.00 | 0.00 | 0.00 | 0.00 | 0.00 |
| 124 | 120 | 4.00 | 0.00 | 0.00 | 0.00 | 0.00 |
| 125 | 120 | 5.00 | 0.00 | 0.00 | 0.00 | 0.00 |
| 126 | 120 | 6.00 | 0.00 | 0.00 | 0.00 | 0.00 |
| 127 | 120 | 7.00 | 0.00 | 0.00 | 0.00 | 0.00 |
| 128 | 120 | 8.00 | 0.00 | 0.00 | 0.00 | 0.00 |
| 129 | 120 | 9.00 | 0.00 | 0.00 | 0.00 | 0.00 |
| 130 | 120 | 10.00 | 0.00 | 0.00 | 0.00 | 0.00 |
| 131 | 120 | 11.00 | 0.00 | 0.00 | 0.00 | 0.00 |
| 132 | 120 | 12.00 | 0.00 | 0.00 | 0.00 | 0.00 |
| 133 | 120 | 13.00 | 0.00 | 0.00 | 0.00 | 0.00 |
| 134 | 120 | 14.00 | 0.00 | 0.00 | 0.00 | 0.00 |
| 135 | 120 | 15.00 | 0.00 | 0.00 | 0.00 | 0.00 |
| 136 | 120 | 16.00 | 0.00 | 0.00 | 0.00 | 0.00 |
| 137 | 120 | 17.00 | 0.00 | 0.00 | 0.00 | 0.00 |
| 138 | 120 | 18.00 | 0.00 | 0.00 | 0.00 | 0.00 |
| 139 | 120 | 19.00 | 0.00 | 0.00 | 0.00 | 0.00 |
| 140 | 120 | 20.00 | 0.00 | 0.00 | 0.00 | 0.00 |
| 141 | 120 | 21.00 | 0.00 | 0.00 | 0.00 | 0.00 |
| 142 | 120 | 22.00 | 0.00 | 0.00 | 0.00 | 0.00 |
| 143 | 120 | 23.00 | 0.00 | 0.00 | 0.00 | 0.00 |
| 144 | 120 | 24.00 | 0.00 | 0.00 | 0.00 | 0.00 |

**Weekly table**

**Table letter M**

| Employee's earnings up to and including the UEL | Earnings at the LEL (where earnings are equal to or exceed the LEL) 1a | Earnings above the LEL, up to and including the PT 1b | Earnings above the PT, up to and including the UEL 1c | Employer's NICs due on all earnings above the ST 1d | Employee's NICs due on all earnings above the PT 1e | Total of employee's and employer's NICs (for information only) |
|---|---|---|---|---|---|---|
| £ | £ | £ p | £ p | £ p | £ p | £ p |
| 145 | 120 | 25.00 | 0.00 | 0.00 | 0.00 | 0.00 |
| 146 | 120 | 26.00 | 0.00 | 0.00 | 0.00 | 0.00 |
| 147 | 120 | 27.00 | 0.00 | 0.00 | 0.00 | 0.00 |
| 148 | 120 | 28.00 | 0.00 | 0.00 | 0.00 | 0.00 |
| 149 | 120 | 29.00 | 0.00 | 0.00 | 0.00 | 0.00 |
| 150 | 120 | 30.00 | 0.00 | 0.00 | 0.00 | 0.00 |
| 151 | 120 | 31.00 | 0.00 | 0.00 | 0.00 | 0.00 |
| 152 | 120 | 32.00 | 0.00 | 0.00 | 0.00 | 0.00 |
| 153 | 120 | 33.00 | 0.00 | 0.00 | 0.00 | 0.00 |
| 154 | 120 | 34.00 | 0.00 | 0.00 | 0.00 | 0.00 |
| 155 | 120 | 35.00 | 0.00 | 0.00 | 0.00 | 0.00 |
| 156 | 120 | 36.00 | 0.00 | 0.00 | 0.00 | 0.00 |
| 157 | 120 | 37.00 | 0.00 | 0.00 | 0.00 | 0.00 |
| 158 | 120 | 38.00 | 0.00 | 0.00 | 0.00 | 0.00 |
| 159 | 120 | 39.00 | 0.00 | 0.00 | 0.00 | 0.00 |
| 160 | 120 | 40.00 | 0.00 | 0.00 | 0.00 | 0.00 |
| 161 | 120 | 41.00 | 0.00 | 0.00 | 0.00 | 0.00 |
| 162 | 120 | 42.00 | 0.00 | 0.00 | 0.00 | 0.00 |
| 163 | 120 | 43.00 | 0.00 | 0.00 | 0.00 | 0.00 |
| 164 | 120 | 44.00 | 0.00 | 0.00 | 0.00 | 0.00 |
| 165 | 120 | 45.00 | 0.00 | 0.00 | 0.00 | 0.00 |
| 166 | 120 | 46.00 | 0.00 | 0.00 | 0.00 | 0.00 |
| 167 | 120 | 47.00 | 0.00 | 0.00 | 0.00 | 0.00 |
| 168 | 120 | 48.00 | 0.00 | 0.00 | 0.00 | 0.00 |
| 169 | 120 | 49.00 | 0.00 | 0.00 | 0.00 | 0.00 |
| 170 | 120 | 50.00 | 0.00 | 0.00 | 0.00 | 0.00 |
| 171 | 120 | 51.00 | 0.00 | 0.00 | 0.00 | 0.00 |
| 172 | 120 | 52.00 | 0.00 | 0.00 | 0.00 | 0.00 |
| 173 | 120 | 53.00 | 0.00 | 0.00 | 0.00 | 0.00 |
| 174 | 120 | 54.00 | 0.00 | 0.00 | 0.00 | 0.00 |
| 175 | 120 | 55.00 | 0.00 | 0.00 | 0.00 | 0.00 |
| 176 | 120 | 56.00 | 0.00 | 0.00 | 0.00 | 0.00 |
| 177 | 120 | 57.00 | 0.00 | 0.00 | 0.00 | 0.00 |
| 178 | 120 | 58.00 | 0.00 | 0.00 | 0.00 | 0.00 |
| 179 | 120 | 59.00 | 0.00 | 0.00 | 0.00 | 0.00 |
| 180 | 120 | 60.00 | 0.00 | 0.00 | 0.00 | 0.00 |
| 181 | 120 | 61.00 | 0.00 | 0.00 | 0.00 | 0.00 |
| 182 | 120 | 62.00 | 0.00 | 0.00 | 0.00 | 0.00 |
| 183 | 120 | 63.00 | 0.00 | 0.00 | 0.00 | 0.00 |
| 184 | 120 | 63.00 | 1.00 | 0.00 | 0.18 | 0.18 |
| 185 | 120 | 63.00 | 2.00 | 0.00 | 0.30 | 0.30 |
| 186 | 120 | 63.00 | 3.00 | 0.00 | 0.42 | 0.42 |
| 187 | 120 | 63.00 | 4.00 | 0.00 | 0.54 | 0.54 |
| 188 | 120 | 63.00 | 5.00 | 0.00 | 0.66 | 0.66 |
| 189 | 120 | 63.00 | 6.00 | 0.00 | 0.78 | 0.78 |
| 190 | 120 | 63.00 | 7.00 | 0.00 | 0.90 | 0.90 |
| 191 | 120 | 63.00 | 8.00 | 0.00 | 1.02 | 1.02 |
| 192 | 120 | 63.00 | 9.00 | 0.00 | 1.14 | 1.14 |
| 193 | 120 | 63.00 | 10.00 | 0.00 | 1.26 | 1.26 |
| 194 | 120 | 63.00 | 11.00 | 0.00 | 1.38 | 1.38 |
| 195 | 120 | 63.00 | 12.00 | 0.00 | 1.50 | 1.50 |
| 196 | 120 | 63.00 | 13.00 | 0.00 | 1.62 | 1.62 |
| 197 | 120 | 63.00 | 14.00 | 0.00 | 1.74 | 1.74 |
| 198 | 120 | 63.00 | 15.00 | 0.00 | 1.86 | 1.86 |
| 199 | 120 | 63.00 | 16.00 | 0.00 | 1.98 | 1.98 |

# Table letter M

**Weekly table**

| Employee's earnings up to and including the UEL | Earnings at the LEL (where earnings are equal to or exceed the LEL) | Earnings above the LEL, up to and including the PT | Earnings above the PT, up to and including the UEL | Employer's NICs due on all earnings above the ST | Employee's NICs due on all earnings above the PT | Total of employee's and employer's NICs (for information only) |
|---|---|---|---|---|---|---|
| | 1a | 1b | 1c | 1d | 1e | |
| £ | £ | £ p | £ p | £ p | £ p | £ p |
| 200 | 120 | 63.00 | 17.00 | 0.00 | 2.10 | 2.10 |
| 201 | 120 | 63.00 | 18.00 | 0.00 | 2.22 | 2.22 |
| 202 | 120 | 63.00 | 19.00 | 0.00 | 2.34 | 2.34 |
| 203 | 120 | 63.00 | 20.00 | 0.00 | 2.46 | 2.46 |
| 204 | 120 | 63.00 | 21.00 | 0.00 | 2.58 | 2.58 |
| 205 | 120 | 63.00 | 22.00 | 0.00 | 2.70 | 2.70 |
| 206 | 120 | 63.00 | 23.00 | 0.00 | 2.82 | 2.82 |
| 207 | 120 | 63.00 | 24.00 | 0.00 | 2.94 | 2.94 |
| 208 | 120 | 63.00 | 25.00 | 0.00 | 3.06 | 3.06 |
| 209 | 120 | 63.00 | 26.00 | 0.00 | 3.18 | 3.18 |
| 210 | 120 | 63.00 | 27.00 | 0.00 | 3.30 | 3.30 |
| 211 | 120 | 63.00 | 28.00 | 0.00 | 3.42 | 3.42 |
| 212 | 120 | 63.00 | 29.00 | 0.00 | 3.54 | 3.54 |
| 213 | 120 | 63.00 | 30.00 | 0.00 | 3.66 | 3.66 |
| 214 | 120 | 63.00 | 31.00 | 0.00 | 3.78 | 3.78 |
| 215 | 120 | 63.00 | 32.00 | 0.00 | 3.90 | 3.90 |
| 216 | 120 | 63.00 | 33.00 | 0.00 | 4.02 | 4.02 |
| 217 | 120 | 63.00 | 34.00 | 0.00 | 4.14 | 4.14 |
| 218 | 120 | 63.00 | 35.00 | 0.00 | 4.26 | 4.26 |
| 219 | 120 | 63.00 | 36.00 | 0.00 | 4.38 | 4.38 |
| 220 | 120 | 63.00 | 37.00 | 0.00 | 4.50 | 4.50 |
| 221 | 120 | 63.00 | 38.00 | 0.00 | 4.62 | 4.62 |
| 222 | 120 | 63.00 | 39.00 | 0.00 | 4.74 | 4.74 |
| 223 | 120 | 63.00 | 40.00 | 0.00 | 4.86 | 4.86 |
| 224 | 120 | 63.00 | 41.00 | 0.00 | 4.98 | 4.98 |
| 225 | 120 | 63.00 | 42.00 | 0.00 | 5.10 | 5.10 |
| 226 | 120 | 63.00 | 43.00 | 0.00 | 5.22 | 5.22 |
| 227 | 120 | 63.00 | 44.00 | 0.00 | 5.34 | 5.34 |
| 228 | 120 | 63.00 | 45.00 | 0.00 | 5.46 | 5.46 |
| 229 | 120 | 63.00 | 46.00 | 0.00 | 5.58 | 5.58 |
| 230 | 120 | 63.00 | 47.00 | 0.00 | 5.70 | 5.70 |
| 231 | 120 | 63.00 | 48.00 | 0.00 | 5.82 | 5.82 |
| 232 | 120 | 63.00 | 49.00 | 0.00 | 5.94 | 5.94 |
| 233 | 120 | 63.00 | 50.00 | 0.00 | 6.06 | 6.06 |
| 234 | 120 | 63.00 | 51.00 | 0.00 | 6.18 | 6.18 |
| 235 | 120 | 63.00 | 52.00 | 0.00 | 6.30 | 6.30 |
| 236 | 120 | 63.00 | 53.00 | 0.00 | 6.42 | 6.42 |
| 237 | 120 | 63.00 | 54.00 | 0.00 | 6.54 | 6.54 |
| 238 | 120 | 63.00 | 55.00 | 0.00 | 6.66 | 6.66 |
| 239 | 120 | 63.00 | 56.00 | 0.00 | 6.78 | 6.78 |
| 240 | 120 | 63.00 | 57.00 | 0.00 | 6.90 | 6.90 |
| 241 | 120 | 63.00 | 58.00 | 0.00 | 7.02 | 7.02 |
| 242 | 120 | 63.00 | 59.00 | 0.00 | 7.14 | 7.14 |
| 243 | 120 | 63.00 | 60.00 | 0.00 | 7.26 | 7.26 |
| 244 | 120 | 63.00 | 61.00 | 0.00 | 7.38 | 7.38 |
| 245 | 120 | 63.00 | 62.00 | 0.00 | 7.50 | 7.50 |
| 246 | 120 | 63.00 | 63.00 | 0.00 | 7.62 | 7.62 |
| 247 | 120 | 63.00 | 64.00 | 0.00 | 7.74 | 7.74 |
| 248 | 120 | 63.00 | 65.00 | 0.00 | 7.86 | 7.86 |
| 249 | 120 | 63.00 | 66.00 | 0.00 | 7.98 | 7.98 |
| 250 | 120 | 63.00 | 67.00 | 0.00 | 8.10 | 8.10 |
| 251 | 120 | 63.00 | 68.00 | 0.00 | 8.22 | 8.22 |
| 252 | 120 | 63.00 | 69.00 | 0.00 | 8.34 | 8.34 |
| 253 | 120 | 63.00 | 70.00 | 0.00 | 8.46 | 8.46 |
| 254 | 120 | 63.00 | 71.00 | 0.00 | 8.58 | 8.58 |

**Weekly table**      **Table letter M**

| Employee's earnings up to and including the UEL | Earnings at the LEL (where earnings are equal to or exceed the LEL) 1a | Earnings above the LEL, up to and including the PT 1b | Earnings above the PT, up to and including the UEL 1c | Employer's NICs due on all earnings above the ST 1d | Employee's NICs due on all earnings above the PT 1e | Total of employee's and employer's NICs (for information only) |
|---|---|---|---|---|---|---|
| £ | £ | £ p | £ p | £ p | £ p | £ p |
| 255 | 120 | 63.00 | 72.00 | 0.00 | 8.70 | 8.70 |
| 256 | 120 | 63.00 | 73.00 | 0.00 | 8.82 | 8.82 |
| 257 | 120 | 63.00 | 74.00 | 0.00 | 8.94 | 8.94 |
| 258 | 120 | 63.00 | 75.00 | 0.00 | 9.06 | 9.06 |
| 259 | 120 | 63.00 | 76.00 | 0.00 | 9.18 | 9.18 |
| 260 | 120 | 63.00 | 77.00 | 0.00 | 9.30 | 9.30 |
| 261 | 120 | 63.00 | 78.00 | 0.00 | 9.42 | 9.42 |
| 262 | 120 | 63.00 | 79.00 | 0.00 | 9.54 | 9.54 |
| 263 | 120 | 63.00 | 80.00 | 0.00 | 9.66 | 9.66 |
| 264 | 120 | 63.00 | 81.00 | 0.00 | 9.78 | 9.78 |
| 265 | 120 | 63.00 | 82.00 | 0.00 | 9.90 | 9.90 |
| 266 | 120 | 63.00 | 83.00 | 0.00 | 10.02 | 10.02 |
| 267 | 120 | 63.00 | 84.00 | 0.00 | 10.14 | 10.14 |
| 268 | 120 | 63.00 | 85.00 | 0.00 | 10.26 | 10.26 |
| 269 | 120 | 63.00 | 86.00 | 0.00 | 10.38 | 10.38 |
| 270 | 120 | 63.00 | 87.00 | 0.00 | 10.50 | 10.50 |
| 271 | 120 | 63.00 | 88.00 | 0.00 | 10.62 | 10.62 |
| 272 | 120 | 63.00 | 89.00 | 0.00 | 10.74 | 10.74 |
| 273 | 120 | 63.00 | 90.00 | 0.00 | 10.86 | 10.86 |
| 274 | 120 | 63.00 | 91.00 | 0.00 | 10.98 | 10.98 |
| 275 | 120 | 63.00 | 92.00 | 0.00 | 11.10 | 11.10 |
| 276 | 120 | 63.00 | 93.00 | 0.00 | 11.22 | 11.22 |
| 277 | 120 | 63.00 | 94.00 | 0.00 | 11.34 | 11.34 |
| 278 | 120 | 63.00 | 95.00 | 0.00 | 11.46 | 11.46 |
| 279 | 120 | 63.00 | 96.00 | 0.00 | 11.58 | 11.58 |
| 280 | 120 | 63.00 | 97.00 | 0.00 | 11.70 | 11.70 |
| 281 | 120 | 63.00 | 98.00 | 0.00 | 11.82 | 11.82 |
| 282 | 120 | 63.00 | 99.00 | 0.00 | 11.94 | 11.94 |
| 283 | 120 | 63.00 | 100.00 | 0.00 | 12.06 | 12.06 |
| 284 | 120 | 63.00 | 101.00 | 0.00 | 12.18 | 12.18 |
| 285 | 120 | 63.00 | 102.00 | 0.00 | 12.30 | 12.30 |
| 286 | 120 | 63.00 | 103.00 | 0.00 | 12.42 | 12.42 |
| 287 | 120 | 63.00 | 104.00 | 0.00 | 12.54 | 12.54 |
| 288 | 120 | 63.00 | 105.00 | 0.00 | 12.66 | 12.66 |
| 289 | 120 | 63.00 | 106.00 | 0.00 | 12.78 | 12.78 |
| 290 | 120 | 63.00 | 107.00 | 0.00 | 12.90 | 12.90 |
| 291 | 120 | 63.00 | 108.00 | 0.00 | 13.02 | 13.02 |
| 292 | 120 | 63.00 | 109.00 | 0.00 | 13.14 | 13.14 |
| 293 | 120 | 63.00 | 110.00 | 0.00 | 13.26 | 13.26 |
| 294 | 120 | 63.00 | 111.00 | 0.00 | 13.38 | 13.38 |
| 295 | 120 | 63.00 | 112.00 | 0.00 | 13.50 | 13.50 |
| 296 | 120 | 63.00 | 113.00 | 0.00 | 13.62 | 13.62 |
| 297 | 120 | 63.00 | 114.00 | 0.00 | 13.74 | 13.74 |
| 298 | 120 | 63.00 | 115.00 | 0.00 | 13.86 | 13.86 |
| 299 | 120 | 63.00 | 116.00 | 0.00 | 13.98 | 13.98 |
| 300 | 120 | 63.00 | 117.00 | 0.00 | 14.10 | 14.10 |
| 301 | 120 | 63.00 | 118.00 | 0.00 | 14.22 | 14.22 |
| 302 | 120 | 63.00 | 119.00 | 0.00 | 14.34 | 14.34 |
| 303 | 120 | 63.00 | 120.00 | 0.00 | 14.46 | 14.46 |
| 304 | 120 | 63.00 | 121.00 | 0.00 | 14.58 | 14.58 |
| 305 | 120 | 63.00 | 122.00 | 0.00 | 14.70 | 14.70 |
| 306 | 120 | 63.00 | 123.00 | 0.00 | 14.82 | 14.82 |
| 307 | 120 | 63.00 | 124.00 | 0.00 | 14.94 | 14.94 |
| 308 | 120 | 63.00 | 125.00 | 0.00 | 15.06 | 15.06 |
| 309 | 120 | 63.00 | 126.00 | 0.00 | 15.18 | 15.18 |

# Table letter M

**Weekly table**

| Employee's earnings up to and including the UEL | Earnings at the LEL (where earnings are equal to or exceed the LEL) | Earnings above the LEL, up to and including the PT | Earnings above the PT, up to and including the UEL | Employer's NICs due on all earnings above the ST | Employee's NICs due on all earnings above the PT | Total of employee's and employer's NICs (for information only) |
|---|---|---|---|---|---|---|
| | | 1a | 1b | 1c | 1d | 1e |
| £ | £ | £ p | £ p | £ p | £ p | £ p |
| 310 | 120 | 63.00 | 127.00 | 0.00 | 15.30 | 15.30 |
| 311 | 120 | 63.00 | 128.00 | 0.00 | 15.42 | 15.42 |
| 312 | 120 | 63.00 | 129.00 | 0.00 | 15.54 | 15.54 |
| 313 | 120 | 63.00 | 130.00 | 0.00 | 15.66 | 15.66 |
| 314 | 120 | 63.00 | 131.00 | 0.00 | 15.78 | 15.78 |
| 315 | 120 | 63.00 | 132.00 | 0.00 | 15.90 | 15.90 |
| 316 | 120 | 63.00 | 133.00 | 0.00 | 16.02 | 16.02 |
| 317 | 120 | 63.00 | 134.00 | 0.00 | 16.14 | 16.14 |
| 318 | 120 | 63.00 | 135.00 | 0.00 | 16.26 | 16.26 |
| 319 | 120 | 63.00 | 136.00 | 0.00 | 16.38 | 16.38 |
| 320 | 120 | 63.00 | 137.00 | 0.00 | 16.50 | 16.50 |
| 321 | 120 | 63.00 | 138.00 | 0.00 | 16.62 | 16.62 |
| 322 | 120 | 63.00 | 139.00 | 0.00 | 16.74 | 16.74 |
| 323 | 120 | 63.00 | 140.00 | 0.00 | 16.86 | 16.86 |
| 324 | 120 | 63.00 | 141.00 | 0.00 | 16.98 | 16.98 |
| 325 | 120 | 63.00 | 142.00 | 0.00 | 17.10 | 17.10 |
| 326 | 120 | 63.00 | 143.00 | 0.00 | 17.22 | 17.22 |
| 327 | 120 | 63.00 | 144.00 | 0.00 | 17.34 | 17.34 |
| 328 | 120 | 63.00 | 145.00 | 0.00 | 17.46 | 17.46 |
| 329 | 120 | 63.00 | 146.00 | 0.00 | 17.58 | 17.58 |
| 330 | 120 | 63.00 | 147.00 | 0.00 | 17.70 | 17.70 |
| 331 | 120 | 63.00 | 148.00 | 0.00 | 17.82 | 17.82 |
| 332 | 120 | 63.00 | 149.00 | 0.00 | 17.94 | 17.94 |
| 333 | 120 | 63.00 | 150.00 | 0.00 | 18.06 | 18.06 |
| 334 | 120 | 63.00 | 151.00 | 0.00 | 18.18 | 18.18 |
| 335 | 120 | 63.00 | 152.00 | 0.00 | 18.30 | 18.30 |
| 336 | 120 | 63.00 | 153.00 | 0.00 | 18.42 | 18.42 |
| 337 | 120 | 63.00 | 154.00 | 0.00 | 18.54 | 18.54 |
| 338 | 120 | 63.00 | 155.00 | 0.00 | 18.66 | 18.66 |
| 339 | 120 | 63.00 | 156.00 | 0.00 | 18.78 | 18.78 |
| 340 | 120 | 63.00 | 157.00 | 0.00 | 18.90 | 18.90 |
| 341 | 120 | 63.00 | 158.00 | 0.00 | 19.02 | 19.02 |
| 342 | 120 | 63.00 | 159.00 | 0.00 | 19.14 | 19.14 |
| 343 | 120 | 63.00 | 160.00 | 0.00 | 19.26 | 19.26 |
| 344 | 120 | 63.00 | 161.00 | 0.00 | 19.38 | 19.38 |
| 345 | 120 | 63.00 | 162.00 | 0.00 | 19.50 | 19.50 |
| 346 | 120 | 63.00 | 163.00 | 0.00 | 19.62 | 19.62 |
| 347 | 120 | 63.00 | 164.00 | 0.00 | 19.74 | 19.74 |
| 348 | 120 | 63.00 | 165.00 | 0.00 | 19.86 | 19.86 |
| 349 | 120 | 63.00 | 166.00 | 0.00 | 19.98 | 19.98 |
| 350 | 120 | 63.00 | 167.00 | 0.00 | 20.10 | 20.10 |
| 351 | 120 | 63.00 | 168.00 | 0.00 | 20.22 | 20.22 |
| 352 | 120 | 63.00 | 169.00 | 0.00 | 20.34 | 20.34 |
| 353 | 120 | 63.00 | 170.00 | 0.00 | 20.46 | 20.46 |
| 354 | 120 | 63.00 | 171.00 | 0.00 | 20.58 | 20.58 |
| 355 | 120 | 63.00 | 172.00 | 0.00 | 20.70 | 20.70 |
| 356 | 120 | 63.00 | 173.00 | 0.00 | 20.82 | 20.82 |
| 357 | 120 | 63.00 | 174.00 | 0.00 | 20.94 | 20.94 |
| 358 | 120 | 63.00 | 175.00 | 0.00 | 21.06 | 21.06 |
| 359 | 120 | 63.00 | 176.00 | 0.00 | 21.18 | 21.18 |
| 360 | 120 | 63.00 | 177.00 | 0.00 | 21.30 | 21.30 |
| 361 | 120 | 63.00 | 178.00 | 0.00 | 21.42 | 21.42 |
| 362 | 120 | 63.00 | 179.00 | 0.00 | 21.54 | 21.54 |
| 363 | 120 | 63.00 | 180.00 | 0.00 | 21.66 | 21.66 |
| 364 | 120 | 63.00 | 181.00 | 0.00 | 21.78 | 21.78 |

**Weekly table**

**Table letter M**

| Employee's earnings up to and including the UEL | Earnings at the LEL (where earnings are equal to or exceed the LEL) | Earnings above the LEL, up to and including the PT | Earnings above the PT, up to and including the UEL | Employer's NICs due on all earnings above the ST | Employee's NICs due on all earnings above the PT | Total of employee's and employer's NICs (for information only) |
|---|---|---|---|---|---|---|
| | | 1a | 1b | 1c | 1d | 1e |
| £ | £ | £ p | £ p | £ p | £ p | £ p |
| 365 | 120 | 63.00 | 182.00 | 0.00 | 21.90 | 21.90 |
| 366 | 120 | 63.00 | 183.00 | 0.00 | 22.02 | 22.02 |
| 367 | 120 | 63.00 | 184.00 | 0.00 | 22.14 | 22.14 |
| 368 | 120 | 63.00 | 185.00 | 0.00 | 22.26 | 22.26 |
| 369 | 120 | 63.00 | 186.00 | 0.00 | 22.38 | 22.38 |
| 370 | 120 | 63.00 | 187.00 | 0.00 | 22.50 | 22.50 |
| 371 | 120 | 63.00 | 188.00 | 0.00 | 22.62 | 22.62 |
| 372 | 120 | 63.00 | 189.00 | 0.00 | 22.74 | 22.74 |
| 373 | 120 | 63.00 | 190.00 | 0.00 | 22.86 | 22.86 |
| 374 | 120 | 63.00 | 191.00 | 0.00 | 22.98 | 22.98 |
| 375 | 120 | 63.00 | 192.00 | 0.00 | 23.10 | 23.10 |
| 376 | 120 | 63.00 | 193.00 | 0.00 | 23.22 | 23.22 |
| 377 | 120 | 63.00 | 194.00 | 0.00 | 23.34 | 23.34 |
| 378 | 120 | 63.00 | 195.00 | 0.00 | 23.46 | 23.46 |
| 379 | 120 | 63.00 | 196.00 | 0.00 | 23.58 | 23.58 |
| 380 | 120 | 63.00 | 197.00 | 0.00 | 23.70 | 23.70 |
| 381 | 120 | 63.00 | 198.00 | 0.00 | 23.82 | 23.82 |
| 382 | 120 | 63.00 | 199.00 | 0.00 | 23.94 | 23.94 |
| 383 | 120 | 63.00 | 200.00 | 0.00 | 24.06 | 24.06 |
| 384 | 120 | 63.00 | 201.00 | 0.00 | 24.18 | 24.18 |
| 385 | 120 | 63.00 | 202.00 | 0.00 | 24.30 | 24.30 |
| 386 | 120 | 63.00 | 203.00 | 0.00 | 24.42 | 24.42 |
| 387 | 120 | 63.00 | 204.00 | 0.00 | 24.54 | 24.54 |
| 388 | 120 | 63.00 | 205.00 | 0.00 | 24.66 | 24.66 |
| 389 | 120 | 63.00 | 206.00 | 0.00 | 24.78 | 24.78 |
| 390 | 120 | 63.00 | 207.00 | 0.00 | 24.90 | 24.90 |
| 391 | 120 | 63.00 | 208.00 | 0.00 | 25.02 | 25.02 |
| 392 | 120 | 63.00 | 209.00 | 0.00 | 25.14 | 25.14 |
| 393 | 120 | 63.00 | 210.00 | 0.00 | 25.26 | 25.26 |
| 394 | 120 | 63.00 | 211.00 | 0.00 | 25.38 | 25.38 |
| 395 | 120 | 63.00 | 212.00 | 0.00 | 25.50 | 25.50 |
| 396 | 120 | 63.00 | 213.00 | 0.00 | 25.62 | 25.62 |
| 397 | 120 | 63.00 | 214.00 | 0.00 | 25.74 | 25.74 |
| 398 | 120 | 63.00 | 215.00 | 0.00 | 25.86 | 25.86 |
| 399 | 120 | 63.00 | 216.00 | 0.00 | 25.98 | 25.98 |
| 400 | 120 | 63.00 | 217.00 | 0.00 | 26.10 | 26.10 |
| 401 | 120 | 63.00 | 218.00 | 0.00 | 26.22 | 26.22 |
| 402 | 120 | 63.00 | 219.00 | 0.00 | 26.34 | 26.34 |
| 403 | 120 | 63.00 | 220.00 | 0.00 | 26.46 | 26.46 |
| 404 | 120 | 63.00 | 221.00 | 0.00 | 26.58 | 26.58 |
| 405 | 120 | 63.00 | 222.00 | 0.00 | 26.70 | 26.70 |
| 406 | 120 | 63.00 | 223.00 | 0.00 | 26.82 | 26.82 |
| 407 | 120 | 63.00 | 224.00 | 0.00 | 26.94 | 26.94 |
| 408 | 120 | 63.00 | 225.00 | 0.00 | 27.06 | 27.06 |
| 409 | 120 | 63.00 | 226.00 | 0.00 | 27.18 | 27.18 |
| 410 | 120 | 63.00 | 227.00 | 0.00 | 27.30 | 27.30 |
| 411 | 120 | 63.00 | 228.00 | 0.00 | 27.42 | 27.42 |
| 412 | 120 | 63.00 | 229.00 | 0.00 | 27.54 | 27.54 |
| 413 | 120 | 63.00 | 230.00 | 0.00 | 27.66 | 27.66 |
| 414 | 120 | 63.00 | 231.00 | 0.00 | 27.78 | 27.78 |
| 415 | 120 | 63.00 | 232.00 | 0.00 | 27.90 | 27.90 |
| 416 | 120 | 63.00 | 233.00 | 0.00 | 28.02 | 28.02 |
| 417 | 120 | 63.00 | 234.00 | 0.00 | 28.14 | 28.14 |
| 418 | 120 | 63.00 | 235.00 | 0.00 | 28.26 | 28.26 |
| 419 | 120 | 63.00 | 236.00 | 0.00 | 28.38 | 28.38 |

## Table letter M

**Weekly table**

| Employee's earnings up to and including the UEL | Earnings at the LEL (where earnings are equal to or exceed the LEL) | Earnings above the LEL, up to and including the PT | Earnings above the PT, up to and including the UEL | Employer's NICs due on all earnings above the ST | Employee's NICs due on all earnings above the PT | Total of employee's and employer's NICs (for information only) |
|---|---|---|---|---|---|---|
| | 1a | 1b | 1c | 1d | 1e | |
| £ | £ | £ p | £ p | £ p | £ p | £ p |
| 420 | 120 | 63.00 | 237.00 | 0.00 | 28.50 | 28.50 |
| 421 | 120 | 63.00 | 238.00 | 0.00 | 28.62 | 28.62 |
| 422 | 120 | 63.00 | 239.00 | 0.00 | 28.74 | 28.74 |
| 423 | 120 | 63.00 | 240.00 | 0.00 | 28.86 | 28.86 |
| 424 | 120 | 63.00 | 241.00 | 0.00 | 28.98 | 28.98 |
| 425 | 120 | 63.00 | 242.00 | 0.00 | 29.10 | 29.10 |
| 426 | 120 | 63.00 | 243.00 | 0.00 | 29.22 | 29.22 |
| 427 | 120 | 63.00 | 244.00 | 0.00 | 29.34 | 29.34 |
| 428 | 120 | 63.00 | 245.00 | 0.00 | 29.46 | 29.46 |
| 429 | 120 | 63.00 | 246.00 | 0.00 | 29.58 | 29.58 |
| 430 | 120 | 63.00 | 247.00 | 0.00 | 29.70 | 29.70 |
| 431 | 120 | 63.00 | 248.00 | 0.00 | 29.82 | 29.82 |
| 432 | 120 | 63.00 | 249.00 | 0.00 | 29.94 | 29.94 |
| 433 | 120 | 63.00 | 250.00 | 0.00 | 30.06 | 30.06 |
| 434 | 120 | 63.00 | 251.00 | 0.00 | 30.18 | 30.18 |
| 435 | 120 | 63.00 | 252.00 | 0.00 | 30.30 | 30.30 |
| 436 | 120 | 63.00 | 253.00 | 0.00 | 30.42 | 30.42 |
| 437 | 120 | 63.00 | 254.00 | 0.00 | 30.54 | 30.54 |
| 438 | 120 | 63.00 | 255.00 | 0.00 | 30.66 | 30.66 |
| 439 | 120 | 63.00 | 256.00 | 0.00 | 30.78 | 30.78 |
| 440 | 120 | 63.00 | 257.00 | 0.00 | 30.90 | 30.90 |
| 441 | 120 | 63.00 | 258.00 | 0.00 | 31.02 | 31.02 |
| 442 | 120 | 63.00 | 259.00 | 0.00 | 31.14 | 31.14 |
| 443 | 120 | 63.00 | 260.00 | 0.00 | 31.26 | 31.26 |
| 444 | 120 | 63.00 | 261.00 | 0.00 | 31.38 | 31.38 |
| 445 | 120 | 63.00 | 262.00 | 0.00 | 31.50 | 31.50 |
| 446 | 120 | 63.00 | 263.00 | 0.00 | 31.62 | 31.62 |
| 447 | 120 | 63.00 | 264.00 | 0.00 | 31.74 | 31.74 |
| 448 | 120 | 63.00 | 265.00 | 0.00 | 31.86 | 31.86 |
| 449 | 120 | 63.00 | 266.00 | 0.00 | 31.98 | 31.98 |
| 450 | 120 | 63.00 | 267.00 | 0.00 | 32.10 | 32.10 |
| 451 | 120 | 63.00 | 268.00 | 0.00 | 32.22 | 32.22 |
| 452 | 120 | 63.00 | 269.00 | 0.00 | 32.34 | 32.34 |
| 453 | 120 | 63.00 | 270.00 | 0.00 | 32.46 | 32.46 |
| 454 | 120 | 63.00 | 271.00 | 0.00 | 32.58 | 32.58 |
| 455 | 120 | 63.00 | 272.00 | 0.00 | 32.70 | 32.70 |
| 456 | 120 | 63.00 | 273.00 | 0.00 | 32.82 | 32.82 |
| 457 | 120 | 63.00 | 274.00 | 0.00 | 32.94 | 32.94 |
| 458 | 120 | 63.00 | 275.00 | 0.00 | 33.06 | 33.06 |
| 459 | 120 | 63.00 | 276.00 | 0.00 | 33.18 | 33.18 |
| 460 | 120 | 63.00 | 277.00 | 0.00 | 33.30 | 33.30 |
| 461 | 120 | 63.00 | 278.00 | 0.00 | 33.42 | 33.42 |
| 462 | 120 | 63.00 | 279.00 | 0.00 | 33.54 | 33.54 |
| 463 | 120 | 63.00 | 280.00 | 0.00 | 33.66 | 33.66 |
| 464 | 120 | 63.00 | 281.00 | 0.00 | 33.78 | 33.78 |
| 465 | 120 | 63.00 | 282.00 | 0.00 | 33.90 | 33.90 |
| 466 | 120 | 63.00 | 283.00 | 0.00 | 34.02 | 34.02 |
| 467 | 120 | 63.00 | 284.00 | 0.00 | 34.14 | 34.14 |
| 468 | 120 | 63.00 | 285.00 | 0.00 | 34.26 | 34.26 |
| 469 | 120 | 63.00 | 286.00 | 0.00 | 34.38 | 34.38 |
| 470 | 120 | 63.00 | 287.00 | 0.00 | 34.50 | 34.50 |
| 471 | 120 | 63.00 | 288.00 | 0.00 | 34.62 | 34.62 |
| 472 | 120 | 63.00 | 289.00 | 0.00 | 34.74 | 34.74 |
| 473 | 120 | 63.00 | 290.00 | 0.00 | 34.86 | 34.86 |
| 474 | 120 | 63.00 | 291.00 | 0.00 | 34.98 | 34.98 |

**Weekly table**

**Table letter M**

| Employee's earnings up to and including the UEL | Earnings at the LEL (where earnings are equal to or exceed the LEL) | Earnings above the LEL, up to and including the PT | Earnings above the PT, up to and including the UEL | Employer's NICs due on all earnings above the ST | Employee's NICs due on all earnings above the PT | Total of employee's and employer's NICs (for information only) |
|---|---|---|---|---|---|---|
| | 1a | 1b | 1c | 1d | 1e | |
| £ | £ | £ p | £ p | £ p | £ p | £ p |
| 475 | 120 | 63.00 | 292.00 | 0.00 | 35.10 | 35.10 |
| 476 | 120 | 63.00 | 293.00 | 0.00 | 35.22 | 35.22 |
| 477 | 120 | 63.00 | 294.00 | 0.00 | 35.34 | 35.34 |
| 478 | 120 | 63.00 | 295.00 | 0.00 | 35.46 | 35.46 |
| 479 | 120 | 63.00 | 296.00 | 0.00 | 35.58 | 35.58 |
| 480 | 120 | 63.00 | 297.00 | 0.00 | 35.70 | 35.70 |
| 481 | 120 | 63.00 | 298.00 | 0.00 | 35.82 | 35.82 |
| 482 | 120 | 63.00 | 299.00 | 0.00 | 35.94 | 35.94 |
| 483 | 120 | 63.00 | 300.00 | 0.00 | 36.06 | 36.06 |
| 484 | 120 | 63.00 | 301.00 | 0.00 | 36.18 | 36.18 |
| 485 | 120 | 63.00 | 302.00 | 0.00 | 36.30 | 36.30 |
| 486 | 120 | 63.00 | 303.00 | 0.00 | 36.42 | 36.42 |
| 487 | 120 | 63.00 | 304.00 | 0.00 | 36.54 | 36.54 |
| 488 | 120 | 63.00 | 305.00 | 0.00 | 36.66 | 36.66 |
| 489 | 120 | 63.00 | 306.00 | 0.00 | 36.78 | 36.78 |
| 490 | 120 | 63.00 | 307.00 | 0.00 | 36.90 | 36.90 |
| 491 | 120 | 63.00 | 308.00 | 0.00 | 37.02 | 37.02 |
| 492 | 120 | 63.00 | 309.00 | 0.00 | 37.14 | 37.14 |
| 493 | 120 | 63.00 | 310.00 | 0.00 | 37.26 | 37.26 |
| 494 | 120 | 63.00 | 311.00 | 0.00 | 37.38 | 37.38 |
| 495 | 120 | 63.00 | 312.00 | 0.00 | 37.50 | 37.50 |
| 496 | 120 | 63.00 | 313.00 | 0.00 | 37.62 | 37.62 |
| 497 | 120 | 63.00 | 314.00 | 0.00 | 37.74 | 37.74 |
| 498 | 120 | 63.00 | 315.00 | 0.00 | 37.86 | 37.86 |
| 499 | 120 | 63.00 | 316.00 | 0.00 | 37.98 | 37.98 |
| 500 | 120 | 63.00 | 317.00 | 0.00 | 38.10 | 38.10 |
| 501 | 120 | 63.00 | 318.00 | 0.00 | 38.22 | 38.22 |
| 502 | 120 | 63.00 | 319.00 | 0.00 | 38.34 | 38.34 |
| 503 | 120 | 63.00 | 320.00 | 0.00 | 38.46 | 38.46 |
| 504 | 120 | 63.00 | 321.00 | 0.00 | 38.58 | 38.58 |
| 505 | 120 | 63.00 | 322.00 | 0.00 | 38.70 | 38.70 |
| 506 | 120 | 63.00 | 323.00 | 0.00 | 38.82 | 38.82 |
| 507 | 120 | 63.00 | 324.00 | 0.00 | 38.94 | 38.94 |
| 508 | 120 | 63.00 | 325.00 | 0.00 | 39.06 | 39.06 |
| 509 | 120 | 63.00 | 326.00 | 0.00 | 39.18 | 39.18 |
| 510 | 120 | 63.00 | 327.00 | 0.00 | 39.30 | 39.30 |
| 511 | 120 | 63.00 | 328.00 | 0.00 | 39.42 | 39.42 |
| 512 | 120 | 63.00 | 329.00 | 0.00 | 39.54 | 39.54 |
| 513 | 120 | 63.00 | 330.00 | 0.00 | 39.66 | 39.66 |
| 514 | 120 | 63.00 | 331.00 | 0.00 | 39.78 | 39.78 |
| 515 | 120 | 63.00 | 332.00 | 0.00 | 39.90 | 39.90 |
| 516 | 120 | 63.00 | 333.00 | 0.00 | 40.02 | 40.02 |
| 517 | 120 | 63.00 | 334.00 | 0.00 | 40.14 | 40.14 |
| 518 | 120 | 63.00 | 335.00 | 0.00 | 40.26 | 40.26 |
| 519 | 120 | 63.00 | 336.00 | 0.00 | 40.38 | 40.38 |
| 520 | 120 | 63.00 | 337.00 | 0.00 | 40.50 | 40.50 |
| 521 | 120 | 63.00 | 338.00 | 0.00 | 40.62 | 40.62 |
| 522 | 120 | 63.00 | 339.00 | 0.00 | 40.74 | 40.74 |
| 523 | 120 | 63.00 | 340.00 | 0.00 | 40.86 | 40.86 |
| 524 | 120 | 63.00 | 341.00 | 0.00 | 40.98 | 40.98 |
| 525 | 120 | 63.00 | 342.00 | 0.00 | 41.10 | 41.10 |
| 526 | 120 | 63.00 | 343.00 | 0.00 | 41.22 | 41.22 |
| 527 | 120 | 63.00 | 344.00 | 0.00 | 41.34 | 41.34 |
| 528 | 120 | 63.00 | 345.00 | 0.00 | 41.46 | 41.46 |
| 529 | 120 | 63.00 | 346.00 | 0.00 | 41.58 | 41.58 |

## Table letter M

**Weekly table**

| Employee's earnings up to and including the UEL | Earnings at the LEL (where earnings are equal to or exceed the LEL) 1a | Earnings above the LEL, up to and including the PT 1b | Earnings above the PT, up to and including the UEL 1c | Employer's NICs due on all earnings above the ST 1d | Employee's NICs due on all earnings above the PT 1e | Total of employee's and employer's NICs (for information only) |
|---|---|---|---|---|---|---|
| £ | £ | £ p | £ p | £ p | £ p | £ p |
| 530 | 120 | 63.00 | 347.00 | 0.00 | 41.70 | 41.70 |
| 531 | 120 | 63.00 | 348.00 | 0.00 | 41.82 | 41.82 |
| 532 | 120 | 63.00 | 349.00 | 0.00 | 41.94 | 41.94 |
| 533 | 120 | 63.00 | 350.00 | 0.00 | 42.06 | 42.06 |
| 534 | 120 | 63.00 | 351.00 | 0.00 | 42.18 | 42.18 |
| 535 | 120 | 63.00 | 352.00 | 0.00 | 42.30 | 42.30 |
| 536 | 120 | 63.00 | 353.00 | 0.00 | 42.42 | 42.42 |
| 537 | 120 | 63.00 | 354.00 | 0.00 | 42.54 | 42.54 |
| 538 | 120 | 63.00 | 355.00 | 0.00 | 42.66 | 42.66 |
| 539 | 120 | 63.00 | 356.00 | 0.00 | 42.78 | 42.78 |
| 540 | 120 | 63.00 | 357.00 | 0.00 | 42.90 | 42.90 |
| 541 | 120 | 63.00 | 358.00 | 0.00 | 43.02 | 43.02 |
| 542 | 120 | 63.00 | 359.00 | 0.00 | 43.14 | 43.14 |
| 543 | 120 | 63.00 | 360.00 | 0.00 | 43.26 | 43.26 |
| 544 | 120 | 63.00 | 361.00 | 0.00 | 43.38 | 43.38 |
| 545 | 120 | 63.00 | 362.00 | 0.00 | 43.50 | 43.50 |
| 546 | 120 | 63.00 | 363.00 | 0.00 | 43.62 | 43.62 |
| 547 | 120 | 63.00 | 364.00 | 0.00 | 43.74 | 43.74 |
| 548 | 120 | 63.00 | 365.00 | 0.00 | 43.86 | 43.86 |
| 549 | 120 | 63.00 | 366.00 | 0.00 | 43.98 | 43.98 |
| 550 | 120 | 63.00 | 367.00 | 0.00 | 44.10 | 44.10 |
| 551 | 120 | 63.00 | 368.00 | 0.00 | 44.22 | 44.22 |
| 552 | 120 | 63.00 | 369.00 | 0.00 | 44.34 | 44.34 |
| 553 | 120 | 63.00 | 370.00 | 0.00 | 44.46 | 44.46 |
| 554 | 120 | 63.00 | 371.00 | 0.00 | 44.58 | 44.58 |
| 555 | 120 | 63.00 | 372.00 | 0.00 | 44.70 | 44.70 |
| 556 | 120 | 63.00 | 373.00 | 0.00 | 44.82 | 44.82 |
| 557 | 120 | 63.00 | 374.00 | 0.00 | 44.94 | 44.94 |
| 558 | 120 | 63.00 | 375.00 | 0.00 | 45.06 | 45.06 |
| 559 | 120 | 63.00 | 376.00 | 0.00 | 45.18 | 45.18 |
| 560 | 120 | 63.00 | 377.00 | 0.00 | 45.30 | 45.30 |
| 561 | 120 | 63.00 | 378.00 | 0.00 | 45.42 | 45.42 |
| 562 | 120 | 63.00 | 379.00 | 0.00 | 45.54 | 45.54 |
| 563 | 120 | 63.00 | 380.00 | 0.00 | 45.66 | 45.66 |
| 564 | 120 | 63.00 | 381.00 | 0.00 | 45.78 | 45.78 |
| 565 | 120 | 63.00 | 382.00 | 0.00 | 45.90 | 45.90 |
| 566 | 120 | 63.00 | 383.00 | 0.00 | 46.02 | 46.02 |
| 567 | 120 | 63.00 | 384.00 | 0.00 | 46.14 | 46.14 |
| 568 | 120 | 63.00 | 385.00 | 0.00 | 46.26 | 46.26 |
| 569 | 120 | 63.00 | 386.00 | 0.00 | 46.38 | 46.38 |
| 570 | 120 | 63.00 | 387.00 | 0.00 | 46.50 | 46.50 |
| 571 | 120 | 63.00 | 388.00 | 0.00 | 46.62 | 46.62 |
| 572 | 120 | 63.00 | 389.00 | 0.00 | 46.74 | 46.74 |
| 573 | 120 | 63.00 | 390.00 | 0.00 | 46.86 | 46.86 |
| 574 | 120 | 63.00 | 391.00 | 0.00 | 46.98 | 46.98 |
| 575 | 120 | 63.00 | 392.00 | 0.00 | 47.10 | 47.10 |
| 576 | 120 | 63.00 | 393.00 | 0.00 | 47.22 | 47.22 |
| 577 | 120 | 63.00 | 394.00 | 0.00 | 47.34 | 47.34 |
| 578 | 120 | 63.00 | 395.00 | 0.00 | 47.46 | 47.46 |
| 579 | 120 | 63.00 | 396.00 | 0.00 | 47.58 | 47.58 |
| 580 | 120 | 63.00 | 397.00 | 0.00 | 47.70 | 47.70 |
| 581 | 120 | 63.00 | 398.00 | 0.00 | 47.82 | 47.82 |
| 582 | 120 | 63.00 | 399.00 | 0.00 | 47.94 | 47.94 |
| 583 | 120 | 63.00 | 400.00 | 0.00 | 48.06 | 48.06 |
| 584 | 120 | 63.00 | 401.00 | 0.00 | 48.18 | 48.18 |

Page 118

**Weekly table**

**Table letter M**

| Employee's earnings up to and including the UEL | Earnings at the LEL (where earnings are equal to or exceed the LEL) | Earnings above the LEL, up to and including the PT | Earnings above the PT, up to and including the UEL | Employer's NICs due on all earnings above the ST | Employee's NICs due on all earnings above the PT | Total of employee's and employer's NICs (for information only) |
|---|---|---|---|---|---|---|
| | 1a | 1b | 1c | 1d | 1e | |
| £ | £ | £ p | £ p | £ p | £ p | £ p |
| 585 | 120 | 63.00 | 402.00 | 0.00 | 48.30 | 48.30 |
| 586 | 120 | 63.00 | 403.00 | 0.00 | 48.42 | 48.42 |
| 587 | 120 | 63.00 | 404.00 | 0.00 | 48.54 | 48.54 |
| 588 | 120 | 63.00 | 405.00 | 0.00 | 48.66 | 48.66 |
| 589 | 120 | 63.00 | 406.00 | 0.00 | 48.78 | 48.78 |
| 590 | 120 | 63.00 | 407.00 | 0.00 | 48.90 | 48.90 |
| 591 | 120 | 63.00 | 408.00 | 0.00 | 49.02 | 49.02 |
| 592 | 120 | 63.00 | 409.00 | 0.00 | 49.14 | 49.14 |
| 593 | 120 | 63.00 | 410.00 | 0.00 | 49.26 | 49.26 |
| 594 | 120 | 63.00 | 411.00 | 0.00 | 49.38 | 49.38 |
| 595 | 120 | 63.00 | 412.00 | 0.00 | 49.50 | 49.50 |
| 596 | 120 | 63.00 | 413.00 | 0.00 | 49.62 | 49.62 |
| 597 | 120 | 63.00 | 414.00 | 0.00 | 49.74 | 49.74 |
| 598 | 120 | 63.00 | 415.00 | 0.00 | 49.86 | 49.86 |
| 599 | 120 | 63.00 | 416.00 | 0.00 | 49.98 | 49.98 |
| 600 | 120 | 63.00 | 417.00 | 0.00 | 50.10 | 50.10 |
| 601 | 120 | 63.00 | 418.00 | 0.00 | 50.22 | 50.22 |
| 602 | 120 | 63.00 | 419.00 | 0.00 | 50.34 | 50.34 |
| 603 | 120 | 63.00 | 420.00 | 0.00 | 50.46 | 50.46 |
| 604 | 120 | 63.00 | 421.00 | 0.00 | 50.58 | 50.58 |
| 605 | 120 | 63.00 | 422.00 | 0.00 | 50.70 | 50.70 |
| 606 | 120 | 63.00 | 423.00 | 0.00 | 50.82 | 50.82 |
| 607 | 120 | 63.00 | 424.00 | 0.00 | 50.94 | 50.94 |
| 608 | 120 | 63.00 | 425.00 | 0.00 | 51.06 | 51.06 |
| 609 | 120 | 63.00 | 426.00 | 0.00 | 51.18 | 51.18 |
| 610 | 120 | 63.00 | 427.00 | 0.00 | 51.30 | 51.30 |
| 611 | 120 | 63.00 | 428.00 | 0.00 | 51.42 | 51.42 |
| 612 | 120 | 63.00 | 429.00 | 0.00 | 51.54 | 51.54 |
| 613 | 120 | 63.00 | 430.00 | 0.00 | 51.66 | 51.66 |
| 614 | 120 | 63.00 | 431.00 | 0.00 | 51.78 | 51.78 |
| 615 | 120 | 63.00 | 432.00 | 0.00 | 51.90 | 51.90 |
| 616 | 120 | 63.00 | 433.00 | 0.00 | 52.02 | 52.02 |
| 617 | 120 | 63.00 | 434.00 | 0.00 | 52.14 | 52.14 |
| 618 | 120 | 63.00 | 435.00 | 0.00 | 52.26 | 52.26 |
| 619 | 120 | 63.00 | 436.00 | 0.00 | 52.38 | 52.38 |
| 620 | 120 | 63.00 | 437.00 | 0.00 | 52.50 | 52.50 |
| 621 | 120 | 63.00 | 438.00 | 0.00 | 52.62 | 52.62 |
| 622 | 120 | 63.00 | 439.00 | 0.00 | 52.74 | 52.74 |
| 623 | 120 | 63.00 | 440.00 | 0.00 | 52.86 | 52.86 |
| 624 | 120 | 63.00 | 441.00 | 0.00 | 52.98 | 52.98 |
| 625 | 120 | 63.00 | 442.00 | 0.00 | 53.10 | 53.10 |
| 626 | 120 | 63.00 | 443.00 | 0.00 | 53.22 | 53.22 |
| 627 | 120 | 63.00 | 444.00 | 0.00 | 53.34 | 53.34 |
| 628 | 120 | 63.00 | 445.00 | 0.00 | 53.46 | 53.46 |
| 629 | 120 | 63.00 | 446.00 | 0.00 | 53.58 | 53.58 |
| 630 | 120 | 63.00 | 447.00 | 0.00 | 53.70 | 53.70 |
| 631 | 120 | 63.00 | 448.00 | 0.00 | 53.82 | 53.82 |
| 632 | 120 | 63.00 | 449.00 | 0.00 | 53.94 | 53.94 |
| 633 | 120 | 63.00 | 450.00 | 0.00 | 54.06 | 54.06 |
| 634 | 120 | 63.00 | 451.00 | 0.00 | 54.18 | 54.18 |
| 635 | 120 | 63.00 | 452.00 | 0.00 | 54.30 | 54.30 |
| 636 | 120 | 63.00 | 453.00 | 0.00 | 54.42 | 54.42 |
| 637 | 120 | 63.00 | 454.00 | 0.00 | 54.54 | 54.54 |
| 638 | 120 | 63.00 | 455.00 | 0.00 | 54.66 | 54.66 |
| 639 | 120 | 63.00 | 456.00 | 0.00 | 54.78 | 54.78 |

## Table letter M

**Weekly table**

| Employee's earnings up to and including the UEL | Earnings at the LEL (where earnings are equal to or exceed the LEL) | Earnings above the LEL, up to and including the PT | Earnings above the PT, up to and including the UEL | Employer's NICs due on all earnings above the ST | Employee's NICs due on all earnings above the PT | Total of employee's and employer's NICs (for information only) |
|---|---|---|---|---|---|---|
| | 1a | 1b | 1c | 1d | 1e | |
| £ | £ | £ p | £ p | £ p | £ p | £ p |
| 640 | 120 | 63.00 | 457.00 | 0.00 | 54.90 | 54.90 |
| 641 | 120 | 63.00 | 458.00 | 0.00 | 55.02 | 55.02 |
| 642 | 120 | 63.00 | 459.00 | 0.00 | 55.14 | 55.14 |
| 643 | 120 | 63.00 | 460.00 | 0.00 | 55.26 | 55.26 |
| 644 | 120 | 63.00 | 461.00 | 0.00 | 55.38 | 55.38 |
| 645 | 120 | 63.00 | 462.00 | 0.00 | 55.50 | 55.50 |
| 646 | 120 | 63.00 | 463.00 | 0.00 | 55.62 | 55.62 |
| 647 | 120 | 63.00 | 464.00 | 0.00 | 55.74 | 55.74 |
| 648 | 120 | 63.00 | 465.00 | 0.00 | 55.86 | 55.86 |
| 649 | 120 | 63.00 | 466.00 | 0.00 | 55.98 | 55.98 |
| 650 | 120 | 63.00 | 467.00 | 0.00 | 56.10 | 56.10 |
| 651 | 120 | 63.00 | 468.00 | 0.00 | 56.22 | 56.22 |
| 652 | 120 | 63.00 | 469.00 | 0.00 | 56.34 | 56.34 |
| 653 | 120 | 63.00 | 470.00 | 0.00 | 56.46 | 56.46 |
| 654 | 120 | 63.00 | 471.00 | 0.00 | 56.58 | 56.58 |
| 655 | 120 | 63.00 | 472.00 | 0.00 | 56.70 | 56.70 |
| 656 | 120 | 63.00 | 473.00 | 0.00 | 56.82 | 56.82 |
| 657 | 120 | 63.00 | 474.00 | 0.00 | 56.94 | 56.94 |
| 658 | 120 | 63.00 | 475.00 | 0.00 | 57.06 | 57.06 |
| 659 | 120 | 63.00 | 476.00 | 0.00 | 57.18 | 57.18 |
| 660 | 120 | 63.00 | 477.00 | 0.00 | 57.30 | 57.30 |
| 661 | 120 | 63.00 | 478.00 | 0.00 | 57.42 | 57.42 |
| 662 | 120 | 63.00 | 479.00 | 0.00 | 57.54 | 57.54 |
| 663 | 120 | 63.00 | 480.00 | 0.00 | 57.66 | 57.66 |
| 664 | 120 | 63.00 | 481.00 | 0.00 | 57.78 | 57.78 |
| 665 | 120 | 63.00 | 482.00 | 0.00 | 57.90 | 57.90 |
| 666 | 120 | 63.00 | 483.00 | 0.00 | 58.02 | 58.02 |
| 667 | 120 | 63.00 | 484.00 | 0.00 | 58.14 | 58.14 |
| 668 | 120 | 63.00 | 485.00 | 0.00 | 58.26 | 58.26 |
| 669 | 120 | 63.00 | 486.00 | 0.00 | 58.38 | 58.38 |
| 670 | 120 | 63.00 | 487.00 | 0.00 | 58.50 | 58.50 |
| 671 | 120 | 63.00 | 488.00 | 0.00 | 58.62 | 58.62 |
| 672 | 120 | 63.00 | 489.00 | 0.00 | 58.74 | 58.74 |
| 673 | 120 | 63.00 | 490.00 | 0.00 | 58.86 | 58.86 |
| 674 | 120 | 63.00 | 491.00 | 0.00 | 58.98 | 58.98 |
| 675 | 120 | 63.00 | 492.00 | 0.00 | 59.10 | 59.10 |
| 676 | 120 | 63.00 | 493.00 | 0.00 | 59.22 | 59.22 |
| 677 | 120 | 63.00 | 494.00 | 0.00 | 59.34 | 59.34 |
| 678 | 120 | 63.00 | 495.00 | 0.00 | 59.46 | 59.46 |
| 679 | 120 | 63.00 | 496.00 | 0.00 | 59.58 | 59.58 |
| 680 | 120 | 63.00 | 497.00 | 0.00 | 59.70 | 59.70 |
| 681 | 120 | 63.00 | 498.00 | 0.00 | 59.82 | 59.82 |
| 682 | 120 | 63.00 | 499.00 | 0.00 | 59.94 | 59.94 |
| 683 | 120 | 63.00 | 500.00 | 0.00 | 60.06 | 60.06 |
| 684 | 120 | 63.00 | 501.00 | 0.00 | 60.18 | 60.18 |
| 685 | 120 | 63.00 | 502.00 | 0.00 | 60.30 | 60.30 |
| 686 | 120 | 63.00 | 503.00 | 0.00 | 60.42 | 60.42 |
| 687 | 120 | 63.00 | 504.00 | 0.00 | 60.54 | 60.54 |
| 688 | 120 | 63.00 | 505.00 | 0.00 | 60.66 | 60.66 |
| 689 | 120 | 63.00 | 506.00 | 0.00 | 60.78 | 60.78 |
| 690 | 120 | 63.00 | 507.00 | 0.00 | 60.90 | 60.90 |
| 691 | 120 | 63.00 | 508.00 | 0.00 | 61.02 | 61.02 |
| 692 | 120 | 63.00 | 509.00 | 0.00 | 61.14 | 61.14 |
| 693 | 120 | 63.00 | 510.00 | 0.00 | 61.26 | 61.26 |
| 694 | 120 | 63.00 | 511.00 | 0.00 | 61.38 | 61.38 |

**Weekly table**

**Table letter M**

| Employee's earnings up to and including the UEL | Earnings at the LEL (where earnings are equal to or exceed the LEL) | Earnings above the LEL, up to and including the PT | Earnings above the PT, up to and including the UEL | Employer's NICs due on all earnings above the ST | Employee's NICs due on all earnings above the PT | Total of employee's and employer's NICs (for information only) |
|---|---|---|---|---|---|---|
| | | 1a | 1b | 1c | 1d | 1e |
| £ | £ | £ p | £ p | £ p | £ p | £ p |
| 695 | 120 | 63.00 | 512.00 | 0.00 | 61.50 | 61.50 |
| 696 | 120 | 63.00 | 513.00 | 0.00 | 61.62 | 61.62 |
| 697 | 120 | 63.00 | 514.00 | 0.00 | 61.74 | 61.74 |
| 698 | 120 | 63.00 | 515.00 | 0.00 | 61.86 | 61.86 |
| 699 | 120 | 63.00 | 516.00 | 0.00 | 61.98 | 61.98 |
| 700 | 120 | 63.00 | 517.00 | 0.00 | 62.10 | 62.10 |
| 701 | 120 | 63.00 | 518.00 | 0.00 | 62.22 | 62.22 |
| 702 | 120 | 63.00 | 519.00 | 0.00 | 62.34 | 62.34 |
| 703 | 120 | 63.00 | 520.00 | 0.00 | 62.46 | 62.46 |
| 704 | 120 | 63.00 | 521.00 | 0.00 | 62.58 | 62.58 |
| 705 | 120 | 63.00 | 522.00 | 0.00 | 62.70 | 62.70 |
| 706 | 120 | 63.00 | 523.00 | 0.00 | 62.82 | 62.82 |
| 707 | 120 | 63.00 | 524.00 | 0.00 | 62.94 | 62.94 |
| 708 | 120 | 63.00 | 525.00 | 0.00 | 63.06 | 63.06 |
| 709 | 120 | 63.00 | 526.00 | 0.00 | 63.18 | 63.18 |
| 710 | 120 | 63.00 | 527.00 | 0.00 | 63.30 | 63.30 |
| 711 | 120 | 63.00 | 528.00 | 0.00 | 63.42 | 63.42 |
| 712 | 120 | 63.00 | 529.00 | 0.00 | 63.54 | 63.54 |
| 713 | 120 | 63.00 | 530.00 | 0.00 | 63.66 | 63.66 |
| 714 | 120 | 63.00 | 531.00 | 0.00 | 63.78 | 63.78 |
| 715 | 120 | 63.00 | 532.00 | 0.00 | 63.90 | 63.90 |
| 716 | 120 | 63.00 | 533.00 | 0.00 | 64.02 | 64.02 |
| 717 | 120 | 63.00 | 534.00 | 0.00 | 64.14 | 64.14 |
| 718 | 120 | 63.00 | 535.00 | 0.00 | 64.26 | 64.26 |
| 719 | 120 | 63.00 | 536.00 | 0.00 | 64.38 | 64.38 |
| 720 | 120 | 63.00 | 537.00 | 0.00 | 64.50 | 64.50 |
| 721 | 120 | 63.00 | 538.00 | 0.00 | 64.62 | 64.62 |
| 722 | 120 | 63.00 | 539.00 | 0.00 | 64.74 | 64.74 |
| 723 | 120 | 63.00 | 540.00 | 0.00 | 64.86 | 64.86 |
| 724 | 120 | 63.00 | 541.00 | 0.00 | 64.98 | 64.98 |
| 725 | 120 | 63.00 | 542.00 | 0.00 | 65.10 | 65.10 |
| 726 | 120 | 63.00 | 543.00 | 0.00 | 65.22 | 65.22 |
| 727 | 120 | 63.00 | 544.00 | 0.00 | 65.34 | 65.34 |
| 728 | 120 | 63.00 | 545.00 | 0.00 | 65.46 | 65.46 |
| 729 | 120 | 63.00 | 546.00 | 0.00 | 65.58 | 65.58 |
| 730 | 120 | 63.00 | 547.00 | 0.00 | 65.70 | 65.70 |
| 731 | 120 | 63.00 | 548.00 | 0.00 | 65.82 | 65.82 |
| 732 | 120 | 63.00 | 549.00 | 0.00 | 65.94 | 65.94 |
| 733 | 120 | 63.00 | 550.00 | 0.00 | 66.06 | 66.06 |
| 734 | 120 | 63.00 | 551.00 | 0.00 | 66.18 | 66.18 |
| 735 | 120 | 63.00 | 552.00 | 0.00 | 66.30 | 66.30 |
| 736 | 120 | 63.00 | 553.00 | 0.00 | 66.42 | 66.42 |
| 737 | 120 | 63.00 | 554.00 | 0.00 | 66.54 | 66.54 |
| 738 | 120 | 63.00 | 555.00 | 0.00 | 66.66 | 66.66 |
| 739 | 120 | 63.00 | 556.00 | 0.00 | 66.78 | 66.78 |
| 740 | 120 | 63.00 | 557.00 | 0.00 | 66.90 | 66.90 |
| 741 | 120 | 63.00 | 558.00 | 0.00 | 67.02 | 67.02 |
| 742 | 120 | 63.00 | 559.00 | 0.00 | 67.14 | 67.14 |
| 743 | 120 | 63.00 | 560.00 | 0.00 | 67.26 | 67.26 |
| 744 | 120 | 63.00 | 561.00 | 0.00 | 67.38 | 67.38 |
| 745 | 120 | 63.00 | 562.00 | 0.00 | 67.50 | 67.50 |
| 746 | 120 | 63.00 | 563.00 | 0.00 | 67.62 | 67.62 |
| 747 | 120 | 63.00 | 564.00 | 0.00 | 67.74 | 67.74 |
| 748 | 120 | 63.00 | 565.00 | 0.00 | 67.86 | 67.86 |
| 749 | 120 | 63.00 | 566.00 | 0.00 | 67.98 | 67.98 |

## Table letter M

**Weekly table**

| Employee's earnings up to and including the UEL | Earnings at the LEL (where earnings are equal to or exceed the LEL) 1a | Earnings above the LEL, up to and including the PT 1b | Earnings above the PT, up to and including the UEL 1c | Employer's NICs due on all earnings above the ST 1d | Employee's NICs due on all earnings above the PT 1e | Total of employee's and employer's NICs (for information only) |
|---|---|---|---|---|---|---|
| £ | £ | £ p | £ p | £ p | £ p | £ p |
| 750 | 120 | 63.00 | 567.00 | 0.00 | 68.10 | 68.10 |
| 751 | 120 | 63.00 | 568.00 | 0.00 | 68.22 | 68.22 |
| 752 | 120 | 63.00 | 569.00 | 0.00 | 68.34 | 68.34 |
| 753 | 120 | 63.00 | 570.00 | 0.00 | 68.46 | 68.46 |
| 754 | 120 | 63.00 | 571.00 | 0.00 | 68.58 | 68.58 |
| 755 | 120 | 63.00 | 572.00 | 0.00 | 68.70 | 68.70 |
| 756 | 120 | 63.00 | 573.00 | 0.00 | 68.82 | 68.82 |
| 757 | 120 | 63.00 | 574.00 | 0.00 | 68.94 | 68.94 |
| 758 | 120 | 63.00 | 575.00 | 0.00 | 69.06 | 69.06 |
| 759 | 120 | 63.00 | 576.00 | 0.00 | 69.18 | 69.18 |
| 760 | 120 | 63.00 | 577.00 | 0.00 | 69.30 | 69.30 |
| 761 | 120 | 63.00 | 578.00 | 0.00 | 69.42 | 69.42 |
| 762 | 120 | 63.00 | 579.00 | 0.00 | 69.54 | 69.54 |
| 763 | 120 | 63.00 | 580.00 | 0.00 | 69.66 | 69.66 |
| 764 | 120 | 63.00 | 581.00 | 0.00 | 69.78 | 69.78 |
| 765 | 120 | 63.00 | 582.00 | 0.00 | 69.90 | 69.90 |
| 766 | 120 | 63.00 | 583.00 | 0.00 | 70.02 | 70.02 |
| 767 | 120 | 63.00 | 584.00 | 0.00 | 70.14 | 70.14 |
| 768 | 120 | 63.00 | 585.00 | 0.00 | 70.26 | 70.26 |
| 769 | 120 | 63.00 | 586.00 | 0.00 | 70.38 | 70.38 |
| 770 | 120 | 63.00 | 587.00 | 0.00 | 70.50 | 70.50 |
| 771 | 120 | 63.00 | 588.00 | 0.00 | 70.62 | 70.62 |
| 772 | 120 | 63.00 | 589.00 | 0.00 | 70.74 | 70.74 |
| 773 | 120 | 63.00 | 590.00 | 0.00 | 70.86 | 70.86 |
| 774 | 120 | 63.00 | 591.00 | 0.00 | 70.98 | 70.98 |
| 775 | 120 | 63.00 | 592.00 | 0.00 | 71.10 | 71.10 |
| 776 | 120 | 63.00 | 593.00 | 0.00 | 71.22 | 71.22 |
| 777 | 120 | 63.00 | 594.00 | 0.00 | 71.34 | 71.34 |
| 778 | 120 | 63.00 | 595.00 | 0.00 | 71.46 | 71.46 |
| 779 | 120 | 63.00 | 596.00 | 0.00 | 71.58 | 71.58 |
| 780 | 120 | 63.00 | 597.00 | 0.00 | 71.70 | 71.70 |
| 781 | 120 | 63.00 | 598.00 | 0.00 | 71.82 | 71.82 |
| 782 | 120 | 63.00 | 599.00 | 0.00 | 71.94 | 71.94 |
| 783 | 120 | 63.00 | 600.00 | 0.00 | 72.06 | 72.06 |
| 784 | 120 | 63.00 | 601.00 | 0.00 | 72.18 | 72.18 |
| 785 | 120 | 63.00 | 602.00 | 0.00 | 72.30 | 72.30 |
| 786 | 120 | 63.00 | 603.00 | 0.00 | 72.42 | 72.42 |
| 787 | 120 | 63.00 | 604.00 | 0.00 | 72.54 | 72.54 |
| 788 | 120 | 63.00 | 605.00 | 0.00 | 72.66 | 72.66 |
| 789 | 120 | 63.00 | 606.00 | 0.00 | 72.78 | 72.78 |
| 790 | 120 | 63.00 | 607.00 | 0.00 | 72.90 | 72.90 |
| 791 | 120 | 63.00 | 608.00 | 0.00 | 73.02 | 73.02 |
| 792 | 120 | 63.00 | 609.00 | 0.00 | 73.14 | 73.14 |
| 793 | 120 | 63.00 | 610.00 | 0.00 | 73.26 | 73.26 |
| 794 | 120 | 63.00 | 611.00 | 0.00 | 73.38 | 73.38 |
| 795 | 120 | 63.00 | 612.00 | 0.00 | 73.50 | 73.50 |
| 796 | 120 | 63.00 | 613.00 | 0.00 | 73.62 | 73.62 |
| 797 | 120 | 63.00 | 614.00 | 0.00 | 73.74 | 73.74 |
| 798 | 120 | 63.00 | 615.00 | 0.00 | 73.86 | 73.86 |
| 799 | 120 | 63.00 | 616.00 | 0.00 | 73.98 | 73.98 |
| 800 | 120 | 63.00 | 617.00 | 0.00 | 74.10 | 74.10 |
| 801 | 120 | 63.00 | 618.00 | 0.00 | 74.22 | 74.22 |
| 802 | 120 | 63.00 | 619.00 | 0.00 | 74.34 | 74.34 |
| 803 | 120 | 63.00 | 620.00 | 0.00 | 74.46 | 74.46 |
| 804 | 120 | 63.00 | 621.00 | 0.00 | 74.58 | 74.58 |

Page 122

## Table letter M

**Weekly table**

| Employee's earnings up to and including the UEL | Earnings at the LEL (where earnings are equal to or exceed the LEL) | Earnings above the LEL, up to and including the PT | Earnings above the PT, up to and including the UEL | Employer's NICs due on all earnings above the ST | Employee's NICs due on all earnings above the PT | Total of employee's and employer's NICs (for information only) |
|---|---|---|---|---|---|---|
|  |  | 1a | 1b | 1c | 1d | 1e |
| £ | £ | £ p | £ p | £ p | £ p | £ p |
| 805 | 120 | 63.00 | 622.00 | 0.00 | 74.70 | 74.70 |
| 806 | 120 | 63.00 | 623.00 | 0.00 | 74.82 | 74.82 |
| 807 | 120 | 63.00 | 624.00 | 0.00 | 74.94 | 74.94 |
| 808 | 120 | 63.00 | 625.00 | 0.00 | 75.06 | 75.06 |
| 809 | 120 | 63.00 | 626.00 | 0.00 | 75.18 | 75.18 |
| 810 | 120 | 63.00 | 627.00 | 0.00 | 75.30 | 75.30 |
| 811 | 120 | 63.00 | 628.00 | 0.00 | 75.42 | 75.42 |
| 812 | 120 | 63.00 | 629.00 | 0.00 | 75.54 | 75.54 |
| 813 | 120 | 63.00 | 630.00 | 0.00 | 75.66 | 75.66 |
| 814 | 120 | 63.00 | 631.00 | 0.00 | 75.78 | 75.78 |
| 815 | 120 | 63.00 | 632.00 | 0.00 | 75.90 | 75.90 |
| 816 | 120 | 63.00 | 633.00 | 0.00 | 76.02 | 76.02 |
| 817 | 120 | 63.00 | 634.00 | 0.00 | 76.14 | 76.14 |
| 818 | 120 | 63.00 | 635.00 | 0.00 | 76.26 | 76.26 |
| 819 | 120 | 63.00 | 636.00 | 0.00 | 76.38 | 76.38 |
| 820 | 120 | 63.00 | 637.00 | 0.00 | 76.50 | 76.50 |
| 821 | 120 | 63.00 | 638.00 | 0.00 | 76.62 | 76.62 |
| 822 | 120 | 63.00 | 639.00 | 0.00 | 76.74 | 76.74 |
| 823 | 120 | 63.00 | 640.00 | 0.00 | 76.86 | 76.86 |
| 824 | 120 | 63.00 | 641.00 | 0.00 | 76.98 | 76.98 |
| 825 | 120 | 63.00 | 642.00 | 0.00 | 77.10 | 77.10 |
| 826 | 120 | 63.00 | 643.00 | 0.00 | 77.22 | 77.22 |
| 827 | 120 | 63.00 | 644.00 | 0.00 | 77.34 | 77.34 |
| 828 | 120 | 63.00 | 645.00 | 0.00 | 77.46 | 77.46 |
| 829 | 120 | 63.00 | 646.00 | 0.00 | 77.58 | 77.58 |
| 830 | 120 | 63.00 | 647.00 | 0.00 | 77.70 | 77.70 |
| 831 | 120 | 63.00 | 648.00 | 0.00 | 77.82 | 77.82 |
| 832 | 120 | 63.00 | 649.00 | 0.00 | 77.94 | 77.94 |
| 833 | 120 | 63.00 | 650.00 | 0.00 | 78.06 | 78.06 |
| 834 | 120 | 63.00 | 651.00 | 0.00 | 78.18 | 78.18 |
| 835 | 120 | 63.00 | 652.00 | 0.00 | 78.30 | 78.30 |
| 836 | 120 | 63.00 | 653.00 | 0.00 | 78.42 | 78.42 |
| 837 | 120 | 63.00 | 654.00 | 0.00 | 78.54 | 78.54 |
| 838 | 120 | 63.00 | 655.00 | 0.00 | 78.66 | 78.66 |
| 839 | 120 | 63.00 | 656.00 | 0.00 | 78.78 | 78.78 |
| 840 | 120 | 63.00 | 657.00 | 0.00 | 78.90 | 78.90 |
| 841 | 120 | 63.00 | 658.00 | 0.00 | 79.02 | 79.02 |
| 842 | 120 | 63.00 | 659.00 | 0.00 | 79.14 | 79.14 |
| 843 | 120 | 63.00 | 660.00 | 0.00 | 79.26 | 79.26 |
| 844 | 120 | 63.00 | 661.00 | 0.00 | 79.38 | 79.38 |
| 845 | 120 | 63.00 | 662.00 | 0.00 | 79.50 | 79.50 |
| 846 | 120 | 63.00 | 663.00 | 0.00 | 79.62 | 79.62 |
| 847 | 120 | 63.00 | 664.00 | 0.00 | 79.74 | 79.74 |
| 848 | 120 | 63.00 | 665.00 | 0.00 | 79.86 | 79.86 |
| 849 | 120 | 63.00 | 666.00 | 0.00 | 79.98 | 79.98 |
| 850 | 120 | 63.00 | 667.00 | 0.00 | 80.10 | 80.10 |
| 851 | 120 | 63.00 | 668.00 | 0.00 | 80.22 | 80.22 |
| 852 | 120 | 63.00 | 669.00 | 0.00 | 80.34 | 80.34 |
| 853 | 120 | 63.00 | 670.00 | 0.00 | 80.46 | 80.46 |
| 854 | 120 | 63.00 | 671.00 | 0.00 | 80.58 | 80.58 |
| 855 | 120 | 63.00 | 672.00 | 0.00 | 80.70 | 80.70 |
| 856 | 120 | 63.00 | 673.00 | 0.00 | 80.82 | 80.82 |
| 857 | 120 | 63.00 | 674.00 | 0.00 | 80.94 | 80.94 |
| 858 | 120 | 63.00 | 675.00 | 0.00 | 81.06 | 81.06 |
| 859 | 120 | 63.00 | 676.00 | 0.00 | 81.18 | 81.18 |

# Weekly table

## Table letter M

| Employee's earnings up to and including the UEL | Earnings at the LEL (where earnings are equal to or exceed the LEL) | Earnings above the LEL, up to and including the PT | Earnings above the PT, up to and including the UEL | Employer's NICs due on all earnings above the ST | Employee's NICs due on all earnings above the PT | Total of employee's and employer's NICs (for information only) |
|---|---|---|---|---|---|---|
| | 1a | 1b | 1c | 1d | 1e | |
| £ | £ | £ p | £ p | £ p | £ p | £ p |
| 860 | 120 | 63.00 | 677.00 | 0.00 | 81.30 | 81.30 |
| 861 | 120 | 63.00 | 678.00 | 0.00 | 81.42 | 81.42 |
| 862 | 120 | 63.00 | 679.00 | 0.00 | 81.54 | 81.54 |
| 863 | 120 | 63.00 | 680.00 | 0.00 | 81.66 | 81.66 |
| 864 | 120 | 63.00 | 681.00 | 0.00 | 81.78 | 81.78 |
| 865 | 120 | 63.00 | 682.00 | 0.00 | 81.90 | 81.90 |
| 866 | 120 | 63.00 | 683.00 | 0.00 | 82.02 | 82.02 |
| 867 | 120 | 63.00 | 684.00 | 0.00 | 82.14 | 82.14 |
| 868 | 120 | 63.00 | 685.00 | 0.00 | 82.26 | 82.26 |
| 869 | 120 | 63.00 | 686.00 | 0.00 | 82.38 | 82.38 |
| 870 | 120 | 63.00 | 687.00 | 0.00 | 82.50 | 82.50 |
| 871 | 120 | 63.00 | 688.00 | 0.00 | 82.62 | 82.62 |
| 872 | 120 | 63.00 | 689.00 | 0.00 | 82.74 | 82.74 |
| 873 | 120 | 63.00 | 690.00 | 0.00 | 82.86 | 82.86 |
| 874 | 120 | 63.00 | 691.00 | 0.00 | 82.98 | 82.98 |
| 875 | 120 | 63.00 | 692.00 | 0.00 | 83.10 | 83.10 |
| 876 | 120 | 63.00 | 693.00 | 0.00 | 83.22 | 83.22 |
| 877 | 120 | 63.00 | 694.00 | 0.00 | 83.34 | 83.34 |
| 878 | 120 | 63.00 | 695.00 | 0.00 | 83.46 | 83.46 |
| 879 | 120 | 63.00 | 696.00 | 0.00 | 83.58 | 83.58 |
| 880 | 120 | 63.00 | 697.00 | 0.00 | 83.70 | 83.70 |
| 881 | 120 | 63.00 | 698.00 | 0.00 | 83.82 | 83.82 |
| 882 | 120 | 63.00 | 699.00 | 0.00 | 83.94 | 83.94 |
| 883 | 120 | 63.00 | 700.00 | 0.00 | 84.06 | 84.06 |
| 884 | 120 | 63.00 | 701.00 | 0.00 | 84.18 | 84.18 |
| 885 | 120 | 63.00 | 702.00 | 0.00 | 84.30 | 84.30 |
| 886 | 120 | 63.00 | 703.00 | 0.00 | 84.42 | 84.42 |
| 887 | 120 | 63.00 | 704.00 | 0.00 | 84.54 | 84.54 |
| 888 | 120 | 63.00 | 705.00 | 0.00 | 84.66 | 84.66 |
| 889 | 120 | 63.00 | 706.00 | 0.00 | 84.78 | 84.78 |
| 890 | 120 | 63.00 | 707.00 | 0.00 | 84.90 | 84.90 |
| 891 | 120 | 63.00 | 708.00 | 0.00 | 85.02 | 85.02 |
| 892 | 120 | 63.00 | 709.00 | 0.00 | 85.14 | 85.14 |
| 893 | 120 | 63.00 | 710.00 | 0.00 | 85.26 | 85.26 |
| 894 | 120 | 63.00 | 711.00 | 0.00 | 85.38 | 85.38 |
| 895 | 120 | 63.00 | 712.00 | 0.00 | 85.50 | 85.50 |
| 896 | 120 | 63.00 | 713.00 | 0.00 | 85.62 | 85.62 |
| 897 | 120 | 63.00 | 714.00 | 0.00 | 85.74 | 85.74 |
| 898 | 120 | 63.00 | 715.00 | 0.00 | 85.86 | 85.86 |
| 899 | 120 | 63.00 | 716.00 | 0.00 | 85.98 | 85.98 |
| 900 | 120 | 63.00 | 717.00 | 0.00 | 86.10 | 86.10 |
| 901 | 120 | 63.00 | 718.00 | 0.00 | 86.22 | 86.22 |
| 902 | 120 | 63.00 | 719.00 | 0.00 | 86.34 | 86.34 |
| 903 | 120 | 63.00 | 720.00 | 0.00 | 86.46 | 86.46 |
| 904 | 120 | 63.00 | 721.00 | 0.00 | 86.58 | 86.58 |
| 905 | 120 | 63.00 | 722.00 | 0.00 | 86.70 | 86.70 |
| 906 | 120 | 63.00 | 723.00 | 0.00 | 86.82 | 86.82 |
| 907 | 120 | 63.00 | 724.00 | 0.00 | 86.94 | 86.94 |
| 908 | 120 | 63.00 | 725.00 | 0.00 | 87.06 | 87.06 |
| 909 | 120 | 63.00 | 726.00 | 0.00 | 87.18 | 87.18 |
| 910 | 120 | 63.00 | 727.00 | 0.00 | 87.30 | 87.30 |
| 911 | 120 | 63.00 | 728.00 | 0.00 | 87.42 | 87.42 |
| 912 | 120 | 63.00 | 729.00 | 0.00 | 87.54 | 87.54 |
| 913 | 120 | 63.00 | 730.00 | 0.00 | 87.66 | 87.66 |
| 914 | 120 | 63.00 | 731.00 | 0.00 | 87.78 | 87.78 |

**Weekly table**        **Table letter M**

| Employee's earnings up to and including the UEL | Earnings at the LEL (where earnings are equal to or exceed the LEL) | Earnings above the LEL, up to and including the PT | Earnings above the PT, up to and including the UEL | Employer's NICs due on all earnings above the ST | Employee's NICs due on all earnings above the PT | Total of employee's and employer's NICs (for information only) |
|---|---|---|---|---|---|---|
| | | 1a | 1b | 1c | 1d | 1e |
| £ | £ | £ p | £ p | £ p | £ p | £ p |
| 915 | 120 | 63.00 | 732.00 | 0.00 | 87.90 | 87.90 |
| 916 | 120 | 63.00 | 733.00 | 0.00 | 88.02 | 88.02 |
| 917 | 120 | 63.00 | 734.00 | 0.00 | 88.14 | 88.14 |
| 918 | 120 | 63.00 | 735.00 | 0.00 | 88.26 | 88.26 |
| 919 | 120 | 63.00 | 736.00 | 0.00 | 88.38 | 88.38 |
| 920 | 120 | 63.00 | 737.00 | 0.00 | 88.50 | 88.50 |
| 921 | 120 | 63.00 | 738.00 | 0.00 | 88.62 | 88.62 |
| 922 | 120 | 63.00 | 739.00 | 0.00 | 88.74 | 88.74 |
| 923 | 120 | 63.00 | 740.00 | 0.00 | 88.86 | 88.86 |
| 924 | 120 | 63.00 | 741.00 | 0.00 | 88.98 | 88.98 |
| 925 | 120 | 63.00 | 742.00 | 0.00 | 89.10 | 89.10 |
| 926 | 120 | 63.00 | 743.00 | 0.00 | 89.22 | 89.22 |
| 927 | 120 | 63.00 | 744.00 | 0.00 | 89.34 | 89.34 |
| 928 | 120 | 63.00 | 745.00 | 0.00 | 89.46 | 89.46 |
| 929 | 120 | 63.00 | 746.00 | 0.00 | 89.58 | 89.58 |
| 930 | 120 | 63.00 | 747.00 | 0.00 | 89.70 | 89.70 |
| 931 | 120 | 63.00 | 748.00 | 0.00 | 89.82 | 89.82 |
| 932 | 120 | 63.00 | 749.00 | 0.00 | 89.94 | 89.94 |
| 933 | 120 | 63.00 | 750.00 | 0.00 | 90.06 | 90.06 |
| 934 | 120 | 63.00 | 751.00 | 0.00 | 90.18 | 90.18 |
| 935 | 120 | 63.00 | 752.00 | 0.00 | 90.30 | 90.30 |
| 936 | 120 | 63.00 | 753.00 | 0.00 | 90.42 | 90.42 |
| 937 | 120 | 63.00 | 754.00 | 0.00 | 90.54 | 90.54 |
| 938 | 120 | 63.00 | 755.00 | 0.00 | 90.66 | 90.66 |
| 939 | 120 | 63.00 | 756.00 | 0.00 | 90.78 | 90.78 |
| 940 | 120 | 63.00 | 757.00 | 0.00 | 90.90 | 90.90 |
| 941 | 120 | 63.00 | 758.00 | 0.00 | 91.02 | 91.02 |
| 942 | 120 | 63.00 | 759.00 | 0.00 | 91.14 | 91.14 |
| 943 | 120 | 63.00 | 760.00 | 0.00 | 91.26 | 91.26 |
| 944 | 120 | 63.00 | 761.00 | 0.00 | 91.38 | 91.38 |
| 945 | 120 | 63.00 | 762.00 | 0.00 | 91.50 | 91.50 |
| 946 | 120 | 63.00 | 763.00 | 0.00 | 91.62 | 91.62 |
| 947 | 120 | 63.00 | 764.00 | 0.00 | 91.74 | 91.74 |
| 948 | 120 | 63.00 | 765.00 | 0.00 | 91.86 | 91.86 |
| 949 | 120 | 63.00 | 766.00 | 0.00 | 91.98 | 91.98 |
| 950 | 120 | 63.00 | 767.00 | 0.00 | 92.10 | 92.10 |
| 951 | 120 | 63.00 | 768.00 | 0.00 | 92.22 | 92.22 |
| 952 | 120 | 63.00 | 769.00 | 0.00 | 92.34 | 92.34 |
| 953 | 120 | 63.00 | 770.00 | 0.00 | 92.46 | 92.46 |
| 954 | 120 | 63.00 | 771.00 | 0.00 | 92.58 | 92.58 |
| 955 | 120 | 63.00 | 772.00 | 0.00 | 92.70 | 92.70 |
| 956 | 120 | 63.00 | 773.00 | 0.00 | 92.82 | 92.82 |
| 957 | 120 | 63.00 | 774.00 | 0.00 | 92.94 | 92.94 |
| 958 | 120 | 63.00 | 775.00 | 0.00 | 93.06 | 93.06 |
| 959 | 120 | 63.00 | 776.00 | 0.00 | 93.18 | 93.18 |
| 960 | 120 | 63.00 | 777.00 | 0.00 | 93.30 | 93.30 |
| 961 | 120 | 63.00 | 778.00 | 0.00 | 93.42 | 93.42 |
| 962 | 120 | 63.00 | 779.00 | 0.00 | 93.48 | 93.48 |

If the employee's gross pay is over £962, go to page 178.

# Monthly table for standard rate NICs for use from 6 April 2020 to 5 April 2021

**Table letter M**

Use this table for employees who are under the age of 21.

Do not use this table for:

- any tax year other than 2020 to 2021
- employees who are aged 21 or over and under State Pension age (go to Table letter A)
- married women or widows who have the right to pay reduced rate employee's NICs (go to Table letter B in booklet CA41)
- employees who are State Pension age or over (go to Table letter C in booklet CA41)
- employees on an ApprovedApprenticeship scheme under the age of 25 (go to Table letter H)
- employees who are aged 21 or over, for whom you hold form CA2700 (go to Table letter J)
- employees who are under the age of 21, for whom you hold form CA2700 (go to Table letter Z)

**Completing form RT11, 'Deductions working sheet' or substitute**

1 Enter 'M' in the NICs Category Letter column on form RT11.

2 Copy the figures in columns 1a – 1e of the table to columns 1a – 1e on the line next to the tax month in which the employee is paid, on form RT11.

If the employee's total earnings fall between the LEL and the UEL/UST/AUST and the exact gross pay is not shown in the table, use the next smaller figure shown. If the employee's total earnings exceed the UEL/UST/AUST, go to page 163.

The figures in the left-hand column of each table show steps between the LEL and the UEL/UST/AUST. The NICs liability for each step, with the exception of the LEL, ST, PT, UEL, UST and AUST, is worked out at the mid-point of the steps so you and your employee may pay slightly more or less than if you used the exact percentage method.

| Employee's earnings up to and including the UEL | Earnings at the LEL (where earnings are equal to or exceed the LEL) | Earnings above the LEL, up to and including the PT | Earnings above the PT, up to and including the UEL | Employer's NICs due on all earnings above the ST | Employee's NICs due on all earnings above the PT | Total of employee's and employer's NICs (for information only) |
|---|---|---|---|---|---|---|
| | 1a | 1b | 1c | 1d | 1e | |
| £ | £ | £ p | £ p | £ p | £ p | £ p |
| Up to and including £519.99 | No NICs liability, make no entries on form RT11 | | | | | |
| 520 | 520 | 0.00 | 0.00 | 0.00 | 0.00 | 0.00 |
| 524 | 520 | 4.00 | 0.00 | 0.00 | 0.00 | 0.00 |
| 528 | 520 | 8.00 | 0.00 | 0.00 | 0.00 | 0.00 |
| 532 | 520 | 12.00 | 0.00 | 0.00 | 0.00 | 0.00 |
| 536 | 520 | 16.00 | 0.00 | 0.00 | 0.00 | 0.00 |
| 540 | 520 | 20.00 | 0.00 | 0.00 | 0.00 | 0.00 |
| 544 | 520 | 24.00 | 0.00 | 0.00 | 0.00 | 0.00 |
| 548 | 520 | 28.00 | 0.00 | 0.00 | 0.00 | 0.00 |
| 552 | 520 | 32.00 | 0.00 | 0.00 | 0.00 | 0.00 |
| 556 | 520 | 36.00 | 0.00 | 0.00 | 0.00 | 0.00 |
| 560 | 520 | 40.00 | 0.00 | 0.00 | 0.00 | 0.00 |
| 564 | 520 | 44.00 | 0.00 | 0.00 | 0.00 | 0.00 |
| 568 | 520 | 48.00 | 0.00 | 0.00 | 0.00 | 0.00 |
| 572 | 520 | 52.00 | 0.00 | 0.00 | 0.00 | 0.00 |
| 576 | 520 | 56.00 | 0.00 | 0.00 | 0.00 | 0.00 |
| 580 | 520 | 60.00 | 0.00 | 0.00 | 0.00 | 0.00 |
| 584 | 520 | 64.00 | 0.00 | 0.00 | 0.00 | 0.00 |
| 588 | 520 | 68.00 | 0.00 | 0.00 | 0.00 | 0.00 |
| 592 | 520 | 72.00 | 0.00 | 0.00 | 0.00 | 0.00 |
| 596 | 520 | 76.00 | 0.00 | 0.00 | 0.00 | 0.00 |
| 600 | 520 | 80.00 | 0.00 | 0.00 | 0.00 | 0.00 |
| 604 | 520 | 84.00 | 0.00 | 0.00 | 0.00 | 0.00 |
| 608 | 520 | 88.00 | 0.00 | 0.00 | 0.00 | 0.00 |
| 612 | 520 | 92.00 | 0.00 | 0.00 | 0.00 | 0.00 |
| 616 | 520 | 96.00 | 0.00 | 0.00 | 0.00 | 0.00 |

Page 126

**Monthly table**

**Table letter M**

| Employee's earnings up to and including the UEL £ | Earnings at the LEL (where earnings are equal to or exceed the LEL) 1a £ | Earnings above the LEL, up to and including the PT 1b £ p | Earnings above the PT, up to and including the UEL 1c £ p | Employer's NICs due on all earnings above the ST 1d £ p | Employee's NICs due on all earnings above the PT 1e £ p | Total of employee's and employer's NICs (for information only) £ p |
|---|---|---|---|---|---|---|
| 620 | 520 | 100.00 | 0.00 | 0.00 | 0.00 | 0.00 |
| 624 | 520 | 104.00 | 0.00 | 0.00 | 0.00 | 0.00 |
| 628 | 520 | 108.00 | 0.00 | 0.00 | 0.00 | 0.00 |
| 632 | 520 | 112.00 | 0.00 | 0.00 | 0.00 | 0.00 |
| 636 | 520 | 116.00 | 0.00 | 0.00 | 0.00 | 0.00 |
| 640 | 520 | 120.00 | 0.00 | 0.00 | 0.00 | 0.00 |
| 644 | 520 | 124.00 | 0.00 | 0.00 | 0.00 | 0.00 |
| 648 | 520 | 128.00 | 0.00 | 0.00 | 0.00 | 0.00 |
| 652 | 520 | 132.00 | 0.00 | 0.00 | 0.00 | 0.00 |
| 656 | 520 | 136.00 | 0.00 | 0.00 | 0.00 | 0.00 |
| 660 | 520 | 140.00 | 0.00 | 0.00 | 0.00 | 0.00 |
| 664 | 520 | 144.00 | 0.00 | 0.00 | 0.00 | 0.00 |
| 668 | 520 | 148.00 | 0.00 | 0.00 | 0.00 | 0.00 |
| 672 | 520 | 152.00 | 0.00 | 0.00 | 0.00 | 0.00 |
| 676 | 520 | 156.00 | 0.00 | 0.00 | 0.00 | 0.00 |
| 680 | 520 | 160.00 | 0.00 | 0.00 | 0.00 | 0.00 |
| 684 | 520 | 164.00 | 0.00 | 0.00 | 0.00 | 0.00 |
| 688 | 520 | 168.00 | 0.00 | 0.00 | 0.00 | 0.00 |
| 692 | 520 | 172.00 | 0.00 | 0.00 | 0.00 | 0.00 |
| 696 | 520 | 176.00 | 0.00 | 0.00 | 0.00 | 0.00 |
| 700 | 520 | 180.00 | 0.00 | 0.00 | 0.00 | 0.00 |
| 704 | 520 | 184.00 | 0.00 | 0.00 | 0.00 | 0.00 |
| 708 | 520 | 188.00 | 0.00 | 0.00 | 0.00 | 0.00 |
| 712 | 520 | 192.00 | 0.00 | 0.00 | 0.00 | 0.00 |
| 716 | 520 | 196.00 | 0.00 | 0.00 | 0.00 | 0.00 |
| 720 | 520 | 200.00 | 0.00 | 0.00 | 0.00 | 0.00 |
| 724 | 520 | 204.00 | 0.00 | 0.00 | 0.00 | 0.00 |
| 728 | 520 | 208.00 | 0.00 | 0.00 | 0.00 | 0.00 |
| 732 | 520 | 212.00 | 0.00 | 0.00 | 0.00 | 0.00 |
| 736 | 520 | 216.00 | 0.00 | 0.00 | 0.00 | 0.00 |
| 740 | 520 | 220.00 | 0.00 | 0.00 | 0.00 | 0.00 |
| 744 | 520 | 224.00 | 0.00 | 0.00 | 0.00 | 0.00 |
| 748 | 520 | 228.00 | 0.00 | 0.00 | 0.00 | 0.00 |
| 752 | 520 | 232.00 | 0.00 | 0.00 | 0.00 | 0.00 |
| 756 | 520 | 236.00 | 0.00 | 0.00 | 0.00 | 0.00 |
| 760 | 520 | 240.00 | 0.00 | 0.00 | 0.00 | 0.00 |
| 764 | 520 | 244.00 | 0.00 | 0.00 | 0.00 | 0.00 |
| 768 | 520 | 248.00 | 0.00 | 0.00 | 0.00 | 0.00 |
| 772 | 520 | 252.00 | 0.00 | 0.00 | 0.00 | 0.00 |
| 776 | 520 | 256.00 | 0.00 | 0.00 | 0.00 | 0.00 |
| 780 | 520 | 260.00 | 0.00 | 0.00 | 0.00 | 0.00 |
| 784 | 520 | 264.00 | 0.00 | 0.00 | 0.00 | 0.00 |
| 788 | 520 | 268.00 | 0.00 | 0.00 | 0.00 | 0.00 |
| 792 | 520 | 272.00 | 0.00 | 0.00 | 0.00 | 0.00 |
| 796 | 520 | 272.00 | 4.00 | 0.00 | 0.72 | 0.72 |
| 800 | 520 | 272.00 | 8.00 | 0.00 | 1.20 | 1.20 |
| 804 | 520 | 272.00 | 12.00 | 0.00 | 1.68 | 1.68 |
| 808 | 520 | 272.00 | 16.00 | 0.00 | 2.16 | 2.16 |
| 812 | 520 | 272.00 | 20.00 | 0.00 | 2.64 | 2.64 |
| 816 | 520 | 272.00 | 24.00 | 0.00 | 3.12 | 3.12 |
| 820 | 520 | 272.00 | 28.00 | 0.00 | 3.60 | 3.60 |
| 824 | 520 | 272.00 | 32.00 | 0.00 | 4.08 | 4.08 |
| 828 | 520 | 272.00 | 36.00 | 0.00 | 4.56 | 4.56 |
| 832 | 520 | 272.00 | 40.00 | 0.00 | 5.04 | 5.04 |
| 836 | 520 | 272.00 | 44.00 | 0.00 | 5.52 | 5.52 |

## Table letter M

**Monthly table**

| Employee's earnings up to and including the UEL | Earnings at the LEL (where earnings are equal to or exceed the LEL) | Earnings above the LEL, up to and including the PT | Earnings above the PT, up to and including the UEL | Employer's NICs due on all earnings above the ST | Employee's NICs due on all earnings above the PT | Total of employee's and employer's NICs (for information only) |
|---|---|---|---|---|---|---|
| | 1a | 1b | 1c | 1d | 1e | |
| £ | £ | £ p | £ p | £ p | £ p | £ p |
| 840 | 520 | 272.00 | 48.00 | 0.00 | 6.00 | 6.00 |
| 844 | 520 | 272.00 | 52.00 | 0.00 | 6.48 | 6.48 |
| 848 | 520 | 272.00 | 56.00 | 0.00 | 6.96 | 6.96 |
| 852 | 520 | 272.00 | 60.00 | 0.00 | 7.44 | 7.44 |
| 856 | 520 | 272.00 | 64.00 | 0.00 | 7.92 | 7.92 |
| 860 | 520 | 272.00 | 68.00 | 0.00 | 8.40 | 8.40 |
| 864 | 520 | 272.00 | 72.00 | 0.00 | 8.88 | 8.88 |
| 868 | 520 | 272.00 | 76.00 | 0.00 | 9.36 | 9.36 |
| 872 | 520 | 272.00 | 80.00 | 0.00 | 9.84 | 9.84 |
| 876 | 520 | 272.00 | 84.00 | 0.00 | 10.32 | 10.32 |
| 880 | 520 | 272.00 | 88.00 | 0.00 | 10.80 | 10.80 |
| 884 | 520 | 272.00 | 92.00 | 0.00 | 11.28 | 11.28 |
| 888 | 520 | 272.00 | 96.00 | 0.00 | 11.76 | 11.76 |
| 892 | 520 | 272.00 | 100.00 | 0.00 | 12.24 | 12.24 |
| 896 | 520 | 272.00 | 104.00 | 0.00 | 12.72 | 12.72 |
| 900 | 520 | 272.00 | 108.00 | 0.00 | 13.20 | 13.20 |
| 904 | 520 | 272.00 | 112.00 | 0.00 | 13.68 | 13.68 |
| 908 | 520 | 272.00 | 116.00 | 0.00 | 14.16 | 14.16 |
| 912 | 520 | 272.00 | 120.00 | 0.00 | 14.64 | 14.64 |
| 916 | 520 | 272.00 | 124.00 | 0.00 | 15.12 | 15.12 |
| 920 | 520 | 272.00 | 128.00 | 0.00 | 15.60 | 15.60 |
| 924 | 520 | 272.00 | 132.00 | 0.00 | 16.08 | 16.08 |
| 928 | 520 | 272.00 | 136.00 | 0.00 | 16.56 | 16.56 |
| 932 | 520 | 272.00 | 140.00 | 0.00 | 17.04 | 17.04 |
| 936 | 520 | 272.00 | 144.00 | 0.00 | 17.52 | 17.52 |
| 940 | 520 | 272.00 | 148.00 | 0.00 | 18.00 | 18.00 |
| 944 | 520 | 272.00 | 152.00 | 0.00 | 18.48 | 18.48 |
| 948 | 520 | 272.00 | 156.00 | 0.00 | 18.96 | 18.96 |
| 952 | 520 | 272.00 | 160.00 | 0.00 | 19.44 | 19.44 |
| 956 | 520 | 272.00 | 164.00 | 0.00 | 19.92 | 19.92 |
| 960 | 520 | 272.00 | 168.00 | 0.00 | 20.40 | 20.40 |
| 964 | 520 | 272.00 | 172.00 | 0.00 | 20.88 | 20.88 |
| 968 | 520 | 272.00 | 176.00 | 0.00 | 21.36 | 21.36 |
| 972 | 520 | 272.00 | 180.00 | 0.00 | 21.84 | 21.84 |
| 976 | 520 | 272.00 | 184.00 | 0.00 | 22.32 | 22.32 |
| 980 | 520 | 272.00 | 188.00 | 0.00 | 22.80 | 22.80 |
| 984 | 520 | 272.00 | 192.00 | 0.00 | 23.28 | 23.28 |
| 988 | 520 | 272.00 | 196.00 | 0.00 | 23.76 | 23.76 |
| 992 | 520 | 272.00 | 200.00 | 0.00 | 24.24 | 24.24 |
| 996 | 520 | 272.00 | 204.00 | 0.00 | 24.72 | 24.72 |
| 1000 | 520 | 272.00 | 208.00 | 0.00 | 25.20 | 25.20 |
| 1004 | 520 | 272.00 | 212.00 | 0.00 | 25.68 | 25.68 |
| 1008 | 520 | 272.00 | 216.00 | 0.00 | 26.16 | 26.16 |
| 1012 | 520 | 272.00 | 220.00 | 0.00 | 26.64 | 26.64 |
| 1016 | 520 | 272.00 | 224.00 | 0.00 | 27.12 | 27.12 |
| 1020 | 520 | 272.00 | 228.00 | 0.00 | 27.60 | 27.60 |
| 1024 | 520 | 272.00 | 232.00 | 0.00 | 28.08 | 28.08 |
| 1028 | 520 | 272.00 | 236.00 | 0.00 | 28.56 | 28.56 |
| 1032 | 520 | 272.00 | 240.00 | 0.00 | 29.04 | 29.04 |
| 1036 | 520 | 272.00 | 244.00 | 0.00 | 29.52 | 29.52 |
| 1040 | 520 | 272.00 | 248.00 | 0.00 | 30.00 | 30.00 |
| 1044 | 520 | 272.00 | 252.00 | 0.00 | 30.48 | 30.48 |
| 1048 | 520 | 272.00 | 256.00 | 0.00 | 30.96 | 30.96 |
| 1052 | 520 | 272.00 | 260.00 | 0.00 | 31.44 | 31.44 |
| 1056 | 520 | 272.00 | 264.00 | 0.00 | 31.92 | 31.92 |

**Monthly table**

**Table letter M**

| Employee's earnings up to and including the UEL | Earnings at the LEL (where earnings are equal to or exceed the LEL) 1a | Earnings above the LEL, up to and including the PT 1b | Earnings above the PT, up to and including the UEL 1c | Employer's NICs due on all earnings above the ST 1d | Employee's NICs due on all earnings above the PT 1e | Total of employee's and employer's NICs (for information only) |
|---|---|---|---|---|---|---|
| £ | £ | £ p | £ p | £ p | £ p | £ p |
| 1060 | 520 | 272.00 | 268.00 | 0.00 | 32.40 | 32.40 |
| 1064 | 520 | 272.00 | 272.00 | 0.00 | 32.88 | 32.88 |
| 1068 | 520 | 272.00 | 276.00 | 0.00 | 33.36 | 33.36 |
| 1072 | 520 | 272.00 | 280.00 | 0.00 | 33.84 | 33.84 |
| 1076 | 520 | 272.00 | 284.00 | 0.00 | 34.32 | 34.32 |
| 1080 | 520 | 272.00 | 288.00 | 0.00 | 34.80 | 34.80 |
| 1084 | 520 | 272.00 | 292.00 | 0.00 | 35.28 | 35.28 |
| 1088 | 520 | 272.00 | 296.00 | 0.00 | 35.76 | 35.76 |
| 1092 | 520 | 272.00 | 300.00 | 0.00 | 36.24 | 36.24 |
| 1096 | 520 | 272.00 | 304.00 | 0.00 | 36.72 | 36.72 |
| 1100 | 520 | 272.00 | 308.00 | 0.00 | 37.20 | 37.20 |
| 1104 | 520 | 272.00 | 312.00 | 0.00 | 37.68 | 37.68 |
| 1108 | 520 | 272.00 | 316.00 | 0.00 | 38.16 | 38.16 |
| 1112 | 520 | 272.00 | 320.00 | 0.00 | 38.64 | 38.64 |
| 1116 | 520 | 272.00 | 324.00 | 0.00 | 39.12 | 39.12 |
| 1120 | 520 | 272.00 | 328.00 | 0.00 | 39.60 | 39.60 |
| 1124 | 520 | 272.00 | 332.00 | 0.00 | 40.08 | 40.08 |
| 1128 | 520 | 272.00 | 336.00 | 0.00 | 40.56 | 40.56 |
| 1132 | 520 | 272.00 | 340.00 | 0.00 | 41.04 | 41.04 |
| 1136 | 520 | 272.00 | 344.00 | 0.00 | 41.52 | 41.52 |
| 1140 | 520 | 272.00 | 348.00 | 0.00 | 42.00 | 42.00 |
| 1144 | 520 | 272.00 | 352.00 | 0.00 | 42.48 | 42.48 |
| 1148 | 520 | 272.00 | 356.00 | 0.00 | 42.96 | 42.96 |
| 1152 | 520 | 272.00 | 360.00 | 0.00 | 43.44 | 43.44 |
| 1156 | 520 | 272.00 | 364.00 | 0.00 | 43.92 | 43.92 |
| 1160 | 520 | 272.00 | 368.00 | 0.00 | 44.40 | 44.40 |
| 1164 | 520 | 272.00 | 372.00 | 0.00 | 44.88 | 44.88 |
| 1168 | 520 | 272.00 | 376.00 | 0.00 | 45.36 | 45.36 |
| 1172 | 520 | 272.00 | 380.00 | 0.00 | 45.84 | 45.84 |
| 1176 | 520 | 272.00 | 384.00 | 0.00 | 46.32 | 46.32 |
| 1180 | 520 | 272.00 | 388.00 | 0.00 | 46.80 | 46.80 |
| 1184 | 520 | 272.00 | 392.00 | 0.00 | 47.28 | 47.28 |
| 1188 | 520 | 272.00 | 396.00 | 0.00 | 47.76 | 47.76 |
| 1192 | 520 | 272.00 | 400.00 | 0.00 | 48.24 | 48.24 |
| 1196 | 520 | 272.00 | 404.00 | 0.00 | 48.72 | 48.72 |
| 1200 | 520 | 272.00 | 408.00 | 0.00 | 49.20 | 49.20 |
| 1204 | 520 | 272.00 | 412.00 | 0.00 | 49.68 | 49.68 |
| 1208 | 520 | 272.00 | 416.00 | 0.00 | 50.16 | 50.16 |
| 1212 | 520 | 272.00 | 420.00 | 0.00 | 50.64 | 50.64 |
| 1216 | 520 | 272.00 | 424.00 | 0.00 | 51.12 | 51.12 |
| 1220 | 520 | 272.00 | 428.00 | 0.00 | 51.60 | 51.60 |
| 1224 | 520 | 272.00 | 432.00 | 0.00 | 52.08 | 52.08 |
| 1228 | 520 | 272.00 | 436.00 | 0.00 | 52.56 | 52.56 |
| 1232 | 520 | 272.00 | 440.00 | 0.00 | 53.04 | 53.04 |
| 1236 | 520 | 272.00 | 444.00 | 0.00 | 53.52 | 53.52 |
| 1240 | 520 | 272.00 | 448.00 | 0.00 | 54.00 | 54.00 |
| 1244 | 520 | 272.00 | 452.00 | 0.00 | 54.48 | 54.48 |
| 1248 | 520 | 272.00 | 456.00 | 0.00 | 54.96 | 54.96 |
| 1252 | 520 | 272.00 | 460.00 | 0.00 | 55.44 | 55.44 |
| 1256 | 520 | 272.00 | 464.00 | 0.00 | 55.92 | 55.92 |
| 1260 | 520 | 272.00 | 468.00 | 0.00 | 56.40 | 56.40 |
| 1264 | 520 | 272.00 | 472.00 | 0.00 | 56.88 | 56.88 |
| 1268 | 520 | 272.00 | 476.00 | 0.00 | 57.36 | 57.36 |
| 1272 | 520 | 272.00 | 480.00 | 0.00 | 57.84 | 57.84 |
| 1276 | 520 | 272.00 | 484.00 | 0.00 | 58.32 | 58.32 |

## Table letter M                                                                      Monthly table

| Employee's earnings up to and including the UEL | Earnings at the LEL (where earnings are equal to or exceed the LEL) | Earnings above the LEL, up to and including the PT | Earnings above the PT, up to and including the UEL | Employer's NICs due on all earnings above the ST | Employee's NICs due on all earnings above the PT | Total of employee's and employer's NICs (for information only) |
|---|---|---|---|---|---|---|
| | 1a | 1b | 1c | 1d | 1e | |
| £ | £ | £ p | £ p | £ p | £ p | £ p |
| 1280 | 520 | 272.00 | 488.00 | 0.00 | 58.80 | 58.80 |
| 1284 | 520 | 272.00 | 492.00 | 0.00 | 59.28 | 59.28 |
| 1288 | 520 | 272.00 | 496.00 | 0.00 | 59.76 | 59.76 |
| 1292 | 520 | 272.00 | 500.00 | 0.00 | 60.24 | 60.24 |
| 1296 | 520 | 272.00 | 504.00 | 0.00 | 60.72 | 60.72 |
| 1300 | 520 | 272.00 | 508.00 | 0.00 | 61.20 | 61.20 |
| 1304 | 520 | 272.00 | 512.00 | 0.00 | 61.68 | 61.68 |
| 1308 | 520 | 272.00 | 516.00 | 0.00 | 62.16 | 62.16 |
| 1312 | 520 | 272.00 | 520.00 | 0.00 | 62.64 | 62.64 |
| 1316 | 520 | 272.00 | 524.00 | 0.00 | 63.12 | 63.12 |
| 1320 | 520 | 272.00 | 528.00 | 0.00 | 63.60 | 63.60 |
| 1324 | 520 | 272.00 | 532.00 | 0.00 | 64.08 | 64.08 |
| 1328 | 520 | 272.00 | 536.00 | 0.00 | 64.56 | 64.56 |
| 1332 | 520 | 272.00 | 540.00 | 0.00 | 65.04 | 65.04 |
| 1336 | 520 | 272.00 | 544.00 | 0.00 | 65.52 | 65.52 |
| 1340 | 520 | 272.00 | 548.00 | 0.00 | 66.00 | 66.00 |
| 1344 | 520 | 272.00 | 552.00 | 0.00 | 66.48 | 66.48 |
| 1348 | 520 | 272.00 | 556.00 | 0.00 | 66.96 | 66.96 |
| 1352 | 520 | 272.00 | 560.00 | 0.00 | 67.44 | 67.44 |
| 1356 | 520 | 272.00 | 564.00 | 0.00 | 67.92 | 67.92 |
| 1360 | 520 | 272.00 | 568.00 | 0.00 | 68.40 | 68.40 |
| 1364 | 520 | 272.00 | 572.00 | 0.00 | 68.88 | 68.88 |
| 1368 | 520 | 272.00 | 576.00 | 0.00 | 69.36 | 69.36 |
| 1372 | 520 | 272.00 | 580.00 | 0.00 | 69.84 | 69.84 |
| 1376 | 520 | 272.00 | 584.00 | 0.00 | 70.32 | 70.32 |
| 1380 | 520 | 272.00 | 588.00 | 0.00 | 70.80 | 70.80 |
| 1384 | 520 | 272.00 | 592.00 | 0.00 | 71.28 | 71.28 |
| 1388 | 520 | 272.00 | 596.00 | 0.00 | 71.76 | 71.76 |
| 1392 | 520 | 272.00 | 600.00 | 0.00 | 72.24 | 72.24 |
| 1396 | 520 | 272.00 | 604.00 | 0.00 | 72.72 | 72.72 |
| 1400 | 520 | 272.00 | 608.00 | 0.00 | 73.20 | 73.20 |
| 1404 | 520 | 272.00 | 612.00 | 0.00 | 73.68 | 73.68 |
| 1408 | 520 | 272.00 | 616.00 | 0.00 | 74.16 | 74.16 |
| 1412 | 520 | 272.00 | 620.00 | 0.00 | 74.64 | 74.64 |
| 1416 | 520 | 272.00 | 624.00 | 0.00 | 75.12 | 75.12 |
| 1420 | 520 | 272.00 | 628.00 | 0.00 | 75.60 | 75.60 |
| 1424 | 520 | 272.00 | 632.00 | 0.00 | 76.08 | 76.08 |
| 1428 | 520 | 272.00 | 636.00 | 0.00 | 76.56 | 76.56 |
| 1432 | 520 | 272.00 | 640.00 | 0.00 | 77.04 | 77.04 |
| 1436 | 520 | 272.00 | 644.00 | 0.00 | 77.52 | 77.52 |
| 1440 | 520 | 272.00 | 648.00 | 0.00 | 78.00 | 78.00 |
| 1444 | 520 | 272.00 | 652.00 | 0.00 | 78.48 | 78.48 |
| 1448 | 520 | 272.00 | 656.00 | 0.00 | 78.96 | 78.96 |
| 1452 | 520 | 272.00 | 660.00 | 0.00 | 79.44 | 79.44 |
| 1456 | 520 | 272.00 | 664.00 | 0.00 | 79.92 | 79.92 |
| 1460 | 520 | 272.00 | 668.00 | 0.00 | 80.40 | 80.40 |
| 1464 | 520 | 272.00 | 672.00 | 0.00 | 80.88 | 80.88 |
| 1468 | 520 | 272.00 | 676.00 | 0.00 | 81.36 | 81.36 |
| 1472 | 520 | 272.00 | 680.00 | 0.00 | 81.84 | 81.84 |
| 1476 | 520 | 272.00 | 684.00 | 0.00 | 82.32 | 82.32 |
| 1480 | 520 | 272.00 | 688.00 | 0.00 | 82.80 | 82.80 |
| 1484 | 520 | 272.00 | 692.00 | 0.00 | 83.28 | 83.28 |
| 1488 | 520 | 272.00 | 696.00 | 0.00 | 83.76 | 83.76 |
| 1492 | 520 | 272.00 | 700.00 | 0.00 | 84.24 | 84.24 |
| 1496 | 520 | 272.00 | 704.00 | 0.00 | 84.72 | 84.72 |

**Monthly table**                                                                                     **Table letter M**

| Employee's earnings up to and including the UEL | Earnings at the LEL (where earnings are equal to or exceed the LEL) 1a | Earnings above the LEL, up to and including the PT 1b | Earnings above the PT, up to and including the UEL 1c | Employer's NICs due on all earnings above the ST 1d | Employee's NICs due on all earnings above the PT 1e | Total of employee's and employer's NICs (for information only) |
|---|---|---|---|---|---|---|
| £ | £ | £ p | £ p | £ p | £ p | £ p |
| 1500 | 520 | 272.00 | 708.00 | 0.00 | 85.20 | 85.20 |
| 1504 | 520 | 272.00 | 712.00 | 0.00 | 85.68 | 85.68 |
| 1508 | 520 | 272.00 | 716.00 | 0.00 | 86.16 | 86.16 |
| 1512 | 520 | 272.00 | 720.00 | 0.00 | 86.64 | 86.64 |
| 1516 | 520 | 272.00 | 724.00 | 0.00 | 87.12 | 87.12 |
| 1520 | 520 | 272.00 | 728.00 | 0.00 | 87.60 | 87.60 |
| 1524 | 520 | 272.00 | 732.00 | 0.00 | 88.08 | 88.08 |
| 1528 | 520 | 272.00 | 736.00 | 0.00 | 88.56 | 88.56 |
| 1532 | 520 | 272.00 | 740.00 | 0.00 | 89.04 | 89.04 |
| 1536 | 520 | 272.00 | 744.00 | 0.00 | 89.52 | 89.52 |
| 1540 | 520 | 272.00 | 748.00 | 0.00 | 90.00 | 90.00 |
| 1544 | 520 | 272.00 | 752.00 | 0.00 | 90.48 | 90.48 |
| 1548 | 520 | 272.00 | 756.00 | 0.00 | 90.96 | 90.96 |
| 1552 | 520 | 272.00 | 760.00 | 0.00 | 91.44 | 91.44 |
| 1556 | 520 | 272.00 | 764.00 | 0.00 | 91.92 | 91.92 |
| 1560 | 520 | 272.00 | 768.00 | 0.00 | 92.40 | 92.40 |
| 1564 | 520 | 272.00 | 772.00 | 0.00 | 92.88 | 92.88 |
| 1568 | 520 | 272.00 | 776.00 | 0.00 | 93.36 | 93.36 |
| 1572 | 520 | 272.00 | 780.00 | 0.00 | 93.84 | 93.84 |
| 1576 | 520 | 272.00 | 784.00 | 0.00 | 94.32 | 94.32 |
| 1580 | 520 | 272.00 | 788.00 | 0.00 | 94.80 | 94.80 |
| 1584 | 520 | 272.00 | 792.00 | 0.00 | 95.28 | 95.28 |
| 1588 | 520 | 272.00 | 796.00 | 0.00 | 95.76 | 95.76 |
| 1592 | 520 | 272.00 | 800.00 | 0.00 | 96.24 | 96.24 |
| 1596 | 520 | 272.00 | 804.00 | 0.00 | 96.72 | 96.72 |
| 1600 | 520 | 272.00 | 808.00 | 0.00 | 97.20 | 97.20 |
| 1604 | 520 | 272.00 | 812.00 | 0.00 | 97.68 | 97.68 |
| 1608 | 520 | 272.00 | 816.00 | 0.00 | 98.16 | 98.16 |
| 1612 | 520 | 272.00 | 820.00 | 0.00 | 98.64 | 98.64 |
| 1616 | 520 | 272.00 | 824.00 | 0.00 | 99.12 | 99.12 |
| 1620 | 520 | 272.00 | 828.00 | 0.00 | 99.60 | 99.60 |
| 1624 | 520 | 272.00 | 832.00 | 0.00 | 100.08 | 100.08 |
| 1628 | 520 | 272.00 | 836.00 | 0.00 | 100.56 | 100.56 |
| 1632 | 520 | 272.00 | 840.00 | 0.00 | 101.04 | 101.04 |
| 1636 | 520 | 272.00 | 844.00 | 0.00 | 101.52 | 101.52 |
| 1640 | 520 | 272.00 | 848.00 | 0.00 | 102.00 | 102.00 |
| 1644 | 520 | 272.00 | 852.00 | 0.00 | 102.48 | 102.48 |
| 1648 | 520 | 272.00 | 856.00 | 0.00 | 102.96 | 102.96 |
| 1652 | 520 | 272.00 | 860.00 | 0.00 | 103.44 | 103.44 |
| 1656 | 520 | 272.00 | 864.00 | 0.00 | 103.92 | 103.92 |
| 1660 | 520 | 272.00 | 868.00 | 0.00 | 104.40 | 104.40 |
| 1664 | 520 | 272.00 | 872.00 | 0.00 | 104.88 | 104.88 |
| 1668 | 520 | 272.00 | 876.00 | 0.00 | 105.36 | 105.36 |
| 1672 | 520 | 272.00 | 880.00 | 0.00 | 105.84 | 105.84 |
| 1676 | 520 | 272.00 | 884.00 | 0.00 | 106.32 | 106.32 |
| 1680 | 520 | 272.00 | 888.00 | 0.00 | 106.80 | 106.80 |
| 1684 | 520 | 272.00 | 892.00 | 0.00 | 107.28 | 107.28 |
| 1688 | 520 | 272.00 | 896.00 | 0.00 | 107.76 | 107.76 |
| 1692 | 520 | 272.00 | 900.00 | 0.00 | 108.24 | 108.24 |
| 1696 | 520 | 272.00 | 904.00 | 0.00 | 108.72 | 108.72 |
| 1700 | 520 | 272.00 | 908.00 | 0.00 | 109.20 | 109.20 |
| 1704 | 520 | 272.00 | 912.00 | 0.00 | 109.68 | 109.68 |
| 1708 | 520 | 272.00 | 916.00 | 0.00 | 110.16 | 110.16 |
| 1712 | 520 | 272.00 | 920.00 | 0.00 | 110.64 | 110.64 |
| 1716 | 520 | 272.00 | 924.00 | 0.00 | 111.12 | 111.12 |

# Table letter M

**Monthly table**

| Employee's earnings up to and including the UEL | Earnings at the LEL (where earnings are equal to or exceed the LEL) | Earnings above the LEL, up to and including the PT | Earnings above the PT, up to and including the UEL | Employer's NICs due on all earnings above the ST | Employee's NICs due on all earnings above the PT | Total of employee's and employer's NICs (for information only) |
|---|---|---|---|---|---|---|
| | 1a | 1b | 1c | 1d | 1e | |
| £ | £ | £ p | £ p | £ p | £ p | £ p |
| 1720 | 520 | 272.00 | 928.00 | 0.00 | 111.60 | 111.60 |
| 1724 | 520 | 272.00 | 932.00 | 0.00 | 112.08 | 112.08 |
| 1728 | 520 | 272.00 | 936.00 | 0.00 | 112.56 | 112.56 |
| 1732 | 520 | 272.00 | 940.00 | 0.00 | 113.04 | 113.04 |
| 1736 | 520 | 272.00 | 944.00 | 0.00 | 113.52 | 113.52 |
| 1740 | 520 | 272.00 | 948.00 | 0.00 | 114.00 | 114.00 |
| 1744 | 520 | 272.00 | 952.00 | 0.00 | 114.48 | 114.48 |
| 1748 | 520 | 272.00 | 956.00 | 0.00 | 114.96 | 114.96 |
| 1752 | 520 | 272.00 | 960.00 | 0.00 | 115.44 | 115.44 |
| 1756 | 520 | 272.00 | 964.00 | 0.00 | 115.92 | 115.92 |
| 1760 | 520 | 272.00 | 968.00 | 0.00 | 116.40 | 116.40 |
| 1764 | 520 | 272.00 | 972.00 | 0.00 | 116.88 | 116.88 |
| 1768 | 520 | 272.00 | 976.00 | 0.00 | 117.36 | 117.36 |
| 1772 | 520 | 272.00 | 980.00 | 0.00 | 117.84 | 117.84 |
| 1776 | 520 | 272.00 | 984.00 | 0.00 | 118.32 | 118.32 |
| 1780 | 520 | 272.00 | 988.00 | 0.00 | 118.80 | 118.80 |
| 1784 | 520 | 272.00 | 992.00 | 0.00 | 119.28 | 119.28 |
| 1788 | 520 | 272.00 | 996.00 | 0.00 | 119.76 | 119.76 |
| 1792 | 520 | 272.00 | 1000.00 | 0.00 | 120.24 | 120.24 |
| 1796 | 520 | 272.00 | 1004.00 | 0.00 | 120.72 | 120.72 |
| 1800 | 520 | 272.00 | 1008.00 | 0.00 | 121.20 | 121.20 |
| 1804 | 520 | 272.00 | 1012.00 | 0.00 | 121.68 | 121.68 |
| 1808 | 520 | 272.00 | 1016.00 | 0.00 | 122.16 | 122.16 |
| 1812 | 520 | 272.00 | 1020.00 | 0.00 | 122.64 | 122.64 |
| 1816 | 520 | 272.00 | 1024.00 | 0.00 | 123.12 | 123.12 |
| 1820 | 520 | 272.00 | 1028.00 | 0.00 | 123.60 | 123.60 |
| 1824 | 520 | 272.00 | 1032.00 | 0.00 | 124.08 | 124.08 |
| 1828 | 520 | 272.00 | 1036.00 | 0.00 | 124.56 | 124.56 |
| 1832 | 520 | 272.00 | 1040.00 | 0.00 | 125.04 | 125.04 |
| 1836 | 520 | 272.00 | 1044.00 | 0.00 | 125.52 | 125.52 |
| 1840 | 520 | 272.00 | 1048.00 | 0.00 | 126.00 | 126.00 |
| 1844 | 520 | 272.00 | 1052.00 | 0.00 | 126.48 | 126.48 |
| 1848 | 520 | 272.00 | 1056.00 | 0.00 | 126.96 | 126.96 |
| 1852 | 520 | 272.00 | 1060.00 | 0.00 | 127.44 | 127.44 |
| 1856 | 520 | 272.00 | 1064.00 | 0.00 | 127.92 | 127.92 |
| 1860 | 520 | 272.00 | 1068.00 | 0.00 | 128.40 | 128.40 |
| 1864 | 520 | 272.00 | 1072.00 | 0.00 | 128.88 | 128.88 |
| 1868 | 520 | 272.00 | 1076.00 | 0.00 | 129.36 | 129.36 |
| 1872 | 520 | 272.00 | 1080.00 | 0.00 | 129.84 | 129.84 |
| 1876 | 520 | 272.00 | 1084.00 | 0.00 | 130.32 | 130.32 |
| 1880 | 520 | 272.00 | 1088.00 | 0.00 | 130.80 | 130.80 |
| 1884 | 520 | 272.00 | 1092.00 | 0.00 | 131.28 | 131.28 |
| 1888 | 520 | 272.00 | 1096.00 | 0.00 | 131.76 | 131.76 |
| 1892 | 520 | 272.00 | 1100.00 | 0.00 | 132.24 | 132.24 |
| 1896 | 520 | 272.00 | 1104.00 | 0.00 | 132.72 | 132.72 |
| 1900 | 520 | 272.00 | 1108.00 | 0.00 | 133.20 | 133.20 |
| 1904 | 520 | 272.00 | 1112.00 | 0.00 | 133.68 | 133.68 |
| 1908 | 520 | 272.00 | 1116.00 | 0.00 | 134.16 | 134.16 |
| 1912 | 520 | 272.00 | 1120.00 | 0.00 | 134.64 | 134.64 |
| 1916 | 520 | 272.00 | 1124.00 | 0.00 | 135.12 | 135.12 |
| 1920 | 520 | 272.00 | 1128.00 | 0.00 | 135.60 | 135.60 |
| 1924 | 520 | 272.00 | 1132.00 | 0.00 | 136.08 | 136.08 |
| 1928 | 520 | 272.00 | 1136.00 | 0.00 | 136.56 | 136.56 |
| 1932 | 520 | 272.00 | 1140.00 | 0.00 | 137.04 | 137.04 |
| 1936 | 520 | 272.00 | 1144.00 | 0.00 | 137.52 | 137.52 |

# Monthly table

**Table letter M**

| Employee's earnings up to and including the UEL | Earnings at the LEL (where earnings are equal to or exceed the LEL) 1a | Earnings above the LEL, up to and including the PT 1b | Earnings above the PT, up to and including the UEL 1c | Employer's NICs due on all earnings above the ST 1d | Employee's NICs due on all earnings above the PT 1e | Total of employee's and employer's NICs (for information only) |
|---|---|---|---|---|---|---|
| £ | £ | £ p | £ p | £ p | £ p | £ p |
| 1940 | 520 | 272.00 | 1148.00 | 0.00 | 138.00 | 138.00 |
| 1944 | 520 | 272.00 | 1152.00 | 0.00 | 138.48 | 138.48 |
| 1948 | 520 | 272.00 | 1156.00 | 0.00 | 138.96 | 138.96 |
| 1952 | 520 | 272.00 | 1160.00 | 0.00 | 139.44 | 139.44 |
| 1956 | 520 | 272.00 | 1164.00 | 0.00 | 139.92 | 139.92 |
| 1960 | 520 | 272.00 | 1168.00 | 0.00 | 140.40 | 140.40 |
| 1964 | 520 | 272.00 | 1172.00 | 0.00 | 140.88 | 140.88 |
| 1968 | 520 | 272.00 | 1176.00 | 0.00 | 141.36 | 141.36 |
| 1972 | 520 | 272.00 | 1180.00 | 0.00 | 141.84 | 141.84 |
| 1976 | 520 | 272.00 | 1184.00 | 0.00 | 142.32 | 142.32 |
| 1980 | 520 | 272.00 | 1188.00 | 0.00 | 142.80 | 142.80 |
| 1984 | 520 | 272.00 | 1192.00 | 0.00 | 143.28 | 143.28 |
| 1988 | 520 | 272.00 | 1196.00 | 0.00 | 143.76 | 143.76 |
| 1992 | 520 | 272.00 | 1200.00 | 0.00 | 144.24 | 144.24 |
| 1996 | 520 | 272.00 | 1204.00 | 0.00 | 144.72 | 144.72 |
| 2000 | 520 | 272.00 | 1208.00 | 0.00 | 145.20 | 145.20 |
| 2004 | 520 | 272.00 | 1212.00 | 0.00 | 145.68 | 145.68 |
| 2008 | 520 | 272.00 | 1216.00 | 0.00 | 146.16 | 146.16 |
| 2012 | 520 | 272.00 | 1220.00 | 0.00 | 146.64 | 146.64 |
| 2016 | 520 | 272.00 | 1224.00 | 0.00 | 147.12 | 147.12 |
| 2020 | 520 | 272.00 | 1228.00 | 0.00 | 147.60 | 147.60 |
| 2024 | 520 | 272.00 | 1232.00 | 0.00 | 148.08 | 148.08 |
| 2028 | 520 | 272.00 | 1236.00 | 0.00 | 148.56 | 148.56 |
| 2032 | 520 | 272.00 | 1240.00 | 0.00 | 149.04 | 149.04 |
| 2036 | 520 | 272.00 | 1244.00 | 0.00 | 149.52 | 149.52 |
| 2040 | 520 | 272.00 | 1248.00 | 0.00 | 150.00 | 150.00 |
| 2044 | 520 | 272.00 | 1252.00 | 0.00 | 150.48 | 150.48 |
| 2048 | 520 | 272.00 | 1256.00 | 0.00 | 150.96 | 150.96 |
| 2052 | 520 | 272.00 | 1260.00 | 0.00 | 151.44 | 151.44 |
| 2056 | 520 | 272.00 | 1264.00 | 0.00 | 151.92 | 151.92 |
| 2060 | 520 | 272.00 | 1268.00 | 0.00 | 152.40 | 152.40 |
| 2064 | 520 | 272.00 | 1272.00 | 0.00 | 152.88 | 152.88 |
| 2068 | 520 | 272.00 | 1276.00 | 0.00 | 153.36 | 153.36 |
| 2072 | 520 | 272.00 | 1280.00 | 0.00 | 153.84 | 153.84 |
| 2076 | 520 | 272.00 | 1284.00 | 0.00 | 154.32 | 154.32 |
| 2080 | 520 | 272.00 | 1288.00 | 0.00 | 154.80 | 154.80 |
| 2084 | 520 | 272.00 | 1292.00 | 0.00 | 155.28 | 155.28 |
| 2088 | 520 | 272.00 | 1296.00 | 0.00 | 155.76 | 155.76 |
| 2092 | 520 | 272.00 | 1300.00 | 0.00 | 156.24 | 156.24 |
| 2096 | 520 | 272.00 | 1304.00 | 0.00 | 156.72 | 156.72 |
| 2100 | 520 | 272.00 | 1308.00 | 0.00 | 157.20 | 157.20 |
| 2104 | 520 | 272.00 | 1312.00 | 0.00 | 157.68 | 157.68 |
| 2108 | 520 | 272.00 | 1316.00 | 0.00 | 158.16 | 158.16 |
| 2112 | 520 | 272.00 | 1320.00 | 0.00 | 158.64 | 158.64 |
| 2116 | 520 | 272.00 | 1324.00 | 0.00 | 159.12 | 159.12 |
| 2120 | 520 | 272.00 | 1328.00 | 0.00 | 159.60 | 159.60 |
| 2124 | 520 | 272.00 | 1332.00 | 0.00 | 160.08 | 160.08 |
| 2128 | 520 | 272.00 | 1336.00 | 0.00 | 160.56 | 160.56 |
| 2132 | 520 | 272.00 | 1340.00 | 0.00 | 161.04 | 161.04 |
| 2136 | 520 | 272.00 | 1344.00 | 0.00 | 161.52 | 161.52 |
| 2140 | 520 | 272.00 | 1348.00 | 0.00 | 162.00 | 162.00 |
| 2144 | 520 | 272.00 | 1352.00 | 0.00 | 162.48 | 162.48 |
| 2148 | 520 | 272.00 | 1356.00 | 0.00 | 162.96 | 162.96 |
| 2152 | 520 | 272.00 | 1360.00 | 0.00 | 163.44 | 163.44 |
| 2156 | 520 | 272.00 | 1364.00 | 0.00 | 163.92 | 163.92 |

## Table letter M

**Monthly table**

| Employee's earnings up to and including the UEL | Earnings at the LEL (where earnings are equal to or exceed the LEL) 1a | Earnings above the LEL, up to and including the PT 1b | Earnings above the PT, up to and including the UEL 1c | Employer's NICs due on all earnings above the ST 1d | Employee's NICs due on all earnings above the PT 1e | Total of employee's and employer's NICs (for information only) |
|---|---|---|---|---|---|---|
| £ | £ | £ p | £ p | £ p | £ p | £ p |
| 2160 | 520 | 272.00 | 1368.00 | 0.00 | 164.40 | 164.40 |
| 2164 | 520 | 272.00 | 1372.00 | 0.00 | 164.88 | 164.88 |
| 2168 | 520 | 272.00 | 1376.00 | 0.00 | 165.36 | 165.36 |
| 2172 | 520 | 272.00 | 1380.00 | 0.00 | 165.84 | 165.84 |
| 2176 | 520 | 272.00 | 1384.00 | 0.00 | 166.32 | 166.32 |
| 2180 | 520 | 272.00 | 1388.00 | 0.00 | 166.80 | 166.80 |
| 2184 | 520 | 272.00 | 1392.00 | 0.00 | 167.28 | 167.28 |
| 2188 | 520 | 272.00 | 1396.00 | 0.00 | 167.76 | 167.76 |
| 2192 | 520 | 272.00 | 1400.00 | 0.00 | 168.24 | 168.24 |
| 2196 | 520 | 272.00 | 1404.00 | 0.00 | 168.72 | 168.72 |
| 2200 | 520 | 272.00 | 1408.00 | 0.00 | 169.20 | 169.20 |
| 2204 | 520 | 272.00 | 1412.00 | 0.00 | 169.68 | 169.68 |
| 2208 | 520 | 272.00 | 1416.00 | 0.00 | 170.16 | 170.16 |
| 2212 | 520 | 272.00 | 1420.00 | 0.00 | 170.64 | 170.64 |
| 2216 | 520 | 272.00 | 1424.00 | 0.00 | 171.12 | 171.12 |
| 2220 | 520 | 272.00 | 1428.00 | 0.00 | 171.60 | 171.60 |
| 2224 | 520 | 272.00 | 1432.00 | 0.00 | 172.08 | 172.08 |
| 2228 | 520 | 272.00 | 1436.00 | 0.00 | 172.56 | 172.56 |
| 2232 | 520 | 272.00 | 1440.00 | 0.00 | 173.04 | 173.04 |
| 2236 | 520 | 272.00 | 1444.00 | 0.00 | 173.52 | 173.52 |
| 2240 | 520 | 272.00 | 1448.00 | 0.00 | 174.00 | 174.00 |
| 2244 | 520 | 272.00 | 1452.00 | 0.00 | 174.48 | 174.48 |
| 2248 | 520 | 272.00 | 1456.00 | 0.00 | 174.96 | 174.96 |
| 2252 | 520 | 272.00 | 1460.00 | 0.00 | 175.44 | 175.44 |
| 2256 | 520 | 272.00 | 1464.00 | 0.00 | 175.92 | 175.92 |
| 2260 | 520 | 272.00 | 1468.00 | 0.00 | 176.40 | 176.40 |
| 2264 | 520 | 272.00 | 1472.00 | 0.00 | 176.88 | 176.88 |
| 2268 | 520 | 272.00 | 1476.00 | 0.00 | 177.36 | 177.36 |
| 2272 | 520 | 272.00 | 1480.00 | 0.00 | 177.84 | 177.84 |
| 2276 | 520 | 272.00 | 1484.00 | 0.00 | 178.32 | 178.32 |
| 2280 | 520 | 272.00 | 1488.00 | 0.00 | 178.80 | 178.80 |
| 2284 | 520 | 272.00 | 1492.00 | 0.00 | 179.28 | 179.28 |
| 2288 | 520 | 272.00 | 1496.00 | 0.00 | 179.76 | 179.76 |
| 2292 | 520 | 272.00 | 1500.00 | 0.00 | 180.24 | 180.24 |
| 2296 | 520 | 272.00 | 1504.00 | 0.00 | 180.72 | 180.72 |
| 2300 | 520 | 272.00 | 1508.00 | 0.00 | 181.20 | 181.20 |
| 2304 | 520 | 272.00 | 1512.00 | 0.00 | 181.68 | 181.68 |
| 2308 | 520 | 272.00 | 1516.00 | 0.00 | 182.16 | 182.16 |
| 2312 | 520 | 272.00 | 1520.00 | 0.00 | 182.64 | 182.64 |
| 2316 | 520 | 272.00 | 1524.00 | 0.00 | 183.12 | 183.12 |
| 2320 | 520 | 272.00 | 1528.00 | 0.00 | 183.60 | 183.60 |
| 2324 | 520 | 272.00 | 1532.00 | 0.00 | 184.08 | 184.08 |
| 2328 | 520 | 272.00 | 1536.00 | 0.00 | 184.56 | 184.56 |
| 2332 | 520 | 272.00 | 1540.00 | 0.00 | 185.04 | 185.04 |
| 2336 | 520 | 272.00 | 1544.00 | 0.00 | 185.52 | 185.52 |
| 2340 | 520 | 272.00 | 1548.00 | 0.00 | 186.00 | 186.00 |
| 2344 | 520 | 272.00 | 1552.00 | 0.00 | 186.48 | 186.48 |
| 2348 | 520 | 272.00 | 1556.00 | 0.00 | 186.96 | 186.96 |
| 2352 | 520 | 272.00 | 1560.00 | 0.00 | 187.44 | 187.44 |
| 2356 | 520 | 272.00 | 1564.00 | 0.00 | 187.92 | 187.92 |
| 2360 | 520 | 272.00 | 1568.00 | 0.00 | 188.40 | 188.40 |
| 2364 | 520 | 272.00 | 1572.00 | 0.00 | 188.88 | 188.88 |
| 2368 | 520 | 272.00 | 1576.00 | 0.00 | 189.36 | 189.36 |
| 2372 | 520 | 272.00 | 1580.00 | 0.00 | 189.84 | 189.84 |
| 2376 | 520 | 272.00 | 1584.00 | 0.00 | 190.32 | 190.32 |

## Monthly table

**Table letter M**

| Employee's earnings up to and including the UEL | Earnings at the LEL (where earnings are equal to or exceed the LEL) | Earnings above the LEL, up to and including the PT | Earnings above the PT, up to and including the UEL | Employer's NICs due on all earnings above the ST | Employee's NICs due on all earnings above the PT | Total of employee's and employer's NICs (for information only) |
|---|---|---|---|---|---|---|
| | | 1a | 1b | 1c | 1d | 1e |
| £ | £ | £ p | £ p | £ p | £ p | £ p |
| 2380 | 520 | 272.00 | 1588.00 | 0.00 | 190.80 | 190.80 |
| 2384 | 520 | 272.00 | 1592.00 | 0.00 | 191.28 | 191.28 |
| 2388 | 520 | 272.00 | 1596.00 | 0.00 | 191.76 | 191.76 |
| 2392 | 520 | 272.00 | 1600.00 | 0.00 | 192.24 | 192.24 |
| 2396 | 520 | 272.00 | 1604.00 | 0.00 | 192.72 | 192.72 |
| 2400 | 520 | 272.00 | 1608.00 | 0.00 | 193.20 | 193.20 |
| 2404 | 520 | 272.00 | 1612.00 | 0.00 | 193.68 | 193.68 |
| 2408 | 520 | 272.00 | 1616.00 | 0.00 | 194.16 | 194.16 |
| 2412 | 520 | 272.00 | 1620.00 | 0.00 | 194.64 | 194.64 |
| 2416 | 520 | 272.00 | 1624.00 | 0.00 | 195.12 | 195.12 |
| 2420 | 520 | 272.00 | 1628.00 | 0.00 | 195.60 | 195.60 |
| 2424 | 520 | 272.00 | 1632.00 | 0.00 | 196.08 | 196.08 |
| 2428 | 520 | 272.00 | 1636.00 | 0.00 | 196.56 | 196.56 |
| 2432 | 520 | 272.00 | 1640.00 | 0.00 | 197.04 | 197.04 |
| 2436 | 520 | 272.00 | 1644.00 | 0.00 | 197.52 | 197.52 |
| 2440 | 520 | 272.00 | 1648.00 | 0.00 | 198.00 | 198.00 |
| 2444 | 520 | 272.00 | 1652.00 | 0.00 | 198.48 | 198.48 |
| 2448 | 520 | 272.00 | 1656.00 | 0.00 | 198.96 | 198.96 |
| 2452 | 520 | 272.00 | 1660.00 | 0.00 | 199.44 | 199.44 |
| 2456 | 520 | 272.00 | 1664.00 | 0.00 | 199.92 | 199.92 |
| 2460 | 520 | 272.00 | 1668.00 | 0.00 | 200.40 | 200.40 |
| 2464 | 520 | 272.00 | 1672.00 | 0.00 | 200.88 | 200.88 |
| 2468 | 520 | 272.00 | 1676.00 | 0.00 | 201.36 | 201.36 |
| 2472 | 520 | 272.00 | 1680.00 | 0.00 | 201.84 | 201.84 |
| 2476 | 520 | 272.00 | 1684.00 | 0.00 | 202.32 | 202.32 |
| 2480 | 520 | 272.00 | 1688.00 | 0.00 | 202.80 | 202.80 |
| 2484 | 520 | 272.00 | 1692.00 | 0.00 | 203.28 | 203.28 |
| 2488 | 520 | 272.00 | 1696.00 | 0.00 | 203.76 | 203.76 |
| 2492 | 520 | 272.00 | 1700.00 | 0.00 | 204.24 | 204.24 |
| 2496 | 520 | 272.00 | 1704.00 | 0.00 | 204.72 | 204.72 |
| 2500 | 520 | 272.00 | 1708.00 | 0.00 | 205.20 | 205.20 |
| 2504 | 520 | 272.00 | 1712.00 | 0.00 | 205.68 | 205.68 |
| 2508 | 520 | 272.00 | 1716.00 | 0.00 | 206.16 | 206.16 |
| 2512 | 520 | 272.00 | 1720.00 | 0.00 | 206.64 | 206.64 |
| 2516 | 520 | 272.00 | 1724.00 | 0.00 | 207.12 | 207.12 |
| 2520 | 520 | 272.00 | 1728.00 | 0.00 | 207.60 | 207.60 |
| 2524 | 520 | 272.00 | 1732.00 | 0.00 | 208.08 | 208.08 |
| 2528 | 520 | 272.00 | 1736.00 | 0.00 | 208.56 | 208.56 |
| 2532 | 520 | 272.00 | 1740.00 | 0.00 | 209.04 | 209.04 |
| 2536 | 520 | 272.00 | 1744.00 | 0.00 | 209.52 | 209.52 |
| 2540 | 520 | 272.00 | 1748.00 | 0.00 | 210.00 | 210.00 |
| 2544 | 520 | 272.00 | 1752.00 | 0.00 | 210.48 | 210.48 |
| 2548 | 520 | 272.00 | 1756.00 | 0.00 | 210.96 | 210.96 |
| 2552 | 520 | 272.00 | 1760.00 | 0.00 | 211.44 | 211.44 |
| 2556 | 520 | 272.00 | 1764.00 | 0.00 | 211.92 | 211.92 |
| 2560 | 520 | 272.00 | 1768.00 | 0.00 | 212.40 | 212.40 |
| 2564 | 520 | 272.00 | 1772.00 | 0.00 | 212.88 | 212.88 |
| 2568 | 520 | 272.00 | 1776.00 | 0.00 | 213.36 | 213.36 |
| 2572 | 520 | 272.00 | 1780.00 | 0.00 | 213.84 | 213.84 |
| 2576 | 520 | 272.00 | 1784.00 | 0.00 | 214.32 | 214.32 |
| 2580 | 520 | 272.00 | 1788.00 | 0.00 | 214.80 | 214.80 |
| 2584 | 520 | 272.00 | 1792.00 | 0.00 | 215.28 | 215.28 |
| 2588 | 520 | 272.00 | 1796.00 | 0.00 | 215.76 | 215.76 |
| 2592 | 520 | 272.00 | 1800.00 | 0.00 | 216.24 | 216.24 |
| 2596 | 520 | 272.00 | 1804.00 | 0.00 | 216.72 | 216.72 |

## Table letter M

## Monthly table

| Employee's earnings up to and including the UEL | Earnings at the LEL (where earnings are equal to or exceed the LEL) | Earnings above the LEL, up to and including the PT | Earnings above the PT, up to and including the UEL | Employer's NICs due on all earnings above the ST | Employee's NICs due on all earnings above the PT | Total of employee's and employer's NICs (for information only) |
|---|---|---|---|---|---|---|
| | 1a | 1b | 1c | 1d | 1e | |
| £ | £ | £ p | £ p | £ p | £ p | £ p |
| 2600 | 520 | 272.00 | 1808.00 | 0.00 | 217.20 | 217.20 |
| 2604 | 520 | 272.00 | 1812.00 | 0.00 | 217.68 | 217.68 |
| 2608 | 520 | 272.00 | 1816.00 | 0.00 | 218.16 | 218.16 |
| 2612 | 520 | 272.00 | 1820.00 | 0.00 | 218.64 | 218.64 |
| 2616 | 520 | 272.00 | 1824.00 | 0.00 | 219.12 | 219.12 |
| 2620 | 520 | 272.00 | 1828.00 | 0.00 | 219.60 | 219.60 |
| 2624 | 520 | 272.00 | 1832.00 | 0.00 | 220.08 | 220.08 |
| 2628 | 520 | 272.00 | 1836.00 | 0.00 | 220.56 | 220.56 |
| 2632 | 520 | 272.00 | 1840.00 | 0.00 | 221.04 | 221.04 |
| 2636 | 520 | 272.00 | 1844.00 | 0.00 | 221.52 | 221.52 |
| 2640 | 520 | 272.00 | 1848.00 | 0.00 | 222.00 | 222.00 |
| 2644 | 520 | 272.00 | 1852.00 | 0.00 | 222.48 | 222.48 |
| 2648 | 520 | 272.00 | 1856.00 | 0.00 | 222.96 | 222.96 |
| 2652 | 520 | 272.00 | 1860.00 | 0.00 | 223.44 | 223.44 |
| 2656 | 520 | 272.00 | 1864.00 | 0.00 | 223.92 | 223.92 |
| 2660 | 520 | 272.00 | 1868.00 | 0.00 | 224.40 | 224.40 |
| 2664 | 520 | 272.00 | 1872.00 | 0.00 | 224.88 | 224.88 |
| 2668 | 520 | 272.00 | 1876.00 | 0.00 | 225.36 | 225.36 |
| 2672 | 520 | 272.00 | 1880.00 | 0.00 | 225.84 | 225.84 |
| 2676 | 520 | 272.00 | 1884.00 | 0.00 | 226.32 | 226.32 |
| 2680 | 520 | 272.00 | 1888.00 | 0.00 | 226.80 | 226.80 |
| 2684 | 520 | 272.00 | 1892.00 | 0.00 | 227.28 | 227.28 |
| 2688 | 520 | 272.00 | 1896.00 | 0.00 | 227.76 | 227.76 |
| 2692 | 520 | 272.00 | 1900.00 | 0.00 | 228.24 | 228.24 |
| 2696 | 520 | 272.00 | 1904.00 | 0.00 | 228.72 | 228.72 |
| 2700 | 520 | 272.00 | 1908.00 | 0.00 | 229.20 | 229.20 |
| 2704 | 520 | 272.00 | 1912.00 | 0.00 | 229.68 | 229.68 |
| 2708 | 520 | 272.00 | 1916.00 | 0.00 | 230.16 | 230.16 |
| 2712 | 520 | 272.00 | 1920.00 | 0.00 | 230.64 | 230.64 |
| 2716 | 520 | 272.00 | 1924.00 | 0.00 | 231.12 | 231.12 |
| 2720 | 520 | 272.00 | 1928.00 | 0.00 | 231.60 | 231.60 |
| 2724 | 520 | 272.00 | 1932.00 | 0.00 | 232.08 | 232.08 |
| 2728 | 520 | 272.00 | 1936.00 | 0.00 | 232.56 | 232.56 |
| 2732 | 520 | 272.00 | 1940.00 | 0.00 | 233.04 | 233.04 |
| 2736 | 520 | 272.00 | 1944.00 | 0.00 | 233.52 | 233.52 |
| 2740 | 520 | 272.00 | 1948.00 | 0.00 | 234.00 | 234.00 |
| 2744 | 520 | 272.00 | 1952.00 | 0.00 | 234.48 | 234.48 |
| 2748 | 520 | 272.00 | 1956.00 | 0.00 | 234.96 | 234.96 |
| 2752 | 520 | 272.00 | 1960.00 | 0.00 | 235.44 | 235.44 |
| 2756 | 520 | 272.00 | 1964.00 | 0.00 | 235.92 | 235.92 |
| 2760 | 520 | 272.00 | 1968.00 | 0.00 | 236.40 | 236.40 |
| 2764 | 520 | 272.00 | 1972.00 | 0.00 | 236.88 | 236.88 |
| 2768 | 520 | 272.00 | 1976.00 | 0.00 | 237.36 | 237.36 |
| 2772 | 520 | 272.00 | 1980.00 | 0.00 | 237.84 | 237.84 |
| 2776 | 520 | 272.00 | 1984.00 | 0.00 | 238.32 | 238.32 |
| 2780 | 520 | 272.00 | 1988.00 | 0.00 | 238.80 | 238.80 |
| 2784 | 520 | 272.00 | 1992.00 | 0.00 | 239.28 | 239.28 |
| 2788 | 520 | 272.00 | 1996.00 | 0.00 | 239.76 | 239.76 |
| 2792 | 520 | 272.00 | 2000.00 | 0.00 | 240.24 | 240.24 |
| 2796 | 520 | 272.00 | 2004.00 | 0.00 | 240.72 | 240.72 |
| 2800 | 520 | 272.00 | 2008.00 | 0.00 | 241.20 | 241.20 |
| 2804 | 520 | 272.00 | 2012.00 | 0.00 | 241.68 | 241.68 |
| 2808 | 520 | 272.00 | 2016.00 | 0.00 | 242.16 | 242.16 |
| 2812 | 520 | 272.00 | 2020.00 | 0.00 | 242.64 | 242.64 |
| 2816 | 520 | 272.00 | 2024.00 | 0.00 | 243.12 | 243.12 |

## Monthly table

## Table letter M

| Employee's earnings up to and including the UEL | Earnings at the LEL (where earnings are equal to or exceed the LEL) | Earnings above the LEL, up to and including the PT | Earnings above the PT, up to and including the UEL | Employer's NICs due on all earnings above the ST | Employee's NICs due on all earnings above the PT | Total of employee's and employer's NICs (for information only) |
|---|---|---|---|---|---|---|
| | | 1a | 1b | 1c | 1d | 1e |
| £ | £ | £ p | £ p | £ p | £ p | £ p |
| 2820 | 520 | 272.00 | 2028.00 | 0.00 | 243.60 | 243.60 |
| 2824 | 520 | 272.00 | 2032.00 | 0.00 | 244.08 | 244.08 |
| 2828 | 520 | 272.00 | 2036.00 | 0.00 | 244.56 | 244.56 |
| 2832 | 520 | 272.00 | 2040.00 | 0.00 | 245.04 | 245.04 |
| 2836 | 520 | 272.00 | 2044.00 | 0.00 | 245.52 | 245.52 |
| 2840 | 520 | 272.00 | 2048.00 | 0.00 | 246.00 | 246.00 |
| 2844 | 520 | 272.00 | 2052.00 | 0.00 | 246.48 | 246.48 |
| 2848 | 520 | 272.00 | 2056.00 | 0.00 | 246.96 | 246.96 |
| 2852 | 520 | 272.00 | 2060.00 | 0.00 | 247.44 | 247.44 |
| 2856 | 520 | 272.00 | 2064.00 | 0.00 | 247.92 | 247.92 |
| 2860 | 520 | 272.00 | 2068.00 | 0.00 | 248.40 | 248.40 |
| 2864 | 520 | 272.00 | 2072.00 | 0.00 | 248.88 | 248.88 |
| 2868 | 520 | 272.00 | 2076.00 | 0.00 | 249.36 | 249.36 |
| 2872 | 520 | 272.00 | 2080.00 | 0.00 | 249.84 | 249.84 |
| 2876 | 520 | 272.00 | 2084.00 | 0.00 | 250.32 | 250.32 |
| 2880 | 520 | 272.00 | 2088.00 | 0.00 | 250.80 | 250.80 |
| 2884 | 520 | 272.00 | 2092.00 | 0.00 | 251.28 | 251.28 |
| 2888 | 520 | 272.00 | 2096.00 | 0.00 | 251.76 | 251.76 |
| 2892 | 520 | 272.00 | 2100.00 | 0.00 | 252.24 | 252.24 |
| 2896 | 520 | 272.00 | 2104.00 | 0.00 | 252.72 | 252.72 |
| 2900 | 520 | 272.00 | 2108.00 | 0.00 | 253.20 | 253.20 |
| 2904 | 520 | 272.00 | 2112.00 | 0.00 | 253.68 | 253.68 |
| 2908 | 520 | 272.00 | 2116.00 | 0.00 | 254.16 | 254.16 |
| 2912 | 520 | 272.00 | 2120.00 | 0.00 | 254.64 | 254.64 |
| 2916 | 520 | 272.00 | 2124.00 | 0.00 | 255.12 | 255.12 |
| 2920 | 520 | 272.00 | 2128.00 | 0.00 | 255.60 | 255.60 |
| 2924 | 520 | 272.00 | 2132.00 | 0.00 | 256.08 | 256.08 |
| 2928 | 520 | 272.00 | 2136.00 | 0.00 | 256.56 | 256.56 |
| 2932 | 520 | 272.00 | 2140.00 | 0.00 | 257.04 | 257.04 |
| 2936 | 520 | 272.00 | 2144.00 | 0.00 | 257.52 | 257.52 |
| 2940 | 520 | 272.00 | 2148.00 | 0.00 | 258.00 | 258.00 |
| 2944 | 520 | 272.00 | 2152.00 | 0.00 | 258.48 | 258.48 |
| 2948 | 520 | 272.00 | 2156.00 | 0.00 | 258.96 | 258.96 |
| 2952 | 520 | 272.00 | 2160.00 | 0.00 | 259.44 | 259.44 |
| 2956 | 520 | 272.00 | 2164.00 | 0.00 | 259.92 | 259.92 |
| 2960 | 520 | 272.00 | 2168.00 | 0.00 | 260.40 | 260.40 |
| 2964 | 520 | 272.00 | 2172.00 | 0.00 | 260.88 | 260.88 |
| 2968 | 520 | 272.00 | 2176.00 | 0.00 | 261.36 | 261.36 |
| 2972 | 520 | 272.00 | 2180.00 | 0.00 | 261.84 | 261.84 |
| 2976 | 520 | 272.00 | 2184.00 | 0.00 | 262.32 | 262.32 |
| 2980 | 520 | 272.00 | 2188.00 | 0.00 | 262.80 | 262.80 |
| 2984 | 520 | 272.00 | 2192.00 | 0.00 | 263.28 | 263.28 |
| 2988 | 520 | 272.00 | 2196.00 | 0.00 | 263.76 | 263.76 |
| 2992 | 520 | 272.00 | 2200.00 | 0.00 | 264.24 | 264.24 |
| 2996 | 520 | 272.00 | 2204.00 | 0.00 | 264.72 | 264.72 |
| 3000 | 520 | 272.00 | 2208.00 | 0.00 | 265.20 | 265.20 |
| 3004 | 520 | 272.00 | 2212.00 | 0.00 | 265.68 | 265.68 |
| 3008 | 520 | 272.00 | 2216.00 | 0.00 | 266.16 | 266.16 |
| 3012 | 520 | 272.00 | 2220.00 | 0.00 | 266.64 | 266.64 |
| 3016 | 520 | 272.00 | 2224.00 | 0.00 | 267.12 | 267.12 |
| 3020 | 520 | 272.00 | 2228.00 | 0.00 | 267.60 | 267.60 |
| 3024 | 520 | 272.00 | 2232.00 | 0.00 | 268.08 | 268.08 |
| 3028 | 520 | 272.00 | 2236.00 | 0.00 | 268.56 | 268.56 |
| 3032 | 520 | 272.00 | 2240.00 | 0.00 | 269.04 | 269.04 |
| 3036 | 520 | 272.00 | 2244.00 | 0.00 | 269.52 | 269.52 |

## Table letter M

## Monthly table

| Employee's earnings up to and including the UEL | Earnings at the LEL (where earnings are equal to or exceed the LEL) | Earnings above the LEL, up to and including the PT | Earnings above the PT, up to and including the UEL | Employer's NICs due on all earnings above the ST | Employee's NICs due on all earnings above the PT | Total of employee's and employer's NICs (for information only) |
|---|---|---|---|---|---|---|
| | 1a | 1b | 1c | 1d | 1e | |
| £ | £ | £ p | £ p | £ p | £ p | £ p |
| 3040 | 520 | 272.00 | 2248.00 | 0.00 | 270.00 | 270.00 |
| 3044 | 520 | 272.00 | 2252.00 | 0.00 | 270.48 | 270.48 |
| 3048 | 520 | 272.00 | 2256.00 | 0.00 | 270.96 | 270.96 |
| 3052 | 520 | 272.00 | 2260.00 | 0.00 | 271.44 | 271.44 |
| 3056 | 520 | 272.00 | 2264.00 | 0.00 | 271.92 | 271.92 |
| 3060 | 520 | 272.00 | 2268.00 | 0.00 | 272.40 | 272.40 |
| 3064 | 520 | 272.00 | 2272.00 | 0.00 | 272.88 | 272.88 |
| 3068 | 520 | 272.00 | 2276.00 | 0.00 | 273.36 | 273.36 |
| 3072 | 520 | 272.00 | 2280.00 | 0.00 | 273.84 | 273.84 |
| 3076 | 520 | 272.00 | 2284.00 | 0.00 | 274.32 | 274.32 |
| 3080 | 520 | 272.00 | 2288.00 | 0.00 | 274.80 | 274.80 |
| 3084 | 520 | 272.00 | 2292.00 | 0.00 | 275.28 | 275.28 |
| 3088 | 520 | 272.00 | 2296.00 | 0.00 | 275.76 | 275.76 |
| 3092 | 520 | 272.00 | 2300.00 | 0.00 | 276.24 | 276.24 |
| 3096 | 520 | 272.00 | 2304.00 | 0.00 | 276.72 | 276.72 |
| 3100 | 520 | 272.00 | 2308.00 | 0.00 | 277.20 | 277.20 |
| 3104 | 520 | 272.00 | 2312.00 | 0.00 | 277.68 | 277.68 |
| 3108 | 520 | 272.00 | 2316.00 | 0.00 | 278.16 | 278.16 |
| 3112 | 520 | 272.00 | 2320.00 | 0.00 | 278.64 | 278.64 |
| 3116 | 520 | 272.00 | 2324.00 | 0.00 | 279.12 | 279.12 |
| 3120 | 520 | 272.00 | 2328.00 | 0.00 | 279.60 | 279.60 |
| 3124 | 520 | 272.00 | 2332.00 | 0.00 | 280.08 | 280.08 |
| 3128 | 520 | 272.00 | 2336.00 | 0.00 | 280.56 | 280.56 |
| 3132 | 520 | 272.00 | 2340.00 | 0.00 | 281.04 | 281.04 |
| 3136 | 520 | 272.00 | 2344.00 | 0.00 | 281.52 | 281.52 |
| 3140 | 520 | 272.00 | 2348.00 | 0.00 | 282.00 | 282.00 |
| 3144 | 520 | 272.00 | 2352.00 | 0.00 | 282.48 | 282.48 |
| 3148 | 520 | 272.00 | 2356.00 | 0.00 | 282.96 | 282.96 |
| 3152 | 520 | 272.00 | 2360.00 | 0.00 | 283.44 | 283.44 |
| 3156 | 520 | 272.00 | 2364.00 | 0.00 | 283.92 | 283.92 |
| 3160 | 520 | 272.00 | 2368.00 | 0.00 | 284.40 | 284.40 |
| 3164 | 520 | 272.00 | 2372.00 | 0.00 | 284.88 | 284.88 |
| 3168 | 520 | 272.00 | 2376.00 | 0.00 | 285.36 | 285.36 |
| 3172 | 520 | 272.00 | 2380.00 | 0.00 | 285.84 | 285.84 |
| 3176 | 520 | 272.00 | 2384.00 | 0.00 | 286.32 | 286.32 |
| 3180 | 520 | 272.00 | 2388.00 | 0.00 | 286.80 | 286.80 |
| 3184 | 520 | 272.00 | 2392.00 | 0.00 | 287.28 | 287.28 |
| 3188 | 520 | 272.00 | 2396.00 | 0.00 | 287.76 | 287.76 |
| 3192 | 520 | 272.00 | 2400.00 | 0.00 | 288.24 | 288.24 |
| 3196 | 520 | 272.00 | 2404.00 | 0.00 | 288.72 | 288.72 |
| 3200 | 520 | 272.00 | 2408.00 | 0.00 | 289.20 | 289.20 |
| 3204 | 520 | 272.00 | 2412.00 | 0.00 | 289.68 | 289.68 |
| 3208 | 520 | 272.00 | 2416.00 | 0.00 | 290.16 | 290.16 |
| 3212 | 520 | 272.00 | 2420.00 | 0.00 | 290.64 | 290.64 |
| 3216 | 520 | 272.00 | 2424.00 | 0.00 | 291.12 | 291.12 |
| 3220 | 520 | 272.00 | 2428.00 | 0.00 | 291.60 | 291.60 |
| 3224 | 520 | 272.00 | 2432.00 | 0.00 | 292.08 | 292.08 |
| 3228 | 520 | 272.00 | 2436.00 | 0.00 | 292.56 | 292.56 |
| 3232 | 520 | 272.00 | 2440.00 | 0.00 | 293.04 | 293.04 |
| 3236 | 520 | 272.00 | 2444.00 | 0.00 | 293.52 | 293.52 |
| 3240 | 520 | 272.00 | 2448.00 | 0.00 | 294.00 | 294.00 |
| 3244 | 520 | 272.00 | 2452.00 | 0.00 | 294.48 | 294.48 |
| 3248 | 520 | 272.00 | 2456.00 | 0.00 | 294.96 | 294.96 |
| 3252 | 520 | 272.00 | 2460.00 | 0.00 | 295.44 | 295.44 |
| 3256 | 520 | 272.00 | 2464.00 | 0.00 | 295.92 | 295.92 |

## Monthly table

**Table letter M**

| Employee's earnings up to and including the UEL | Earnings at the LEL (where earnings are equal to or exceed the LEL) 1a | Earnings above the LEL, up to and including the PT 1b | Earnings above the PT, up to and including the UEL 1c | Employer's NICs due on all earnings above the ST 1d | Employee's NICs due on all earnings above the PT 1e | Total of employee's and employer's NICs (for information only) |
|---|---|---|---|---|---|---|
| £ | £ | £ p | £ p | £ p | £ p | £ p |
| 3260 | 520 | 272.00 | 2468.00 | 0.00 | 296.40 | 296.40 |
| 3264 | 520 | 272.00 | 2472.00 | 0.00 | 296.88 | 296.88 |
| 3268 | 520 | 272.00 | 2476.00 | 0.00 | 297.36 | 297.36 |
| 3272 | 520 | 272.00 | 2480.00 | 0.00 | 297.84 | 297.84 |
| 3276 | 520 | 272.00 | 2484.00 | 0.00 | 298.32 | 298.32 |
| 3280 | 520 | 272.00 | 2488.00 | 0.00 | 298.80 | 298.80 |
| 3284 | 520 | 272.00 | 2492.00 | 0.00 | 299.28 | 299.28 |
| 3288 | 520 | 272.00 | 2496.00 | 0.00 | 299.76 | 299.76 |
| 3292 | 520 | 272.00 | 2500.00 | 0.00 | 300.24 | 300.24 |
| 3296 | 520 | 272.00 | 2504.00 | 0.00 | 300.72 | 300.72 |
| 3300 | 520 | 272.00 | 2508.00 | 0.00 | 301.20 | 301.20 |
| 3304 | 520 | 272.00 | 2512.00 | 0.00 | 301.68 | 301.68 |
| 3308 | 520 | 272.00 | 2516.00 | 0.00 | 302.16 | 302.16 |
| 3312 | 520 | 272.00 | 2520.00 | 0.00 | 302.64 | 302.64 |
| 3316 | 520 | 272.00 | 2524.00 | 0.00 | 303.12 | 303.12 |
| 3320 | 520 | 272.00 | 2528.00 | 0.00 | 303.60 | 303.60 |
| 3324 | 520 | 272.00 | 2532.00 | 0.00 | 304.08 | 304.08 |
| 3328 | 520 | 272.00 | 2536.00 | 0.00 | 304.56 | 304.56 |
| 3332 | 520 | 272.00 | 2540.00 | 0.00 | 305.04 | 305.04 |
| 3336 | 520 | 272.00 | 2544.00 | 0.00 | 305.52 | 305.52 |
| 3340 | 520 | 272.00 | 2548.00 | 0.00 | 306.00 | 306.00 |
| 3344 | 520 | 272.00 | 2552.00 | 0.00 | 306.48 | 306.48 |
| 3348 | 520 | 272.00 | 2556.00 | 0.00 | 306.96 | 306.96 |
| 3352 | 520 | 272.00 | 2560.00 | 0.00 | 307.44 | 307.44 |
| 3356 | 520 | 272.00 | 2564.00 | 0.00 | 307.92 | 307.92 |
| 3360 | 520 | 272.00 | 2568.00 | 0.00 | 308.40 | 308.40 |
| 3364 | 520 | 272.00 | 2572.00 | 0.00 | 308.88 | 308.88 |
| 3368 | 520 | 272.00 | 2576.00 | 0.00 | 309.36 | 309.36 |
| 3372 | 520 | 272.00 | 2580.00 | 0.00 | 309.84 | 309.84 |
| 3376 | 520 | 272.00 | 2584.00 | 0.00 | 310.32 | 310.32 |
| 3380 | 520 | 272.00 | 2588.00 | 0.00 | 310.80 | 310.80 |
| 3384 | 520 | 272.00 | 2592.00 | 0.00 | 311.28 | 311.28 |
| 3388 | 520 | 272.00 | 2596.00 | 0.00 | 311.76 | 311.76 |
| 3392 | 520 | 272.00 | 2600.00 | 0.00 | 312.24 | 312.24 |
| 3396 | 520 | 272.00 | 2604.00 | 0.00 | 312.72 | 312.72 |
| 3400 | 520 | 272.00 | 2608.00 | 0.00 | 313.20 | 313.20 |
| 3404 | 520 | 272.00 | 2612.00 | 0.00 | 313.68 | 313.68 |
| 3408 | 520 | 272.00 | 2616.00 | 0.00 | 314.16 | 314.16 |
| 3412 | 520 | 272.00 | 2620.00 | 0.00 | 314.64 | 314.64 |
| 3416 | 520 | 272.00 | 2624.00 | 0.00 | 315.12 | 315.12 |
| 3420 | 520 | 272.00 | 2628.00 | 0.00 | 315.60 | 315.60 |
| 3424 | 520 | 272.00 | 2632.00 | 0.00 | 316.08 | 316.08 |
| 3428 | 520 | 272.00 | 2636.00 | 0.00 | 316.56 | 316.56 |
| 3432 | 520 | 272.00 | 2640.00 | 0.00 | 317.04 | 317.04 |
| 3436 | 520 | 272.00 | 2644.00 | 0.00 | 317.52 | 317.52 |
| 3440 | 520 | 272.00 | 2648.00 | 0.00 | 318.00 | 318.00 |
| 3444 | 520 | 272.00 | 2652.00 | 0.00 | 318.48 | 318.48 |
| 3448 | 520 | 272.00 | 2656.00 | 0.00 | 318.96 | 318.96 |
| 3452 | 520 | 272.00 | 2660.00 | 0.00 | 319.44 | 319.44 |
| 3456 | 520 | 272.00 | 2664.00 | 0.00 | 319.92 | 319.92 |
| 3460 | 520 | 272.00 | 2668.00 | 0.00 | 320.40 | 320.40 |
| 3464 | 520 | 272.00 | 2672.00 | 0.00 | 320.88 | 320.88 |
| 3468 | 520 | 272.00 | 2676.00 | 0.00 | 321.36 | 321.36 |
| 3472 | 520 | 272.00 | 2680.00 | 0.00 | 321.84 | 321.84 |
| 3476 | 520 | 272.00 | 2684.00 | 0.00 | 322.32 | 322.32 |

## Table letter M — Monthly table

| Employee's earnings up to and including the UEL | Earnings at the LEL (where earnings are equal to or exceed the LEL) 1a | Earnings above the LEL, up to and including the PT 1b | Earnings above the PT, up to and including the UEL 1c | Employer's NICs due on all earnings above the ST 1d | Employee's NICs due on all earnings above the PT 1e | Total of employee's and employer's NICs (for information only) |
|---|---|---|---|---|---|---|
| £ | £ | £ p | £ p | £ p | £ p | £ p |
| 3480 | 520 | 272.00 | 2688.00 | 0.00 | 322.80 | 322.80 |
| 3484 | 520 | 272.00 | 2692.00 | 0.00 | 323.28 | 323.28 |
| 3488 | 520 | 272.00 | 2696.00 | 0.00 | 323.76 | 323.76 |
| 3492 | 520 | 272.00 | 2700.00 | 0.00 | 324.24 | 324.24 |
| 3496 | 520 | 272.00 | 2704.00 | 0.00 | 324.72 | 324.72 |
| 3500 | 520 | 272.00 | 2708.00 | 0.00 | 325.20 | 325.20 |
| 3504 | 520 | 272.00 | 2712.00 | 0.00 | 325.68 | 325.68 |
| 3508 | 520 | 272.00 | 2716.00 | 0.00 | 326.16 | 326.16 |
| 3512 | 520 | 272.00 | 2720.00 | 0.00 | 326.64 | 326.64 |
| 3516 | 520 | 272.00 | 2724.00 | 0.00 | 327.12 | 327.12 |
| 3520 | 520 | 272.00 | 2728.00 | 0.00 | 327.60 | 327.60 |
| 3524 | 520 | 272.00 | 2732.00 | 0.00 | 328.08 | 328.08 |
| 3528 | 520 | 272.00 | 2736.00 | 0.00 | 328.56 | 328.56 |
| 3532 | 520 | 272.00 | 2740.00 | 0.00 | 329.04 | 329.04 |
| 3536 | 520 | 272.00 | 2744.00 | 0.00 | 329.52 | 329.52 |
| 3540 | 520 | 272.00 | 2748.00 | 0.00 | 330.00 | 330.00 |
| 3544 | 520 | 272.00 | 2752.00 | 0.00 | 330.48 | 330.48 |
| 3548 | 520 | 272.00 | 2756.00 | 0.00 | 330.96 | 330.96 |
| 3552 | 520 | 272.00 | 2760.00 | 0.00 | 331.44 | 331.44 |
| 3556 | 520 | 272.00 | 2764.00 | 0.00 | 331.92 | 331.92 |
| 3560 | 520 | 272.00 | 2768.00 | 0.00 | 332.40 | 332.40 |
| 3564 | 520 | 272.00 | 2772.00 | 0.00 | 332.88 | 332.88 |
| 3568 | 520 | 272.00 | 2776.00 | 0.00 | 333.36 | 333.36 |
| 3572 | 520 | 272.00 | 2780.00 | 0.00 | 333.84 | 333.84 |
| 3576 | 520 | 272.00 | 2784.00 | 0.00 | 334.32 | 334.32 |
| 3580 | 520 | 272.00 | 2788.00 | 0.00 | 334.80 | 334.80 |
| 3584 | 520 | 272.00 | 2792.00 | 0.00 | 335.28 | 335.28 |
| 3588 | 520 | 272.00 | 2796.00 | 0.00 | 335.76 | 335.76 |
| 3592 | 520 | 272.00 | 2800.00 | 0.00 | 336.24 | 336.24 |
| 3596 | 520 | 272.00 | 2804.00 | 0.00 | 336.72 | 336.72 |
| 3600 | 520 | 272.00 | 2808.00 | 0.00 | 337.20 | 337.20 |
| 3604 | 520 | 272.00 | 2812.00 | 0.00 | 337.68 | 337.68 |
| 3608 | 520 | 272.00 | 2816.00 | 0.00 | 338.16 | 338.16 |
| 3612 | 520 | 272.00 | 2820.00 | 0.00 | 338.64 | 338.64 |
| 3616 | 520 | 272.00 | 2824.00 | 0.00 | 339.12 | 339.12 |
| 3620 | 520 | 272.00 | 2828.00 | 0.00 | 339.60 | 339.60 |
| 3624 | 520 | 272.00 | 2832.00 | 0.00 | 340.08 | 340.08 |
| 3628 | 520 | 272.00 | 2836.00 | 0.00 | 340.56 | 340.56 |
| 3632 | 520 | 272.00 | 2840.00 | 0.00 | 341.04 | 341.04 |
| 3636 | 520 | 272.00 | 2844.00 | 0.00 | 341.52 | 341.52 |
| 3640 | 520 | 272.00 | 2848.00 | 0.00 | 342.00 | 342.00 |
| 3644 | 520 | 272.00 | 2852.00 | 0.00 | 342.48 | 342.48 |
| 3648 | 520 | 272.00 | 2856.00 | 0.00 | 342.96 | 342.96 |
| 3652 | 520 | 272.00 | 2860.00 | 0.00 | 343.44 | 343.44 |
| 3656 | 520 | 272.00 | 2864.00 | 0.00 | 343.92 | 343.92 |
| 3660 | 520 | 272.00 | 2868.00 | 0.00 | 344.40 | 344.40 |
| 3664 | 520 | 272.00 | 2872.00 | 0.00 | 344.88 | 344.88 |
| 3668 | 520 | 272.00 | 2876.00 | 0.00 | 345.36 | 345.36 |
| 3672 | 520 | 272.00 | 2880.00 | 0.00 | 345.84 | 345.84 |
| 3676 | 520 | 272.00 | 2884.00 | 0.00 | 346.32 | 346.32 |
| 3680 | 520 | 272.00 | 2888.00 | 0.00 | 346.80 | 346.80 |
| 3684 | 520 | 272.00 | 2892.00 | 0.00 | 347.28 | 347.28 |
| 3688 | 520 | 272.00 | 2896.00 | 0.00 | 347.76 | 347.76 |
| 3692 | 520 | 272.00 | 2900.00 | 0.00 | 348.24 | 348.24 |
| 3696 | 520 | 272.00 | 2904.00 | 0.00 | 348.72 | 348.72 |

**Monthly table**                                                                    **Table letter M**

| Employee's earnings up to and including the UEL | Earnings at the LEL (where earnings are equal to or exceed the LEL) 1a | Earnings above the LEL, up to and including the PT 1b | Earnings above the PT, up to and including the UEL 1c | Employer's NICs due on all earnings above the ST 1d | Employee's NICs due on all earnings above the PT 1e | Total of employee's and employer's NICs (for information only) |
|---|---|---|---|---|---|---|
| £ | £ | £ p | £ p | £ p | £ p | £ p |
| 3700 | 520 | 272.00 | 2908.00 | 0.00 | 349.20 | 349.20 |
| 3704 | 520 | 272.00 | 2912.00 | 0.00 | 349.68 | 349.68 |
| 3708 | 520 | 272.00 | 2916.00 | 0.00 | 350.16 | 350.16 |
| 3712 | 520 | 272.00 | 2920.00 | 0.00 | 350.64 | 350.64 |
| 3716 | 520 | 272.00 | 2924.00 | 0.00 | 351.12 | 351.12 |
| 3720 | 520 | 272.00 | 2928.00 | 0.00 | 351.60 | 351.60 |
| 3724 | 520 | 272.00 | 2932.00 | 0.00 | 352.08 | 352.08 |
| 3728 | 520 | 272.00 | 2936.00 | 0.00 | 352.56 | 352.56 |
| 3732 | 520 | 272.00 | 2940.00 | 0.00 | 353.04 | 353.04 |
| 3736 | 520 | 272.00 | 2944.00 | 0.00 | 353.52 | 353.52 |
| 3740 | 520 | 272.00 | 2948.00 | 0.00 | 354.00 | 354.00 |
| 3744 | 520 | 272.00 | 2952.00 | 0.00 | 354.48 | 354.48 |
| 3748 | 520 | 272.00 | 2956.00 | 0.00 | 354.96 | 354.96 |
| 3752 | 520 | 272.00 | 2960.00 | 0.00 | 355.44 | 355.44 |
| 3756 | 520 | 272.00 | 2964.00 | 0.00 | 355.92 | 355.92 |
| 3760 | 520 | 272.00 | 2968.00 | 0.00 | 356.40 | 356.40 |
| 3764 | 520 | 272.00 | 2972.00 | 0.00 | 356.88 | 356.88 |
| 3768 | 520 | 272.00 | 2976.00 | 0.00 | 357.36 | 357.36 |
| 3772 | 520 | 272.00 | 2980.00 | 0.00 | 357.84 | 357.84 |
| 3776 | 520 | 272.00 | 2984.00 | 0.00 | 358.32 | 358.32 |
| 3780 | 520 | 272.00 | 2988.00 | 0.00 | 358.80 | 358.80 |
| 3784 | 520 | 272.00 | 2992.00 | 0.00 | 359.28 | 359.28 |
| 3788 | 520 | 272.00 | 2996.00 | 0.00 | 359.76 | 359.76 |
| 3792 | 520 | 272.00 | 3000.00 | 0.00 | 360.24 | 360.24 |
| 3796 | 520 | 272.00 | 3004.00 | 0.00 | 360.72 | 360.72 |
| 3800 | 520 | 272.00 | 3008.00 | 0.00 | 361.20 | 361.20 |
| 3804 | 520 | 272.00 | 3012.00 | 0.00 | 361.68 | 361.68 |
| 3808 | 520 | 272.00 | 3016.00 | 0.00 | 362.16 | 362.16 |
| 3812 | 520 | 272.00 | 3020.00 | 0.00 | 362.64 | 362.64 |
| 3816 | 520 | 272.00 | 3024.00 | 0.00 | 363.12 | 363.12 |
| 3820 | 520 | 272.00 | 3028.00 | 0.00 | 363.60 | 363.60 |
| 3824 | 520 | 272.00 | 3032.00 | 0.00 | 364.08 | 364.08 |
| 3828 | 520 | 272.00 | 3036.00 | 0.00 | 364.56 | 364.56 |
| 3832 | 520 | 272.00 | 3040.00 | 0.00 | 365.04 | 365.04 |
| 3836 | 520 | 272.00 | 3044.00 | 0.00 | 365.52 | 365.52 |
| 3840 | 520 | 272.00 | 3048.00 | 0.00 | 366.00 | 366.00 |
| 3844 | 520 | 272.00 | 3052.00 | 0.00 | 366.48 | 366.48 |
| 3848 | 520 | 272.00 | 3056.00 | 0.00 | 366.96 | 366.96 |
| 3852 | 520 | 272.00 | 3060.00 | 0.00 | 367.44 | 367.44 |
| 3856 | 520 | 272.00 | 3064.00 | 0.00 | 367.92 | 367.92 |
| 3860 | 520 | 272.00 | 3068.00 | 0.00 | 368.40 | 368.40 |
| 3864 | 520 | 272.00 | 3072.00 | 0.00 | 368.88 | 368.88 |
| 3868 | 520 | 272.00 | 3076.00 | 0.00 | 369.36 | 369.36 |
| 3872 | 520 | 272.00 | 3080.00 | 0.00 | 369.84 | 369.84 |
| 3876 | 520 | 272.00 | 3084.00 | 0.00 | 370.32 | 370.32 |
| 3880 | 520 | 272.00 | 3088.00 | 0.00 | 370.80 | 370.80 |
| 3884 | 520 | 272.00 | 3092.00 | 0.00 | 371.28 | 371.28 |
| 3888 | 520 | 272.00 | 3096.00 | 0.00 | 371.76 | 371.76 |
| 3892 | 520 | 272.00 | 3100.00 | 0.00 | 372.24 | 372.24 |
| 3896 | 520 | 272.00 | 3104.00 | 0.00 | 372.72 | 372.72 |
| 3900 | 520 | 272.00 | 3108.00 | 0.00 | 373.20 | 373.20 |
| 3904 | 520 | 272.00 | 3112.00 | 0.00 | 373.68 | 373.68 |
| 3908 | 520 | 272.00 | 3116.00 | 0.00 | 374.16 | 374.16 |
| 3912 | 520 | 272.00 | 3120.00 | 0.00 | 374.64 | 374.64 |
| 3916 | 520 | 272.00 | 3124.00 | 0.00 | 375.12 | 375.12 |

# Table letter M

**Monthly table**

| Employee's earnings up to and including the UEL | Earnings at the LEL (where earnings are equal to or exceed the LEL) 1a | Earnings above the LEL, up to and including the PT 1b | Earnings above the PT, up to and including the UEL 1c | Employer's NICs due on all earnings above the ST 1d | Employee's NICs due on all earnings above the PT 1e | Total of employee's and employer's NICs (for information only) |
|---|---|---|---|---|---|---|
| £ | £ | £ p | £ p | £ p | £ p | £ p |
| 3920 | 520 | 272.00 | 3128.00 | 0.00 | 375.60 | 375.60 |
| 3924 | 520 | 272.00 | 3132.00 | 0.00 | 376.08 | 376.08 |
| 3928 | 520 | 272.00 | 3136.00 | 0.00 | 376.56 | 376.56 |
| 3932 | 520 | 272.00 | 3140.00 | 0.00 | 377.04 | 377.04 |
| 3936 | 520 | 272.00 | 3144.00 | 0.00 | 377.52 | 377.52 |
| 3940 | 520 | 272.00 | 3148.00 | 0.00 | 378.00 | 378.00 |
| 3944 | 520 | 272.00 | 3152.00 | 0.00 | 378.48 | 378.48 |
| 3948 | 520 | 272.00 | 3156.00 | 0.00 | 378.96 | 378.96 |
| 3952 | 520 | 272.00 | 3160.00 | 0.00 | 379.44 | 379.44 |
| 3956 | 520 | 272.00 | 3164.00 | 0.00 | 379.92 | 379.92 |
| 3960 | 520 | 272.00 | 3168.00 | 0.00 | 380.40 | 380.40 |
| 3964 | 520 | 272.00 | 3172.00 | 0.00 | 380.88 | 380.88 |
| 3968 | 520 | 272.00 | 3176.00 | 0.00 | 381.36 | 381.36 |
| 3972 | 520 | 272.00 | 3180.00 | 0.00 | 381.84 | 381.84 |
| 3976 | 520 | 272.00 | 3184.00 | 0.00 | 382.32 | 382.32 |
| 3980 | 520 | 272.00 | 3188.00 | 0.00 | 382.80 | 382.80 |
| 3984 | 520 | 272.00 | 3192.00 | 0.00 | 383.28 | 383.28 |
| 3988 | 520 | 272.00 | 3196.00 | 0.00 | 383.76 | 383.76 |
| 3992 | 520 | 272.00 | 3200.00 | 0.00 | 384.24 | 384.24 |
| 3996 | 520 | 272.00 | 3204.00 | 0.00 | 384.72 | 384.72 |
| 4000 | 520 | 272.00 | 3208.00 | 0.00 | 385.20 | 385.20 |
| 4004 | 520 | 272.00 | 3212.00 | 0.00 | 385.68 | 385.68 |
| 4008 | 520 | 272.00 | 3216.00 | 0.00 | 386.16 | 386.16 |
| 4012 | 520 | 272.00 | 3220.00 | 0.00 | 386.64 | 386.64 |
| 4016 | 520 | 272.00 | 3224.00 | 0.00 | 387.12 | 387.12 |
| 4020 | 520 | 272.00 | 3228.00 | 0.00 | 387.60 | 387.60 |
| 4024 | 520 | 272.00 | 3232.00 | 0.00 | 388.08 | 388.08 |
| 4028 | 520 | 272.00 | 3236.00 | 0.00 | 388.56 | 388.56 |
| 4032 | 520 | 272.00 | 3240.00 | 0.00 | 389.04 | 389.04 |
| 4036 | 520 | 272.00 | 3244.00 | 0.00 | 389.52 | 389.52 |
| 4040 | 520 | 272.00 | 3248.00 | 0.00 | 390.00 | 390.00 |
| 4044 | 520 | 272.00 | 3252.00 | 0.00 | 390.48 | 390.48 |
| 4048 | 520 | 272.00 | 3256.00 | 0.00 | 390.96 | 390.96 |
| 4052 | 520 | 272.00 | 3260.00 | 0.00 | 391.44 | 391.44 |
| 4056 | 520 | 272.00 | 3264.00 | 0.00 | 391.92 | 391.92 |
| 4060 | 520 | 272.00 | 3268.00 | 0.00 | 392.40 | 392.40 |
| 4064 | 520 | 272.00 | 3272.00 | 0.00 | 392.88 | 392.88 |
| 4068 | 520 | 272.00 | 3276.00 | 0.00 | 393.36 | 393.36 |
| 4072 | 520 | 272.00 | 3280.00 | 0.00 | 393.84 | 393.84 |
| 4076 | 520 | 272.00 | 3284.00 | 0.00 | 394.32 | 394.32 |
| 4080 | 520 | 272.00 | 3288.00 | 0.00 | 394.80 | 394.80 |
| 4084 | 520 | 272.00 | 3292.00 | 0.00 | 395.28 | 395.28 |
| 4088 | 520 | 272.00 | 3296.00 | 0.00 | 395.76 | 395.76 |
| 4092 | 520 | 272.00 | 3300.00 | 0.00 | 396.24 | 396.24 |
| 4096 | 520 | 272.00 | 3304.00 | 0.00 | 396.72 | 396.72 |
| 4100 | 520 | 272.00 | 3308.00 | 0.00 | 397.20 | 397.20 |
| 4104 | 520 | 272.00 | 3312.00 | 0.00 | 397.68 | 397.68 |
| 4108 | 520 | 272.00 | 3316.00 | 0.00 | 398.16 | 398.16 |
| 4112 | 520 | 272.00 | 3320.00 | 0.00 | 398.64 | 398.64 |
| 4116 | 520 | 272.00 | 3324.00 | 0.00 | 399.12 | 399.12 |
| 4120 | 520 | 272.00 | 3328.00 | 0.00 | 399.60 | 399.60 |
| 4124 | 520 | 272.00 | 3332.00 | 0.00 | 400.08 | 400.08 |
| 4128 | 520 | 272.00 | 3336.00 | 0.00 | 400.56 | 400.56 |
| 4132 | 520 | 272.00 | 3340.00 | 0.00 | 401.04 | 401.04 |
| 4136 | 520 | 272.00 | 3344.00 | 0.00 | 401.52 | 401.52 |

**Monthly table**

**Table letter M**

| Employee's earnings up to and including the UEL | Earnings at the LEL (where earnings are equal to or exceed the LEL) | Earnings above the LEL, up to and including the PT | Earnings above the PT, up to and including the UEL | Employer's NICs due on all earnings above the ST | Employee's NICs due on all earnings above the PT | Total of employee's and employer's NICs (for information only) |
|---|---|---|---|---|---|---|
| | | 1a | 1b | 1c | 1d | 1e |
| £ | £ | £ p | £ p | £ p | £ p | £ p |
| 4140 | 520 | 272.00 | 3348.00 | 0.00 | 402.00 | 402.00 |
| 4144 | 520 | 272.00 | 3352.00 | 0.00 | 402.48 | 402.48 |
| 4148 | 520 | 272.00 | 3356.00 | 0.00 | 402.96 | 402.96 |
| 4152 | 520 | 272.00 | 3360.00 | 0.00 | 403.44 | 403.44 |
| 4156 | 520 | 272.00 | 3364.00 | 0.00 | 403.92 | 403.92 |
| 4160 | 520 | 272.00 | 3368.00 | 0.00 | 404.40 | 404.40 |
| 4164 | 520 | 272.00 | 3372.00 | 0.00 | 404.82 | 404.82 |
| 4167 | 520 | 272.00 | 3375.00 | 0.00 | 405.00 | 405.00 |

If the employee's gross pay is over £4,167, go to page 178.

## Weekly table for NICs where employee has deferment for use from 6 April 2020 to 5 April 2021

**Table letter Z**

Use this table for employees who are under the age of 21, for whom you hold form CA2700.

Do not use this table for:

- any tax year other than 2020 to 2021
- employees who are aged 21 or over, for whom you hold form CA2700 (go to Table letter J)
- employees who are State Pension age or over (go to Table letter C in booklet CA41)

**Completing form RT11, 'Deductions working sheet' or substitute**

1  Enter 'Z' in the NICs Category Letter column on form RT11.

2  Copy the figures in columns 1a – 1e of the table to columns 1a – 1e on the line next to the tax week in which the employee is paid, on form RT11.

If the employee's total earnings fall between the LEL and the UEL/UST/AUST and the exact gross pay is not shown in the table, use the next smaller figure shown. If the employee's total earnings exceed the UEL/UST/AUST, go to page 163.

The figures in the left-hand column of each table show steps between the LEL and the UEL/UST/AUST. The NICs liability for each step, with the exception of the LEL, ST, PT, UEL, UST and AUST, is worked out at the mid-point of the steps so you and your employee may pay slightly more or less than if you used the exact percentage method.

| Employee's earnings up to and including the UEL | Earnings at the LEL (where earnings are equal to or exceed the LEL) | Earnings above the LEL, up to and including the PT | Earnings above the PT, up to and including the UEL | Employer's NICs due on all earnings above the ST | Employee's NICs due on all earnings above the PT | Total of employee's and employer's NICs (for information only) |
|---|---|---|---|---|---|---|
| | | 1a | 1b | 1c | 1d | 1e |
| £ | £ | £ p | £ p | £ p | £ p | £ p |
| Up to and including £119.99 | | No NICs liability, make no entry on form RT11 | | | | |
| 120 | 120 | 0.00 | 0.00 | 0.00 | 0.00 | 0.00 |
| 121 | 120 | 1.00 | 0.00 | 0.00 | 0.00 | 0.00 |
| 122 | 120 | 2.00 | 0.00 | 0.00 | 0.00 | 0.00 |
| 123 | 120 | 3.00 | 0.00 | 0.00 | 0.00 | 0.00 |
| 124 | 120 | 4.00 | 0.00 | 0.00 | 0.00 | 0.00 |
| 125 | 120 | 5.00 | 0.00 | 0.00 | 0.00 | 0.00 |
| 126 | 120 | 6.00 | 0.00 | 0.00 | 0.00 | 0.00 |
| 127 | 120 | 7.00 | 0.00 | 0.00 | 0.00 | 0.00 |
| 128 | 120 | 8.00 | 0.00 | 0.00 | 0.00 | 0.00 |
| 129 | 120 | 9.00 | 0.00 | 0.00 | 0.00 | 0.00 |
| 130 | 120 | 10.00 | 0.00 | 0.00 | 0.00 | 0.00 |
| 131 | 120 | 11.00 | 0.00 | 0.00 | 0.00 | 0.00 |
| 132 | 120 | 12.00 | 0.00 | 0.00 | 0.00 | 0.00 |
| 133 | 120 | 13.00 | 0.00 | 0.00 | 0.00 | 0.00 |
| 134 | 120 | 14.00 | 0.00 | 0.00 | 0.00 | 0.00 |
| 135 | 120 | 15.00 | 0.00 | 0.00 | 0.00 | 0.00 |
| 136 | 120 | 16.00 | 0.00 | 0.00 | 0.00 | 0.00 |
| 137 | 120 | 17.00 | 0.00 | 0.00 | 0.00 | 0.00 |
| 138 | 120 | 18.00 | 0.00 | 0.00 | 0.00 | 0.00 |
| 139 | 120 | 19.00 | 0.00 | 0.00 | 0.00 | 0.00 |
| 140 | 120 | 20.00 | 0.00 | 0.00 | 0.00 | 0.00 |
| 141 | 120 | 21.00 | 0.00 | 0.00 | 0.00 | 0.00 |
| 142 | 120 | 22.00 | 0.00 | 0.00 | 0.00 | 0.00 |
| 143 | 120 | 23.00 | 0.00 | 0.00 | 0.00 | 0.00 |
| 144 | 120 | 24.00 | 0.00 | 0.00 | 0.00 | 0.00 |

**Weekly table**

| Employee's earnings up to and including the UEL | Earnings at the LEL (where earnings are equal to or exceed the LEL) 1a | Earnings above the LEL, up to and including the PT 1b | Earnings above the PT, up to and including the UEL 1c | Employer's NICs due on all earnings above the ST 1d | Employee's NICs due on all earnings above the PT 1e | Total of employee's and employer's NICs (for information only) |
|---|---|---|---|---|---|---|
| £ | £ | £ p | £ p | £ p | £ p | £ p |
| 145 | 120 | 25.00 | 0.00 | 0.00 | 0.00 | 0.00 |
| 146 | 120 | 26.00 | 0.00 | 0.00 | 0.00 | 0.00 |
| 147 | 120 | 27.00 | 0.00 | 0.00 | 0.00 | 0.00 |
| 148 | 120 | 28.00 | 0.00 | 0.00 | 0.00 | 0.00 |
| 149 | 120 | 29.00 | 0.00 | 0.00 | 0.00 | 0.00 |
| 150 | 120 | 30.00 | 0.00 | 0.00 | 0.00 | 0.00 |
| 151 | 120 | 31.00 | 0.00 | 0.00 | 0.00 | 0.00 |
| 152 | 120 | 32.00 | 0.00 | 0.00 | 0.00 | 0.00 |
| 153 | 120 | 33.00 | 0.00 | 0.00 | 0.00 | 0.00 |
| 154 | 120 | 34.00 | 0.00 | 0.00 | 0.00 | 0.00 |
| 155 | 120 | 35.00 | 0.00 | 0.00 | 0.00 | 0.00 |
| 156 | 120 | 36.00 | 0.00 | 0.00 | 0.00 | 0.00 |
| 157 | 120 | 37.00 | 0.00 | 0.00 | 0.00 | 0.00 |
| 158 | 120 | 38.00 | 0.00 | 0.00 | 0.00 | 0.00 |
| 159 | 120 | 39.00 | 0.00 | 0.00 | 0.00 | 0.00 |
| 160 | 120 | 40.00 | 0.00 | 0.00 | 0.00 | 0.00 |
| 161 | 120 | 41.00 | 0.00 | 0.00 | 0.00 | 0.00 |
| 162 | 120 | 42.00 | 0.00 | 0.00 | 0.00 | 0.00 |
| 163 | 120 | 43.00 | 0.00 | 0.00 | 0.00 | 0.00 |
| 164 | 120 | 44.00 | 0.00 | 0.00 | 0.00 | 0.00 |
| 165 | 120 | 45.00 | 0.00 | 0.00 | 0.00 | 0.00 |
| 166 | 120 | 46.00 | 0.00 | 0.00 | 0.00 | 0.00 |
| 167 | 120 | 47.00 | 0.00 | 0.00 | 0.00 | 0.00 |
| 168 | 120 | 48.00 | 0.00 | 0.00 | 0.00 | 0.00 |
| 169 | 120 | 49.00 | 0.00 | 0.00 | 0.00 | 0.00 |
| 170 | 120 | 50.00 | 0.00 | 0.00 | 0.00 | 0.00 |
| 171 | 120 | 51.00 | 0.00 | 0.00 | 0.00 | 0.00 |
| 172 | 120 | 52.00 | 0.00 | 0.00 | 0.00 | 0.00 |
| 173 | 120 | 53.00 | 0.00 | 0.00 | 0.00 | 0.00 |
| 174 | 120 | 54.00 | 0.00 | 0.00 | 0.00 | 0.00 |
| 175 | 120 | 55.00 | 0.00 | 0.00 | 0.00 | 0.00 |
| 176 | 120 | 56.00 | 0.00 | 0.00 | 0.00 | 0.00 |
| 177 | 120 | 57.00 | 0.00 | 0.00 | 0.00 | 0.00 |
| 178 | 120 | 58.00 | 0.00 | 0.00 | 0.00 | 0.00 |
| 179 | 120 | 59.00 | 0.00 | 0.00 | 0.00 | 0.00 |
| 180 | 120 | 60.00 | 0.00 | 0.00 | 0.00 | 0.00 |
| 181 | 120 | 61.00 | 0.00 | 0.00 | 0.00 | 0.00 |
| 182 | 120 | 62.00 | 0.00 | 0.00 | 0.00 | 0.00 |
| 183 | 120 | 63.00 | 0.00 | 0.00 | 0.00 | 0.00 |
| 184 | 120 | 63.00 | 1.00 | 0.00 | 0.03 | 0.03 |
| 185 | 120 | 63.00 | 2.00 | 0.00 | 0.05 | 0.05 |
| 186 | 120 | 63.00 | 3.00 | 0.00 | 0.07 | 0.07 |
| 187 | 120 | 63.00 | 4.00 | 0.00 | 0.09 | 0.09 |
| 188 | 120 | 63.00 | 5.00 | 0.00 | 0.11 | 0.11 |
| 189 | 120 | 63.00 | 6.00 | 0.00 | 0.13 | 0.13 |
| 190 | 120 | 63.00 | 7.00 | 0.00 | 0.15 | 0.15 |
| 191 | 120 | 63.00 | 8.00 | 0.00 | 0.17 | 0.17 |
| 192 | 120 | 63.00 | 9.00 | 0.00 | 0.19 | 0.19 |
| 193 | 120 | 63.00 | 10.00 | 0.00 | 0.21 | 0.21 |
| 194 | 120 | 63.00 | 11.00 | 0.00 | 0.23 | 0.23 |
| 195 | 120 | 63.00 | 12.00 | 0.00 | 0.25 | 0.25 |
| 196 | 120 | 63.00 | 13.00 | 0.00 | 0.27 | 0.27 |
| 197 | 120 | 63.00 | 14.00 | 0.00 | 0.29 | 0.29 |
| 198 | 120 | 63.00 | 15.00 | 0.00 | 0.31 | 0.31 |
| 199 | 120 | 63.00 | 16.00 | 0.00 | 0.33 | 0.33 |

Page 145

## Table letter Z

**Weekly table**

| Employee's earnings up to and including the UEL | Earnings at the LEL (where earnings are equal to or exceed the LEL) 1a | Earnings above the LEL, up to and including the PT 1b | Earnings above the PT, up to and including the UEL 1c | Employer's NICs due on all earnings above the ST 1d | Employee's NICs due on all earnings above the PT 1e | Total of employee's and employer's NICs (for information only) |
|---|---|---|---|---|---|---|
| £ | £ | £ p | £ p | £ p | £ p | £ p |
| 200 | 120 | 63.00 | 17.00 | 0.00 | 0.35 | 0.35 |
| 201 | 120 | 63.00 | 18.00 | 0.00 | 0.37 | 0.37 |
| 202 | 120 | 63.00 | 19.00 | 0.00 | 0.39 | 0.39 |
| 203 | 120 | 63.00 | 20.00 | 0.00 | 0.41 | 0.41 |
| 204 | 120 | 63.00 | 21.00 | 0.00 | 0.43 | 0.43 |
| 205 | 120 | 63.00 | 22.00 | 0.00 | 0.45 | 0.45 |
| 206 | 120 | 63.00 | 23.00 | 0.00 | 0.47 | 0.47 |
| 207 | 120 | 63.00 | 24.00 | 0.00 | 0.49 | 0.49 |
| 208 | 120 | 63.00 | 25.00 | 0.00 | 0.51 | 0.51 |
| 209 | 120 | 63.00 | 26.00 | 0.00 | 0.53 | 0.53 |
| 210 | 120 | 63.00 | 27.00 | 0.00 | 0.55 | 0.55 |
| 211 | 120 | 63.00 | 28.00 | 0.00 | 0.57 | 0.57 |
| 212 | 120 | 63.00 | 29.00 | 0.00 | 0.59 | 0.59 |
| 213 | 120 | 63.00 | 30.00 | 0.00 | 0.61 | 0.61 |
| 214 | 120 | 63.00 | 31.00 | 0.00 | 0.63 | 0.63 |
| 215 | 120 | 63.00 | 32.00 | 0.00 | 0.65 | 0.65 |
| 216 | 120 | 63.00 | 33.00 | 0.00 | 0.67 | 0.67 |
| 217 | 120 | 63.00 | 34.00 | 0.00 | 0.69 | 0.69 |
| 218 | 120 | 63.00 | 35.00 | 0.00 | 0.71 | 0.71 |
| 219 | 120 | 63.00 | 36.00 | 0.00 | 0.73 | 0.73 |
| 220 | 120 | 63.00 | 37.00 | 0.00 | 0.75 | 0.75 |
| 221 | 120 | 63.00 | 38.00 | 0.00 | 0.77 | 0.77 |
| 222 | 120 | 63.00 | 39.00 | 0.00 | 0.79 | 0.79 |
| 223 | 120 | 63.00 | 40.00 | 0.00 | 0.81 | 0.81 |
| 224 | 120 | 63.00 | 41.00 | 0.00 | 0.83 | 0.83 |
| 225 | 120 | 63.00 | 42.00 | 0.00 | 0.85 | 0.85 |
| 226 | 120 | 63.00 | 43.00 | 0.00 | 0.87 | 0.87 |
| 227 | 120 | 63.00 | 44.00 | 0.00 | 0.89 | 0.89 |
| 228 | 120 | 63.00 | 45.00 | 0.00 | 0.91 | 0.91 |
| 229 | 120 | 63.00 | 46.00 | 0.00 | 0.93 | 0.93 |
| 230 | 120 | 63.00 | 47.00 | 0.00 | 0.95 | 0.95 |
| 231 | 120 | 63.00 | 48.00 | 0.00 | 0.97 | 0.97 |
| 232 | 120 | 63.00 | 49.00 | 0.00 | 0.99 | 0.99 |
| 233 | 120 | 63.00 | 50.00 | 0.00 | 1.01 | 1.01 |
| 234 | 120 | 63.00 | 51.00 | 0.00 | 1.03 | 1.03 |
| 235 | 120 | 63.00 | 52.00 | 0.00 | 1.05 | 1.05 |
| 236 | 120 | 63.00 | 53.00 | 0.00 | 1.07 | 1.07 |
| 237 | 120 | 63.00 | 54.00 | 0.00 | 1.09 | 1.09 |
| 238 | 120 | 63.00 | 55.00 | 0.00 | 1.11 | 1.11 |
| 239 | 120 | 63.00 | 56.00 | 0.00 | 1.13 | 1.13 |
| 240 | 120 | 63.00 | 57.00 | 0.00 | 1.15 | 1.15 |
| 241 | 120 | 63.00 | 58.00 | 0.00 | 1.17 | 1.17 |
| 242 | 120 | 63.00 | 59.00 | 0.00 | 1.19 | 1.19 |
| 243 | 120 | 63.00 | 60.00 | 0.00 | 1.21 | 1.21 |
| 244 | 120 | 63.00 | 61.00 | 0.00 | 1.23 | 1.23 |
| 245 | 120 | 63.00 | 62.00 | 0.00 | 1.25 | 1.25 |
| 246 | 120 | 63.00 | 63.00 | 0.00 | 1.27 | 1.27 |
| 247 | 120 | 63.00 | 64.00 | 0.00 | 1.29 | 1.29 |
| 248 | 120 | 63.00 | 65.00 | 0.00 | 1.31 | 1.31 |
| 249 | 120 | 63.00 | 66.00 | 0.00 | 1.33 | 1.33 |
| 250 | 120 | 63.00 | 67.00 | 0.00 | 1.35 | 1.35 |
| 251 | 120 | 63.00 | 68.00 | 0.00 | 1.37 | 1.37 |
| 252 | 120 | 63.00 | 69.00 | 0.00 | 1.39 | 1.39 |
| 253 | 120 | 63.00 | 70.00 | 0.00 | 1.41 | 1.41 |
| 254 | 120 | 63.00 | 71.00 | 0.00 | 1.43 | 1.43 |

**Weekly table**

| Employee's earnings up to and including the UEL | Earnings at the LEL (where earnings are equal to or exceed the LEL) 1a | Earnings above the LEL, up to and including the PT 1b | Earnings above the PT, up to and including the UEL 1c | Employer's NICs due on all earnings above the ST 1d | Employee's NICs due on all earnings above the PT 1e | Total of employee's and employer's NICs (for information only) |
|---|---|---|---|---|---|---|
| £ | £ | £ p | £ p | £ p | £ p | £ p |
| 255 | 120 | 63.00 | 72.00 | 0.00 | 1.45 | 1.45 |
| 256 | 120 | 63.00 | 73.00 | 0.00 | 1.47 | 1.47 |
| 257 | 120 | 63.00 | 74.00 | 0.00 | 1.49 | 1.49 |
| 258 | 120 | 63.00 | 75.00 | 0.00 | 1.51 | 1.51 |
| 259 | 120 | 63.00 | 76.00 | 0.00 | 1.53 | 1.53 |
| 260 | 120 | 63.00 | 77.00 | 0.00 | 1.55 | 1.55 |
| 261 | 120 | 63.00 | 78.00 | 0.00 | 1.57 | 1.57 |
| 262 | 120 | 63.00 | 79.00 | 0.00 | 1.59 | 1.59 |
| 263 | 120 | 63.00 | 80.00 | 0.00 | 1.61 | 1.61 |
| 264 | 120 | 63.00 | 81.00 | 0.00 | 1.63 | 1.63 |
| 265 | 120 | 63.00 | 82.00 | 0.00 | 1.65 | 1.65 |
| 266 | 120 | 63.00 | 83.00 | 0.00 | 1.67 | 1.67 |
| 267 | 120 | 63.00 | 84.00 | 0.00 | 1.69 | 1.69 |
| 268 | 120 | 63.00 | 85.00 | 0.00 | 1.71 | 1.71 |
| 269 | 120 | 63.00 | 86.00 | 0.00 | 1.73 | 1.73 |
| 270 | 120 | 63.00 | 87.00 | 0.00 | 1.75 | 1.75 |
| 271 | 120 | 63.00 | 88.00 | 0.00 | 1.77 | 1.77 |
| 272 | 120 | 63.00 | 89.00 | 0.00 | 1.79 | 1.79 |
| 273 | 120 | 63.00 | 90.00 | 0.00 | 1.81 | 1.81 |
| 274 | 120 | 63.00 | 91.00 | 0.00 | 1.83 | 1.83 |
| 275 | 120 | 63.00 | 92.00 | 0.00 | 1.85 | 1.85 |
| 276 | 120 | 63.00 | 93.00 | 0.00 | 1.87 | 1.87 |
| 277 | 120 | 63.00 | 94.00 | 0.00 | 1.89 | 1.89 |
| 278 | 120 | 63.00 | 95.00 | 0.00 | 1.91 | 1.91 |
| 279 | 120 | 63.00 | 96.00 | 0.00 | 1.93 | 1.93 |
| 280 | 120 | 63.00 | 97.00 | 0.00 | 1.95 | 1.95 |
| 281 | 120 | 63.00 | 98.00 | 0.00 | 1.97 | 1.97 |
| 282 | 120 | 63.00 | 99.00 | 0.00 | 1.99 | 1.99 |
| 283 | 120 | 63.00 | 100.00 | 0.00 | 2.01 | 2.01 |
| 284 | 120 | 63.00 | 101.00 | 0.00 | 2.03 | 2.03 |
| 285 | 120 | 63.00 | 102.00 | 0.00 | 2.05 | 2.05 |
| 286 | 120 | 63.00 | 103.00 | 0.00 | 2.07 | 2.07 |
| 287 | 120 | 63.00 | 104.00 | 0.00 | 2.09 | 2.09 |
| 288 | 120 | 63.00 | 105.00 | 0.00 | 2.11 | 2.11 |
| 289 | 120 | 63.00 | 106.00 | 0.00 | 2.13 | 2.13 |
| 290 | 120 | 63.00 | 107.00 | 0.00 | 2.15 | 2.15 |
| 291 | 120 | 63.00 | 108.00 | 0.00 | 2.17 | 2.17 |
| 292 | 120 | 63.00 | 109.00 | 0.00 | 2.19 | 2.19 |
| 293 | 120 | 63.00 | 110.00 | 0.00 | 2.21 | 2.21 |
| 294 | 120 | 63.00 | 111.00 | 0.00 | 2.23 | 2.23 |
| 295 | 120 | 63.00 | 112.00 | 0.00 | 2.25 | 2.25 |
| 296 | 120 | 63.00 | 113.00 | 0.00 | 2.27 | 2.27 |
| 297 | 120 | 63.00 | 114.00 | 0.00 | 2.29 | 2.29 |
| 298 | 120 | 63.00 | 115.00 | 0.00 | 2.31 | 2.31 |
| 299 | 120 | 63.00 | 116.00 | 0.00 | 2.33 | 2.33 |
| 300 | 120 | 63.00 | 117.00 | 0.00 | 2.35 | 2.35 |
| 301 | 120 | 63.00 | 118.00 | 0.00 | 2.37 | 2.37 |
| 302 | 120 | 63.00 | 119.00 | 0.00 | 2.39 | 2.39 |
| 303 | 120 | 63.00 | 120.00 | 0.00 | 2.41 | 2.41 |
| 304 | 120 | 63.00 | 121.00 | 0.00 | 2.43 | 2.43 |
| 305 | 120 | 63.00 | 122.00 | 0.00 | 2.45 | 2.45 |
| 306 | 120 | 63.00 | 123.00 | 0.00 | 2.47 | 2.47 |
| 307 | 120 | 63.00 | 124.00 | 0.00 | 2.49 | 2.49 |
| 308 | 120 | 63.00 | 125.00 | 0.00 | 2.51 | 2.51 |
| 309 | 120 | 63.00 | 126.00 | 0.00 | 2.53 | 2.53 |

# Table letter Z

**Weekly table**

| Employee's earnings up to and including the UEL | Earnings at the LEL (where earnings are equal to or exceed the LEL) | Earnings above the LEL, up to and including the PT | Earnings above the PT, up to and including the UEL | Employer's NICs due on all earnings above the ST | Employee's NICs due on all earnings above the PT | Total of employee's and employer's NICs (for information only) |
|---|---|---|---|---|---|---|
| | 1a | 1b | 1c | 1d | 1e | |
| £ | £ | £ p | £ p | £ p | £ p | £ p |
| 310 | 120 | 63.00 | 127.00 | 0.00 | 2.55 | 2.55 |
| 311 | 120 | 63.00 | 128.00 | 0.00 | 2.57 | 2.57 |
| 312 | 120 | 63.00 | 129.00 | 0.00 | 2.59 | 2.59 |
| 313 | 120 | 63.00 | 130.00 | 0.00 | 2.61 | 2.61 |
| 314 | 120 | 63.00 | 131.00 | 0.00 | 2.63 | 2.63 |
| 315 | 120 | 63.00 | 132.00 | 0.00 | 2.65 | 2.65 |
| 316 | 120 | 63.00 | 133.00 | 0.00 | 2.67 | 2.67 |
| 317 | 120 | 63.00 | 134.00 | 0.00 | 2.69 | 2.69 |
| 318 | 120 | 63.00 | 135.00 | 0.00 | 2.71 | 2.71 |
| 319 | 120 | 63.00 | 136.00 | 0.00 | 2.73 | 2.73 |
| 320 | 120 | 63.00 | 137.00 | 0.00 | 2.75 | 2.75 |
| 321 | 120 | 63.00 | 138.00 | 0.00 | 2.77 | 2.77 |
| 322 | 120 | 63.00 | 139.00 | 0.00 | 2.79 | 2.79 |
| 323 | 120 | 63.00 | 140.00 | 0.00 | 2.81 | 2.81 |
| 324 | 120 | 63.00 | 141.00 | 0.00 | 2.83 | 2.83 |
| 325 | 120 | 63.00 | 142.00 | 0.00 | 2.85 | 2.85 |
| 326 | 120 | 63.00 | 143.00 | 0.00 | 2.87 | 2.87 |
| 327 | 120 | 63.00 | 144.00 | 0.00 | 2.89 | 2.89 |
| 328 | 120 | 63.00 | 145.00 | 0.00 | 2.91 | 2.91 |
| 329 | 120 | 63.00 | 146.00 | 0.00 | 2.93 | 2.93 |
| 330 | 120 | 63.00 | 147.00 | 0.00 | 2.95 | 2.95 |
| 331 | 120 | 63.00 | 148.00 | 0.00 | 2.97 | 2.97 |
| 332 | 120 | 63.00 | 149.00 | 0.00 | 2.99 | 2.99 |
| 333 | 120 | 63.00 | 150.00 | 0.00 | 3.01 | 3.01 |
| 334 | 120 | 63.00 | 151.00 | 0.00 | 3.03 | 3.03 |
| 335 | 120 | 63.00 | 152.00 | 0.00 | 3.05 | 3.05 |
| 336 | 120 | 63.00 | 153.00 | 0.00 | 3.07 | 3.07 |
| 337 | 120 | 63.00 | 154.00 | 0.00 | 3.09 | 3.09 |
| 338 | 120 | 63.00 | 155.00 | 0.00 | 3.11 | 3.11 |
| 339 | 120 | 63.00 | 156.00 | 0.00 | 3.13 | 3.13 |
| 340 | 120 | 63.00 | 157.00 | 0.00 | 3.15 | 3.15 |
| 341 | 120 | 63.00 | 158.00 | 0.00 | 3.17 | 3.17 |
| 342 | 120 | 63.00 | 159.00 | 0.00 | 3.19 | 3.19 |
| 343 | 120 | 63.00 | 160.00 | 0.00 | 3.21 | 3.21 |
| 344 | 120 | 63.00 | 161.00 | 0.00 | 3.23 | 3.23 |
| 345 | 120 | 63.00 | 162.00 | 0.00 | 3.25 | 3.25 |
| 346 | 120 | 63.00 | 163.00 | 0.00 | 3.27 | 3.27 |
| 347 | 120 | 63.00 | 164.00 | 0.00 | 3.29 | 3.29 |
| 348 | 120 | 63.00 | 165.00 | 0.00 | 3.31 | 3.31 |
| 349 | 120 | 63.00 | 166.00 | 0.00 | 3.33 | 3.33 |
| 350 | 120 | 63.00 | 167.00 | 0.00 | 3.35 | 3.35 |
| 351 | 120 | 63.00 | 168.00 | 0.00 | 3.37 | 3.37 |
| 352 | 120 | 63.00 | 169.00 | 0.00 | 3.39 | 3.39 |
| 353 | 120 | 63.00 | 170.00 | 0.00 | 3.41 | 3.41 |
| 354 | 120 | 63.00 | 171.00 | 0.00 | 3.43 | 3.43 |
| 355 | 120 | 63.00 | 172.00 | 0.00 | 3.45 | 3.45 |
| 356 | 120 | 63.00 | 173.00 | 0.00 | 3.47 | 3.47 |
| 357 | 120 | 63.00 | 174.00 | 0.00 | 3.49 | 3.49 |
| 358 | 120 | 63.00 | 175.00 | 0.00 | 3.51 | 3.51 |
| 359 | 120 | 63.00 | 176.00 | 0.00 | 3.53 | 3.53 |
| 360 | 120 | 63.00 | 177.00 | 0.00 | 3.55 | 3.55 |
| 361 | 120 | 63.00 | 178.00 | 0.00 | 3.57 | 3.57 |
| 362 | 120 | 63.00 | 179.00 | 0.00 | 3.59 | 3.59 |
| 363 | 120 | 63.00 | 180.00 | 0.00 | 3.61 | 3.61 |
| 364 | 120 | 63.00 | 181.00 | 0.00 | 3.63 | 3.63 |

**Weekly table**

**Table letter Z**

| Employee's earnings up to and including the UEL | Earnings at the LEL (where earnings are equal to or exceed the LEL) | Earnings above the LEL, up to and including the PT | Earnings above the PT, up to and including the UEL | Employer's NICs due on all earnings above the ST | Employee's NICs due on all earnings above the PT | Total of employee's and employer's NICs (for information only) |
|---|---|---|---|---|---|---|
| | | 1a | 1b | 1c | 1d | 1e |
| £ | £ | £ p | £ p | £ p | £ p | £ p |
| 365 | 120 | 63.00 | 182.00 | 0.00 | 3.65 | 3.65 |
| 366 | 120 | 63.00 | 183.00 | 0.00 | 3.67 | 3.67 |
| 367 | 120 | 63.00 | 184.00 | 0.00 | 3.69 | 3.69 |
| 368 | 120 | 63.00 | 185.00 | 0.00 | 3.71 | 3.71 |
| 369 | 120 | 63.00 | 186.00 | 0.00 | 3.73 | 3.73 |
| 370 | 120 | 63.00 | 187.00 | 0.00 | 3.75 | 3.75 |
| 371 | 120 | 63.00 | 188.00 | 0.00 | 3.77 | 3.77 |
| 372 | 120 | 63.00 | 189.00 | 0.00 | 3.79 | 3.79 |
| 373 | 120 | 63.00 | 190.00 | 0.00 | 3.81 | 3.81 |
| 374 | 120 | 63.00 | 191.00 | 0.00 | 3.83 | 3.83 |
| 375 | 120 | 63.00 | 192.00 | 0.00 | 3.85 | 3.85 |
| 376 | 120 | 63.00 | 193.00 | 0.00 | 3.87 | 3.87 |
| 377 | 120 | 63.00 | 194.00 | 0.00 | 3.89 | 3.89 |
| 378 | 120 | 63.00 | 195.00 | 0.00 | 3.91 | 3.91 |
| 379 | 120 | 63.00 | 196.00 | 0.00 | 3.93 | 3.93 |
| 380 | 120 | 63.00 | 197.00 | 0.00 | 3.95 | 3.95 |
| 381 | 120 | 63.00 | 198.00 | 0.00 | 3.97 | 3.97 |
| 382 | 120 | 63.00 | 199.00 | 0.00 | 3.99 | 3.99 |
| 383 | 120 | 63.00 | 200.00 | 0.00 | 4.01 | 4.01 |
| 384 | 120 | 63.00 | 201.00 | 0.00 | 4.03 | 4.03 |
| 385 | 120 | 63.00 | 202.00 | 0.00 | 4.05 | 4.05 |
| 386 | 120 | 63.00 | 203.00 | 0.00 | 4.07 | 4.07 |
| 387 | 120 | 63.00 | 204.00 | 0.00 | 4.09 | 4.09 |
| 388 | 120 | 63.00 | 205.00 | 0.00 | 4.11 | 4.11 |
| 389 | 120 | 63.00 | 206.00 | 0.00 | 4.13 | 4.13 |
| 390 | 120 | 63.00 | 207.00 | 0.00 | 4.15 | 4.15 |
| 391 | 120 | 63.00 | 208.00 | 0.00 | 4.17 | 4.17 |
| 392 | 120 | 63.00 | 209.00 | 0.00 | 4.19 | 4.19 |
| 393 | 120 | 63.00 | 210.00 | 0.00 | 4.21 | 4.21 |
| 394 | 120 | 63.00 | 211.00 | 0.00 | 4.23 | 4.23 |
| 395 | 120 | 63.00 | 212.00 | 0.00 | 4.25 | 4.25 |
| 396 | 120 | 63.00 | 213.00 | 0.00 | 4.27 | 4.27 |
| 397 | 120 | 63.00 | 214.00 | 0.00 | 4.29 | 4.29 |
| 398 | 120 | 63.00 | 215.00 | 0.00 | 4.31 | 4.31 |
| 399 | 120 | 63.00 | 216.00 | 0.00 | 4.33 | 4.33 |
| 400 | 120 | 63.00 | 217.00 | 0.00 | 4.35 | 4.35 |
| 401 | 120 | 63.00 | 218.00 | 0.00 | 4.37 | 4.37 |
| 402 | 120 | 63.00 | 219.00 | 0.00 | 4.39 | 4.39 |
| 403 | 120 | 63.00 | 220.00 | 0.00 | 4.41 | 4.41 |
| 404 | 120 | 63.00 | 221.00 | 0.00 | 4.43 | 4.43 |
| 405 | 120 | 63.00 | 222.00 | 0.00 | 4.45 | 4.45 |
| 406 | 120 | 63.00 | 223.00 | 0.00 | 4.47 | 4.47 |
| 407 | 120 | 63.00 | 224.00 | 0.00 | 4.49 | 4.49 |
| 408 | 120 | 63.00 | 225.00 | 0.00 | 4.51 | 4.51 |
| 409 | 120 | 63.00 | 226.00 | 0.00 | 4.53 | 4.53 |
| 410 | 120 | 63.00 | 227.00 | 0.00 | 4.55 | 4.55 |
| 411 | 120 | 63.00 | 228.00 | 0.00 | 4.57 | 4.57 |
| 412 | 120 | 63.00 | 229.00 | 0.00 | 4.59 | 4.59 |
| 413 | 120 | 63.00 | 230.00 | 0.00 | 4.61 | 4.61 |
| 414 | 120 | 63.00 | 231.00 | 0.00 | 4.63 | 4.63 |
| 415 | 120 | 63.00 | 232.00 | 0.00 | 4.65 | 4.65 |
| 416 | 120 | 63.00 | 233.00 | 0.00 | 4.67 | 4.67 |
| 417 | 120 | 63.00 | 234.00 | 0.00 | 4.69 | 4.69 |
| 418 | 120 | 63.00 | 235.00 | 0.00 | 4.71 | 4.71 |
| 419 | 120 | 63.00 | 236.00 | 0.00 | 4.73 | 4.73 |

## Table letter Z

**Weekly table**

| Employee's earnings up to and including the UEL | Earnings at the LEL (where earnings are equal to or exceed the LEL) 1a | Earnings above the LEL, up to and including the PT 1b | Earnings above the PT, up to and including the UEL 1c | Employer's NICs due on all earnings above the ST 1d | Employee's NICs due on all earnings above the PT 1e | Total of employee's and employer's NICs (for information only) |
|---|---|---|---|---|---|---|
| £ | £ | £ p | £ p | £ p | £ p | £ p |
| 420 | 120 | 63.00 | 237.00 | 0.00 | 4.75 | 4.75 |
| 421 | 120 | 63.00 | 238.00 | 0.00 | 4.77 | 4.77 |
| 422 | 120 | 63.00 | 239.00 | 0.00 | 4.79 | 4.79 |
| 423 | 120 | 63.00 | 240.00 | 0.00 | 4.81 | 4.81 |
| 424 | 120 | 63.00 | 241.00 | 0.00 | 4.83 | 4.83 |
| 425 | 120 | 63.00 | 242.00 | 0.00 | 4.85 | 4.85 |
| 426 | 120 | 63.00 | 243.00 | 0.00 | 4.87 | 4.87 |
| 427 | 120 | 63.00 | 244.00 | 0.00 | 4.89 | 4.89 |
| 428 | 120 | 63.00 | 245.00 | 0.00 | 4.91 | 4.91 |
| 429 | 120 | 63.00 | 246.00 | 0.00 | 4.93 | 4.93 |
| 430 | 120 | 63.00 | 247.00 | 0.00 | 4.95 | 4.95 |
| 431 | 120 | 63.00 | 248.00 | 0.00 | 4.97 | 4.97 |
| 432 | 120 | 63.00 | 249.00 | 0.00 | 4.99 | 4.99 |
| 433 | 120 | 63.00 | 250.00 | 0.00 | 5.01 | 5.01 |
| 434 | 120 | 63.00 | 251.00 | 0.00 | 5.03 | 5.03 |
| 435 | 120 | 63.00 | 252.00 | 0.00 | 5.05 | 5.05 |
| 436 | 120 | 63.00 | 253.00 | 0.00 | 5.07 | 5.07 |
| 437 | 120 | 63.00 | 254.00 | 0.00 | 5.09 | 5.09 |
| 438 | 120 | 63.00 | 255.00 | 0.00 | 5.11 | 5.11 |
| 439 | 120 | 63.00 | 256.00 | 0.00 | 5.13 | 5.13 |
| 440 | 120 | 63.00 | 257.00 | 0.00 | 5.15 | 5.15 |
| 441 | 120 | 63.00 | 258.00 | 0.00 | 5.17 | 5.17 |
| 442 | 120 | 63.00 | 259.00 | 0.00 | 5.19 | 5.19 |
| 443 | 120 | 63.00 | 260.00 | 0.00 | 5.21 | 5.21 |
| 444 | 120 | 63.00 | 261.00 | 0.00 | 5.23 | 5.23 |
| 445 | 120 | 63.00 | 262.00 | 0.00 | 5.25 | 5.25 |
| 446 | 120 | 63.00 | 263.00 | 0.00 | 5.27 | 5.27 |
| 447 | 120 | 63.00 | 264.00 | 0.00 | 5.29 | 5.29 |
| 448 | 120 | 63.00 | 265.00 | 0.00 | 5.31 | 5.31 |
| 449 | 120 | 63.00 | 266.00 | 0.00 | 5.33 | 5.33 |
| 450 | 120 | 63.00 | 267.00 | 0.00 | 5.35 | 5.35 |
| 451 | 120 | 63.00 | 268.00 | 0.00 | 5.37 | 5.37 |
| 452 | 120 | 63.00 | 269.00 | 0.00 | 5.39 | 5.39 |
| 453 | 120 | 63.00 | 270.00 | 0.00 | 5.41 | 5.41 |
| 454 | 120 | 63.00 | 271.00 | 0.00 | 5.43 | 5.43 |
| 455 | 120 | 63.00 | 272.00 | 0.00 | 5.45 | 5.45 |
| 456 | 120 | 63.00 | 273.00 | 0.00 | 5.47 | 5.47 |
| 457 | 120 | 63.00 | 274.00 | 0.00 | 5.49 | 5.49 |
| 458 | 120 | 63.00 | 275.00 | 0.00 | 5.51 | 5.51 |
| 459 | 120 | 63.00 | 276.00 | 0.00 | 5.53 | 5.53 |
| 460 | 120 | 63.00 | 277.00 | 0.00 | 5.55 | 5.55 |
| 461 | 120 | 63.00 | 278.00 | 0.00 | 5.57 | 5.57 |
| 462 | 120 | 63.00 | 279.00 | 0.00 | 5.59 | 5.59 |
| 463 | 120 | 63.00 | 280.00 | 0.00 | 5.61 | 5.61 |
| 464 | 120 | 63.00 | 281.00 | 0.00 | 5.63 | 5.63 |
| 465 | 120 | 63.00 | 282.00 | 0.00 | 5.65 | 5.65 |
| 466 | 120 | 63.00 | 283.00 | 0.00 | 5.67 | 5.67 |
| 467 | 120 | 63.00 | 284.00 | 0.00 | 5.69 | 5.69 |
| 468 | 120 | 63.00 | 285.00 | 0.00 | 5.71 | 5.71 |
| 469 | 120 | 63.00 | 286.00 | 0.00 | 5.73 | 5.73 |
| 470 | 120 | 63.00 | 287.00 | 0.00 | 5.75 | 5.75 |
| 471 | 120 | 63.00 | 288.00 | 0.00 | 5.77 | 5.77 |
| 472 | 120 | 63.00 | 289.00 | 0.00 | 5.79 | 5.79 |
| 473 | 120 | 63.00 | 290.00 | 0.00 | 5.81 | 5.81 |
| 474 | 120 | 63.00 | 291.00 | 0.00 | 5.83 | 5.83 |

**Weekly table**

Table letter Z

| Employee's earnings up to and including the UEL | Earnings at the LEL (where earnings are equal to or exceed the LEL) | Earnings above the LEL, up to and including the PT | Earnings above the PT, up to and including the UEL | Employer's NICs due on all earnings above the ST | Employee's NICs due on all earnings above the PT | Total of employee's and employer's NICs (for information only) |
|---|---|---|---|---|---|---|
| | 1a | 1b | 1c | 1d | 1e | |
| £ | £ | £ p | £ p | £ p | £ p | £ p |
| 475 | 120 | 63.00 | 292.00 | 0.00 | 5.85 | 5.85 |
| 476 | 120 | 63.00 | 293.00 | 0.00 | 5.87 | 5.87 |
| 477 | 120 | 63.00 | 294.00 | 0.00 | 5.89 | 5.89 |
| 478 | 120 | 63.00 | 295.00 | 0.00 | 5.91 | 5.91 |
| 479 | 120 | 63.00 | 296.00 | 0.00 | 5.93 | 5.93 |
| 480 | 120 | 63.00 | 297.00 | 0.00 | 5.95 | 5.95 |
| 481 | 120 | 63.00 | 298.00 | 0.00 | 5.97 | 5.97 |
| 482 | 120 | 63.00 | 299.00 | 0.00 | 5.99 | 5.99 |
| 483 | 120 | 63.00 | 300.00 | 0.00 | 6.01 | 6.01 |
| 484 | 120 | 63.00 | 301.00 | 0.00 | 6.03 | 6.03 |
| 485 | 120 | 63.00 | 302.00 | 0.00 | 6.05 | 6.05 |
| 486 | 120 | 63.00 | 303.00 | 0.00 | 6.07 | 6.07 |
| 487 | 120 | 63.00 | 304.00 | 0.00 | 6.09 | 6.09 |
| 488 | 120 | 63.00 | 305.00 | 0.00 | 6.11 | 6.11 |
| 489 | 120 | 63.00 | 306.00 | 0.00 | 6.13 | 6.13 |
| 490 | 120 | 63.00 | 307.00 | 0.00 | 6.15 | 6.15 |
| 491 | 120 | 63.00 | 308.00 | 0.00 | 6.17 | 6.17 |
| 492 | 120 | 63.00 | 309.00 | 0.00 | 6.19 | 6.19 |
| 493 | 120 | 63.00 | 310.00 | 0.00 | 6.21 | 6.21 |
| 494 | 120 | 63.00 | 311.00 | 0.00 | 6.23 | 6.23 |
| 495 | 120 | 63.00 | 312.00 | 0.00 | 6.25 | 6.25 |
| 496 | 120 | 63.00 | 313.00 | 0.00 | 6.27 | 6.27 |
| 497 | 120 | 63.00 | 314.00 | 0.00 | 6.29 | 6.29 |
| 498 | 120 | 63.00 | 315.00 | 0.00 | 6.31 | 6.31 |
| 499 | 120 | 63.00 | 316.00 | 0.00 | 6.33 | 6.33 |
| 500 | 120 | 63.00 | 317.00 | 0.00 | 6.35 | 6.35 |
| 501 | 120 | 63.00 | 318.00 | 0.00 | 6.37 | 6.37 |
| 502 | 120 | 63.00 | 319.00 | 0.00 | 6.39 | 6.39 |
| 503 | 120 | 63.00 | 320.00 | 0.00 | 6.41 | 6.41 |
| 504 | 120 | 63.00 | 321.00 | 0.00 | 6.43 | 6.43 |
| 505 | 120 | 63.00 | 322.00 | 0.00 | 6.45 | 6.45 |
| 506 | 120 | 63.00 | 323.00 | 0.00 | 6.47 | 6.47 |
| 507 | 120 | 63.00 | 324.00 | 0.00 | 6.49 | 6.49 |
| 508 | 120 | 63.00 | 325.00 | 0.00 | 6.51 | 6.51 |
| 509 | 120 | 63.00 | 326.00 | 0.00 | 6.53 | 6.53 |
| 510 | 120 | 63.00 | 327.00 | 0.00 | 6.55 | 6.55 |
| 511 | 120 | 63.00 | 328.00 | 0.00 | 6.57 | 6.57 |
| 512 | 120 | 63.00 | 329.00 | 0.00 | 6.59 | 6.59 |
| 513 | 120 | 63.00 | 330.00 | 0.00 | 6.61 | 6.61 |
| 514 | 120 | 63.00 | 331.00 | 0.00 | 6.63 | 6.63 |
| 515 | 120 | 63.00 | 332.00 | 0.00 | 6.65 | 6.65 |
| 516 | 120 | 63.00 | 333.00 | 0.00 | 6.67 | 6.67 |
| 517 | 120 | 63.00 | 334.00 | 0.00 | 6.69 | 6.69 |
| 518 | 120 | 63.00 | 335.00 | 0.00 | 6.71 | 6.71 |
| 519 | 120 | 63.00 | 336.00 | 0.00 | 6.73 | 6.73 |
| 520 | 120 | 63.00 | 337.00 | 0.00 | 6.75 | 6.75 |
| 521 | 120 | 63.00 | 338.00 | 0.00 | 6.77 | 6.77 |
| 522 | 120 | 63.00 | 339.00 | 0.00 | 6.79 | 6.79 |
| 523 | 120 | 63.00 | 340.00 | 0.00 | 6.81 | 6.81 |
| 524 | 120 | 63.00 | 341.00 | 0.00 | 6.83 | 6.83 |
| 525 | 120 | 63.00 | 342.00 | 0.00 | 6.85 | 6.85 |
| 526 | 120 | 63.00 | 343.00 | 0.00 | 6.87 | 6.87 |
| 527 | 120 | 63.00 | 344.00 | 0.00 | 6.89 | 6.89 |
| 528 | 120 | 63.00 | 345.00 | 0.00 | 6.91 | 6.91 |
| 529 | 120 | 63.00 | 346.00 | 0.00 | 6.93 | 6.93 |

## Table letter Z

**Weekly table**

| Employee's earnings up to and including the UEL | Earnings at the LEL (where earnings are equal to or exceed the LEL) | Earnings above the LEL, up to and including the PT | Earnings above the PT, up to and including the UEL | Employer's NICs due on all earnings above the ST | Employee's NICs due on all earnings above the PT | Total of employee's and employer's NICs (for information only) |
|---|---|---|---|---|---|---|
| | | 1a | 1b | 1c | 1d | 1e |
| £ | £ | £ p | £ p | £ p | £ p | £ p |
| 530 | 120 | 63.00 | 347.00 | 0.00 | 6.95 | 6.95 |
| 531 | 120 | 63.00 | 348.00 | 0.00 | 6.97 | 6.97 |
| 532 | 120 | 63.00 | 349.00 | 0.00 | 6.99 | 6.99 |
| 533 | 120 | 63.00 | 350.00 | 0.00 | 7.01 | 7.01 |
| 534 | 120 | 63.00 | 351.00 | 0.00 | 7.03 | 7.03 |
| 535 | 120 | 63.00 | 352.00 | 0.00 | 7.05 | 7.05 |
| 536 | 120 | 63.00 | 353.00 | 0.00 | 7.07 | 7.07 |
| 537 | 120 | 63.00 | 354.00 | 0.00 | 7.09 | 7.09 |
| 538 | 120 | 63.00 | 355.00 | 0.00 | 7.11 | 7.11 |
| 539 | 120 | 63.00 | 356.00 | 0.00 | 7.13 | 7.13 |
| 540 | 120 | 63.00 | 357.00 | 0.00 | 7.15 | 7.15 |
| 541 | 120 | 63.00 | 358.00 | 0.00 | 7.17 | 7.17 |
| 542 | 120 | 63.00 | 359.00 | 0.00 | 7.19 | 7.19 |
| 543 | 120 | 63.00 | 360.00 | 0.00 | 7.21 | 7.21 |
| 544 | 120 | 63.00 | 361.00 | 0.00 | 7.23 | 7.23 |
| 545 | 120 | 63.00 | 362.00 | 0.00 | 7.25 | 7.25 |
| 546 | 120 | 63.00 | 363.00 | 0.00 | 7.27 | 7.27 |
| 547 | 120 | 63.00 | 364.00 | 0.00 | 7.29 | 7.29 |
| 548 | 120 | 63.00 | 365.00 | 0.00 | 7.31 | 7.31 |
| 549 | 120 | 63.00 | 366.00 | 0.00 | 7.33 | 7.33 |
| 550 | 120 | 63.00 | 367.00 | 0.00 | 7.35 | 7.35 |
| 551 | 120 | 63.00 | 368.00 | 0.00 | 7.37 | 7.37 |
| 552 | 120 | 63.00 | 369.00 | 0.00 | 7.39 | 7.39 |
| 553 | 120 | 63.00 | 370.00 | 0.00 | 7.41 | 7.41 |
| 554 | 120 | 63.00 | 371.00 | 0.00 | 7.43 | 7.43 |
| 555 | 120 | 63.00 | 372.00 | 0.00 | 7.45 | 7.45 |
| 556 | 120 | 63.00 | 373.00 | 0.00 | 7.47 | 7.47 |
| 557 | 120 | 63.00 | 374.00 | 0.00 | 7.49 | 7.49 |
| 558 | 120 | 63.00 | 375.00 | 0.00 | 7.51 | 7.51 |
| 559 | 120 | 63.00 | 376.00 | 0.00 | 7.53 | 7.53 |
| 560 | 120 | 63.00 | 377.00 | 0.00 | 7.55 | 7.55 |
| 561 | 120 | 63.00 | 378.00 | 0.00 | 7.57 | 7.57 |
| 562 | 120 | 63.00 | 379.00 | 0.00 | 7.59 | 7.59 |
| 563 | 120 | 63.00 | 380.00 | 0.00 | 7.61 | 7.61 |
| 564 | 120 | 63.00 | 381.00 | 0.00 | 7.63 | 7.63 |
| 565 | 120 | 63.00 | 382.00 | 0.00 | 7.65 | 7.65 |
| 566 | 120 | 63.00 | 383.00 | 0.00 | 7.67 | 7.67 |
| 567 | 120 | 63.00 | 384.00 | 0.00 | 7.69 | 7.69 |
| 568 | 120 | 63.00 | 385.00 | 0.00 | 7.71 | 7.71 |
| 569 | 120 | 63.00 | 386.00 | 0.00 | 7.73 | 7.73 |
| 570 | 120 | 63.00 | 387.00 | 0.00 | 7.75 | 7.75 |
| 571 | 120 | 63.00 | 388.00 | 0.00 | 7.77 | 7.77 |
| 572 | 120 | 63.00 | 389.00 | 0.00 | 7.79 | 7.79 |
| 573 | 120 | 63.00 | 390.00 | 0.00 | 7.81 | 7.81 |
| 574 | 120 | 63.00 | 391.00 | 0.00 | 7.83 | 7.83 |
| 575 | 120 | 63.00 | 392.00 | 0.00 | 7.85 | 7.85 |
| 576 | 120 | 63.00 | 393.00 | 0.00 | 7.87 | 7.87 |
| 577 | 120 | 63.00 | 394.00 | 0.00 | 7.89 | 7.89 |
| 578 | 120 | 63.00 | 395.00 | 0.00 | 7.91 | 7.91 |
| 579 | 120 | 63.00 | 396.00 | 0.00 | 7.93 | 7.93 |
| 580 | 120 | 63.00 | 397.00 | 0.00 | 7.95 | 7.95 |
| 581 | 120 | 63.00 | 398.00 | 0.00 | 7.97 | 7.97 |
| 582 | 120 | 63.00 | 399.00 | 0.00 | 7.99 | 7.99 |
| 583 | 120 | 63.00 | 400.00 | 0.00 | 8.01 | 8.01 |
| 584 | 120 | 63.00 | 401.00 | 0.00 | 8.03 | 8.03 |

**Weekly table**

**Table letter Z**

| Employee's earnings up to and including the UEL | Earnings at the LEL (where earnings are equal to or exceed the LEL) | Earnings above the LEL, up to and including the PT | Earnings above the PT, up to and including the UEL | Employer's NICs due on all earnings above the ST | Employee's NICs due on all earnings above the PT | Total of employee's and employer's NICs (for information only) |
|---|---|---|---|---|---|---|
| | 1a | 1b | 1c | 1d | 1e | |
| £ | £ | £ p | £ p | £ p | £ p | £ p |
| 585 | 120 | 63.00 | 402.00 | 0.00 | 8.05 | 8.05 |
| 586 | 120 | 63.00 | 403.00 | 0.00 | 8.07 | 8.07 |
| 587 | 120 | 63.00 | 404.00 | 0.00 | 8.09 | 8.09 |
| 588 | 120 | 63.00 | 405.00 | 0.00 | 8.11 | 8.11 |
| 589 | 120 | 63.00 | 406.00 | 0.00 | 8.13 | 8.13 |
| 590 | 120 | 63.00 | 407.00 | 0.00 | 8.15 | 8.15 |
| 591 | 120 | 63.00 | 408.00 | 0.00 | 8.17 | 8.17 |
| 592 | 120 | 63.00 | 409.00 | 0.00 | 8.19 | 8.19 |
| 593 | 120 | 63.00 | 410.00 | 0.00 | 8.21 | 8.21 |
| 594 | 120 | 63.00 | 411.00 | 0.00 | 8.23 | 8.23 |
| 595 | 120 | 63.00 | 412.00 | 0.00 | 8.25 | 8.25 |
| 596 | 120 | 63.00 | 413.00 | 0.00 | 8.27 | 8.27 |
| 597 | 120 | 63.00 | 414.00 | 0.00 | 8.29 | 8.29 |
| 598 | 120 | 63.00 | 415.00 | 0.00 | 8.31 | 8.31 |
| 599 | 120 | 63.00 | 416.00 | 0.00 | 8.33 | 8.33 |
| 600 | 120 | 63.00 | 417.00 | 0.00 | 8.35 | 8.35 |
| 601 | 120 | 63.00 | 418.00 | 0.00 | 8.37 | 8.37 |
| 602 | 120 | 63.00 | 419.00 | 0.00 | 8.39 | 8.39 |
| 603 | 120 | 63.00 | 420.00 | 0.00 | 8.41 | 8.41 |
| 604 | 120 | 63.00 | 421.00 | 0.00 | 8.43 | 8.43 |
| 605 | 120 | 63.00 | 422.00 | 0.00 | 8.45 | 8.45 |
| 606 | 120 | 63.00 | 423.00 | 0.00 | 8.47 | 8.47 |
| 607 | 120 | 63.00 | 424.00 | 0.00 | 8.49 | 8.49 |
| 608 | 120 | 63.00 | 425.00 | 0.00 | 8.51 | 8.51 |
| 609 | 120 | 63.00 | 426.00 | 0.00 | 8.53 | 8.53 |
| 610 | 120 | 63.00 | 427.00 | 0.00 | 8.55 | 8.55 |
| 611 | 120 | 63.00 | 428.00 | 0.00 | 8.57 | 8.57 |
| 612 | 120 | 63.00 | 429.00 | 0.00 | 8.59 | 8.59 |
| 613 | 120 | 63.00 | 430.00 | 0.00 | 8.61 | 8.61 |
| 614 | 120 | 63.00 | 431.00 | 0.00 | 8.63 | 8.63 |
| 615 | 120 | 63.00 | 432.00 | 0.00 | 8.65 | 8.65 |
| 616 | 120 | 63.00 | 433.00 | 0.00 | 8.67 | 8.67 |
| 617 | 120 | 63.00 | 434.00 | 0.00 | 8.69 | 8.69 |
| 618 | 120 | 63.00 | 435.00 | 0.00 | 8.71 | 8.71 |
| 619 | 120 | 63.00 | 436.00 | 0.00 | 8.73 | 8.73 |
| 620 | 120 | 63.00 | 437.00 | 0.00 | 8.75 | 8.75 |
| 621 | 120 | 63.00 | 438.00 | 0.00 | 8.77 | 8.77 |
| 622 | 120 | 63.00 | 439.00 | 0.00 | 8.79 | 8.79 |
| 623 | 120 | 63.00 | 440.00 | 0.00 | 8.81 | 8.81 |
| 624 | 120 | 63.00 | 441.00 | 0.00 | 8.83 | 8.83 |
| 625 | 120 | 63.00 | 442.00 | 0.00 | 8.85 | 8.85 |
| 626 | 120 | 63.00 | 443.00 | 0.00 | 8.87 | 8.87 |
| 627 | 120 | 63.00 | 444.00 | 0.00 | 8.89 | 8.89 |
| 628 | 120 | 63.00 | 445.00 | 0.00 | 8.91 | 8.91 |
| 629 | 120 | 63.00 | 446.00 | 0.00 | 8.93 | 8.93 |
| 630 | 120 | 63.00 | 447.00 | 0.00 | 8.95 | 8.95 |
| 631 | 120 | 63.00 | 448.00 | 0.00 | 8.97 | 8.97 |
| 632 | 120 | 63.00 | 449.00 | 0.00 | 8.99 | 8.99 |
| 633 | 120 | 63.00 | 450.00 | 0.00 | 9.01 | 9.01 |
| 634 | 120 | 63.00 | 451.00 | 0.00 | 9.03 | 9.03 |
| 635 | 120 | 63.00 | 452.00 | 0.00 | 9.05 | 9.05 |
| 636 | 120 | 63.00 | 453.00 | 0.00 | 9.07 | 9.07 |
| 637 | 120 | 63.00 | 454.00 | 0.00 | 9.09 | 9.09 |
| 638 | 120 | 63.00 | 455.00 | 0.00 | 9.11 | 9.11 |
| 639 | 120 | 63.00 | 456.00 | 0.00 | 9.13 | 9.13 |

# Table letter Z

**Weekly table**

| Employee's earnings up to and including the UEL | Earnings at the LEL (where earnings are equal to or exceed the LEL) 1a | Earnings above the LEL, up to and including the PT 1b | Earnings above the PT, up to and including the UEL 1c | Employer's NICs due on all earnings above the ST 1d | Employee's NICs due on all earnings above the PT 1e | Total of employee's and employer's NICs (for information only) |
|---|---|---|---|---|---|---|
| £ | £ | £ p | £ p | £ p | £ p | £ p |
| 640 | 120 | 63.00 | 457.00 | 0.00 | 9.15 | 9.15 |
| 641 | 120 | 63.00 | 458.00 | 0.00 | 9.17 | 9.17 |
| 642 | 120 | 63.00 | 459.00 | 0.00 | 9.19 | 9.19 |
| 643 | 120 | 63.00 | 460.00 | 0.00 | 9.21 | 9.21 |
| 644 | 120 | 63.00 | 461.00 | 0.00 | 9.23 | 9.23 |
| 645 | 120 | 63.00 | 462.00 | 0.00 | 9.25 | 9.25 |
| 646 | 120 | 63.00 | 463.00 | 0.00 | 9.27 | 9.27 |
| 647 | 120 | 63.00 | 464.00 | 0.00 | 9.29 | 9.29 |
| 648 | 120 | 63.00 | 465.00 | 0.00 | 9.31 | 9.31 |
| 649 | 120 | 63.00 | 466.00 | 0.00 | 9.33 | 9.33 |
| 650 | 120 | 63.00 | 467.00 | 0.00 | 9.35 | 9.35 |
| 651 | 120 | 63.00 | 468.00 | 0.00 | 9.37 | 9.37 |
| 652 | 120 | 63.00 | 469.00 | 0.00 | 9.39 | 9.39 |
| 653 | 120 | 63.00 | 470.00 | 0.00 | 9.41 | 9.41 |
| 654 | 120 | 63.00 | 471.00 | 0.00 | 9.43 | 9.43 |
| 655 | 120 | 63.00 | 472.00 | 0.00 | 9.45 | 9.45 |
| 656 | 120 | 63.00 | 473.00 | 0.00 | 9.47 | 9.47 |
| 657 | 120 | 63.00 | 474.00 | 0.00 | 9.49 | 9.49 |
| 658 | 120 | 63.00 | 475.00 | 0.00 | 9.51 | 9.51 |
| 659 | 120 | 63.00 | 476.00 | 0.00 | 9.53 | 9.53 |
| 660 | 120 | 63.00 | 477.00 | 0.00 | 9.55 | 9.55 |
| 661 | 120 | 63.00 | 478.00 | 0.00 | 9.57 | 9.57 |
| 662 | 120 | 63.00 | 479.00 | 0.00 | 9.59 | 9.59 |
| 663 | 120 | 63.00 | 480.00 | 0.00 | 9.61 | 9.61 |
| 664 | 120 | 63.00 | 481.00 | 0.00 | 9.63 | 9.63 |
| 665 | 120 | 63.00 | 482.00 | 0.00 | 9.65 | 9.65 |
| 666 | 120 | 63.00 | 483.00 | 0.00 | 9.67 | 9.67 |
| 667 | 120 | 63.00 | 484.00 | 0.00 | 9.69 | 9.69 |
| 668 | 120 | 63.00 | 485.00 | 0.00 | 9.71 | 9.71 |
| 669 | 120 | 63.00 | 486.00 | 0.00 | 9.73 | 9.73 |
| 670 | 120 | 63.00 | 487.00 | 0.00 | 9.75 | 9.75 |
| 671 | 120 | 63.00 | 488.00 | 0.00 | 9.77 | 9.77 |
| 672 | 120 | 63.00 | 489.00 | 0.00 | 9.79 | 9.79 |
| 673 | 120 | 63.00 | 490.00 | 0.00 | 9.81 | 9.81 |
| 674 | 120 | 63.00 | 491.00 | 0.00 | 9.83 | 9.83 |
| 675 | 120 | 63.00 | 492.00 | 0.00 | 9.85 | 9.85 |
| 676 | 120 | 63.00 | 493.00 | 0.00 | 9.87 | 9.87 |
| 677 | 120 | 63.00 | 494.00 | 0.00 | 9.89 | 9.89 |
| 678 | 120 | 63.00 | 495.00 | 0.00 | 9.91 | 9.91 |
| 679 | 120 | 63.00 | 496.00 | 0.00 | 9.93 | 9.93 |
| 680 | 120 | 63.00 | 497.00 | 0.00 | 9.95 | 9.95 |
| 681 | 120 | 63.00 | 498.00 | 0.00 | 9.97 | 9.97 |
| 682 | 120 | 63.00 | 499.00 | 0.00 | 9.99 | 9.99 |
| 683 | 120 | 63.00 | 500.00 | 0.00 | 10.01 | 10.01 |
| 684 | 120 | 63.00 | 501.00 | 0.00 | 10.03 | 10.03 |
| 685 | 120 | 63.00 | 502.00 | 0.00 | 10.05 | 10.05 |
| 686 | 120 | 63.00 | 503.00 | 0.00 | 10.07 | 10.07 |
| 687 | 120 | 63.00 | 504.00 | 0.00 | 10.09 | 10.09 |
| 688 | 120 | 63.00 | 505.00 | 0.00 | 10.11 | 10.11 |
| 689 | 120 | 63.00 | 506.00 | 0.00 | 10.13 | 10.13 |
| 690 | 120 | 63.00 | 507.00 | 0.00 | 10.15 | 10.15 |
| 691 | 120 | 63.00 | 508.00 | 0.00 | 10.17 | 10.17 |
| 692 | 120 | 63.00 | 509.00 | 0.00 | 10.19 | 10.19 |
| 693 | 120 | 63.00 | 510.00 | 0.00 | 10.21 | 10.21 |
| 694 | 120 | 63.00 | 511.00 | 0.00 | 10.23 | 10.23 |

**Weekly table**

**Table letter Z**

| Employee's earnings up to and including the UEL | Earnings at the LEL (where earnings are equal to or exceed the LEL) | Earnings above the LEL, up to and including the PT | Earnings above the PT, up to and including the UEL | Employer's NICs due on all earnings above the ST | Employee's NICs due on all earnings above the PT | Total of employee's and employer's NICs (for information only) |
|---|---|---|---|---|---|---|
| | 1a | 1b | 1c | 1d | 1e | |
| £ | £ | £ p | £ p | £ p | £ p | £ p |
| 695 | 120 | 63.00 | 512.00 | 0.00 | 10.25 | 10.25 |
| 696 | 120 | 63.00 | 513.00 | 0.00 | 10.27 | 10.27 |
| 697 | 120 | 63.00 | 514.00 | 0.00 | 10.29 | 10.29 |
| 698 | 120 | 63.00 | 515.00 | 0.00 | 10.31 | 10.31 |
| 699 | 120 | 63.00 | 516.00 | 0.00 | 10.33 | 10.33 |
| 700 | 120 | 63.00 | 517.00 | 0.00 | 10.35 | 10.35 |
| 701 | 120 | 63.00 | 518.00 | 0.00 | 10.37 | 10.37 |
| 702 | 120 | 63.00 | 519.00 | 0.00 | 10.39 | 10.39 |
| 703 | 120 | 63.00 | 520.00 | 0.00 | 10.41 | 10.41 |
| 704 | 120 | 63.00 | 521.00 | 0.00 | 10.43 | 10.43 |
| 705 | 120 | 63.00 | 522.00 | 0.00 | 10.45 | 10.45 |
| 706 | 120 | 63.00 | 523.00 | 0.00 | 10.47 | 10.47 |
| 707 | 120 | 63.00 | 524.00 | 0.00 | 10.49 | 10.49 |
| 708 | 120 | 63.00 | 525.00 | 0.00 | 10.51 | 10.51 |
| 709 | 120 | 63.00 | 526.00 | 0.00 | 10.53 | 10.53 |
| 710 | 120 | 63.00 | 527.00 | 0.00 | 10.55 | 10.55 |
| 711 | 120 | 63.00 | 528.00 | 0.00 | 10.57 | 10.57 |
| 712 | 120 | 63.00 | 529.00 | 0.00 | 10.59 | 10.59 |
| 713 | 120 | 63.00 | 530.00 | 0.00 | 10.61 | 10.61 |
| 714 | 120 | 63.00 | 531.00 | 0.00 | 10.63 | 10.63 |
| 715 | 120 | 63.00 | 532.00 | 0.00 | 10.65 | 10.65 |
| 716 | 120 | 63.00 | 533.00 | 0.00 | 10.67 | 10.67 |
| 717 | 120 | 63.00 | 534.00 | 0.00 | 10.69 | 10.69 |
| 718 | 120 | 63.00 | 535.00 | 0.00 | 10.71 | 10.71 |
| 719 | 120 | 63.00 | 536.00 | 0.00 | 10.73 | 10.73 |
| 720 | 120 | 63.00 | 537.00 | 0.00 | 10.75 | 10.75 |
| 721 | 120 | 63.00 | 538.00 | 0.00 | 10.77 | 10.77 |
| 722 | 120 | 63.00 | 539.00 | 0.00 | 10.79 | 10.79 |
| 723 | 120 | 63.00 | 540.00 | 0.00 | 10.81 | 10.81 |
| 724 | 120 | 63.00 | 541.00 | 0.00 | 10.83 | 10.83 |
| 725 | 120 | 63.00 | 542.00 | 0.00 | 10.85 | 10.85 |
| 726 | 120 | 63.00 | 543.00 | 0.00 | 10.87 | 10.87 |
| 727 | 120 | 63.00 | 544.00 | 0.00 | 10.89 | 10.89 |
| 728 | 120 | 63.00 | 545.00 | 0.00 | 10.91 | 10.91 |
| 729 | 120 | 63.00 | 546.00 | 0.00 | 10.93 | 10.93 |
| 730 | 120 | 63.00 | 547.00 | 0.00 | 10.95 | 10.95 |
| 731 | 120 | 63.00 | 548.00 | 0.00 | 10.97 | 10.97 |
| 732 | 120 | 63.00 | 549.00 | 0.00 | 10.99 | 10.99 |
| 733 | 120 | 63.00 | 550.00 | 0.00 | 11.01 | 11.01 |
| 734 | 120 | 63.00 | 551.00 | 0.00 | 11.03 | 11.03 |
| 735 | 120 | 63.00 | 552.00 | 0.00 | 11.05 | 11.05 |
| 736 | 120 | 63.00 | 553.00 | 0.00 | 11.07 | 11.07 |
| 737 | 120 | 63.00 | 554.00 | 0.00 | 11.09 | 11.09 |
| 738 | 120 | 63.00 | 555.00 | 0.00 | 11.11 | 11.11 |
| 739 | 120 | 63.00 | 556.00 | 0.00 | 11.13 | 11.13 |
| 740 | 120 | 63.00 | 557.00 | 0.00 | 11.15 | 11.15 |
| 741 | 120 | 63.00 | 558.00 | 0.00 | 11.17 | 11.17 |
| 742 | 120 | 63.00 | 559.00 | 0.00 | 11.19 | 11.19 |
| 743 | 120 | 63.00 | 560.00 | 0.00 | 11.21 | 11.21 |
| 744 | 120 | 63.00 | 561.00 | 0.00 | 11.23 | 11.23 |
| 745 | 120 | 63.00 | 562.00 | 0.00 | 11.25 | 11.25 |
| 746 | 120 | 63.00 | 563.00 | 0.00 | 11.27 | 11.27 |
| 747 | 120 | 63.00 | 564.00 | 0.00 | 11.29 | 11.29 |
| 748 | 120 | 63.00 | 565.00 | 0.00 | 11.31 | 11.31 |
| 749 | 120 | 63.00 | 566.00 | 0.00 | 11.33 | 11.33 |

# Table letter Z

**Weekly table**

| Employee's earnings up to and including the UEL | Earnings at the LEL (where earnings are equal to or exceed the LEL) 1a | Earnings above the LEL, up to and including the PT 1b | Earnings above the PT, up to and including the UEL 1c | Employer's NICs due on all earnings above the ST 1d | Employee's NICs due on all earnings above the PT 1e | Total of employee's and employer's NICs (for information only) |
|---|---|---|---|---|---|---|
| £ | £ | £ p | £ p | £ p | £ p | £ p |
| 750 | 120 | 63.00 | 567.00 | 0.00 | 11.35 | 11.35 |
| 751 | 120 | 63.00 | 568.00 | 0.00 | 11.37 | 11.37 |
| 752 | 120 | 63.00 | 569.00 | 0.00 | 11.39 | 11.39 |
| 753 | 120 | 63.00 | 570.00 | 0.00 | 11.41 | 11.41 |
| 754 | 120 | 63.00 | 571.00 | 0.00 | 11.43 | 11.43 |
| 755 | 120 | 63.00 | 572.00 | 0.00 | 11.45 | 11.45 |
| 756 | 120 | 63.00 | 573.00 | 0.00 | 11.47 | 11.47 |
| 757 | 120 | 63.00 | 574.00 | 0.00 | 11.49 | 11.49 |
| 758 | 120 | 63.00 | 575.00 | 0.00 | 11.51 | 11.51 |
| 759 | 120 | 63.00 | 576.00 | 0.00 | 11.53 | 11.53 |
| 760 | 120 | 63.00 | 577.00 | 0.00 | 11.55 | 11.55 |
| 761 | 120 | 63.00 | 578.00 | 0.00 | 11.57 | 11.57 |
| 762 | 120 | 63.00 | 579.00 | 0.00 | 11.59 | 11.59 |
| 763 | 120 | 63.00 | 580.00 | 0.00 | 11.61 | 11.61 |
| 764 | 120 | 63.00 | 581.00 | 0.00 | 11.63 | 11.63 |
| 765 | 120 | 63.00 | 582.00 | 0.00 | 11.65 | 11.65 |
| 766 | 120 | 63.00 | 583.00 | 0.00 | 11.67 | 11.67 |
| 767 | 120 | 63.00 | 584.00 | 0.00 | 11.69 | 11.69 |
| 768 | 120 | 63.00 | 585.00 | 0.00 | 11.71 | 11.71 |
| 769 | 120 | 63.00 | 586.00 | 0.00 | 11.73 | 11.73 |
| 770 | 120 | 63.00 | 587.00 | 0.00 | 11.75 | 11.75 |
| 771 | 120 | 63.00 | 588.00 | 0.00 | 11.77 | 11.77 |
| 772 | 120 | 63.00 | 589.00 | 0.00 | 11.79 | 11.79 |
| 773 | 120 | 63.00 | 590.00 | 0.00 | 11.81 | 11.81 |
| 774 | 120 | 63.00 | 591.00 | 0.00 | 11.83 | 11.83 |
| 775 | 120 | 63.00 | 592.00 | 0.00 | 11.85 | 11.85 |
| 776 | 120 | 63.00 | 593.00 | 0.00 | 11.87 | 11.87 |
| 777 | 120 | 63.00 | 594.00 | 0.00 | 11.89 | 11.89 |
| 778 | 120 | 63.00 | 595.00 | 0.00 | 11.91 | 11.91 |
| 779 | 120 | 63.00 | 596.00 | 0.00 | 11.93 | 11.93 |
| 780 | 120 | 63.00 | 597.00 | 0.00 | 11.95 | 11.95 |
| 781 | 120 | 63.00 | 598.00 | 0.00 | 11.97 | 11.97 |
| 782 | 120 | 63.00 | 599.00 | 0.00 | 11.99 | 11.99 |
| 783 | 120 | 63.00 | 600.00 | 0.00 | 12.01 | 12.01 |
| 784 | 120 | 63.00 | 601.00 | 0.00 | 12.03 | 12.03 |
| 785 | 120 | 63.00 | 602.00 | 0.00 | 12.05 | 12.05 |
| 786 | 120 | 63.00 | 603.00 | 0.00 | 12.07 | 12.07 |
| 787 | 120 | 63.00 | 604.00 | 0.00 | 12.09 | 12.09 |
| 788 | 120 | 63.00 | 605.00 | 0.00 | 12.11 | 12.11 |
| 789 | 120 | 63.00 | 606.00 | 0.00 | 12.13 | 12.13 |
| 790 | 120 | 63.00 | 607.00 | 0.00 | 12.15 | 12.15 |
| 791 | 120 | 63.00 | 608.00 | 0.00 | 12.17 | 12.17 |
| 792 | 120 | 63.00 | 609.00 | 0.00 | 12.19 | 12.19 |
| 793 | 120 | 63.00 | 610.00 | 0.00 | 12.21 | 12.21 |
| 794 | 120 | 63.00 | 611.00 | 0.00 | 12.23 | 12.23 |
| 795 | 120 | 63.00 | 612.00 | 0.00 | 12.25 | 12.25 |
| 796 | 120 | 63.00 | 613.00 | 0.00 | 12.27 | 12.27 |
| 797 | 120 | 63.00 | 614.00 | 0.00 | 12.29 | 12.29 |
| 798 | 120 | 63.00 | 615.00 | 0.00 | 12.31 | 12.31 |
| 799 | 120 | 63.00 | 616.00 | 0.00 | 12.33 | 12.33 |
| 800 | 120 | 63.00 | 617.00 | 0.00 | 12.35 | 12.35 |
| 801 | 120 | 63.00 | 618.00 | 0.00 | 12.37 | 12.37 |
| 802 | 120 | 63.00 | 619.00 | 0.00 | 12.39 | 12.39 |
| 803 | 120 | 63.00 | 620.00 | 0.00 | 12.41 | 12.41 |
| 804 | 120 | 63.00 | 621.00 | 0.00 | 12.43 | 12.43 |

**Weekly table**                                                                                    **Table letter Z**

| Employee's earnings up to and including the UEL | Earnings at the LEL (where earnings are equal to or exceed the LEL) | Earnings above the LEL, up to and including the PT | Earnings above the PT, up to and including the UEL | Employer's NICs due on all earnings above the ST | Employee's NICs due on all earnings above the PT | Total of employee's and employer's NICs (for information only) |
|---|---|---|---|---|---|---|
| | 1a | 1b | 1c | 1d | 1e | |
| £ | £ | £ p | £ p | £ p | £ p | £ p |
| 805 | 120 | 63.00 | 622.00 | 0.00 | 12.45 | 12.45 |
| 806 | 120 | 63.00 | 623.00 | 0.00 | 12.47 | 12.47 |
| 807 | 120 | 63.00 | 624.00 | 0.00 | 12.49 | 12.49 |
| 808 | 120 | 63.00 | 625.00 | 0.00 | 12.51 | 12.51 |
| 809 | 120 | 63.00 | 626.00 | 0.00 | 12.53 | 12.53 |
| 810 | 120 | 63.00 | 627.00 | 0.00 | 12.55 | 12.55 |
| 811 | 120 | 63.00 | 628.00 | 0.00 | 12.57 | 12.57 |
| 812 | 120 | 63.00 | 629.00 | 0.00 | 12.59 | 12.59 |
| 813 | 120 | 63.00 | 630.00 | 0.00 | 12.61 | 12.61 |
| 814 | 120 | 63.00 | 631.00 | 0.00 | 12.63 | 12.63 |
| 815 | 120 | 63.00 | 632.00 | 0.00 | 12.65 | 12.65 |
| 816 | 120 | 63.00 | 633.00 | 0.00 | 12.67 | 12.67 |
| 817 | 120 | 63.00 | 634.00 | 0.00 | 12.69 | 12.69 |
| 818 | 120 | 63.00 | 635.00 | 0.00 | 12.71 | 12.71 |
| 819 | 120 | 63.00 | 636.00 | 0.00 | 12.73 | 12.73 |
| 820 | 120 | 63.00 | 637.00 | 0.00 | 12.75 | 12.75 |
| 821 | 120 | 63.00 | 638.00 | 0.00 | 12.77 | 12.77 |
| 822 | 120 | 63.00 | 639.00 | 0.00 | 12.79 | 12.79 |
| 823 | 120 | 63.00 | 640.00 | 0.00 | 12.81 | 12.81 |
| 824 | 120 | 63.00 | 641.00 | 0.00 | 12.83 | 12.83 |
| 825 | 120 | 63.00 | 642.00 | 0.00 | 12.85 | 12.85 |
| 826 | 120 | 63.00 | 643.00 | 0.00 | 12.87 | 12.87 |
| 827 | 120 | 63.00 | 644.00 | 0.00 | 12.89 | 12.89 |
| 828 | 120 | 63.00 | 645.00 | 0.00 | 12.91 | 12.91 |
| 829 | 120 | 63.00 | 646.00 | 0.00 | 12.93 | 12.93 |
| 830 | 120 | 63.00 | 647.00 | 0.00 | 12.95 | 12.95 |
| 831 | 120 | 63.00 | 648.00 | 0.00 | 12.97 | 12.97 |
| 832 | 120 | 63.00 | 649.00 | 0.00 | 12.99 | 12.99 |
| 833 | 120 | 63.00 | 650.00 | 0.00 | 13.01 | 13.01 |
| 834 | 120 | 63.00 | 651.00 | 0.00 | 13.03 | 13.03 |
| 835 | 120 | 63.00 | 652.00 | 0.00 | 13.05 | 13.05 |
| 836 | 120 | 63.00 | 653.00 | 0.00 | 13.07 | 13.07 |
| 837 | 120 | 63.00 | 654.00 | 0.00 | 13.09 | 13.09 |
| 838 | 120 | 63.00 | 655.00 | 0.00 | 13.11 | 13.11 |
| 839 | 120 | 63.00 | 656.00 | 0.00 | 13.13 | 13.13 |
| 840 | 120 | 63.00 | 657.00 | 0.00 | 13.15 | 13.15 |
| 841 | 120 | 63.00 | 658.00 | 0.00 | 13.17 | 13.17 |
| 842 | 120 | 63.00 | 659.00 | 0.00 | 13.19 | 13.19 |
| 843 | 120 | 63.00 | 660.00 | 0.00 | 13.21 | 13.21 |
| 844 | 120 | 63.00 | 661.00 | 0.00 | 13.23 | 13.23 |
| 845 | 120 | 63.00 | 662.00 | 0.00 | 13.25 | 13.25 |
| 846 | 120 | 63.00 | 663.00 | 0.00 | 13.27 | 13.27 |
| 847 | 120 | 63.00 | 664.00 | 0.00 | 13.29 | 13.29 |
| 848 | 120 | 63.00 | 665.00 | 0.00 | 13.31 | 13.31 |
| 849 | 120 | 63.00 | 666.00 | 0.00 | 13.33 | 13.33 |
| 850 | 120 | 63.00 | 667.00 | 0.00 | 13.35 | 13.35 |
| 851 | 120 | 63.00 | 668.00 | 0.00 | 13.37 | 13.37 |
| 852 | 120 | 63.00 | 669.00 | 0.00 | 13.39 | 13.39 |
| 853 | 120 | 63.00 | 670.00 | 0.00 | 13.41 | 13.41 |
| 854 | 120 | 63.00 | 671.00 | 0.00 | 13.43 | 13.43 |
| 855 | 120 | 63.00 | 672.00 | 0.00 | 13.45 | 13.45 |
| 856 | 120 | 63.00 | 673.00 | 0.00 | 13.47 | 13.47 |
| 857 | 120 | 63.00 | 674.00 | 0.00 | 13.49 | 13.49 |
| 858 | 120 | 63.00 | 675.00 | 0.00 | 13.51 | 13.51 |
| 859 | 120 | 63.00 | 676.00 | 0.00 | 13.53 | 13.53 |

## Table letter Z
## Weekly table

| Employee's earnings up to and including the UEL | Earnings at the LEL (where earnings are equal to or exceed the LEL) | Earnings above the LEL, up to and including the PT | Earnings above the PT, up to and including the UEL | Employer's NICs due on all earnings above the ST | Employee's NICs due on all earnings above the PT | Total of employee's and employer's NICs (for information only) |
|---|---|---|---|---|---|---|
| | 1a | 1b | 1c | 1d | 1e | |
| £ | £ | £ p | £ p | £ p | £ p | £ p |
| 860 | 120 | 63.00 | 677.00 | 0.00 | 13.55 | 13.55 |
| 861 | 120 | 63.00 | 678.00 | 0.00 | 13.57 | 13.57 |
| 862 | 120 | 63.00 | 679.00 | 0.00 | 13.59 | 13.59 |
| 863 | 120 | 63.00 | 680.00 | 0.00 | 13.61 | 13.61 |
| 864 | 120 | 63.00 | 681.00 | 0.00 | 13.63 | 13.63 |
| 865 | 120 | 63.00 | 682.00 | 0.00 | 13.65 | 13.65 |
| 866 | 120 | 63.00 | 683.00 | 0.00 | 13.67 | 13.67 |
| 867 | 120 | 63.00 | 684.00 | 0.00 | 13.69 | 13.69 |
| 868 | 120 | 63.00 | 685.00 | 0.00 | 13.71 | 13.71 |
| 869 | 120 | 63.00 | 686.00 | 0.00 | 13.73 | 13.73 |
| 870 | 120 | 63.00 | 687.00 | 0.00 | 13.75 | 13.75 |
| 871 | 120 | 63.00 | 688.00 | 0.00 | 13.77 | 13.77 |
| 872 | 120 | 63.00 | 689.00 | 0.00 | 13.79 | 13.79 |
| 873 | 120 | 63.00 | 690.00 | 0.00 | 13.81 | 13.81 |
| 874 | 120 | 63.00 | 691.00 | 0.00 | 13.83 | 13.83 |
| 875 | 120 | 63.00 | 692.00 | 0.00 | 13.85 | 13.85 |
| 876 | 120 | 63.00 | 693.00 | 0.00 | 13.87 | 13.87 |
| 877 | 120 | 63.00 | 694.00 | 0.00 | 13.89 | 13.89 |
| 878 | 120 | 63.00 | 695.00 | 0.00 | 13.91 | 13.91 |
| 879 | 120 | 63.00 | 696.00 | 0.00 | 13.93 | 13.93 |
| 880 | 120 | 63.00 | 697.00 | 0.00 | 13.95 | 13.95 |
| 881 | 120 | 63.00 | 698.00 | 0.00 | 13.97 | 13.97 |
| 882 | 120 | 63.00 | 699.00 | 0.00 | 13.99 | 13.99 |
| 883 | 120 | 63.00 | 700.00 | 0.00 | 14.01 | 14.01 |
| 884 | 120 | 63.00 | 701.00 | 0.00 | 14.03 | 14.03 |
| 885 | 120 | 63.00 | 702.00 | 0.00 | 14.05 | 14.05 |
| 886 | 120 | 63.00 | 703.00 | 0.00 | 14.07 | 14.07 |
| 887 | 120 | 63.00 | 704.00 | 0.00 | 14.09 | 14.09 |
| 888 | 120 | 63.00 | 705.00 | 0.00 | 14.11 | 14.11 |
| 889 | 120 | 63.00 | 706.00 | 0.00 | 14.13 | 14.13 |
| 890 | 120 | 63.00 | 707.00 | 0.00 | 14.15 | 14.15 |
| 891 | 120 | 63.00 | 708.00 | 0.00 | 14.17 | 14.17 |
| 892 | 120 | 63.00 | 709.00 | 0.00 | 14.19 | 14.19 |
| 893 | 120 | 63.00 | 710.00 | 0.00 | 14.21 | 14.21 |
| 894 | 120 | 63.00 | 711.00 | 0.00 | 14.23 | 14.23 |
| 895 | 120 | 63.00 | 712.00 | 0.00 | 14.25 | 14.25 |
| 896 | 120 | 63.00 | 713.00 | 0.00 | 14.27 | 14.27 |
| 897 | 120 | 63.00 | 714.00 | 0.00 | 14.29 | 14.29 |
| 898 | 120 | 63.00 | 715.00 | 0.00 | 14.31 | 14.31 |
| 899 | 120 | 63.00 | 716.00 | 0.00 | 14.33 | 14.33 |
| 900 | 120 | 63.00 | 717.00 | 0.00 | 14.35 | 14.35 |
| 901 | 120 | 63.00 | 718.00 | 0.00 | 14.37 | 14.37 |
| 902 | 120 | 63.00 | 719.00 | 0.00 | 14.39 | 14.39 |
| 903 | 120 | 63.00 | 720.00 | 0.00 | 14.41 | 14.41 |
| 904 | 120 | 63.00 | 721.00 | 0.00 | 14.43 | 14.43 |
| 905 | 120 | 63.00 | 722.00 | 0.00 | 14.45 | 14.45 |
| 906 | 120 | 63.00 | 723.00 | 0.00 | 14.47 | 14.47 |
| 907 | 120 | 63.00 | 724.00 | 0.00 | 14.49 | 14.49 |
| 908 | 120 | 63.00 | 725.00 | 0.00 | 14.51 | 14.51 |
| 909 | 120 | 63.00 | 726.00 | 0.00 | 14.53 | 14.53 |
| 910 | 120 | 63.00 | 727.00 | 0.00 | 14.55 | 14.55 |
| 911 | 120 | 63.00 | 728.00 | 0.00 | 14.57 | 14.57 |
| 912 | 120 | 63.00 | 729.00 | 0.00 | 14.59 | 14.59 |
| 913 | 120 | 63.00 | 730.00 | 0.00 | 14.61 | 14.61 |
| 914 | 120 | 63.00 | 731.00 | 0.00 | 14.63 | 14.63 |

**Weekly table**

**Table letter Z**

| Employee's earnings up to and including the UEL | Earnings at the LEL (where earnings are equal to or exceed the LEL) 1a | Earnings above the LEL, up to and including the PT 1b | Earnings above the PT, up to and including the UEL 1c | Employer's NICs due on all earnings above the ST 1d | Employee's NICs due on all earnings above the PT 1e | Total of employee's and employer's NICs (for information only) |
|---|---|---|---|---|---|---|
| £ | £ | £ p | £ p | £ p | £ p | £ p |
| 915 | 120 | 63.00 | 732.00 | 0.00 | 14.65 | 14.65 |
| 916 | 120 | 63.00 | 733.00 | 0.00 | 14.67 | 14.67 |
| 917 | 120 | 63.00 | 734.00 | 0.00 | 14.69 | 14.69 |
| 918 | 120 | 63.00 | 735.00 | 0.00 | 14.71 | 14.71 |
| 919 | 120 | 63.00 | 736.00 | 0.00 | 14.73 | 14.73 |
| 920 | 120 | 63.00 | 737.00 | 0.00 | 14.75 | 14.75 |
| 921 | 120 | 63.00 | 738.00 | 0.00 | 14.77 | 14.77 |
| 922 | 120 | 63.00 | 739.00 | 0.00 | 14.79 | 14.79 |
| 923 | 120 | 63.00 | 740.00 | 0.00 | 14.81 | 14.81 |
| 924 | 120 | 63.00 | 741.00 | 0.00 | 14.83 | 14.83 |
| 925 | 120 | 63.00 | 742.00 | 0.00 | 14.85 | 14.85 |
| 926 | 120 | 63.00 | 743.00 | 0.00 | 14.87 | 14.87 |
| 927 | 120 | 63.00 | 744.00 | 0.00 | 14.89 | 14.89 |
| 928 | 120 | 63.00 | 745.00 | 0.00 | 14.91 | 14.91 |
| 929 | 120 | 63.00 | 746.00 | 0.00 | 14.93 | 14.93 |
| 930 | 120 | 63.00 | 747.00 | 0.00 | 14.95 | 14.95 |
| 931 | 120 | 63.00 | 748.00 | 0.00 | 14.97 | 14.97 |
| 932 | 120 | 63.00 | 749.00 | 0.00 | 14.99 | 14.99 |
| 933 | 120 | 63.00 | 750.00 | 0.00 | 15.01 | 15.01 |
| 934 | 120 | 63.00 | 751.00 | 0.00 | 15.03 | 15.03 |
| 935 | 120 | 63.00 | 752.00 | 0.00 | 15.05 | 15.05 |
| 936 | 120 | 63.00 | 753.00 | 0.00 | 15.07 | 15.07 |
| 937 | 120 | 63.00 | 754.00 | 0.00 | 15.09 | 15.09 |
| 938 | 120 | 63.00 | 755.00 | 0.00 | 15.11 | 15.11 |
| 939 | 120 | 63.00 | 756.00 | 0.00 | 15.13 | 15.13 |
| 940 | 120 | 63.00 | 757.00 | 0.00 | 15.15 | 15.15 |
| 941 | 120 | 63.00 | 758.00 | 0.00 | 15.17 | 15.17 |
| 942 | 120 | 63.00 | 759.00 | 0.00 | 15.19 | 15.19 |
| 943 | 120 | 63.00 | 760.00 | 0.00 | 15.21 | 15.21 |
| 944 | 120 | 63.00 | 761.00 | 0.00 | 15.23 | 15.23 |
| 945 | 120 | 63.00 | 762.00 | 0.00 | 15.25 | 15.25 |
| 946 | 120 | 63.00 | 763.00 | 0.00 | 15.27 | 15.27 |
| 947 | 120 | 63.00 | 764.00 | 0.00 | 15.29 | 15.29 |
| 948 | 120 | 63.00 | 765.00 | 0.00 | 15.31 | 15.31 |
| 949 | 120 | 63.00 | 766.00 | 0.00 | 15.33 | 15.33 |
| 950 | 120 | 63.00 | 767.00 | 0.00 | 15.35 | 15.35 |
| 951 | 120 | 63.00 | 768.00 | 0.00 | 15.37 | 15.37 |
| 952 | 120 | 63.00 | 769.00 | 0.00 | 15.39 | 15.39 |
| 953 | 120 | 63.00 | 770.00 | 0.00 | 15.41 | 15.41 |
| 954 | 120 | 63.00 | 771.00 | 0.00 | 15.43 | 15.43 |
| 955 | 120 | 63.00 | 772.00 | 0.00 | 15.45 | 15.45 |
| 956 | 120 | 63.00 | 773.00 | 0.00 | 15.47 | 15.47 |
| 957 | 120 | 63.00 | 774.00 | 0.00 | 15.49 | 15.49 |
| 958 | 120 | 63.00 | 775.00 | 0.00 | 15.51 | 15.51 |
| 959 | 120 | 63.00 | 776.00 | 0.00 | 15.53 | 15.53 |
| 960 | 120 | 63.00 | 777.00 | 0.00 | 15.55 | 15.55 |
| 961 | 120 | 63.00 | 778.00 | 0.00 | 15.57 | 15.57 |
| 962 | 120 | 63.00 | 779.00 | 0.00 | 15.58 | 15.58 |

If the employee's gross pay is over £962, go to page 178.

# Monthly table for NICs where employee has deferment for use from 6 April 2020 to 5 April 2021

**Table letter Z**

Use this table for employees who are under the age of 21 for whom you hold form CA2700.

Do not use this table for:

- any tax year other than 2020 to 2021
- employees who are aged 21 or over, for whom you hold form CA2700 (go to Table letter J)
- employees who are State Pension age or over (go to Table letter C in booklet CA41)

**Completing form RT11, 'Deductions working sheet' or substitute**

1 Enter 'Z' in the NICs Category Letter column on form RT11.

2 Copy the figures in columns 1a – 1e of the table to columns 1a – 1e on the line next to the tax month in which the employee is paid, on form RT11.

If the employee's total earnings fall between the LEL and the UEL/UST/AUST and the exact gross pay is not shown in the table, use the next smaller figure shown. If the employee's total earnings exceed the UEL/UST/AUST, go to page 163.

The figures in the left-hand column of each table show steps between the LEL and the UEL/UST/AUST. The NICs liability for each step, with the exception of the LEL, ST, PT, UEL, UST and AUST is worked out at the mid-point of the steps so you and your employee may pay slightly more or less than if you used the exact percentage method.

| Employee's earnings up to and including the UEL | Earnings at the LEL (where earnings are equal to or exceed the LEL) | Earnings above the LEL, up to and including the PT | Earnings above the PT, up to and including the UEL | Employer's NICs due on all earnings above the ST | Employee's NICs due on all earnings above the PT | Total of employee's and employer's NICs (for information only) |
|---|---|---|---|---|---|---|
| | 1a | 1b | 1c | 1d | 1e | |
| £ | £ | £ p | £ p | £ p | £ p | £ p |
| Up to and including £519.99 | No NICs liability, make no entries on form RT11 | | | | | |
| 520 | 520 | 0.00 | 0.00 | 0.00 | 0.00 | 0.00 |
| 524 | 520 | 4.00 | 0.00 | 0.00 | 0.00 | 0.00 |
| 528 | 520 | 8.00 | 0.00 | 0.00 | 0.00 | 0.00 |
| 532 | 520 | 12.00 | 0.00 | 0.00 | 0.00 | 0.00 |
| 536 | 520 | 16.00 | 0.00 | 0.00 | 0.00 | 0.00 |
| 540 | 520 | 20.00 | 0.00 | 0.00 | 0.00 | 0.00 |
| 544 | 520 | 24.00 | 0.00 | 0.00 | 0.00 | 0.00 |
| 548 | 520 | 28.00 | 0.00 | 0.00 | 0.00 | 0.00 |
| 552 | 520 | 32.00 | 0.00 | 0.00 | 0.00 | 0.00 |
| 556 | 520 | 36.00 | 0.00 | 0.00 | 0.00 | 0.00 |
| 560 | 520 | 40.00 | 0.00 | 0.00 | 0.00 | 0.00 |
| 564 | 520 | 44.00 | 0.00 | 0.00 | 0.00 | 0.00 |
| 568 | 520 | 48.00 | 0.00 | 0.00 | 0.00 | 0.00 |
| 572 | 520 | 52.00 | 0.00 | 0.00 | 0.00 | 0.00 |
| 576 | 520 | 56.00 | 0.00 | 0.00 | 0.00 | 0.00 |
| 580 | 520 | 60.00 | 0.00 | 0.00 | 0.00 | 0.00 |
| 584 | 520 | 64.00 | 0.00 | 0.00 | 0.00 | 0.00 |
| 588 | 520 | 68.00 | 0.00 | 0.00 | 0.00 | 0.00 |
| 592 | 520 | 72.00 | 0.00 | 0.00 | 0.00 | 0.00 |
| 596 | 520 | 76.00 | 0.00 | 0.00 | 0.00 | 0.00 |
| 600 | 520 | 80.00 | 0.00 | 0.00 | 0.00 | 0.00 |
| 604 | 520 | 84.00 | 0.00 | 0.00 | 0.00 | 0.00 |
| 608 | 520 | 88.00 | 0.00 | 0.00 | 0.00 | 0.00 |
| 612 | 520 | 92.00 | 0.00 | 0.00 | 0.00 | 0.00 |
| 616 | 520 | 96.00 | 0.00 | 0.00 | 0.00 | 0.00 |

## Table letter Z

**Monthly table**

| Employee's earnings up to and including the UEL | Earnings at the LEL (where earnings are equal to or exceed the LEL) | Earnings above the LEL, up to and including the PT | Earnings above the PT, up to and including the UEL | Employer's NICs due on all earnings above the ST | Employee's NICs due on all earnings above the PT | Total of employee's and employer's NICs (for information only) |
|---|---|---|---|---|---|---|
| | | 1a | 1b | 1c | 1d | 1e |
| £ | £ | £ p | £ p | £ p | £ p | £ p |
| 620 | 520 | 100.00 | 0.00 | 0.00 | 0.00 | 0.00 |
| 624 | 520 | 104.00 | 0.00 | 0.00 | 0.00 | 0.00 |
| 628 | 520 | 108.00 | 0.00 | 0.00 | 0.00 | 0.00 |
| 632 | 520 | 112.00 | 0.00 | 0.00 | 0.00 | 0.00 |
| 636 | 520 | 116.00 | 0.00 | 0.00 | 0.00 | 0.00 |
| 640 | 520 | 120.00 | 0.00 | 0.00 | 0.00 | 0.00 |
| 644 | 520 | 124.00 | 0.00 | 0.00 | 0.00 | 0.00 |
| 648 | 520 | 128.00 | 0.00 | 0.00 | 0.00 | 0.00 |
| 652 | 520 | 132.00 | 0.00 | 0.00 | 0.00 | 0.00 |
| 656 | 520 | 136.00 | 0.00 | 0.00 | 0.00 | 0.00 |
| 660 | 520 | 140.00 | 0.00 | 0.00 | 0.00 | 0.00 |
| 664 | 520 | 144.00 | 0.00 | 0.00 | 0.00 | 0.00 |
| 668 | 520 | 148.00 | 0.00 | 0.00 | 0.00 | 0.00 |
| 672 | 520 | 152.00 | 0.00 | 0.00 | 0.00 | 0.00 |
| 676 | 520 | 156.00 | 0.00 | 0.00 | 0.00 | 0.00 |
| 680 | 520 | 160.00 | 0.00 | 0.00 | 0.00 | 0.00 |
| 684 | 520 | 164.00 | 0.00 | 0.00 | 0.00 | 0.00 |
| 688 | 520 | 168.00 | 0.00 | 0.00 | 0.00 | 0.00 |
| 692 | 520 | 172.00 | 0.00 | 0.00 | 0.00 | 0.00 |
| 696 | 520 | 176.00 | 0.00 | 0.00 | 0.00 | 0.00 |
| 700 | 520 | 180.00 | 0.00 | 0.00 | 0.00 | 0.00 |
| 704 | 520 | 184.00 | 0.00 | 0.00 | 0.00 | 0.00 |
| 708 | 520 | 188.00 | 0.00 | 0.00 | 0.00 | 0.00 |
| 712 | 520 | 192.00 | 0.00 | 0.00 | 0.00 | 0.00 |
| 716 | 520 | 196.00 | 0.00 | 0.00 | 0.00 | 0.00 |
| 720 | 520 | 200.00 | 0.00 | 0.00 | 0.00 | 0.00 |
| 724 | 520 | 204.00 | 0.00 | 0.00 | 0.00 | 0.00 |
| 728 | 520 | 208.00 | 0.00 | 0.00 | 0.00 | 0.00 |
| 732 | 520 | 212.00 | 0.00 | 0.00 | 0.00 | 0.00 |
| 736 | 520 | 216.00 | 0.00 | 0.00 | 0.00 | 0.00 |
| 740 | 520 | 220.00 | 0.00 | 0.00 | 0.00 | 0.00 |
| 744 | 520 | 224.00 | 0.00 | 0.00 | 0.00 | 0.00 |
| 748 | 520 | 228.00 | 0.00 | 0.00 | 0.00 | 0.00 |
| 752 | 520 | 232.00 | 0.00 | 0.00 | 0.00 | 0.00 |
| 756 | 520 | 236.00 | 0.00 | 0.00 | 0.00 | 0.00 |
| 760 | 520 | 240.00 | 0.00 | 0.00 | 0.00 | 0.00 |
| 764 | 520 | 244.00 | 0.00 | 0.00 | 0.00 | 0.00 |
| 768 | 520 | 248.00 | 0.00 | 0.00 | 0.00 | 0.00 |
| 772 | 520 | 252.00 | 0.00 | 0.00 | 0.00 | 0.00 |
| 776 | 520 | 256.00 | 0.00 | 0.00 | 0.00 | 0.00 |
| 780 | 520 | 260.00 | 0.00 | 0.00 | 0.00 | 0.00 |
| 784 | 520 | 264.00 | 0.00 | 0.00 | 0.00 | 0.00 |
| 788 | 520 | 268.00 | 0.00 | 0.00 | 0.00 | 0.00 |
| 792 | 520 | 272.00 | 0.00 | 0.00 | 0.00 | 0.00 |
| 796 | 520 | 272.00 | 4.00 | 0.00 | 0.12 | 0.12 |
| 800 | 520 | 272.00 | 8.00 | 0.00 | 0.20 | 0.20 |
| 804 | 520 | 272.00 | 12.00 | 0.00 | 0.28 | 0.28 |
| 808 | 520 | 272.00 | 16.00 | 0.00 | 0.36 | 0.36 |
| 812 | 520 | 272.00 | 20.00 | 0.00 | 0.44 | 0.44 |
| 816 | 520 | 272.00 | 24.00 | 0.00 | 0.52 | 0.52 |
| 820 | 520 | 272.00 | 28.00 | 0.00 | 0.60 | 0.60 |
| 824 | 520 | 272.00 | 32.00 | 0.00 | 0.68 | 0.68 |
| 828 | 520 | 272.00 | 36.00 | 0.00 | 0.76 | 0.76 |
| 832 | 520 | 272.00 | 40.00 | 0.00 | 0.84 | 0.84 |
| 836 | 520 | 272.00 | 44.00 | 0.00 | 0.92 | 0.92 |

## Table letter Z

**Monthly table**

| Employee's earnings up to and including the UEL | Earnings at the LEL (where earnings are equal to or exceed the LEL) | Earnings above the LEL, up to and including the PT | Earnings above the PT, up to and including the UEL | Employer's NICs due on all earnings above the ST | Employee's NICs due on all earnings above the PT | Total of employee's and employer's NICs (for information only) |
|---|---|---|---|---|---|---|
| | 1a | 1b | 1c | 1d | 1e | |
| £ | £ | £ p | £ p | £ p | £ p | £ p |
| 840 | 520 | 272.00 | 48.00 | 0.00 | 1.00 | 1.00 |
| 844 | 520 | 272.00 | 52.00 | 0.00 | 1.08 | 1.08 |
| 848 | 520 | 272.00 | 56.00 | 0.00 | 1.16 | 1.16 |
| 852 | 520 | 272.00 | 60.00 | 0.00 | 1.24 | 1.24 |
| 856 | 520 | 272.00 | 64.00 | 0.00 | 1.32 | 1.32 |
| 860 | 520 | 272.00 | 68.00 | 0.00 | 1.40 | 1.40 |
| 864 | 520 | 272.00 | 72.00 | 0.00 | 1.48 | 1.48 |
| 868 | 520 | 272.00 | 76.00 | 0.00 | 1.56 | 1.56 |
| 872 | 520 | 272.00 | 80.00 | 0.00 | 1.64 | 1.64 |
| 876 | 520 | 272.00 | 84.00 | 0.00 | 1.72 | 1.72 |
| 880 | 520 | 272.00 | 88.00 | 0.00 | 1.80 | 1.80 |
| 884 | 520 | 272.00 | 92.00 | 0.00 | 1.88 | 1.88 |
| 888 | 520 | 272.00 | 96.00 | 0.00 | 1.96 | 1.96 |
| 892 | 520 | 272.00 | 100.00 | 0.00 | 2.04 | 2.04 |
| 896 | 520 | 272.00 | 104.00 | 0.00 | 2.12 | 2.12 |
| 900 | 520 | 272.00 | 108.00 | 0.00 | 2.20 | 2.20 |
| 904 | 520 | 272.00 | 112.00 | 0.00 | 2.28 | 2.28 |
| 908 | 520 | 272.00 | 116.00 | 0.00 | 2.36 | 2.36 |
| 912 | 520 | 272.00 | 120.00 | 0.00 | 2.44 | 2.44 |
| 916 | 520 | 272.00 | 124.00 | 0.00 | 2.52 | 2.52 |
| 920 | 520 | 272.00 | 128.00 | 0.00 | 2.60 | 2.60 |
| 924 | 520 | 272.00 | 132.00 | 0.00 | 2.68 | 2.68 |
| 928 | 520 | 272.00 | 136.00 | 0.00 | 2.76 | 2.76 |
| 932 | 520 | 272.00 | 140.00 | 0.00 | 2.84 | 2.84 |
| 936 | 520 | 272.00 | 144.00 | 0.00 | 2.92 | 2.92 |
| 940 | 520 | 272.00 | 148.00 | 0.00 | 3.00 | 3.00 |
| 944 | 520 | 272.00 | 152.00 | 0.00 | 3.08 | 3.08 |
| 948 | 520 | 272.00 | 156.00 | 0.00 | 3.16 | 3.16 |
| 952 | 520 | 272.00 | 160.00 | 0.00 | 3.24 | 3.24 |
| 956 | 520 | 272.00 | 164.00 | 0.00 | 3.32 | 3.32 |
| 960 | 520 | 272.00 | 168.00 | 0.00 | 3.40 | 3.40 |
| 964 | 520 | 272.00 | 172.00 | 0.00 | 3.48 | 3.48 |
| 968 | 520 | 272.00 | 176.00 | 0.00 | 3.56 | 3.56 |
| 972 | 520 | 272.00 | 180.00 | 0.00 | 3.64 | 3.64 |
| 976 | 520 | 272.00 | 184.00 | 0.00 | 3.72 | 3.72 |
| 980 | 520 | 272.00 | 188.00 | 0.00 | 3.80 | 3.80 |
| 984 | 520 | 272.00 | 192.00 | 0.00 | 3.88 | 3.88 |
| 988 | 520 | 272.00 | 196.00 | 0.00 | 3.96 | 3.96 |
| 992 | 520 | 272.00 | 200.00 | 0.00 | 4.04 | 4.04 |
| 996 | 520 | 272.00 | 204.00 | 0.00 | 4.12 | 4.12 |
| 1000 | 520 | 272.00 | 208.00 | 0.00 | 4.20 | 4.20 |
| 1004 | 520 | 272.00 | 212.00 | 0.00 | 4.28 | 4.28 |
| 1008 | 520 | 272.00 | 216.00 | 0.00 | 4.36 | 4.36 |
| 1012 | 520 | 272.00 | 220.00 | 0.00 | 4.44 | 4.44 |
| 1016 | 520 | 272.00 | 224.00 | 0.00 | 4.52 | 4.52 |
| 1020 | 520 | 272.00 | 228.00 | 0.00 | 4.60 | 4.60 |
| 1024 | 520 | 272.00 | 232.00 | 0.00 | 4.68 | 4.68 |
| 1028 | 520 | 272.00 | 236.00 | 0.00 | 4.76 | 4.76 |
| 1032 | 520 | 272.00 | 240.00 | 0.00 | 4.84 | 4.84 |
| 1036 | 520 | 272.00 | 244.00 | 0.00 | 4.92 | 4.92 |
| 1040 | 520 | 272.00 | 248.00 | 0.00 | 5.00 | 5.00 |
| 1044 | 520 | 272.00 | 252.00 | 0.00 | 5.08 | 5.08 |
| 1048 | 520 | 272.00 | 256.00 | 0.00 | 5.16 | 5.16 |
| 1052 | 520 | 272.00 | 260.00 | 0.00 | 5.24 | 5.24 |
| 1056 | 520 | 272.00 | 264.00 | 0.00 | 5.32 | 5.32 |

**Monthly table**

**Table letter Z**

| Employee's earnings up to and including the UEL | Earnings at the LEL (where earnings are equal to or exceed the LEL) 1a | Earnings above the LEL, up to and including the PT 1b | Earnings above the PT, up to and including the UEL 1c | Employer's NICs due on all earnings above the ST 1d | Employee's NICs due on all earnings above the PT 1e | Total of employee's and employer's NICs (for information only) |
|---|---|---|---|---|---|---|
| £ | £ | £ p | £ p | £ p | £ p | £ p |
| 1060 | 520 | 272.00 | 268.00 | 0.00 | 5.40 | 5.40 |
| 1064 | 520 | 272.00 | 272.00 | 0.00 | 5.48 | 5.48 |
| 1068 | 520 | 272.00 | 276.00 | 0.00 | 5.56 | 5.56 |
| 1072 | 520 | 272.00 | 280.00 | 0.00 | 5.64 | 5.64 |
| 1076 | 520 | 272.00 | 284.00 | 0.00 | 5.72 | 5.72 |
| 1080 | 520 | 272.00 | 288.00 | 0.00 | 5.80 | 5.80 |
| 1084 | 520 | 272.00 | 292.00 | 0.00 | 5.88 | 5.88 |
| 1088 | 520 | 272.00 | 296.00 | 0.00 | 5.96 | 5.96 |
| 1092 | 520 | 272.00 | 300.00 | 0.00 | 6.04 | 6.04 |
| 1096 | 520 | 272.00 | 304.00 | 0.00 | 6.12 | 6.12 |
| 1100 | 520 | 272.00 | 308.00 | 0.00 | 6.20 | 6.20 |
| 1104 | 520 | 272.00 | 312.00 | 0.00 | 6.28 | 6.28 |
| 1108 | 520 | 272.00 | 316.00 | 0.00 | 6.36 | 6.36 |
| 1112 | 520 | 272.00 | 320.00 | 0.00 | 6.44 | 6.44 |
| 1116 | 520 | 272.00 | 324.00 | 0.00 | 6.52 | 6.52 |
| 1120 | 520 | 272.00 | 328.00 | 0.00 | 6.60 | 6.60 |
| 1124 | 520 | 272.00 | 332.00 | 0.00 | 6.68 | 6.68 |
| 1128 | 520 | 272.00 | 336.00 | 0.00 | 6.76 | 6.76 |
| 1132 | 520 | 272.00 | 340.00 | 0.00 | 6.84 | 6.84 |
| 1136 | 520 | 272.00 | 344.00 | 0.00 | 6.92 | 6.92 |
| 1140 | 520 | 272.00 | 348.00 | 0.00 | 7.00 | 7.00 |
| 1144 | 520 | 272.00 | 352.00 | 0.00 | 7.08 | 7.08 |
| 1148 | 520 | 272.00 | 356.00 | 0.00 | 7.16 | 7.16 |
| 1152 | 520 | 272.00 | 360.00 | 0.00 | 7.24 | 7.24 |
| 1156 | 520 | 272.00 | 364.00 | 0.00 | 7.32 | 7.32 |
| 1160 | 520 | 272.00 | 368.00 | 0.00 | 7.40 | 7.40 |
| 1164 | 520 | 272.00 | 372.00 | 0.00 | 7.48 | 7.48 |
| 1168 | 520 | 272.00 | 376.00 | 0.00 | 7.56 | 7.56 |
| 1172 | 520 | 272.00 | 380.00 | 0.00 | 7.64 | 7.64 |
| 1176 | 520 | 272.00 | 384.00 | 0.00 | 7.72 | 7.72 |
| 1180 | 520 | 272.00 | 388.00 | 0.00 | 7.80 | 7.80 |
| 1184 | 520 | 272.00 | 392.00 | 0.00 | 7.88 | 7.88 |
| 1188 | 520 | 272.00 | 396.00 | 0.00 | 7.96 | 7.96 |
| 1192 | 520 | 272.00 | 400.00 | 0.00 | 8.04 | 8.04 |
| 1196 | 520 | 272.00 | 404.00 | 0.00 | 8.12 | 8.12 |
| 1200 | 520 | 272.00 | 408.00 | 0.00 | 8.20 | 8.20 |
| 1204 | 520 | 272.00 | 412.00 | 0.00 | 8.28 | 8.28 |
| 1208 | 520 | 272.00 | 416.00 | 0.00 | 8.36 | 8.36 |
| 1212 | 520 | 272.00 | 420.00 | 0.00 | 8.44 | 8.44 |
| 1216 | 520 | 272.00 | 424.00 | 0.00 | 8.52 | 8.52 |
| 1220 | 520 | 272.00 | 428.00 | 0.00 | 8.60 | 8.60 |
| 1224 | 520 | 272.00 | 432.00 | 0.00 | 8.68 | 8.68 |
| 1228 | 520 | 272.00 | 436.00 | 0.00 | 8.76 | 8.76 |
| 1232 | 520 | 272.00 | 440.00 | 0.00 | 8.84 | 8.84 |
| 1236 | 520 | 272.00 | 444.00 | 0.00 | 8.92 | 8.92 |
| 1240 | 520 | 272.00 | 448.00 | 0.00 | 9.00 | 9.00 |
| 1244 | 520 | 272.00 | 452.00 | 0.00 | 9.08 | 9.08 |
| 1248 | 520 | 272.00 | 456.00 | 0.00 | 9.16 | 9.16 |
| 1252 | 520 | 272.00 | 460.00 | 0.00 | 9.24 | 9.24 |
| 1256 | 520 | 272.00 | 464.00 | 0.00 | 9.32 | 9.32 |
| 1260 | 520 | 272.00 | 468.00 | 0.00 | 9.40 | 9.40 |
| 1264 | 520 | 272.00 | 472.00 | 0.00 | 9.48 | 9.48 |
| 1268 | 520 | 272.00 | 476.00 | 0.00 | 9.56 | 9.56 |
| 1272 | 520 | 272.00 | 480.00 | 0.00 | 9.64 | 9.64 |
| 1276 | 520 | 272.00 | 484.00 | 0.00 | 9.72 | 9.72 |

## Table letter Z

## Monthly table

| Employee's earnings up to and including the UEL | Earnings at the LEL (where earnings are equal to or exceed the LEL) 1a | Earnings above the LEL, up to and including the PT 1b | Earnings above the PT, up to and including the UEL 1c | Employer's NICs due on all earnings above the ST 1d | Employee's NICs due on all earnings above the PT 1e | Total of employee's and employer's NICs (for information only) |
|---|---|---|---|---|---|---|
| £ | £ | £ p | £ p | £ p | £ p | £ p |
| 1280 | 520 | 272.00 | 488.00 | 0.00 | 9.80 | 9.80 |
| 1284 | 520 | 272.00 | 492.00 | 0.00 | 9.88 | 9.88 |
| 1288 | 520 | 272.00 | 496.00 | 0.00 | 9.96 | 9.96 |
| 1292 | 520 | 272.00 | 500.00 | 0.00 | 10.04 | 10.04 |
| 1296 | 520 | 272.00 | 504.00 | 0.00 | 10.12 | 10.12 |
| 1300 | 520 | 272.00 | 508.00 | 0.00 | 10.20 | 10.20 |
| 1304 | 520 | 272.00 | 512.00 | 0.00 | 10.28 | 10.28 |
| 1308 | 520 | 272.00 | 516.00 | 0.00 | 10.36 | 10.36 |
| 1312 | 520 | 272.00 | 520.00 | 0.00 | 10.44 | 10.44 |
| 1316 | 520 | 272.00 | 524.00 | 0.00 | 10.52 | 10.52 |
| 1320 | 520 | 272.00 | 528.00 | 0.00 | 10.60 | 10.60 |
| 1324 | 520 | 272.00 | 532.00 | 0.00 | 10.68 | 10.68 |
| 1328 | 520 | 272.00 | 536.00 | 0.00 | 10.76 | 10.76 |
| 1332 | 520 | 272.00 | 540.00 | 0.00 | 10.84 | 10.84 |
| 1336 | 520 | 272.00 | 544.00 | 0.00 | 10.92 | 10.92 |
| 1340 | 520 | 272.00 | 548.00 | 0.00 | 11.00 | 11.00 |
| 1344 | 520 | 272.00 | 552.00 | 0.00 | 11.08 | 11.08 |
| 1348 | 520 | 272.00 | 556.00 | 0.00 | 11.16 | 11.16 |
| 1352 | 520 | 272.00 | 560.00 | 0.00 | 11.24 | 11.24 |
| 1356 | 520 | 272.00 | 564.00 | 0.00 | 11.32 | 11.32 |
| 1360 | 520 | 272.00 | 568.00 | 0.00 | 11.40 | 11.40 |
| 1364 | 520 | 272.00 | 572.00 | 0.00 | 11.48 | 11.48 |
| 1368 | 520 | 272.00 | 576.00 | 0.00 | 11.56 | 11.56 |
| 1372 | 520 | 272.00 | 580.00 | 0.00 | 11.64 | 11.64 |
| 1376 | 520 | 272.00 | 584.00 | 0.00 | 11.72 | 11.72 |
| 1380 | 520 | 272.00 | 588.00 | 0.00 | 11.80 | 11.80 |
| 1384 | 520 | 272.00 | 592.00 | 0.00 | 11.88 | 11.88 |
| 1388 | 520 | 272.00 | 596.00 | 0.00 | 11.96 | 11.96 |
| 1392 | 520 | 272.00 | 600.00 | 0.00 | 12.04 | 12.04 |
| 1396 | 520 | 272.00 | 604.00 | 0.00 | 12.12 | 12.12 |
| 1400 | 520 | 272.00 | 608.00 | 0.00 | 12.20 | 12.20 |
| 1404 | 520 | 272.00 | 612.00 | 0.00 | 12.28 | 12.28 |
| 1408 | 520 | 272.00 | 616.00 | 0.00 | 12.36 | 12.36 |
| 1412 | 520 | 272.00 | 620.00 | 0.00 | 12.44 | 12.44 |
| 1416 | 520 | 272.00 | 624.00 | 0.00 | 12.52 | 12.52 |
| 1420 | 520 | 272.00 | 628.00 | 0.00 | 12.60 | 12.60 |
| 1424 | 520 | 272.00 | 632.00 | 0.00 | 12.68 | 12.68 |
| 1428 | 520 | 272.00 | 636.00 | 0.00 | 12.76 | 12.76 |
| 1432 | 520 | 272.00 | 640.00 | 0.00 | 12.84 | 12.84 |
| 1436 | 520 | 272.00 | 644.00 | 0.00 | 12.92 | 12.92 |
| 1440 | 520 | 272.00 | 648.00 | 0.00 | 13.00 | 13.00 |
| 1444 | 520 | 272.00 | 652.00 | 0.00 | 13.08 | 13.08 |
| 1448 | 520 | 272.00 | 656.00 | 0.00 | 13.16 | 13.16 |
| 1452 | 520 | 272.00 | 660.00 | 0.00 | 13.24 | 13.24 |
| 1456 | 520 | 272.00 | 664.00 | 0.00 | 13.32 | 13.32 |
| 1460 | 520 | 272.00 | 668.00 | 0.00 | 13.40 | 13.40 |
| 1464 | 520 | 272.00 | 672.00 | 0.00 | 13.48 | 13.48 |
| 1468 | 520 | 272.00 | 676.00 | 0.00 | 13.56 | 13.56 |
| 1472 | 520 | 272.00 | 680.00 | 0.00 | 13.64 | 13.64 |
| 1476 | 520 | 272.00 | 684.00 | 0.00 | 13.72 | 13.72 |
| 1480 | 520 | 272.00 | 688.00 | 0.00 | 13.80 | 13.80 |
| 1484 | 520 | 272.00 | 692.00 | 0.00 | 13.88 | 13.88 |
| 1488 | 520 | 272.00 | 696.00 | 0.00 | 13.96 | 13.96 |
| 1492 | 520 | 272.00 | 700.00 | 0.00 | 14.04 | 14.04 |
| 1496 | 520 | 272.00 | 704.00 | 0.00 | 14.12 | 14.12 |

## Monthly table

**Table letter Z**

| Employee's earnings up to and including the UEL | Earnings at the LEL (where earnings are equal to or exceed the LEL) | Earnings above the LEL, up to and including the PT | Earnings above the PT, up to and including the UEL | Employer's NICs due on all earnings above the ST | Employee's NICs due on all earnings above the PT | Total of employee's and employer's NICs (for information only) |
|---|---|---|---|---|---|---|
| | 1a | 1b | 1c | 1d | 1e | |
| £ | £ | £ p | £ p | £ p | £ p | £ p |
| 1500 | 520 | 272.00 | 708.00 | 0.00 | 14.20 | 14.20 |
| 1504 | 520 | 272.00 | 712.00 | 0.00 | 14.28 | 14.28 |
| 1508 | 520 | 272.00 | 716.00 | 0.00 | 14.36 | 14.36 |
| 1512 | 520 | 272.00 | 720.00 | 0.00 | 14.44 | 14.44 |
| 1516 | 520 | 272.00 | 724.00 | 0.00 | 14.52 | 14.52 |
| 1520 | 520 | 272.00 | 728.00 | 0.00 | 14.60 | 14.60 |
| 1524 | 520 | 272.00 | 732.00 | 0.00 | 14.68 | 14.68 |
| 1528 | 520 | 272.00 | 736.00 | 0.00 | 14.76 | 14.76 |
| 1532 | 520 | 272.00 | 740.00 | 0.00 | 14.84 | 14.84 |
| 1536 | 520 | 272.00 | 744.00 | 0.00 | 14.92 | 14.92 |
| 1540 | 520 | 272.00 | 748.00 | 0.00 | 15.00 | 15.00 |
| 1544 | 520 | 272.00 | 752.00 | 0.00 | 15.08 | 15.08 |
| 1548 | 520 | 272.00 | 756.00 | 0.00 | 15.16 | 15.16 |
| 1552 | 520 | 272.00 | 760.00 | 0.00 | 15.24 | 15.24 |
| 1556 | 520 | 272.00 | 764.00 | 0.00 | 15.32 | 15.32 |
| 1560 | 520 | 272.00 | 768.00 | 0.00 | 15.40 | 15.40 |
| 1564 | 520 | 272.00 | 772.00 | 0.00 | 15.48 | 15.48 |
| 1568 | 520 | 272.00 | 776.00 | 0.00 | 15.56 | 15.56 |
| 1572 | 520 | 272.00 | 780.00 | 0.00 | 15.64 | 15.64 |
| 1576 | 520 | 272.00 | 784.00 | 0.00 | 15.72 | 15.72 |
| 1580 | 520 | 272.00 | 788.00 | 0.00 | 15.80 | 15.80 |
| 1584 | 520 | 272.00 | 792.00 | 0.00 | 15.88 | 15.88 |
| 1588 | 520 | 272.00 | 796.00 | 0.00 | 15.96 | 15.96 |
| 1592 | 520 | 272.00 | 800.00 | 0.00 | 16.04 | 16.04 |
| 1596 | 520 | 272.00 | 804.00 | 0.00 | 16.12 | 16.12 |
| 1600 | 520 | 272.00 | 808.00 | 0.00 | 16.20 | 16.20 |
| 1604 | 520 | 272.00 | 812.00 | 0.00 | 16.28 | 16.28 |
| 1608 | 520 | 272.00 | 816.00 | 0.00 | 16.36 | 16.36 |
| 1612 | 520 | 272.00 | 820.00 | 0.00 | 16.44 | 16.44 |
| 1616 | 520 | 272.00 | 824.00 | 0.00 | 16.52 | 16.52 |
| 1620 | 520 | 272.00 | 828.00 | 0.00 | 16.60 | 16.60 |
| 1624 | 520 | 272.00 | 832.00 | 0.00 | 16.68 | 16.68 |
| 1628 | 520 | 272.00 | 836.00 | 0.00 | 16.76 | 16.76 |
| 1632 | 520 | 272.00 | 840.00 | 0.00 | 16.84 | 16.84 |
| 1636 | 520 | 272.00 | 844.00 | 0.00 | 16.92 | 16.92 |
| 1640 | 520 | 272.00 | 848.00 | 0.00 | 17.00 | 17.00 |
| 1644 | 520 | 272.00 | 852.00 | 0.00 | 17.08 | 17.08 |
| 1648 | 520 | 272.00 | 856.00 | 0.00 | 17.16 | 17.16 |
| 1652 | 520 | 272.00 | 860.00 | 0.00 | 17.24 | 17.24 |
| 1656 | 520 | 272.00 | 864.00 | 0.00 | 17.32 | 17.32 |
| 1660 | 520 | 272.00 | 868.00 | 0.00 | 17.40 | 17.40 |
| 1664 | 520 | 272.00 | 872.00 | 0.00 | 17.48 | 17.48 |
| 1668 | 520 | 272.00 | 876.00 | 0.00 | 17.56 | 17.56 |
| 1672 | 520 | 272.00 | 880.00 | 0.00 | 17.64 | 17.64 |
| 1676 | 520 | 272.00 | 884.00 | 0.00 | 17.72 | 17.72 |
| 1680 | 520 | 272.00 | 888.00 | 0.00 | 17.80 | 17.80 |
| 1684 | 520 | 272.00 | 892.00 | 0.00 | 17.88 | 17.88 |
| 1688 | 520 | 272.00 | 896.00 | 0.00 | 17.96 | 17.96 |
| 1692 | 520 | 272.00 | 900.00 | 0.00 | 18.04 | 18.04 |
| 1696 | 520 | 272.00 | 904.00 | 0.00 | 18.12 | 18.12 |
| 1700 | 520 | 272.00 | 908.00 | 0.00 | 18.20 | 18.20 |
| 1704 | 520 | 272.00 | 912.00 | 0.00 | 18.28 | 18.28 |
| 1708 | 520 | 272.00 | 916.00 | 0.00 | 18.36 | 18.36 |
| 1712 | 520 | 272.00 | 920.00 | 0.00 | 18.44 | 18.44 |
| 1716 | 520 | 272.00 | 924.00 | 0.00 | 18.52 | 18.52 |

## Table letter Z

**Monthly table**

| Employee's earnings up to and including the UEL | Earnings at the LEL (where earnings are equal to or exceed the LEL) | Earnings above the LEL, up to and including the PT | Earnings above the PT, up to and including the UEL | Employer's NICs due on all earnings above the ST | Employee's NICs due on all earnings above the PT | Total of employee's and employer's NICs (for information only) |
|---|---|---|---|---|---|---|
| | 1a | 1b | 1c | 1d | 1e | |
| £ | £ | £ p | £ p | £ p | £ p | £ p |
| 1720 | 520 | 272.00 | 928.00 | 0.00 | 18.60 | 18.60 |
| 1724 | 520 | 272.00 | 932.00 | 0.00 | 18.68 | 18.68 |
| 1728 | 520 | 272.00 | 936.00 | 0.00 | 18.76 | 18.76 |
| 1732 | 520 | 272.00 | 940.00 | 0.00 | 18.84 | 18.84 |
| 1736 | 520 | 272.00 | 944.00 | 0.00 | 18.92 | 18.92 |
| 1740 | 520 | 272.00 | 948.00 | 0.00 | 19.00 | 19.00 |
| 1744 | 520 | 272.00 | 952.00 | 0.00 | 19.08 | 19.08 |
| 1748 | 520 | 272.00 | 956.00 | 0.00 | 19.16 | 19.16 |
| 1752 | 520 | 272.00 | 960.00 | 0.00 | 19.24 | 19.24 |
| 1756 | 520 | 272.00 | 964.00 | 0.00 | 19.32 | 19.32 |
| 1760 | 520 | 272.00 | 968.00 | 0.00 | 19.40 | 19.40 |
| 1764 | 520 | 272.00 | 972.00 | 0.00 | 19.48 | 19.48 |
| 1768 | 520 | 272.00 | 976.00 | 0.00 | 19.56 | 19.56 |
| 1772 | 520 | 272.00 | 980.00 | 0.00 | 19.64 | 19.64 |
| 1776 | 520 | 272.00 | 984.00 | 0.00 | 19.72 | 19.72 |
| 1780 | 520 | 272.00 | 988.00 | 0.00 | 19.80 | 19.80 |
| 1784 | 520 | 272.00 | 992.00 | 0.00 | 19.88 | 19.88 |
| 1788 | 520 | 272.00 | 996.00 | 0.00 | 19.96 | 19.96 |
| 1792 | 520 | 272.00 | 1000.00 | 0.00 | 20.04 | 20.04 |
| 1796 | 520 | 272.00 | 1004.00 | 0.00 | 20.12 | 20.12 |
| 1800 | 520 | 272.00 | 1008.00 | 0.00 | 20.20 | 20.20 |
| 1804 | 520 | 272.00 | 1012.00 | 0.00 | 20.28 | 20.28 |
| 1808 | 520 | 272.00 | 1016.00 | 0.00 | 20.36 | 20.36 |
| 1812 | 520 | 272.00 | 1020.00 | 0.00 | 20.44 | 20.44 |
| 1816 | 520 | 272.00 | 1024.00 | 0.00 | 20.52 | 20.52 |
| 1820 | 520 | 272.00 | 1028.00 | 0.00 | 20.60 | 20.60 |
| 1824 | 520 | 272.00 | 1032.00 | 0.00 | 20.68 | 20.68 |
| 1828 | 520 | 272.00 | 1036.00 | 0.00 | 20.76 | 20.76 |
| 1832 | 520 | 272.00 | 1040.00 | 0.00 | 20.84 | 20.84 |
| 1836 | 520 | 272.00 | 1044.00 | 0.00 | 20.92 | 20.92 |
| 1840 | 520 | 272.00 | 1048.00 | 0.00 | 21.00 | 21.00 |
| 1844 | 520 | 272.00 | 1052.00 | 0.00 | 21.08 | 21.08 |
| 1848 | 520 | 272.00 | 1056.00 | 0.00 | 21.16 | 21.16 |
| 1852 | 520 | 272.00 | 1060.00 | 0.00 | 21.24 | 21.24 |
| 1856 | 520 | 272.00 | 1064.00 | 0.00 | 21.32 | 21.32 |
| 1860 | 520 | 272.00 | 1068.00 | 0.00 | 21.40 | 21.40 |
| 1864 | 520 | 272.00 | 1072.00 | 0.00 | 21.48 | 21.48 |
| 1868 | 520 | 272.00 | 1076.00 | 0.00 | 21.56 | 21.56 |
| 1872 | 520 | 272.00 | 1080.00 | 0.00 | 21.64 | 21.64 |
| 1876 | 520 | 272.00 | 1084.00 | 0.00 | 21.72 | 21.72 |
| 1880 | 520 | 272.00 | 1088.00 | 0.00 | 21.80 | 21.80 |
| 1884 | 520 | 272.00 | 1092.00 | 0.00 | 21.88 | 21.88 |
| 1888 | 520 | 272.00 | 1096.00 | 0.00 | 21.96 | 21.96 |
| 1892 | 520 | 272.00 | 1100.00 | 0.00 | 22.04 | 22.04 |
| 1896 | 520 | 272.00 | 1104.00 | 0.00 | 22.12 | 22.12 |
| 1900 | 520 | 272.00 | 1108.00 | 0.00 | 22.20 | 22.20 |
| 1904 | 520 | 272.00 | 1112.00 | 0.00 | 22.28 | 22.28 |
| 1908 | 520 | 272.00 | 1116.00 | 0.00 | 22.36 | 22.36 |
| 1912 | 520 | 272.00 | 1120.00 | 0.00 | 22.44 | 22.44 |
| 1916 | 520 | 272.00 | 1124.00 | 0.00 | 22.52 | 22.52 |
| 1920 | 520 | 272.00 | 1128.00 | 0.00 | 22.60 | 22.60 |
| 1924 | 520 | 272.00 | 1132.00 | 0.00 | 22.68 | 22.68 |
| 1928 | 520 | 272.00 | 1136.00 | 0.00 | 22.76 | 22.76 |
| 1932 | 520 | 272.00 | 1140.00 | 0.00 | 22.84 | 22.84 |
| 1936 | 520 | 272.00 | 1144.00 | 0.00 | 22.92 | 22.92 |

## Monthly table

**Table letter Z**

| Employee's earnings up to and including the UEL | Earnings at the LEL (where earnings are equal to or exceed the LEL) 1a | Earnings above the LEL, up to and including the PT 1b | Earnings above the PT, up to and including the UEL 1c | Employer's NICs due on all earnings above the ST 1d | Employee's NICs due on all earnings above the PT 1e | Total of employee's and employer's NICs (for information only) |
|---|---|---|---|---|---|---|
| £ | £ | £ p | £ p | £ p | £ p | £ p |
| 1940 | 520 | 272.00 | 1148.00 | 0.00 | 23.00 | 23.00 |
| 1944 | 520 | 272.00 | 1152.00 | 0.00 | 23.08 | 23.08 |
| 1948 | 520 | 272.00 | 1156.00 | 0.00 | 23.16 | 23.16 |
| 1952 | 520 | 272.00 | 1160.00 | 0.00 | 23.24 | 23.24 |
| 1956 | 520 | 272.00 | 1164.00 | 0.00 | 23.32 | 23.32 |
| 1960 | 520 | 272.00 | 1168.00 | 0.00 | 23.40 | 23.40 |
| 1964 | 520 | 272.00 | 1172.00 | 0.00 | 23.48 | 23.48 |
| 1968 | 520 | 272.00 | 1176.00 | 0.00 | 23.56 | 23.56 |
| 1972 | 520 | 272.00 | 1180.00 | 0.00 | 23.64 | 23.64 |
| 1976 | 520 | 272.00 | 1184.00 | 0.00 | 23.72 | 23.72 |
| 1980 | 520 | 272.00 | 1188.00 | 0.00 | 23.80 | 23.80 |
| 1984 | 520 | 272.00 | 1192.00 | 0.00 | 23.88 | 23.88 |
| 1988 | 520 | 272.00 | 1196.00 | 0.00 | 23.96 | 23.96 |
| 1992 | 520 | 272.00 | 1200.00 | 0.00 | 24.04 | 24.04 |
| 1996 | 520 | 272.00 | 1204.00 | 0.00 | 24.12 | 24.12 |
| 2000 | 520 | 272.00 | 1208.00 | 0.00 | 24.20 | 24.20 |
| 2004 | 520 | 272.00 | 1212.00 | 0.00 | 24.28 | 24.28 |
| 2008 | 520 | 272.00 | 1216.00 | 0.00 | 24.36 | 24.36 |
| 2012 | 520 | 272.00 | 1220.00 | 0.00 | 24.44 | 24.44 |
| 2016 | 520 | 272.00 | 1224.00 | 0.00 | 24.52 | 24.52 |
| 2020 | 520 | 272.00 | 1228.00 | 0.00 | 24.60 | 24.60 |
| 2024 | 520 | 272.00 | 1232.00 | 0.00 | 24.68 | 24.68 |
| 2028 | 520 | 272.00 | 1236.00 | 0.00 | 24.76 | 24.76 |
| 2032 | 520 | 272.00 | 1240.00 | 0.00 | 24.84 | 24.84 |
| 2036 | 520 | 272.00 | 1244.00 | 0.00 | 24.92 | 24.92 |
| 2040 | 520 | 272.00 | 1248.00 | 0.00 | 25.00 | 25.00 |
| 2044 | 520 | 272.00 | 1252.00 | 0.00 | 25.08 | 25.08 |
| 2048 | 520 | 272.00 | 1256.00 | 0.00 | 25.16 | 25.16 |
| 2052 | 520 | 272.00 | 1260.00 | 0.00 | 25.24 | 25.24 |
| 2056 | 520 | 272.00 | 1264.00 | 0.00 | 25.32 | 25.32 |
| 2060 | 520 | 272.00 | 1268.00 | 0.00 | 25.40 | 25.40 |
| 2064 | 520 | 272.00 | 1272.00 | 0.00 | 25.48 | 25.48 |
| 2068 | 520 | 272.00 | 1276.00 | 0.00 | 25.56 | 25.56 |
| 2072 | 520 | 272.00 | 1280.00 | 0.00 | 25.64 | 25.64 |
| 2076 | 520 | 272.00 | 1284.00 | 0.00 | 25.72 | 25.72 |
| 2080 | 520 | 272.00 | 1288.00 | 0.00 | 25.80 | 25.80 |
| 2084 | 520 | 272.00 | 1292.00 | 0.00 | 25.88 | 25.88 |
| 2088 | 520 | 272.00 | 1296.00 | 0.00 | 25.96 | 25.96 |
| 2092 | 520 | 272.00 | 1300.00 | 0.00 | 26.04 | 26.04 |
| 2096 | 520 | 272.00 | 1304.00 | 0.00 | 26.12 | 26.12 |
| 2100 | 520 | 272.00 | 1308.00 | 0.00 | 26.20 | 26.20 |
| 2104 | 520 | 272.00 | 1312.00 | 0.00 | 26.28 | 26.28 |
| 2108 | 520 | 272.00 | 1316.00 | 0.00 | 26.36 | 26.36 |
| 2112 | 520 | 272.00 | 1320.00 | 0.00 | 26.44 | 26.44 |
| 2116 | 520 | 272.00 | 1324.00 | 0.00 | 26.52 | 26.52 |
| 2120 | 520 | 272.00 | 1328.00 | 0.00 | 26.60 | 26.60 |
| 2124 | 520 | 272.00 | 1332.00 | 0.00 | 26.68 | 26.68 |
| 2128 | 520 | 272.00 | 1336.00 | 0.00 | 26.76 | 26.76 |
| 2132 | 520 | 272.00 | 1340.00 | 0.00 | 26.84 | 26.84 |
| 2136 | 520 | 272.00 | 1344.00 | 0.00 | 26.92 | 26.92 |
| 2140 | 520 | 272.00 | 1348.00 | 0.00 | 27.00 | 27.00 |
| 2144 | 520 | 272.00 | 1352.00 | 0.00 | 27.08 | 27.08 |
| 2148 | 520 | 272.00 | 1356.00 | 0.00 | 27.16 | 27.16 |
| 2152 | 520 | 272.00 | 1360.00 | 0.00 | 27.24 | 27.24 |
| 2156 | 520 | 272.00 | 1364.00 | 0.00 | 27.32 | 27.32 |

## Table letter Z                                                                        Monthly table

| Employee's earnings up to and including the UEL | Earnings at the LEL (where earnings are equal to or exceed the LEL) | Earnings above the LEL, up to and including the PT | Earnings above the PT, up to and including the UEL | Employer's NICs due on all earnings above the ST | Employee's NICs due on all earnings above the PT | Total of employee's and employer's NICs (for information only) |
|---|---|---|---|---|---|---|
| | | 1a | 1b | 1c | 1d | 1e |
| £ | £ | £ p | £ p | £ p | £ p | £ p |
| 2160 | 520 | 272.00 | 1368.00 | 0.00 | 27.40 | 27.40 |
| 2164 | 520 | 272.00 | 1372.00 | 0.00 | 27.48 | 27.48 |
| 2168 | 520 | 272.00 | 1376.00 | 0.00 | 27.56 | 27.56 |
| 2172 | 520 | 272.00 | 1380.00 | 0.00 | 27.64 | 27.64 |
| 2176 | 520 | 272.00 | 1384.00 | 0.00 | 27.72 | 27.72 |
| 2180 | 520 | 272.00 | 1388.00 | 0.00 | 27.80 | 27.80 |
| 2184 | 520 | 272.00 | 1392.00 | 0.00 | 27.88 | 27.88 |
| 2188 | 520 | 272.00 | 1396.00 | 0.00 | 27.96 | 27.96 |
| 2192 | 520 | 272.00 | 1400.00 | 0.00 | 28.04 | 28.04 |
| 2196 | 520 | 272.00 | 1404.00 | 0.00 | 28.12 | 28.12 |
| 2200 | 520 | 272.00 | 1408.00 | 0.00 | 28.20 | 28.20 |
| 2204 | 520 | 272.00 | 1412.00 | 0.00 | 28.28 | 28.28 |
| 2208 | 520 | 272.00 | 1416.00 | 0.00 | 28.36 | 28.36 |
| 2212 | 520 | 272.00 | 1420.00 | 0.00 | 28.44 | 28.44 |
| 2216 | 520 | 272.00 | 1424.00 | 0.00 | 28.52 | 28.52 |
| 2220 | 520 | 272.00 | 1428.00 | 0.00 | 28.60 | 28.60 |
| 2224 | 520 | 272.00 | 1432.00 | 0.00 | 28.68 | 28.68 |
| 2228 | 520 | 272.00 | 1436.00 | 0.00 | 28.76 | 28.76 |
| 2232 | 520 | 272.00 | 1440.00 | 0.00 | 28.84 | 28.84 |
| 2236 | 520 | 272.00 | 1444.00 | 0.00 | 28.92 | 28.92 |
| 2240 | 520 | 272.00 | 1448.00 | 0.00 | 29.00 | 29.00 |
| 2244 | 520 | 272.00 | 1452.00 | 0.00 | 29.08 | 29.08 |
| 2248 | 520 | 272.00 | 1456.00 | 0.00 | 29.16 | 29.16 |
| 2252 | 520 | 272.00 | 1460.00 | 0.00 | 29.24 | 29.24 |
| 2256 | 520 | 272.00 | 1464.00 | 0.00 | 29.32 | 29.32 |
| 2260 | 520 | 272.00 | 1468.00 | 0.00 | 29.40 | 29.40 |
| 2264 | 520 | 272.00 | 1472.00 | 0.00 | 29.48 | 29.48 |
| 2268 | 520 | 272.00 | 1476.00 | 0.00 | 29.56 | 29.56 |
| 2272 | 520 | 272.00 | 1480.00 | 0.00 | 29.64 | 29.64 |
| 2276 | 520 | 272.00 | 1484.00 | 0.00 | 29.72 | 29.72 |
| 2280 | 520 | 272.00 | 1488.00 | 0.00 | 29.80 | 29.80 |
| 2284 | 520 | 272.00 | 1492.00 | 0.00 | 29.88 | 29.88 |
| 2288 | 520 | 272.00 | 1496.00 | 0.00 | 29.96 | 29.96 |
| 2292 | 520 | 272.00 | 1500.00 | 0.00 | 30.04 | 30.04 |
| 2296 | 520 | 272.00 | 1504.00 | 0.00 | 30.12 | 30.12 |
| 2300 | 520 | 272.00 | 1508.00 | 0.00 | 30.20 | 30.20 |
| 2304 | 520 | 272.00 | 1512.00 | 0.00 | 30.28 | 30.28 |
| 2308 | 520 | 272.00 | 1516.00 | 0.00 | 30.36 | 30.36 |
| 2312 | 520 | 272.00 | 1520.00 | 0.00 | 30.44 | 30.44 |
| 2316 | 520 | 272.00 | 1524.00 | 0.00 | 30.52 | 30.52 |
| 2320 | 520 | 272.00 | 1528.00 | 0.00 | 30.60 | 30.60 |
| 2324 | 520 | 272.00 | 1532.00 | 0.00 | 30.68 | 30.68 |
| 2328 | 520 | 272.00 | 1536.00 | 0.00 | 30.76 | 30.76 |
| 2332 | 520 | 272.00 | 1540.00 | 0.00 | 30.84 | 30.84 |
| 2336 | 520 | 272.00 | 1544.00 | 0.00 | 30.92 | 30.92 |
| 2340 | 520 | 272.00 | 1548.00 | 0.00 | 31.00 | 31.00 |
| 2344 | 520 | 272.00 | 1552.00 | 0.00 | 31.08 | 31.08 |
| 2348 | 520 | 272.00 | 1556.00 | 0.00 | 31.16 | 31.16 |
| 2352 | 520 | 272.00 | 1560.00 | 0.00 | 31.24 | 31.24 |
| 2356 | 520 | 272.00 | 1564.00 | 0.00 | 31.32 | 31.32 |
| 2360 | 520 | 272.00 | 1568.00 | 0.00 | 31.40 | 31.40 |
| 2364 | 520 | 272.00 | 1572.00 | 0.00 | 31.48 | 31.48 |
| 2368 | 520 | 272.00 | 1576.00 | 0.00 | 31.56 | 31.56 |
| 2372 | 520 | 272.00 | 1580.00 | 0.00 | 31.64 | 31.64 |
| 2376 | 520 | 272.00 | 1584.00 | 0.00 | 31.72 | 31.72 |

## Monthly table

**Table letter Z**

| Employee's earnings up to and including the UEL | Earnings at the LEL (where earnings are equal to or exceed the LEL) 1a | Earnings above the LEL, up to and including the PT 1b | Earnings above the PT, up to and including the UEL 1c | Employer's NICs due on all earnings above the ST 1d | Employee's NICs due on all earnings above the PT 1e | Total of employee's and employer's NICs (for information only) |
|---|---|---|---|---|---|---|
| £ | £ | £ p | £ p | £ p | £ p | £ p |
| 2380 | 520 | 272.00 | 1588.00 | 0.00 | 31.80 | 31.80 |
| 2384 | 520 | 272.00 | 1592.00 | 0.00 | 31.88 | 31.88 |
| 2388 | 520 | 272.00 | 1596.00 | 0.00 | 31.96 | 31.96 |
| 2392 | 520 | 272.00 | 1600.00 | 0.00 | 32.04 | 32.04 |
| 2396 | 520 | 272.00 | 1604.00 | 0.00 | 32.12 | 32.12 |
| 2400 | 520 | 272.00 | 1608.00 | 0.00 | 32.20 | 32.20 |
| 2404 | 520 | 272.00 | 1612.00 | 0.00 | 32.28 | 32.28 |
| 2408 | 520 | 272.00 | 1616.00 | 0.00 | 32.36 | 32.36 |
| 2412 | 520 | 272.00 | 1620.00 | 0.00 | 32.44 | 32.44 |
| 2416 | 520 | 272.00 | 1624.00 | 0.00 | 32.52 | 32.52 |
| 2420 | 520 | 272.00 | 1628.00 | 0.00 | 32.60 | 32.60 |
| 2424 | 520 | 272.00 | 1632.00 | 0.00 | 32.68 | 32.68 |
| 2428 | 520 | 272.00 | 1636.00 | 0.00 | 32.76 | 32.76 |
| 2432 | 520 | 272.00 | 1640.00 | 0.00 | 32.84 | 32.84 |
| 2436 | 520 | 272.00 | 1644.00 | 0.00 | 32.92 | 32.92 |
| 2440 | 520 | 272.00 | 1648.00 | 0.00 | 33.00 | 33.00 |
| 2444 | 520 | 272.00 | 1652.00 | 0.00 | 33.08 | 33.08 |
| 2448 | 520 | 272.00 | 1656.00 | 0.00 | 33.16 | 33.16 |
| 2452 | 520 | 272.00 | 1660.00 | 0.00 | 33.24 | 33.24 |
| 2456 | 520 | 272.00 | 1664.00 | 0.00 | 33.32 | 33.32 |
| 2460 | 520 | 272.00 | 1668.00 | 0.00 | 33.40 | 33.40 |
| 2464 | 520 | 272.00 | 1672.00 | 0.00 | 33.48 | 33.48 |
| 2468 | 520 | 272.00 | 1676.00 | 0.00 | 33.56 | 33.56 |
| 2472 | 520 | 272.00 | 1680.00 | 0.00 | 33.64 | 33.64 |
| 2476 | 520 | 272.00 | 1684.00 | 0.00 | 33.72 | 33.72 |
| 2480 | 520 | 272.00 | 1688.00 | 0.00 | 33.80 | 33.80 |
| 2484 | 520 | 272.00 | 1692.00 | 0.00 | 33.88 | 33.88 |
| 2488 | 520 | 272.00 | 1696.00 | 0.00 | 33.96 | 33.96 |
| 2492 | 520 | 272.00 | 1700.00 | 0.00 | 34.04 | 34.04 |
| 2496 | 520 | 272.00 | 1704.00 | 0.00 | 34.12 | 34.12 |
| 2500 | 520 | 272.00 | 1708.00 | 0.00 | 34.20 | 34.20 |
| 2504 | 520 | 272.00 | 1712.00 | 0.00 | 34.28 | 34.28 |
| 2508 | 520 | 272.00 | 1716.00 | 0.00 | 34.36 | 34.36 |
| 2512 | 520 | 272.00 | 1720.00 | 0.00 | 34.44 | 34.44 |
| 2516 | 520 | 272.00 | 1724.00 | 0.00 | 34.52 | 34.52 |
| 2520 | 520 | 272.00 | 1728.00 | 0.00 | 34.60 | 34.60 |
| 2524 | 520 | 272.00 | 1732.00 | 0.00 | 34.68 | 34.68 |
| 2528 | 520 | 272.00 | 1736.00 | 0.00 | 34.76 | 34.76 |
| 2532 | 520 | 272.00 | 1740.00 | 0.00 | 34.84 | 34.84 |
| 2536 | 520 | 272.00 | 1744.00 | 0.00 | 34.92 | 34.92 |
| 2540 | 520 | 272.00 | 1748.00 | 0.00 | 35.00 | 35.00 |
| 2544 | 520 | 272.00 | 1752.00 | 0.00 | 35.08 | 35.08 |
| 2548 | 520 | 272.00 | 1756.00 | 0.00 | 35.16 | 35.16 |
| 2552 | 520 | 272.00 | 1760.00 | 0.00 | 35.24 | 35.24 |
| 2556 | 520 | 272.00 | 1764.00 | 0.00 | 35.32 | 35.32 |
| 2560 | 520 | 272.00 | 1768.00 | 0.00 | 35.40 | 35.40 |
| 2564 | 520 | 272.00 | 1772.00 | 0.00 | 35.48 | 35.48 |
| 2568 | 520 | 272.00 | 1776.00 | 0.00 | 35.56 | 35.56 |
| 2572 | 520 | 272.00 | 1780.00 | 0.00 | 35.64 | 35.64 |
| 2576 | 520 | 272.00 | 1784.00 | 0.00 | 35.72 | 35.72 |
| 2580 | 520 | 272.00 | 1788.00 | 0.00 | 35.80 | 35.80 |
| 2584 | 520 | 272.00 | 1792.00 | 0.00 | 35.88 | 35.88 |
| 2588 | 520 | 272.00 | 1796.00 | 0.00 | 35.96 | 35.96 |
| 2592 | 520 | 272.00 | 1800.00 | 0.00 | 36.04 | 36.04 |
| 2596 | 520 | 272.00 | 1804.00 | 0.00 | 36.12 | 36.12 |

# Table letter Z

**Monthly table**

| Employee's earnings up to and including the UEL | Earnings at the LEL (where earnings are equal to or exceed the LEL) 1a | Earnings above the LEL, up to and including the PT 1b | Earnings above the PT, up to and including the UEL 1c | Employer's NICs due on all earnings above the ST 1d | Employee's NICs due on all earnings above the PT 1e | Total of employee's and employer's NICs (for information only) |
|---|---|---|---|---|---|---|
| £ | £ | £ p | £ p | £ p | £ p | £ p |
| 2600 | 520 | 272.00 | 1808.00 | 0.00 | 36.20 | 36.20 |
| 2604 | 520 | 272.00 | 1812.00 | 0.00 | 36.28 | 36.28 |
| 2608 | 520 | 272.00 | 1816.00 | 0.00 | 36.36 | 36.36 |
| 2612 | 520 | 272.00 | 1820.00 | 0.00 | 36.44 | 36.44 |
| 2616 | 520 | 272.00 | 1824.00 | 0.00 | 36.52 | 36.52 |
| 2620 | 520 | 272.00 | 1828.00 | 0.00 | 36.60 | 36.60 |
| 2624 | 520 | 272.00 | 1832.00 | 0.00 | 36.68 | 36.68 |
| 2628 | 520 | 272.00 | 1836.00 | 0.00 | 36.76 | 36.76 |
| 2632 | 520 | 272.00 | 1840.00 | 0.00 | 36.84 | 36.84 |
| 2636 | 520 | 272.00 | 1844.00 | 0.00 | 36.92 | 36.92 |
| 2640 | 520 | 272.00 | 1848.00 | 0.00 | 37.00 | 37.00 |
| 2644 | 520 | 272.00 | 1852.00 | 0.00 | 37.08 | 37.08 |
| 2648 | 520 | 272.00 | 1856.00 | 0.00 | 37.16 | 37.16 |
| 2652 | 520 | 272.00 | 1860.00 | 0.00 | 37.24 | 37.24 |
| 2656 | 520 | 272.00 | 1864.00 | 0.00 | 37.32 | 37.32 |
| 2660 | 520 | 272.00 | 1868.00 | 0.00 | 37.40 | 37.40 |
| 2664 | 520 | 272.00 | 1872.00 | 0.00 | 37.48 | 37.48 |
| 2668 | 520 | 272.00 | 1876.00 | 0.00 | 37.56 | 37.56 |
| 2672 | 520 | 272.00 | 1880.00 | 0.00 | 37.64 | 37.64 |
| 2676 | 520 | 272.00 | 1884.00 | 0.00 | 37.72 | 37.72 |
| 2680 | 520 | 272.00 | 1888.00 | 0.00 | 37.80 | 37.80 |
| 2684 | 520 | 272.00 | 1892.00 | 0.00 | 37.88 | 37.88 |
| 2688 | 520 | 272.00 | 1896.00 | 0.00 | 37.96 | 37.96 |
| 2692 | 520 | 272.00 | 1900.00 | 0.00 | 38.04 | 38.04 |
| 2696 | 520 | 272.00 | 1904.00 | 0.00 | 38.12 | 38.12 |
| 2700 | 520 | 272.00 | 1908.00 | 0.00 | 38.20 | 38.20 |
| 2704 | 520 | 272.00 | 1912.00 | 0.00 | 38.28 | 38.28 |
| 2708 | 520 | 272.00 | 1916.00 | 0.00 | 38.36 | 38.36 |
| 2712 | 520 | 272.00 | 1920.00 | 0.00 | 38.44 | 38.44 |
| 2716 | 520 | 272.00 | 1924.00 | 0.00 | 38.52 | 38.52 |
| 2720 | 520 | 272.00 | 1928.00 | 0.00 | 38.60 | 38.60 |
| 2724 | 520 | 272.00 | 1932.00 | 0.00 | 38.68 | 38.68 |
| 2728 | 520 | 272.00 | 1936.00 | 0.00 | 38.76 | 38.76 |
| 2732 | 520 | 272.00 | 1940.00 | 0.00 | 38.84 | 38.84 |
| 2736 | 520 | 272.00 | 1944.00 | 0.00 | 38.92 | 38.92 |
| 2740 | 520 | 272.00 | 1948.00 | 0.00 | 39.00 | 39.00 |
| 2744 | 520 | 272.00 | 1952.00 | 0.00 | 39.08 | 39.08 |
| 2748 | 520 | 272.00 | 1956.00 | 0.00 | 39.16 | 39.16 |
| 2752 | 520 | 272.00 | 1960.00 | 0.00 | 39.24 | 39.24 |
| 2756 | 520 | 272.00 | 1964.00 | 0.00 | 39.32 | 39.32 |
| 2760 | 520 | 272.00 | 1968.00 | 0.00 | 39.40 | 39.40 |
| 2764 | 520 | 272.00 | 1972.00 | 0.00 | 39.48 | 39.48 |
| 2768 | 520 | 272.00 | 1976.00 | 0.00 | 39.56 | 39.56 |
| 2772 | 520 | 272.00 | 1980.00 | 0.00 | 39.64 | 39.64 |
| 2776 | 520 | 272.00 | 1984.00 | 0.00 | 39.72 | 39.72 |
| 2780 | 520 | 272.00 | 1988.00 | 0.00 | 39.80 | 39.80 |
| 2784 | 520 | 272.00 | 1992.00 | 0.00 | 39.88 | 39.88 |
| 2788 | 520 | 272.00 | 1996.00 | 0.00 | 39.96 | 39.96 |
| 2792 | 520 | 272.00 | 2000.00 | 0.00 | 40.04 | 40.04 |
| 2796 | 520 | 272.00 | 2004.00 | 0.00 | 40.12 | 40.12 |
| 2800 | 520 | 272.00 | 2008.00 | 0.00 | 40.20 | 40.20 |
| 2804 | 520 | 272.00 | 2012.00 | 0.00 | 40.28 | 40.28 |
| 2808 | 520 | 272.00 | 2016.00 | 0.00 | 40.36 | 40.36 |
| 2812 | 520 | 272.00 | 2020.00 | 0.00 | 40.44 | 40.44 |
| 2816 | 520 | 272.00 | 2024.00 | 0.00 | 40.52 | 40.52 |

**Monthly table**                                                                                            **Table letter Z**

| Employee's earnings up to and including the UEL | Earnings at the LEL (where earnings are equal to or exceed the LEL) 1a | Earnings above the LEL, up to and including the PT 1b | Earnings above the PT, up to and including the UEL 1c | Employer's NICs due on all earnings above the ST 1d | Employee's NICs due on all earnings above the PT 1e | Total of employee's and employer's NICs (for information only) |
|---|---|---|---|---|---|---|
| £ | £ | £ p | £ p | £ p | £ p | £ p |
| 2820 | 520 | 272.00 | 2028.00 | 0.00 | 40.60 | 40.60 |
| 2824 | 520 | 272.00 | 2032.00 | 0.00 | 40.68 | 40.68 |
| 2828 | 520 | 272.00 | 2036.00 | 0.00 | 40.76 | 40.76 |
| 2832 | 520 | 272.00 | 2040.00 | 0.00 | 40.84 | 40.84 |
| 2836 | 520 | 272.00 | 2044.00 | 0.00 | 40.92 | 40.92 |
| 2840 | 520 | 272.00 | 2048.00 | 0.00 | 41.00 | 41.00 |
| 2844 | 520 | 272.00 | 2052.00 | 0.00 | 41.08 | 41.08 |
| 2848 | 520 | 272.00 | 2056.00 | 0.00 | 41.16 | 41.16 |
| 2852 | 520 | 272.00 | 2060.00 | 0.00 | 41.24 | 41.24 |
| 2856 | 520 | 272.00 | 2064.00 | 0.00 | 41.32 | 41.32 |
| 2860 | 520 | 272.00 | 2068.00 | 0.00 | 41.40 | 41.40 |
| 2864 | 520 | 272.00 | 2072.00 | 0.00 | 41.48 | 41.48 |
| 2868 | 520 | 272.00 | 2076.00 | 0.00 | 41.56 | 41.56 |
| 2872 | 520 | 272.00 | 2080.00 | 0.00 | 41.64 | 41.64 |
| 2876 | 520 | 272.00 | 2084.00 | 0.00 | 41.72 | 41.72 |
| 2880 | 520 | 272.00 | 2088.00 | 0.00 | 41.80 | 41.80 |
| 2884 | 520 | 272.00 | 2092.00 | 0.00 | 41.88 | 41.88 |
| 2888 | 520 | 272.00 | 2096.00 | 0.00 | 41.96 | 41.96 |
| 2892 | 520 | 272.00 | 2100.00 | 0.00 | 42.04 | 42.04 |
| 2896 | 520 | 272.00 | 2104.00 | 0.00 | 42.12 | 42.12 |
| 2900 | 520 | 272.00 | 2108.00 | 0.00 | 42.20 | 42.20 |
| 2904 | 520 | 272.00 | 2112.00 | 0.00 | 42.28 | 42.28 |
| 2908 | 520 | 272.00 | 2116.00 | 0.00 | 42.36 | 42.36 |
| 2912 | 520 | 272.00 | 2120.00 | 0.00 | 42.44 | 42.44 |
| 2916 | 520 | 272.00 | 2124.00 | 0.00 | 42.52 | 42.52 |
| 2920 | 520 | 272.00 | 2128.00 | 0.00 | 42.60 | 42.60 |
| 2924 | 520 | 272.00 | 2132.00 | 0.00 | 42.68 | 42.68 |
| 2928 | 520 | 272.00 | 2136.00 | 0.00 | 42.76 | 42.76 |
| 2932 | 520 | 272.00 | 2140.00 | 0.00 | 42.84 | 42.84 |
| 2936 | 520 | 272.00 | 2144.00 | 0.00 | 42.92 | 42.92 |
| 2940 | 520 | 272.00 | 2148.00 | 0.00 | 43.00 | 43.00 |
| 2944 | 520 | 272.00 | 2152.00 | 0.00 | 43.08 | 43.08 |
| 2948 | 520 | 272.00 | 2156.00 | 0.00 | 43.16 | 43.16 |
| 2952 | 520 | 272.00 | 2160.00 | 0.00 | 43.24 | 43.24 |
| 2956 | 520 | 272.00 | 2164.00 | 0.00 | 43.32 | 43.32 |
| 2960 | 520 | 272.00 | 2168.00 | 0.00 | 43.40 | 43.40 |
| 2964 | 520 | 272.00 | 2172.00 | 0.00 | 43.48 | 43.48 |
| 2968 | 520 | 272.00 | 2176.00 | 0.00 | 43.56 | 43.56 |
| 2972 | 520 | 272.00 | 2180.00 | 0.00 | 43.64 | 43.64 |
| 2976 | 520 | 272.00 | 2184.00 | 0.00 | 43.72 | 43.72 |
| 2980 | 520 | 272.00 | 2188.00 | 0.00 | 43.80 | 43.80 |
| 2984 | 520 | 272.00 | 2192.00 | 0.00 | 43.88 | 43.88 |
| 2988 | 520 | 272.00 | 2196.00 | 0.00 | 43.96 | 43.96 |
| 2992 | 520 | 272.00 | 2200.00 | 0.00 | 44.04 | 44.04 |
| 2996 | 520 | 272.00 | 2204.00 | 0.00 | 44.12 | 44.12 |
| 3000 | 520 | 272.00 | 2208.00 | 0.00 | 44.20 | 44.20 |
| 3004 | 520 | 272.00 | 2212.00 | 0.00 | 44.28 | 44.28 |
| 3008 | 520 | 272.00 | 2216.00 | 0.00 | 44.36 | 44.36 |
| 3012 | 520 | 272.00 | 2220.00 | 0.00 | 44.44 | 44.44 |
| 3016 | 520 | 272.00 | 2224.00 | 0.00 | 44.52 | 44.52 |
| 3020 | 520 | 272.00 | 2228.00 | 0.00 | 44.60 | 44.60 |
| 3024 | 520 | 272.00 | 2232.00 | 0.00 | 44.68 | 44.68 |
| 3028 | 520 | 272.00 | 2236.00 | 0.00 | 44.76 | 44.76 |
| 3032 | 520 | 272.00 | 2240.00 | 0.00 | 44.84 | 44.84 |
| 3036 | 520 | 272.00 | 2244.00 | 0.00 | 44.92 | 44.92 |

## Table letter Z

**Monthly table**

| Employee's earnings up to and including the UEL £ | Earnings at the LEL (where earnings are equal to or exceed the LEL) 1a £ | Earnings above the LEL, up to and including the PT 1b £ p | Earnings above the PT, up to and including the UEL 1c £ p | Employer's NICs due on all earnings above the ST 1d £ p | Employee's NICs due on all earnings above the PT 1e £ p | Total of employee's and employer's NICs (for information only) £ p |
|---|---|---|---|---|---|---|
| 3040 | 520 | 272.00 | 2248.00 | 0.00 | 45.00 | 45.00 |
| 3044 | 520 | 272.00 | 2252.00 | 0.00 | 45.08 | 45.08 |
| 3048 | 520 | 272.00 | 2256.00 | 0.00 | 45.16 | 45.16 |
| 3052 | 520 | 272.00 | 2260.00 | 0.00 | 45.24 | 45.24 |
| 3056 | 520 | 272.00 | 2264.00 | 0.00 | 45.32 | 45.32 |
| 3060 | 520 | 272.00 | 2268.00 | 0.00 | 45.40 | 45.40 |
| 3064 | 520 | 272.00 | 2272.00 | 0.00 | 45.48 | 45.48 |
| 3068 | 520 | 272.00 | 2276.00 | 0.00 | 45.56 | 45.56 |
| 3072 | 520 | 272.00 | 2280.00 | 0.00 | 45.64 | 45.64 |
| 3076 | 520 | 272.00 | 2284.00 | 0.00 | 45.72 | 45.72 |
| 3080 | 520 | 272.00 | 2288.00 | 0.00 | 45.80 | 45.80 |
| 3084 | 520 | 272.00 | 2292.00 | 0.00 | 45.88 | 45.88 |
| 3088 | 520 | 272.00 | 2296.00 | 0.00 | 45.96 | 45.96 |
| 3092 | 520 | 272.00 | 2300.00 | 0.00 | 46.04 | 46.04 |
| 3096 | 520 | 272.00 | 2304.00 | 0.00 | 46.12 | 46.12 |
| 3100 | 520 | 272.00 | 2308.00 | 0.00 | 46.20 | 46.20 |
| 3104 | 520 | 272.00 | 2312.00 | 0.00 | 46.28 | 46.28 |
| 3108 | 520 | 272.00 | 2316.00 | 0.00 | 46.36 | 46.36 |
| 3112 | 520 | 272.00 | 2320.00 | 0.00 | 46.44 | 46.44 |
| 3116 | 520 | 272.00 | 2324.00 | 0.00 | 46.52 | 46.52 |
| 3120 | 520 | 272.00 | 2328.00 | 0.00 | 46.60 | 46.60 |
| 3124 | 520 | 272.00 | 2332.00 | 0.00 | 46.68 | 46.68 |
| 3128 | 520 | 272.00 | 2336.00 | 0.00 | 46.76 | 46.76 |
| 3132 | 520 | 272.00 | 2340.00 | 0.00 | 46.84 | 46.84 |
| 3136 | 520 | 272.00 | 2344.00 | 0.00 | 46.92 | 46.92 |
| 3140 | 520 | 272.00 | 2348.00 | 0.00 | 47.00 | 47.00 |
| 3144 | 520 | 272.00 | 2352.00 | 0.00 | 47.08 | 47.08 |
| 3148 | 520 | 272.00 | 2356.00 | 0.00 | 47.16 | 47.16 |
| 3152 | 520 | 272.00 | 2360.00 | 0.00 | 47.24 | 47.24 |
| 3156 | 520 | 272.00 | 2364.00 | 0.00 | 47.32 | 47.32 |
| 3160 | 520 | 272.00 | 2368.00 | 0.00 | 47.40 | 47.40 |
| 3164 | 520 | 272.00 | 2372.00 | 0.00 | 47.48 | 47.48 |
| 3168 | 520 | 272.00 | 2376.00 | 0.00 | 47.56 | 47.56 |
| 3172 | 520 | 272.00 | 2380.00 | 0.00 | 47.64 | 47.64 |
| 3176 | 520 | 272.00 | 2384.00 | 0.00 | 47.72 | 47.72 |
| 3180 | 520 | 272.00 | 2388.00 | 0.00 | 47.80 | 47.80 |
| 3184 | 520 | 272.00 | 2392.00 | 0.00 | 47.88 | 47.88 |
| 3188 | 520 | 272.00 | 2396.00 | 0.00 | 47.96 | 47.96 |
| 3192 | 520 | 272.00 | 2400.00 | 0.00 | 48.04 | 48.04 |
| 3196 | 520 | 272.00 | 2404.00 | 0.00 | 48.12 | 48.12 |
| 3200 | 520 | 272.00 | 2408.00 | 0.00 | 48.20 | 48.20 |
| 3204 | 520 | 272.00 | 2412.00 | 0.00 | 48.28 | 48.28 |
| 3208 | 520 | 272.00 | 2416.00 | 0.00 | 48.36 | 48.36 |
| 3212 | 520 | 272.00 | 2420.00 | 0.00 | 48.44 | 48.44 |
| 3216 | 520 | 272.00 | 2424.00 | 0.00 | 48.52 | 48.52 |
| 3220 | 520 | 272.00 | 2428.00 | 0.00 | 48.60 | 48.60 |
| 3224 | 520 | 272.00 | 2432.00 | 0.00 | 48.68 | 48.68 |
| 3228 | 520 | 272.00 | 2436.00 | 0.00 | 48.76 | 48.76 |
| 3232 | 520 | 272.00 | 2440.00 | 0.00 | 48.84 | 48.84 |
| 3236 | 520 | 272.00 | 2444.00 | 0.00 | 48.92 | 48.92 |
| 3240 | 520 | 272.00 | 2448.00 | 0.00 | 49.00 | 49.00 |
| 3244 | 520 | 272.00 | 2452.00 | 0.00 | 49.08 | 49.08 |
| 3248 | 520 | 272.00 | 2456.00 | 0.00 | 49.16 | 49.16 |
| 3252 | 520 | 272.00 | 2460.00 | 0.00 | 49.24 | 49.24 |
| 3256 | 520 | 272.00 | 2464.00 | 0.00 | 49.32 | 49.32 |

**Monthly table**

| Employee's earnings up to and including the UEL | Earnings at the LEL (where earnings are equal to or exceed the LEL) | Earnings above the LEL, up to and including the PT | Earnings above the PT, up to and including the UEL | Employer's NICs due on all earnings above the ST | Employee's NICs due on all earnings above the PT | Total of employee's and employer's NICs (for information only) |
|---|---|---|---|---|---|---|
| | | 1a | 1b | 1c | 1d | 1e |
| £ | £ | £ p | £ p | £ p | £ p | £ p |
| 3260 | 520 | 272.00 | 2468.00 | 0.00 | 49.40 | 49.40 |
| 3264 | 520 | 272.00 | 2472.00 | 0.00 | 49.48 | 49.48 |
| 3268 | 520 | 272.00 | 2476.00 | 0.00 | 49.56 | 49.56 |
| 3272 | 520 | 272.00 | 2480.00 | 0.00 | 49.64 | 49.64 |
| 3276 | 520 | 272.00 | 2484.00 | 0.00 | 49.72 | 49.72 |
| 3280 | 520 | 272.00 | 2488.00 | 0.00 | 49.80 | 49.80 |
| 3284 | 520 | 272.00 | 2492.00 | 0.00 | 49.88 | 49.88 |
| 3288 | 520 | 272.00 | 2496.00 | 0.00 | 49.96 | 49.96 |
| 3292 | 520 | 272.00 | 2500.00 | 0.00 | 50.04 | 50.04 |
| 3296 | 520 | 272.00 | 2504.00 | 0.00 | 50.12 | 50.12 |
| 3300 | 520 | 272.00 | 2508.00 | 0.00 | 50.20 | 50.20 |
| 3304 | 520 | 272.00 | 2512.00 | 0.00 | 50.28 | 50.28 |
| 3308 | 520 | 272.00 | 2516.00 | 0.00 | 50.36 | 50.36 |
| 3312 | 520 | 272.00 | 2520.00 | 0.00 | 50.44 | 50.44 |
| 3316 | 520 | 272.00 | 2524.00 | 0.00 | 50.52 | 50.52 |
| 3320 | 520 | 272.00 | 2528.00 | 0.00 | 50.60 | 50.60 |
| 3324 | 520 | 272.00 | 2532.00 | 0.00 | 50.68 | 50.68 |
| 3328 | 520 | 272.00 | 2536.00 | 0.00 | 50.76 | 50.76 |
| 3332 | 520 | 272.00 | 2540.00 | 0.00 | 50.84 | 50.84 |
| 3336 | 520 | 272.00 | 2544.00 | 0.00 | 50.92 | 50.92 |
| 3340 | 520 | 272.00 | 2548.00 | 0.00 | 51.00 | 51.00 |
| 3344 | 520 | 272.00 | 2552.00 | 0.00 | 51.08 | 51.08 |
| 3348 | 520 | 272.00 | 2556.00 | 0.00 | 51.16 | 51.16 |
| 3352 | 520 | 272.00 | 2560.00 | 0.00 | 51.24 | 51.24 |
| 3356 | 520 | 272.00 | 2564.00 | 0.00 | 51.32 | 51.32 |
| 3360 | 520 | 272.00 | 2568.00 | 0.00 | 51.40 | 51.40 |
| 3364 | 520 | 272.00 | 2572.00 | 0.00 | 51.48 | 51.48 |
| 3368 | 520 | 272.00 | 2576.00 | 0.00 | 51.56 | 51.56 |
| 3372 | 520 | 272.00 | 2580.00 | 0.00 | 51.64 | 51.64 |
| 3376 | 520 | 272.00 | 2584.00 | 0.00 | 51.72 | 51.72 |
| 3380 | 520 | 272.00 | 2588.00 | 0.00 | 51.80 | 51.80 |
| 3384 | 520 | 272.00 | 2592.00 | 0.00 | 51.88 | 51.88 |
| 3388 | 520 | 272.00 | 2596.00 | 0.00 | 51.96 | 51.96 |
| 3392 | 520 | 272.00 | 2600.00 | 0.00 | 52.04 | 52.04 |
| 3396 | 520 | 272.00 | 2604.00 | 0.00 | 52.12 | 52.12 |
| 3400 | 520 | 272.00 | 2608.00 | 0.00 | 52.20 | 52.20 |
| 3404 | 520 | 272.00 | 2612.00 | 0.00 | 52.28 | 52.28 |
| 3408 | 520 | 272.00 | 2616.00 | 0.00 | 52.36 | 52.36 |
| 3412 | 520 | 272.00 | 2620.00 | 0.00 | 52.44 | 52.44 |
| 3416 | 520 | 272.00 | 2624.00 | 0.00 | 52.52 | 52.52 |
| 3420 | 520 | 272.00 | 2628.00 | 0.00 | 52.60 | 52.60 |
| 3424 | 520 | 272.00 | 2632.00 | 0.00 | 52.68 | 52.68 |
| 3428 | 520 | 272.00 | 2636.00 | 0.00 | 52.76 | 52.76 |
| 3432 | 520 | 272.00 | 2640.00 | 0.00 | 52.84 | 52.84 |
| 3436 | 520 | 272.00 | 2644.00 | 0.00 | 52.92 | 52.92 |
| 3440 | 520 | 272.00 | 2648.00 | 0.00 | 53.00 | 53.00 |
| 3444 | 520 | 272.00 | 2652.00 | 0.00 | 53.08 | 53.08 |
| 3448 | 520 | 272.00 | 2656.00 | 0.00 | 53.16 | 53.16 |
| 3452 | 520 | 272.00 | 2660.00 | 0.00 | 53.24 | 53.24 |
| 3456 | 520 | 272.00 | 2664.00 | 0.00 | 53.32 | 53.32 |
| 3460 | 520 | 272.00 | 2668.00 | 0.00 | 53.40 | 53.40 |
| 3464 | 520 | 272.00 | 2672.00 | 0.00 | 53.48 | 53.48 |
| 3468 | 520 | 272.00 | 2676.00 | 0.00 | 53.56 | 53.56 |
| 3472 | 520 | 272.00 | 2680.00 | 0.00 | 53.64 | 53.64 |
| 3476 | 520 | 272.00 | 2684.00 | 0.00 | 53.72 | 53.72 |

# Monthly table

**Table letter Z**

| Employee's earnings up to and including the UEL | Earnings at the LEL (where earnings are equal to or exceed the LEL) | Earnings above the LEL, up to and including the PT | Earnings above the PT, up to and including the UEL | Employer's NICs due on all earnings above the ST | Employee's NICs due on all earnings above the PT | Total of employee's and employer's NICs (for information only) |
|---|---|---|---|---|---|---|
| | 1a | 1b | 1c | 1d | 1e | |
| £ | £ | £ p | £ p | £ p | £ p | £ p |
| 3480 | 520 | 272.00 | 2688.00 | 0.00 | 53.80 | 53.80 |
| 3484 | 520 | 272.00 | 2692.00 | 0.00 | 53.88 | 53.88 |
| 3488 | 520 | 272.00 | 2696.00 | 0.00 | 53.96 | 53.96 |
| 3492 | 520 | 272.00 | 2700.00 | 0.00 | 54.04 | 54.04 |
| 3496 | 520 | 272.00 | 2704.00 | 0.00 | 54.12 | 54.12 |
| 3500 | 520 | 272.00 | 2708.00 | 0.00 | 54.20 | 54.20 |
| 3504 | 520 | 272.00 | 2712.00 | 0.00 | 54.28 | 54.28 |
| 3508 | 520 | 272.00 | 2716.00 | 0.00 | 54.36 | 54.36 |
| 3512 | 520 | 272.00 | 2720.00 | 0.00 | 54.44 | 54.44 |
| 3516 | 520 | 272.00 | 2724.00 | 0.00 | 54.52 | 54.52 |
| 3520 | 520 | 272.00 | 2728.00 | 0.00 | 54.60 | 54.60 |
| 3524 | 520 | 272.00 | 2732.00 | 0.00 | 54.68 | 54.68 |
| 3528 | 520 | 272.00 | 2736.00 | 0.00 | 54.76 | 54.76 |
| 3532 | 520 | 272.00 | 2740.00 | 0.00 | 54.84 | 54.84 |
| 3536 | 520 | 272.00 | 2744.00 | 0.00 | 54.92 | 54.92 |
| 3540 | 520 | 272.00 | 2748.00 | 0.00 | 55.00 | 55.00 |
| 3544 | 520 | 272.00 | 2752.00 | 0.00 | 55.08 | 55.08 |
| 3548 | 520 | 272.00 | 2756.00 | 0.00 | 55.16 | 55.16 |
| 3552 | 520 | 272.00 | 2760.00 | 0.00 | 55.24 | 55.24 |
| 3556 | 520 | 272.00 | 2764.00 | 0.00 | 55.32 | 55.32 |
| 3560 | 520 | 272.00 | 2768.00 | 0.00 | 55.40 | 55.40 |
| 3564 | 520 | 272.00 | 2772.00 | 0.00 | 55.48 | 55.48 |
| 3568 | 520 | 272.00 | 2776.00 | 0.00 | 55.56 | 55.56 |
| 3572 | 520 | 272.00 | 2780.00 | 0.00 | 55.64 | 55.64 |
| 3576 | 520 | 272.00 | 2784.00 | 0.00 | 55.72 | 55.72 |
| 3580 | 520 | 272.00 | 2788.00 | 0.00 | 55.80 | 55.80 |
| 3584 | 520 | 272.00 | 2792.00 | 0.00 | 55.88 | 55.88 |
| 3588 | 520 | 272.00 | 2796.00 | 0.00 | 55.96 | 55.96 |
| 3592 | 520 | 272.00 | 2800.00 | 0.00 | 56.04 | 56.04 |
| 3596 | 520 | 272.00 | 2804.00 | 0.00 | 56.12 | 56.12 |
| 3600 | 520 | 272.00 | 2808.00 | 0.00 | 56.20 | 56.20 |
| 3604 | 520 | 272.00 | 2812.00 | 0.00 | 56.28 | 56.28 |
| 3608 | 520 | 272.00 | 2816.00 | 0.00 | 56.36 | 56.36 |
| 3612 | 520 | 272.00 | 2820.00 | 0.00 | 56.44 | 56.44 |
| 3616 | 520 | 272.00 | 2824.00 | 0.00 | 56.52 | 56.52 |
| 3620 | 520 | 272.00 | 2828.00 | 0.00 | 56.60 | 56.60 |
| 3624 | 520 | 272.00 | 2832.00 | 0.00 | 56.68 | 56.68 |
| 3628 | 520 | 272.00 | 2836.00 | 0.00 | 56.76 | 56.76 |
| 3632 | 520 | 272.00 | 2840.00 | 0.00 | 56.84 | 56.84 |
| 3636 | 520 | 272.00 | 2844.00 | 0.00 | 56.92 | 56.92 |
| 3640 | 520 | 272.00 | 2848.00 | 0.00 | 57.00 | 57.00 |
| 3644 | 520 | 272.00 | 2852.00 | 0.00 | 57.08 | 57.08 |
| 3648 | 520 | 272.00 | 2856.00 | 0.00 | 57.16 | 57.16 |
| 3652 | 520 | 272.00 | 2860.00 | 0.00 | 57.24 | 57.24 |
| 3656 | 520 | 272.00 | 2864.00 | 0.00 | 57.32 | 57.32 |
| 3660 | 520 | 272.00 | 2868.00 | 0.00 | 57.40 | 57.40 |
| 3664 | 520 | 272.00 | 2872.00 | 0.00 | 57.48 | 57.48 |
| 3668 | 520 | 272.00 | 2876.00 | 0.00 | 57.56 | 57.56 |
| 3672 | 520 | 272.00 | 2880.00 | 0.00 | 57.64 | 57.64 |
| 3676 | 520 | 272.00 | 2884.00 | 0.00 | 57.72 | 57.72 |
| 3680 | 520 | 272.00 | 2888.00 | 0.00 | 57.80 | 57.80 |
| 3684 | 520 | 272.00 | 2892.00 | 0.00 | 57.88 | 57.88 |
| 3688 | 520 | 272.00 | 2896.00 | 0.00 | 57.96 | 57.96 |
| 3692 | 520 | 272.00 | 2900.00 | 0.00 | 58.04 | 58.04 |
| 3696 | 520 | 272.00 | 2904.00 | 0.00 | 58.12 | 58.12 |

**Table letter Z**                                                                      **Monthly table**

| Employee's earnings up to and including the UEL | Earnings at the LEL (where earnings are equal to or exceed the LEL) | Earnings above the LEL, up to and including the PT | Earnings above the PT, up to and including the UEL | Employer's NICs due on all earnings above the ST | Employee's NICs due on all earnings above the PT | Total of employee's and employer's NICs (for information only) |
|---|---|---|---|---|---|---|
| | 1a | 1b | 1c | 1d | 1e | |
| £ | £ | £ p | £ p | £ p | £ p | £ p |
| 3700 | 520 | 272.00 | 2908.00 | 0.00 | 58.20 | 58.20 |
| 3704 | 520 | 272.00 | 2912.00 | 0.00 | 58.28 | 58.28 |
| 3708 | 520 | 272.00 | 2916.00 | 0.00 | 58.36 | 58.36 |
| 3712 | 520 | 272.00 | 2920.00 | 0.00 | 58.44 | 58.44 |
| 3716 | 520 | 272.00 | 2924.00 | 0.00 | 58.52 | 58.52 |
| 3720 | 520 | 272.00 | 2928.00 | 0.00 | 58.60 | 58.60 |
| 3724 | 520 | 272.00 | 2932.00 | 0.00 | 58.68 | 58.68 |
| 3728 | 520 | 272.00 | 2936.00 | 0.00 | 58.76 | 58.76 |
| 3732 | 520 | 272.00 | 2940.00 | 0.00 | 58.84 | 58.84 |
| 3736 | 520 | 272.00 | 2944.00 | 0.00 | 58.92 | 58.92 |
| 3740 | 520 | 272.00 | 2948.00 | 0.00 | 59.00 | 59.00 |
| 3744 | 520 | 272.00 | 2952.00 | 0.00 | 59.08 | 59.08 |
| 3748 | 520 | 272.00 | 2956.00 | 0.00 | 59.16 | 59.16 |
| 3752 | 520 | 272.00 | 2960.00 | 0.00 | 59.24 | 59.24 |
| 3756 | 520 | 272.00 | 2964.00 | 0.00 | 59.32 | 59.32 |
| 3760 | 520 | 272.00 | 2968.00 | 0.00 | 59.40 | 59.40 |
| 3764 | 520 | 272.00 | 2972.00 | 0.00 | 59.48 | 59.48 |
| 3768 | 520 | 272.00 | 2976.00 | 0.00 | 59.56 | 59.56 |
| 3772 | 520 | 272.00 | 2980.00 | 0.00 | 59.64 | 59.64 |
| 3776 | 520 | 272.00 | 2984.00 | 0.00 | 59.72 | 59.72 |
| 3780 | 520 | 272.00 | 2988.00 | 0.00 | 59.80 | 59.80 |
| 3784 | 520 | 272.00 | 2992.00 | 0.00 | 59.88 | 59.88 |
| 3788 | 520 | 272.00 | 2996.00 | 0.00 | 59.96 | 59.96 |
| 3792 | 520 | 272.00 | 3000.00 | 0.00 | 60.04 | 60.04 |
| 3796 | 520 | 272.00 | 3004.00 | 0.00 | 60.12 | 60.12 |
| 3800 | 520 | 272.00 | 3008.00 | 0.00 | 60.20 | 60.20 |
| 3804 | 520 | 272.00 | 3012.00 | 0.00 | 60.28 | 60.28 |
| 3808 | 520 | 272.00 | 3016.00 | 0.00 | 60.36 | 60.36 |
| 3812 | 520 | 272.00 | 3020.00 | 0.00 | 60.44 | 60.44 |
| 3816 | 520 | 272.00 | 3024.00 | 0.00 | 60.52 | 60.52 |
| 3820 | 520 | 272.00 | 3028.00 | 0.00 | 60.60 | 60.60 |
| 3824 | 520 | 272.00 | 3032.00 | 0.00 | 60.68 | 60.68 |
| 3828 | 520 | 272.00 | 3036.00 | 0.00 | 60.76 | 60.76 |
| 3832 | 520 | 272.00 | 3040.00 | 0.00 | 60.84 | 60.84 |
| 3836 | 520 | 272.00 | 3044.00 | 0.00 | 60.92 | 60.92 |
| 3840 | 520 | 272.00 | 3048.00 | 0.00 | 61.00 | 61.00 |
| 3844 | 520 | 272.00 | 3052.00 | 0.00 | 61.08 | 61.08 |
| 3848 | 520 | 272.00 | 3056.00 | 0.00 | 61.16 | 61.16 |
| 3852 | 520 | 272.00 | 3060.00 | 0.00 | 61.24 | 61.24 |
| 3856 | 520 | 272.00 | 3064.00 | 0.00 | 61.32 | 61.32 |
| 3860 | 520 | 272.00 | 3068.00 | 0.00 | 61.40 | 61.40 |
| 3864 | 520 | 272.00 | 3072.00 | 0.00 | 61.48 | 61.48 |
| 3868 | 520 | 272.00 | 3076.00 | 0.00 | 61.56 | 61.56 |
| 3872 | 520 | 272.00 | 3080.00 | 0.00 | 61.64 | 61.64 |
| 3876 | 520 | 272.00 | 3084.00 | 0.00 | 61.72 | 61.72 |
| 3880 | 520 | 272.00 | 3088.00 | 0.00 | 61.80 | 61.80 |
| 3884 | 520 | 272.00 | 3092.00 | 0.00 | 61.88 | 61.88 |
| 3888 | 520 | 272.00 | 3096.00 | 0.00 | 61.96 | 61.96 |
| 3892 | 520 | 272.00 | 3100.00 | 0.00 | 62.04 | 62.04 |
| 3896 | 520 | 272.00 | 3104.00 | 0.00 | 62.12 | 62.12 |
| 3900 | 520 | 272.00 | 3108.00 | 0.00 | 62.20 | 62.20 |
| 3904 | 520 | 272.00 | 3112.00 | 0.00 | 62.28 | 62.28 |
| 3908 | 520 | 272.00 | 3116.00 | 0.00 | 62.36 | 62.36 |
| 3912 | 520 | 272.00 | 3120.00 | 0.00 | 62.44 | 62.44 |
| 3916 | 520 | 272.00 | 3124.00 | 0.00 | 62.52 | 62.52 |

# Table letter Z

## Monthly table

| Employee's earnings up to and including the UEL | Earnings at the LEL (where earnings are equal to or exceed the LEL) | Earnings above the LEL, up to and including the PT | Earnings above the PT, up to and including the UEL | Employer's NICs due on all earnings above the ST | Employee's NICs due on all earnings above the PT | Total of employee's and employer's NICs (for information only) |
|---|---|---|---|---|---|---|
| | 1a | 1b | 1c | 1d | 1e | |
| £ | £ | £ p | £ p | £ p | £ p | £ p |
| 3920 | 520 | 272.00 | 3128.00 | 0.00 | 62.60 | 62.60 |
| 3924 | 520 | 272.00 | 3132.00 | 0.00 | 62.68 | 62.68 |
| 3928 | 520 | 272.00 | 3136.00 | 0.00 | 62.76 | 62.76 |
| 3932 | 520 | 272.00 | 3140.00 | 0.00 | 62.84 | 62.84 |
| 3936 | 520 | 272.00 | 3144.00 | 0.00 | 62.92 | 62.92 |
| 3940 | 520 | 272.00 | 3148.00 | 0.00 | 63.00 | 63.00 |
| 3944 | 520 | 272.00 | 3152.00 | 0.00 | 63.08 | 63.08 |
| 3948 | 520 | 272.00 | 3156.00 | 0.00 | 63.16 | 63.16 |
| 3952 | 520 | 272.00 | 3160.00 | 0.00 | 63.24 | 63.24 |
| 3956 | 520 | 272.00 | 3164.00 | 0.00 | 63.32 | 63.32 |
| 3960 | 520 | 272.00 | 3168.00 | 0.00 | 63.40 | 63.40 |
| 3964 | 520 | 272.00 | 3172.00 | 0.00 | 63.48 | 63.48 |
| 3968 | 520 | 272.00 | 3176.00 | 0.00 | 63.56 | 63.56 |
| 3972 | 520 | 272.00 | 3180.00 | 0.00 | 63.64 | 63.64 |
| 3976 | 520 | 272.00 | 3184.00 | 0.00 | 63.72 | 63.72 |
| 3980 | 520 | 272.00 | 3188.00 | 0.00 | 63.80 | 63.80 |
| 3984 | 520 | 272.00 | 3192.00 | 0.00 | 63.88 | 63.88 |
| 3988 | 520 | 272.00 | 3196.00 | 0.00 | 63.96 | 63.96 |
| 3992 | 520 | 272.00 | 3200.00 | 0.00 | 64.04 | 64.04 |
| 3996 | 520 | 272.00 | 3204.00 | 0.00 | 64.12 | 64.12 |
| 4000 | 520 | 272.00 | 3208.00 | 0.00 | 64.20 | 64.20 |
| 4004 | 520 | 272.00 | 3212.00 | 0.00 | 64.28 | 64.28 |
| 4008 | 520 | 272.00 | 3216.00 | 0.00 | 64.36 | 64.36 |
| 4012 | 520 | 272.00 | 3220.00 | 0.00 | 64.44 | 64.44 |
| 4016 | 520 | 272.00 | 3224.00 | 0.00 | 64.52 | 64.52 |
| 4020 | 520 | 272.00 | 3228.00 | 0.00 | 64.60 | 64.60 |
| 4024 | 520 | 272.00 | 3232.00 | 0.00 | 64.68 | 64.68 |
| 4028 | 520 | 272.00 | 3236.00 | 0.00 | 64.76 | 64.76 |
| 4032 | 520 | 272.00 | 3240.00 | 0.00 | 64.84 | 64.84 |
| 4036 | 520 | 272.00 | 3244.00 | 0.00 | 64.92 | 64.92 |
| 4040 | 520 | 272.00 | 3248.00 | 0.00 | 65.00 | 65.00 |
| 4044 | 520 | 272.00 | 3252.00 | 0.00 | 65.08 | 65.08 |
| 4048 | 520 | 272.00 | 3256.00 | 0.00 | 65.16 | 65.16 |
| 4052 | 520 | 272.00 | 3260.00 | 0.00 | 65.24 | 65.24 |
| 4056 | 520 | 272.00 | 3264.00 | 0.00 | 65.32 | 65.32 |
| 4060 | 520 | 272.00 | 3268.00 | 0.00 | 65.40 | 65.40 |
| 4064 | 520 | 272.00 | 3272.00 | 0.00 | 65.48 | 65.48 |
| 4068 | 520 | 272.00 | 3276.00 | 0.00 | 65.56 | 65.56 |
| 4072 | 520 | 272.00 | 3280.00 | 0.00 | 65.64 | 65.64 |
| 4076 | 520 | 272.00 | 3284.00 | 0.00 | 65.72 | 65.72 |
| 4080 | 520 | 272.00 | 3288.00 | 0.00 | 65.80 | 65.80 |
| 4084 | 520 | 272.00 | 3292.00 | 0.00 | 65.88 | 65.88 |
| 4088 | 520 | 272.00 | 3296.00 | 0.00 | 65.96 | 65.96 |
| 4092 | 520 | 272.00 | 3300.00 | 0.00 | 66.04 | 66.04 |
| 4096 | 520 | 272.00 | 3304.00 | 0.00 | 66.12 | 66.12 |
| 4100 | 520 | 272.00 | 3308.00 | 0.00 | 66.20 | 66.20 |
| 4104 | 520 | 272.00 | 3312.00 | 0.00 | 66.28 | 66.28 |
| 4108 | 520 | 272.00 | 3316.00 | 0.00 | 66.36 | 66.36 |
| 4112 | 520 | 272.00 | 3320.00 | 0.00 | 66.44 | 66.44 |
| 4116 | 520 | 272.00 | 3324.00 | 0.00 | 66.52 | 66.52 |
| 4120 | 520 | 272.00 | 3328.00 | 0.00 | 66.60 | 66.60 |
| 4124 | 520 | 272.00 | 3332.00 | 0.00 | 66.68 | 66.68 |
| 4128 | 520 | 272.00 | 3336.00 | 0.00 | 66.76 | 66.76 |
| 4132 | 520 | 272.00 | 3340.00 | 0.00 | 66.84 | 66.84 |
| 4136 | 520 | 272.00 | 3344.00 | 0.00 | 66.92 | 66.92 |

## Monthly table

**Table letter Z**

| Employee's earnings up to and including the UEL | Earnings at the LEL (where earnings are equal to or exceed the LEL) | Earnings above the LEL, up to and including the PT | Earnings above the PT, up to and including the UEL | Employer's NICs due on all earnings above the ST | Employee's NICs due on all earnings above the PT | Total of employee's and employer's NICs (for information only) |
|---|---|---|---|---|---|---|
| | | 1a | 1b | 1c | 1d | 1e |
| £ | £ | £ p | £ p | £ p | £ p | £ p |
| 4140 | 520 | 272.00 | 3348.00 | 0.00 | 67.00 | 67.00 |
| 4144 | 520 | 272.00 | 3352.00 | 0.00 | 67.08 | 67.08 |
| 4148 | 520 | 272.00 | 3356.00 | 0.00 | 67.16 | 67.16 |
| 4152 | 520 | 272.00 | 3360.00 | 0.00 | 67.24 | 67.24 |
| 4156 | 520 | 272.00 | 3364.00 | 0.00 | 67.32 | 67.32 |
| 4160 | 520 | 272.00 | 3368.00 | 0.00 | 67.40 | 67.40 |
| 4164 | 520 | 272.00 | 3372.00 | 0.00 | 67.47 | 67.47 |
| 4167 | 520 | 272.00 | 3375.00 | 0.00 | 67.50 | 67.50 |

If the employee's gross pay is over £4,167, go to page 178.

# Working out and recording NICs where employee's total earnings exceed the Upper Earnings Limit (UEL)/Upper Secondary Threshold (UST)/ Apprentice Upper Secondary Threshold (AUST)

Where the employee's total earnings exceed the UEL/UST/AUST, only the earnings between the PT and the UEL/UST/AUST should be recorded in column 1c of form RT11.

Use the main table to work out the employer's NICs and the employee's NICs due on the earnings up to the UEL/UST/AUST.

To work out the employer's NICs and the employee's NICs due on the earnings above the UEL/UST/AUST, take the following action.

| Step | Action | Example (based on Table letter A with total monthly earnings of £5,483.29) | | |
|---|---|---|---|---|
| 1 | Subtract the UEL/UST/AUST figure from the total gross pay. | £5,483.29 − £4,167 = £1,316.29 | | |
| 2 | Round the answer down to the nearest whole £. | Rounded down to £1,316 | | |
| 3 | Look this figure up in the Additional gross pay table on page 179. | Look up £1,316 | | |

| Step | Action | Amount | Employer's NICs payable | Employee's NICs payable |
|---|---|---|---|---|
| 4 | If the figure is not shown in the table, build up to it by adding together as few entries as possible. | £1000 | £138.00 | £20.00 |
| | | £300 | + £41.40 | + £6.00 |
| | | £16 | + £2.21 | +£0.32 |
| | | **Totals** | **= £181.61** | **= £26.32** |

| Step | Action | | Total payable by employer | Total payable by employee |
|---|---|---|---|---|
| 5 | Add the further employer's NICs and employee's NICs worked out on the earnings above the UEL/UST/AUST (columns 1d and 1e of the Additional gross pay table) to employer's NICs and employee's NICs due for earnings at the UEL/UST/AUST (columns 1d and 1e of the main table). | | £181.61 (further employer NICs) | £26.32 (further employee NICs) |
| | | | + £474.03 (due for employer on earnings at UEL/UST/AUST) | + £405.00 (due for employee on earnings at UEL/UST/AUST) |
| | | **Totals** | **= £655.64** | **= £431.32** |
| 6 | Record the figures resulting from Step 5 in columns 1d and 1e of form RT11. | | | |

On form RT11 or equivalent record:

| Col 1a | Col 1b | Col 1c | Col 1d | Col 1e |
|---|---|---|---|---|
| 520 | 272 | 3375 | 655.64 | 431.32 |

## Additional gross pay table

| Earnings on which NICs payable | Employer's NICs payable | Employee's NICs payable | Total of employee's and employer's NICs payable (for information only) |
|---|---|---|---|
| | 1d | 1e | |
| £ | £ p | £ p | £ p |
| 1 | 0.14 | 0.02 | 0.16 |
| 2 | 0.28 | 0.04 | 0.32 |
| 3 | 0.41 | 0.06 | 0.47 |
| 4 | 0.55 | 0.08 | 0.63 |
| 5 | 0.69 | 0.10 | 0.79 |
| 6 | 0.83 | 0.12 | 0.95 |
| 7 | 0.97 | 0.14 | 1.11 |
| 8 | 1.10 | 0.16 | 1.26 |
| 9 | 1.24 | 0.18 | 1.42 |
| 10 | 1.38 | 0.20 | 1.58 |
| 11 | 1.52 | 0.22 | 1.74 |
| 12 | 1.66 | 0.24 | 1.90 |
| 13 | 1.79 | 0.26 | 2.05 |
| 14 | 1.93 | 0.28 | 2.21 |
| 15 | 2.07 | 0.30 | 2.37 |
| 16 | 2.21 | 0.32 | 2.53 |
| 17 | 2.35 | 0.34 | 2.69 |
| 18 | 2.48 | 0.36 | 2.84 |
| 19 | 2.62 | 0.38 | 3.00 |
| 20 | 2.76 | 0.40 | 3.16 |
| 21 | 2.90 | 0.42 | 3.32 |
| 22 | 3.04 | 0.44 | 3.48 |
| 23 | 3.17 | 0.46 | 3.63 |
| 24 | 3.31 | 0.48 | 3.79 |
| 25 | 3.45 | 0.50 | 3.95 |
| 26 | 3.59 | 0.52 | 4.11 |
| 27 | 3.73 | 0.54 | 4.27 |
| 28 | 3.86 | 0.56 | 4.42 |
| 29 | 4.00 | 0.58 | 4.58 |
| 30 | 4.14 | 0.60 | 4.74 |
| 31 | 4.28 | 0.62 | 4.90 |
| 32 | 4.42 | 0.64 | 5.06 |
| 33 | 4.55 | 0.66 | 5.21 |
| 34 | 4.69 | 0.68 | 5.37 |
| 35 | 4.83 | 0.70 | 5.53 |
| 36 | 4.97 | 0.72 | 5.69 |
| 37 | 5.11 | 0.74 | 5.85 |
| 38 | 5.24 | 0.76 | 6.00 |
| 39 | 5.38 | 0.78 | 6.16 |
| 40 | 5.52 | 0.80 | 6.32 |
| 41 | 5.66 | 0.82 | 6.48 |
| 42 | 5.80 | 0.84 | 6.64 |
| 43 | 5.93 | 0.86 | 6.79 |
| 44 | 6.07 | 0.88 | 6.95 |
| 45 | 6.21 | 0.90 | 7.11 |
| 46 | 6.35 | 0.92 | 7.27 |
| 47 | 6.49 | 0.94 | 7.43 |
| 48 | 6.62 | 0.96 | 7.58 |
| 49 | 6.76 | 0.98 | 7.74 |
| 50 | 6.90 | 1.00 | 7.90 |
| 51 | 7.04 | 1.02 | 8.06 |
| 52 | 7.18 | 1.04 | 8.22 |
| 53 | 7.31 | 1.06 | 8.37 |
| 54 | 7.45 | 1.08 | 8.53 |
| 55 | 7.59 | 1.10 | 8.69 |

## Additional gross pay table

| Earnings on which NICs payable | Employer's NICs payable | Employee's NICs payable | Total of employee's and employer's NICs payable (for information only) | Earnings on which NICs payable | Employer's NICs payable | Employee's NICs payable | Total of employee's and employer's NICs payable (for information only) |
|---|---|---|---|---|---|---|---|
| | 1d | 1e | | | 1d | 1e | |
| £ | £ p | £ p | £ p | £ | £ p | £ p | £ p |
| 56 | 7.73 | 1.12 | 8.85 | 3000 | 414.00 | 60.00 | 474.00 |
| 57 | 7.87 | 1.14 | 9.01 | 4000 | 552.00 | 80.00 | 632.00 |
| 58 | 8.00 | 1.16 | 9.16 | 5000 | 690.00 | 100.00 | 790.00 |
| 59 | 8.14 | 1.18 | 9.32 | 6000 | 828.00 | 120.00 | 948.00 |
| 60 | 8.28 | 1.20 | 9.48 | 7000 | 966.00 | 140.00 | 1106.00 |
| 61 | 8.42 | 1.22 | 9.64 | 8000 | 1104.00 | 160.00 | 1264.00 |
| 62 | 8.56 | 1.24 | 9.80 | 9000 | 1242.00 | 180.00 | 1422.00 |
| 63 | 8.69 | 1.26 | 9.95 | 10000 | 1380.00 | 200.00 | 1580.00 |
| 64 | 8.83 | 1.28 | 10.11 | 20000 | 2760.00 | 400.00 | 3160.00 |
| 65 | 8.97 | 1.30 | 10.27 | 30000 | 4140.00 | 600.00 | 4740.00 |
| 66 | 9.11 | 1.32 | 10.43 | 40000 | 5520.00 | 800.00 | 6320.00 |
| 67 | 9.25 | 1.34 | 10.59 | 50000 | 6900.00 | 1000.00 | 7900.00 |
| 68 | 9.38 | 1.36 | 10.74 | 60000 | 8280.00 | 1200.00 | 9480.00 |
| 69 | 9.52 | 1.38 | 10.90 | 70000 | 9660.00 | 1400.00 | 11060.00 |
| 70 | 9.66 | 1.40 | 11.06 | 80000 | 11040.00 | 1600.00 | 12640.00 |
| 71 | 9.80 | 1.42 | 11.22 | 90000 | 12420.00 | 1800.00 | 14220.00 |
| 72 | 9.94 | 1.44 | 11.38 | 100000 | 13800.00 | 2000.00 | 15800.00 |
| 73 | 10.07 | 1.46 | 11.53 | | | | |
| 74 | 10.21 | 1.48 | 11.69 | | | | |
| 75 | 10.35 | 1.50 | 11.85 | | | | |
| 76 | 10.49 | 1.52 | 12.01 | | | | |
| 77 | 10.63 | 1.54 | 12.17 | | | | |
| 78 | 10.76 | 1.56 | 12.32 | | | | |
| 79 | 10.90 | 1.58 | 12.48 | | | | |
| 80 | 11.04 | 1.60 | 12.64 | | | | |
| 81 | 11.18 | 1.62 | 12.80 | | | | |
| 82 | 11.32 | 1.64 | 12.96 | | | | |
| 83 | 11.45 | 1.66 | 13.11 | | | | |
| 84 | 11.59 | 1.68 | 13.27 | | | | |
| 85 | 11.73 | 1.70 | 13.43 | | | | |
| 86 | 11.87 | 1.72 | 13.59 | | | | |
| 87 | 12.01 | 1.74 | 13.75 | | | | |
| 88 | 12.14 | 1.76 | 13.90 | | | | |
| 89 | 12.28 | 1.78 | 14.06 | | | | |
| 90 | 12.42 | 1.80 | 14.22 | | | | |
| 91 | 12.56 | 1.82 | 14.38 | | | | |
| 92 | 12.70 | 1.84 | 14.54 | | | | |
| 93 | 12.83 | 1.86 | 14.69 | | | | |
| 94 | 12.97 | 1.88 | 14.85 | | | | |
| 95 | 13.11 | 1.90 | 15.01 | | | | |
| 96 | 13.25 | 1.92 | 15.17 | | | | |
| 97 | 13.39 | 1.94 | 15.33 | | | | |
| 98 | 13.52 | 1.96 | 15.48 | | | | |
| 99 | 13.66 | 1.98 | 15.64 | | | | |
| 100 | 13.80 | 2.00 | 15.80 | | | | |
| 200 | 27.60 | 4.00 | 31.60 | | | | |
| 300 | 41.40 | 6.00 | 47.40 | | | | |
| 400 | 55.20 | 8.00 | 63.20 | | | | |
| 500 | 69.00 | 10.00 | 79.00 | | | | |
| 600 | 82.80 | 12.00 | 94.80 | | | | |
| 700 | 96.60 | 14.00 | 110.60 | | | | |
| 800 | 110.40 | 16.00 | 126.40 | | | | |
| 900 | 124.20 | 18.00 | 142.20 | | | | |
| 1000 | 138.00 | 20.00 | 158.00 | | | | |
| 2000 | 276.00 | 40.00 | 316.00 | | | | |

# Which National Insurance contributions (NICs) tables to use

You must use the correct tables when working out the NICs due on your employee's earnings.

NICs tables are renewed every tax year.

Check you're using the tables for the tax year 2020 to 2021.

If your employee is under 16 years of age, there's no NICs liability.

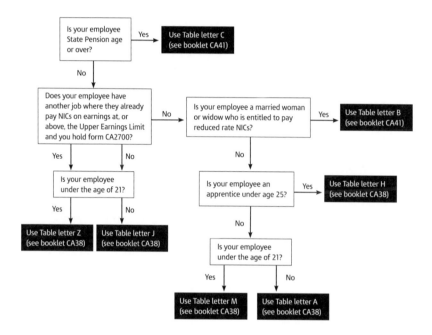

If you employ mariners, the CA42 'National Insurance contributions for employers of foreign-going mariners and deep-sea fishermen' gives details of category letters, rates and limits to use.

Page 2

## Layout of these tables

The first earnings figure in each table is the Lower Earnings Limit (LEL) (£120 weekly or £520 monthly). This is because NICs liability only arises when the employee's total earnings in the earnings period reach the LEL, even though no NICs are actually payable on those earnings. The employer pays NICs only when the employee's earnings exceed the Secondary Threshold (ST) (£169 weekly or £732 monthly). The employee pays NICs only when the employee's earnings exceed the Primary Threshold (PT) (£183 weekly or £792 monthly). But, for standard rate NICs, earnings between the LEL and the PT are used to protect the employee's entitlement to benefit.

Employees and their employers continue to pay NICs at the appropriate main percentage rate on earnings between ST and PT respectively up to the Upper Earnings Limit (UEL). The last earnings figure in each table is the UEL (£962 weekly or £4,167 monthly). This is because employee's NICs are due only at a rate of 2% on earnings above the UEL. The employer pays NICs at the rate of 13.8% on earnings above the UEL.

The figures in the left-hand column of each table show steps between the LEL and the UEL. The NICs liability for each step is based on the earnings limits and percentage rates shown on page 5 and with the exception of the LEL, ST, PT and UEL is worked out at the mid-point of the steps. Therefore, you and your employee may pay slightly more or less than if you used the exact percentage method to work out the NICs due.

Where the employee's total earnings fall between the LEL and the UEL, if the exact figure is not shown in the tables, use the next smaller figure shown.

Where the employee's total earnings exceed the UEL, see pages 75 or 76.

For instructions on how to complete form RT11, 'Deductions working sheet' read the helpbook RT7, 'Guidance for employers exempt from filing Real Time Information online'.

An example form RT11 is also shown on page 6.

# Using these tables to work out NICs

## Introduction

These tables are aimed at the small number of employers exempt from filing payroll information online and the guidance on how to record the figures displayed within the tables is for employers who are operating a manual payroll. Form RT11, 'Deductions working sheet' replaces form P11 for the purposes of operating a manual payroll. You can work out NICs by using either:

- these tables
- the exact percentage method

For general information about NICs, see the employer helpbooks.

## Are you using the correct tables?

Only use these tables between 6 April 2020 and 5 April 2021 (the tax year 2020 to 2021).

Only use the tables in this booklet for employees who are employed in the tax year 2020 to 2021, and for whom NICs are payable under NICs Table letter B or C.

If there's no table in this booklet for a particular employee, you must use a table from a different booklet.

## About these tables

The tables under letters B and C contain 2 tables for:

- weekly pay intervals
- monthly pay intervals

The letters B and C correspond with the NICs table letters under which NICs are payable.

## Identifying the correct table to use

### Table B

Use this table for married women and widows:

- under State Pension age
- who are entitled to pay employee's NICs at the reduced rate

For these women, you must have either a valid:

- form CA4139 or CF383 Certificate of Election
- form CF380A Certificate of Reduced Liability

### Table C

Use this table for all men and women who are State Pension age or over, for whom you hold a copy of either their birth certificate or passport as evidence of their date of birth.

## How to use these tables

1. Decide which table, B or C, and then apply the earnings period (weekly or monthly) to work out the NICs liability.
2. Look up the employee's gross pay in the left-hand column of the table. If the employee's total earnings fall between the LEL and the UEL and the exact amount is not shown, use the lower amount closest to the exact gross pay. If the employee's total earnings exceed the UEL, see pages 75 or 76.
3. Record the figures in each column of the table onto the employee's form RT11, 'Deductions working sheet'. See the example on page 6.

## Adapting these tables for pay intervals other than weekly or monthly

If the employee is paid in multiples of a week or month:

- divide the pay into equal weekly or monthly amounts to get an average weekly or monthly amount
- find the amount of NICs due for the average weekly or monthly amount
- multiply the amount of NICs by the number of weeks or months that the earnings are paid for
- record the multiplied amounts on their form RT11, 'Deductions working sheet'

# Earnings limits and NICs rates

| Earnings limits | Employee's NICs | | Employer's NICs |
| --- | --- | --- | --- |
| | NICs table letter B | NICs table letter C | NICs table letters B and C |
| below £120 weekly, or below £520 monthly, or below £6,240 yearly | Nil | Nil | Nil |
| £120 to £169 weekly, or £520 to £732 monthly, or £6,240 to £8,788 yearly | 0% | Nil | 0% |
| £169.01 to £183 weekly, or £732.01 to £792 monthly, or £8,788 to £9,500 yearly | 0% | Nil | 13.8% |
| £183.01 to £962 weekly, or £792.01 to £4,167 monthly, or £9,500.01 to £50,000 yearly | 5.85% | Nil | 13.8% |
| Over £962 weekly, or over £4,167 monthly, or over £50,000 yearly | 2% | Nil | 13.8% |

# An example of working out NICs using these tables and recording figures on form RT11, 'Deductions working sheet'

## Example

A monthly paid female employee earns £888.15, payable on 29 April 2020 (tax month 1).

NICs are due under monthly Table letter B. The nearest lower figure to £888.15 is £888. Record the figures shown in the table onto the employee's form RT11 .

## Extract from monthly Table letter B

| Employee's earnings up to and including the UEL | Earnings at the LEL (where earnings are equal to or exceed the LEL) | Earnings above the LEL, up to and including the PT | Earnings above the PT, up to and including the UEL | Employer's NICs due on all earnings above the ST | Employee's NICs due on all earnings above the PT | Total of employee's and employer's NICs (for information only) |
|---|---|---|---|---|---|---|
| | | 1a | 1b | 1c | 1d | 1e |
| £ | £ | £ p | £ p | £ p | £ p | £ p |
| 888 | 520 | 272.00 | 96.00 | 21.80 | 5.73 | 27.53 |

## Extract from form RT11

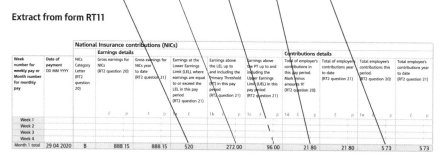

| Week number for weekly pay or Month number for monthly pay | Date of payment DD MM YYYY | NICs Category Letter (RT2 question 20) | Gross earnings for NICs (RT2 question 20) | Gross earnings for NICs year to date (RT2 question 21) | Earnings at the Lower Earnings Limit (LEL), where earnings are equal to or exceed the LEL in this pay period (RT2 question 21) | Earnings above the LEL up to and including the Primary Threshold (PT) in this pay period (RT2 question 21) | Earnings above the PT up to and including the Upper Earnings Limit (UEL) in this pay period (RT2 question 21) | Total of employer's contributions in this pay period. Mark 'minus' amounts 'R' (RT2 question 20) | Total of employer's contributions year to date (RT2 question 21) | Total employee's contributions this period. (RT2 question 20) | Total employee's contributions year to date (RT2 question 21) |
|---|---|---|---|---|---|---|---|---|---|---|---|
| | | | £ p | £ p | £ 1b p | 1c £ p | 1d £ p | £ p | 1e p | £ p | £ p |
| Week 1 | | | | | | | | | | | |
| Week 2 | | | | | | | | | | | |
| Week 3 | | | | | | | | | | | |
| Week 4 | | | | | | | | | | | |
| Month 1 total | 29 04 2020 | B | 888 15 | 888 15 | 520 | 272 00 | 96 00 | 21 80 | 21 80 | 5 73 | 5 73 |

For tips on filling in form RT11 and examples of filled in RT11s, read the helpbook RT7, 'Guidance for employers exempt from Real Time Information online'.

Page 6

457

## Weekly table for reduced rate NICs for use from 6 April 2020 to 5 April 2021

**Table letter B**

Use this table for married women or widows who have a right to pay reduced rate employee's NICs for whom you hold a valid certificate CA4139, CF383 or CF380A.

Do not use this table for:

- any tax year other than 2020 to 2021
- women who are State Pension age or over (see Table letter C)
- women for whom you hold form CA2700 (see Table letter J in booklet CA38)

### Filling in form RT11, 'Deductions working sheet' or substitute

1. Enter 'B' in the NICs category letter column on form RT11.
2. Copy the figures in columns 1a – 1e of the table to columns 1a – 1e on the line next to the tax week in which the employee is paid, on form RT11.

If the employee's total earnings fall between the LEL and the UEL and the exact gross pay is not shown in the table, use the next smaller figure shown. If the employee's total earnings exceed the UEL, see page 75.

The figures in the left-hand column of each table show steps between the LEL and the UEL. The NICs liability for each step, with the exception of the LEL, ST, PT and UEL is worked out at the mid-point of the steps, so you and your employee may pay slightly more or less than if you used the exact percentage method.

| Employee's earnings up to and including the UEL | Earnings at the LEL (where earnings are equal to or exceed the LEL) | Earnings above the LEL, up to and including the PT | Earnings above the PT, up to and including the UEL | Employer's NICs due on all earnings above the ST | Employee's NICs due on all earnings above the PT | Total of employee's and employers NICs (for information only) |
|---|---|---|---|---|---|---|
| | 1a | 1b | 1c | 1d | 1e | |
| £ | £ | £ p | £ p | £ p | £ p | £ p |
| Up to and including £119.99 | No NICs liability, make no entries on form RT11 | | | | | |
| 120 | 120 | 0.00 | 0.00 | 0.00 | 0.00 | 0.00 |
| 121 | 120 | 1.00 | 0.00 | 0.00 | 0.00 | 0.00 |
| 122 | 120 | 2.00 | 0.00 | 0.00 | 0.00 | 0.00 |
| 123 | 120 | 3.00 | 0.00 | 0.00 | 0.00 | 0.00 |
| 124 | 120 | 4.00 | 0.00 | 0.00 | 0.00 | 0.00 |
| 125 | 120 | 5.00 | 0.00 | 0.00 | 0.00 | 0.00 |
| 126 | 120 | 6.00 | 0.00 | 0.00 | 0.00 | 0.00 |
| 127 | 120 | 7.00 | 0.00 | 0.00 | 0.00 | 0.00 |
| 128 | 120 | 8.00 | 0.00 | 0.00 | 0.00 | 0.00 |
| 129 | 120 | 9.00 | 0.00 | 0.00 | 0.00 | 0.00 |
| 130 | 120 | 10.00 | 0.00 | 0.00 | 0.00 | 0.00 |
| 131 | 120 | 11.00 | 0.00 | 0.00 | 0.00 | 0.00 |
| 132 | 120 | 12.00 | 0.00 | 0.00 | 0.00 | 0.00 |
| 133 | 120 | 13.00 | 0.00 | 0.00 | 0.00 | 0.00 |
| 134 | 120 | 14.00 | 0.00 | 0.00 | 0.00 | 0.00 |
| 135 | 120 | 15.00 | 0.00 | 0.00 | 0.00 | 0.00 |
| 136 | 120 | 16.00 | 0.00 | 0.00 | 0.00 | 0.00 |
| 137 | 120 | 17.00 | 0.00 | 0.00 | 0.00 | 0.00 |
| 138 | 120 | 18.00 | 0.00 | 0.00 | 0.00 | 0.00 |
| 139 | 120 | 19.00 | 0.00 | 0.00 | 0.00 | 0.00 |
| 140 | 120 | 20.00 | 0.00 | 0.00 | 0.00 | 0.00 |
| 141 | 120 | 21.00 | 0.00 | 0.00 | 0.00 | 0.00 |
| 142 | 120 | 22.00 | 0.00 | 0.00 | 0.00 | 0.00 |
| 143 | 120 | 23.00 | 0.00 | 0.00 | 0.00 | 0.00 |
| 144 | 120 | 24.00 | 0.00 | 0.00 | 0.00 | 0.00 |
| 145 | 120 | 25.00 | 0.00 | 0.00 | 0.00 | 0.00 |
| 146 | 120 | 26.00 | 0.00 | 0.00 | 0.00 | 0.00 |
| 147 | 120 | 27.00 | 0.00 | 0.00 | 0.00 | 0.00 |
| 148 | 120 | 28.00 | 0.00 | 0.00 | 0.00 | 0.00 |
| 149 | 120 | 29.00 | 0.00 | 0.00 | 0.00 | 0.00 |

Page 7

## Weekly table

**Table letter B**

| Employee's earnings up to and including the UEL | Earnings at the LEL (where earnings are equal to or exceed the LEL) | Earnings above the LEL, up to and including the PT | Earnings above the PT, up to and including the UEL | Employer's NICs due on all earnings above the ST | Employee's NICs due on all earnings above the PT | Total of employee's and employer's NICs (for information only) |
|---|---|---|---|---|---|---|
| | | 1a | 1b | 1c | 1d | 1e |
| £ | £ | £ p | £ p | £ p | £ p | £ p |
| 150 | 120 | 30.00 | 0.00 | 0.00 | 0.00 | 0.00 |
| 151 | 120 | 31.00 | 0.00 | 0.00 | 0.00 | 0.00 |
| 152 | 120 | 32.00 | 0.00 | 0.00 | 0.00 | 0.00 |
| 153 | 120 | 33.00 | 0.00 | 0.00 | 0.00 | 0.00 |
| 154 | 120 | 34.00 | 0.00 | 0.00 | 0.00 | 0.00 |
| 155 | 120 | 35.00 | 0.00 | 0.00 | 0.00 | 0.00 |
| 156 | 120 | 36.00 | 0.00 | 0.00 | 0.00 | 0.00 |
| 157 | 120 | 37.00 | 0.00 | 0.00 | 0.00 | 0.00 |
| 158 | 120 | 38.00 | 0.00 | 0.00 | 0.00 | 0.00 |
| 159 | 120 | 39.00 | 0.00 | 0.00 | 0.00 | 0.00 |
| 160 | 120 | 40.00 | 0.00 | 0.00 | 0.00 | 0.00 |
| 161 | 120 | 41.00 | 0.00 | 0.00 | 0.00 | 0.00 |
| 162 | 120 | 42.00 | 0.00 | 0.00 | 0.00 | 0.00 |
| 163 | 120 | 43.00 | 0.00 | 0.00 | 0.00 | 0.00 |
| 164 | 120 | 44.00 | 0.00 | 0.00 | 0.00 | 0.00 |
| 165 | 120 | 45.00 | 0.00 | 0.00 | 0.00 | 0.00 |
| 166 | 120 | 46.00 | 0.00 | 0.00 | 0.00 | 0.00 |
| 167 | 120 | 47.00 | 0.00 | 0.00 | 0.00 | 0.00 |
| 168 | 120 | 48.00 | 0.00 | 0.00 | 0.00 | 0.00 |
| 169 | 120 | 49.00 | 0.00 | 0.00 | 0.00 | 0.00 |
| 170 | 120 | 50.00 | 0.00 | 0.21 | 0.00 | 0.21 |
| 171 | 120 | 51.00 | 0.00 | 0.34 | 0.00 | 0.34 |
| 172 | 120 | 52.00 | 0.00 | 0.48 | 0.00 | 0.48 |
| 173 | 120 | 53.00 | 0.00 | 0.62 | 0.00 | 0.62 |
| 174 | 120 | 54.00 | 0.00 | 0.76 | 0.00 | 0.76 |
| 175 | 120 | 55.00 | 0.00 | 0.90 | 0.00 | 0.90 |
| 176 | 120 | 56.00 | 0.00 | 1.03 | 0.00 | 1.03 |
| 177 | 120 | 57.00 | 0.00 | 1.17 | 0.00 | 1.17 |
| 178 | 120 | 58.00 | 0.00 | 1.31 | 0.00 | 1.31 |
| 179 | 120 | 59.00 | 0.00 | 1.45 | 0.00 | 1.45 |
| 180 | 120 | 60.00 | 0.00 | 1.59 | 0.00 | 1.59 |
| 181 | 120 | 61.00 | 0.00 | 1.72 | 0.00 | 1.72 |
| 182 | 120 | 62.00 | 0.00 | 1.86 | 0.00 | 1.86 |
| 183 | 120 | 63.00 | 0.00 | 1.93 | 0.00 | 1.93 |
| 184 | 120 | 63.00 | 1.00 | 2.14 | 0.09 | 2.23 |
| 185 | 120 | 63.00 | 2.00 | 2.27 | 0.15 | 2.42 |
| 186 | 120 | 63.00 | 3.00 | 2.41 | 0.20 | 2.61 |
| 187 | 120 | 63.00 | 4.00 | 2.55 | 0.26 | 2.81 |
| 188 | 120 | 63.00 | 5.00 | 2.69 | 0.32 | 3.01 |
| 189 | 120 | 63.00 | 6.00 | 2.83 | 0.38 | 3.21 |
| 190 | 120 | 63.00 | 7.00 | 2.96 | 0.44 | 3.40 |
| 191 | 120 | 63.00 | 8.00 | 3.10 | 0.50 | 3.60 |
| 192 | 120 | 63.00 | 9.00 | 3.24 | 0.55 | 3.79 |
| 193 | 120 | 63.00 | 10.00 | 3.38 | 0.61 | 3.99 |
| 194 | 120 | 63.00 | 11.00 | 3.52 | 0.67 | 4.19 |
| 195 | 120 | 63.00 | 12.00 | 3.65 | 0.73 | 4.38 |
| 196 | 120 | 63.00 | 13.00 | 3.79 | 0.79 | 4.58 |
| 197 | 120 | 63.00 | 14.00 | 3.93 | 0.85 | 4.78 |
| 198 | 120 | 63.00 | 15.00 | 4.07 | 0.91 | 4.98 |
| 199 | 120 | 63.00 | 16.00 | 4.21 | 0.96 | 5.17 |
| 200 | 120 | 63.00 | 17.00 | 4.34 | 1.02 | 5.36 |
| 201 | 120 | 63.00 | 18.00 | 4.48 | 1.08 | 5.56 |
| 202 | 120 | 63.00 | 19.00 | 4.62 | 1.14 | 5.76 |
| 203 | 120 | 63.00 | 20.00 | 4.76 | 1.20 | 5.96 |
| 204 | 120 | 63.00 | 21.00 | 4.90 | 1.26 | 6.16 |

Page 8

## Weekly table

**Table letter B**

| Employee's earnings up to and including the UEL | Earnings at the LEL (where earnings are equal to or exceed the LEL) | Earnings above the LEL, up to and including the PT | Earnings above the PT, up to and including the UEL | Employer's NICs due on all earnings above the ST | Employee's NICs due on all earnings above the PT | Total of employee's and employer's NICs (for information only) |
|---|---|---|---|---|---|---|
| | | 1a | 1b | 1c | 1d | 1e |
| £ | £ | £ p | £ p | £ p | £ p | £ p |
| 205 | 120 | 63.00 | 22.00 | 5.03 | 1.32 | 6.35 |
| 206 | 120 | 63.00 | 23.00 | 5.17 | 1.37 | 6.54 |
| 207 | 120 | 63.00 | 24.00 | 5.31 | 1.43 | 6.74 |
| 208 | 120 | 63.00 | 25.00 | 5.45 | 1.49 | 6.94 |
| 209 | 120 | 63.00 | 26.00 | 5.59 | 1.55 | 7.14 |
| 210 | 120 | 63.00 | 27.00 | 5.72 | 1.61 | 7.33 |
| 211 | 120 | 63.00 | 28.00 | 5.86 | 1.67 | 7.53 |
| 212 | 120 | 63.00 | 29.00 | 6.00 | 1.72 | 7.72 |
| 213 | 120 | 63.00 | 30.00 | 6.14 | 1.78 | 7.92 |
| 214 | 120 | 63.00 | 31.00 | 6.28 | 1.84 | 8.12 |
| 215 | 120 | 63.00 | 32.00 | 6.41 | 1.90 | 8.31 |
| 216 | 120 | 63.00 | 33.00 | 6.55 | 1.96 | 8.51 |
| 217 | 120 | 63.00 | 34.00 | 6.69 | 2.02 | 8.71 |
| 218 | 120 | 63.00 | 35.00 | 6.83 | 2.08 | 8.91 |
| 219 | 120 | 63.00 | 36.00 | 6.97 | 2.13 | 9.10 |
| 220 | 120 | 63.00 | 37.00 | 7.10 | 2.19 | 9.29 |
| 221 | 120 | 63.00 | 38.00 | 7.24 | 2.25 | 9.49 |
| 222 | 120 | 63.00 | 39.00 | 7.38 | 2.31 | 9.69 |
| 223 | 120 | 63.00 | 40.00 | 7.52 | 2.37 | 9.89 |
| 224 | 120 | 63.00 | 41.00 | 7.66 | 2.43 | 10.09 |
| 225 | 120 | 63.00 | 42.00 | 7.79 | 2.49 | 10.28 |
| 226 | 120 | 63.00 | 43.00 | 7.93 | 2.54 | 10.47 |
| 227 | 120 | 63.00 | 44.00 | 8.07 | 2.60 | 10.67 |
| 228 | 120 | 63.00 | 45.00 | 8.21 | 2.66 | 10.87 |
| 229 | 120 | 63.00 | 46.00 | 8.35 | 2.72 | 11.07 |
| 230 | 120 | 63.00 | 47.00 | 8.48 | 2.78 | 11.26 |
| 231 | 120 | 63.00 | 48.00 | 8.62 | 2.84 | 11.46 |
| 232 | 120 | 63.00 | 49.00 | 8.76 | 2.89 | 11.65 |
| 233 | 120 | 63.00 | 50.00 | 8.90 | 2.95 | 11.85 |
| 234 | 120 | 63.00 | 51.00 | 9.04 | 3.01 | 12.05 |
| 235 | 120 | 63.00 | 52.00 | 9.17 | 3.07 | 12.24 |
| 236 | 120 | 63.00 | 53.00 | 9.31 | 3.13 | 12.44 |
| 237 | 120 | 63.00 | 54.00 | 9.45 | 3.19 | 12.64 |
| 238 | 120 | 63.00 | 55.00 | 9.59 | 3.25 | 12.84 |
| 239 | 120 | 63.00 | 56.00 | 9.73 | 3.30 | 13.03 |
| 240 | 120 | 63.00 | 57.00 | 9.86 | 3.36 | 13.22 |
| 241 | 120 | 63.00 | 58.00 | 10.00 | 3.42 | 13.42 |
| 242 | 120 | 63.00 | 59.00 | 10.14 | 3.48 | 13.62 |
| 243 | 120 | 63.00 | 60.00 | 10.28 | 3.54 | 13.82 |
| 244 | 120 | 63.00 | 61.00 | 10.42 | 3.60 | 14.02 |
| 245 | 120 | 63.00 | 62.00 | 10.55 | 3.66 | 14.21 |
| 246 | 120 | 63.00 | 63.00 | 10.69 | 3.71 | 14.40 |
| 247 | 120 | 63.00 | 64.00 | 10.83 | 3.77 | 14.60 |
| 248 | 120 | 63.00 | 65.00 | 10.97 | 3.83 | 14.80 |
| 249 | 120 | 63.00 | 66.00 | 11.11 | 3.89 | 15.00 |
| 250 | 120 | 63.00 | 67.00 | 11.24 | 3.95 | 15.19 |
| 251 | 120 | 63.00 | 68.00 | 11.38 | 4.01 | 15.39 |
| 252 | 120 | 63.00 | 69.00 | 11.52 | 4.06 | 15.58 |
| 253 | 120 | 63.00 | 70.00 | 11.66 | 4.12 | 15.78 |
| 254 | 120 | 63.00 | 71.00 | 11.80 | 4.18 | 15.98 |
| 255 | 120 | 63.00 | 72.00 | 11.93 | 4.24 | 16.17 |
| 256 | 120 | 63.00 | 73.00 | 12.07 | 4.30 | 16.37 |
| 257 | 120 | 63.00 | 74.00 | 12.21 | 4.36 | 16.57 |
| 258 | 120 | 63.00 | 75.00 | 12.35 | 4.42 | 16.77 |
| 259 | 120 | 63.00 | 76.00 | 12.49 | 4.47 | 16.96 |

# Weekly table

**Table letter B**

| Employee's earnings up to and including the UEL | Earnings at the LEL (where earnings are equal to or exceed the LEL) | Earnings above the LEL, up to and including the PT | Earnings above the PT, up to and including the UEL | Employer's NICs due on all earnings above the ST | Employee's NICs due on all earnings above the PT | Total of employee's and employer's NICs (for information only) |
|---|---|---|---|---|---|---|
| | 1a | 1b | 1c | 1d | 1e | |
| £ | £ | £ p | £ p | £ p | £ p | £ p |
| 260 | 120 | 63.00 | 77.00 | 12.62 | 4.53 | 17.15 |
| 261 | 120 | 63.00 | 78.00 | 12.76 | 4.59 | 17.35 |
| 262 | 120 | 63.00 | 79.00 | 12.90 | 4.65 | 17.55 |
| 263 | 120 | 63.00 | 80.00 | 13.04 | 4.71 | 17.75 |
| 264 | 120 | 63.00 | 81.00 | 13.18 | 4.77 | 17.95 |
| 265 | 120 | 63.00 | 82.00 | 13.31 | 4.83 | 18.14 |
| 266 | 120 | 63.00 | 83.00 | 13.45 | 4.88 | 18.33 |
| 267 | 120 | 63.00 | 84.00 | 13.59 | 4.94 | 18.53 |
| 268 | 120 | 63.00 | 85.00 | 13.73 | 5.00 | 18.73 |
| 269 | 120 | 63.00 | 86.00 | 13.87 | 5.06 | 18.93 |
| 270 | 120 | 63.00 | 87.00 | 14.00 | 5.12 | 19.12 |
| 271 | 120 | 63.00 | 88.00 | 14.14 | 5.18 | 19.32 |
| 272 | 120 | 63.00 | 89.00 | 14.28 | 5.23 | 19.51 |
| 273 | 120 | 63.00 | 90.00 | 14.42 | 5.29 | 19.71 |
| 274 | 120 | 63.00 | 91.00 | 14.56 | 5.35 | 19.91 |
| 275 | 120 | 63.00 | 92.00 | 14.69 | 5.41 | 20.10 |
| 276 | 120 | 63.00 | 93.00 | 14.83 | 5.47 | 20.30 |
| 277 | 120 | 63.00 | 94.00 | 14.97 | 5.53 | 20.50 |
| 278 | 120 | 63.00 | 95.00 | 15.11 | 5.59 | 20.70 |
| 279 | 120 | 63.00 | 96.00 | 15.25 | 5.64 | 20.89 |
| 280 | 120 | 63.00 | 97.00 | 15.38 | 5.70 | 21.08 |
| 281 | 120 | 63.00 | 98.00 | 15.52 | 5.76 | 21.28 |
| 282 | 120 | 63.00 | 99.00 | 15.66 | 5.82 | 21.48 |
| 283 | 120 | 63.00 | 100.00 | 15.80 | 5.88 | 21.68 |
| 284 | 120 | 63.00 | 101.00 | 15.94 | 5.94 | 21.88 |
| 285 | 120 | 63.00 | 102.00 | 16.07 | 6.00 | 22.07 |
| 286 | 120 | 63.00 | 103.00 | 16.21 | 6.05 | 22.26 |
| 287 | 120 | 63.00 | 104.00 | 16.35 | 6.11 | 22.46 |
| 288 | 120 | 63.00 | 105.00 | 16.49 | 6.17 | 22.66 |
| 289 | 120 | 63.00 | 106.00 | 16.63 | 6.23 | 22.86 |
| 290 | 120 | 63.00 | 107.00 | 16.76 | 6.29 | 23.05 |
| 291 | 120 | 63.00 | 108.00 | 16.90 | 6.35 | 23.25 |
| 292 | 120 | 63.00 | 109.00 | 17.04 | 6.40 | 23.44 |
| 293 | 120 | 63.00 | 110.00 | 17.18 | 6.46 | 23.64 |
| 294 | 120 | 63.00 | 111.00 | 17.32 | 6.52 | 23.84 |
| 295 | 120 | 63.00 | 112.00 | 17.45 | 6.58 | 24.03 |
| 296 | 120 | 63.00 | 113.00 | 17.59 | 6.64 | 24.23 |
| 297 | 120 | 63.00 | 114.00 | 17.73 | 6.70 | 24.43 |
| 298 | 120 | 63.00 | 115.00 | 17.87 | 6.76 | 24.63 |
| 299 | 120 | 63.00 | 116.00 | 18.01 | 6.81 | 24.82 |
| 300 | 120 | 63.00 | 117.00 | 18.14 | 6.87 | 25.01 |
| 301 | 120 | 63.00 | 118.00 | 18.28 | 6.93 | 25.21 |
| 302 | 120 | 63.00 | 119.00 | 18.42 | 6.99 | 25.41 |
| 303 | 120 | 63.00 | 120.00 | 18.56 | 7.05 | 25.61 |
| 304 | 120 | 63.00 | 121.00 | 18.70 | 7.11 | 25.81 |
| 305 | 120 | 63.00 | 122.00 | 18.83 | 7.17 | 26.00 |
| 306 | 120 | 63.00 | 123.00 | 18.97 | 7.22 | 26.19 |
| 307 | 120 | 63.00 | 124.00 | 19.11 | 7.28 | 26.39 |
| 308 | 120 | 63.00 | 125.00 | 19.25 | 7.34 | 26.59 |
| 309 | 120 | 63.00 | 126.00 | 19.39 | 7.40 | 26.79 |
| 310 | 120 | 63.00 | 127.00 | 19.52 | 7.46 | 26.98 |
| 311 | 120 | 63.00 | 128.00 | 19.66 | 7.52 | 27.18 |
| 312 | 120 | 63.00 | 129.00 | 19.80 | 7.57 | 27.37 |
| 313 | 120 | 63.00 | 130.00 | 19.94 | 7.63 | 27.57 |
| 314 | 120 | 63.00 | 131.00 | 20.08 | 7.69 | 27.77 |

## Weekly table

**Table letter B**

| Employee's earnings up to and including the UEL | Earnings at the LEL (where earnings are equal to or exceed the LEL) | Earnings above the LEL, up to and including the PT | Earnings above the PT, up to and including the UEL | Employer's NICs due on all earnings above the ST | Employee's NICs due on all earnings above the PT | Total of employee's and employer's NICs (for information only) |
|---|---|---|---|---|---|---|
| | | 1a | 1b | 1c | 1d | 1e | |
| £ | £ | £ p | £ p | £ p | £ p | £ p |
| 315 | 120 | 63.00 | 132.00 | 20.21 | 7.75 | 27.96 |
| 316 | 120 | 63.00 | 133.00 | 20.35 | 7.81 | 28.16 |
| 317 | 120 | 63.00 | 134.00 | 20.49 | 7.87 | 28.36 |
| 318 | 120 | 63.00 | 135.00 | 20.63 | 7.93 | 28.56 |
| 319 | 120 | 63.00 | 136.00 | 20.77 | 7.98 | 28.75 |
| 320 | 120 | 63.00 | 137.00 | 20.90 | 8.04 | 28.94 |
| 321 | 120 | 63.00 | 138.00 | 21.04 | 8.10 | 29.14 |
| 322 | 120 | 63.00 | 139.00 | 21.18 | 8.16 | 29.34 |
| 323 | 120 | 63.00 | 140.00 | 21.32 | 8.22 | 29.54 |
| 324 | 120 | 63.00 | 141.00 | 21.46 | 8.28 | 29.74 |
| 325 | 120 | 63.00 | 142.00 | 21.59 | 8.34 | 29.93 |
| 326 | 120 | 63.00 | 143.00 | 21.73 | 8.39 | 30.12 |
| 327 | 120 | 63.00 | 144.00 | 21.87 | 8.45 | 30.32 |
| 328 | 120 | 63.00 | 145.00 | 22.01 | 8.51 | 30.52 |
| 329 | 120 | 63.00 | 146.00 | 22.15 | 8.57 | 30.72 |
| 330 | 120 | 63.00 | 147.00 | 22.28 | 8.63 | 30.91 |
| 331 | 120 | 63.00 | 148.00 | 22.42 | 8.69 | 31.11 |
| 332 | 120 | 63.00 | 149.00 | 22.56 | 8.74 | 31.30 |
| 333 | 120 | 63.00 | 150.00 | 22.70 | 8.80 | 31.50 |
| 334 | 120 | 63.00 | 151.00 | 22.84 | 8.86 | 31.70 |
| 335 | 120 | 63.00 | 152.00 | 22.97 | 8.92 | 31.89 |
| 336 | 120 | 63.00 | 153.00 | 23.11 | 8.98 | 32.09 |
| 337 | 120 | 63.00 | 154.00 | 23.25 | 9.04 | 32.29 |
| 338 | 120 | 63.00 | 155.00 | 23.39 | 9.10 | 32.49 |
| 339 | 120 | 63.00 | 156.00 | 23.53 | 9.15 | 32.68 |
| 340 | 120 | 63.00 | 157.00 | 23.66 | 9.21 | 32.87 |
| 341 | 120 | 63.00 | 158.00 | 23.80 | 9.27 | 33.07 |
| 342 | 120 | 63.00 | 159.00 | 23.94 | 9.33 | 33.27 |
| 343 | 120 | 63.00 | 160.00 | 24.08 | 9.39 | 33.47 |
| 344 | 120 | 63.00 | 161.00 | 24.22 | 9.45 | 33.67 |
| 345 | 120 | 63.00 | 162.00 | 24.35 | 9.51 | 33.86 |
| 346 | 120 | 63.00 | 163.00 | 24.49 | 9.56 | 34.05 |
| 347 | 120 | 63.00 | 164.00 | 24.63 | 9.62 | 34.25 |
| 348 | 120 | 63.00 | 165.00 | 24.77 | 9.68 | 34.45 |
| 349 | 120 | 63.00 | 166.00 | 24.91 | 9.74 | 34.65 |
| 350 | 120 | 63.00 | 167.00 | 25.04 | 9.80 | 34.84 |
| 351 | 120 | 63.00 | 168.00 | 25.18 | 9.86 | 35.04 |
| 352 | 120 | 63.00 | 169.00 | 25.32 | 9.91 | 35.23 |
| 353 | 120 | 63.00 | 170.00 | 25.46 | 9.97 | 35.43 |
| 354 | 120 | 63.00 | 171.00 | 25.60 | 10.03 | 35.63 |
| 355 | 120 | 63.00 | 172.00 | 25.73 | 10.09 | 35.82 |
| 356 | 120 | 63.00 | 173.00 | 25.87 | 10.15 | 36.02 |
| 357 | 120 | 63.00 | 174.00 | 26.01 | 10.21 | 36.22 |
| 358 | 120 | 63.00 | 175.00 | 26.15 | 10.27 | 36.42 |
| 359 | 120 | 63.00 | 176.00 | 26.29 | 10.32 | 36.61 |
| 360 | 120 | 63.00 | 177.00 | 26.42 | 10.38 | 36.80 |
| 361 | 120 | 63.00 | 178.00 | 26.56 | 10.44 | 37.00 |
| 362 | 120 | 63.00 | 179.00 | 26.70 | 10.50 | 37.20 |
| 363 | 120 | 63.00 | 180.00 | 26.84 | 10.56 | 37.40 |
| 364 | 120 | 63.00 | 181.00 | 26.98 | 10.62 | 37.60 |
| 365 | 120 | 63.00 | 182.00 | 27.11 | 10.68 | 37.79 |
| 366 | 120 | 63.00 | 183.00 | 27.25 | 10.73 | 37.98 |
| 367 | 120 | 63.00 | 184.00 | 27.39 | 10.79 | 38.18 |
| 368 | 120 | 63.00 | 185.00 | 27.53 | 10.85 | 38.38 |
| 369 | 120 | 63.00 | 186.00 | 27.67 | 10.91 | 38.58 |

## Weekly table

**Table letter B**

| Employee's earnings up to and including the UEL | Earnings at the LEL (where earnings are equal to or exceed the LEL) | Earnings above the LEL, up to and including the PT | Earnings above the PT, up to and including the UEL | Employer's NICs due on all earnings above the ST | Employee's NICs due on all earnings above the PT | Total of employee's and employer's NICs (for information only) |
|---|---|---|---|---|---|---|
| | | 1a | 1b | 1c | 1d | 1e |
| £ | £ | £ p | £ p | £ p | £ p | £ p |
| 370 | 120 | 63.00 | 187.00 | 27.80 | 10.97 | 38.77 |
| 371 | 120 | 63.00 | 188.00 | 27.94 | 11.03 | 38.97 |
| 372 | 120 | 63.00 | 189.00 | 28.08 | 11.08 | 39.16 |
| 373 | 120 | 63.00 | 190.00 | 28.22 | 11.14 | 39.36 |
| 374 | 120 | 63.00 | 191.00 | 28.36 | 11.20 | 39.56 |
| 375 | 120 | 63.00 | 192.00 | 28.49 | 11.26 | 39.75 |
| 376 | 120 | 63.00 | 193.00 | 28.63 | 11.32 | 39.95 |
| 377 | 120 | 63.00 | 194.00 | 28.77 | 11.38 | 40.15 |
| 378 | 120 | 63.00 | 195.00 | 28.91 | 11.44 | 40.35 |
| 379 | 120 | 63.00 | 196.00 | 29.05 | 11.49 | 40.54 |
| 380 | 120 | 63.00 | 197.00 | 29.18 | 11.55 | 40.73 |
| 381 | 120 | 63.00 | 198.00 | 29.32 | 11.61 | 40.93 |
| 382 | 120 | 63.00 | 199.00 | 29.46 | 11.67 | 41.13 |
| 383 | 120 | 63.00 | 200.00 | 29.60 | 11.73 | 41.33 |
| 384 | 120 | 63.00 | 201.00 | 29.74 | 11.79 | 41.53 |
| 385 | 120 | 63.00 | 202.00 | 29.87 | 11.85 | 41.72 |
| 386 | 120 | 63.00 | 203.00 | 30.01 | 11.90 | 41.91 |
| 387 | 120 | 63.00 | 204.00 | 30.15 | 11.96 | 42.11 |
| 388 | 120 | 63.00 | 205.00 | 30.29 | 12.02 | 42.31 |
| 389 | 120 | 63.00 | 206.00 | 30.43 | 12.08 | 42.51 |
| 390 | 120 | 63.00 | 207.00 | 30.56 | 12.14 | 42.70 |
| 391 | 120 | 63.00 | 208.00 | 30.70 | 12.20 | 42.90 |
| 392 | 120 | 63.00 | 209.00 | 30.84 | 12.25 | 43.09 |
| 393 | 120 | 63.00 | 210.00 | 30.98 | 12.31 | 43.29 |
| 394 | 120 | 63.00 | 211.00 | 31.12 | 12.37 | 43.49 |
| 395 | 120 | 63.00 | 212.00 | 31.25 | 12.43 | 43.68 |
| 396 | 120 | 63.00 | 213.00 | 31.39 | 12.49 | 43.88 |
| 397 | 120 | 63.00 | 214.00 | 31.53 | 12.55 | 44.08 |
| 398 | 120 | 63.00 | 215.00 | 31.67 | 12.61 | 44.28 |
| 399 | 120 | 63.00 | 216.00 | 31.81 | 12.66 | 44.47 |
| 400 | 120 | 63.00 | 217.00 | 31.94 | 12.72 | 44.66 |
| 401 | 120 | 63.00 | 218.00 | 32.08 | 12.78 | 44.86 |
| 402 | 120 | 63.00 | 219.00 | 32.22 | 12.84 | 45.06 |
| 403 | 120 | 63.00 | 220.00 | 32.36 | 12.90 | 45.26 |
| 404 | 120 | 63.00 | 221.00 | 32.50 | 12.96 | 45.46 |
| 405 | 120 | 63.00 | 222.00 | 32.63 | 13.02 | 45.65 |
| 406 | 120 | 63.00 | 223.00 | 32.77 | 13.07 | 45.84 |
| 407 | 120 | 63.00 | 224.00 | 32.91 | 13.13 | 46.04 |
| 408 | 120 | 63.00 | 225.00 | 33.05 | 13.19 | 46.24 |
| 409 | 120 | 63.00 | 226.00 | 33.19 | 13.25 | 46.44 |
| 410 | 120 | 63.00 | 227.00 | 33.32 | 13.31 | 46.63 |
| 411 | 120 | 63.00 | 228.00 | 33.46 | 13.37 | 46.83 |
| 412 | 120 | 63.00 | 229.00 | 33.60 | 13.42 | 47.02 |
| 413 | 120 | 63.00 | 230.00 | 33.74 | 13.48 | 47.22 |
| 414 | 120 | 63.00 | 231.00 | 33.88 | 13.54 | 47.42 |
| 415 | 120 | 63.00 | 232.00 | 34.01 | 13.60 | 47.61 |
| 416 | 120 | 63.00 | 233.00 | 34.15 | 13.66 | 47.81 |
| 417 | 120 | 63.00 | 234.00 | 34.29 | 13.72 | 48.01 |
| 418 | 120 | 63.00 | 235.00 | 34.43 | 13.78 | 48.21 |
| 419 | 120 | 63.00 | 236.00 | 34.57 | 13.83 | 48.40 |
| 420 | 120 | 63.00 | 237.00 | 34.70 | 13.89 | 48.59 |
| 421 | 120 | 63.00 | 238.00 | 34.84 | 13.95 | 48.79 |
| 422 | 120 | 63.00 | 239.00 | 34.98 | 14.01 | 48.99 |
| 423 | 120 | 63.00 | 240.00 | 35.12 | 14.07 | 49.19 |
| 424 | 120 | 63.00 | 241.00 | 35.26 | 14.13 | 49.39 |

## Weekly table

**Table letter B**

| Employee's earnings up to and including the UEL | Earnings at the LEL (where earnings are equal to or exceed the LEL) | Earnings above the LEL, up to and including the PT | Earnings above the PT, up to and including the UEL | Employer's NICs due on all earnings above the ST | Employee's NICs due on all earnings above the PT | Total of employee's and employer's NICs (for information only) |
|---|---|---|---|---|---|---|
| | | 1a | 1b | 1c | 1d | 1e |
| £ | £ | £ p | £ p | £ p | £ p | £ p |
| 425 | 120 | 63.00 | 242.00 | 35.39 | 14.19 | 49.58 |
| 426 | 120 | 63.00 | 243.00 | 35.53 | 14.24 | 49.77 |
| 427 | 120 | 63.00 | 244.00 | 35.67 | 14.30 | 49.97 |
| 428 | 120 | 63.00 | 245.00 | 35.81 | 14.36 | 50.17 |
| 429 | 120 | 63.00 | 246.00 | 35.95 | 14.42 | 50.37 |
| 430 | 120 | 63.00 | 247.00 | 36.08 | 14.48 | 50.56 |
| 431 | 120 | 63.00 | 248.00 | 36.22 | 14.54 | 50.76 |
| 432 | 120 | 63.00 | 249.00 | 36.36 | 14.59 | 50.95 |
| 433 | 120 | 63.00 | 250.00 | 36.50 | 14.65 | 51.15 |
| 434 | 120 | 63.00 | 251.00 | 36.64 | 14.71 | 51.35 |
| 435 | 120 | 63.00 | 252.00 | 36.77 | 14.77 | 51.54 |
| 436 | 120 | 63.00 | 253.00 | 36.91 | 14.83 | 51.74 |
| 437 | 120 | 63.00 | 254.00 | 37.05 | 14.89 | 51.94 |
| 438 | 120 | 63.00 | 255.00 | 37.19 | 14.95 | 52.14 |
| 439 | 120 | 63.00 | 256.00 | 37.33 | 15.00 | 52.33 |
| 440 | 120 | 63.00 | 257.00 | 37.46 | 15.06 | 52.52 |
| 441 | 120 | 63.00 | 258.00 | 37.60 | 15.12 | 52.72 |
| 442 | 120 | 63.00 | 259.00 | 37.74 | 15.18 | 52.92 |
| 443 | 120 | 63.00 | 260.00 | 37.88 | 15.24 | 53.12 |
| 444 | 120 | 63.00 | 261.00 | 38.02 | 15.30 | 53.32 |
| 445 | 120 | 63.00 | 262.00 | 38.15 | 15.36 | 53.51 |
| 446 | 120 | 63.00 | 263.00 | 38.29 | 15.41 | 53.70 |
| 447 | 120 | 63.00 | 264.00 | 38.43 | 15.47 | 53.90 |
| 448 | 120 | 63.00 | 265.00 | 38.57 | 15.53 | 54.10 |
| 449 | 120 | 63.00 | 266.00 | 38.71 | 15.59 | 54.30 |
| 450 | 120 | 63.00 | 267.00 | 38.84 | 15.65 | 54.49 |
| 451 | 120 | 63.00 | 268.00 | 38.98 | 15.71 | 54.69 |
| 452 | 120 | 63.00 | 269.00 | 39.12 | 15.76 | 54.88 |
| 453 | 120 | 63.00 | 270.00 | 39.26 | 15.82 | 55.08 |
| 454 | 120 | 63.00 | 271.00 | 39.40 | 15.88 | 55.28 |
| 455 | 120 | 63.00 | 272.00 | 39.53 | 15.94 | 55.47 |
| 456 | 120 | 63.00 | 273.00 | 39.67 | 16.00 | 55.67 |
| 457 | 120 | 63.00 | 274.00 | 39.81 | 16.06 | 55.87 |
| 458 | 120 | 63.00 | 275.00 | 39.95 | 16.12 | 56.07 |
| 459 | 120 | 63.00 | 276.00 | 40.09 | 16.17 | 56.26 |
| 460 | 120 | 63.00 | 277.00 | 40.22 | 16.23 | 56.45 |
| 461 | 120 | 63.00 | 278.00 | 40.36 | 16.29 | 56.65 |
| 462 | 120 | 63.00 | 279.00 | 40.50 | 16.35 | 56.85 |
| 463 | 120 | 63.00 | 280.00 | 40.64 | 16.41 | 57.05 |
| 464 | 120 | 63.00 | 281.00 | 40.78 | 16.47 | 57.25 |
| 465 | 120 | 63.00 | 282.00 | 40.91 | 16.53 | 57.44 |
| 466 | 120 | 63.00 | 283.00 | 41.05 | 16.58 | 57.63 |
| 467 | 120 | 63.00 | 284.00 | 41.19 | 16.64 | 57.83 |
| 468 | 120 | 63.00 | 285.00 | 41.33 | 16.70 | 58.03 |
| 469 | 120 | 63.00 | 286.00 | 41.47 | 16.76 | 58.23 |
| 470 | 120 | 63.00 | 287.00 | 41.60 | 16.82 | 58.42 |
| 471 | 120 | 63.00 | 288.00 | 41.74 | 16.88 | 58.62 |
| 472 | 120 | 63.00 | 289.00 | 41.88 | 16.93 | 58.81 |
| 473 | 120 | 63.00 | 290.00 | 42.02 | 16.99 | 59.01 |
| 474 | 120 | 63.00 | 291.00 | 42.16 | 17.05 | 59.21 |
| 475 | 120 | 63.00 | 292.00 | 42.29 | 17.11 | 59.40 |
| 476 | 120 | 63.00 | 293.00 | 42.43 | 17.17 | 59.60 |
| 477 | 120 | 63.00 | 294.00 | 42.57 | 17.23 | 59.80 |
| 478 | 120 | 63.00 | 295.00 | 42.71 | 17.29 | 60.00 |
| 479 | 120 | 63.00 | 296.00 | 42.85 | 17.34 | 60.19 |

**Weekly table**

**Table letter B**

| Employee's earnings up to and including the UEL | Earnings at the LEL (where earnings are equal to or exceed the LEL) | Earnings above the LEL, up to and including the PT | Earnings above the PT, up to and including the UEL | Employer's NICs due on all earnings above the ST | Employee's NICs due on all earnings above the PT | Total of employee's and employer's NICs (for information only) |
|---|---|---|---|---|---|---|
| | | 1a | 1b | 1c | 1d | 1e |
| £ | £ | £ p | £ p | £ p | £ p | £ p |
| 480 | 120 | 63.00 | 297.00 | 42.98 | 17.40 | 60.38 |
| 481 | 120 | 63.00 | 298.00 | 43.12 | 17.46 | 60.58 |
| 482 | 120 | 63.00 | 299.00 | 43.26 | 17.52 | 60.78 |
| 483 | 120 | 63.00 | 300.00 | 43.40 | 17.58 | 60.98 |
| 484 | 120 | 63.00 | 301.00 | 43.54 | 17.64 | 61.18 |
| 485 | 120 | 63.00 | 302.00 | 43.67 | 17.70 | 61.37 |
| 486 | 120 | 63.00 | 303.00 | 43.81 | 17.75 | 61.56 |
| 487 | 120 | 63.00 | 304.00 | 43.95 | 17.81 | 61.76 |
| 488 | 120 | 63.00 | 305.00 | 44.09 | 17.87 | 61.96 |
| 489 | 120 | 63.00 | 306.00 | 44.23 | 17.93 | 62.16 |
| 490 | 120 | 63.00 | 307.00 | 44.36 | 17.99 | 62.35 |
| 491 | 120 | 63.00 | 308.00 | 44.50 | 18.05 | 62.55 |
| 492 | 120 | 63.00 | 309.00 | 44.64 | 18.10 | 62.74 |
| 493 | 120 | 63.00 | 310.00 | 44.78 | 18.16 | 62.94 |
| 494 | 120 | 63.00 | 311.00 | 44.92 | 18.22 | 63.14 |
| 495 | 120 | 63.00 | 312.00 | 45.05 | 18.28 | 63.33 |
| 496 | 120 | 63.00 | 313.00 | 45.19 | 18.34 | 63.53 |
| 497 | 120 | 63.00 | 314.00 | 45.33 | 18.40 | 63.73 |
| 498 | 120 | 63.00 | 315.00 | 45.47 | 18.46 | 63.93 |
| 499 | 120 | 63.00 | 316.00 | 45.61 | 18.51 | 64.12 |
| 500 | 120 | 63.00 | 317.00 | 45.74 | 18.57 | 64.31 |
| 501 | 120 | 63.00 | 318.00 | 45.88 | 18.63 | 64.51 |
| 502 | 120 | 63.00 | 319.00 | 46.02 | 18.69 | 64.71 |
| 503 | 120 | 63.00 | 320.00 | 46.16 | 18.75 | 64.91 |
| 504 | 120 | 63.00 | 321.00 | 46.30 | 18.81 | 65.11 |
| 505 | 120 | 63.00 | 322.00 | 46.43 | 18.87 | 65.30 |
| 506 | 120 | 63.00 | 323.00 | 46.57 | 18.92 | 65.49 |
| 507 | 120 | 63.00 | 324.00 | 46.71 | 18.98 | 65.69 |
| 508 | 120 | 63.00 | 325.00 | 46.85 | 19.04 | 65.89 |
| 509 | 120 | 63.00 | 326.00 | 46.99 | 19.10 | 66.09 |
| 510 | 120 | 63.00 | 327.00 | 47.12 | 19.16 | 66.28 |
| 511 | 120 | 63.00 | 328.00 | 47.26 | 19.22 | 66.48 |
| 512 | 120 | 63.00 | 329.00 | 47.40 | 19.27 | 66.67 |
| 513 | 120 | 63.00 | 330.00 | 47.54 | 19.33 | 66.87 |
| 514 | 120 | 63.00 | 331.00 | 47.68 | 19.39 | 67.07 |
| 515 | 120 | 63.00 | 332.00 | 47.81 | 19.45 | 67.26 |
| 516 | 120 | 63.00 | 333.00 | 47.95 | 19.51 | 67.46 |
| 517 | 120 | 63.00 | 334.00 | 48.09 | 19.57 | 67.66 |
| 518 | 120 | 63.00 | 335.00 | 48.23 | 19.63 | 67.86 |
| 519 | 120 | 63.00 | 336.00 | 48.37 | 19.68 | 68.05 |
| 520 | 120 | 63.00 | 337.00 | 48.50 | 19.74 | 68.24 |
| 521 | 120 | 63.00 | 338.00 | 48.64 | 19.80 | 68.44 |
| 522 | 120 | 63.00 | 339.00 | 48.78 | 19.86 | 68.64 |
| 523 | 120 | 63.00 | 340.00 | 48.92 | 19.92 | 68.84 |
| 524 | 120 | 63.00 | 341.00 | 49.06 | 19.98 | 69.04 |
| 525 | 120 | 63.00 | 342.00 | 49.19 | 20.04 | 69.23 |
| 526 | 120 | 63.00 | 343.00 | 49.33 | 20.09 | 69.42 |
| 527 | 120 | 63.00 | 344.00 | 49.47 | 20.15 | 69.62 |
| 528 | 120 | 63.00 | 345.00 | 49.61 | 20.21 | 69.82 |
| 529 | 120 | 63.00 | 346.00 | 49.75 | 20.27 | 70.02 |
| 530 | 120 | 63.00 | 347.00 | 49.88 | 20.33 | 70.21 |
| 531 | 120 | 63.00 | 348.00 | 50.02 | 20.39 | 70.41 |
| 532 | 120 | 63.00 | 349.00 | 50.16 | 20.44 | 70.60 |
| 533 | 120 | 63.00 | 350.00 | 50.30 | 20.50 | 70.80 |
| 534 | 120 | 63.00 | 351.00 | 50.44 | 20.56 | 71.00 |

Page 14

## Weekly table

**Table letter B**

| Employee's earnings up to and including the UEL | Earnings at the LEL (where earnings are equal to or exceed the LEL) | Earnings above the LEL, up to and including the PT | Earnings above the PT, up to and including the UEL | Employer's NICs due on all earnings above the ST | Employee's NICs due on all earnings above the PT | Total of employee's and employer's NICs (for information only) |
|---|---|---|---|---|---|---|
| | | 1a | 1b | 1c | 1d | 1e |
| £ | £ | £ p | £ p | £ p | £ p | £ p |
| 535 | 120 | 63.00 | 352.00 | 50.57 | 20.62 | 71.19 |
| 536 | 120 | 63.00 | 353.00 | 50.71 | 20.68 | 71.39 |
| 537 | 120 | 63.00 | 354.00 | 50.85 | 20.74 | 71.59 |
| 538 | 120 | 63.00 | 355.00 | 50.99 | 20.80 | 71.79 |
| 539 | 120 | 63.00 | 356.00 | 51.13 | 20.85 | 71.98 |
| 540 | 120 | 63.00 | 357.00 | 51.26 | 20.91 | 72.17 |
| 541 | 120 | 63.00 | 358.00 | 51.40 | 20.97 | 72.37 |
| 542 | 120 | 63.00 | 359.00 | 51.54 | 21.03 | 72.57 |
| 543 | 120 | 63.00 | 360.00 | 51.68 | 21.09 | 72.77 |
| 544 | 120 | 63.00 | 361.00 | 51.82 | 21.15 | 72.97 |
| 545 | 120 | 63.00 | 362.00 | 51.95 | 21.21 | 73.16 |
| 546 | 120 | 63.00 | 363.00 | 52.09 | 21.26 | 73.35 |
| 547 | 120 | 63.00 | 364.00 | 52.23 | 21.32 | 73.55 |
| 548 | 120 | 63.00 | 365.00 | 52.37 | 21.38 | 73.75 |
| 549 | 120 | 63.00 | 366.00 | 52.51 | 21.44 | 73.95 |
| 550 | 120 | 63.00 | 367.00 | 52.64 | 21.50 | 74.14 |
| 551 | 120 | 63.00 | 368.00 | 52.78 | 21.56 | 74.34 |
| 552 | 120 | 63.00 | 369.00 | 52.92 | 21.61 | 74.53 |
| 553 | 120 | 63.00 | 370.00 | 53.06 | 21.67 | 74.73 |
| 554 | 120 | 63.00 | 371.00 | 53.20 | 21.73 | 74.93 |
| 555 | 120 | 63.00 | 372.00 | 53.33 | 21.79 | 75.12 |
| 556 | 120 | 63.00 | 373.00 | 53.47 | 21.85 | 75.32 |
| 557 | 120 | 63.00 | 374.00 | 53.61 | 21.91 | 75.52 |
| 558 | 120 | 63.00 | 375.00 | 53.75 | 21.97 | 75.72 |
| 559 | 120 | 63.00 | 376.00 | 53.89 | 22.02 | 75.91 |
| 560 | 120 | 63.00 | 377.00 | 54.02 | 22.08 | 76.10 |
| 561 | 120 | 63.00 | 378.00 | 54.16 | 22.14 | 76.30 |
| 562 | 120 | 63.00 | 379.00 | 54.30 | 22.20 | 76.50 |
| 563 | 120 | 63.00 | 380.00 | 54.44 | 22.26 | 76.70 |
| 564 | 120 | 63.00 | 381.00 | 54.58 | 22.32 | 76.90 |
| 565 | 120 | 63.00 | 382.00 | 54.71 | 22.38 | 77.09 |
| 566 | 120 | 63.00 | 383.00 | 54.85 | 22.43 | 77.28 |
| 567 | 120 | 63.00 | 384.00 | 54.99 | 22.49 | 77.48 |
| 568 | 120 | 63.00 | 385.00 | 55.13 | 22.55 | 77.68 |
| 569 | 120 | 63.00 | 386.00 | 55.27 | 22.61 | 77.88 |
| 570 | 120 | 63.00 | 387.00 | 55.40 | 22.67 | 78.07 |
| 571 | 120 | 63.00 | 388.00 | 55.54 | 22.73 | 78.27 |
| 572 | 120 | 63.00 | 389.00 | 55.68 | 22.78 | 78.46 |
| 573 | 120 | 63.00 | 390.00 | 55.82 | 22.84 | 78.66 |
| 574 | 120 | 63.00 | 391.00 | 55.96 | 22.90 | 78.86 |
| 575 | 120 | 63.00 | 392.00 | 56.09 | 22.96 | 79.05 |
| 576 | 120 | 63.00 | 393.00 | 56.23 | 23.02 | 79.25 |
| 577 | 120 | 63.00 | 394.00 | 56.37 | 23.08 | 79.45 |
| 578 | 120 | 63.00 | 395.00 | 56.51 | 23.14 | 79.65 |
| 579 | 120 | 63.00 | 396.00 | 56.65 | 23.19 | 79.84 |
| 580 | 120 | 63.00 | 397.00 | 56.78 | 23.25 | 80.03 |
| 581 | 120 | 63.00 | 398.00 | 56.92 | 23.31 | 80.23 |
| 582 | 120 | 63.00 | 399.00 | 57.06 | 23.37 | 80.43 |
| 583 | 120 | 63.00 | 400.00 | 57.20 | 23.43 | 80.63 |
| 584 | 120 | 63.00 | 401.00 | 57.34 | 23.49 | 80.83 |
| 585 | 120 | 63.00 | 402.00 | 57.47 | 23.55 | 81.02 |
| 586 | 120 | 63.00 | 403.00 | 57.61 | 23.60 | 81.21 |
| 587 | 120 | 63.00 | 404.00 | 57.75 | 23.66 | 81.41 |
| 588 | 120 | 63.00 | 405.00 | 57.89 | 23.72 | 81.61 |
| 589 | 120 | 63.00 | 406.00 | 58.03 | 23.78 | 81.81 |

## Weekly table

## Table letter B

| Employee's earnings up to and including the UEL | Earnings at the LEL (where earnings are equal to or exceed the LEL) | Earnings above the LEL, up to and including the PT | Earnings above the PT, up to and including the UEL | Employer's NICs due on all earnings above the ST | Employee's NICs due on all earnings above the PT | Total of employee's and employer's NICs (for information only) |
|---|---|---|---|---|---|---|
| | 1a | 1b | 1c | 1d | 1e | |
| £ | £ | £ p | £ p | £ p | £ p | £ p |
| 590 | 120 | 63.00 | 407.00 | 58.16 | 23.84 | 82.00 |
| 591 | 120 | 63.00 | 408.00 | 58.30 | 23.90 | 82.20 |
| 592 | 120 | 63.00 | 409.00 | 58.44 | 23.95 | 82.39 |
| 593 | 120 | 63.00 | 410.00 | 58.58 | 24.01 | 82.59 |
| 594 | 120 | 63.00 | 411.00 | 58.72 | 24.07 | 82.79 |
| 595 | 120 | 63.00 | 412.00 | 58.85 | 24.13 | 82.98 |
| 596 | 120 | 63.00 | 413.00 | 58.99 | 24.19 | 83.18 |
| 597 | 120 | 63.00 | 414.00 | 59.13 | 24.25 | 83.38 |
| 598 | 120 | 63.00 | 415.00 | 59.27 | 24.31 | 83.58 |
| 599 | 120 | 63.00 | 416.00 | 59.41 | 24.36 | 83.77 |
| 600 | 120 | 63.00 | 417.00 | 59.54 | 24.42 | 83.96 |
| 601 | 120 | 63.00 | 418.00 | 59.68 | 24.48 | 84.16 |
| 602 | 120 | 63.00 | 419.00 | 59.82 | 24.54 | 84.36 |
| 603 | 120 | 63.00 | 420.00 | 59.96 | 24.60 | 84.56 |
| 604 | 120 | 63.00 | 421.00 | 60.10 | 24.66 | 84.76 |
| 605 | 120 | 63.00 | 422.00 | 60.23 | 24.72 | 84.95 |
| 606 | 120 | 63.00 | 423.00 | 60.37 | 24.77 | 85.14 |
| 607 | 120 | 63.00 | 424.00 | 60.51 | 24.83 | 85.34 |
| 608 | 120 | 63.00 | 425.00 | 60.65 | 24.89 | 85.54 |
| 609 | 120 | 63.00 | 426.00 | 60.79 | 24.95 | 85.74 |
| 610 | 120 | 63.00 | 427.00 | 60.92 | 25.01 | 85.93 |
| 611 | 120 | 63.00 | 428.00 | 61.06 | 25.07 | 86.13 |
| 612 | 120 | 63.00 | 429.00 | 61.20 | 25.12 | 86.32 |
| 613 | 120 | 63.00 | 430.00 | 61.34 | 25.18 | 86.52 |
| 614 | 120 | 63.00 | 431.00 | 61.48 | 25.24 | 86.72 |
| 615 | 120 | 63.00 | 432.00 | 61.61 | 25.30 | 86.91 |
| 616 | 120 | 63.00 | 433.00 | 61.75 | 25.36 | 87.11 |
| 617 | 120 | 63.00 | 434.00 | 61.89 | 25.42 | 87.31 |
| 618 | 120 | 63.00 | 435.00 | 62.03 | 25.48 | 87.51 |
| 619 | 120 | 63.00 | 436.00 | 62.17 | 25.53 | 87.70 |
| 620 | 120 | 63.00 | 437.00 | 62.30 | 25.59 | 87.89 |
| 621 | 120 | 63.00 | 438.00 | 62.44 | 25.65 | 88.09 |
| 622 | 120 | 63.00 | 439.00 | 62.58 | 25.71 | 88.29 |
| 623 | 120 | 63.00 | 440.00 | 62.72 | 25.77 | 88.49 |
| 624 | 120 | 63.00 | 441.00 | 62.86 | 25.83 | 88.69 |
| 625 | 120 | 63.00 | 442.00 | 62.99 | 25.89 | 88.88 |
| 626 | 120 | 63.00 | 443.00 | 63.13 | 25.94 | 89.07 |
| 627 | 120 | 63.00 | 444.00 | 63.27 | 26.00 | 89.27 |
| 628 | 120 | 63.00 | 445.00 | 63.41 | 26.06 | 89.47 |
| 629 | 120 | 63.00 | 446.00 | 63.55 | 26.12 | 89.67 |
| 630 | 120 | 63.00 | 447.00 | 63.68 | 26.18 | 89.86 |
| 631 | 120 | 63.00 | 448.00 | 63.82 | 26.24 | 90.06 |
| 632 | 120 | 63.00 | 449.00 | 63.96 | 26.29 | 90.25 |
| 633 | 120 | 63.00 | 450.00 | 64.10 | 26.35 | 90.45 |
| 634 | 120 | 63.00 | 451.00 | 64.24 | 26.41 | 90.65 |
| 635 | 120 | 63.00 | 452.00 | 64.37 | 26.47 | 90.84 |
| 636 | 120 | 63.00 | 453.00 | 64.51 | 26.53 | 91.04 |
| 637 | 120 | 63.00 | 454.00 | 64.65 | 26.59 | 91.24 |
| 638 | 120 | 63.00 | 455.00 | 64.79 | 26.65 | 91.44 |
| 639 | 120 | 63.00 | 456.00 | 64.93 | 26.70 | 91.63 |
| 640 | 120 | 63.00 | 457.00 | 65.06 | 26.76 | 91.82 |
| 641 | 120 | 63.00 | 458.00 | 65.20 | 26.82 | 92.02 |
| 642 | 120 | 63.00 | 459.00 | 65.34 | 26.88 | 92.22 |
| 643 | 120 | 63.00 | 460.00 | 65.48 | 26.94 | 92.42 |
| 644 | 120 | 63.00 | 461.00 | 65.62 | 27.00 | 92.62 |

## Weekly table

**Table letter B**

| Employee's earnings up to and including the UEL | Earnings at the LEL (where earnings are equal to or exceed the LEL) | Earnings above the LEL, up to and including the PT | Earnings above the PT, up to and including the UEL | Employer's NICs due on all earnings above the ST | Employee's NICs due on all earnings above the PT | Total of employee's and employer's NICs (for information only) |
|---|---|---|---|---|---|---|
| | | 1a | 1b | 1c | 1d | 1e |
| £ | £ | £ p | £ p | £ p | £ p | £ p |
| 645 | 120 | 63.00 | 462.00 | 65.75 | 27.06 | 92.81 |
| 646 | 120 | 63.00 | 463.00 | 65.89 | 27.11 | 93.00 |
| 647 | 120 | 63.00 | 464.00 | 66.03 | 27.17 | 93.20 |
| 648 | 120 | 63.00 | 465.00 | 66.17 | 27.23 | 93.40 |
| 649 | 120 | 63.00 | 466.00 | 66.31 | 27.29 | 93.60 |
| 650 | 120 | 63.00 | 467.00 | 66.44 | 27.35 | 93.79 |
| 651 | 120 | 63.00 | 468.00 | 66.58 | 27.41 | 93.99 |
| 652 | 120 | 63.00 | 469.00 | 66.72 | 27.46 | 94.18 |
| 653 | 120 | 63.00 | 470.00 | 66.86 | 27.52 | 94.38 |
| 654 | 120 | 63.00 | 471.00 | 67.00 | 27.58 | 94.58 |
| 655 | 120 | 63.00 | 472.00 | 67.13 | 27.64 | 94.77 |
| 656 | 120 | 63.00 | 473.00 | 67.27 | 27.70 | 94.97 |
| 657 | 120 | 63.00 | 474.00 | 67.41 | 27.76 | 95.17 |
| 658 | 120 | 63.00 | 475.00 | 67.55 | 27.82 | 95.37 |
| 659 | 120 | 63.00 | 476.00 | 67.69 | 27.87 | 95.56 |
| 660 | 120 | 63.00 | 477.00 | 67.82 | 27.93 | 95.75 |
| 661 | 120 | 63.00 | 478.00 | 67.96 | 27.99 | 95.95 |
| 662 | 120 | 63.00 | 479.00 | 68.10 | 28.05 | 96.15 |
| 663 | 120 | 63.00 | 480.00 | 68.24 | 28.11 | 96.35 |
| 664 | 120 | 63.00 | 481.00 | 68.38 | 28.17 | 96.55 |
| 665 | 120 | 63.00 | 482.00 | 68.51 | 28.23 | 96.74 |
| 666 | 120 | 63.00 | 483.00 | 68.65 | 28.28 | 96.93 |
| 667 | 120 | 63.00 | 484.00 | 68.79 | 28.34 | 97.13 |
| 668 | 120 | 63.00 | 485.00 | 68.93 | 28.40 | 97.33 |
| 669 | 120 | 63.00 | 486.00 | 69.07 | 28.46 | 97.53 |
| 670 | 120 | 63.00 | 487.00 | 69.20 | 28.52 | 97.72 |
| 671 | 120 | 63.00 | 488.00 | 69.34 | 28.58 | 97.92 |
| 672 | 120 | 63.00 | 489.00 | 69.48 | 28.63 | 98.11 |
| 673 | 120 | 63.00 | 490.00 | 69.62 | 28.69 | 98.31 |
| 674 | 120 | 63.00 | 491.00 | 69.76 | 28.75 | 98.51 |
| 675 | 120 | 63.00 | 492.00 | 69.89 | 28.81 | 98.70 |
| 676 | 120 | 63.00 | 493.00 | 70.03 | 28.87 | 98.90 |
| 677 | 120 | 63.00 | 494.00 | 70.17 | 28.93 | 99.10 |
| 678 | 120 | 63.00 | 495.00 | 70.31 | 28.99 | 99.30 |
| 679 | 120 | 63.00 | 496.00 | 70.45 | 29.04 | 99.49 |
| 680 | 120 | 63.00 | 497.00 | 70.58 | 29.10 | 99.68 |
| 681 | 120 | 63.00 | 498.00 | 70.72 | 29.16 | 99.88 |
| 682 | 120 | 63.00 | 499.00 | 70.86 | 29.22 | 100.08 |
| 683 | 120 | 63.00 | 500.00 | 71.00 | 29.28 | 100.28 |
| 684 | 120 | 63.00 | 501.00 | 71.14 | 29.34 | 100.48 |
| 685 | 120 | 63.00 | 502.00 | 71.27 | 29.40 | 100.67 |
| 686 | 120 | 63.00 | 503.00 | 71.41 | 29.45 | 100.86 |
| 687 | 120 | 63.00 | 504.00 | 71.55 | 29.51 | 101.06 |
| 688 | 120 | 63.00 | 505.00 | 71.69 | 29.57 | 101.26 |
| 689 | 120 | 63.00 | 506.00 | 71.83 | 29.63 | 101.46 |
| 690 | 120 | 63.00 | 507.00 | 71.96 | 29.69 | 101.65 |
| 691 | 120 | 63.00 | 508.00 | 72.10 | 29.75 | 101.85 |
| 692 | 120 | 63.00 | 509.00 | 72.24 | 29.80 | 102.04 |
| 693 | 120 | 63.00 | 510.00 | 72.38 | 29.86 | 102.24 |
| 694 | 120 | 63.00 | 511.00 | 72.52 | 29.92 | 102.44 |
| 695 | 120 | 63.00 | 512.00 | 72.65 | 29.98 | 102.63 |
| 696 | 120 | 63.00 | 513.00 | 72.79 | 30.04 | 102.83 |
| 697 | 120 | 63.00 | 514.00 | 72.93 | 30.10 | 103.03 |
| 698 | 120 | 63.00 | 515.00 | 73.07 | 30.16 | 103.23 |
| 699 | 120 | 63.00 | 516.00 | 73.21 | 30.21 | 103.42 |

## Weekly table

**Table letter B**

| Employee's earnings up to and including the UEL | Earnings at the LEL (where earnings are equal to or exceed the LEL) | Earnings above the LEL, up to and including the PT | Earnings above the PT, up to and including the UEL | Employer's NICs due on all earnings above the ST | Employee's NICs due on all earnings above the PT | Total of employee's and employer's NICs (for information only) |
|---|---|---|---|---|---|---|
| | 1a | 1b | 1c | 1d | 1e | |
| £ | £ | £ p | £ p | £ p | £ p | £ p |
| 700 | 120 | 63.00 | 517.00 | 73.34 | 30.27 | 103.61 |
| 701 | 120 | 63.00 | 518.00 | 73.48 | 30.33 | 103.81 |
| 702 | 120 | 63.00 | 519.00 | 73.62 | 30.39 | 104.01 |
| 703 | 120 | 63.00 | 520.00 | 73.76 | 30.45 | 104.21 |
| 704 | 120 | 63.00 | 521.00 | 73.90 | 30.51 | 104.41 |
| 705 | 120 | 63.00 | 522.00 | 74.03 | 30.57 | 104.60 |
| 706 | 120 | 63.00 | 523.00 | 74.17 | 30.62 | 104.79 |
| 707 | 120 | 63.00 | 524.00 | 74.31 | 30.68 | 104.99 |
| 708 | 120 | 63.00 | 525.00 | 74.45 | 30.74 | 105.19 |
| 709 | 120 | 63.00 | 526.00 | 74.59 | 30.80 | 105.39 |
| 710 | 120 | 63.00 | 527.00 | 74.72 | 30.86 | 105.58 |
| 711 | 120 | 63.00 | 528.00 | 74.86 | 30.92 | 105.78 |
| 712 | 120 | 63.00 | 529.00 | 75.00 | 30.97 | 105.97 |
| 713 | 120 | 63.00 | 530.00 | 75.14 | 31.03 | 106.17 |
| 714 | 120 | 63.00 | 531.00 | 75.28 | 31.09 | 106.37 |
| 715 | 120 | 63.00 | 532.00 | 75.41 | 31.15 | 106.56 |
| 716 | 120 | 63.00 | 533.00 | 75.55 | 31.21 | 106.76 |
| 717 | 120 | 63.00 | 534.00 | 75.69 | 31.27 | 106.96 |
| 718 | 120 | 63.00 | 535.00 | 75.83 | 31.33 | 107.16 |
| 719 | 120 | 63.00 | 536.00 | 75.97 | 31.38 | 107.35 |
| 720 | 120 | 63.00 | 537.00 | 76.10 | 31.44 | 107.54 |
| 721 | 120 | 63.00 | 538.00 | 76.24 | 31.50 | 107.74 |
| 722 | 120 | 63.00 | 539.00 | 76.38 | 31.56 | 107.94 |
| 723 | 120 | 63.00 | 540.00 | 76.52 | 31.62 | 108.14 |
| 724 | 120 | 63.00 | 541.00 | 76.66 | 31.68 | 108.34 |
| 725 | 120 | 63.00 | 542.00 | 76.79 | 31.74 | 108.53 |
| 726 | 120 | 63.00 | 543.00 | 76.93 | 31.79 | 108.72 |
| 727 | 120 | 63.00 | 544.00 | 77.07 | 31.85 | 108.92 |
| 728 | 120 | 63.00 | 545.00 | 77.21 | 31.91 | 109.12 |
| 729 | 120 | 63.00 | 546.00 | 77.35 | 31.97 | 109.32 |
| 730 | 120 | 63.00 | 547.00 | 77.48 | 32.03 | 109.51 |
| 731 | 120 | 63.00 | 548.00 | 77.62 | 32.09 | 109.71 |
| 732 | 120 | 63.00 | 549.00 | 77.76 | 32.14 | 109.90 |
| 733 | 120 | 63.00 | 550.00 | 77.90 | 32.20 | 110.10 |
| 734 | 120 | 63.00 | 551.00 | 78.04 | 32.26 | 110.30 |
| 735 | 120 | 63.00 | 552.00 | 78.17 | 32.32 | 110.49 |
| 736 | 120 | 63.00 | 553.00 | 78.31 | 32.38 | 110.69 |
| 737 | 120 | 63.00 | 554.00 | 78.45 | 32.44 | 110.89 |
| 738 | 120 | 63.00 | 555.00 | 78.59 | 32.50 | 111.09 |
| 739 | 120 | 63.00 | 556.00 | 78.73 | 32.55 | 111.28 |
| 740 | 120 | 63.00 | 557.00 | 78.86 | 32.61 | 111.47 |
| 741 | 120 | 63.00 | 558.00 | 79.00 | 32.67 | 111.67 |
| 742 | 120 | 63.00 | 559.00 | 79.14 | 32.73 | 111.87 |
| 743 | 120 | 63.00 | 560.00 | 79.28 | 32.79 | 112.07 |
| 744 | 120 | 63.00 | 561.00 | 79.42 | 32.85 | 112.27 |
| 745 | 120 | 63.00 | 562.00 | 79.55 | 32.91 | 112.46 |
| 746 | 120 | 63.00 | 563.00 | 79.69 | 32.96 | 112.65 |
| 747 | 120 | 63.00 | 564.00 | 79.83 | 33.02 | 112.85 |
| 748 | 120 | 63.00 | 565.00 | 79.97 | 33.08 | 113.05 |
| 749 | 120 | 63.00 | 566.00 | 80.11 | 33.14 | 113.25 |
| 750 | 120 | 63.00 | 567.00 | 80.24 | 33.20 | 113.44 |
| 751 | 120 | 63.00 | 568.00 | 80.38 | 33.26 | 113.64 |
| 752 | 120 | 63.00 | 569.00 | 80.52 | 33.31 | 113.83 |
| 753 | 120 | 63.00 | 570.00 | 80.66 | 33.37 | 114.03 |
| 754 | 120 | 63.00 | 571.00 | 80.80 | 33.43 | 114.23 |

Page 18

## Weekly table

**Table letter B**

| Employee's earnings up to and including the UEL | Earnings at the LEL (where earnings are equal to or exceed the LEL) | Earnings above the LEL, up to and including the PT | Earnings above the PT, up to and including the UEL | Employer's NICs due on all earnings above the ST | Employee's NICs due on all earnings above the PT | Total of employee's and employers NICs (for information only) |
|---|---|---|---|---|---|---|
| | | 1a | 1b | 1c | 1d | 1e | |
| £ | £ | £ p | £ p | £ p | £ p | £ p |
| 755 | 120 | 63.00 | 572.00 | 80.93 | 33.49 | 114.42 |
| 756 | 120 | 63.00 | 573.00 | 81.07 | 33.55 | 114.62 |
| 757 | 120 | 63.00 | 574.00 | 81.21 | 33.61 | 114.82 |
| 758 | 120 | 63.00 | 575.00 | 81.35 | 33.67 | 115.02 |
| 759 | 120 | 63.00 | 576.00 | 81.49 | 33.72 | 115.21 |
| 760 | 120 | 63.00 | 577.00 | 81.62 | 33.78 | 115.40 |
| 761 | 120 | 63.00 | 578.00 | 81.76 | 33.84 | 115.60 |
| 762 | 120 | 63.00 | 579.00 | 81.90 | 33.90 | 115.80 |
| 763 | 120 | 63.00 | 580.00 | 82.04 | 33.96 | 116.00 |
| 764 | 120 | 63.00 | 581.00 | 82.18 | 34.02 | 116.20 |
| 765 | 120 | 63.00 | 582.00 | 82.31 | 34.08 | 116.39 |
| 766 | 120 | 63.00 | 583.00 | 82.45 | 34.13 | 116.58 |
| 767 | 120 | 63.00 | 584.00 | 82.59 | 34.19 | 116.78 |
| 768 | 120 | 63.00 | 585.00 | 82.73 | 34.25 | 116.98 |
| 769 | 120 | 63.00 | 586.00 | 82.87 | 34.31 | 117.18 |
| 770 | 120 | 63.00 | 587.00 | 83.00 | 34.37 | 117.37 |
| 771 | 120 | 63.00 | 588.00 | 83.14 | 34.43 | 117.57 |
| 772 | 120 | 63.00 | 589.00 | 83.28 | 34.48 | 117.76 |
| 773 | 120 | 63.00 | 590.00 | 83.42 | 34.54 | 117.96 |
| 774 | 120 | 63.00 | 591.00 | 83.56 | 34.60 | 118.16 |
| 775 | 120 | 63.00 | 592.00 | 83.69 | 34.66 | 118.35 |
| 776 | 120 | 63.00 | 593.00 | 83.83 | 34.72 | 118.55 |
| 777 | 120 | 63.00 | 594.00 | 83.97 | 34.78 | 118.75 |
| 778 | 120 | 63.00 | 595.00 | 84.11 | 34.84 | 118.95 |
| 779 | 120 | 63.00 | 596.00 | 84.25 | 34.89 | 119.14 |
| 780 | 120 | 63.00 | 597.00 | 84.38 | 34.95 | 119.33 |
| 781 | 120 | 63.00 | 598.00 | 84.52 | 35.01 | 119.53 |
| 782 | 120 | 63.00 | 599.00 | 84.66 | 35.07 | 119.73 |
| 783 | 120 | 63.00 | 600.00 | 84.80 | 35.13 | 119.93 |
| 784 | 120 | 63.00 | 601.00 | 84.94 | 35.19 | 120.13 |
| 785 | 120 | 63.00 | 602.00 | 85.07 | 35.25 | 120.32 |
| 786 | 120 | 63.00 | 603.00 | 85.21 | 35.30 | 120.51 |
| 787 | 120 | 63.00 | 604.00 | 85.35 | 35.36 | 120.71 |
| 788 | 120 | 63.00 | 605.00 | 85.49 | 35.42 | 120.91 |
| 789 | 120 | 63.00 | 606.00 | 85.63 | 35.48 | 121.11 |
| 790 | 120 | 63.00 | 607.00 | 85.76 | 35.54 | 121.30 |
| 791 | 120 | 63.00 | 608.00 | 85.90 | 35.60 | 121.50 |
| 792 | 120 | 63.00 | 609.00 | 86.04 | 35.65 | 121.69 |
| 793 | 120 | 63.00 | 610.00 | 86.18 | 35.71 | 121.89 |
| 794 | 120 | 63.00 | 611.00 | 86.32 | 35.77 | 122.09 |
| 795 | 120 | 63.00 | 612.00 | 86.45 | 35.83 | 122.28 |
| 796 | 120 | 63.00 | 613.00 | 86.59 | 35.89 | 122.48 |
| 797 | 120 | 63.00 | 614.00 | 86.73 | 35.95 | 122.68 |
| 798 | 120 | 63.00 | 615.00 | 86.87 | 36.01 | 122.88 |
| 799 | 120 | 63.00 | 616.00 | 87.01 | 36.06 | 123.07 |
| 800 | 120 | 63.00 | 617.00 | 87.14 | 36.12 | 123.26 |
| 801 | 120 | 63.00 | 618.00 | 87.28 | 36.18 | 123.46 |
| 802 | 120 | 63.00 | 619.00 | 87.42 | 36.24 | 123.66 |
| 803 | 120 | 63.00 | 620.00 | 87.56 | 36.30 | 123.86 |
| 804 | 120 | 63.00 | 621.00 | 87.70 | 36.36 | 124.06 |
| 805 | 120 | 63.00 | 622.00 | 87.83 | 36.42 | 124.25 |
| 806 | 120 | 63.00 | 623.00 | 87.97 | 36.47 | 124.44 |
| 807 | 120 | 63.00 | 624.00 | 88.11 | 36.53 | 124.64 |
| 808 | 120 | 63.00 | 625.00 | 88.25 | 36.59 | 124.84 |
| 809 | 120 | 63.00 | 626.00 | 88.39 | 36.65 | 125.04 |

Page 19

## Weekly table

**Table letter B**

| Employee's earnings up to and including the UEL | Earnings at the LEL (where earnings are equal to or exceed the LEL) | Earnings above the LEL, up to and including the PT | Earnings above the PT, up to and including the UEL | Employer's NICs due on all earnings above the ST | Employee's NICs due on all earnings above the PT | Total of employee's and employers NICs (for information only) |
|---|---|---|---|---|---|---|
| | | 1a | 1b | 1c | 1d | 1e |
| £ | £ | £ p | £ p | £ p | £ p | £ p |
| 810 | 120 | 63.00 | 627.00 | 88.52 | 36.71 | 125.23 |
| 811 | 120 | 63.00 | 628.00 | 88.66 | 36.77 | 125.43 |
| 812 | 120 | 63.00 | 629.00 | 88.80 | 36.82 | 125.62 |
| 813 | 120 | 63.00 | 630.00 | 88.94 | 36.88 | 125.82 |
| 814 | 120 | 63.00 | 631.00 | 89.08 | 36.94 | 126.02 |
| 815 | 120 | 63.00 | 632.00 | 89.21 | 37.00 | 126.21 |
| 816 | 120 | 63.00 | 633.00 | 89.35 | 37.06 | 126.41 |
| 817 | 120 | 63.00 | 634.00 | 89.49 | 37.12 | 126.61 |
| 818 | 120 | 63.00 | 635.00 | 89.63 | 37.18 | 126.81 |
| 819 | 120 | 63.00 | 636.00 | 89.77 | 37.23 | 127.00 |
| 820 | 120 | 63.00 | 637.00 | 89.90 | 37.29 | 127.19 |
| 821 | 120 | 63.00 | 638.00 | 90.04 | 37.35 | 127.39 |
| 822 | 120 | 63.00 | 639.00 | 90.18 | 37.41 | 127.59 |
| 823 | 120 | 63.00 | 640.00 | 90.32 | 37.47 | 127.79 |
| 824 | 120 | 63.00 | 641.00 | 90.46 | 37.53 | 127.99 |
| 825 | 120 | 63.00 | 642.00 | 90.59 | 37.59 | 128.18 |
| 826 | 120 | 63.00 | 643.00 | 90.73 | 37.64 | 128.37 |
| 827 | 120 | 63.00 | 644.00 | 90.87 | 37.70 | 128.57 |
| 828 | 120 | 63.00 | 645.00 | 91.01 | 37.76 | 128.77 |
| 829 | 120 | 63.00 | 646.00 | 91.15 | 37.82 | 128.97 |
| 830 | 120 | 63.00 | 647.00 | 91.28 | 37.88 | 129.16 |
| 831 | 120 | 63.00 | 648.00 | 91.42 | 37.94 | 129.36 |
| 832 | 120 | 63.00 | 649.00 | 91.56 | 37.99 | 129.55 |
| 833 | 120 | 63.00 | 650.00 | 91.70 | 38.05 | 129.75 |
| 834 | 120 | 63.00 | 651.00 | 91.84 | 38.11 | 129.95 |
| 835 | 120 | 63.00 | 652.00 | 91.97 | 38.17 | 130.14 |
| 836 | 120 | 63.00 | 653.00 | 92.11 | 38.23 | 130.34 |
| 837 | 120 | 63.00 | 654.00 | 92.25 | 38.29 | 130.54 |
| 838 | 120 | 63.00 | 655.00 | 92.39 | 38.35 | 130.74 |
| 839 | 120 | 63.00 | 656.00 | 92.53 | 38.40 | 130.93 |
| 840 | 120 | 63.00 | 657.00 | 92.66 | 38.46 | 131.12 |
| 841 | 120 | 63.00 | 658.00 | 92.80 | 38.52 | 131.32 |
| 842 | 120 | 63.00 | 659.00 | 92.94 | 38.58 | 131.52 |
| 843 | 120 | 63.00 | 660.00 | 93.08 | 38.64 | 131.72 |
| 844 | 120 | 63.00 | 661.00 | 93.22 | 38.70 | 131.92 |
| 845 | 120 | 63.00 | 662.00 | 93.35 | 38.76 | 132.11 |
| 846 | 120 | 63.00 | 663.00 | 93.49 | 38.81 | 132.30 |
| 847 | 120 | 63.00 | 664.00 | 93.63 | 38.87 | 132.50 |
| 848 | 120 | 63.00 | 665.00 | 93.77 | 38.93 | 132.70 |
| 849 | 120 | 63.00 | 666.00 | 93.91 | 38.99 | 132.90 |
| 850 | 120 | 63.00 | 667.00 | 94.04 | 39.05 | 133.09 |
| 851 | 120 | 63.00 | 668.00 | 94.18 | 39.11 | 133.29 |
| 852 | 120 | 63.00 | 669.00 | 94.32 | 39.16 | 133.48 |
| 853 | 120 | 63.00 | 670.00 | 94.46 | 39.22 | 133.68 |
| 854 | 120 | 63.00 | 671.00 | 94.60 | 39.28 | 133.88 |
| 855 | 120 | 63.00 | 672.00 | 94.73 | 39.34 | 134.07 |
| 856 | 120 | 63.00 | 673.00 | 94.87 | 39.40 | 134.27 |
| 857 | 120 | 63.00 | 674.00 | 95.01 | 39.46 | 134.47 |
| 858 | 120 | 63.00 | 675.00 | 95.15 | 39.52 | 134.67 |
| 859 | 120 | 63.00 | 676.00 | 95.29 | 39.57 | 134.86 |
| 860 | 120 | 63.00 | 677.00 | 95.42 | 39.63 | 135.05 |
| 861 | 120 | 63.00 | 678.00 | 95.56 | 39.69 | 135.25 |
| 862 | 120 | 63.00 | 679.00 | 95.70 | 39.75 | 135.45 |
| 863 | 120 | 63.00 | 680.00 | 95.84 | 39.81 | 135.65 |
| 864 | 120 | 63.00 | 681.00 | 95.98 | 39.87 | 135.85 |

**Weekly table**                                                                                    **Table letter B**

| Employee's earnings up to and including the UEL | Earnings at the LEL (where earnings are equal to or exceed the LEL) | Earnings above the LEL, up to and including the PT | Earnings above the PT, up to and including the UEL | Employer's NICs due on all earnings above the ST | Employee's NICs due on all earnings above the PT | Total of employee's and employer's NICs (for information only) |
|---|---|---|---|---|---|---|
|  | 1a | 1b | 1c | 1d | 1e |  |
| £ | £ | £ p | £ p | £ p | £ p | £ p |
| 865 | 120 | 63.00 | 682.00 | 96.11 | 39.93 | 136.04 |
| 866 | 120 | 63.00 | 683.00 | 96.25 | 39.98 | 136.23 |
| 867 | 120 | 63.00 | 684.00 | 96.39 | 40.04 | 136.43 |
| 868 | 120 | 63.00 | 685.00 | 96.53 | 40.10 | 136.63 |
| 869 | 120 | 63.00 | 686.00 | 96.67 | 40.16 | 136.83 |
| 870 | 120 | 63.00 | 687.00 | 96.80 | 40.22 | 137.02 |
| 871 | 120 | 63.00 | 688.00 | 96.94 | 40.28 | 137.22 |
| 872 | 120 | 63.00 | 689.00 | 97.08 | 40.33 | 137.41 |
| 873 | 120 | 63.00 | 690.00 | 97.22 | 40.39 | 137.61 |
| 874 | 120 | 63.00 | 691.00 | 97.36 | 40.45 | 137.81 |
| 875 | 120 | 63.00 | 692.00 | 97.49 | 40.51 | 138.00 |
| 876 | 120 | 63.00 | 693.00 | 97.63 | 40.57 | 138.20 |
| 877 | 120 | 63.00 | 694.00 | 97.77 | 40.63 | 138.40 |
| 878 | 120 | 63.00 | 695.00 | 97.91 | 40.69 | 138.60 |
| 879 | 120 | 63.00 | 696.00 | 98.05 | 40.74 | 138.79 |
| 880 | 120 | 63.00 | 697.00 | 98.18 | 40.80 | 138.98 |
| 881 | 120 | 63.00 | 698.00 | 98.32 | 40.86 | 139.18 |
| 882 | 120 | 63.00 | 699.00 | 98.46 | 40.92 | 139.38 |
| 883 | 120 | 63.00 | 700.00 | 98.60 | 40.98 | 139.58 |
| 884 | 120 | 63.00 | 701.00 | 98.74 | 41.04 | 139.78 |
| 885 | 120 | 63.00 | 702.00 | 98.87 | 41.10 | 139.97 |
| 886 | 120 | 63.00 | 703.00 | 99.01 | 41.15 | 140.16 |
| 887 | 120 | 63.00 | 704.00 | 99.15 | 41.21 | 140.36 |
| 888 | 120 | 63.00 | 705.00 | 99.29 | 41.27 | 140.56 |
| 889 | 120 | 63.00 | 706.00 | 99.43 | 41.33 | 140.76 |
| 890 | 120 | 63.00 | 707.00 | 99.56 | 41.39 | 140.95 |
| 891 | 120 | 63.00 | 708.00 | 99.70 | 41.45 | 141.15 |
| 892 | 120 | 63.00 | 709.00 | 99.84 | 41.50 | 141.34 |
| 893 | 120 | 63.00 | 710.00 | 99.98 | 41.56 | 141.54 |
| 894 | 120 | 63.00 | 711.00 | 100.12 | 41.62 | 141.74 |
| 895 | 120 | 63.00 | 712.00 | 100.25 | 41.68 | 141.93 |
| 896 | 120 | 63.00 | 713.00 | 100.39 | 41.74 | 142.13 |
| 897 | 120 | 63.00 | 714.00 | 100.53 | 41.80 | 142.33 |
| 898 | 120 | 63.00 | 715.00 | 100.67 | 41.86 | 142.53 |
| 899 | 120 | 63.00 | 716.00 | 100.81 | 41.91 | 142.72 |
| 900 | 120 | 63.00 | 717.00 | 100.94 | 41.97 | 142.91 |
| 901 | 120 | 63.00 | 718.00 | 101.08 | 42.03 | 143.11 |
| 902 | 120 | 63.00 | 719.00 | 101.22 | 42.09 | 143.31 |
| 903 | 120 | 63.00 | 720.00 | 101.36 | 42.15 | 143.51 |
| 904 | 120 | 63.00 | 721.00 | 101.50 | 42.21 | 143.71 |
| 905 | 120 | 63.00 | 722.00 | 101.63 | 42.27 | 143.90 |
| 906 | 120 | 63.00 | 723.00 | 101.77 | 42.32 | 144.09 |
| 907 | 120 | 63.00 | 724.00 | 101.91 | 42.38 | 144.29 |
| 908 | 120 | 63.00 | 725.00 | 102.05 | 42.44 | 144.49 |
| 909 | 120 | 63.00 | 726.00 | 102.19 | 42.50 | 144.69 |
| 910 | 120 | 63.00 | 727.00 | 102.32 | 42.56 | 144.88 |
| 911 | 120 | 63.00 | 728.00 | 102.46 | 42.62 | 145.08 |
| 912 | 120 | 63.00 | 729.00 | 102.60 | 42.67 | 145.27 |
| 913 | 120 | 63.00 | 730.00 | 102.74 | 42.73 | 145.47 |
| 914 | 120 | 63.00 | 731.00 | 102.88 | 42.79 | 145.67 |
| 915 | 120 | 63.00 | 732.00 | 103.01 | 42.85 | 145.86 |
| 916 | 120 | 63.00 | 733.00 | 103.15 | 42.91 | 146.06 |
| 917 | 120 | 63.00 | 734.00 | 103.29 | 42.97 | 146.26 |
| 918 | 120 | 63.00 | 735.00 | 103.43 | 43.03 | 146.46 |
| 919 | 120 | 63.00 | 736.00 | 103.57 | 43.08 | 146.65 |

Page 21

## Weekly table

**Table letter B**

| Employee's earnings up to and including the UEL | Earnings at the LEL (where earnings are equal to or exceed the LEL) | Earnings above the LEL, up to and including the PT | Earnings above the PT, up to and including the UEL | Employer's NICs due on all earnings above the ST | Employee's NICs due on all earnings above the PT | Total of employee's and employers NICs (for information only) |
|---|---|---|---|---|---|---|
| | | 1a | 1b | 1c | 1d | 1e |
| £ | £ | £ p | £ p | £ p | £ p | £ p |
| 920 | 120 | 63.00 | 737.00 | 103.70 | 43.14 | 146.84 |
| 921 | 120 | 63.00 | 738.00 | 103.84 | 43.20 | 147.04 |
| 922 | 120 | 63.00 | 739.00 | 103.98 | 43.26 | 147.24 |
| 923 | 120 | 63.00 | 740.00 | 104.12 | 43.32 | 147.44 |
| 924 | 120 | 63.00 | 741.00 | 104.26 | 43.38 | 147.64 |
| 925 | 120 | 63.00 | 742.00 | 104.39 | 43.44 | 147.83 |
| 926 | 120 | 63.00 | 743.00 | 104.53 | 43.49 | 148.02 |
| 927 | 120 | 63.00 | 744.00 | 104.67 | 43.55 | 148.22 |
| 928 | 120 | 63.00 | 745.00 | 104.81 | 43.61 | 148.42 |
| 929 | 120 | 63.00 | 746.00 | 104.95 | 43.67 | 148.62 |
| 930 | 120 | 63.00 | 747.00 | 105.08 | 43.73 | 148.81 |
| 931 | 120 | 63.00 | 748.00 | 105.22 | 43.79 | 149.01 |
| 932 | 120 | 63.00 | 749.00 | 105.36 | 43.84 | 149.20 |
| 933 | 120 | 63.00 | 750.00 | 105.50 | 43.90 | 149.40 |
| 934 | 120 | 63.00 | 751.00 | 105.64 | 43.96 | 149.60 |
| 935 | 120 | 63.00 | 752.00 | 105.77 | 44.02 | 149.79 |
| 936 | 120 | 63.00 | 753.00 | 105.91 | 44.08 | 149.99 |
| 937 | 120 | 63.00 | 754.00 | 106.05 | 44.14 | 150.19 |
| 938 | 120 | 63.00 | 755.00 | 106.19 | 44.20 | 150.39 |
| 939 | 120 | 63.00 | 756.00 | 106.33 | 44.25 | 150.58 |
| 940 | 120 | 63.00 | 757.00 | 106.46 | 44.31 | 150.77 |
| 941 | 120 | 63.00 | 758.00 | 106.60 | 44.37 | 150.97 |
| 942 | 120 | 63.00 | 759.00 | 106.74 | 44.43 | 151.17 |
| 943 | 120 | 63.00 | 760.00 | 106.88 | 44.49 | 151.37 |
| 944 | 120 | 63.00 | 761.00 | 107.02 | 44.55 | 151.57 |
| 945 | 120 | 63.00 | 762.00 | 107.15 | 44.61 | 151.76 |
| 946 | 120 | 63.00 | 763.00 | 107.29 | 44.66 | 151.95 |
| 947 | 120 | 63.00 | 764.00 | 107.43 | 44.72 | 152.15 |
| 948 | 120 | 63.00 | 765.00 | 107.57 | 44.78 | 152.35 |
| 949 | 120 | 63.00 | 766.00 | 107.71 | 44.84 | 152.55 |
| 950 | 120 | 63.00 | 767.00 | 107.84 | 44.90 | 152.74 |
| 951 | 120 | 63.00 | 768.00 | 107.98 | 44.96 | 152.94 |
| 952 | 120 | 63.00 | 769.00 | 108.12 | 45.01 | 153.13 |
| 953 | 120 | 63.00 | 770.00 | 108.26 | 45.07 | 153.33 |
| 954 | 120 | 63.00 | 771.00 | 108.40 | 45.13 | 153.53 |
| 955 | 120 | 63.00 | 772.00 | 108.53 | 45.19 | 153.72 |
| 956 | 120 | 63.00 | 773.00 | 108.67 | 45.25 | 153.92 |
| 957 | 120 | 63.00 | 774.00 | 108.81 | 45.31 | 154.12 |
| 958 | 120 | 63.00 | 775.00 | 108.95 | 45.37 | 154.32 |
| 959 | 120 | 63.00 | 776.00 | 109.09 | 45.42 | 154.51 |
| 960 | 120 | 63.00 | 777.00 | 109.22 | 45.48 | 154.70 |
| 961 | 120 | 63.00 | 778.00 | 109.36 | 45.54 | 154.90 |
| 962 | 120 | 63.00 | 779.00 | 109.43 | 45.57 | 155.00 |

If the employee's gross pay is over £962, go to page 75.

Page 22

## Monthly table for reduced rate NICs for use from 6 April 2020 to 5 April 2021

**Table letter B**

Use this table for married women or widows who have a right to pay reduced rate employee's NICs for whom you hold a valid certificate CA4139, CF383 or CF380A.

Do not use this table for:

- any tax year other than 2020 to 2021
- women who are State Pension age or over (see Table letter C)
- women for whom you hold form CA2700 (see Table letter J in booklet CA38)

### Filling in form RT11, 'Deductions working sheet' or substitute

1. Enter 'B' in the NICs category letter column on form RT11.

2. Copy the figures in columns 1a – 1e of the table to columns 1a – 1e on the line next to the tax month in which the employee is paid, on form RT11.

If the employee's total earnings fall between the LEL and the UEL and the exact gross pay is not shown in the table, use the next smaller figure shown. If the employee's total earnings exceed the UEL, see page 75.

The figures in the left-hand column of each table show steps between the LEL and the UEL. The NICs liability for each step, with the exception of the LEL, ST, PT and UEL, is worked out at the mid-point of the steps, so you and your employee may pay slightly more or less than if you used the exact percentage method.

| Employee's earnings up to and including the UEL | Earnings at the LEL (where earnings are equal to or exceed the LEL) | Earnings above the LEL, up to and including the PT | Earnings above the PT, up to and including the UEL | Employer's NICs due on all earnings above the ST | Employee's NICs due on all earnings above the PT | Total of employee's and employer's NICs (for information only) |
|---|---|---|---|---|---|---|
| | 1a | 1b | 1c | 1d | 1e | |
| £ | £ | £ p | £ p | £ p | £ p | £ p |
| Up to and including £519.99 | No NICs liability, make no entries on form RT11 | | | | | |
| 520 | 520 | 0.00 | 0.00 | 0.00 | 0.00 | 0.00 |
| 524 | 520 | 4.00 | 0.00 | 0.00 | 0.00 | 0.00 |
| 528 | 520 | 8.00 | 0.00 | 0.00 | 0.00 | 0.00 |
| 532 | 520 | 12.00 | 0.00 | 0.00 | 0.00 | 0.00 |
| 536 | 520 | 16.00 | 0.00 | 0.00 | 0.00 | 0.00 |
| 540 | 520 | 20.00 | 0.00 | 0.00 | 0.00 | 0.00 |
| 544 | 520 | 24.00 | 0.00 | 0.00 | 0.00 | 0.00 |
| 548 | 520 | 28.00 | 0.00 | 0.00 | 0.00 | 0.00 |
| 552 | 520 | 32.00 | 0.00 | 0.00 | 0.00 | 0.00 |
| 556 | 520 | 36.00 | 0.00 | 0.00 | 0.00 | 0.00 |
| 560 | 520 | 40.00 | 0.00 | 0.00 | 0.00 | 0.00 |
| 564 | 520 | 44.00 | 0.00 | 0.00 | 0.00 | 0.00 |
| 568 | 520 | 48.00 | 0.00 | 0.00 | 0.00 | 0.00 |
| 572 | 520 | 52.00 | 0.00 | 0.00 | 0.00 | 0.00 |
| 576 | 520 | 56.00 | 0.00 | 0.00 | 0.00 | 0.00 |
| 580 | 520 | 60.00 | 0.00 | 0.00 | 0.00 | 0.00 |
| 584 | 520 | 64.00 | 0.00 | 0.00 | 0.00 | 0.00 |
| 588 | 520 | 68.00 | 0.00 | 0.00 | 0.00 | 0.00 |
| 592 | 520 | 72.00 | 0.00 | 0.00 | 0.00 | 0.00 |
| 596 | 520 | 76.00 | 0.00 | 0.00 | 0.00 | 0.00 |
| 600 | 520 | 80.00 | 0.00 | 0.00 | 0.00 | 0.00 |
| 604 | 520 | 84.00 | 0.00 | 0.00 | 0.00 | 0.00 |
| 608 | 520 | 88.00 | 0.00 | 0.00 | 0.00 | 0.00 |
| 612 | 520 | 92.00 | 0.00 | 0.00 | 0.00 | 0.00 |
| 616 | 520 | 96.00 | 0.00 | 0.00 | 0.00 | 0.00 |
| 620 | 520 | 100.00 | 0.00 | 0.00 | 0.00 | 0.00 |
| 624 | 520 | 104.00 | 0.00 | 0.00 | 0.00 | 0.00 |
| 628 | 520 | 108.00 | 0.00 | 0.00 | 0.00 | 0.00 |
| 632 | 520 | 112.00 | 0.00 | 0.00 | 0.00 | 0.00 |
| 636 | 520 | 116.00 | 0.00 | 0.00 | 0.00 | 0.00 |

Page 23

## Monthly table

**Table letter B**

| Employee's earnings up to and including the UEL | Earnings at the LEL (where earnings are equal to or exceed the LEL) | Earnings above the LEL, up to and including the PT | Earnings above the PT, up to and including the UEL | Employer's NICs due on all earnings above the ST | Employee's NICs due on all earnings above the PT | Total of employee's and employer's NICs (for information only) |
|---|---|---|---|---|---|---|
| | 1a | 1b | 1c | 1d | 1e | |
| £ | £ | £ p | £ p | £ p | £ p | £ p |
| 640 | 520 | 120.00 | 0.00 | 0.00 | 0.00 | 0.00 |
| 644 | 520 | 124.00 | 0.00 | 0.00 | 0.00 | 0.00 |
| 648 | 520 | 128.00 | 0.00 | 0.00 | 0.00 | 0.00 |
| 652 | 520 | 132.00 | 0.00 | 0.00 | 0.00 | 0.00 |
| 656 | 520 | 136.00 | 0.00 | 0.00 | 0.00 | 0.00 |
| 660 | 520 | 140.00 | 0.00 | 0.00 | 0.00 | 0.00 |
| 664 | 520 | 144.00 | 0.00 | 0.00 | 0.00 | 0.00 |
| 668 | 520 | 148.00 | 0.00 | 0.00 | 0.00 | 0.00 |
| 672 | 520 | 152.00 | 0.00 | 0.00 | 0.00 | 0.00 |
| 676 | 520 | 156.00 | 0.00 | 0.00 | 0.00 | 0.00 |
| 680 | 520 | 160.00 | 0.00 | 0.00 | 0.00 | 0.00 |
| 684 | 520 | 164.00 | 0.00 | 0.00 | 0.00 | 0.00 |
| 688 | 520 | 168.00 | 0.00 | 0.00 | 0.00 | 0.00 |
| 692 | 520 | 172.00 | 0.00 | 0.00 | 0.00 | 0.00 |
| 696 | 520 | 176.00 | 0.00 | 0.00 | 0.00 | 0.00 |
| 700 | 520 | 180.00 | 0.00 | 0.00 | 0.00 | 0.00 |
| 704 | 520 | 184.00 | 0.00 | 0.00 | 0.00 | 0.00 |
| 708 | 520 | 188.00 | 0.00 | 0.00 | 0.00 | 0.00 |
| 712 | 520 | 192.00 | 0.00 | 0.00 | 0.00 | 0.00 |
| 716 | 520 | 196.00 | 0.00 | 0.00 | 0.00 | 0.00 |
| 720 | 520 | 200.00 | 0.00 | 0.00 | 0.00 | 0.00 |
| 724 | 520 | 204.00 | 0.00 | 0.00 | 0.00 | 0.00 |
| 728 | 520 | 208.00 | 0.00 | 0.00 | 0.00 | 0.00 |
| 732 | 520 | 212.00 | 0.00 | 0.00 | 0.00 | 0.00 |
| 736 | 520 | 216.00 | 0.00 | 0.83 | 0.00 | 0.83 |
| 740 | 520 | 220.00 | 0.00 | 1.38 | 0.00 | 1.38 |
| 744 | 520 | 224.00 | 0.00 | 1.93 | 0.00 | 1.93 |
| 748 | 520 | 228.00 | 0.00 | 2.48 | 0.00 | 2.48 |
| 752 | 520 | 232.00 | 0.00 | 3.04 | 0.00 | 3.04 |
| 756 | 520 | 236.00 | 0.00 | 3.59 | 0.00 | 3.59 |
| 760 | 520 | 240.00 | 0.00 | 4.14 | 0.00 | 4.14 |
| 764 | 520 | 244.00 | 0.00 | 4.69 | 0.00 | 4.69 |
| 768 | 520 | 248.00 | 0.00 | 5.24 | 0.00 | 5.24 |
| 772 | 520 | 252.00 | 0.00 | 5.80 | 0.00 | 5.80 |
| 776 | 520 | 256.00 | 0.00 | 6.35 | 0.00 | 6.35 |
| 780 | 520 | 260.00 | 0.00 | 6.90 | 0.00 | 6.90 |
| 784 | 520 | 264.00 | 0.00 | 7.45 | 0.00 | 7.45 |
| 788 | 520 | 268.00 | 0.00 | 8.00 | 0.00 | 8.00 |
| 792 | 520 | 272.00 | 0.00 | 8.28 | 0.00 | 8.28 |
| 796 | 520 | 272.00 | 4.00 | 9.11 | 0.35 | 9.46 |
| 800 | 520 | 272.00 | 8.00 | 9.66 | 0.58 | 10.24 |
| 804 | 520 | 272.00 | 12.00 | 10.21 | 0.82 | 11.03 |
| 808 | 520 | 272.00 | 16.00 | 10.76 | 1.05 | 11.81 |
| 812 | 520 | 272.00 | 20.00 | 11.32 | 1.29 | 12.61 |
| 816 | 520 | 272.00 | 24.00 | 11.87 | 1.52 | 13.39 |
| 820 | 520 | 272.00 | 28.00 | 12.42 | 1.75 | 14.17 |
| 824 | 520 | 272.00 | 32.00 | 12.97 | 1.99 | 14.96 |
| 828 | 520 | 272.00 | 36.00 | 13.52 | 2.22 | 15.74 |
| 832 | 520 | 272.00 | 40.00 | 14.08 | 2.46 | 16.54 |
| 836 | 520 | 272.00 | 44.00 | 14.63 | 2.69 | 17.32 |
| 840 | 520 | 272.00 | 48.00 | 15.18 | 2.92 | 18.10 |
| 844 | 520 | 272.00 | 52.00 | 15.73 | 3.16 | 18.89 |
| 848 | 520 | 272.00 | 56.00 | 16.28 | 3.39 | 19.67 |
| 852 | 520 | 272.00 | 60.00 | 16.84 | 3.63 | 20.47 |
| 856 | 520 | 272.00 | 64.00 | 17.39 | 3.86 | 21.25 |

## Monthly table

**Table letter B**

| Employee's earnings up to and including the UEL | Earnings at the LEL (where earnings are equal to or exceed the LEL) | Earnings above the LEL, up to and including the PT | Earnings above the PT, up to and including the UEL | Employer's NICs due on all earnings above the ST | Employee's NICs due on all earnings above the PT | Total of employee's and employer's NICs (for information only) |
|---|---|---|---|---|---|---|
| | 1a | 1b | 1c | 1d | 1e | |
| £ | £ | £ p | £ p | £ p | £ p | £ p |
| 860 | 520 | 272.00 | 68.00 | 17.94 | 4.09 | 22.03 |
| 864 | 520 | 272.00 | 72.00 | 18.49 | 4.33 | 22.82 |
| 868 | 520 | 272.00 | 76.00 | 19.04 | 4.56 | 23.60 |
| 872 | 520 | 272.00 | 80.00 | 19.60 | 4.80 | 24.40 |
| 876 | 520 | 272.00 | 84.00 | 20.15 | 5.03 | 25.18 |
| 880 | 520 | 272.00 | 88.00 | 20.70 | 5.26 | 25.96 |
| 884 | 520 | 272.00 | 92.00 | 21.25 | 5.50 | 26.75 |
| 888 | 520 | 272.00 | 96.00 | 21.80 | 5.73 | 27.53 |
| 892 | 520 | 272.00 | 100.00 | 22.36 | 5.97 | 28.33 |
| 896 | 520 | 272.00 | 104.00 | 22.91 | 6.20 | 29.11 |
| 900 | 520 | 272.00 | 108.00 | 23.46 | 6.43 | 29.89 |
| 904 | 520 | 272.00 | 112.00 | 24.01 | 6.67 | 30.68 |
| 908 | 520 | 272.00 | 116.00 | 24.56 | 6.90 | 31.46 |
| 912 | 520 | 272.00 | 120.00 | 25.12 | 7.14 | 32.26 |
| 916 | 520 | 272.00 | 124.00 | 25.67 | 7.37 | 33.04 |
| 920 | 520 | 272.00 | 128.00 | 26.22 | 7.60 | 33.82 |
| 924 | 520 | 272.00 | 132.00 | 26.77 | 7.84 | 34.61 |
| 928 | 520 | 272.00 | 136.00 | 27.32 | 8.07 | 35.39 |
| 932 | 520 | 272.00 | 140.00 | 27.88 | 8.31 | 36.19 |
| 936 | 520 | 272.00 | 144.00 | 28.43 | 8.54 | 36.97 |
| 940 | 520 | 272.00 | 148.00 | 28.98 | 8.77 | 37.75 |
| 944 | 520 | 272.00 | 152.00 | 29.53 | 9.01 | 38.54 |
| 948 | 520 | 272.00 | 156.00 | 30.08 | 9.24 | 39.32 |
| 952 | 520 | 272.00 | 160.00 | 30.64 | 9.48 | 40.12 |
| 956 | 520 | 272.00 | 164.00 | 31.19 | 9.71 | 40.90 |
| 960 | 520 | 272.00 | 168.00 | 31.74 | 9.94 | 41.68 |
| 964 | 520 | 272.00 | 172.00 | 32.29 | 10.18 | 42.47 |
| 968 | 520 | 272.00 | 176.00 | 32.84 | 10.41 | 43.25 |
| 972 | 520 | 272.00 | 180.00 | 33.40 | 10.65 | 44.05 |
| 976 | 520 | 272.00 | 184.00 | 33.95 | 10.88 | 44.83 |
| 980 | 520 | 272.00 | 188.00 | 34.50 | 11.11 | 45.61 |
| 984 | 520 | 272.00 | 192.00 | 35.05 | 11.35 | 46.40 |
| 988 | 520 | 272.00 | 196.00 | 35.60 | 11.58 | 47.18 |
| 992 | 520 | 272.00 | 200.00 | 36.16 | 11.82 | 47.98 |
| 996 | 520 | 272.00 | 204.00 | 36.71 | 12.05 | 48.76 |
| 1000 | 520 | 272.00 | 208.00 | 37.26 | 12.28 | 49.54 |
| 1004 | 520 | 272.00 | 212.00 | 37.81 | 12.52 | 50.33 |
| 1008 | 520 | 272.00 | 216.00 | 38.36 | 12.75 | 51.11 |
| 1012 | 520 | 272.00 | 220.00 | 38.92 | 12.99 | 51.91 |
| 1016 | 520 | 272.00 | 224.00 | 39.47 | 13.22 | 52.69 |
| 1020 | 520 | 272.00 | 228.00 | 40.02 | 13.45 | 53.47 |
| 1024 | 520 | 272.00 | 232.00 | 40.57 | 13.69 | 54.26 |
| 1028 | 520 | 272.00 | 236.00 | 41.12 | 13.92 | 55.04 |
| 1032 | 520 | 272.00 | 240.00 | 41.68 | 14.16 | 55.84 |
| 1036 | 520 | 272.00 | 244.00 | 42.23 | 14.39 | 56.62 |
| 1040 | 520 | 272.00 | 248.00 | 42.78 | 14.62 | 57.40 |
| 1044 | 520 | 272.00 | 252.00 | 43.33 | 14.86 | 58.19 |
| 1048 | 520 | 272.00 | 256.00 | 43.88 | 15.09 | 58.97 |
| 1052 | 520 | 272.00 | 260.00 | 44.44 | 15.33 | 59.77 |
| 1056 | 520 | 272.00 | 264.00 | 44.99 | 15.56 | 60.55 |
| 1060 | 520 | 272.00 | 268.00 | 45.54 | 15.79 | 61.33 |
| 1064 | 520 | 272.00 | 272.00 | 46.09 | 16.03 | 62.12 |
| 1068 | 520 | 272.00 | 276.00 | 46.64 | 16.26 | 62.90 |
| 1072 | 520 | 272.00 | 280.00 | 47.20 | 16.50 | 63.70 |
| 1076 | 520 | 272.00 | 284.00 | 47.75 | 16.73 | 64.48 |

## Monthly table

**Table letter B**

| Employee's earnings up to and including the UEL | Earnings at the LEL (where earnings are equal to or exceed the LEL) | Earnings above the LEL, up to and including the PT | Earnings above the PT, up to and including the UEL | Employer's NICs due on all earnings above the ST | Employee's NICs due on all earnings above the PT | Total of employee's and employer's NICs (for information only) |
|---|---|---|---|---|---|---|
| | | 1a | 1b | 1c | 1d | 1e |
| £ | £ | £ p | £ p | £ p | £ p | £ p |
| 1080 | 520 | 272.00 | 288.00 | 48.30 | 16.96 | 65.26 |
| 1084 | 520 | 272.00 | 292.00 | 48.85 | 17.20 | 66.05 |
| 1088 | 520 | 272.00 | 296.00 | 49.40 | 17.43 | 66.83 |
| 1092 | 520 | 272.00 | 300.00 | 49.96 | 17.67 | 67.63 |
| 1096 | 520 | 272.00 | 304.00 | 50.51 | 17.90 | 68.41 |
| 1100 | 520 | 272.00 | 308.00 | 51.06 | 18.13 | 69.19 |
| 1104 | 520 | 272.00 | 312.00 | 51.61 | 18.37 | 69.98 |
| 1108 | 520 | 272.00 | 316.00 | 52.16 | 18.60 | 70.76 |
| 1112 | 520 | 272.00 | 320.00 | 52.72 | 18.84 | 71.56 |
| 1116 | 520 | 272.00 | 324.00 | 53.27 | 19.07 | 72.34 |
| 1120 | 520 | 272.00 | 328.00 | 53.82 | 19.30 | 73.12 |
| 1124 | 520 | 272.00 | 332.00 | 54.37 | 19.54 | 73.91 |
| 1128 | 520 | 272.00 | 336.00 | 54.92 | 19.77 | 74.69 |
| 1132 | 520 | 272.00 | 340.00 | 55.48 | 20.01 | 75.49 |
| 1136 | 520 | 272.00 | 344.00 | 56.03 | 20.24 | 76.27 |
| 1140 | 520 | 272.00 | 348.00 | 56.58 | 20.47 | 77.05 |
| 1144 | 520 | 272.00 | 352.00 | 57.13 | 20.71 | 77.84 |
| 1148 | 520 | 272.00 | 356.00 | 57.68 | 20.94 | 78.62 |
| 1152 | 520 | 272.00 | 360.00 | 58.24 | 21.18 | 79.42 |
| 1156 | 520 | 272.00 | 364.00 | 58.79 | 21.41 | 80.20 |
| 1160 | 520 | 272.00 | 368.00 | 59.34 | 21.64 | 80.98 |
| 1164 | 520 | 272.00 | 372.00 | 59.89 | 21.88 | 81.77 |
| 1168 | 520 | 272.00 | 376.00 | 60.44 | 22.11 | 82.55 |
| 1172 | 520 | 272.00 | 380.00 | 61.00 | 22.35 | 83.35 |
| 1176 | 520 | 272.00 | 384.00 | 61.55 | 22.58 | 84.13 |
| 1180 | 520 | 272.00 | 388.00 | 62.10 | 22.81 | 84.91 |
| 1184 | 520 | 272.00 | 392.00 | 62.65 | 23.05 | 85.70 |
| 1188 | 520 | 272.00 | 396.00 | 63.20 | 23.28 | 86.48 |
| 1192 | 520 | 272.00 | 400.00 | 63.76 | 23.52 | 87.28 |
| 1196 | 520 | 272.00 | 404.00 | 64.31 | 23.75 | 88.06 |
| 1200 | 520 | 272.00 | 408.00 | 64.86 | 23.98 | 88.84 |
| 1204 | 520 | 272.00 | 412.00 | 65.41 | 24.22 | 89.63 |
| 1208 | 520 | 272.00 | 416.00 | 65.96 | 24.45 | 90.41 |
| 1212 | 520 | 272.00 | 420.00 | 66.52 | 24.69 | 91.21 |
| 1216 | 520 | 272.00 | 424.00 | 67.07 | 24.92 | 91.99 |
| 1220 | 520 | 272.00 | 428.00 | 67.62 | 25.15 | 92.77 |
| 1224 | 520 | 272.00 | 432.00 | 68.17 | 25.39 | 93.56 |
| 1228 | 520 | 272.00 | 436.00 | 68.72 | 25.62 | 94.34 |
| 1232 | 520 | 272.00 | 440.00 | 69.28 | 25.86 | 95.14 |
| 1236 | 520 | 272.00 | 444.00 | 69.83 | 26.09 | 95.92 |
| 1240 | 520 | 272.00 | 448.00 | 70.38 | 26.32 | 96.70 |
| 1244 | 520 | 272.00 | 452.00 | 70.93 | 26.56 | 97.49 |
| 1248 | 520 | 272.00 | 456.00 | 71.48 | 26.79 | 98.27 |
| 1252 | 520 | 272.00 | 460.00 | 72.04 | 27.03 | 99.07 |
| 1256 | 520 | 272.00 | 464.00 | 72.59 | 27.26 | 99.85 |
| 1260 | 520 | 272.00 | 468.00 | 73.14 | 27.49 | 100.63 |
| 1264 | 520 | 272.00 | 472.00 | 73.69 | 27.73 | 101.42 |
| 1268 | 520 | 272.00 | 476.00 | 74.24 | 27.96 | 102.20 |
| 1272 | 520 | 272.00 | 480.00 | 74.80 | 28.20 | 103.00 |
| 1276 | 520 | 272.00 | 484.00 | 75.35 | 28.43 | 103.78 |
| 1280 | 520 | 272.00 | 488.00 | 75.90 | 28.66 | 104.56 |
| 1284 | 520 | 272.00 | 492.00 | 76.45 | 28.90 | 105.35 |
| 1288 | 520 | 272.00 | 496.00 | 77.00 | 29.13 | 106.13 |
| 1292 | 520 | 272.00 | 500.00 | 77.56 | 29.37 | 106.93 |
| 1296 | 520 | 272.00 | 504.00 | 78.11 | 29.60 | 107.71 |

## Monthly table

**Table letter B**

| Employee's earnings up to and including the UEL | Earnings at the LEL (where earnings are equal to or exceed the LEL) | Earnings above the LEL, up to and including the PT | Earnings above the PT, up to and including the UEL | Employer's NICs due on all earnings above the ST | Employee's NICs due on all earnings above the PT | Total of employee's and employer's NICs (for information only) |
|---|---|---|---|---|---|---|
| | | 1a | 1b | 1c | 1d | 1e |
| £ | £ | £ p | £ p | £ p | £ p | £ p |
| 1300 | 520 | 272.00 | 508.00 | 78.66 | 29.83 | 108.49 |
| 1304 | 520 | 272.00 | 512.00 | 79.21 | 30.07 | 109.28 |
| 1308 | 520 | 272.00 | 516.00 | 79.76 | 30.30 | 110.06 |
| 1312 | 520 | 272.00 | 520.00 | 80.32 | 30.54 | 110.86 |
| 1316 | 520 | 272.00 | 524.00 | 80.87 | 30.77 | 111.64 |
| 1320 | 520 | 272.00 | 528.00 | 81.42 | 31.00 | 112.42 |
| 1324 | 520 | 272.00 | 532.00 | 81.97 | 31.24 | 113.21 |
| 1328 | 520 | 272.00 | 536.00 | 82.52 | 31.47 | 113.99 |
| 1332 | 520 | 272.00 | 540.00 | 83.08 | 31.71 | 114.79 |
| 1336 | 520 | 272.00 | 544.00 | 83.63 | 31.94 | 115.57 |
| 1340 | 520 | 272.00 | 548.00 | 84.18 | 32.17 | 116.35 |
| 1344 | 520 | 272.00 | 552.00 | 84.73 | 32.41 | 117.14 |
| 1348 | 520 | 272.00 | 556.00 | 85.28 | 32.64 | 117.92 |
| 1352 | 520 | 272.00 | 560.00 | 85.84 | 32.88 | 118.72 |
| 1356 | 520 | 272.00 | 564.00 | 86.39 | 33.11 | 119.50 |
| 1360 | 520 | 272.00 | 568.00 | 86.94 | 33.34 | 120.28 |
| 1364 | 520 | 272.00 | 572.00 | 87.49 | 33.58 | 121.07 |
| 1368 | 520 | 272.00 | 576.00 | 88.04 | 33.81 | 121.85 |
| 1372 | 520 | 272.00 | 580.00 | 88.60 | 34.05 | 122.65 |
| 1376 | 520 | 272.00 | 584.00 | 89.15 | 34.28 | 123.43 |
| 1380 | 520 | 272.00 | 588.00 | 89.70 | 34.51 | 124.21 |
| 1384 | 520 | 272.00 | 592.00 | 90.25 | 34.75 | 125.00 |
| 1388 | 520 | 272.00 | 596.00 | 90.80 | 34.98 | 125.78 |
| 1392 | 520 | 272.00 | 600.00 | 91.36 | 35.22 | 126.58 |
| 1396 | 520 | 272.00 | 604.00 | 91.91 | 35.45 | 127.36 |
| 1400 | 520 | 272.00 | 608.00 | 92.46 | 35.68 | 128.14 |
| 1404 | 520 | 272.00 | 612.00 | 93.01 | 35.92 | 128.93 |
| 1408 | 520 | 272.00 | 616.00 | 93.56 | 36.15 | 129.71 |
| 1412 | 520 | 272.00 | 620.00 | 94.12 | 36.39 | 130.51 |
| 1416 | 520 | 272.00 | 624.00 | 94.67 | 36.62 | 131.29 |
| 1420 | 520 | 272.00 | 628.00 | 95.22 | 36.85 | 132.07 |
| 1424 | 520 | 272.00 | 632.00 | 95.77 | 37.09 | 132.86 |
| 1428 | 520 | 272.00 | 636.00 | 96.32 | 37.32 | 133.64 |
| 1432 | 520 | 272.00 | 640.00 | 96.88 | 37.56 | 134.44 |
| 1436 | 520 | 272.00 | 644.00 | 97.43 | 37.79 | 135.22 |
| 1440 | 520 | 272.00 | 648.00 | 97.98 | 38.02 | 136.00 |
| 1444 | 520 | 272.00 | 652.00 | 98.53 | 38.26 | 136.79 |
| 1448 | 520 | 272.00 | 656.00 | 99.08 | 38.49 | 137.57 |
| 1452 | 520 | 272.00 | 660.00 | 99.64 | 38.73 | 138.37 |
| 1456 | 520 | 272.00 | 664.00 | 100.19 | 38.96 | 139.15 |
| 1460 | 520 | 272.00 | 668.00 | 100.74 | 39.19 | 139.93 |
| 1464 | 520 | 272.00 | 672.00 | 101.29 | 39.43 | 140.72 |
| 1468 | 520 | 272.00 | 676.00 | 101.84 | 39.66 | 141.50 |
| 1472 | 520 | 272.00 | 680.00 | 102.40 | 39.90 | 142.30 |
| 1476 | 520 | 272.00 | 684.00 | 102.95 | 40.13 | 143.08 |
| 1480 | 520 | 272.00 | 688.00 | 103.50 | 40.36 | 143.86 |
| 1484 | 520 | 272.00 | 692.00 | 104.05 | 40.60 | 144.65 |
| 1488 | 520 | 272.00 | 696.00 | 104.60 | 40.83 | 145.43 |
| 1492 | 520 | 272.00 | 700.00 | 105.16 | 41.07 | 146.23 |
| 1496 | 520 | 272.00 | 704.00 | 105.71 | 41.30 | 147.01 |
| 1500 | 520 | 272.00 | 708.00 | 106.26 | 41.53 | 147.79 |
| 1504 | 520 | 272.00 | 712.00 | 106.81 | 41.77 | 148.58 |
| 1508 | 520 | 272.00 | 716.00 | 107.36 | 42.00 | 149.36 |
| 1512 | 520 | 272.00 | 720.00 | 107.92 | 42.24 | 150.16 |
| 1516 | 520 | 272.00 | 724.00 | 108.47 | 42.47 | 150.94 |

## Monthly table

**Table letter B**

| Employee's earnings up to and including the UEL | Earnings at the LEL (where earnings are equal to or exceed the LEL) | Earnings above the LEL, up to and including the PT | Earnings above the PT, up to and including the UEL | Employer's NICs due on all earnings above the ST | Employee's NICs due on all earnings above the PT | Total of employee's and employer's NICs (for information only) |
|---|---|---|---|---|---|---|
| | | 1a | 1b | 1c | 1d | 1e |
| £ | £ | £ p | £ p | £ p | £ p | £ p |
| 1520 | 520 | 272.00 | 728.00 | 109.02 | 42.70 | 151.72 |
| 1524 | 520 | 272.00 | 732.00 | 109.57 | 42.94 | 152.51 |
| 1528 | 520 | 272.00 | 736.00 | 110.12 | 43.17 | 153.29 |
| 1532 | 520 | 272.00 | 740.00 | 110.68 | 43.41 | 154.09 |
| 1536 | 520 | 272.00 | 744.00 | 111.23 | 43.64 | 154.87 |
| 1540 | 520 | 272.00 | 748.00 | 111.78 | 43.87 | 155.65 |
| 1544 | 520 | 272.00 | 752.00 | 112.33 | 44.11 | 156.44 |
| 1548 | 520 | 272.00 | 756.00 | 112.88 | 44.34 | 157.22 |
| 1552 | 520 | 272.00 | 760.00 | 113.44 | 44.58 | 158.02 |
| 1556 | 520 | 272.00 | 764.00 | 113.99 | 44.81 | 158.80 |
| 1560 | 520 | 272.00 | 768.00 | 114.54 | 45.04 | 159.58 |
| 1564 | 520 | 272.00 | 772.00 | 115.09 | 45.28 | 160.37 |
| 1568 | 520 | 272.00 | 776.00 | 115.64 | 45.51 | 161.15 |
| 1572 | 520 | 272.00 | 780.00 | 116.20 | 45.75 | 161.95 |
| 1576 | 520 | 272.00 | 784.00 | 116.75 | 45.98 | 162.73 |
| 1580 | 520 | 272.00 | 788.00 | 117.30 | 46.21 | 163.51 |
| 1584 | 520 | 272.00 | 792.00 | 117.85 | 46.45 | 164.30 |
| 1588 | 520 | 272.00 | 796.00 | 118.40 | 46.68 | 165.08 |
| 1592 | 520 | 272.00 | 800.00 | 118.96 | 46.92 | 165.88 |
| 1596 | 520 | 272.00 | 804.00 | 119.51 | 47.15 | 166.66 |
| 1600 | 520 | 272.00 | 808.00 | 120.06 | 47.38 | 167.44 |
| 1604 | 520 | 272.00 | 812.00 | 120.61 | 47.62 | 168.23 |
| 1608 | 520 | 272.00 | 816.00 | 121.16 | 47.85 | 169.01 |
| 1612 | 520 | 272.00 | 820.00 | 121.72 | 48.09 | 169.81 |
| 1616 | 520 | 272.00 | 824.00 | 122.27 | 48.32 | 170.59 |
| 1620 | 520 | 272.00 | 828.00 | 122.82 | 48.55 | 171.37 |
| 1624 | 520 | 272.00 | 832.00 | 123.37 | 48.79 | 172.16 |
| 1628 | 520 | 272.00 | 836.00 | 123.92 | 49.02 | 172.94 |
| 1632 | 520 | 272.00 | 840.00 | 124.48 | 49.26 | 173.74 |
| 1636 | 520 | 272.00 | 844.00 | 125.03 | 49.49 | 174.52 |
| 1640 | 520 | 272.00 | 848.00 | 125.58 | 49.72 | 175.30 |
| 1644 | 520 | 272.00 | 852.00 | 126.13 | 49.96 | 176.09 |
| 1648 | 520 | 272.00 | 856.00 | 126.68 | 50.19 | 176.87 |
| 1652 | 520 | 272.00 | 860.00 | 127.24 | 50.43 | 177.67 |
| 1656 | 520 | 272.00 | 864.00 | 127.79 | 50.66 | 178.45 |
| 1660 | 520 | 272.00 | 868.00 | 128.34 | 50.89 | 179.23 |
| 1664 | 520 | 272.00 | 872.00 | 128.89 | 51.13 | 180.02 |
| 1668 | 520 | 272.00 | 876.00 | 129.44 | 51.36 | 180.80 |
| 1672 | 520 | 272.00 | 880.00 | 130.00 | 51.60 | 181.60 |
| 1676 | 520 | 272.00 | 884.00 | 130.55 | 51.83 | 182.38 |
| 1680 | 520 | 272.00 | 888.00 | 131.10 | 52.06 | 183.16 |
| 1684 | 520 | 272.00 | 892.00 | 131.65 | 52.30 | 183.95 |
| 1688 | 520 | 272.00 | 896.00 | 132.20 | 52.53 | 184.73 |
| 1692 | 520 | 272.00 | 900.00 | 132.76 | 52.77 | 185.53 |
| 1696 | 520 | 272.00 | 904.00 | 133.31 | 53.00 | 186.31 |
| 1700 | 520 | 272.00 | 908.00 | 133.86 | 53.23 | 187.09 |
| 1704 | 520 | 272.00 | 912.00 | 134.41 | 53.47 | 187.88 |
| 1708 | 520 | 272.00 | 916.00 | 134.96 | 53.70 | 188.66 |
| 1712 | 520 | 272.00 | 920.00 | 135.52 | 53.94 | 189.46 |
| 1716 | 520 | 272.00 | 924.00 | 136.07 | 54.17 | 190.24 |
| 1720 | 520 | 272.00 | 928.00 | 136.62 | 54.40 | 191.02 |
| 1724 | 520 | 272.00 | 932.00 | 137.17 | 54.64 | 191.81 |
| 1728 | 520 | 272.00 | 936.00 | 137.72 | 54.87 | 192.59 |
| 1732 | 520 | 272.00 | 940.00 | 138.28 | 55.11 | 193.39 |
| 1736 | 520 | 272.00 | 944.00 | 138.83 | 55.34 | 194.17 |

Page 28

## Monthly table

**Table letter B**

| Employee's earnings up to and including the UEL | Earnings at the LEL (where earnings are equal to or exceed the LEL) | Earnings above the LEL, up to and including the PT | Earnings above the PT, up to and including the UEL | Employer's NICs due on all earnings above the ST | Employee's NICs due on all earnings above the PT | Total of employee's and employer's NICs (for information only) |
|---|---|---|---|---|---|---|
| | | 1a | 1b | 1c | 1d | 1e |
| £ | £ | £ p | £ p | £ p | £ p | £ p |
| 1740 | 520 | 272.00 | 948.00 | 139.38 | 55.57 | 194.95 |
| 1744 | 520 | 272.00 | 952.00 | 139.93 | 55.81 | 195.74 |
| 1748 | 520 | 272.00 | 956.00 | 140.48 | 56.04 | 196.52 |
| 1752 | 520 | 272.00 | 960.00 | 141.04 | 56.28 | 197.32 |
| 1756 | 520 | 272.00 | 964.00 | 141.59 | 56.51 | 198.10 |
| 1760 | 520 | 272.00 | 968.00 | 142.14 | 56.74 | 198.88 |
| 1764 | 520 | 272.00 | 972.00 | 142.69 | 56.98 | 199.67 |
| 1768 | 520 | 272.00 | 976.00 | 143.24 | 57.21 | 200.45 |
| 1772 | 520 | 272.00 | 980.00 | 143.80 | 57.45 | 201.25 |
| 1776 | 520 | 272.00 | 984.00 | 144.35 | 57.68 | 202.03 |
| 1780 | 520 | 272.00 | 988.00 | 144.90 | 57.91 | 202.81 |
| 1784 | 520 | 272.00 | 992.00 | 145.45 | 58.15 | 203.60 |
| 1788 | 520 | 272.00 | 996.00 | 146.00 | 58.38 | 204.38 |
| 1792 | 520 | 272.00 | 1000.00 | 146.56 | 58.62 | 205.18 |
| 1796 | 520 | 272.00 | 1004.00 | 147.11 | 58.85 | 205.96 |
| 1800 | 520 | 272.00 | 1008.00 | 147.66 | 59.08 | 206.74 |
| 1804 | 520 | 272.00 | 1012.00 | 148.21 | 59.32 | 207.53 |
| 1808 | 520 | 272.00 | 1016.00 | 148.76 | 59.55 | 208.31 |
| 1812 | 520 | 272.00 | 1020.00 | 149.32 | 59.79 | 209.11 |
| 1816 | 520 | 272.00 | 1024.00 | 149.87 | 60.02 | 209.89 |
| 1820 | 520 | 272.00 | 1028.00 | 150.42 | 60.25 | 210.67 |
| 1824 | 520 | 272.00 | 1032.00 | 150.97 | 60.49 | 211.46 |
| 1828 | 520 | 272.00 | 1036.00 | 151.52 | 60.72 | 212.24 |
| 1832 | 520 | 272.00 | 1040.00 | 152.08 | 60.96 | 213.04 |
| 1836 | 520 | 272.00 | 1044.00 | 152.63 | 61.19 | 213.82 |
| 1840 | 520 | 272.00 | 1048.00 | 153.18 | 61.42 | 214.60 |
| 1844 | 520 | 272.00 | 1052.00 | 153.73 | 61.66 | 215.39 |
| 1848 | LEL | 272.00 | 1056.00 | 154.28 | 61.89 | 216.17 |
| 1852 | 520 | 272.00 | 1060.00 | 154.84 | 62.13 | 216.97 |
| 1856 | 520 | 272.00 | 1064.00 | 155.39 | 62.36 | 217.75 |
| 1860 | 520 | 272.00 | 1068.00 | 155.94 | 62.59 | 218.53 |
| 1864 | 520 | 272.00 | 1072.00 | 156.49 | 62.83 | 219.32 |
| 1868 | 520 | 272.00 | 1076.00 | 157.04 | 63.06 | 220.10 |
| 1872 | 520 | 272.00 | 1080.00 | 157.60 | 63.30 | 220.90 |
| 1876 | 520 | 272.00 | 1084.00 | 158.15 | 63.53 | 221.68 |
| 1880 | 520 | 272.00 | 1088.00 | 158.70 | 63.76 | 222.46 |
| 1884 | 520 | 272.00 | 1092.00 | 159.25 | 64.00 | 223.25 |
| 1888 | 520 | 272.00 | 1096.00 | 159.80 | 64.23 | 224.03 |
| 1892 | 520 | 272.00 | 1100.00 | 160.36 | 64.47 | 224.83 |
| 1896 | 520 | 272.00 | 1104.00 | 160.91 | 64.70 | 225.61 |
| 1900 | 520 | 272.00 | 1108.00 | 161.46 | 64.93 | 226.39 |
| 1904 | 520 | 272.00 | 1112.00 | 162.01 | 65.17 | 227.18 |
| 1908 | 520 | 272.00 | 1116.00 | 162.56 | 65.40 | 227.96 |
| 1912 | 520 | 272.00 | 1120.00 | 163.12 | 65.64 | 228.76 |
| 1916 | 520 | 272.00 | 1124.00 | 163.67 | 65.87 | 229.54 |
| 1920 | 520 | 272.00 | 1128.00 | 164.22 | 66.10 | 230.32 |
| 1924 | 520 | 272.00 | 1132.00 | 164.77 | 66.34 | 231.11 |
| 1928 | 520 | 272.00 | 1136.00 | 165.32 | 66.57 | 231.89 |
| 1932 | 520 | 272.00 | 1140.00 | 165.88 | 66.81 | 232.69 |
| 1936 | 520 | 272.00 | 1144.00 | 166.43 | 67.04 | 233.47 |
| 1940 | 520 | 272.00 | 1148.00 | 166.98 | 67.27 | 234.25 |
| 1944 | 520 | 272.00 | 1152.00 | 167.53 | 67.51 | 235.04 |
| 1948 | 520 | 272.00 | 1156.00 | 168.08 | 67.74 | 235.82 |
| 1952 | 520 | 272.00 | 1160.00 | 168.64 | 67.98 | 236.62 |
| 1956 | 520 | 272.00 | 1164.00 | 169.19 | 68.21 | 237.40 |

Page 29

## Monthly table

**Table letter B**

| Employee's earnings up to and including the UEL | Earnings at the LEL (where earnings are equal to or exceed the LEL) | Earnings above the LEL, up to and including the PT | Earnings above the PT, up to and including the UEL | Employer's NICs due on all earnings above the ST | Employee's NICs due on all earnings above the PT | Total of employee's and employer's NICs (for information only) |
|---|---|---|---|---|---|---|
| | 1a | 1b | 1c | 1d | 1e | |
| £ | £ | £ p | £ p | £ p | £ p | £ p |
| 1960 | 520 | 272.00 | 1168.00 | 169.74 | 68.44 | 238.18 |
| 1964 | 520 | 272.00 | 1172.00 | 170.29 | 68.68 | 238.97 |
| 1968 | 520 | 272.00 | 1176.00 | 170.84 | 68.91 | 239.75 |
| 1972 | 520 | 272.00 | 1180.00 | 171.40 | 69.15 | 240.55 |
| 1976 | 520 | 272.00 | 1184.00 | 171.95 | 69.38 | 241.33 |
| 1980 | 520 | 272.00 | 1188.00 | 172.50 | 69.61 | 242.11 |
| 1984 | 520 | 272.00 | 1192.00 | 173.05 | 69.85 | 242.90 |
| 1988 | 520 | 272.00 | 1196.00 | 173.60 | 70.08 | 243.68 |
| 1992 | 520 | 272.00 | 1200.00 | 174.16 | 70.32 | 244.48 |
| 1996 | 520 | 272.00 | 1204.00 | 174.71 | 70.55 | 245.26 |
| 2000 | 520 | 272.00 | 1208.00 | 175.26 | 70.78 | 246.04 |
| 2004 | 520 | 272.00 | 1212.00 | 175.81 | 71.02 | 246.83 |
| 2008 | 520 | 272.00 | 1216.00 | 176.36 | 71.25 | 247.61 |
| 2012 | 520 | 272.00 | 1220.00 | 176.92 | 71.49 | 248.41 |
| 2016 | 520 | 272.00 | 1224.00 | 177.47 | 71.72 | 249.19 |
| 2020 | 520 | 272.00 | 1228.00 | 178.02 | 71.95 | 249.97 |
| 2024 | 520 | 272.00 | 1232.00 | 178.57 | 72.19 | 250.76 |
| 2028 | 520 | 272.00 | 1236.00 | 179.12 | 72.42 | 251.54 |
| 2032 | 520 | 272.00 | 1240.00 | 179.68 | 72.66 | 252.34 |
| 2036 | 520 | 272.00 | 1244.00 | 180.23 | 72.89 | 253.12 |
| 2040 | 520 | 272.00 | 1248.00 | 180.78 | 73.12 | 253.90 |
| 2044 | 520 | 272.00 | 1252.00 | 181.33 | 73.36 | 254.69 |
| 2048 | 520 | 272.00 | 1256.00 | 181.88 | 73.59 | 255.47 |
| 2052 | 520 | 272.00 | 1260.00 | 182.44 | 73.83 | 256.27 |
| 2056 | 520 | 272.00 | 1264.00 | 182.99 | 74.06 | 257.05 |
| 2060 | 520 | 272.00 | 1268.00 | 183.54 | 74.29 | 257.83 |
| 2064 | 520 | 272.00 | 1272.00 | 184.09 | 74.53 | 258.62 |
| 2068 | 520 | 272.00 | 1276.00 | 184.64 | 74.76 | 259.40 |
| 2072 | 520 | 272.00 | 1280.00 | 185.20 | 75.00 | 260.20 |
| 2076 | 520 | 272.00 | 1284.00 | 185.75 | 75.23 | 260.98 |
| 2080 | 520 | 272.00 | 1288.00 | 186.30 | 75.46 | 261.76 |
| 2084 | 520 | 272.00 | 1292.00 | 186.85 | 75.70 | 262.55 |
| 2088 | 520 | 272.00 | 1296.00 | 187.40 | 75.93 | 263.33 |
| 2092 | 520 | 272.00 | 1300.00 | 187.96 | 76.17 | 264.13 |
| 2096 | 520 | 272.00 | 1304.00 | 188.51 | 76.40 | 264.91 |
| 2100 | 520 | 272.00 | 1308.00 | 189.06 | 76.63 | 265.69 |
| 2104 | 520 | 272.00 | 1312.00 | 189.61 | 76.87 | 266.48 |
| 2108 | 520 | 272.00 | 1316.00 | 190.16 | 77.10 | 267.26 |
| 2112 | 520 | 272.00 | 1320.00 | 190.72 | 77.34 | 268.06 |
| 2116 | 520 | 272.00 | 1324.00 | 191.27 | 77.57 | 268.84 |
| 2120 | 520 | 272.00 | 1328.00 | 191.82 | 77.80 | 269.62 |
| 2124 | 520 | 272.00 | 1332.00 | 192.37 | 78.04 | 270.41 |
| 2128 | 520 | 272.00 | 1336.00 | 192.92 | 78.27 | 271.19 |
| 2132 | 520 | 272.00 | 1340.00 | 193.48 | 78.51 | 271.99 |
| 2136 | 520 | 272.00 | 1344.00 | 194.03 | 78.74 | 272.77 |
| 2140 | 520 | 272.00 | 1348.00 | 194.58 | 78.97 | 273.55 |
| 2144 | 520 | 272.00 | 1352.00 | 195.13 | 79.21 | 274.34 |
| 2148 | 520 | 272.00 | 1356.00 | 195.68 | 79.44 | 275.12 |
| 2152 | 520 | 272.00 | 1360.00 | 196.24 | 79.68 | 275.92 |
| 2156 | 520 | 272.00 | 1364.00 | 196.79 | 79.91 | 276.70 |
| 2160 | 520 | 272.00 | 1368.00 | 197.34 | 80.14 | 277.48 |
| 2164 | 520 | 272.00 | 1372.00 | 197.89 | 80.38 | 278.27 |
| 2168 | 520 | 272.00 | 1376.00 | 198.44 | 80.61 | 279.05 |
| 2172 | 520 | 272.00 | 1380.00 | 199.00 | 80.85 | 279.85 |
| 2176 | 520 | 272.00 | 1384.00 | 199.55 | 81.08 | 280.63 |

## Monthly table

**Table letter B**

| Employee's earnings up to and including the UEL | Earnings at the LEL (where earnings are equal to or exceed the LEL) | Earnings above the LEL, up to and including the PT | Earnings above the PT, up to and including the UEL | Employer's NICs due on all earnings above the ST | Employee's NICs due on all earnings above the PT | Total of employee's and employer's NICs (for information only) |
|---|---|---|---|---|---|---|
| | | 1a | 1b | 1c | 1d | 1e |
| £ | £ | £ p | £ p | £ p | £ p | £ p |
| 2180 | 520 | 272.00 | 1388.00 | 200.10 | 81.31 | 281.41 |
| 2184 | 520 | 272.00 | 1392.00 | 200.65 | 81.55 | 282.20 |
| 2188 | 520 | 272.00 | 1396.00 | 201.20 | 81.78 | 282.98 |
| 2192 | 520 | 272.00 | 1400.00 | 201.76 | 82.02 | 283.78 |
| 2196 | 520 | 272.00 | 1404.00 | 202.31 | 82.25 | 284.56 |
| 2200 | 520 | 272.00 | 1408.00 | 202.86 | 82.48 | 285.34 |
| 2204 | 520 | 272.00 | 1412.00 | 203.41 | 82.72 | 286.13 |
| 2208 | 520 | 272.00 | 1416.00 | 203.96 | 82.95 | 286.91 |
| 2212 | 520 | 272.00 | 1420.00 | 204.52 | 83.19 | 287.71 |
| 2216 | 520 | 272.00 | 1424.00 | 205.07 | 83.42 | 288.49 |
| 2220 | 520 | 272.00 | 1428.00 | 205.62 | 83.65 | 289.27 |
| 2224 | 520 | 272.00 | 1432.00 | 206.17 | 83.89 | 290.06 |
| 2228 | 520 | 272.00 | 1436.00 | 206.72 | 84.12 | 290.84 |
| 2232 | 520 | 272.00 | 1440.00 | 207.28 | 84.36 | 291.64 |
| 2236 | 520 | 272.00 | 1444.00 | 207.83 | 84.59 | 292.42 |
| 2240 | 520 | 272.00 | 1448.00 | 208.38 | 84.82 | 293.20 |
| 2244 | 520 | 272.00 | 1452.00 | 208.93 | 85.06 | 293.99 |
| 2248 | 520 | 272.00 | 1456.00 | 209.48 | 85.29 | 294.77 |
| 2252 | 520 | 272.00 | 1460.00 | 210.04 | 85.53 | 295.57 |
| 2256 | 520 | 272.00 | 1464.00 | 210.59 | 85.76 | 296.35 |
| 2260 | 520 | 272.00 | 1468.00 | 211.14 | 85.99 | 297.13 |
| 2264 | 520 | 272.00 | 1472.00 | 211.69 | 86.23 | 297.92 |
| 2268 | 520 | 272.00 | 1476.00 | 212.24 | 86.46 | 298.70 |
| 2272 | 520 | 272.00 | 1480.00 | 212.80 | 86.70 | 299.50 |
| 2276 | 520 | 272.00 | 1484.00 | 213.35 | 86.93 | 300.28 |
| 2280 | 520 | 272.00 | 1488.00 | 213.90 | 87.16 | 301.06 |
| 2284 | 520 | 272.00 | 1492.00 | 214.45 | 87.40 | 301.85 |
| 2288 | 520 | 272.00 | 1496.00 | 215.00 | 87.63 | 302.63 |
| 2292 | 520 | 272.00 | 1500.00 | 215.56 | 87.87 | 303.43 |
| 2296 | 520 | 272.00 | 1504.00 | 216.11 | 88.10 | 304.21 |
| 2300 | 520 | 272.00 | 1508.00 | 216.66 | 88.33 | 304.99 |
| 2304 | 520 | 272.00 | 1512.00 | 217.21 | 88.57 | 305.78 |
| 2308 | 520 | 272.00 | 1516.00 | 217.76 | 88.80 | 306.56 |
| 2312 | 520 | 272.00 | 1520.00 | 218.32 | 89.04 | 307.36 |
| 2316 | 520 | 272.00 | 1524.00 | 218.87 | 89.27 | 308.14 |
| 2320 | 520 | 272.00 | 1528.00 | 219.42 | 89.50 | 308.92 |
| 2324 | 520 | 272.00 | 1532.00 | 219.97 | 89.74 | 309.71 |
| 2328 | 520 | 272.00 | 1536.00 | 220.52 | 89.97 | 310.49 |
| 2332 | 520 | 272.00 | 1540.00 | 221.08 | 90.21 | 311.29 |
| 2336 | 520 | 272.00 | 1544.00 | 221.63 | 90.44 | 312.07 |
| 2340 | 520 | 272.00 | 1548.00 | 222.18 | 90.67 | 312.85 |
| 2344 | 520 | 272.00 | 1552.00 | 222.73 | 90.91 | 313.64 |
| 2348 | 520 | 272.00 | 1556.00 | 223.28 | 91.14 | 314.42 |
| 2352 | 520 | 272.00 | 1560.00 | 223.84 | 91.38 | 315.22 |
| 2356 | 520 | 272.00 | 1564.00 | 224.39 | 91.61 | 316.00 |
| 2360 | 520 | 272.00 | 1568.00 | 224.94 | 91.84 | 316.78 |
| 2364 | 520 | 272.00 | 1572.00 | 225.49 | 92.08 | 317.57 |
| 2368 | 520 | 272.00 | 1576.00 | 226.04 | 92.31 | 318.35 |
| 2372 | 520 | 272.00 | 1580.00 | 226.60 | 92.55 | 319.15 |
| 2376 | 520 | 272.00 | 1584.00 | 227.15 | 92.78 | 319.93 |
| 2380 | 520 | 272.00 | 1588.00 | 227.70 | 93.01 | 320.71 |
| 2384 | 520 | 272.00 | 1592.00 | 228.25 | 93.25 | 321.50 |
| 2388 | 520 | 272.00 | 1596.00 | 228.80 | 93.48 | 322.28 |
| 2392 | 520 | 272.00 | 1600.00 | 229.36 | 93.72 | 323.08 |
| 2396 | 520 | 272.00 | 1604.00 | 229.91 | 93.95 | 323.86 |

## Monthly table

**Table letter B**

| Employee's earnings up to and including the UEL £ | Earnings at the LEL (where earnings are equal to or exceed the LEL) £ | Earnings above the LEL, up to and including the PT £ p | Earnings above the PT, up to and including the UEL £ p | Employer's NICs due on all earnings above the ST £ p | Employee's NICs due on all earnings above the PT £ p | Total of employee's and employer's NICs (for information only) £ p |
|---|---|---|---|---|---|---|
| | | **1a** | **1b** | **1c** | **1d** | **1e** |
| 2400 | 520 | 272.00 | 1608.00 | 230.46 | 94.18 | 324.64 |
| 2404 | 520 | 272.00 | 1612.00 | 231.01 | 94.42 | 325.43 |
| 2408 | 520 | 272.00 | 1616.00 | 231.56 | 94.65 | 326.21 |
| 2412 | 520 | 272.00 | 1620.00 | 232.12 | 94.89 | 327.01 |
| 2416 | 520 | 272.00 | 1624.00 | 232.67 | 95.12 | 327.79 |
| 2420 | 520 | 272.00 | 1628.00 | 233.22 | 95.35 | 328.57 |
| 2424 | 520 | 272.00 | 1632.00 | 233.77 | 95.59 | 329.36 |
| 2428 | 520 | 272.00 | 1636.00 | 234.32 | 95.82 | 330.14 |
| 2432 | 520 | 272.00 | 1640.00 | 234.88 | 96.06 | 330.94 |
| 2436 | 520 | 272.00 | 1644.00 | 235.43 | 96.29 | 331.72 |
| 2440 | 520 | 272.00 | 1648.00 | 235.98 | 96.52 | 332.50 |
| 2444 | 520 | 272.00 | 1652.00 | 236.53 | 96.76 | 333.29 |
| 2448 | 520 | 272.00 | 1656.00 | 237.08 | 96.99 | 334.07 |
| 2452 | 520 | 272.00 | 1660.00 | 237.64 | 97.23 | 334.87 |
| 2456 | 520 | 272.00 | 1664.00 | 238.19 | 97.46 | 335.65 |
| 2460 | 520 | 272.00 | 1668.00 | 238.74 | 97.69 | 336.43 |
| 2464 | 520 | 272.00 | 1672.00 | 239.29 | 97.93 | 337.22 |
| 2468 | 520 | 272.00 | 1676.00 | 239.84 | 98.16 | 338.00 |
| 2472 | 520 | 272.00 | 1680.00 | 240.40 | 98.40 | 338.80 |
| 2476 | 520 | 272.00 | 1684.00 | 240.95 | 98.63 | 339.58 |
| 2480 | 520 | 272.00 | 1688.00 | 241.50 | 98.86 | 340.36 |
| 2484 | 520 | 272.00 | 1692.00 | 242.05 | 99.10 | 341.15 |
| 2488 | 520 | 272.00 | 1696.00 | 242.60 | 99.33 | 341.93 |
| 2492 | 520 | 272.00 | 1700.00 | 243.16 | 99.57 | 342.73 |
| 2496 | 520 | 272.00 | 1704.00 | 243.71 | 99.80 | 343.51 |
| 2500 | 520 | 272.00 | 1708.00 | 244.26 | 100.03 | 344.29 |
| 2504 | 520 | 272.00 | 1712.00 | 244.81 | 100.27 | 345.08 |
| 2508 | 520 | 272.00 | 1716.00 | 245.36 | 100.50 | 345.86 |
| 2512 | 520 | 272.00 | 1720.00 | 245.92 | 100.74 | 346.66 |
| 2516 | 520 | 272.00 | 1724.00 | 246.47 | 100.97 | 347.44 |
| 2520 | 520 | 272.00 | 1728.00 | 247.02 | 101.20 | 348.22 |
| 2524 | 520 | 272.00 | 1732.00 | 247.57 | 101.44 | 349.01 |
| 2528 | 520 | 272.00 | 1736.00 | 248.12 | 101.67 | 349.79 |
| 2532 | 520 | 272.00 | 1740.00 | 248.68 | 101.91 | 350.59 |
| 2536 | 520 | 272.00 | 1744.00 | 249.23 | 102.14 | 351.37 |
| 2540 | 520 | 272.00 | 1748.00 | 249.78 | 102.37 | 352.15 |
| 2544 | 520 | 272.00 | 1752.00 | 250.33 | 102.61 | 352.94 |
| 2548 | 520 | 272.00 | 1756.00 | 250.88 | 102.84 | 353.72 |
| 2552 | 520 | 272.00 | 1760.00 | 251.44 | 103.08 | 354.52 |
| 2556 | 520 | 272.00 | 1764.00 | 251.99 | 103.31 | 355.30 |
| 2560 | 520 | 272.00 | 1768.00 | 252.54 | 103.54 | 356.08 |
| 2564 | 520 | 272.00 | 1772.00 | 253.09 | 103.78 | 356.87 |
| 2568 | 520 | 272.00 | 1776.00 | 253.64 | 104.01 | 357.65 |
| 2572 | 520 | 272.00 | 1780.00 | 254.20 | 104.25 | 358.45 |
| 2576 | 520 | 272.00 | 1784.00 | 254.75 | 104.48 | 359.23 |
| 2580 | 520 | 272.00 | 1788.00 | 255.30 | 104.71 | 360.01 |
| 2584 | 520 | 272.00 | 1792.00 | 255.85 | 104.95 | 360.80 |
| 2588 | 520 | 272.00 | 1796.00 | 256.40 | 105.18 | 361.58 |
| 2592 | 520 | 272.00 | 1800.00 | 256.96 | 105.42 | 362.38 |
| 2596 | 520 | 272.00 | 1804.00 | 257.51 | 105.65 | 363.16 |
| 2600 | 520 | 272.00 | 1808.00 | 258.06 | 105.88 | 363.94 |
| 2604 | 520 | 272.00 | 1812.00 | 258.61 | 106.12 | 364.73 |
| 2608 | 520 | 272.00 | 1816.00 | 259.16 | 106.35 | 365.51 |
| 2612 | 520 | 272.00 | 1820.00 | 259.72 | 106.59 | 366.31 |
| 2616 | 520 | 272.00 | 1824.00 | 260.27 | 106.82 | 367.09 |

## Monthly table

**Table letter B**

| Employee's earnings up to and including the UEL | Earnings at the LEL (where earnings are equal to or exceed the LEL) | Earnings above the LEL, up to and including the PT | Earnings above the PT, up to and including the UEL | Employer's NICs due on all earnings above the ST | Employee's NICs due on all earnings above the PT | Total of employee's and employer's NICs (for information only) |
|---|---|---|---|---|---|---|
| | 1a | 1b | 1c | 1d | 1e | |
| £ | £ | £ p | £ p | £ p | £ p | £ p |
| 2620 | 520 | 272.00 | 1828.00 | 260.82 | 107.05 | 367.87 |
| 2624 | 520 | 272.00 | 1832.00 | 261.37 | 107.29 | 368.66 |
| 2628 | 520 | 272.00 | 1836.00 | 261.92 | 107.52 | 369.44 |
| 2632 | 520 | 272.00 | 1840.00 | 262.48 | 107.76 | 370.24 |
| 2636 | 520 | 272.00 | 1844.00 | 263.03 | 107.99 | 371.02 |
| 2640 | 520 | 272.00 | 1848.00 | 263.58 | 108.22 | 371.80 |
| 2644 | 520 | 272.00 | 1852.00 | 264.13 | 108.46 | 372.59 |
| 2648 | 520 | 272.00 | 1856.00 | 264.68 | 108.69 | 373.37 |
| 2652 | 520 | 272.00 | 1860.00 | 265.24 | 108.93 | 374.17 |
| 2656 | 520 | 272.00 | 1864.00 | 265.79 | 109.16 | 374.95 |
| 2660 | 520 | 272.00 | 1868.00 | 266.34 | 109.39 | 375.73 |
| 2664 | 520 | 272.00 | 1872.00 | 266.89 | 109.63 | 376.52 |
| 2668 | 520 | 272.00 | 1876.00 | 267.44 | 109.86 | 377.30 |
| 2672 | 520 | 272.00 | 1880.00 | 268.00 | 110.10 | 378.10 |
| 2676 | 520 | 272.00 | 1884.00 | 268.55 | 110.33 | 378.88 |
| 2680 | 520 | 272.00 | 1888.00 | 269.10 | 110.56 | 379.66 |
| 2684 | 520 | 272.00 | 1892.00 | 269.65 | 110.80 | 380.45 |
| 2688 | 520 | 272.00 | 1896.00 | 270.20 | 111.03 | 381.23 |
| 2692 | 520 | 272.00 | 1900.00 | 270.76 | 111.27 | 382.03 |
| 2696 | 520 | 272.00 | 1904.00 | 271.31 | 111.50 | 382.81 |
| 2700 | 520 | 272.00 | 1908.00 | 271.86 | 111.73 | 383.59 |
| 2704 | 520 | 272.00 | 1912.00 | 272.41 | 111.97 | 384.38 |
| 2708 | 520 | 272.00 | 1916.00 | 272.96 | 112.20 | 385.16 |
| 2712 | 520 | 272.00 | 1920.00 | 273.52 | 112.44 | 385.96 |
| 2716 | 520 | 272.00 | 1924.00 | 274.07 | 112.67 | 386.74 |
| 2720 | 520 | 272.00 | 1928.00 | 274.62 | 112.90 | 387.52 |
| 2724 | 520 | 272.00 | 1932.00 | 275.17 | 113.14 | 388.31 |
| 2728 | 520 | 272.00 | 1936.00 | 275.72 | 113.37 | 389.09 |
| 2732 | 520 | 272.00 | 1940.00 | 276.28 | 113.61 | 389.89 |
| 2736 | 520 | 272.00 | 1944.00 | 276.83 | 113.84 | 390.67 |
| 2740 | 520 | 272.00 | 1948.00 | 277.38 | 114.07 | 391.45 |
| 2744 | 520 | 272.00 | 1952.00 | 277.93 | 114.31 | 392.24 |
| 2748 | 520 | 272.00 | 1956.00 | 278.48 | 114.54 | 393.02 |
| 2752 | 520 | 272.00 | 1960.00 | 279.04 | 114.78 | 393.82 |
| 2756 | 520 | 272.00 | 1964.00 | 279.59 | 115.01 | 394.60 |
| 2760 | 520 | 272.00 | 1968.00 | 280.14 | 115.24 | 395.38 |
| 2764 | 520 | 272.00 | 1972.00 | 280.69 | 115.48 | 396.17 |
| 2768 | 520 | 272.00 | 1976.00 | 281.24 | 115.71 | 396.95 |
| 2772 | 520 | 272.00 | 1980.00 | 281.80 | 115.95 | 397.75 |
| 2776 | 520 | 272.00 | 1984.00 | 282.35 | 116.18 | 398.53 |
| 2780 | 520 | 272.00 | 1988.00 | 282.90 | 116.41 | 399.31 |
| 2784 | 520 | 272.00 | 1992.00 | 283.45 | 116.65 | 400.10 |
| 2788 | 520 | 272.00 | 1996.00 | 284.00 | 116.88 | 400.88 |
| 2792 | 520 | 272.00 | 2000.00 | 284.56 | 117.12 | 401.68 |
| 2796 | 520 | 272.00 | 2004.00 | 285.11 | 117.35 | 402.46 |
| 2800 | 520 | 272.00 | 2008.00 | 285.66 | 117.58 | 403.24 |
| 2804 | 520 | 272.00 | 2012.00 | 286.21 | 117.82 | 404.03 |
| 2808 | 520 | 272.00 | 2016.00 | 286.76 | 118.05 | 404.81 |
| 2812 | 520 | 272.00 | 2020.00 | 287.32 | 118.29 | 405.61 |
| 2816 | 520 | 272.00 | 2024.00 | 287.87 | 118.52 | 406.39 |
| 2820 | 520 | 272.00 | 2028.00 | 288.42 | 118.75 | 407.17 |
| 2824 | 520 | 272.00 | 2032.00 | 288.97 | 118.99 | 407.96 |
| 2828 | 520 | 272.00 | 2036.00 | 289.52 | 119.22 | 408.74 |
| 2832 | 520 | 272.00 | 2040.00 | 290.08 | 119.46 | 409.54 |
| 2836 | 520 | 272.00 | 2044.00 | 290.63 | 119.69 | 410.32 |

Page 33

## Monthly table

**Table letter B**

| Employee's earnings up to and including the UEL | Earnings at the LEL (where earnings are equal to or exceed the LEL) | Earnings above the LEL, up to and including the PT | Earnings above the PT, up to and including the UEL | Employer's NICs due on all earnings above the ST | Employee's NICs due on all earnings above the PT | Total of employee's and employer's NICs (for information only) |
|---|---|---|---|---|---|---|
| | | 1a | 1b | 1c | 1d | 1e |
| £ | £ | £ p | £ p | £ p | £ p | £ p |
| 2840 | 520 | 272.00 | 2048.00 | 291.18 | 119.92 | 411.10 |
| 2844 | 520 | 272.00 | 2052.00 | 291.73 | 120.16 | 411.89 |
| 2848 | 520 | 272.00 | 2056.00 | 292.28 | 120.39 | 412.67 |
| 2852 | 520 | 272.00 | 2060.00 | 292.84 | 120.63 | 413.47 |
| 2856 | 520 | 272.00 | 2064.00 | 293.39 | 120.86 | 414.25 |
| 2860 | 520 | 272.00 | 2068.00 | 293.94 | 121.09 | 415.03 |
| 2864 | 520 | 272.00 | 2072.00 | 294.49 | 121.33 | 415.82 |
| 2868 | 520 | 272.00 | 2076.00 | 295.04 | 121.56 | 416.60 |
| 2872 | 520 | 272.00 | 2080.00 | 295.60 | 121.80 | 417.40 |
| 2876 | 520 | 272.00 | 2084.00 | 296.15 | 122.03 | 418.18 |
| 2880 | 520 | 272.00 | 2088.00 | 296.70 | 122.26 | 418.96 |
| 2884 | 520 | 272.00 | 2092.00 | 297.25 | 122.50 | 419.75 |
| 2888 | 520 | 272.00 | 2096.00 | 297.80 | 122.73 | 420.53 |
| 2892 | 520 | 272.00 | 2100.00 | 298.36 | 122.97 | 421.33 |
| 2896 | 520 | 272.00 | 2104.00 | 298.91 | 123.20 | 422.11 |
| 2900 | 520 | 272.00 | 2108.00 | 299.46 | 123.43 | 422.89 |
| 2904 | 520 | 272.00 | 2112.00 | 300.01 | 123.67 | 423.68 |
| 2908 | 520 | 272.00 | 2116.00 | 300.56 | 123.90 | 424.46 |
| 2912 | 520 | 272.00 | 2120.00 | 301.12 | 124.14 | 425.26 |
| 2916 | 520 | 272.00 | 2124.00 | 301.67 | 124.37 | 426.04 |
| 2920 | 520 | 272.00 | 2128.00 | 302.22 | 124.60 | 426.82 |
| 2924 | 520 | 272.00 | 2132.00 | 302.77 | 124.84 | 427.61 |
| 2928 | 520 | 272.00 | 2136.00 | 303.32 | 125.07 | 428.39 |
| 2932 | 520 | 272.00 | 2140.00 | 303.88 | 125.31 | 429.19 |
| 2936 | 520 | 272.00 | 2144.00 | 304.43 | 125.54 | 429.97 |
| 2940 | 520 | 272.00 | 2148.00 | 304.98 | 125.77 | 430.75 |
| 2944 | 520 | 272.00 | 2152.00 | 305.53 | 126.01 | 431.54 |
| 2948 | 520 | 272.00 | 2156.00 | 306.08 | 126.24 | 432.32 |
| 2952 | 520 | 272.00 | 2160.00 | 306.64 | 126.48 | 433.12 |
| 2956 | 520 | 272.00 | 2164.00 | 307.19 | 126.71 | 433.90 |
| 2960 | 520 | 272.00 | 2168.00 | 307.74 | 126.94 | 434.68 |
| 2964 | 520 | 272.00 | 2172.00 | 308.29 | 127.18 | 435.47 |
| 2968 | 520 | 272.00 | 2176.00 | 308.84 | 127.41 | 436.25 |
| 2972 | 520 | 272.00 | 2180.00 | 309.40 | 127.65 | 437.05 |
| 2976 | 520 | 272.00 | 2184.00 | 309.95 | 127.88 | 437.83 |
| 2980 | 520 | 272.00 | 2188.00 | 310.50 | 128.11 | 438.61 |
| 2984 | 520 | 272.00 | 2192.00 | 311.05 | 128.35 | 439.40 |
| 2988 | 520 | 272.00 | 2196.00 | 311.60 | 128.58 | 440.18 |
| 2992 | 520 | 272.00 | 2200.00 | 312.16 | 128.82 | 440.98 |
| 2996 | 520 | 272.00 | 2204.00 | 312.71 | 129.05 | 441.76 |
| 3000 | 520 | 272.00 | 2208.00 | 313.26 | 129.28 | 442.54 |
| 3004 | 520 | 272.00 | 2212.00 | 313.81 | 129.52 | 443.33 |
| 3008 | 520 | 272.00 | 2216.00 | 314.36 | 129.75 | 444.11 |
| 3012 | 520 | 272.00 | 2220.00 | 314.92 | 129.99 | 444.91 |
| 3016 | 520 | 272.00 | 2224.00 | 315.47 | 130.22 | 445.69 |
| 3020 | 520 | 272.00 | 2228.00 | 316.02 | 130.45 | 446.47 |
| 3024 | 520 | 272.00 | 2232.00 | 316.57 | 130.69 | 447.26 |
| 3028 | 520 | 272.00 | 2236.00 | 317.12 | 130.92 | 448.04 |
| 3032 | 520 | 272.00 | 2240.00 | 317.68 | 131.16 | 448.84 |
| 3036 | 520 | 272.00 | 2244.00 | 318.23 | 131.39 | 449.62 |
| 3040 | 520 | 272.00 | 2248.00 | 318.78 | 131.62 | 450.40 |
| 3044 | 520 | 272.00 | 2252.00 | 319.33 | 131.86 | 451.19 |
| 3048 | 520 | 272.00 | 2256.00 | 319.88 | 132.09 | 451.97 |
| 3052 | 520 | 272.00 | 2260.00 | 320.44 | 132.33 | 452.77 |
| 3056 | 520 | 272.00 | 2264.00 | 320.99 | 132.56 | 453.55 |

Page 34

## Monthly table

**Table letter B**

| Employee's earnings up to and including the UEL | Earnings at the LEL (where earnings are equal to or exceed the LEL) | Earnings above the LEL, up to and including the PT | Earnings above the PT, up to and including the UEL | Employer's NICs due on all earnings above the ST | Employee's NICs due on all earnings above the PT | Total of employee's and employer's NICs (for information only) |
|---|---|---|---|---|---|---|
| | 1a | 1b | 1c | 1d | 1e | |
| £ | £ | £ p | £ p | £ p | £ p | £ p |
| 3060 | 520 | 272.00 | 2268.00 | 321.54 | 132.79 | 454.33 |
| 3064 | 520 | 272.00 | 2272.00 | 322.09 | 133.03 | 455.12 |
| 3068 | 520 | 272.00 | 2276.00 | 322.64 | 133.26 | 455.90 |
| 3072 | 520 | 272.00 | 2280.00 | 323.20 | 133.50 | 456.70 |
| 3076 | 520 | 272.00 | 2284.00 | 323.75 | 133.73 | 457.48 |
| 3080 | 520 | 272.00 | 2288.00 | 324.30 | 133.96 | 458.26 |
| 3084 | 520 | 272.00 | 2292.00 | 324.85 | 134.20 | 459.05 |
| 3088 | 520 | 272.00 | 2296.00 | 325.40 | 134.43 | 459.83 |
| 3092 | 520 | 272.00 | 2300.00 | 325.96 | 134.67 | 460.63 |
| 3096 | 520 | 272.00 | 2304.00 | 326.51 | 134.90 | 461.41 |
| 3100 | 520 | 272.00 | 2308.00 | 327.06 | 135.13 | 462.19 |
| 3104 | 520 | 272.00 | 2312.00 | 327.61 | 135.37 | 462.98 |
| 3108 | 520 | 272.00 | 2316.00 | 328.16 | 135.60 | 463.76 |
| 3112 | 520 | 272.00 | 2320.00 | 328.72 | 135.84 | 464.56 |
| 3116 | 520 | 272.00 | 2324.00 | 329.27 | 136.07 | 465.34 |
| 3120 | 520 | 272.00 | 2328.00 | 329.82 | 136.30 | 466.12 |
| 3124 | 520 | 272.00 | 2332.00 | 330.37 | 136.54 | 466.91 |
| 3128 | 520 | 272.00 | 2336.00 | 330.92 | 136.77 | 467.69 |
| 3132 | 520 | 272.00 | 2340.00 | 331.48 | 137.01 | 468.49 |
| 3136 | 520 | 272.00 | 2344.00 | 332.03 | 137.24 | 469.27 |
| 3140 | 520 | 272.00 | 2348.00 | 332.58 | 137.47 | 470.05 |
| 3144 | 520 | 272.00 | 2352.00 | 333.13 | 137.71 | 470.84 |
| 3148 | 520 | 272.00 | 2356.00 | 333.68 | 137.94 | 471.62 |
| 3152 | 520 | 272.00 | 2360.00 | 334.24 | 138.18 | 472.42 |
| 3156 | 520 | 272.00 | 2364.00 | 334.79 | 138.41 | 473.20 |
| 3160 | 520 | 272.00 | 2368.00 | 335.34 | 138.64 | 473.98 |
| 3164 | 520 | 272.00 | 2372.00 | 335.89 | 138.88 | 474.77 |
| 3168 | 520 | 272.00 | 2376.00 | 336.44 | 139.11 | 475.55 |
| 3172 | 520 | 272.00 | 2380.00 | 337.00 | 139.35 | 476.35 |
| 3176 | 520 | 272.00 | 2384.00 | 337.55 | 139.58 | 477.13 |
| 3180 | 520 | 272.00 | 2388.00 | 338.10 | 139.81 | 477.91 |
| 3184 | 520 | 272.00 | 2392.00 | 338.65 | 140.05 | 478.70 |
| 3188 | 520 | 272.00 | 2396.00 | 339.20 | 140.28 | 479.48 |
| 3192 | 520 | 272.00 | 2400.00 | 339.76 | 140.52 | 480.28 |
| 3196 | 520 | 272.00 | 2404.00 | 340.31 | 140.75 | 481.06 |
| 3200 | 520 | 272.00 | 2408.00 | 340.86 | 140.98 | 481.84 |
| 3204 | 520 | 272.00 | 2412.00 | 341.41 | 141.22 | 482.63 |
| 3208 | 520 | 272.00 | 2416.00 | 341.96 | 141.45 | 483.41 |
| 3212 | 520 | 272.00 | 2420.00 | 342.52 | 141.69 | 484.21 |
| 3216 | 520 | 272.00 | 2424.00 | 343.07 | 141.92 | 484.99 |
| 3220 | 520 | 272.00 | 2428.00 | 343.62 | 142.15 | 485.77 |
| 3224 | 520 | 272.00 | 2432.00 | 344.17 | 142.39 | 486.56 |
| 3228 | 520 | 272.00 | 2436.00 | 344.72 | 142.62 | 487.34 |
| 3232 | 520 | 272.00 | 2440.00 | 345.28 | 142.86 | 488.14 |
| 3236 | 520 | 272.00 | 2444.00 | 345.83 | 143.09 | 488.92 |
| 3240 | 520 | 272.00 | 2448.00 | 346.38 | 143.32 | 489.70 |
| 3244 | 520 | 272.00 | 2452.00 | 346.93 | 143.56 | 490.49 |
| 3248 | 520 | 272.00 | 2456.00 | 347.48 | 143.79 | 491.27 |
| 3252 | 520 | 272.00 | 2460.00 | 348.04 | 144.03 | 492.07 |
| 3256 | 520 | 272.00 | 2464.00 | 348.59 | 144.26 | 492.85 |
| 3260 | 520 | 272.00 | 2468.00 | 349.14 | 144.49 | 493.63 |
| 3264 | 520 | 272.00 | 2472.00 | 349.69 | 144.73 | 494.42 |
| 3268 | 520 | 272.00 | 2476.00 | 350.24 | 144.96 | 495.20 |
| 3272 | 520 | 272.00 | 2480.00 | 350.80 | 145.20 | 496.00 |
| 3276 | 520 | 272.00 | 2484.00 | 351.35 | 145.43 | 496.78 |

**Monthly table**                                                       **Table letter B**

| Employee's earnings up to and including the UEL | Earnings at the LEL (where earnings are equal to or exceed the LEL) | Earnings above the LEL, up to and including the PT | Earnings above the PT, up to and including the UEL | Employer's NICs due on all earnings above the ST | Employee's NICs due on all earnings above the PT | Total of employee's and employer's NICs (for information only) |
|---|---|---|---|---|---|---|
|  |  | 1a | 1b | 1c | 1d | 1e |
| £ | £ | £ p | £ p | £ p | £ p | £ p |
| 3280 | 520 | 272.00 | 2488.00 | 351.90 | 145.66 | 497.56 |
| 3284 | 520 | 272.00 | 2492.00 | 352.45 | 145.90 | 498.35 |
| 3288 | 520 | 272.00 | 2496.00 | 353.00 | 146.13 | 499.13 |
| 3292 | 520 | 272.00 | 2500.00 | 353.56 | 146.37 | 499.93 |
| 3296 | 520 | 272.00 | 2504.00 | 354.11 | 146.60 | 500.71 |
| 3300 | 520 | 272.00 | 2508.00 | 354.66 | 146.83 | 501.49 |
| 3304 | 520 | 272.00 | 2512.00 | 355.21 | 147.07 | 502.28 |
| 3308 | 520 | 272.00 | 2516.00 | 355.76 | 147.30 | 503.06 |
| 3312 | 520 | 272.00 | 2520.00 | 356.32 | 147.54 | 503.86 |
| 3316 | 520 | 272.00 | 2524.00 | 356.87 | 147.77 | 504.64 |
| 3320 | 520 | 272.00 | 2528.00 | 357.42 | 148.00 | 505.42 |
| 3324 | 520 | 272.00 | 2532.00 | 357.97 | 148.24 | 506.21 |
| 3328 | 520 | 272.00 | 2536.00 | 358.52 | 148.47 | 506.99 |
| 3332 | 520 | 272.00 | 2540.00 | 359.08 | 148.71 | 507.79 |
| 3336 | 520 | 272.00 | 2544.00 | 359.63 | 148.94 | 508.57 |
| 3340 | 520 | 272.00 | 2548.00 | 360.18 | 149.17 | 509.35 |
| 3344 | 520 | 272.00 | 2552.00 | 360.73 | 149.41 | 510.14 |
| 3348 | 520 | 272.00 | 2556.00 | 361.28 | 149.64 | 510.92 |
| 3352 | 520 | 272.00 | 2560.00 | 361.84 | 149.88 | 511.72 |
| 3356 | 520 | 272.00 | 2564.00 | 362.39 | 150.11 | 512.50 |
| 3360 | 520 | 272.00 | 2568.00 | 362.94 | 150.34 | 513.28 |
| 3364 | 520 | 272.00 | 2572.00 | 363.49 | 150.58 | 514.07 |
| 3368 | 520 | 272.00 | 2576.00 | 364.04 | 150.81 | 514.85 |
| 3372 | 520 | 272.00 | 2580.00 | 364.60 | 151.05 | 515.65 |
| 3376 | 520 | 272.00 | 2584.00 | 365.15 | 151.28 | 516.43 |
| 3380 | 520 | 272.00 | 2588.00 | 365.70 | 151.51 | 517.21 |
| 3384 | 520 | 272.00 | 2592.00 | 366.25 | 151.75 | 518.00 |
| 3388 | 520 | 272.00 | 2596.00 | 366.80 | 151.98 | 518.78 |
| 3392 | 520 | 272.00 | 2600.00 | 367.36 | 152.22 | 519.58 |
| 3396 | 520 | 272.00 | 2604.00 | 367.91 | 152.45 | 520.36 |
| 3400 | 520 | 272.00 | 2608.00 | 368.46 | 152.68 | 521.14 |
| 3404 | 520 | 272.00 | 2612.00 | 369.01 | 152.92 | 521.93 |
| 3408 | 520 | 272.00 | 2616.00 | 369.56 | 153.15 | 522.71 |
| 3412 | 520 | 272.00 | 2620.00 | 370.12 | 153.39 | 523.51 |
| 3416 | 520 | 272.00 | 2624.00 | 370.67 | 153.62 | 524.29 |
| 3420 | 520 | 272.00 | 2628.00 | 371.22 | 153.85 | 525.07 |
| 3424 | 520 | 272.00 | 2632.00 | 371.77 | 154.09 | 525.86 |
| 3428 | 520 | 272.00 | 2636.00 | 372.32 | 154.32 | 526.64 |
| 3432 | 520 | 272.00 | 2640.00 | 372.88 | 154.56 | 527.44 |
| 3436 | 520 | 272.00 | 2644.00 | 373.43 | 154.79 | 528.22 |
| 3440 | 520 | 272.00 | 2648.00 | 373.98 | 155.02 | 529.00 |
| 3444 | 520 | 272.00 | 2652.00 | 374.53 | 155.26 | 529.79 |
| 3448 | 520 | 272.00 | 2656.00 | 375.08 | 155.49 | 530.57 |
| 3452 | 520 | 272.00 | 2660.00 | 375.64 | 155.73 | 531.37 |
| 3456 | 520 | 272.00 | 2664.00 | 376.19 | 155.96 | 532.15 |
| 3460 | 520 | 272.00 | 2668.00 | 376.74 | 156.19 | 532.93 |
| 3464 | 520 | 272.00 | 2672.00 | 377.29 | 156.43 | 533.72 |
| 3468 | 520 | 272.00 | 2676.00 | 377.84 | 156.66 | 534.50 |
| 3472 | 520 | 272.00 | 2680.00 | 378.40 | 156.90 | 535.30 |
| 3476 | 520 | 272.00 | 2684.00 | 378.95 | 157.13 | 536.08 |
| 3480 | 520 | 272.00 | 2688.00 | 379.50 | 157.36 | 536.86 |
| 3484 | 520 | 272.00 | 2692.00 | 380.05 | 157.60 | 537.65 |
| 3488 | 520 | 272.00 | 2696.00 | 380.60 | 157.83 | 538.43 |
| 3492 | 520 | 272.00 | 2700.00 | 381.16 | 158.07 | 539.23 |
| 3496 | 520 | 272.00 | 2704.00 | 381.71 | 158.30 | 540.01 |

## Monthly table

**Table letter B**

| Employee's earnings up to and including the UEL | Earnings at the LEL (where earnings are equal to or exceed the LEL) | Earnings above the LEL, up to and including the PT | Earnings above the PT, up to and including the UEL | Employer's NICs due on all earnings above the ST | Employee's NICs due on all earnings above the PT | Total of employee's and employer's NICs (for information only) |
|---|---|---|---|---|---|---|
| | | 1a | 1b | 1c | 1d | 1e |
| £ | £ | £ p | £ p | £ p | £ p | £ p |
| 3500 | 520 | 272.00 | 2708.00 | 382.26 | 158.53 | 540.79 |
| 3504 | 520 | 272.00 | 2712.00 | 382.81 | 158.77 | 541.58 |
| 3508 | 520 | 272.00 | 2716.00 | 383.36 | 159.00 | 542.36 |
| 3512 | 520 | 272.00 | 2720.00 | 383.92 | 159.24 | 543.16 |
| 3516 | 520 | 272.00 | 2724.00 | 384.47 | 159.47 | 543.94 |
| 3520 | 520 | 272.00 | 2728.00 | 385.02 | 159.70 | 544.72 |
| 3524 | 520 | 272.00 | 2732.00 | 385.57 | 159.94 | 545.51 |
| 3528 | 520 | 272.00 | 2736.00 | 386.12 | 160.17 | 546.29 |
| 3532 | 520 | 272.00 | 2740.00 | 386.68 | 160.41 | 547.09 |
| 3536 | 520 | 272.00 | 2744.00 | 387.23 | 160.64 | 547.87 |
| 3540 | 520 | 272.00 | 2748.00 | 387.78 | 160.87 | 548.65 |
| 3544 | 520 | 272.00 | 2752.00 | 388.33 | 161.11 | 549.44 |
| 3548 | 520 | 272.00 | 2756.00 | 388.88 | 161.34 | 550.22 |
| 3552 | 520 | 272.00 | 2760.00 | 389.44 | 161.58 | 551.02 |
| 3556 | 520 | 272.00 | 2764.00 | 389.99 | 161.81 | 551.80 |
| 3560 | 520 | 272.00 | 2768.00 | 390.54 | 162.04 | 552.58 |
| 3564 | 520 | 272.00 | 2772.00 | 391.09 | 162.28 | 553.37 |
| 3568 | 520 | 272.00 | 2776.00 | 391.64 | 162.51 | 554.15 |
| 3572 | 520 | 272.00 | 2780.00 | 392.20 | 162.75 | 554.95 |
| 3576 | 520 | 272.00 | 2784.00 | 392.75 | 162.98 | 555.73 |
| 3580 | 520 | 272.00 | 2788.00 | 393.30 | 163.21 | 556.51 |
| 3584 | 520 | 272.00 | 2792.00 | 393.85 | 163.45 | 557.30 |
| 3588 | 520 | 272.00 | 2796.00 | 394.40 | 163.68 | 558.08 |
| 3592 | 520 | 272.00 | 2800.00 | 394.96 | 163.92 | 558.88 |
| 3596 | 520 | 272.00 | 2804.00 | 395.51 | 164.15 | 559.66 |
| 3600 | 520 | 272.00 | 2808.00 | 396.06 | 164.38 | 560.44 |
| 3604 | 520 | 272.00 | 2812.00 | 396.61 | 164.62 | 561.23 |
| 3608 | 520 | 272.00 | 2816.00 | 397.16 | 164.85 | 562.01 |
| 3612 | 520 | 272.00 | 2820.00 | 397.72 | 165.09 | 562.81 |
| 3616 | 520 | 272.00 | 2824.00 | 398.27 | 165.32 | 563.59 |
| 3620 | 520 | 272.00 | 2828.00 | 398.82 | 165.55 | 564.37 |
| 3624 | 520 | 272.00 | 2832.00 | 399.37 | 165.79 | 565.16 |
| 3628 | 520 | 272.00 | 2836.00 | 399.92 | 166.02 | 565.94 |
| 3632 | 520 | 272.00 | 2840.00 | 400.48 | 166.26 | 566.74 |
| 3636 | 520 | 272.00 | 2844.00 | 401.03 | 166.49 | 567.52 |
| 3640 | 520 | 272.00 | 2848.00 | 401.58 | 166.72 | 568.30 |
| 3644 | 520 | 272.00 | 2852.00 | 402.13 | 166.96 | 569.09 |
| 3648 | 520 | 272.00 | 2856.00 | 402.68 | 167.19 | 569.87 |
| 3652 | 520 | 272.00 | 2860.00 | 403.24 | 167.43 | 570.67 |
| 3656 | 520 | 272.00 | 2864.00 | 403.79 | 167.66 | 571.45 |
| 3660 | 520 | 272.00 | 2868.00 | 404.34 | 167.89 | 572.23 |
| 3664 | 520 | 272.00 | 2872.00 | 404.89 | 168.13 | 573.02 |
| 3668 | 520 | 272.00 | 2876.00 | 405.44 | 168.36 | 573.80 |
| 3672 | 520 | 272.00 | 2880.00 | 406.00 | 168.60 | 574.60 |
| 3676 | 520 | 272.00 | 2884.00 | 406.55 | 168.83 | 575.38 |
| 3680 | 520 | 272.00 | 2888.00 | 407.10 | 169.06 | 576.16 |
| 3684 | 520 | 272.00 | 2892.00 | 407.65 | 169.30 | 576.95 |
| 3688 | 520 | 272.00 | 2896.00 | 408.20 | 169.53 | 577.73 |
| 3692 | 520 | 272.00 | 2900.00 | 408.76 | 169.77 | 578.53 |
| 3696 | 520 | 272.00 | 2904.00 | 409.31 | 170.00 | 579.31 |
| 3700 | 520 | 272.00 | 2908.00 | 409.86 | 170.23 | 580.09 |
| 3704 | 520 | 272.00 | 2912.00 | 410.41 | 170.47 | 580.88 |
| 3708 | 520 | 272.00 | 2916.00 | 410.96 | 170.70 | 581.66 |
| 3712 | 520 | 272.00 | 2920.00 | 411.52 | 170.94 | 582.46 |
| 3716 | 520 | 272.00 | 2924.00 | 412.07 | 171.17 | 583.24 |

**Monthly table**

**Table letter B**

| Employee's earnings up to and including the UEL | Earnings at the LEL (where earnings are equal to or exceed the LEL) | Earnings above the LEL, up to and including the PT | Earnings above the PT, up to and including the UEL | Employer's NICs due on all earnings above the ST | Employee's NICs due on all earnings above the PT | Total of employee's and employer's NICs (for information only) |
|---|---|---|---|---|---|---|
| | | 1a | 1b | 1c | 1d | 1e |
| £ | £ | £ p | £ p | £ p | £ p | £ p |
| 3720 | 520 | 272.00 | 2928.00 | 412.62 | 171.40 | 584.02 |
| 3724 | 520 | 272.00 | 2932.00 | 413.17 | 171.64 | 584.81 |
| 3728 | 520 | 272.00 | 2936.00 | 413.72 | 171.87 | 585.59 |
| 3732 | 520 | 272.00 | 2940.00 | 414.28 | 172.11 | 586.39 |
| 3736 | 520 | 272.00 | 2944.00 | 414.83 | 172.34 | 587.17 |
| 3740 | 520 | 272.00 | 2948.00 | 415.38 | 172.57 | 587.95 |
| 3744 | 520 | 272.00 | 2952.00 | 415.93 | 172.81 | 588.74 |
| 3748 | 520 | 272.00 | 2956.00 | 416.48 | 173.04 | 589.52 |
| 3752 | 520 | 272.00 | 2960.00 | 417.04 | 173.28 | 590.32 |
| 3756 | 520 | 272.00 | 2964.00 | 417.59 | 173.51 | 591.10 |
| 3760 | 520 | 272.00 | 2968.00 | 418.14 | 173.74 | 591.88 |
| 3764 | 520 | 272.00 | 2972.00 | 418.69 | 173.98 | 592.67 |
| 3768 | 520 | 272.00 | 2976.00 | 419.24 | 174.21 | 593.45 |
| 3772 | 520 | 272.00 | 2980.00 | 419.80 | 174.45 | 594.25 |
| 3776 | 520 | 272.00 | 2984.00 | 420.35 | 174.68 | 595.03 |
| 3780 | 520 | 272.00 | 2988.00 | 420.90 | 174.91 | 595.81 |
| 3784 | 520 | 272.00 | 2992.00 | 421.45 | 175.15 | 596.60 |
| 3788 | 520 | 272.00 | 2996.00 | 422.00 | 175.38 | 597.38 |
| 3792 | 520 | 272.00 | 3000.00 | 422.56 | 175.62 | 598.18 |
| 3796 | 520 | 272.00 | 3004.00 | 423.11 | 175.85 | 598.96 |
| 3800 | 520 | 272.00 | 3008.00 | 423.66 | 176.08 | 599.74 |
| 3804 | 520 | 272.00 | 3012.00 | 424.21 | 176.32 | 600.53 |
| 3808 | 520 | 272.00 | 3016.00 | 424.76 | 176.55 | 601.31 |
| 3812 | 520 | 272.00 | 3020.00 | 425.32 | 176.79 | 602.11 |
| 3816 | 520 | 272.00 | 3024.00 | 425.87 | 177.02 | 602.89 |
| 3820 | 520 | 272.00 | 3028.00 | 426.42 | 177.25 | 603.67 |
| 3824 | 520 | 272.00 | 3032.00 | 426.97 | 177.49 | 604.46 |
| 3828 | 520 | 272.00 | 3036.00 | 427.52 | 177.72 | 605.24 |
| 3832 | 520 | 272.00 | 3040.00 | 428.08 | 177.96 | 606.04 |
| 3836 | 520 | 272.00 | 3044.00 | 428.63 | 178.19 | 606.82 |
| 3840 | 520 | 272.00 | 3048.00 | 429.18 | 178.42 | 607.60 |
| 3844 | 520 | 272.00 | 3052.00 | 429.73 | 178.66 | 608.39 |
| 3848 | 520 | 272.00 | 3056.00 | 430.28 | 178.89 | 609.17 |
| 3852 | 520 | 272.00 | 3060.00 | 430.84 | 179.13 | 609.97 |
| 3856 | 520 | 272.00 | 3064.00 | 431.39 | 179.36 | 610.75 |
| 3860 | 520 | 272.00 | 3068.00 | 431.94 | 179.59 | 611.53 |
| 3864 | 520 | 272.00 | 3072.00 | 432.49 | 179.83 | 612.32 |
| 3868 | 520 | 272.00 | 3076.00 | 433.04 | 180.06 | 613.10 |
| 3872 | 520 | 272.00 | 3080.00 | 433.60 | 180.30 | 613.90 |
| 3876 | 520 | 272.00 | 3084.00 | 434.15 | 180.53 | 614.68 |
| 3880 | 520 | 272.00 | 3088.00 | 434.70 | 180.76 | 615.46 |
| 3884 | 520 | 272.00 | 3092.00 | 435.25 | 181.00 | 616.25 |
| 3888 | 520 | 272.00 | 3096.00 | 435.80 | 181.23 | 617.03 |
| 3892 | 520 | 272.00 | 3100.00 | 436.36 | 181.47 | 617.83 |
| 3896 | 520 | 272.00 | 3104.00 | 436.91 | 181.70 | 618.61 |
| 3900 | 520 | 272.00 | 3108.00 | 437.46 | 181.93 | 619.39 |
| 3904 | 520 | 272.00 | 3112.00 | 438.01 | 182.17 | 620.18 |
| 3908 | 520 | 272.00 | 3116.00 | 438.56 | 182.40 | 620.96 |
| 3912 | 520 | 272.00 | 3120.00 | 439.12 | 182.64 | 621.76 |
| 3916 | 520 | 272.00 | 3124.00 | 439.67 | 182.87 | 622.54 |
| 3920 | 520 | 272.00 | 3128.00 | 440.22 | 183.10 | 623.32 |
| 3924 | 520 | 272.00 | 3132.00 | 440.77 | 183.34 | 624.11 |
| 3928 | 520 | 272.00 | 3136.00 | 441.32 | 183.57 | 624.89 |
| 3932 | 520 | 272.00 | 3140.00 | 441.88 | 183.81 | 625.69 |
| 3936 | 520 | 272.00 | 3144.00 | 442.43 | 184.04 | 626.47 |

## Monthly table

**Table letter B**

| Employee's earnings up to and including the UEL | Earnings at the LEL (where earnings are equal to or exceed the LEL) | Earnings above the LEL, up to and including the PT | Earnings above the PT, up to and including the UEL | Employer's NICs due on all earnings above the ST | Employee's NICs due on all earnings above the PT | Total of employee's and employer's NICs (for information only) |
|---|---|---|---|---|---|---|
| | | 1a | 1b | 1c | 1d | 1e |
| £ | £ | £ p | £ p | £ p | £ p | £ p |
| 3940 | 520 | 272.00 | 3148.00 | 442.98 | 184.27 | 627.25 |
| 3944 | 520 | 272.00 | 3152.00 | 443.53 | 184.51 | 628.04 |
| 3948 | 520 | 272.00 | 3156.00 | 444.08 | 184.74 | 628.82 |
| 3952 | 520 | 272.00 | 3160.00 | 444.64 | 184.98 | 629.62 |
| 3956 | 520 | 272.00 | 3164.00 | 445.19 | 185.21 | 630.40 |
| 3960 | 520 | 272.00 | 3168.00 | 445.74 | 185.44 | 631.18 |
| 3964 | 520 | 272.00 | 3172.00 | 446.29 | 185.68 | 631.97 |
| 3968 | 520 | 272.00 | 3176.00 | 446.84 | 185.91 | 632.75 |
| 3972 | 520 | 272.00 | 3180.00 | 447.40 | 186.15 | 633.55 |
| 3976 | 520 | 272.00 | 3184.00 | 447.95 | 186.38 | 634.33 |
| 3980 | 520 | 272.00 | 3188.00 | 448.50 | 186.61 | 635.11 |
| 3984 | 520 | 272.00 | 3192.00 | 449.05 | 186.85 | 635.90 |
| 3988 | 520 | 272.00 | 3196.00 | 449.60 | 187.08 | 636.68 |
| 3992 | 520 | 272.00 | 3200.00 | 450.16 | 187.32 | 637.48 |
| 3996 | 520 | 272.00 | 3204.00 | 450.71 | 187.55 | 638.26 |
| 4000 | 520 | 272.00 | 3208.00 | 451.26 | 187.78 | 639.04 |
| 4004 | 520 | 272.00 | 3212.00 | 451.81 | 188.02 | 639.83 |
| 4008 | 520 | 272.00 | 3216.00 | 452.36 | 188.25 | 640.61 |
| 4012 | 520 | 272.00 | 3220.00 | 452.92 | 188.49 | 641.41 |
| 4016 | 520 | 272.00 | 3224.00 | 453.47 | 188.72 | 642.19 |
| 4020 | 520 | 272.00 | 3228.00 | 454.02 | 188.95 | 642.97 |
| 4024 | 520 | 272.00 | 3232.00 | 454.57 | 189.19 | 643.76 |
| 4028 | 520 | 272.00 | 3236.00 | 455.12 | 189.42 | 644.54 |
| 4032 | 520 | 272.00 | 3240.00 | 455.68 | 189.66 | 645.34 |
| 4036 | 520 | 272.00 | 3244.00 | 456.23 | 189.89 | 646.12 |
| 4040 | 520 | 272.00 | 3248.00 | 456.78 | 190.12 | 646.90 |
| 4044 | 520 | 272.00 | 3252.00 | 457.33 | 190.36 | 647.69 |
| 4048 | 520 | 272.00 | 3256.00 | 457.88 | 190.59 | 648.47 |
| 4052 | 520 | 272.00 | 3260.00 | 458.44 | 190.83 | 649.27 |
| 4056 | 520 | 272.00 | 3264.00 | 458.99 | 191.06 | 650.05 |
| 4060 | 520 | 272.00 | 3268.00 | 459.54 | 191.29 | 650.83 |
| 4064 | 520 | 272.00 | 3272.00 | 460.09 | 191.53 | 651.62 |
| 4068 | 520 | 272.00 | 3276.00 | 460.64 | 191.76 | 652.40 |
| 4072 | 520 | 272.00 | 3280.00 | 461.20 | 192.00 | 653.20 |
| 4076 | 520 | 272.00 | 3284.00 | 461.75 | 192.23 | 653.98 |
| 4080 | 520 | 272.00 | 3288.00 | 462.30 | 192.46 | 654.76 |
| 4084 | 520 | 272.00 | 3292.00 | 462.85 | 192.70 | 655.55 |
| 4088 | 520 | 272.00 | 3296.00 | 463.40 | 192.93 | 656.33 |
| 4092 | 520 | 272.00 | 3300.00 | 463.96 | 193.17 | 657.13 |
| 4096 | 520 | 272.00 | 3304.00 | 464.51 | 193.40 | 657.91 |
| 4100 | 520 | 272.00 | 3308.00 | 465.06 | 193.63 | 658.69 |
| 4104 | 520 | 272.00 | 3312.00 | 465.61 | 193.87 | 659.48 |
| 4108 | 520 | 272.00 | 3316.00 | 466.16 | 194.10 | 660.26 |
| 4112 | 520 | 272.00 | 3320.00 | 466.72 | 194.34 | 661.06 |
| 4116 | 520 | 272.00 | 3324.00 | 467.27 | 194.57 | 661.84 |
| 4120 | 520 | 272.00 | 3328.00 | 467.82 | 194.80 | 662.62 |
| 4124 | 520 | 272.00 | 3332.00 | 468.37 | 195.04 | 663.41 |
| 4128 | 520 | 272.00 | 3336.00 | 468.92 | 195.27 | 664.19 |
| 4132 | 520 | 272.00 | 3340.00 | 469.48 | 195.51 | 664.99 |
| 4136 | 520 | 272.00 | 3344.00 | 470.03 | 195.74 | 665.77 |
| 4140 | 520 | 272.00 | 3348.00 | 470.58 | 195.97 | 666.55 |
| 4144 | 520 | 272.00 | 3352.00 | 471.13 | 196.21 | 667.34 |
| 4148 | 520 | 272.00 | 3356.00 | 471.68 | 196.44 | 668.12 |
| 4152 | 520 | 272.00 | 3360.00 | 472.24 | 196.68 | 668.92 |
| 4156 | 520 | 272.00 | 3364.00 | 472.79 | 196.91 | 669.70 |

## Monthly table

**Table letter B**

| Employee's earnings up to and including the UEL | Earnings at the LEL (where earnings are equal to or exceed the LEL) | Earnings above the LEL, up to and including the PT | Earnings above the PT, up to and including the UEL | Employer's NICs due on all earnings above the ST | Employee's NICs due on all earnings above the PT | Total of employee's and employers NICs (for information only) |
|---|---|---|---|---|---|---|
|  | 1a | 1b | 1c | 1d | 1e |  |
| £ | £ | £ p | £ p | £ p | £ p | £ p |
| 4160 | 520 | 272.00 | 3368.00 | 473.34 | 197.14 | 670.48 |
| 4164 | 520 | 272.00 | 3372.00 | 473.82 | 197.35 | 671.17 |
| 4167 | 520 | 272.00 | 3375.00 | 474.03 | 197.44 | 671.47 |

If the employee's gross pay is over £4,167, go to page 75.

## Weekly table for employees who are State Pension age or over – employer only NICs for use from 6 April 2020 to 5 April 2021

**Table letter C**

Use this table for employees who are State Pension age or over, for whom you hold a copy of either their birth certificate or passport as evidence of their date of birth.

### Filling in form RT11, 'Deductions working sheet' or substitute

1. Enter 'C' in the NICs category letter column on form RT11.

2. Copy the figures in columns 1a – 1e of the table to columns 1a – 1e on the line next to the tax week in which the employee is paid, on form RT11.

If the employee's total earnings fall between the LEL and the UEL and the exact gross pay is not shown in the table, use the next smaller figure shown. If the employee's total earnings exceed the UEL, see page 76.

The figures in the left-hand column of each table show steps between the LEL and the UEL. The NICs liability for each step, with the exception of the LEL, ST, PT and UEL, is worked out at the mid-point of the steps, so you and your employee may pay slightly more or less than if you used the exact percentage method.

| Employee's earnings up to and including the UEL | Earnings at the LEL (where earnings are equal to or exceed the LEL) | Earnings above the LEL, up to and including the PT | Earnings above the PT, up to and including the UEL | Employer's NICs due on all earnings above the ST | Employee's NICs due on all earnings above the PT |
|---|---|---|---|---|---|
| | 1a | 1b | 1c | 1d | 1e |
| £ | £ | £ p | £ p | £ p | £ p |
| Up to and including £119.99 | No NICs liability, make no entries on form RT11 | | | | |
| 120 | 120 | 0.00 | 0.00 | 0.00 | 0.00 |
| 121 | 120 | 1.00 | 0.00 | 0.00 | 0.00 |
| 122 | 120 | 2.00 | 0.00 | 0.00 | 0.00 |
| 123 | 120 | 3.00 | 0.00 | 0.00 | 0.00 |
| 124 | 120 | 4.00 | 0.00 | 0.00 | 0.00 |
| 125 | 120 | 5.00 | 0.00 | 0.00 | 0.00 |
| 126 | 120 | 6.00 | 0.00 | 0.00 | 0.00 |
| 127 | 120 | 7.00 | 0.00 | 0.00 | 0.00 |
| 128 | 120 | 8.00 | 0.00 | 0.00 | 0.00 |
| 129 | 120 | 9.00 | 0.00 | 0.00 | 0.00 |
| 130 | 120 | 10.00 | 0.00 | 0.00 | 0.00 |
| 131 | 120 | 11.00 | 0.00 | 0.00 | 0.00 |
| 132 | 120 | 12.00 | 0.00 | 0.00 | 0.00 |
| 133 | 120 | 13.00 | 0.00 | 0.00 | 0.00 |
| 134 | 120 | 14.00 | 0.00 | 0.00 | 0.00 |
| 135 | 120 | 15.00 | 0.00 | 0.00 | 0.00 |
| 136 | 120 | 16.00 | 0.00 | 0.00 | 0.00 |
| 137 | 120 | 17.00 | 0.00 | 0.00 | 0.00 |
| 138 | 120 | 18.00 | 0.00 | 0.00 | 0.00 |
| 139 | 120 | 19.00 | 0.00 | 0.00 | 0.00 |
| 140 | 120 | 20.00 | 0.00 | 0.00 | 0.00 |
| 141 | 120 | 21.00 | 0.00 | 0.00 | 0.00 |
| 142 | 120 | 22.00 | 0.00 | 0.00 | 0.00 |
| 143 | 120 | 23.00 | 0.00 | 0.00 | 0.00 |
| 144 | 120 | 24.00 | 0.00 | 0.00 | 0.00 |
| 145 | 120 | 25.00 | 0.00 | 0.00 | 0.00 |
| 146 | 120 | 26.00 | 0.00 | 0.00 | 0.00 |
| 147 | 120 | 27.00 | 0.00 | 0.00 | 0.00 |
| 148 | 120 | 28.00 | 0.00 | 0.00 | 0.00 |
| 149 | 120 | 29.00 | 0.00 | 0.00 | 0.00 |
| 150 | 120 | 30.00 | 0.00 | 0.00 | 0.00 |
| 151 | 120 | 31.00 | 0.00 | 0.00 | 0.00 |
| 152 | 120 | 32.00 | 0.00 | 0.00 | 0.00 |
| 153 | 120 | 33.00 | 0.00 | 0.00 | 0.00 |
| 154 | 120 | 34.00 | 0.00 | 0.00 | 0.00 |

**Weekly table**　　　　　　　　　　　　　　　　　　　　**Table letter C**

| Employee's earnings up to and including the UEL | Earnings at the LEL (where earnings are equal to or exceed the LEL) | Earnings above the LEL, up to and including the PT | Earnings above the PT, up to and including the UEL | Employer's NICs due on all earnings above the ST | Employee's NICs due on all earnings above the PT |
|---|---|---|---|---|---|
| | | 1a | 1b | 1c | 1d | 1e |
| £ | £ | £ p | £ p | £ p | £ p |
| 155 | 120 | 35.00 | 0.00 | 0.00 | 0.00 |
| 156 | 120 | 36.00 | 0.00 | 0.00 | 0.00 |
| 157 | 120 | 37.00 | 0.00 | 0.00 | 0.00 |
| 158 | 120 | 38.00 | 0.00 | 0.00 | 0.00 |
| 159 | 120 | 39.00 | 0.00 | 0.00 | 0.00 |
| 160 | 120 | 40.00 | 0.00 | 0.00 | 0.00 |
| 161 | 120 | 41.00 | 0.00 | 0.00 | 0.00 |
| 162 | 120 | 42.00 | 0.00 | 0.00 | 0.00 |
| 163 | 120 | 43.00 | 0.00 | 0.00 | 0.00 |
| 164 | 120 | 44.00 | 0.00 | 0.00 | 0.00 |
| 165 | 120 | 45.00 | 0.00 | 0.00 | 0.00 |
| 166 | 120 | 46.00 | 0.00 | 0.00 | 0.00 |
| 167 | 120 | 47.00 | 0.00 | 0.00 | 0.00 |
| 168 | 120 | 48.00 | 0.00 | 0.00 | 0.00 |
| 169 | 120 | 49.00 | 0.00 | 0.00 | 0.00 |
| 170 | 120 | 50.00 | 0.00 | 0.21 | 0.00 |
| 171 | 120 | 51.00 | 0.00 | 0.34 | 0.00 |
| 172 | 120 | 52.00 | 0.00 | 0.48 | 0.00 |
| 173 | 120 | 53.00 | 0.00 | 0.62 | 0.00 |
| 174 | 120 | 54.00 | 0.00 | 0.76 | 0.00 |
| 175 | 120 | 55.00 | 0.00 | 0.90 | 0.00 |
| 176 | 120 | 56.00 | 0.00 | 1.03 | 0.00 |
| 177 | 120 | 57.00 | 0.00 | 1.17 | 0.00 |
| 178 | 120 | 58.00 | 0.00 | 1.31 | 0.00 |
| 179 | 120 | 59.00 | 0.00 | 1.45 | 0.00 |
| 180 | 120 | 60.00 | 0.00 | 1.59 | 0.00 |
| 181 | 120 | 61.00 | 0.00 | 1.72 | 0.00 |
| 182 | 120 | 62.00 | 0.00 | 1.86 | 0.00 |
| 183 | 120 | 63.00 | 0.00 | 1.93 | 0.00 |
| 184 | 120 | 63.00 | 1.00 | 2.14 | 0.00 |
| 185 | 120 | 63.00 | 2.00 | 2.27 | 0.00 |
| 186 | 120 | 63.00 | 3.00 | 2.41 | 0.00 |
| 187 | 120 | 63.00 | 4.00 | 2.55 | 0.00 |
| 188 | 120 | 63.00 | 5.00 | 2.69 | 0.00 |
| 189 | 120 | 63.00 | 6.00 | 2.83 | 0.00 |
| 190 | 120 | 63.00 | 7.00 | 2.96 | 0.00 |
| 191 | 120 | 63.00 | 8.00 | 3.10 | 0.00 |
| 192 | 120 | 63.00 | 9.00 | 3.24 | 0.00 |
| 193 | 120 | 63.00 | 10.00 | 3.38 | 0.00 |
| 194 | 120 | 63.00 | 11.00 | 3.52 | 0.00 |
| 195 | 120 | 63.00 | 12.00 | 3.65 | 0.00 |
| 196 | 120 | 63.00 | 13.00 | 3.79 | 0.00 |
| 197 | 120 | 63.00 | 14.00 | 3.93 | 0.00 |
| 198 | 120 | 63.00 | 15.00 | 4.07 | 0.00 |
| 199 | 120 | 63.00 | 16.00 | 4.21 | 0.00 |
| 200 | 120 | 63.00 | 17.00 | 4.34 | 0.00 |
| 201 | 120 | 63.00 | 18.00 | 4.48 | 0.00 |
| 202 | 120 | 63.00 | 19.00 | 4.62 | 0.00 |
| 203 | 120 | 63.00 | 20.00 | 4.76 | 0.00 |
| 204 | 120 | 63.00 | 21.00 | 4.90 | 0.00 |
| 205 | 120 | 63.00 | 22.00 | 5.03 | 0.00 |
| 206 | 120 | 63.00 | 23.00 | 5.17 | 0.00 |
| 207 | 120 | 63.00 | 24.00 | 5.31 | 0.00 |
| 208 | 120 | 63.00 | 25.00 | 5.45 | 0.00 |
| 209 | 120 | 63.00 | 26.00 | 5.59 | 0.00 |

Page 42

**Weekly table**                                                                 **Table letter C**

| Employee's earnings up to and including the UEL | Earnings at the LEL (where earnings are equal to or exceed the LEL) | Earnings above the LEL, up to and including the PT | Earnings above the PT, up to and including the UEL | Employer's NICs due on all earnings above the ST | Employee's NICs due on all earnings above the PT |
|---|---|---|---|---|---|
| 1a | 1b | 1c | 1d | 1e |
| £ | £ | £ p | £ p | £ p | £ p |
| 210 | 120 | 63.00 | 27.00 | 5.72 | 0.00 |
| 211 | 120 | 63.00 | 28.00 | 5.86 | 0.00 |
| 212 | 120 | 63.00 | 29.00 | 6.00 | 0.00 |
| 213 | 120 | 63.00 | 30.00 | 6.14 | 0.00 |
| 214 | 120 | 63.00 | 31.00 | 6.28 | 0.00 |
| 215 | 120 | 63.00 | 32.00 | 6.41 | 0.00 |
| 216 | 120 | 63.00 | 33.00 | 6.55 | 0.00 |
| 217 | 120 | 63.00 | 34.00 | 6.69 | 0.00 |
| 218 | 120 | 63.00 | 35.00 | 6.83 | 0.00 |
| 219 | 120 | 63.00 | 36.00 | 6.97 | 0.00 |
| 220 | 120 | 63.00 | 37.00 | 7.10 | 0.00 |
| 221 | 120 | 63.00 | 38.00 | 7.24 | 0.00 |
| 222 | 120 | 63.00 | 39.00 | 7.38 | 0.00 |
| 223 | 120 | 63.00 | 40.00 | 7.52 | 0.00 |
| 224 | 120 | 63.00 | 41.00 | 7.66 | 0.00 |
| 225 | 120 | 63.00 | 42.00 | 7.79 | 0.00 |
| 226 | 120 | 63.00 | 43.00 | 7.93 | 0.00 |
| 227 | 120 | 63.00 | 44.00 | 8.07 | 0.00 |
| 228 | 120 | 63.00 | 45.00 | 8.21 | 0.00 |
| 229 | 120 | 63.00 | 46.00 | 8.35 | 0.00 |
| 230 | 120 | 63.00 | 47.00 | 8.48 | 0.00 |
| 231 | 120 | 63.00 | 48.00 | 8.62 | 0.00 |
| 232 | 120 | 63.00 | 49.00 | 8.76 | 0.00 |
| 233 | 120 | 63.00 | 50.00 | 8.90 | 0.00 |
| 234 | 120 | 63.00 | 51.00 | 9.04 | 0.00 |
| 235 | 120 | 63.00 | 52.00 | 9.17 | 0.00 |
| 236 | 120 | 63.00 | 53.00 | 9.31 | 0.00 |
| 237 | 120 | 63.00 | 54.00 | 9.45 | 0.00 |
| 238 | 120 | 63.00 | 55.00 | 9.59 | 0.00 |
| 239 | 120 | 63.00 | 56.00 | 9.73 | 0.00 |
| 240 | 120 | 63.00 | 57.00 | 9.86 | 0.00 |
| 241 | 120 | 63.00 | 58.00 | 10.00 | 0.00 |
| 242 | 120 | 63.00 | 59.00 | 10.14 | 0.00 |
| 243 | 120 | 63.00 | 60.00 | 10.28 | 0.00 |
| 244 | 120 | 63.00 | 61.00 | 10.42 | 0.00 |
| 245 | 120 | 63.00 | 62.00 | 10.55 | 0.00 |
| 246 | 120 | 63.00 | 63.00 | 10.69 | 0.00 |
| 247 | 120 | 63.00 | 64.00 | 10.83 | 0.00 |
| 248 | 120 | 63.00 | 65.00 | 10.97 | 0.00 |
| 249 | 120 | 63.00 | 66.00 | 11.11 | 0.00 |
| 250 | 120 | 63.00 | 67.00 | 11.24 | 0.00 |
| 251 | 120 | 63.00 | 68.00 | 11.38 | 0.00 |
| 252 | 120 | 63.00 | 69.00 | 11.52 | 0.00 |
| 253 | 120 | 63.00 | 70.00 | 11.66 | 0.00 |
| 254 | 120 | 63.00 | 71.00 | 11.80 | 0.00 |
| 255 | 120 | 63.00 | 72.00 | 11.93 | 0.00 |
| 256 | 120 | 63.00 | 73.00 | 12.07 | 0.00 |
| 257 | 120 | 63.00 | 74.00 | 12.21 | 0.00 |
| 258 | 120 | 63.00 | 75.00 | 12.35 | 0.00 |
| 259 | 120 | 63.00 | 76.00 | 12.49 | 0.00 |
| 260 | 120 | 63.00 | 77.00 | 12.62 | 0.00 |
| 261 | 120 | 63.00 | 78.00 | 12.76 | 0.00 |
| 262 | 120 | 63.00 | 79.00 | 12.90 | 0.00 |
| 263 | 120 | 63.00 | 80.00 | 13.04 | 0.00 |
| 264 | 120 | 63.00 | 81.00 | 13.18 | 0.00 |

**Weekly table**  **Table letter C**

| Employee's earnings up to and including the UEL | Earnings at the LEL (where earnings are equal to or exceed the LEL) | Earnings above the LEL, up to and including the PT | Earnings above the PT, up to and including the UEL | Employer's NICs due on all earnings above the ST | Employee's NICs due on all earnings above the PT |
|---|---|---|---|---|---|
| | | 1a | 1b | 1c | 1d | 1e |
| £ | £ | £ p | £ p | £ p | £ p |
| 265 | 120 | 63.00 | 82.00 | 13.31 | 0.00 |
| 266 | 120 | 63.00 | 83.00 | 13.45 | 0.00 |
| 267 | 120 | 63.00 | 84.00 | 13.59 | 0.00 |
| 268 | 120 | 63.00 | 85.00 | 13.73 | 0.00 |
| 269 | 120 | 63.00 | 86.00 | 13.87 | 0.00 |
| 270 | 120 | 63.00 | 87.00 | 14.00 | 0.00 |
| 271 | 120 | 63.00 | 88.00 | 14.14 | 0.00 |
| 272 | 120 | 63.00 | 89.00 | 14.28 | 0.00 |
| 273 | 120 | 63.00 | 90.00 | 14.42 | 0.00 |
| 274 | 120 | 63.00 | 91.00 | 14.56 | 0.00 |
| 275 | 120 | 63.00 | 92.00 | 14.69 | 0.00 |
| 276 | 120 | 63.00 | 93.00 | 14.83 | 0.00 |
| 277 | 120 | 63.00 | 94.00 | 14.97 | 0.00 |
| 278 | 120 | 63.00 | 95.00 | 15.11 | 0.00 |
| 279 | 120 | 63.00 | 96.00 | 15.25 | 0.00 |
| 280 | 120 | 63.00 | 97.00 | 15.38 | 0.00 |
| 281 | 120 | 63.00 | 98.00 | 15.52 | 0.00 |
| 282 | 120 | 63.00 | 99.00 | 15.66 | 0.00 |
| 283 | 120 | 63.00 | 100.00 | 15.80 | 0.00 |
| 284 | 120 | 63.00 | 101.00 | 15.94 | 0.00 |
| 285 | 120 | 63.00 | 102.00 | 16.07 | 0.00 |
| 286 | 120 | 63.00 | 103.00 | 16.21 | 0.00 |
| 287 | 120 | 63.00 | 104.00 | 16.35 | 0.00 |
| 288 | 120 | 63.00 | 105.00 | 16.49 | 0.00 |
| 289 | 120 | 63.00 | 106.00 | 16.63 | 0.00 |
| 290 | 120 | 63.00 | 107.00 | 16.76 | 0.00 |
| 291 | 120 | 63.00 | 108.00 | 16.90 | 0.00 |
| 292 | 120 | 63.00 | 109.00 | 17.04 | 0.00 |
| 293 | 120 | 63.00 | 110.00 | 17.18 | 0.00 |
| 294 | 120 | 63.00 | 111.00 | 17.32 | 0.00 |
| 295 | 120 | 63.00 | 112.00 | 17.45 | 0.00 |
| 296 | 120 | 63.00 | 113.00 | 17.59 | 0.00 |
| 297 | 120 | 63.00 | 114.00 | 17.73 | 0.00 |
| 298 | 120 | 63.00 | 115.00 | 17.87 | 0.00 |
| 299 | 120 | 63.00 | 116.00 | 18.01 | 0.00 |
| 300 | 120 | 63.00 | 117.00 | 18.14 | 0.00 |
| 301 | 120 | 63.00 | 118.00 | 18.28 | 0.00 |
| 302 | 120 | 63.00 | 119.00 | 18.42 | 0.00 |
| 303 | 120 | 63.00 | 120.00 | 18.56 | 0.00 |
| 304 | 120 | 63.00 | 121.00 | 18.70 | 0.00 |
| 305 | 120 | 63.00 | 122.00 | 18.83 | 0.00 |
| 306 | 120 | 63.00 | 123.00 | 18.97 | 0.00 |
| 307 | 120 | 63.00 | 124.00 | 19.11 | 0.00 |
| 308 | 120 | 63.00 | 125.00 | 19.25 | 0.00 |
| 309 | 120 | 63.00 | 126.00 | 19.39 | 0.00 |
| 310 | 120 | 63.00 | 127.00 | 19.52 | 0.00 |
| 311 | 120 | 63.00 | 128.00 | 19.66 | 0.00 |
| 312 | 120 | 63.00 | 129.00 | 19.80 | 0.00 |
| 313 | 120 | 63.00 | 130.00 | 19.94 | 0.00 |
| 314 | 120 | 63.00 | 131.00 | 20.08 | 0.00 |
| 315 | 120 | 63.00 | 132.00 | 20.21 | 0.00 |
| 316 | 120 | 63.00 | 133.00 | 20.35 | 0.00 |
| 317 | 120 | 63.00 | 134.00 | 20.49 | 0.00 |
| 318 | 120 | 63.00 | 135.00 | 20.63 | 0.00 |
| 319 | 120 | 63.00 | 136.00 | 20.77 | 0.00 |

**Weekly table**                                             **Table letter C**

| Employee's earnings up to and including the UEL | Earnings at the LEL (where earnings are equal to or exceed the LEL) | Earnings above the LEL, up to and including the PT | Earnings above the PT, up to and including the UEL | Employer's NICs due on all earnings above the ST | Employee's NICs due on all earnings above the PT |
|---|---|---|---|---|---|
| | 1a | 1b | 1c | 1d | 1e |
| £ | £ | £ p | £ p | £ p | £ p |
| 320 | 120 | 63.00 | 137.00 | 20.90 | 0.00 |
| 321 | 120 | 63.00 | 138.00 | 21.04 | 0.00 |
| 322 | 120 | 63.00 | 139.00 | 21.18 | 0.00 |
| 323 | 120 | 63.00 | 140.00 | 21.32 | 0.00 |
| 324 | 120 | 63.00 | 141.00 | 21.46 | 0.00 |
| 325 | 120 | 63.00 | 142.00 | 21.59 | 0.00 |
| 326 | 120 | 63.00 | 143.00 | 21.73 | 0.00 |
| 327 | 120 | 63.00 | 144.00 | 21.87 | 0.00 |
| 328 | 120 | 63.00 | 145.00 | 22.01 | 0.00 |
| 329 | 120 | 63.00 | 146.00 | 22.15 | 0.00 |
| 330 | 120 | 63.00 | 147.00 | 22.28 | 0.00 |
| 331 | 120 | 63.00 | 148.00 | 22.42 | 0.00 |
| 332 | 120 | 63.00 | 149.00 | 22.56 | 0.00 |
| 333 | 120 | 63.00 | 150.00 | 22.70 | 0.00 |
| 334 | 120 | 63.00 | 151.00 | 22.84 | 0.00 |
| 335 | 120 | 63.00 | 152.00 | 22.97 | 0.00 |
| 336 | 120 | 63.00 | 153.00 | 23.11 | 0.00 |
| 337 | 120 | 63.00 | 154.00 | 23.25 | 0.00 |
| 338 | 120 | 63.00 | 155.00 | 23.39 | 0.00 |
| 339 | 120 | 63.00 | 156.00 | 23.53 | 0.00 |
| 340 | 120 | 63.00 | 157.00 | 23.66 | 0.00 |
| 341 | 120 | 63.00 | 158.00 | 23.80 | 0.00 |
| 342 | 120 | 63.00 | 159.00 | 23.94 | 0.00 |
| 343 | 120 | 63.00 | 160.00 | 24.08 | 0.00 |
| 344 | 120 | 63.00 | 161.00 | 24.22 | 0.00 |
| 345 | 120 | 63.00 | 162.00 | 24.35 | 0.00 |
| 346 | 120 | 63.00 | 163.00 | 24.49 | 0.00 |
| 347 | 120 | 63.00 | 164.00 | 24.63 | 0.00 |
| 348 | 120 | 63.00 | 165.00 | 24.77 | 0.00 |
| 349 | 120 | 63.00 | 166.00 | 24.91 | 0.00 |
| 350 | 120 | 63.00 | 167.00 | 25.04 | 0.00 |
| 351 | 120 | 63.00 | 168.00 | 25.18 | 0.00 |
| 352 | 120 | 63.00 | 169.00 | 25.32 | 0.00 |
| 353 | 120 | 63.00 | 170.00 | 25.46 | 0.00 |
| 354 | 120 | 63.00 | 171.00 | 25.60 | 0.00 |
| 355 | 120 | 63.00 | 172.00 | 25.73 | 0.00 |
| 356 | 120 | 63.00 | 173.00 | 25.87 | 0.00 |
| 357 | 120 | 63.00 | 174.00 | 26.01 | 0.00 |
| 358 | 120 | 63.00 | 175.00 | 26.15 | 0.00 |
| 359 | 120 | 63.00 | 176.00 | 26.29 | 0.00 |
| 360 | 120 | 63.00 | 177.00 | 26.42 | 0.00 |
| 361 | 120 | 63.00 | 178.00 | 26.56 | 0.00 |
| 362 | 120 | 63.00 | 179.00 | 26.70 | 0.00 |
| 363 | 120 | 63.00 | 180.00 | 26.84 | 0.00 |
| 364 | 120 | 63.00 | 181.00 | 26.98 | 0.00 |
| 365 | 120 | 63.00 | 182.00 | 27.11 | 0.00 |
| 366 | 120 | 63.00 | 183.00 | 27.25 | 0.00 |
| 367 | 120 | 63.00 | 184.00 | 27.39 | 0.00 |
| 368 | 120 | 63.00 | 185.00 | 27.53 | 0.00 |
| 369 | 120 | 63.00 | 186.00 | 27.67 | 0.00 |
| 370 | 120 | 63.00 | 187.00 | 27.80 | 0.00 |
| 371 | 120 | 63.00 | 188.00 | 27.94 | 0.00 |
| 372 | 120 | 63.00 | 189.00 | 28.08 | 0.00 |
| 373 | 120 | 63.00 | 190.00 | 28.22 | 0.00 |
| 374 | 120 | 63.00 | 191.00 | 28.36 | 0.00 |

**Weekly table**                                                                                           **Table letter C**

| Employee's earnings up to and including the UEL | Earnings at the LEL (where earnings are equal to or exceed the LEL) | Earnings above the LEL, up to and including the PT | Earnings above the PT, up to and including the UEL | Employer's NICs due on all earnings above the ST | Employee's NICs due on all earnings above the PT |
|---|---|---|---|---|---|
| | | 1a | 1b | 1c | 1d | 1e |
| £ | £ | £ p | £ p | £ p | £ p |
| 375 | 120 | 63.00 | 192.00 | 28.49 | 0.00 |
| 376 | 120 | 63.00 | 193.00 | 28.63 | 0.00 |
| 377 | 120 | 63.00 | 194.00 | 28.77 | 0.00 |
| 378 | 120 | 63.00 | 195.00 | 28.91 | 0.00 |
| 379 | 120 | 63.00 | 196.00 | 29.05 | 0.00 |
| 380 | 120 | 63.00 | 197.00 | 29.18 | 0.00 |
| 381 | 120 | 63.00 | 198.00 | 29.32 | 0.00 |
| 382 | 120 | 63.00 | 199.00 | 29.46 | 0.00 |
| 383 | 120 | 63.00 | 200.00 | 29.60 | 0.00 |
| 384 | 120 | 63.00 | 201.00 | 29.74 | 0.00 |
| 385 | 120 | 63.00 | 202.00 | 29.87 | 0.00 |
| 386 | 120 | 63.00 | 203.00 | 30.01 | 0.00 |
| 387 | 120 | 63.00 | 204.00 | 30.15 | 0.00 |
| 388 | 120 | 63.00 | 205.00 | 30.29 | 0.00 |
| 389 | 120 | 63.00 | 206.00 | 30.43 | 0.00 |
| 390 | 120 | 63.00 | 207.00 | 30.56 | 0.00 |
| 391 | 120 | 63.00 | 208.00 | 30.70 | 0.00 |
| 392 | 120 | 63.00 | 209.00 | 30.84 | 0.00 |
| 393 | 120 | 63.00 | 210.00 | 30.98 | 0.00 |
| 394 | 120 | 63.00 | 211.00 | 31.12 | 0.00 |
| 395 | 120 | 63.00 | 212.00 | 31.25 | 0.00 |
| 396 | 120 | 63.00 | 213.00 | 31.39 | 0.00 |
| 397 | 120 | 63.00 | 214.00 | 31.53 | 0.00 |
| 398 | 120 | 63.00 | 215.00 | 31.67 | 0.00 |
| 399 | 120 | 63.00 | 216.00 | 31.81 | 0.00 |
| 400 | 120 | 63.00 | 217.00 | 31.94 | 0.00 |
| 401 | 120 | 63.00 | 218.00 | 32.08 | 0.00 |
| 402 | 120 | 63.00 | 219.00 | 32.22 | 0.00 |
| 403 | 120 | 63.00 | 220.00 | 32.36 | 0.00 |
| 404 | 120 | 63.00 | 221.00 | 32.50 | 0.00 |
| 405 | 120 | 63.00 | 222.00 | 32.63 | 0.00 |
| 406 | 120 | 63.00 | 223.00 | 32.77 | 0.00 |
| 407 | 120 | 63.00 | 224.00 | 32.91 | 0.00 |
| 408 | 120 | 63.00 | 225.00 | 33.05 | 0.00 |
| 409 | 120 | 63.00 | 226.00 | 33.19 | 0.00 |
| 410 | 120 | 63.00 | 227.00 | 33.32 | 0.00 |
| 411 | 120 | 63.00 | 228.00 | 33.46 | 0.00 |
| 412 | 120 | 63.00 | 229.00 | 33.60 | 0.00 |
| 413 | 120 | 63.00 | 230.00 | 33.74 | 0.00 |
| 414 | 120 | 63.00 | 231.00 | 33.88 | 0.00 |
| 415 | 120 | 63.00 | 232.00 | 34.01 | 0.00 |
| 416 | 120 | 63.00 | 233.00 | 34.15 | 0.00 |
| 417 | 120 | 63.00 | 234.00 | 34.29 | 0.00 |
| 418 | 120 | 63.00 | 235.00 | 34.43 | 0.00 |
| 419 | 120 | 63.00 | 236.00 | 34.57 | 0.00 |
| 420 | 120 | 63.00 | 237.00 | 34.70 | 0.00 |
| 421 | 120 | 63.00 | 238.00 | 34.84 | 0.00 |
| 422 | 120 | 63.00 | 239.00 | 34.98 | 0.00 |
| 423 | 120 | 63.00 | 240.00 | 35.12 | 0.00 |
| 424 | 120 | 63.00 | 241.00 | 35.26 | 0.00 |
| 425 | 120 | 63.00 | 242.00 | 35.39 | 0.00 |
| 426 | 120 | 63.00 | 243.00 | 35.53 | 0.00 |
| 427 | 120 | 63.00 | 244.00 | 35.67 | 0.00 |
| 428 | 120 | 63.00 | 245.00 | 35.81 | 0.00 |
| 429 | 120 | 63.00 | 246.00 | 35.95 | 0.00 |

**Weekly table**                                                                                    **Table letter C**

| Employee's earnings up to and including the UEL | Earnings at the LEL (where earnings are equal to or exceed the LEL) | Earnings above the LEL, up to and including the PT | Earnings above the PT, up to and including the UEL | Employer's NICs due on all earnings above the ST | Employee's NICs due on all earnings above the PT |
|---|---|---|---|---|---|
| 1a | 1b | 1c | 1d | 1e |
| £ | £ | £ p | £ p | £ p | £ p |
| 430 | 120 | 63.00 | 247.00 | 36.08 | 0.00 |
| 431 | 120 | 63.00 | 248.00 | 36.22 | 0.00 |
| 432 | 120 | 63.00 | 249.00 | 36.36 | 0.00 |
| 433 | 120 | 63.00 | 250.00 | 36.50 | 0.00 |
| 434 | 120 | 63.00 | 251.00 | 36.64 | 0.00 |
| 435 | 120 | 63.00 | 252.00 | 36.77 | 0.00 |
| 436 | 120 | 63.00 | 253.00 | 36.91 | 0.00 |
| 437 | 120 | 63.00 | 254.00 | 37.05 | 0.00 |
| 438 | 120 | 63.00 | 255.00 | 37.19 | 0.00 |
| 439 | 120 | 63.00 | 256.00 | 37.33 | 0.00 |
| 440 | 120 | 63.00 | 257.00 | 37.46 | 0.00 |
| 441 | 120 | 63.00 | 258.00 | 37.60 | 0.00 |
| 442 | 120 | 63.00 | 259.00 | 37.74 | 0.00 |
| 443 | 120 | 63.00 | 260.00 | 37.88 | 0.00 |
| 444 | 120 | 63.00 | 261.00 | 38.02 | 0.00 |
| 445 | 120 | 63.00 | 262.00 | 38.15 | 0.00 |
| 446 | 120 | 63.00 | 263.00 | 38.29 | 0.00 |
| 447 | 120 | 63.00 | 264.00 | 38.43 | 0.00 |
| 448 | 120 | 63.00 | 265.00 | 38.57 | 0.00 |
| 449 | 120 | 63.00 | 266.00 | 38.71 | 0.00 |
| 450 | 120 | 63.00 | 267.00 | 38.84 | 0.00 |
| 451 | 120 | 63.00 | 268.00 | 38.98 | 0.00 |
| 452 | 120 | 63.00 | 269.00 | 39.12 | 0.00 |
| 453 | 120 | 63.00 | 270.00 | 39.26 | 0.00 |
| 454 | 120 | 63.00 | 271.00 | 39.40 | 0.00 |
| 455 | 120 | 63.00 | 272.00 | 39.53 | 0.00 |
| 456 | 120 | 63.00 | 273.00 | 39.67 | 0.00 |
| 457 | 120 | 63.00 | 274.00 | 39.81 | 0.00 |
| 458 | 120 | 63.00 | 275.00 | 39.95 | 0.00 |
| 459 | 120 | 63.00 | 276.00 | 40.09 | 0.00 |
| 460 | 120 | 63.00 | 277.00 | 40.22 | 0.00 |
| 461 | 120 | 63.00 | 278.00 | 40.36 | 0.00 |
| 462 | 120 | 63.00 | 279.00 | 40.50 | 0.00 |
| 463 | 120 | 63.00 | 280.00 | 40.64 | 0.00 |
| 464 | 120 | 63.00 | 281.00 | 40.78 | 0.00 |
| 465 | 120 | 63.00 | 282.00 | 40.91 | 0.00 |
| 466 | 120 | 63.00 | 283.00 | 41.05 | 0.00 |
| 467 | 120 | 63.00 | 284.00 | 41.19 | 0.00 |
| 468 | 120 | 63.00 | 285.00 | 41.33 | 0.00 |
| 469 | 120 | 63.00 | 286.00 | 41.47 | 0.00 |
| 470 | 120 | 63.00 | 287.00 | 41.60 | 0.00 |
| 471 | 120 | 63.00 | 288.00 | 41.74 | 0.00 |
| 472 | 120 | 63.00 | 289.00 | 41.88 | 0.00 |
| 473 | 120 | 63.00 | 290.00 | 42.02 | 0.00 |
| 474 | 120 | 63.00 | 291.00 | 42.16 | 0.00 |
| 475 | 120 | 63.00 | 292.00 | 42.29 | 0.00 |
| 476 | 120 | 63.00 | 293.00 | 42.43 | 0.00 |
| 477 | 120 | 63.00 | 294.00 | 42.57 | 0.00 |
| 478 | 120 | 63.00 | 295.00 | 42.71 | 0.00 |
| 479 | 120 | 63.00 | 296.00 | 42.85 | 0.00 |
| 480 | 120 | 63.00 | 297.00 | 42.98 | 0.00 |
| 481 | 120 | 63.00 | 298.00 | 43.12 | 0.00 |
| 482 | 120 | 63.00 | 299.00 | 43.26 | 0.00 |
| 483 | 120 | 63.00 | 300.00 | 43.40 | 0.00 |
| 484 | 120 | 63.00 | 301.00 | 43.54 | 0.00 |

**Weekly table**

**Table letter C**

| Employee's earnings up to and including the UEL | Earnings at the LEL (where earnings are equal to or exceed the LEL) | Earnings above the LEL, up to and including the PT | Earnings above the PT, up to and including the UEL | Employer's NICs due on all earnings above the ST | Employee's NICs due on all earnings above the PT |
|---|---|---|---|---|---|
| 1a | 1b | 1c | 1d | 1e | |
| £ | £ | £ p | £ p | £ p | £ p |
| 485 | 120 | 63.00 | 302.00 | 43.67 | 0.00 |
| 486 | 120 | 63.00 | 303.00 | 43.81 | 0.00 |
| 487 | 120 | 63.00 | 304.00 | 43.95 | 0.00 |
| 488 | 120 | 63.00 | 305.00 | 44.09 | 0.00 |
| 489 | 120 | 63.00 | 306.00 | 44.23 | 0.00 |
| 490 | 120 | 63.00 | 307.00 | 44.36 | 0.00 |
| 491 | 120 | 63.00 | 308.00 | 44.50 | 0.00 |
| 492 | 120 | 63.00 | 309.00 | 44.64 | 0.00 |
| 493 | 120 | 63.00 | 310.00 | 44.78 | 0.00 |
| 494 | 120 | 63.00 | 311.00 | 44.92 | 0.00 |
| 495 | 120 | 63.00 | 312.00 | 45.05 | 0.00 |
| 496 | 120 | 63.00 | 313.00 | 45.19 | 0.00 |
| 497 | 120 | 63.00 | 314.00 | 45.33 | 0.00 |
| 498 | 120 | 63.00 | 315.00 | 45.47 | 0.00 |
| 499 | 120 | 63.00 | 316.00 | 45.61 | 0.00 |
| 500 | 120 | 63.00 | 317.00 | 45.74 | 0.00 |
| 501 | 120 | 63.00 | 318.00 | 45.88 | 0.00 |
| 502 | 120 | 63.00 | 319.00 | 46.02 | 0.00 |
| 503 | 120 | 63.00 | 320.00 | 46.16 | 0.00 |
| 504 | 120 | 63.00 | 321.00 | 46.30 | 0.00 |
| 505 | 120 | 63.00 | 322.00 | 46.43 | 0.00 |
| 506 | 120 | 63.00 | 323.00 | 46.57 | 0.00 |
| 507 | 120 | 63.00 | 324.00 | 46.71 | 0.00 |
| 508 | 120 | 63.00 | 325.00 | 46.85 | 0.00 |
| 509 | 120 | 63.00 | 326.00 | 46.99 | 0.00 |
| 510 | 120 | 63.00 | 327.00 | 47.12 | 0.00 |
| 511 | 120 | 63.00 | 328.00 | 47.26 | 0.00 |
| 512 | 120 | 63.00 | 329.00 | 47.40 | 0.00 |
| 513 | 120 | 63.00 | 330.00 | 47.54 | 0.00 |
| 514 | 120 | 63.00 | 331.00 | 47.68 | 0.00 |
| 515 | 120 | 63.00 | 332.00 | 47.81 | 0.00 |
| 516 | 120 | 63.00 | 333.00 | 47.95 | 0.00 |
| 517 | 120 | 63.00 | 334.00 | 48.09 | 0.00 |
| 518 | 120 | 63.00 | 335.00 | 48.23 | 0.00 |
| 519 | 120 | 63.00 | 336.00 | 48.37 | 0.00 |
| 520 | 120 | 63.00 | 337.00 | 48.50 | 0.00 |
| 521 | 120 | 63.00 | 338.00 | 48.64 | 0.00 |
| 522 | 120 | 63.00 | 339.00 | 48.78 | 0.00 |
| 523 | 120 | 63.00 | 340.00 | 48.92 | 0.00 |
| 524 | 120 | 63.00 | 341.00 | 49.06 | 0.00 |
| 525 | 120 | 63.00 | 342.00 | 49.19 | 0.00 |
| 526 | 120 | 63.00 | 343.00 | 49.33 | 0.00 |
| 527 | 120 | 63.00 | 344.00 | 49.47 | 0.00 |
| 528 | 120 | 63.00 | 345.00 | 49.61 | 0.00 |
| 529 | 120 | 63.00 | 346.00 | 49.75 | 0.00 |
| 530 | 120 | 63.00 | 347.00 | 49.88 | 0.00 |
| 531 | 120 | 63.00 | 348.00 | 50.02 | 0.00 |
| 532 | 120 | 63.00 | 349.00 | 50.16 | 0.00 |
| 533 | 120 | 63.00 | 350.00 | 50.30 | 0.00 |
| 534 | 120 | 63.00 | 351.00 | 50.44 | 0.00 |
| 535 | 120 | 63.00 | 352.00 | 50.57 | 0.00 |
| 536 | 120 | 63.00 | 353.00 | 50.71 | 0.00 |
| 537 | 120 | 63.00 | 354.00 | 50.85 | 0.00 |
| 538 | 120 | 63.00 | 355.00 | 50.99 | 0.00 |
| 539 | 120 | 63.00 | 356.00 | 51.13 | 0.00 |

**Weekly table**

**Table letter C**

| Employee's earnings up to and including the UEL | Earnings at the LEL (where earnings are equal to or exceed the LEL) | Earnings above the LEL, up to and including the PT | Earnings above the PT, up to and including the UEL | Employer's NICs due on all earnings above the ST | Employee's NICs due on all earnings above the PT |
|---|---|---|---|---|---|
| | 1a | 1b | 1c | 1d | 1e |
| £ | £ | £ p | £ p | £ p | £ p |
| 540 | 120 | 63.00 | 357.00 | 51.26 | 0.00 |
| 541 | 120 | 63.00 | 358.00 | 51.40 | 0.00 |
| 542 | 120 | 63.00 | 359.00 | 51.54 | 0.00 |
| 543 | 120 | 63.00 | 360.00 | 51.68 | 0.00 |
| 544 | 120 | 63.00 | 361.00 | 51.82 | 0.00 |
| 545 | 120 | 63.00 | 362.00 | 51.95 | 0.00 |
| 546 | 120 | 63.00 | 363.00 | 52.09 | 0.00 |
| 547 | 120 | 63.00 | 364.00 | 52.23 | 0.00 |
| 548 | 120 | 63.00 | 365.00 | 52.37 | 0.00 |
| 549 | 120 | 63.00 | 366.00 | 52.51 | 0.00 |
| 550 | 120 | 63.00 | 367.00 | 52.64 | 0.00 |
| 551 | 120 | 63.00 | 368.00 | 52.78 | 0.00 |
| 552 | 120 | 63.00 | 369.00 | 52.92 | 0.00 |
| 553 | 120 | 63.00 | 370.00 | 53.06 | 0.00 |
| 554 | 120 | 63.00 | 371.00 | 53.20 | 0.00 |
| 555 | 120 | 63.00 | 372.00 | 53.33 | 0.00 |
| 556 | 120 | 63.00 | 373.00 | 53.47 | 0.00 |
| 557 | 120 | 63.00 | 374.00 | 53.61 | 0.00 |
| 558 | 120 | 63.00 | 375.00 | 53.75 | 0.00 |
| 559 | 120 | 63.00 | 376.00 | 53.89 | 0.00 |
| 560 | 120 | 63.00 | 377.00 | 54.02 | 0.00 |
| 561 | 120 | 63.00 | 378.00 | 54.16 | 0.00 |
| 562 | 120 | 63.00 | 379.00 | 54.30 | 0.00 |
| 563 | 120 | 63.00 | 380.00 | 54.44 | 0.00 |
| 564 | 120 | 63.00 | 381.00 | 54.58 | 0.00 |
| 565 | 120 | 63.00 | 382.00 | 54.71 | 0.00 |
| 566 | 120 | 63.00 | 383.00 | 54.85 | 0.00 |
| 567 | 120 | 63.00 | 384.00 | 54.99 | 0.00 |
| 568 | 120 | 63.00 | 385.00 | 55.13 | 0.00 |
| 569 | 120 | 63.00 | 386.00 | 55.27 | 0.00 |
| 570 | 120 | 63.00 | 387.00 | 55.40 | 0.00 |
| 571 | 120 | 63.00 | 388.00 | 55.54 | 0.00 |
| 572 | 120 | 63.00 | 389.00 | 55.68 | 0.00 |
| 573 | 120 | 63.00 | 390.00 | 55.82 | 0.00 |
| 574 | 120 | 63.00 | 391.00 | 55.96 | 0.00 |
| 575 | 120 | 63.00 | 392.00 | 56.09 | 0.00 |
| 576 | 120 | 63.00 | 393.00 | 56.23 | 0.00 |
| 577 | 120 | 63.00 | 394.00 | 56.37 | 0.00 |
| 578 | 120 | 63.00 | 395.00 | 56.51 | 0.00 |
| 579 | 120 | 63.00 | 396.00 | 56.65 | 0.00 |
| 580 | 120 | 63.00 | 397.00 | 56.78 | 0.00 |
| 581 | 120 | 63.00 | 398.00 | 56.92 | 0.00 |
| 582 | 120 | 63.00 | 399.00 | 57.06 | 0.00 |
| 583 | 120 | 63.00 | 400.00 | 57.20 | 0.00 |
| 584 | 120 | 63.00 | 401.00 | 57.34 | 0.00 |
| 585 | 120 | 63.00 | 402.00 | 57.47 | 0.00 |
| 586 | 120 | 63.00 | 403.00 | 57.61 | 0.00 |
| 587 | 120 | 63.00 | 404.00 | 57.75 | 0.00 |
| 588 | 120 | 63.00 | 405.00 | 57.89 | 0.00 |
| 589 | 120 | 63.00 | 406.00 | 58.03 | 0.00 |
| 590 | 120 | 63.00 | 407.00 | 58.16 | 0.00 |
| 591 | 120 | 63.00 | 408.00 | 58.30 | 0.00 |
| 592 | 120 | 63.00 | 409.00 | 58.44 | 0.00 |
| 593 | 120 | 63.00 | 410.00 | 58.58 | 0.00 |
| 594 | 120 | 63.00 | 411.00 | 58.72 | 0.00 |

**Weekly table**

**Table letter C**

| Employee's earnings up to and including the UEL | Earnings at the LEL (where earnings are equal to or exceed the LEL) | Earnings above the LEL, up to and including the PT | Earnings above the PT, up to and including the UEL | Employer's NICs due on all earnings above the ST | Employee's NICs due on all earnings above the PT |
|---|---|---|---|---|---|
| | 1a | 1b | 1c | 1d | 1e |
| £ | £ | £ p | £ p | £ p | £ p |
| 595 | 120 | 63.00 | 412.00 | 58.85 | 0.00 |
| 596 | 120 | 63.00 | 413.00 | 58.99 | 0.00 |
| 597 | 120 | 63.00 | 414.00 | 59.13 | 0.00 |
| 598 | 120 | 63.00 | 415.00 | 59.27 | 0.00 |
| 599 | 120 | 63.00 | 416.00 | 59.41 | 0.00 |
| 600 | 120 | 63.00 | 417.00 | 59.54 | 0.00 |
| 601 | 120 | 63.00 | 418.00 | 59.68 | 0.00 |
| 602 | 120 | 63.00 | 419.00 | 59.82 | 0.00 |
| 603 | 120 | 63.00 | 420.00 | 59.96 | 0.00 |
| 604 | 120 | 63.00 | 421.00 | 60.10 | 0.00 |
| 605 | 120 | 63.00 | 422.00 | 60.23 | 0.00 |
| 606 | 120 | 63.00 | 423.00 | 60.37 | 0.00 |
| 607 | 120 | 63.00 | 424.00 | 60.51 | 0.00 |
| 608 | 120 | 63.00 | 425.00 | 60.65 | 0.00 |
| 609 | 120 | 63.00 | 426.00 | 60.79 | 0.00 |
| 610 | 120 | 63.00 | 427.00 | 60.92 | 0.00 |
| 611 | 120 | 63.00 | 428.00 | 61.06 | 0.00 |
| 612 | 120 | 63.00 | 429.00 | 61.20 | 0.00 |
| 613 | 120 | 63.00 | 430.00 | 61.34 | 0.00 |
| 614 | 120 | 63.00 | 431.00 | 61.48 | 0.00 |
| 615 | 120 | 63.00 | 432.00 | 61.61 | 0.00 |
| 616 | 120 | 63.00 | 433.00 | 61.75 | 0.00 |
| 617 | 120 | 63.00 | 434.00 | 61.89 | 0.00 |
| 618 | 120 | 63.00 | 435.00 | 62.03 | 0.00 |
| 619 | 120 | 63.00 | 436.00 | 62.17 | 0.00 |
| 620 | 120 | 63.00 | 437.00 | 62.30 | 0.00 |
| 621 | 120 | 63.00 | 438.00 | 62.44 | 0.00 |
| 622 | 120 | 63.00 | 439.00 | 62.58 | 0.00 |
| 623 | 120 | 63.00 | 440.00 | 62.72 | 0.00 |
| 624 | 120 | 63.00 | 441.00 | 62.86 | 0.00 |
| 625 | 120 | 63.00 | 442.00 | 62.99 | 0.00 |
| 626 | 120 | 63.00 | 443.00 | 63.13 | 0.00 |
| 627 | 120 | 63.00 | 444.00 | 63.27 | 0.00 |
| 628 | 120 | 63.00 | 445.00 | 63.41 | 0.00 |
| 629 | 120 | 63.00 | 446.00 | 63.55 | 0.00 |
| 630 | 120 | 63.00 | 447.00 | 63.68 | 0.00 |
| 631 | 120 | 63.00 | 448.00 | 63.82 | 0.00 |
| 632 | 120 | 63.00 | 449.00 | 63.96 | 0.00 |
| 633 | 120 | 63.00 | 450.00 | 64.10 | 0.00 |
| 634 | 120 | 63.00 | 451.00 | 64.24 | 0.00 |
| 635 | 120 | 63.00 | 452.00 | 64.37 | 0.00 |
| 636 | 120 | 63.00 | 453.00 | 64.51 | 0.00 |
| 637 | 120 | 63.00 | 454.00 | 64.65 | 0.00 |
| 638 | 120 | 63.00 | 455.00 | 64.79 | 0.00 |
| 639 | 120 | 63.00 | 456.00 | 64.93 | 0.00 |
| 640 | 120 | 63.00 | 457.00 | 65.06 | 0.00 |
| 641 | 120 | 63.00 | 458.00 | 65.20 | 0.00 |
| 642 | 120 | 63.00 | 459.00 | 65.34 | 0.00 |
| 643 | 120 | 63.00 | 460.00 | 65.48 | 0.00 |
| 644 | 120 | 63.00 | 461.00 | 65.62 | 0.00 |
| 645 | 120 | 63.00 | 462.00 | 65.75 | 0.00 |
| 646 | 120 | 63.00 | 463.00 | 65.89 | 0.00 |
| 647 | 120 | 63.00 | 464.00 | 66.03 | 0.00 |
| 648 | 120 | 63.00 | 465.00 | 66.17 | 0.00 |
| 649 | 120 | 63.00 | 466.00 | 66.31 | 0.00 |

**Weekly table**

**Table letter C**

| Employee's earnings up to and including the UEL | Earnings at the LEL (where earnings are equal to or exceed the LEL) | Earnings above the LEL, up to and including the PT | Earnings above the PT, up to and including the UEL | Employer's NICs due on all earnings above the ST | Employee's NICs due on all earnings above the PT |
|---|---|---|---|---|---|
| | | 1a | 1b | 1c | 1d | 1e |
| £ | £ | £ p | £ p | £ p | £ p |
| 650 | 120 | 63.00 | 467.00 | 66.44 | 0.00 |
| 651 | 120 | 63.00 | 468.00 | 66.58 | 0.00 |
| 652 | 120 | 63.00 | 469.00 | 66.72 | 0.00 |
| 653 | 120 | 63.00 | 470.00 | 66.86 | 0.00 |
| 654 | 120 | 63.00 | 471.00 | 67.00 | 0.00 |
| 655 | 120 | 63.00 | 472.00 | 67.13 | 0.00 |
| 656 | 120 | 63.00 | 473.00 | 67.27 | 0.00 |
| 657 | 120 | 63.00 | 474.00 | 67.41 | 0.00 |
| 658 | 120 | 63.00 | 475.00 | 67.55 | 0.00 |
| 659 | 120 | 63.00 | 476.00 | 67.69 | 0.00 |
| 660 | 120 | 63.00 | 477.00 | 67.82 | 0.00 |
| 661 | 120 | 63.00 | 478.00 | 67.96 | 0.00 |
| 662 | 120 | 63.00 | 479.00 | 68.10 | 0.00 |
| 663 | 120 | 63.00 | 480.00 | 68.24 | 0.00 |
| 664 | 120 | 63.00 | 481.00 | 68.38 | 0.00 |
| 665 | 120 | 63.00 | 482.00 | 68.51 | 0.00 |
| 666 | 120 | 63.00 | 483.00 | 68.65 | 0.00 |
| 667 | 120 | 63.00 | 484.00 | 68.79 | 0.00 |
| 668 | 120 | 63.00 | 485.00 | 68.93 | 0.00 |
| 669 | 120 | 63.00 | 486.00 | 69.07 | 0.00 |
| 670 | 120 | 63.00 | 487.00 | 69.20 | 0.00 |
| 671 | 120 | 63.00 | 488.00 | 69.34 | 0.00 |
| 672 | 120 | 63.00 | 489.00 | 69.48 | 0.00 |
| 673 | 120 | 63.00 | 490.00 | 69.62 | 0.00 |
| 674 | 120 | 63.00 | 491.00 | 69.76 | 0.00 |
| 675 | 120 | 63.00 | 492.00 | 69.89 | 0.00 |
| 676 | 120 | 63.00 | 493.00 | 70.03 | 0.00 |
| 677 | 120 | 63.00 | 494.00 | 70.17 | 0.00 |
| 678 | 120 | 63.00 | 495.00 | 70.31 | 0.00 |
| 679 | 120 | 63.00 | 496.00 | 70.45 | 0.00 |
| 680 | 120 | 63.00 | 497.00 | 70.58 | 0.00 |
| 681 | 120 | 63.00 | 498.00 | 70.72 | 0.00 |
| 682 | 120 | 63.00 | 499.00 | 70.86 | 0.00 |
| 683 | 120 | 63.00 | 500.00 | 71.00 | 0.00 |
| 684 | 120 | 63.00 | 501.00 | 71.14 | 0.00 |
| 685 | 120 | 63.00 | 502.00 | 71.27 | 0.00 |
| 686 | 120 | 63.00 | 503.00 | 71.41 | 0.00 |
| 687 | 120 | 63.00 | 504.00 | 71.55 | 0.00 |
| 688 | 120 | 63.00 | 505.00 | 71.69 | 0.00 |
| 689 | 120 | 63.00 | 506.00 | 71.83 | 0.00 |
| 690 | 120 | 63.00 | 507.00 | 71.96 | 0.00 |
| 691 | 120 | 63.00 | 508.00 | 72.10 | 0.00 |
| 692 | 120 | 63.00 | 509.00 | 72.24 | 0.00 |
| 693 | 120 | 63.00 | 510.00 | 72.38 | 0.00 |
| 694 | 120 | 63.00 | 511.00 | 72.52 | 0.00 |
| 695 | 120 | 63.00 | 512.00 | 72.65 | 0.00 |
| 696 | 120 | 63.00 | 513.00 | 72.79 | 0.00 |
| 697 | 120 | 63.00 | 514.00 | 72.93 | 0.00 |
| 698 | 120 | 63.00 | 515.00 | 73.07 | 0.00 |
| 699 | 120 | 63.00 | 516.00 | 73.21 | 0.00 |
| 700 | 120 | 63.00 | 517.00 | 73.34 | 0.00 |
| 701 | 120 | 63.00 | 518.00 | 73.48 | 0.00 |
| 702 | 120 | 63.00 | 519.00 | 73.62 | 0.00 |
| 703 | 120 | 63.00 | 520.00 | 73.76 | 0.00 |
| 704 | 120 | 63.00 | 521.00 | 73.90 | 0.00 |

**Weekly table**

**Table letter C**

| Employee's earnings up to and including the UEL | Earnings at the LEL (where earnings are equal to or exceed the LEL) | Earnings above the LEL, up to and including the PT | Earnings above the PT, up to and including the UEL | Employer's NICs due on all earnings above the ST | Employee's NICs due on all earnings above the PT |
|---|---|---|---|---|---|
| 1a | 1b | 1c | 1d | 1e | |
| £ | £ | £ p | £ p | £ p | £ p |
| 705 | 120 | 63.00 | 522.00 | 74.03 | 0.00 |
| 706 | 120 | 63.00 | 523.00 | 74.17 | 0.00 |
| 707 | 120 | 63.00 | 524.00 | 74.31 | 0.00 |
| 708 | 120 | 63.00 | 525.00 | 74.45 | 0.00 |
| 709 | 120 | 63.00 | 526.00 | 74.59 | 0.00 |
| 710 | 120 | 63.00 | 527.00 | 74.72 | 0.00 |
| 711 | 120 | 63.00 | 528.00 | 74.86 | 0.00 |
| 712 | 120 | 63.00 | 529.00 | 75.00 | 0.00 |
| 713 | 120 | 63.00 | 530.00 | 75.14 | 0.00 |
| 714 | 120 | 63.00 | 531.00 | 75.28 | 0.00 |
| 715 | 120 | 63.00 | 532.00 | 75.41 | 0.00 |
| 716 | 120 | 63.00 | 533.00 | 75.55 | 0.00 |
| 717 | 120 | 63.00 | 534.00 | 75.69 | 0.00 |
| 718 | 120 | 63.00 | 535.00 | 75.83 | 0.00 |
| 719 | 120 | 63.00 | 536.00 | 75.97 | 0.00 |
| 720 | 120 | 63.00 | 537.00 | 76.10 | 0.00 |
| 721 | 120 | 63.00 | 538.00 | 76.24 | 0.00 |
| 722 | 120 | 63.00 | 539.00 | 76.38 | 0.00 |
| 723 | 120 | 63.00 | 540.00 | 76.52 | 0.00 |
| 724 | 120 | 63.00 | 541.00 | 76.66 | 0.00 |
| 725 | 120 | 63.00 | 542.00 | 76.79 | 0.00 |
| 726 | 120 | 63.00 | 543.00 | 76.93 | 0.00 |
| 727 | 120 | 63.00 | 544.00 | 77.07 | 0.00 |
| 728 | 120 | 63.00 | 545.00 | 77.21 | 0.00 |
| 729 | 120 | 63.00 | 546.00 | 77.35 | 0.00 |
| 730 | 120 | 63.00 | 547.00 | 77.48 | 0.00 |
| 731 | 120 | 63.00 | 548.00 | 77.62 | 0.00 |
| 732 | 120 | 63.00 | 549.00 | 77.76 | 0.00 |
| 733 | 120 | 63.00 | 550.00 | 77.90 | 0.00 |
| 734 | 120 | 63.00 | 551.00 | 78.04 | 0.00 |
| 735 | 120 | 63.00 | 552.00 | 78.17 | 0.00 |
| 736 | 120 | 63.00 | 553.00 | 78.31 | 0.00 |
| 737 | 120 | 63.00 | 554.00 | 78.45 | 0.00 |
| 738 | 120 | 63.00 | 555.00 | 78.59 | 0.00 |
| 739 | 120 | 63.00 | 556.00 | 78.73 | 0.00 |
| 740 | 120 | 63.00 | 557.00 | 78.86 | 0.00 |
| 741 | 120 | 63.00 | 558.00 | 79.00 | 0.00 |
| 742 | 120 | 63.00 | 559.00 | 79.14 | 0.00 |
| 743 | 120 | 63.00 | 560.00 | 79.28 | 0.00 |
| 744 | 120 | 63.00 | 561.00 | 79.42 | 0.00 |
| 745 | 120 | 63.00 | 562.00 | 79.55 | 0.00 |
| 746 | 120 | 63.00 | 563.00 | 79.69 | 0.00 |
| 747 | 120 | 63.00 | 564.00 | 79.83 | 0.00 |
| 748 | 120 | 63.00 | 565.00 | 79.97 | 0.00 |
| 749 | 120 | 63.00 | 566.00 | 80.11 | 0.00 |
| 750 | 120 | 63.00 | 567.00 | 80.24 | 0.00 |
| 751 | 120 | 63.00 | 568.00 | 80.38 | 0.00 |
| 752 | 120 | 63.00 | 569.00 | 80.52 | 0.00 |
| 753 | 120 | 63.00 | 570.00 | 80.66 | 0.00 |
| 754 | 120 | 63.00 | 571.00 | 80.80 | 0.00 |
| 755 | 120 | 63.00 | 572.00 | 80.93 | 0.00 |
| 756 | 120 | 63.00 | 573.00 | 81.07 | 0.00 |
| 757 | 120 | 63.00 | 574.00 | 81.21 | 0.00 |
| 758 | 120 | 63.00 | 575.00 | 81.35 | 0.00 |
| 759 | 120 | 63.00 | 576.00 | 81.49 | 0.00 |

**Weekly table**

**Table letter C**

| Employee's earnings up to and including the UEL | Earnings at the LEL (where earnings are equal to or exceed the LEL) | Earnings above the LEL, up to and including the PT | Earnings above the PT, up to and including the UEL | Employer's NICs due on all earnings above the ST | Employee's NICs due on all earnings above the PT |
|---|---|---|---|---|---|
| | 1a | 1b | 1c | 1d | 1e |
| £ | £ | £ p | £ p | £ p | £ p |
| 760 | 120 | 63.00 | 577.00 | 81.62 | 0.00 |
| 761 | 120 | 63.00 | 578.00 | 81.76 | 0.00 |
| 762 | 120 | 63.00 | 579.00 | 81.90 | 0.00 |
| 763 | 120 | 63.00 | 580.00 | 82.04 | 0.00 |
| 764 | 120 | 63.00 | 581.00 | 82.18 | 0.00 |
| 765 | 120 | 63.00 | 582.00 | 82.31 | 0.00 |
| 766 | 120 | 63.00 | 583.00 | 82.45 | 0.00 |
| 767 | 120 | 63.00 | 584.00 | 82.59 | 0.00 |
| 768 | 120 | 63.00 | 585.00 | 82.73 | 0.00 |
| 769 | 120 | 63.00 | 586.00 | 82.87 | 0.00 |
| 770 | 120 | 63.00 | 587.00 | 83.00 | 0.00 |
| 771 | 120 | 63.00 | 588.00 | 83.14 | 0.00 |
| 772 | 120 | 63.00 | 589.00 | 83.28 | 0.00 |
| 773 | 120 | 63.00 | 590.00 | 83.42 | 0.00 |
| 774 | 120 | 63.00 | 591.00 | 83.56 | 0.00 |
| 775 | 120 | 63.00 | 592.00 | 83.69 | 0.00 |
| 776 | 120 | 63.00 | 593.00 | 83.83 | 0.00 |
| 777 | 120 | 63.00 | 594.00 | 83.97 | 0.00 |
| 778 | 120 | 63.00 | 595.00 | 84.11 | 0.00 |
| 779 | 120 | 63.00 | 596.00 | 84.25 | 0.00 |
| 780 | 120 | 63.00 | 597.00 | 84.38 | 0.00 |
| 781 | 120 | 63.00 | 598.00 | 84.52 | 0.00 |
| 782 | 120 | 63.00 | 599.00 | 84.66 | 0.00 |
| 783 | 120 | 63.00 | 600.00 | 84.80 | 0.00 |
| 784 | 120 | 63.00 | 601.00 | 84.94 | 0.00 |
| 785 | 120 | 63.00 | 602.00 | 85.07 | 0.00 |
| 786 | 120 | 63.00 | 603.00 | 85.21 | 0.00 |
| 787 | 120 | 63.00 | 604.00 | 85.35 | 0.00 |
| 788 | 120 | 63.00 | 605.00 | 85.49 | 0.00 |
| 789 | 120 | 63.00 | 606.00 | 85.63 | 0.00 |
| 790 | 120 | 63.00 | 607.00 | 85.76 | 0.00 |
| 791 | 120 | 63.00 | 608.00 | 85.90 | 0.00 |
| 792 | 120 | 63.00 | 609.00 | 86.04 | 0.00 |
| 793 | 120 | 63.00 | 610.00 | 86.18 | 0.00 |
| 794 | 120 | 63.00 | 611.00 | 86.32 | 0.00 |
| 795 | 120 | 63.00 | 612.00 | 86.45 | 0.00 |
| 796 | 120 | 63.00 | 613.00 | 86.59 | 0.00 |
| 797 | 120 | 63.00 | 614.00 | 86.73 | 0.00 |
| 798 | 120 | 63.00 | 615.00 | 86.87 | 0.00 |
| 799 | 120 | 63.00 | 616.00 | 87.01 | 0.00 |
| 800 | 120 | 63.00 | 617.00 | 87.14 | 0.00 |
| 801 | 120 | 63.00 | 618.00 | 87.28 | 0.00 |
| 802 | 120 | 63.00 | 619.00 | 87.42 | 0.00 |
| 803 | 120 | 63.00 | 620.00 | 87.56 | 0.00 |
| 804 | 120 | 63.00 | 621.00 | 87.70 | 0.00 |
| 805 | 120 | 63.00 | 622.00 | 87.83 | 0.00 |
| 806 | 120 | 63.00 | 623.00 | 87.97 | 0.00 |
| 807 | 120 | 63.00 | 624.00 | 88.11 | 0.00 |
| 808 | 120 | 63.00 | 625.00 | 88.25 | 0.00 |
| 809 | 120 | 63.00 | 626.00 | 88.39 | 0.00 |
| 810 | 120 | 63.00 | 627.00 | 88.52 | 0.00 |
| 811 | 120 | 63.00 | 628.00 | 88.66 | 0.00 |
| 812 | 120 | 63.00 | 629.00 | 88.80 | 0.00 |
| 813 | 120 | 63.00 | 630.00 | 88.94 | 0.00 |
| 814 | 120 | 63.00 | 631.00 | 89.08 | 0.00 |

**Weekly table**

| Employee's earnings up to and including the UEL | Earnings at the LEL (where earnings are equal to or exceed the LEL) | Earnings above the LEL, up to and including the PT | Earnings above the PT, up to and including the UEL | Employer's NICs due on all earnings above the ST | Employee's NICs due on all earnings above the PT |
|---|---|---|---|---|---|
| | 1a | 1b | 1c | 1d | 1e |
| £ | £ | £ p | £ p | £ p | £ p |
| 815 | 120 | 63.00 | 632.00 | 89.21 | 0.00 |
| 816 | 120 | 63.00 | 633.00 | 89.35 | 0.00 |
| 817 | 120 | 63.00 | 634.00 | 89.49 | 0.00 |
| 818 | 120 | 63.00 | 635.00 | 89.63 | 0.00 |
| 819 | 120 | 63.00 | 636.00 | 89.77 | 0.00 |
| 820 | 120 | 63.00 | 637.00 | 89.90 | 0.00 |
| 821 | 120 | 63.00 | 638.00 | 90.04 | 0.00 |
| 822 | 120 | 63.00 | 639.00 | 90.18 | 0.00 |
| 823 | 120 | 63.00 | 640.00 | 90.32 | 0.00 |
| 824 | 120 | 63.00 | 641.00 | 90.46 | 0.00 |
| 825 | 120 | 63.00 | 642.00 | 90.59 | 0.00 |
| 826 | 120 | 63.00 | 643.00 | 90.73 | 0.00 |
| 827 | 120 | 63.00 | 644.00 | 90.87 | 0.00 |
| 828 | 120 | 63.00 | 645.00 | 91.01 | 0.00 |
| 829 | 120 | 63.00 | 646.00 | 91.15 | 0.00 |
| 830 | 120 | 63.00 | 647.00 | 91.28 | 0.00 |
| 831 | 120 | 63.00 | 648.00 | 91.42 | 0.00 |
| 832 | 120 | 63.00 | 649.00 | 91.56 | 0.00 |
| 833 | 120 | 63.00 | 650.00 | 91.70 | 0.00 |
| 834 | 120 | 63.00 | 651.00 | 91.84 | 0.00 |
| 835 | 120 | 63.00 | 652.00 | 91.97 | 0.00 |
| 836 | 120 | 63.00 | 653.00 | 92.11 | 0.00 |
| 837 | 120 | 63.00 | 654.00 | 92.25 | 0.00 |
| 838 | 120 | 63.00 | 655.00 | 92.39 | 0.00 |
| 839 | 120 | 63.00 | 656.00 | 92.53 | 0.00 |
| 840 | 120 | 63.00 | 657.00 | 92.66 | 0.00 |
| 841 | 120 | 63.00 | 658.00 | 92.80 | 0.00 |
| 842 | 120 | 63.00 | 659.00 | 92.94 | 0.00 |
| 843 | 120 | 63.00 | 660.00 | 93.08 | 0.00 |
| 844 | 120 | 63.00 | 661.00 | 93.22 | 0.00 |
| 845 | 120 | 63.00 | 662.00 | 93.35 | 0.00 |
| 846 | 120 | 63.00 | 663.00 | 93.49 | 0.00 |
| 847 | 120 | 63.00 | 664.00 | 93.63 | 0.00 |
| 848 | 120 | 63.00 | 665.00 | 93.77 | 0.00 |
| 849 | 120 | 63.00 | 666.00 | 93.91 | 0.00 |
| 850 | 120 | 63.00 | 667.00 | 94.04 | 0.00 |
| 851 | 120 | 63.00 | 668.00 | 94.18 | 0.00 |
| 852 | 120 | 63.00 | 669.00 | 94.32 | 0.00 |
| 853 | 120 | 63.00 | 670.00 | 94.46 | 0.00 |
| 854 | 120 | 63.00 | 671.00 | 94.60 | 0.00 |
| 855 | 120 | 63.00 | 672.00 | 94.73 | 0.00 |
| 856 | 120 | 63.00 | 673.00 | 94.87 | 0.00 |
| 857 | 120 | 63.00 | 674.00 | 95.01 | 0.00 |
| 858 | 120 | 63.00 | 675.00 | 95.15 | 0.00 |
| 859 | 120 | 63.00 | 676.00 | 95.29 | 0.00 |
| 860 | 120 | 63.00 | 677.00 | 95.42 | 0.00 |
| 861 | 120 | 63.00 | 678.00 | 95.56 | 0.00 |
| 862 | 120 | 63.00 | 679.00 | 95.70 | 0.00 |
| 863 | 120 | 63.00 | 680.00 | 95.84 | 0.00 |
| 864 | 120 | 63.00 | 681.00 | 95.98 | 0.00 |
| 865 | 120 | 63.00 | 682.00 | 96.11 | 0.00 |
| 866 | 120 | 63.00 | 683.00 | 96.25 | 0.00 |
| 867 | 120 | 63.00 | 684.00 | 96.39 | 0.00 |
| 868 | 120 | 63.00 | 685.00 | 96.53 | 0.00 |
| 869 | 120 | 63.00 | 686.00 | 96.67 | 0.00 |

**Weekly table**

| Employee's earnings up to and including the UEL | Earnings at the LEL (where earnings are equal to or exceed the LEL) | Earnings above the LEL, up to and including the PT | Earnings above the PT, up to and including the UEL | Employer's NICs due on all earnings above the ST | Employee's NICs due on all earnings above the PT |
|---|---|---|---|---|---|
| | 1a | 1b | 1c | 1d | 1e |
| £ | £ | £ p | £ p | £ p | £ p |
| 870 | 120 | 63.00 | 687.00 | 96.80 | 0.00 |
| 871 | 120 | 63.00 | 688.00 | 96.94 | 0.00 |
| 872 | 120 | 63.00 | 689.00 | 97.08 | 0.00 |
| 873 | 120 | 63.00 | 690.00 | 97.22 | 0.00 |
| 874 | 120 | 63.00 | 691.00 | 97.36 | 0.00 |
| 875 | 120 | 63.00 | 692.00 | 97.49 | 0.00 |
| 876 | 120 | 63.00 | 693.00 | 97.63 | 0.00 |
| 877 | 120 | 63.00 | 694.00 | 97.77 | 0.00 |
| 878 | 120 | 63.00 | 695.00 | 97.91 | 0.00 |
| 879 | 120 | 63.00 | 696.00 | 98.05 | 0.00 |
| 880 | 120 | 63.00 | 697.00 | 98.18 | 0.00 |
| 881 | 120 | 63.00 | 698.00 | 98.32 | 0.00 |
| 882 | 120 | 63.00 | 699.00 | 98.46 | 0.00 |
| 883 | 120 | 63.00 | 700.00 | 98.60 | 0.00 |
| 884 | 120 | 63.00 | 701.00 | 98.74 | 0.00 |
| 885 | 120 | 63.00 | 702.00 | 98.87 | 0.00 |
| 886 | 120 | 63.00 | 703.00 | 99.01 | 0.00 |
| 887 | 120 | 63.00 | 704.00 | 99.15 | 0.00 |
| 888 | 120 | 63.00 | 705.00 | 99.29 | 0.00 |
| 889 | 120 | 63.00 | 706.00 | 99.43 | 0.00 |
| 890 | 120 | 63.00 | 707.00 | 99.56 | 0.00 |
| 891 | 120 | 63.00 | 708.00 | 99.70 | 0.00 |
| 892 | 120 | 63.00 | 709.00 | 99.84 | 0.00 |
| 893 | 120 | 63.00 | 710.00 | 99.98 | 0.00 |
| 894 | 120 | 63.00 | 711.00 | 100.12 | 0.00 |
| 895 | 120 | 63.00 | 712.00 | 100.25 | 0.00 |
| 896 | 120 | 63.00 | 713.00 | 100.39 | 0.00 |
| 897 | 120 | 63.00 | 714.00 | 100.53 | 0.00 |
| 898 | 120 | 63.00 | 715.00 | 100.67 | 0.00 |
| 899 | 120 | 63.00 | 716.00 | 100.81 | 0.00 |
| 900 | 120 | 63.00 | 717.00 | 100.94 | 0.00 |
| 901 | 120 | 63.00 | 718.00 | 101.08 | 0.00 |
| 902 | 120 | 63.00 | 719.00 | 101.22 | 0.00 |
| 903 | 120 | 63.00 | 720.00 | 101.36 | 0.00 |
| 904 | 120 | 63.00 | 721.00 | 101.50 | 0.00 |
| 905 | 120 | 63.00 | 722.00 | 101.63 | 0.00 |
| 906 | 120 | 63.00 | 723.00 | 101.77 | 0.00 |
| 907 | 120 | 63.00 | 724.00 | 101.91 | 0.00 |
| 908 | 120 | 63.00 | 725.00 | 102.05 | 0.00 |
| 909 | 120 | 63.00 | 726.00 | 102.19 | 0.00 |
| 910 | 120 | 63.00 | 727.00 | 102.32 | 0.00 |
| 911 | 120 | 63.00 | 728.00 | 102.46 | 0.00 |
| 912 | 120 | 63.00 | 729.00 | 102.60 | 0.00 |
| 913 | 120 | 63.00 | 730.00 | 102.74 | 0.00 |
| 914 | 120 | 63.00 | 731.00 | 102.88 | 0.00 |
| 915 | 120 | 63.00 | 732.00 | 103.01 | 0.00 |
| 916 | 120 | 63.00 | 733.00 | 103.15 | 0.00 |
| 917 | 120 | 63.00 | 734.00 | 103.29 | 0.00 |
| 918 | 120 | 63.00 | 735.00 | 103.43 | 0.00 |
| 919 | 120 | 63.00 | 736.00 | 103.57 | 0.00 |
| 920 | 120 | 63.00 | 737.00 | 103.70 | 0.00 |
| 921 | 120 | 63.00 | 738.00 | 103.84 | 0.00 |
| 922 | 120 | 63.00 | 739.00 | 103.98 | 0.00 |
| 923 | 120 | 63.00 | 740.00 | 104.12 | 0.00 |
| 924 | 120 | 63.00 | 741.00 | 104.26 | 0.00 |

**Weekly table**

| Employee's earnings up to and including the UEL | Earnings at the LEL (where earnings are equal to or exceed the LEL) | Earnings above the LEL, up to and including the PT | Earnings above the PT, up to and including the UEL | Employer's NICs due on all earnings above the ST | Employee's NICs due on all earnings above the PT |
|---|---|---|---|---|---|
| | | 1a | 1b | 1c | 1d | 1e |
| £ | £ | £ p | £ p | £ p | £ p |
| 925 | 120 | 63.00 | 742.00 | 104.39 | 0.00 |
| 926 | 120 | 63.00 | 743.00 | 104.53 | 0.00 |
| 927 | 120 | 63.00 | 744.00 | 104.67 | 0.00 |
| 928 | 120 | 63.00 | 745.00 | 104.81 | 0.00 |
| 929 | 120 | 63.00 | 746.00 | 104.95 | 0.00 |
| 930 | 120 | 63.00 | 747.00 | 105.08 | 0.00 |
| 931 | 120 | 63.00 | 748.00 | 105.22 | 0.00 |
| 932 | 120 | 63.00 | 749.00 | 105.36 | 0.00 |
| 933 | 120 | 63.00 | 750.00 | 105.50 | 0.00 |
| 934 | 120 | 63.00 | 751.00 | 105.64 | 0.00 |
| 935 | 120 | 63.00 | 752.00 | 105.77 | 0.00 |
| 936 | 120 | 63.00 | 753.00 | 105.91 | 0.00 |
| 937 | 120 | 63.00 | 754.00 | 106.05 | 0.00 |
| 938 | 120 | 63.00 | 755.00 | 106.19 | 0.00 |
| 939 | 120 | 63.00 | 756.00 | 106.33 | 0.00 |
| 940 | 120 | 63.00 | 757.00 | 106.46 | 0.00 |
| 941 | 120 | 63.00 | 758.00 | 106.60 | 0.00 |
| 942 | 120 | 63.00 | 759.00 | 106.74 | 0.00 |
| 943 | 120 | 63.00 | 760.00 | 106.88 | 0.00 |
| 944 | 120 | 63.00 | 761.00 | 107.02 | 0.00 |
| 945 | 120 | 63.00 | 762.00 | 107.15 | 0.00 |
| 946 | 120 | 63.00 | 763.00 | 107.29 | 0.00 |
| 947 | 120 | 63.00 | 764.00 | 107.43 | 0.00 |
| 948 | 120 | 63.00 | 765.00 | 107.57 | 0.00 |
| 949 | 120 | 63.00 | 766.00 | 107.71 | 0.00 |
| 950 | 120 | 63.00 | 767.00 | 107.84 | 0.00 |
| 951 | 120 | 63.00 | 768.00 | 107.98 | 0.00 |
| 952 | 120 | 63.00 | 769.00 | 108.12 | 0.00 |
| 953 | 120 | 63.00 | 770.00 | 108.26 | 0.00 |
| 954 | 120 | 63.00 | 771.00 | 108.40 | 0.00 |
| 955 | 120 | 63.00 | 772.00 | 108.53 | 0.00 |
| 956 | 120 | 63.00 | 773.00 | 108.67 | 0.00 |
| 957 | 120 | 63.00 | 774.00 | 108.81 | 0.00 |
| 958 | 120 | 63.00 | 775.00 | 108.95 | 0.00 |
| 959 | 120 | 63.00 | 776.00 | 109.09 | 0.00 |
| 960 | 120 | 63.00 | 777.00 | 109.22 | 0.00 |
| 961 | 120 | 63.00 | 778.00 | 109.36 | 0.00 |
| 962 | 120 | 63.00 | 779.00 | 109.43 | 0.00 |

If the employee's gross pay is over £962, go to page 76.

## Monthly table for employees who are State Pension age or over – employer only NICs for use from 6 April 2020 to 5 April 2021

Use this table for employees who are State Pension age or over, for whom you hold a copy of either their birth certificate or passport as evidence of their date of birth.

### Filling in form RT11, 'Deductions working sheet' or substitute

1. Enter 'C' in the NICs category letter column on form RT11.
2. Copy the figures in columns 1a – 1e of the table to columns 1a – 1e on the line next to the tax month in which the employee is paid, on form RT11.

If the employee's total earnings fall between the LEL and the UEL and the exact gross pay is not shown in the table, use the next smaller figure shown. If the employee's total earnings exceed the UEL, see page 76.

The figures in the left-hand column of each table show steps between the LEL and the UEL. The NICs liability for each step, with the exception of the LEL, ST, PT and UEL, is worked out at the mid-point of the steps, so you and your employee may pay slightly more or less than if you used the exact percentage method.

| Employee's earnings up to and including the UEL | Earnings at the LEL (where earnings are equal to or exceed the LEL) | Earnings above the LEL, up to and including the PT | Earnings above the PT, up to and including the UEL | Employer's NICs due on all earnings above the ST | Employee's NICs due on all earnings above the PT |
|---|---|---|---|---|---|
| 1a | 1a | 1b | 1c | 1d | 1e |
| £ | £ | £  p | £  p | £  p | £  p |
| Up to and including £519.99 | No NICs liability, make no entries on form RT11 | | | | |
| 520 | 520 | 0.00 | 0.00 | 0.00 | 0.00 |
| 524 | 520 | 4.00 | 0.00 | 0.00 | 0.00 |
| 528 | 520 | 8.00 | 0.00 | 0.00 | 0.00 |
| 532 | 520 | 12.00 | 0.00 | 0.00 | 0.00 |
| 536 | 520 | 16.00 | 0.00 | 0.00 | 0.00 |
| 540 | 520 | 20.00 | 0.00 | 0.00 | 0.00 |
| 544 | 520 | 24.00 | 0.00 | 0.00 | 0.00 |
| 548 | 520 | 28.00 | 0.00 | 0.00 | 0.00 |
| 552 | 520 | 32.00 | 0.00 | 0.00 | 0.00 |
| 556 | 520 | 36.00 | 0.00 | 0.00 | 0.00 |
| 560 | 520 | 40.00 | 0.00 | 0.00 | 0.00 |
| 564 | 520 | 44.00 | 0.00 | 0.00 | 0.00 |
| 568 | 520 | 48.00 | 0.00 | 0.00 | 0.00 |
| 572 | 520 | 52.00 | 0.00 | 0.00 | 0.00 |
| 576 | 520 | 56.00 | 0.00 | 0.00 | 0.00 |
| 580 | 520 | 60.00 | 0.00 | 0.00 | 0.00 |
| 584 | 520 | 64.00 | 0.00 | 0.00 | 0.00 |
| 588 | 520 | 68.00 | 0.00 | 0.00 | 0.00 |
| 592 | 520 | 72.00 | 0.00 | 0.00 | 0.00 |
| 596 | 520 | 76.00 | 0.00 | 0.00 | 0.00 |
| 600 | 520 | 80.00 | 0.00 | 0.00 | 0.00 |
| 604 | 520 | 84.00 | 0.00 | 0.00 | 0.00 |
| 608 | 520 | 88.00 | 0.00 | 0.00 | 0.00 |
| 612 | 520 | 92.00 | 0.00 | 0.00 | 0.00 |
| 616 | 520 | 96.00 | 0.00 | 0.00 | 0.00 |
| 620 | 520 | 100.00 | 0.00 | 0.00 | 0.00 |
| 624 | 520 | 104.00 | 0.00 | 0.00 | 0.00 |
| 628 | 520 | 108.00 | 0.00 | 0.00 | 0.00 |
| 632 | 520 | 112.00 | 0.00 | 0.00 | 0.00 |
| 636 | 520 | 116.00 | 0.00 | 0.00 | 0.00 |
| 640 | 520 | 120.00 | 0.00 | 0.00 | 0.00 |
| 644 | 520 | 124.00 | 0.00 | 0.00 | 0.00 |
| 648 | 520 | 128.00 | 0.00 | 0.00 | 0.00 |
| 652 | 520 | 132.00 | 0.00 | 0.00 | 0.00 |
| 656 | 520 | 136.00 | 0.00 | 0.00 | 0.00 |

**Monthly table**

**Table letter C**

| Employee's earnings up to and including the UEL | Earnings at the LEL (where earnings are equal to or exceed the LEL) | Earnings above the LEL, up to and including the PT | Earnings above the PT, up to and including the UEL | Employer's NICs due on all earnings above the ST | Employee's NICs due on all earnings above the PT |
|---|---|---|---|---|---|
| | 1a | 1b | 1c | 1d | 1e |
| £ | £ | £ p | £ p | £ p | £ p |
| 660 | 520 | 140.00 | 0.00 | 0.00 | 0.00 |
| 664 | 520 | 144.00 | 0.00 | 0.00 | 0.00 |
| 668 | 520 | 148.00 | 0.00 | 0.00 | 0.00 |
| 672 | 520 | 152.00 | 0.00 | 0.00 | 0.00 |
| 676 | 520 | 156.00 | 0.00 | 0.00 | 0.00 |
| 680 | 520 | 160.00 | 0.00 | 0.00 | 0.00 |
| 684 | 520 | 164.00 | 0.00 | 0.00 | 0.00 |
| 688 | 520 | 168.00 | 0.00 | 0.00 | 0.00 |
| 692 | 520 | 172.00 | 0.00 | 0.00 | 0.00 |
| 696 | 520 | 176.00 | 0.00 | 0.00 | 0.00 |
| 700 | 520 | 180.00 | 0.00 | 0.00 | 0.00 |
| 704 | 520 | 184.00 | 0.00 | 0.00 | 0.00 |
| 708 | 520 | 188.00 | 0.00 | 0.00 | 0.00 |
| 712 | 520 | 192.00 | 0.00 | 0.00 | 0.00 |
| 716 | 520 | 196.00 | 0.00 | 0.00 | 0.00 |
| 720 | 520 | 200.00 | 0.00 | 0.00 | 0.00 |
| 724 | 520 | 204.00 | 0.00 | 0.00 | 0.00 |
| 728 | 520 | 208.00 | 0.00 | 0.00 | 0.00 |
| 732 | 520 | 212.00 | 0.00 | 0.00 | 0.00 |
| 736 | 520 | 216.00 | 0.00 | 0.83 | 0.00 |
| 740 | 520 | 220.00 | 0.00 | 1.38 | 0.00 |
| 744 | 520 | 224.00 | 0.00 | 1.93 | 0.00 |
| 748 | 520 | 228.00 | 0.00 | 2.48 | 0.00 |
| 752 | 520 | 232.00 | 0.00 | 3.04 | 0.00 |
| 756 | 520 | 236.00 | 0.00 | 3.59 | 0.00 |
| 760 | 520 | 240.00 | 0.00 | 4.14 | 0.00 |
| 764 | 520 | 244.00 | 0.00 | 4.69 | 0.00 |
| 768 | 520 | 248.00 | 0.00 | 5.24 | 0.00 |
| 772 | 520 | 252.00 | 0.00 | 5.80 | 0.00 |
| 776 | 520 | 256.00 | 0.00 | 6.35 | 0.00 |
| 780 | 520 | 260.00 | 0.00 | 6.90 | 0.00 |
| 784 | 520 | 264.00 | 0.00 | 7.45 | 0.00 |
| 788 | 520 | 268.00 | 0.00 | 8.00 | 0.00 |
| 792 | 520 | 272.00 | 0.00 | 8.28 | 0.00 |
| 796 | 520 | 272.00 | 4.00 | 9.11 | 0.00 |
| 800 | 520 | 272.00 | 8.00 | 9.66 | 0.00 |
| 804 | 520 | 272.00 | 12.00 | 10.21 | 0.00 |
| 808 | 520 | 272.00 | 16.00 | 10.76 | 0.00 |
| 812 | 520 | 272.00 | 20.00 | 11.32 | 0.00 |
| 816 | 520 | 272.00 | 24.00 | 11.87 | 0.00 |
| 820 | 520 | 272.00 | 28.00 | 12.42 | 0.00 |
| 824 | 520 | 272.00 | 32.00 | 12.97 | 0.00 |
| 828 | 520 | 272.00 | 36.00 | 13.52 | 0.00 |
| 832 | 520 | 272.00 | 40.00 | 14.08 | 0.00 |
| 836 | 520 | 272.00 | 44.00 | 14.63 | 0.00 |
| 840 | 520 | 272.00 | 48.00 | 15.18 | 0.00 |
| 844 | 520 | 272.00 | 52.00 | 15.73 | 0.00 |
| 848 | 520 | 272.00 | 56.00 | 16.28 | 0.00 |
| 852 | 520 | 272.00 | 60.00 | 16.84 | 0.00 |
| 856 | 520 | 272.00 | 64.00 | 17.39 | 0.00 |
| 860 | 520 | 272.00 | 68.00 | 17.94 | 0.00 |
| 864 | 520 | 272.00 | 72.00 | 18.49 | 0.00 |
| 868 | 520 | 272.00 | 76.00 | 19.04 | 0.00 |
| 872 | 520 | 272.00 | 80.00 | 19.60 | 0.00 |
| 876 | 520 | 272.00 | 84.00 | 20.15 | 0.00 |

**Monthly table**

| Employee's earnings up to and including the UEL | Earnings at the LEL (where earnings are equal to or exceed the LEL) 1a | Earnings above the LEL, up to and including the PT 1b | Earnings above the PT, up to and including the UEL 1c | Employer's NICs due on all earnings above the ST 1d | Employee's NICs due on all earnings above the PT 1e |
|---|---|---|---|---|---|
| £ | £ | £ p | £ p | £ p | £ p |
| 880 | 520 | 272.00 | 88.00 | 20.70 | 0.00 |
| 884 | 520 | 272.00 | 92.00 | 21.25 | 0.00 |
| 888 | 520 | 272.00 | 96.00 | 21.80 | 0.00 |
| 892 | 520 | 272.00 | 100.00 | 22.36 | 0.00 |
| 896 | 520 | 272.00 | 104.00 | 22.91 | 0.00 |
| 900 | 520 | 272.00 | 108.00 | 23.46 | 0.00 |
| 904 | 520 | 272.00 | 112.00 | 24.01 | 0.00 |
| 908 | 520 | 272.00 | 116.00 | 24.56 | 0.00 |
| 912 | 520 | 272.00 | 120.00 | 25.12 | 0.00 |
| 916 | 520 | 272.00 | 124.00 | 25.67 | 0.00 |
| 920 | 520 | 272.00 | 128.00 | 26.22 | 0.00 |
| 924 | 520 | 272.00 | 132.00 | 26.77 | 0.00 |
| 928 | 520 | 272.00 | 136.00 | 27.32 | 0.00 |
| 932 | 520 | 272.00 | 140.00 | 27.88 | 0.00 |
| 936 | 520 | 272.00 | 144.00 | 28.43 | 0.00 |
| 940 | 520 | 272.00 | 148.00 | 28.98 | 0.00 |
| 944 | 520 | 272.00 | 152.00 | 29.53 | 0.00 |
| 948 | 520 | 272.00 | 156.00 | 30.08 | 0.00 |
| 952 | 520 | 272.00 | 160.00 | 30.64 | 0.00 |
| 956 | 520 | 272.00 | 164.00 | 31.19 | 0.00 |
| 960 | 520 | 272.00 | 168.00 | 31.74 | 0.00 |
| 964 | 520 | 272.00 | 172.00 | 32.29 | 0.00 |
| 968 | 520 | 272.00 | 176.00 | 32.84 | 0.00 |
| 972 | 520 | 272.00 | 180.00 | 33.40 | 0.00 |
| 976 | 520 | 272.00 | 184.00 | 33.95 | 0.00 |
| 980 | 520 | 272.00 | 188.00 | 34.50 | 0.00 |
| 984 | 520 | 272.00 | 192.00 | 35.05 | 0.00 |
| 988 | 520 | 272.00 | 196.00 | 35.60 | 0.00 |
| 992 | 520 | 272.00 | 200.00 | 36.16 | 0.00 |
| 996 | 520 | 272.00 | 204.00 | 36.71 | 0.00 |
| 1000 | 520 | 272.00 | 208.00 | 37.26 | 0.00 |
| 1004 | 520 | 272.00 | 212.00 | 37.81 | 0.00 |
| 1008 | 520 | 272.00 | 216.00 | 38.36 | 0.00 |
| 1012 | 520 | 272.00 | 220.00 | 38.92 | 0.00 |
| 1016 | 520 | 272.00 | 224.00 | 39.47 | 0.00 |
| 1020 | 520 | 272.00 | 228.00 | 40.02 | 0.00 |
| 1024 | 520 | 272.00 | 232.00 | 40.57 | 0.00 |
| 1028 | 520 | 272.00 | 236.00 | 41.12 | 0.00 |
| 1032 | 520 | 272.00 | 240.00 | 41.68 | 0.00 |
| 1036 | 520 | 272.00 | 244.00 | 42.23 | 0.00 |
| 1040 | 520 | 272.00 | 248.00 | 42.78 | 0.00 |
| 1044 | 520 | 272.00 | 252.00 | 43.33 | 0.00 |
| 1048 | 520 | 272.00 | 256.00 | 43.88 | 0.00 |
| 1052 | 520 | 272.00 | 260.00 | 44.44 | 0.00 |
| 1056 | 520 | 272.00 | 264.00 | 44.99 | 0.00 |
| 1060 | 520 | 272.00 | 268.00 | 45.54 | 0.00 |
| 1064 | 520 | 272.00 | 272.00 | 46.09 | 0.00 |
| 1068 | 520 | 272.00 | 276.00 | 46.64 | 0.00 |
| 1072 | 520 | 272.00 | 280.00 | 47.20 | 0.00 |
| 1076 | 520 | 272.00 | 284.00 | 47.75 | 0.00 |
| 1080 | 520 | 272.00 | 288.00 | 48.30 | 0.00 |
| 1084 | 520 | 272.00 | 292.00 | 48.85 | 0.00 |
| 1088 | 520 | 272.00 | 296.00 | 49.40 | 0.00 |
| 1092 | 520 | 272.00 | 300.00 | 49.96 | 0.00 |
| 1096 | 520 | 272.00 | 304.00 | 50.51 | 0.00 |

## Monthly table

**Table letter C**

| Employee's earnings up to and including the UEL | Earnings at the LEL (where earnings are equal to or exceed the LEL) | Earnings above the LEL, up to and including the PT | Earnings above the PT, up to and including the UEL | Employer's NICs due on all earnings above the ST | Employee's NICs due on all earnings above the PT |
|---|---|---|---|---|---|
| | 1a | 1b | 1c | 1d | 1e |
| £ | £ | £ p | £ p | £ p | £ p |
| 1100 | 520 | 272.00 | 308.00 | 51.06 | 0.00 |
| 1104 | 520 | 272.00 | 312.00 | 51.61 | 0.00 |
| 1108 | 520 | 272.00 | 316.00 | 52.16 | 0.00 |
| 1112 | 520 | 272.00 | 320.00 | 52.72 | 0.00 |
| 1116 | 520 | 272.00 | 324.00 | 53.27 | 0.00 |
| 1120 | 520 | 272.00 | 328.00 | 53.82 | 0.00 |
| 1124 | 520 | 272.00 | 332.00 | 54.37 | 0.00 |
| 1128 | 520 | 272.00 | 336.00 | 54.92 | 0.00 |
| 1132 | 520 | 272.00 | 340.00 | 55.48 | 0.00 |
| 1136 | 520 | 272.00 | 344.00 | 56.03 | 0.00 |
| 1140 | 520 | 272.00 | 348.00 | 56.58 | 0.00 |
| 1144 | 520 | 272.00 | 352.00 | 57.13 | 0.00 |
| 1148 | 520 | 272.00 | 356.00 | 57.68 | 0.00 |
| 1152 | 520 | 272.00 | 360.00 | 58.24 | 0.00 |
| 1156 | 520 | 272.00 | 364.00 | 58.79 | 0.00 |
| 1160 | 520 | 272.00 | 368.00 | 59.34 | 0.00 |
| 1164 | 520 | 272.00 | 372.00 | 59.89 | 0.00 |
| 1168 | 520 | 272.00 | 376.00 | 60.44 | 0.00 |
| 1172 | 520 | 272.00 | 380.00 | 61.00 | 0.00 |
| 1176 | 520 | 272.00 | 384.00 | 61.55 | 0.00 |
| 1180 | 520 | 272.00 | 388.00 | 62.10 | 0.00 |
| 1184 | 520 | 272.00 | 392.00 | 62.65 | 0.00 |
| 1188 | 520 | 272.00 | 396.00 | 63.20 | 0.00 |
| 1192 | 520 | 272.00 | 400.00 | 63.76 | 0.00 |
| 1196 | 520 | 272.00 | 404.00 | 64.31 | 0.00 |
| 1200 | 520 | 272.00 | 408.00 | 64.86 | 0.00 |
| 1204 | 520 | 272.00 | 412.00 | 65.41 | 0.00 |
| 1208 | 520 | 272.00 | 416.00 | 65.96 | 0.00 |
| 1212 | 520 | 272.00 | 420.00 | 66.52 | 0.00 |
| 1216 | 520 | 272.00 | 424.00 | 67.07 | 0.00 |
| 1220 | 520 | 272.00 | 428.00 | 67.62 | 0.00 |
| 1224 | 520 | 272.00 | 432.00 | 68.17 | 0.00 |
| 1228 | 520 | 272.00 | 436.00 | 68.72 | 0.00 |
| 1232 | 520 | 272.00 | 440.00 | 69.28 | 0.00 |
| 1236 | 520 | 272.00 | 444.00 | 69.83 | 0.00 |
| 1240 | 520 | 272.00 | 448.00 | 70.38 | 0.00 |
| 1244 | 520 | 272.00 | 452.00 | 70.93 | 0.00 |
| 1248 | 520 | 272.00 | 456.00 | 71.48 | 0.00 |
| 1252 | 520 | 272.00 | 460.00 | 72.04 | 0.00 |
| 1256 | 520 | 272.00 | 464.00 | 72.59 | 0.00 |
| 1260 | 520 | 272.00 | 468.00 | 73.14 | 0.00 |
| 1264 | 520 | 272.00 | 472.00 | 73.69 | 0.00 |
| 1268 | 520 | 272.00 | 476.00 | 74.24 | 0.00 |
| 1272 | 520 | 272.00 | 480.00 | 74.80 | 0.00 |
| 1276 | 520 | 272.00 | 484.00 | 75.35 | 0.00 |
| 1280 | 520 | 272.00 | 488.00 | 75.90 | 0.00 |
| 1284 | 520 | 272.00 | 492.00 | 76.45 | 0.00 |
| 1288 | 520 | 272.00 | 496.00 | 77.00 | 0.00 |
| 1292 | 520 | 272.00 | 500.00 | 77.56 | 0.00 |
| 1296 | 520 | 272.00 | 504.00 | 78.11 | 0.00 |
| 1300 | 520 | 272.00 | 508.00 | 78.66 | 0.00 |
| 1304 | 520 | 272.00 | 512.00 | 79.21 | 0.00 |
| 1308 | 520 | 272.00 | 516.00 | 79.76 | 0.00 |
| 1312 | 520 | 272.00 | 520.00 | 80.32 | 0.00 |
| 1316 | 520 | 272.00 | 524.00 | 80.87 | 0.00 |

## Monthly table

| Employee's earnings up to and including the UEL | Earnings at the LEL (where earnings are equal to or exceed the LEL) | Earnings above the LEL, up to and including the PT | Earnings above the PT, up to and including the UEL | Employer's NICs due on all earnings above the ST | Employee's NICs due on all earnings above the PT |
|---|---|---|---|---|---|
| 1a | 1b | 1c | 1d | 1e | |
| £ | £ | £ p | £ p | £ p | £ p |
| 1320 | 520 | 272.00 | 528.00 | 81.42 | 0.00 |
| 1324 | 520 | 272.00 | 532.00 | 81.97 | 0.00 |
| 1328 | 520 | 272.00 | 536.00 | 82.52 | 0.00 |
| 1332 | 520 | 272.00 | 540.00 | 83.08 | 0.00 |
| 1336 | 520 | 272.00 | 544.00 | 83.63 | 0.00 |
| 1340 | 520 | 272.00 | 548.00 | 84.18 | 0.00 |
| 1344 | 520 | 272.00 | 552.00 | 84.73 | 0.00 |
| 1348 | 520 | 272.00 | 556.00 | 85.28 | 0.00 |
| 1352 | 520 | 272.00 | 560.00 | 85.84 | 0.00 |
| 1356 | 520 | 272.00 | 564.00 | 86.39 | 0.00 |
| 1360 | 520 | 272.00 | 568.00 | 86.94 | 0.00 |
| 1364 | 520 | 272.00 | 572.00 | 87.49 | 0.00 |
| 1368 | 520 | 272.00 | 576.00 | 88.04 | 0.00 |
| 1372 | 520 | 272.00 | 580.00 | 88.60 | 0.00 |
| 1376 | 520 | 272.00 | 584.00 | 89.15 | 0.00 |
| 1380 | 520 | 272.00 | 588.00 | 89.70 | 0.00 |
| 1384 | 520 | 272.00 | 592.00 | 90.25 | 0.00 |
| 1388 | 520 | 272.00 | 596.00 | 90.80 | 0.00 |
| 1392 | 520 | 272.00 | 600.00 | 91.36 | 0.00 |
| 1396 | 520 | 272.00 | 604.00 | 91.91 | 0.00 |
| 1400 | 520 | 272.00 | 608.00 | 92.46 | 0.00 |
| 1404 | 520 | 272.00 | 612.00 | 93.01 | 0.00 |
| 1408 | 520 | 272.00 | 616.00 | 93.56 | 0.00 |
| 1412 | 520 | 272.00 | 620.00 | 94.12 | 0.00 |
| 1416 | 520 | 272.00 | 624.00 | 94.67 | 0.00 |
| 1420 | 520 | 272.00 | 628.00 | 95.22 | 0.00 |
| 1424 | 520 | 272.00 | 632.00 | 95.77 | 0.00 |
| 1428 | 520 | 272.00 | 636.00 | 96.32 | 0.00 |
| 1432 | 520 | 272.00 | 640.00 | 96.88 | 0.00 |
| 1436 | 520 | 272.00 | 644.00 | 97.43 | 0.00 |
| 1440 | 520 | 272.00 | 648.00 | 97.98 | 0.00 |
| 1444 | 520 | 272.00 | 652.00 | 98.53 | 0.00 |
| 1448 | 520 | 272.00 | 656.00 | 99.08 | 0.00 |
| 1452 | 520 | 272.00 | 660.00 | 99.64 | 0.00 |
| 1456 | 520 | 272.00 | 664.00 | 100.19 | 0.00 |
| 1460 | 520 | 272.00 | 668.00 | 100.74 | 0.00 |
| 1464 | 520 | 272.00 | 672.00 | 101.29 | 0.00 |
| 1468 | 520 | 272.00 | 676.00 | 101.84 | 0.00 |
| 1472 | 520 | 272.00 | 680.00 | 102.40 | 0.00 |
| 1476 | 520 | 272.00 | 684.00 | 102.95 | 0.00 |
| 1480 | 520 | 272.00 | 688.00 | 103.50 | 0.00 |
| 1484 | 520 | 272.00 | 692.00 | 104.05 | 0.00 |
| 1488 | 520 | 272.00 | 696.00 | 104.60 | 0.00 |
| 1492 | 520 | 272.00 | 700.00 | 105.16 | 0.00 |
| 1496 | 520 | 272.00 | 704.00 | 105.71 | 0.00 |
| 1500 | 520 | 272.00 | 708.00 | 106.26 | 0.00 |
| 1504 | 520 | 272.00 | 712.00 | 106.81 | 0.00 |
| 1508 | 520 | 272.00 | 716.00 | 107.36 | 0.00 |
| 1512 | 520 | 272.00 | 720.00 | 107.92 | 0.00 |
| 1516 | 520 | 272.00 | 724.00 | 108.47 | 0.00 |
| 1520 | 520 | 272.00 | 728.00 | 109.02 | 0.00 |
| 1524 | 520 | 272.00 | 732.00 | 109.57 | 0.00 |
| 1528 | 520 | 272.00 | 736.00 | 110.12 | 0.00 |
| 1532 | 520 | 272.00 | 740.00 | 110.68 | 0.00 |
| 1536 | 520 | 272.00 | 744.00 | 111.23 | 0.00 |

**Monthly table**

**Table letter C**

| Employee's earnings up to and including the UEL | Earnings at the LEL (where earnings are equal to or exceed the LEL) | Earnings above the LEL, up to and including the PT | Earnings above the PT, up to and including the UEL | Employer's NICs due on all earnings above the ST | Employee's NICs due on all earnings above the PT |
|---|---|---|---|---|---|
| | 1a | 1b | 1c | 1d | 1e |
| £ | £ | £ p | £ p | £ p | £ p |
| 1540 | 520 | 272.00 | 748.00 | 111.78 | 0.00 |
| 1544 | 520 | 272.00 | 752.00 | 112.33 | 0.00 |
| 1548 | 520 | 272.00 | 756.00 | 112.88 | 0.00 |
| 1552 | 520 | 272.00 | 760.00 | 113.44 | 0.00 |
| 1556 | 520 | 272.00 | 764.00 | 113.99 | 0.00 |
| 1560 | 520 | 272.00 | 768.00 | 114.54 | 0.00 |
| 1564 | 520 | 272.00 | 772.00 | 115.09 | 0.00 |
| 1568 | 520 | 272.00 | 776.00 | 115.64 | 0.00 |
| 1572 | 520 | 272.00 | 780.00 | 116.20 | 0.00 |
| 1576 | 520 | 272.00 | 784.00 | 116.75 | 0.00 |
| 1580 | 520 | 272.00 | 788.00 | 117.30 | 0.00 |
| 1584 | 520 | 272.00 | 792.00 | 117.85 | 0.00 |
| 1588 | 520 | 272.00 | 796.00 | 118.40 | 0.00 |
| 1592 | 520 | 272.00 | 800.00 | 118.96 | 0.00 |
| 1596 | 520 | 272.00 | 804.00 | 119.51 | 0.00 |
| 1600 | 520 | 272.00 | 808.00 | 120.06 | 0.00 |
| 1604 | 520 | 272.00 | 812.00 | 120.61 | 0.00 |
| 1608 | 520 | 272.00 | 816.00 | 121.16 | 0.00 |
| 1612 | 520 | 272.00 | 820.00 | 121.72 | 0.00 |
| 1616 | 520 | 272.00 | 824.00 | 122.27 | 0.00 |
| 1620 | 520 | 272.00 | 828.00 | 122.82 | 0.00 |
| 1624 | 520 | 272.00 | 832.00 | 123.37 | 0.00 |
| 1628 | 520 | 272.00 | 836.00 | 123.92 | 0.00 |
| 1632 | 520 | 272.00 | 840.00 | 124.48 | 0.00 |
| 1636 | 520 | 272.00 | 844.00 | 125.03 | 0.00 |
| 1640 | 520 | 272.00 | 848.00 | 125.58 | 0.00 |
| 1644 | 520 | 272.00 | 852.00 | 126.13 | 0.00 |
| 1648 | 520 | 272.00 | 856.00 | 126.68 | 0.00 |
| 1652 | 520 | 272.00 | 860.00 | 127.24 | 0.00 |
| 1656 | 520 | 272.00 | 864.00 | 127.79 | 0.00 |
| 1660 | 520 | 272.00 | 868.00 | 128.34 | 0.00 |
| 1664 | 520 | 272.00 | 872.00 | 128.89 | 0.00 |
| 1668 | 520 | 272.00 | 876.00 | 129.44 | 0.00 |
| 1672 | 520 | 272.00 | 880.00 | 130.00 | 0.00 |
| 1676 | 520 | 272.00 | 884.00 | 130.55 | 0.00 |
| 1680 | 520 | 272.00 | 888.00 | 131.10 | 0.00 |
| 1684 | 520 | 272.00 | 892.00 | 131.65 | 0.00 |
| 1688 | 520 | 272.00 | 896.00 | 132.20 | 0.00 |
| 1692 | 520 | 272.00 | 900.00 | 132.76 | 0.00 |
| 1696 | 520 | 272.00 | 904.00 | 133.31 | 0.00 |
| 1700 | 520 | 272.00 | 908.00 | 133.86 | 0.00 |
| 1704 | 520 | 272.00 | 912.00 | 134.41 | 0.00 |
| 1708 | 520 | 272.00 | 916.00 | 134.96 | 0.00 |
| 1712 | 520 | 272.00 | 920.00 | 135.52 | 0.00 |
| 1716 | 520 | 272.00 | 924.00 | 136.07 | 0.00 |
| 1720 | 520 | 272.00 | 928.00 | 136.62 | 0.00 |
| 1724 | 520 | 272.00 | 932.00 | 137.17 | 0.00 |
| 1728 | 520 | 272.00 | 936.00 | 137.72 | 0.00 |
| 1732 | 520 | 272.00 | 940.00 | 138.28 | 0.00 |
| 1736 | 520 | 272.00 | 944.00 | 138.83 | 0.00 |
| 1740 | 520 | 272.00 | 948.00 | 139.38 | 0.00 |
| 1744 | 520 | 272.00 | 952.00 | 139.93 | 0.00 |
| 1748 | 520 | 272.00 | 956.00 | 140.48 | 0.00 |
| 1752 | 520 | 272.00 | 960.00 | 141.04 | 0.00 |
| 1756 | 520 | 272.00 | 964.00 | 141.59 | 0.00 |

## Monthly table

**Table letter C**

| Employee's earnings up to and including the UEL | Earnings at the LEL (where earnings are equal to or exceed the LEL) | Earnings above the LEL, up to and including the PT | Earnings above the PT, up to and including the UEL | Employer's NICs due on all earnings above the ST | Employee's NICs due on all earnings above the PT |
|---|---|---|---|---|---|
| | 1a | 1b | 1c | 1d | 1e |
| £ | £ | £ p | £ p | £ p | £ p |
| 1760 | 520 | 272.00 | 968.00 | 142.14 | 0.00 |
| 1764 | 520 | 272.00 | 972.00 | 142.69 | 0.00 |
| 1768 | 520 | 272.00 | 976.00 | 143.24 | 0.00 |
| 1772 | 520 | 272.00 | 980.00 | 143.80 | 0.00 |
| 1776 | 520 | 272.00 | 984.00 | 144.35 | 0.00 |
| 1780 | 520 | 272.00 | 988.00 | 144.90 | 0.00 |
| 1784 | 520 | 272.00 | 992.00 | 145.45 | 0.00 |
| 1788 | 520 | 272.00 | 996.00 | 146.00 | 0.00 |
| 1792 | 520 | 272.00 | 1000.00 | 146.56 | 0.00 |
| 1796 | 520 | 272.00 | 1004.00 | 147.11 | 0.00 |
| 1800 | 520 | 272.00 | 1008.00 | 147.66 | 0.00 |
| 1804 | 520 | 272.00 | 1012.00 | 148.21 | 0.00 |
| 1808 | 520 | 272.00 | 1016.00 | 148.76 | 0.00 |
| 1812 | 520 | 272.00 | 1020.00 | 149.32 | 0.00 |
| 1816 | 520 | 272.00 | 1024.00 | 149.87 | 0.00 |
| 1820 | 520 | 272.00 | 1028.00 | 150.42 | 0.00 |
| 1824 | 520 | 272.00 | 1032.00 | 150.97 | 0.00 |
| 1828 | 520 | 272.00 | 1036.00 | 151.52 | 0.00 |
| 1832 | 520 | 272.00 | 1040.00 | 152.08 | 0.00 |
| 1836 | 520 | 272.00 | 1044.00 | 152.63 | 0.00 |
| 1840 | 520 | 272.00 | 1048.00 | 153.18 | 0.00 |
| 1844 | 520 | 272.00 | 1052.00 | 153.73 | 0.00 |
| 1848 | 520 | 272.00 | 1056.00 | 154.28 | 0.00 |
| 1852 | 520 | 272.00 | 1060.00 | 154.84 | 0.00 |
| 1856 | 520 | 272.00 | 1064.00 | 155.39 | 0.00 |
| 1860 | 520 | 272.00 | 1068.00 | 155.94 | 0.00 |
| 1864 | 520 | 272.00 | 1072.00 | 156.49 | 0.00 |
| 1868 | 520 | 272.00 | 1076.00 | 157.04 | 0.00 |
| 1872 | 520 | 272.00 | 1080.00 | 157.60 | 0.00 |
| 1876 | 520 | 272.00 | 1084.00 | 158.15 | 0.00 |
| 1880 | 520 | 272.00 | 1088.00 | 158.70 | 0.00 |
| 1884 | 520 | 272.00 | 1092.00 | 159.25 | 0.00 |
| 1888 | 520 | 272.00 | 1096.00 | 159.80 | 0.00 |
| 1892 | 520 | 272.00 | 1100.00 | 160.36 | 0.00 |
| 1896 | 520 | 272.00 | 1104.00 | 160.91 | 0.00 |
| 1900 | 520 | 272.00 | 1108.00 | 161.46 | 0.00 |
| 1904 | 520 | 272.00 | 1112.00 | 162.01 | 0.00 |
| 1908 | 520 | 272.00 | 1116.00 | 162.56 | 0.00 |
| 1912 | 520 | 272.00 | 1120.00 | 163.12 | 0.00 |
| 1916 | 520 | 272.00 | 1124.00 | 163.67 | 0.00 |
| 1920 | 520 | 272.00 | 1128.00 | 164.22 | 0.00 |
| 1924 | 520 | 272.00 | 1132.00 | 164.77 | 0.00 |
| 1928 | 520 | 272.00 | 1136.00 | 165.32 | 0.00 |
| 1932 | 520 | 272.00 | 1140.00 | 165.88 | 0.00 |
| 1936 | 520 | 272.00 | 1144.00 | 166.43 | 0.00 |
| 1940 | 520 | 272.00 | 1148.00 | 166.98 | 0.00 |
| 1944 | 520 | 272.00 | 1152.00 | 167.53 | 0.00 |
| 1948 | 520 | 272.00 | 1156.00 | 168.08 | 0.00 |
| 1952 | 520 | 272.00 | 1160.00 | 168.64 | 0.00 |
| 1956 | 520 | 272.00 | 1164.00 | 169.19 | 0.00 |
| 1960 | 520 | 272.00 | 1168.00 | 169.74 | 0.00 |
| 1964 | 520 | 272.00 | 1172.00 | 170.29 | 0.00 |
| 1968 | 520 | 272.00 | 1176.00 | 170.84 | 0.00 |
| 1972 | 520 | 272.00 | 1180.00 | 171.40 | 0.00 |
| 1976 | 520 | 272.00 | 1184.00 | 171.95 | 0.00 |

**Monthly table**  **Table letter C**

| Employee's earnings up to and including the UEL | Earnings at the LEL (where earnings are equal to or exceed the LEL) | Earnings above the LEL, up to and including the PT | Earnings above the PT, up to and including the UEL | Employer's NICs due on all earnings above the ST | Employee's NICs due on all earnings above the PT |
|---|---|---|---|---|---|
| | | 1a | 1b | 1c | 1d | 1e |
| £ | £ | £ p | £ p | £ p | £ p |
| 1980 | 520 | 272.00 | 1188.00 | 172.50 | 0.00 |
| 1984 | 520 | 272.00 | 1192.00 | 173.05 | 0.00 |
| 1988 | 520 | 272.00 | 1196.00 | 173.60 | 0.00 |
| 1992 | 520 | 272.00 | 1200.00 | 174.16 | 0.00 |
| 1996 | 520 | 272.00 | 1204.00 | 174.71 | 0.00 |
| 2000 | 520 | 272.00 | 1208.00 | 175.26 | 0.00 |
| 2004 | 520 | 272.00 | 1212.00 | 175.81 | 0.00 |
| 2008 | 520 | 272.00 | 1216.00 | 176.36 | 0.00 |
| 2012 | 520 | 272.00 | 1220.00 | 176.92 | 0.00 |
| 2016 | 520 | 272.00 | 1224.00 | 177.47 | 0.00 |
| 2020 | 520 | 272.00 | 1228.00 | 178.02 | 0.00 |
| 2024 | 520 | 272.00 | 1232.00 | 178.57 | 0.00 |
| 2028 | 520 | 272.00 | 1236.00 | 179.12 | 0.00 |
| 2032 | 520 | 272.00 | 1240.00 | 179.68 | 0.00 |
| 2036 | 520 | 272.00 | 1244.00 | 180.23 | 0.00 |
| 2040 | 520 | 272.00 | 1248.00 | 180.78 | 0.00 |
| 2044 | 520 | 272.00 | 1252.00 | 181.33 | 0.00 |
| 2048 | 520 | 272.00 | 1256.00 | 181.88 | 0.00 |
| 2052 | 520 | 272.00 | 1260.00 | 182.44 | 0.00 |
| 2056 | 520 | 272.00 | 1264.00 | 182.99 | 0.00 |
| 2060 | 520 | 272.00 | 1268.00 | 183.54 | 0.00 |
| 2064 | 520 | 272.00 | 1272.00 | 184.09 | 0.00 |
| 2068 | 520 | 272.00 | 1276.00 | 184.64 | 0.00 |
| 2072 | 520 | 272.00 | 1280.00 | 185.20 | 0.00 |
| 2076 | 520 | 272.00 | 1284.00 | 185.75 | 0.00 |
| 2080 | 520 | 272.00 | 1288.00 | 186.30 | 0.00 |
| 2084 | 520 | 272.00 | 1292.00 | 186.85 | 0.00 |
| 2088 | 520 | 272.00 | 1296.00 | 187.40 | 0.00 |
| 2092 | 520 | 272.00 | 1300.00 | 187.96 | 0.00 |
| 2096 | 520 | 272.00 | 1304.00 | 188.51 | 0.00 |
| 2100 | 520 | 272.00 | 1308.00 | 189.06 | 0.00 |
| 2104 | 520 | 272.00 | 1312.00 | 189.61 | 0.00 |
| 2108 | 520 | 272.00 | 1316.00 | 190.16 | 0.00 |
| 2112 | 520 | 272.00 | 1320.00 | 190.72 | 0.00 |
| 2116 | 520 | 272.00 | 1324.00 | 191.27 | 0.00 |
| 2120 | 520 | 272.00 | 1328.00 | 191.82 | 0.00 |
| 2124 | 520 | 272.00 | 1332.00 | 192.37 | 0.00 |
| 2128 | 520 | 272.00 | 1336.00 | 192.92 | 0.00 |
| 2132 | 520 | 272.00 | 1340.00 | 193.48 | 0.00 |
| 2136 | 520 | 272.00 | 1344.00 | 194.03 | 0.00 |
| 2140 | 520 | 272.00 | 1348.00 | 194.58 | 0.00 |
| 2144 | 520 | 272.00 | 1352.00 | 195.13 | 0.00 |
| 2148 | 520 | 272.00 | 1356.00 | 195.68 | 0.00 |
| 2152 | 520 | 272.00 | 1360.00 | 196.24 | 0.00 |
| 2156 | 520 | 272.00 | 1364.00 | 196.79 | 0.00 |
| 2160 | 520 | 272.00 | 1368.00 | 197.34 | 0.00 |
| 2164 | 520 | 272.00 | 1372.00 | 197.89 | 0.00 |
| 2168 | 520 | 272.00 | 1376.00 | 198.44 | 0.00 |
| 2172 | 520 | 272.00 | 1380.00 | 199.00 | 0.00 |
| 2176 | 520 | 272.00 | 1384.00 | 199.55 | 0.00 |
| 2180 | 520 | 272.00 | 1388.00 | 200.10 | 0.00 |
| 2184 | 520 | 272.00 | 1392.00 | 200.65 | 0.00 |
| 2188 | 520 | 272.00 | 1396.00 | 201.20 | 0.00 |
| 2192 | 520 | 272.00 | 1400.00 | 201.76 | 0.00 |
| 2196 | 520 | 272.00 | 1404.00 | 202.31 | 0.00 |

**Monthly table**                                                                       **Table letter C**

| Employee's earnings up to and including the UEL | Earnings at the LEL (where earnings are equal to or exceed the LEL) | Earnings above the LEL, up to and including the PT | Earnings above the PT, up to and including the UEL | Employer's NICs due on all earnings above the ST | Employee's NICs due on all earnings above the PT |
|---|---|---|---|---|---|
| | 1a | 1b | 1c | 1d | 1e |
| £ | £ | £ p | £ p | £ p | £ p |
| 2200 | 520 | 272.00 | 1408.00 | 202.86 | 0.00 |
| 2204 | 520 | 272.00 | 1412.00 | 203.41 | 0.00 |
| 2208 | 520 | 272.00 | 1416.00 | 203.96 | 0.00 |
| 2212 | 520 | 272.00 | 1420.00 | 204.52 | 0.00 |
| 2216 | 520 | 272.00 | 1424.00 | 205.07 | 0.00 |
| 2220 | 520 | 272.00 | 1428.00 | 205.62 | 0.00 |
| 2224 | 520 | 272.00 | 1432.00 | 206.17 | 0.00 |
| 2228 | 520 | 272.00 | 1436.00 | 206.72 | 0.00 |
| 2232 | 520 | 272.00 | 1440.00 | 207.28 | 0.00 |
| 2236 | 520 | 272.00 | 1444.00 | 207.83 | 0.00 |
| 2240 | 520 | 272.00 | 1448.00 | 208.38 | 0.00 |
| 2244 | 520 | 272.00 | 1452.00 | 208.93 | 0.00 |
| 2248 | 520 | 272.00 | 1456.00 | 209.48 | 0.00 |
| 2252 | 520 | 272.00 | 1460.00 | 210.04 | 0.00 |
| 2256 | 520 | 272.00 | 1464.00 | 210.59 | 0.00 |
| 2260 | 520 | 272.00 | 1468.00 | 211.14 | 0.00 |
| 2264 | 520 | 272.00 | 1472.00 | 211.69 | 0.00 |
| 2268 | 520 | 272.00 | 1476.00 | 212.24 | 0.00 |
| 2272 | 520 | 272.00 | 1480.00 | 212.80 | 0.00 |
| 2276 | 520 | 272.00 | 1484.00 | 213.35 | 0.00 |
| 2280 | 520 | 272.00 | 1488.00 | 213.90 | 0.00 |
| 2284 | 520 | 272.00 | 1492.00 | 214.45 | 0.00 |
| 2288 | 520 | 272.00 | 1496.00 | 215.00 | 0.00 |
| 2292 | 520 | 272.00 | 1500.00 | 215.56 | 0.00 |
| 2296 | 520 | 272.00 | 1504.00 | 216.11 | 0.00 |
| 2300 | 520 | 272.00 | 1508.00 | 216.66 | 0.00 |
| 2304 | 520 | 272.00 | 1512.00 | 217.21 | 0.00 |
| 2308 | 520 | 272.00 | 1516.00 | 217.76 | 0.00 |
| 2312 | 520 | 272.00 | 1520.00 | 218.32 | 0.00 |
| 2316 | 520 | 272.00 | 1524.00 | 218.87 | 0.00 |
| 2320 | 520 | 272.00 | 1528.00 | 219.42 | 0.00 |
| 2324 | 520 | 272.00 | 1532.00 | 219.97 | 0.00 |
| 2328 | 520 | 272.00 | 1536.00 | 220.52 | 0.00 |
| 2332 | 520 | 272.00 | 1540.00 | 221.08 | 0.00 |
| 2336 | 520 | 272.00 | 1544.00 | 221.63 | 0.00 |
| 2340 | 520 | 272.00 | 1548.00 | 222.18 | 0.00 |
| 2344 | 520 | 272.00 | 1552.00 | 222.73 | 0.00 |
| 2348 | 520 | 272.00 | 1556.00 | 223.28 | 0.00 |
| 2352 | 520 | 272.00 | 1560.00 | 223.84 | 0.00 |
| 2356 | 520 | 272.00 | 1564.00 | 224.39 | 0.00 |
| 2360 | 520 | 272.00 | 1568.00 | 224.94 | 0.00 |
| 2364 | 520 | 272.00 | 1572.00 | 225.49 | 0.00 |
| 2368 | 520 | 272.00 | 1576.00 | 226.04 | 0.00 |
| 2372 | 520 | 272.00 | 1580.00 | 226.60 | 0.00 |
| 2376 | 520 | 272.00 | 1584.00 | 227.15 | 0.00 |
| 2380 | 520 | 272.00 | 1588.00 | 227.70 | 0.00 |
| 2384 | 520 | 272.00 | 1592.00 | 228.25 | 0.00 |
| 2388 | 520 | 272.00 | 1596.00 | 228.80 | 0.00 |
| 2392 | 520 | 272.00 | 1600.00 | 229.36 | 0.00 |
| 2396 | 520 | 272.00 | 1604.00 | 229.91 | 0.00 |
| 2400 | 520 | 272.00 | 1608.00 | 230.46 | 0.00 |
| 2404 | 520 | 272.00 | 1612.00 | 231.01 | 0.00 |
| 2408 | 520 | 272.00 | 1616.00 | 231.56 | 0.00 |
| 2412 | 520 | 272.00 | 1620.00 | 232.12 | 0.00 |
| 2416 | 520 | 272.00 | 1624.00 | 232.67 | 0.00 |

**Monthly table**                                                                                  **Table letter C**

| Employee's earnings up to and including the UEL | Earnings at the LEL (where earnings are equal to or exceed the LEL) | Earnings above the LEL, up to and including the PT | Earnings above the PT, up to and including the UEL | Employer's NICs due on all earnings above the ST | Employee's NICs due on all earnings above the PT |
|---|---|---|---|---|---|
| | | 1a | 1b | 1c | 1d | 1e |
| £ | £ | £ p | £ p | £ p | £ p |
| 2420 | 520 | 272.00 | 1628.00 | 233.22 | 0.00 |
| 2424 | 520 | 272.00 | 1632.00 | 233.77 | 0.00 |
| 2428 | 520 | 272.00 | 1636.00 | 234.32 | 0.00 |
| 2432 | 520 | 272.00 | 1640.00 | 234.88 | 0.00 |
| 2436 | 520 | 272.00 | 1644.00 | 235.43 | 0.00 |
| 2440 | 520 | 272.00 | 1648.00 | 235.98 | 0.00 |
| 2444 | 520 | 272.00 | 1652.00 | 236.53 | 0.00 |
| 2448 | 520 | 272.00 | 1656.00 | 237.08 | 0.00 |
| 2452 | 520 | 272.00 | 1660.00 | 237.64 | 0.00 |
| 2456 | 520 | 272.00 | 1664.00 | 238.19 | 0.00 |
| 2460 | 520 | 272.00 | 1668.00 | 238.74 | 0.00 |
| 2464 | 520 | 272.00 | 1672.00 | 239.29 | 0.00 |
| 2468 | 520 | 272.00 | 1676.00 | 239.84 | 0.00 |
| 2472 | 520 | 272.00 | 1680.00 | 240.40 | 0.00 |
| 2476 | 520 | 272.00 | 1684.00 | 240.95 | 0.00 |
| 2480 | 520 | 272.00 | 1688.00 | 241.50 | 0.00 |
| 2484 | 520 | 272.00 | 1692.00 | 242.05 | 0.00 |
| 2488 | 520 | 272.00 | 1696.00 | 242.60 | 0.00 |
| 2492 | 520 | 272.00 | 1700.00 | 243.16 | 0.00 |
| 2496 | 520 | 272.00 | 1704.00 | 243.71 | 0.00 |
| 2500 | 520 | 272.00 | 1708.00 | 244.26 | 0.00 |
| 2504 | 520 | 272.00 | 1712.00 | 244.81 | 0.00 |
| 2508 | 520 | 272.00 | 1716.00 | 245.36 | 0.00 |
| 2512 | 520 | 272.00 | 1720.00 | 245.92 | 0.00 |
| 2516 | 520 | 272.00 | 1724.00 | 246.47 | 0.00 |
| 2520 | 520 | 272.00 | 1728.00 | 247.02 | 0.00 |
| 2524 | 520 | 272.00 | 1732.00 | 247.57 | 0.00 |
| 2528 | 520 | 272.00 | 1736.00 | 248.12 | 0.00 |
| 2532 | 520 | 272.00 | 1740.00 | 248.68 | 0.00 |
| 2536 | 520 | 272.00 | 1744.00 | 249.23 | 0.00 |
| 2540 | 520 | 272.00 | 1748.00 | 249.78 | 0.00 |
| 2544 | 520 | 272.00 | 1752.00 | 250.33 | 0.00 |
| 2548 | 520 | 272.00 | 1756.00 | 250.88 | 0.00 |
| 2552 | 520 | 272.00 | 1760.00 | 251.44 | 0.00 |
| 2556 | 520 | 272.00 | 1764.00 | 251.99 | 0.00 |
| 2560 | 520 | 272.00 | 1768.00 | 252.54 | 0.00 |
| 2564 | 520 | 272.00 | 1772.00 | 253.09 | 0.00 |
| 2568 | 520 | 272.00 | 1776.00 | 253.64 | 0.00 |
| 2572 | 520 | 272.00 | 1780.00 | 254.20 | 0.00 |
| 2576 | 520 | 272.00 | 1784.00 | 254.75 | 0.00 |
| 2580 | 520 | 272.00 | 1788.00 | 255.30 | 0.00 |
| 2584 | 520 | 272.00 | 1792.00 | 255.85 | 0.00 |
| 2588 | 520 | 272.00 | 1796.00 | 256.40 | 0.00 |
| 2592 | 520 | 272.00 | 1800.00 | 256.96 | 0.00 |
| 2596 | 520 | 272.00 | 1804.00 | 257.51 | 0.00 |
| 2600 | 520 | 272.00 | 1808.00 | 258.06 | 0.00 |
| 2604 | 520 | 272.00 | 1812.00 | 258.61 | 0.00 |
| 2608 | 520 | 272.00 | 1816.00 | 259.16 | 0.00 |
| 2612 | 520 | 272.00 | 1820.00 | 259.72 | 0.00 |
| 2616 | 520 | 272.00 | 1824.00 | 260.27 | 0.00 |
| 2620 | 520 | 272.00 | 1828.00 | 260.82 | 0.00 |
| 2624 | 520 | 272.00 | 1832.00 | 261.37 | 0.00 |
| 2628 | 520 | 272.00 | 1836.00 | 261.92 | 0.00 |
| 2632 | 520 | 272.00 | 1840.00 | 262.48 | 0.00 |
| 2636 | 520 | 272.00 | 1844.00 | 263.03 | 0.00 |

**Monthly table**                                                                    **Table letter C**

| Employee's earnings up to and including the UEL | Earnings at the LEL (where earnings are equal to or exceed the LEL) | Earnings above the LEL, up to and including the PT | Earnings above the PT, up to and including the UEL | Employer's NICs due on all earnings above the ST | Employee's NICs due on all earnings above the PT |
|---|---|---|---|---|---|
| | 1a | 1b | 1c | 1d | 1e |
| £ | £ | £ p | £ p | £ p | £ p |
| 2640 | 520 | 272.00 | 1848.00 | 263.58 | 0.00 |
| 2644 | 520 | 272.00 | 1852.00 | 264.13 | 0.00 |
| 2648 | 520 | 272.00 | 1856.00 | 264.68 | 0.00 |
| 2652 | 520 | 272.00 | 1860.00 | 265.24 | 0.00 |
| 2656 | 520 | 272.00 | 1864.00 | 265.79 | 0.00 |
| 2660 | 520 | 272.00 | 1868.00 | 266.34 | 0.00 |
| 2664 | 520 | 272.00 | 1872.00 | 266.89 | 0.00 |
| 2668 | 520 | 272.00 | 1876.00 | 267.44 | 0.00 |
| 2672 | 520 | 272.00 | 1880.00 | 268.00 | 0.00 |
| 2676 | 520 | 272.00 | 1884.00 | 268.55 | 0.00 |
| 2680 | 520 | 272.00 | 1888.00 | 269.10 | 0.00 |
| 2684 | 520 | 272.00 | 1892.00 | 269.65 | 0.00 |
| 2688 | 520 | 272.00 | 1896.00 | 270.20 | 0.00 |
| 2692 | 520 | 272.00 | 1900.00 | 270.76 | 0.00 |
| 2696 | 520 | 272.00 | 1904.00 | 271.31 | 0.00 |
| 2700 | 520 | 272.00 | 1908.00 | 271.86 | 0.00 |
| 2704 | 520 | 272.00 | 1912.00 | 272.41 | 0.00 |
| 2708 | 520 | 272.00 | 1916.00 | 272.96 | 0.00 |
| 2712 | 520 | 272.00 | 1920.00 | 273.52 | 0.00 |
| 2716 | 520 | 272.00 | 1924.00 | 274.07 | 0.00 |
| 2720 | 520 | 272.00 | 1928.00 | 274.62 | 0.00 |
| 2724 | 520 | 272.00 | 1932.00 | 275.17 | 0.00 |
| 2728 | 520 | 272.00 | 1936.00 | 275.72 | 0.00 |
| 2732 | 520 | 272.00 | 1940.00 | 276.28 | 0.00 |
| 2736 | 520 | 272.00 | 1944.00 | 276.83 | 0.00 |
| 2740 | 520 | 272.00 | 1948.00 | 277.38 | 0.00 |
| 2744 | 520 | 272.00 | 1952.00 | 277.93 | 0.00 |
| 2748 | 520 | 272.00 | 1956.00 | 278.48 | 0.00 |
| 2752 | 520 | 272.00 | 1960.00 | 279.04 | 0.00 |
| 2756 | 520 | 272.00 | 1964.00 | 279.59 | 0.00 |
| 2760 | 520 | 272.00 | 1968.00 | 280.14 | 0.00 |
| 2764 | 520 | 272.00 | 1972.00 | 280.69 | 0.00 |
| 2768 | 520 | 272.00 | 1976.00 | 281.24 | 0.00 |
| 2772 | 520 | 272.00 | 1980.00 | 281.80 | 0.00 |
| 2776 | 520 | 272.00 | 1984.00 | 282.35 | 0.00 |
| 2780 | 520 | 272.00 | 1988.00 | 282.90 | 0.00 |
| 2784 | 520 | 272.00 | 1992.00 | 283.45 | 0.00 |
| 2788 | 520 | 272.00 | 1996.00 | 284.00 | 0.00 |
| 2792 | 520 | 272.00 | 2000.00 | 284.56 | 0.00 |
| 2796 | 520 | 272.00 | 2004.00 | 285.11 | 0.00 |
| 2800 | 520 | 272.00 | 2008.00 | 285.66 | 0.00 |
| 2804 | 520 | 272.00 | 2012.00 | 286.21 | 0.00 |
| 2808 | 520 | 272.00 | 2016.00 | 286.76 | 0.00 |
| 2812 | 520 | 272.00 | 2020.00 | 287.32 | 0.00 |
| 2816 | 520 | 272.00 | 2024.00 | 287.87 | 0.00 |
| 2820 | 520 | 272.00 | 2028.00 | 288.42 | 0.00 |
| 2824 | 520 | 272.00 | 2032.00 | 288.97 | 0.00 |
| 2828 | 520 | 272.00 | 2036.00 | 289.52 | 0.00 |
| 2832 | 520 | 272.00 | 2040.00 | 290.08 | 0.00 |
| 2836 | 520 | 272.00 | 2044.00 | 290.63 | 0.00 |
| 2840 | 520 | 272.00 | 2048.00 | 291.18 | 0.00 |
| 2844 | 520 | 272.00 | 2052.00 | 291.73 | 0.00 |
| 2848 | 520 | 272.00 | 2056.00 | 292.28 | 0.00 |
| 2852 | 520 | 272.00 | 2060.00 | 292.84 | 0.00 |
| 2856 | 520 | 272.00 | 2064.00 | 293.39 | 0.00 |

## Monthly table

**Table letter C**

| Employee's earnings up to and including the UEL | Earnings at the LEL (where earnings are equal to or exceed the LEL) | Earnings above the LEL, up to and including the PT | Earnings above the PT, up to and including the UEL | Employer's NICs due on all earnings above the ST | Employee's NICs due on all earnings above the PT |
|---|---|---|---|---|---|
| | 1a | 1b | 1c | 1d | 1e |
| £ | £ | £ p | £ p | £ p | £ p |
| 2860 | 520 | 272.00 | 2068.00 | 293.94 | 0.00 |
| 2864 | 520 | 272.00 | 2072.00 | 294.49 | 0.00 |
| 2868 | 520 | 272.00 | 2076.00 | 295.04 | 0.00 |
| 2872 | 520 | 272.00 | 2080.00 | 295.60 | 0.00 |
| 2876 | 520 | 272.00 | 2084.00 | 296.15 | 0.00 |
| 2880 | 520 | 272.00 | 2088.00 | 296.70 | 0.00 |
| 2884 | 520 | 272.00 | 2092.00 | 297.25 | 0.00 |
| 2888 | 520 | 272.00 | 2096.00 | 297.80 | 0.00 |
| 2892 | 520 | 272.00 | 2100.00 | 298.36 | 0.00 |
| 2896 | 520 | 272.00 | 2104.00 | 298.91 | 0.00 |
| 2900 | 520 | 272.00 | 2108.00 | 299.46 | 0.00 |
| 2904 | 520 | 272.00 | 2112.00 | 300.01 | 0.00 |
| 2908 | 520 | 272.00 | 2116.00 | 300.56 | 0.00 |
| 2912 | 520 | 272.00 | 2120.00 | 301.12 | 0.00 |
| 2916 | 520 | 272.00 | 2124.00 | 301.67 | 0.00 |
| 2920 | 520 | 272.00 | 2128.00 | 302.22 | 0.00 |
| 2924 | 520 | 272.00 | 2132.00 | 302.77 | 0.00 |
| 2928 | 520 | 272.00 | 2136.00 | 303.32 | 0.00 |
| 2932 | 520 | 272.00 | 2140.00 | 303.88 | 0.00 |
| 2936 | 520 | 272.00 | 2144.00 | 304.43 | 0.00 |
| 2940 | 520 | 272.00 | 2148.00 | 304.98 | 0.00 |
| 2944 | 520 | 272.00 | 2152.00 | 305.53 | 0.00 |
| 2948 | 520 | 272.00 | 2156.00 | 306.08 | 0.00 |
| 2952 | 520 | 272.00 | 2160.00 | 306.64 | 0.00 |
| 2956 | 520 | 272.00 | 2164.00 | 307.19 | 0.00 |
| 2960 | 520 | 272.00 | 2168.00 | 307.74 | 0.00 |
| 2964 | 520 | 272.00 | 2172.00 | 308.29 | 0.00 |
| 2968 | 520 | 272.00 | 2176.00 | 308.84 | 0.00 |
| 2972 | 520 | 272.00 | 2180.00 | 309.40 | 0.00 |
| 2976 | 520 | 272.00 | 2184.00 | 309.95 | 0.00 |
| 2980 | 520 | 272.00 | 2188.00 | 310.50 | 0.00 |
| 2984 | 520 | 272.00 | 2192.00 | 311.05 | 0.00 |
| 2988 | 520 | 272.00 | 2196.00 | 311.60 | 0.00 |
| 2992 | 520 | 272.00 | 2200.00 | 312.16 | 0.00 |
| 2996 | 520 | 272.00 | 2204.00 | 312.71 | 0.00 |
| 3000 | 520 | 272.00 | 2208.00 | 313.26 | 0.00 |
| 3004 | 520 | 272.00 | 2212.00 | 313.81 | 0.00 |
| 3008 | 520 | 272.00 | 2216.00 | 314.36 | 0.00 |
| 3012 | 520 | 272.00 | 2220.00 | 314.92 | 0.00 |
| 3016 | 520 | 272.00 | 2224.00 | 315.47 | 0.00 |
| 3020 | 520 | 272.00 | 2228.00 | 316.02 | 0.00 |
| 3024 | 520 | 272.00 | 2232.00 | 316.57 | 0.00 |
| 3028 | 520 | 272.00 | 2236.00 | 317.12 | 0.00 |
| 3032 | 520 | 272.00 | 2240.00 | 317.68 | 0.00 |
| 3036 | 520 | 272.00 | 2244.00 | 318.23 | 0.00 |
| 3040 | 520 | 272.00 | 2248.00 | 318.78 | 0.00 |
| 3044 | 520 | 272.00 | 2252.00 | 319.33 | 0.00 |
| 3048 | 520 | 272.00 | 2256.00 | 319.88 | 0.00 |
| 3052 | 520 | 272.00 | 2260.00 | 320.44 | 0.00 |
| 3056 | 520 | 272.00 | 2264.00 | 320.99 | 0.00 |
| 3060 | 520 | 272.00 | 2268.00 | 321.54 | 0.00 |
| 3064 | 520 | 272.00 | 2272.00 | 322.09 | 0.00 |
| 3068 | 520 | 272.00 | 2276.00 | 322.64 | 0.00 |
| 3072 | 520 | 272.00 | 2280.00 | 323.20 | 0.00 |
| 3076 | 520 | 272.00 | 2284.00 | 323.75 | 0.00 |

## Monthly table

| Employee's earnings up to and including the UEL | Earnings at the LEL (where earnings are equal to or exceed the LEL) | Earnings above the LEL, up to and including the PT | Earnings above the PT, up to and including the UEL | Employer's NICs due on all earnings above the ST | Employee's NICs due on all earnings above the PT |
|---|---|---|---|---|---|
| | 1a | 1b | 1c | 1d | 1e |
| £ | £ | £ p | £ p | £ p | £ p |
| 3080 | 520 | 272.00 | 2288.00 | 324.30 | 0.00 |
| 3084 | 520 | 272.00 | 2292.00 | 324.85 | 0.00 |
| 3088 | 520 | 272.00 | 2296.00 | 325.40 | 0.00 |
| 3092 | 520 | 272.00 | 2300.00 | 325.96 | 0.00 |
| 3096 | 520 | 272.00 | 2304.00 | 326.51 | 0.00 |
| 3100 | 520 | 272.00 | 2308.00 | 327.06 | 0.00 |
| 3104 | 520 | 272.00 | 2312.00 | 327.61 | 0.00 |
| 3108 | 520 | 272.00 | 2316.00 | 328.16 | 0.00 |
| 3112 | 520 | 272.00 | 2320.00 | 328.72 | 0.00 |
| 3116 | 520 | 272.00 | 2324.00 | 329.27 | 0.00 |
| 3120 | 520 | 272.00 | 2328.00 | 329.82 | 0.00 |
| 3124 | 520 | 272.00 | 2332.00 | 330.37 | 0.00 |
| 3128 | 520 | 272.00 | 2336.00 | 330.92 | 0.00 |
| 3132 | 520 | 272.00 | 2340.00 | 331.48 | 0.00 |
| 3136 | 520 | 272.00 | 2344.00 | 332.03 | 0.00 |
| 3140 | 520 | 272.00 | 2348.00 | 332.58 | 0.00 |
| 3144 | 520 | 272.00 | 2352.00 | 333.13 | 0.00 |
| 3148 | 520 | 272.00 | 2356.00 | 333.68 | 0.00 |
| 3152 | 520 | 272.00 | 2360.00 | 334.24 | 0.00 |
| 3156 | 520 | 272.00 | 2364.00 | 334.79 | 0.00 |
| 3160 | 520 | 272.00 | 2368.00 | 335.34 | 0.00 |
| 3164 | 520 | 272.00 | 2372.00 | 335.89 | 0.00 |
| 3168 | 520 | 272.00 | 2376.00 | 336.44 | 0.00 |
| 3172 | 520 | 272.00 | 2380.00 | 337.00 | 0.00 |
| 3176 | 520 | 272.00 | 2384.00 | 337.55 | 0.00 |
| 3180 | 520 | 272.00 | 2388.00 | 338.10 | 0.00 |
| 3184 | 520 | 272.00 | 2392.00 | 338.65 | 0.00 |
| 3188 | 520 | 272.00 | 2396.00 | 339.20 | 0.00 |
| 3192 | 520 | 272.00 | 2400.00 | 339.76 | 0.00 |
| 3196 | 520 | 272.00 | 2404.00 | 340.31 | 0.00 |
| 3200 | 520 | 272.00 | 2408.00 | 340.86 | 0.00 |
| 3204 | 520 | 272.00 | 2412.00 | 341.41 | 0.00 |
| 3208 | 520 | 272.00 | 2416.00 | 341.96 | 0.00 |
| 3212 | 520 | 272.00 | 2420.00 | 342.52 | 0.00 |
| 3216 | 520 | 272.00 | 2424.00 | 343.07 | 0.00 |
| 3220 | 520 | 272.00 | 2428.00 | 343.62 | 0.00 |
| 3224 | 520 | 272.00 | 2432.00 | 344.17 | 0.00 |
| 3228 | 520 | 272.00 | 2436.00 | 344.72 | 0.00 |
| 3232 | 520 | 272.00 | 2440.00 | 345.28 | 0.00 |
| 3236 | 520 | 272.00 | 2444.00 | 345.83 | 0.00 |
| 3240 | 520 | 272.00 | 2448.00 | 346.38 | 0.00 |
| 3244 | 520 | 272.00 | 2452.00 | 346.93 | 0.00 |
| 3248 | 520 | 272.00 | 2456.00 | 347.48 | 0.00 |
| 3252 | 520 | 272.00 | 2460.00 | 348.04 | 0.00 |
| 3256 | 520 | 272.00 | 2464.00 | 348.59 | 0.00 |
| 3260 | 520 | 272.00 | 2468.00 | 349.14 | 0.00 |
| 3264 | 520 | 272.00 | 2472.00 | 349.69 | 0.00 |
| 3268 | 520 | 272.00 | 2476.00 | 350.24 | 0.00 |
| 3272 | 520 | 272.00 | 2480.00 | 350.80 | 0.00 |
| 3276 | 520 | 272.00 | 2484.00 | 351.35 | 0.00 |
| 3280 | 520 | 272.00 | 2488.00 | 351.90 | 0.00 |
| 3284 | 520 | 272.00 | 2492.00 | 352.45 | 0.00 |
| 3288 | 520 | 272.00 | 2496.00 | 353.00 | 0.00 |
| 3292 | 520 | 272.00 | 2500.00 | 353.56 | 0.00 |
| 3296 | 520 | 272.00 | 2504.00 | 354.11 | 0.00 |

**Monthly table**

**Table letter C**

| Employee's earnings up to and including the UEL | Earnings at the LEL (where earnings are equal to or exceed the LEL) | Earnings above the LEL, up to and including the PT | Earnings above the PT, up to and including the UEL | Employer's NICs due on all earnings above the ST | Employee's NICs due on all earnings above the PT |
|---|---|---|---|---|---|
| | 1a | 1b | 1c | 1d | 1e |
| £ | £ | £ p | £ p | £ p | £ p |
| 3300 | 520 | 272.00 | 2508.00 | 354.66 | 0.00 |
| 3304 | 520 | 272.00 | 2512.00 | 355.21 | 0.00 |
| 3308 | 520 | 272.00 | 2516.00 | 355.76 | 0.00 |
| 3312 | 520 | 272.00 | 2520.00 | 356.32 | 0.00 |
| 3316 | 520 | 272.00 | 2524.00 | 356.87 | 0.00 |
| 3320 | 520 | 272.00 | 2528.00 | 357.42 | 0.00 |
| 3324 | 520 | 272.00 | 2532.00 | 357.97 | 0.00 |
| 3328 | 520 | 272.00 | 2536.00 | 358.52 | 0.00 |
| 3332 | 520 | 272.00 | 2540.00 | 359.08 | 0.00 |
| 3336 | 520 | 272.00 | 2544.00 | 359.63 | 0.00 |
| 3340 | 520 | 272.00 | 2548.00 | 360.18 | 0.00 |
| 3344 | 520 | 272.00 | 2552.00 | 360.73 | 0.00 |
| 3348 | 520 | 272.00 | 2556.00 | 361.28 | 0.00 |
| 3352 | 520 | 272.00 | 2560.00 | 361.84 | 0.00 |
| 3356 | 520 | 272.00 | 2564.00 | 362.39 | 0.00 |
| 3360 | 520 | 272.00 | 2568.00 | 362.94 | 0.00 |
| 3364 | 520 | 272.00 | 2572.00 | 363.49 | 0.00 |
| 3368 | 520 | 272.00 | 2576.00 | 364.04 | 0.00 |
| 3372 | 520 | 272.00 | 2580.00 | 364.60 | 0.00 |
| 3376 | 520 | 272.00 | 2584.00 | 365.15 | 0.00 |
| 3380 | 520 | 272.00 | 2588.00 | 365.70 | 0.00 |
| 3384 | 520 | 272.00 | 2592.00 | 366.25 | 0.00 |
| 3388 | 520 | 272.00 | 2596.00 | 366.80 | 0.00 |
| 3392 | 520 | 272.00 | 2600.00 | 367.36 | 0.00 |
| 3396 | 520 | 272.00 | 2604.00 | 367.91 | 0.00 |
| 3400 | 520 | 272.00 | 2608.00 | 368.46 | 0.00 |
| 3404 | 520 | 272.00 | 2612.00 | 369.01 | 0.00 |
| 3408 | 520 | 272.00 | 2616.00 | 369.56 | 0.00 |
| 3412 | 520 | 272.00 | 2620.00 | 370.12 | 0.00 |
| 3416 | 520 | 272.00 | 2624.00 | 370.67 | 0.00 |
| 3420 | 520 | 272.00 | 2628.00 | 371.22 | 0.00 |
| 3424 | 520 | 272.00 | 2632.00 | 371.77 | 0.00 |
| 3428 | 520 | 272.00 | 2636.00 | 372.32 | 0.00 |
| 3432 | 520 | 272.00 | 2640.00 | 372.88 | 0.00 |
| 3436 | 520 | 272.00 | 2644.00 | 373.43 | 0.00 |
| 3440 | 520 | 272.00 | 2648.00 | 373.98 | 0.00 |
| 3444 | 520 | 272.00 | 2652.00 | 374.53 | 0.00 |
| 3448 | 520 | 272.00 | 2656.00 | 375.08 | 0.00 |
| 3452 | 520 | 272.00 | 2660.00 | 375.64 | 0.00 |
| 3456 | 520 | 272.00 | 2664.00 | 376.19 | 0.00 |
| 3460 | 520 | 272.00 | 2668.00 | 376.74 | 0.00 |
| 3464 | 520 | 272.00 | 2672.00 | 377.29 | 0.00 |
| 3468 | 520 | 272.00 | 2676.00 | 377.84 | 0.00 |
| 3472 | 520 | 272.00 | 2680.00 | 378.40 | 0.00 |
| 3476 | 520 | 272.00 | 2684.00 | 378.95 | 0.00 |
| 3480 | 520 | 272.00 | 2688.00 | 379.50 | 0.00 |
| 3484 | 520 | 272.00 | 2692.00 | 380.05 | 0.00 |
| 3488 | 520 | 272.00 | 2696.00 | 380.60 | 0.00 |
| 3492 | 520 | 272.00 | 2700.00 | 381.16 | 0.00 |
| 3496 | 520 | 272.00 | 2704.00 | 381.71 | 0.00 |
| 3500 | 520 | 272.00 | 2708.00 | 382.26 | 0.00 |
| 3504 | 520 | 272.00 | 2712.00 | 382.81 | 0.00 |
| 3508 | 520 | 272.00 | 2716.00 | 383.36 | 0.00 |
| 3512 | 520 | 272.00 | 2720.00 | 383.92 | 0.00 |
| 3516 | 520 | 272.00 | 2724.00 | 384.47 | 0.00 |

## Monthly table

| Employee's earnings up to and including the UEL | Earnings at the LEL (where earnings are equal to or exceed the LEL) | Earnings above the LEL, up to and including the PT | Earnings above the PT, up to and including the UEL | Employer's NICs due on all earnings above the ST | Employee's NICs due on all earnings above the PT |
|---|---|---|---|---|---|
| | 1a | 1b | 1c | 1d | 1e |
| £ | £ | £ p | £ p | £ p | £ p |
| 3520 | 520 | 272.00 | 2728.00 | 385.02 | 0.00 |
| 3524 | 520 | 272.00 | 2732.00 | 385.57 | 0.00 |
| 3528 | 520 | 272.00 | 2736.00 | 386.12 | 0.00 |
| 3532 | 520 | 272.00 | 2740.00 | 386.68 | 0.00 |
| 3536 | 520 | 272.00 | 2744.00 | 387.23 | 0.00 |
| 3540 | 520 | 272.00 | 2748.00 | 387.78 | 0.00 |
| 3544 | 520 | 272.00 | 2752.00 | 388.33 | 0.00 |
| 3548 | 520 | 272.00 | 2756.00 | 388.88 | 0.00 |
| 3552 | 520 | 272.00 | 2760.00 | 389.44 | 0.00 |
| 3556 | 520 | 272.00 | 2764.00 | 389.99 | 0.00 |
| 3560 | 520 | 272.00 | 2768.00 | 390.54 | 0.00 |
| 3564 | 520 | 272.00 | 2772.00 | 391.09 | 0.00 |
| 3568 | 520 | 272.00 | 2776.00 | 391.64 | 0.00 |
| 3572 | 520 | 272.00 | 2780.00 | 392.20 | 0.00 |
| 3576 | 520 | 272.00 | 2784.00 | 392.75 | 0.00 |
| 3580 | 520 | 272.00 | 2788.00 | 393.30 | 0.00 |
| 3584 | 520 | 272.00 | 2792.00 | 393.85 | 0.00 |
| 3588 | 520 | 272.00 | 2796.00 | 394.40 | 0.00 |
| 3592 | 520 | 272.00 | 2800.00 | 394.96 | 0.00 |
| 3596 | 520 | 272.00 | 2804.00 | 395.51 | 0.00 |
| 3600 | 520 | 272.00 | 2808.00 | 396.06 | 0.00 |
| 3604 | 520 | 272.00 | 2812.00 | 396.61 | 0.00 |
| 3608 | 520 | 272.00 | 2816.00 | 397.16 | 0.00 |
| 3612 | 520 | 272.00 | 2820.00 | 397.72 | 0.00 |
| 3616 | 520 | 272.00 | 2824.00 | 398.27 | 0.00 |
| 3620 | 520 | 272.00 | 2828.00 | 398.82 | 0.00 |
| 3624 | 520 | 272.00 | 2832.00 | 399.37 | 0.00 |
| 3628 | 520 | 272.00 | 2836.00 | 399.92 | 0.00 |
| 3632 | 520 | 272.00 | 2840.00 | 400.48 | 0.00 |
| 3636 | 520 | 272.00 | 2844.00 | 401.03 | 0.00 |
| 3640 | 520 | 272.00 | 2848.00 | 401.58 | 0.00 |
| 3644 | 520 | 272.00 | 2852.00 | 402.13 | 0.00 |
| 3648 | 520 | 272.00 | 2856.00 | 402.68 | 0.00 |
| 3652 | 520 | 272.00 | 2860.00 | 403.24 | 0.00 |
| 3656 | 520 | 272.00 | 2864.00 | 403.79 | 0.00 |
| 3660 | 520 | 272.00 | 2868.00 | 404.34 | 0.00 |
| 3664 | 520 | 272.00 | 2872.00 | 404.89 | 0.00 |
| 3668 | 520 | 272.00 | 2876.00 | 405.44 | 0.00 |
| 3672 | 520 | 272.00 | 2880.00 | 406.00 | 0.00 |
| 3676 | 520 | 272.00 | 2884.00 | 406.55 | 0.00 |
| 3680 | 520 | 272.00 | 2888.00 | 407.10 | 0.00 |
| 3684 | 520 | 272.00 | 2892.00 | 407.65 | 0.00 |
| 3688 | 520 | 272.00 | 2896.00 | 408.20 | 0.00 |
| 3692 | 520 | 272.00 | 2900.00 | 408.76 | 0.00 |
| 3696 | 520 | 272.00 | 2904.00 | 409.31 | 0.00 |
| 3700 | 520 | 272.00 | 2908.00 | 409.86 | 0.00 |
| 3704 | 520 | 272.00 | 2912.00 | 410.41 | 0.00 |
| 3708 | 520 | 272.00 | 2916.00 | 410.96 | 0.00 |
| 3712 | 520 | 272.00 | 2920.00 | 411.52 | 0.00 |
| 3716 | 520 | 272.00 | 2924.00 | 412.07 | 0.00 |
| 3720 | 520 | 272.00 | 2928.00 | 412.62 | 0.00 |
| 3724 | 520 | 272.00 | 2932.00 | 413.17 | 0.00 |
| 3728 | 520 | 272.00 | 2936.00 | 413.72 | 0.00 |
| 3732 | 520 | 272.00 | 2940.00 | 414.28 | 0.00 |
| 3736 | 520 | 272.00 | 2944.00 | 414.83 | 0.00 |

**Monthly table**                                                                          **Table letter C**

| Employee's earnings up to and including the UEL | Earnings at the LEL (where earnings are equal to or exceed the LEL) | Earnings above the LEL, up to and including the PT | Earnings above the PT, up to and including the UEL | Employer's NICs due on all earnings above the ST | Employee's NICs due on all earnings above the PT |
|---|---|---|---|---|---|
| | 1a | 1b | 1c | 1d | 1e |
| £ | £ | £ p | £ p | £ p | £ p |
| 3740 | 520 | 272.00 | 2948.00 | 415.38 | 0.00 |
| 3744 | 520 | 272.00 | 2952.00 | 415.93 | 0.00 |
| 3748 | 520 | 272.00 | 2956.00 | 416.48 | 0.00 |
| 3752 | 520 | 272.00 | 2960.00 | 417.04 | 0.00 |
| 3756 | 520 | 272.00 | 2964.00 | 417.59 | 0.00 |
| 3760 | 520 | 272.00 | 2968.00 | 418.14 | 0.00 |
| 3764 | 520 | 272.00 | 2972.00 | 418.69 | 0.00 |
| 3768 | 520 | 272.00 | 2976.00 | 419.24 | 0.00 |
| 3772 | 520 | 272.00 | 2980.00 | 419.80 | 0.00 |
| 3776 | 520 | 272.00 | 2984.00 | 420.35 | 0.00 |
| 3780 | 520 | 272.00 | 2988.00 | 420.90 | 0.00 |
| 3784 | 520 | 272.00 | 2992.00 | 421.45 | 0.00 |
| 3788 | 520 | 272.00 | 2996.00 | 422.00 | 0.00 |
| 3792 | 520 | 272.00 | 3000.00 | 422.56 | 0.00 |
| 3796 | 520 | 272.00 | 3004.00 | 423.11 | 0.00 |
| 3800 | 520 | 272.00 | 3008.00 | 423.66 | 0.00 |
| 3804 | 520 | 272.00 | 3012.00 | 424.21 | 0.00 |
| 3808 | 520 | 272.00 | 3016.00 | 424.76 | 0.00 |
| 3812 | 520 | 272.00 | 3020.00 | 425.32 | 0.00 |
| 3816 | 520 | 272.00 | 3024.00 | 425.87 | 0.00 |
| 3820 | 520 | 272.00 | 3028.00 | 426.42 | 0.00 |
| 3824 | 520 | 272.00 | 3032.00 | 426.97 | 0.00 |
| 3828 | 520 | 272.00 | 3036.00 | 427.52 | 0.00 |
| 3832 | 520 | 272.00 | 3040.00 | 428.08 | 0.00 |
| 3836 | 520 | 272.00 | 3044.00 | 428.63 | 0.00 |
| 3840 | 520 | 272.00 | 3048.00 | 429.18 | 0.00 |
| 3844 | 520 | 272.00 | 3052.00 | 429.73 | 0.00 |
| 3848 | 520 | 272.00 | 3056.00 | 430.28 | 0.00 |
| 3852 | 520 | 272.00 | 3060.00 | 430.84 | 0.00 |
| 3856 | 520 | 272.00 | 3064.00 | 431.39 | 0.00 |
| 3860 | 520 | 272.00 | 3068.00 | 431.94 | 0.00 |
| 3864 | 520 | 272.00 | 3072.00 | 432.49 | 0.00 |
| 3868 | 520 | 272.00 | 3076.00 | 433.04 | 0.00 |
| 3872 | 520 | 272.00 | 3080.00 | 433.60 | 0.00 |
| 3876 | 520 | 272.00 | 3084.00 | 434.15 | 0.00 |
| 3880 | 520 | 272.00 | 3088.00 | 434.70 | 0.00 |
| 3884 | 520 | 272.00 | 3092.00 | 435.25 | 0.00 |
| 3888 | 520 | 272.00 | 3096.00 | 435.80 | 0.00 |
| 3892 | 520 | 272.00 | 3100.00 | 436.36 | 0.00 |
| 3896 | 520 | 272.00 | 3104.00 | 436.91 | 0.00 |
| 3900 | 520 | 272.00 | 3108.00 | 437.46 | 0.00 |
| 3904 | 520 | 272.00 | 3112.00 | 438.01 | 0.00 |
| 3908 | 520 | 272.00 | 3116.00 | 438.56 | 0.00 |
| 3912 | 520 | 272.00 | 3120.00 | 439.12 | 0.00 |
| 3916 | 520 | 272.00 | 3124.00 | 439.67 | 0.00 |
| 3920 | 520 | 272.00 | 3128.00 | 440.22 | 0.00 |
| 3924 | 520 | 272.00 | 3132.00 | 440.77 | 0.00 |
| 3928 | 520 | 272.00 | 3136.00 | 441.32 | 0.00 |
| 3932 | 520 | 272.00 | 3140.00 | 441.88 | 0.00 |
| 3936 | 520 | 272.00 | 3144.00 | 442.43 | 0.00 |
| 3940 | 520 | 272.00 | 3148.00 | 442.98 | 0.00 |
| 3944 | 520 | 272.00 | 3152.00 | 443.53 | 0.00 |
| 3948 | 520 | 272.00 | 3156.00 | 444.08 | 0.00 |
| 3952 | 520 | 272.00 | 3160.00 | 444.64 | 0.00 |
| 3956 | 520 | 272.00 | 3164.00 | 445.19 | 0.00 |

## Monthly table

**Table letter C**

| Employee's earnings up to and including the UEL | Earnings at the LEL (where earnings are equal to or exceed the LEL) | Earnings above the LEL, up to and including the PT | Earnings above the PT, up to and including the UEL | Employer's NICs due on all earnings above the ST | Employee's NICs due on all earnings above the PT |
|---|---|---|---|---|---|
| | 1a | 1b | 1c | 1d | 1e |
| £ | £ | £ p | £ p | £ p | £ p |
| 3960 | 520 | 272.00 | 3168.00 | 445.74 | 0.00 |
| 3964 | 520 | 272.00 | 3172.00 | 446.29 | 0.00 |
| 3968 | 520 | 272.00 | 3176.00 | 446.84 | 0.00 |
| 3972 | 520 | 272.00 | 3180.00 | 447.40 | 0.00 |
| 3976 | 520 | 272.00 | 3184.00 | 447.95 | 0.00 |
| 3980 | 520 | 272.00 | 3188.00 | 448.50 | 0.00 |
| 3984 | 520 | 272.00 | 3192.00 | 449.05 | 0.00 |
| 3988 | 520 | 272.00 | 3196.00 | 449.60 | 0.00 |
| 3992 | 520 | 272.00 | 3200.00 | 450.16 | 0.00 |
| 3996 | 520 | 272.00 | 3204.00 | 450.71 | 0.00 |
| 4000 | 520 | 272.00 | 3208.00 | 451.26 | 0.00 |
| 4004 | 520 | 272.00 | 3212.00 | 451.81 | 0.00 |
| 4008 | 520 | 272.00 | 3216.00 | 452.36 | 0.00 |
| 4012 | 520 | 272.00 | 3220.00 | 452.92 | 0.00 |
| 4016 | 520 | 272.00 | 3224.00 | 453.47 | 0.00 |
| 4020 | 520 | 272.00 | 3228.00 | 454.02 | 0.00 |
| 4024 | 520 | 272.00 | 3232.00 | 454.57 | 0.00 |
| 4028 | 520 | 272.00 | 3236.00 | 455.12 | 0.00 |
| 4032 | 520 | 272.00 | 3240.00 | 455.68 | 0.00 |
| 4036 | 520 | 272.00 | 3244.00 | 456.23 | 0.00 |
| 4040 | 520 | 272.00 | 3248.00 | 456.78 | 0.00 |
| 4044 | 520 | 272.00 | 3252.00 | 457.33 | 0.00 |
| 4048 | 520 | 272.00 | 3256.00 | 457.88 | 0.00 |
| 4052 | 520 | 272.00 | 3260.00 | 458.44 | 0.00 |
| 4056 | 520 | 272.00 | 3264.00 | 458.99 | 0.00 |
| 4060 | 520 | 272.00 | 3268.00 | 459.54 | 0.00 |
| 4064 | 520 | 272.00 | 3272.00 | 460.09 | 0.00 |
| 4068 | 520 | 272.00 | 3276.00 | 460.64 | 0.00 |
| 4072 | 520 | 272.00 | 3280.00 | 461.20 | 0.00 |
| 4076 | 520 | 272.00 | 3284.00 | 461.75 | 0.00 |
| 4080 | 520 | 272.00 | 3288.00 | 462.30 | 0.00 |
| 4084 | 520 | 272.00 | 3292.00 | 462.85 | 0.00 |
| 4088 | 520 | 272.00 | 3296.00 | 463.40 | 0.00 |
| 4092 | 520 | 272.00 | 3300.00 | 463.96 | 0.00 |
| 4096 | 520 | 272.00 | 3304.00 | 464.51 | 0.00 |
| 4100 | 520 | 272.00 | 3308.00 | 465.06 | 0.00 |
| 4104 | 520 | 272.00 | 3312.00 | 465.61 | 0.00 |
| 4108 | 520 | 272.00 | 3316.00 | 466.16 | 0.00 |
| 4112 | 520 | 272.00 | 3320.00 | 466.72 | 0.00 |
| 4116 | 520 | 272.00 | 3324.00 | 467.27 | 0.00 |
| 4120 | 520 | 272.00 | 3328.00 | 467.82 | 0.00 |
| 4124 | 520 | 272.00 | 3332.00 | 468.37 | 0.00 |
| 4128 | 520 | 272.00 | 3336.00 | 468.92 | 0.00 |
| 4132 | 520 | 272.00 | 3340.00 | 469.48 | 0.00 |
| 4136 | 520 | 272.00 | 3344.00 | 470.03 | 0.00 |
| 4140 | 520 | 272.00 | 3348.00 | 470.58 | 0.00 |
| 4144 | 520 | 272.00 | 3352.00 | 471.13 | 0.00 |
| 4148 | 520 | 272.00 | 3356.00 | 471.68 | 0.00 |
| 4152 | 520 | 272.00 | 3360.00 | 472.24 | 0.00 |
| 4156 | 520 | 272.00 | 3364.00 | 472.79 | 0.00 |

## Monthly table

**Table letter C**

| Employee's earnings up to and including the UEL | Earnings at the LEL (where earnings are equal to or exceed the LEL) 1a | Earnings above the LEL, up to and including the PT 1b | Earnings above the PT, up to and including the UEL 1c | Employer's NICs due on all earnings above the ST 1d | Employee's NICs due on all earnings above the PT 1e |
|---|---|---|---|---|---|
| £ | £ | £ p | £ p | £ p | £ p |
| 4160 | 520 | 272.00 | 3368.00 | 473.34 | 0.00 |
| 4164 | 520 | 272.00 | 3372.00 | 473.82 | 0.00 |
| 4167 | 520 | 272.00 | 3375.00 | 474.03 | 0.00 |

If the employee's gross pay is over £4,167, go to page 76.

# Working out and recording NICs where employee's total earnings exceed the UEL – Table letter B

Where the employee's total earnings exceed the UEL, only the earnings between the PT and the UEL should be recorded in column 1c of form RT11.

Use the main table to work out the employer's NICs and the employee's NICs due on the earnings up to the UEL.

To work out the employer's NICs and the employee's NICs due on the earnings above the UEL, take the following action:

| Step | Action | Example (based on Table letter B with total monthly earnings of £5,483.29) | | |
|------|--------|------|------|------|
| 1. | Subtract the UEL figure from the total gross pay. | £5,483.29 - £4,167 = £1,316.29 | | |
| 2. | Round the answer down to the nearest whole £. | Rounded down to £1,316 | | |
| 3. | Look this figure up in the Additional gross pay table on page 77. | Look up £1,316 | | |

| Step | Action | Amount | Employer's NICs payable | Employee's NICs payable |
|------|--------|--------|------|------|
| 4. | If the figure is not shown in the table, build up to it by adding together as few entries as possible. | £1000 | £138.00 | £20.00 |
| | | £300 | + £41.40 | + £6.00 |
| | | £16 | + £2.21 | + £0.32 |
| | | **Totals** | **= £181.61** | **= £26.32** |

| Step | Action | | Total payable by employer | Total payable by employee |
|------|--------|--|------|------|
| 5. | Add the further employer's NICs and employee's NICs worked out on the earnings above the UEL (columns 1d and 1e of the Additional gross pay table) to the employer's NICs and employee's NICs due for earnings at the UEL (columns 1d and 1e of the main table). | | £181.61 (further employer NICs) | £26.32 (further employee NICs) |
| | | | + £474.03 (due for employer on earnings at UEL) | + £197.44 (due for employee on earnings at UEL) |
| | | **Totals** | **= £655.64** | **= £223.76** |

| Step | Action |
|------|--------|
| 6. | Record the figures resulting from Step 5 in columns 1d and 1e of form RT11. |

On form RT11 or equivalent record

| Col 1a | Col 1b | Col 1c | Col 1d | Col 1e |
|--------|--------|--------|--------|--------|
| 520 | 272 | 3375 | 655.64 | 223.76 |

## Working out and recording NICs where employee's total earnings exceed the UEL - Table letter C

Where the employee's total earnings exceed the UEL, only the earnings between the PT and the UEL should be recorded in column 1c of form RT11.

Use the main table to work out the employer's NICs due on the earnings up to the UEL.

To work out the employer's NICs due on the earnings above the UEL, take the following action:

| Step | Action | Example (based on Table letter C with total monthly earnings of £5,483.29) |
|---|---|---|
| 1. | Subtract the UEL figure from the total gross pay. | £5,483.29 - £4,167 = £1,316.29 |
| 2. | Round the answer down to the nearest whole £. | Rounded down to £1,316 |
| 3. | Look this figure up in the Additional gross pay table on page 80. | Look up £1,316 |
| 4. | If the figure is not shown in the table, build up to it by adding together as few entries as possible. | |

| Amount | Employer's NICs payable |
|---|---|
| £1000 | £138.00 |
| £300 | + £41.40 |
| £16 | + £2.21 |
| Total | = £181.61 |

| Step | Action | |
|---|---|---|
| 5. | Add the employer's NICs worked out on the earnings above the UEL (column 1d of the Additional gross pay table) to the employer NICs due for earnings at the UEL (column 1d of the main table). | **Total payable by employer** |

| | |
|---|---|
| | £181.61 (further employer NICs) |
| | + £474.03 (due for employer on earnings at UEL) |
| Total | = £655.64 |

| Step | Action |
|---|---|
| 6. | Record the figure resulting from Step 5 in column 1d of form RT11. |

On form RT11 or equivalent record

| Col 1a | Col 1b | Col 1c | Col 1d | Col 1e |
|---|---|---|---|---|
| 520 | 272 | 3375 | 655.64 | 0.00 |

## Additional gross pay table – Table letter B

| Earnings on which NICs payable | Employer's NICs payable | Employee's NICs payable | Total of employee's and employer's NICs payable (for information only) |
|---|---|---|---|
| | 1d | 1e | |
| £ | £ p | £ p | £ p |
| 1 | 0.14 | 0.02 | 0.16 |
| 2 | 0.28 | 0.04 | 0.32 |
| 3 | 0.41 | 0.06 | 0.47 |
| 4 | 0.55 | 0.08 | 0.63 |
| 5 | 0.69 | 0.10 | 0.79 |
| 6 | 0.83 | 0.12 | 0.95 |
| 7 | 0.97 | 0.14 | 1.11 |
| 8 | 1.10 | 0.16 | 1.26 |
| 9 | 1.24 | 0.18 | 1.42 |
| 10 | 1.38 | 0.20 | 1.58 |
| 11 | 1.52 | 0.22 | 1.74 |
| 12 | 1.66 | 0.24 | 1.90 |
| 13 | 1.79 | 0.26 | 2.05 |
| 14 | 1.93 | 0.28 | 2.21 |
| 15 | 2.07 | 0.30 | 2.37 |
| 16 | 2.21 | 0.32 | 2.53 |
| 17 | 2.35 | 0.34 | 2.69 |
| 18 | 2.48 | 0.36 | 2.84 |
| 19 | 2.62 | 0.38 | 3.00 |
| 20 | 2.76 | 0.40 | 3.16 |
| 21 | 2.90 | 0.42 | 3.32 |
| 22 | 3.04 | 0.44 | 3.48 |
| 23 | 3.17 | 0.46 | 3.63 |
| 24 | 3.31 | 0.48 | 3.79 |
| 25 | 3.45 | 0.50 | 3.95 |
| 26 | 3.59 | 0.52 | 4.11 |
| 27 | 3.73 | 0.54 | 4.27 |
| 28 | 3.86 | 0.56 | 4.42 |
| 29 | 4.00 | 0.58 | 4.58 |
| 30 | 4.14 | 0.60 | 4.74 |
| 31 | 4.28 | 0.62 | 4.90 |
| 32 | 4.42 | 0.64 | 5.06 |
| 33 | 4.55 | 0.66 | 5.21 |
| 34 | 4.69 | 0.68 | 5.37 |
| 35 | 4.83 | 0.70 | 5.53 |
| 36 | 4.97 | 0.72 | 5.69 |
| 37 | 5.11 | 0.74 | 5.85 |
| 38 | 5.24 | 0.76 | 6.00 |
| 39 | 5.38 | 0.78 | 6.16 |
| 40 | 5.52 | 0.80 | 6.32 |
| 41 | 5.66 | 0.82 | 6.48 |
| 42 | 5.80 | 0.84 | 6.64 |
| 43 | 5.93 | 0.86 | 6.79 |
| 44 | 6.07 | 0.88 | 6.95 |
| 45 | 6.21 | 0.90 | 7.11 |
| 46 | 6.35 | 0.92 | 7.27 |
| 47 | 6.49 | 0.94 | 7.43 |
| 48 | 6.62 | 0.96 | 7.58 |
| 49 | 6.76 | 0.98 | 7.74 |
| 50 | 6.90 | 1.00 | 7.90 |
| 51 | 7.04 | 1.02 | 8.06 |
| 52 | 7.18 | 1.04 | 8.22 |
| 53 | 7.31 | 1.06 | 8.37 |
| 54 | 7.45 | 1.08 | 8.53 |
| 55 | 7.59 | 1.10 | 8.69 |

## Additional gross pay table – Table letter B

| Earnings on which NICs payable | Employer's NICs payable | Employee's NICs payable | Total of employee's and employer's NICs payable (for information only) |
|---|---|---|---|
| | 1d | 1e | |
| £ | £ p | £ p | £ p |
| 56 | 7.73 | 1.12 | 8.85 |
| 57 | 7.87 | 1.14 | 9.01 |
| 58 | 8.00 | 1.16 | 9.16 |
| 59 | 8.14 | 1.18 | 9.32 |
| 60 | 8.28 | 1.20 | 9.48 |
| 61 | 8.42 | 1.22 | 9.64 |
| 62 | 8.56 | 1.24 | 9.80 |
| 63 | 8.69 | 1.26 | 9.95 |
| 64 | 8.83 | 1.28 | 10.11 |
| 65 | 8.97 | 1.30 | 10.27 |
| 66 | 9.11 | 1.32 | 10.43 |
| 67 | 9.25 | 1.34 | 10.59 |
| 68 | 9.38 | 1.36 | 10.74 |
| 69 | 9.52 | 1.38 | 10.90 |
| 70 | 9.66 | 1.40 | 11.06 |
| 71 | 9.80 | 1.42 | 11.22 |
| 72 | 9.94 | 1.44 | 11.38 |
| 73 | 10.07 | 1.46 | 11.53 |
| 74 | 10.21 | 1.48 | 11.69 |
| 75 | 10.35 | 1.50 | 11.85 |
| 76 | 10.49 | 1.52 | 12.01 |
| 77 | 10.63 | 1.54 | 12.17 |
| 78 | 10.76 | 1.56 | 12.32 |
| 79 | 10.90 | 1.58 | 12.48 |
| 80 | 11.04 | 1.60 | 12.64 |
| 81 | 11.18 | 1.62 | 12.80 |
| 82 | 11.32 | 1.64 | 12.96 |
| 83 | 11.45 | 1.66 | 13.11 |
| 84 | 11.59 | 1.68 | 13.27 |
| 85 | 11.73 | 1.70 | 13.43 |
| 86 | 11.87 | 1.72 | 13.59 |
| 87 | 12.01 | 1.74 | 13.75 |
| 88 | 12.14 | 1.76 | 13.90 |
| 89 | 12.28 | 1.78 | 14.06 |
| 90 | 12.42 | 1.80 | 14.22 |
| 91 | 12.56 | 1.82 | 14.38 |
| 92 | 12.70 | 1.84 | 14.54 |
| 93 | 12.83 | 1.86 | 14.69 |
| 94 | 12.97 | 1.88 | 14.85 |
| 95 | 13.11 | 1.90 | 15.01 |
| 96 | 13.25 | 1.92 | 15.17 |
| 97 | 13.39 | 1.94 | 15.33 |
| 98 | 13.52 | 1.96 | 15.48 |
| 99 | 13.66 | 1.98 | 15.64 |
| 100 | 13.80 | 2.00 | 15.80 |
| 200 | 27.60 | 4.00 | 31.60 |
| 300 | 41.40 | 6.00 | 47.40 |
| 400 | 55.20 | 8.00 | 63.20 |
| 500 | 69.00 | 10.00 | 79.00 |
| 600 | 82.80 | 12.00 | 94.80 |
| 700 | 96.60 | 14.00 | 110.60 |
| 800 | 110.40 | 16.00 | 126.40 |
| 900 | 124.20 | 18.00 | 142.20 |
| 1000 | 138.00 | 20.00 | 158.00 |
| 2000 | 276.00 | 40.00 | 316.00 |

Page 78

## Additional gross pay table – Table letter B

| Earnings on which NICs payable | Employer's NICs payable | Employee's NICs payable | Total of employee's and employer's NICs payable (for information only) |
|---|---|---|---|
| | 1d | 1e | |
| £ | £ p | £ p | £ p |
| 3000 | 414.00 | 60.00 | 474.00 |
| 4000 | 552.00 | 80.00 | 632.00 |
| 5000 | 690.00 | 100.00 | 790.00 |
| 6000 | 828.00 | 120.00 | 948.00 |
| 7000 | 966.00 | 140.00 | 1106.00 |
| 8000 | 1104.00 | 160.00 | 1264.00 |
| 9000 | 1242.00 | 180.00 | 1422.00 |
| 10000 | 1380.00 | 200.00 | 1580.00 |
| 20000 | 2760.00 | 400.00 | 3160.00 |
| 30000 | 4140.00 | 600.00 | 4740.00 |
| 40000 | 5520.00 | 800.00 | 6320.00 |
| 50000 | 6900.00 | 1000.00 | 7900.00 |
| 60000 | 8280.00 | 1200.00 | 9480.00 |
| 70000 | 9660.00 | 1400.00 | 11060.00 |
| 80000 | 11040.00 | 1600.00 | 12640.00 |
| 90000 | 12420.00 | 1800.00 | 14220.00 |
| 100000 | 13800.00 | 2000.00 | 15800.00 |

## Additional gross pay table – Table letter C

| Earnings on which NICs payable | Employer's NICs payable | Earnings on which NICs payable | Employer's NICs payable | Earnings on which NICs payable | Employer's NICs payable |
|---|---|---|---|---|---|
| | 1d | | 1d | | 1d |
| £ | £ p | £ | £ p | £ | £ p |
| 1 | 0.14 | 56 | 7.73 | 3000 | 414.00 |
| 2 | 0.28 | 57 | 7.87 | 4000 | 552.00 |
| 3 | 0.41 | 58 | 8.00 | 5000 | 690.00 |
| 4 | 0.55 | 59 | 8.14 | 6000 | 828.00 |
| 5 | 0.69 | 60 | 8.28 | 7000 | 966.00 |
| 6 | 0.83 | 61 | 8.42 | 8000 | 1104.00 |
| 7 | 0.97 | 62 | 8.56 | 9000 | 1242.00 |
| 8 | 1.10 | 63 | 8.69 | 10000 | 1380.00 |
| 9 | 1.24 | 64 | 8.83 | 20000 | 2760.00 |
| 10 | 1.38 | 65 | 8.97 | 30000 | 4140.00 |
| 11 | 1.52 | 66 | 9.11 | 40000 | 5520.00 |
| 12 | 1.66 | 67 | 9.25 | 50000 | 6900.00 |
| 13 | 1.79 | 68 | 9.38 | 60000 | 8280.00 |
| 14 | 1.93 | 69 | 9.52 | 70000 | 9660.00 |
| 15 | 2.07 | 70 | 9.66 | 80000 | 11040.00 |
| 16 | 2.21 | 71 | 9.80 | 90000 | 12420.00 |
| 17 | 2.35 | 72 | 9.94 | 100000 | 13800.00 |
| 18 | 2.48 | 73 | 10.07 | | |
| 19 | 2.62 | 74 | 10.21 | | |
| 20 | 2.76 | 75 | 10.35 | | |
| 21 | 2.90 | 76 | 10.49 | | |
| 22 | 3.04 | 77 | 10.63 | | |
| 23 | 3.17 | 78 | 10.76 | | |
| 24 | 3.31 | 79 | 10.90 | | |
| 25 | 3.45 | 80 | 11.04 | | |
| 26 | 3.59 | 81 | 11.18 | | |
| 27 | 3.73 | 82 | 11.32 | | |
| 28 | 3.86 | 83 | 11.45 | | |
| 29 | 4.00 | 84 | 11.59 | | |
| 30 | 4.14 | 85 | 11.73 | | |
| 31 | 4.28 | 86 | 11.87 | | |
| 32 | 4.42 | 87 | 12.01 | | |
| 33 | 4.55 | 88 | 12.14 | | |
| 34 | 4.69 | 89 | 12.28 | | |
| 35 | 4.83 | 90 | 12.42 | | |
| 36 | 4.97 | 91 | 12.56 | | |
| 37 | 5.11 | 92 | 12.70 | | |
| 38 | 5.24 | 93 | 12.83 | | |
| 39 | 5.38 | 94 | 12.97 | | |
| 40 | 5.52 | 95 | 13.11 | | |
| 41 | 5.66 | 96 | 13.25 | | |
| 42 | 5.80 | 97 | 13.39 | | |
| 43 | 5.93 | 98 | 13.52 | | |
| 44 | 6.07 | 99 | 13.66 | | |
| 45 | 6.21 | 100 | 13.80 | | |
| 46 | 6.35 | 200 | 27.60 | | |
| 47 | 6.49 | 300 | 41.40 | | |
| 48 | 6.62 | 400 | 55.20 | | |
| 49 | 6.76 | 500 | 69.00 | | |
| 50 | 6.90 | 600 | 82.80 | | |
| 51 | 7.04 | 700 | 96.60 | | |
| 52 | 7.18 | 800 | 110.40 | | |
| 53 | 7.31 | 900 | 124.20 | | |
| 54 | 7.45 | 1000 | 138.00 | | |
| 55 | 7.59 | 2000 | 276.00 | | |

HM Revenue
& Customs

Pay Adjustment Tables

# Tables A

These tables are intended for the very small number of
employers who are exempt from the requirement to file
Real Time information online.

If you are an employer operating PAYE in real time you are no
longer able to run your payroll manually and you do not need to
use these manual tables. Instead you should be using software that
is capable of filing payroll information online.

# Contents

These Tables show the weekly and monthly
• free pay for each suffix code, including S prefix codes (except NT)
• 'additional pay' for codes with a K, or SK prefix
Use these Tables together with the Taxable Pay Tables.

These Tables were brought into use from 6 April 1993.

**You should continue to use these Tables until we tell you to destroy them.**

From 6 April 2016 Scottish rates of tax have been introduced. If an employee has a tax code with prefix S the Scottish rates of tax must be used.

## Tables A – the Pay Adjustment Tables

Use these Tables to work out the free pay to date of employees whose codes have the suffix L, M, N, P or T, and S prefix tax codes (not NT); and to work out the 'additional pay' to date of employees whose codes have the prefix K or SK.

## How to work out free pay

After turning to the Table appropriate to the pay day use it in this way:

- In the column headed 'Code' find the number of the employee's PAYE code (ignore the suffix letter and the S prefix). The amount of free pay to date is shown to the right of the code.
- If the code exceeds 500 the free pay is obtained by adding together two or more amounts of pay adjustment calculated as follows:
  - divide the code into units of 500 and note the number of units and the amount left over. For example, for code 1567 the number of units of 500 is three and the remainder is 67.

The free pay is then calculated in two stages:

1 look up the amount of pay adjustment from the main look-up Table for the remainder (67 in this example)
2 multiply the figure given in the box marked '*' at the bottom of the page by the number of units of 500.

Add these two amounts together.

| Example | |
|---|---|
| For code **1567** at **week 35** the free pay is worked out like this: | |
| • Amount in respect of the **remainder of 67** | £ 457.10 |
| • Amount in respect of the **units of 500** (3 x £3365.60) | £ 10096.80 |
| • **Total Free Pay** | £ 10553 .90 |

One amount of pay adjustment, but only one amount, should be taken from the main look-up Table.

If the code divides **exactly** into units of 500 with no balance over (for example, 1500, 2000, 2500) **divide** the code into units of 500 and note the number of units (for example, **1500** is **3** units of 500, **2000** is **4** units of 500. Calculate the free pay like this:

1 **look up** the amount for **one unit** of 500 from the main look-up Table
2 **multiply** the figure given in the box marked '*' at the bottom of the page by the number of **remaining** units of 500.

Add these two amounts together.

| Example | |
|---|---|
| For code **1500** at **week 35** the free pay is worked out like this: | |
| • Amount in respect of **one unit** of 500 (500 on the main look-up Table) | £ 3371.55 |
| • Amount in respect of the **two remaining** units (3 x £3365.60) | £ 6731.20 |
| • **Total Free Pay** | £ 10102.75 |

## How to work out 'additional pay'

This is worked out in the same way as free pay. The only point you must remember is that you enter the amount in the shaded column 4b on the RT11 Deductions working sheet and add it to the Total Pay to date. For guidance on how to complete form RT11 in PAYE code K, and SK cases see Guidance for Employers exempt from filing Real Time Information online.

If you have any questions please call the Employer's Helpline on **0300 200 3200** for advice.

**Week 1** Apr 6 to Apr 12    **Tables A** - Pay Adjustment Tables

| Code | Total pay adjustment to date | Code | Total pay adjustment to date | Code | Total pay adjustment to date | Code | Total pay adjustment to date | Code | Total pay adjustment to date | Code | Total pay adjustment to date | Code | Total pay adjustment to date | Code | Total pay adjustment to date | Code | Total pay adjustment to date |
|---|---|---|---|---|---|---|---|---|---|---|---|---|---|---|---|---|---|
| | £ | | £ | | £ | | £ | | £ | | £ | | £ | | £ | | £ |
| 0 | NIL | 61 | 11.91 | 121 | 23.45 | 181 | 34.99 | 241 | 46.52 | 301 | 58.06 | 351 | 67.68 | 401 | 77.29 | 451 | 86.91 |
| 1 | 0.37 | 62 | 12.10 | 122 | 23.64 | 182 | 35.18 | 242 | 46.72 | 302 | 58.25 | 352 | 67.87 | 402 | 77.49 | 452 | 87.10 |
| 2 | 0.56 | 63 | 12.29 | 123 | 23.83 | 183 | 35.37 | 243 | 46.91 | 303 | 58.45 | 353 | 68.06 | 403 | 77.68 | 453 | 87.29 |
| 3 | 0.75 | 64 | 12.49 | 124 | 24.02 | 184 | 35.56 | 244 | 47.10 | 304 | 58.64 | 354 | 68.25 | 404 | 77.87 | 454 | 87.49 |
| 4 | 0.95 | 65 | 12.68 | 125 | 24.22 | 185 | 35.75 | 245 | 47.29 | 305 | 58.83 | 355 | 68.45 | 405 | 78.06 | 455 | 87.68 |
| 5 | 1.14 | | | | | | | | | | | | | | | | |
| 6 | 1.33 | 66 | 12.87 | 126 | 24.41 | 186 | 35.95 | 246 | 47.49 | 306 | 59.02 | 356 | 68.64 | 406 | 78.25 | 456 | 87.87 |
| 7 | 1.52 | 67 | 13.06 | 127 | 24.60 | 187 | 36.14 | 247 | 47.68 | 307 | 59.22 | 357 | 68.83 | 407 | 78.45 | 457 | 88.06 |
| 8 | 1.72 | 68 | 13.25 | 128 | 24.79 | 188 | 36.33 | 248 | 47.87 | 308 | 59.41 | 358 | 69.02 | 408 | 78.64 | 458 | 88.25 |
| 9 | 1.91 | 69 | 13.45 | 129 | 24.99 | 189 | 36.52 | 249 | 48.06 | 309 | 59.60 | 359 | 69.22 | 409 | 78.83 | 459 | 88.45 |
| 10 | 2.10 | 70 | 13.64 | 130 | 25.18 | 190 | 36.72 | 250 | 48.25 | 310 | 59.79 | 360 | 69.41 | 410 | 79.02 | 460 | 88.64 |
| 11 | 2.29 | 71 | 13.83 | 131 | 25.37 | 191 | 36.91 | 251 | 48.45 | 311 | 59.99 | 361 | 69.60 | 411 | 79.22 | 461 | 88.83 |
| 12 | 2.49 | 72 | 14.02 | 132 | 25.56 | 192 | 37.10 | 252 | 48.64 | 312 | 60.18 | 362 | 69.79 | 412 | 79.41 | 462 | 89.02 |
| 13 | 2.68 | 73 | 14.22 | 133 | 25.75 | 193 | 37.29 | 253 | 48.83 | 313 | 60.37 | 363 | 69.99 | 413 | 79.60 | 463 | 89.22 |
| 14 | 2.87 | 74 | 14.41 | 134 | 25.95 | 194 | 37.49 | 254 | 49.02 | 314 | 60.56 | 364 | 70.18 | 414 | 79.79 | 464 | 89.41 |
| 15 | 3.06 | 75 | 14.60 | 135 | 26.14 | 195 | 37.68 | 255 | 49.22 | 315 | 60.75 | 365 | 70.37 | 415 | 79.99 | 465 | 89.60 |
| 16 | 3.25 | 76 | 14.79 | 136 | 26.33 | 196 | 37.87 | 256 | 49.41 | 316 | 60.95 | 366 | 70.56 | 416 | 80.18 | 466 | 89.79 |
| 17 | 3.45 | 77 | 14.99 | 137 | 26.52 | 197 | 38.06 | 257 | 49.60 | 317 | 61.14 | 367 | 70.75 | 417 | 80.37 | 467 | 89.99 |
| 18 | 3.64 | 78 | 15.18 | 138 | 26.72 | 198 | 38.25 | 258 | 49.79 | 318 | 61.33 | 368 | 70.95 | 418 | 80.56 | 468 | 90.18 |
| 19 | 3.83 | 79 | 15.37 | 139 | 26.91 | 199 | 38.45 | 259 | 49.99 | 319 | 61.52 | 369 | 71.14 | 419 | 80.75 | 469 | 90.37 |
| 20 | 4.02 | 80 | 15.56 | 140 | 27.10 | 200 | 38.64 | 260 | 50.18 | 320 | 61.72 | 370 | 71.33 | 420 | 80.95 | 470 | 90.56 |
| 21 | 4.22 | 81 | 15.75 | 141 | 27.29 | 201 | 38.83 | 261 | 50.37 | 321 | 61.91 | 371 | 71.52 | 421 | 81.14 | 471 | 90.75 |
| 22 | 4.41 | 82 | 15.95 | 142 | 27.49 | 202 | 39.02 | 262 | 50.56 | 322 | 62.10 | 372 | 71.72 | 422 | 81.33 | 472 | 90.95 |
| 23 | 4.60 | 83 | 16.14 | 143 | 27.68 | 203 | 39.22 | 263 | 50.75 | 323 | 62.29 | 373 | 71.91 | 423 | 81.52 | 473 | 91.14 |
| 24 | 4.79 | 84 | 16.33 | 144 | 27.87 | 204 | 39.41 | 264 | 50.95 | 324 | 62.49 | 374 | 72.10 | 424 | 81.72 | 474 | 91.33 |
| 25 | 4.99 | 85 | 16.52 | 145 | 28.06 | 205 | 39.60 | 265 | 51.14 | 325 | 62.68 | 375 | 72.29 | 425 | 81.91 | 475 | 91.52 |
| 26 | 5.18 | 86 | 16.72 | 146 | 28.25 | 206 | 39.79 | 266 | 51.33 | 326 | 62.87 | 376 | 72.49 | 426 | 82.10 | 476 | 91.72 |
| 27 | 5.37 | 87 | 16.91 | 147 | 28.45 | 207 | 39.99 | 267 | 51.52 | 327 | 63.06 | 377 | 72.68 | 427 | 82.29 | 477 | 91.91 |
| 28 | 5.56 | 88 | 17.10 | 148 | 28.64 | 208 | 40.18 | 268 | 51.72 | 328 | 63.25 | 378 | 72.87 | 428 | 82.49 | 478 | 92.10 |
| 29 | 5.75 | 89 | 17.29 | 149 | 28.83 | 209 | 40.37 | 269 | 51.91 | 329 | 63.45 | 379 | 73.06 | 429 | 82.68 | 479 | 92.29 |
| 30 | 5.95 | 90 | 17.49 | 150 | 29.02 | 210 | 40.56 | 270 | 52.10 | 330 | 63.64 | 380 | 73.25 | 430 | 82.87 | 480 | 92.49 |
| 31 | 6.14 | 91 | 17.68 | 151 | 29.22 | 211 | 40.75 | 271 | 52.29 | 331 | 63.83 | 381 | 73.45 | 431 | 83.06 | 481 | 92.68 |
| 32 | 6.33 | 92 | 17.87 | 152 | 29.41 | 212 | 40.95 | 272 | 52.49 | 332 | 64.02 | 382 | 73.64 | 432 | 83.25 | 482 | 92.87 |
| 33 | 6.52 | 93 | 18.06 | 153 | 29.60 | 213 | 41.14 | 273 | 52.68 | 333 | 64.22 | 383 | 73.83 | 433 | 83.45 | 483 | 93.06 |
| 34 | 6.72 | 94 | 18.25 | 154 | 29.79 | 214 | 41.33 | 274 | 52.87 | 334 | 64.41 | 384 | 74.02 | 434 | 83.64 | 484 | 93.25 |
| 35 | 6.91 | 95 | 18.45 | 155 | 29.99 | 215 | 41.52 | 275 | 53.06 | 335 | 64.60 | 385 | 74.22 | 435 | 83.83 | 485 | 93.45 |
| 36 | 7.10 | 96 | 18.64 | 156 | 30.18 | 216 | 41.72 | 276 | 53.25 | 336 | 64.79 | 386 | 74.41 | 436 | 84.02 | 486 | 93.64 |
| 37 | 7.29 | 97 | 18.83 | 157 | 30.37 | 217 | 41.91 | 277 | 53.45 | 337 | 64.99 | 387 | 74.60 | 437 | 84.22 | 487 | 93.83 |
| 38 | 7.49 | 98 | 19.02 | 158 | 30.56 | 218 | 42.10 | 278 | 53.64 | 338 | 65.18 | 388 | 74.79 | 438 | 84.41 | 488 | 94.02 |
| 39 | 7.68 | 99 | 19.22 | 159 | 30.75 | 219 | 42.29 | 279 | 53.83 | 339 | 65.37 | 389 | 74.99 | 439 | 84.60 | 489 | 94.22 |
| 40 | 7.87 | 100 | 19.41 | 160 | 30.95 | 220 | 42.49 | 280 | 54.02 | 340 | 65.56 | 390 | 75.18 | 440 | 84.79 | 490 | 94.41 |
| 41 | 8.06 | 101 | 19.60 | 161 | 31.14 | 221 | 42.68 | 281 | 54.22 | 341 | 65.75 | 391 | 75.37 | 441 | 84.99 | 491 | 94.60 |
| 42 | 8.25 | 102 | 19.79 | 162 | 31.33 | 222 | 42.87 | 282 | 54.41 | 342 | 65.95 | 392 | 75.56 | 442 | 85.18 | 492 | 94.79 |
| 43 | 8.45 | 103 | 19.99 | 163 | 31.52 | 223 | 43.06 | 283 | 54.60 | 343 | 66.14 | 393 | 75.75 | 443 | 85.37 | 493 | 94.99 |
| 44 | 8.64 | 104 | 20.18 | 164 | 31.72 | 224 | 43.25 | 284 | 54.79 | 344 | 66.33 | 394 | 75.95 | 444 | 85.56 | 494 | 95.18 |
| 45 | 8.83 | 105 | 20.37 | 165 | 31.91 | 225 | 43.45 | 285 | 54.99 | 345 | 66.52 | 395 | 76.14 | 445 | 85.75 | 495 | 95.37 |
| 46 | 9.02 | 106 | 20.56 | 166 | 32.10 | 226 | 43.64 | 286 | 55.18 | 346 | 66.72 | 396 | 76.33 | 446 | 85.95 | 496 | 95.56 |
| 47 | 9.22 | 107 | 20.75 | 167 | 32.29 | 227 | 43.83 | 287 | 55.37 | 347 | 66.91 | 397 | 76.52 | 447 | 86.14 | 497 | 95.75 |
| 48 | 9.41 | 108 | 20.95 | 168 | 32.49 | 228 | 44.02 | 288 | 55.56 | 348 | 67.10 | 398 | 76.72 | 448 | 86.33 | 498 | 95.95 |
| 49 | 9.60 | 109 | 21.14 | 169 | 32.68 | 229 | 44.22 | 289 | 55.75 | 349 | 67.29 | 399 | 76.91 | 449 | 86.52 | 499 | 96.14 |
| 50 | 9.79 | 110 | 21.33 | 170 | 32.87 | 230 | 44.41 | 290 | 55.95 | 350 | 67.49 | 400 | 77.10 | 450 | 86.72 | 500 | 96.33 |
| 51 | 9.99 | 111 | 21.52 | 171 | 33.06 | 231 | 44.60 | 291 | 56.14 | | | | | | | | |
| 52 | 10.18 | 112 | 21.72 | 172 | 33.25 | 232 | 44.79 | 292 | 56.33 | | | | | | | | |
| 53 | 10.37 | 113 | 21.91 | 173 | 33.45 | 233 | 44.99 | 293 | 56.52 | | | | | | | | |
| 54 | 10.56 | 114 | 22.10 | 174 | 33.64 | 234 | 45.18 | 294 | 56.72 | | | | | | | | |
| 55 | 10.75 | 115 | 22.29 | 175 | 33.83 | 235 | 45.37 | 295 | 56.91 | | | | | | | | |
| 56 | 10.95 | 116 | 22.49 | 176 | 34.02 | 236 | 45.56 | 296 | 57.10 | | | | | | | | |
| 57 | 11.14 | 117 | 22.68 | 177 | 34.22 | 237 | 45.75 | 297 | 57.29 | | | | | | | | |
| 58 | 11.33 | 118 | 22.87 | 178 | 34.41 | 238 | 45.95 | 298 | 57.49 | | | | | | | | |
| 59 | 11.52 | 119 | 23.06 | 179 | 34.60 | 239 | 46.14 | 299 | 57.68 | | | | | | | | |
| 60 | 11.72 | 120 | 23.25 | 180 | 34.79 | 240 | 46.33 | 300 | 57.87 | | | | | | | | |

**Code more than 500**

1 Where the code is in the range **501 to 1000** inclusive:

a. Subtract **500** from the code and use the balance of the code to obtain a pay adjustment figure from the table above.

b. Add this pay adjustment figure to the figure given in the box alongside to obtain the figure of total pay adjustment to date * | 96.16 |

2 Where the code **exceeds 1000** follow the instructions on **page 3**.

4

# Tables A - Pay Adjustment Tables

Apr 13 to Apr 19  **Week 2**

| Code | Total pay adjustment to date | Code | Total pay adjustment to date | Code | Total pay adjustment to date | Code | Total pay adjustment to date | Code | Total pay adjustment to date | Code | Total pay adjustment to date | Code | Total pay adjustment to date | Code | Total pay adjustment to date | Code | Total pay adjustment to date |
|---|---|---|---|---|---|---|---|---|---|---|---|---|---|---|---|---|---|
| | £ | | £ | | £ | | £ | | £ | | £ | | £ | | £ | | £ |
| 0 | NIL | 61 | 23.82 | 121 | 46.90 | 181 | 69.98 | 241 | 93.04 | 301 | 116.12 | 351 | 135.36 | 401 | 154.58 | 451 | 173.82 |
| 1 | 0.74 | 62 | 24.20 | 122 | 47.28 | 182 | 70.36 | 242 | 93.44 | 302 | 116.50 | 352 | 135.74 | 402 | 154.98 | 452 | 174.20 |
| 2 | 1.12 | 63 | 24.58 | 123 | 47.66 | 183 | 70.74 | 243 | 93.82 | 303 | 116.90 | 353 | 136.12 | 403 | 155.36 | 453 | 174.58 |
| 3 | 1.50 | 64 | 24.98 | 124 | 48.04 | 184 | 71.12 | 244 | 94.20 | 304 | 117.28 | 354 | 136.50 | 404 | 155.74 | 454 | 174.98 |
| 4 | 1.90 | 65 | 25.36 | 125 | 48.44 | 185 | 71.50 | 245 | 94.58 | 305 | 117.66 | 355 | 136.90 | 405 | 156.12 | 455 | 175.36 |
| 5 | 2.28 | 66 | 25.74 | 126 | 48.82 | 186 | 71.90 | 246 | 94.98 | 306 | 118.04 | 356 | 137.28 | 406 | 156.50 | 456 | 175.74 |
| 6 | 2.66 | 67 | 26.12 | 127 | 49.20 | 187 | 72.28 | 247 | 95.36 | 307 | 118.44 | 357 | 137.66 | 407 | 156.90 | 457 | 176.12 |
| 7 | 3.04 | 68 | 26.50 | 128 | 49.58 | 188 | 72.66 | 248 | 95.74 | 308 | 118.82 | 358 | 138.04 | 408 | 157.28 | 458 | 176.50 |
| 8 | 3.44 | 69 | 26.90 | 129 | 49.98 | 189 | 73.04 | 249 | 96.12 | 309 | 119.20 | 359 | 138.44 | 409 | 157.66 | 459 | 176.90 |
| 9 | 3.82 | 70 | 27.28 | 130 | 50.36 | 190 | 73.44 | 250 | 96.50 | 310 | 119.58 | 360 | 138.82 | 410 | 158.04 | 460 | 177.28 |
| 10 | 4.20 | 71 | 27.66 | 131 | 50.74 | 191 | 73.82 | 251 | 96.90 | 311 | 119.98 | 361 | 139.20 | 411 | 158.44 | 461 | 177.66 |
| 11 | 4.58 | 72 | 28.04 | 132 | 51.12 | 192 | 74.20 | 252 | 97.28 | 312 | 120.36 | 362 | 139.58 | 412 | 158.82 | 462 | 178.04 |
| 12 | 4.98 | 73 | 28.44 | 133 | 51.50 | 193 | 74.58 | 253 | 97.66 | 313 | 120.74 | 363 | 139.98 | 413 | 159.20 | 463 | 178.44 |
| 13 | 5.36 | 74 | 28.82 | 134 | 51.90 | 194 | 74.98 | 254 | 98.04 | 314 | 121.12 | 364 | 140.36 | 414 | 159.58 | 464 | 178.82 |
| 14 | 5.74 | 75 | 29.20 | 135 | 52.28 | 195 | 75.36 | 255 | 98.44 | 315 | 121.50 | 365 | 140.74 | 415 | 159.98 | 465 | 179.20 |
| 15 | 6.12 | 76 | 29.58 | 136 | 52.66 | 196 | 75.74 | 256 | 98.82 | 316 | 121.90 | 366 | 141.12 | 416 | 160.36 | 466 | 179.58 |
| 16 | 6.50 | 77 | 29.98 | 137 | 53.04 | 197 | 76.12 | 257 | 99.20 | 317 | 122.28 | 367 | 141.50 | 417 | 160.74 | 467 | 179.98 |
| 17 | 6.90 | 78 | 30.36 | 138 | 53.44 | 198 | 76.50 | 258 | 99.58 | 318 | 122.66 | 368 | 141.90 | 418 | 161.12 | 468 | 180.36 |
| 18 | 7.28 | 79 | 30.74 | 139 | 53.82 | 199 | 76.90 | 259 | 99.98 | 319 | 123.04 | 369 | 142.28 | 419 | 161.50 | 469 | 180.74 |
| 19 | 7.66 | 80 | 31.12 | 140 | 54.20 | 200 | 77.28 | 260 | 100.36 | 320 | 123.44 | 370 | 142.66 | 420 | 161.90 | 470 | 181.12 |
| 20 | 8.04 | 81 | 31.50 | 141 | 54.58 | 201 | 77.66 | 261 | 100.74 | 321 | 123.82 | 371 | 143.04 | 421 | 162.28 | 471 | 181.50 |
| 21 | 8.44 | 82 | 31.90 | 142 | 54.98 | 202 | 78.04 | 262 | 101.12 | 322 | 124.20 | 372 | 143.42 | 422 | 162.66 | 472 | 181.90 |
| 22 | 8.82 | 83 | 32.28 | 143 | 55.36 | 203 | 78.44 | 263 | 101.50 | 323 | 124.58 | 373 | 143.82 | 423 | 163.04 | 473 | 182.28 |
| 23 | 9.20 | 84 | 32.66 | 144 | 55.74 | 204 | 78.82 | 264 | 101.90 | 324 | 124.98 | 374 | 144.20 | 424 | 163.44 | 474 | 182.66 |
| 24 | 9.58 | 85 | 33.04 | 145 | 56.12 | 205 | 79.20 | 265 | 102.28 | 325 | 125.36 | 375 | 144.58 | 425 | 163.82 | 475 | 183.04 |
| 25 | 9.98 | 86 | 33.44 | 146 | 56.50 | 206 | 79.58 | 266 | 102.66 | 326 | 125.74 | 376 | 144.98 | 426 | 164.20 | 476 | 183.44 |
| 26 | 10.36 | 87 | 33.82 | 147 | 56.90 | 207 | 79.98 | 267 | 103.04 | 327 | 126.12 | 377 | 145.36 | 427 | 164.58 | 477 | 183.82 |
| 27 | 10.74 | 88 | 34.20 | 148 | 57.28 | 208 | 80.36 | 268 | 103.44 | 328 | 126.50 | 378 | 145.74 | 428 | 164.98 | 478 | 184.20 |
| 28 | 11.12 | 89 | 34.58 | 149 | 57.66 | 209 | 80.74 | 269 | 103.82 | 329 | 126.90 | 379 | 146.12 | 429 | 165.36 | 479 | 184.58 |
| 29 | 11.50 | 90 | 34.98 | 150 | 58.04 | 210 | 81.12 | 270 | 104.20 | 330 | 127.28 | 380 | 146.50 | 430 | 165.74 | 480 | 184.98 |
| 30 | 11.90 | 91 | 35.36 | 151 | 58.44 | 211 | 81.50 | 271 | 104.58 | 331 | 127.66 | 381 | 146.90 | 431 | 166.12 | 481 | 185.36 |
| 31 | 12.28 | 92 | 35.74 | 152 | 58.82 | 212 | 81.90 | 272 | 104.98 | 332 | 128.04 | 382 | 147.28 | 432 | 166.50 | 482 | 185.74 |
| 32 | 12.66 | 93 | 36.12 | 153 | 59.20 | 213 | 82.28 | 273 | 105.36 | 333 | 128.44 | 383 | 147.66 | 433 | 166.90 | 483 | 186.12 |
| 33 | 13.04 | 94 | 36.50 | 154 | 59.58 | 214 | 82.66 | 274 | 105.74 | 334 | 128.82 | 384 | 148.04 | 434 | 167.28 | 484 | 186.50 |
| 34 | 13.44 | 95 | 36.90 | 155 | 59.98 | 215 | 83.04 | 275 | 106.12 | 335 | 129.20 | 385 | 148.44 | 435 | 167.66 | 485 | 186.90 |
| 35 | 13.82 | 96 | 37.28 | 156 | 60.36 | 216 | 83.44 | 276 | 106.50 | 336 | 129.58 | 386 | 148.82 | 436 | 168.04 | 486 | 187.28 |
| 36 | 14.20 | 97 | 37.66 | 157 | 60.74 | 217 | 83.82 | 277 | 106.90 | 337 | 129.98 | 387 | 149.20 | 437 | 168.44 | 487 | 187.66 |
| 37 | 14.58 | 98 | 38.04 | 158 | 61.12 | 218 | 84.20 | 278 | 107.28 | 338 | 130.36 | 388 | 149.58 | 438 | 168.82 | 488 | 188.04 |
| 38 | 14.98 | 99 | 38.44 | 159 | 61.50 | 219 | 84.58 | 279 | 107.66 | 339 | 130.74 | 389 | 149.98 | 439 | 169.20 | 489 | 188.44 |
| 39 | 15.36 | 100 | 38.82 | 160 | 61.90 | 220 | 84.98 | 280 | 108.04 | 340 | 131.12 | 390 | 150.36 | 440 | 169.58 | 490 | 188.82 |
| 40 | 15.74 | 101 | 39.20 | 161 | 62.28 | 221 | 85.36 | 281 | 108.44 | 341 | 131.50 | 391 | 150.74 | 441 | 169.98 | 491 | 189.20 |
| 41 | 16.12 | 102 | 39.58 | 162 | 62.66 | 222 | 85.74 | 282 | 108.82 | 342 | 131.90 | 392 | 151.12 | 442 | 170.36 | 492 | 189.58 |
| 42 | 16.50 | 103 | 39.98 | 163 | 63.04 | 223 | 86.12 | 283 | 109.20 | 343 | 132.28 | 393 | 151.50 | 443 | 170.74 | 493 | 189.98 |
| 43 | 16.90 | 104 | 40.36 | 164 | 63.44 | 224 | 86.50 | 284 | 109.58 | 344 | 132.66 | 394 | 151.90 | 444 | 171.12 | 494 | 190.36 |
| 44 | 17.28 | 105 | 40.74 | 165 | 63.82 | 225 | 86.90 | 285 | 109.98 | 345 | 133.04 | 395 | 152.28 | 445 | 171.50 | 495 | 190.74 |
| 45 | 17.66 | 106 | 41.12 | 166 | 64.20 | 226 | 87.28 | 286 | 110.36 | 346 | 133.44 | 396 | 152.66 | 446 | 171.90 | 496 | 191.12 |
| 46 | 18.04 | 107 | 41.50 | 167 | 64.58 | 227 | 87.66 | 287 | 110.74 | 347 | 133.82 | 397 | 153.04 | 447 | 172.28 | 497 | 191.50 |
| 47 | 18.44 | 108 | 41.90 | 168 | 64.98 | 228 | 88.04 | 288 | 111.12 | 348 | 134.20 | 398 | 153.44 | 448 | 172.66 | 498 | 191.90 |
| 48 | 18.82 | 109 | 42.28 | 169 | 65.36 | 229 | 88.44 | 289 | 111.50 | 349 | 134.58 | 399 | 153.82 | 449 | 173.04 | 499 | 192.28 |
| 49 | 19.20 | 110 | 42.66 | 170 | 65.74 | 230 | 88.82 | 290 | 111.90 | 350 | 134.98 | 400 | 154.20 | 450 | 173.44 | 500 | 192.66 |
| 50 | 19.58 | 111 | 43.04 | 171 | 66.12 | 231 | 89.20 | 291 | 112.28 | | | | | | | | |
| 51 | 19.98 | 112 | 43.44 | 172 | 66.50 | 232 | 89.58 | 292 | 112.66 | | | | | | | | |
| 52 | 20.36 | 113 | 43.82 | 173 | 66.90 | 233 | 89.98 | 293 | 113.04 | | | | | | | | |
| 53 | 20.74 | 114 | 44.20 | 174 | 67.28 | 234 | 90.36 | 294 | 113.44 | | | | | | | | |
| 54 | 21.12 | 115 | 44.58 | 175 | 67.66 | 235 | 90.74 | 295 | 113.82 | | | | | | | | |
| 55 | 21.50 | 116 | 44.98 | 176 | 68.04 | 236 | 91.12 | 296 | 114.20 | | | | | | | | |
| 56 | 21.90 | 117 | 45.36 | 177 | 68.44 | 237 | 91.50 | 297 | 114.58 | | | | | | | | |
| 57 | 22.28 | 118 | 45.74 | 178 | 68.82 | 238 | 91.90 | 298 | 114.98 | | | | | | | | |
| 58 | 22.66 | 119 | 46.12 | 179 | 69.20 | 239 | 92.28 | 299 | 115.36 | | | | | | | | |
| 59 | 23.04 | 120 | 46.50 | 180 | 69.58 | 240 | 92.66 | 300 | 115.74 | | | | | | | | |
| 60 | 23.44 | | | | | | | | | | | | | | | | |

### Code more than 500

1  Where the code is in the range 501 to **1000** inclusive:

  a. Subtract 500 from the code and use the balance of the code to obtain a pay adjustment figure from the table above.

  b. Add this pay adjustment figure to the figure given in the box alongside to obtain the figure of total pay adjustment to date *  | **192.32** |

2  Where the code **exceeds 1000** follow the instructions on **page 3**.

5

**Week 3**  Apr 20 to Apr 26

**Tables A** - Pay Adjustment Tables

| Code | Total pay adjustment to date | Code | Total pay adjustment to date | Code | Total pay adjustment to date | Code | Total pay adjustment to date | Code | Total pay adjustment to date | Code | Total pay adjustment to date | Code | Total pay adjustment to date | Code | Total pay adjustment to date | Code | Total pay adjustment to date |
|---|---|---|---|---|---|---|---|---|---|---|---|---|---|---|---|---|---|
| | £ | | £ | | £ | | £ | | £ | | £ | | £ | | £ | | £ |
| 0 | NIL | 61 | 35.73 | 121 | 70.35 | 181 | 104.97 | 241 | 139.56 | 301 | 174.18 | 351 | 203.04 | 401 | 231.87 | 451 | 260.73 |
| 1 | 1.11 | 62 | 36.30 | 122 | 70.92 | 182 | 105.54 | 242 | 140.16 | 302 | 174.75 | 352 | 203.61 | 402 | 232.47 | 452 | 261.30 |
| 2 | 1.68 | 63 | 36.87 | 123 | 71.49 | 183 | 106.11 | 243 | 140.73 | 303 | 175.35 | 353 | 204.18 | 403 | 233.04 | 453 | 261.87 |
| 3 | 2.25 | 64 | 37.47 | 124 | 72.06 | 184 | 106.68 | 244 | 141.30 | 304 | 175.92 | 354 | 204.75 | 404 | 233.61 | 454 | 262.47 |
| 4 | 2.85 | 65 | 38.04 | 125 | 72.66 | 185 | 107.25 | 245 | 141.87 | 305 | 176.49 | 355 | 205.35 | 405 | 234.18 | 455 | 263.04 |
| 5 | 3.42 | | | | | | | | | | | | | | | | |
| 6 | 3.99 | 66 | 38.61 | 126 | 73.23 | 186 | 107.85 | 246 | 142.47 | 306 | 177.06 | 356 | 205.92 | 406 | 234.75 | 456 | 263.61 |
| 7 | 4.56 | 67 | 39.18 | 127 | 73.80 | 187 | 108.42 | 247 | 143.04 | 307 | 177.66 | 357 | 206.49 | 407 | 235.35 | 457 | 264.18 |
| 8 | 5.16 | 68 | 39.75 | 128 | 74.37 | 188 | 108.99 | 248 | 143.61 | 308 | 178.23 | 358 | 207.06 | 408 | 235.92 | 458 | 264.75 |
| 9 | 5.73 | 69 | 40.35 | 129 | 74.97 | 189 | 109.56 | 249 | 144.18 | 309 | 178.80 | 359 | 207.66 | 409 | 236.49 | 459 | 265.35 |
| 10 | 6.30 | 70 | 40.92 | 130 | 75.54 | 190 | 110.16 | 250 | 144.75 | 310 | 179.37 | 360 | 208.23 | 410 | 237.06 | 460 | 265.92 |
| 11 | 6.87 | 71 | 41.49 | 131 | 76.11 | 191 | 110.73 | 251 | 145.35 | 311 | 179.97 | 361 | 208.80 | 411 | 237.66 | 461 | 266.49 |
| 12 | 7.47 | 72 | 42.06 | 132 | 76.68 | 192 | 111.30 | 252 | 145.92 | 312 | 180.54 | 362 | 209.37 | 412 | 238.23 | 462 | 267.06 |
| 13 | 8.04 | 73 | 42.66 | 133 | 77.25 | 193 | 111.87 | 253 | 146.49 | 313 | 181.11 | 363 | 209.97 | 413 | 238.80 | 463 | 267.66 |
| 14 | 8.61 | 74 | 43.23 | 134 | 77.85 | 194 | 112.47 | 254 | 147.06 | 314 | 181.68 | 364 | 210.54 | 414 | 239.37 | 464 | 268.23 |
| 15 | 9.18 | 75 | 43.80 | 135 | 78.42 | 195 | 113.04 | 255 | 147.66 | 315 | 182.25 | 365 | 211.11 | 415 | 239.97 | 465 | 268.80 |
| 16 | 9.75 | 76 | 44.37 | 136 | 78.99 | 196 | 113.61 | 256 | 148.23 | 316 | 182.85 | 366 | 211.68 | 416 | 240.54 | 466 | 269.37 |
| 17 | 10.35 | 77 | 44.97 | 137 | 79.56 | 197 | 114.18 | 257 | 148.80 | 317 | 183.42 | 367 | 212.25 | 417 | 241.11 | 467 | 269.97 |
| 18 | 10.92 | 78 | 45.54 | 138 | 80.16 | 198 | 114.75 | 258 | 149.37 | 318 | 183.99 | 368 | 212.85 | 418 | 241.68 | 468 | 270.54 |
| 19 | 11.49 | 79 | 46.11 | 139 | 80.73 | 199 | 115.35 | 259 | 149.97 | 319 | 184.56 | 369 | 213.42 | 419 | 242.25 | 469 | 271.11 |
| 20 | 12.06 | 80 | 46.68 | 140 | 81.30 | 200 | 115.92 | 260 | 150.54 | 320 | 185.16 | 370 | 213.99 | 420 | 242.85 | 470 | 271.68 |
| 21 | 12.66 | 81 | 47.25 | 141 | 81.87 | 201 | 116.49 | 261 | 151.11 | 321 | 185.73 | 371 | 214.56 | 421 | 243.42 | 471 | 272.25 |
| 22 | 13.23 | 82 | 47.85 | 142 | 82.47 | 202 | 117.06 | 262 | 151.68 | 322 | 186.30 | 372 | 215.16 | 422 | 243.99 | 472 | 272.85 |
| 23 | 13.80 | 83 | 48.42 | 143 | 83.04 | 203 | 117.66 | 263 | 152.25 | 323 | 186.87 | 373 | 215.73 | 423 | 244.56 | 473 | 273.42 |
| 24 | 14.37 | 84 | 48.99 | 144 | 83.61 | 204 | 118.23 | 264 | 152.85 | 324 | 187.47 | 374 | 216.30 | 424 | 245.16 | 474 | 273.99 |
| 25 | 14.97 | 85 | 49.56 | 145 | 84.18 | 205 | 118.80 | 265 | 153.42 | 325 | 188.04 | 375 | 216.87 | 425 | 245.73 | 475 | 274.56 |
| 26 | 15.54 | 86 | 50.16 | 146 | 84.75 | 206 | 119.37 | 266 | 153.99 | 326 | 188.61 | 376 | 217.47 | 426 | 246.30 | 476 | 275.16 |
| 27 | 16.11 | 87 | 50.73 | 147 | 85.35 | 207 | 119.97 | 267 | 154.56 | 327 | 189.18 | 377 | 218.04 | 427 | 246.87 | 477 | 275.73 |
| 28 | 16.68 | 88 | 51.30 | 148 | 85.92 | 208 | 120.54 | 268 | 155.16 | 328 | 189.75 | 378 | 218.61 | 428 | 247.47 | 478 | 276.30 |
| 29 | 17.25 | 89 | 51.87 | 149 | 86.49 | 209 | 121.11 | 269 | 155.73 | 329 | 190.35 | 379 | 219.18 | 429 | 248.04 | 479 | 276.87 |
| 30 | 17.85 | 90 | 52.47 | 150 | 87.06 | 210 | 121.68 | 270 | 156.30 | 330 | 190.92 | 380 | 219.75 | 430 | 248.61 | 480 | 277.47 |
| 31 | 18.42 | 91 | 53.04 | 151 | 87.66 | 211 | 122.25 | 271 | 156.87 | 331 | 191.49 | 381 | 220.35 | 431 | 249.18 | 481 | 278.04 |
| 32 | 18.99 | 92 | 53.61 | 152 | 88.23 | 212 | 122.85 | 272 | 157.47 | 332 | 192.06 | 382 | 220.92 | 432 | 249.75 | 482 | 278.61 |
| 33 | 19.56 | 93 | 54.15 | 153 | 88.80 | 213 | 123.42 | 273 | 158.04 | 333 | 192.66 | 383 | 221.49 | 433 | 250.35 | 483 | 279.18 |
| 34 | 20.16 | 94 | 54.75 | 154 | 89.37 | 214 | 123.99 | 274 | 158.61 | 334 | 193.23 | 384 | 222.06 | 434 | 250.92 | 484 | 279.75 |
| 35 | 20.73 | 95 | 55.35 | 155 | 89.97 | 215 | 124.56 | 275 | 159.18 | 335 | 193.80 | 385 | 222.66 | 435 | 251.49 | 485 | 280.35 |
| 36 | 21.30 | 96 | 55.92 | 156 | 90.54 | 216 | 125.16 | 276 | 159.75 | 336 | 194.37 | 386 | 223.23 | 436 | 252.06 | 486 | 280.92 |
| 37 | 21.87 | 97 | 56.49 | 157 | 91.11 | 217 | 125.73 | 277 | 160.35 | 337 | 194.97 | 387 | 223.80 | 437 | 252.66 | 487 | 281.49 |
| 38 | 22.47 | 98 | 57.06 | 158 | 91.68 | 218 | 126.30 | 278 | 160.92 | 338 | 195.54 | 388 | 224.37 | 438 | 253.23 | 488 | 282.06 |
| 39 | 23.04 | 99 | 57.66 | 159 | 92.25 | 219 | 126.87 | 279 | 161.49 | 339 | 196.11 | 389 | 224.97 | 439 | 253.80 | 489 | 282.66 |
| 40 | 23.61 | 100 | 58.23 | 160 | 92.85 | 220 | 127.47 | 280 | 162.06 | 340 | 196.68 | 390 | 225.54 | 440 | 254.37 | 490 | 283.23 |
| 41 | 24.18 | 101 | 58.80 | 161 | 93.42 | 221 | 128.04 | 281 | 162.66 | 341 | 197.25 | 391 | 226.11 | 441 | 254.97 | 491 | 283.80 |
| 42 | 24.75 | 102 | 59.37 | 162 | 93.99 | 222 | 128.61 | 282 | 163.23 | 342 | 197.85 | 392 | 226.68 | 442 | 255.54 | 492 | 284.37 |
| 43 | 25.35 | 103 | 59.97 | 163 | 94.56 | 223 | 129.18 | 283 | 163.80 | 343 | 198.42 | 393 | 227.25 | 443 | 256.11 | 493 | 284.97 |
| 44 | 25.92 | 104 | 60.54 | 164 | 95.16 | 224 | 129.75 | 284 | 164.37 | 344 | 198.99 | 394 | 227.85 | 444 | 256.68 | 494 | 285.54 |
| 45 | 26.49 | 105 | 61.11 | 165 | 95.73 | 225 | 130.35 | 285 | 164.97 | 345 | 199.56 | 395 | 228.42 | 445 | 257.25 | 495 | 286.11 |
| 46 | 27.06 | 106 | 61.68 | 166 | 96.30 | 226 | 130.92 | 286 | 165.54 | 346 | 200.16 | 396 | 228.99 | 446 | 257.85 | 496 | 286.68 |
| 47 | 27.66 | 107 | 62.25 | 167 | 96.87 | 227 | 131.49 | 287 | 166.11 | 347 | 200.73 | 397 | 229.56 | 447 | 258.42 | 497 | 287.25 |
| 48 | 28.23 | 108 | 62.85 | 168 | 97.47 | 228 | 132.08 | 288 | 166.68 | 348 | 201.30 | 398 | 230.16 | 448 | 258.99 | 498 | 287.85 |
| 49 | 28.80 | 109 | 63.42 | 169 | 98.04 | 229 | 132.66 | 289 | 167.25 | 349 | 201.87 | 399 | 230.73 | 449 | 259.56 | 499 | 288.42 |
| 50 | 29.37 | 110 | 63.99 | 170 | 98.61 | 230 | 133.23 | 290 | 167.85 | 350 | 202.47 | 400 | 231.30 | 450 | 260.16 | 500 | 288.99 |
| 51 | 29.97 | 111 | 64.56 | 171 | 99.18 | 231 | 133.80 | 291 | 168.42 | | | | | | | | |
| 52 | 30.54 | 112 | 65.16 | 172 | 99.75 | 232 | 134.37 | 292 | 168.99 | | | | | | | | |
| 53 | 31.11 | 113 | 65.73 | 173 | 100.35 | 233 | 134.97 | 293 | 169.56 | | | | | | | | |
| 54 | 31.68 | 114 | 66.30 | 174 | 100.92 | 234 | 135.54 | 294 | 170.16 | | | | | | | | |
| 55 | 32.25 | 115 | 66.87 | 175 | 101.49 | 235 | 136.11 | 295 | 170.73 | | | | | | | | |
| 56 | 32.85 | 116 | 67.47 | 176 | 102.06 | 236 | 136.68 | 296 | 171.30 | | | | | | | | |
| 57 | 33.42 | 117 | 68.04 | 177 | 102.66 | 237 | 137.25 | 297 | 171.87 | | | | | | | | |
| 58 | 33.99 | 118 | 68.61 | 178 | 103.23 | 238 | 137.85 | 298 | 172.47 | | | | | | | | |
| 59 | 34.56 | 119 | 69.18 | 179 | 103.80 | 239 | 138.42 | 299 | 173.04 | | | | | | | | |
| 60 | 35.16 | 120 | 69.75 | 180 | 104.37 | 240 | 138.99 | 300 | 173.61 | | | | | | | | |

**Code more than 500**

1 Where the code is in the range 501 to 1000 inclusive:

  a. Subtract **500** from the code and use the balance of the code to obtain a pay adjustment figure from the table above.

  b. Add this pay adjustment figure to the figure given in the box alongside to obtain the figure of total pay adjustment to date * | **288.48** |

2 Where the code **exceeds 1000** follow the instructions on **page 3**.

6

# Tables A - Pay Adjustment Tables

Apr 27 to May 3 **Week 4**

| Code | Total pay adjustment to date £ | Code | Total pay adjustment to date £ | Code | Total pay adjustment to date £ | Code | Total pay adjustment to date £ | Code | Total pay adjustment to date £ | Code | Total pay adjustment to date £ | Code | Total pay adjustment to date £ | Code | Total pay adjustment to date £ | Code | Total pay adjustment to date £ |
|---|---|---|---|---|---|---|---|---|---|---|---|---|---|---|---|---|---|
| 0 | NIL | 61 | 47.64 | 121 | 93.80 | 181 | 139.96 | 241 | 186.08 | 301 | 232.24 | 351 | 270.72 | 401 | 309.16 | 451 | 347.64 |
| 1 | 1.48 | 62 | 48.40 | 122 | 94.56 | 182 | 140.72 | 242 | 186.88 | 302 | 233.00 | 352 | 271.48 | 402 | 309.96 | 452 | 348.40 |
| 2 | 2.24 | 63 | 49.16 | 123 | 95.32 | 183 | 141.48 | 243 | 187.64 | 303 | 233.80 | 353 | 272.24 | 403 | 310.72 | 453 | 349.16 |
| 3 | 3.00 | 64 | 49.96 | 124 | 96.08 | 184 | 142.24 | 244 | 188.40 | 304 | 234.56 | 354 | 273.00 | 404 | 311.48 | 454 | 349.96 |
| 4 | 3.80 | 65 | 50.72 | 125 | 96.88 | 185 | 143.00 | 245 | 189.16 | 305 | 235.32 | 355 | 273.80 | 405 | 312.24 | 455 | 350.72 |
| 5 | 4.56 | 66 | 51.48 | 126 | 97.64 | 186 | 143.80 | 246 | 189.96 | 306 | 236.08 | 356 | 274.56 | 406 | 313.00 | 456 | 351.48 |
| 6 | 5.32 | 67 | 52.24 | 127 | 98.40 | 187 | 144.56 | 247 | 190.72 | 307 | 236.88 | 357 | 275.32 | 407 | 313.80 | 457 | 352.24 |
| 7 | 6.08 | 68 | 53.00 | 128 | 99.16 | 188 | 145.32 | 248 | 191.48 | 308 | 237.64 | 358 | 276.08 | 408 | 314.56 | 458 | 353.00 |
| 8 | 6.88 | 69 | 53.80 | 129 | 99.96 | 189 | 146.08 | 249 | 192.24 | 309 | 238.40 | 359 | 276.88 | 409 | 315.32 | 459 | 353.80 |
| 9 | 7.64 | 70 | 54.56 | 130 | 100.72 | 190 | 146.88 | 250 | 193.00 | 310 | 239.16 | 360 | 277.64 | 410 | 316.08 | 460 | 354.56 |
| 10 | 8.40 | 71 | 55.32 | 131 | 101.48 | 191 | 147.64 | 251 | 193.80 | 311 | 239.96 | 361 | 278.40 | 411 | 316.88 | 461 | 355.32 |
| 11 | 9.16 | 72 | 56.08 | 132 | 102.24 | 192 | 148.40 | 252 | 194.56 | 312 | 240.72 | 362 | 279.16 | 412 | 317.64 | 462 | 356.08 |
| 12 | 9.96 | 73 | 56.88 | 133 | 103.00 | 193 | 149.16 | 253 | 195.32 | 313 | 241.48 | 363 | 279.96 | 413 | 318.40 | 463 | 356.88 |
| 13 | 10.72 | 74 | 57.64 | 134 | 103.80 | 194 | 149.96 | 254 | 196.08 | 314 | 242.24 | 364 | 280.72 | 414 | 319.16 | 464 | 357.64 |
| 14 | 11.48 | 75 | 58.40 | 135 | 104.56 | 195 | 150.72 | 255 | 196.88 | 315 | 243.00 | 365 | 281.48 | 415 | 319.96 | 465 | 358.40 |
| 15 | 12.24 | 76 | 59.16 | 136 | 105.32 | 196 | 151.48 | 256 | 197.64 | 316 | 243.80 | 366 | 282.24 | 416 | 320.72 | 466 | 359.16 |
| 16 | 13.00 | 77 | 59.96 | 137 | 106.08 | 197 | 152.24 | 257 | 198.40 | 317 | 244.56 | 367 | 283.00 | 417 | 321.48 | 467 | 359.96 |
| 17 | 13.80 | 78 | 60.72 | 138 | 106.88 | 198 | 153.00 | 258 | 199.16 | 318 | 245.32 | 368 | 283.80 | 418 | 322.24 | 468 | 360.72 |
| 18 | 14.56 | 79 | 61.48 | 139 | 107.64 | 199 | 153.80 | 259 | 199.96 | 319 | 246.08 | 369 | 284.56 | 419 | 323.00 | 469 | 361.48 |
| 19 | 15.32 | 80 | 62.24 | 140 | 108.40 | 200 | 154.56 | 260 | 200.72 | 320 | 246.88 | 370 | 285.32 | 420 | 323.80 | 470 | 362.24 |
| 20 | 16.08 | 81 | 63.00 | 141 | 109.16 | 201 | 155.32 | 261 | 201.48 | 321 | 247.64 | 371 | 286.08 | 421 | 324.56 | 471 | 363.00 |
| 21 | 16.88 | 82 | 63.80 | 142 | 109.96 | 202 | 156.08 | 262 | 202.24 | 322 | 248.40 | 372 | 286.88 | 422 | 325.32 | 472 | 363.80 |
| 22 | 17.64 | 83 | 64.56 | 143 | 110.72 | 203 | 156.88 | 263 | 203.00 | 323 | 249.16 | 373 | 287.64 | 423 | 326.08 | 473 | 364.56 |
| 23 | 18.40 | 84 | 65.32 | 144 | 111.48 | 204 | 157.64 | 264 | 203.80 | 324 | 249.96 | 374 | 288.40 | 424 | 326.88 | 474 | 365.32 |
| 24 | 19.16 | 85 | 66.08 | 145 | 112.24 | 205 | 158.40 | 265 | 204.56 | 325 | 250.72 | 375 | 289.16 | 425 | 327.64 | 475 | 366.08 |
| 25 | 19.96 | 86 | 66.88 | 146 | 113.00 | 206 | 159.16 | 266 | 205.32 | 326 | 251.48 | 376 | 289.96 | 426 | 328.40 | 476 | 366.88 |
| 26 | 20.72 | 87 | 67.64 | 147 | 113.80 | 207 | 159.96 | 267 | 206.08 | 327 | 252.24 | 377 | 290.72 | 427 | 329.16 | 477 | 367.64 |
| 27 | 21.48 | 88 | 68.40 | 148 | 114.56 | 208 | 160.72 | 268 | 206.88 | 328 | 253.00 | 378 | 291.48 | 428 | 329.96 | 478 | 368.40 |
| 28 | 22.24 | 89 | 69.16 | 149 | 115.32 | 209 | 161.48 | 269 | 207.64 | 329 | 253.80 | 379 | 292.24 | 429 | 330.72 | 479 | 369.16 |
| 29 | 23.00 | 90 | 69.96 | 150 | 116.08 | 210 | 162.24 | 270 | 208.40 | 330 | 254.56 | 380 | 293.00 | 430 | 331.48 | 480 | 369.96 |
| 30 | 23.80 | 91 | 70.72 | 151 | 116.88 | 211 | 163.00 | 271 | 209.16 | 331 | 255.32 | 381 | 293.80 | 431 | 332.24 | 481 | 370.72 |
| 31 | 24.56 | 92 | 71.48 | 152 | 117.64 | 212 | 163.80 | 272 | 209.96 | 332 | 256.08 | 382 | 294.56 | 432 | 333.00 | 482 | 371.48 |
| 32 | 25.32 | 93 | 72.24 | 153 | 118.40 | 213 | 164.56 | 273 | 210.72 | 333 | 256.88 | 383 | 295.32 | 433 | 333.80 | 483 | 372.24 |
| 33 | 26.08 | 94 | 73.00 | 154 | 119.16 | 214 | 165.32 | 274 | 211.48 | 334 | 257.64 | 384 | 296.08 | 434 | 334.56 | 484 | 373.00 |
| 34 | 26.88 | 95 | 73.80 | 155 | 119.96 | 215 | 166.08 | 275 | 212.24 | 335 | 258.40 | 385 | 296.88 | 435 | 335.32 | 485 | 373.80 |
| 35 | 27.64 | 96 | 74.56 | 156 | 120.72 | 216 | 166.88 | 276 | 213.00 | 336 | 259.16 | 386 | 297.64 | 436 | 336.08 | 486 | 374.56 |
| 36 | 28.40 | 97 | 75.32 | 157 | 121.48 | 217 | 167.64 | 277 | 213.80 | 337 | 259.96 | 387 | 298.40 | 437 | 336.88 | 487 | 375.32 |
| 37 | 29.16 | 98 | 76.08 | 158 | 122.24 | 218 | 168.40 | 278 | 214.56 | 338 | 260.72 | 388 | 299.16 | 438 | 337.64 | 488 | 376.08 |
| 38 | 29.96 | 99 | 76.88 | 159 | 123.00 | 219 | 169.16 | 279 | 215.32 | 339 | 261.48 | 389 | 299.96 | 439 | 338.40 | 489 | 376.88 |
| 39 | 30.72 | 100 | 77.64 | 160 | 123.80 | 220 | 169.96 | 280 | 216.08 | 340 | 262.24 | 390 | 300.72 | 440 | 339.16 | 490 | 377.64 |
| 40 | 31.48 | 101 | 78.40 | 161 | 124.56 | 221 | 170.72 | 281 | 216.88 | 341 | 263.00 | 391 | 301.48 | 441 | 339.96 | 491 | 378.40 |
| 41 | 32.24 | 102 | 79.16 | 162 | 125.32 | 222 | 171.48 | 282 | 217.64 | 342 | 263.80 | 392 | 302.24 | 442 | 340.72 | 492 | 379.16 |
| 42 | 33.00 | 103 | 79.96 | 163 | 126.08 | 223 | 172.24 | 283 | 218.40 | 343 | 264.56 | 393 | 303.00 | 443 | 341.48 | 493 | 379.96 |
| 43 | 33.80 | 104 | 80.72 | 164 | 126.88 | 224 | 173.00 | 284 | 219.16 | 344 | 265.32 | 394 | 303.80 | 444 | 342.24 | 494 | 380.72 |
| 44 | 34.56 | 105 | 81.48 | 165 | 127.64 | 225 | 173.80 | 285 | 219.96 | 345 | 266.08 | 395 | 304.56 | 445 | 343.00 | 495 | 381.48 |
| 45 | 35.32 | 106 | 82.24 | 166 | 128.40 | 226 | 174.56 | 286 | 220.72 | 346 | 266.88 | 396 | 305.32 | 446 | 343.80 | 496 | 382.24 |
| 46 | 36.08 | 107 | 83.00 | 167 | 129.16 | 227 | 175.32 | 287 | 221.48 | 347 | 267.64 | 397 | 306.08 | 447 | 344.56 | 497 | 383.00 |
| 47 | 36.88 | 108 | 83.80 | 168 | 129.96 | 228 | 176.08 | 288 | 222.24 | 348 | 268.40 | 398 | 306.88 | 448 | 345.32 | 498 | 383.80 |
| 48 | 37.64 | 109 | 84.56 | 169 | 130.72 | 229 | 176.88 | 289 | 223.00 | 349 | 269.16 | 399 | 307.64 | 449 | 346.08 | 499 | 384.56 |
| 49 | 38.40 | 110 | 85.32 | 170 | 131.48 | 230 | 177.64 | 290 | 223.80 | 350 | 269.96 | 400 | 308.40 | 450 | 346.88 | 500 | 385.32 |
| 50 | 39.16 | 111 | 86.08 | 171 | 132.24 | 231 | 178.40 | 291 | 224.56 | | | | | | | | |
| 51 | 39.96 | 112 | 86.88 | 172 | 133.00 | 232 | 179.16 | 292 | 225.32 | | | | | | | | |
| 52 | 40.72 | 113 | 87.64 | 173 | 133.80 | 233 | 179.96 | 293 | 226.08 | | | | | | | | |
| 53 | 41.48 | 114 | 88.40 | 174 | 134.56 | 234 | 180.72 | 294 | 226.88 | | | | | | | | |
| 54 | 42.24 | 115 | 89.16 | 175 | 135.32 | 235 | 181.48 | 295 | 227.64 | | | | | | | | |
| 55 | 43.00 | | | | | | | | | | | | | | | | |
| 56 | 43.80 | 116 | 89.96 | 176 | 136.08 | 236 | 182.24 | 296 | 228.40 | | | | | | | | |
| 57 | 44.56 | 117 | 90.72 | 177 | 136.88 | 237 | 183.00 | 297 | 229.16 | | | | | | | | |
| 58 | 45.32 | 118 | 91.48 | 178 | 137.64 | 238 | 183.80 | 298 | 229.96 | | | | | | | | |
| 59 | 46.08 | 119 | 92.24 | 179 | 138.40 | 239 | 184.56 | 299 | 230.72 | | | | | | | | |
| 60 | 46.88 | 120 | 93.00 | 180 | 139.16 | 240 | 185.32 | 300 | 231.48 | | | | | | | | |

**Code more than 500**

1 Where the code is in the range 501 to **1000** inclusive:

   a. Subtract **500** from the code and use the balance of the code to obtain a pay adjustment figure from the table above.

   b. Add this pay adjustment figure to the figure given in the box alongside to obtain the figure of total pay adjustment to date * | **384.64**

2 Where the code **exceeds 1000** follow the instructions on **page 3**.

**Week 5**  May 4 to May 10                    **Tables A** - Pay Adjustment Tables

| Code | Total pay adjustment to date £ | Code | Total pay adjustment to date £ | Code | Total pay adjustment to date £ | Code | Total pay adjustment to date £ | Code | Total pay adjustment to date £ | Code | Total pay adjustment to date £ | Code | Total pay adjustment to date £ | Code | Total pay adjustment to date £ | Code | Total pay adjustment to date £ |
|---|---|---|---|---|---|---|---|---|---|---|---|---|---|---|---|---|---|
| 0 | NIL | 61 | 59.55 | 121 | 117.25 | 181 | 174.95 | 241 | 232.60 | 301 | 290.30 | 351 | 338.40 | 401 | 386.45 | 451 | 434.55 |
| 1 | 1.85 | 62 | 60.50 | 122 | 118.20 | 182 | 175.90 | 242 | 233.60 | 302 | 291.25 | 352 | 339.35 | 402 | 387.45 | 452 | 435.50 |
| 2 | 2.80 | 63 | 61.45 | 123 | 119.15 | 183 | 176.85 | 243 | 234.55 | 303 | 292.25 | 353 | 340.30 | 403 | 388.40 | 453 | 436.45 |
| 3 | 3.75 | 64 | 62.45 | 124 | 120.10 | 184 | 177.80 | 244 | 235.50 | 304 | 293.20 | 354 | 341.25 | 404 | 389.35 | 454 | 437.45 |
| 4 | 4.75 | 65 | 63.40 | 125 | 121.10 | 185 | 178.75 | 245 | 236.45 | 305 | 294.15 | 355 | 342.25 | 405 | 390.30 | 455 | 438.40 |
| 5 | 5.70 | 66 | 64.35 | 126 | 122.05 | 186 | 179.75 | 246 | 237.45 | 306 | 295.10 | 356 | 343.20 | 406 | 391.25 | 456 | 439.35 |
| 6 | 6.65 | 67 | 65.30 | 127 | 123.00 | 187 | 180.70 | 247 | 238.40 | 307 | 296.10 | 357 | 344.15 | 407 | 392.25 | 457 | 440.30 |
| 7 | 7.60 | 68 | 66.25 | 128 | 123.95 | 188 | 181.65 | 248 | 239.35 | 308 | 297.05 | 358 | 345.10 | 408 | 393.20 | 458 | 441.25 |
| 8 | 8.60 | 69 | 67.25 | 129 | 124.95 | 189 | 182.60 | 249 | 240.30 | 309 | 298.00 | 359 | 346.10 | 409 | 394.15 | 459 | 442.25 |
| 9 | 9.55 | 70 | 68.20 | 130 | 125.90 | 190 | 183.60 | 250 | 241.25 | 310 | 298.95 | 360 | 347.05 | 410 | 395.10 | 460 | 443.20 |
| 10 | 10.50 | 71 | 69.15 | 131 | 126.85 | 191 | 184.55 | 251 | 242.25 | 311 | 299.95 | 361 | 348.00 | 411 | 396.10 | 461 | 444.15 |
| 11 | 11.45 | 72 | 70.10 | 132 | 127.80 | 192 | 185.50 | 252 | 243.20 | 312 | 300.90 | 362 | 348.95 | 412 | 397.05 | 462 | 445.10 |
| 12 | 12.45 | 73 | 71.10 | 133 | 128.75 | 193 | 186.45 | 253 | 244.15 | 313 | 301.85 | 363 | 349.95 | 413 | 398.00 | 463 | 446.10 |
| 13 | 13.40 | 74 | 72.05 | 134 | 129.75 | 194 | 187.45 | 254 | 245.10 | 314 | 302.80 | 364 | 350.90 | 414 | 398.95 | 464 | 447.05 |
| 14 | 14.35 | 75 | 73.00 | 135 | 130.70 | 195 | 188.40 | 255 | 246.10 | 315 | 303.75 | 365 | 351.85 | 415 | 399.95 | 465 | 448.00 |
| 15 | 15.30 | 76 | 73.95 | 136 | 131.65 | 196 | 189.35 | 256 | 247.05 | 316 | 304.75 | 366 | 352.80 | 416 | 400.90 | 466 | 448.95 |
| 16 | 16.25 | 77 | 74.95 | 137 | 132.60 | 197 | 190.30 | 257 | 248.00 | 317 | 305.70 | 367 | 353.75 | 417 | 401.85 | 467 | 449.95 |
| 17 | 17.25 | 78 | 75.90 | 138 | 133.60 | 198 | 191.25 | 258 | 248.95 | 318 | 306.65 | 368 | 354.75 | 418 | 402.80 | 468 | 450.90 |
| 18 | 18.20 | 79 | 76.85 | 139 | 134.55 | 199 | 192.25 | 259 | 249.95 | 319 | 307.60 | 369 | 355.70 | 419 | 403.75 | 469 | 451.85 |
| 19 | 19.15 | 80 | 77.80 | 140 | 135.50 | 200 | 193.20 | 260 | 250.90 | 320 | 308.60 | 370 | 356.65 | 420 | 404.75 | 470 | 452.80 |
| 20 | 20.10 | 81 | 78.75 | 141 | 136.45 | 201 | 194.15 | 261 | 251.85 | 321 | 309.55 | 371 | 357.60 | 421 | 405.70 | 471 | 453.75 |
| 21 | 21.10 | 82 | 79.75 | 142 | 137.45 | 202 | 195.10 | 262 | 252.80 | 322 | 310.50 | 372 | 358.60 | 422 | 406.65 | 472 | 454.75 |
| 22 | 22.05 | 83 | 80.70 | 143 | 138.40 | 203 | 196.05 | 263 | 253.75 | 323 | 311.45 | 373 | 359.55 | 423 | 407.60 | 473 | 455.70 |
| 23 | 23.00 | 84 | 81.65 | 144 | 139.35 | 204 | 197.05 | 264 | 254.75 | 324 | 312.45 | 374 | 360.50 | 424 | 408.60 | 474 | 456.65 |
| 24 | 23.95 | 85 | 82.60 | 145 | 140.30 | 205 | 198.00 | 265 | 255.70 | 325 | 313.40 | 375 | 361.45 | 425 | 409.55 | 475 | 457.60 |
| 25 | 24.95 | 86 | 83.60 | 146 | 141.25 | 206 | 198.95 | 266 | 256.65 | 326 | 314.35 | 376 | 362.45 | 426 | 410.50 | 476 | 458.60 |
| 26 | 25.90 | 87 | 84.55 | 147 | 142.25 | 207 | 199.95 | 267 | 257.60 | 327 | 315.30 | 377 | 363.40 | 427 | 411.45 | 477 | 459.55 |
| 27 | 26.85 | 88 | 85.50 | 148 | 143.20 | 208 | 200.90 | 268 | 258.60 | 328 | 316.25 | 378 | 364.35 | 428 | 412.45 | 478 | 460.50 |
| 28 | 27.80 | 89 | 86.45 | 149 | 144.15 | 209 | 201.85 | 269 | 259.55 | 329 | 317.25 | 379 | 365.30 | 429 | 413.40 | 479 | 461.45 |
| 29 | 28.75 | 90 | 87.45 | 150 | 145.10 | 210 | 202.80 | 270 | 260.50 | 330 | 318.20 | 380 | 366.25 | 430 | 414.35 | 480 | 462.45 |
| 30 | 29.75 | 91 | 88.40 | 151 | 146.10 | 211 | 203.75 | 271 | 261.45 | 331 | 319.15 | 381 | 367.25 | 431 | 415.30 | 481 | 463.40 |
| 31 | 30.70 | 92 | 89.35 | 152 | 147.05 | 212 | 204.75 | 272 | 262.45 | 332 | 320.10 | 382 | 368.20 | 432 | 416.25 | 482 | 464.35 |
| 32 | 31.65 | 93 | 90.30 | 153 | 148.00 | 213 | 205.70 | 273 | 263.40 | 333 | 321.10 | 383 | 369.15 | 433 | 417.25 | 483 | 465.30 |
| 33 | 32.60 | 94 | 91.25 | 154 | 148.95 | 214 | 206.65 | 274 | 264.35 | 334 | 322.05 | 384 | 370.10 | 434 | 418.20 | 484 | 466.25 |
| 34 | 33.60 | 95 | 92.25 | 155 | 149.95 | 215 | 207.60 | 275 | 265.30 | 335 | 323.00 | 385 | 371.10 | 435 | 419.15 | 485 | 467.25 |
| 35 | 34.55 | 96 | 93.20 | 156 | 150.90 | 216 | 208.60 | 276 | 266.25 | 336 | 323.95 | 386 | 372.05 | 436 | 420.10 | 486 | 468.20 |
| 36 | 35.50 | 97 | 94.15 | 157 | 151.85 | 217 | 209.55 | 277 | 267.25 | 337 | 324.95 | 387 | 373.00 | 437 | 421.10 | 487 | 469.15 |
| 37 | 36.45 | 98 | 95.10 | 158 | 152.80 | 218 | 210.50 | 278 | 268.20 | 338 | 325.90 | 388 | 373.95 | 438 | 422.05 | 488 | 470.10 |
| 38 | 37.45 | 99 | 96.10 | 159 | 153.75 | 219 | 211.45 | 279 | 269.15 | 339 | 326.85 | 389 | 374.95 | 439 | 423.00 | 489 | 471.10 |
| 39 | 38.40 | 100 | 97.05 | 160 | 154.75 | 220 | 212.45 | 280 | 270.10 | 340 | 327.80 | 390 | 375.90 | 440 | 423.95 | 490 | 472.05 |
| 40 | 39.35 | 101 | 98.00 | 161 | 155.70 | 221 | 213.40 | 281 | 271.10 | 341 | 328.75 | 391 | 376.85 | 441 | 424.95 | 491 | 473.00 |
| 41 | 40.30 | 102 | 98.95 | 162 | 156.65 | 222 | 214.35 | 282 | 272.05 | 342 | 329.75 | 392 | 377.80 | 442 | 425.90 | 492 | 473.95 |
| 42 | 41.25 | 103 | 99.95 | 163 | 157.60 | 223 | 215.30 | 283 | 273.00 | 343 | 330.70 | 393 | 378.75 | 443 | 426.85 | 493 | 474.95 |
| 43 | 42.25 | 104 | 100.90 | 164 | 158.60 | 224 | 216.25 | 284 | 273.95 | 344 | 331.65 | 394 | 379.75 | 444 | 427.80 | 494 | 475.90 |
| 44 | 43.20 | 105 | 101.85 | 165 | 159.55 | 225 | 217.25 | 285 | 274.95 | 345 | 332.60 | 395 | 380.70 | 445 | 428.75 | 495 | 476.85 |
| 45 | 44.15 | 106 | 102.80 | 166 | 160.50 | 226 | 218.20 | 286 | 275.90 | 346 | 333.60 | 396 | 381.65 | 446 | 429.75 | 496 | 477.80 |
| 46 | 45.10 | 107 | 103.75 | 167 | 161.45 | 227 | 219.15 | 287 | 276.85 | 347 | 334.55 | 397 | 382.60 | 447 | 430.70 | 497 | 478.75 |
| 47 | 46.10 | 108 | 104.70 | 168 | 162.45 | 228 | 220.10 | 288 | 277.80 | 348 | 335.50 | 398 | 383.60 | 448 | 431.65 | 498 | 479.75 |
| 48 | 47.05 | 109 | 105.70 | 169 | 163.40 | 229 | 221.10 | 289 | 278.75 | 349 | 336.45 | 399 | 384.55 | 449 | 432.60 | 499 | 480.70 |
| 49 | 48.00 | 110 | 106.65 | 170 | 164.35 | 230 | 222.05 | 290 | 279.75 | 350 | 337.45 | 400 | 385.50 | 450 | 433.60 | 500 | 481.65 |
| 50 | 48.95 | 111 | 107.60 | 171 | 165.30 | 231 | 223.00 | 291 | 280.70 | | | | | | | | |
| 51 | 49.95 | 112 | 108.60 | 172 | 166.25 | 232 | 223.95 | 292 | 281.65 | | | | | | | | |
| 52 | 50.90 | 113 | 109.55 | 173 | 167.25 | 233 | 224.95 | 293 | 282.60 | | | | | | | | |
| 53 | 51.85 | 114 | 110.50 | 174 | 168.20 | 234 | 225.90 | 294 | 283.60 | | | | | | | | |
| 54 | 52.80 | 115 | 111.45 | 175 | 169.15 | 235 | 226.85 | 295 | 284.55 | | | | | | | | |
| 55 | 53.75 | 116 | 112.45 | 176 | 170.10 | 236 | 227.80 | 296 | 285.50 | | | | | | | | |
| 56 | 54.75 | 117 | 113.40 | 177 | 171.10 | 237 | 228.75 | 297 | 286.45 | | | | | | | | |
| 57 | 55.70 | 118 | 114.35 | 178 | 172.05 | 238 | 229.75 | 298 | 287.45 | | | | | | | | |
| 58 | 56.65 | 119 | 115.30 | 179 | 173.00 | 239 | 230.70 | 299 | 288.40 | | | | | | | | |
| 59 | 57.60 | 120 | 116.25 | 180 | 173.95 | 240 | 231.65 | 300 | 289.35 | | | | | | | | |
| 60 | 58.60 | | | | | | | | | | | | | | | | |

**Code more than 500**

1  Where the code is in the range **501 to 1000** inclusive:

a. Subtract **500** from the code and use the balance of the code to obtain a pay adjustment figure from the table above.

b. Add this pay adjustment figure to the figure given in the box alongside to obtain the figure of total pay adjustment to date * **480.80**

2  Where the code **exceeds 1000** follow the instructions on **page 3**.

# Tables A - Pay Adjustment Tables

May 11 to May 17 **Week 6**

| Code | Total pay adjustment to date £ | Code | Total pay adjustment to date £ | Code | Total pay adjustment to date £ | Code | Total pay adjustment to date £ | Code | Total pay adjustment to date £ | Code | Total pay adjustment to date £ | Code | Total pay adjustment to date £ | Code | Total pay adjustment to date £ | Code | Total pay adjustment to date £ |
|---|---|---|---|---|---|---|---|---|---|---|---|---|---|---|---|---|---|
| 0 | NIL | 61 | 71.46 | 121 | 140.70 | 181 | 209.94 | 241 | 279.12 | 301 | 348.36 | 351 | 406.08 | 401 | 463.74 | 451 | 521.46 |
| 1 | 2.22 | 62 | 72.60 | 122 | 141.84 | 182 | 211.08 | 242 | 280.32 | 302 | 349.50 | 352 | 407.22 | 402 | 464.94 | 452 | 522.60 |
| 2 | 3.36 | 63 | 73.74 | 123 | 142.98 | 183 | 212.22 | 243 | 281.46 | 303 | 350.70 | 353 | 408.36 | 403 | 466.08 | 453 | 523.74 |
| 3 | 4.50 | 64 | 74.94 | 124 | 144.12 | 184 | 213.36 | 244 | 282.60 | 304 | 351.84 | 354 | 409.50 | 404 | 467.22 | 454 | 524.94 |
| 4 | 5.70 | 65 | 76.08 | 125 | 145.32 | 185 | 214.50 | 245 | 283.74 | 305 | 352.98 | 355 | 410.70 | 405 | 468.36 | 455 | 526.08 |
| 5 | 6.84 | 66 | 77.22 | 126 | 146.46 | 186 | 215.70 | 246 | 284.94 | 306 | 354.12 | 356 | 411.84 | 406 | 469.50 | 456 | 527.22 |
| 6 | 7.98 | 67 | 78.36 | 127 | 147.60 | 187 | 216.84 | 247 | 286.08 | 307 | 355.32 | 357 | 412.98 | 407 | 470.70 | 457 | 528.36 |
| 7 | 9.12 | 68 | 79.50 | 128 | 148.74 | 188 | 217.98 | 248 | 287.22 | 308 | 356.46 | 358 | 414.12 | 408 | 471.84 | 458 | 529.50 |
| 8 | 10.32 | 69 | 80.70 | 129 | 149.94 | 189 | 219.12 | 249 | 288.36 | 309 | 357.60 | 359 | 415.32 | 409 | 472.98 | 459 | 530.70 |
| 9 | 11.46 | 70 | 81.84 | 130 | 151.08 | 190 | 220.32 | 250 | 289.50 | 310 | 358.74 | 360 | 416.46 | 410 | 474.12 | 460 | 531.84 |
| 10 | 12.60 | 71 | 82.98 | 131 | 152.22 | 191 | 221.46 | 251 | 290.70 | 311 | 359.94 | 361 | 417.60 | 411 | 475.32 | 461 | 532.98 |
| 11 | 13.74 | 72 | 84.12 | 132 | 153.36 | 192 | 222.60 | 252 | 291.84 | 312 | 361.08 | 362 | 418.74 | 412 | 476.46 | 462 | 534.12 |
| 12 | 14.94 | 73 | 85.32 | 133 | 154.50 | 193 | 223.74 | 253 | 292.98 | 313 | 362.22 | 363 | 419.94 | 413 | 477.60 | 463 | 535.32 |
| 13 | 16.08 | 74 | 86.46 | 134 | 155.70 | 194 | 224.94 | 254 | 294.12 | 314 | 363.36 | 364 | 421.08 | 414 | 478.74 | 464 | 536.46 |
| 14 | 17.22 | 75 | 87.60 | 135 | 156.84 | 195 | 226.08 | 255 | 295.32 | 315 | 364.50 | 365 | 422.22 | 415 | 479.94 | 465 | 537.60 |
| 15 | 18.36 | 76 | 88.74 | 136 | 157.98 | 196 | 227.22 | 256 | 296.46 | 316 | 365.70 | 366 | 423.36 | 416 | 481.08 | 466 | 538.74 |
| 16 | 19.50 | 77 | 89.94 | 137 | 159.12 | 197 | 228.36 | 257 | 297.60 | 317 | 366.84 | 367 | 424.50 | 417 | 482.22 | 467 | 539.94 |
| 17 | 20.70 | 78 | 91.08 | 138 | 160.32 | 198 | 229.50 | 258 | 298.74 | 318 | 367.98 | 368 | 425.70 | 418 | 483.36 | 468 | 541.08 |
| 18 | 21.84 | 79 | 92.22 | 139 | 161.46 | 199 | 230.70 | 259 | 299.94 | 319 | 369.12 | 369 | 426.84 | 419 | 484.50 | 469 | 542.22 |
| 19 | 22.98 | 80 | 93.36 | 140 | 162.60 | 200 | 231.84 | 260 | 301.08 | 320 | 370.32 | 370 | 427.98 | 420 | 485.70 | 470 | 543.36 |
| 20 | 24.12 | 81 | 94.50 | 141 | 163.74 | 201 | 232.98 | 261 | 302.22 | 321 | 371.46 | 371 | 429.12 | 421 | 486.84 | 471 | 544.50 |
| 21 | 25.32 | 82 | 95.70 | 142 | 164.94 | 202 | 234.12 | 262 | 303.36 | 322 | 372.60 | 372 | 430.32 | 422 | 487.98 | 472 | 545.70 |
| 22 | 26.46 | 83 | 96.84 | 143 | 166.08 | 203 | 235.32 | 263 | 304.50 | 323 | 373.74 | 373 | 431.46 | 423 | 489.12 | 473 | 546.84 |
| 23 | 27.60 | 84 | 97.98 | 144 | 167.22 | 204 | 236.46 | 264 | 305.70 | 324 | 374.94 | 374 | 432.60 | 424 | 490.32 | 474 | 547.98 |
| 24 | 28.74 | 85 | 99.12 | 145 | 168.36 | 205 | 237.60 | 265 | 306.84 | 325 | 376.08 | 375 | 433.74 | 425 | 491.46 | 475 | 549.12 |
| 25 | 29.94 | 86 | 100.32 | 146 | 169.50 | 206 | 238.74 | 266 | 307.98 | 326 | 377.22 | 376 | 434.94 | 426 | 492.60 | 476 | 550.32 |
| 26 | 31.08 | 87 | 101.46 | 147 | 170.70 | 207 | 239.94 | 267 | 309.12 | 327 | 378.36 | 377 | 436.08 | 427 | 493.74 | 477 | 551.46 |
| 27 | 32.22 | 88 | 102.60 | 148 | 171.84 | 208 | 241.08 | 268 | 310.32 | 328 | 379.50 | 378 | 437.22 | 428 | 494.94 | 478 | 552.60 |
| 28 | 33.36 | 89 | 103.74 | 149 | 172.98 | 209 | 242.22 | 269 | 311.46 | 329 | 380.70 | 379 | 438.36 | 429 | 496.08 | 479 | 553.74 |
| 29 | 34.50 | 90 | 104.94 | 150 | 174.12 | 210 | 243.36 | 270 | 312.60 | 330 | 381.84 | 380 | 439.50 | 430 | 497.22 | 480 | 554.94 |
| 30 | 35.70 | 91 | 106.08 | 151 | 175.32 | 211 | 244.50 | 271 | 313.74 | 331 | 382.98 | 381 | 440.70 | 431 | 498.36 | 481 | 556.08 |
| 31 | 36.84 | 92 | 107.22 | 152 | 176.46 | 212 | 245.70 | 272 | 314.94 | 332 | 384.12 | 382 | 441.84 | 432 | 499.50 | 482 | 557.22 |
| 32 | 37.98 | 93 | 108.36 | 153 | 177.60 | 213 | 246.84 | 273 | 316.08 | 333 | 385.32 | 383 | 442.98 | 433 | 500.70 | 483 | 558.36 |
| 33 | 39.12 | 94 | 109.50 | 154 | 178.74 | 214 | 247.98 | 274 | 317.22 | 334 | 386.46 | 384 | 444.12 | 434 | 501.84 | 484 | 559.50 |
| 34 | 40.32 | 95 | 110.70 | 155 | 179.94 | 215 | 249.12 | 275 | 318.36 | 335 | 387.60 | 385 | 445.32 | 435 | 502.98 | 485 | 560.70 |
| 35 | 41.46 | 96 | 111.84 | 156 | 181.08 | 216 | 250.32 | 276 | 319.50 | 336 | 388.74 | 386 | 446.46 | 436 | 504.12 | 486 | 561.84 |
| 36 | 42.60 | 97 | 112.98 | 157 | 182.22 | 217 | 251.46 | 277 | 320.70 | 337 | 389.94 | 387 | 447.60 | 437 | 505.32 | 487 | 562.98 |
| 37 | 43.74 | 98 | 114.12 | 158 | 183.36 | 218 | 252.60 | 278 | 321.84 | 338 | 391.08 | 388 | 448.74 | 438 | 506.46 | 488 | 564.12 |
| 38 | 44.94 | 99 | 115.32 | 159 | 184.50 | 219 | 253.74 | 279 | 322.98 | 339 | 392.22 | 389 | 449.94 | 439 | 507.60 | 489 | 565.32 |
| 39 | 46.08 | 100 | 116.46 | 160 | 185.70 | 220 | 254.94 | 280 | 324.12 | 340 | 393.36 | 390 | 451.08 | 440 | 508.74 | 490 | 566.46 |
| 40 | 47.22 | 101 | 117.60 | 161 | 186.84 | 221 | 256.08 | 281 | 325.32 | 341 | 394.50 | 391 | 452.22 | 441 | 509.94 | 491 | 567.60 |
| 41 | 48.36 | 102 | 118.74 | 162 | 187.98 | 222 | 257.22 | 282 | 326.46 | 342 | 395.70 | 392 | 453.36 | 442 | 511.08 | 492 | 568.74 |
| 42 | 49.50 | 103 | 119.94 | 163 | 189.12 | 223 | 258.36 | 283 | 327.60 | 343 | 396.84 | 393 | 454.50 | 443 | 512.22 | 493 | 569.94 |
| 43 | 50.70 | 104 | 121.08 | 164 | 190.32 | 224 | 259.50 | 284 | 328.74 | 344 | 397.98 | 394 | 455.70 | 444 | 513.36 | 494 | 571.08 |
| 44 | 51.84 | 105 | 122.22 | 165 | 191.46 | 225 | 260.70 | 285 | 329.94 | 345 | 399.12 | 395 | 456.84 | 445 | 514.50 | 495 | 572.22 |
| 45 | 52.98 | 106 | 123.36 | 166 | 192.60 | 226 | 261.84 | 286 | 331.08 | 346 | 400.32 | 396 | 457.98 | 446 | 515.70 | 496 | 573.36 |
| 46 | 54.12 | 107 | 124.50 | 167 | 193.74 | 227 | 262.98 | 287 | 332.22 | 347 | 401.46 | 397 | 459.12 | 447 | 516.84 | 497 | 574.50 |
| 47 | 55.32 | 108 | 125.70 | 168 | 194.94 | 228 | 264.12 | 288 | 333.36 | 348 | 402.60 | 398 | 460.32 | 448 | 517.98 | 498 | 575.70 |
| 48 | 56.46 | 109 | 126.84 | 169 | 196.08 | 229 | 265.32 | 289 | 334.50 | 349 | 403.74 | 399 | 461.46 | 449 | 519.12 | 499 | 576.84 |
| 49 | 57.60 | 110 | 127.98 | 170 | 197.22 | 230 | 266.46 | 290 | 335.70 | 350 | 404.94 | 400 | 462.60 | 450 | 520.32 | 500 | 577.98 |
| 50 | 58.74 | 111 | 129.12 | 171 | 198.36 | 231 | 267.60 | 291 | 336.84 | | | | | | | | |
| 51 | 59.94 | 112 | 130.32 | 172 | 199.50 | 232 | 268.74 | 292 | 337.98 | | | | | | | | |
| 52 | 61.08 | 113 | 131.46 | 173 | 200.70 | 233 | 269.94 | 293 | 339.12 | | | | | | | | |
| 53 | 62.22 | 114 | 132.60 | 174 | 201.84 | 234 | 271.08 | 294 | 340.32 | | | | | | | | |
| 54 | 63.36 | 115 | 133.74 | 175 | 202.98 | 235 | 272.22 | 295 | 341.46 | | | | | | | | |
| 55 | 64.50 | 116 | 134.94 | 176 | 204.12 | 236 | 273.36 | 296 | 342.60 | | | | | | | | |
| 56 | 65.70 | 117 | 136.08 | 177 | 205.32 | 237 | 274.50 | 297 | 343.74 | | | | | | | | |
| 57 | 66.84 | 118 | 137.22 | 178 | 206.46 | 238 | 275.70 | 298 | 344.94 | | | | | | | | |
| 58 | 67.98 | 119 | 138.36 | 179 | 207.60 | 239 | 276.84 | 299 | 346.08 | | | | | | | | |
| 59 | 69.12 | 120 | 139.50 | 180 | 208.74 | 240 | 277.98 | 300 | 347.22 | | | | | | | | |
| 60 | 70.32 | | | | | | | | | | | | | | | | |

## Code more than 500

1 Where the code is in the range 501 to **1000** inclusive:

  a. Subtract **500** from the code and use the balance of the code to obtain a pay adjustment figure from the table above.

  b. Add this pay adjustment figure to the figure given in the box alongside to obtain the figure of total pay adjustment to date * | **576.96**

2 Where the code **exceeds 1000** follow the instructions on **page 3**.

# APPENDIX 4: PAYE TAX TABLES – PAY ADJUSTMENT TABLES

**Week 7**   May 18 to May 24                    **Tables A** - Pay Adjustment Tables

| Code | Total pay adjustment to date | Code | Total pay adjustment to date | Code | Total pay adjustment to date | Code | Total pay adjustment to date | Code | Total pay adjustment to date | Code | Total pay adjustment to date | Code | Total pay adjustment to date | Code | Total pay adjustment to date | Code | Total pay adjustment to date |
|---|---|---|---|---|---|---|---|---|---|---|---|---|---|---|---|---|---|
|  | £ |  | £ |  | £ |  | £ |  | £ |  | £ |  | £ |  | £ |  | £ |
| 0 | NIL |  |  |  |  |  |  |  |  |  |  |  |  |  |  |  |  |
| 1 | 2.59 | 61 | 83.37 | 121 | 164.15 | 181 | 244.93 | 241 | 325.64 | 301 | 406.42 | 351 | 473.76 | 401 | 541.03 | 451 | 608.37 |
| 2 | 3.92 | 62 | 84.70 | 122 | 165.48 | 182 | 246.26 | 242 | 327.04 | 302 | 407.75 | 352 | 475.09 | 402 | 542.43 | 452 | 609.70 |
| 3 | 5.25 | 63 | 86.03 | 123 | 166.81 | 183 | 247.59 | 243 | 328.37 | 303 | 409.15 | 353 | 476.42 | 403 | 543.76 | 453 | 611.03 |
| 4 | 6.65 | 64 | 87.43 | 124 | 168.14 | 184 | 248.92 | 244 | 329.70 | 304 | 410.48 | 354 | 477.75 | 404 | 545.09 | 454 | 612.43 |
| 5 | 7.98 | 65 | 88.76 | 125 | 169.54 | 185 | 250.25 | 245 | 331.03 | 305 | 411.81 | 355 | 479.15 | 405 | 546.42 | 455 | 613.76 |
| 6 | 9.31 | 66 | 90.09 | 126 | 170.87 | 186 | 251.65 | 246 | 332.43 | 306 | 413.14 | 356 | 480.48 | 406 | 547.75 | 456 | 615.09 |
| 7 | 10.64 | 67 | 91.42 | 127 | 172.20 | 187 | 252.98 | 247 | 333.76 | 307 | 414.54 | 357 | 481.81 | 407 | 549.15 | 457 | 616.42 |
| 8 | 12.04 | 68 | 92.75 | 128 | 173.53 | 188 | 254.31 | 248 | 335.09 | 308 | 415.87 | 358 | 483.14 | 408 | 550.48 | 458 | 617.75 |
| 9 | 13.37 | 69 | 94.15 | 129 | 174.93 | 189 | 255.64 | 249 | 336.42 | 309 | 417.20 | 359 | 484.54 | 409 | 551.81 | 459 | 619.15 |
| 10 | 14.70 | 70 | 95.48 | 130 | 176.26 | 190 | 257.04 | 250 | 337.75 | 310 | 418.53 | 360 | 485.87 | 410 | 553.14 | 460 | 620.48 |
| 11 | 16.03 | 71 | 96.81 | 131 | 177.59 | 191 | 258.37 | 251 | 339.15 | 311 | 419.93 | 361 | 487.20 | 411 | 554.54 | 461 | 621.81 |
| 12 | 17.43 | 72 | 98.14 | 132 | 178.92 | 192 | 259.70 | 252 | 340.48 | 312 | 421.26 | 362 | 488.53 | 412 | 555.87 | 462 | 623.14 |
| 13 | 18.76 | 73 | 99.54 | 133 | 180.25 | 193 | 261.03 | 253 | 341.81 | 313 | 422.59 | 363 | 489.93 | 413 | 557.20 | 463 | 624.54 |
| 14 | 20.09 | 74 | 100.87 | 134 | 181.65 | 194 | 262.43 | 254 | 343.14 | 314 | 423.92 | 364 | 491.26 | 414 | 558.53 | 464 | 625.87 |
| 15 | 21.42 | 75 | 102.20 | 135 | 182.98 | 195 | 263.76 | 255 | 344.54 | 315 | 425.25 | 365 | 492.59 | 415 | 559.93 | 465 | 627.20 |
| 16 | 22.75 | 76 | 103.53 | 136 | 184.31 | 196 | 265.09 | 256 | 345.87 | 316 | 426.65 | 366 | 493.92 | 416 | 561.26 | 466 | 628.53 |
| 17 | 24.15 | 77 | 104.93 | 137 | 185.64 | 197 | 266.42 | 257 | 347.20 | 317 | 427.98 | 367 | 495.25 | 417 | 562.59 | 467 | 629.93 |
| 18 | 25.48 | 78 | 106.26 | 138 | 187.04 | 198 | 267.75 | 258 | 348.53 | 318 | 429.31 | 368 | 496.65 | 418 | 563.92 | 468 | 631.26 |
| 19 | 26.81 | 79 | 107.59 | 139 | 188.37 | 199 | 269.15 | 259 | 349.93 | 319 | 430.64 | 369 | 497.98 | 419 | 565.25 | 469 | 632.59 |
| 20 | 28.14 | 80 | 108.92 | 140 | 189.70 | 200 | 270.48 | 260 | 351.26 | 320 | 432.04 | 370 | 499.31 | 420 | 566.65 | 470 | 633.92 |
| 21 | 29.54 | 81 | 110.25 | 141 | 191.03 | 201 | 271.81 | 261 | 352.59 | 321 | 433.37 | 371 | 500.64 | 421 | 567.98 | 471 | 635.25 |
| 22 | 30.87 | 82 | 111.65 | 142 | 192.43 | 202 | 273.14 | 262 | 353.92 | 322 | 434.70 | 372 | 502.04 | 422 | 569.31 | 472 | 636.65 |
| 23 | 32.20 | 83 | 112.98 | 143 | 193.76 | 203 | 274.54 | 263 | 355.25 | 323 | 436.03 | 373 | 503.37 | 423 | 570.64 | 473 | 637.98 |
| 24 | 33.53 | 84 | 114.31 | 144 | 195.09 | 204 | 275.87 | 264 | 356.65 | 324 | 437.43 | 374 | 504.70 | 424 | 572.04 | 474 | 639.31 |
| 25 | 34.93 | 85 | 115.64 | 145 | 196.42 | 205 | 277.20 | 265 | 357.98 | 325 | 438.76 | 375 | 506.03 | 425 | 573.37 | 475 | 640.64 |
| 26 | 36.26 | 86 | 117.04 | 146 | 197.75 | 206 | 278.53 | 266 | 359.31 | 326 | 440.09 | 376 | 507.43 | 426 | 574.70 | 476 | 642.04 |
| 27 | 37.59 | 87 | 118.37 | 147 | 199.15 | 207 | 279.93 | 267 | 360.64 | 327 | 441.42 | 377 | 508.76 | 427 | 576.03 | 477 | 643.37 |
| 28 | 38.92 | 88 | 119.70 | 148 | 200.48 | 208 | 281.26 | 268 | 362.04 | 328 | 442.75 | 378 | 510.09 | 428 | 577.43 | 478 | 644.70 |
| 29 | 40.25 | 89 | 121.03 | 149 | 201.81 | 209 | 282.59 | 269 | 363.37 | 329 | 444.15 | 379 | 511.42 | 429 | 578.76 | 479 | 646.03 |
| 30 | 41.65 | 90 | 122.43 | 150 | 203.14 | 210 | 283.92 | 270 | 364.70 | 330 | 445.48 | 380 | 512.75 | 430 | 580.09 | 480 | 647.43 |
| 31 | 42.98 | 91 | 123.76 | 151 | 204.54 | 211 | 285.25 | 271 | 366.03 | 331 | 446.81 | 381 | 514.15 | 431 | 581.42 | 481 | 648.76 |
| 32 | 44.31 | 92 | 125.09 | 152 | 205.87 | 212 | 286.65 | 272 | 367.43 | 332 | 448.14 | 382 | 515.48 | 432 | 582.75 | 482 | 650.09 |
| 33 | 45.64 | 93 | 126.42 | 153 | 207.20 | 213 | 287.98 | 273 | 368.76 | 333 | 449.54 | 383 | 516.81 | 433 | 584.15 | 483 | 651.42 |
| 34 | 47.04 | 94 | 127.75 | 154 | 208.53 | 214 | 289.31 | 274 | 370.09 | 334 | 450.87 | 384 | 518.14 | 434 | 585.48 | 484 | 652.75 |
| 35 | 48.37 | 95 | 129.15 | 155 | 209.93 | 215 | 290.64 | 275 | 371.42 | 335 | 452.20 | 385 | 519.54 | 435 | 586.81 | 485 | 654.15 |
| 36 | 49.70 | 96 | 130.48 | 156 | 211.26 | 216 | 292.04 | 276 | 372.75 | 336 | 453.53 | 386 | 520.87 | 436 | 588.14 | 486 | 655.48 |
| 37 | 51.03 | 97 | 131.81 | 157 | 212.59 | 217 | 293.37 | 277 | 374.15 | 337 | 454.93 | 387 | 522.20 | 437 | 589.54 | 487 | 656.81 |
| 38 | 52.43 | 98 | 133.14 | 158 | 213.92 | 218 | 294.70 | 278 | 375.48 | 338 | 456.26 | 388 | 523.53 | 438 | 590.87 | 488 | 658.14 |
| 39 | 53.76 | 99 | 134.54 | 159 | 215.25 | 219 | 296.03 | 279 | 376.81 | 339 | 457.59 | 389 | 524.93 | 439 | 592.20 | 489 | 659.54 |
| 40 | 55.09 | 100 | 135.87 | 160 | 216.65 | 220 | 297.43 | 280 | 378.14 | 340 | 458.92 | 390 | 526.26 | 440 | 593.53 | 490 | 660.87 |
| 41 | 56.42 | 101 | 137.20 | 161 | 217.98 | 221 | 298.76 | 281 | 379.54 | 341 | 460.25 | 391 | 527.59 | 441 | 594.93 | 491 | 662.20 |
| 42 | 57.75 | 102 | 138.53 | 162 | 219.31 | 222 | 300.09 | 282 | 380.87 | 342 | 461.65 | 392 | 528.92 | 442 | 596.26 | 492 | 663.53 |
| 43 | 59.15 | 103 | 139.93 | 163 | 220.64 | 223 | 301.42 | 283 | 382.20 | 343 | 462.98 | 393 | 530.25 | 443 | 597.59 | 493 | 664.93 |
| 44 | 60.48 | 104 | 141.26 | 164 | 222.04 | 224 | 302.75 | 284 | 383.53 | 344 | 464.31 | 394 | 531.65 | 444 | 598.92 | 494 | 666.26 |
| 45 | 61.81 | 105 | 142.59 | 165 | 223.37 | 225 | 304.15 | 285 | 384.93 | 345 | 465.64 | 395 | 532.98 | 445 | 600.25 | 495 | 667.59 |
| 46 | 63.14 | 106 | 143.92 | 166 | 224.70 | 226 | 305.48 | 286 | 386.26 | 346 | 467.04 | 396 | 534.31 | 446 | 601.65 | 496 | 668.92 |
| 47 | 64.54 | 107 | 145.25 | 167 | 226.03 | 227 | 306.81 | 287 | 387.59 | 347 | 468.37 | 397 | 535.64 | 447 | 602.98 | 497 | 670.25 |
| 48 | 65.87 | 108 | 146.65 | 168 | 227.43 | 228 | 308.14 | 288 | 388.92 | 348 | 469.70 | 398 | 537.04 | 448 | 604.31 | 498 | 671.65 |
| 49 | 67.20 | 109 | 147.98 | 169 | 228.76 | 229 | 309.54 | 289 | 390.25 | 349 | 471.03 | 399 | 538.37 | 449 | 605.64 | 499 | 672.98 |
| 50 | 68.53 | 110 | 149.31 | 170 | 230.09 | 230 | 310.87 | 290 | 391.65 | 350 | 472.43 | 400 | 539.70 | 450 | 607.04 | 500 | 674.31 |
| 51 | 69.93 | 111 | 150.64 | 171 | 231.42 | 231 | 312.20 | 291 | 392.98 |  |  |  |  |  |  |  |  |
| 52 | 71.26 | 112 | 152.04 | 172 | 232.75 | 232 | 313.53 | 292 | 394.31 |  |  |  |  |  |  |  |  |
| 53 | 72.59 | 113 | 153.37 | 173 | 234.15 | 233 | 314.93 | 293 | 395.64 |  |  |  |  |  |  |  |  |
| 54 | 73.92 | 114 | 154.70 | 174 | 235.48 | 234 | 316.26 | 294 | 397.04 |  |  |  |  |  |  |  |  |
| 55 | 75.25 | 115 | 156.03 | 175 | 236.81 | 235 | 317.59 | 295 | 398.37 |  |  |  |  |  |  |  |  |
| 56 | 76.65 | 116 | 157.43 | 176 | 238.14 | 236 | 318.92 | 296 | 399.70 |  |  |  |  |  |  |  |  |
| 57 | 77.98 | 117 | 158.76 | 177 | 239.54 | 237 | 320.25 | 297 | 401.03 |  |  |  |  |  |  |  |  |
| 58 | 79.31 | 118 | 160.09 | 178 | 240.87 | 238 | 321.65 | 298 | 402.43 |  |  |  |  |  |  |  |  |
| 59 | 80.64 | 119 | 161.42 | 179 | 242.20 | 239 | 322.98 | 299 | 403.76 |  |  |  |  |  |  |  |  |
| 60 | 82.04 | 120 | 162.75 | 180 | 243.53 | 240 | 324.31 | 300 | 405.09 |  |  |  |  |  |  |  |  |

**Code more than 500**

1  Where the code is in the range 501 to 1000 inclusive:

  a. Subtract **500** from the code and use the balance of the code to obtain a pay adjustment figure from the table above.

  b. Add this pay adjustment figure to the figure given in the box alongside to obtain the figure of total pay adjustment to date *   | 673.12 |

2  Where the code **exceeds 1000** follow the instructions on **page 3**.

## Tables A - Pay Adjustment Tables

May 25 to May 31 **Week 8**

| Code | Total pay adjustment to date £ | Code | Total pay adjustment to date £ | Code | Total pay adjustment to date £ | Code | Total pay adjustment to date £ | Code | Total pay adjustment to date £ | Code | Total pay adjustment to date £ | Code | Total pay adjustment to date £ | Code | Total pay adjustment to date £ | Code | Total pay adjustment to date £ |
|---|---|---|---|---|---|---|---|---|---|---|---|---|---|---|---|---|---|
| 0 | NIL | | | | | | | | | | | | | | | | |
| 1 | 2.96 | 61 | 95.28 | 121 | 187.60 | 181 | 279.92 | 241 | 372.16 | 301 | 464.48 | 351 | 541.44 | 401 | 618.32 | 451 | 695.28 |
| 2 | 4.48 | 62 | 96.80 | 122 | 189.12 | 182 | 281.44 | 242 | 373.76 | 302 | 466.00 | 352 | 542.96 | 402 | 619.92 | 452 | 696.80 |
| 3 | 6.00 | 63 | 98.32 | 123 | 190.64 | 183 | 282.96 | 243 | 375.28 | 303 | 467.60 | 353 | 544.48 | 403 | 621.44 | 453 | 698.32 |
| 4 | 7.60 | 64 | 99.92 | 124 | 192.16 | 184 | 284.48 | 244 | 376.80 | 304 | 469.12 | 354 | 546.00 | 404 | 622.96 | 454 | 699.92 |
| 5 | 9.12 | 65 | 101.44 | 125 | 193.76 | 185 | 286.00 | 245 | 378.32 | 305 | 470.64 | 355 | 547.60 | 405 | 624.48 | 455 | 701.44 |
| 6 | 10.64 | 66 | 102.96 | 126 | 195.28 | 186 | 287.60 | 246 | 379.92 | 306 | 472.16 | 356 | 549.12 | 406 | 626.00 | 456 | 702.96 |
| 7 | 12.16 | 67 | 104.48 | 127 | 196.80 | 187 | 289.12 | 247 | 381.44 | 307 | 473.76 | 357 | 550.64 | 407 | 627.60 | 457 | 704.48 |
| 8 | 13.76 | 68 | 106.00 | 128 | 198.32 | 188 | 290.64 | 248 | 382.96 | 308 | 475.28 | 358 | 552.16 | 408 | 629.12 | 458 | 706.00 |
| 9 | 15.28 | 69 | 107.60 | 129 | 199.92 | 189 | 292.16 | 249 | 384.48 | 309 | 476.80 | 359 | 553.76 | 409 | 630.64 | 459 | 707.60 |
| 10 | 16.80 | 70 | 109.12 | 130 | 201.44 | 190 | 293.76 | 250 | 386.00 | 310 | 478.32 | 360 | 555.28 | 410 | 632.16 | 460 | 709.12 |
| 11 | 18.32 | 71 | 110.64 | 131 | 202.96 | 191 | 295.28 | 251 | 387.60 | 311 | 479.92 | 361 | 556.80 | 411 | 633.76 | 461 | 710.64 |
| 12 | 19.92 | 72 | 112.16 | 132 | 204.48 | 192 | 296.80 | 252 | 389.12 | 312 | 481.44 | 362 | 558.32 | 412 | 635.28 | 462 | 712.16 |
| 13 | 21.44 | 73 | 113.76 | 133 | 206.00 | 193 | 298.32 | 253 | 390.64 | 313 | 482.96 | 363 | 559.92 | 413 | 636.80 | 463 | 713.76 |
| 14 | 22.96 | 74 | 115.28 | 134 | 207.60 | 194 | 299.92 | 254 | 392.16 | 314 | 484.48 | 364 | 561.44 | 414 | 638.32 | 464 | 715.28 |
| 15 | 24.48 | 75 | 116.80 | 135 | 209.12 | 195 | 301.44 | 255 | 393.76 | 315 | 486.00 | 365 | 562.96 | 415 | 639.92 | 465 | 716.80 |
| 16 | 26.00 | 76 | 118.32 | 136 | 210.64 | 196 | 302.96 | 256 | 395.28 | 316 | 487.60 | 366 | 564.48 | 416 | 641.44 | 466 | 718.32 |
| 17 | 27.60 | 77 | 119.92 | 137 | 212.16 | 197 | 304.48 | 257 | 396.80 | 317 | 489.12 | 367 | 566.00 | 417 | 642.96 | 467 | 719.92 |
| 18 | 29.12 | 78 | 121.44 | 138 | 213.76 | 198 | 306.00 | 258 | 398.32 | 318 | 490.64 | 368 | 567.60 | 418 | 644.48 | 468 | 721.44 |
| 19 | 30.64 | 79 | 122.96 | 139 | 215.28 | 199 | 307.60 | 259 | 399.92 | 319 | 492.16 | 369 | 569.12 | 419 | 646.00 | 469 | 722.96 |
| 20 | 32.16 | 80 | 124.48 | 140 | 216.80 | 200 | 309.12 | 260 | 401.44 | 320 | 493.76 | 370 | 570.64 | 420 | 647.60 | 470 | 724.48 |
| 21 | 33.76 | 81 | 126.00 | 141 | 218.32 | 201 | 310.64 | 261 | 402.96 | 321 | 495.28 | 371 | 572.16 | 421 | 649.12 | 471 | 726.00 |
| 22 | 35.28 | 82 | 127.60 | 142 | 219.92 | 202 | 312.16 | 262 | 404.48 | 322 | 496.80 | 372 | 573.76 | 422 | 650.64 | 472 | 727.60 |
| 23 | 36.80 | 83 | 129.12 | 143 | 221.44 | 203 | 313.76 | 263 | 406.00 | 323 | 498.32 | 373 | 575.28 | 423 | 652.16 | 473 | 729.12 |
| 24 | 38.32 | 84 | 130.64 | 144 | 222.96 | 204 | 315.28 | 264 | 407.60 | 324 | 499.92 | 374 | 576.80 | 424 | 653.76 | 474 | 730.64 |
| 25 | 39.92 | 85 | 132.16 | 145 | 224.48 | 205 | 316.80 | 265 | 409.12 | 325 | 501.44 | 375 | 578.32 | 425 | 655.28 | 475 | 732.16 |
| 26 | 41.44 | 86 | 133.76 | 146 | 226.00 | 206 | 318.32 | 266 | 410.64 | 326 | 502.96 | 376 | 579.92 | 426 | 656.80 | 476 | 733.76 |
| 27 | 42.96 | 87 | 135.28 | 147 | 227.60 | 207 | 319.92 | 267 | 412.16 | 327 | 504.48 | 377 | 581.44 | 427 | 658.32 | 477 | 735.28 |
| 28 | 44.48 | 88 | 136.80 | 148 | 229.12 | 208 | 321.44 | 268 | 413.76 | 328 | 506.00 | 378 | 582.96 | 428 | 659.92 | 478 | 736.80 |
| 29 | 46.00 | 89 | 138.32 | 149 | 230.64 | 209 | 322.96 | 269 | 415.28 | 329 | 507.60 | 379 | 584.48 | 429 | 661.44 | 479 | 738.32 |
| 30 | 47.60 | 90 | 139.92 | 150 | 232.16 | 210 | 324.48 | 270 | 416.80 | 330 | 509.12 | 380 | 586.00 | 430 | 662.96 | 480 | 739.92 |
| 31 | 49.12 | 91 | 141.44 | 151 | 233.76 | 211 | 326.00 | 271 | 418.32 | 331 | 510.64 | 381 | 587.60 | 431 | 664.48 | 481 | 741.44 |
| 32 | 50.64 | 92 | 142.96 | 152 | 235.28 | 212 | 327.60 | 272 | 419.92 | 332 | 512.16 | 382 | 589.12 | 432 | 666.00 | 482 | 742.96 |
| 33 | 52.16 | 93 | 144.48 | 153 | 236.80 | 213 | 329.12 | 273 | 421.44 | 333 | 513.76 | 383 | 590.64 | 433 | 667.60 | 483 | 744.48 |
| 34 | 53.76 | 94 | 146.00 | 154 | 238.32 | 214 | 330.64 | 274 | 422.96 | 334 | 515.28 | 384 | 592.16 | 434 | 669.12 | 484 | 746.00 |
| 35 | 55.28 | 95 | 147.60 | 155 | 239.92 | 215 | 332.16 | 275 | 424.48 | 335 | 516.80 | 385 | 593.76 | 435 | 670.64 | 485 | 747.60 |
| 36 | 56.80 | 96 | 149.12 | 156 | 241.44 | 216 | 333.76 | 276 | 426.00 | 336 | 518.32 | 386 | 595.28 | 436 | 672.16 | 486 | 749.12 |
| 37 | 58.32 | 97 | 150.64 | 157 | 242.96 | 217 | 335.28 | 277 | 427.60 | 337 | 519.92 | 387 | 596.80 | 437 | 673.76 | 487 | 750.64 |
| 38 | 59.92 | 98 | 152.16 | 158 | 244.48 | 218 | 336.80 | 278 | 429.12 | 338 | 521.44 | 388 | 598.32 | 438 | 675.28 | 488 | 752.16 |
| 39 | 61.44 | 99 | 153.76 | 159 | 246.00 | 219 | 338.32 | 279 | 430.64 | 339 | 522.96 | 389 | 599.92 | 439 | 676.80 | 489 | 753.76 |
| 40 | 62.96 | 100 | 155.28 | 160 | 247.60 | 220 | 339.92 | 280 | 432.16 | 340 | 524.48 | 390 | 601.44 | 440 | 678.32 | 490 | 755.28 |
| 41 | 64.48 | 101 | 156.80 | 161 | 249.12 | 221 | 341.44 | 281 | 433.76 | 341 | 526.00 | 391 | 602.96 | 441 | 679.92 | 491 | 756.80 |
| 42 | 66.00 | 102 | 158.32 | 162 | 250.64 | 222 | 342.96 | 282 | 435.28 | 342 | 527.60 | 392 | 604.48 | 442 | 681.44 | 492 | 758.32 |
| 43 | 67.60 | 103 | 159.92 | 163 | 252.16 | 223 | 344.48 | 283 | 436.80 | 343 | 529.12 | 393 | 606.00 | 443 | 682.96 | 493 | 759.92 |
| 44 | 69.12 | 104 | 161.44 | 164 | 253.76 | 224 | 346.00 | 284 | 438.32 | 344 | 530.64 | 394 | 607.60 | 444 | 684.48 | 494 | 761.44 |
| 45 | 70.64 | 105 | 162.96 | 165 | 255.28 | 225 | 347.60 | 285 | 439.92 | 345 | 532.16 | 395 | 609.12 | 445 | 686.00 | 495 | 762.96 |
| 46 | 72.16 | 106 | 164.48 | 166 | 256.80 | 226 | 349.12 | 286 | 441.44 | 346 | 533.76 | 396 | 610.64 | 446 | 687.60 | 496 | 764.48 |
| 47 | 73.76 | 107 | 166.00 | 167 | 258.32 | 227 | 350.64 | 287 | 442.96 | 347 | 535.28 | 397 | 612.16 | 447 | 689.12 | 497 | 766.00 |
| 48 | 75.28 | 108 | 167.60 | 168 | 259.92 | 228 | 352.16 | 288 | 444.48 | 348 | 536.80 | 398 | 613.76 | 448 | 690.64 | 498 | 767.60 |
| 49 | 76.80 | 109 | 169.12 | 169 | 261.44 | 229 | 353.76 | 289 | 446.00 | 349 | 538.32 | 399 | 615.28 | 449 | 692.16 | 499 | 769.12 |
| 50 | 78.32 | 110 | 170.64 | 170 | 262.96 | 230 | 355.28 | 290 | 447.60 | 350 | 539.92 | 400 | 616.80 | 450 | 693.76 | 500 | 770.64 |
| 51 | 79.92 | 111 | 172.16 | 171 | 264.48 | 231 | 356.80 | 291 | 449.12 | | | | | | | | |
| 52 | 81.44 | 112 | 173.76 | 172 | 266.00 | 232 | 358.32 | 292 | 450.64 | | | | | | | | |
| 53 | 82.96 | 113 | 175.28 | 173 | 267.60 | 233 | 359.92 | 293 | 452.16 | | | | | | | | |
| 54 | 84.48 | 114 | 176.80 | 174 | 269.12 | 234 | 361.44 | 294 | 453.76 | | | | | | | | |
| 55 | 86.00 | 115 | 178.32 | 175 | 270.64 | 235 | 362.96 | 295 | 455.28 | | | | | | | | |
| 56 | 87.60 | 116 | 179.92 | 176 | 272.16 | 236 | 364.48 | 296 | 456.80 | | | | | | | | |
| 57 | 89.12 | 117 | 181.44 | 177 | 273.76 | 237 | 366.00 | 297 | 458.32 | | | | | | | | |
| 58 | 90.64 | 118 | 182.96 | 178 | 275.28 | 238 | 367.60 | 298 | 459.92 | | | | | | | | |
| 59 | 92.16 | 119 | 184.48 | 179 | 276.80 | 239 | 369.12 | 299 | 461.44 | | | | | | | | |
| 60 | 93.76 | 120 | 186.00 | 180 | 278.32 | 240 | 370.64 | 300 | 462.96 | | | | | | | | |

**Code more than 500**

1 Where the code is in the range **501 to 1000** inclusive:

a. Subtract **500** from the code and use the balance of the code to obtain a pay adjustment figure from the table above.

b. Add this pay adjustment figure to the figure given in the box alongside to obtain the figure of total pay adjustment to date * 769.28

2 Where the code **exceeds 1000** follow the instructions on **page 3**.

11

**Week 9**  Jun 1 to Jun 7

**Tables A** - Pay Adjustment Tables

| Code | Total pay adjustment to date | Code | Total pay adjustment to date | Code | Total pay adjustment to date | Code | Total pay adjustment to date | Code | Total pay adjustment to date | Code | Total pay adjustment to date | Code | Total pay adjustment to date | Code | Total pay adjustment to date | Code | Total pay adjustment to date |
|---|---|---|---|---|---|---|---|---|---|---|---|---|---|---|---|---|---|
| | £ | | £ | | £ | | £ | | £ | | £ | | £ | | £ | | £ |
| 0 | NIL | 61 | 107.19 | 121 | 211.05 | 181 | 314.91 | 241 | 418.68 | 301 | 522.54 | 351 | 609.12 | 401 | 695.61 | 451 | 782.19 |
| 1 | 3.33 | 62 | 108.90 | 122 | 212.76 | 182 | 316.62 | 242 | 420.48 | 302 | 524.25 | 352 | 610.83 | 402 | 697.41 | 452 | 783.90 |
| 2 | 5.04 | 63 | 110.61 | 123 | 214.47 | 183 | 318.33 | 243 | 422.19 | 303 | 526.05 | 353 | 612.54 | 403 | 699.12 | 453 | 785.61 |
| 3 | 6.75 | 64 | 112.41 | 124 | 216.18 | 184 | 320.04 | 244 | 423.90 | 304 | 527.76 | 354 | 614.25 | 404 | 700.83 | 454 | 787.41 |
| 4 | 8.55 | 65 | 114.12 | 125 | 217.98 | 185 | 321.75 | 245 | 425.61 | 305 | 529.47 | 355 | 616.05 | 405 | 702.54 | 455 | 789.12 |
| 5 | 10.26 | | | | | | | | | | | | | | | | |
| 6 | 11.97 | 66 | 115.83 | 126 | 219.69 | 186 | 323.55 | 246 | 427.41 | 306 | 531.18 | 356 | 617.76 | 406 | 704.25 | 456 | 790.83 |
| 7 | 13.68 | 67 | 117.54 | 127 | 221.40 | 187 | 325.26 | 247 | 429.12 | 307 | 532.98 | 357 | 619.47 | 407 | 706.05 | 457 | 792.54 |
| 8 | 15.48 | 68 | 119.25 | 128 | 223.11 | 188 | 326.97 | 248 | 430.83 | 308 | 534.69 | 358 | 621.18 | 408 | 707.76 | 458 | 794.25 |
| 9 | 17.19 | 69 | 121.05 | 129 | 224.91 | 189 | 328.68 | 249 | 432.54 | 309 | 536.40 | 359 | 622.98 | 409 | 709.47 | 459 | 796.05 |
| 10 | 18.90 | 70 | 122.76 | 130 | 226.62 | 190 | 330.48 | 250 | 434.25 | 310 | 538.11 | 360 | 624.69 | 410 | 711.18 | 460 | 797.76 |
| 11 | 20.61 | 71 | 124.47 | 131 | 228.33 | 191 | 332.19 | 251 | 436.05 | 311 | 539.91 | 361 | 626.40 | 411 | 712.98 | 461 | 799.47 |
| 12 | 22.41 | 72 | 126.18 | 132 | 230.04 | 192 | 333.90 | 252 | 437.76 | 312 | 541.62 | 362 | 628.11 | 412 | 714.69 | 462 | 801.18 |
| 13 | 24.12 | 73 | 127.98 | 133 | 231.75 | 193 | 335.61 | 253 | 439.47 | 313 | 543.33 | 363 | 629.91 | 413 | 716.40 | 463 | 802.98 |
| 14 | 25.83 | 74 | 129.69 | 134 | 233.55 | 194 | 337.41 | 254 | 441.18 | 314 | 545.04 | 364 | 631.62 | 414 | 718.11 | 464 | 804.69 |
| 15 | 27.54 | 75 | 131.40 | 135 | 235.26 | 195 | 339.12 | 255 | 442.98 | 315 | 546.75 | 365 | 633.33 | 415 | 719.91 | 465 | 806.40 |
| 16 | 29.25 | 76 | 133.11 | 136 | 236.97 | 196 | 340.83 | 256 | 444.69 | 316 | 548.55 | 366 | 635.04 | 416 | 721.62 | 466 | 808.11 |
| 17 | 31.05 | 77 | 134.91 | 137 | 238.68 | 197 | 342.54 | 257 | 446.40 | 317 | 550.26 | 367 | 636.75 | 417 | 723.33 | 467 | 809.91 |
| 18 | 32.76 | 78 | 136.62 | 138 | 240.48 | 198 | 344.25 | 258 | 448.11 | 318 | 551.97 | 368 | 638.55 | 418 | 725.04 | 468 | 811.62 |
| 19 | 34.47 | 79 | 138.33 | 139 | 242.19 | 199 | 346.05 | 259 | 449.91 | 319 | 553.68 | 369 | 640.26 | 419 | 726.75 | 469 | 813.33 |
| 20 | 36.18 | 80 | 140.04 | 140 | 243.90 | 200 | 347.76 | 260 | 451.62 | 320 | 555.48 | 370 | 641.97 | 420 | 728.55 | 470 | 815.04 |
| 21 | 37.98 | 81 | 141.75 | 141 | 245.61 | 201 | 349.47 | 261 | 453.33 | 321 | 557.19 | 371 | 643.68 | 421 | 730.26 | 471 | 816.75 |
| 22 | 39.69 | 82 | 143.55 | 142 | 247.41 | 202 | 351.18 | 262 | 455.04 | 322 | 558.90 | 372 | 645.48 | 422 | 731.97 | 472 | 818.55 |
| 23 | 41.40 | 83 | 145.26 | 143 | 249.12 | 203 | 352.98 | 263 | 456.75 | 323 | 560.61 | 373 | 647.19 | 423 | 733.68 | 473 | 820.26 |
| 24 | 43.11 | 84 | 146.97 | 144 | 250.83 | 204 | 354.69 | 264 | 458.55 | 324 | 562.41 | 374 | 648.90 | 424 | 735.48 | 474 | 821.97 |
| 25 | 44.91 | 85 | 148.68 | 145 | 252.54 | 205 | 356.40 | 265 | 460.26 | 325 | 564.12 | 375 | 650.61 | 425 | 737.19 | 475 | 823.68 |
| 26 | 46.62 | 86 | 150.48 | 146 | 254.25 | 206 | 358.11 | 266 | 461.97 | 326 | 565.83 | 376 | 652.41 | 426 | 738.90 | 476 | 825.48 |
| 27 | 48.33 | 87 | 152.19 | 147 | 256.05 | 207 | 359.91 | 267 | 463.68 | 327 | 567.54 | 377 | 654.12 | 427 | 740.61 | 477 | 827.19 |
| 28 | 50.04 | 88 | 153.90 | 148 | 257.76 | 208 | 361.62 | 268 | 465.48 | 328 | 569.25 | 378 | 655.83 | 428 | 742.41 | 478 | 828.90 |
| 29 | 51.75 | 89 | 155.61 | 149 | 259.47 | 209 | 363.33 | 269 | 467.19 | 329 | 571.05 | 379 | 657.54 | 429 | 744.12 | 479 | 830.61 |
| 30 | 53.55 | 90 | 157.41 | 150 | 261.18 | 210 | 365.04 | 270 | 468.90 | 330 | 572.76 | 380 | 659.25 | 430 | 745.83 | 480 | 832.41 |
| 31 | 55.26 | 91 | 159.12 | 151 | 262.98 | 211 | 366.75 | 271 | 470.61 | 331 | 574.47 | 381 | 661.05 | 431 | 747.54 | 481 | 834.12 |
| 32 | 56.97 | 92 | 160.83 | 152 | 264.69 | 212 | 368.55 | 272 | 472.41 | 332 | 576.18 | 382 | 662.76 | 432 | 749.25 | 482 | 835.83 |
| 33 | 58.68 | 93 | 162.54 | 153 | 266.40 | 213 | 370.26 | 273 | 474.12 | 333 | 577.98 | 383 | 664.47 | 433 | 751.05 | 483 | 837.54 |
| 34 | 60.48 | 94 | 164.25 | 154 | 268.11 | 214 | 371.97 | 274 | 475.83 | 334 | 579.69 | 384 | 666.18 | 434 | 752.76 | 484 | 839.25 |
| 35 | 62.19 | 95 | 166.05 | 155 | 269.91 | 215 | 373.68 | 275 | 477.54 | 335 | 581.40 | 385 | 667.98 | 435 | 754.47 | 485 | 841.05 |
| 36 | 63.90 | 96 | 167.76 | 156 | 271.62 | 216 | 375.48 | 276 | 479.25 | 336 | 583.11 | 386 | 669.69 | 436 | 756.18 | 486 | 842.76 |
| 37 | 65.61 | 97 | 169.47 | 157 | 273.33 | 217 | 377.19 | 277 | 481.05 | 337 | 584.91 | 387 | 671.40 | 437 | 757.98 | 487 | 844.47 |
| 38 | 67.41 | 98 | 171.18 | 158 | 275.04 | 218 | 378.90 | 278 | 482.76 | 338 | 586.62 | 388 | 673.11 | 438 | 759.69 | 488 | 846.18 |
| 39 | 69.12 | 99 | 172.98 | 159 | 276.75 | 219 | 380.61 | 279 | 484.47 | 339 | 588.33 | 389 | 674.91 | 439 | 761.40 | 489 | 847.98 |
| 40 | 70.83 | 100 | 174.69 | 160 | 278.55 | 220 | 382.41 | 280 | 486.18 | 340 | 590.04 | 390 | 676.62 | 440 | 763.11 | 490 | 849.69 |
| 41 | 72.54 | 101 | 176.40 | 161 | 280.26 | 221 | 384.12 | 281 | 487.98 | 341 | 591.75 | 391 | 678.33 | 441 | 764.91 | 491 | 851.40 |
| 42 | 74.25 | 102 | 178.11 | 162 | 281.97 | 222 | 385.83 | 282 | 489.69 | 342 | 593.55 | 392 | 680.04 | 442 | 766.62 | 492 | 853.11 |
| 43 | 76.05 | 103 | 179.91 | 163 | 283.68 | 223 | 387.54 | 283 | 491.40 | 343 | 595.26 | 393 | 681.75 | 443 | 768.33 | 493 | 854.91 |
| 44 | 77.76 | 104 | 181.62 | 164 | 285.48 | 224 | 389.25 | 284 | 493.11 | 344 | 596.97 | 394 | 683.55 | 444 | 770.04 | 494 | 856.62 |
| 45 | 79.47 | 105 | 183.33 | 165 | 287.19 | 225 | 391.05 | 285 | 494.91 | 345 | 598.68 | 395 | 685.26 | 445 | 771.75 | 495 | 858.33 |
| 46 | 81.18 | 106 | 185.04 | 166 | 288.90 | 226 | 392.76 | 286 | 496.62 | 346 | 600.48 | 396 | 686.97 | 446 | 773.55 | 496 | 860.04 |
| 47 | 82.98 | 107 | 186.75 | 167 | 290.61 | 227 | 394.47 | 287 | 498.33 | 347 | 602.19 | 397 | 688.68 | 447 | 775.26 | 497 | 861.75 |
| 48 | 84.69 | 108 | 188.55 | 168 | 292.41 | 228 | 396.18 | 288 | 500.04 | 348 | 603.90 | 398 | 690.48 | 448 | 776.97 | 498 | 863.55 |
| 49 | 86.40 | 109 | 190.26 | 169 | 294.12 | 229 | 397.98 | 289 | 501.75 | 349 | 605.61 | 399 | 692.19 | 449 | 778.68 | 499 | 865.26 |
| 50 | 88.11 | 110 | 191.97 | 170 | 295.83 | 230 | 399.69 | 290 | 503.55 | 350 | 607.41 | 400 | 693.90 | 450 | 780.48 | 500 | 866.97 |
| 51 | 89.91 | 111 | 193.68 | 171 | 297.54 | 231 | 401.40 | 291 | 505.26 | | | | | | | | |
| 52 | 91.62 | 112 | 195.48 | 172 | 299.25 | 232 | 403.11 | 292 | 506.97 | | | | | | | | |
| 53 | 93.33 | 113 | 197.19 | 173 | 301.05 | 233 | 404.91 | 293 | 508.68 | | | | | | | | |
| 54 | 95.04 | 114 | 198.90 | 174 | 302.76 | 234 | 406.62 | 294 | 510.48 | | | | | | | | |
| 55 | 96.75 | 115 | 200.61 | 175 | 304.47 | 235 | 408.33 | 295 | 512.19 | | | | | | | | |
| 56 | 98.55 | 116 | 202.41 | 176 | 306.18 | 236 | 410.04 | 296 | 513.90 | | | | | | | | |
| 57 | 100.26 | 117 | 204.12 | 177 | 307.98 | 237 | 411.75 | 297 | 515.61 | | | | | | | | |
| 58 | 101.97 | 118 | 205.83 | 178 | 309.69 | 238 | 413.55 | 298 | 517.41 | | | | | | | | |
| 59 | 103.68 | 119 | 207.54 | 179 | 311.40 | 239 | 415.26 | 299 | 519.12 | | | | | | | | |
| 60 | 105.48 | 120 | 209.25 | 180 | 313.11 | 240 | 416.97 | 300 | 520.83 | | | | | | | | |

**Code more than 500**

1 Where the code is in the range **501** to **1000** inclusive:

a. Subtract **500** from the code and use the balance of the code to obtain a pay adjustment figure from the table above.

b. Add this pay adjustment figure to the figure given in the box alongside to obtain the figure of total pay adjustment to date * **865.44**

2 Where the code **exceeds 1000** follow the instructions on **page 3**.

12

# Tables A - Pay Adjustment Tables

Jun 8 to Jun 14 **Week 10**

| Code | Total pay adjustment to date | Code | Total pay adjustment to date | Code | Total pay adjustment to date | Code | Total pay adjustment to date | Code | Total pay adjustment to date | Code | Total pay adjustment to date | Code | Total pay adjustment to date | Code | Total pay adjustment to date | Code | Total pay adjustment to date |
|---|---|---|---|---|---|---|---|---|---|---|---|---|---|---|---|---|---|
| | £ | | £ | | £ | | £ | | £ | | £ | | £ | | £ | | £ |
| 0 | NIL | | | | | | | | | | | | | | | | |
| 1 | 3.70 | 61 | 119.10 | 121 | 234.50 | 181 | 349.90 | 241 | 465.20 | 301 | 580.60 | 351 | 676.80 | 401 | 772.90 | 451 | 869.10 |
| 2 | 5.60 | 62 | 121.00 | 122 | 236.40 | 182 | 351.80 | 242 | 467.20 | 302 | 582.50 | 352 | 678.70 | 402 | 774.90 | 452 | 871.00 |
| 3 | 7.50 | 63 | 122.90 | 123 | 238.30 | 183 | 353.70 | 243 | 469.10 | 303 | 584.50 | 353 | 680.60 | 403 | 776.80 | 453 | 872.90 |
| 4 | 9.50 | 64 | 124.90 | 124 | 240.20 | 184 | 355.60 | 244 | 471.00 | 304 | 586.40 | 354 | 682.50 | 404 | 778.70 | 454 | 874.90 |
| 5 | 11.40 | 65 | 126.80 | 125 | 242.20 | 185 | 357.50 | 245 | 472.90 | 305 | 588.30 | 355 | 684.50 | 405 | 780.60 | 455 | 876.80 |
| 6 | 13.30 | 66 | 128.70 | 126 | 244.10 | 186 | 359.50 | 246 | 474.90 | 306 | 590.20 | 356 | 686.40 | 406 | 782.50 | 456 | 878.70 |
| 7 | 15.20 | 67 | 130.60 | 127 | 246.00 | 187 | 361.40 | 247 | 476.80 | 307 | 592.20 | 357 | 688.30 | 407 | 784.50 | 457 | 880.60 |
| 8 | 17.20 | 68 | 132.50 | 128 | 247.90 | 188 | 363.30 | 248 | 478.70 | 308 | 594.10 | 358 | 690.20 | 408 | 786.40 | 458 | 882.50 |
| 9 | 19.10 | 69 | 134.50 | 129 | 249.90 | 189 | 365.20 | 249 | 480.60 | 309 | 596.00 | 359 | 692.20 | 409 | 788.30 | 459 | 884.50 |
| 10 | 21.00 | 70 | 136.40 | 130 | 251.80 | 190 | 367.20 | 250 | 482.50 | 310 | 597.90 | 360 | 694.10 | 410 | 790.20 | 460 | 886.40 |
| 11 | 22.90 | 71 | 138.30 | 131 | 253.70 | 191 | 369.10 | 251 | 484.50 | 311 | 599.90 | 361 | 696.00 | 411 | 792.20 | 461 | 888.30 |
| 12 | 24.90 | 72 | 140.20 | 132 | 255.60 | 192 | 371.00 | 252 | 486.40 | 312 | 601.80 | 362 | 697.90 | 412 | 794.10 | 462 | 890.20 |
| 13 | 26.80 | 73 | 142.20 | 133 | 257.50 | 193 | 372.90 | 253 | 488.30 | 313 | 603.70 | 363 | 699.90 | 413 | 796.00 | 463 | 892.20 |
| 14 | 28.70 | 74 | 144.10 | 134 | 259.50 | 194 | 374.90 | 254 | 490.20 | 314 | 605.60 | 364 | 701.80 | 414 | 797.90 | 464 | 894.10 |
| 15 | 30.60 | 75 | 146.00 | 135 | 261.40 | 195 | 376.80 | 255 | 492.20 | 315 | 607.50 | 365 | 703.70 | 415 | 799.90 | 465 | 896.00 |
| 16 | 32.50 | 76 | 147.90 | 136 | 263.30 | 196 | 378.70 | 256 | 494.10 | 316 | 609.50 | 366 | 705.60 | 416 | 801.80 | 466 | 897.90 |
| 17 | 34.50 | 77 | 149.90 | 137 | 265.20 | 197 | 380.60 | 257 | 496.00 | 317 | 611.40 | 367 | 707.50 | 417 | 803.70 | 467 | 899.90 |
| 18 | 36.40 | 78 | 151.80 | 138 | 267.20 | 198 | 382.50 | 258 | 497.90 | 318 | 613.30 | 368 | 709.50 | 418 | 805.60 | 468 | 901.80 |
| 19 | 38.30 | 79 | 153.70 | 139 | 269.10 | 199 | 384.50 | 259 | 499.90 | 319 | 615.20 | 369 | 711.40 | 419 | 807.50 | 469 | 903.70 |
| 20 | 40.20 | 80 | 155.60 | 140 | 271.00 | 200 | 386.40 | 260 | 501.80 | 320 | 617.20 | 370 | 713.30 | 420 | 809.50 | 470 | 905.60 |
| 21 | 42.20 | 81 | 157.50 | 141 | 272.90 | 201 | 388.30 | 261 | 503.70 | 321 | 619.10 | 371 | 715.20 | 421 | 811.40 | 471 | 907.50 |
| 22 | 44.10 | 82 | 159.50 | 142 | 274.90 | 202 | 390.20 | 262 | 505.60 | 322 | 621.00 | 372 | 717.20 | 422 | 813.30 | 472 | 909.50 |
| 23 | 46.00 | 83 | 161.40 | 143 | 276.80 | 203 | 392.20 | 263 | 507.50 | 323 | 622.90 | 373 | 719.10 | 423 | 815.20 | 473 | 911.40 |
| 24 | 47.90 | 84 | 163.30 | 144 | 278.70 | 204 | 394.10 | 264 | 509.50 | 324 | 624.90 | 374 | 721.00 | 424 | 817.20 | 474 | 913.30 |
| 25 | 49.90 | 85 | 165.20 | 145 | 280.60 | 205 | 396.00 | 265 | 511.40 | 325 | 626.80 | 375 | 722.90 | 425 | 819.10 | 475 | 915.20 |
| 26 | 51.80 | 86 | 167.20 | 146 | 282.50 | 206 | 397.90 | 266 | 513.30 | 326 | 628.70 | 376 | 724.90 | 426 | 821.00 | 476 | 917.20 |
| 27 | 53.70 | 87 | 169.10 | 147 | 284.50 | 207 | 399.90 | 267 | 515.20 | 327 | 630.60 | 377 | 726.80 | 427 | 822.90 | 477 | 919.10 |
| 28 | 55.60 | 88 | 171.00 | 148 | 286.40 | 208 | 401.80 | 268 | 517.20 | 328 | 632.50 | 378 | 728.70 | 428 | 824.90 | 478 | 921.00 |
| 29 | 57.50 | 89 | 172.90 | 149 | 288.30 | 209 | 403.70 | 269 | 519.10 | 329 | 634.50 | 379 | 730.60 | 429 | 826.80 | 479 | 922.90 |
| 30 | 59.50 | 90 | 174.90 | 150 | 290.20 | 210 | 405.60 | 270 | 521.00 | 330 | 636.40 | 380 | 732.50 | 430 | 828.70 | 480 | 924.90 |
| 31 | 61.40 | 91 | 176.80 | 151 | 292.20 | 211 | 407.50 | 271 | 522.90 | 331 | 638.30 | 381 | 734.50 | 431 | 830.60 | 481 | 926.80 |
| 32 | 63.30 | 92 | 178.70 | 152 | 294.10 | 212 | 409.50 | 272 | 524.90 | 332 | 640.20 | 382 | 736.40 | 432 | 832.50 | 482 | 928.70 |
| 33 | 65.20 | 93 | 180.60 | 153 | 296.00 | 213 | 411.40 | 273 | 526.80 | 333 | 642.20 | 383 | 738.30 | 433 | 834.50 | 483 | 930.60 |
| 34 | 67.20 | 94 | 182.50 | 154 | 297.90 | 214 | 413.30 | 274 | 528.70 | 334 | 644.10 | 384 | 740.20 | 434 | 836.40 | 484 | 932.50 |
| 35 | 69.10 | 95 | 184.50 | 155 | 299.90 | 215 | 415.20 | 275 | 530.60 | 335 | 646.00 | 385 | 742.20 | 435 | 838.30 | 485 | 934.50 |
| 36 | 71.00 | 96 | 186.40 | 156 | 301.80 | 216 | 417.20 | 276 | 532.50 | 336 | 647.90 | 386 | 744.10 | 436 | 840.20 | 486 | 936.40 |
| 37 | 72.90 | 97 | 188.30 | 157 | 303.70 | 217 | 419.10 | 277 | 534.50 | 337 | 649.90 | 387 | 746.00 | 437 | 842.20 | 487 | 938.30 |
| 38 | 74.90 | 98 | 190.20 | 158 | 305.60 | 218 | 421.00 | 278 | 536.40 | 338 | 651.80 | 388 | 747.90 | 438 | 844.10 | 488 | 940.20 |
| 39 | 76.80 | 99 | 192.20 | 159 | 307.50 | 219 | 422.90 | 279 | 538.30 | 339 | 653.70 | 389 | 749.90 | 439 | 846.00 | 489 | 942.20 |
| 40 | 78.70 | 100 | 194.10 | 160 | 309.50 | 220 | 424.90 | 280 | 540.20 | 340 | 655.60 | 390 | 751.80 | 440 | 847.90 | 490 | 944.10 |
| 41 | 80.60 | 101 | 196.00 | 161 | 311.40 | 221 | 426.80 | 281 | 542.20 | 341 | 657.50 | 391 | 753.70 | 441 | 849.90 | 491 | 946.00 |
| 42 | 82.50 | 102 | 197.90 | 162 | 313.30 | 222 | 428.70 | 282 | 544.10 | 342 | 659.50 | 392 | 755.60 | 442 | 851.80 | 492 | 947.90 |
| 43 | 84.50 | 103 | 199.90 | 163 | 315.20 | 223 | 430.60 | 283 | 546.00 | 343 | 661.40 | 393 | 757.50 | 443 | 853.70 | 493 | 949.90 |
| 44 | 86.40 | 104 | 201.80 | 164 | 317.20 | 224 | 432.50 | 284 | 547.90 | 344 | 663.30 | 394 | 759.50 | 444 | 855.60 | 494 | 951.80 |
| 45 | 88.30 | 105 | 203.70 | 165 | 319.10 | 225 | 434.50 | 285 | 549.90 | 345 | 665.20 | 395 | 761.40 | 445 | 857.50 | 495 | 953.70 |
| 46 | 90.20 | 106 | 205.60 | 166 | 321.00 | 226 | 436.40 | 286 | 551.80 | 346 | 667.20 | 396 | 763.30 | 446 | 859.50 | 496 | 955.60 |
| 47 | 92.20 | 107 | 207.50 | 167 | 322.90 | 227 | 438.30 | 287 | 553.70 | 347 | 669.10 | 397 | 765.20 | 447 | 861.40 | 497 | 957.50 |
| 48 | 94.10 | 108 | 209.50 | 168 | 324.90 | 228 | 440.20 | 288 | 555.60 | 348 | 671.00 | 398 | 767.20 | 448 | 863.30 | 498 | 959.50 |
| 49 | 96.00 | 109 | 211.40 | 169 | 326.80 | 229 | 442.20 | 289 | 557.50 | 349 | 672.90 | 399 | 769.10 | 449 | 865.20 | 499 | 961.40 |
| 50 | 97.90 | 110 | 213.30 | 170 | 328.70 | 230 | 444.10 | 290 | 559.50 | 350 | 674.90 | 400 | 771.00 | 450 | 867.20 | 500 | 963.30 |
| 51 | 99.90 | 111 | 215.20 | 171 | 330.60 | 231 | 446.00 | 291 | 561.40 | | | | | | | | |
| 52 | 101.80 | 112 | 217.20 | 172 | 332.50 | 232 | 447.90 | 292 | 563.30 | | | | | | | | |
| 53 | 103.70 | 113 | 219.10 | 173 | 334.50 | 233 | 449.90 | 293 | 565.20 | | | | | | | | |
| 54 | 105.60 | 114 | 221.00 | 174 | 336.40 | 234 | 451.80 | 294 | 567.20 | | | | | | | | |
| 55 | 107.50 | 115 | 222.90 | 175 | 338.30 | 235 | 453.70 | 295 | 569.10 | | | | | | | | |
| 56 | 109.50 | 116 | 224.90 | 176 | 340.20 | 236 | 455.60 | 296 | 571.00 | | | | | | | | |
| 57 | 111.40 | 117 | 226.80 | 177 | 342.20 | 237 | 457.50 | 297 | 572.90 | | | | | | | | |
| 58 | 113.30 | 118 | 228.70 | 178 | 344.10 | 238 | 459.50 | 298 | 574.90 | | | | | | | | |
| 59 | 115.20 | 119 | 230.60 | 179 | 346.00 | 239 | 461.40 | 299 | 576.80 | | | | | | | | |
| 60 | 117.20 | 120 | 232.50 | 180 | 347.90 | 240 | 463.30 | 300 | 578.70 | | | | | | | | |

**Code more than 500**

1 Where the code is in the range **501** to **1000** inclusive:

  a. Subtract **500** from the code and use the balance of the code to obtain a pay adjustment figure from the table above.

  b. Add this pay adjustment figure to the figure given in the box alongside to obtain the figure of total pay adjustment to date *   | 961.60 |

2 Where the code **exceeds 1000** follow the instructions on **page 3**.

13

# APPENDIX 4: PAYE TAX TABLES – PAY ADJUSTMENT TABLES

**Week 11**  Jun 15 to Jun 21                                        **Tables A** - Pay Adjustment Tables

| Code | Total pay adjustment to date | Code | Total pay adjustment to date | Code | Total pay adjustment to date | Code | Total pay adjustment to date | Code | Total pay adjustment to date | Code | Total pay adjustment to date | Code | Total pay adjustment to date | Code | Total pay adjustment to date | Code | Total pay adjustment to date |
|---|---|---|---|---|---|---|---|---|---|---|---|---|---|---|---|---|---|
| | £ | | £ | | £ | | £ | | £ | | £ | | £ | | £ | | £ |
| 0 | NIL | 61 | 131.01 | 121 | 257.95 | 181 | 384.89 | 241 | 511.72 | 301 | 638.66 | 351 | 744.48 | 401 | 850.19 | 451 | 956.01 |
| 1 | 4.07 | 62 | 133.10 | 122 | 260.04 | 182 | 386.98 | 242 | 513.92 | 302 | 640.75 | 352 | 746.57 | 402 | 852.39 | 452 | 958.10 |
| 2 | 6.16 | 63 | 135.19 | 123 | 262.13 | 183 | 389.07 | 243 | 516.01 | 303 | 642.95 | 353 | 748.66 | 403 | 854.48 | 453 | 960.19 |
| 3 | 8.25 | 64 | 137.39 | 124 | 264.22 | 184 | 391.16 | 244 | 518.10 | 304 | 645.04 | 354 | 750.75 | 404 | 856.57 | 454 | 962.39 |
| 4 | 10.45 | 65 | 139.48 | 125 | 266.42 | 185 | 393.25 | 245 | 520.19 | 305 | 647.13 | 355 | 752.95 | 405 | 858.66 | 455 | 964.48 |
| 5 | 12.54 | | | | | | | | | | | | | | | | |
| 6 | 14.63 | 66 | 141.57 | 126 | 268.51 | 186 | 395.45 | 246 | 522.39 | 306 | 649.22 | 356 | 755.04 | 406 | 860.75 | 456 | 966.57 |
| 7 | 16.72 | 67 | 143.66 | 127 | 270.60 | 187 | 397.54 | 247 | 524.48 | 307 | 651.42 | 357 | 757.13 | 407 | 862.95 | 457 | 968.66 |
| 8 | 18.92 | 68 | 145.75 | 128 | 272.69 | 188 | 399.63 | 248 | 526.57 | 308 | 653.51 | 358 | 759.22 | 408 | 865.04 | 458 | 970.75 |
| 9 | 21.01 | 69 | 147.95 | 129 | 274.89 | 189 | 401.72 | 249 | 528.66 | 309 | 655.60 | 359 | 761.42 | 409 | 867.13 | 459 | 972.95 |
| 10 | 23.10 | 70 | 150.04 | 130 | 276.98 | 190 | 403.92 | 250 | 530.75 | 310 | 657.69 | 360 | 763.51 | 410 | 869.22 | 460 | 975.04 |
| 11 | 25.19 | 71 | 152.13 | 131 | 279.07 | 191 | 406.01 | 251 | 532.95 | 311 | 659.89 | 361 | 765.60 | 411 | 871.42 | 461 | 977.13 |
| 12 | 27.39 | 72 | 154.22 | 132 | 281.16 | 192 | 408.10 | 252 | 535.04 | 312 | 661.98 | 362 | 767.69 | 412 | 873.51 | 462 | 979.22 |
| 13 | 29.48 | 73 | 156.42 | 133 | 283.25 | 193 | 410.19 | 253 | 537.13 | 313 | 664.07 | 363 | 769.89 | 413 | 875.60 | 463 | 981.42 |
| 14 | 31.57 | 74 | 158.51 | 134 | 285.45 | 194 | 412.39 | 254 | 539.22 | 314 | 666.16 | 364 | 771.98 | 414 | 877.69 | 464 | 983.51 |
| 15 | 33.66 | 75 | 160.60 | 135 | 287.54 | 195 | 414.48 | 255 | 541.42 | 315 | 668.25 | 365 | 774.07 | 415 | 879.89 | 465 | 985.60 |
| 16 | 35.75 | 76 | 162.69 | 136 | 289.63 | 196 | 416.57 | 256 | 543.51 | 316 | 670.45 | 366 | 776.16 | 416 | 881.98 | 466 | 987.69 |
| 17 | 37.95 | 77 | 164.89 | 137 | 291.72 | 197 | 418.66 | 257 | 545.60 | 317 | 672.54 | 367 | 778.25 | 417 | 884.07 | 467 | 989.89 |
| 18 | 40.04 | 78 | 166.98 | 138 | 293.92 | 198 | 420.75 | 258 | 547.69 | 318 | 674.63 | 368 | 780.45 | 418 | 886.16 | 468 | 991.98 |
| 19 | 42.13 | 79 | 169.07 | 139 | 296.01 | 199 | 422.95 | 259 | 549.89 | 319 | 676.72 | 369 | 782.54 | 419 | 888.25 | 469 | 994.07 |
| 20 | 44.22 | 80 | 171.16 | 140 | 298.10 | 200 | 425.04 | 260 | 551.98 | 320 | 678.92 | 370 | 784.63 | 420 | 890.45 | 470 | 996.16 |
| 21 | 46.42 | 81 | 173.25 | 141 | 300.19 | 201 | 427.13 | 261 | 554.07 | 321 | 681.01 | 371 | 786.72 | 421 | 892.54 | 471 | 998.25 |
| 22 | 48.51 | 82 | 175.45 | 142 | 302.39 | 202 | 429.22 | 262 | 556.16 | 322 | 683.10 | 372 | 788.92 | 422 | 894.63 | 472 | 1000.45 |
| 23 | 50.60 | 83 | 177.54 | 143 | 304.48 | 203 | 431.42 | 263 | 558.25 | 323 | 685.19 | 373 | 791.01 | 423 | 896.72 | 473 | 1002.54 |
| 24 | 52.69 | 84 | 179.63 | 144 | 306.57 | 204 | 433.51 | 264 | 560.45 | 324 | 687.39 | 374 | 793.10 | 424 | 898.92 | 474 | 1004.63 |
| 25 | 54.89 | 85 | 181.72 | 145 | 308.66 | 205 | 435.60 | 265 | 562.54 | 325 | 689.48 | 375 | 795.19 | 425 | 901.01 | 475 | 1006.72 |
| 26 | 56.98 | 86 | 183.92 | 146 | 310.75 | 206 | 437.69 | 266 | 564.63 | 326 | 691.57 | 376 | 797.39 | 426 | 903.10 | 476 | 1008.92 |
| 27 | 59.07 | 87 | 186.01 | 147 | 312.95 | 207 | 439.89 | 267 | 566.72 | 327 | 693.66 | 377 | 799.48 | 427 | 905.19 | 477 | 1011.01 |
| 28 | 61.16 | 88 | 188.10 | 148 | 315.04 | 208 | 441.98 | 268 | 568.92 | 328 | 695.75 | 378 | 801.57 | 428 | 907.39 | 478 | 1013.10 |
| 29 | 63.25 | 89 | 190.19 | 149 | 317.13 | 209 | 444.07 | 269 | 571.01 | 329 | 697.95 | 379 | 803.66 | 429 | 909.48 | 479 | 1015.19 |
| 30 | 65.45 | 90 | 192.39 | 150 | 319.22 | 210 | 446.16 | 270 | 573.10 | 330 | 700.04 | 380 | 805.75 | 430 | 911.57 | 480 | 1017.39 |
| 31 | 67.54 | 91 | 194.48 | 151 | 321.42 | 211 | 448.25 | 271 | 575.19 | 331 | 702.13 | 381 | 807.95 | 431 | 913.66 | 481 | 1019.48 |
| 32 | 69.63 | 92 | 196.57 | 152 | 323.51 | 212 | 450.45 | 272 | 577.39 | 332 | 704.22 | 382 | 810.04 | 432 | 915.75 | 482 | 1021.57 |
| 33 | 71.72 | 93 | 198.66 | 153 | 325.60 | 213 | 452.54 | 273 | 579.48 | 333 | 706.42 | 383 | 812.13 | 433 | 917.95 | 483 | 1023.66 |
| 34 | 73.92 | 94 | 200.75 | 154 | 327.69 | 214 | 454.63 | 274 | 581.57 | 334 | 708.51 | 384 | 814.22 | 434 | 920.04 | 484 | 1025.75 |
| 35 | 76.01 | 95 | 202.95 | 155 | 329.89 | 215 | 456.72 | 275 | 583.66 | 335 | 710.60 | 385 | 816.42 | 435 | 922.13 | 485 | 1027.95 |
| 36 | 78.10 | 96 | 205.04 | 156 | 331.98 | 216 | 458.92 | 276 | 585.75 | 336 | 712.69 | 386 | 818.51 | 436 | 924.22 | 486 | 1030.04 |
| 37 | 80.19 | 97 | 207.13 | 157 | 334.07 | 217 | 461.01 | 277 | 587.95 | 337 | 714.89 | 387 | 820.60 | 437 | 926.42 | 487 | 1032.13 |
| 38 | 82.39 | 98 | 209.22 | 158 | 336.16 | 218 | 463.10 | 278 | 590.04 | 338 | 716.98 | 388 | 822.69 | 438 | 928.51 | 488 | 1034.22 |
| 39 | 84.48 | 99 | 211.42 | 159 | 338.25 | 219 | 465.19 | 279 | 592.13 | 339 | 719.07 | 389 | 824.89 | 439 | 930.60 | 489 | 1036.42 |
| 40 | 86.57 | 100 | 213.51 | 160 | 340.45 | 220 | 467.39 | 280 | 594.22 | 340 | 721.16 | 390 | 826.98 | 440 | 932.69 | 490 | 1038.51 |
| 41 | 88.66 | 101 | 215.60 | 161 | 342.54 | 221 | 469.48 | 281 | 596.42 | 341 | 723.25 | 391 | 829.07 | 441 | 934.89 | 491 | 1040.60 |
| 42 | 90.75 | 102 | 217.69 | 162 | 344.63 | 222 | 471.57 | 282 | 598.51 | 342 | 725.45 | 392 | 831.16 | 442 | 936.98 | 492 | 1042.69 |
| 43 | 92.95 | 103 | 219.89 | 163 | 346.72 | 223 | 473.66 | 283 | 600.60 | 343 | 727.54 | 393 | 833.25 | 443 | 939.07 | 493 | 1044.89 |
| 44 | 95.04 | 104 | 221.98 | 164 | 348.92 | 224 | 475.75 | 284 | 602.69 | 344 | 729.63 | 394 | 835.45 | 444 | 941.16 | 494 | 1046.98 |
| 45 | 97.13 | 105 | 224.07 | 165 | 351.01 | 225 | 477.95 | 285 | 604.89 | 345 | 731.72 | 395 | 837.54 | 445 | 943.25 | 495 | 1049.07 |
| 46 | 99.22 | 106 | 226.16 | 166 | 353.10 | 226 | 480.04 | 286 | 606.98 | 346 | 733.92 | 396 | 839.63 | 446 | 945.45 | 496 | 1051.16 |
| 47 | 101.42 | 107 | 228.25 | 167 | 355.19 | 227 | 482.13 | 287 | 609.07 | 347 | 736.01 | 397 | 841.72 | 447 | 947.54 | 497 | 1053.25 |
| 48 | 103.51 | 108 | 230.45 | 168 | 357.39 | 228 | 484.22 | 288 | 611.16 | 348 | 738.10 | 398 | 843.92 | 448 | 949.63 | 498 | 1055.45 |
| 49 | 105.60 | 109 | 232.54 | 169 | 359.48 | 229 | 486.42 | 289 | 613.25 | 349 | 740.19 | 399 | 846.01 | 449 | 951.72 | 499 | 1057.54 |
| 50 | 107.69 | 110 | 234.63 | 170 | 361.57 | 230 | 488.51 | 290 | 615.45 | 350 | 742.39 | 400 | 848.10 | 450 | 953.92 | 500 | 1059.63 |
| 51 | 109.89 | 111 | 236.72 | 171 | 363.66 | 231 | 490.60 | 291 | 617.54 | | | | | | | | |
| 52 | 111.98 | 112 | 238.92 | 172 | 365.75 | 232 | 492.69 | 292 | 619.63 | | | | | | | | |
| 53 | 114.07 | 113 | 241.01 | 173 | 367.95 | 233 | 494.89 | 293 | 621.72 | | | | | | | | |
| 54 | 116.16 | 114 | 243.10 | 174 | 370.04 | 234 | 496.98 | 294 | 623.92 | | | | | | | | |
| 55 | 118.25 | 115 | 245.19 | 175 | 372.13 | 235 | 499.07 | 295 | 626.01 | | | | | | | | |
| 56 | 120.45 | 116 | 247.39 | 176 | 374.22 | 236 | 501.16 | 296 | 628.10 | | | | | | | | |
| 57 | 122.54 | 117 | 249.48 | 177 | 376.42 | 237 | 503.25 | 297 | 630.19 | | | | | | | | |
| 58 | 124.63 | 118 | 251.57 | 178 | 378.51 | 238 | 505.45 | 298 | 632.39 | | | | | | | | |
| 59 | 126.72 | 119 | 253.66 | 179 | 380.60 | 239 | 507.54 | 299 | 634.48 | | | | | | | | |
| 60 | 128.92 | 120 | 255.75 | 180 | 382.69 | 240 | 509.63 | 300 | 636.57 | | | | | | | | |

**Code more than 500**

1 Where the code is in the range 501 to **1000** inclusive:

  a. Subtract **500** from the code and use the balance of the code to obtain a pay adjustment figure from the table above.

  b. Add this pay adjustment figure to the figure given in the box alongside to obtain the figure of total pay adjustment to date *  | **1057.76** |

2 Where the code **exceeds 1000** follow the instructions on **page 3**.

## Tables A - Pay Adjustment Tables

Jun 22 to Jun 28 **Week 12**

| Code | Total pay adjustment to date £ | Code | Total pay adjustment to date £ | Code | Total pay adjustment to date £ | Code | Total pay adjustment to date £ | Code | Total pay adjustment to date £ | Code | Total pay adjustment to date £ | Code | Total pay adjustment to date £ | Code | Total pay adjustment to date £ | Code | Total pay adjustment to date £ |
|---|---|---|---|---|---|---|---|---|---|---|---|---|---|---|---|---|---|
| 0 | NIL | | | | | | | | | | | | | | | | |
| 1 | 4.44 | 61 | 142.92 | 121 | 281.40 | 181 | 419.88 | 241 | 558.24 | 301 | 696.72 | 351 | 812.16 | 401 | 927.48 | 451 | 1042.92 |
| 2 | 6.72 | 62 | 145.20 | 122 | 283.68 | 182 | 422.16 | 242 | 560.64 | 302 | 699.00 | 352 | 814.44 | 402 | 929.88 | 452 | 1045.20 |
| 3 | 9.00 | 63 | 147.48 | 123 | 285.96 | 183 | 424.44 | 243 | 562.92 | 303 | 701.40 | 353 | 816.72 | 403 | 932.16 | 453 | 1047.48 |
| 4 | 11.40 | 64 | 149.88 | 124 | 288.24 | 184 | 426.72 | 244 | 565.20 | 304 | 703.68 | 354 | 819.00 | 404 | 934.44 | 454 | 1049.88 |
| 5 | 13.68 | 65 | 152.16 | 125 | 290.64 | 185 | 429.00 | 245 | 567.48 | 305 | 705.96 | 355 | 821.40 | 405 | 936.72 | 455 | 1052.16 |
| 6 | 15.96 | 66 | 154.44 | 126 | 292.92 | 186 | 431.40 | 246 | 569.88 | 306 | 708.24 | 356 | 823.68 | 406 | 939.00 | 456 | 1054.44 |
| 7 | 18.24 | 67 | 156.72 | 127 | 295.20 | 187 | 433.68 | 247 | 572.16 | 307 | 710.64 | 357 | 825.96 | 407 | 941.40 | 457 | 1056.72 |
| 8 | 20.64 | 68 | 159.00 | 128 | 297.48 | 188 | 435.96 | 248 | 574.44 | 308 | 712.92 | 358 | 828.24 | 408 | 943.68 | 458 | 1059.00 |
| 9 | 22.92 | 69 | 161.40 | 129 | 299.88 | 189 | 438.24 | 249 | 576.72 | 309 | 715.20 | 359 | 830.64 | 409 | 945.96 | 459 | 1061.40 |
| 10 | 25.20 | 70 | 163.68 | 130 | 302.16 | 190 | 440.64 | 250 | 579.00 | 310 | 717.48 | 360 | 832.92 | 410 | 948.24 | 460 | 1063.68 |
| 11 | 27.48 | 71 | 165.96 | 131 | 304.44 | 191 | 442.92 | 251 | 581.40 | 311 | 719.88 | 361 | 835.20 | 411 | 950.64 | 461 | 1065.96 |
| 12 | 29.88 | 72 | 168.24 | 132 | 306.72 | 192 | 445.20 | 252 | 583.68 | 312 | 722.16 | 362 | 837.48 | 412 | 952.92 | 462 | 1068.24 |
| 13 | 32.16 | 73 | 170.64 | 133 | 309.00 | 193 | 447.48 | 253 | 585.96 | 313 | 724.44 | 363 | 839.88 | 413 | 955.20 | 463 | 1070.64 |
| 14 | 34.44 | 74 | 172.92 | 134 | 311.40 | 194 | 449.88 | 254 | 588.24 | 314 | 726.72 | 364 | 842.16 | 414 | 957.48 | 464 | 1072.92 |
| 15 | 36.72 | 75 | 175.20 | 135 | 313.68 | 195 | 452.16 | 255 | 590.64 | 315 | 729.00 | 365 | 844.44 | 415 | 959.88 | 465 | 1075.20 |
| 16 | 39.00 | 76 | 177.48 | 136 | 315.96 | 196 | 454.44 | 256 | 592.92 | 316 | 731.40 | 366 | 846.72 | 416 | 962.16 | 466 | 1077.48 |
| 17 | 41.40 | 77 | 179.88 | 137 | 318.24 | 197 | 456.72 | 257 | 595.20 | 317 | 733.68 | 367 | 849.00 | 417 | 964.44 | 467 | 1079.88 |
| 18 | 43.68 | 78 | 182.16 | 138 | 320.64 | 198 | 459.00 | 258 | 597.48 | 318 | 735.96 | 368 | 851.40 | 418 | 966.72 | 468 | 1082.16 |
| 19 | 45.96 | 79 | 184.44 | 139 | 322.92 | 199 | 461.40 | 259 | 599.88 | 319 | 738.24 | 369 | 853.68 | 419 | 969.00 | 469 | 1084.44 |
| 20 | 48.24 | 80 | 186.72 | 140 | 325.20 | 200 | 463.68 | 260 | 602.16 | 320 | 740.64 | 370 | 855.96 | 420 | 971.40 | 470 | 1086.72 |
| 21 | 50.64 | 81 | 189.00 | 141 | 327.48 | 201 | 465.96 | 261 | 604.44 | 321 | 742.92 | 371 | 858.24 | 421 | 973.68 | 471 | 1089.00 |
| 22 | 52.92 | 82 | 191.40 | 142 | 329.88 | 202 | 468.24 | 262 | 606.72 | 322 | 745.20 | 372 | 860.64 | 422 | 975.96 | 472 | 1091.40 |
| 23 | 55.20 | 83 | 193.68 | 143 | 332.16 | 203 | 470.64 | 263 | 609.00 | 323 | 747.48 | 373 | 862.92 | 423 | 978.24 | 473 | 1093.68 |
| 24 | 57.48 | 84 | 195.96 | 144 | 334.44 | 204 | 472.92 | 264 | 611.40 | 324 | 749.88 | 374 | 865.20 | 424 | 980.64 | 474 | 1095.96 |
| 25 | 59.88 | 85 | 198.24 | 145 | 336.72 | 205 | 475.20 | 265 | 613.68 | 325 | 752.16 | 375 | 867.48 | 425 | 982.92 | 475 | 1098.24 |
| 26 | 62.16 | 86 | 200.64 | 146 | 339.00 | 206 | 477.48 | 266 | 615.96 | 326 | 754.44 | 376 | 869.88 | 426 | 985.20 | 476 | 1100.64 |
| 27 | 64.44 | 87 | 202.92 | 147 | 341.40 | 207 | 479.88 | 267 | 618.24 | 327 | 756.72 | 377 | 872.16 | 427 | 987.48 | 477 | 1102.92 |
| 28 | 66.72 | 88 | 205.20 | 148 | 343.68 | 208 | 482.16 | 268 | 620.64 | 328 | 759.00 | 378 | 874.44 | 428 | 989.88 | 478 | 1105.20 |
| 29 | 69.00 | 89 | 207.48 | 149 | 345.96 | 209 | 484.44 | 269 | 622.92 | 329 | 761.40 | 379 | 876.72 | 429 | 992.16 | 479 | 1107.48 |
| 30 | 71.40 | 90 | 209.88 | 150 | 348.24 | 210 | 486.72 | 270 | 625.20 | 330 | 763.68 | 380 | 879.00 | 430 | 994.44 | 480 | 1109.88 |
| 31 | 73.68 | 91 | 212.16 | 151 | 350.64 | 211 | 489.00 | 271 | 627.48 | 331 | 765.96 | 381 | 881.40 | 431 | 996.72 | 481 | 1112.16 |
| 32 | 75.96 | 92 | 214.44 | 152 | 352.92 | 212 | 491.40 | 272 | 629.88 | 332 | 768.24 | 382 | 883.68 | 432 | 999.00 | 482 | 1114.44 |
| 33 | 78.24 | 93 | 216.72 | 153 | 355.20 | 213 | 493.68 | 273 | 632.16 | 333 | 770.64 | 383 | 885.96 | 433 | 1001.40 | 483 | 1116.72 |
| 34 | 80.64 | 94 | 219.00 | 154 | 357.48 | 214 | 495.96 | 274 | 634.44 | 334 | 772.92 | 384 | 888.24 | 434 | 1003.68 | 484 | 1119.00 |
| 35 | 82.92 | 95 | 221.40 | 155 | 359.88 | 215 | 498.24 | 275 | 636.72 | 335 | 775.20 | 385 | 890.64 | 435 | 1005.96 | 485 | 1121.40 |
| 36 | 85.20 | 96 | 223.68 | 156 | 362.16 | 216 | 500.64 | 276 | 639.00 | 336 | 777.48 | 386 | 892.92 | 436 | 1008.24 | 486 | 1123.68 |
| 37 | 87.48 | 97 | 225.96 | 157 | 364.44 | 217 | 502.92 | 277 | 641.40 | 337 | 779.88 | 387 | 895.20 | 437 | 1010.64 | 487 | 1125.96 |
| 38 | 89.88 | 98 | 228.24 | 158 | 366.72 | 218 | 505.20 | 278 | 643.68 | 338 | 782.16 | 388 | 897.48 | 438 | 1012.92 | 488 | 1128.24 |
| 39 | 92.16 | 99 | 230.64 | 159 | 369.00 | 219 | 507.48 | 279 | 645.96 | 339 | 784.44 | 389 | 899.88 | 439 | 1015.20 | 489 | 1130.64 |
| 40 | 94.44 | 100 | 232.92 | 160 | 371.40 | 220 | 509.88 | 280 | 648.24 | 340 | 786.72 | 390 | 902.16 | 440 | 1017.48 | 490 | 1132.92 |
| 41 | 96.72 | 101 | 235.20 | 161 | 373.68 | 221 | 512.16 | 281 | 650.64 | 341 | 789.00 | 391 | 904.44 | 441 | 1019.88 | 491 | 1135.20 |
| 42 | 99.00 | 102 | 237.48 | 162 | 375.96 | 222 | 514.44 | 282 | 652.92 | 342 | 791.40 | 392 | 906.72 | 442 | 1022.16 | 492 | 1137.48 |
| 43 | 101.40 | 103 | 239.88 | 163 | 378.24 | 223 | 516.72 | 283 | 655.20 | 343 | 793.68 | 393 | 909.00 | 443 | 1024.44 | 493 | 1139.88 |
| 44 | 103.68 | 104 | 242.16 | 164 | 380.64 | 224 | 519.00 | 284 | 657.48 | 344 | 795.96 | 394 | 911.40 | 444 | 1026.72 | 494 | 1142.16 |
| 45 | 105.96 | 105 | 244.44 | 165 | 382.92 | 225 | 521.40 | 285 | 659.88 | 345 | 798.24 | 395 | 913.68 | 445 | 1029.00 | 495 | 1144.44 |
| 46 | 108.24 | 106 | 246.72 | 166 | 385.20 | 226 | 523.68 | 286 | 662.16 | 346 | 800.64 | 396 | 915.96 | 446 | 1031.40 | 496 | 1146.72 |
| 47 | 110.64 | 107 | 249.00 | 167 | 387.48 | 227 | 525.96 | 287 | 664.44 | 347 | 802.92 | 397 | 918.24 | 447 | 1033.68 | 497 | 1149.00 |
| 48 | 112.92 | 108 | 251.40 | 168 | 389.88 | 228 | 528.24 | 288 | 666.72 | 348 | 805.20 | 398 | 920.64 | 448 | 1035.96 | 498 | 1151.40 |
| 49 | 115.20 | 109 | 253.68 | 169 | 392.16 | 229 | 530.64 | 289 | 669.00 | 349 | 807.48 | 399 | 922.92 | 449 | 1038.24 | 499 | 1153.68 |
| 50 | 117.48 | 110 | 255.96 | 170 | 394.44 | 230 | 532.92 | 290 | 671.40 | 350 | 809.88 | 400 | 925.20 | 450 | 1040.64 | 500 | 1155.96 |
| 51 | 119.88 | 111 | 258.24 | 171 | 396.72 | 231 | 535.20 | 291 | 673.68 | | | | | | | | |
| 52 | 122.16 | 112 | 260.64 | 172 | 399.00 | 232 | 537.48 | 292 | 675.96 | | | | | | | | |
| 53 | 124.44 | 113 | 262.92 | 173 | 401.40 | 233 | 539.88 | 293 | 678.24 | | | | | | | | |
| 54 | 126.72 | 114 | 265.20 | 174 | 403.68 | 234 | 542.16 | 294 | 680.64 | | | | | | | | |
| 55 | 129.00 | 115 | 267.48 | 175 | 405.96 | 235 | 544.44 | 295 | 682.92 | | | | | | | | |
| 56 | 131.40 | 116 | 269.88 | 176 | 408.24 | 236 | 546.72 | 296 | 685.20 | | | | | | | | |
| 57 | 133.68 | 117 | 272.16 | 177 | 410.64 | 237 | 549.00 | 297 | 687.48 | | | | | | | | |
| 58 | 135.96 | 118 | 274.44 | 178 | 412.92 | 238 | 551.40 | 298 | 689.88 | | | | | | | | |
| 59 | 138.24 | 119 | 276.72 | 179 | 415.20 | 239 | 553.68 | 299 | 692.16 | | | | | | | | |
| 60 | 140.64 | 120 | 279.00 | 180 | 417.48 | 240 | 555.96 | 300 | 694.44 | | | | | | | | |

### Code more than 500

1 Where the code is in the range 501 to 1000 inclusive:

  a. Subtract 500 from the code and use the balance of the code to obtain a pay adjustment figure from the table above.

  b. Add this pay adjustment figure to the figure given in the box alongside to obtain the figure of total pay adjustment to date *  | 1153.92 |

2 Where the code exceeds 1000 follow the instructions on page 3.

**Week 13** Jun 29 to Jul 5                    **Tables A** - Pay Adjustment Tables

| Code | Total pay adjustment to date | Code | Total pay adjustment to date | Code | Total pay adjustment to date | Code | Total pay adjustment to date | Code | Total pay adjustment to date | Code | Total pay adjustment to date | Code | Total pay adjustment to date | Code | Total pay adjustment to date | Code | Total pay adjustment to date |
|---|---|---|---|---|---|---|---|---|---|---|---|---|---|---|---|---|---|
| | £ | | £ | | £ | | £ | | £ | | £ | | £ | | £ | | £ |
| 0 | NIL | 61 | 154.83 | 121 | 304.85 | 181 | 454.87 | 241 | 604.76 | 301 | 754.78 | 351 | 879.84 | 401 | 1004.77 | 451 | 1129.83 |
| 1 | 4.81 | 62 | 157.30 | 122 | 307.32 | 182 | 457.34 | 242 | 607.36 | 302 | 757.25 | 352 | 882.31 | 402 | 1007.37 | 452 | 1132.30 |
| 2 | 7.28 | 63 | 159.77 | 123 | 309.79 | 183 | 459.81 | 243 | 609.83 | 303 | 759.85 | 353 | 884.78 | 403 | 1009.84 | 453 | 1134.77 |
| 3 | 9.75 | 64 | 162.37 | 124 | 312.26 | 184 | 462.28 | 244 | 612.30 | 304 | 762.32 | 354 | 887.25 | 404 | 1012.31 | 454 | 1137.37 |
| 4 | 12.35 | 65 | 164.84 | 125 | 314.86 | 185 | 464.75 | 245 | 614.77 | 305 | 764.79 | 355 | 889.85 | 405 | 1014.78 | 455 | 1139.84 |
| 5 | 14.82 | | | | | | | | | | | | | | | | |
| 6 | 17.29 | 66 | 167.31 | 126 | 317.33 | 186 | 467.35 | 246 | 617.37 | 306 | 767.26 | 356 | 892.32 | 406 | 1017.25 | 456 | 1142.31 |
| 7 | 19.76 | 67 | 169.78 | 127 | 319.80 | 187 | 469.82 | 247 | 619.84 | 307 | 769.86 | 357 | 894.79 | 407 | 1019.85 | 457 | 1144.78 |
| 8 | 22.36 | 68 | 172.25 | 128 | 322.27 | 188 | 472.29 | 248 | 622.31 | 308 | 772.33 | 358 | 897.26 | 408 | 1022.32 | 458 | 1147.25 |
| 9 | 24.83 | 69 | 174.85 | 129 | 324.87 | 189 | 474.76 | 249 | 624.78 | 309 | 774.80 | 359 | 899.86 | 409 | 1024.79 | 459 | 1149.85 |
| 10 | 27.30 | 70 | 177.32 | 130 | 327.34 | 190 | 477.36 | 250 | 627.25 | 310 | 777.27 | 360 | 902.33 | 410 | 1027.26 | 460 | 1152.32 |
| 11 | 29.77 | 71 | 179.79 | 131 | 329.81 | 191 | 479.83 | 251 | 629.85 | 311 | 779.87 | 361 | 904.80 | 411 | 1029.86 | 461 | 1154.79 |
| 12 | 32.37 | 72 | 182.26 | 132 | 332.28 | 192 | 482.30 | 252 | 632.32 | 312 | 782.34 | 362 | 907.27 | 412 | 1032.33 | 462 | 1157.26 |
| 13 | 34.84 | 73 | 184.86 | 133 | 334.75 | 193 | 484.77 | 253 | 634.79 | 313 | 784.81 | 363 | 909.87 | 413 | 1034.80 | 463 | 1159.86 |
| 14 | 37.31 | 74 | 187.33 | 134 | 337.35 | 194 | 487.37 | 254 | 637.26 | 314 | 787.28 | 364 | 912.34 | 414 | 1037.27 | 464 | 1162.33 |
| 15 | 39.78 | 75 | 189.80 | 135 | 339.82 | 195 | 489.84 | 255 | 639.86 | 315 | 789.75 | 365 | 914.81 | 415 | 1039.87 | 465 | 1164.80 |
| 16 | 42.25 | 76 | 192.27 | 136 | 342.29 | 196 | 492.31 | 256 | 642.33 | 316 | 792.35 | 366 | 917.28 | 416 | 1042.34 | 466 | 1167.27 |
| 17 | 44.85 | 77 | 194.87 | 137 | 344.76 | 197 | 494.78 | 257 | 644.80 | 317 | 794.82 | 367 | 919.75 | 417 | 1044.81 | 467 | 1169.87 |
| 18 | 47.32 | 78 | 197.34 | 138 | 347.36 | 198 | 497.25 | 258 | 647.27 | 318 | 797.29 | 368 | 922.35 | 418 | 1047.28 | 468 | 1172.34 |
| 19 | 49.79 | 79 | 199.81 | 139 | 349.83 | 199 | 499.85 | 259 | 649.87 | 319 | 799.76 | 369 | 924.82 | 419 | 1049.75 | 469 | 1174.81 |
| 20 | 52.26 | 80 | 202.28 | 140 | 352.30 | 200 | 502.32 | 260 | 652.34 | 320 | 802.36 | 370 | 927.29 | 420 | 1052.35 | 470 | 1177.28 |
| 21 | 54.86 | 81 | 204.75 | 141 | 354.77 | 201 | 504.79 | 261 | 654.81 | 321 | 804.83 | 371 | 929.76 | 421 | 1054.82 | 471 | 1179.75 |
| 22 | 57.33 | 82 | 207.25 | 142 | 357.37 | 202 | 507.26 | 262 | 657.28 | 322 | 807.30 | 372 | 932.36 | 422 | 1057.29 | 472 | 1182.35 |
| 23 | 59.80 | 83 | 209.82 | 143 | 359.84 | 203 | 509.86 | 263 | 659.75 | 323 | 809.77 | 373 | 934.83 | 423 | 1059.76 | 473 | 1184.82 |
| 24 | 62.27 | 84 | 212.29 | 144 | 362.31 | 204 | 512.33 | 264 | 662.35 | 324 | 812.37 | 374 | 937.30 | 424 | 1062.36 | 474 | 1187.29 |
| 25 | 64.87 | 85 | 214.76 | 145 | 364.78 | 205 | 514.80 | 265 | 664.82 | 325 | 814.84 | 375 | 939.77 | 425 | 1064.83 | 475 | 1189.76 |
| 26 | 67.34 | 86 | 217.36 | 146 | 367.25 | 206 | 517.27 | 266 | 667.29 | 326 | 817.31 | 376 | 942.37 | 426 | 1067.30 | 476 | 1192.36 |
| 27 | 69.81 | 87 | 219.83 | 147 | 369.85 | 207 | 519.87 | 267 | 669.76 | 327 | 819.78 | 377 | 944.84 | 427 | 1069.77 | 477 | 1194.83 |
| 28 | 72.28 | 88 | 222.30 | 148 | 372.32 | 208 | 522.34 | 268 | 672.36 | 328 | 822.25 | 378 | 947.31 | 428 | 1072.37 | 478 | 1197.30 |
| 29 | 74.75 | 89 | 224.77 | 149 | 374.79 | 209 | 524.81 | 269 | 674.83 | 329 | 824.85 | 379 | 949.78 | 429 | 1074.84 | 479 | 1199.77 |
| 30 | 77.35 | 90 | 227.37 | 150 | 377.26 | 210 | 527.28 | 270 | 677.30 | 330 | 827.32 | 380 | 952.25 | 430 | 1077.31 | 480 | 1202.37 |
| 31 | 79.82 | 91 | 229.84 | 151 | 379.86 | 211 | 529.75 | 271 | 679.77 | 331 | 829.79 | 381 | 954.85 | 431 | 1079.78 | 481 | 1204.84 |
| 32 | 82.29 | 92 | 232.31 | 152 | 382.33 | 212 | 532.35 | 272 | 682.37 | 332 | 832.26 | 382 | 957.32 | 432 | 1082.25 | 482 | 1207.31 |
| 33 | 84.76 | 93 | 234.78 | 153 | 384.80 | 213 | 534.82 | 273 | 684.84 | 333 | 834.86 | 383 | 959.79 | 433 | 1084.85 | 483 | 1209.78 |
| 34 | 87.36 | 94 | 237.25 | 154 | 387.27 | 214 | 537.29 | 274 | 687.31 | 334 | 837.33 | 384 | 962.26 | 434 | 1087.32 | 484 | 1212.25 |
| 35 | 89.83 | 95 | 239.85 | 155 | 389.87 | 215 | 539.76 | 275 | 689.78 | 335 | 839.80 | 385 | 964.86 | 435 | 1089.79 | 485 | 1214.85 |
| 36 | 92.30 | 96 | 242.32 | 156 | 392.34 | 216 | 542.36 | 276 | 692.25 | 336 | 842.27 | 386 | 967.33 | 436 | 1092.26 | 486 | 1217.32 |
| 37 | 94.77 | 97 | 244.79 | 157 | 394.81 | 217 | 544.83 | 277 | 694.85 | 337 | 844.87 | 387 | 969.80 | 437 | 1094.86 | 487 | 1219.79 |
| 38 | 97.37 | 98 | 247.26 | 158 | 397.28 | 218 | 547.30 | 278 | 697.32 | 338 | 847.34 | 388 | 972.27 | 438 | 1097.33 | 488 | 1222.26 |
| 39 | 99.84 | 99 | 249.86 | 159 | 399.75 | 219 | 549.77 | 279 | 699.79 | 339 | 849.81 | 389 | 974.87 | 439 | 1099.80 | 489 | 1224.86 |
| 40 | 102.31 | 100 | 252.33 | 160 | 402.35 | 220 | 552.37 | 280 | 702.26 | 340 | 852.28 | 390 | 977.34 | 440 | 1102.27 | 490 | 1227.33 |
| 41 | 104.78 | 101 | 254.80 | 161 | 404.82 | 221 | 554.84 | 281 | 704.86 | 341 | 854.75 | 391 | 979.81 | 441 | 1104.87 | 491 | 1229.80 |
| 42 | 107.25 | 102 | 257.27 | 162 | 407.29 | 222 | 557.31 | 282 | 707.33 | 342 | 857.35 | 392 | 982.28 | 442 | 1107.34 | 492 | 1232.27 |
| 43 | 109.85 | 103 | 259.87 | 163 | 409.76 | 223 | 559.78 | 283 | 709.80 | 343 | 859.82 | 393 | 984.75 | 443 | 1109.81 | 493 | 1234.87 |
| 44 | 112.32 | 104 | 262.34 | 164 | 412.36 | 224 | 562.25 | 284 | 712.27 | 344 | 862.29 | 394 | 987.35 | 444 | 1112.28 | 494 | 1237.34 |
| 45 | 114.79 | 105 | 264.81 | 165 | 414.83 | 225 | 564.85 | 285 | 714.87 | 345 | 864.76 | 395 | 989.82 | 445 | 1114.75 | 495 | 1239.81 |
| 46 | 117.26 | 106 | 267.28 | 166 | 417.30 | 226 | 567.32 | 286 | 717.34 | 346 | 867.36 | 396 | 992.29 | 446 | 1117.35 | 496 | 1242.28 |
| 47 | 119.86 | 107 | 269.75 | 167 | 419.77 | 227 | 569.79 | 287 | 719.81 | 347 | 869.83 | 397 | 994.76 | 447 | 1119.82 | 497 | 1244.75 |
| 48 | 122.33 | 108 | 272.35 | 168 | 422.37 | 228 | 572.26 | 288 | 722.28 | 348 | 872.30 | 398 | 997.36 | 448 | 1122.29 | 498 | 1247.35 |
| 49 | 124.80 | 109 | 274.82 | 169 | 424.84 | 229 | 574.86 | 289 | 724.75 | 349 | 874.77 | 399 | 999.83 | 449 | 1124.76 | 499 | 1249.82 |
| 50 | 127.27 | 110 | 277.29 | 170 | 427.31 | 230 | 577.33 | 290 | 727.35 | 350 | 877.37 | 400 | 1002.30 | 450 | 1127.36 | 500 | 1252.29 |
| 51 | 129.87 | 111 | 279.76 | 171 | 429.78 | 231 | 579.80 | 291 | 729.82 | | | | | | | | |
| 52 | 132.34 | 112 | 282.36 | 172 | 432.25 | 232 | 582.27 | 292 | 732.29 | | | | | | | | |
| 53 | 134.81 | 113 | 284.83 | 173 | 434.85 | 233 | 584.87 | 293 | 734.76 | | | | | | | | |
| 54 | 137.28 | 114 | 287.30 | 174 | 437.32 | 234 | 587.34 | 294 | 737.36 | | | | | | | | |
| 55 | 139.75 | 115 | 289.77 | 175 | 439.79 | 235 | 589.81 | 295 | 739.83 | | | | | | | | |
| 56 | 142.35 | 116 | 292.37 | 176 | 442.26 | 236 | 592.28 | 296 | 742.30 | | | | | | | | |
| 57 | 144.82 | 117 | 294.84 | 177 | 444.86 | 237 | 594.75 | 297 | 744.77 | | | | | | | | |
| 58 | 147.29 | 118 | 297.31 | 178 | 447.33 | 238 | 597.35 | 298 | 747.37 | | | | | | | | |
| 59 | 149.76 | 119 | 299.78 | 179 | 449.80 | 239 | 599.82 | 299 | 749.84 | | | | | | | | |
| 60 | 152.36 | 120 | 302.25 | 180 | 452.27 | 240 | 602.29 | 300 | 752.31 | | | | | | | | |

**Code more than 500**

1 Where the code is in the range 501 to **1000** inclusive:

  a. Subtract **500** from the code and use the balance of the table to obtain a pay adjustment figure from the table above.

  b. Add this pay adjustment figure to the figure given in the box alongside to obtain the figure of total pay adjustment to date * | **1250.08** |

2 Where the code **exceeds 1000** follow the instructions on **page 3**.

16

## Tables A - Pay Adjustment Tables

Jul 6 to Jul 12 **Week 14**

| Code | Total pay adjustment to date £ | Code | Total pay adjustment to date £ | Code | Total pay adjustment to date £ | Code | Total pay adjustment to date £ | Code | Total pay adjustment to date £ | Code | Total pay adjustment to date £ | Code | Total pay adjustment to date £ | Code | Total pay adjustment to date £ | Code | Total pay adjustment to date £ |
|---|---|---|---|---|---|---|---|---|---|---|---|---|---|---|---|---|---|
| 0 | NIL | | | | | | | | | | | | | | | | |
| 1 | 5.18 | 61 | 166.74 | 121 | 328.30 | 181 | 489.86 | 241 | 651.28 | 301 | 812.84 | 351 | 947.52 | 401 | 1082.06 | 451 | 1216.74 |
| 2 | 7.84 | 62 | 169.40 | 122 | 330.96 | 182 | 492.52 | 242 | 654.08 | 302 | 815.50 | 352 | 950.18 | 402 | 1084.86 | 452 | 1219.40 |
| 3 | 10.50 | 63 | 172.06 | 123 | 333.62 | 183 | 495.18 | 243 | 656.74 | 303 | 818.30 | 353 | 952.84 | 403 | 1087.52 | 453 | 1222.06 |
| 4 | 13.30 | 64 | 174.86 | 124 | 336.28 | 184 | 497.84 | 244 | 659.40 | 304 | 820.96 | 354 | 955.50 | 404 | 1090.18 | 454 | 1224.86 |
| 5 | 15.96 | 65 | 177.52 | 125 | 339.08 | 185 | 500.50 | 245 | 662.06 | 305 | 823.62 | 355 | 958.30 | 405 | 1092.84 | 455 | 1227.52 |
| 6 | 18.62 | 66 | 180.18 | 126 | 341.74 | 186 | 503.30 | 246 | 664.86 | 306 | 826.28 | 356 | 960.96 | 406 | 1095.50 | 456 | 1230.18 |
| 7 | 21.28 | 67 | 182.84 | 127 | 344.40 | 187 | 505.96 | 247 | 667.52 | 307 | 829.08 | 357 | 963.62 | 407 | 1098.30 | 457 | 1232.84 |
| 8 | 24.08 | 68 | 185.50 | 128 | 347.06 | 188 | 508.62 | 248 | 670.18 | 308 | 831.74 | 358 | 966.28 | 408 | 1100.96 | 458 | 1235.50 |
| 9 | 26.74 | 69 | 188.30 | 129 | 349.86 | 189 | 511.28 | 249 | 672.84 | 309 | 834.40 | 359 | 969.08 | 409 | 1103.62 | 459 | 1238.30 |
| 10 | 29.40 | 70 | 190.96 | 130 | 352.52 | 190 | 514.08 | 250 | 675.50 | 310 | 837.06 | 360 | 971.74 | 410 | 1106.28 | 460 | 1240.96 |
| 11 | 32.06 | 71 | 193.62 | 131 | 355.18 | 191 | 516.74 | 251 | 678.30 | 311 | 839.86 | 361 | 974.40 | 411 | 1109.08 | 461 | 1243.62 |
| 12 | 34.86 | 72 | 196.28 | 132 | 357.84 | 192 | 519.40 | 252 | 680.96 | 312 | 842.52 | 362 | 977.06 | 412 | 1111.74 | 462 | 1246.28 |
| 13 | 37.52 | 73 | 199.08 | 133 | 360.50 | 193 | 522.06 | 253 | 683.62 | 313 | 845.18 | 363 | 979.86 | 413 | 1114.40 | 463 | 1249.08 |
| 14 | 40.18 | 74 | 201.74 | 134 | 363.30 | 194 | 524.86 | 254 | 686.28 | 314 | 847.84 | 364 | 982.52 | 414 | 1117.06 | 464 | 1251.74 |
| 15 | 42.84 | 75 | 204.40 | 135 | 365.96 | 195 | 527.52 | 255 | 689.08 | 315 | 850.50 | 365 | 985.18 | 415 | 1119.86 | 465 | 1254.40 |
| 16 | 45.50 | 76 | 207.06 | 136 | 368.62 | 196 | 530.18 | 256 | 691.74 | 316 | 853.30 | 366 | 987.84 | 416 | 1122.52 | 466 | 1257.06 |
| 17 | 48.30 | 77 | 209.86 | 137 | 371.28 | 197 | 532.84 | 257 | 694.40 | 317 | 855.96 | 367 | 990.50 | 417 | 1125.18 | 467 | 1259.86 |
| 18 | 50.96 | 78 | 212.52 | 138 | 374.08 | 198 | 535.50 | 258 | 697.06 | 318 | 858.62 | 368 | 993.30 | 418 | 1127.84 | 468 | 1262.52 |
| 19 | 53.62 | 79 | 215.18 | 139 | 376.74 | 199 | 538.30 | 259 | 699.86 | 319 | 861.28 | 369 | 995.96 | 419 | 1130.50 | 469 | 1265.18 |
| 20 | 56.28 | 80 | 217.84 | 140 | 379.40 | 200 | 540.96 | 260 | 702.52 | 320 | 864.08 | 370 | 998.62 | 420 | 1133.30 | 470 | 1267.84 |
| 21 | 59.08 | 81 | 220.50 | 141 | 382.06 | 201 | 543.62 | 261 | 705.18 | 321 | 866.74 | 371 | 1001.28 | 421 | 1135.96 | 471 | 1270.50 |
| 22 | 61.74 | 82 | 223.30 | 142 | 384.86 | 202 | 546.28 | 262 | 707.84 | 322 | 869.40 | 372 | 1004.08 | 422 | 1138.62 | 472 | 1273.30 |
| 23 | 64.40 | 83 | 225.96 | 143 | 387.52 | 203 | 549.08 | 263 | 710.50 | 323 | 872.06 | 373 | 1006.74 | 423 | 1141.28 | 473 | 1275.96 |
| 24 | 67.06 | 84 | 228.62 | 144 | 390.18 | 204 | 551.74 | 264 | 713.30 | 324 | 874.86 | 374 | 1009.40 | 424 | 1144.08 | 474 | 1278.62 |
| 25 | 69.86 | 85 | 231.28 | 145 | 392.84 | 205 | 554.40 | 265 | 715.96 | 325 | 877.52 | 375 | 1012.06 | 425 | 1146.74 | 475 | 1281.28 |
| 26 | 72.52 | 86 | 234.08 | 146 | 395.50 | 206 | 557.06 | 266 | 718.62 | 326 | 880.18 | 376 | 1014.86 | 426 | 1149.40 | 476 | 1284.08 |
| 27 | 75.18 | 87 | 236.74 | 147 | 398.30 | 207 | 559.86 | 267 | 721.28 | 327 | 882.84 | 377 | 1017.52 | 427 | 1152.06 | 477 | 1286.74 |
| 28 | 77.84 | 88 | 239.40 | 148 | 400.96 | 208 | 562.52 | 268 | 724.08 | 328 | 885.50 | 378 | 1020.18 | 428 | 1154.86 | 478 | 1289.40 |
| 29 | 80.50 | 89 | 242.06 | 149 | 403.62 | 209 | 565.18 | 269 | 726.74 | 329 | 888.30 | 379 | 1022.84 | 429 | 1157.52 | 479 | 1292.06 |
| 30 | 83.30 | 90 | 244.86 | 150 | 406.28 | 210 | 567.84 | 270 | 729.40 | 330 | 890.96 | 380 | 1025.50 | 430 | 1160.18 | 480 | 1294.86 |
| 31 | 85.96 | 91 | 247.52 | 151 | 409.08 | 211 | 570.50 | 271 | 732.06 | 331 | 893.62 | 381 | 1028.30 | 431 | 1162.84 | 481 | 1297.52 |
| 32 | 88.62 | 92 | 250.18 | 152 | 411.74 | 212 | 573.30 | 272 | 734.86 | 332 | 896.28 | 382 | 1030.96 | 432 | 1165.50 | 482 | 1300.18 |
| 33 | 91.28 | 93 | 252.84 | 153 | 414.40 | 213 | 575.96 | 273 | 737.52 | 333 | 899.08 | 383 | 1033.62 | 433 | 1168.30 | 483 | 1302.84 |
| 34 | 94.08 | 94 | 255.50 | 154 | 417.06 | 214 | 578.62 | 274 | 740.18 | 334 | 901.74 | 384 | 1036.28 | 434 | 1170.96 | 484 | 1305.50 |
| 35 | 96.74 | 95 | 258.30 | 155 | 419.86 | 215 | 581.28 | 275 | 742.84 | 335 | 904.40 | 385 | 1039.08 | 435 | 1173.62 | 485 | 1308.30 |
| 36 | 99.40 | 96 | 260.96 | 156 | 422.52 | 216 | 584.08 | 276 | 745.50 | 336 | 907.06 | 386 | 1041.74 | 436 | 1176.28 | 486 | 1310.96 |
| 37 | 102.06 | 97 | 263.62 | 157 | 425.18 | 217 | 586.74 | 277 | 748.30 | 337 | 909.86 | 387 | 1044.40 | 437 | 1179.08 | 487 | 1313.62 |
| 38 | 104.86 | 98 | 266.28 | 158 | 427.84 | 218 | 589.40 | 278 | 750.96 | 338 | 912.52 | 388 | 1047.06 | 438 | 1181.74 | 488 | 1316.28 |
| 39 | 107.52 | 99 | 269.08 | 159 | 430.50 | 219 | 592.06 | 279 | 753.62 | 339 | 915.18 | 389 | 1049.86 | 439 | 1184.40 | 489 | 1319.08 |
| 40 | 110.18 | 100 | 271.74 | 160 | 433.30 | 220 | 594.86 | 280 | 756.28 | 340 | 917.84 | 390 | 1052.52 | 440 | 1187.06 | 490 | 1321.74 |
| 41 | 112.84 | 101 | 274.40 | 161 | 435.96 | 221 | 597.52 | 281 | 759.08 | 341 | 920.50 | 391 | 1055.18 | 441 | 1189.86 | 491 | 1324.40 |
| 42 | 115.50 | 102 | 277.06 | 162 | 438.62 | 222 | 600.18 | 282 | 761.74 | 342 | 923.30 | 392 | 1057.84 | 442 | 1192.52 | 492 | 1327.06 |
| 43 | 118.30 | 103 | 279.86 | 163 | 441.28 | 223 | 602.84 | 283 | 764.40 | 343 | 925.96 | 393 | 1060.50 | 443 | 1195.18 | 493 | 1329.86 |
| 44 | 120.96 | 104 | 282.52 | 164 | 444.08 | 224 | 605.50 | 284 | 767.06 | 344 | 928.62 | 394 | 1063.30 | 444 | 1197.84 | 494 | 1332.52 |
| 45 | 123.62 | 105 | 285.18 | 165 | 446.74 | 225 | 608.30 | 285 | 769.86 | 345 | 931.28 | 395 | 1065.96 | 445 | 1200.50 | 495 | 1335.18 |
| 46 | 126.28 | 106 | 287.84 | 166 | 449.40 | 226 | 610.96 | 286 | 772.52 | 346 | 934.08 | 396 | 1068.62 | 446 | 1203.30 | 496 | 1337.84 |
| 47 | 129.08 | 107 | 290.50 | 167 | 452.06 | 227 | 613.62 | 287 | 775.18 | 347 | 936.74 | 397 | 1071.28 | 447 | 1205.96 | 497 | 1340.50 |
| 48 | 131.74 | 108 | 293.30 | 168 | 454.86 | 228 | 616.28 | 288 | 777.84 | 348 | 939.40 | 398 | 1074.08 | 448 | 1208.62 | 498 | 1343.30 |
| 49 | 134.40 | 109 | 295.96 | 169 | 457.52 | 229 | 619.08 | 289 | 780.50 | 349 | 942.06 | 399 | 1076.74 | 449 | 1211.28 | 499 | 1345.96 |
| 50 | 137.06 | 110 | 298.62 | 170 | 460.18 | 230 | 621.74 | 290 | 783.30 | 350 | 944.86 | 400 | 1079.40 | 450 | 1214.08 | 500 | 1348.62 |
| 51 | 139.86 | 111 | 301.28 | 171 | 462.84 | 231 | 624.40 | 291 | 785.96 | | | | | | | | |
| 52 | 142.52 | 112 | 304.08 | 172 | 465.50 | 232 | 627.06 | 292 | 788.62 | | | | | | | | |
| 53 | 145.18 | 113 | 306.74 | 173 | 468.30 | 233 | 629.86 | 293 | 791.28 | | | | | | | | |
| 54 | 147.84 | 114 | 309.40 | 174 | 470.96 | 234 | 632.52 | 294 | 794.08 | | | | | | | | |
| 55 | 150.50 | 115 | 312.06 | 175 | 473.62 | 235 | 635.18 | 295 | 796.74 | | | | | | | | |
| 56 | 153.30 | 116 | 314.86 | 176 | 476.28 | 236 | 637.84 | 296 | 799.40 | | | | | | | | |
| 57 | 155.96 | 117 | 317.52 | 177 | 479.08 | 237 | 640.50 | 297 | 802.06 | | | | | | | | |
| 58 | 158.62 | 118 | 320.18 | 178 | 481.74 | 238 | 643.30 | 298 | 804.86 | | | | | | | | |
| 59 | 161.28 | 119 | 322.84 | 179 | 484.40 | 239 | 645.96 | 299 | 807.52 | | | | | | | | |
| 60 | 164.08 | 120 | 325.50 | 180 | 487.06 | 240 | 648.62 | 300 | 810.18 | | | | | | | | |

### Code more than 500

1 Where the code is in the range **501 to 1000** inclusive:

  a. Subtract **500** from the code and use the balance of the code to obtain a pay adjustment figure from the table above.

  b. Add this pay adjustment figure to the figure given in the box alongside to obtain the figure of total pay adjustment to date * | **1346.24**

2 Where the code **exceeds 1000** follow the instructions on **page 3**.

17

**Week 15**  Jul 13 to Jul 19                     **Tables A** - Pay Adjustment Table

| Code | Total pay adjustment to date | Code | Total pay adjustment to date | Code | Total pay adjustment to date | Code | Total pay adjustment to date | Code | Total pay adjustment to date | Code | Total pay adjustment to date | Code | Total pay adjustment to date | Code | Total pay adjustment to date | Code | Total pay adjustment to date |
|---|---|---|---|---|---|---|---|---|---|---|---|---|---|---|---|---|---|
| | £ | | £ | | £ | | £ | | £ | | £ | | £ | | £ | | £ |
| 0 | NIL | 61 | 178.65 | 121 | 351.75 | 181 | 524.85 | 241 | 697.80 | 301 | 870.90 | 351 | 1015.20 | 401 | 1159.35 | 451 | 1303.65 |
| 1 | 5.55 | 62 | 181.50 | 122 | 354.60 | 182 | 527.70 | 242 | 700.80 | 302 | 873.75 | 352 | 1018.05 | 402 | 1162.35 | 452 | 1306.50 |
| 2 | 8.40 | 63 | 184.35 | 123 | 357.45 | 183 | 530.55 | 243 | 703.65 | 303 | 876.75 | 353 | 1020.90 | 403 | 1165.20 | 453 | 1309.35 |
| 3 | 11.25 | 64 | 187.35 | 124 | 360.30 | 184 | 533.40 | 244 | 706.50 | 304 | 879.60 | 354 | 1023.75 | 404 | 1168.05 | 454 | 1312.35 |
| 4 | 14.25 | 65 | 190.20 | 125 | 363.30 | 185 | 536.25 | 245 | 709.35 | 305 | 882.45 | 355 | 1026.75 | 405 | 1170.90 | 455 | 1315.20 |
| 5 | 17.10 | | | | | | | | | | | | | | | | |
| 6 | 19.95 | 66 | 193.05 | 126 | 366.15 | 186 | 539.25 | 246 | 712.35 | 306 | 885.30 | 356 | 1029.60 | 406 | 1173.75 | 456 | 1318.05 |
| 7 | 22.80 | 67 | 195.90 | 127 | 369.00 | 187 | 542.10 | 247 | 715.20 | 307 | 888.30 | 357 | 1032.45 | 407 | 1176.75 | 457 | 1320.90 |
| 8 | 25.80 | 68 | 198.75 | 128 | 371.85 | 188 | 544.95 | 248 | 718.05 | 308 | 891.15 | 358 | 1035.30 | 408 | 1179.60 | 458 | 1323.75 |
| 9 | 28.65 | 69 | 201.75 | 129 | 374.85 | 189 | 547.80 | 249 | 720.90 | 309 | 894.00 | 359 | 1038.30 | 409 | 1182.45 | 459 | 1326.75 |
| 10 | 31.50 | 70 | 204.60 | 130 | 377.70 | 190 | 550.80 | 250 | 723.75 | 310 | 896.85 | 360 | 1041.15 | 410 | 1185.30 | 460 | 1329.60 |
| 11 | 34.35 | 71 | 207.45 | 131 | 380.55 | 191 | 553.65 | 251 | 726.75 | 311 | 899.85 | 361 | 1044.00 | 411 | 1188.30 | 461 | 1332.45 |
| 12 | 37.35 | 72 | 210.30 | 132 | 383.40 | 192 | 556.50 | 252 | 729.60 | 312 | 902.70 | 362 | 1046.85 | 412 | 1191.15 | 462 | 1335.30 |
| 13 | 40.20 | 73 | 213.30 | 133 | 386.25 | 193 | 559.35 | 253 | 732.45 | 313 | 905.55 | 363 | 1049.85 | 413 | 1194.00 | 463 | 1338.30 |
| 14 | 43.05 | 74 | 216.15 | 134 | 389.25 | 194 | 562.35 | 254 | 735.30 | 314 | 908.40 | 364 | 1052.70 | 414 | 1196.85 | 464 | 1341.15 |
| 15 | 45.90 | 75 | 219.00 | 135 | 392.10 | 195 | 565.20 | 255 | 738.30 | 315 | 911.25 | 365 | 1055.55 | 415 | 1199.85 | 465 | 1344.00 |
| 16 | 48.75 | 76 | 221.85 | 136 | 394.95 | 196 | 568.05 | 256 | 741.15 | 316 | 914.25 | 366 | 1058.40 | 416 | 1202.70 | 466 | 1346.85 |
| 17 | 51.75 | 77 | 224.85 | 137 | 397.80 | 197 | 570.90 | 257 | 744.00 | 317 | 917.10 | 367 | 1061.25 | 417 | 1205.55 | 467 | 1349.85 |
| 18 | 54.60 | 78 | 227.70 | 138 | 400.80 | 198 | 573.75 | 258 | 746.85 | 318 | 919.95 | 368 | 1064.25 | 418 | 1208.40 | 468 | 1352.70 |
| 19 | 57.45 | 79 | 230.55 | 139 | 403.65 | 199 | 576.75 | 259 | 749.85 | 319 | 922.80 | 369 | 1067.10 | 419 | 1211.25 | 469 | 1355.55 |
| 20 | 60.30 | 80 | 233.40 | 140 | 406.50 | 200 | 579.60 | 260 | 752.70 | 320 | 925.80 | 370 | 1069.95 | 420 | 1214.25 | 470 | 1358.40 |
| 21 | 63.30 | 81 | 236.25 | 141 | 409.35 | 201 | 582.45 | 261 | 755.55 | 321 | 928.65 | 371 | 1072.80 | 421 | 1217.10 | 471 | 1361.25 |
| 22 | 66.15 | 82 | 239.25 | 142 | 412.35 | 202 | 585.30 | 262 | 758.40 | 322 | 931.50 | 372 | 1075.80 | 422 | 1219.95 | 472 | 1364.25 |
| 23 | 69.00 | 83 | 242.10 | 143 | 415.20 | 203 | 588.30 | 263 | 761.25 | 323 | 934.35 | 373 | 1078.65 | 423 | 1222.80 | 473 | 1367.10 |
| 24 | 71.85 | 84 | 244.95 | 144 | 418.05 | 204 | 591.15 | 264 | 764.25 | 324 | 937.35 | 374 | 1081.50 | 424 | 1225.80 | 474 | 1369.95 |
| 25 | 74.85 | 85 | 247.80 | 145 | 420.90 | 205 | 594.00 | 265 | 767.10 | 325 | 940.20 | 375 | 1084.35 | 425 | 1228.65 | 475 | 1372.80 |
| 26 | 77.70 | 86 | 250.80 | 146 | 423.75 | 206 | 596.85 | 266 | 769.95 | 326 | 943.05 | 376 | 1087.35 | 426 | 1231.50 | 476 | 1375.80 |
| 27 | 80.55 | 87 | 253.65 | 147 | 426.75 | 207 | 599.85 | 267 | 772.80 | 327 | 945.90 | 377 | 1090.20 | 427 | 1234.35 | 477 | 1378.65 |
| 28 | 83.40 | 88 | 256.50 | 148 | 429.60 | 208 | 602.70 | 268 | 775.80 | 328 | 948.75 | 378 | 1093.05 | 428 | 1237.35 | 478 | 1381.50 |
| 29 | 86.25 | 89 | 259.35 | 149 | 432.45 | 209 | 605.55 | 269 | 778.65 | 329 | 951.75 | 379 | 1095.90 | 429 | 1240.20 | 479 | 1384.35 |
| 30 | 89.25 | 90 | 262.35 | 150 | 435.30 | 210 | 608.40 | 270 | 781.50 | 330 | 954.60 | 380 | 1098.75 | 430 | 1243.05 | 480 | 1387.35 |
| 31 | 92.10 | 91 | 265.20 | 151 | 438.30 | 211 | 611.25 | 271 | 784.35 | 331 | 957.45 | 381 | 1101.75 | 431 | 1245.90 | 481 | 1390.20 |
| 32 | 94.95 | 92 | 268.05 | 152 | 441.15 | 212 | 614.25 | 272 | 787.35 | 332 | 960.30 | 382 | 1104.60 | 432 | 1248.75 | 482 | 1393.05 |
| 33 | 97.80 | 93 | 270.90 | 153 | 444.00 | 213 | 617.10 | 273 | 790.20 | 333 | 963.30 | 383 | 1107.45 | 433 | 1251.75 | 483 | 1395.90 |
| 34 | 100.80 | 94 | 273.75 | 154 | 446.85 | 214 | 619.95 | 274 | 793.05 | 334 | 966.15 | 384 | 1110.30 | 434 | 1254.60 | 484 | 1398.75 |
| 35 | 103.65 | 95 | 276.75 | 155 | 449.85 | 215 | 622.80 | 275 | 795.90 | 335 | 969.00 | 385 | 1113.30 | 435 | 1257.45 | 485 | 1401.75 |
| 36 | 106.50 | 96 | 279.60 | 156 | 452.70 | 216 | 625.80 | 276 | 798.75 | 336 | 971.85 | 386 | 1116.15 | 436 | 1260.30 | 486 | 1404.60 |
| 37 | 109.35 | 97 | 282.45 | 157 | 455.55 | 217 | 628.65 | 277 | 801.75 | 337 | 974.85 | 387 | 1119.00 | 437 | 1263.30 | 487 | 1407.45 |
| 38 | 112.35 | 98 | 285.30 | 158 | 458.40 | 218 | 631.50 | 278 | 804.60 | 338 | 977.70 | 388 | 1121.85 | 438 | 1266.15 | 488 | 1410.30 |
| 39 | 115.20 | 99 | 288.15 | 159 | 461.25 | 219 | 634.35 | 279 | 807.45 | 339 | 980.55 | 389 | 1124.85 | 439 | 1269.00 | 489 | 1413.30 |
| 40 | 118.05 | 100 | 291.15 | 160 | 464.25 | 220 | 637.35 | 280 | 810.30 | 340 | 983.40 | 390 | 1127.70 | 440 | 1271.85 | 490 | 1416.15 |
| 41 | 120.90 | 101 | 294.00 | 161 | 467.10 | 221 | 640.20 | 281 | 813.30 | 341 | 986.25 | 391 | 1130.55 | 441 | 1274.85 | 491 | 1419.00 |
| 42 | 123.75 | 102 | 296.85 | 162 | 469.95 | 222 | 643.05 | 282 | 816.15 | 342 | 989.25 | 392 | 1133.40 | 442 | 1277.70 | 492 | 1421.85 |
| 43 | 126.75 | 103 | 299.85 | 163 | 472.80 | 223 | 645.90 | 283 | 819.00 | 343 | 992.10 | 393 | 1136.25 | 443 | 1280.55 | 493 | 1424.85 |
| 44 | 129.60 | 104 | 302.70 | 164 | 475.80 | 224 | 648.75 | 284 | 821.85 | 344 | 994.95 | 394 | 1139.25 | 444 | 1283.40 | 494 | 1427.70 |
| 45 | 132.45 | 105 | 305.55 | 165 | 478.65 | 225 | 651.75 | 285 | 824.85 | 345 | 997.80 | 395 | 1142.10 | 445 | 1286.25 | 495 | 1430.55 |
| 46 | 135.30 | 106 | 308.40 | 166 | 481.50 | 226 | 654.60 | 286 | 827.70 | 346 | 1000.80 | 396 | 1144.95 | 446 | 1289.25 | 496 | 1433.40 |
| 47 | 138.30 | 107 | 311.25 | 167 | 484.35 | 227 | 657.45 | 287 | 830.55 | 347 | 1003.65 | 397 | 1147.80 | 447 | 1292.10 | 497 | 1436.25 |
| 48 | 141.15 | 108 | 314.25 | 168 | 487.35 | 228 | 660.30 | 288 | 833.40 | 348 | 1006.50 | 398 | 1150.80 | 448 | 1294.95 | 498 | 1439.25 |
| 49 | 144.00 | 109 | 317.10 | 169 | 490.20 | 229 | 663.30 | 289 | 836.25 | 349 | 1009.35 | 399 | 1153.65 | 449 | 1297.80 | 499 | 1442.10 |
| 50 | 146.85 | 110 | 319.95 | 170 | 493.05 | 230 | 666.15 | 290 | 839.25 | 350 | 1012.35 | 400 | 1156.50 | 450 | 1300.80 | 500 | 1444.95 |
| 51 | 149.85 | 111 | 322.80 | 171 | 495.90 | 231 | 669.00 | 291 | 842.10 | | | | | | | | |
| 52 | 152.70 | 112 | 325.80 | 172 | 498.75 | 232 | 671.85 | 292 | 844.95 | | | | | | | | |
| 53 | 155.55 | 113 | 328.65 | 173 | 501.75 | 233 | 674.85 | 293 | 847.80 | | | | | | | | |
| 54 | 158.40 | 114 | 331.50 | 174 | 504.60 | 234 | 677.70 | 294 | 850.80 | | | | | | | | |
| 55 | 161.25 | 115 | 334.35 | 175 | 507.45 | 235 | 680.55 | 295 | 853.65 | | | | | | | | |
| 56 | 164.25 | 116 | 337.35 | 176 | 510.30 | 236 | 683.40 | 296 | 856.50 | | | | | | | | |
| 57 | 167.10 | 117 | 340.20 | 177 | 513.30 | 237 | 686.25 | 297 | 859.35 | | | | | | | | |
| 58 | 169.95 | 118 | 343.05 | 178 | 516.15 | 238 | 689.25 | 298 | 862.35 | | | | | | | | |
| 59 | 172.80 | 119 | 345.90 | 179 | 519.00 | 239 | 692.10 | 299 | 865.20 | | | | | | | | |
| 60 | 175.80 | 120 | 348.75 | 180 | 521.85 | 240 | 694.95 | 300 | 868.05 | | | | | | | | |

**Code more than 500**

1 Where the code is in the range 501 to 1000 inclusive:
  a. Subtract **500** from the code and use the balance of the code to obtain a pay adjustment figure from the table above.
  b. Add this pay adjustment figure to the figure given in the box alongside to obtain the figure of total pay adjustment to date *   **1442.40**

2 Where the code **exceeds 1000** follow the instructions on **page 3**.

# Tables A - Pay Adjustment Tables

Jul 20 to Jul 26  **Week 16**

| Code | Total pay adjustment to date | Code | Total pay adjustment to date | Code | Total pay adjustment to date | Code | Total pay adjustment to date | Code | Total pay adjustment to date | Code | Total pay adjustment to date | Code | Total pay adjustment to date | Code | Total pay adjustment to date | Code | Total pay adjustment to date |
|---|---|---|---|---|---|---|---|---|---|---|---|---|---|---|---|---|---|
| | £ | | £ | | £ | | £ | | £ | | £ | | £ | | £ | | £ |
| 0 | NIL | | | | | | | | | | | | | | | | |
| 1 | 5.92 | 61 | 190.56 | 121 | 375.20 | 181 | 559.84 | 241 | 744.32 | 301 | 928.96 | 351 | 1082.88 | 401 | 1236.64 | 451 | 1390.56 |
| 2 | 8.96 | 62 | 193.60 | 122 | 378.24 | 182 | 562.88 | 242 | 747.52 | 302 | 932.00 | 352 | 1085.92 | 402 | 1239.84 | 452 | 1393.60 |
| 3 | 12.00 | 63 | 196.64 | 123 | 381.28 | 183 | 565.92 | 243 | 750.56 | 303 | 935.20 | 353 | 1088.96 | 403 | 1242.88 | 453 | 1396.64 |
| 4 | 15.20 | 64 | 199.84 | 124 | 384.32 | 184 | 568.96 | 244 | 753.60 | 304 | 938.24 | 354 | 1092.00 | 404 | 1245.92 | 454 | 1399.84 |
| 5 | 18.24 | 65 | 202.88 | 125 | 387.52 | 185 | 572.00 | 245 | 756.64 | 305 | 941.28 | 355 | 1095.20 | 405 | 1248.96 | 455 | 1402.88 |
| 6 | 21.28 | 66 | 205.92 | 126 | 390.56 | 186 | 575.20 | 246 | 759.84 | 306 | 944.32 | 356 | 1098.24 | 406 | 1252.00 | 456 | 1405.92 |
| 7 | 24.32 | 67 | 208.96 | 127 | 393.60 | 187 | 578.24 | 247 | 762.88 | 307 | 947.52 | 357 | 1101.28 | 407 | 1255.20 | 457 | 1408.96 |
| 8 | 27.52 | 68 | 212.00 | 128 | 396.64 | 188 | 581.28 | 248 | 765.92 | 308 | 950.56 | 358 | 1104.32 | 408 | 1258.24 | 458 | 1412.00 |
| 9 | 30.56 | 69 | 215.20 | 129 | 399.84 | 189 | 584.32 | 249 | 768.96 | 309 | 953.60 | 359 | 1107.52 | 409 | 1261.28 | 459 | 1415.20 |
| 10 | 33.60 | 70 | 218.24 | 130 | 402.88 | 190 | 587.52 | 250 | 772.00 | 310 | 956.64 | 360 | 1110.56 | 410 | 1264.32 | 460 | 1418.24 |
| 11 | 36.64 | 71 | 221.28 | 131 | 405.92 | 191 | 590.56 | 251 | 775.20 | 311 | 959.84 | 361 | 1113.60 | 411 | 1267.52 | 461 | 1421.28 |
| 12 | 39.84 | 72 | 224.32 | 132 | 408.96 | 192 | 593.60 | 252 | 778.24 | 312 | 962.88 | 362 | 1116.64 | 412 | 1270.56 | 462 | 1424.32 |
| 13 | 42.88 | 73 | 227.52 | 133 | 412.00 | 193 | 596.64 | 253 | 781.28 | 313 | 965.92 | 363 | 1119.84 | 413 | 1273.60 | 463 | 1427.52 |
| 14 | 45.92 | 74 | 230.56 | 134 | 415.20 | 194 | 599.84 | 254 | 784.32 | 314 | 968.96 | 364 | 1122.88 | 414 | 1276.64 | 464 | 1430.56 |
| 15 | 48.96 | 75 | 233.60 | 135 | 418.24 | 195 | 602.88 | 255 | 787.52 | 315 | 972.00 | 365 | 1125.92 | 415 | 1279.84 | 465 | 1433.60 |
| 16 | 52.00 | 76 | 236.64 | 136 | 421.28 | 196 | 605.92 | 256 | 790.56 | 316 | 975.20 | 366 | 1128.96 | 416 | 1282.88 | 466 | 1436.64 |
| 17 | 55.20 | 77 | 239.84 | 137 | 424.32 | 197 | 608.96 | 257 | 793.60 | 317 | 978.24 | 367 | 1132.00 | 417 | 1285.92 | 467 | 1439.84 |
| 18 | 58.24 | 78 | 242.88 | 138 | 427.52 | 198 | 612.00 | 258 | 796.64 | 318 | 981.28 | 368 | 1135.20 | 418 | 1288.96 | 468 | 1442.88 |
| 19 | 61.28 | 79 | 245.92 | 139 | 430.56 | 199 | 615.20 | 259 | 799.84 | 319 | 984.32 | 369 | 1138.24 | 419 | 1292.00 | 469 | 1445.92 |
| 20 | 64.32 | 80 | 248.96 | 140 | 433.60 | 200 | 618.24 | 260 | 802.88 | 320 | 987.52 | 370 | 1141.28 | 420 | 1295.20 | 470 | 1448.96 |
| 21 | 67.52 | 81 | 252.00 | 141 | 436.64 | 201 | 621.28 | 261 | 805.92 | 321 | 990.56 | 371 | 1144.32 | 421 | 1298.24 | 471 | 1452.00 |
| 22 | 70.56 | 82 | 255.20 | 142 | 439.84 | 202 | 624.32 | 262 | 808.96 | 322 | 993.60 | 372 | 1147.52 | 422 | 1301.28 | 472 | 1455.20 |
| 23 | 73.60 | 83 | 258.24 | 143 | 442.88 | 203 | 627.52 | 263 | 812.00 | 323 | 996.64 | 373 | 1150.56 | 423 | 1304.32 | 473 | 1458.24 |
| 24 | 76.64 | 84 | 261.28 | 144 | 445.92 | 204 | 630.56 | 264 | 815.20 | 324 | 999.84 | 374 | 1153.60 | 424 | 1307.52 | 474 | 1461.28 |
| 25 | 79.84 | 85 | 264.32 | 145 | 448.96 | 205 | 633.60 | 265 | 818.24 | 325 | 1002.88 | 375 | 1156.64 | 425 | 1310.56 | 475 | 1464.32 |
| 26 | 82.88 | 86 | 267.52 | 146 | 452.00 | 206 | 636.64 | 266 | 821.28 | 326 | 1005.92 | 376 | 1159.84 | 426 | 1313.60 | 476 | 1467.52 |
| 27 | 85.92 | 87 | 270.56 | 147 | 455.20 | 207 | 639.84 | 267 | 824.32 | 327 | 1008.96 | 377 | 1162.88 | 427 | 1316.64 | 477 | 1470.56 |
| 28 | 88.96 | 88 | 273.60 | 148 | 458.24 | 208 | 642.88 | 268 | 827.52 | 328 | 1012.00 | 378 | 1165.92 | 428 | 1319.84 | 478 | 1473.60 |
| 29 | 92.00 | 89 | 276.64 | 149 | 461.28 | 209 | 645.92 | 269 | 830.56 | 329 | 1015.20 | 379 | 1168.96 | 429 | 1322.88 | 479 | 1476.64 |
| 30 | 95.20 | 90 | 279.84 | 150 | 464.32 | 210 | 648.96 | 270 | 833.60 | 330 | 1018.24 | 380 | 1172.00 | 430 | 1325.92 | 480 | 1479.84 |
| 31 | 98.24 | 91 | 282.88 | 151 | 467.52 | 211 | 652.00 | 271 | 836.64 | 331 | 1021.28 | 381 | 1175.20 | 431 | 1328.96 | 481 | 1482.88 |
| 32 | 101.28 | 92 | 285.92 | 152 | 470.56 | 212 | 655.20 | 272 | 839.84 | 332 | 1024.32 | 382 | 1178.24 | 432 | 1332.00 | 482 | 1485.92 |
| 33 | 104.32 | 93 | 288.96 | 153 | 473.60 | 213 | 658.24 | 273 | 842.88 | 333 | 1027.52 | 383 | 1181.28 | 433 | 1335.20 | 483 | 1488.96 |
| 34 | 107.52 | 94 | 292.00 | 154 | 476.64 | 214 | 661.28 | 274 | 845.92 | 334 | 1030.56 | 384 | 1184.32 | 434 | 1338.24 | 484 | 1492.00 |
| 35 | 110.56 | 95 | 295.20 | 155 | 479.84 | 215 | 664.32 | 275 | 848.96 | 335 | 1033.60 | 385 | 1187.52 | 435 | 1341.28 | 485 | 1495.20 |
| 36 | 113.60 | 96 | 298.24 | 156 | 482.88 | 216 | 667.52 | 276 | 852.00 | 336 | 1036.64 | 386 | 1190.56 | 436 | 1344.32 | 486 | 1498.24 |
| 37 | 116.64 | 97 | 301.28 | 157 | 485.92 | 217 | 670.56 | 277 | 855.20 | 337 | 1039.84 | 387 | 1193.60 | 437 | 1347.52 | 487 | 1501.28 |
| 38 | 119.84 | 98 | 304.32 | 158 | 488.96 | 218 | 673.60 | 278 | 858.24 | 338 | 1042.88 | 388 | 1196.64 | 438 | 1350.56 | 488 | 1504.32 |
| 39 | 122.88 | 99 | 307.52 | 159 | 492.00 | 219 | 676.64 | 279 | 861.28 | 339 | 1045.92 | 389 | 1199.84 | 439 | 1353.60 | 489 | 1507.52 |
| 40 | 125.92 | 100 | 310.56 | 160 | 495.20 | 220 | 679.84 | 280 | 864.32 | 340 | 1048.96 | 390 | 1202.88 | 440 | 1356.64 | 490 | 1510.56 |
| 41 | 128.96 | 101 | 313.60 | 161 | 498.24 | 221 | 682.88 | 281 | 867.52 | 341 | 1052.00 | 391 | 1205.92 | 441 | 1359.84 | 491 | 1513.60 |
| 42 | 132.00 | 102 | 316.64 | 162 | 501.28 | 222 | 685.92 | 282 | 870.56 | 342 | 1055.20 | 392 | 1208.96 | 442 | 1362.88 | 492 | 1516.64 |
| 43 | 135.20 | 103 | 319.84 | 163 | 504.32 | 223 | 688.96 | 283 | 873.60 | 343 | 1058.24 | 393 | 1212.00 | 443 | 1365.92 | 493 | 1519.84 |
| 44 | 138.24 | 104 | 322.88 | 164 | 507.52 | 224 | 692.00 | 284 | 876.64 | 344 | 1061.28 | 394 | 1215.20 | 444 | 1368.96 | 494 | 1522.88 |
| 45 | 141.28 | 105 | 325.92 | 165 | 510.56 | 225 | 695.20 | 285 | 879.84 | 345 | 1064.32 | 395 | 1218.24 | 445 | 1372.00 | 495 | 1525.92 |
| 46 | 144.32 | 106 | 328.96 | 166 | 513.60 | 226 | 698.24 | 286 | 882.88 | 346 | 1067.52 | 396 | 1221.28 | 446 | 1375.20 | 496 | 1528.96 |
| 47 | 147.52 | 107 | 332.00 | 167 | 516.64 | 227 | 701.28 | 287 | 885.92 | 347 | 1070.56 | 397 | 1224.32 | 447 | 1378.24 | 497 | 1532.00 |
| 48 | 150.56 | 108 | 335.20 | 168 | 519.84 | 228 | 704.32 | 288 | 888.96 | 348 | 1073.60 | 398 | 1227.52 | 448 | 1381.28 | 498 | 1535.20 |
| 49 | 153.60 | 109 | 338.24 | 169 | 522.88 | 229 | 707.52 | 289 | 892.00 | 349 | 1076.64 | 399 | 1230.56 | 449 | 1384.32 | 499 | 1538.24 |
| 50 | 156.64 | 110 | 341.28 | 170 | 525.92 | 230 | 710.56 | 290 | 895.20 | 350 | 1079.84 | 400 | 1233.60 | 450 | 1387.52 | 500 | 1541.28 |
| 51 | 159.84 | 111 | 344.32 | 171 | 528.96 | 231 | 713.60 | 291 | 898.24 | | | | | | | | |
| 52 | 162.88 | 112 | 347.52 | 172 | 532.00 | 232 | 716.64 | 292 | 901.28 | | | | | | | | |
| 53 | 165.92 | 113 | 350.56 | 173 | 535.20 | 233 | 719.84 | 293 | 904.32 | | | | | | | | |
| 54 | 168.96 | 114 | 353.60 | 174 | 538.24 | 234 | 722.88 | 294 | 907.52 | | | | | | | | |
| 55 | 172.00 | 115 | 356.64 | 175 | 541.28 | 235 | 725.92 | 295 | 910.56 | | | | | | | | |
| 56 | 175.20 | 116 | 359.84 | 176 | 544.32 | 236 | 728.96 | 296 | 913.60 | | | | | | | | |
| 57 | 178.24 | 117 | 362.88 | 177 | 547.52 | 237 | 732.00 | 297 | 916.64 | | | | | | | | |
| 58 | 181.28 | 118 | 365.92 | 178 | 550.56 | 238 | 735.20 | 298 | 919.84 | | | | | | | | |
| 59 | 184.32 | 119 | 368.96 | 179 | 553.60 | 239 | 738.24 | 299 | 922.88 | | | | | | | | |
| 60 | 187.52 | 120 | 372.00 | 180 | 556.64 | 240 | 741.28 | 300 | 925.92 | | | | | | | | |

## Code more than 500

1 Where the code is in the range **501** to **1000** inclusive:

  a. Subtract **500** from the code and use the balance of the code to obtain a pay adjustment figure from the table above.

  b. Add this pay adjustment figure to the figure given in the box alongside to obtain the figure of total pay adjustment to date *  | **1538.56** |

2 Where the code **exceeds 1000** follow the instructions on **page 3**.

19

# APPENDIX 4: PAYE TAX TABLES – PAY ADJUSTMENT TABLES

**Week 17**   Jul 27 to Aug 2                     **Tables A** - Pay Adjustment Tables

| Code | Total pay adjustment to date | Code | Total pay adjustment to date | Code | Total pay adjustment to date | Code | Total pay adjustment to date | Code | Total pay adjustment to date | Code | Total pay adjustment to date | Code | Total pay adjustment to date | Code | Total pay adjustment to date | Code | Total pay adjustment to date |
|---|---|---|---|---|---|---|---|---|---|---|---|---|---|---|---|---|---|
| | £ | | £ | | £ | | £ | | £ | | £ | | £ | | £ | | £ |
| 0 | NIL | | | | | | | | | | | | | | | | |
| 1 | 6.29 | 61 | 202.47 | 121 | 398.65 | 181 | 594.83 | 241 | 790.84 | 301 | 987.02 | 351 | 1150.56 | 401 | 1313.93 | 451 | 1477.47 |
| 2 | 9.52 | 62 | 205.70 | 122 | 401.88 | 182 | 598.06 | 242 | 794.24 | 302 | 990.25 | 352 | 1153.79 | 402 | 1317.33 | 452 | 1480.70 |
| 3 | 12.75 | 63 | 208.93 | 123 | 405.11 | 183 | 601.29 | 243 | 797.47 | 303 | 993.65 | 353 | 1157.02 | 403 | 1320.56 | 453 | 1483.93 |
| 4 | 16.15 | 64 | 212.33 | 124 | 408.34 | 184 | 604.52 | 244 | 800.70 | 304 | 996.88 | 354 | 1160.25 | 404 | 1323.79 | 454 | 1487.33 |
| 5 | 19.38 | 65 | 215.56 | 125 | 411.74 | 185 | 607.75 | 245 | 803.93 | 305 | 1000.11 | 355 | 1163.65 | 405 | 1327.02 | 455 | 1490.56 |
| 6 | 22.61 | 66 | 218.79 | 126 | 414.97 | 186 | 611.15 | 246 | 807.33 | 306 | 1003.34 | 356 | 1166.88 | 406 | 1330.25 | 456 | 1493.79 |
| 7 | 25.84 | 67 | 222.02 | 127 | 418.20 | 187 | 614.38 | 247 | 810.56 | 307 | 1006.74 | 357 | 1170.11 | 407 | 1333.65 | 457 | 1497.02 |
| 8 | 29.24 | 68 | 225.25 | 128 | 421.43 | 188 | 617.61 | 248 | 813.79 | 308 | 1009.97 | 358 | 1173.34 | 408 | 1336.88 | 458 | 1500.25 |
| 9 | 32.47 | 69 | 228.65 | 129 | 424.83 | 189 | 620.84 | 249 | 817.02 | 309 | 1013.20 | 359 | 1176.74 | 409 | 1340.11 | 459 | 1503.65 |
| 10 | 35.70 | 70 | 231.88 | 130 | 428.06 | 190 | 624.24 | 250 | 820.25 | 310 | 1016.43 | 360 | 1179.97 | 410 | 1343.34 | 460 | 1506.88 |
| 11 | 38.93 | 71 | 235.11 | 131 | 431.29 | 191 | 627.47 | 251 | 823.65 | 311 | 1019.83 | 361 | 1183.20 | 411 | 1346.74 | 461 | 1510.11 |
| 12 | 42.33 | 72 | 238.34 | 132 | 434.52 | 192 | 630.70 | 252 | 826.88 | 312 | 1023.06 | 362 | 1186.43 | 412 | 1349.97 | 462 | 1513.34 |
| 13 | 45.56 | 73 | 241.74 | 133 | 437.75 | 193 | 633.93 | 253 | 830.11 | 313 | 1026.29 | 363 | 1189.83 | 413 | 1353.20 | 463 | 1516.74 |
| 14 | 48.79 | 74 | 244.97 | 134 | 441.15 | 194 | 637.33 | 254 | 833.34 | 314 | 1029.52 | 364 | 1193.06 | 414 | 1356.43 | 464 | 1519.97 |
| 15 | 52.02 | 75 | 248.20 | 135 | 444.38 | 195 | 640.56 | 255 | 836.74 | 315 | 1032.75 | 365 | 1196.29 | 415 | 1359.83 | 465 | 1523.20 |
| 16 | 55.25 | 76 | 251.43 | 136 | 447.61 | 196 | 643.79 | 256 | 839.97 | 316 | 1036.15 | 366 | 1199.52 | 416 | 1363.06 | 466 | 1526.43 |
| 17 | 58.65 | 77 | 254.83 | 137 | 450.84 | 197 | 647.02 | 257 | 843.20 | 317 | 1039.38 | 367 | 1202.75 | 417 | 1366.29 | 467 | 1529.83 |
| 18 | 61.88 | 78 | 258.06 | 138 | 454.24 | 198 | 650.25 | 258 | 846.43 | 318 | 1042.61 | 368 | 1206.15 | 418 | 1369.52 | 468 | 1533.06 |
| 19 | 65.11 | 79 | 261.29 | 139 | 457.47 | 199 | 653.65 | 259 | 849.83 | 319 | 1045.84 | 369 | 1209.38 | 419 | 1372.75 | 469 | 1536.29 |
| 20 | 68.34 | 80 | 264.52 | 140 | 460.70 | 200 | 656.88 | 260 | 853.06 | 320 | 1049.24 | 370 | 1212.61 | 420 | 1376.15 | 470 | 1539.52 |
| 21 | 71.74 | 81 | 267.75 | 141 | 463.93 | 201 | 660.11 | 261 | 856.29 | 321 | 1052.47 | 371 | 1215.84 | 421 | 1379.38 | 471 | 1542.75 |
| 22 | 74.97 | 82 | 271.15 | 142 | 467.33 | 202 | 663.34 | 262 | 859.52 | 322 | 1055.70 | 372 | 1219.24 | 422 | 1382.61 | 472 | 1546.15 |
| 23 | 78.20 | 83 | 274.38 | 143 | 470.56 | 203 | 666.74 | 263 | 862.75 | 323 | 1058.93 | 373 | 1222.47 | 423 | 1385.84 | 473 | 1549.38 |
| 24 | 81.43 | 84 | 277.61 | 144 | 473.79 | 204 | 669.97 | 264 | 866.15 | 324 | 1062.33 | 374 | 1225.70 | 424 | 1389.24 | 474 | 1552.61 |
| 25 | 84.83 | 85 | 280.84 | 145 | 477.02 | 205 | 673.20 | 265 | 869.38 | 325 | 1065.56 | 375 | 1228.93 | 425 | 1392.47 | 475 | 1555.84 |
| 26 | 88.06 | 86 | 284.24 | 146 | 480.25 | 206 | 676.43 | 266 | 872.61 | 326 | 1068.79 | 376 | 1232.33 | 426 | 1395.70 | 476 | 1559.24 |
| 27 | 91.29 | 87 | 287.47 | 147 | 483.65 | 207 | 679.83 | 267 | 875.84 | 327 | 1072.02 | 377 | 1235.56 | 427 | 1398.93 | 477 | 1562.47 |
| 28 | 94.52 | 88 | 290.70 | 148 | 486.88 | 208 | 683.06 | 268 | 879.24 | 328 | 1075.25 | 378 | 1238.79 | 428 | 1402.33 | 478 | 1565.70 |
| 29 | 97.75 | 89 | 293.93 | 149 | 490.11 | 209 | 686.29 | 269 | 882.47 | 329 | 1078.65 | 379 | 1242.02 | 429 | 1405.56 | 479 | 1568.93 |
| 30 | 101.15 | 90 | 297.33 | 150 | 493.34 | 210 | 689.52 | 270 | 885.70 | 330 | 1081.88 | 380 | 1245.25 | 430 | 1408.79 | 480 | 1572.33 |
| 31 | 104.38 | 91 | 300.56 | 151 | 496.74 | 211 | 692.75 | 271 | 888.93 | 331 | 1085.11 | 381 | 1248.65 | 431 | 1412.02 | 481 | 1575.56 |
| 32 | 107.61 | 92 | 303.79 | 152 | 499.97 | 212 | 696.15 | 272 | 892.33 | 332 | 1088.34 | 382 | 1251.88 | 432 | 1415.25 | 482 | 1578.79 |
| 33 | 110.84 | 93 | 307.02 | 153 | 503.20 | 213 | 699.38 | 273 | 895.56 | 333 | 1091.74 | 383 | 1255.11 | 433 | 1418.65 | 483 | 1582.02 |
| 34 | 114.24 | 94 | 310.25 | 154 | 506.43 | 214 | 702.61 | 274 | 898.79 | 334 | 1094.97 | 384 | 1258.34 | 434 | 1421.88 | 484 | 1585.25 |
| 35 | 117.47 | 95 | 313.65 | 155 | 509.83 | 215 | 705.84 | 275 | 902.02 | 335 | 1098.20 | 385 | 1261.74 | 435 | 1425.11 | 485 | 1588.65 |
| 36 | 120.70 | 96 | 316.88 | 156 | 513.06 | 216 | 709.24 | 276 | 905.25 | 336 | 1101.43 | 386 | 1264.97 | 436 | 1428.34 | 486 | 1591.88 |
| 37 | 123.93 | 97 | 320.11 | 157 | 516.29 | 217 | 712.47 | 277 | 908.65 | 337 | 1104.83 | 387 | 1268.20 | 437 | 1431.74 | 487 | 1595.11 |
| 38 | 127.33 | 98 | 323.34 | 158 | 519.52 | 218 | 715.70 | 278 | 911.88 | 338 | 1108.06 | 388 | 1271.43 | 438 | 1434.97 | 488 | 1598.34 |
| 39 | 130.56 | 99 | 326.74 | 159 | 522.75 | 219 | 718.93 | 279 | 915.11 | 339 | 1111.29 | 389 | 1274.83 | 439 | 1438.20 | 489 | 1601.74 |
| 40 | 133.79 | 100 | 329.97 | 160 | 526.15 | 220 | 722.33 | 280 | 918.34 | 340 | 1114.52 | 390 | 1278.06 | 440 | 1441.43 | 490 | 1604.97 |
| 41 | 137.02 | 101 | 333.20 | 161 | 529.38 | 221 | 725.56 | 281 | 921.74 | 341 | 1117.75 | 391 | 1281.29 | 441 | 1444.83 | 491 | 1608.20 |
| 42 | 140.25 | 102 | 336.43 | 162 | 532.61 | 222 | 728.79 | 282 | 924.97 | 342 | 1121.15 | 392 | 1284.52 | 442 | 1448.06 | 492 | 1611.43 |
| 43 | 143.65 | 103 | 339.83 | 163 | 535.84 | 223 | 732.02 | 283 | 928.20 | 343 | 1124.38 | 393 | 1287.75 | 443 | 1451.29 | 493 | 1614.83 |
| 44 | 146.88 | 104 | 343.06 | 164 | 539.24 | 224 | 735.25 | 284 | 931.43 | 344 | 1127.61 | 394 | 1291.15 | 444 | 1454.52 | 494 | 1618.06 |
| 45 | 150.11 | 105 | 346.29 | 165 | 542.47 | 225 | 738.65 | 285 | 934.83 | 345 | 1130.84 | 395 | 1294.38 | 445 | 1457.75 | 495 | 1621.29 |
| 46 | 153.34 | 106 | 349.52 | 166 | 545.70 | 226 | 741.88 | 286 | 938.06 | 346 | 1134.24 | 396 | 1297.61 | 446 | 1461.15 | 496 | 1624.52 |
| 47 | 156.74 | 107 | 352.75 | 167 | 548.93 | 227 | 745.11 | 287 | 941.29 | 347 | 1137.47 | 397 | 1300.84 | 447 | 1464.38 | 497 | 1627.75 |
| 48 | 159.97 | 108 | 356.15 | 168 | 552.33 | 228 | 748.34 | 288 | 944.52 | 348 | 1140.70 | 398 | 1304.24 | 448 | 1467.61 | 498 | 1631.15 |
| 49 | 163.20 | 109 | 359.38 | 169 | 555.56 | 229 | 751.74 | 289 | 947.75 | 349 | 1143.93 | 399 | 1307.47 | 449 | 1470.84 | 499 | 1634.38 |
| 50 | 166.43 | 110 | 362.61 | 170 | 558.79 | 230 | 754.97 | 290 | 951.15 | 350 | 1147.33 | 400 | 1310.70 | 450 | 1474.24 | 500 | 1637.61 |
| 51 | 169.83 | 111 | 365.84 | 171 | 562.02 | 231 | 758.20 | 291 | 954.38 | | | | | | |
| 52 | 173.06 | 112 | 369.24 | 172 | 565.25 | 232 | 761.43 | 292 | 957.61 | | | | | | |
| 53 | 176.29 | 113 | 372.47 | 173 | 568.65 | 233 | 764.83 | 293 | 960.84 | | | | | | |
| 54 | 179.52 | 114 | 375.70 | 174 | 571.88 | 234 | 768.06 | 294 | 964.24 | | | | | | |
| 55 | 182.75 | 115 | 378.93 | 175 | 575.11 | 235 | 771.29 | 295 | 967.47 | | | | | | |
| 56 | 186.15 | 116 | 382.33 | 176 | 578.34 | 236 | 774.52 | 296 | 970.70 | | | | | | |
| 57 | 189.38 | 117 | 385.56 | 177 | 581.74 | 237 | 777.75 | 297 | 973.93 | | | | | | |
| 58 | 192.61 | 118 | 388.79 | 178 | 584.97 | 238 | 781.15 | 298 | 977.33 | | | | | | |
| 59 | 195.84 | 119 | 392.02 | 179 | 588.20 | 239 | 784.38 | 299 | 980.56 | | | | | | |
| 60 | 199.24 | 120 | 395.25 | 180 | 591.43 | 240 | 787.61 | 300 | 983.79 | | | | | | |

### Code more than 500

1  Where the code is in the range **501** to **1000** inclusive:

  a. Subtract **500** from the code and use the balance of the code to obtain a pay adjustment figure from the table above.

  b. Add this pay adjustment figure to the figure given in the box alongside to obtain the figure of total pay adjustment to date *

| 1634.72 |
|---|

2  Where the code **exceeds 1000** follow the instructions on **page 3**.

# Tables A - Pay Adjustment Tables

Aug 3 to Aug 9  **Week 18**

| Code | Total pay adjustment to date £ | Code | Total pay adjustment to date £ | Code | Total pay adjustment to date £ | Code | Total pay adjustment to date £ | Code | Total pay adjustment to date £ | Code | Total pay adjustment to date £ | Code | Total pay adjustment to date £ | Code | Total pay adjustment to date £ | Code | Total pay adjustment to date £ |
|---|---|---|---|---|---|---|---|---|---|---|---|---|---|---|---|---|---|
| 0 | NIL | | | | | | | | | | | | | | | | |
| 1 | 6.66 | 61 | 214.38 | 121 | 422.10 | 181 | 629.82 | 241 | 837.36 | 301 | 1045.08 | 351 | 1218.24 | 401 | 1391.22 | 451 | 1564.38 |
| 2 | 10.08 | 62 | 217.80 | 122 | 425.52 | 182 | 633.24 | 242 | 840.96 | 302 | 1048.50 | 352 | 1221.66 | 402 | 1394.82 | 452 | 1567.80 |
| 3 | 13.50 | 63 | 221.22 | 123 | 428.94 | 183 | 636.66 | 243 | 844.38 | 303 | 1052.10 | 353 | 1225.08 | 403 | 1398.24 | 453 | 1571.22 |
| 4 | 17.10 | 64 | 224.82 | 124 | 432.36 | 184 | 640.08 | 244 | 847.80 | 304 | 1055.52 | 354 | 1228.50 | 404 | 1401.66 | 454 | 1574.82 |
| 5 | 20.52 | 65 | 228.24 | 125 | 435.96 | 185 | 643.50 | 245 | 851.22 | 305 | 1058.94 | 355 | 1232.10 | 405 | 1405.08 | 455 | 1578.24 |
| 6 | 23.94 | 66 | 231.66 | 126 | 439.38 | 186 | 647.10 | 246 | 854.82 | 306 | 1062.36 | 356 | 1235.52 | 406 | 1408.50 | 456 | 1581.66 |
| 7 | 27.36 | 67 | 235.08 | 127 | 442.80 | 187 | 650.52 | 247 | 858.24 | 307 | 1065.96 | 357 | 1238.94 | 407 | 1412.10 | 457 | 1585.08 |
| 8 | 30.96 | 68 | 238.50 | 128 | 446.22 | 188 | 653.94 | 248 | 861.66 | 308 | 1069.38 | 358 | 1242.36 | 408 | 1415.52 | 458 | 1588.50 |
| 9 | 34.38 | 69 | 242.10 | 129 | 449.82 | 189 | 657.36 | 249 | 865.08 | 309 | 1072.80 | 359 | 1245.96 | 409 | 1418.94 | 459 | 1592.10 |
| 10 | 37.80 | 70 | 245.52 | 130 | 453.24 | 190 | 660.96 | 250 | 868.50 | 310 | 1076.22 | 360 | 1249.38 | 410 | 1422.36 | 460 | 1595.52 |
| 11 | 41.22 | 71 | 248.94 | 131 | 456.66 | 191 | 664.38 | 251 | 872.10 | 311 | 1079.82 | 361 | 1252.80 | 411 | 1425.96 | 461 | 1598.94 |
| 12 | 44.82 | 72 | 252.36 | 132 | 460.08 | 192 | 667.80 | 252 | 875.52 | 312 | 1083.24 | 362 | 1256.22 | 412 | 1429.38 | 462 | 1602.36 |
| 13 | 48.24 | 73 | 255.96 | 133 | 463.50 | 193 | 671.22 | 253 | 878.94 | 313 | 1086.66 | 363 | 1259.82 | 413 | 1432.80 | 463 | 1605.96 |
| 14 | 51.66 | 74 | 259.38 | 134 | 467.10 | 194 | 674.82 | 254 | 882.36 | 314 | 1090.08 | 364 | 1263.24 | 414 | 1436.22 | 464 | 1609.38 |
| 15 | 55.08 | 75 | 262.80 | 135 | 470.52 | 195 | 678.24 | 255 | 885.96 | 315 | 1093.50 | 365 | 1266.66 | 415 | 1439.82 | 465 | 1612.80 |
| 16 | 58.50 | 76 | 266.22 | 136 | 473.94 | 196 | 681.66 | 256 | 889.38 | 316 | 1097.10 | 366 | 1270.08 | 416 | 1443.24 | 466 | 1616.22 |
| 17 | 62.10 | 77 | 269.82 | 137 | 477.36 | 197 | 685.08 | 257 | 892.80 | 317 | 1100.52 | 367 | 1273.50 | 417 | 1446.66 | 467 | 1619.82 |
| 18 | 65.52 | 78 | 273.24 | 138 | 480.96 | 198 | 688.50 | 258 | 896.22 | 318 | 1103.94 | 368 | 1277.10 | 418 | 1450.08 | 468 | 1623.24 |
| 19 | 68.94 | 79 | 276.66 | 139 | 484.38 | 199 | 692.10 | 259 | 899.82 | 319 | 1107.36 | 369 | 1280.52 | 419 | 1453.50 | 469 | 1626.66 |
| 20 | 72.36 | 80 | 280.08 | 140 | 487.80 | 200 | 695.52 | 260 | 903.24 | 320 | 1110.96 | 370 | 1283.94 | 420 | 1457.10 | 470 | 1630.08 |
| 21 | 75.96 | 81 | 283.50 | 141 | 491.22 | 201 | 698.94 | 261 | 906.66 | 321 | 1114.38 | 371 | 1287.36 | 421 | 1460.52 | 471 | 1633.50 |
| 22 | 79.38 | 82 | 287.10 | 142 | 494.82 | 202 | 702.36 | 262 | 910.08 | 322 | 1117.80 | 372 | 1290.96 | 422 | 1463.94 | 472 | 1637.10 |
| 23 | 82.80 | 83 | 290.52 | 143 | 498.24 | 203 | 705.96 | 263 | 913.50 | 323 | 1121.22 | 373 | 1294.38 | 423 | 1467.36 | 473 | 1640.52 |
| 24 | 86.22 | 84 | 293.94 | 144 | 501.66 | 204 | 709.38 | 264 | 917.10 | 324 | 1124.82 | 374 | 1297.80 | 424 | 1470.96 | 474 | 1643.94 |
| 25 | 89.82 | 85 | 297.36 | 145 | 505.08 | 205 | 712.80 | 265 | 920.52 | 325 | 1128.24 | 375 | 1301.22 | 425 | 1474.38 | 475 | 1647.36 |
| 26 | 93.24 | 86 | 300.96 | 146 | 508.50 | 206 | 716.22 | 266 | 923.94 | 326 | 1131.66 | 376 | 1304.82 | 426 | 1477.80 | 476 | 1650.96 |
| 27 | 96.66 | 87 | 304.38 | 147 | 512.10 | 207 | 719.82 | 267 | 927.36 | 327 | 1135.08 | 377 | 1308.24 | 427 | 1481.22 | 477 | 1654.38 |
| 28 | 100.08 | 88 | 307.80 | 148 | 515.52 | 208 | 723.24 | 268 | 930.96 | 328 | 1138.50 | 378 | 1311.66 | 428 | 1484.82 | 478 | 1657.80 |
| 29 | 103.50 | 89 | 311.22 | 149 | 518.94 | 209 | 726.66 | 269 | 934.38 | 329 | 1142.10 | 379 | 1315.08 | 429 | 1488.24 | 479 | 1661.22 |
| 30 | 107.10 | 90 | 314.82 | 150 | 522.36 | 210 | 730.08 | 270 | 937.80 | 330 | 1145.52 | 380 | 1318.50 | 430 | 1491.66 | 480 | 1664.82 |
| 31 | 110.52 | 91 | 318.24 | 151 | 525.96 | 211 | 733.50 | 271 | 941.22 | 331 | 1148.94 | 381 | 1322.10 | 431 | 1495.08 | 481 | 1668.24 |
| 32 | 113.94 | 92 | 321.66 | 152 | 529.38 | 212 | 737.10 | 272 | 944.82 | 332 | 1152.36 | 382 | 1325.52 | 432 | 1498.50 | 482 | 1671.66 |
| 33 | 117.36 | 93 | 325.08 | 153 | 532.80 | 213 | 740.52 | 273 | 948.24 | 333 | 1155.96 | 383 | 1328.94 | 433 | 1502.10 | 483 | 1675.08 |
| 34 | 120.96 | 94 | 328.50 | 154 | 536.22 | 214 | 743.94 | 274 | 951.66 | 334 | 1159.38 | 384 | 1332.36 | 434 | 1505.52 | 484 | 1678.50 |
| 35 | 124.38 | 95 | 332.10 | 155 | 539.82 | 215 | 747.36 | 275 | 955.08 | 335 | 1162.80 | 385 | 1335.96 | 435 | 1508.94 | 485 | 1682.10 |
| 36 | 127.80 | 96 | 335.52 | 156 | 543.24 | 216 | 750.96 | 276 | 958.50 | 336 | 1166.22 | 386 | 1339.38 | 436 | 1512.36 | 486 | 1685.52 |
| 37 | 131.22 | 97 | 338.94 | 157 | 546.66 | 217 | 754.38 | 277 | 962.10 | 337 | 1169.82 | 387 | 1342.80 | 437 | 1515.96 | 487 | 1688.94 |
| 38 | 134.82 | 98 | 342.36 | 158 | 550.08 | 218 | 757.80 | 278 | 965.52 | 338 | 1173.24 | 388 | 1346.22 | 438 | 1519.38 | 488 | 1692.36 |
| 39 | 138.24 | 99 | 345.96 | 159 | 553.50 | 219 | 761.22 | 279 | 968.94 | 339 | 1176.66 | 389 | 1349.82 | 439 | 1522.80 | 489 | 1695.96 |
| 40 | 141.66 | 100 | 349.38 | 160 | 557.10 | 220 | 764.82 | 280 | 972.36 | 340 | 1180.08 | 390 | 1353.24 | 440 | 1526.22 | 490 | 1699.38 |
| 41 | 145.08 | 101 | 352.80 | 161 | 560.52 | 221 | 768.24 | 281 | 975.96 | 341 | 1183.50 | 391 | 1356.66 | 441 | 1529.82 | 491 | 1702.80 |
| 42 | 148.50 | 102 | 356.22 | 162 | 563.94 | 222 | 771.66 | 282 | 979.38 | 342 | 1187.10 | 392 | 1360.08 | 442 | 1533.24 | 492 | 1706.22 |
| 43 | 152.10 | 103 | 359.82 | 163 | 567.36 | 223 | 775.08 | 283 | 982.80 | 343 | 1190.52 | 393 | 1363.50 | 443 | 1536.66 | 493 | 1709.82 |
| 44 | 155.52 | 104 | 363.24 | 164 | 570.96 | 224 | 778.50 | 284 | 986.22 | 344 | 1193.94 | 394 | 1367.10 | 444 | 1540.08 | 494 | 1713.24 |
| 45 | 158.94 | 105 | 366.66 | 165 | 574.38 | 225 | 782.10 | 285 | 989.82 | 345 | 1197.36 | 395 | 1370.52 | 445 | 1543.50 | 495 | 1716.66 |
| 46 | 162.36 | 106 | 370.08 | 166 | 577.80 | 226 | 785.52 | 286 | 993.24 | 346 | 1200.96 | 396 | 1373.94 | 446 | 1547.10 | 496 | 1720.08 |
| 47 | 165.96 | 107 | 373.50 | 167 | 581.22 | 227 | 788.94 | 287 | 996.66 | 347 | 1204.38 | 397 | 1377.36 | 447 | 1550.52 | 497 | 1723.50 |
| 48 | 169.38 | 108 | 377.10 | 168 | 584.82 | 228 | 792.36 | 288 | 1000.08 | 348 | 1207.80 | 398 | 1380.96 | 448 | 1553.94 | 498 | 1727.10 |
| 49 | 172.80 | 109 | 380.52 | 169 | 588.24 | 229 | 795.96 | 289 | 1003.50 | 349 | 1211.22 | 399 | 1384.38 | 449 | 1557.36 | 499 | 1730.52 |
| 50 | 176.22 | 110 | 383.94 | 170 | 591.66 | 230 | 799.38 | 290 | 1007.10 | 350 | 1214.82 | 400 | 1387.80 | 450 | 1560.96 | 500 | 1733.94 |
| 51 | 179.82 | 111 | 387.36 | 171 | 595.08 | 231 | 802.80 | 291 | 1010.52 | | | | | | | | |
| 52 | 183.24 | 112 | 390.96 | 172 | 598.50 | 232 | 806.22 | 292 | 1013.94 | | | | | | | | |
| 53 | 186.66 | 113 | 394.38 | 173 | 602.10 | 233 | 809.82 | 293 | 1017.36 | | | | | | | | |
| 54 | 190.08 | 114 | 397.80 | 174 | 605.52 | 234 | 813.24 | 294 | 1020.96 | | | | | | | | |
| 55 | 193.50 | 115 | 401.22 | 175 | 608.94 | 235 | 816.66 | 295 | 1024.38 | | | | | | | | |
| 56 | 197.10 | 116 | 404.82 | 176 | 612.36 | 236 | 820.08 | 296 | 1027.80 | | | | | | | | |
| 57 | 200.52 | 117 | 408.24 | 177 | 615.96 | 237 | 823.50 | 297 | 1031.22 | | | | | | | | |
| 58 | 203.94 | 118 | 411.66 | 178 | 619.38 | 238 | 827.10 | 298 | 1034.82 | | | | | | | | |
| 59 | 207.36 | 119 | 415.08 | 179 | 622.80 | 239 | 830.52 | 299 | 1038.24 | | | | | | | | |
| 60 | 210.96 | 120 | 418.50 | 180 | 626.22 | 240 | 833.94 | 300 | 1041.66 | | | | | | | | |

**Code more than 500**

1 Where the code is in the range **501 to 1000** inclusive:

  a. Subtract **500** from the code and use the balance of the code to obtain a pay adjustment figure from the table above.

  b. Add this pay adjustment figure to the figure given in the box alongside to obtain the figure of total pay adjustment to date *   **1730.88**

2 Where the code **exceeds 1000** follow the instructions on **page 3**.

21

**Week 19**  Aug 10 to Aug 16                                   **Tables A** - Pay Adjustment Tables

| Code | Total pay adjustment to date | Code | Total pay adjustment to date | Code | Total pay adjustment to date | Code | Total pay adjustment to date | Code | Total pay adjustment to date | Code | Total pay adjustment to date | Code | Total pay adjustment to date | Code | Total pay adjustment to date | Code | Total pay adjustment to date |
|---|---|---|---|---|---|---|---|---|---|---|---|---|---|---|---|---|---|
| | £ | | £ | | £ | | £ | | £ | | £ | | £ | | £ | | £ |
| 0 | NIL | 61 | 226.29 | 121 | 445.55 | 181 | 664.81 | 241 | 883.88 | 301 | 1103.14 | 351 | 1285.92 | 401 | 1468.51 | 451 | 1651.29 |
| 1 | 7.03 | 62 | 229.90 | 122 | 449.16 | 182 | 668.42 | 242 | 887.68 | 302 | 1106.75 | 352 | 1289.53 | 402 | 1472.31 | 452 | 1654.90 |
| 2 | 10.64 | 63 | 233.51 | 123 | 452.77 | 183 | 672.03 | 243 | 891.29 | 303 | 1110.55 | 353 | 1293.14 | 403 | 1475.92 | 453 | 1658.51 |
| 3 | 14.25 | 64 | 237.31 | 124 | 456.38 | 184 | 675.64 | 244 | 894.90 | 304 | 1114.16 | 354 | 1296.75 | 404 | 1479.53 | 454 | 1662.31 |
| 4 | 18.05 | 65 | 240.92 | 125 | 460.18 | 185 | 679.25 | 245 | 898.51 | 305 | 1117.77 | 355 | 1300.55 | 405 | 1483.14 | 455 | 1665.92 |
| 5 | 21.66 | 66 | 244.53 | 126 | 463.79 | 186 | 683.05 | 246 | 902.31 | 306 | 1121.38 | 356 | 1304.16 | 406 | 1486.75 | 456 | 1669.53 |
| 6 | 25.27 | 67 | 248.14 | 127 | 467.40 | 187 | 686.66 | 247 | 905.92 | 307 | 1125.18 | 357 | 1307.77 | 407 | 1490.55 | 457 | 1673.14 |
| 7 | 28.88 | 68 | 251.75 | 128 | 471.01 | 188 | 690.27 | 248 | 909.53 | 308 | 1128.79 | 358 | 1311.38 | 408 | 1494.16 | 458 | 1676.75 |
| 8 | 32.68 | 69 | 255.55 | 129 | 474.81 | 189 | 693.88 | 249 | 913.14 | 309 | 1132.40 | 359 | 1315.18 | 409 | 1497.77 | 459 | 1680.55 |
| 9 | 36.29 | 70 | 259.16 | 130 | 478.42 | 190 | 697.68 | 250 | 916.75 | 310 | 1136.01 | 360 | 1318.79 | 410 | 1501.38 | 460 | 1684.16 |
| 10 | 39.90 | 71 | 262.77 | 131 | 482.03 | 191 | 701.29 | 251 | 920.55 | 311 | 1139.81 | 361 | 1322.40 | 411 | 1505.18 | 461 | 1687.77 |
| 11 | 43.51 | 72 | 266.38 | 132 | 485.64 | 192 | 704.90 | 252 | 924.16 | 312 | 1143.42 | 362 | 1326.01 | 412 | 1508.79 | 462 | 1691.38 |
| 12 | 47.31 | 73 | 270.18 | 133 | 489.25 | 193 | 708.51 | 253 | 927.77 | 313 | 1147.03 | 363 | 1329.81 | 413 | 1512.40 | 463 | 1695.18 |
| 13 | 50.92 | 74 | 273.79 | 134 | 493.05 | 194 | 712.31 | 254 | 931.38 | 314 | 1150.64 | 364 | 1333.42 | 414 | 1516.01 | 464 | 1698.79 |
| 14 | 54.53 | 75 | 277.40 | 135 | 496.66 | 195 | 715.92 | 255 | 935.18 | 315 | 1154.25 | 365 | 1337.03 | 415 | 1519.81 | 465 | 1702.40 |
| 15 | 58.14 | 76 | 281.01 | 136 | 500.27 | 196 | 719.53 | 256 | 938.79 | 316 | 1158.05 | 366 | 1340.64 | 416 | 1523.42 | 466 | 1706.01 |
| 16 | 61.75 | 77 | 284.81 | 137 | 503.88 | 197 | 723.14 | 257 | 942.40 | 317 | 1161.66 | 367 | 1344.25 | 417 | 1527.03 | 467 | 1709.81 |
| 17 | 65.55 | 78 | 288.42 | 138 | 507.68 | 198 | 726.75 | 258 | 946.01 | 318 | 1165.27 | 368 | 1348.05 | 418 | 1530.64 | 468 | 1713.42 |
| 18 | 69.16 | 79 | 292.03 | 139 | 511.29 | 199 | 730.55 | 259 | 949.81 | 319 | 1168.88 | 369 | 1351.66 | 419 | 1534.25 | 469 | 1717.03 |
| 19 | 72.77 | 80 | 295.64 | 140 | 514.90 | 200 | 734.16 | 260 | 953.42 | 320 | 1172.68 | 370 | 1355.27 | 420 | 1538.05 | 470 | 1720.64 |
| 20 | 76.38 | 81 | 299.25 | 141 | 518.51 | 201 | 737.77 | 261 | 957.03 | 321 | 1176.29 | 371 | 1358.88 | 421 | 1541.66 | 471 | 1724.25 |
| 21 | 80.18 | 82 | 303.05 | 142 | 522.31 | 202 | 741.38 | 262 | 960.64 | 322 | 1179.90 | 372 | 1362.68 | 422 | 1545.27 | 472 | 1728.05 |
| 22 | 83.79 | 83 | 306.66 | 143 | 525.92 | 203 | 745.18 | 263 | 964.25 | 323 | 1183.51 | 373 | 1366.29 | 423 | 1548.88 | 473 | 1731.66 |
| 23 | 87.40 | 84 | 310.27 | 144 | 529.53 | 204 | 748.79 | 264 | 968.05 | 324 | 1187.31 | 374 | 1369.90 | 424 | 1552.68 | 474 | 1735.27 |
| 24 | 91.01 | 85 | 313.88 | 145 | 533.14 | 205 | 752.40 | 265 | 971.66 | 325 | 1190.92 | 375 | 1373.51 | 425 | 1556.29 | 475 | 1738.88 |
| 25 | 94.81 | 86 | 317.68 | 146 | 536.75 | 206 | 756.01 | 266 | 975.27 | 326 | 1194.53 | 376 | 1377.31 | 426 | 1559.90 | 476 | 1742.68 |
| 26 | 98.42 | 87 | 321.29 | 147 | 540.55 | 207 | 759.81 | 267 | 978.88 | 327 | 1198.14 | 377 | 1380.92 | 427 | 1563.51 | 477 | 1746.29 |
| 27 | 102.03 | 88 | 324.90 | 148 | 544.16 | 208 | 763.42 | 268 | 982.68 | 328 | 1201.75 | 378 | 1384.53 | 428 | 1567.31 | 478 | 1749.90 |
| 28 | 105.64 | 89 | 328.51 | 149 | 547.77 | 209 | 767.03 | 269 | 986.29 | 329 | 1205.55 | 379 | 1388.14 | 429 | 1570.92 | 479 | 1753.51 |
| 29 | 109.25 | 90 | 332.31 | 150 | 551.38 | 210 | 770.64 | 270 | 989.90 | 330 | 1209.16 | 380 | 1391.75 | 430 | 1574.53 | 480 | 1757.31 |
| 30 | 113.05 | 91 | 335.92 | 151 | 555.18 | 211 | 774.25 | 271 | 993.51 | 331 | 1212.77 | 381 | 1395.55 | 431 | 1578.14 | 481 | 1760.92 |
| 31 | 116.66 | 92 | 339.53 | 152 | 558.79 | 212 | 778.05 | 272 | 997.31 | 332 | 1216.38 | 382 | 1399.16 | 432 | 1581.75 | 482 | 1764.53 |
| 32 | 120.27 | 93 | 343.14 | 153 | 562.40 | 213 | 781.66 | 273 | 1000.92 | 333 | 1220.18 | 383 | 1402.77 | 433 | 1585.55 | 483 | 1768.14 |
| 33 | 123.88 | 94 | 346.75 | 154 | 566.01 | 214 | 785.27 | 274 | 1004.53 | 334 | 1223.79 | 384 | 1406.38 | 434 | 1589.16 | 484 | 1771.75 |
| 34 | 127.68 | 95 | 350.55 | 155 | 569.81 | 215 | 788.88 | 275 | 1008.14 | 335 | 1227.40 | 385 | 1410.18 | 435 | 1592.77 | 485 | 1775.55 |
| 35 | 131.29 | 96 | 354.16 | 156 | 573.42 | 216 | 792.68 | 276 | 1011.75 | 336 | 1231.01 | 386 | 1413.79 | 436 | 1596.38 | 486 | 1779.16 |
| 36 | 134.90 | 97 | 357.77 | 157 | 577.03 | 217 | 796.29 | 277 | 1015.55 | 337 | 1234.81 | 387 | 1417.40 | 437 | 1600.18 | 487 | 1782.77 |
| 37 | 138.51 | 98 | 361.38 | 158 | 580.64 | 218 | 799.90 | 278 | 1019.16 | 338 | 1238.42 | 388 | 1421.01 | 438 | 1603.79 | 488 | 1786.38 |
| 38 | 142.31 | 99 | 365.18 | 159 | 584.25 | 219 | 803.51 | 279 | 1022.77 | 339 | 1242.03 | 389 | 1424.81 | 439 | 1607.40 | 489 | 1790.18 |
| 39 | 145.92 | 100 | 368.79 | 160 | 588.05 | 220 | 807.31 | 280 | 1026.38 | 340 | 1245.64 | 390 | 1428.42 | 440 | 1611.01 | 490 | 1793.79 |
| 40 | 149.53 | 101 | 372.40 | 161 | 591.66 | 221 | 810.92 | 281 | 1030.18 | 341 | 1249.25 | 391 | 1432.03 | 441 | 1614.81 | 491 | 1797.40 |
| 41 | 153.14 | 102 | 376.01 | 162 | 595.27 | 222 | 814.53 | 282 | 1033.79 | 342 | 1253.05 | 392 | 1435.64 | 442 | 1618.42 | 492 | 1801.01 |
| 42 | 156.75 | 103 | 379.81 | 163 | 598.88 | 223 | 818.14 | 283 | 1037.40 | 343 | 1256.66 | 393 | 1439.25 | 443 | 1622.03 | 493 | 1804.81 |
| 43 | 160.55 | 104 | 383.42 | 164 | 602.68 | 224 | 821.75 | 284 | 1041.01 | 344 | 1260.27 | 394 | 1443.05 | 444 | 1625.64 | 494 | 1808.42 |
| 44 | 164.16 | 105 | 387.03 | 165 | 606.29 | 225 | 825.55 | 285 | 1044.81 | 345 | 1263.88 | 395 | 1446.66 | 445 | 1629.25 | 495 | 1812.03 |
| 45 | 167.77 | 106 | 390.64 | 166 | 609.90 | 226 | 829.16 | 286 | 1048.42 | 346 | 1267.68 | 396 | 1450.27 | 446 | 1633.05 | 496 | 1815.64 |
| 46 | 171.38 | 107 | 394.25 | 167 | 613.51 | 227 | 832.77 | 287 | 1052.03 | 347 | 1271.29 | 397 | 1453.88 | 447 | 1636.66 | 497 | 1819.25 |
| 47 | 175.18 | 108 | 398.05 | 168 | 617.31 | 228 | 836.38 | 288 | 1055.64 | 348 | 1274.90 | 398 | 1457.68 | 448 | 1640.27 | 498 | 1823.05 |
| 48 | 178.79 | 109 | 401.66 | 169 | 620.92 | 229 | 840.18 | 289 | 1059.25 | 349 | 1278.51 | 399 | 1461.29 | 449 | 1643.88 | 499 | 1826.66 |
| 49 | 182.40 | 110 | 405.27 | 170 | 624.53 | 230 | 843.79 | 290 | 1063.05 | 350 | 1282.31 | 400 | 1464.90 | 450 | 1647.68 | 500 | 1830.27 |
| 50 | 186.01 | 111 | 408.88 | 171 | 628.14 | 231 | 847.40 | 291 | 1066.66 | | | | | | | | |
| 51 | 189.81 | 112 | 412.68 | 172 | 631.75 | 232 | 851.01 | 292 | 1070.27 | | | | | | | | |
| 52 | 193.42 | 113 | 416.29 | 173 | 635.55 | 233 | 854.81 | 293 | 1073.88 | | | | | | | | |
| 53 | 197.03 | 114 | 419.90 | 174 | 639.16 | 234 | 858.42 | 294 | 1077.68 | | | | | | | | |
| 54 | 200.64 | 115 | 423.51 | 175 | 642.77 | 235 | 862.03 | 295 | 1081.29 | | | | | | | | |
| 55 | 204.25 | 116 | 427.31 | 176 | 646.38 | 236 | 865.64 | 296 | 1084.90 | | | | | | | | |
| 56 | 208.05 | 117 | 430.92 | 177 | 650.18 | 237 | 869.25 | 297 | 1088.51 | | | | | | | | |
| 57 | 211.66 | 118 | 434.53 | 178 | 653.79 | 238 | 873.05 | 298 | 1092.31 | | | | | | | | |
| 58 | 215.27 | 119 | 438.14 | 179 | 657.40 | 239 | 876.66 | 299 | 1095.92 | | | | | | | | |
| 59 | 218.88 | 120 | 441.75 | 180 | 661.01 | 240 | 880.27 | 300 | 1099.53 | | | | | | | | |
| 60 | 222.68 | | | | | | | | | | | | | | | | |

**Code more than 500**

1 Where the code is in the range 501 to 1000 inclusive:

   a. Subtract **500** from the code and use the balance of the code to obtain a pay adjustment figure from the table above.

   b. Add this pay adjustment figure to the figure given in the box alongside to obtain the figure of total pay adjustment to date *   | 1827.04 |

2 Where the code **exceeds 1000** follow the instructions on **page 3**.

22

**Tables A** - Pay Adjustment Tables        Aug 17 to Aug 23  **Week 20**

| Code | Total pay adjustment to date £ | Code | Total pay adjustment to date £ | Code | Total pay adjustment to date £ | Code | Total pay adjustment to date £ | Code | Total pay adjustment to date £ | Code | Total pay adjustment to date £ | Code | Total pay adjustment to date £ | Code | Total pay adjustment to date £ | Code | Total pay adjustment to date £ |
|---|---|---|---|---|---|---|---|---|---|---|---|---|---|---|---|---|---|
| 0 | NIL | 61 | 238.20 | 121 | 469.00 | 181 | 699.80 | 241 | 930.40 | 301 | 1161.20 | 351 | 1353.60 | 401 | 1545.80 | 451 | 1738.20 |
| 1 | 7.40 | 62 | 242.00 | 122 | 472.80 | 182 | 703.60 | 242 | 934.40 | 302 | 1165.00 | 352 | 1357.40 | 402 | 1549.80 | 452 | 1742.00 |
| 2 | 11.20 | 63 | 245.80 | 123 | 476.60 | 183 | 707.40 | 243 | 938.20 | 303 | 1169.00 | 353 | 1361.20 | 403 | 1553.60 | 453 | 1745.80 |
| 3 | 15.00 | 64 | 249.80 | 124 | 480.40 | 184 | 711.20 | 244 | 942.00 | 304 | 1172.80 | 354 | 1365.00 | 404 | 1557.40 | 454 | 1749.80 |
| 4 | 19.00 | 65 | 253.60 | 125 | 484.40 | 185 | 715.00 | 245 | 945.80 | 305 | 1176.60 | 355 | 1369.00 | 405 | 1561.20 | 455 | 1753.60 |
| 5 | 22.80 | 66 | 257.40 | 126 | 488.20 | 186 | 719.00 | 246 | 949.80 | 306 | 1180.40 | 356 | 1372.80 | 406 | 1565.00 | 456 | 1757.40 |
| 6 | 26.60 | 67 | 261.20 | 127 | 492.00 | 187 | 722.80 | 247 | 953.60 | 307 | 1184.40 | 357 | 1376.60 | 407 | 1569.00 | 457 | 1761.20 |
| 7 | 30.40 | 68 | 265.00 | 128 | 495.80 | 188 | 726.60 | 248 | 957.40 | 308 | 1188.20 | 358 | 1380.40 | 408 | 1572.80 | 458 | 1765.00 |
| 8 | 34.40 | 69 | 269.00 | 129 | 499.80 | 189 | 730.40 | 249 | 961.20 | 309 | 1192.00 | 359 | 1384.40 | 409 | 1576.60 | 459 | 1769.00 |
| 9 | 38.20 | 70 | 272.80 | 130 | 503.60 | 190 | 734.40 | 250 | 965.00 | 310 | 1195.80 | 360 | 1388.20 | 410 | 1580.40 | 460 | 1772.80 |
| 10 | 42.00 | 71 | 276.60 | 131 | 507.40 | 191 | 738.20 | 251 | 969.00 | 311 | 1199.80 | 361 | 1392.00 | 411 | 1584.40 | 461 | 1776.60 |
| 11 | 45.80 | 72 | 280.40 | 132 | 511.20 | 192 | 742.00 | 252 | 972.80 | 312 | 1203.60 | 362 | 1395.80 | 412 | 1588.20 | 462 | 1780.40 |
| 12 | 49.80 | 73 | 284.40 | 133 | 515.00 | 193 | 745.80 | 253 | 976.60 | 313 | 1207.40 | 363 | 1399.80 | 413 | 1592.00 | 463 | 1784.40 |
| 13 | 53.60 | 74 | 288.20 | 134 | 519.00 | 194 | 749.80 | 254 | 980.40 | 314 | 1211.20 | 364 | 1403.60 | 414 | 1595.80 | 464 | 1788.20 |
| 14 | 57.40 | 75 | 292.00 | 135 | 522.80 | 195 | 753.60 | 255 | 984.40 | 315 | 1215.00 | 365 | 1407.40 | 415 | 1599.80 | 465 | 1792.00 |
| 15 | 61.20 | 76 | 295.80 | 136 | 526.60 | 196 | 757.40 | 256 | 988.20 | 316 | 1219.00 | 366 | 1411.20 | 416 | 1603.60 | 466 | 1795.80 |
| 16 | 65.00 | 77 | 299.80 | 137 | 530.40 | 197 | 761.20 | 257 | 992.00 | 317 | 1222.80 | 367 | 1415.00 | 417 | 1607.40 | 467 | 1799.80 |
| 17 | 69.00 | 78 | 303.60 | 138 | 534.40 | 198 | 765.00 | 258 | 995.80 | 318 | 1226.60 | 368 | 1419.00 | 418 | 1611.20 | 468 | 1803.60 |
| 18 | 72.80 | 79 | 307.40 | 139 | 538.20 | 199 | 769.00 | 259 | 999.80 | 319 | 1230.40 | 369 | 1422.80 | 419 | 1615.00 | 469 | 1807.40 |
| 19 | 76.60 | 80 | 311.20 | 140 | 542.00 | 200 | 772.80 | 260 | 1003.60 | 320 | 1234.40 | 370 | 1426.60 | 420 | 1619.00 | 470 | 1811.20 |
| 20 | 80.40 | 81 | 315.00 | 141 | 545.80 | 201 | 776.60 | 261 | 1007.40 | 321 | 1238.20 | 371 | 1430.40 | 421 | 1622.80 | 471 | 1815.00 |
| 21 | 84.40 | 82 | 319.00 | 142 | 549.80 | 202 | 780.40 | 262 | 1011.20 | 322 | 1242.00 | 372 | 1434.40 | 422 | 1626.60 | 472 | 1819.00 |
| 22 | 88.20 | 83 | 322.80 | 143 | 553.60 | 203 | 784.40 | 263 | 1015.00 | 323 | 1245.80 | 373 | 1438.20 | 423 | 1630.40 | 473 | 1822.80 |
| 23 | 92.00 | 84 | 326.60 | 144 | 557.40 | 204 | 788.20 | 264 | 1019.00 | 324 | 1249.80 | 374 | 1442.00 | 424 | 1634.40 | 474 | 1826.60 |
| 24 | 95.80 | 85 | 330.40 | 145 | 561.20 | 205 | 792.00 | 265 | 1022.80 | 325 | 1253.60 | 375 | 1445.80 | 425 | 1638.20 | 475 | 1830.40 |
| 25 | 99.80 | 86 | 334.40 | 146 | 565.00 | 206 | 795.80 | 266 | 1026.60 | 326 | 1257.40 | 376 | 1449.80 | 426 | 1642.00 | 476 | 1834.40 |
| 26 | 103.60 | 87 | 338.20 | 147 | 569.00 | 207 | 799.80 | 267 | 1030.40 | 327 | 1261.20 | 377 | 1453.60 | 427 | 1645.80 | 477 | 1838.20 |
| 27 | 107.40 | 88 | 342.00 | 148 | 572.80 | 208 | 803.60 | 268 | 1034.40 | 328 | 1265.00 | 378 | 1457.40 | 428 | 1649.80 | 478 | 1842.00 |
| 28 | 111.20 | 89 | 345.80 | 149 | 576.60 | 209 | 807.40 | 269 | 1038.20 | 329 | 1269.00 | 379 | 1461.20 | 429 | 1653.60 | 479 | 1845.80 |
| 29 | 115.00 | 90 | 349.80 | 150 | 580.40 | 210 | 811.20 | 270 | 1042.00 | 330 | 1272.80 | 380 | 1465.00 | 430 | 1657.40 | 480 | 1849.80 |
| 30 | 119.00 | 91 | 353.60 | 151 | 584.40 | 211 | 815.00 | 271 | 1045.80 | 331 | 1276.60 | 381 | 1469.00 | 431 | 1661.20 | 481 | 1853.60 |
| 31 | 122.80 | 92 | 357.40 | 152 | 588.20 | 212 | 819.00 | 272 | 1049.80 | 332 | 1280.40 | 382 | 1472.80 | 432 | 1665.00 | 482 | 1857.40 |
| 32 | 126.60 | 93 | 361.20 | 153 | 592.00 | 213 | 822.80 | 273 | 1053.60 | 333 | 1284.40 | 383 | 1476.60 | 433 | 1669.00 | 483 | 1861.20 |
| 33 | 130.40 | 94 | 365.00 | 154 | 595.80 | 214 | 826.60 | 274 | 1057.40 | 334 | 1288.20 | 384 | 1480.40 | 434 | 1672.80 | 484 | 1865.00 |
| 34 | 134.40 | 95 | 369.00 | 155 | 599.80 | 215 | 830.40 | 275 | 1061.20 | 335 | 1292.00 | 385 | 1484.40 | 435 | 1676.60 | 485 | 1869.00 |
| 35 | 138.20 | 96 | 372.80 | 156 | 603.60 | 216 | 834.40 | 276 | 1065.00 | 336 | 1295.80 | 386 | 1488.20 | 436 | 1680.40 | 486 | 1872.80 |
| 36 | 142.00 | 97 | 376.60 | 157 | 607.40 | 217 | 838.20 | 277 | 1069.00 | 337 | 1299.80 | 387 | 1492.00 | 437 | 1684.40 | 487 | 1876.60 |
| 37 | 145.80 | 98 | 380.40 | 158 | 611.20 | 218 | 842.00 | 278 | 1072.80 | 338 | 1303.60 | 388 | 1495.80 | 438 | 1688.20 | 488 | 1880.40 |
| 38 | 149.80 | 99 | 384.40 | 159 | 615.00 | 219 | 845.80 | 279 | 1076.60 | 339 | 1307.40 | 389 | 1499.80 | 439 | 1692.00 | 489 | 1884.40 |
| 39 | 153.60 | 100 | 388.20 | 160 | 619.00 | 220 | 849.80 | 280 | 1080.40 | 340 | 1311.20 | 390 | 1503.60 | 440 | 1695.80 | 490 | 1888.20 |
| 40 | 157.40 | 101 | 392.00 | 161 | 622.80 | 221 | 853.60 | 281 | 1084.40 | 341 | 1315.00 | 391 | 1507.40 | 441 | 1699.80 | 491 | 1892.00 |
| 41 | 161.20 | 102 | 395.80 | 162 | 626.60 | 222 | 857.40 | 282 | 1088.20 | 342 | 1319.00 | 392 | 1511.20 | 442 | 1703.60 | 492 | 1895.80 |
| 42 | 165.00 | 103 | 399.80 | 163 | 630.40 | 223 | 861.20 | 283 | 1092.00 | 343 | 1322.80 | 393 | 1515.00 | 443 | 1707.40 | 493 | 1899.80 |
| 43 | 169.00 | 104 | 403.60 | 164 | 634.40 | 224 | 865.00 | 284 | 1095.80 | 344 | 1326.60 | 394 | 1519.00 | 444 | 1711.20 | 494 | 1903.60 |
| 44 | 172.80 | 105 | 407.40 | 165 | 638.20 | 225 | 869.00 | 285 | 1099.80 | 345 | 1330.40 | 395 | 1522.80 | 445 | 1715.00 | 495 | 1907.40 |
| 45 | 176.60 | 106 | 411.20 | 166 | 642.00 | 226 | 872.80 | 286 | 1103.60 | 346 | 1334.40 | 396 | 1526.60 | 446 | 1719.00 | 496 | 1911.20 |
| 46 | 180.40 | 107 | 415.00 | 167 | 645.80 | 227 | 876.60 | 287 | 1107.40 | 347 | 1338.20 | 397 | 1530.40 | 447 | 1722.80 | 497 | 1915.00 |
| 47 | 184.40 | 108 | 419.00 | 168 | 649.80 | 228 | 880.40 | 288 | 1111.20 | 348 | 1342.00 | 398 | 1534.40 | 448 | 1726.60 | 498 | 1919.00 |
| 48 | 188.20 | 109 | 422.80 | 169 | 653.60 | 229 | 884.40 | 289 | 1115.00 | 349 | 1345.80 | 399 | 1538.20 | 449 | 1730.40 | 499 | 1922.80 |
| 49 | 192.00 | 110 | 426.60 | 170 | 657.40 | 230 | 888.20 | 290 | 1119.00 | 350 | 1349.80 | 400 | 1542.00 | 450 | 1734.40 | 500 | 1926.60 |
| 50 | 195.80 | | | | | | | | | | | | | | | | |
| 51 | 199.80 | 111 | 430.40 | 171 | 661.20 | 231 | 892.00 | 291 | 1122.80 | | | | | | | | |
| 52 | 203.60 | 112 | 434.40 | 172 | 665.00 | 232 | 895.80 | 292 | 1126.60 | | | | | | | | |
| 53 | 207.40 | 113 | 438.20 | 173 | 669.00 | 233 | 899.80 | 293 | 1130.40 | | | | | | | | |
| 54 | 211.20 | 114 | 442.00 | 174 | 672.80 | 234 | 903.60 | 294 | 1134.40 | | | | | | | | |
| 55 | 215.00 | 115 | 445.80 | 175 | 676.60 | 235 | 907.40 | 295 | 1138.20 | | | | | | | | |
| 56 | 219.00 | 116 | 449.80 | 176 | 680.40 | 236 | 911.20 | 296 | 1142.00 | | | | | | | | |
| 57 | 222.80 | 117 | 453.60 | 177 | 684.40 | 237 | 915.00 | 297 | 1145.80 | | | | | | | | |
| 58 | 226.60 | 118 | 457.40 | 178 | 688.20 | 238 | 919.00 | 298 | 1149.80 | | | | | | | | |
| 59 | 230.40 | 119 | 461.20 | 179 | 692.00 | 239 | 922.80 | 299 | 1153.60 | | | | | | | | |
| 60 | 234.40 | 120 | 465.00 | 180 | 695.80 | 240 | 926.60 | 300 | 1157.40 | | | | | | | | |

### Code more than 500

1 Where the code is in the range 501 to **1000** inclusive:

  a. Subtract **500** from the code and use the balance of the code to obtain a pay adjustment figure from the table above.

  b. Add this pay adjustment figure to the figure given in the box alongside to obtain the figure of total pay adjustment to date *  | **1923.20** |

2 Where the code **exceeds 1000** follow the instructions on **page 3**.

23

**Week 21**  Aug 24 to Aug 30                    **Tables A** - Pay Adjustment Tables

| Code | Total pay adjustment to date | Code | Total pay adjustment to date | Code | Total pay adjustment to date | Code | Total pay adjustment to date | Code | Total pay adjustment to date | Code | Total pay adjustment to date | Code | Total pay adjustment to date | Code | Total pay adjustment to date | Code | Total pay adjustment to date |
|---|---|---|---|---|---|---|---|---|---|---|---|---|---|---|---|---|---|
| | £ | | £ | | £ | | £ | | £ | | £ | | £ | | £ | | £ |
| 0 | NIL | | | | | | | | | | | | | | | | |
| 1 | 7.77 | 61 | 250.11 | 121 | 492.45 | 181 | 734.79 | 241 | 976.92 | 301 | 1219.26 | 351 | 1421.28 | 401 | 1623.09 | 451 | 1825.11 |
| 2 | 11.76 | 62 | 254.10 | 122 | 496.44 | 182 | 738.78 | 242 | 981.12 | 302 | 1223.25 | 352 | 1425.27 | 402 | 1627.29 | 452 | 1829.10 |
| 3 | 15.75 | 63 | 258.09 | 123 | 500.43 | 183 | 742.77 | 243 | 985.11 | 303 | 1227.45 | 353 | 1429.26 | 403 | 1631.28 | 453 | 1833.09 |
| 4 | 19.95 | 64 | 262.29 | 124 | 504.42 | 184 | 746.76 | 244 | 989.10 | 304 | 1231.44 | 354 | 1433.25 | 404 | 1635.27 | 454 | 1837.29 |
| 5 | 23.94 | 65 | 266.28 | 125 | 508.62 | 185 | 750.75 | 245 | 993.09 | 305 | 1235.43 | 355 | 1437.45 | 405 | 1639.26 | 455 | 1841.28 |
| 6 | 27.93 | 66 | 270.27 | 126 | 512.61 | 186 | 754.95 | 246 | 997.29 | 306 | 1239.42 | 356 | 1441.44 | 406 | 1643.25 | 456 | 1845.27 |
| 7 | 31.92 | 67 | 274.26 | 127 | 516.60 | 187 | 758.94 | 247 | 1001.28 | 307 | 1243.62 | 357 | 1445.43 | 407 | 1647.45 | 457 | 1849.26 |
| 8 | 36.12 | 68 | 278.25 | 128 | 520.59 | 188 | 762.93 | 248 | 1005.27 | 308 | 1247.61 | 358 | 1449.42 | 408 | 1651.44 | 458 | 1853.25 |
| 9 | 40.11 | 69 | 282.45 | 129 | 524.79 | 189 | 766.92 | 249 | 1009.26 | 309 | 1251.60 | 359 | 1453.62 | 409 | 1655.43 | 459 | 1857.45 |
| 10 | 44.10 | 70 | 286.44 | 130 | 528.78 | 190 | 771.12 | 250 | 1013.25 | 310 | 1255.59 | 360 | 1457.61 | 410 | 1659.42 | 460 | 1861.44 |
| 11 | 48.09 | 71 | 290.43 | 131 | 532.77 | 191 | 775.11 | 251 | 1017.45 | 311 | 1259.79 | 361 | 1461.60 | 411 | 1663.62 | 461 | 1865.43 |
| 12 | 52.29 | 72 | 294.42 | 132 | 536.76 | 192 | 779.10 | 252 | 1021.44 | 312 | 1263.78 | 362 | 1465.59 | 412 | 1667.61 | 462 | 1869.42 |
| 13 | 56.28 | 73 | 298.62 | 133 | 540.75 | 193 | 783.09 | 253 | 1025.43 | 313 | 1267.77 | 363 | 1469.79 | 413 | 1671.60 | 463 | 1873.62 |
| 14 | 60.27 | 74 | 302.61 | 134 | 544.95 | 194 | 787.29 | 254 | 1029.42 | 314 | 1271.76 | 364 | 1473.78 | 414 | 1675.59 | 464 | 1877.61 |
| 15 | 64.26 | 75 | 306.60 | 135 | 548.94 | 195 | 791.28 | 255 | 1033.62 | 315 | 1275.95 | 365 | 1477.77 | 415 | 1679.79 | 465 | 1881.60 |
| 16 | 68.25 | 76 | 310.59 | 136 | 552.93 | 196 | 795.27 | 256 | 1037.61 | 316 | 1279.95 | 366 | 1481.76 | 416 | 1683.78 | 466 | 1885.59 |
| 17 | 72.45 | 77 | 314.79 | 137 | 556.92 | 197 | 799.26 | 257 | 1041.60 | 317 | 1283.94 | 367 | 1485.75 | 417 | 1687.77 | 467 | 1889.79 |
| 18 | 76.44 | 78 | 318.78 | 138 | 561.12 | 198 | 803.25 | 258 | 1045.59 | 318 | 1287.93 | 368 | 1489.95 | 418 | 1691.76 | 468 | 1893.78 |
| 19 | 80.43 | 79 | 322.77 | 139 | 565.11 | 199 | 807.45 | 259 | 1049.79 | 319 | 1291.92 | 369 | 1493.94 | 419 | 1695.75 | 469 | 1897.77 |
| 20 | 84.42 | 80 | 326.76 | 140 | 569.10 | 200 | 811.44 | 260 | 1053.78 | 320 | 1296.12 | 370 | 1497.93 | 420 | 1699.95 | 470 | 1901.76 |
| 21 | 88.62 | 81 | 330.75 | 141 | 573.09 | 201 | 815.43 | 261 | 1057.77 | 321 | 1300.11 | 371 | 1501.92 | 421 | 1703.94 | 471 | 1905.75 |
| 22 | 92.61 | 82 | 334.95 | 142 | 577.29 | 202 | 819.42 | 262 | 1061.76 | 322 | 1304.10 | 372 | 1506.12 | 422 | 1707.93 | 472 | 1909.95 |
| 23 | 96.60 | 83 | 338.94 | 143 | 581.28 | 203 | 823.62 | 263 | 1065.75 | 323 | 1308.09 | 373 | 1510.11 | 423 | 1711.92 | 473 | 1913.94 |
| 24 | 100.59 | 84 | 342.93 | 144 | 585.27 | 204 | 827.61 | 264 | 1069.95 | 324 | 1312.29 | 374 | 1514.10 | 424 | 1716.12 | 474 | 1917.93 |
| 25 | 104.79 | 85 | 346.92 | 145 | 589.26 | 205 | 831.60 | 265 | 1073.94 | 325 | 1316.28 | 375 | 1518.09 | 425 | 1720.11 | 475 | 1921.92 |
| 26 | 108.78 | 86 | 351.12 | 146 | 593.25 | 206 | 835.59 | 266 | 1077.93 | 326 | 1320.27 | 376 | 1522.29 | 426 | 1724.10 | 476 | 1926.12 |
| 27 | 112.77 | 87 | 355.11 | 147 | 597.45 | 207 | 839.79 | 267 | 1081.92 | 327 | 1324.26 | 377 | 1526.28 | 427 | 1728.09 | 477 | 1930.11 |
| 28 | 116.76 | 88 | 359.10 | 148 | 601.44 | 208 | 843.78 | 268 | 1086.12 | 328 | 1328.25 | 378 | 1530.27 | 428 | 1732.29 | 478 | 1934.10 |
| 29 | 120.75 | 89 | 363.09 | 149 | 605.43 | 209 | 847.77 | 269 | 1090.11 | 329 | 1332.45 | 379 | 1534.26 | 429 | 1736.28 | 479 | 1938.09 |
| 30 | 124.95 | 90 | 367.29 | 150 | 609.42 | 210 | 851.76 | 270 | 1094.10 | 330 | 1336.44 | 380 | 1538.25 | 430 | 1740.27 | 480 | 1942.29 |
| 31 | 128.94 | 91 | 371.28 | 151 | 613.62 | 211 | 855.75 | 271 | 1098.09 | 331 | 1340.43 | 381 | 1542.45 | 431 | 1744.26 | 481 | 1946.28 |
| 32 | 132.93 | 92 | 375.27 | 152 | 617.61 | 212 | 859.95 | 272 | 1102.29 | 332 | 1344.42 | 382 | 1546.44 | 432 | 1748.25 | 482 | 1950.27 |
| 33 | 136.92 | 93 | 379.26 | 153 | 621.60 | 213 | 863.94 | 273 | 1106.28 | 333 | 1348.62 | 383 | 1550.43 | 433 | 1752.45 | 483 | 1954.26 |
| 34 | 141.12 | 94 | 383.25 | 154 | 625.59 | 214 | 867.93 | 274 | 1110.27 | 334 | 1352.61 | 384 | 1554.42 | 434 | 1756.44 | 484 | 1958.25 |
| 35 | 145.11 | 95 | 387.45 | 155 | 629.79 | 215 | 871.92 | 275 | 1114.26 | 335 | 1356.60 | 385 | 1558.62 | 435 | 1760.43 | 485 | 1962.45 |
| 36 | 149.10 | 96 | 391.44 | 156 | 633.78 | 216 | 876.12 | 276 | 1118.25 | 336 | 1360.59 | 386 | 1562.61 | 436 | 1764.42 | 486 | 1966.44 |
| 37 | 153.09 | 97 | 395.43 | 157 | 637.77 | 217 | 880.11 | 277 | 1122.45 | 337 | 1364.79 | 387 | 1566.60 | 437 | 1768.62 | 487 | 1970.43 |
| 38 | 157.29 | 98 | 399.42 | 158 | 641.76 | 218 | 884.10 | 278 | 1126.44 | 338 | 1368.78 | 388 | 1570.59 | 438 | 1772.61 | 488 | 1974.42 |
| 39 | 161.28 | 99 | 403.62 | 159 | 645.75 | 219 | 888.09 | 279 | 1130.43 | 339 | 1372.77 | 389 | 1574.79 | 439 | 1776.60 | 489 | 1978.62 |
| 40 | 165.27 | 100 | 407.61 | 160 | 649.95 | 220 | 892.29 | 280 | 1134.42 | 340 | 1376.76 | 390 | 1578.78 | 440 | 1780.59 | 490 | 1982.61 |
| 41 | 169.26 | 101 | 411.60 | 161 | 653.94 | 221 | 896.28 | 281 | 1138.62 | 341 | 1380.75 | 391 | 1582.77 | 441 | 1784.79 | 491 | 1986.60 |
| 42 | 173.25 | 102 | 415.59 | 162 | 657.93 | 222 | 900.27 | 282 | 1142.61 | 342 | 1384.95 | 392 | 1586.76 | 442 | 1788.78 | 492 | 1990.59 |
| 43 | 177.45 | 103 | 419.79 | 163 | 661.92 | 223 | 904.26 | 283 | 1146.60 | 343 | 1388.94 | 393 | 1590.75 | 443 | 1792.77 | 493 | 1994.79 |
| 44 | 181.44 | 104 | 423.78 | 164 | 666.12 | 224 | 908.25 | 284 | 1150.59 | 344 | 1392.93 | 394 | 1594.95 | 444 | 1796.76 | 494 | 1998.78 |
| 45 | 185.43 | 105 | 427.77 | 165 | 670.11 | 225 | 912.45 | 285 | 1154.79 | 345 | 1396.92 | 395 | 1598.94 | 445 | 1800.75 | 495 | 2002.77 |
| 46 | 189.42 | 106 | 431.76 | 166 | 674.10 | 226 | 916.44 | 286 | 1158.78 | 346 | 1401.12 | 396 | 1602.93 | 446 | 1804.95 | 496 | 2006.76 |
| 47 | 193.62 | 107 | 435.95 | 167 | 678.09 | 227 | 920.43 | 287 | 1162.77 | 347 | 1405.11 | 397 | 1606.92 | 447 | 1808.94 | 497 | 2010.75 |
| 48 | 197.61 | 108 | 439.95 | 168 | 682.29 | 228 | 924.42 | 288 | 1166.76 | 348 | 1409.10 | 398 | 1611.12 | 448 | 1812.93 | 498 | 2014.95 |
| 49 | 201.60 | 109 | 443.94 | 169 | 686.28 | 229 | 928.62 | 289 | 1170.75 | 349 | 1413.09 | 399 | 1615.11 | 449 | 1816.92 | 499 | 2018.94 |
| 50 | 205.59 | 110 | 447.93 | 170 | 690.27 | 230 | 932.61 | 290 | 1174.95 | 350 | 1417.29 | 400 | 1619.10 | 450 | 1821.12 | 500 | 2022.93 |
| 51 | 209.79 | 111 | 451.92 | 171 | 694.26 | 231 | 936.60 | 291 | 1178.94 | | | | | | | | |
| 52 | 213.78 | 112 | 456.12 | 172 | 698.25 | 232 | 940.59 | 292 | 1182.93 | | | | | | | | |
| 53 | 217.77 | 113 | 460.11 | 173 | 702.45 | 233 | 944.79 | 293 | 1186.92 | | | | | | | | |
| 54 | 221.76 | 114 | 464.10 | 174 | 706.44 | 234 | 948.78 | 294 | 1191.12 | | | | | | | | |
| 55 | 225.75 | 115 | 468.09 | 175 | 710.43 | 235 | 952.77 | 295 | 1195.11 | | | | | | | | |
| 56 | 229.95 | 116 | 472.29 | 176 | 714.42 | 236 | 956.76 | 296 | 1199.10 | | | | | | | | |
| 57 | 233.94 | 117 | 476.28 | 177 | 718.62 | 237 | 960.75 | 297 | 1203.09 | | | | | | | | |
| 58 | 237.93 | 118 | 480.27 | 178 | 722.61 | 238 | 964.95 | 298 | 1207.29 | | | | | | | | |
| 59 | 241.92 | 119 | 484.26 | 179 | 726.60 | 239 | 968.94 | 299 | 1211.28 | | | | | | | | |
| 60 | 246.12 | 120 | 488.25 | 180 | 730.59 | 240 | 972.93 | 300 | 1215.27 | | | | | | | | |

**Code more than 500**

1  Where the code is in the range **501** to **1000** inclusive:

   a. Subtract **500** from the code and use the balance of the code to obtain a pay adjustment figure from the table above.

   b. Add this pay adjustment figure to the figure given in the box alongside to obtain the figure of total pay adjustment to date *   | 2019.36 |

2  Where the code **exceeds 1000** follow the instructions on **page 3**.

24

# Tables A - Pay Adjustment Tables

Aug 31 to Sep 6  **Week 22**

| Code | Total pay adjustment to date | Code | Total pay adjustment to date | Code | Total pay adjustment to date | Code | Total pay adjustment to date | Code | Total pay adjustment to date | Code | Total pay adjustment to date | Code | Total pay adjustment to date | Code | Total pay adjustment to date | Code | Total pay adjustment to date |
|---|---|---|---|---|---|---|---|---|---|---|---|---|---|---|---|---|---|
| | £ | | £ | | £ | | £ | | £ | | £ | | £ | | £ | | £ |
| 0 | NIL | | | | | | | | | | | | | | | | |
| 1 | 8.14 | 61 | 262.02 | 121 | 515.90 | 181 | 769.78 | 241 | 1023.44 | 301 | 1277.32 | 351 | 1488.96 | 401 | 1700.38 | 451 | 1912.02 |
| 2 | 12.32 | 62 | 266.20 | 122 | 520.08 | 182 | 773.96 | 242 | 1027.84 | 302 | 1281.50 | 352 | 1493.14 | 402 | 1704.78 | 452 | 1916.20 |
| 3 | 16.50 | 63 | 270.38 | 123 | 524.26 | 183 | 778.14 | 243 | 1032.02 | 303 | 1285.90 | 353 | 1497.32 | 403 | 1708.96 | 453 | 1920.38 |
| 4 | 20.90 | 64 | 274.78 | 124 | 528.44 | 184 | 782.32 | 244 | 1036.20 | 304 | 1290.08 | 354 | 1501.50 | 404 | 1713.14 | 454 | 1924.78 |
| 5 | 25.08 | 65 | 278.96 | 125 | 532.84 | 185 | 786.50 | 245 | 1040.38 | 305 | 1294.26 | 355 | 1505.90 | 405 | 1717.32 | 455 | 1928.96 |
| 6 | 29.26 | 66 | 283.14 | 126 | 537.02 | 186 | 790.90 | 246 | 1044.78 | 306 | 1298.44 | 356 | 1510.08 | 406 | 1721.50 | 456 | 1933.14 |
| 7 | 33.44 | 67 | 287.32 | 127 | 541.20 | 187 | 795.08 | 247 | 1048.96 | 307 | 1302.84 | 357 | 1514.26 | 407 | 1725.90 | 457 | 1937.32 |
| 8 | 37.84 | 68 | 291.50 | 128 | 545.38 | 188 | 799.26 | 248 | 1053.14 | 308 | 1307.02 | 358 | 1518.44 | 408 | 1730.08 | 458 | 1941.50 |
| 9 | 42.02 | 69 | 295.90 | 129 | 549.78 | 189 | 803.44 | 249 | 1057.32 | 309 | 1311.20 | 359 | 1522.84 | 409 | 1734.26 | 459 | 1945.90 |
| 10 | 46.20 | 70 | 300.08 | 130 | 553.96 | 190 | 807.84 | 250 | 1061.50 | 310 | 1315.38 | 360 | 1527.02 | 410 | 1738.44 | 460 | 1950.08 |
| 11 | 50.38 | 71 | 304.26 | 131 | 558.14 | 191 | 812.02 | 251 | 1065.90 | 311 | 1319.78 | 361 | 1531.20 | 411 | 1742.84 | 461 | 1954.26 |
| 12 | 54.78 | 72 | 308.44 | 132 | 562.32 | 192 | 816.20 | 252 | 1070.08 | 312 | 1323.96 | 362 | 1535.38 | 412 | 1747.02 | 462 | 1958.44 |
| 13 | 58.96 | 73 | 312.84 | 133 | 566.50 | 193 | 820.38 | 253 | 1074.26 | 313 | 1328.14 | 363 | 1539.78 | 413 | 1751.20 | 463 | 1962.84 |
| 14 | 63.14 | 74 | 317.02 | 134 | 570.90 | 194 | 824.78 | 254 | 1078.44 | 314 | 1332.32 | 364 | 1543.96 | 414 | 1755.38 | 464 | 1967.02 |
| 15 | 67.32 | 75 | 321.20 | 135 | 575.08 | 195 | 828.96 | 255 | 1082.84 | 315 | 1336.50 | 365 | 1548.14 | 415 | 1759.78 | 465 | 1971.20 |
| 16 | 71.50 | 76 | 325.38 | 136 | 579.26 | 196 | 833.14 | 256 | 1087.02 | 316 | 1340.90 | 366 | 1552.32 | 416 | 1763.96 | 466 | 1975.38 |
| 17 | 75.90 | 77 | 329.78 | 137 | 583.44 | 197 | 837.32 | 257 | 1091.20 | 317 | 1345.08 | 367 | 1556.50 | 417 | 1768.14 | 467 | 1979.78 |
| 18 | 80.08 | 78 | 333.96 | 138 | 587.84 | 198 | 841.50 | 258 | 1095.38 | 318 | 1349.26 | 368 | 1560.90 | 418 | 1772.32 | 468 | 1983.96 |
| 19 | 84.26 | 79 | 338.14 | 139 | 592.02 | 199 | 845.90 | 259 | 1099.78 | 319 | 1353.44 | 369 | 1565.08 | 419 | 1776.50 | 469 | 1988.14 |
| 20 | 88.44 | 80 | 342.32 | 140 | 596.20 | 200 | 850.08 | 260 | 1103.96 | 320 | 1357.84 | 370 | 1569.26 | 420 | 1780.90 | 470 | 1992.32 |
| 21 | 92.84 | 81 | 346.50 | 141 | 600.38 | 201 | 854.26 | 261 | 1108.14 | 321 | 1362.02 | 371 | 1573.44 | 421 | 1785.08 | 471 | 1996.50 |
| 22 | 97.02 | 82 | 350.90 | 142 | 604.78 | 202 | 858.44 | 262 | 1112.32 | 322 | 1366.20 | 372 | 1577.84 | 422 | 1789.26 | 472 | 2000.90 |
| 23 | 101.20 | 83 | 355.08 | 143 | 608.96 | 203 | 862.84 | 263 | 1116.50 | 323 | 1370.38 | 373 | 1582.02 | 423 | 1793.44 | 473 | 2005.08 |
| 24 | 105.38 | 84 | 359.26 | 144 | 613.14 | 204 | 867.02 | 264 | 1120.90 | 324 | 1374.78 | 374 | 1586.20 | 424 | 1797.84 | 474 | 2009.26 |
| 25 | 109.78 | 85 | 363.44 | 145 | 617.32 | 205 | 871.20 | 265 | 1125.08 | 325 | 1378.96 | 375 | 1590.38 | 425 | 1802.02 | 475 | 2013.44 |
| 26 | 113.96 | 86 | 367.84 | 146 | 621.50 | 206 | 875.38 | 266 | 1129.26 | 326 | 1383.14 | 376 | 1594.78 | 426 | 1806.20 | 476 | 2017.84 |
| 27 | 118.14 | 87 | 372.02 | 147 | 625.90 | 207 | 879.78 | 267 | 1133.44 | 327 | 1387.32 | 377 | 1598.96 | 427 | 1810.38 | 477 | 2022.02 |
| 28 | 122.32 | 88 | 376.20 | 148 | 630.08 | 208 | 883.96 | 268 | 1137.84 | 328 | 1391.50 | 378 | 1603.14 | 428 | 1814.78 | 478 | 2026.20 |
| 29 | 126.50 | 89 | 380.38 | 149 | 634.26 | 209 | 888.14 | 269 | 1142.02 | 329 | 1395.90 | 379 | 1607.32 | 429 | 1818.96 | 479 | 2030.38 |
| 30 | 130.90 | 90 | 384.78 | 150 | 638.44 | 210 | 892.32 | 270 | 1146.20 | 330 | 1400.08 | 380 | 1611.50 | 430 | 1823.14 | 480 | 2034.78 |
| 31 | 135.08 | 91 | 388.96 | 151 | 642.84 | 211 | 896.50 | 271 | 1150.38 | 331 | 1404.26 | 381 | 1615.90 | 431 | 1827.32 | 481 | 2038.96 |
| 32 | 139.26 | 92 | 393.14 | 152 | 647.02 | 212 | 900.90 | 272 | 1154.78 | 332 | 1408.44 | 382 | 1620.08 | 432 | 1831.50 | 482 | 2043.14 |
| 33 | 143.44 | 93 | 397.32 | 153 | 651.20 | 213 | 905.08 | 273 | 1158.96 | 333 | 1412.84 | 383 | 1624.26 | 433 | 1835.90 | 483 | 2047.32 |
| 34 | 147.84 | 94 | 401.50 | 154 | 655.38 | 214 | 909.26 | 274 | 1163.14 | 334 | 1417.02 | 384 | 1628.44 | 434 | 1840.08 | 484 | 2051.50 |
| 35 | 152.02 | 95 | 405.90 | 155 | 659.78 | 215 | 913.44 | 275 | 1167.32 | 335 | 1421.20 | 385 | 1632.84 | 435 | 1844.26 | 485 | 2055.90 |
| 36 | 156.20 | 96 | 410.08 | 156 | 663.96 | 216 | 917.84 | 276 | 1171.50 | 336 | 1425.38 | 386 | 1637.02 | 436 | 1848.44 | 486 | 2060.08 |
| 37 | 160.38 | 97 | 414.26 | 157 | 668.14 | 217 | 922.02 | 277 | 1175.90 | 337 | 1429.78 | 387 | 1641.20 | 437 | 1852.84 | 487 | 2064.26 |
| 38 | 164.78 | 98 | 418.44 | 158 | 672.32 | 218 | 926.20 | 278 | 1180.08 | 338 | 1433.96 | 388 | 1645.38 | 438 | 1857.02 | 488 | 2068.44 |
| 39 | 168.96 | 99 | 422.84 | 159 | 676.50 | 219 | 930.38 | 279 | 1184.26 | 339 | 1438.14 | 389 | 1649.78 | 439 | 1861.20 | 489 | 2072.84 |
| 40 | 173.14 | 100 | 427.02 | 160 | 680.90 | 220 | 934.78 | 280 | 1188.44 | 340 | 1442.32 | 390 | 1653.96 | 440 | 1865.38 | 490 | 2077.02 |
| 41 | 177.32 | 101 | 431.20 | 161 | 685.08 | 221 | 938.96 | 281 | 1192.84 | 341 | 1446.50 | 391 | 1658.14 | 441 | 1869.78 | 491 | 2081.20 |
| 42 | 181.50 | 102 | 435.38 | 162 | 689.26 | 222 | 943.14 | 282 | 1197.02 | 342 | 1450.90 | 392 | 1662.32 | 442 | 1873.96 | 492 | 2085.38 |
| 43 | 185.90 | 103 | 439.78 | 163 | 693.44 | 223 | 947.32 | 283 | 1201.20 | 343 | 1455.08 | 393 | 1666.50 | 443 | 1878.14 | 493 | 2089.78 |
| 44 | 190.08 | 104 | 443.96 | 164 | 697.84 | 224 | 951.50 | 284 | 1205.38 | 344 | 1459.26 | 394 | 1670.90 | 444 | 1882.32 | 494 | 2093.96 |
| 45 | 194.26 | 105 | 448.14 | 165 | 702.02 | 225 | 955.90 | 285 | 1209.78 | 345 | 1463.44 | 395 | 1675.08 | 445 | 1886.50 | 495 | 2098.14 |
| 46 | 198.44 | 106 | 452.32 | 166 | 706.20 | 226 | 960.08 | 286 | 1213.96 | 346 | 1467.84 | 396 | 1679.26 | 446 | 1890.90 | 496 | 2102.32 |
| 47 | 202.84 | 107 | 456.50 | 167 | 710.38 | 227 | 964.26 | 287 | 1218.14 | 347 | 1472.02 | 397 | 1683.44 | 447 | 1895.08 | 497 | 2106.50 |
| 48 | 207.02 | 108 | 460.90 | 168 | 714.78 | 228 | 968.44 | 288 | 1222.32 | 348 | 1476.20 | 398 | 1687.84 | 448 | 1899.26 | 498 | 2110.90 |
| 49 | 211.20 | 109 | 465.08 | 169 | 718.96 | 229 | 972.84 | 289 | 1226.50 | 349 | 1480.38 | 399 | 1692.02 | 449 | 1903.44 | 499 | 2115.08 |
| 50 | 215.38 | 110 | 469.26 | 170 | 723.14 | 230 | 977.02 | 290 | 1230.90 | 350 | 1484.78 | 400 | 1696.20 | 450 | 1907.84 | 500 | 2119.26 |
| 51 | 219.78 | 111 | 473.44 | 171 | 727.32 | 231 | 981.20 | 291 | 1235.08 | | | | | | | | |
| 52 | 223.96 | 112 | 477.84 | 172 | 731.50 | 232 | 985.38 | 292 | 1239.26 | | | | | | | | |
| 53 | 228.14 | 113 | 482.02 | 173 | 735.90 | 233 | 989.78 | 293 | 1243.44 | | | | | | | | |
| 54 | 232.32 | 114 | 486.20 | 174 | 740.08 | 234 | 993.96 | 294 | 1247.84 | | | | | | | | |
| 55 | 236.50 | 115 | 490.38 | 175 | 744.26 | 235 | 998.14 | 295 | 1252.02 | | | | | | | | |
| 56 | 240.90 | 116 | 494.78 | 176 | 748.44 | 236 | 1002.32 | 296 | 1256.20 | | | | | | | | |
| 57 | 245.08 | 117 | 498.96 | 177 | 752.84 | 237 | 1006.50 | 297 | 1260.38 | | | | | | | | |
| 58 | 249.26 | 118 | 503.14 | 178 | 757.02 | 238 | 1010.90 | 298 | 1264.78 | | | | | | | | |
| 59 | 253.44 | 119 | 507.32 | 179 | 761.20 | 239 | 1015.08 | 299 | 1268.96 | | | | | | | | |
| 60 | 257.84 | 120 | 511.50 | 180 | 765.38 | 240 | 1019.26 | 300 | 1273.14 | | | | | | | | |

### Code more than 500

1 Where the code is in the range 501 to **1000** inclusive:

  a. Subtract **500** from the code and use the balance of the code to obtain a pay adjustment figure from the table above.

  b. Add this pay adjustment figure to the figure given in the box alongside to obtain the figure of total pay adjustment to date * | 2115.52 |

2 Where the code **exceeds 1000** follow the instructions on **page 3**.

25

**Week 23**  Sep 7 to Sep 13                    **Tables A** - Pay Adjustment Tables

| Code | Total pay adjustment to date | Code | Total pay adjustment to date | Code | Total pay adjustment to date | Code | Total pay adjustment to date | Code | Total pay adjustment to date | Code | Total pay adjustment to date | Code | Total pay adjustment to date | Code | Total pay adjustment to date | Code | Total pay adjustment to date |
|---|---|---|---|---|---|---|---|---|---|---|---|---|---|---|---|---|---|
| | £ | | £ | | £ | | £ | | £ | | £ | | £ | | £ | | £ |
| 0 | NIL | | | | | | | | | | | | | | | | |
| 1 | 8.51 | 61 | 273.93 | 121 | 539.35 | 181 | 804.77 | 241 | 1069.96 | 301 | 1335.38 | 351 | 1556.64 | 401 | 1777.67 | 451 | 1998.93 |
| 2 | 12.88 | 62 | 278.30 | 122 | 543.72 | 182 | 809.14 | 242 | 1074.56 | 302 | 1339.75 | 352 | 1561.01 | 402 | 1782.27 | 452 | 2003.30 |
| 3 | 17.25 | 63 | 282.67 | 123 | 548.09 | 183 | 813.51 | 243 | 1078.93 | 303 | 1344.35 | 353 | 1565.38 | 403 | 1786.64 | 453 | 2007.67 |
| 4 | 21.85 | 64 | 287.27 | 124 | 552.46 | 184 | 817.88 | 244 | 1083.30 | 304 | 1348.72 | 354 | 1569.75 | 404 | 1791.01 | 454 | 2012.27 |
| 5 | 26.22 | 65 | 291.64 | 125 | 557.06 | 185 | 822.25 | 245 | 1087.67 | 305 | 1353.09 | 355 | 1574.35 | 405 | 1795.38 | 455 | 2016.64 |
| 6 | 30.59 | 66 | 296.01 | 126 | 561.43 | 186 | 826.85 | 246 | 1092.27 | 306 | 1357.46 | 356 | 1578.72 | 406 | 1799.75 | 456 | 2021.01 |
| 7 | 34.96 | 67 | 300.38 | 127 | 565.80 | 187 | 831.22 | 247 | 1096.64 | 307 | 1362.06 | 357 | 1583.09 | 407 | 1804.35 | 457 | 2025.38 |
| 8 | 39.56 | 68 | 304.75 | 128 | 570.17 | 188 | 835.59 | 248 | 1101.01 | 308 | 1366.43 | 358 | 1587.46 | 408 | 1808.72 | 458 | 2029.75 |
| 9 | 43.93 | 69 | 309.35 | 129 | 574.77 | 189 | 839.96 | 249 | 1105.38 | 309 | 1370.80 | 359 | 1592.06 | 409 | 1813.09 | 459 | 2034.35 |
| 10 | 48.30 | 70 | 313.72 | 130 | 579.14 | 190 | 844.56 | 250 | 1109.75 | 310 | 1375.17 | 360 | 1596.43 | 410 | 1817.46 | 460 | 2038.72 |
| 11 | 52.67 | 71 | 318.09 | 131 | 583.51 | 191 | 848.93 | 251 | 1114.35 | 311 | 1379.77 | 361 | 1600.80 | 411 | 1822.06 | 461 | 2043.09 |
| 12 | 57.27 | 72 | 322.46 | 132 | 587.88 | 192 | 853.30 | 252 | 1118.72 | 312 | 1384.14 | 362 | 1605.17 | 412 | 1826.43 | 462 | 2047.46 |
| 13 | 61.64 | 73 | 327.06 | 133 | 592.25 | 193 | 857.67 | 253 | 1123.09 | 313 | 1388.51 | 363 | 1609.77 | 413 | 1830.80 | 463 | 2052.06 |
| 14 | 66.01 | 74 | 331.43 | 134 | 596.85 | 194 | 862.27 | 254 | 1127.46 | 314 | 1392.88 | 364 | 1614.14 | 414 | 1835.17 | 464 | 2056.43 |
| 15 | 70.38 | 75 | 335.80 | 135 | 601.22 | 195 | 866.64 | 255 | 1132.06 | 315 | 1397.25 | 365 | 1618.51 | 415 | 1839.77 | 465 | 2060.80 |
| 16 | 74.75 | 76 | 340.17 | 136 | 605.59 | 196 | 871.01 | 256 | 1136.43 | 316 | 1401.85 | 366 | 1622.88 | 416 | 1844.14 | 466 | 2065.17 |
| 17 | 79.35 | 77 | 344.77 | 137 | 609.96 | 197 | 875.38 | 257 | 1140.80 | 317 | 1406.22 | 367 | 1627.25 | 417 | 1848.51 | 467 | 2069.77 |
| 18 | 83.72 | 78 | 349.14 | 138 | 614.56 | 198 | 879.75 | 258 | 1145.17 | 318 | 1410.59 | 368 | 1631.85 | 418 | 1852.88 | 468 | 2074.14 |
| 19 | 88.09 | 79 | 353.51 | 139 | 618.93 | 199 | 884.35 | 259 | 1149.77 | 319 | 1414.96 | 369 | 1636.22 | 419 | 1857.25 | 469 | 2078.51 |
| 20 | 92.46 | 80 | 357.88 | 140 | 623.30 | 200 | 888.72 | 260 | 1154.14 | 320 | 1419.56 | 370 | 1640.59 | 420 | 1861.85 | 470 | 2082.88 |
| 21 | 97.06 | 81 | 362.25 | 141 | 627.67 | 201 | 893.09 | 261 | 1158.51 | 321 | 1423.93 | 371 | 1644.96 | 421 | 1866.22 | 471 | 2087.25 |
| 22 | 101.43 | 82 | 366.85 | 142 | 632.27 | 202 | 897.46 | 262 | 1162.88 | 322 | 1428.30 | 372 | 1649.56 | 422 | 1870.59 | 472 | 2091.85 |
| 23 | 105.80 | 83 | 371.22 | 143 | 636.64 | 203 | 902.06 | 263 | 1167.25 | 323 | 1432.67 | 373 | 1653.93 | 423 | 1874.96 | 473 | 2096.22 |
| 24 | 110.17 | 84 | 375.59 | 144 | 641.01 | 204 | 906.43 | 264 | 1171.85 | 324 | 1437.27 | 374 | 1658.30 | 424 | 1879.56 | 474 | 2100.59 |
| 25 | 114.77 | 85 | 379.96 | 145 | 645.38 | 205 | 910.80 | 265 | 1176.22 | 325 | 1441.64 | 375 | 1662.67 | 425 | 1883.93 | 475 | 2104.96 |
| 26 | 119.14 | 86 | 384.56 | 146 | 649.75 | 206 | 915.17 | 266 | 1180.59 | 326 | 1446.01 | 376 | 1667.27 | 426 | 1888.30 | 476 | 2109.56 |
| 27 | 123.51 | 87 | 388.93 | 147 | 654.35 | 207 | 919.77 | 267 | 1184.96 | 327 | 1450.38 | 377 | 1671.64 | 427 | 1892.67 | 477 | 2113.93 |
| 28 | 127.88 | 88 | 393.30 | 148 | 658.72 | 208 | 924.14 | 268 | 1189.56 | 328 | 1454.75 | 378 | 1676.01 | 428 | 1897.27 | 478 | 2118.30 |
| 29 | 132.25 | 89 | 397.67 | 149 | 663.09 | 209 | 928.51 | 269 | 1193.93 | 329 | 1459.35 | 379 | 1680.38 | 429 | 1901.64 | 479 | 2122.67 |
| 30 | 136.85 | 90 | 402.27 | 150 | 667.46 | 210 | 932.88 | 270 | 1198.30 | 330 | 1463.72 | 380 | 1684.75 | 430 | 1906.01 | 480 | 2127.27 |
| 31 | 141.22 | 91 | 406.64 | 151 | 672.06 | 211 | 937.25 | 271 | 1202.67 | 331 | 1468.09 | 381 | 1689.35 | 431 | 1910.38 | 481 | 2131.64 |
| 32 | 145.59 | 92 | 411.01 | 152 | 676.43 | 212 | 941.85 | 272 | 1207.27 | 332 | 1472.46 | 382 | 1693.72 | 432 | 1914.75 | 482 | 2136.01 |
| 33 | 149.96 | 93 | 415.38 | 153 | 680.80 | 213 | 946.22 | 273 | 1211.64 | 333 | 1477.06 | 383 | 1698.09 | 433 | 1919.35 | 483 | 2140.38 |
| 34 | 154.56 | 94 | 419.75 | 154 | 685.17 | 214 | 950.59 | 274 | 1216.01 | 334 | 1481.43 | 384 | 1702.46 | 434 | 1923.72 | 484 | 2144.75 |
| 35 | 158.93 | 95 | 424.35 | 155 | 689.77 | 215 | 954.96 | 275 | 1220.38 | 335 | 1485.80 | 385 | 1707.06 | 435 | 1928.09 | 485 | 2149.35 |
| 36 | 163.30 | 96 | 428.72 | 156 | 694.14 | 216 | 959.56 | 276 | 1224.75 | 336 | 1490.17 | 386 | 1711.43 | 436 | 1932.46 | 486 | 2153.72 |
| 37 | 167.67 | 97 | 433.09 | 157 | 698.51 | 217 | 963.93 | 277 | 1229.35 | 337 | 1494.77 | 387 | 1715.80 | 437 | 1937.06 | 487 | 2158.09 |
| 38 | 172.27 | 98 | 437.46 | 158 | 702.88 | 218 | 968.30 | 278 | 1233.72 | 338 | 1499.14 | 388 | 1720.17 | 438 | 1941.43 | 488 | 2162.46 |
| 39 | 176.64 | 99 | 442.06 | 159 | 707.25 | 219 | 972.67 | 279 | 1238.09 | 339 | 1503.51 | 389 | 1724.77 | 439 | 1945.80 | 489 | 2167.06 |
| 40 | 181.01 | 100 | 446.43 | 160 | 711.85 | 220 | 977.27 | 280 | 1242.46 | 340 | 1507.88 | 390 | 1729.14 | 440 | 1950.17 | 490 | 2171.43 |
| 41 | 185.38 | 101 | 450.80 | 161 | 716.22 | 221 | 981.64 | 281 | 1247.06 | 341 | 1512.25 | 391 | 1733.51 | 441 | 1954.77 | 491 | 2175.80 |
| 42 | 189.75 | 102 | 455.17 | 162 | 720.59 | 222 | 986.01 | 282 | 1251.43 | 342 | 1516.85 | 392 | 1737.88 | 442 | 1959.14 | 492 | 2180.17 |
| 43 | 194.35 | 103 | 459.77 | 163 | 724.96 | 223 | 990.38 | 283 | 1255.80 | 343 | 1521.22 | 393 | 1742.25 | 443 | 1963.51 | 493 | 2184.77 |
| 44 | 198.72 | 104 | 464.14 | 164 | 729.56 | 224 | 994.75 | 284 | 1260.17 | 344 | 1525.59 | 394 | 1746.85 | 444 | 1967.88 | 494 | 2189.14 |
| 45 | 203.09 | 105 | 468.51 | 165 | 733.93 | 225 | 999.35 | 285 | 1264.77 | 345 | 1529.96 | 395 | 1751.22 | 445 | 1972.25 | 495 | 2193.51 |
| 46 | 207.46 | 106 | 472.88 | 166 | 738.30 | 226 | 1003.72 | 286 | 1269.14 | 346 | 1534.56 | 396 | 1755.59 | 446 | 1976.85 | 496 | 2197.88 |
| 47 | 212.06 | 107 | 477.25 | 167 | 742.67 | 227 | 1008.09 | 287 | 1273.51 | 347 | 1538.93 | 397 | 1759.96 | 447 | 1981.22 | 497 | 2202.25 |
| 48 | 216.43 | 108 | 481.85 | 168 | 747.27 | 228 | 1012.46 | 288 | 1277.88 | 348 | 1543.30 | 398 | 1764.56 | 448 | 1985.59 | 498 | 2206.85 |
| 49 | 220.80 | 109 | 486.22 | 169 | 751.64 | 229 | 1017.06 | 289 | 1282.25 | 349 | 1547.67 | 399 | 1768.93 | 449 | 1989.96 | 499 | 2211.22 |
| 50 | 225.17 | 110 | 490.59 | 170 | 756.01 | 230 | 1021.43 | 290 | 1286.85 | 350 | 1552.27 | 400 | 1773.30 | 450 | 1994.56 | 500 | 2215.59 |
| 51 | 229.77 | 111 | 494.96 | 171 | 760.38 | 231 | 1025.80 | 291 | 1291.22 | | | | | | | | |
| 52 | 234.14 | 112 | 499.56 | 172 | 764.75 | 232 | 1030.17 | 292 | 1295.59 | | | | | | | | |
| 53 | 238.51 | 113 | 503.93 | 173 | 769.35 | 233 | 1034.77 | 293 | 1299.96 | | | | | | | | |
| 54 | 242.88 | 114 | 508.30 | 174 | 773.72 | 234 | 1039.14 | 294 | 1304.56 | | | | | | | | |
| 55 | 247.25 | 115 | 512.67 | 175 | 778.09 | 235 | 1043.51 | 295 | 1308.93 | | | | | | | | |
| 56 | 251.85 | 116 | 517.27 | 176 | 782.46 | 236 | 1047.88 | 296 | 1313.30 | | | | | | | | |
| 57 | 256.22 | 117 | 521.64 | 177 | 787.06 | 237 | 1052.25 | 297 | 1317.67 | | | | | | | | |
| 58 | 260.59 | 118 | 526.01 | 178 | 791.43 | 238 | 1056.85 | 298 | 1322.27 | | | | | | | | |
| 59 | 264.96 | 119 | 530.38 | 179 | 795.80 | 239 | 1061.22 | 299 | 1326.64 | | | | | | | | |
| 60 | 269.56 | 120 | 534.75 | 180 | 800.17 | 240 | 1065.59 | 300 | 1331.01 | | | | | | | | |

**Code more than 500**

1  Where the code is in the range **501 to 1000** inclusive:

a. Subtract **500** from the code and use the balance of the code to obtain a pay adjustment figure from the table above.

b. Add this pay adjustment figure to the figure given in the box alongside to obtain the figure of total pay adjustment to date *  **2211.68**

2  Where the code **exceeds 1000** follow the instructions on **page 3**.

26

# Tables A - Pay Adjustment Tables

Sep 14 to Sep 20 **Week 24**

| Code | Total pay adjustment to date £ | Code | Total pay adjustment to date £ | Code | Total pay adjustment to date £ | Code | Total pay adjustment to date £ | Code | Total pay adjustment to date £ | Code | Total pay adjustment to date £ | Code | Total pay adjustment to date £ | Code | Total pay adjustment to date £ | Code | Total pay adjustment to date £ |
|---|---|---|---|---|---|---|---|---|---|---|---|---|---|---|---|---|---|
| 0 | NIL | 61 | 285.84 | 121 | 562.80 | 181 | 839.76 | 241 | 1116.48 | 301 | 1393.44 | 351 | 1624.32 | 401 | 1854.96 | 451 | 2085.84 |
| 1 | 8.88 | 62 | 290.40 | 122 | 567.36 | 182 | 844.32 | 242 | 1121.28 | 302 | 1398.00 | 352 | 1628.88 | 402 | 1859.76 | 452 | 2090.40 |
| 2 | 13.44 | 63 | 294.96 | 123 | 571.92 | 183 | 848.88 | 243 | 1125.84 | 303 | 1402.80 | 353 | 1633.44 | 403 | 1864.32 | 453 | 2094.96 |
| 3 | 18.00 | 64 | 299.76 | 124 | 576.48 | 184 | 853.44 | 244 | 1130.40 | 304 | 1407.36 | 354 | 1638.00 | 404 | 1868.88 | 454 | 2099.76 |
| 4 | 22.80 | 65 | 304.32 | 125 | 581.28 | 185 | 858.00 | 245 | 1134.96 | 305 | 1411.92 | 355 | 1642.80 | 405 | 1873.44 | 455 | 2104.32 |
| 5 | 27.36 | | | | | | | | | | | | | | | | |
| 6 | 31.92 | 66 | 308.88 | 126 | 585.84 | 186 | 862.80 | 246 | 1139.76 | 306 | 1416.48 | 356 | 1647.36 | 406 | 1878.00 | 456 | 2108.88 |
| 7 | 36.48 | 67 | 313.44 | 127 | 590.40 | 187 | 867.36 | 247 | 1144.32 | 307 | 1421.28 | 357 | 1651.92 | 407 | 1882.80 | 457 | 2113.44 |
| 8 | 41.28 | 68 | 318.00 | 128 | 594.96 | 188 | 871.92 | 248 | 1148.88 | 308 | 1425.84 | 358 | 1656.48 | 408 | 1887.36 | 458 | 2118.00 |
| 9 | 45.84 | 69 | 322.80 | 129 | 599.76 | 189 | 876.48 | 249 | 1153.44 | 309 | 1430.40 | 359 | 1661.28 | 409 | 1891.92 | 459 | 2122.80 |
| 10 | 50.40 | 70 | 327.36 | 130 | 604.32 | 190 | 881.28 | 250 | 1158.00 | 310 | 1434.96 | 360 | 1665.84 | 410 | 1896.48 | 460 | 2127.36 |
| 11 | 54.96 | 71 | 331.92 | 131 | 608.88 | 191 | 885.84 | 251 | 1162.80 | 311 | 1439.76 | 361 | 1670.40 | 411 | 1901.28 | 461 | 2131.92 |
| 12 | 59.76 | 72 | 336.48 | 132 | 613.44 | 192 | 890.40 | 252 | 1167.36 | 312 | 1444.32 | 362 | 1674.96 | 412 | 1905.84 | 462 | 2136.48 |
| 13 | 64.32 | 73 | 341.28 | 133 | 618.00 | 193 | 894.96 | 253 | 1171.92 | 313 | 1448.88 | 363 | 1679.76 | 413 | 1910.40 | 463 | 2141.28 |
| 14 | 68.88 | 74 | 345.84 | 134 | 622.80 | 194 | 899.76 | 254 | 1176.48 | 314 | 1453.44 | 364 | 1684.32 | 414 | 1914.96 | 464 | 2145.84 |
| 15 | 73.44 | 75 | 350.40 | 135 | 627.36 | 195 | 904.32 | 255 | 1181.28 | 315 | 1458.00 | 365 | 1688.88 | 415 | 1919.76 | 465 | 2150.40 |
| 16 | 78.00 | 76 | 354.96 | 136 | 631.92 | 196 | 908.88 | 256 | 1185.84 | 316 | 1462.80 | 366 | 1693.44 | 416 | 1924.32 | 466 | 2154.96 |
| 17 | 82.80 | 77 | 359.76 | 137 | 636.48 | 197 | 913.44 | 257 | 1190.40 | 317 | 1467.36 | 367 | 1698.00 | 417 | 1928.88 | 467 | 2159.76 |
| 18 | 87.36 | 78 | 364.32 | 138 | 641.28 | 198 | 918.00 | 258 | 1194.96 | 318 | 1471.92 | 368 | 1702.80 | 418 | 1933.44 | 468 | 2164.32 |
| 19 | 91.92 | 79 | 368.88 | 139 | 645.84 | 199 | 922.80 | 259 | 1199.76 | 319 | 1476.48 | 369 | 1707.36 | 419 | 1938.00 | 469 | 2168.88 |
| 20 | 96.48 | 80 | 373.44 | 140 | 650.40 | 200 | 927.36 | 260 | 1204.32 | 320 | 1481.28 | 370 | 1711.92 | 420 | 1942.80 | 470 | 2173.44 |
| 21 | 101.28 | 81 | 378.00 | 141 | 654.96 | 201 | 931.92 | 261 | 1208.88 | 321 | 1485.84 | 371 | 1716.48 | 421 | 1947.36 | 471 | 2178.00 |
| 22 | 105.84 | 82 | 382.80 | 142 | 659.76 | 202 | 936.48 | 262 | 1213.44 | 322 | 1490.40 | 372 | 1721.28 | 422 | 1951.92 | 472 | 2182.80 |
| 23 | 110.40 | 83 | 387.36 | 143 | 664.32 | 203 | 941.28 | 263 | 1218.00 | 323 | 1494.96 | 373 | 1725.84 | 423 | 1956.48 | 473 | 2187.36 |
| 24 | 114.96 | 84 | 391.92 | 144 | 668.88 | 204 | 945.84 | 264 | 1222.80 | 324 | 1499.76 | 374 | 1730.40 | 424 | 1961.28 | 474 | 2191.92 |
| 25 | 119.76 | 85 | 396.48 | 145 | 673.44 | 205 | 950.40 | 265 | 1227.36 | 325 | 1504.32 | 375 | 1734.96 | 425 | 1965.84 | 475 | 2196.48 |
| 26 | 124.32 | 86 | 401.28 | 146 | 678.00 | 206 | 954.96 | 266 | 1231.92 | 326 | 1508.88 | 376 | 1739.76 | 426 | 1970.40 | 476 | 2201.28 |
| 27 | 128.88 | 87 | 405.84 | 147 | 682.80 | 207 | 959.76 | 267 | 1236.48 | 327 | 1513.44 | 377 | 1744.32 | 427 | 1974.96 | 477 | 2205.84 |
| 28 | 133.44 | 88 | 410.40 | 148 | 687.36 | 208 | 964.32 | 268 | 1241.28 | 328 | 1518.00 | 378 | 1748.88 | 428 | 1979.76 | 478 | 2210.40 |
| 29 | 138.00 | 89 | 414.96 | 149 | 691.92 | 209 | 968.88 | 269 | 1245.84 | 329 | 1522.80 | 379 | 1753.44 | 429 | 1984.32 | 479 | 2214.96 |
| 30 | 142.80 | 90 | 419.76 | 150 | 696.48 | 210 | 973.44 | 270 | 1250.40 | 330 | 1527.36 | 380 | 1758.00 | 430 | 1988.88 | 480 | 2219.76 |
| 31 | 147.36 | 91 | 424.32 | 151 | 701.28 | 211 | 978.00 | 271 | 1254.96 | 331 | 1531.92 | 381 | 1762.80 | 431 | 1993.44 | 481 | 2224.32 |
| 32 | 151.92 | 92 | 428.88 | 152 | 705.84 | 212 | 982.80 | 272 | 1259.76 | 332 | 1536.48 | 382 | 1767.36 | 432 | 1998.00 | 482 | 2228.88 |
| 33 | 156.48 | 93 | 433.44 | 153 | 710.40 | 213 | 987.36 | 273 | 1264.32 | 333 | 1541.28 | 383 | 1771.92 | 433 | 2002.80 | 483 | 2233.44 |
| 34 | 161.28 | 94 | 438.00 | 154 | 714.96 | 214 | 991.92 | 274 | 1268.88 | 334 | 1545.84 | 384 | 1776.48 | 434 | 2007.36 | 484 | 2238.00 |
| 35 | 165.84 | 95 | 442.80 | 155 | 719.76 | 215 | 996.48 | 275 | 1273.44 | 335 | 1550.40 | 385 | 1781.28 | 435 | 2011.92 | 485 | 2242.80 |
| 36 | 170.40 | 96 | 447.36 | 156 | 724.32 | 216 | 1001.28 | 276 | 1278.00 | 336 | 1554.96 | 386 | 1785.84 | 436 | 2016.48 | 486 | 2247.36 |
| 37 | 174.96 | 97 | 451.92 | 157 | 728.88 | 217 | 1005.84 | 277 | 1282.80 | 337 | 1559.76 | 387 | 1790.40 | 437 | 2021.28 | 487 | 2251.92 |
| 38 | 179.76 | 98 | 456.48 | 158 | 733.44 | 218 | 1010.40 | 278 | 1287.36 | 338 | 1564.32 | 388 | 1794.96 | 438 | 2025.84 | 488 | 2256.48 |
| 39 | 184.32 | 99 | 461.28 | 159 | 738.00 | 219 | 1014.96 | 279 | 1291.92 | 339 | 1568.88 | 389 | 1799.76 | 439 | 2030.40 | 489 | 2261.28 |
| 40 | 188.88 | 100 | 465.84 | 160 | 742.80 | 220 | 1019.76 | 280 | 1296.48 | 340 | 1573.44 | 390 | 1804.32 | 440 | 2034.96 | 490 | 2265.84 |
| 41 | 193.44 | 101 | 470.40 | 161 | 747.36 | 221 | 1024.32 | 281 | 1301.28 | 341 | 1578.00 | 391 | 1808.88 | 441 | 2039.76 | 491 | 2270.40 |
| 42 | 198.00 | 102 | 474.96 | 162 | 751.92 | 222 | 1028.88 | 282 | 1305.84 | 342 | 1582.80 | 392 | 1813.44 | 442 | 2044.32 | 492 | 2274.96 |
| 43 | 202.80 | 103 | 479.76 | 163 | 756.48 | 223 | 1033.44 | 283 | 1310.40 | 343 | 1587.36 | 393 | 1818.00 | 443 | 2048.88 | 493 | 2279.76 |
| 44 | 207.36 | 104 | 484.32 | 164 | 761.28 | 224 | 1038.00 | 284 | 1314.96 | 344 | 1591.92 | 394 | 1822.80 | 444 | 2053.44 | 494 | 2284.32 |
| 45 | 211.92 | 105 | 488.88 | 165 | 765.84 | 225 | 1042.80 | 285 | 1319.76 | 345 | 1596.48 | 395 | 1827.36 | 445 | 2058.00 | 495 | 2288.88 |
| 46 | 216.48 | 106 | 493.44 | 166 | 770.40 | 226 | 1047.36 | 286 | 1324.32 | 346 | 1601.28 | 396 | 1831.92 | 446 | 2062.80 | 496 | 2293.44 |
| 47 | 221.28 | 107 | 498.00 | 167 | 774.96 | 227 | 1051.92 | 287 | 1328.88 | 347 | 1605.84 | 397 | 1836.48 | 447 | 2067.36 | 497 | 2298.00 |
| 48 | 225.84 | 108 | 502.80 | 168 | 779.76 | 228 | 1056.48 | 288 | 1333.44 | 348 | 1610.40 | 398 | 1841.28 | 448 | 2071.92 | 498 | 2302.80 |
| 49 | 230.40 | 109 | 507.36 | 169 | 784.32 | 229 | 1061.28 | 289 | 1338.00 | 349 | 1614.96 | 399 | 1845.84 | 449 | 2076.48 | 499 | 2307.36 |
| 50 | 234.96 | 110 | 511.92 | 170 | 788.88 | 230 | 1065.84 | 290 | 1342.80 | 350 | 1619.76 | 400 | 1850.40 | 450 | 2081.28 | 500 | 2311.92 |
| 51 | 239.76 | 111 | 516.48 | 171 | 793.44 | 231 | 1070.40 | 291 | 1347.36 | | | | | | | | |
| 52 | 244.32 | 112 | 521.28 | 172 | 798.00 | 232 | 1074.96 | 292 | 1351.92 | | | | | | | | |
| 53 | 248.88 | 113 | 525.84 | 173 | 802.80 | 233 | 1079.76 | 293 | 1356.48 | | | | | | | | |
| 54 | 253.44 | 114 | 530.40 | 174 | 807.36 | 234 | 1084.32 | 294 | 1361.28 | | | | | | | | |
| 55 | 258.00 | 115 | 534.96 | 175 | 811.92 | 235 | 1088.88 | 295 | 1365.84 | | | | | | | | |
| 56 | 262.80 | 116 | 539.76 | 176 | 816.48 | 236 | 1093.44 | 296 | 1370.40 | | | | | | | | |
| 57 | 267.36 | 117 | 544.32 | 177 | 821.28 | 237 | 1098.00 | 297 | 1374.96 | | | | | | | | |
| 58 | 271.92 | 118 | 548.88 | 178 | 825.84 | 238 | 1102.80 | 298 | 1379.76 | | | | | | | | |
| 59 | 276.48 | 119 | 553.44 | 179 | 830.40 | 239 | 1107.36 | 299 | 1384.32 | | | | | | | | |
| 60 | 281.28 | 120 | 558.00 | 180 | 834.96 | 240 | 1111.92 | 300 | 1388.88 | | | | | | | | |

## Code more than 500

1 Where the code is in the range **501** to **1000** inclusive:

 a. Subtract **500** from the code and use the balance of the code to obtain a pay adjustment figure from the table above.

 b. Add this pay adjustment figure to the figure given in the box alongside to obtain the figure of total pay adjustment to date * | **2307.84** |

2 Where the code **exceeds 1000** follow the instructions on **page 3**.

## Week 25   Sep21 to Sep 27                                              Tables A - Pay Adjustment Tables

| Code | Total pay adjustment to date | Code | Total pay adjustment to date | Code | Total pay adjustment to date | Code | Total pay adjustment to date | Code | Total pay adjustment to date | Code | Total pay adjustment to date | Code | Total pay adjustment to date | Code | Total pay adjustment to date | Code | Total pay adjustment to date |
|---|---|---|---|---|---|---|---|---|---|---|---|---|---|---|---|---|---|
| | £ | | £ | | £ | | £ | | £ | | £ | | £ | | £ | | £ |
| 0 | NIL | | | | | | | | | | | | | | | | |
| 1 | 9.25 | 61 | 297.75 | 121 | 586.25 | 181 | 874.75 | 241 | 1163.00 | 301 | 1451.50 | 351 | 1692.00 | 401 | 1932.25 | 451 | 2172.75 |
| 2 | 14.00 | 62 | 302.50 | 122 | 591.00 | 182 | 879.50 | 242 | 1168.00 | 302 | 1456.25 | 352 | 1696.75 | 402 | 1937.25 | 452 | 2177.50 |
| 3 | 18.75 | 63 | 307.25 | 123 | 595.75 | 183 | 884.25 | 243 | 1172.75 | 303 | 1461.25 | 353 | 1701.50 | 403 | 1942.00 | 453 | 2182.25 |
| 4 | 23.75 | 64 | 312.25 | 124 | 600.50 | 184 | 889.00 | 244 | 1177.50 | 304 | 1466.00 | 354 | 1706.25 | 404 | 1946.75 | 454 | 2187.25 |
| 5 | 28.50 | 65 | 317.00 | 125 | 605.50 | 185 | 893.75 | 245 | 1182.25 | 305 | 1470.75 | 355 | 1711.25 | 405 | 1951.50 | 455 | 2192.00 |
| 6 | 33.25 | 66 | 321.75 | 126 | 610.25 | 186 | 898.75 | 246 | 1187.25 | 306 | 1475.50 | 356 | 1716.00 | 406 | 1956.25 | 456 | 2196.75 |
| 7 | 38.00 | 67 | 326.50 | 127 | 615.00 | 187 | 903.50 | 247 | 1192.00 | 307 | 1480.50 | 357 | 1720.75 | 407 | 1961.25 | 457 | 2201.50 |
| 8 | 43.00 | 68 | 331.25 | 128 | 619.75 | 188 | 908.25 | 248 | 1196.75 | 308 | 1485.25 | 358 | 1725.50 | 408 | 1966.00 | 458 | 2206.25 |
| 9 | 47.75 | 69 | 336.25 | 129 | 624.75 | 189 | 913.00 | 249 | 1201.50 | 309 | 1490.00 | 359 | 1730.50 | 409 | 1970.75 | 459 | 2211.25 |
| 10 | 52.50 | 70 | 341.00 | 130 | 629.50 | 190 | 918.00 | 250 | 1206.25 | 310 | 1494.75 | 360 | 1735.25 | 410 | 1975.50 | 460 | 2216.00 |
| 11 | 57.25 | 71 | 345.75 | 131 | 634.25 | 191 | 922.75 | 251 | 1211.25 | 311 | 1499.75 | 361 | 1740.00 | 411 | 1980.50 | 461 | 2220.75 |
| 12 | 62.25 | 72 | 350.50 | 132 | 639.00 | 192 | 927.50 | 252 | 1216.00 | 312 | 1504.50 | 362 | 1744.75 | 412 | 1985.25 | 462 | 2225.50 |
| 13 | 67.00 | 73 | 355.50 | 133 | 643.75 | 193 | 932.25 | 253 | 1220.75 | 313 | 1509.25 | 363 | 1749.75 | 413 | 1990.00 | 463 | 2230.50 |
| 14 | 71.75 | 74 | 360.25 | 134 | 648.75 | 194 | 937.25 | 254 | 1225.50 | 314 | 1514.00 | 364 | 1754.50 | 414 | 1994.75 | 464 | 2235.25 |
| 15 | 76.50 | 75 | 365.00 | 135 | 653.50 | 195 | 942.00 | 255 | 1230.50 | 315 | 1518.75 | 365 | 1759.25 | 415 | 1999.75 | 465 | 2240.00 |
| 16 | 81.25 | 76 | 369.75 | 136 | 658.25 | 196 | 946.75 | 256 | 1235.25 | 316 | 1523.75 | 366 | 1764.00 | 416 | 2004.50 | 466 | 2244.75 |
| 17 | 86.25 | 77 | 374.75 | 137 | 663.00 | 197 | 951.50 | 257 | 1240.00 | 317 | 1528.50 | 367 | 1768.75 | 417 | 2009.25 | 467 | 2249.75 |
| 18 | 91.00 | 78 | 379.50 | 138 | 668.00 | 198 | 956.25 | 258 | 1244.75 | 318 | 1533.25 | 368 | 1773.75 | 418 | 2014.00 | 468 | 2254.50 |
| 19 | 95.75 | 79 | 384.25 | 139 | 672.75 | 199 | 961.25 | 259 | 1249.75 | 319 | 1538.00 | 369 | 1778.50 | 419 | 2018.75 | 469 | 2259.25 |
| 20 | 100.50 | 80 | 389.00 | 140 | 677.50 | 200 | 966.00 | 260 | 1254.50 | 320 | 1543.00 | 370 | 1783.25 | 420 | 2023.75 | 470 | 2264.00 |
| 21 | 105.50 | 81 | 393.75 | 141 | 682.25 | 201 | 970.75 | 261 | 1259.25 | 321 | 1547.75 | 371 | 1788.00 | 421 | 2028.50 | 471 | 2268.75 |
| 22 | 110.25 | 82 | 398.75 | 142 | 687.25 | 202 | 975.50 | 262 | 1264.00 | 322 | 1552.50 | 372 | 1793.00 | 422 | 2033.25 | 472 | 2273.75 |
| 23 | 115.00 | 83 | 403.50 | 143 | 692.00 | 203 | 980.50 | 263 | 1268.75 | 323 | 1557.25 | 373 | 1797.75 | 423 | 2038.00 | 473 | 2278.50 |
| 24 | 119.75 | 84 | 408.25 | 144 | 696.75 | 204 | 985.25 | 264 | 1273.75 | 324 | 1562.25 | 374 | 1802.50 | 424 | 2043.00 | 474 | 2283.25 |
| 25 | 124.75 | 85 | 413.00 | 145 | 701.50 | 205 | 990.00 | 265 | 1278.50 | 325 | 1567.00 | 375 | 1807.25 | 425 | 2047.75 | 475 | 2288.00 |
| 26 | 129.50 | 86 | 418.00 | 146 | 706.25 | 206 | 994.75 | 266 | 1283.25 | 326 | 1571.75 | 376 | 1812.25 | 426 | 2052.50 | 476 | 2293.00 |
| 27 | 134.25 | 87 | 422.75 | 147 | 711.25 | 207 | 999.75 | 267 | 1288.00 | 327 | 1576.50 | 377 | 1817.00 | 427 | 2057.25 | 477 | 2297.75 |
| 28 | 139.00 | 88 | 427.50 | 148 | 716.00 | 208 | 1004.50 | 268 | 1293.00 | 328 | 1581.25 | 378 | 1821.75 | 428 | 2062.25 | 478 | 2302.50 |
| 29 | 143.75 | 89 | 432.25 | 149 | 720.75 | 209 | 1009.25 | 269 | 1297.75 | 329 | 1586.25 | 379 | 1826.50 | 429 | 2067.00 | 479 | 2307.25 |
| 30 | 148.75 | 90 | 437.25 | 150 | 725.50 | 210 | 1014.00 | 270 | 1302.50 | 330 | 1591.00 | 380 | 1831.25 | 430 | 2071.75 | 480 | 2312.25 |
| 31 | 153.50 | 91 | 442.00 | 151 | 730.50 | 211 | 1018.75 | 271 | 1307.25 | 331 | 1595.75 | 381 | 1836.25 | 431 | 2076.50 | 481 | 2317.00 |
| 32 | 158.25 | 92 | 446.75 | 152 | 735.25 | 212 | 1023.75 | 272 | 1312.25 | 332 | 1600.50 | 382 | 1841.00 | 432 | 2081.25 | 482 | 2321.75 |
| 33 | 163.00 | 93 | 451.50 | 153 | 740.00 | 213 | 1028.50 | 273 | 1317.00 | 333 | 1605.50 | 383 | 1845.75 | 433 | 2086.25 | 483 | 2326.50 |
| 34 | 168.00 | 94 | 456.25 | 154 | 744.75 | 214 | 1033.25 | 274 | 1321.75 | 334 | 1610.25 | 384 | 1850.50 | 434 | 2091.00 | 484 | 2331.25 |
| 35 | 172.75 | 95 | 461.25 | 155 | 749.75 | 215 | 1038.00 | 275 | 1326.50 | 335 | 1615.00 | 385 | 1855.50 | 435 | 2095.75 | 485 | 2336.25 |
| 36 | 177.50 | 96 | 466.00 | 156 | 754.50 | 216 | 1043.00 | 276 | 1331.25 | 336 | 1619.75 | 386 | 1860.25 | 436 | 2100.50 | 486 | 2341.00 |
| 37 | 182.25 | 97 | 470.75 | 157 | 759.25 | 217 | 1047.75 | 277 | 1336.25 | 337 | 1624.75 | 387 | 1865.00 | 437 | 2105.50 | 487 | 2345.75 |
| 38 | 187.25 | 98 | 475.50 | 158 | 764.00 | 218 | 1052.50 | 278 | 1341.00 | 338 | 1629.50 | 388 | 1869.75 | 438 | 2110.25 | 488 | 2350.50 |
| 39 | 192.00 | 99 | 480.50 | 159 | 768.75 | 219 | 1057.25 | 279 | 1345.75 | 339 | 1634.25 | 389 | 1874.75 | 439 | 2115.00 | 489 | 2355.50 |
| 40 | 196.75 | 100 | 485.25 | 160 | 773.75 | 220 | 1062.25 | 280 | 1350.50 | 340 | 1639.00 | 390 | 1879.50 | 440 | 2119.75 | 490 | 2360.25 |
| 41 | 201.50 | 101 | 490.00 | 161 | 778.50 | 221 | 1067.00 | 281 | 1355.50 | 341 | 1643.75 | 391 | 1884.25 | 441 | 2124.75 | 491 | 2365.00 |
| 42 | 206.25 | 102 | 494.75 | 162 | 783.25 | 222 | 1071.75 | 282 | 1360.25 | 342 | 1648.75 | 392 | 1889.00 | 442 | 2129.50 | 492 | 2369.75 |
| 43 | 211.25 | 103 | 499.75 | 163 | 788.00 | 223 | 1076.50 | 283 | 1365.00 | 343 | 1653.50 | 393 | 1893.75 | 443 | 2134.25 | 493 | 2374.75 |
| 44 | 216.00 | 104 | 504.50 | 164 | 793.00 | 224 | 1081.25 | 284 | 1369.75 | 344 | 1658.25 | 394 | 1898.75 | 444 | 2139.00 | 494 | 2379.50 |
| 45 | 220.75 | 105 | 509.25 | 165 | 797.75 | 225 | 1086.25 | 285 | 1374.75 | 345 | 1663.00 | 395 | 1903.50 | 445 | 2143.75 | 495 | 2384.25 |
| 46 | 225.50 | 106 | 514.00 | 166 | 802.50 | 226 | 1091.00 | 286 | 1379.50 | 346 | 1668.00 | 396 | 1908.25 | 446 | 2148.75 | 496 | 2389.00 |
| 47 | 230.50 | 107 | 518.75 | 167 | 807.25 | 227 | 1095.75 | 287 | 1384.25 | 347 | 1672.75 | 397 | 1913.00 | 447 | 2153.50 | 497 | 2393.75 |
| 48 | 235.25 | 108 | 523.75 | 168 | 812.25 | 228 | 1100.50 | 288 | 1389.00 | 348 | 1677.50 | 398 | 1918.00 | 448 | 2158.25 | 498 | 2398.75 |
| 49 | 240.00 | 109 | 528.50 | 169 | 817.00 | 229 | 1105.50 | 289 | 1393.75 | 349 | 1682.25 | 399 | 1922.75 | 449 | 2163.00 | 499 | 2403.50 |
| 50 | 244.75 | 110 | 533.25 | 170 | 821.75 | 230 | 1110.25 | 290 | 1398.75 | 350 | 1687.25 | 400 | 1927.50 | 450 | 2168.00 | 500 | 2408.25 |
| 51 | 249.75 | 111 | 538.00 | 171 | 826.50 | 231 | 1115.00 | 291 | 1403.50 | | | | | | |
| 52 | 254.50 | 112 | 543.00 | 172 | 831.25 | 232 | 1119.75 | 292 | 1408.25 | | | | | | |
| 53 | 259.25 | 113 | 547.75 | 173 | 836.25 | 233 | 1124.75 | 293 | 1413.00 | | | | | | |
| 54 | 264.00 | 114 | 552.50 | 174 | 841.00 | 234 | 1129.50 | 294 | 1418.00 | | | | | | |
| 55 | 268.75 | 115 | 557.25 | 175 | 845.75 | 235 | 1134.25 | 295 | 1422.75 | | | | | | |
| 56 | 273.75 | 116 | 562.25 | 176 | 850.50 | 236 | 1139.00 | 296 | 1427.50 | | | | | | |
| 57 | 278.50 | 117 | 567.00 | 177 | 855.50 | 237 | 1143.75 | 297 | 1432.25 | | | | | | |
| 58 | 283.25 | 118 | 571.75 | 178 | 860.25 | 238 | 1148.75 | 298 | 1437.25 | | | | | | |
| 59 | 288.00 | 119 | 576.50 | 179 | 865.00 | 239 | 1153.50 | 299 | 1442.00 | | | | | | |
| 60 | 293.00 | 120 | 581.25 | 180 | 869.75 | 240 | 1158.25 | 300 | 1446.75 | | | | | | |

**Code more than 500**

1 Where the code is in the range **501 to 1000** inclusive:

  a. Subtract **500** from the code and use the balance of the code to obtain a pay adjustment figure from the table above.

  b. Add this pay adjustment figure to the figure given in the box alongside to obtain the figure of total pay adjustment to date *   **2404.00**

2 Where the code **exceeds 1000** follow the instructions on **page 3**.

28

# Tables A - Pay Adjustment Tables

Sep 28 to Oct 4 **Week 26**

| Code | Total pay adjustment to date £ | Code | Total pay adjustment to date £ | Code | Total pay adjustment to date £ | Code | Total pay adjustment to date £ | Code | Total pay adjustment to date £ | Code | Total pay adjustment to date £ | Code | Total pay adjustment to date £ | Code | Total pay adjustment to date £ | Code | Total pay adjustment to date £ |
|---|---|---|---|---|---|---|---|---|---|---|---|---|---|---|---|---|---|
| 0 | NIL | | | | | | | | | | | | | | | | |
| 1 | 9.62 | 61 | 309.66 | 121 | 609.70 | 181 | 909.74 | 241 | 1209.52 | 301 | 1509.56 | 351 | 1759.68 | 401 | 2009.54 | 451 | 2259.66 |
| 2 | 14.56 | 62 | 314.60 | 122 | 614.64 | 182 | 914.68 | 242 | 1214.72 | 302 | 1514.50 | 352 | 1764.62 | 402 | 2014.74 | 452 | 2264.60 |
| 3 | 19.50 | 63 | 319.54 | 123 | 619.58 | 183 | 919.62 | 243 | 1219.66 | 303 | 1519.70 | 353 | 1769.56 | 403 | 2019.68 | 453 | 2269.54 |
| 4 | 24.70 | 64 | 324.74 | 124 | 624.52 | 184 | 924.56 | 244 | 1224.60 | 304 | 1524.64 | 354 | 1774.50 | 404 | 2024.62 | 454 | 2274.74 |
| 5 | 29.64 | 65 | 329.68 | 125 | 629.72 | 185 | 929.50 | 245 | 1229.54 | 305 | 1529.58 | 355 | 1779.70 | 405 | 2029.56 | 455 | 2279.68 |
| 6 | 34.58 | 66 | 334.62 | 126 | 634.66 | 186 | 934.70 | 246 | 1234.74 | 306 | 1534.52 | 356 | 1784.64 | 406 | 2034.50 | 456 | 2284.62 |
| 7 | 39.52 | 67 | 339.56 | 127 | 639.60 | 187 | 939.64 | 247 | 1239.68 | 307 | 1539.72 | 357 | 1789.58 | 407 | 2039.70 | 457 | 2289.56 |
| 8 | 44.72 | 68 | 344.50 | 128 | 644.54 | 188 | 944.58 | 248 | 1244.62 | 308 | 1544.66 | 358 | 1794.52 | 408 | 2044.64 | 458 | 2294.50 |
| 9 | 49.66 | 69 | 349.70 | 129 | 649.74 | 189 | 949.52 | 249 | 1249.56 | 309 | 1549.60 | 359 | 1799.72 | 409 | 2049.58 | 459 | 2299.70 |
| 10 | 54.60 | 70 | 354.64 | 130 | 654.68 | 190 | 954.72 | 250 | 1254.50 | 310 | 1554.54 | 360 | 1804.66 | 410 | 2054.52 | 460 | 2304.64 |
| 11 | 59.54 | 71 | 359.58 | 131 | 659.62 | 191 | 959.66 | 251 | 1259.70 | 311 | 1559.74 | 361 | 1809.60 | 411 | 2059.72 | 461 | 2309.58 |
| 12 | 64.74 | 72 | 364.52 | 132 | 664.56 | 192 | 964.60 | 252 | 1264.64 | 312 | 1564.68 | 362 | 1814.54 | 412 | 2064.66 | 462 | 2314.52 |
| 13 | 69.68 | 73 | 369.72 | 133 | 669.50 | 193 | 969.54 | 253 | 1269.58 | 313 | 1569.62 | 363 | 1819.74 | 413 | 2069.60 | 463 | 2319.72 |
| 14 | 74.62 | 74 | 374.66 | 134 | 674.70 | 194 | 974.74 | 254 | 1274.52 | 314 | 1574.56 | 364 | 1824.68 | 414 | 2074.54 | 464 | 2324.66 |
| 15 | 79.56 | 75 | 379.60 | 135 | 679.64 | 195 | 979.68 | 255 | 1279.72 | 315 | 1579.50 | 365 | 1829.62 | 415 | 2079.74 | 465 | 2329.60 |
| 16 | 84.50 | 76 | 384.54 | 136 | 684.58 | 196 | 984.62 | 256 | 1284.66 | 316 | 1584.70 | 366 | 1834.56 | 416 | 2084.68 | 466 | 2334.54 |
| 17 | 89.70 | 77 | 389.74 | 137 | 689.52 | 197 | 989.56 | 257 | 1289.60 | 317 | 1589.64 | 367 | 1839.50 | 417 | 2089.62 | 467 | 2339.74 |
| 18 | 94.64 | 78 | 394.68 | 138 | 694.72 | 198 | 994.50 | 258 | 1294.54 | 318 | 1594.58 | 368 | 1844.70 | 418 | 2094.56 | 468 | 2344.68 |
| 19 | 99.58 | 79 | 399.62 | 139 | 699.66 | 199 | 999.70 | 259 | 1299.74 | 319 | 1599.52 | 369 | 1849.64 | 419 | 2099.50 | 469 | 2349.62 |
| 20 | 104.52 | 80 | 404.56 | 140 | 704.60 | 200 | 1004.64 | 260 | 1304.68 | 320 | 1604.72 | 370 | 1854.58 | 420 | 2104.70 | 470 | 2354.56 |
| 21 | 109.72 | 81 | 409.50 | 141 | 709.54 | 201 | 1009.58 | 261 | 1309.62 | 321 | 1609.66 | 371 | 1859.52 | 421 | 2109.64 | 471 | 2359.50 |
| 22 | 114.66 | 82 | 414.70 | 142 | 714.74 | 202 | 1014.52 | 262 | 1314.56 | 322 | 1614.60 | 372 | 1864.72 | 422 | 2114.58 | 472 | 2364.70 |
| 23 | 119.60 | 83 | 419.64 | 143 | 719.68 | 203 | 1019.72 | 263 | 1319.50 | 323 | 1619.54 | 373 | 1869.66 | 423 | 2119.52 | 473 | 2369.64 |
| 24 | 124.54 | 84 | 424.58 | 144 | 724.62 | 204 | 1024.66 | 264 | 1324.70 | 324 | 1624.74 | 374 | 1874.60 | 424 | 2124.72 | 474 | 2374.58 |
| 25 | 129.74 | 85 | 429.52 | 145 | 729.56 | 205 | 1029.60 | 265 | 1329.64 | 325 | 1629.68 | 375 | 1879.54 | 425 | 2129.66 | 475 | 2379.52 |
| 26 | 134.68 | 86 | 434.72 | 146 | 734.50 | 206 | 1034.54 | 266 | 1334.58 | 326 | 1634.62 | 376 | 1884.74 | 426 | 2134.60 | 476 | 2384.72 |
| 27 | 139.62 | 87 | 439.66 | 147 | 739.70 | 207 | 1039.74 | 267 | 1339.52 | 327 | 1639.56 | 377 | 1889.68 | 427 | 2139.54 | 477 | 2389.66 |
| 28 | 144.56 | 88 | 444.60 | 148 | 744.64 | 208 | 1044.68 | 268 | 1344.72 | 328 | 1644.50 | 378 | 1894.62 | 428 | 2144.74 | 478 | 2394.60 |
| 29 | 149.50 | 89 | 449.54 | 149 | 749.58 | 209 | 1049.62 | 269 | 1349.66 | 329 | 1649.70 | 379 | 1899.56 | 429 | 2149.68 | 479 | 2399.54 |
| 30 | 154.70 | 90 | 454.74 | 150 | 754.52 | 210 | 1054.56 | 270 | 1354.60 | 330 | 1654.64 | 380 | 1904.50 | 430 | 2154.62 | 480 | 2404.74 |
| 31 | 159.64 | 91 | 459.68 | 151 | 759.72 | 211 | 1059.50 | 271 | 1359.54 | 331 | 1659.58 | 381 | 1909.70 | 431 | 2159.56 | 481 | 2409.68 |
| 32 | 164.58 | 92 | 464.62 | 152 | 764.66 | 212 | 1064.70 | 272 | 1364.74 | 332 | 1664.52 | 382 | 1914.64 | 432 | 2164.50 | 482 | 2414.62 |
| 33 | 169.52 | 93 | 469.56 | 153 | 769.60 | 213 | 1069.64 | 273 | 1369.68 | 333 | 1669.72 | 383 | 1919.58 | 433 | 2169.70 | 483 | 2419.56 |
| 34 | 174.72 | 94 | 474.50 | 154 | 774.54 | 214 | 1074.58 | 274 | 1374.62 | 334 | 1674.66 | 384 | 1924.52 | 434 | 2174.64 | 484 | 2424.50 |
| 35 | 179.66 | 95 | 479.70 | 155 | 779.74 | 215 | 1079.52 | 275 | 1379.56 | 335 | 1679.60 | 385 | 1929.72 | 435 | 2179.58 | 485 | 2429.70 |
| 36 | 184.60 | 96 | 484.64 | 156 | 784.68 | 216 | 1084.72 | 276 | 1384.50 | 336 | 1684.54 | 386 | 1934.66 | 436 | 2184.52 | 486 | 2434.64 |
| 37 | 189.54 | 97 | 489.58 | 157 | 789.62 | 217 | 1089.66 | 277 | 1389.70 | 337 | 1689.74 | 387 | 1939.60 | 437 | 2189.72 | 487 | 2439.58 |
| 38 | 194.74 | 98 | 494.52 | 158 | 794.56 | 218 | 1094.60 | 278 | 1394.64 | 338 | 1694.68 | 388 | 1944.54 | 438 | 2194.66 | 488 | 2444.52 |
| 39 | 199.68 | 99 | 499.72 | 159 | 799.50 | 219 | 1099.54 | 279 | 1399.58 | 339 | 1699.62 | 389 | 1949.74 | 439 | 2199.60 | 489 | 2449.72 |
| 40 | 204.62 | 100 | 504.66 | 160 | 804.70 | 220 | 1104.74 | 280 | 1404.52 | 340 | 1704.56 | 390 | 1954.68 | 440 | 2204.54 | 490 | 2454.66 |
| 41 | 209.56 | 101 | 509.60 | 161 | 809.64 | 221 | 1109.68 | 281 | 1409.72 | 341 | 1709.50 | 391 | 1959.62 | 441 | 2209.74 | 491 | 2459.60 |
| 42 | 214.50 | 102 | 514.54 | 162 | 814.58 | 222 | 1114.62 | 282 | 1414.66 | 342 | 1714.70 | 392 | 1964.56 | 442 | 2214.68 | 492 | 2464.54 |
| 43 | 219.70 | 103 | 519.74 | 163 | 819.74 | 223 | 1119.56 | 283 | 1419.60 | 343 | 1719.64 | 393 | 1969.50 | 443 | 2219.62 | 493 | 2469.74 |
| 44 | 224.64 | 104 | 524.68 | 164 | 824.72 | 224 | 1124.50 | 284 | 1424.54 | 344 | 1724.58 | 394 | 1974.70 | 444 | 2224.56 | 494 | 2474.68 |
| 45 | 229.58 | 105 | 529.62 | 165 | 829.66 | 225 | 1129.70 | 285 | 1429.74 | 345 | 1729.52 | 395 | 1979.64 | 445 | 2229.50 | 495 | 2479.62 |
| 46 | 234.52 | 106 | 534.56 | 166 | 834.60 | 226 | 1134.64 | 286 | 1434.68 | 346 | 1734.72 | 396 | 1984.58 | 446 | 2234.70 | 496 | 2484.56 |
| 47 | 239.72 | 107 | 539.50 | 167 | 839.54 | 227 | 1139.58 | 287 | 1439.62 | 347 | 1739.66 | 397 | 1989.52 | 447 | 2239.64 | 497 | 2489.50 |
| 48 | 244.66 | 108 | 544.70 | 168 | 844.74 | 228 | 1144.52 | 288 | 1444.56 | 348 | 1744.60 | 398 | 1994.72 | 448 | 2244.58 | 498 | 2494.70 |
| 49 | 249.60 | 109 | 549.64 | 169 | 849.68 | 229 | 1149.72 | 289 | 1449.50 | 349 | 1749.54 | 399 | 1999.66 | 449 | 2249.52 | 499 | 2499.64 |
| 50 | 254.54 | 110 | 554.58 | 170 | 854.62 | 230 | 1154.66 | 290 | 1454.70 | 350 | 1754.74 | 400 | 2004.60 | 450 | 2254.72 | 500 | 2504.58 |
| 51 | 259.74 | 111 | 559.52 | 171 | 859.56 | 231 | 1159.60 | 291 | 1459.64 | | | | | | | | |
| 52 | 264.68 | 112 | 564.72 | 172 | 864.50 | 232 | 1164.54 | 292 | 1464.58 | | | | | | | | |
| 53 | 269.62 | 113 | 569.66 | 173 | 869.70 | 233 | 1169.74 | 293 | 1469.52 | | | | | | | | |
| 54 | 274.56 | 114 | 574.60 | 174 | 874.64 | 234 | 1174.68 | 294 | 1474.72 | | | | | | | | |
| 55 | 279.50 | 115 | 579.54 | 175 | 879.58 | 235 | 1179.62 | 295 | 1479.66 | | | | | | | | |
| 56 | 284.70 | 116 | 584.74 | 176 | 884.52 | 236 | 1184.56 | 296 | 1484.60 | | | | | | | | |
| 57 | 289.64 | 117 | 589.68 | 177 | 889.72 | 237 | 1189.50 | 297 | 1489.54 | | | | | | | | |
| 58 | 294.58 | 118 | 594.62 | 178 | 894.66 | 238 | 1194.70 | 298 | 1494.74 | | | | | | | | |
| 59 | 299.52 | 119 | 599.56 | 179 | 899.60 | 239 | 1199.64 | 299 | 1499.68 | | | | | | | | |
| 60 | 304.72 | 120 | 604.50 | 180 | 904.54 | 240 | 1204.58 | 300 | 1504.62 | | | | | | | | |

**Code more than 500**

1 Where the code is in the range **501** to **1000** inclusive:

a. Subtract **500** from the code and use the balance of the code to obtain a pay adjustment figure from the table above.

b. Add this pay adjustment figure to the figure given in the box alongside to obtain the figure of total pay adjustment to date * **2500.16**

2 Where the code **exceeds 1000** follow the instructions on **page 3**.

29

**Week 27**   Oct 5 to Oct 11                                                     **Tables A** - Pay Adjustment Tables

| Code | Total pay adj. to date (£) | Code | Total pay adj. to date (£) | Code | Total pay adj. to date (£) | Code | Total pay adj. to date (£) | Code | Total pay adj. to date (£) | Code | Total pay adj. to date (£) | Code | Total pay adj. to date (£) | Code | Total pay adj. to date (£) | Code | Total pay adj. to date (£) |
|---|---|---|---|---|---|---|---|---|---|---|---|---|---|---|---|---|---|
| 0 | NIL | | | | | | | | | | | | | | | | |
| 1 | 9.99 | 61 | 321.57 | 121 | 633.15 | 181 | 944.73 | 241 | 1256.04 | 301 | 1567.62 | 351 | 1827.36 | 401 | 2086.83 | 451 | 2346.57 |
| 2 | 15.12 | 62 | 326.70 | 122 | 638.28 | 182 | 949.86 | 242 | 1261.44 | 302 | 1572.75 | 352 | 1832.49 | 402 | 2092.23 | 452 | 2351.70 |
| 3 | 20.25 | 63 | 331.83 | 123 | 643.41 | 183 | 954.99 | 243 | 1266.57 | 303 | 1578.15 | 353 | 1837.62 | 403 | 2097.36 | 453 | 2356.83 |
| 4 | 25.65 | 64 | 337.23 | 124 | 648.54 | 184 | 960.12 | 244 | 1271.70 | 304 | 1583.28 | 354 | 1842.75 | 404 | 2102.49 | 454 | 2362.23 |
| 5 | 30.78 | 65 | 342.36 | 125 | 653.94 | 185 | 965.25 | 245 | 1276.83 | 305 | 1588.41 | 355 | 1848.15 | 405 | 2107.62 | 455 | 2367.36 |
| 6 | 35.91 | 66 | 347.49 | 126 | 659.07 | 186 | 970.65 | 246 | 1282.23 | 306 | 1593.54 | 356 | 1853.28 | 406 | 2112.75 | 456 | 2372.49 |
| 7 | 41.04 | 67 | 352.62 | 127 | 664.20 | 187 | 975.78 | 247 | 1287.36 | 307 | 1598.94 | 357 | 1858.41 | 407 | 2118.15 | 457 | 2377.62 |
| 8 | 46.44 | 68 | 357.75 | 128 | 669.33 | 188 | 980.91 | 248 | 1292.49 | 308 | 1604.07 | 358 | 1863.54 | 408 | 2123.28 | 458 | 2382.75 |
| 9 | 51.57 | 69 | 363.15 | 129 | 674.73 | 189 | 986.04 | 249 | 1297.62 | 309 | 1609.20 | 359 | 1868.94 | 409 | 2128.41 | 459 | 2388.15 |
| 10 | 56.70 | 70 | 368.28 | 130 | 679.86 | 190 | 991.44 | 250 | 1302.75 | 310 | 1614.33 | 360 | 1874.07 | 410 | 2133.54 | 460 | 2393.28 |
| 11 | 61.83 | 71 | 373.41 | 131 | 684.99 | 191 | 996.57 | 251 | 1308.15 | 311 | 1619.73 | 361 | 1879.20 | 411 | 2138.94 | 461 | 2398.41 |
| 12 | 67.23 | 72 | 378.54 | 132 | 690.12 | 192 | 1001.70 | 252 | 1313.28 | 312 | 1624.86 | 362 | 1884.33 | 412 | 2144.07 | 462 | 2403.54 |
| 13 | 72.36 | 73 | 383.94 | 133 | 695.25 | 193 | 1006.83 | 253 | 1318.41 | 313 | 1629.99 | 363 | 1889.73 | 413 | 2149.20 | 463 | 2408.94 |
| 14 | 77.49 | 74 | 389.07 | 134 | 700.65 | 194 | 1012.23 | 254 | 1323.54 | 314 | 1635.12 | 364 | 1894.86 | 414 | 2154.33 | 464 | 2414.07 |
| 15 | 82.62 | 75 | 394.20 | 135 | 705.78 | 195 | 1017.36 | 255 | 1328.94 | 315 | 1640.25 | 365 | 1899.99 | 415 | 2159.73 | 465 | 2419.20 |
| 16 | 87.75 | 76 | 399.33 | 136 | 710.91 | 196 | 1022.49 | 256 | 1334.07 | 316 | 1645.65 | 366 | 1905.12 | 416 | 2164.86 | 466 | 2424.33 |
| 17 | 93.15 | 77 | 404.73 | 137 | 716.04 | 197 | 1027.62 | 257 | 1339.20 | 317 | 1650.78 | 367 | 1910.25 | 417 | 2169.99 | 467 | 2429.73 |
| 18 | 98.28 | 78 | 409.86 | 138 | 721.44 | 198 | 1032.75 | 258 | 1344.33 | 318 | 1655.91 | 368 | 1915.65 | 418 | 2175.12 | 468 | 2434.86 |
| 19 | 103.41 | 79 | 414.99 | 139 | 726.57 | 199 | 1038.15 | 259 | 1349.73 | 319 | 1661.04 | 369 | 1920.78 | 419 | 2180.25 | 469 | 2439.99 |
| 20 | 108.54 | 80 | 420.12 | 140 | 731.70 | 200 | 1043.28 | 260 | 1354.86 | 320 | 1666.44 | 370 | 1925.91 | 420 | 2185.65 | 470 | 2445.12 |
| 21 | 113.94 | 81 | 425.25 | 141 | 736.83 | 201 | 1048.41 | 261 | 1359.99 | 321 | 1671.57 | 371 | 1931.04 | 421 | 2190.78 | 471 | 2450.25 |
| 22 | 119.07 | 82 | 430.65 | 142 | 742.23 | 202 | 1053.54 | 262 | 1365.12 | 322 | 1676.70 | 372 | 1936.44 | 422 | 2195.91 | 472 | 2455.65 |
| 23 | 124.20 | 83 | 435.78 | 143 | 747.36 | 203 | 1058.94 | 263 | 1370.25 | 323 | 1681.83 | 373 | 1941.57 | 423 | 2201.04 | 473 | 2460.78 |
| 24 | 129.33 | 84 | 440.91 | 144 | 752.49 | 204 | 1064.07 | 264 | 1375.65 | 324 | 1687.23 | 374 | 1946.70 | 424 | 2206.44 | 474 | 2465.91 |
| 25 | 134.73 | 85 | 446.04 | 145 | 757.62 | 205 | 1069.20 | 265 | 1380.78 | 325 | 1692.36 | 375 | 1951.83 | 425 | 2211.57 | 475 | 2471.04 |
| 26 | 139.86 | 86 | 451.44 | 146 | 762.75 | 206 | 1074.33 | 266 | 1385.91 | 326 | 1697.49 | 376 | 1957.23 | 426 | 2216.70 | 476 | 2476.44 |
| 27 | 144.99 | 87 | 456.57 | 147 | 768.15 | 207 | 1079.73 | 267 | 1391.04 | 327 | 1702.62 | 377 | 1962.36 | 427 | 2221.83 | 477 | 2481.57 |
| 28 | 150.12 | 88 | 461.70 | 148 | 773.28 | 208 | 1084.86 | 268 | 1396.44 | 328 | 1707.75 | 378 | 1967.49 | 428 | 2227.23 | 478 | 2486.70 |
| 29 | 155.25 | 89 | 466.83 | 149 | 778.41 | 209 | 1089.99 | 269 | 1401.57 | 329 | 1713.15 | 379 | 1972.62 | 429 | 2232.36 | 479 | 2491.83 |
| 30 | 160.65 | 90 | 472.23 | 150 | 783.54 | 210 | 1095.12 | 270 | 1406.70 | 330 | 1718.28 | 380 | 1977.75 | 430 | 2237.49 | 480 | 2497.23 |
| 31 | 165.78 | 91 | 477.36 | 151 | 788.94 | 211 | 1100.25 | 271 | 1411.83 | 331 | 1723.41 | 381 | 1983.15 | 431 | 2242.62 | 481 | 2502.36 |
| 32 | 170.91 | 92 | 482.49 | 152 | 794.07 | 212 | 1105.65 | 272 | 1417.23 | 332 | 1728.54 | 382 | 1988.28 | 432 | 2247.75 | 482 | 2507.49 |
| 33 | 176.04 | 93 | 487.62 | 153 | 799.20 | 213 | 1110.78 | 273 | 1422.36 | 333 | 1733.94 | 383 | 1993.41 | 433 | 2253.15 | 483 | 2512.62 |
| 34 | 181.44 | 94 | 492.75 | 154 | 804.33 | 214 | 1115.91 | 274 | 1427.49 | 334 | 1739.07 | 384 | 1998.54 | 434 | 2258.28 | 484 | 2517.75 |
| 35 | 186.57 | 95 | 498.15 | 155 | 809.73 | 215 | 1121.04 | 275 | 1432.62 | 335 | 1744.20 | 385 | 2003.94 | 435 | 2263.41 | 485 | 2523.15 |
| 36 | 191.70 | 96 | 503.28 | 156 | 814.86 | 216 | 1126.44 | 276 | 1437.75 | 336 | 1749.33 | 386 | 2009.07 | 436 | 2268.54 | 486 | 2528.28 |
| 37 | 196.83 | 97 | 508.41 | 157 | 819.99 | 217 | 1131.57 | 277 | 1443.15 | 337 | 1754.73 | 387 | 2014.20 | 437 | 2273.94 | 487 | 2533.41 |
| 38 | 202.23 | 98 | 513.54 | 158 | 825.12 | 218 | 1136.70 | 278 | 1448.28 | 338 | 1759.86 | 388 | 2019.33 | 438 | 2279.07 | 488 | 2538.54 |
| 39 | 207.36 | 99 | 518.94 | 159 | 830.25 | 219 | 1141.83 | 279 | 1453.41 | 339 | 1764.99 | 389 | 2024.73 | 439 | 2284.20 | 489 | 2543.94 |
| 40 | 212.49 | 100 | 524.07 | 160 | 835.65 | 220 | 1147.23 | 280 | 1458.54 | 340 | 1770.12 | 390 | 2029.86 | 440 | 2289.33 | 490 | 2549.07 |
| 41 | 217.62 | 101 | 529.20 | 161 | 840.78 | 221 | 1152.36 | 281 | 1463.94 | 341 | 1775.25 | 391 | 2034.99 | 441 | 2294.73 | 491 | 2554.20 |
| 42 | 222.75 | 102 | 534.33 | 162 | 845.91 | 222 | 1157.49 | 282 | 1469.07 | 342 | 1780.65 | 392 | 2040.12 | 442 | 2299.86 | 492 | 2559.33 |
| 43 | 228.15 | 103 | 539.73 | 163 | 851.04 | 223 | 1162.62 | 283 | 1474.20 | 343 | 1785.78 | 393 | 2045.25 | 443 | 2304.99 | 493 | 2564.73 |
| 44 | 233.28 | 104 | 544.86 | 164 | 856.44 | 224 | 1167.75 | 284 | 1479.33 | 344 | 1790.91 | 394 | 2050.65 | 444 | 2310.12 | 494 | 2569.86 |
| 45 | 238.41 | 105 | 549.99 | 165 | 861.57 | 225 | 1173.15 | 285 | 1484.73 | 345 | 1796.04 | 395 | 2055.78 | 445 | 2315.25 | 495 | 2574.99 |
| 46 | 243.54 | 106 | 555.12 | 166 | 866.70 | 226 | 1178.28 | 286 | 1489.86 | 346 | 1801.44 | 396 | 2060.91 | 446 | 2320.65 | 496 | 2580.12 |
| 47 | 248.94 | 107 | 560.25 | 167 | 871.83 | 227 | 1183.41 | 287 | 1494.99 | 347 | 1806.57 | 397 | 2066.04 | 447 | 2325.78 | 497 | 2585.25 |
| 48 | 254.07 | 108 | 565.65 | 168 | 877.23 | 228 | 1188.54 | 288 | 1500.12 | 348 | 1811.70 | 398 | 2071.44 | 448 | 2330.91 | 498 | 2590.65 |
| 49 | 259.20 | 109 | 570.78 | 169 | 882.36 | 229 | 1193.94 | 289 | 1505.25 | 349 | 1816.83 | 399 | 2076.57 | 449 | 2336.04 | 499 | 2595.78 |
| 50 | 264.33 | 110 | 575.91 | 170 | 887.49 | 230 | 1199.07 | 290 | 1510.65 | 350 | 1822.23 | 400 | 2081.70 | 450 | 2341.44 | 500 | 2600.91 |
| 51 | 269.73 | 111 | 581.04 | 171 | 892.62 | 231 | 1204.20 | 291 | 1515.78 | | | | | | | | |
| 52 | 274.86 | 112 | 586.44 | 172 | 897.75 | 232 | 1209.33 | 292 | 1520.91 | | | | | | | | |
| 53 | 279.99 | 113 | 591.57 | 173 | 903.15 | 233 | 1214.73 | 293 | 1526.04 | | | | | | | | |
| 54 | 285.12 | 114 | 596.70 | 174 | 908.28 | 234 | 1219.86 | 294 | 1531.44 | | | | | | | | |
| 55 | 290.25 | 115 | 601.83 | 175 | 913.41 | 235 | 1224.99 | 295 | 1536.57 | | | | | | | | |
| 56 | 295.65 | 116 | 607.23 | 176 | 918.54 | 236 | 1230.12 | 296 | 1541.70 | | | | | | | | |
| 57 | 300.78 | 117 | 612.36 | 177 | 923.94 | 237 | 1235.25 | 297 | 1546.83 | | | | | | | | |
| 58 | 305.91 | 118 | 617.49 | 178 | 929.07 | 238 | 1240.65 | 298 | 1552.23 | | | | | | | | |
| 59 | 311.04 | 119 | 622.62 | 179 | 934.20 | 239 | 1245.78 | 299 | 1557.36 | | | | | | | | |
| 60 | 316.44 | 120 | 627.75 | 180 | 939.33 | 240 | 1250.91 | 300 | 1562.49 | | | | | | | | |

**Code more than 500**

1 Where the code is in the range **501** to **1000** inclusive:

 a. Subtract **500** from the code and use the balance of the code to obtain a pay adjustment figure from the table above.

 b. Add this pay adjustment figure to the figure given in the box alongside to obtain the figure of total pay adjustment to date *  **2596.32**

2 Where the code **exceeds 1000** follow the instructions on **page 3**.

30

## Tables A - Pay Adjustment Tables

Oct 12 to Oct 18   **Week 28**

| Code | Total pay adjustment to date £ | Code | Total pay adjustment to date £ | Code | Total pay adjustment to date £ | Code | Total pay adjustment to date £ | Code | Total pay adjustment to date £ | Code | Total pay adjustment to date £ | Code | Total pay adjustment to date £ | Code | Total pay adjustment to date £ | Code | Total pay adjustment to date £ |
|---|---|---|---|---|---|---|---|---|---|---|---|---|---|---|---|---|---|
| 0 | NIL | 61 | 333.48 | 121 | 656.60 | 181 | 979.72 | 241 | 1302.56 | 301 | 1625.68 | 351 | 1895.04 | 401 | 2164.12 | 451 | 2433.48 |
| 1 | 10.36 | 62 | 338.80 | 122 | 661.92 | 182 | 985.04 | 242 | 1308.16 | 302 | 1631.00 | 352 | 1900.36 | 402 | 2169.72 | 452 | 2438.80 |
| 2 | 15.68 | 63 | 344.12 | 123 | 667.24 | 183 | 990.36 | 243 | 1313.48 | 303 | 1636.60 | 353 | 1905.68 | 403 | 2175.04 | 453 | 2444.12 |
| 3 | 21.00 | 64 | 349.72 | 124 | 672.56 | 184 | 995.68 | 244 | 1318.80 | 304 | 1641.92 | 354 | 1911.00 | 404 | 2180.36 | 454 | 2449.72 |
| 4 | 26.60 | 65 | 355.04 | 125 | 678.16 | 185 | 1001.00 | 245 | 1324.12 | 305 | 1647.24 | 355 | 1916.60 | 405 | 2185.68 | 455 | 2455.04 |
| 5 | 31.92 | | | | | | | | | | | | | | | | |
| 6 | 37.24 | 66 | 360.36 | 126 | 683.48 | 186 | 1006.60 | 246 | 1329.72 | 306 | 1652.56 | 356 | 1921.92 | 406 | 2191.00 | 456 | 2460.36 |
| 7 | 42.56 | 67 | 365.68 | 127 | 688.80 | 187 | 1011.92 | 247 | 1335.04 | 307 | 1658.16 | 357 | 1927.24 | 407 | 2196.60 | 457 | 2465.68 |
| 8 | 48.16 | 68 | 371.00 | 128 | 694.12 | 188 | 1017.24 | 248 | 1340.36 | 308 | 1663.48 | 358 | 1932.56 | 408 | 2201.92 | 458 | 2471.00 |
| 9 | 53.48 | 69 | 376.60 | 129 | 699.72 | 189 | 1022.56 | 249 | 1345.68 | 309 | 1668.80 | 359 | 1938.16 | 409 | 2207.24 | 459 | 2476.60 |
| 10 | 58.80 | 70 | 381.92 | 130 | 705.04 | 190 | 1028.16 | 250 | 1351.00 | 310 | 1674.12 | 360 | 1943.48 | 410 | 2212.56 | 460 | 2481.92 |
| 11 | 64.12 | 71 | 387.24 | 131 | 710.36 | 191 | 1033.48 | 251 | 1356.60 | 311 | 1679.72 | 361 | 1948.80 | 411 | 2218.16 | 461 | 2487.24 |
| 12 | 69.72 | 72 | 392.56 | 132 | 715.68 | 192 | 1038.80 | 252 | 1361.92 | 312 | 1685.04 | 362 | 1954.12 | 412 | 2223.48 | 462 | 2492.56 |
| 13 | 75.04 | 73 | 398.16 | 133 | 721.00 | 193 | 1044.12 | 253 | 1367.24 | 313 | 1690.36 | 363 | 1959.72 | 413 | 2228.80 | 463 | 2498.16 |
| 14 | 80.36 | 74 | 403.48 | 134 | 726.60 | 194 | 1049.72 | 254 | 1372.56 | 314 | 1695.68 | 364 | 1965.04 | 414 | 2234.12 | 464 | 2503.48 |
| 15 | 85.68 | 75 | 408.80 | 135 | 731.92 | 195 | 1055.04 | 255 | 1378.16 | 315 | 1701.00 | 365 | 1970.36 | 415 | 2239.72 | 465 | 2508.80 |
| 16 | 91.00 | 76 | 414.12 | 136 | 737.24 | 196 | 1060.36 | 256 | 1383.48 | 316 | 1706.60 | 366 | 1975.68 | 416 | 2245.04 | 466 | 2514.12 |
| 17 | 96.60 | 77 | 419.72 | 137 | 742.56 | 197 | 1065.68 | 257 | 1388.80 | 317 | 1711.92 | 367 | 1981.00 | 417 | 2250.36 | 467 | 2519.72 |
| 18 | 101.92 | 78 | 425.04 | 138 | 748.16 | 198 | 1071.00 | 258 | 1394.12 | 318 | 1717.24 | 368 | 1986.60 | 418 | 2255.68 | 468 | 2525.04 |
| 19 | 107.24 | 79 | 430.36 | 139 | 753.48 | 199 | 1076.60 | 259 | 1399.72 | 319 | 1722.56 | 369 | 1991.92 | 419 | 2261.00 | 469 | 2530.36 |
| 20 | 112.56 | 80 | 435.68 | 140 | 758.80 | 200 | 1081.92 | 260 | 1405.04 | 320 | 1728.16 | 370 | 1997.24 | 420 | 2266.60 | 470 | 2535.68 |
| 21 | 118.16 | 81 | 441.00 | 141 | 764.12 | 201 | 1087.24 | 261 | 1410.36 | 321 | 1733.48 | 371 | 2002.56 | 421 | 2271.92 | 471 | 2541.00 |
| 22 | 123.48 | 82 | 446.60 | 142 | 769.72 | 202 | 1092.56 | 262 | 1415.68 | 322 | 1738.80 | 372 | 2008.16 | 422 | 2277.24 | 472 | 2546.60 |
| 23 | 128.80 | 83 | 451.92 | 143 | 775.04 | 203 | 1098.16 | 263 | 1421.00 | 323 | 1744.12 | 373 | 2013.48 | 423 | 2282.56 | 473 | 2551.92 |
| 24 | 134.12 | 84 | 457.24 | 144 | 780.36 | 204 | 1103.48 | 264 | 1426.60 | 324 | 1749.72 | 374 | 2018.80 | 424 | 2288.16 | 474 | 2557.24 |
| 25 | 139.72 | 85 | 462.56 | 145 | 785.68 | 205 | 1108.80 | 265 | 1431.92 | 325 | 1755.04 | 375 | 2024.12 | 425 | 2293.48 | 475 | 2562.56 |
| 26 | 145.04 | 86 | 468.16 | 146 | 791.00 | 206 | 1114.12 | 266 | 1437.24 | 326 | 1760.36 | 376 | 2029.72 | 426 | 2298.80 | 476 | 2568.16 |
| 27 | 150.36 | 87 | 473.48 | 147 | 796.60 | 207 | 1119.72 | 267 | 1442.56 | 327 | 1765.68 | 377 | 2035.04 | 427 | 2304.12 | 477 | 2573.48 |
| 28 | 155.68 | 88 | 478.80 | 148 | 801.92 | 208 | 1125.04 | 268 | 1448.16 | 328 | 1771.00 | 378 | 2040.36 | 428 | 2309.72 | 478 | 2578.80 |
| 29 | 161.00 | 89 | 484.12 | 149 | 807.24 | 209 | 1130.36 | 269 | 1453.48 | 329 | 1776.60 | 379 | 2045.68 | 429 | 2315.04 | 479 | 2584.12 |
| 30 | 166.60 | 90 | 489.72 | 150 | 812.56 | 210 | 1135.68 | 270 | 1458.80 | 330 | 1781.92 | 380 | 2051.00 | 430 | 2320.36 | 480 | 2589.72 |
| 31 | 171.92 | 91 | 495.04 | 151 | 818.16 | 211 | 1141.00 | 271 | 1464.12 | 331 | 1787.24 | 381 | 2056.60 | 431 | 2325.68 | 481 | 2595.04 |
| 32 | 177.24 | 92 | 500.36 | 152 | 823.48 | 212 | 1146.60 | 272 | 1469.72 | 332 | 1792.56 | 382 | 2061.92 | 432 | 2331.00 | 482 | 2600.36 |
| 33 | 182.56 | 93 | 505.68 | 153 | 828.80 | 213 | 1151.92 | 273 | 1475.04 | 333 | 1798.16 | 383 | 2067.24 | 433 | 2336.60 | 483 | 2605.68 |
| 34 | 188.16 | 94 | 511.00 | 154 | 834.12 | 214 | 1157.24 | 274 | 1480.36 | 334 | 1803.48 | 384 | 2072.56 | 434 | 2341.92 | 484 | 2611.00 |
| 35 | 193.48 | 95 | 516.60 | 155 | 839.72 | 215 | 1162.56 | 275 | 1485.68 | 335 | 1808.80 | 385 | 2078.16 | 435 | 2347.24 | 485 | 2616.60 |
| 36 | 198.80 | 96 | 521.92 | 156 | 845.04 | 216 | 1168.16 | 276 | 1491.00 | 336 | 1814.12 | 386 | 2083.48 | 436 | 2352.56 | 486 | 2621.92 |
| 37 | 204.12 | 97 | 527.24 | 157 | 850.36 | 217 | 1173.48 | 277 | 1496.60 | 337 | 1819.72 | 387 | 2088.80 | 437 | 2358.16 | 487 | 2627.24 |
| 38 | 209.72 | 98 | 532.56 | 158 | 855.68 | 218 | 1178.80 | 278 | 1501.92 | 338 | 1825.04 | 388 | 2094.12 | 438 | 2363.48 | 488 | 2632.56 |
| 39 | 215.04 | 99 | 538.16 | 159 | 861.00 | 219 | 1184.12 | 279 | 1507.24 | 339 | 1830.36 | 389 | 2099.72 | 439 | 2368.80 | 489 | 2638.16 |
| 40 | 220.36 | 100 | 543.48 | 160 | 866.60 | 220 | 1189.72 | 280 | 1512.56 | 340 | 1835.68 | 390 | 2105.04 | 440 | 2374.12 | 490 | 2643.48 |
| 41 | 225.68 | 101 | 548.80 | 161 | 871.92 | 221 | 1195.04 | 281 | 1518.16 | 341 | 1841.00 | 391 | 2110.36 | 441 | 2379.72 | 491 | 2648.80 |
| 42 | 231.00 | 102 | 554.12 | 162 | 877.24 | 222 | 1200.36 | 282 | 1523.48 | 342 | 1846.60 | 392 | 2115.68 | 442 | 2385.04 | 492 | 2654.12 |
| 43 | 236.60 | 103 | 559.72 | 163 | 882.56 | 223 | 1205.68 | 283 | 1528.80 | 343 | 1851.92 | 393 | 2121.00 | 443 | 2390.36 | 493 | 2659.72 |
| 44 | 241.92 | 104 | 565.04 | 164 | 888.16 | 224 | 1211.00 | 284 | 1534.12 | 344 | 1857.24 | 394 | 2126.60 | 444 | 2395.68 | 494 | 2665.04 |
| 45 | 247.24 | 105 | 570.36 | 165 | 893.48 | 225 | 1216.60 | 285 | 1539.72 | 345 | 1862.56 | 395 | 2131.92 | 445 | 2401.00 | 495 | 2670.36 |
| 46 | 252.56 | 106 | 575.68 | 166 | 898.80 | 226 | 1221.92 | 286 | 1545.04 | 346 | 1868.16 | 396 | 2137.24 | 446 | 2406.60 | 496 | 2675.68 |
| 47 | 258.16 | 107 | 581.00 | 167 | 904.12 | 227 | 1227.24 | 287 | 1550.36 | 347 | 1873.48 | 397 | 2142.56 | 447 | 2411.92 | 497 | 2681.00 |
| 48 | 263.48 | 108 | 586.60 | 168 | 909.72 | 228 | 1232.56 | 288 | 1555.68 | 348 | 1878.80 | 398 | 2148.16 | 448 | 2417.24 | 498 | 2686.60 |
| 49 | 268.80 | 109 | 591.92 | 169 | 915.04 | 229 | 1238.16 | 289 | 1561.00 | 349 | 1884.12 | 399 | 2153.48 | 449 | 2422.56 | 499 | 2691.92 |
| 50 | 274.12 | 110 | 597.24 | 170 | 920.36 | 230 | 1243.48 | 290 | 1566.60 | 350 | 1889.72 | 400 | 2158.80 | 450 | 2428.16 | 500 | 2697.24 |
| 51 | 279.72 | 111 | 602.56 | 171 | 925.68 | 231 | 1248.80 | 291 | 1571.92 | | | | | | | | |
| 52 | 285.04 | 112 | 608.16 | 172 | 931.00 | 232 | 1254.12 | 292 | 1577.24 | | | | | | | | |
| 53 | 290.36 | 113 | 613.48 | 173 | 936.60 | 233 | 1259.72 | 293 | 1582.56 | | | | | | | | |
| 54 | 295.68 | 114 | 618.80 | 174 | 941.92 | 234 | 1265.04 | 294 | 1588.16 | | | | | | | | |
| 55 | 301.00 | 115 | 624.12 | 175 | 947.24 | 235 | 1270.36 | 295 | 1593.48 | | | | | | | | |
| 56 | 306.60 | 116 | 629.72 | 176 | 952.56 | 236 | 1275.68 | 296 | 1598.80 | | | | | | | | |
| 57 | 311.92 | 117 | 635.04 | 177 | 958.16 | 237 | 1281.00 | 297 | 1604.12 | | | | | | | | |
| 58 | 317.24 | 118 | 640.36 | 178 | 963.48 | 238 | 1286.60 | 298 | 1609.72 | | | | | | | | |
| 59 | 322.56 | 119 | 645.68 | 179 | 968.80 | 239 | 1291.92 | 299 | 1615.04 | | | | | | | | |
| 60 | 328.16 | 120 | 651.00 | 180 | 974.12 | 240 | 1297.24 | 300 | 1620.36 | | | | | | | | |

### Code more than 500

1 Where the code is in the range **501** to **1000** inclusive:

 a. Subtract **500** from the code and use the balance of the code to obtain a pay adjustment figure from the table above.

 b. Add this pay adjustment figure to the figure given in the box alongside to obtain the figure of total pay adjustment to date *   | **2692.48** |

2 Where the code **exceeds 1000** follow the instructions on **page 3**.

**Week 29**   Oct 19 to Oct 25                                   **Tables A** - Pay Adjustment Tables

| Code | Total pay adjustment to date | Code | Total pay adjustment to date | Code | Total pay adjustment to date | Code | Total pay adjustment to date | Code | Total pay adjustment to date | Code | Total pay adjustment to date | Code | Total pay adjustment to date | Code | Total pay adjustment to date | Code | Total pay adjustment to date |
|---|---|---|---|---|---|---|---|---|---|---|---|---|---|---|---|---|---|
| | £ | | £ | | £ | | £ | | £ | | £ | | £ | | £ | | £ |
| 0 | NIL | 61 | 345.39 | 121 | 680.05 | 181 | 1014.71 | 241 | 1349.08 | 301 | 1683.74 | 351 | 1962.72 | 401 | 2241.41 | 451 | 2520.39 |
| 1 | 10.73 | 62 | 350.90 | 122 | 685.56 | 182 | 1020.22 | 242 | 1354.88 | 302 | 1689.25 | 352 | 1968.23 | 402 | 2247.21 | 452 | 2525.90 |
| 2 | 16.24 | 63 | 356.41 | 123 | 691.07 | 183 | 1025.73 | 243 | 1360.39 | 303 | 1695.05 | 353 | 1973.74 | 403 | 2252.72 | 453 | 2531.41 |
| 3 | 21.75 | 64 | 362.21 | 124 | 696.58 | 184 | 1031.24 | 244 | 1365.90 | 304 | 1700.56 | 354 | 1979.25 | 404 | 2258.23 | 454 | 2537.21 |
| 4 | 27.55 | 65 | 367.72 | 125 | 702.38 | 185 | 1036.75 | 245 | 1371.41 | 305 | 1706.07 | 355 | 1985.05 | 405 | 2263.74 | 455 | 2542.72 |
| 5 | 33.06 | | | | | | | | | | | | | | | | |
| 6 | 38.57 | 66 | 373.23 | 126 | 707.89 | 186 | 1042.55 | 246 | 1377.21 | 306 | 1711.58 | 356 | 1990.56 | 406 | 2269.25 | 456 | 2548.23 |
| 7 | 44.08 | 67 | 378.74 | 127 | 713.40 | 187 | 1048.06 | 247 | 1382.72 | 307 | 1717.38 | 357 | 1996.07 | 407 | 2275.05 | 457 | 2553.74 |
| 8 | 49.88 | 68 | 384.25 | 128 | 718.91 | 188 | 1053.57 | 248 | 1388.23 | 308 | 1722.89 | 358 | 2001.58 | 408 | 2280.56 | 458 | 2559.25 |
| 9 | 55.39 | 69 | 390.05 | 129 | 724.71 | 189 | 1059.08 | 249 | 1393.74 | 309 | 1728.40 | 359 | 2007.38 | 409 | 2286.07 | 459 | 2565.05 |
| 10 | 60.90 | 70 | 395.56 | 130 | 730.22 | 190 | 1064.88 | 250 | 1399.25 | 310 | 1733.91 | 360 | 2012.89 | 410 | 2291.58 | 460 | 2570.56 |
| 11 | 66.41 | 71 | 401.07 | 131 | 735.73 | 191 | 1070.39 | 251 | 1405.05 | 311 | 1739.71 | 361 | 2018.40 | 411 | 2297.38 | 461 | 2576.07 |
| 12 | 72.21 | 72 | 406.58 | 132 | 741.24 | 192 | 1075.90 | 252 | 1410.56 | 312 | 1745.22 | 362 | 2023.91 | 412 | 2302.89 | 462 | 2581.58 |
| 13 | 77.72 | 73 | 412.38 | 133 | 746.75 | 193 | 1081.41 | 253 | 1416.07 | 313 | 1750.73 | 363 | 2029.71 | 413 | 2308.40 | 463 | 2587.38 |
| 14 | 83.23 | 74 | 417.89 | 134 | 752.55 | 194 | 1087.21 | 254 | 1421.58 | 314 | 1756.24 | 364 | 2035.22 | 414 | 2313.91 | 464 | 2592.89 |
| 15 | 88.74 | 75 | 423.40 | 135 | 758.06 | 195 | 1092.72 | 255 | 1427.38 | 315 | 1761.75 | 365 | 2040.73 | 415 | 2319.71 | 465 | 2598.40 |
| 16 | 94.25 | 76 | 428.91 | 136 | 763.57 | 196 | 1098.23 | 256 | 1432.89 | 316 | 1767.55 | 366 | 2046.24 | 416 | 2325.22 | 466 | 2603.91 |
| 17 | 100.05 | 77 | 434.71 | 137 | 769.08 | 197 | 1103.74 | 257 | 1438.40 | 317 | 1773.06 | 367 | 2051.75 | 417 | 2330.73 | 467 | 2609.71 |
| 18 | 105.56 | 78 | 440.22 | 138 | 774.88 | 198 | 1109.25 | 258 | 1443.91 | 318 | 1778.57 | 368 | 2057.55 | 418 | 2336.24 | 468 | 2615.22 |
| 19 | 111.07 | 79 | 445.73 | 139 | 780.39 | 199 | 1115.05 | 259 | 1449.71 | 319 | 1784.08 | 369 | 2063.06 | 419 | 2341.75 | 469 | 2620.73 |
| 20 | 116.58 | 80 | 451.24 | 140 | 785.90 | 200 | 1120.56 | 260 | 1455.22 | 320 | 1789.88 | 370 | 2068.57 | 420 | 2347.55 | 470 | 2626.24 |
| 21 | 122.38 | 81 | 456.75 | 141 | 791.41 | 201 | 1126.07 | 261 | 1460.73 | 321 | 1795.39 | 371 | 2074.08 | 421 | 2353.06 | 471 | 2631.75 |
| 22 | 127.89 | 82 | 462.55 | 142 | 797.21 | 202 | 1131.58 | 262 | 1466.24 | 322 | 1800.90 | 372 | 2079.88 | 422 | 2358.57 | 472 | 2637.55 |
| 23 | 133.40 | 83 | 468.06 | 143 | 802.72 | 203 | 1137.38 | 263 | 1471.75 | 323 | 1806.41 | 373 | 2085.39 | 423 | 2364.08 | 473 | 2643.06 |
| 24 | 138.91 | 84 | 473.57 | 144 | 808.23 | 204 | 1142.89 | 264 | 1477.55 | 324 | 1812.21 | 374 | 2090.90 | 424 | 2369.88 | 474 | 2648.57 |
| 25 | 144.71 | 85 | 479.08 | 145 | 813.74 | 205 | 1148.40 | 265 | 1483.06 | 325 | 1817.72 | 375 | 2096.41 | 425 | 2375.39 | 475 | 2654.08 |
| 26 | 150.22 | 86 | 484.88 | 146 | 819.25 | 206 | 1153.91 | 266 | 1488.57 | 326 | 1823.23 | 376 | 2102.21 | 426 | 2380.90 | 476 | 2659.88 |
| 27 | 155.73 | 87 | 490.39 | 147 | 825.05 | 207 | 1159.71 | 267 | 1494.08 | 327 | 1828.74 | 377 | 2107.72 | 427 | 2386.41 | 477 | 2665.39 |
| 28 | 161.24 | 88 | 495.90 | 148 | 830.56 | 208 | 1165.22 | 268 | 1499.88 | 328 | 1834.25 | 378 | 2113.23 | 428 | 2392.21 | 478 | 2670.90 |
| 29 | 166.75 | 89 | 501.41 | 149 | 836.07 | 209 | 1170.73 | 269 | 1505.39 | 329 | 1840.05 | 379 | 2118.74 | 429 | 2397.72 | 479 | 2676.41 |
| 30 | 172.55 | 90 | 507.21 | 150 | 841.58 | 210 | 1176.24 | 270 | 1510.90 | 330 | 1845.56 | 380 | 2124.25 | 430 | 2403.23 | 480 | 2682.21 |
| 31 | 178.06 | 91 | 512.72 | 151 | 847.38 | 211 | 1181.75 | 271 | 1516.41 | 331 | 1851.07 | 381 | 2130.05 | 431 | 2408.74 | 481 | 2687.72 |
| 32 | 183.57 | 92 | 518.23 | 152 | 852.89 | 212 | 1187.55 | 272 | 1522.21 | 332 | 1856.58 | 382 | 2135.56 | 432 | 2414.25 | 482 | 2693.23 |
| 33 | 189.08 | 93 | 523.74 | 153 | 858.40 | 213 | 1193.06 | 273 | 1527.72 | 333 | 1862.38 | 383 | 2141.07 | 433 | 2420.05 | 483 | 2698.74 |
| 34 | 194.88 | 94 | 529.25 | 154 | 863.91 | 214 | 1198.57 | 274 | 1533.23 | 334 | 1867.89 | 384 | 2146.58 | 434 | 2425.56 | 484 | 2704.25 |
| 35 | 200.39 | 95 | 535.05 | 155 | 869.71 | 215 | 1204.08 | 275 | 1538.74 | 335 | 1873.40 | 385 | 2152.38 | 435 | 2431.07 | 485 | 2710.05 |
| 36 | 205.90 | 96 | 540.56 | 156 | 875.22 | 216 | 1209.88 | 276 | 1544.25 | 336 | 1878.91 | 386 | 2157.89 | 436 | 2436.58 | 486 | 2715.56 |
| 37 | 211.41 | 97 | 546.07 | 157 | 880.73 | 217 | 1215.39 | 277 | 1550.05 | 337 | 1884.71 | 387 | 2163.40 | 437 | 2442.38 | 487 | 2721.07 |
| 38 | 217.21 | 98 | 551.58 | 158 | 886.24 | 218 | 1220.90 | 278 | 1555.56 | 338 | 1890.22 | 388 | 2168.91 | 438 | 2447.89 | 488 | 2726.58 |
| 39 | 222.72 | 99 | 557.38 | 159 | 891.75 | 219 | 1226.41 | 279 | 1561.07 | 339 | 1895.73 | 389 | 2174.71 | 439 | 2453.40 | 489 | 2732.38 |
| 40 | 228.23 | 100 | 562.89 | 160 | 897.55 | 220 | 1232.21 | 280 | 1566.58 | 340 | 1901.24 | 390 | 2180.22 | 440 | 2458.91 | 490 | 2737.89 |
| 41 | 233.74 | 101 | 568.40 | 161 | 903.06 | 221 | 1237.72 | 281 | 1572.38 | 341 | 1906.75 | 391 | 2185.73 | 441 | 2464.71 | 491 | 2743.40 |
| 42 | 239.25 | 102 | 573.91 | 162 | 908.57 | 222 | 1243.23 | 282 | 1577.89 | 342 | 1912.55 | 392 | 2191.24 | 442 | 2470.22 | 492 | 2748.91 |
| 43 | 245.05 | 103 | 579.71 | 163 | 914.08 | 223 | 1248.74 | 283 | 1583.40 | 343 | 1918.06 | 393 | 2196.75 | 443 | 2475.73 | 493 | 2754.71 |
| 44 | 250.56 | 104 | 585.22 | 164 | 919.88 | 224 | 1254.25 | 284 | 1588.91 | 344 | 1923.57 | 394 | 2202.55 | 444 | 2481.24 | 494 | 2760.22 |
| 45 | 256.07 | 105 | 590.73 | 165 | 925.39 | 225 | 1260.05 | 285 | 1594.71 | 345 | 1929.08 | 395 | 2208.06 | 445 | 2486.75 | 495 | 2765.73 |
| 46 | 261.58 | 106 | 596.24 | 166 | 930.90 | 226 | 1265.56 | 286 | 1600.22 | 346 | 1934.88 | 396 | 2213.57 | 446 | 2492.55 | 496 | 2771.24 |
| 47 | 267.38 | 107 | 601.75 | 167 | 936.41 | 227 | 1271.07 | 287 | 1605.73 | 347 | 1940.39 | 397 | 2219.08 | 447 | 2498.06 | 497 | 2776.75 |
| 48 | 272.89 | 108 | 607.55 | 168 | 942.21 | 228 | 1276.58 | 288 | 1611.24 | 348 | 1945.90 | 398 | 2224.88 | 448 | 2503.57 | 498 | 2782.55 |
| 49 | 278.40 | 109 | 613.06 | 169 | 947.72 | 229 | 1282.38 | 289 | 1616.75 | 349 | 1951.41 | 399 | 2230.39 | 449 | 2509.08 | 499 | 2788.06 |
| 50 | 283.91 | 110 | 618.57 | 170 | 953.23 | 230 | 1287.89 | 290 | 1622.55 | 350 | 1957.21 | 400 | 2235.90 | 450 | 2514.88 | 500 | 2793.57 |
| 51 | 289.71 | 111 | 624.08 | 171 | 958.74 | 231 | 1293.40 | 291 | 1628.06 | | | | | | | | |
| 52 | 295.22 | 112 | 629.88 | 172 | 964.25 | 232 | 1298.91 | 292 | 1633.57 | | | | | | | | |
| 53 | 300.73 | 113 | 635.39 | 173 | 970.05 | 233 | 1304.71 | 293 | 1639.08 | | | | | | | | |
| 54 | 306.24 | 114 | 640.90 | 174 | 975.56 | 234 | 1310.22 | 294 | 1644.88 | | | | | | | | |
| 55 | 311.75 | 115 | 646.41 | 175 | 981.07 | 235 | 1315.73 | 295 | 1650.39 | | | | | | | | |
| 56 | 317.55 | 116 | 652.21 | 176 | 986.58 | 236 | 1321.24 | 296 | 1655.90 | | | | | | | | |
| 57 | 323.06 | 117 | 657.72 | 177 | 992.38 | 237 | 1326.75 | 297 | 1661.41 | | | | | | | | |
| 58 | 328.57 | 118 | 663.23 | 178 | 997.89 | 238 | 1332.55 | 298 | 1667.21 | | | | | | | | |
| 59 | 334.08 | 119 | 668.74 | 179 | 1003.40 | 239 | 1338.06 | 299 | 1672.72 | | | | | | | | |
| 60 | 339.88 | 120 | 674.29 | 180 | 1008.91 | 240 | 1343.57 | 300 | 1678.23 | | | | | | | | |

**Code more than 500**

1 Where the code is in the range **501** to **1000** inclusive:

a. Subtract **500** from the code and use the balance of the code to obtain a pay adjustment figure from the table above.

b. Add this pay adjustment figure to the figure given in the box alongside to obtain the figure of total pay adjustment to date *    **2788.64**

2 Where the code **exceeds 1000** follow the instructions on **page 3**.

32

## Tables A - Pay Adjustment Tables      Oct 26 to Nov 1 **Week 30**

| Code | Total pay adjustment to date £ | Code | Total pay adjustment to date £ | Code | Total pay adjustment to date £ | Code | Total pay adjustment to date £ | Code | Total pay adjustment to date £ | Code | Total pay adjustment to date £ | Code | Total pay adjustment to date £ | Code | Total pay adjustment to date £ | Code | Total pay adjustment to date £ |
|---|---|---|---|---|---|---|---|---|---|---|---|---|---|---|---|---|---|
| 0 | NIL | | | | | | | | | | | | | | | | |
| 1 | 11.10 | 61 | 357.30 | 121 | 703.50 | 181 | 1049.70 | 241 | 1395.60 | 301 | 1741.80 | 351 | 2030.40 | 401 | 2318.70 | 451 | 2607.30 |
| 2 | 16.80 | 62 | 363.00 | 122 | 709.20 | 182 | 1055.40 | 242 | 1401.60 | 302 | 1747.50 | 352 | 2036.10 | 402 | 2324.70 | 452 | 2613.00 |
| 3 | 22.50 | 63 | 368.70 | 123 | 714.90 | 183 | 1061.10 | 243 | 1407.30 | 303 | 1753.50 | 353 | 2041.80 | 403 | 2330.40 | 453 | 2618.70 |
| 4 | 28.50 | 64 | 374.70 | 124 | 720.60 | 184 | 1066.80 | 244 | 1413.00 | 304 | 1759.20 | 354 | 2047.50 | 404 | 2336.10 | 454 | 2624.70 |
| 5 | 34.20 | 65 | 380.40 | 125 | 726.60 | 185 | 1072.50 | 245 | 1418.70 | 305 | 1764.90 | 355 | 2053.50 | 405 | 2341.80 | 455 | 2630.40 |
| 6 | 39.90 | 66 | 386.10 | 126 | 732.30 | 186 | 1078.50 | 246 | 1424.70 | 306 | 1770.60 | 356 | 2059.20 | 406 | 2347.50 | 456 | 2636.10 |
| 7 | 45.60 | 67 | 391.80 | 127 | 738.00 | 187 | 1084.20 | 247 | 1430.40 | 307 | 1776.60 | 357 | 2064.90 | 407 | 2353.50 | 457 | 2641.80 |
| 8 | 51.60 | 68 | 397.50 | 128 | 743.70 | 188 | 1089.90 | 248 | 1436.10 | 308 | 1782.30 | 358 | 2070.60 | 408 | 2359.20 | 458 | 2647.50 |
| 9 | 57.30 | 69 | 403.50 | 129 | 749.70 | 189 | 1095.60 | 249 | 1441.80 | 309 | 1788.00 | 359 | 2076.60 | 409 | 2364.90 | 459 | 2653.50 |
| 10 | 63.00 | 70 | 409.20 | 130 | 755.40 | 190 | 1101.60 | 250 | 1447.50 | 310 | 1793.70 | 360 | 2082.30 | 410 | 2370.60 | 460 | 2659.20 |
| 11 | 68.70 | 71 | 414.90 | 131 | 761.10 | 191 | 1107.30 | 251 | 1453.50 | 311 | 1799.70 | 361 | 2088.00 | 411 | 2376.60 | 461 | 2664.90 |
| 12 | 74.70 | 72 | 420.60 | 132 | 766.80 | 192 | 1113.00 | 252 | 1459.20 | 312 | 1805.40 | 362 | 2093.70 | 412 | 2382.30 | 462 | 2670.60 |
| 13 | 80.40 | 73 | 426.60 | 133 | 772.50 | 193 | 1118.70 | 253 | 1464.90 | 313 | 1811.10 | 363 | 2099.70 | 413 | 2388.00 | 463 | 2676.60 |
| 14 | 86.10 | 74 | 432.30 | 134 | 778.50 | 194 | 1124.70 | 254 | 1470.60 | 314 | 1816.80 | 364 | 2105.40 | 414 | 2393.70 | 464 | 2682.30 |
| 15 | 91.80 | 75 | 438.00 | 135 | 784.20 | 195 | 1130.40 | 255 | 1476.60 | 315 | 1822.50 | 365 | 2111.10 | 415 | 2399.70 | 465 | 2688.00 |
| 16 | 97.50 | 76 | 443.70 | 136 | 789.90 | 196 | 1136.10 | 256 | 1482.30 | 316 | 1828.50 | 366 | 2116.80 | 416 | 2405.40 | 466 | 2693.70 |
| 17 | 103.50 | 77 | 449.70 | 137 | 795.60 | 197 | 1141.80 | 257 | 1488.00 | 317 | 1834.20 | 367 | 2122.50 | 417 | 2411.10 | 467 | 2699.70 |
| 18 | 109.20 | 78 | 455.40 | 138 | 801.60 | 198 | 1147.50 | 258 | 1493.70 | 318 | 1839.90 | 368 | 2128.50 | 418 | 2416.80 | 468 | 2705.40 |
| 19 | 114.90 | 79 | 461.10 | 139 | 807.30 | 199 | 1153.50 | 259 | 1499.70 | 319 | 1845.60 | 369 | 2134.20 | 419 | 2422.50 | 469 | 2711.10 |
| 20 | 120.60 | 80 | 466.80 | 140 | 813.00 | 200 | 1159.20 | 260 | 1505.40 | 320 | 1851.60 | 370 | 2139.90 | 420 | 2428.50 | 470 | 2716.80 |
| 21 | 126.60 | 81 | 472.50 | 141 | 818.70 | 201 | 1164.90 | 261 | 1511.10 | 321 | 1857.30 | 371 | 2145.60 | 421 | 2434.20 | 471 | 2722.50 |
| 22 | 132.30 | 82 | 478.50 | 142 | 824.70 | 202 | 1170.60 | 262 | 1516.80 | 322 | 1863.00 | 372 | 2151.60 | 422 | 2439.90 | 472 | 2728.50 |
| 23 | 138.00 | 83 | 484.20 | 143 | 830.40 | 203 | 1176.60 | 263 | 1522.50 | 323 | 1868.70 | 373 | 2157.30 | 423 | 2445.60 | 473 | 2734.20 |
| 24 | 143.70 | 84 | 489.90 | 144 | 836.10 | 204 | 1182.30 | 264 | 1528.50 | 324 | 1874.70 | 374 | 2163.00 | 424 | 2451.60 | 474 | 2739.90 |
| 25 | 149.70 | 85 | 495.60 | 145 | 841.80 | 205 | 1188.00 | 265 | 1534.20 | 325 | 1880.40 | 375 | 2168.70 | 425 | 2457.30 | 475 | 2745.60 |
| 26 | 155.40 | 86 | 501.60 | 146 | 847.50 | 206 | 1193.70 | 266 | 1539.90 | 326 | 1886.10 | 376 | 2174.70 | 426 | 2463.00 | 476 | 2751.60 |
| 27 | 161.10 | 87 | 507.30 | 147 | 853.50 | 207 | 1199.70 | 267 | 1545.60 | 327 | 1891.80 | 377 | 2180.40 | 427 | 2468.70 | 477 | 2757.30 |
| 28 | 166.80 | 88 | 513.00 | 148 | 859.20 | 208 | 1205.40 | 268 | 1551.60 | 328 | 1897.50 | 378 | 2186.10 | 428 | 2474.70 | 478 | 2763.00 |
| 29 | 172.50 | 89 | 518.70 | 149 | 864.90 | 209 | 1211.10 | 269 | 1557.30 | 329 | 1903.50 | 379 | 2191.80 | 429 | 2480.40 | 479 | 2768.70 |
| 30 | 178.50 | 90 | 524.70 | 150 | 870.60 | 210 | 1216.80 | 270 | 1563.00 | 330 | 1909.20 | 380 | 2197.50 | 430 | 2486.10 | 480 | 2774.70 |
| 31 | 184.20 | 91 | 530.40 | 151 | 876.60 | 211 | 1222.50 | 271 | 1568.70 | 331 | 1914.90 | 381 | 2203.50 | 431 | 2491.80 | 481 | 2780.40 |
| 32 | 189.90 | 92 | 536.10 | 152 | 882.30 | 212 | 1228.50 | 272 | 1574.70 | 332 | 1920.60 | 382 | 2209.20 | 432 | 2497.50 | 482 | 2786.10 |
| 33 | 195.60 | 93 | 541.80 | 153 | 888.00 | 213 | 1234.20 | 273 | 1580.40 | 333 | 1926.60 | 383 | 2214.90 | 433 | 2503.50 | 483 | 2791.80 |
| 34 | 201.60 | 94 | 547.50 | 154 | 893.70 | 214 | 1239.90 | 274 | 1586.10 | 334 | 1932.30 | 384 | 2220.60 | 434 | 2509.20 | 484 | 2797.50 |
| 35 | 207.30 | 95 | 553.50 | 155 | 899.70 | 215 | 1245.60 | 275 | 1591.80 | 335 | 1938.00 | 385 | 2226.60 | 435 | 2514.90 | 485 | 2803.50 |
| 36 | 213.00 | 96 | 559.20 | 156 | 905.40 | 216 | 1251.60 | 276 | 1597.50 | 336 | 1943.70 | 386 | 2232.30 | 436 | 2520.60 | 486 | 2809.20 |
| 37 | 218.90 | 97 | 564.90 | 157 | 911.10 | 217 | 1257.30 | 277 | 1603.50 | 337 | 1949.70 | 387 | 2238.00 | 437 | 2526.60 | 487 | 2814.90 |
| 38 | 224.70 | 98 | 570.60 | 158 | 916.80 | 218 | 1263.00 | 278 | 1609.20 | 338 | 1955.40 | 388 | 2243.70 | 438 | 2532.30 | 488 | 2820.60 |
| 39 | 230.40 | 99 | 576.60 | 159 | 922.50 | 219 | 1268.70 | 279 | 1614.90 | 339 | 1961.10 | 389 | 2249.70 | 439 | 2538.00 | 489 | 2826.60 |
| 40 | 236.10 | 100 | 582.30 | 160 | 928.50 | 220 | 1274.70 | 280 | 1620.60 | 340 | 1966.80 | 390 | 2255.40 | 440 | 2543.70 | 490 | 2832.30 |
| 41 | 241.80 | 101 | 588.00 | 161 | 934.20 | 221 | 1280.40 | 281 | 1626.60 | 341 | 1972.50 | 391 | 2261.10 | 441 | 2549.70 | 491 | 2838.00 |
| 42 | 247.50 | 102 | 593.70 | 162 | 939.90 | 222 | 1286.10 | 282 | 1632.30 | 342 | 1978.50 | 392 | 2266.80 | 442 | 2555.40 | 492 | 2843.70 |
| 43 | 253.50 | 103 | 599.70 | 163 | 945.60 | 223 | 1291.80 | 283 | 1638.00 | 343 | 1984.20 | 393 | 2272.50 | 443 | 2561.10 | 493 | 2849.70 |
| 44 | 259.20 | 104 | 605.40 | 164 | 951.60 | 224 | 1297.50 | 284 | 1643.70 | 344 | 1989.90 | 394 | 2278.50 | 444 | 2566.80 | 494 | 2855.40 |
| 45 | 264.90 | 105 | 611.10 | 165 | 957.30 | 225 | 1303.50 | 285 | 1649.70 | 345 | 1995.60 | 395 | 2284.20 | 445 | 2572.50 | 495 | 2861.10 |
| 46 | 270.60 | 106 | 616.80 | 166 | 963.00 | 226 | 1309.20 | 286 | 1655.40 | 346 | 2001.60 | 396 | 2289.90 | 446 | 2578.50 | 496 | 2866.80 |
| 47 | 276.60 | 107 | 622.50 | 167 | 968.70 | 227 | 1314.90 | 287 | 1661.10 | 347 | 2007.30 | 397 | 2295.60 | 447 | 2584.20 | 497 | 2872.50 |
| 48 | 282.30 | 108 | 628.50 | 168 | 974.70 | 228 | 1320.60 | 288 | 1666.80 | 348 | 2013.00 | 398 | 2301.60 | 448 | 2589.90 | 498 | 2878.50 |
| 49 | 288.00 | 109 | 634.20 | 169 | 980.40 | 229 | 1326.60 | 289 | 1672.50 | 349 | 2018.70 | 399 | 2307.30 | 449 | 2595.60 | 499 | 2884.20 |
| 50 | 293.70 | 110 | 639.90 | 170 | 986.10 | 230 | 1332.30 | 290 | 1678.50 | 350 | 2024.70 | 400 | 2313.00 | 450 | 2601.60 | 500 | 2889.90 |
| 51 | 299.70 | 111 | 645.60 | 171 | 991.80 | 231 | 1338.00 | 291 | 1684.20 | | | | | | | | |
| 52 | 305.40 | 112 | 651.60 | 172 | 997.50 | 232 | 1343.70 | 292 | 1689.90 | | | | | | | | |
| 53 | 311.10 | 113 | 657.30 | 173 | 1003.50 | 233 | 1349.70 | 293 | 1695.60 | | | | | | | | |
| 54 | 316.80 | 114 | 663.00 | 174 | 1009.20 | 234 | 1355.40 | 294 | 1701.60 | | | | | | | | |
| 55 | 322.50 | 115 | 668.70 | 175 | 1014.90 | 235 | 1361.10 | 295 | 1707.30 | | | | | | | | |
| 56 | 328.50 | 116 | 674.70 | 176 | 1020.60 | 236 | 1366.80 | 296 | 1713.00 | | | | | | | | |
| 57 | 334.20 | 117 | 680.40 | 177 | 1026.60 | 237 | 1372.50 | 297 | 1718.70 | | | | | | | | |
| 58 | 339.90 | 118 | 686.10 | 178 | 1032.30 | 238 | 1378.50 | 298 | 1724.70 | | | | | | | | |
| 59 | 345.60 | 119 | 691.80 | 179 | 1038.00 | 239 | 1384.20 | 299 | 1730.40 | | | | | | | | |
| 60 | 351.60 | 120 | 697.50 | 180 | 1043.70 | 240 | 1389.90 | 300 | 1736.10 | | | | | | | | |

**Code more than 500**

1 Where the code is in the range **501** to **1000** inclusive:

  a. Subtract **500** from the code and use the balance of the code to obtain a pay adjustment figure from the table above.

  b. Add this pay adjustment figure to the figure given in the box alongside to obtain the figure of total pay adjustment to date *    **2884.80**

2 Where the code **exceeds 1000** follow the instructions on **page 3**.

33

**Week 31**  Nov 2 to Nov 8                                   **Tables A** - Pay Adjustment Tables

| Code | Total pay adjustment to date | Code | Total pay adjustment to date | Code | Total pay adjustment to date | Code | Total pay adjustment to date | Code | Total pay adjustment to date | Code | Total pay adjustment to date | Code | Total pay adjustment to date | Code | Total pay adjustment to date | Code | Total pay adjustment to date |
|---|---|---|---|---|---|---|---|---|---|---|---|---|---|---|---|---|---|
| | £ | | £ | | £ | | £ | | £ | | £ | | £ | | £ | | £ |
| 0 | NIL | | | | | | | | | | | | | | | | |
| 1 | 11.47 | 61 | 369.21 | 121 | 726.95 | 181 | 1084.69 | 241 | 1442.12 | 301 | 1799.86 | 351 | 2098.08 | 401 | 2395.99 | 451 | 2694.21 |
| 2 | 17.36 | 62 | 375.10 | 122 | 732.84 | 182 | 1090.58 | 242 | 1448.32 | 302 | 1805.75 | 352 | 2103.97 | 402 | 2402.19 | 452 | 2700.10 |
| 3 | 23.25 | 63 | 380.99 | 123 | 738.73 | 183 | 1096.47 | 243 | 1454.21 | 303 | 1811.95 | 353 | 2109.86 | 403 | 2408.08 | 453 | 2705.99 |
| 4 | 29.45 | 64 | 387.19 | 124 | 744.62 | 184 | 1102.36 | 244 | 1460.10 | 304 | 1817.84 | 354 | 2115.75 | 404 | 2413.97 | 454 | 2712.19 |
| 5 | 35.34 | 65 | 393.08 | 125 | 750.82 | 185 | 1108.25 | 245 | 1465.99 | 305 | 1823.73 | 355 | 2121.95 | 405 | 2419.86 | 455 | 2718.08 |
| 6 | 41.23 | 66 | 398.97 | 126 | 756.71 | 186 | 1114.45 | 246 | 1472.19 | 306 | 1829.62 | 356 | 2127.84 | 406 | 2425.75 | 456 | 2723.97 |
| 7 | 47.12 | 67 | 404.86 | 127 | 762.60 | 187 | 1120.34 | 247 | 1478.08 | 307 | 1835.82 | 357 | 2133.73 | 407 | 2431.95 | 457 | 2729.86 |
| 8 | 53.32 | 68 | 410.75 | 128 | 768.49 | 188 | 1126.23 | 248 | 1483.97 | 308 | 1841.71 | 358 | 2139.62 | 408 | 2437.84 | 458 | 2735.75 |
| 9 | 59.21 | 69 | 416.95 | 129 | 774.69 | 189 | 1132.12 | 249 | 1489.86 | 309 | 1847.60 | 359 | 2145.82 | 409 | 2443.73 | 459 | 2741.95 |
| 10 | 65.10 | 70 | 422.84 | 130 | 780.58 | 190 | 1138.32 | 250 | 1495.75 | 310 | 1853.49 | 360 | 2151.71 | 410 | 2449.62 | 460 | 2747.84 |
| 11 | 70.99 | 71 | 428.73 | 131 | 786.47 | 191 | 1144.21 | 251 | 1501.95 | 311 | 1859.69 | 361 | 2157.60 | 411 | 2455.82 | 461 | 2753.73 |
| 12 | 77.19 | 72 | 434.62 | 132 | 792.36 | 192 | 1150.10 | 252 | 1507.84 | 312 | 1865.58 | 362 | 2163.49 | 412 | 2461.71 | 462 | 2759.62 |
| 13 | 83.08 | 73 | 440.82 | 133 | 798.25 | 193 | 1155.99 | 253 | 1513.73 | 313 | 1871.47 | 363 | 2169.69 | 413 | 2467.60 | 463 | 2765.82 |
| 14 | 88.97 | 74 | 446.71 | 134 | 804.45 | 194 | 1162.19 | 254 | 1519.62 | 314 | 1877.36 | 364 | 2175.58 | 414 | 2473.49 | 464 | 2771.71 |
| 15 | 94.86 | 75 | 452.60 | 135 | 810.34 | 195 | 1168.08 | 255 | 1525.82 | 315 | 1883.25 | 365 | 2181.47 | 415 | 2479.69 | 465 | 2777.60 |
| 16 | 100.75 | 76 | 458.49 | 136 | 816.23 | 196 | 1173.97 | 256 | 1531.71 | 316 | 1889.45 | 366 | 2187.36 | 416 | 2485.58 | 466 | 2783.49 |
| 17 | 106.95 | 77 | 464.69 | 137 | 822.12 | 197 | 1179.86 | 257 | 1537.60 | 317 | 1895.34 | 367 | 2193.25 | 417 | 2491.47 | 467 | 2789.69 |
| 18 | 112.84 | 78 | 470.58 | 138 | 828.32 | 198 | 1185.75 | 258 | 1543.49 | 318 | 1901.23 | 368 | 2199.45 | 418 | 2497.36 | 468 | 2795.58 |
| 19 | 118.73 | 79 | 476.47 | 139 | 834.21 | 199 | 1191.95 | 259 | 1549.69 | 319 | 1907.12 | 369 | 2205.34 | 419 | 2503.25 | 469 | 2801.47 |
| 20 | 124.62 | 80 | 482.36 | 140 | 840.10 | 200 | 1197.84 | 260 | 1555.58 | 320 | 1913.32 | 370 | 2211.23 | 420 | 2509.45 | 470 | 2807.36 |
| 21 | 130.82 | 81 | 488.25 | 141 | 845.99 | 201 | 1203.73 | 261 | 1561.47 | 321 | 1919.21 | 371 | 2217.12 | 421 | 2515.34 | 471 | 2813.25 |
| 22 | 136.71 | 82 | 494.45 | 142 | 852.19 | 202 | 1209.62 | 262 | 1567.36 | 322 | 1925.10 | 372 | 2223.32 | 422 | 2521.23 | 472 | 2819.45 |
| 23 | 142.60 | 83 | 500.34 | 143 | 858.08 | 203 | 1215.82 | 263 | 1573.25 | 323 | 1930.99 | 373 | 2229.21 | 423 | 2527.12 | 473 | 2825.34 |
| 24 | 148.49 | 84 | 506.23 | 144 | 863.97 | 204 | 1221.71 | 264 | 1579.45 | 324 | 1937.19 | 374 | 2235.10 | 424 | 2533.32 | 474 | 2831.23 |
| 25 | 154.69 | 85 | 512.12 | 145 | 869.86 | 205 | 1227.60 | 265 | 1585.34 | 325 | 1943.08 | 375 | 2240.99 | 425 | 2539.21 | 475 | 2837.12 |
| 26 | 160.58 | 86 | 518.32 | 146 | 875.75 | 206 | 1233.49 | 266 | 1591.23 | 326 | 1948.97 | 376 | 2247.19 | 426 | 2545.10 | 476 | 2843.32 |
| 27 | 166.47 | 87 | 524.21 | 147 | 881.95 | 207 | 1239.69 | 267 | 1597.12 | 327 | 1954.86 | 377 | 2253.08 | 427 | 2550.99 | 477 | 2849.21 |
| 28 | 172.36 | 88 | 530.10 | 148 | 887.84 | 208 | 1245.58 | 268 | 1603.32 | 328 | 1960.75 | 378 | 2258.97 | 428 | 2557.19 | 478 | 2855.10 |
| 29 | 178.25 | 89 | 535.99 | 149 | 893.73 | 209 | 1251.47 | 269 | 1609.21 | 329 | 1966.95 | 379 | 2264.86 | 429 | 2563.08 | 479 | 2860.99 |
| 30 | 184.45 | 90 | 542.19 | 150 | 899.62 | 210 | 1257.36 | 270 | 1615.10 | 330 | 1972.84 | 380 | 2270.75 | 430 | 2568.97 | 480 | 2867.19 |
| 31 | 190.34 | 91 | 548.08 | 151 | 905.82 | 211 | 1263.25 | 271 | 1620.99 | 331 | 1978.73 | 381 | 2276.95 | 431 | 2574.86 | 481 | 2873.08 |
| 32 | 196.23 | 92 | 553.97 | 152 | 911.71 | 212 | 1269.45 | 272 | 1627.19 | 332 | 1984.62 | 382 | 2282.84 | 432 | 2580.75 | 482 | 2878.97 |
| 33 | 202.12 | 93 | 559.86 | 153 | 917.60 | 213 | 1275.34 | 273 | 1633.08 | 333 | 1990.82 | 383 | 2288.73 | 433 | 2586.95 | 483 | 2884.86 |
| 34 | 208.32 | 94 | 565.75 | 154 | 923.49 | 214 | 1281.23 | 274 | 1638.97 | 334 | 1996.71 | 384 | 2294.62 | 434 | 2592.84 | 484 | 2890.75 |
| 35 | 214.21 | 95 | 571.95 | 155 | 929.69 | 215 | 1287.12 | 275 | 1644.86 | 335 | 2002.60 | 385 | 2300.82 | 435 | 2598.73 | 485 | 2896.95 |
| 36 | 220.10 | 96 | 577.84 | 156 | 935.58 | 216 | 1293.32 | 276 | 1650.75 | 336 | 2008.49 | 386 | 2306.71 | 436 | 2604.62 | 486 | 2902.84 |
| 37 | 225.99 | 97 | 583.73 | 157 | 941.47 | 217 | 1299.21 | 277 | 1656.95 | 337 | 2014.69 | 387 | 2312.60 | 437 | 2610.82 | 487 | 2908.73 |
| 38 | 232.19 | 98 | 589.62 | 158 | 947.36 | 218 | 1305.10 | 278 | 1662.84 | 338 | 2020.58 | 388 | 2318.49 | 438 | 2616.71 | 488 | 2914.62 |
| 39 | 238.08 | 99 | 595.82 | 159 | 953.25 | 219 | 1310.99 | 279 | 1668.73 | 339 | 2026.47 | 389 | 2324.69 | 439 | 2622.60 | 489 | 2920.82 |
| 40 | 243.97 | 100 | 601.71 | 160 | 959.45 | 220 | 1317.19 | 280 | 1674.62 | 340 | 2032.36 | 390 | 2330.58 | 440 | 2628.49 | 490 | 2926.71 |
| 41 | 249.86 | 101 | 607.60 | 161 | 965.34 | 221 | 1323.08 | 281 | 1680.82 | 341 | 2038.25 | 391 | 2336.47 | 441 | 2634.69 | 491 | 2932.60 |
| 42 | 255.75 | 102 | 613.49 | 162 | 971.23 | 222 | 1328.97 | 282 | 1686.71 | 342 | 2044.45 | 392 | 2342.36 | 442 | 2640.58 | 492 | 2938.49 |
| 43 | 261.95 | 103 | 619.69 | 163 | 977.12 | 223 | 1334.86 | 283 | 1692.60 | 343 | 2050.34 | 393 | 2348.25 | 443 | 2646.47 | 493 | 2944.69 |
| 44 | 267.84 | 104 | 625.58 | 164 | 983.32 | 224 | 1340.75 | 284 | 1698.49 | 344 | 2056.23 | 394 | 2354.45 | 444 | 2652.36 | 494 | 2950.58 |
| 45 | 273.73 | 105 | 631.47 | 165 | 989.21 | 225 | 1346.95 | 285 | 1704.69 | 345 | 2062.12 | 395 | 2360.34 | 445 | 2658.25 | 495 | 2956.47 |
| 46 | 279.62 | 106 | 637.36 | 166 | 995.10 | 226 | 1352.84 | 286 | 1710.58 | 346 | 2068.32 | 396 | 2366.23 | 446 | 2664.45 | 496 | 2962.36 |
| 47 | 285.82 | 107 | 643.25 | 167 | 1000.99 | 227 | 1358.73 | 287 | 1716.47 | 347 | 2074.21 | 397 | 2372.12 | 447 | 2670.34 | 497 | 2968.25 |
| 48 | 291.71 | 108 | 649.45 | 168 | 1007.19 | 228 | 1364.62 | 288 | 1722.36 | 348 | 2080.10 | 398 | 2378.32 | 448 | 2676.23 | 498 | 2974.45 |
| 49 | 297.60 | 109 | 655.34 | 169 | 1013.08 | 229 | 1370.82 | 289 | 1728.25 | 349 | 2085.99 | 399 | 2384.21 | 449 | 2682.12 | 499 | 2980.34 |
| 50 | 303.49 | 110 | 661.23 | 170 | 1018.97 | 230 | 1376.71 | 290 | 1734.45 | 350 | 2092.19 | 400 | 2390.10 | 450 | 2688.32 | 500 | 2986.23 |
| 51 | 309.69 | 111 | 667.12 | 171 | 1024.86 | 231 | 1382.60 | 291 | 1740.34 | | | | | | | | |
| 52 | 315.58 | 112 | 673.32 | 172 | 1030.75 | 232 | 1388.49 | 292 | 1746.23 | | | | | | | | |
| 53 | 321.47 | 113 | 679.21 | 173 | 1036.95 | 233 | 1394.69 | 293 | 1752.12 | | | | | | | | |
| 54 | 327.36 | 114 | 685.10 | 174 | 1042.84 | 234 | 1400.58 | 294 | 1758.32 | | | | | | | | |
| 55 | 333.25 | 115 | 690.99 | 175 | 1048.73 | 235 | 1406.47 | 295 | 1764.21 | | | | | | | | |
| 56 | 339.45 | 116 | 697.19 | 176 | 1054.62 | 236 | 1412.36 | 296 | 1770.10 | | | | | | | | |
| 57 | 345.34 | 117 | 703.08 | 177 | 1060.82 | 237 | 1418.25 | 297 | 1775.99 | | | | | | | | |
| 58 | 351.23 | 118 | 708.97 | 178 | 1066.71 | 238 | 1424.45 | 298 | 1782.19 | | | | | | | | |
| 59 | 357.12 | 119 | 714.86 | 179 | 1072.60 | 239 | 1430.34 | 299 | 1788.08 | | | | | | | | |
| 60 | 363.32 | 120 | 720.75 | 180 | 1078.49 | 240 | 1436.23 | 300 | 1793.97 | | | | | | | | |

**Code more than 500**

1 Where the code is in the range **501** to **1000** inclusive:

   a. Subtract **500** from the code and use the balance of the code to obtain a pay adjustment figure from the table above.

   b. Add this pay adjustment figure to the figure given in the box alongside to obtain the figure of total pay adjustment to date *    **2980.96**

2 Where the code **exceeds 1000** follow the instructions on **page 3**.

## Tables A - Pay Adjustment Tables

Nov 9 to Nov 15 **Week 32**

| Code | Total pay adjustment to date | Code | Total pay adjustment to date | Code | Total pay adjustment to date | Code | Total pay adjustment to date | Code | Total pay adjustment to date | Code | Total pay adjustment to date | Code | Total pay adjustment to date | Code | Total pay adjustment to date | Code | Total pay adjustment to date |
|---|---|---|---|---|---|---|---|---|---|---|---|---|---|---|---|---|---|
| | £ | | £ | | £ | | £ | | £ | | £ | | £ | | £ | | £ |
| 0 | NIL | | | | | | | | | | | | | | | | |
| 1 | 11.84 | 61 | 381.12 | 121 | 750.40 | 181 | 1119.68 | 241 | 1488.64 | 301 | 1857.92 | 351 | 2165.76 | 401 | 2473.28 | 451 | 2781.12 |
| 2 | 17.92 | 62 | 387.20 | 122 | 756.48 | 182 | 1125.76 | 242 | 1495.04 | 302 | 1864.00 | 352 | 2171.84 | 402 | 2479.68 | 452 | 2787.20 |
| 3 | 24.00 | 63 | 393.28 | 123 | 762.56 | 183 | 1131.84 | 243 | 1501.12 | 303 | 1870.40 | 353 | 2177.92 | 403 | 2485.76 | 453 | 2793.28 |
| 4 | 30.40 | 64 | 399.68 | 124 | 768.64 | 184 | 1137.92 | 244 | 1507.20 | 304 | 1876.48 | 354 | 2184.00 | 404 | 2491.84 | 454 | 2799.68 |
| 5 | 36.48 | 65 | 405.76 | 125 | 775.04 | 185 | 1144.00 | 245 | 1513.28 | 305 | 1882.56 | 355 | 2190.40 | 405 | 2497.92 | 455 | 2805.76 |
| 6 | 42.56 | 66 | 411.84 | 126 | 781.12 | 186 | 1150.40 | 246 | 1519.68 | 306 | 1888.64 | 356 | 2196.48 | 406 | 2504.00 | 456 | 2811.84 |
| 7 | 48.64 | 67 | 417.92 | 127 | 787.20 | 187 | 1156.48 | 247 | 1525.76 | 307 | 1895.04 | 357 | 2202.56 | 407 | 2510.40 | 457 | 2817.92 |
| 8 | 55.04 | 68 | 424.00 | 128 | 793.28 | 188 | 1162.56 | 248 | 1531.84 | 308 | 1901.12 | 358 | 2208.64 | 408 | 2516.48 | 458 | 2824.00 |
| 9 | 61.12 | 69 | 430.40 | 129 | 799.68 | 189 | 1168.64 | 249 | 1537.92 | 309 | 1907.20 | 359 | 2215.04 | 409 | 2522.56 | 459 | 2830.40 |
| 10 | 67.20 | 70 | 436.48 | 130 | 805.76 | 190 | 1175.04 | 250 | 1544.00 | 310 | 1913.28 | 360 | 2221.12 | 410 | 2528.64 | 460 | 2836.48 |
| 11 | 73.28 | 71 | 442.56 | 131 | 811.84 | 191 | 1181.12 | 251 | 1550.40 | 311 | 1919.68 | 361 | 2227.20 | 411 | 2535.04 | 461 | 2842.56 |
| 12 | 79.68 | 72 | 448.64 | 132 | 817.92 | 192 | 1187.20 | 252 | 1556.48 | 312 | 1925.76 | 362 | 2233.28 | 412 | 2541.12 | 462 | 2848.64 |
| 13 | 85.76 | 73 | 455.04 | 133 | 824.00 | 193 | 1193.28 | 253 | 1562.56 | 313 | 1931.84 | 363 | 2239.68 | 413 | 2547.20 | 463 | 2855.04 |
| 14 | 91.84 | 74 | 461.12 | 134 | 830.40 | 194 | 1199.68 | 254 | 1568.64 | 314 | 1937.92 | 364 | 2245.76 | 414 | 2553.28 | 464 | 2861.12 |
| 15 | 97.92 | 75 | 467.20 | 135 | 836.48 | 195 | 1205.76 | 255 | 1575.04 | 315 | 1944.00 | 365 | 2251.84 | 415 | 2559.68 | 465 | 2867.20 |
| 16 | 104.00 | 76 | 473.28 | 136 | 842.56 | 196 | 1211.84 | 256 | 1581.12 | 316 | 1950.40 | 366 | 2257.92 | 416 | 2565.76 | 466 | 2873.28 |
| 17 | 110.40 | 77 | 479.68 | 137 | 848.64 | 197 | 1217.92 | 257 | 1587.20 | 317 | 1956.48 | 367 | 2264.00 | 417 | 2571.84 | 467 | 2879.68 |
| 18 | 116.48 | 78 | 485.76 | 138 | 855.04 | 198 | 1224.00 | 258 | 1593.28 | 318 | 1962.56 | 368 | 2270.40 | 418 | 2577.92 | 468 | 2885.76 |
| 19 | 122.56 | 79 | 491.84 | 139 | 861.12 | 199 | 1230.40 | 259 | 1599.68 | 319 | 1968.64 | 369 | 2276.48 | 419 | 2584.00 | 469 | 2891.84 |
| 20 | 128.64 | 80 | 497.92 | 140 | 867.20 | 200 | 1236.48 | 260 | 1605.76 | 320 | 1975.04 | 370 | 2282.56 | 420 | 2590.40 | 470 | 2897.92 |
| 21 | 135.04 | 81 | 504.00 | 141 | 873.28 | 201 | 1242.56 | 261 | 1611.84 | 321 | 1981.12 | 371 | 2288.64 | 421 | 2596.48 | 471 | 2904.00 |
| 22 | 141.12 | 82 | 510.40 | 142 | 879.68 | 202 | 1248.64 | 262 | 1617.92 | 322 | 1987.20 | 372 | 2295.04 | 422 | 2602.56 | 472 | 2910.40 |
| 23 | 147.20 | 83 | 516.48 | 143 | 885.76 | 203 | 1255.04 | 263 | 1624.00 | 323 | 1993.28 | 373 | 2301.12 | 423 | 2608.64 | 473 | 2916.48 |
| 24 | 153.28 | 84 | 522.56 | 144 | 891.84 | 204 | 1261.12 | 264 | 1630.40 | 324 | 1999.68 | 374 | 2307.20 | 424 | 2615.04 | 474 | 2922.56 |
| 25 | 159.68 | 85 | 528.64 | 145 | 897.92 | 205 | 1267.20 | 265 | 1636.48 | 325 | 2005.76 | 375 | 2313.28 | 425 | 2621.12 | 475 | 2928.64 |
| 26 | 165.76 | 86 | 535.04 | 146 | 904.00 | 206 | 1273.28 | 266 | 1642.56 | 326 | 2011.84 | 376 | 2319.68 | 426 | 2627.20 | 476 | 2935.04 |
| 27 | 171.84 | 87 | 541.12 | 147 | 910.40 | 207 | 1279.68 | 267 | 1648.64 | 327 | 2017.92 | 377 | 2325.76 | 427 | 2633.28 | 477 | 2941.12 |
| 28 | 177.92 | 88 | 547.20 | 148 | 916.48 | 208 | 1285.76 | 268 | 1655.04 | 328 | 2024.00 | 378 | 2331.84 | 428 | 2639.68 | 478 | 2947.20 |
| 29 | 184.00 | 89 | 553.28 | 149 | 922.56 | 209 | 1291.84 | 269 | 1661.12 | 329 | 2030.40 | 379 | 2337.92 | 429 | 2645.76 | 479 | 2953.28 |
| 30 | 190.40 | 90 | 559.68 | 150 | 928.64 | 210 | 1297.92 | 270 | 1667.20 | 330 | 2036.48 | 380 | 2344.00 | 430 | 2651.84 | 480 | 2959.68 |
| 31 | 196.48 | 91 | 565.76 | 151 | 935.04 | 211 | 1304.00 | 271 | 1673.28 | 331 | 2042.56 | 381 | 2350.40 | 431 | 2657.92 | 481 | 2965.76 |
| 32 | 202.56 | 92 | 571.84 | 152 | 941.12 | 212 | 1310.40 | 272 | 1679.68 | 332 | 2048.64 | 382 | 2356.48 | 432 | 2664.00 | 482 | 2971.84 |
| 33 | 208.64 | 93 | 577.92 | 153 | 947.20 | 213 | 1316.48 | 273 | 1685.76 | 333 | 2055.04 | 383 | 2362.56 | 433 | 2670.40 | 483 | 2977.92 |
| 34 | 215.04 | 94 | 584.00 | 154 | 953.28 | 214 | 1322.56 | 274 | 1691.84 | 334 | 2061.12 | 384 | 2368.64 | 434 | 2676.48 | 484 | 2984.00 |
| 35 | 221.12 | 95 | 590.40 | 155 | 959.68 | 215 | 1328.64 | 275 | 1697.92 | 335 | 2067.20 | 385 | 2375.04 | 435 | 2682.56 | 485 | 2990.40 |
| 36 | 227.20 | 96 | 596.48 | 156 | 965.76 | 216 | 1335.04 | 276 | 1704.00 | 336 | 2073.28 | 386 | 2381.12 | 436 | 2688.64 | 486 | 2996.48 |
| 37 | 233.28 | 97 | 602.56 | 157 | 971.84 | 217 | 1341.12 | 277 | 1710.40 | 337 | 2079.68 | 387 | 2387.20 | 437 | 2695.04 | 487 | 3002.56 |
| 38 | 239.68 | 98 | 608.64 | 158 | 977.92 | 218 | 1347.20 | 278 | 1716.48 | 338 | 2085.76 | 388 | 2393.28 | 438 | 2701.12 | 488 | 3008.64 |
| 39 | 245.76 | 99 | 615.04 | 159 | 984.00 | 219 | 1353.28 | 279 | 1722.56 | 339 | 2091.84 | 389 | 2399.68 | 439 | 2707.20 | 489 | 3015.04 |
| 40 | 251.84 | 100 | 621.12 | 160 | 990.40 | 220 | 1359.68 | 280 | 1728.64 | 340 | 2097.92 | 390 | 2405.76 | 440 | 2713.28 | 490 | 3021.12 |
| 41 | 257.92 | 101 | 627.20 | 161 | 996.48 | 221 | 1365.76 | 281 | 1735.04 | 341 | 2104.00 | 391 | 2411.84 | 441 | 2719.68 | 491 | 3027.20 |
| 42 | 264.00 | 102 | 633.28 | 162 | 1002.56 | 222 | 1371.84 | 282 | 1741.12 | 342 | 2110.40 | 392 | 2417.92 | 442 | 2725.76 | 492 | 3033.28 |
| 43 | 270.40 | 103 | 639.68 | 163 | 1008.64 | 223 | 1377.92 | 283 | 1747.20 | 343 | 2116.48 | 393 | 2424.00 | 443 | 2731.84 | 493 | 3039.68 |
| 44 | 276.48 | 104 | 645.76 | 164 | 1015.04 | 224 | 1384.00 | 284 | 1753.28 | 344 | 2122.56 | 394 | 2430.40 | 444 | 2737.92 | 494 | 3045.76 |
| 45 | 282.56 | 105 | 651.84 | 165 | 1021.12 | 225 | 1390.40 | 285 | 1759.68 | 345 | 2128.64 | 395 | 2436.48 | 445 | 2744.00 | 495 | 3051.84 |
| 46 | 288.64 | 106 | 657.92 | 166 | 1027.20 | 226 | 1396.48 | 286 | 1765.76 | 346 | 2135.04 | 396 | 2442.56 | 446 | 2750.40 | 496 | 3057.92 |
| 47 | 295.04 | 107 | 664.00 | 167 | 1033.28 | 227 | 1402.56 | 287 | 1771.84 | 347 | 2141.12 | 397 | 2448.64 | 447 | 2756.48 | 497 | 3064.00 |
| 48 | 301.12 | 108 | 670.40 | 168 | 1039.68 | 228 | 1408.64 | 288 | 1777.92 | 348 | 2147.20 | 398 | 2455.04 | 448 | 2762.56 | 498 | 3070.40 |
| 49 | 307.20 | 109 | 676.48 | 169 | 1045.76 | 229 | 1415.04 | 289 | 1784.00 | 349 | 2153.28 | 399 | 2461.12 | 449 | 2768.64 | 499 | 3076.48 |
| 50 | 313.28 | 110 | 682.56 | 170 | 1051.84 | 230 | 1421.12 | 290 | 1790.40 | 350 | 2159.68 | 400 | 2467.20 | 450 | 2775.04 | 500 | 3082.56 |
| 51 | 319.68 | 111 | 688.64 | 171 | 1057.92 | 231 | 1427.20 | 291 | 1796.48 | | | | | | | | |
| 52 | 325.76 | 112 | 695.04 | 172 | 1064.00 | 232 | 1433.28 | 292 | 1802.56 | | | | | | | | |
| 53 | 331.84 | 113 | 701.12 | 173 | 1070.40 | 233 | 1439.68 | 293 | 1808.64 | | | | | | | | |
| 54 | 337.92 | 114 | 707.20 | 174 | 1076.48 | 234 | 1445.76 | 294 | 1815.04 | | | | | | | | |
| 55 | 344.00 | 115 | 713.28 | 175 | 1082.56 | 235 | 1451.84 | 295 | 1821.12 | | | | | | | | |
| 56 | 350.40 | 116 | 719.68 | 176 | 1088.64 | 236 | 1457.92 | 296 | 1827.20 | | | | | | | | |
| 57 | 356.48 | 117 | 725.76 | 177 | 1095.04 | 237 | 1464.00 | 297 | 1833.28 | | | | | | | | |
| 58 | 362.56 | 118 | 731.84 | 178 | 1101.12 | 238 | 1470.40 | 298 | 1839.68 | | | | | | | | |
| 59 | 368.64 | 119 | 737.92 | 179 | 1107.20 | 239 | 1476.48 | 299 | 1845.76 | | | | | | | | |
| 60 | 375.04 | 120 | 744.00 | 180 | 1113.28 | 240 | 1482.56 | 300 | 1851.84 | | | | | | | | |

**Code more than 500**

1 Where the code is in the range **501** to **1000** inclusive:

    a. Subtract **500** from the code and use the balance of the code to obtain a pay adjustment figure from the table above.

    b. Add this pay adjustment figure to the figure given in the box alongside to obtain the figure of total pay adjustment to date * **3077.12**

2 Where the code **exceeds 1000** follow the instructions on **page 3**.

35

**Week 33**  Nov 16 to Nov 22 — **Tables A** - Pay Adjustment Tables

| Code | Total pay adjustment to date | Code | Total pay adjustment to date | Code | Total pay adjustment to date | Code | Total pay adjustment to date | Code | Total pay adjustment to date | Code | Total pay adjustment to date | Code | Total pay adjustment to date | Code | Total pay adjustment to date | Code | Total pay adjustment to date |
|---|---|---|---|---|---|---|---|---|---|---|---|---|---|---|---|---|---|
| | £ | | £ | | £ | | £ | | £ | | £ | | £ | | £ | | £ |
| 0 | NIL | | | | | | | | | | | | | | | | |
| 1 | 12.21 | 61 | 393.03 | 121 | 773.85 | 181 | 1154.67 | 241 | 1535.16 | 301 | 1915.98 | 351 | 2233.44 | 401 | 2550.57 | 451 | 2868.03 |
| 2 | 18.48 | 62 | 399.30 | 122 | 780.12 | 182 | 1160.94 | 242 | 1541.76 | 302 | 1922.25 | 352 | 2239.71 | 402 | 2557.17 | 452 | 2874.30 |
| 3 | 24.75 | 63 | 405.57 | 123 | 786.39 | 183 | 1167.21 | 243 | 1548.03 | 303 | 1928.85 | 353 | 2245.98 | 403 | 2563.44 | 453 | 2880.57 |
| 4 | 31.35 | 64 | 412.17 | 124 | 792.66 | 184 | 1173.48 | 244 | 1554.30 | 304 | 1935.12 | 354 | 2252.25 | 404 | 2569.71 | 454 | 2887.17 |
| 5 | 37.62 | 65 | 418.44 | 125 | 799.26 | 185 | 1179.75 | 245 | 1560.57 | 305 | 1941.39 | 355 | 2258.85 | 405 | 2575.98 | 455 | 2893.44 |
| 6 | 43.89 | 66 | 424.71 | 126 | 805.53 | 186 | 1186.35 | 246 | 1567.17 | 306 | 1947.66 | 356 | 2265.12 | 406 | 2582.25 | 456 | 2899.71 |
| 7 | 50.16 | 67 | 430.98 | 127 | 811.80 | 187 | 1192.62 | 247 | 1573.44 | 307 | 1954.26 | 357 | 2271.39 | 407 | 2588.85 | 457 | 2905.98 |
| 8 | 56.76 | 68 | 437.25 | 128 | 818.07 | 188 | 1198.89 | 248 | 1579.71 | 308 | 1960.53 | 358 | 2277.66 | 408 | 2595.12 | 458 | 2912.25 |
| 9 | 63.03 | 69 | 443.85 | 129 | 824.67 | 189 | 1205.16 | 249 | 1585.98 | 309 | 1966.80 | 359 | 2284.26 | 409 | 2601.39 | 459 | 2918.85 |
| 10 | 69.30 | 70 | 450.12 | 130 | 830.94 | 190 | 1211.76 | 250 | 1592.25 | 310 | 1973.07 | 360 | 2290.53 | 410 | 2607.66 | 460 | 2925.12 |
| 11 | 75.57 | 71 | 456.39 | 131 | 837.21 | 191 | 1218.03 | 251 | 1598.85 | 311 | 1979.67 | 361 | 2296.80 | 411 | 2614.26 | 461 | 2931.39 |
| 12 | 82.17 | 72 | 462.66 | 132 | 843.48 | 192 | 1224.30 | 252 | 1605.12 | 312 | 1985.94 | 362 | 2303.07 | 412 | 2620.53 | 462 | 2937.66 |
| 13 | 88.44 | 73 | 469.26 | 133 | 849.75 | 193 | 1230.57 | 253 | 1611.39 | 313 | 1992.21 | 363 | 2309.67 | 413 | 2626.80 | 463 | 2944.26 |
| 14 | 94.71 | 74 | 475.53 | 134 | 856.35 | 194 | 1237.17 | 254 | 1617.66 | 314 | 1998.48 | 364 | 2315.94 | 414 | 2633.07 | 464 | 2950.53 |
| 15 | 100.98 | 75 | 481.80 | 135 | 862.62 | 195 | 1243.44 | 255 | 1624.26 | 315 | 2004.75 | 365 | 2322.21 | 415 | 2639.67 | 465 | 2956.80 |
| 16 | 107.25 | 76 | 488.07 | 136 | 868.89 | 196 | 1249.71 | 256 | 1630.53 | 316 | 2011.35 | 366 | 2328.48 | 416 | 2645.94 | 466 | 2963.07 |
| 17 | 113.85 | 77 | 494.67 | 137 | 875.16 | 197 | 1255.98 | 257 | 1636.80 | 317 | 2017.62 | 367 | 2334.75 | 417 | 2652.21 | 467 | 2969.67 |
| 18 | 120.12 | 78 | 500.94 | 138 | 881.76 | 198 | 1262.25 | 258 | 1643.07 | 318 | 2023.89 | 368 | 2341.35 | 418 | 2658.48 | 468 | 2975.94 |
| 19 | 126.39 | 79 | 507.21 | 139 | 888.03 | 199 | 1268.85 | 259 | 1649.67 | 319 | 2030.16 | 369 | 2347.62 | 419 | 2664.75 | 469 | 2982.21 |
| 20 | 132.66 | 80 | 513.48 | 140 | 894.30 | 200 | 1275.12 | 260 | 1655.94 | 320 | 2036.76 | 370 | 2353.89 | 420 | 2671.35 | 470 | 2988.48 |
| 21 | 139.26 | 81 | 519.75 | 141 | 900.57 | 201 | 1281.39 | 261 | 1662.21 | 321 | 2043.03 | 371 | 2360.16 | 421 | 2677.62 | 471 | 2994.75 |
| 22 | 145.53 | 82 | 526.35 | 142 | 907.17 | 202 | 1287.66 | 262 | 1668.48 | 322 | 2049.30 | 372 | 2366.76 | 422 | 2683.89 | 472 | 3001.35 |
| 23 | 151.80 | 83 | 532.62 | 143 | 913.44 | 203 | 1294.26 | 263 | 1674.75 | 323 | 2055.57 | 373 | 2373.03 | 423 | 2690.16 | 473 | 3007.62 |
| 24 | 158.07 | 84 | 538.89 | 144 | 919.71 | 204 | 1300.53 | 264 | 1681.35 | 324 | 2062.17 | 374 | 2379.30 | 424 | 2696.76 | 474 | 3013.89 |
| 25 | 164.67 | 85 | 545.16 | 145 | 925.98 | 205 | 1306.80 | 265 | 1687.62 | 325 | 2068.44 | 375 | 2385.57 | 425 | 2703.03 | 475 | 3020.16 |
| 26 | 170.94 | 86 | 551.76 | 146 | 932.25 | 206 | 1313.07 | 266 | 1693.89 | 326 | 2074.71 | 376 | 2392.17 | 426 | 2709.30 | 476 | 3026.76 |
| 27 | 177.21 | 87 | 558.03 | 147 | 938.85 | 207 | 1319.67 | 267 | 1700.16 | 327 | 2080.98 | 377 | 2398.44 | 427 | 2715.57 | 477 | 3033.03 |
| 28 | 183.48 | 88 | 564.30 | 148 | 945.12 | 208 | 1325.94 | 268 | 1706.76 | 328 | 2087.25 | 378 | 2404.71 | 428 | 2722.17 | 478 | 3039.30 |
| 29 | 189.75 | 89 | 570.57 | 149 | 951.39 | 209 | 1332.21 | 269 | 1713.03 | 329 | 2093.85 | 379 | 2410.98 | 429 | 2728.44 | 479 | 3045.57 |
| 30 | 196.35 | 90 | 577.17 | 150 | 957.66 | 210 | 1338.48 | 270 | 1719.30 | 330 | 2100.12 | 380 | 2417.25 | 430 | 2734.71 | 480 | 3052.17 |
| 31 | 202.62 | 91 | 583.44 | 151 | 964.26 | 211 | 1344.75 | 271 | 1725.57 | 331 | 2106.39 | 381 | 2423.85 | 431 | 2740.98 | 481 | 3058.44 |
| 32 | 208.89 | 92 | 589.71 | 152 | 970.53 | 212 | 1351.35 | 272 | 1732.17 | 332 | 2112.66 | 382 | 2430.12 | 432 | 2747.25 | 482 | 3064.71 |
| 33 | 215.16 | 93 | 595.98 | 153 | 976.80 | 213 | 1357.62 | 273 | 1738.44 | 333 | 2119.26 | 383 | 2436.39 | 433 | 2753.85 | 483 | 3070.98 |
| 34 | 221.76 | 94 | 602.25 | 154 | 983.07 | 214 | 1363.89 | 274 | 1744.71 | 334 | 2125.53 | 384 | 2442.66 | 434 | 2760.12 | 484 | 3077.25 |
| 35 | 228.03 | 95 | 608.85 | 155 | 989.67 | 215 | 1370.16 | 275 | 1750.98 | 335 | 2131.80 | 385 | 2449.26 | 435 | 2766.39 | 485 | 3083.85 |
| 36 | 234.30 | 96 | 615.12 | 156 | 995.94 | 216 | 1376.76 | 276 | 1757.25 | 336 | 2138.07 | 386 | 2455.53 | 436 | 2772.66 | 486 | 3090.12 |
| 37 | 240.57 | 97 | 621.39 | 157 | 1002.21 | 217 | 1383.03 | 277 | 1763.85 | 337 | 2144.67 | 387 | 2461.80 | 437 | 2779.26 | 487 | 3096.39 |
| 38 | 247.17 | 98 | 627.66 | 158 | 1008.48 | 218 | 1389.30 | 278 | 1770.12 | 338 | 2150.94 | 388 | 2468.07 | 438 | 2785.53 | 488 | 3102.66 |
| 39 | 253.44 | 99 | 634.26 | 159 | 1014.75 | 219 | 1395.57 | 279 | 1776.39 | 339 | 2157.21 | 389 | 2474.67 | 439 | 2791.80 | 489 | 3109.26 |
| 40 | 259.71 | 100 | 640.53 | 160 | 1021.35 | 220 | 1402.17 | 280 | 1782.66 | 340 | 2163.48 | 390 | 2480.94 | 440 | 2798.07 | 490 | 3115.53 |
| 41 | 265.98 | 101 | 646.80 | 161 | 1027.62 | 221 | 1408.44 | 281 | 1789.26 | 341 | 2169.75 | 391 | 2487.21 | 441 | 2804.67 | 491 | 3121.80 |
| 42 | 272.25 | 102 | 653.07 | 162 | 1033.89 | 222 | 1414.71 | 282 | 1795.53 | 342 | 2176.35 | 392 | 2493.48 | 442 | 2810.94 | 492 | 3128.07 |
| 43 | 278.85 | 103 | 659.67 | 163 | 1040.16 | 223 | 1420.98 | 283 | 1801.80 | 343 | 2182.62 | 393 | 2499.75 | 443 | 2817.21 | 493 | 3134.67 |
| 44 | 285.12 | 104 | 665.94 | 164 | 1046.76 | 224 | 1427.25 | 284 | 1808.07 | 344 | 2188.89 | 394 | 2506.35 | 444 | 2823.48 | 494 | 3140.94 |
| 45 | 291.39 | 105 | 672.21 | 165 | 1053.03 | 225 | 1433.85 | 285 | 1814.67 | 345 | 2195.16 | 395 | 2512.62 | 445 | 2829.75 | 495 | 3147.21 |
| 46 | 297.66 | 106 | 678.48 | 166 | 1059.30 | 226 | 1440.12 | 286 | 1820.94 | 346 | 2201.76 | 396 | 2518.89 | 446 | 2836.35 | 496 | 3153.48 |
| 47 | 304.26 | 107 | 684.75 | 167 | 1065.57 | 227 | 1446.39 | 287 | 1827.21 | 347 | 2208.03 | 397 | 2525.16 | 447 | 2842.62 | 497 | 3159.75 |
| 48 | 310.53 | 108 | 691.35 | 168 | 1072.17 | 228 | 1452.66 | 288 | 1833.48 | 348 | 2214.30 | 398 | 2531.76 | 448 | 2848.89 | 498 | 3166.35 |
| 49 | 316.80 | 109 | 697.62 | 169 | 1078.44 | 229 | 1459.26 | 289 | 1839.75 | 349 | 2220.57 | 399 | 2538.03 | 449 | 2855.16 | 499 | 3172.62 |
| 50 | 323.07 | 110 | 703.89 | 170 | 1084.71 | 230 | 1465.53 | 290 | 1846.35 | 350 | 2227.17 | 400 | 2544.30 | 450 | 2861.76 | 500 | 3178.89 |
| 51 | 329.67 | 111 | 710.16 | 171 | 1090.98 | 231 | 1471.80 | 291 | 1852.62 | | | | | | | | |
| 52 | 335.94 | 112 | 716.76 | 172 | 1097.25 | 232 | 1478.07 | 292 | 1858.89 | | | | | | | | |
| 53 | 342.21 | 113 | 723.03 | 173 | 1103.85 | 233 | 1484.67 | 293 | 1865.16 | | | | | | | | |
| 54 | 348.48 | 114 | 729.30 | 174 | 1110.12 | 234 | 1490.94 | 294 | 1871.76 | | | | | | | | |
| 55 | 354.75 | 115 | 735.57 | 175 | 1116.39 | 235 | 1497.21 | 295 | 1878.03 | | | | | | | | |
| 56 | 361.35 | 116 | 742.17 | 176 | 1122.66 | 236 | 1503.48 | 296 | 1884.30 | | | | | | | | |
| 57 | 367.62 | 117 | 748.44 | 177 | 1129.26 | 237 | 1509.75 | 297 | 1890.57 | | | | | | | | |
| 58 | 373.89 | 118 | 754.71 | 178 | 1135.53 | 238 | 1516.35 | 298 | 1897.17 | | | | | | | | |
| 59 | 380.16 | 119 | 760.98 | 179 | 1141.80 | 239 | 1522.62 | 299 | 1903.44 | | | | | | | | |
| 60 | 386.76 | 120 | 767.25 | 180 | 1148.07 | 240 | 1528.89 | 300 | 1909.71 | | | | | | | | |

**Code more than 500**

1 Where the code is in the range **501 to 1000** inclusive:

a. Subtract **500** from the code and use the balance of the code to obtain a pay adjustment figure from the table above.

b. Add this pay adjustment figure to the figure given in the box alongside to obtain the figure of total pay adjustment to date *   **3173.28**

2 Where the code **exceeds 1000** follow the instructions on **page 3**.

## Tables A - Pay Adjustment Tables

Nov 23 to Nov 29 **Week 34**

| Code | Total pay adjustment to date £ | Code | Total pay adjustment to date £ | Code | Total pay adjustment to date £ | Code | Total pay adjustment to date £ | Code | Total pay adjustment to date £ | Code | Total pay adjustment to date £ | Code | Total pay adjustment to date £ | Code | Total pay adjustment to date £ | Code | Total pay adjustment to date £ |
|---|---|---|---|---|---|---|---|---|---|---|---|---|---|---|---|---|---|
| 0 | NIL | 61 | 404.94 | 121 | 797.30 | 181 | 1189.66 | 241 | 1581.68 | 301 | 1974.04 | 351 | 2301.12 | 401 | 2627.86 | 451 | 2954.94 |
| 1 | 12.58 | 62 | 411.40 | 122 | 803.76 | 182 | 1196.12 | 242 | 1588.48 | 302 | 1980.50 | 352 | 2307.58 | 402 | 2634.66 | 452 | 2961.40 |
| 2 | 19.04 | 63 | 417.86 | 123 | 810.22 | 183 | 1202.58 | 243 | 1594.94 | 303 | 1987.30 | 353 | 2314.04 | 403 | 2641.12 | 453 | 2967.86 |
| 3 | 25.50 | 64 | 424.66 | 124 | 816.68 | 184 | 1209.04 | 244 | 1601.40 | 304 | 1993.76 | 354 | 2320.50 | 404 | 2647.58 | 454 | 2974.66 |
| 4 | 32.30 | 65 | 431.12 | 125 | 823.48 | 185 | 1215.50 | 245 | 1607.86 | 305 | 2000.22 | 355 | 2327.30 | 405 | 2654.04 | 455 | 2981.12 |
| 5 | 38.76 | | | | | | | | | | | | | | | | |
| 6 | 45.22 | 66 | 437.58 | 126 | 829.94 | 186 | 1222.30 | 246 | 1614.66 | 306 | 2006.68 | 356 | 2333.76 | 406 | 2660.50 | 456 | 2987.58 |
| 7 | 51.68 | 67 | 444.04 | 127 | 836.40 | 187 | 1228.76 | 247 | 1621.12 | 307 | 2013.48 | 357 | 2340.22 | 407 | 2667.30 | 457 | 2994.04 |
| 8 | 58.48 | 68 | 450.50 | 128 | 842.86 | 188 | 1235.22 | 248 | 1627.58 | 308 | 2019.94 | 358 | 2346.68 | 408 | 2673.76 | 458 | 3000.50 |
| 9 | 64.94 | 69 | 457.30 | 129 | 849.66 | 189 | 1241.68 | 249 | 1634.04 | 309 | 2026.40 | 359 | 2353.48 | 409 | 2680.22 | 459 | 3007.30 |
| 10 | 71.40 | 70 | 463.76 | 130 | 856.12 | 190 | 1248.48 | 250 | 1640.50 | 310 | 2032.86 | 360 | 2359.94 | 410 | 2686.68 | 460 | 3013.76 |
| 11 | 77.86 | 71 | 470.22 | 131 | 862.58 | 191 | 1254.94 | 251 | 1647.30 | 311 | 2039.66 | 361 | 2366.40 | 411 | 2693.48 | 461 | 3020.22 |
| 12 | 84.66 | 72 | 476.68 | 132 | 869.04 | 192 | 1261.40 | 252 | 1653.76 | 312 | 2046.12 | 362 | 2372.86 | 412 | 2699.94 | 462 | 3026.68 |
| 13 | 91.12 | 73 | 483.48 | 133 | 875.50 | 193 | 1267.86 | 253 | 1660.22 | 313 | 2052.58 | 363 | 2379.66 | 413 | 2706.40 | 463 | 3033.48 |
| 14 | 97.58 | 74 | 489.94 | 134 | 882.30 | 194 | 1274.66 | 254 | 1666.68 | 314 | 2059.04 | 364 | 2386.12 | 414 | 2712.86 | 464 | 3039.94 |
| 15 | 104.04 | 75 | 496.40 | 135 | 888.76 | 195 | 1281.12 | 255 | 1673.48 | 315 | 2065.50 | 365 | 2392.58 | 415 | 2719.66 | 465 | 3046.40 |
| 16 | 110.50 | 76 | 502.86 | 136 | 895.22 | 196 | 1287.58 | 256 | 1679.94 | 316 | 2072.30 | 366 | 2399.04 | 416 | 2726.12 | 466 | 3052.86 |
| 17 | 117.30 | 77 | 509.66 | 137 | 901.68 | 197 | 1294.04 | 257 | 1686.40 | 317 | 2078.76 | 367 | 2405.50 | 417 | 2732.58 | 467 | 3059.66 |
| 18 | 123.76 | 78 | 516.12 | 138 | 908.48 | 198 | 1300.50 | 258 | 1692.86 | 318 | 2085.22 | 368 | 2412.30 | 418 | 2739.04 | 468 | 3066.12 |
| 19 | 130.22 | 79 | 522.58 | 139 | 914.94 | 199 | 1307.30 | 259 | 1699.66 | 319 | 2091.68 | 369 | 2418.76 | 419 | 2745.50 | 469 | 3072.58 |
| 20 | 136.68 | 80 | 529.04 | 140 | 921.40 | 200 | 1313.76 | 260 | 1706.12 | 320 | 2098.48 | 370 | 2425.22 | 420 | 2752.30 | 470 | 3079.04 |
| 21 | 143.48 | 81 | 535.50 | 141 | 927.86 | 201 | 1320.22 | 261 | 1712.58 | 321 | 2104.94 | 371 | 2431.68 | 421 | 2758.76 | 471 | 3085.50 |
| 22 | 149.94 | 82 | 542.30 | 142 | 934.66 | 202 | 1326.68 | 262 | 1719.04 | 322 | 2111.40 | 372 | 2438.48 | 422 | 2765.22 | 472 | 3092.30 |
| 23 | 156.40 | 83 | 548.76 | 143 | 941.12 | 203 | 1333.48 | 263 | 1725.50 | 323 | 2117.86 | 373 | 2444.94 | 423 | 2771.68 | 473 | 3098.76 |
| 24 | 162.86 | 84 | 555.22 | 144 | 947.58 | 204 | 1339.94 | 264 | 1732.30 | 324 | 2124.66 | 374 | 2451.40 | 424 | 2778.48 | 474 | 3105.22 |
| 25 | 169.66 | 85 | 561.68 | 145 | 954.04 | 205 | 1346.40 | 265 | 1738.76 | 325 | 2131.12 | 375 | 2457.86 | 425 | 2784.94 | 475 | 3111.68 |
| 26 | 176.12 | 86 | 568.48 | 146 | 960.50 | 206 | 1352.86 | 266 | 1745.22 | 326 | 2137.58 | 376 | 2464.66 | 426 | 2791.40 | 476 | 3118.48 |
| 27 | 182.58 | 87 | 574.94 | 147 | 967.30 | 207 | 1359.66 | 267 | 1751.68 | 327 | 2144.04 | 377 | 2471.12 | 427 | 2797.86 | 477 | 3124.94 |
| 28 | 189.04 | 88 | 581.40 | 148 | 973.76 | 208 | 1366.12 | 268 | 1758.48 | 328 | 2150.50 | 378 | 2477.58 | 428 | 2804.66 | 478 | 3131.40 |
| 29 | 195.50 | 89 | 587.86 | 149 | 980.22 | 209 | 1372.58 | 269 | 1764.94 | 329 | 2157.30 | 379 | 2484.04 | 429 | 2811.12 | 479 | 3137.86 |
| 30 | 202.30 | 90 | 594.66 | 150 | 986.68 | 210 | 1379.04 | 270 | 1771.40 | 330 | 2163.76 | 380 | 2490.50 | 430 | 2817.58 | 480 | 3144.66 |
| 31 | 208.76 | 91 | 601.12 | 151 | 993.48 | 211 | 1385.50 | 271 | 1777.86 | 331 | 2170.22 | 381 | 2497.30 | 431 | 2824.04 | 481 | 3151.12 |
| 32 | 215.22 | 92 | 607.58 | 152 | 999.94 | 212 | 1392.30 | 272 | 1784.66 | 332 | 2176.68 | 382 | 2503.76 | 432 | 2830.50 | 482 | 3157.58 |
| 33 | 221.68 | 93 | 614.04 | 153 | 1006.40 | 213 | 1398.76 | 273 | 1791.12 | 333 | 2183.48 | 383 | 2510.22 | 433 | 2837.30 | 483 | 3164.04 |
| 34 | 228.48 | 94 | 620.50 | 154 | 1012.86 | 214 | 1405.22 | 274 | 1797.58 | 334 | 2189.94 | 384 | 2516.68 | 434 | 2843.76 | 484 | 3170.50 |
| 35 | 234.94 | 95 | 627.30 | 155 | 1019.66 | 215 | 1411.68 | 275 | 1804.04 | 335 | 2196.40 | 385 | 2523.48 | 435 | 2850.22 | 485 | 3177.30 |
| 36 | 241.40 | 96 | 633.76 | 156 | 1026.12 | 216 | 1418.48 | 276 | 1810.50 | 336 | 2202.86 | 386 | 2529.94 | 436 | 2856.68 | 486 | 3183.76 |
| 37 | 247.86 | 97 | 640.22 | 157 | 1032.58 | 217 | 1424.94 | 277 | 1817.30 | 337 | 2209.66 | 387 | 2536.40 | 437 | 2863.48 | 487 | 3190.22 |
| 38 | 254.66 | 98 | 646.68 | 158 | 1039.04 | 218 | 1431.40 | 278 | 1823.76 | 338 | 2216.12 | 388 | 2542.86 | 438 | 2869.94 | 488 | 3196.68 |
| 39 | 261.12 | 99 | 653.48 | 159 | 1045.50 | 219 | 1437.86 | 279 | 1830.22 | 339 | 2222.58 | 389 | 2549.66 | 439 | 2876.40 | 489 | 3203.48 |
| 40 | 267.58 | 100 | 659.94 | 160 | 1052.30 | 220 | 1444.66 | 280 | 1836.68 | 340 | 2229.04 | 390 | 2556.12 | 440 | 2882.86 | 490 | 3209.94 |
| 41 | 274.04 | 101 | 666.40 | 161 | 1058.76 | 221 | 1451.12 | 281 | 1843.48 | 341 | 2235.50 | 391 | 2562.58 | 441 | 2889.66 | 491 | 3216.40 |
| 42 | 280.50 | 102 | 672.86 | 162 | 1065.22 | 222 | 1457.58 | 282 | 1849.94 | 342 | 2242.30 | 392 | 2569.04 | 442 | 2896.12 | 492 | 3222.86 |
| 43 | 287.30 | 103 | 679.66 | 163 | 1071.68 | 223 | 1464.04 | 283 | 1856.40 | 343 | 2248.76 | 393 | 2575.50 | 443 | 2902.58 | 493 | 3229.66 |
| 44 | 293.76 | 104 | 686.12 | 164 | 1078.48 | 224 | 1470.50 | 284 | 1862.86 | 344 | 2255.22 | 394 | 2582.30 | 444 | 2909.04 | 494 | 3236.12 |
| 45 | 300.22 | 105 | 692.58 | 165 | 1084.94 | 225 | 1477.30 | 285 | 1869.66 | 345 | 2261.68 | 395 | 2588.76 | 445 | 2915.50 | 495 | 3242.58 |
| 46 | 306.68 | 106 | 699.04 | 166 | 1091.40 | 226 | 1483.76 | 286 | 1876.12 | 346 | 2268.48 | 396 | 2595.22 | 446 | 2922.30 | 496 | 3249.04 |
| 47 | 313.48 | 107 | 705.50 | 167 | 1097.86 | 227 | 1490.22 | 287 | 1882.58 | 347 | 2274.94 | 397 | 2601.68 | 447 | 2928.76 | 497 | 3255.50 |
| 48 | 319.94 | 108 | 712.30 | 168 | 1104.66 | 228 | 1496.68 | 288 | 1889.04 | 348 | 2281.40 | 398 | 2608.48 | 448 | 2935.22 | 498 | 3262.30 |
| 49 | 326.40 | 109 | 718.76 | 169 | 1111.12 | 229 | 1503.48 | 289 | 1895.50 | 349 | 2287.86 | 399 | 2614.94 | 449 | 2941.68 | 499 | 3268.76 |
| 50 | 332.86 | 110 | 725.22 | 170 | 1117.58 | 230 | 1509.94 | 290 | 1902.30 | 350 | 2294.66 | 400 | 2621.40 | 450 | 2948.48 | 500 | 3275.22 |
| 51 | 339.66 | 111 | 731.68 | 171 | 1124.04 | 231 | 1516.40 | 291 | 1908.76 | | | | | | | | |
| 52 | 346.12 | 112 | 738.48 | 172 | 1130.50 | 232 | 1522.86 | 292 | 1915.22 | | | | | | | | |
| 53 | 352.58 | 113 | 744.94 | 173 | 1137.30 | 233 | 1529.66 | 293 | 1921.68 | | | | | | | | |
| 54 | 359.04 | 114 | 751.40 | 174 | 1143.76 | 234 | 1536.12 | 294 | 1928.48 | | | | | | | | |
| 55 | 365.50 | 115 | 757.86 | 175 | 1150.22 | 235 | 1542.58 | 295 | 1934.94 | | | | | | | | |
| 56 | 372.30 | 116 | 764.66 | 176 | 1156.68 | 236 | 1549.04 | 296 | 1941.40 | | | | | | | | |
| 57 | 378.76 | 117 | 771.12 | 177 | 1163.48 | 237 | 1555.50 | 297 | 1947.86 | | | | | | | | |
| 58 | 385.22 | 118 | 777.58 | 178 | 1169.94 | 238 | 1562.30 | 298 | 1954.66 | | | | | | | | |
| 59 | 391.68 | 119 | 784.04 | 179 | 1176.40 | 239 | 1568.76 | 299 | 1961.12 | | | | | | | | |
| 60 | 398.48 | 120 | 790.50 | 180 | 1182.86 | 240 | 1575.22 | 300 | 1967.58 | | | | | | | | |

### Code more than 500

1 Where the code is in the range 501 to **1000** inclusive:

  a. Subtract **500** from the code and use the balance of the code to obtain a pay adjustment figure from the table above.

  b. Add this pay adjustment figure to the figure given in the box alongside to obtain the figure of total pay adjustment to date * | **3269.44** |

2 Where the code **exceeds 1000** follow the instructions on **page 3**.

**Week 35**  Nov 30 to Dec 6                                    **Tables A** - Pay Adjustment Tables

| Code | Total pay adjustment to date | Code | Total pay adjustment to date | Code | Total pay adjustment to date | Code | Total pay adjustment to date | Code | Total pay adjustment to date | Code | Total pay adjustment to date | Code | Total pay adjustment to date | Code | Total pay adjustment to date | Code | Total pay adjustment to date |
|---|---|---|---|---|---|---|---|---|---|---|---|---|---|---|---|---|---|
| | £ | | £ | | £ | | £ | | £ | | £ | | £ | | £ | | £ |
| 0 | NIL | 61 | 416.85 | 121 | 820.75 | 181 | 1224.65 | 241 | 1628.20 | 301 | 2032.10 | 351 | 2368.80 | 401 | 2705.15 | 451 | 3041.85 |
| 1 | 12.95 | 62 | 423.50 | 122 | 827.40 | 182 | 1231.30 | 242 | 1635.20 | 302 | 2038.75 | 352 | 2375.45 | 402 | 2712.15 | 452 | 3048.50 |
| 2 | 19.60 | 63 | 430.15 | 123 | 834.05 | 183 | 1237.95 | 243 | 1641.85 | 303 | 2045.75 | 353 | 2382.10 | 403 | 2718.80 | 453 | 3055.15 |
| 3 | 26.25 | 64 | 437.15 | 124 | 840.70 | 184 | 1244.60 | 244 | 1648.50 | 304 | 2052.40 | 354 | 2388.75 | 404 | 2725.45 | 454 | 3062.15 |
| 4 | 33.25 | 65 | 443.80 | 125 | 847.70 | 185 | 1251.25 | 245 | 1655.15 | 305 | 2059.05 | 355 | 2395.75 | 405 | 2732.10 | 455 | 3068.80 |
| 5 | 39.90 | | | | | | | | | | | | | | | | |
| 6 | 46.55 | 66 | 450.45 | 126 | 854.35 | 186 | 1258.25 | 246 | 1662.15 | 306 | 2065.70 | 356 | 2402.40 | 406 | 2738.75 | 456 | 3075.45 |
| 7 | 53.20 | 67 | 457.10 | 127 | 861.00 | 187 | 1264.90 | 247 | 1668.80 | 307 | 2072.70 | 357 | 2409.05 | 407 | 2745.75 | 457 | 3082.10 |
| 8 | 60.20 | 68 | 463.75 | 128 | 867.65 | 188 | 1271.55 | 248 | 1675.45 | 308 | 2079.35 | 358 | 2415.70 | 408 | 2752.40 | 458 | 3088.75 |
| 9 | 66.85 | 69 | 470.75 | 129 | 874.65 | 189 | 1278.20 | 249 | 1682.10 | 309 | 2086.00 | 359 | 2422.70 | 409 | 2759.05 | 459 | 3095.75 |
| 10 | 73.50 | 70 | 477.40 | 130 | 881.30 | 190 | 1285.20 | 250 | 1688.75 | 310 | 2092.65 | 360 | 2429.35 | 410 | 2765.70 | 460 | 3102.40 |
| 11 | 80.15 | 71 | 484.05 | 131 | 887.95 | 191 | 1291.85 | 251 | 1695.75 | 311 | 2099.65 | 361 | 2436.00 | 411 | 2772.70 | 461 | 3109.05 |
| 12 | 87.15 | 72 | 490.70 | 132 | 894.60 | 192 | 1298.50 | 252 | 1702.40 | 312 | 2106.30 | 362 | 2442.65 | 412 | 2779.35 | 462 | 3115.70 |
| 13 | 93.80 | 73 | 497.70 | 133 | 901.25 | 193 | 1305.15 | 253 | 1709.05 | 313 | 2112.95 | 363 | 2449.65 | 413 | 2786.00 | 463 | 3122.70 |
| 14 | 100.45 | 74 | 504.35 | 134 | 908.25 | 194 | 1312.15 | 254 | 1715.70 | 314 | 2119.60 | 364 | 2456.30 | 414 | 2792.65 | 464 | 3129.35 |
| 15 | 107.10 | 75 | 511.00 | 135 | 914.90 | 195 | 1318.80 | 255 | 1722.70 | 315 | 2126.25 | 365 | 2462.95 | 415 | 2799.65 | 465 | 3136.00 |
| 16 | 113.75 | 76 | 517.65 | 136 | 921.55 | 196 | 1325.45 | 256 | 1729.35 | 316 | 2133.25 | 366 | 2469.60 | 416 | 2806.30 | 466 | 3142.65 |
| 17 | 120.75 | 77 | 524.65 | 137 | 928.20 | 197 | 1332.10 | 257 | 1736.00 | 317 | 2139.90 | 367 | 2476.25 | 417 | 2812.95 | 467 | 3149.65 |
| 18 | 127.40 | 78 | 531.30 | 138 | 935.20 | 198 | 1338.75 | 258 | 1742.65 | 318 | 2146.55 | 368 | 2483.25 | 418 | 2819.60 | 468 | 3156.30 |
| 19 | 134.05 | 79 | 537.95 | 139 | 941.85 | 199 | 1345.75 | 259 | 1749.65 | 319 | 2153.20 | 369 | 2489.90 | 419 | 2826.25 | 469 | 3162.95 |
| 20 | 140.70 | 80 | 544.60 | 140 | 948.50 | 200 | 1352.40 | 260 | 1756.30 | 320 | 2160.20 | 370 | 2496.55 | 420 | 2833.25 | 470 | 3169.60 |
| 21 | 147.70 | 81 | 551.25 | 141 | 955.15 | 201 | 1359.05 | 261 | 1762.95 | 321 | 2166.85 | 371 | 2503.20 | 421 | 2839.90 | 471 | 3176.25 |
| 22 | 154.35 | 82 | 558.25 | 142 | 962.15 | 202 | 1365.70 | 262 | 1769.60 | 322 | 2173.50 | 372 | 2510.20 | 422 | 2846.55 | 472 | 3183.25 |
| 23 | 161.00 | 83 | 564.90 | 143 | 968.80 | 203 | 1372.70 | 263 | 1776.25 | 323 | 2180.15 | 373 | 2516.85 | 423 | 2853.20 | 473 | 3189.90 |
| 24 | 167.65 | 84 | 571.55 | 144 | 975.45 | 204 | 1379.35 | 264 | 1783.25 | 324 | 2187.15 | 374 | 2523.50 | 424 | 2860.20 | 474 | 3196.55 |
| 25 | 174.65 | 85 | 578.20 | 145 | 982.10 | 205 | 1386.00 | 265 | 1789.90 | 325 | 2193.80 | 375 | 2530.15 | 425 | 2866.85 | 475 | 3203.20 |
| 26 | 181.30 | 86 | 585.20 | 146 | 988.75 | 206 | 1392.65 | 266 | 1796.55 | 326 | 2200.45 | 376 | 2537.15 | 426 | 2873.50 | 476 | 3210.20 |
| 27 | 187.95 | 87 | 591.85 | 147 | 995.75 | 207 | 1399.65 | 267 | 1803.20 | 327 | 2207.10 | 377 | 2543.80 | 427 | 2880.15 | 477 | 3216.85 |
| 28 | 194.60 | 88 | 598.50 | 148 | 1002.40 | 208 | 1406.30 | 268 | 1810.20 | 328 | 2213.75 | 378 | 2550.45 | 428 | 2887.15 | 478 | 3223.50 |
| 29 | 201.25 | 89 | 605.15 | 149 | 1009.05 | 209 | 1412.95 | 269 | 1816.85 | 329 | 2220.75 | 379 | 2557.10 | 429 | 2893.80 | 479 | 3230.15 |
| 30 | 208.25 | 90 | 612.15 | 150 | 1015.70 | 210 | 1419.60 | 270 | 1823.50 | 330 | 2227.40 | 380 | 2563.75 | 430 | 2900.45 | 480 | 3237.15 |
| 31 | 214.90 | 91 | 618.80 | 151 | 1022.70 | 211 | 1426.25 | 271 | 1830.15 | 331 | 2234.05 | 381 | 2570.75 | 431 | 2907.10 | 481 | 3243.60 |
| 32 | 221.55 | 92 | 625.45 | 152 | 1029.35 | 212 | 1433.25 | 272 | 1837.15 | 332 | 2240.70 | 382 | 2577.40 | 432 | 2913.75 | 482 | 3250.45 |
| 33 | 228.20 | 93 | 632.10 | 153 | 1036.00 | 213 | 1439.90 | 273 | 1843.80 | 333 | 2247.70 | 383 | 2584.05 | 433 | 2920.75 | 483 | 3257.10 |
| 34 | 235.20 | 94 | 638.75 | 154 | 1042.65 | 214 | 1446.55 | 274 | 1850.45 | 334 | 2254.35 | 384 | 2590.70 | 434 | 2927.40 | 484 | 3263.75 |
| 35 | 241.85 | 95 | 645.75 | 155 | 1049.65 | 215 | 1453.20 | 275 | 1857.10 | 335 | 2261.00 | 385 | 2597.70 | 435 | 2934.05 | 485 | 3270.75 |
| 36 | 248.50 | 96 | 652.40 | 156 | 1056.30 | 216 | 1460.20 | 276 | 1863.75 | 336 | 2267.65 | 386 | 2604.35 | 436 | 2940.70 | 486 | 3277.40 |
| 37 | 255.15 | 97 | 659.05 | 157 | 1062.95 | 217 | 1466.85 | 277 | 1870.75 | 337 | 2274.65 | 387 | 2611.00 | 437 | 2947.70 | 487 | 3284.05 |
| 38 | 262.15 | 98 | 665.70 | 158 | 1069.60 | 218 | 1473.50 | 278 | 1877.40 | 338 | 2281.30 | 388 | 2617.65 | 438 | 2954.35 | 488 | 3290.70 |
| 39 | 268.80 | 99 | 672.70 | 159 | 1076.25 | 219 | 1480.15 | 279 | 1884.05 | 339 | 2287.95 | 389 | 2624.65 | 439 | 2961.00 | 489 | 3297.70 |
| 40 | 275.45 | 100 | 679.35 | 160 | 1083.25 | 220 | 1487.15 | 280 | 1890.70 | 340 | 2294.60 | 390 | 2631.30 | 440 | 2967.65 | 490 | 3304.35 |
| 41 | 282.10 | 101 | 686.00 | 161 | 1089.90 | 221 | 1493.80 | 281 | 1897.70 | 341 | 2301.25 | 391 | 2637.95 | 441 | 2974.65 | 491 | 3311.00 |
| 42 | 288.75 | 102 | 692.65 | 162 | 1096.55 | 222 | 1500.45 | 282 | 1904.35 | 342 | 2308.25 | 392 | 2644.60 | 442 | 2981.30 | 492 | 3317.65 |
| 43 | 295.75 | 103 | 699.65 | 163 | 1103.20 | 223 | 1507.10 | 283 | 1911.00 | 343 | 2314.90 | 393 | 2651.25 | 443 | 2987.95 | 493 | 3324.65 |
| 44 | 302.40 | 104 | 706.30 | 164 | 1110.20 | 224 | 1513.75 | 284 | 1917.65 | 344 | 2321.55 | 394 | 2658.25 | 444 | 2994.60 | 494 | 3331.30 |
| 45 | 309.05 | 105 | 712.95 | 165 | 1116.85 | 225 | 1520.75 | 285 | 1924.65 | 345 | 2328.20 | 395 | 2664.90 | 445 | 3001.25 | 495 | 3337.95 |
| 46 | 315.70 | 106 | 719.60 | 166 | 1123.50 | 226 | 1527.40 | 286 | 1931.30 | 346 | 2335.20 | 396 | 2671.55 | 446 | 3008.25 | 496 | 3344.60 |
| 47 | 322.70 | 107 | 726.25 | 167 | 1130.15 | 227 | 1534.05 | 287 | 1937.95 | 347 | 2341.85 | 397 | 2678.20 | 447 | 3014.90 | 497 | 3351.25 |
| 48 | 329.35 | 108 | 733.25 | 168 | 1137.15 | 228 | 1540.70 | 288 | 1944.60 | 348 | 2348.50 | 398 | 2685.20 | 448 | 3021.55 | 498 | 3358.25 |
| 49 | 336.00 | 109 | 739.90 | 169 | 1143.80 | 229 | 1547.70 | 289 | 1951.25 | 349 | 2355.15 | 399 | 2691.85 | 449 | 3028.20 | 499 | 3364.90 |
| 50 | 342.65 | 110 | 746.55 | 170 | 1150.45 | 230 | 1554.35 | 290 | 1958.25 | 350 | 2362.15 | 400 | 2698.50 | 450 | 3035.20 | 500 | 3371.55 |
| 51 | 349.65 | 111 | 753.20 | 171 | 1157.10 | 231 | 1561.00 | 291 | 1964.90 | | | | | | | | |
| 52 | 356.30 | 112 | 760.20 | 172 | 1163.75 | 232 | 1567.65 | 292 | 1971.55 | | | | | | | | |
| 53 | 362.95 | 113 | 766.85 | 173 | 1170.75 | 233 | 1574.65 | 293 | 1978.20 | | | | | | | | |
| 54 | 369.60 | 114 | 773.50 | 174 | 1177.40 | 234 | 1581.30 | 294 | 1985.20 | | | | | | | | |
| 55 | 376.25 | 115 | 780.15 | 175 | 1184.05 | 235 | 1587.95 | 295 | 1991.85 | | | | | | | | |
| 56 | 383.25 | 116 | 787.15 | 176 | 1190.70 | 236 | 1594.60 | 296 | 1998.50 | | | | | | | | |
| 57 | 389.90 | 117 | 793.80 | 177 | 1197.70 | 237 | 1601.25 | 297 | 2005.15 | | | | | | | | |
| 58 | 396.55 | 118 | 800.45 | 178 | 1204.35 | 238 | 1608.25 | 298 | 2012.15 | | | | | | | | |
| 59 | 403.20 | 119 | 807.10 | 179 | 1211.00 | 239 | 1614.90 | 299 | 2018.80 | | | | | | | | |
| 60 | 410.20 | 120 | 813.75 | 180 | 1217.65 | 240 | 1621.55 | 300 | 2025.45 | | | | | | | | |

**Code more than 500**

1  Where the code is in the range 501 to 1000 inclusive:

   a. Subtract **500** from the code and use the balance of the code to obtain a pay adjustment figure from the table above.

   b. Add this pay adjustment figure to the figure given in the box alongside to obtain the figure of total pay adjustment to date *  | **3365.60** |

2  Where the code **exceeds 1000** follow the instructions on **page 3**.

**Tables A** - Pay Adjustment Tables                      Dec 7 to Dec 13  **Week 36**

| Code | Total pay adjustment to date | Code | Total pay adjustment to date | Code | Total pay adjustment to date | Code | Total pay adjustment to date | Code | Total pay adjustment to date | Code | Total pay adjustment to date | Code | Total pay adjustment to date | Code | Total pay adjustment to date | Code | Total pay adjustment to date |
|---|---|---|---|---|---|---|---|---|---|---|---|---|---|---|---|---|---|
| | £ | | £ | | £ | | £ | | £ | | £ | | £ | | £ | | £ |
| 0 | NIL | 61 | 428.76 | 121 | 844.20 | 181 | 1259.64 | 241 | 1674.72 | 301 | 2090.16 | 351 | 2436.48 | 401 | 2782.44 | 451 | 3128.76 |
| 1 | 13.32 | 62 | 435.60 | 122 | 851.04 | 182 | 1266.48 | 242 | 1681.92 | 302 | 2097.00 | 352 | 2443.32 | 402 | 2789.64 | 452 | 3135.60 |
| 2 | 20.16 | 63 | 442.44 | 123 | 857.88 | 183 | 1273.32 | 243 | 1688.76 | 303 | 2104.20 | 353 | 2450.16 | 403 | 2796.48 | 453 | 3142.44 |
| 3 | 27.00 | 64 | 449.64 | 124 | 864.72 | 184 | 1280.16 | 244 | 1695.60 | 304 | 2111.04 | 354 | 2457.00 | 404 | 2803.32 | 454 | 3149.64 |
| 4 | 34.20 | 65 | 456.48 | 125 | 871.92 | 185 | 1287.00 | 245 | 1702.44 | 305 | 2117.88 | 355 | 2464.20 | 405 | 2810.16 | 455 | 3156.48 |
| 5 | 41.04 | | | | | | | | | | | | | | | | |
| 6 | 47.88 | 66 | 463.32 | 126 | 878.76 | 186 | 1294.20 | 246 | 1709.64 | 306 | 2124.72 | 356 | 2471.04 | 406 | 2817.00 | 456 | 3163.32 |
| 7 | 54.72 | 67 | 470.16 | 127 | 885.60 | 187 | 1301.04 | 247 | 1716.48 | 307 | 2131.92 | 357 | 2477.88 | 407 | 2824.20 | 457 | 3170.16 |
| 8 | 61.92 | 68 | 477.00 | 128 | 892.44 | 188 | 1307.88 | 248 | 1723.32 | 308 | 2138.76 | 358 | 2484.72 | 408 | 2831.04 | 458 | 3177.00 |
| 9 | 68.76 | 69 | 484.20 | 129 | 899.64 | 189 | 1314.72 | 249 | 1730.16 | 309 | 2145.60 | 359 | 2491.92 | 409 | 2837.88 | 459 | 3184.20 |
| 10 | 75.60 | 70 | 491.04 | 130 | 906.48 | 190 | 1321.92 | 250 | 1737.00 | 310 | 2152.44 | 360 | 2498.76 | 410 | 2844.72 | 460 | 3191.04 |
| 11 | 82.44 | 71 | 497.88 | 131 | 913.32 | 191 | 1328.76 | 251 | 1744.20 | 311 | 2159.64 | 361 | 2505.60 | 411 | 2851.92 | 461 | 3197.88 |
| 12 | 89.64 | 72 | 504.72 | 132 | 920.16 | 192 | 1335.60 | 252 | 1751.04 | 312 | 2166.48 | 362 | 2512.44 | 412 | 2858.76 | 462 | 3204.72 |
| 13 | 96.48 | 73 | 511.92 | 133 | 927.00 | 193 | 1342.44 | 253 | 1757.88 | 313 | 2173.32 | 363 | 2519.64 | 413 | 2865.60 | 463 | 3211.92 |
| 14 | 103.32 | 74 | 518.76 | 134 | 934.20 | 194 | 1349.64 | 254 | 1764.72 | 314 | 2180.16 | 364 | 2526.48 | 414 | 2872.44 | 464 | 3218.76 |
| 15 | 110.16 | 75 | 525.60 | 135 | 941.04 | 195 | 1356.48 | 255 | 1771.92 | 315 | 2187.00 | 365 | 2533.32 | 415 | 2879.64 | 465 | 3225.60 |
| 16 | 117.00 | 76 | 532.44 | 136 | 947.88 | 196 | 1363.32 | 256 | 1778.76 | 316 | 2194.20 | 366 | 2540.16 | 416 | 2886.48 | 466 | 3232.44 |
| 17 | 124.20 | 77 | 539.64 | 137 | 954.72 | 197 | 1370.16 | 257 | 1785.60 | 317 | 2201.04 | 367 | 2547.00 | 417 | 2893.32 | 467 | 3239.64 |
| 18 | 131.04 | 78 | 546.48 | 138 | 961.92 | 198 | 1377.00 | 258 | 1792.44 | 318 | 2207.88 | 368 | 2554.20 | 418 | 2900.16 | 468 | 3246.48 |
| 19 | 137.88 | 79 | 553.32 | 139 | 968.76 | 199 | 1384.20 | 259 | 1799.64 | 319 | 2214.72 | 369 | 2561.04 | 419 | 2907.00 | 469 | 3253.32 |
| 20 | 144.72 | 80 | 560.16 | 140 | 975.60 | 200 | 1391.04 | 260 | 1806.48 | 320 | 2221.92 | 370 | 2567.88 | 420 | 2914.20 | 470 | 3260.16 |
| 21 | 151.92 | 81 | 567.00 | 141 | 982.44 | 201 | 1397.88 | 261 | 1813.32 | 321 | 2228.76 | 371 | 2574.72 | 421 | 2921.04 | 471 | 3267.00 |
| 22 | 158.76 | 82 | 574.20 | 142 | 989.64 | 202 | 1404.72 | 262 | 1820.16 | 322 | 2235.60 | 372 | 2581.92 | 422 | 2927.88 | 472 | 3274.20 |
| 23 | 165.60 | 83 | 581.04 | 143 | 996.48 | 203 | 1411.92 | 263 | 1827.00 | 323 | 2242.44 | 373 | 2588.76 | 423 | 2934.72 | 473 | 3281.04 |
| 24 | 172.44 | 84 | 587.88 | 144 | 1003.32 | 204 | 1418.76 | 264 | 1834.20 | 324 | 2249.64 | 374 | 2595.60 | 424 | 2941.92 | 474 | 3287.88 |
| 25 | 179.64 | 85 | 594.72 | 145 | 1010.16 | 205 | 1425.60 | 265 | 1841.04 | 325 | 2256.48 | 375 | 2602.44 | 425 | 2948.76 | 475 | 3294.72 |
| 26 | 186.48 | 86 | 601.92 | 146 | 1017.00 | 206 | 1432.44 | 266 | 1847.88 | 326 | 2263.32 | 376 | 2609.64 | 426 | 2955.60 | 476 | 3301.92 |
| 27 | 193.32 | 87 | 608.76 | 147 | 1024.20 | 207 | 1439.64 | 267 | 1854.72 | 327 | 2270.16 | 377 | 2616.48 | 427 | 2962.44 | 477 | 3308.76 |
| 28 | 200.16 | 88 | 615.60 | 148 | 1031.04 | 208 | 1446.48 | 268 | 1861.92 | 328 | 2277.00 | 378 | 2623.32 | 428 | 2969.64 | 478 | 3315.60 |
| 29 | 207.00 | 89 | 622.44 | 149 | 1037.88 | 209 | 1453.32 | 269 | 1868.76 | 329 | 2284.20 | 379 | 2630.16 | 429 | 2976.48 | 479 | 3322.44 |
| 30 | 214.20 | 90 | 629.64 | 150 | 1044.72 | 210 | 1460.16 | 270 | 1875.60 | 330 | 2291.04 | 380 | 2637.00 | 430 | 2983.32 | 480 | 3329.64 |
| 31 | 221.04 | 91 | 636.48 | 151 | 1051.92 | 211 | 1467.00 | 271 | 1882.44 | 331 | 2297.88 | 381 | 2644.20 | 431 | 2990.16 | 481 | 3336.48 |
| 32 | 227.88 | 92 | 643.32 | 152 | 1058.76 | 212 | 1474.20 | 272 | 1889.64 | 332 | 2304.72 | 382 | 2651.04 | 432 | 2997.00 | 482 | 3343.32 |
| 33 | 234.72 | 93 | 650.16 | 153 | 1065.60 | 213 | 1481.04 | 273 | 1896.48 | 333 | 2311.92 | 383 | 2657.88 | 433 | 3004.20 | 483 | 3350.16 |
| 34 | 241.92 | 94 | 657.00 | 154 | 1072.44 | 214 | 1487.88 | 274 | 1903.32 | 334 | 2318.76 | 384 | 2664.72 | 434 | 3011.04 | 484 | 3357.00 |
| 35 | 248.76 | 95 | 664.20 | 155 | 1079.64 | 215 | 1494.72 | 275 | 1910.16 | 335 | 2325.60 | 385 | 2671.92 | 435 | 3017.88 | 485 | 3364.20 |
| 36 | 255.60 | 96 | 671.04 | 156 | 1086.48 | 216 | 1501.92 | 276 | 1917.00 | 336 | 2332.44 | 386 | 2678.76 | 436 | 3024.72 | 486 | 3371.04 |
| 37 | 262.44 | 97 | 677.88 | 157 | 1093.32 | 217 | 1508.76 | 277 | 1924.20 | 337 | 2339.64 | 387 | 2685.60 | 437 | 3031.92 | 487 | 3377.88 |
| 38 | 269.64 | 98 | 684.72 | 158 | 1100.16 | 218 | 1515.60 | 278 | 1931.04 | 338 | 2346.48 | 388 | 2692.44 | 438 | 3038.76 | 488 | 3384.72 |
| 39 | 276.48 | 99 | 691.92 | 159 | 1107.00 | 219 | 1522.44 | 279 | 1937.88 | 339 | 2353.32 | 389 | 2699.64 | 439 | 3045.60 | 489 | 3391.92 |
| 40 | 283.32 | 100 | 698.76 | 160 | 1114.20 | 220 | 1529.64 | 280 | 1944.72 | 340 | 2360.16 | 390 | 2706.48 | 440 | 3052.44 | 490 | 3398.76 |
| 41 | 290.16 | 101 | 705.60 | 161 | 1121.04 | 221 | 1536.48 | 281 | 1951.92 | 341 | 2367.00 | 391 | 2713.32 | 441 | 3059.64 | 491 | 3405.60 |
| 42 | 297.00 | 102 | 712.44 | 162 | 1127.88 | 222 | 1543.32 | 282 | 1958.76 | 342 | 2374.20 | 392 | 2720.16 | 442 | 3066.48 | 492 | 3412.44 |
| 43 | 304.20 | 103 | 719.64 | 163 | 1134.72 | 223 | 1550.16 | 283 | 1965.60 | 343 | 2381.04 | 393 | 2727.00 | 443 | 3073.32 | 493 | 3419.64 |
| 44 | 311.04 | 104 | 726.48 | 164 | 1141.92 | 224 | 1557.00 | 284 | 1972.44 | 344 | 2387.88 | 394 | 2734.20 | 444 | 3080.16 | 494 | 3426.48 |
| 45 | 317.88 | 105 | 733.32 | 165 | 1148.76 | 225 | 1564.20 | 285 | 1979.64 | 345 | 2394.72 | 395 | 2741.04 | 445 | 3087.00 | 495 | 3433.32 |
| 46 | 324.72 | 106 | 740.16 | 166 | 1155.60 | 226 | 1571.04 | 286 | 1986.48 | 346 | 2401.92 | 396 | 2747.88 | 446 | 3094.20 | 496 | 3440.16 |
| 47 | 331.92 | 107 | 747.00 | 167 | 1162.44 | 227 | 1577.88 | 287 | 1993.32 | 347 | 2408.76 | 397 | 2754.72 | 447 | 3101.04 | 497 | 3447.00 |
| 48 | 338.76 | 108 | 754.20 | 168 | 1169.64 | 228 | 1584.72 | 288 | 2000.16 | 348 | 2415.60 | 398 | 2761.92 | 448 | 3107.88 | 498 | 3454.20 |
| 49 | 345.60 | 109 | 761.04 | 169 | 1176.48 | 229 | 1591.92 | 289 | 2007.00 | 349 | 2422.44 | 399 | 2768.76 | 449 | 3114.72 | 499 | 3461.04 |
| 50 | 352.44 | 110 | 767.88 | 170 | 1183.32 | 230 | 1598.76 | 290 | 2014.20 | 350 | 2429.64 | 400 | 2775.60 | 450 | 3121.92 | 500 | 3467.88 |
| 51 | 359.64 | 111 | 774.72 | 171 | 1190.16 | 231 | 1605.60 | 291 | 2021.04 | | | | | | | | |
| 52 | 366.48 | 112 | 781.92 | 172 | 1197.00 | 232 | 1612.44 | 292 | 2027.88 | | | | | | | | |
| 53 | 373.32 | 113 | 788.76 | 173 | 1204.20 | 233 | 1619.64 | 293 | 2034.72 | | | | | | | | |
| 54 | 380.16 | 114 | 795.60 | 174 | 1211.04 | 234 | 1626.48 | 294 | 2041.92 | | | | | | | | |
| 55 | 387.00 | 115 | 802.44 | 175 | 1217.88 | 235 | 1633.32 | 295 | 2048.76 | | | | | | | | |
| 56 | 394.20 | 116 | 809.64 | 176 | 1224.72 | 236 | 1640.16 | 296 | 2055.60 | | | | | | | | |
| 57 | 401.04 | 117 | 816.48 | 177 | 1231.92 | 237 | 1647.00 | 297 | 2062.44 | | | | | | | | |
| 58 | 407.88 | 118 | 823.32 | 178 | 1238.76 | 238 | 1654.20 | 298 | 2069.64 | | | | | | | | |
| 59 | 414.72 | 119 | 830.16 | 179 | 1245.60 | 239 | 1661.04 | 299 | 2076.48 | | | | | | | | |
| 60 | 421.92 | 120 | 837.00 | 180 | 1252.44 | 240 | 1667.88 | 300 | 2083.32 | | | | | | | | |

**Code more than 500**

1 Where the code is in the range **501** to **1000** inclusive:

   a. Subtract **500** from the code and use the balance of the code to obtain a pay adjustment figure from the table above.

   b. Add this pay adjustment figure to the figure given in the box alongside to obtain the figure of total pay adjustment to date * | **3461.76** |

2 Where the code **exceeds 1000** follow the instructions on **page 3**.

39

**Week 37**  Dec 14 to Dec 20                                   **Tables A** - Pay Adjustment Tables

| Code | Total pay adjustment to date | Code | Total pay adjustment to date | Code | Total pay adjustment to date | Code | Total pay adjustment to date | Code | Total pay adjustment to date | Code | Total pay adjustment to date | Code | Total pay adjustment to date | Code | Total pay adjustment to date | Code | Total pay adjustment to date |
|---|---|---|---|---|---|---|---|---|---|---|---|---|---|---|---|---|---|
| | £ | | £ | | £ | | £ | | £ | | £ | | £ | | £ | | £ |
| 0 | NIL | | | | | | | | | | | | | | | | |
| 1 | 13.69 | 61 | 440.67 | 121 | 867.65 | 181 | 1294.63 | 241 | 1721.24 | 301 | 2148.22 | 351 | 2504.16 | 401 | 2859.73 | 451 | 3215.67 |
| 2 | 20.72 | 62 | 447.70 | 122 | 874.68 | 182 | 1301.66 | 242 | 1728.64 | 302 | 2155.25 | 352 | 2511.19 | 402 | 2867.13 | 452 | 3222.70 |
| 3 | 27.75 | 63 | 454.73 | 123 | 881.71 | 183 | 1308.69 | 243 | 1735.67 | 303 | 2162.65 | 353 | 2518.22 | 403 | 2874.16 | 453 | 3229.73 |
| 4 | 35.15 | 64 | 462.13 | 124 | 888.74 | 184 | 1315.72 | 244 | 1742.70 | 304 | 2169.68 | 354 | 2525.23 | 404 | 2881.19 | 454 | 3237.13 |
| 5 | 42.18 | 65 | 469.16 | 125 | 896.14 | 185 | 1322.75 | 245 | 1749.73 | 305 | 2176.71 | 355 | 2532.65 | 405 | 2888.22 | 455 | 3244.16 |
| 6 | 49.21 | 66 | 476.19 | 126 | 903.17 | 186 | 1330.15 | 246 | 1757.13 | 306 | 2183.74 | 356 | 2539.68 | 406 | 2895.25 | 456 | 3251.19 |
| 7 | 56.24 | 67 | 483.22 | 127 | 910.20 | 187 | 1337.18 | 247 | 1764.16 | 307 | 2191.14 | 357 | 2546.71 | 407 | 2902.65 | 457 | 3258.22 |
| 8 | 63.64 | 68 | 490.25 | 128 | 917.23 | 188 | 1344.21 | 248 | 1771.19 | 308 | 2198.17 | 358 | 2553.74 | 408 | 2909.68 | 458 | 3265.25 |
| 9 | 70.67 | 69 | 497.65 | 129 | 924.63 | 189 | 1351.24 | 249 | 1778.22 | 309 | 2205.20 | 359 | 2561.14 | 409 | 2916.71 | 459 | 3272.65 |
| 10 | 77.70 | 70 | 504.68 | 130 | 931.66 | 190 | 1358.64 | 250 | 1785.25 | 310 | 2212.23 | 360 | 2568.17 | 410 | 2923.74 | 460 | 3279.68 |
| 11 | 84.73 | 71 | 511.71 | 131 | 938.69 | 191 | 1365.67 | 251 | 1792.65 | 311 | 2219.63 | 361 | 2575.20 | 411 | 2931.14 | 461 | 3286.71 |
| 12 | 92.13 | 72 | 518.74 | 132 | 945.72 | 192 | 1372.70 | 252 | 1799.68 | 312 | 2226.66 | 362 | 2582.23 | 412 | 2938.17 | 462 | 3293.74 |
| 13 | 99.16 | 73 | 526.14 | 133 | 952.75 | 193 | 1379.73 | 253 | 1806.71 | 313 | 2233.69 | 363 | 2589.63 | 413 | 2945.20 | 463 | 3301.14 |
| 14 | 106.19 | 74 | 533.17 | 134 | 960.15 | 194 | 1387.13 | 254 | 1813.74 | 314 | 2240.72 | 364 | 2596.66 | 414 | 2952.23 | 464 | 3308.17 |
| 15 | 113.22 | 75 | 540.20 | 135 | 967.18 | 195 | 1394.16 | 255 | 1821.14 | 315 | 2247.75 | 365 | 2603.69 | 415 | 2959.63 | 465 | 3315.20 |
| 16 | 120.25 | 76 | 547.23 | 136 | 974.21 | 196 | 1401.19 | 256 | 1828.17 | 316 | 2255.15 | 366 | 2610.72 | 416 | 2966.66 | 466 | 3322.23 |
| 17 | 127.65 | 77 | 554.63 | 137 | 981.24 | 197 | 1408.22 | 257 | 1835.20 | 317 | 2262.18 | 367 | 2617.75 | 417 | 2973.69 | 467 | 3329.63 |
| 18 | 134.68 | 78 | 561.66 | 138 | 988.64 | 198 | 1415.25 | 258 | 1842.23 | 318 | 2269.21 | 368 | 2625.15 | 418 | 2980.72 | 468 | 3336.66 |
| 19 | 141.71 | 79 | 568.69 | 139 | 995.67 | 199 | 1422.65 | 259 | 1849.63 | 319 | 2276.24 | 369 | 2632.18 | 419 | 2987.75 | 469 | 3343.69 |
| 20 | 148.74 | 80 | 575.72 | 140 | 1002.70 | 200 | 1429.68 | 260 | 1856.66 | 320 | 2283.64 | 370 | 2639.21 | 420 | 2995.15 | 470 | 3350.72 |
| 21 | 156.14 | 81 | 582.75 | 141 | 1009.73 | 201 | 1436.71 | 261 | 1863.69 | 321 | 2290.67 | 371 | 2646.24 | 421 | 3002.18 | 471 | 3357.75 |
| 22 | 163.17 | 82 | 590.15 | 142 | 1017.13 | 202 | 1443.74 | 262 | 1870.72 | 322 | 2297.70 | 372 | 2653.64 | 422 | 3009.21 | 472 | 3365.15 |
| 23 | 170.20 | 83 | 597.18 | 143 | 1024.16 | 203 | 1451.14 | 263 | 1877.75 | 323 | 2304.73 | 373 | 2660.67 | 423 | 3016.24 | 473 | 3372.18 |
| 24 | 177.23 | 84 | 604.21 | 144 | 1031.19 | 204 | 1458.17 | 264 | 1885.15 | 324 | 2312.13 | 374 | 2667.70 | 424 | 3023.64 | 474 | 3379.21 |
| 25 | 184.63 | 85 | 611.24 | 145 | 1038.22 | 205 | 1465.20 | 265 | 1892.18 | 325 | 2319.16 | 375 | 2674.73 | 425 | 3030.67 | 475 | 3386.24 |
| 26 | 191.66 | 86 | 618.64 | 146 | 1045.25 | 206 | 1472.23 | 266 | 1899.21 | 326 | 2326.19 | 376 | 2682.13 | 426 | 3037.70 | 476 | 3393.64 |
| 27 | 198.69 | 87 | 625.67 | 147 | 1052.65 | 207 | 1479.63 | 267 | 1906.24 | 327 | 2333.22 | 377 | 2689.16 | 427 | 3044.73 | 477 | 3400.67 |
| 28 | 205.72 | 88 | 632.70 | 148 | 1059.68 | 208 | 1486.66 | 268 | 1913.64 | 328 | 2340.25 | 378 | 2696.19 | 428 | 3052.13 | 478 | 3407.70 |
| 29 | 212.75 | 89 | 639.73 | 149 | 1066.71 | 209 | 1493.69 | 269 | 1920.67 | 329 | 2347.65 | 379 | 2703.22 | 429 | 3059.16 | 479 | 3414.73 |
| 30 | 220.15 | 90 | 647.13 | 150 | 1073.74 | 210 | 1500.72 | 270 | 1927.70 | 330 | 2354.68 | 380 | 2710.25 | 430 | 3066.19 | 480 | 3422.13 |
| 31 | 227.18 | 91 | 654.16 | 151 | 1081.14 | 211 | 1507.75 | 271 | 1934.73 | 331 | 2361.71 | 381 | 2717.65 | 431 | 3073.22 | 481 | 3429.16 |
| 32 | 234.21 | 92 | 661.19 | 152 | 1088.17 | 212 | 1515.15 | 272 | 1942.13 | 332 | 2368.74 | 382 | 2724.68 | 432 | 3080.25 | 482 | 3436.19 |
| 33 | 241.24 | 93 | 668.22 | 153 | 1095.20 | 213 | 1522.18 | 273 | 1949.16 | 333 | 2376.14 | 383 | 2731.71 | 433 | 3087.65 | 483 | 3443.22 |
| 34 | 248.64 | 94 | 675.25 | 154 | 1102.23 | 214 | 1529.21 | 274 | 1956.19 | 334 | 2383.17 | 384 | 2738.74 | 434 | 3094.68 | 484 | 3450.25 |
| 35 | 255.67 | 95 | 682.65 | 155 | 1109.63 | 215 | 1536.24 | 275 | 1963.22 | 335 | 2390.20 | 385 | 2746.14 | 435 | 3101.71 | 485 | 3457.65 |
| 36 | 262.70 | 96 | 689.68 | 156 | 1116.66 | 216 | 1543.64 | 276 | 1970.25 | 336 | 2397.23 | 386 | 2753.17 | 436 | 3108.74 | 486 | 3464.68 |
| 37 | 269.73 | 97 | 696.71 | 157 | 1123.69 | 217 | 1550.67 | 277 | 1977.65 | 337 | 2404.63 | 387 | 2760.20 | 437 | 3116.14 | 487 | 3471.71 |
| 38 | 277.13 | 98 | 703.74 | 158 | 1130.72 | 218 | 1557.70 | 278 | 1984.68 | 338 | 2411.66 | 388 | 2767.23 | 438 | 3123.17 | 488 | 3478.74 |
| 39 | 284.16 | 99 | 711.14 | 159 | 1137.75 | 219 | 1564.73 | 279 | 1991.71 | 339 | 2418.69 | 389 | 2774.63 | 439 | 3130.20 | 489 | 3486.14 |
| 40 | 291.19 | 100 | 718.17 | 160 | 1145.15 | 220 | 1572.13 | 280 | 1998.74 | 340 | 2425.72 | 390 | 2781.66 | 440 | 3137.23 | 490 | 3493.17 |
| 41 | 298.22 | 101 | 725.20 | 161 | 1152.18 | 221 | 1579.16 | 281 | 2006.14 | 341 | 2432.75 | 391 | 2788.69 | 441 | 3144.63 | 491 | 3500.20 |
| 42 | 305.25 | 102 | 732.23 | 162 | 1159.21 | 222 | 1586.19 | 282 | 2013.17 | 342 | 2440.15 | 392 | 2795.72 | 442 | 3151.66 | 492 | 3507.23 |
| 43 | 312.65 | 103 | 739.63 | 163 | 1166.24 | 223 | 1593.22 | 283 | 2020.20 | 343 | 2447.18 | 393 | 2802.75 | 443 | 3158.69 | 493 | 3514.63 |
| 44 | 319.68 | 104 | 746.66 | 164 | 1173.64 | 224 | 1600.25 | 284 | 2027.23 | 344 | 2454.21 | 394 | 2810.15 | 444 | 3165.72 | 494 | 3521.66 |
| 45 | 326.71 | 105 | 753.69 | 165 | 1180.67 | 225 | 1607.65 | 285 | 2034.63 | 345 | 2461.24 | 395 | 2817.18 | 445 | 3172.75 | 495 | 3528.69 |
| 46 | 333.74 | 106 | 760.72 | 166 | 1187.70 | 226 | 1614.68 | 286 | 2041.66 | 346 | 2468.64 | 396 | 2824.21 | 446 | 3180.15 | 496 | 3535.72 |
| 47 | 341.14 | 107 | 767.75 | 167 | 1194.73 | 227 | 1621.71 | 287 | 2048.69 | 347 | 2475.67 | 397 | 2831.24 | 447 | 3187.18 | 497 | 3542.75 |
| 48 | 348.17 | 108 | 775.15 | 168 | 1202.13 | 228 | 1628.74 | 288 | 2055.72 | 348 | 2482.70 | 398 | 2838.64 | 448 | 3194.21 | 498 | 3550.15 |
| 49 | 355.20 | 109 | 782.18 | 169 | 1209.16 | 229 | 1636.14 | 289 | 2062.75 | 349 | 2489.73 | 399 | 2845.67 | 449 | 3201.24 | 499 | 3557.18 |
| 50 | 362.23 | 110 | 789.21 | 170 | 1216.19 | 230 | 1643.17 | 290 | 2070.15 | 350 | 2497.13 | 400 | 2852.70 | 450 | 3208.64 | 500 | 3564.21 |
| 51 | 369.63 | 111 | 796.24 | 171 | 1223.22 | 231 | 1650.20 | 291 | 2077.18 | | | | | | | | |
| 52 | 376.66 | 112 | 803.64 | 172 | 1230.25 | 232 | 1657.23 | 292 | 2084.21 | | | | | | | | |
| 53 | 383.69 | 113 | 810.67 | 173 | 1237.65 | 233 | 1664.63 | 293 | 2091.24 | | | | | | | | |
| 54 | 390.72 | 114 | 817.70 | 174 | 1244.68 | 234 | 1671.66 | 294 | 2098.64 | | | | | | | | |
| 55 | 397.75 | 115 | 824.73 | 175 | 1251.71 | 235 | 1678.69 | 295 | 2105.67 | | | | | | | | |
| 56 | 405.14 | 116 | 832.13 | 176 | 1258.74 | 236 | 1685.72 | 296 | 2112.70 | | | | | | | | |
| 57 | 412.18 | 117 | 839.16 | 177 | 1266.14 | 237 | 1692.75 | 297 | 2119.73 | | | | | | | | |
| 58 | 419.21 | 118 | 846.19 | 178 | 1273.17 | 238 | 1700.15 | 298 | 2127.13 | | | | | | | | |
| 59 | 426.24 | 119 | 853.22 | 179 | 1280.20 | 239 | 1707.18 | 299 | 2134.16 | | | | | | | | |
| 60 | 433.64 | 120 | 860.25 | 180 | 1287.23 | 240 | 1714.21 | 300 | 2141.19 | | | | | | | | |

**Code more than 500**

1  Where the code is in the range **501 to 1000** inclusive:

   a. Subtract **500** from the code and use the balance of the code to obtain a pay adjustment figure from the table above.

   b. Add this pay adjustment figure to the figure given in the box alongside to obtain the figure of total pay adjustment to date *  | 3557.92 |

2  Where the code **exceeds 1000** follow the instructions on **page 3**.

# Tables A - Pay Adjustment Tables

Dec21 to Dec 27 **Week 38**

| Code | Total pay adjustment to date £ | Code | Total pay adjustment to date £ | Code | Total pay adjustment to date £ | Code | Total pay adjustment to date £ | Code | Total pay adjustment to date £ | Code | Total pay adjustment to date £ | Code | Total pay adjustment to date £ | Code | Total pay adjustment to date £ | Code | Total pay adjustment to date £ |
|---|---|---|---|---|---|---|---|---|---|---|---|---|---|---|---|---|---|
| 0 | NIL | 61 | 452.58 | 121 | 891.10 | 181 | 1329.62 | 241 | 1767.76 | 301 | 2206.28 | 351 | 2571.84 | 401 | 2937.02 | 451 | 3302.58 |
| 1 | 14.06 | 62 | 459.80 | 122 | 898.32 | 182 | 1336.84 | 242 | 1775.36 | 302 | 2213.50 | 352 | 2579.06 | 402 | 2944.62 | 452 | 3309.80 |
| 2 | 21.28 | 63 | 467.02 | 123 | 905.54 | 183 | 1344.06 | 243 | 1782.58 | 303 | 2221.10 | 353 | 2586.28 | 403 | 2951.84 | 453 | 3317.02 |
| 3 | 28.50 | 64 | 474.62 | 124 | 912.76 | 184 | 1351.28 | 244 | 1789.80 | 304 | 2228.32 | 354 | 2593.50 | 404 | 2959.06 | 454 | 3324.62 |
| 4 | 36.10 | 65 | 481.84 | 125 | 920.36 | 185 | 1358.50 | 245 | 1797.02 | 305 | 2235.54 | 355 | 2601.10 | 405 | 2966.28 | 455 | 3331.84 |
| 5 | 43.32 | 66 | 489.06 | 126 | 927.58 | 186 | 1366.10 | 246 | 1804.62 | 306 | 2242.76 | 356 | 2608.32 | 406 | 2973.50 | 456 | 3339.06 |
| 6 | 50.54 | 67 | 496.28 | 127 | 934.80 | 187 | 1373.32 | 247 | 1811.84 | 307 | 2250.36 | 357 | 2615.54 | 407 | 2981.10 | 457 | 3346.28 |
| 7 | 57.76 | 68 | 503.50 | 128 | 942.02 | 188 | 1380.54 | 248 | 1819.06 | 308 | 2257.58 | 358 | 2622.76 | 408 | 2988.32 | 458 | 3353.50 |
| 8 | 65.36 | 69 | 511.10 | 129 | 949.62 | 189 | 1387.76 | 249 | 1826.28 | 309 | 2264.80 | 359 | 2630.36 | 409 | 2995.54 | 459 | 3361.10 |
| 9 | 72.58 | 70 | 518.32 | 130 | 956.84 | 190 | 1395.36 | 250 | 1833.50 | 310 | 2272.02 | 360 | 2637.58 | 410 | 3002.76 | 460 | 3368.32 |
| 10 | 79.80 | 71 | 525.54 | 131 | 964.06 | 191 | 1402.58 | 251 | 1841.10 | 311 | 2279.62 | 361 | 2644.80 | 411 | 3010.36 | 461 | 3375.54 |
| 11 | 87.02 | 72 | 532.76 | 132 | 971.28 | 192 | 1409.80 | 252 | 1848.32 | 312 | 2286.84 | 362 | 2652.02 | 412 | 3017.58 | 462 | 3382.76 |
| 12 | 94.62 | 73 | 540.36 | 133 | 978.50 | 193 | 1417.02 | 253 | 1855.54 | 313 | 2294.06 | 363 | 2659.62 | 413 | 3024.80 | 463 | 3390.36 |
| 13 | 101.84 | 74 | 547.58 | 134 | 986.10 | 194 | 1424.62 | 254 | 1862.76 | 314 | 2301.28 | 364 | 2666.84 | 414 | 3032.02 | 464 | 3397.58 |
| 14 | 109.06 | 75 | 554.80 | 135 | 993.32 | 195 | 1431.84 | 255 | 1870.36 | 315 | 2308.50 | 365 | 2674.06 | 415 | 3039.62 | 465 | 3404.80 |
| 15 | 116.28 | 76 | 562.02 | 136 | 1000.54 | 196 | 1439.06 | 256 | 1877.58 | 316 | 2316.10 | 366 | 2681.28 | 416 | 3046.84 | 466 | 3412.02 |
| 16 | 123.50 | 77 | 569.62 | 137 | 1007.76 | 197 | 1446.28 | 257 | 1884.80 | 317 | 2323.32 | 367 | 2688.50 | 417 | 3054.06 | 467 | 3419.62 |
| 17 | 131.10 | 78 | 576.84 | 138 | 1015.36 | 198 | 1453.50 | 258 | 1892.02 | 318 | 2330.54 | 368 | 2696.10 | 418 | 3061.28 | 468 | 3426.84 |
| 18 | 138.32 | 79 | 584.06 | 139 | 1022.58 | 199 | 1461.10 | 259 | 1899.62 | 319 | 2337.76 | 369 | 2703.32 | 419 | 3068.50 | 469 | 3434.06 |
| 19 | 145.54 | 80 | 591.28 | 140 | 1029.80 | 200 | 1468.32 | 260 | 1906.84 | 320 | 2345.36 | 370 | 2710.54 | 420 | 3076.10 | 470 | 3441.28 |
| 20 | 152.76 | 81 | 598.50 | 141 | 1037.02 | 201 | 1475.54 | 261 | 1914.06 | 321 | 2352.58 | 371 | 2717.76 | 421 | 3083.32 | 471 | 3448.50 |
| 21 | 160.36 | 82 | 606.10 | 142 | 1044.62 | 202 | 1482.76 | 262 | 1921.28 | 322 | 2359.80 | 372 | 2725.36 | 422 | 3090.54 | 472 | 3456.10 |
| 22 | 167.58 | 83 | 613.32 | 143 | 1051.84 | 203 | 1490.36 | 263 | 1928.50 | 323 | 2367.02 | 373 | 2732.58 | 423 | 3097.76 | 473 | 3463.32 |
| 23 | 174.80 | 84 | 620.54 | 144 | 1059.06 | 204 | 1497.58 | 264 | 1936.10 | 324 | 2374.62 | 374 | 2739.80 | 424 | 3105.36 | 474 | 3470.54 |
| 24 | 182.02 | 85 | 627.76 | 145 | 1066.28 | 205 | 1504.80 | 265 | 1943.32 | 325 | 2381.84 | 375 | 2747.02 | 425 | 3112.58 | 475 | 3477.76 |
| 25 | 189.62 | 86 | 635.36 | 146 | 1073.50 | 206 | 1512.02 | 266 | 1950.54 | 326 | 2389.06 | 376 | 2754.62 | 426 | 3119.80 | 476 | 3485.36 |
| 26 | 196.84 | 87 | 642.58 | 147 | 1081.10 | 207 | 1519.62 | 267 | 1957.76 | 327 | 2396.28 | 377 | 2761.84 | 427 | 3127.02 | 477 | 3492.58 |
| 27 | 204.06 | 88 | 649.80 | 148 | 1088.32 | 208 | 1526.84 | 268 | 1965.36 | 328 | 2403.50 | 378 | 2769.06 | 428 | 3134.62 | 478 | 3499.80 |
| 28 | 211.28 | 89 | 657.02 | 149 | 1095.54 | 209 | 1534.06 | 269 | 1972.58 | 329 | 2411.10 | 379 | 2776.28 | 429 | 3141.84 | 479 | 3507.02 |
| 29 | 218.50 | 90 | 664.62 | 150 | 1102.76 | 210 | 1541.28 | 270 | 1979.80 | 330 | 2418.32 | 380 | 2783.50 | 430 | 3149.06 | 480 | 3514.62 |
| 30 | 226.10 | 91 | 671.84 | 151 | 1110.36 | 211 | 1548.50 | 271 | 1987.02 | 331 | 2425.54 | 381 | 2791.10 | 431 | 3156.28 | 481 | 3521.84 |
| 31 | 233.32 | 92 | 679.06 | 152 | 1117.58 | 212 | 1556.10 | 272 | 1994.62 | 332 | 2432.76 | 382 | 2798.32 | 432 | 3163.50 | 482 | 3529.06 |
| 32 | 240.54 | 93 | 686.28 | 153 | 1124.80 | 213 | 1563.32 | 273 | 2001.84 | 333 | 2440.36 | 383 | 2805.54 | 433 | 3171.10 | 483 | 3536.28 |
| 33 | 247.76 | 94 | 693.50 | 154 | 1132.02 | 214 | 1570.54 | 274 | 2009.06 | 334 | 2447.58 | 384 | 2812.76 | 434 | 3178.32 | 484 | 3543.50 |
| 34 | 255.36 | 95 | 701.10 | 155 | 1139.62 | 215 | 1577.76 | 275 | 2016.28 | 335 | 2454.80 | 385 | 2820.36 | 435 | 3185.54 | 485 | 3551.10 |
| 35 | 262.58 | 96 | 708.32 | 156 | 1146.84 | 216 | 1585.36 | 276 | 2023.50 | 336 | 2462.02 | 386 | 2827.58 | 436 | 3192.76 | 486 | 3558.32 |
| 36 | 269.80 | 97 | 715.54 | 157 | 1154.06 | 217 | 1592.58 | 277 | 2031.10 | 337 | 2469.62 | 387 | 2834.80 | 437 | 3200.36 | 487 | 3565.54 |
| 37 | 277.02 | 98 | 722.76 | 158 | 1161.28 | 218 | 1599.80 | 278 | 2038.32 | 338 | 2476.84 | 388 | 2842.02 | 438 | 3207.58 | 488 | 3572.76 |
| 38 | 284.62 | 99 | 730.36 | 159 | 1168.50 | 219 | 1607.02 | 279 | 2045.54 | 339 | 2484.06 | 389 | 2849.62 | 439 | 3214.80 | 489 | 3580.36 |
| 39 | 291.84 | 100 | 737.58 | 160 | 1176.10 | 220 | 1614.62 | 280 | 2052.76 | 340 | 2491.28 | 390 | 2857.58 | 440 | 3222.02 | 490 | 3587.58 |
| 40 | 299.06 | 101 | 744.80 | 161 | 1183.32 | 221 | 1621.84 | 281 | 2060.36 | 341 | 2498.50 | 391 | 2864.06 | 441 | 3229.62 | 491 | 3594.80 |
| 41 | 306.28 | 102 | 752.02 | 162 | 1190.54 | 222 | 1629.06 | 282 | 2067.58 | 342 | 2506.10 | 392 | 2871.28 | 442 | 3236.84 | 492 | 3602.02 |
| 42 | 313.50 | 103 | 759.62 | 163 | 1197.76 | 223 | 1636.28 | 283 | 2074.80 | 343 | 2513.32 | 393 | 2878.50 | 443 | 3244.06 | 493 | 3609.62 |
| 43 | 321.10 | 104 | 766.84 | 164 | 1205.36 | 224 | 1643.50 | 284 | 2082.02 | 344 | 2520.54 | 394 | 2886.10 | 444 | 3251.28 | 494 | 3616.84 |
| 44 | 328.32 | 105 | 774.06 | 165 | 1212.58 | 225 | 1651.10 | 285 | 2089.62 | 345 | 2527.76 | 395 | 2893.32 | 445 | 3258.50 | 495 | 3624.06 |
| 45 | 335.54 | 106 | 781.28 | 166 | 1219.80 | 226 | 1658.32 | 286 | 2096.84 | 346 | 2535.36 | 396 | 2900.54 | 446 | 3266.10 | 496 | 3631.28 |
| 46 | 342.76 | 107 | 788.50 | 167 | 1227.02 | 227 | 1665.54 | 287 | 2104.06 | 347 | 2542.58 | 397 | 2907.76 | 447 | 3273.32 | 497 | 3638.50 |
| 47 | 350.36 | 108 | 796.10 | 168 | 1234.62 | 228 | 1672.76 | 288 | 2111.28 | 348 | 2549.80 | 398 | 2915.36 | 448 | 3280.54 | 498 | 3646.10 |
| 48 | 357.58 | 109 | 803.32 | 169 | 1241.84 | 229 | 1680.36 | 289 | 2118.50 | 349 | 2557.02 | 399 | 2922.58 | 449 | 3287.76 | 499 | 3653.32 |
| 49 | 364.80 | 110 | 810.54 | 170 | 1249.06 | 230 | 1687.58 | 290 | 2126.10 | 350 | 2564.62 | 400 | 2929.80 | 450 | 3295.36 | 500 | 3660.54 |
| 50 | 372.02 | 111 | 817.76 | 171 | 1256.28 | 231 | 1694.80 | 291 | 2133.32 | | | | | | | | |
| 51 | 379.62 | 112 | 825.36 | 172 | 1263.50 | 232 | 1702.02 | 292 | 2140.54 | | | | | | | | |
| 52 | 386.84 | 113 | 832.58 | 173 | 1271.10 | 233 | 1709.62 | 293 | 2147.76 | | | | | | | | |
| 53 | 394.06 | 114 | 839.80 | 174 | 1278.32 | 234 | 1716.84 | 294 | 2155.36 | | | | | | | | |
| 54 | 401.28 | 115 | 847.02 | 175 | 1285.54 | 235 | 1724.06 | 295 | 2162.58 | | | | | | | | |
| 55 | 408.50 | 116 | 854.62 | 176 | 1292.76 | 236 | 1731.28 | 296 | 2169.80 | | | | | | | | |
| 56 | 416.10 | 117 | 861.84 | 177 | 1300.36 | 237 | 1738.50 | 297 | 2177.02 | | | | | | | | |
| 57 | 423.32 | 118 | 869.06 | 178 | 1307.58 | 238 | 1746.10 | 298 | 2184.62 | | | | | | | | |
| 58 | 430.54 | 119 | 876.28 | 179 | 1314.80 | 239 | 1753.32 | 299 | 2191.84 | | | | | | | | |
| 59 | 437.76 | 120 | 883.50 | 180 | 1322.02 | 240 | 1760.54 | 300 | 2199.06 | | | | | | | | |
| 60 | 445.36 | | | | | | | | | | | | | | | | |

**Code more than 500**

1 Where the code is in the range 501 to **1000** inclusive:

  a. Subtract **500** from the code and use the balance of the code to obtain a pay adjustment figure from the table above.

  b. Add this pay adjustment figure to the figure given in the box alongside to obtain the figure of total pay adjustment to date * **3654.08**

2 Where the code **exceeds 1000** follow the instructions on **page 3**.

## Week 39   Dec 28 to Jan 3

**Tables A** - Pay Adjustment Tables

| Code | Total pay adjustment to date | Code | Total pay adjustment to date | Code | Total pay adjustment to date | Code | Total pay adjustment to date | Code | Total pay adjustment to date | Code | Total pay adjustment to date | Code | Total pay adjustment to date | Code | Total pay adjustment to date | Code | Total pay adjustment to date |
|---|---|---|---|---|---|---|---|---|---|---|---|---|---|---|---|---|---|
| | £ | | £ | | £ | | £ | | £ | | £ | | £ | | £ | | £ |
| 0 | NIL | | | | | | | | | | | | | | | | |
| 1 | 14.43 | 61 | 464.49 | 121 | 914.55 | 181 | 1364.61 | 241 | 1814.28 | 301 | 2264.34 | 351 | 2639.52 | 401 | 3014.31 | 451 | 3389.49 |
| 2 | 21.84 | 62 | 471.90 | 122 | 921.96 | 182 | 1372.02 | 242 | 1822.08 | 302 | 2271.75 | 352 | 2646.93 | 402 | 3022.11 | 452 | 3396.90 |
| 3 | 29.25 | 63 | 479.31 | 123 | 929.37 | 183 | 1379.43 | 243 | 1829.49 | 303 | 2279.55 | 353 | 2654.34 | 403 | 3029.52 | 453 | 3404.31 |
| 4 | 37.05 | 64 | 487.11 | 124 | 936.78 | 184 | 1386.84 | 244 | 1836.90 | 304 | 2286.96 | 354 | 2661.75 | 404 | 3036.93 | 454 | 3412.11 |
| 5 | 44.46 | 65 | 494.52 | 125 | 944.58 | 185 | 1394.25 | 245 | 1844.31 | 305 | 2294.37 | 355 | 2669.55 | 405 | 3044.34 | 455 | 3419.52 |
| 6 | 51.87 | 66 | 501.93 | 126 | 951.99 | 186 | 1402.05 | 246 | 1852.11 | 306 | 2301.78 | 356 | 2676.96 | 406 | 3051.75 | 456 | 3426.93 |
| 7 | 59.28 | 67 | 509.34 | 127 | 959.40 | 187 | 1409.46 | 247 | 1859.52 | 307 | 2309.58 | 357 | 2684.37 | 407 | 3059.55 | 457 | 3434.34 |
| 8 | 67.08 | 68 | 516.75 | 128 | 966.81 | 188 | 1416.87 | 248 | 1866.93 | 308 | 2316.99 | 358 | 2691.78 | 408 | 3066.96 | 458 | 3441.75 |
| 9 | 74.49 | 69 | 524.55 | 129 | 974.61 | 189 | 1424.28 | 249 | 1874.34 | 309 | 2324.40 | 359 | 2699.58 | 409 | 3074.37 | 459 | 3449.55 |
| 10 | 81.90 | 70 | 531.96 | 130 | 982.02 | 190 | 1432.08 | 250 | 1881.75 | 310 | 2331.81 | 360 | 2706.99 | 410 | 3081.78 | 460 | 3456.96 |
| 11 | 89.31 | 71 | 539.37 | 131 | 989.43 | 191 | 1439.49 | 251 | 1889.55 | 311 | 2339.61 | 361 | 2714.40 | 411 | 3089.58 | 461 | 3464.37 |
| 12 | 97.11 | 72 | 546.78 | 132 | 996.84 | 192 | 1446.90 | 252 | 1896.96 | 312 | 2347.02 | 362 | 2721.81 | 412 | 3096.99 | 462 | 3471.78 |
| 13 | 104.52 | 73 | 554.58 | 133 | 1004.25 | 193 | 1454.31 | 253 | 1904.37 | 313 | 2354.43 | 363 | 2729.61 | 413 | 3104.40 | 463 | 3479.58 |
| 14 | 111.93 | 74 | 561.99 | 134 | 1012.05 | 194 | 1462.11 | 254 | 1911.78 | 314 | 2361.84 | 364 | 2737.02 | 414 | 3111.81 | 464 | 3486.99 |
| 15 | 119.34 | 75 | 569.40 | 135 | 1019.46 | 195 | 1469.52 | 255 | 1919.58 | 315 | 2369.25 | 365 | 2744.43 | 415 | 3119.61 | 465 | 3494.40 |
| 16 | 126.75 | 76 | 576.81 | 136 | 1026.87 | 196 | 1476.93 | 256 | 1926.99 | 316 | 2377.05 | 366 | 2751.84 | 416 | 3127.02 | 466 | 3501.81 |
| 17 | 134.55 | 77 | 584.61 | 137 | 1034.28 | 197 | 1484.34 | 257 | 1934.40 | 317 | 2384.46 | 367 | 2759.25 | 417 | 3134.43 | 467 | 3509.61 |
| 18 | 141.96 | 78 | 592.02 | 138 | 1042.08 | 198 | 1491.75 | 258 | 1941.81 | 318 | 2391.87 | 368 | 2767.05 | 418 | 3141.84 | 468 | 3517.02 |
| 19 | 149.37 | 79 | 599.43 | 139 | 1049.49 | 199 | 1499.55 | 259 | 1949.61 | 319 | 2399.28 | 369 | 2774.46 | 419 | 3149.25 | 469 | 3524.43 |
| 20 | 156.78 | 80 | 606.84 | 140 | 1056.90 | 200 | 1506.96 | 260 | 1957.02 | 320 | 2407.08 | 370 | 2781.87 | 420 | 3157.05 | 470 | 3531.84 |
| 21 | 164.58 | 81 | 614.25 | 141 | 1064.31 | 201 | 1514.37 | 261 | 1964.43 | 321 | 2414.49 | 371 | 2789.28 | 421 | 3164.46 | 471 | 3539.25 |
| 22 | 171.99 | 82 | 622.05 | 142 | 1072.11 | 202 | 1521.78 | 262 | 1971.84 | 322 | 2421.90 | 372 | 2797.08 | 422 | 3171.87 | 472 | 3547.05 |
| 23 | 179.40 | 83 | 629.46 | 143 | 1079.52 | 203 | 1529.58 | 263 | 1979.25 | 323 | 2429.31 | 373 | 2804.49 | 423 | 3179.28 | 473 | 3554.46 |
| 24 | 186.81 | 84 | 636.87 | 144 | 1086.93 | 204 | 1536.99 | 264 | 1987.05 | 324 | 2437.11 | 374 | 2811.90 | 424 | 3187.08 | 474 | 3561.87 |
| 25 | 194.61 | 85 | 644.28 | 145 | 1094.34 | 205 | 1544.40 | 265 | 1994.46 | 325 | 2444.52 | 375 | 2819.31 | 425 | 3194.49 | 475 | 3569.28 |
| 26 | 202.02 | 86 | 652.08 | 146 | 1101.75 | 206 | 1551.81 | 266 | 2001.87 | 326 | 2451.93 | 376 | 2827.11 | 426 | 3201.90 | 476 | 3577.08 |
| 27 | 209.43 | 87 | 659.49 | 147 | 1109.55 | 207 | 1559.61 | 267 | 2009.28 | 327 | 2459.34 | 377 | 2834.52 | 427 | 3209.31 | 477 | 3584.49 |
| 28 | 216.84 | 88 | 666.90 | 148 | 1116.96 | 208 | 1567.02 | 268 | 2017.08 | 328 | 2466.75 | 378 | 2841.93 | 428 | 3217.11 | 478 | 3591.90 |
| 29 | 224.25 | 89 | 674.31 | 149 | 1124.37 | 209 | 1574.43 | 269 | 2024.49 | 329 | 2474.55 | 379 | 2849.34 | 429 | 3224.52 | 479 | 3599.31 |
| 30 | 232.05 | 90 | 682.11 | 150 | 1131.78 | 210 | 1581.84 | 270 | 2031.90 | 330 | 2481.96 | 380 | 2856.75 | 430 | 3231.93 | 480 | 3607.11 |
| 31 | 239.46 | 91 | 689.52 | 151 | 1139.58 | 211 | 1589.25 | 271 | 2039.31 | 331 | 2489.37 | 381 | 2864.55 | 431 | 3239.34 | 481 | 3614.52 |
| 32 | 246.87 | 92 | 696.93 | 152 | 1146.99 | 212 | 1597.05 | 272 | 2047.11 | 332 | 2496.78 | 382 | 2871.96 | 432 | 3246.75 | 482 | 3621.93 |
| 33 | 254.28 | 93 | 704.34 | 153 | 1154.40 | 213 | 1604.46 | 273 | 2054.52 | 333 | 2504.58 | 383 | 2879.37 | 433 | 3254.55 | 483 | 3629.34 |
| 34 | 262.08 | 94 | 711.75 | 154 | 1161.81 | 214 | 1611.87 | 274 | 2061.93 | 334 | 2511.99 | 384 | 2886.78 | 434 | 3261.96 | 484 | 3636.75 |
| 35 | 269.49 | 95 | 719.55 | 155 | 1169.61 | 215 | 1619.28 | 275 | 2069.34 | 335 | 2519.40 | 385 | 2894.58 | 435 | 3269.37 | 485 | 3644.55 |
| 36 | 276.90 | 96 | 726.96 | 156 | 1177.02 | 216 | 1627.08 | 276 | 2076.75 | 336 | 2526.81 | 386 | 2901.99 | 436 | 3276.78 | 486 | 3651.96 |
| 37 | 284.31 | 97 | 734.37 | 157 | 1184.43 | 217 | 1634.49 | 277 | 2084.55 | 337 | 2534.61 | 387 | 2909.40 | 437 | 3284.58 | 487 | 3659.37 |
| 38 | 292.11 | 98 | 741.78 | 158 | 1191.84 | 218 | 1641.90 | 278 | 2091.96 | 338 | 2542.02 | 388 | 2916.81 | 438 | 3291.99 | 488 | 3666.78 |
| 39 | 299.52 | 99 | 749.58 | 159 | 1199.25 | 219 | 1649.31 | 279 | 2099.37 | 339 | 2549.43 | 389 | 2924.61 | 439 | 3299.40 | 489 | 3674.58 |
| 40 | 306.93 | 100 | 756.99 | 160 | 1207.05 | 220 | 1657.11 | 280 | 2106.78 | 340 | 2556.84 | 390 | 2932.02 | 440 | 3306.81 | 490 | 3681.99 |
| 41 | 314.34 | 101 | 764.40 | 161 | 1214.46 | 221 | 1664.52 | 281 | 2114.58 | 341 | 2564.25 | 391 | 2939.43 | 441 | 3314.61 | 491 | 3689.40 |
| 42 | 321.75 | 102 | 771.81 | 162 | 1221.87 | 222 | 1671.93 | 282 | 2121.99 | 342 | 2572.05 | 392 | 2946.84 | 442 | 3322.02 | 492 | 3696.81 |
| 43 | 329.55 | 103 | 779.61 | 163 | 1229.28 | 223 | 1679.34 | 283 | 2129.40 | 343 | 2579.46 | 393 | 2954.25 | 443 | 3329.43 | 493 | 3704.61 |
| 44 | 336.96 | 104 | 787.02 | 164 | 1237.08 | 224 | 1686.75 | 284 | 2136.81 | 344 | 2586.87 | 394 | 2962.05 | 444 | 3336.84 | 494 | 3712.02 |
| 45 | 344.37 | 105 | 794.43 | 165 | 1244.49 | 225 | 1694.55 | 285 | 2144.61 | 345 | 2594.28 | 395 | 2969.46 | 445 | 3344.25 | 495 | 3719.43 |
| 46 | 351.78 | 106 | 801.84 | 166 | 1251.90 | 226 | 1701.96 | 286 | 2152.02 | 346 | 2602.08 | 396 | 2976.87 | 446 | 3352.05 | 496 | 3726.84 |
| 47 | 359.58 | 107 | 809.25 | 167 | 1259.31 | 227 | 1709.37 | 287 | 2159.43 | 347 | 2609.49 | 397 | 2984.28 | 447 | 3359.46 | 497 | 3734.25 |
| 48 | 366.99 | 108 | 817.05 | 168 | 1267.11 | 228 | 1716.78 | 288 | 2166.84 | 348 | 2616.90 | 398 | 2992.08 | 448 | 3366.87 | 498 | 3742.05 |
| 49 | 374.40 | 109 | 824.46 | 169 | 1274.52 | 229 | 1724.58 | 289 | 2174.25 | 349 | 2624.31 | 399 | 2999.49 | 449 | 3374.28 | 499 | 3749.46 |
| 50 | 381.81 | 110 | 831.87 | 170 | 1281.93 | 230 | 1731.99 | 290 | 2182.05 | 350 | 2632.11 | 400 | 3006.90 | 450 | 3382.08 | 500 | 3756.87 |
| 51 | 389.61 | 111 | 839.28 | 171 | 1289.34 | 231 | 1739.40 | 291 | 2189.46 | | | | | | | | |
| 52 | 397.02 | 112 | 847.08 | 172 | 1296.75 | 232 | 1746.81 | 292 | 2196.87 | | | | | | | | |
| 53 | 404.43 | 113 | 854.49 | 173 | 1304.55 | 233 | 1754.61 | 293 | 2204.28 | | | | | | | | |
| 54 | 411.84 | 114 | 861.90 | 174 | 1311.96 | 234 | 1762.02 | 294 | 2212.08 | | | | | | | | |
| 55 | 419.25 | 115 | 869.31 | 175 | 1319.37 | 235 | 1769.43 | 295 | 2219.49 | | | | | | | | |
| 56 | 427.04 | 116 | 877.11 | 176 | 1326.78 | 236 | 1776.84 | 296 | 2226.90 | | | | | | | | |
| 57 | 434.46 | 117 | 884.52 | 177 | 1334.58 | 237 | 1784.25 | 297 | 2234.31 | | | | | | | | |
| 58 | 441.87 | 118 | 891.93 | 178 | 1341.99 | 238 | 1792.05 | 298 | 2242.11 | | | | | | | | |
| 59 | 449.28 | 119 | 899.34 | 179 | 1349.40 | 239 | 1799.46 | 299 | 2249.52 | | | | | | | | |
| 60 | 457.08 | 120 | 906.75 | 180 | 1356.81 | 240 | 1806.87 | 300 | 2256.93 | | | | | | | | |

### Code more than 500

1 Where the code is in the range **501 to 1000** inclusive:

a. Subtract **500** from the code and use the balance of the code to obtain a pay adjustment figure from the table above.

b. Add this pay adjustment figure to the figure given in the box alongside to obtain the figure of total pay adjustment to date *   | 3750.24 |

2 Where the code **exceeds 1000** follow the instructions on **page 3**.

42

## Tables A - Pay Adjustment Tables

Jan 4 to Jan 10  **Week 40**

| Code | Total pay adjustment to date | Code | Total pay adjustment to date | Code | Total pay adjustment to date | Code | Total pay adjustment to date | Code | Total pay adjustment to date | Code | Total pay adjustment to date | Code | Total pay adjustment to date | Code | Total pay adjustment to date | Code | Total pay adjustment to date |
|---|---|---|---|---|---|---|---|---|---|---|---|---|---|---|---|---|---|
| | £ | | £ | | £ | | £ | | £ | | £ | | £ | | £ | | £ |
| 0 | NIL | 61 | 476.40 | 121 | 938.00 | 181 | 1399.60 | 241 | 1860.80 | 301 | 2322.40 | 351 | 2707.20 | 401 | 3091.60 | 451 | 3476.40 |
| 1 | 14.80 | 62 | 484.00 | 122 | 945.60 | 182 | 1407.20 | 242 | 1868.80 | 302 | 2330.00 | 352 | 2714.80 | 402 | 3099.60 | 452 | 3484.00 |
| 2 | 22.40 | 63 | 491.60 | 123 | 953.20 | 183 | 1414.80 | 243 | 1876.40 | 303 | 2338.00 | 353 | 2722.40 | 403 | 3107.20 | 453 | 3491.60 |
| 3 | 30.00 | 64 | 499.60 | 124 | 960.80 | 184 | 1422.40 | 244 | 1884.00 | 304 | 2345.60 | 354 | 2730.00 | 404 | 3114.80 | 454 | 3499.60 |
| 4 | 38.00 | 65 | 507.20 | 125 | 968.80 | 185 | 1430.00 | 245 | 1891.60 | 305 | 2353.20 | 355 | 2738.00 | 405 | 3122.40 | 455 | 3507.20 |
| 5 | 45.60 | 66 | 514.80 | 126 | 976.40 | 186 | 1438.00 | 246 | 1899.60 | 306 | 2360.80 | 356 | 2745.60 | 406 | 3130.00 | 456 | 3514.80 |
| 6 | 53.20 | 67 | 522.40 | 127 | 984.00 | 187 | 1445.60 | 247 | 1907.20 | 307 | 2368.80 | 357 | 2753.20 | 407 | 3138.00 | 457 | 3522.40 |
| 7 | 60.80 | 68 | 530.00 | 128 | 991.60 | 188 | 1453.20 | 248 | 1914.80 | 308 | 2376.40 | 358 | 2760.80 | 408 | 3145.60 | 458 | 3530.00 |
| 8 | 68.80 | 69 | 538.00 | 129 | 999.60 | 189 | 1460.80 | 249 | 1922.40 | 309 | 2384.00 | 359 | 2768.80 | 409 | 3153.20 | 459 | 3538.00 |
| 9 | 76.40 | 70 | 545.60 | 130 | 1007.20 | 190 | 1468.80 | 250 | 1930.00 | 310 | 2391.60 | 360 | 2776.40 | 410 | 3160.80 | 460 | 3545.60 |
| 10 | 84.00 | 71 | 553.20 | 131 | 1014.80 | 191 | 1476.40 | 251 | 1938.00 | 311 | 2399.60 | 361 | 2784.00 | 411 | 3168.80 | 461 | 3553.20 |
| 11 | 91.60 | 72 | 560.80 | 132 | 1022.40 | 192 | 1484.00 | 252 | 1945.60 | 312 | 2407.20 | 362 | 2791.60 | 412 | 3176.40 | 462 | 3560.80 |
| 12 | 99.60 | 73 | 568.80 | 133 | 1030.00 | 193 | 1491.60 | 253 | 1953.20 | 313 | 2414.80 | 363 | 2799.60 | 413 | 3184.00 | 463 | 3568.80 |
| 13 | 107.20 | 74 | 576.40 | 134 | 1038.00 | 194 | 1499.60 | 254 | 1960.80 | 314 | 2422.40 | 364 | 2807.20 | 414 | 3191.60 | 464 | 3576.40 |
| 14 | 114.80 | 75 | 584.00 | 135 | 1045.60 | 195 | 1507.20 | 255 | 1968.80 | 315 | 2430.00 | 365 | 2814.80 | 415 | 3199.60 | 465 | 3584.00 |
| 15 | 122.40 | 76 | 591.60 | 136 | 1053.20 | 196 | 1514.80 | 256 | 1976.40 | 316 | 2438.00 | 366 | 2822.40 | 416 | 3207.20 | 466 | 3591.60 |
| 16 | 130.00 | 77 | 599.60 | 137 | 1060.80 | 197 | 1522.40 | 257 | 1984.00 | 317 | 2445.60 | 367 | 2830.00 | 417 | 3214.80 | 467 | 3599.60 |
| 17 | 138.00 | 78 | 607.20 | 138 | 1068.80 | 198 | 1530.00 | 258 | 1991.60 | 318 | 2453.20 | 368 | 2838.00 | 418 | 3222.40 | 468 | 3607.20 |
| 18 | 145.60 | 79 | 614.80 | 139 | 1076.40 | 199 | 1538.00 | 259 | 1999.60 | 319 | 2460.80 | 369 | 2845.60 | 419 | 3230.00 | 469 | 3614.80 |
| 19 | 153.20 | 80 | 622.40 | 140 | 1084.00 | 200 | 1545.60 | 260 | 2007.20 | 320 | 2468.80 | 370 | 2853.20 | 420 | 3238.00 | 470 | 3622.40 |
| 20 | 160.80 | 81 | 630.00 | 141 | 1091.60 | 201 | 1553.20 | 261 | 2014.80 | 321 | 2476.40 | 371 | 2860.80 | 421 | 3245.60 | 471 | 3630.00 |
| 21 | 168.80 | 82 | 638.00 | 142 | 1099.60 | 202 | 1560.80 | 262 | 2022.40 | 322 | 2484.00 | 372 | 2868.80 | 422 | 3253.20 | 472 | 3638.00 |
| 22 | 176.40 | 83 | 645.60 | 143 | 1107.20 | 203 | 1568.80 | 263 | 2030.00 | 323 | 2491.60 | 373 | 2876.40 | 423 | 3260.80 | 473 | 3645.60 |
| 23 | 184.00 | 84 | 653.20 | 144 | 1114.80 | 204 | 1576.40 | 264 | 2038.00 | 324 | 2499.60 | 374 | 2884.00 | 424 | 3268.80 | 474 | 3653.20 |
| 24 | 191.60 | 85 | 660.80 | 145 | 1122.40 | 205 | 1584.00 | 265 | 2045.60 | 325 | 2507.20 | 375 | 2891.60 | 425 | 3276.40 | 475 | 3660.80 |
| 25 | 199.60 | 86 | 668.80 | 146 | 1130.00 | 206 | 1591.60 | 266 | 2053.20 | 326 | 2514.80 | 376 | 2899.60 | 426 | 3284.00 | 476 | 3668.80 |
| 26 | 207.20 | 87 | 676.40 | 147 | 1138.00 | 207 | 1599.60 | 267 | 2060.80 | 327 | 2522.40 | 377 | 2907.20 | 427 | 3291.60 | 477 | 3676.40 |
| 27 | 214.80 | 88 | 684.00 | 148 | 1145.60 | 208 | 1607.20 | 268 | 2068.80 | 328 | 2530.00 | 378 | 2914.80 | 428 | 3299.60 | 478 | 3684.00 |
| 28 | 222.40 | 89 | 691.60 | 149 | 1153.20 | 209 | 1614.80 | 269 | 2076.40 | 329 | 2538.00 | 379 | 2922.40 | 429 | 3307.20 | 479 | 3691.60 |
| 29 | 230.00 | 90 | 699.60 | 150 | 1160.80 | 210 | 1622.40 | 270 | 2084.00 | 330 | 2545.60 | 380 | 2930.00 | 430 | 3314.80 | 480 | 3699.60 |
| 30 | 238.00 | 91 | 707.20 | 151 | 1168.80 | 211 | 1630.00 | 271 | 2091.60 | 331 | 2553.20 | 381 | 2938.00 | 431 | 3322.40 | 481 | 3707.20 |
| 31 | 245.60 | 92 | 714.80 | 152 | 1176.40 | 212 | 1638.00 | 272 | 2099.60 | 332 | 2560.80 | 382 | 2945.60 | 432 | 3330.00 | 482 | 3714.80 |
| 32 | 253.20 | 93 | 722.40 | 153 | 1184.00 | 213 | 1645.60 | 273 | 2107.20 | 333 | 2568.80 | 383 | 2953.20 | 433 | 3338.00 | 483 | 3722.40 |
| 33 | 260.80 | 94 | 730.00 | 154 | 1191.60 | 214 | 1653.20 | 274 | 2114.80 | 334 | 2576.40 | 384 | 2960.80 | 434 | 3345.60 | 484 | 3730.00 |
| 34 | 268.80 | 95 | 738.00 | 155 | 1199.60 | 215 | 1660.80 | 275 | 2122.40 | 335 | 2584.00 | 385 | 2968.80 | 435 | 3353.20 | 485 | 3738.00 |
| 35 | 276.40 | 96 | 745.60 | 156 | 1207.20 | 216 | 1668.80 | 276 | 2130.00 | 336 | 2591.60 | 386 | 2976.40 | 436 | 3360.80 | 486 | 3745.60 |
| 36 | 284.00 | 97 | 753.20 | 157 | 1214.80 | 217 | 1676.40 | 277 | 2138.00 | 337 | 2599.60 | 387 | 2984.00 | 437 | 3368.80 | 487 | 3753.20 |
| 37 | 291.60 | 98 | 760.80 | 158 | 1222.40 | 218 | 1684.00 | 278 | 2145.60 | 338 | 2607.20 | 388 | 2991.60 | 438 | 3376.40 | 488 | 3760.80 |
| 38 | 299.60 | 99 | 768.80 | 159 | 1230.00 | 219 | 1691.60 | 279 | 2153.20 | 339 | 2614.80 | 389 | 2999.60 | 439 | 3384.00 | 489 | 3768.80 |
| 39 | 307.20 | 100 | 776.40 | 160 | 1238.00 | 220 | 1699.60 | 280 | 2160.80 | 340 | 2622.40 | 390 | 3007.20 | 440 | 3391.60 | 490 | 3776.40 |
| 40 | 314.80 | 101 | 784.00 | 161 | 1245.60 | 221 | 1707.20 | 281 | 2168.80 | 341 | 2630.00 | 391 | 3014.80 | 441 | 3399.60 | 491 | 3784.00 |
| 41 | 322.40 | 102 | 791.60 | 162 | 1253.20 | 222 | 1714.80 | 282 | 2176.40 | 342 | 2638.00 | 392 | 3022.40 | 442 | 3407.20 | 492 | 3791.60 |
| 42 | 330.00 | 103 | 799.60 | 163 | 1260.80 | 223 | 1722.40 | 283 | 2184.00 | 343 | 2645.60 | 393 | 3030.00 | 443 | 3414.80 | 493 | 3799.60 |
| 43 | 338.00 | 104 | 807.20 | 164 | 1268.80 | 224 | 1730.00 | 284 | 2191.60 | 344 | 2653.20 | 394 | 3038.00 | 444 | 3422.40 | 494 | 3807.20 |
| 44 | 345.60 | 105 | 814.80 | 165 | 1276.40 | 225 | 1738.00 | 285 | 2199.60 | 345 | 2660.80 | 395 | 3045.60 | 445 | 3430.00 | 495 | 3814.80 |
| 45 | 353.20 | 106 | 822.40 | 166 | 1284.00 | 226 | 1745.60 | 286 | 2207.20 | 346 | 2668.80 | 396 | 3053.20 | 446 | 3438.00 | 496 | 3822.40 |
| 46 | 360.80 | 107 | 830.00 | 167 | 1291.60 | 227 | 1753.20 | 287 | 2214.80 | 347 | 2676.40 | 397 | 3060.80 | 447 | 3445.60 | 497 | 3830.00 |
| 47 | 368.80 | 108 | 838.00 | 168 | 1299.60 | 228 | 1760.80 | 288 | 2222.40 | 348 | 2684.00 | 398 | 3068.80 | 448 | 3453.20 | 498 | 3838.00 |
| 48 | 376.40 | 109 | 845.60 | 169 | 1307.20 | 229 | 1768.80 | 289 | 2230.00 | 349 | 2691.60 | 399 | 3076.40 | 449 | 3460.80 | 499 | 3845.60 |
| 49 | 384.00 | 110 | 853.20 | 170 | 1314.80 | 230 | 1776.40 | 290 | 2238.00 | 350 | 2699.60 | 400 | 3084.00 | 450 | 3468.80 | 500 | 3853.20 |
| 50 | 391.60 | 111 | 860.80 | 171 | 1322.40 | 231 | 1784.00 | 291 | 2245.60 | | | | | | | | |
| 51 | 399.60 | 112 | 868.80 | 172 | 1330.00 | 232 | 1791.60 | 292 | 2253.20 | | | | | | | | |
| 52 | 407.20 | 113 | 876.40 | 173 | 1338.00 | 233 | 1799.60 | 293 | 2260.80 | | | | | | | | |
| 53 | 414.80 | 114 | 884.00 | 174 | 1345.60 | 234 | 1807.20 | 294 | 2268.80 | | | | | | | | |
| 54 | 422.40 | 115 | 891.60 | 175 | 1353.20 | 235 | 1814.80 | 295 | 2276.40 | | | | | | | | |
| 55 | 430.00 | 116 | 899.60 | 176 | 1360.80 | 236 | 1822.40 | 296 | 2284.00 | | | | | | | | |
| 56 | 438.00 | 117 | 907.20 | 177 | 1368.80 | 237 | 1830.00 | 297 | 2291.60 | | | | | | | | |
| 57 | 445.60 | 118 | 914.80 | 178 | 1376.40 | 238 | 1838.00 | 298 | 2299.60 | | | | | | | | |
| 58 | 453.20 | 119 | 922.40 | 179 | 1384.00 | 239 | 1845.60 | 299 | 2307.20 | | | | | | | | |
| 59 | 460.80 | 120 | 930.00 | 180 | 1391.60 | 240 | 1853.20 | 300 | 2314.80 | | | | | | | | |
| 60 | 468.80 | | | | | | | | | | | | | | | | |

**Code more than 500**

1 Where the code is in the range 501 to 1000 inclusive:

  a. Subtract **500** from the code and use the balance of the code to obtain a pay adjustment figure from the table above.

  b. Add this pay adjustment figure to the figure given in the box alongside to obtain the figure of total pay adjustment to date * **3846.40**

2 Where the **code exceeds 1000** follow the instructions on **page 3**.

**Week 41**  Jan 11 to Jan 17      **Tables A** - Pay Adjustment Tables

| Code | Total pay adjustment to date | Code | Total pay adjustment to date | Code | Total pay adjustment to date | Code | Total pay adjustment to date | Code | Total pay adjustment to date | Code | Total pay adjustment to date | Code | Total pay adjustment to date | Code | Total pay adjustment to date | Code | Total pay adjustment to date |
|---|---|---|---|---|---|---|---|---|---|---|---|---|---|---|---|---|---|
| | £ | | £ | | £ | | £ | | £ | | £ | | £ | | £ | | £ |
| 0 | NIL | | | | | | | | | | | | | | | | |
| 1 | 15.17 | 61 | 488.31 | 121 | 961.45 | 181 | 1434.59 | 241 | 1907.32 | 301 | 2380.46 | 351 | 2774.88 | 401 | 3168.89 | 451 | 3563.31 |
| 2 | 22.96 | 62 | 496.10 | 122 | 969.24 | 182 | 1442.38 | 242 | 1915.52 | 302 | 2388.25 | 352 | 2782.67 | 402 | 3177.09 | 452 | 3571.10 |
| 3 | 30.75 | 63 | 503.89 | 123 | 977.03 | 183 | 1450.17 | 243 | 1923.31 | 303 | 2396.45 | 353 | 2790.46 | 403 | 3184.88 | 453 | 3578.89 |
| 4 | 38.95 | 64 | 512.09 | 124 | 984.82 | 184 | 1457.96 | 244 | 1931.10 | 304 | 2404.24 | 354 | 2798.25 | 404 | 3192.67 | 454 | 3587.09 |
| 5 | 46.74 | 65 | 519.88 | 125 | 993.02 | 185 | 1465.75 | 245 | 1938.89 | 305 | 2412.03 | 355 | 2806.45 | 405 | 3200.46 | 455 | 3594.88 |
| 6 | 54.53 | 66 | 527.67 | 126 | 1000.81 | 186 | 1473.95 | 246 | 1947.09 | 306 | 2419.82 | 356 | 2814.24 | 406 | 3208.25 | 456 | 3602.67 |
| 7 | 62.32 | 67 | 535.46 | 127 | 1008.60 | 187 | 1481.74 | 247 | 1954.88 | 307 | 2428.02 | 357 | 2822.03 | 407 | 3216.45 | 457 | 3610.46 |
| 8 | 70.52 | 68 | 543.25 | 128 | 1016.39 | 188 | 1489.53 | 248 | 1962.67 | 308 | 2435.81 | 358 | 2829.82 | 408 | 3224.24 | 458 | 3618.25 |
| 9 | 78.31 | 69 | 551.45 | 129 | 1024.59 | 189 | 1497.32 | 249 | 1970.46 | 309 | 2443.60 | 359 | 2838.02 | 409 | 3232.03 | 459 | 3626.45 |
| 10 | 86.10 | 70 | 559.24 | 130 | 1032.38 | 190 | 1505.52 | 250 | 1978.25 | 310 | 2451.39 | 360 | 2845.81 | 410 | 3239.82 | 460 | 3634.24 |
| 11 | 93.89 | 71 | 567.03 | 131 | 1040.17 | 191 | 1513.31 | 251 | 1986.45 | 311 | 2459.59 | 361 | 2853.60 | 411 | 3248.02 | 461 | 3642.03 |
| 12 | 102.09 | 72 | 574.82 | 132 | 1047.96 | 192 | 1521.10 | 252 | 1994.24 | 312 | 2467.38 | 362 | 2861.39 | 412 | 3255.81 | 462 | 3649.82 |
| 13 | 109.88 | 73 | 583.02 | 133 | 1055.75 | 193 | 1528.89 | 253 | 2002.03 | 313 | 2475.17 | 363 | 2869.59 | 413 | 3263.60 | 463 | 3658.02 |
| 14 | 117.67 | 74 | 590.81 | 134 | 1063.95 | 194 | 1537.09 | 254 | 2009.82 | 314 | 2482.96 | 364 | 2877.38 | 414 | 3271.39 | 464 | 3665.81 |
| 15 | 125.46 | 75 | 598.60 | 135 | 1071.74 | 195 | 1544.88 | 255 | 2018.02 | 315 | 2490.75 | 365 | 2885.17 | 415 | 3279.59 | 465 | 3673.60 |
| 16 | 133.25 | 76 | 606.39 | 136 | 1079.53 | 196 | 1552.67 | 256 | 2025.81 | 316 | 2498.95 | 366 | 2892.96 | 416 | 3287.38 | 466 | 3681.39 |
| 17 | 141.45 | 77 | 614.59 | 137 | 1087.32 | 197 | 1560.46 | 257 | 2033.60 | 317 | 2506.74 | 367 | 2900.75 | 417 | 3295.17 | 467 | 3689.59 |
| 18 | 149.24 | 78 | 622.38 | 138 | 1095.52 | 198 | 1568.25 | 258 | 2041.39 | 318 | 2514.53 | 368 | 2908.95 | 418 | 3302.96 | 468 | 3697.38 |
| 19 | 157.03 | 79 | 630.17 | 139 | 1103.31 | 199 | 1576.45 | 259 | 2049.59 | 319 | 2522.32 | 369 | 2916.74 | 419 | 3310.75 | 469 | 3705.17 |
| 20 | 164.82 | 80 | 637.96 | 140 | 1111.10 | 200 | 1584.24 | 260 | 2057.38 | 320 | 2530.52 | 370 | 2924.53 | 420 | 3318.95 | 470 | 3712.96 |
| 21 | 173.02 | 81 | 645.75 | 141 | 1118.89 | 201 | 1592.03 | 261 | 2065.17 | 321 | 2538.31 | 371 | 2932.32 | 421 | 3326.74 | 471 | 3720.75 |
| 22 | 180.81 | 82 | 653.95 | 142 | 1127.09 | 202 | 1599.82 | 262 | 2072.96 | 322 | 2546.10 | 372 | 2940.52 | 422 | 3334.53 | 472 | 3728.95 |
| 23 | 188.60 | 83 | 661.74 | 143 | 1134.88 | 203 | 1608.02 | 263 | 2080.75 | 323 | 2553.89 | 373 | 2948.31 | 423 | 3342.32 | 473 | 3736.74 |
| 24 | 196.39 | 84 | 669.53 | 144 | 1142.67 | 204 | 1615.81 | 264 | 2088.95 | 324 | 2562.09 | 374 | 2956.10 | 424 | 3350.52 | 474 | 3744.53 |
| 25 | 204.59 | 85 | 677.32 | 145 | 1150.46 | 205 | 1623.60 | 265 | 2096.74 | 325 | 2569.88 | 375 | 2963.89 | 425 | 3358.31 | 475 | 3752.32 |
| 26 | 212.38 | 86 | 685.52 | 146 | 1158.25 | 206 | 1631.39 | 266 | 2104.53 | 326 | 2577.67 | 376 | 2972.09 | 426 | 3366.10 | 476 | 3760.52 |
| 27 | 220.17 | 87 | 693.31 | 147 | 1166.45 | 207 | 1639.59 | 267 | 2112.32 | 327 | 2585.46 | 377 | 2979.88 | 427 | 3373.89 | 477 | 3768.31 |
| 28 | 227.96 | 88 | 701.10 | 148 | 1174.24 | 208 | 1647.38 | 268 | 2120.52 | 328 | 2593.25 | 378 | 2987.67 | 428 | 3382.09 | 478 | 3776.10 |
| 29 | 235.75 | 89 | 708.89 | 149 | 1182.03 | 209 | 1655.17 | 269 | 2128.31 | 329 | 2601.45 | 379 | 2995.46 | 429 | 3389.88 | 479 | 3783.89 |
| 30 | 243.95 | 90 | 717.09 | 150 | 1189.82 | 210 | 1662.96 | 270 | 2136.10 | 330 | 2609.24 | 380 | 3003.25 | 430 | 3397.67 | 480 | 3792.09 |
| 31 | 251.74 | 91 | 724.88 | 151 | 1198.02 | 211 | 1670.75 | 271 | 2143.89 | 331 | 2617.03 | 381 | 3011.45 | 431 | 3405.46 | 481 | 3799.88 |
| 32 | 259.53 | 92 | 732.67 | 152 | 1205.81 | 212 | 1678.95 | 272 | 2152.09 | 332 | 2624.82 | 382 | 3019.24 | 432 | 3413.25 | 482 | 3807.67 |
| 33 | 267.32 | 93 | 740.46 | 153 | 1213.60 | 213 | 1686.74 | 273 | 2159.88 | 333 | 2633.02 | 383 | 3027.03 | 433 | 3421.45 | 483 | 3815.46 |
| 34 | 275.52 | 94 | 748.25 | 154 | 1221.39 | 214 | 1694.53 | 274 | 2167.67 | 334 | 2640.81 | 384 | 3034.82 | 434 | 3429.24 | 484 | 3823.25 |
| 35 | 283.31 | 95 | 756.45 | 155 | 1229.59 | 215 | 1702.32 | 275 | 2175.46 | 335 | 2648.60 | 385 | 3043.02 | 435 | 3437.03 | 485 | 3831.45 |
| 36 | 291.10 | 96 | 764.24 | 156 | 1237.38 | 216 | 1710.52 | 276 | 2183.25 | 336 | 2656.39 | 386 | 3050.81 | 436 | 3444.82 | 486 | 3839.24 |
| 37 | 298.89 | 97 | 772.03 | 157 | 1245.17 | 217 | 1718.31 | 277 | 2191.45 | 337 | 2664.59 | 387 | 3058.60 | 437 | 3453.02 | 487 | 3847.03 |
| 38 | 307.09 | 98 | 779.82 | 158 | 1252.96 | 218 | 1726.10 | 278 | 2199.24 | 338 | 2672.38 | 388 | 3066.39 | 438 | 3460.81 | 488 | 3854.82 |
| 39 | 314.88 | 99 | 788.02 | 159 | 1260.75 | 219 | 1733.89 | 279 | 2207.03 | 339 | 2680.17 | 389 | 3074.59 | 439 | 3468.60 | 489 | 3863.02 |
| 40 | 322.67 | 100 | 795.81 | 160 | 1268.95 | 220 | 1742.09 | 280 | 2214.82 | 340 | 2687.96 | 390 | 3082.38 | 440 | 3476.39 | 490 | 3870.81 |
| 41 | 330.46 | 101 | 803.60 | 161 | 1276.74 | 221 | 1749.88 | 281 | 2223.02 | 341 | 2695.75 | 391 | 3090.17 | 441 | 3484.59 | 491 | 3878.60 |
| 42 | 338.25 | 102 | 811.39 | 162 | 1284.53 | 222 | 1757.67 | 282 | 2230.81 | 342 | 2703.95 | 392 | 3097.96 | 442 | 3492.38 | 492 | 3886.39 |
| 43 | 346.45 | 103 | 819.59 | 163 | 1292.32 | 223 | 1765.46 | 283 | 2238.60 | 343 | 2711.74 | 393 | 3105.75 | 443 | 3500.17 | 493 | 3894.59 |
| 44 | 354.24 | 104 | 827.38 | 164 | 1300.52 | 224 | 1773.25 | 284 | 2246.39 | 344 | 2719.53 | 394 | 3113.95 | 444 | 3507.96 | 494 | 3902.38 |
| 45 | 362.03 | 105 | 835.17 | 165 | 1308.31 | 225 | 1781.45 | 285 | 2254.59 | 345 | 2727.32 | 395 | 3121.74 | 445 | 3515.75 | 495 | 3910.17 |
| 46 | 369.82 | 106 | 842.96 | 166 | 1316.10 | 226 | 1789.24 | 286 | 2262.38 | 346 | 2735.52 | 396 | 3129.53 | 446 | 3523.95 | 496 | 3917.96 |
| 47 | 378.02 | 107 | 850.75 | 167 | 1323.89 | 227 | 1797.03 | 287 | 2270.17 | 347 | 2743.31 | 397 | 3137.32 | 447 | 3531.74 | 497 | 3925.75 |
| 48 | 385.81 | 108 | 858.95 | 168 | 1332.09 | 228 | 1804.82 | 288 | 2277.96 | 348 | 2751.10 | 398 | 3145.52 | 448 | 3539.53 | 498 | 3933.95 |
| 49 | 393.60 | 109 | 866.74 | 169 | 1339.88 | 229 | 1813.02 | 289 | 2285.75 | 349 | 2758.89 | 399 | 3153.31 | 449 | 3547.32 | 499 | 3941.74 |
| 50 | 401.39 | 110 | 874.53 | 170 | 1347.67 | 230 | 1820.81 | 290 | 2293.95 | 350 | 2767.09 | 400 | 3161.10 | 450 | 3555.52 | 500 | 3949.53 |
| 51 | 409.59 | 111 | 882.32 | 171 | 1355.46 | 231 | 1828.60 | 291 | 2301.74 | | | | | | | | |
| 52 | 417.38 | 112 | 890.52 | 172 | 1363.25 | 232 | 1836.39 | 292 | 2309.53 | | | | | | | | |
| 53 | 425.17 | 113 | 898.31 | 173 | 1371.45 | 233 | 1844.59 | 293 | 2317.32 | | | | | | | | |
| 54 | 432.96 | 114 | 906.10 | 174 | 1379.24 | 234 | 1852.38 | 294 | 2325.52 | | | | | | | | |
| 55 | 440.75 | 115 | 913.89 | 175 | 1387.03 | 235 | 1860.17 | 295 | 2333.31 | | | | | | | | |
| 56 | 448.95 | 116 | 922.09 | 176 | 1394.82 | 236 | 1867.96 | 296 | 2341.10 | | | | | | | | |
| 57 | 456.74 | 117 | 929.88 | 177 | 1403.02 | 237 | 1875.75 | 297 | 2348.89 | | | | | | | | |
| 58 | 464.53 | 118 | 937.67 | 178 | 1410.81 | 238 | 1883.95 | 298 | 2357.09 | | | | | | | | |
| 59 | 472.32 | 119 | 945.46 | 179 | 1418.60 | 239 | 1891.74 | 299 | 2364.88 | | | | | | | | |
| 60 | 480.52 | 120 | 953.25 | 180 | 1426.39 | 240 | 1899.53 | 300 | 2372.67 | | | | | | | | |

**Code more than 500**

1 Where the code is in the range **501** to **1000** inclusive:

  a. Subtract **500** from the code and use the balance of the code to obtain a pay adjustment figure from the table above.

  b. Add this pay adjustment figure to the figure given in the box alongside to obtain the figure of total pay adjustment to date *  | 3942.56 |

2 Where the code **exceeds 1000** follow the instructions on **page 3**.

44

## ables A - Pay Adjustment Tables

Jan 18 to Jan 24 **Week 42**

| Code | Total pay adjustment to date | Code | Total pay adjustment to date | Code | Total pay adjustment to date | Code | Total pay adjustment to date | Code | Total pay adjustment to date | Code | Total pay adjustment to date | Code | Total pay adjustment to date | Code | Total pay adjustment to date | Code | Total pay adjustment to date |
|---|---|---|---|---|---|---|---|---|---|---|---|---|---|---|---|---|---|
| | £ | | £ | | £ | | £ | | £ | | £ | | £ | | £ | | £ |
| 0 | NIL | | | | | | | | | | | | | | | | |
| 1 | 15.54 | 61 | 500.22 | 121 | 984.90 | 181 | 1469.58 | 241 | 1953.84 | 301 | 2438.52 | 351 | 2842.56 | 401 | 3246.18 | 451 | 3650.22 |
| 2 | 23.52 | 62 | 508.20 | 122 | 992.88 | 182 | 1477.56 | 242 | 1962.24 | 302 | 2446.50 | 352 | 2850.54 | 402 | 3254.58 | 452 | 3658.20 |
| 3 | 31.50 | 63 | 516.18 | 123 | 1000.86 | 183 | 1485.54 | 243 | 1970.22 | 303 | 2454.90 | 353 | 2858.52 | 403 | 3262.56 | 453 | 3666.18 |
| 4 | 39.90 | 64 | 524.58 | 124 | 1008.84 | 184 | 1493.52 | 244 | 1978.20 | 304 | 2462.88 | 354 | 2866.50 | 404 | 3270.54 | 454 | 3674.58 |
| 5 | 47.88 | 65 | 532.56 | 125 | 1017.24 | 185 | 1501.50 | 245 | 1986.18 | 305 | 2470.86 | 355 | 2874.90 | 405 | 3278.52 | 455 | 3682.56 |
| 6 | 55.86 | 66 | 540.54 | 126 | 1025.22 | 186 | 1509.90 | 246 | 1994.58 | 306 | 2478.84 | 356 | 2882.88 | 406 | 3286.50 | 456 | 3690.54 |
| 7 | 63.84 | 67 | 548.52 | 127 | 1033.20 | 187 | 1517.88 | 247 | 2002.56 | 307 | 2487.24 | 357 | 2890.86 | 407 | 3294.90 | 457 | 3698.52 |
| 8 | 72.24 | 68 | 556.50 | 128 | 1041.18 | 188 | 1525.86 | 248 | 2010.54 | 308 | 2495.22 | 358 | 2898.84 | 408 | 3302.88 | 458 | 3706.50 |
| 9 | 80.22 | 69 | 564.90 | 129 | 1049.58 | 189 | 1533.84 | 249 | 2018.52 | 309 | 2503.20 | 359 | 2907.24 | 409 | 3310.86 | 459 | 3714.90 |
| 10 | 88.20 | 70 | 572.88 | 130 | 1057.56 | 190 | 1542.24 | 250 | 2026.50 | 310 | 2511.18 | 360 | 2915.22 | 410 | 3318.84 | 460 | 3722.88 |
| 11 | 96.18 | 71 | 580.86 | 131 | 1065.54 | 191 | 1550.22 | 251 | 2034.90 | 311 | 2519.58 | 361 | 2923.20 | 411 | 3327.24 | 461 | 3730.86 |
| 12 | 104.58 | 72 | 588.84 | 132 | 1073.52 | 192 | 1558.20 | 252 | 2042.88 | 312 | 2527.56 | 362 | 2931.18 | 412 | 3335.22 | 462 | 3738.84 |
| 13 | 112.56 | 73 | 597.24 | 133 | 1081.50 | 193 | 1566.18 | 253 | 2050.86 | 313 | 2535.54 | 363 | 2939.58 | 413 | 3343.20 | 463 | 3747.24 |
| 14 | 120.54 | 74 | 605.22 | 134 | 1089.90 | 194 | 1574.58 | 254 | 2058.84 | 314 | 2543.52 | 364 | 2947.56 | 414 | 3351.18 | 464 | 3755.22 |
| 15 | 128.52 | 75 | 613.20 | 135 | 1097.88 | 195 | 1582.56 | 255 | 2067.24 | 315 | 2551.50 | 365 | 2955.54 | 415 | 3359.58 | 465 | 3763.20 |
| 16 | 136.50 | 76 | 621.18 | 136 | 1105.86 | 196 | 1590.54 | 256 | 2075.22 | 316 | 2559.90 | 366 | 2963.52 | 416 | 3367.56 | 466 | 3771.18 |
| 17 | 144.90 | 77 | 629.58 | 137 | 1113.84 | 197 | 1598.52 | 257 | 2083.20 | 317 | 2567.88 | 367 | 2971.50 | 417 | 3375.54 | 467 | 3779.58 |
| 18 | 152.88 | 78 | 637.56 | 138 | 1122.24 | 198 | 1606.50 | 258 | 2091.18 | 318 | 2575.86 | 368 | 2979.90 | 418 | 3383.52 | 468 | 3787.56 |
| 19 | 160.86 | 79 | 645.54 | 139 | 1130.22 | 199 | 1614.90 | 259 | 2099.58 | 319 | 2583.84 | 369 | 2987.88 | 419 | 3391.50 | 469 | 3795.54 |
| 20 | 168.84 | 80 | 653.52 | 140 | 1138.20 | 200 | 1622.88 | 260 | 2107.56 | 320 | 2592.24 | 370 | 2995.86 | 420 | 3399.90 | 470 | 3803.52 |
| 21 | 177.24 | 81 | 661.50 | 141 | 1146.18 | 201 | 1630.86 | 261 | 2115.54 | 321 | 2600.22 | 371 | 3003.84 | 421 | 3407.88 | 471 | 3811.50 |
| 22 | 185.22 | 82 | 669.90 | 142 | 1154.58 | 202 | 1638.84 | 262 | 2123.52 | 322 | 2608.20 | 372 | 3012.24 | 422 | 3415.86 | 472 | 3819.90 |
| 23 | 193.20 | 83 | 677.88 | 143 | 1162.56 | 203 | 1647.24 | 263 | 2131.50 | 323 | 2616.18 | 373 | 3020.22 | 423 | 3423.84 | 473 | 3827.88 |
| 24 | 201.18 | 84 | 685.86 | 144 | 1170.54 | 204 | 1655.22 | 264 | 2139.90 | 324 | 2624.58 | 374 | 3028.20 | 424 | 3432.24 | 474 | 3835.86 |
| 25 | 209.58 | 85 | 693.84 | 145 | 1178.52 | 205 | 1663.20 | 265 | 2147.88 | 325 | 2632.56 | 375 | 3036.18 | 425 | 3440.22 | 475 | 3843.84 |
| 26 | 217.56 | 86 | 702.24 | 146 | 1186.50 | 206 | 1671.18 | 266 | 2155.86 | 326 | 2640.54 | 376 | 3044.58 | 426 | 3448.20 | 476 | 3852.24 |
| 27 | 225.54 | 87 | 710.22 | 147 | 1194.90 | 207 | 1679.58 | 267 | 2163.84 | 327 | 2648.52 | 377 | 3052.56 | 427 | 3456.18 | 477 | 3860.22 |
| 28 | 233.52 | 88 | 718.20 | 148 | 1202.88 | 208 | 1687.56 | 268 | 2172.24 | 328 | 2656.50 | 378 | 3060.54 | 428 | 3464.58 | 478 | 3868.20 |
| 29 | 241.50 | 89 | 726.18 | 149 | 1210.86 | 209 | 1695.54 | 269 | 2180.22 | 329 | 2664.90 | 379 | 3068.52 | 429 | 3472.56 | 479 | 3876.18 |
| 30 | 249.90 | 90 | 734.58 | 150 | 1218.84 | 210 | 1703.52 | 270 | 2188.20 | 330 | 2672.88 | 380 | 3076.50 | 430 | 3480.54 | 480 | 3884.58 |
| 31 | 257.88 | 91 | 742.56 | 151 | 1227.24 | 211 | 1711.50 | 271 | 2196.18 | 331 | 2680.86 | 381 | 3084.90 | 431 | 3488.52 | 481 | 3892.56 |
| 32 | 265.86 | 92 | 750.54 | 152 | 1235.22 | 212 | 1719.90 | 272 | 2204.58 | 332 | 2688.84 | 382 | 3092.88 | 432 | 3496.50 | 482 | 3900.54 |
| 33 | 273.84 | 93 | 758.52 | 153 | 1243.20 | 213 | 1727.88 | 273 | 2212.56 | 333 | 2697.24 | 383 | 3100.86 | 433 | 3504.90 | 483 | 3908.52 |
| 34 | 282.24 | 94 | 766.50 | 154 | 1251.18 | 214 | 1735.86 | 274 | 2220.54 | 334 | 2705.22 | 384 | 3108.84 | 434 | 3512.88 | 484 | 3916.50 |
| 35 | 290.22 | 95 | 774.90 | 155 | 1259.58 | 215 | 1743.84 | 275 | 2228.52 | 335 | 2713.20 | 385 | 3117.24 | 435 | 3520.86 | 485 | 3924.90 |
| 36 | 298.20 | 96 | 782.88 | 156 | 1267.56 | 216 | 1752.24 | 276 | 2236.50 | 336 | 2721.18 | 386 | 3125.22 | 436 | 3528.84 | 486 | 3932.88 |
| 37 | 306.18 | 97 | 790.86 | 157 | 1275.54 | 217 | 1760.22 | 277 | 2244.90 | 337 | 2729.58 | 387 | 3133.20 | 437 | 3537.24 | 487 | 3940.86 |
| 38 | 314.58 | 98 | 798.84 | 158 | 1283.52 | 218 | 1768.20 | 278 | 2252.88 | 338 | 2737.56 | 388 | 3141.18 | 438 | 3545.22 | 488 | 3948.84 |
| 39 | 322.56 | 99 | 807.24 | 159 | 1291.50 | 219 | 1776.18 | 279 | 2260.86 | 339 | 2745.54 | 389 | 3149.58 | 439 | 3553.20 | 489 | 3957.24 |
| 40 | 330.54 | 100 | 815.22 | 160 | 1299.90 | 220 | 1784.58 | 280 | 2268.84 | 340 | 2753.52 | 390 | 3157.56 | 440 | 3561.18 | 490 | 3965.22 |
| 41 | 338.52 | 101 | 823.20 | 161 | 1307.88 | 221 | 1792.56 | 281 | 2277.24 | 341 | 2761.50 | 391 | 3165.54 | 441 | 3569.58 | 491 | 3973.20 |
| 42 | 346.50 | 102 | 831.18 | 162 | 1315.86 | 222 | 1800.54 | 282 | 2285.22 | 342 | 2769.90 | 392 | 3173.52 | 442 | 3577.56 | 492 | 3981.18 |
| 43 | 354.90 | 103 | 839.58 | 163 | 1323.84 | 223 | 1808.52 | 283 | 2293.20 | 343 | 2777.88 | 393 | 3181.50 | 443 | 3585.54 | 493 | 3989.58 |
| 44 | 362.88 | 104 | 847.56 | 164 | 1332.24 | 224 | 1816.50 | 284 | 2301.18 | 344 | 2785.86 | 394 | 3189.90 | 444 | 3593.52 | 494 | 3997.56 |
| 45 | 370.86 | 105 | 855.54 | 165 | 1340.22 | 225 | 1824.90 | 285 | 2309.58 | 345 | 2793.84 | 395 | 3197.88 | 445 | 3601.50 | 495 | 4005.54 |
| 46 | 378.84 | 106 | 863.52 | 166 | 1348.20 | 226 | 1832.88 | 286 | 2317.56 | 346 | 2802.24 | 396 | 3205.86 | 446 | 3609.90 | 496 | 4013.52 |
| 47 | 387.24 | 107 | 871.50 | 167 | 1356.18 | 227 | 1840.86 | 287 | 2325.54 | 347 | 2810.22 | 397 | 3213.84 | 447 | 3617.88 | 497 | 4021.50 |
| 48 | 395.22 | 108 | 879.90 | 168 | 1364.58 | 228 | 1848.84 | 288 | 2333.52 | 348 | 2818.20 | 398 | 3222.24 | 448 | 3625.86 | 498 | 4029.90 |
| 49 | 403.20 | 109 | 887.88 | 169 | 1372.56 | 229 | 1857.24 | 289 | 2341.50 | 349 | 2826.18 | 399 | 3230.22 | 449 | 3633.84 | 499 | 4037.88 |
| 50 | 411.18 | 110 | 895.86 | 170 | 1380.54 | 230 | 1865.22 | 290 | 2349.90 | 350 | 2834.58 | 400 | 3238.20 | 450 | 3642.24 | 500 | 4045.86 |
| 51 | 419.58 | 111 | 903.84 | 171 | 1388.52 | 231 | 1873.20 | 291 | 2357.88 | | | | | | | | |
| 52 | 427.56 | 112 | 912.24 | 172 | 1396.50 | 232 | 1881.18 | 292 | 2365.86 | | | | | | | | |
| 53 | 435.54 | 113 | 920.22 | 173 | 1404.90 | 233 | 1889.58 | 293 | 2373.84 | | | | | | | | |
| 54 | 443.52 | 114 | 928.20 | 174 | 1412.88 | 234 | 1897.56 | 294 | 2382.24 | | | | | | | | |
| 55 | 451.50 | 115 | 936.18 | 175 | 1420.86 | 235 | 1905.54 | 295 | 2390.22 | | | | | | | | |
| 56 | 459.90 | 116 | 944.58 | 176 | 1428.84 | 236 | 1913.52 | 296 | 2398.20 | | | | | | | | |
| 57 | 467.88 | 117 | 952.56 | 177 | 1437.24 | 237 | 1921.50 | 297 | 2406.18 | | | | | | | | |
| 58 | 475.86 | 118 | 960.54 | 178 | 1445.22 | 238 | 1929.90 | 298 | 2414.58 | | | | | | | | |
| 59 | 483.84 | 119 | 968.52 | 179 | 1453.20 | 239 | 1937.88 | 299 | 2422.56 | | | | | | | | |
| 60 | 492.24 | 120 | 976.50 | 180 | 1461.18 | 240 | 1945.86 | 300 | 2430.54 | | | | | | | | |

**Code more than 500**

1 Where the code is in the range **501** to **1000** inclusive:

  a. Subtract **500** from the code and use the balance of the code to obtain a pay adjustment figure from the table above.

  b. Add this pay adjustment figure to the figure given in the box alongside to obtain the figure of total pay adjustment to date * | **4038.72** |

2 Where the code **exceeds 1000** follow the instructions on **page 3**.

45

**Week 43**  Jan 25 to Jan 31                    **Tables A** - Pay Adjustment Table

| Code | Total pay adjustment to date | Code | Total pay adjustment to date | Code | Total pay adjustment to date | Code | Total pay adjustment to date | Code | Total pay adjustment to date | Code | Total pay adjustment to date | Code | Total pay adjustment to date | Code | Total pay adjustment to date | Code | Total pay adjustment to date |
|---|---|---|---|---|---|---|---|---|---|---|---|---|---|---|---|---|---|
| | £ | | £ | | £ | | £ | | £ | | £ | | £ | | £ | | £ |
| 0 | NIL | | | | | | | | | | | | | | | | |
| 1 | 15.91 | 61 | 512.13 | 121 | 1008.35 | 181 | 1504.57 | 241 | 2000.36 | 301 | 2496.58 | 351 | 2910.24 | 401 | 3323.47 | 451 | 3737.13 |
| 2 | 24.08 | 62 | 520.30 | 122 | 1016.52 | 182 | 1512.74 | 242 | 2008.96 | 302 | 2504.75 | 352 | 2918.41 | 402 | 3332.07 | 452 | 3745.30 |
| 3 | 32.25 | 63 | 528.47 | 123 | 1024.69 | 183 | 1520.91 | 243 | 2017.13 | 303 | 2513.35 | 353 | 2926.58 | 403 | 3340.24 | 453 | 3753.47 |
| 4 | 40.85 | 64 | 537.07 | 124 | 1032.86 | 184 | 1529.08 | 244 | 2025.30 | 304 | 2521.52 | 354 | 2934.75 | 404 | 3348.41 | 454 | 3762.07 |
| 5 | 49.02 | 65 | 545.24 | 125 | 1041.46 | 185 | 1537.25 | 245 | 2033.47 | 305 | 2529.69 | 355 | 2943.35 | 405 | 3356.58 | 455 | 3770.24 |
| 6 | 57.19 | 66 | 553.41 | 126 | 1049.63 | 186 | 1545.85 | 246 | 2042.07 | 306 | 2537.86 | 356 | 2951.52 | 406 | 3364.75 | 456 | 3778.41 |
| 7 | 65.36 | 67 | 561.58 | 127 | 1057.80 | 187 | 1554.02 | 247 | 2050.24 | 307 | 2546.46 | 357 | 2959.69 | 407 | 3373.35 | 457 | 3786.58 |
| 8 | 73.96 | 68 | 569.75 | 128 | 1065.97 | 188 | 1562.19 | 248 | 2058.41 | 308 | 2554.63 | 358 | 2967.86 | 408 | 3381.52 | 458 | 3794.75 |
| 9 | 82.13 | 69 | 578.35 | 129 | 1074.57 | 189 | 1570.36 | 249 | 2066.58 | 309 | 2562.80 | 359 | 2976.46 | 409 | 3389.69 | 459 | 3803.35 |
| 10 | 90.30 | 70 | 586.52 | 130 | 1082.74 | 190 | 1578.96 | 250 | 2074.75 | 310 | 2570.97 | 360 | 2984.63 | 410 | 3397.86 | 460 | 3811.52 |
| 11 | 98.47 | 71 | 594.69 | 131 | 1090.91 | 191 | 1587.13 | 251 | 2083.35 | 311 | 2579.57 | 361 | 2992.80 | 411 | 3406.46 | 461 | 3819.69 |
| 12 | 107.07 | 72 | 602.86 | 132 | 1099.08 | 192 | 1595.30 | 252 | 2091.52 | 312 | 2587.74 | 362 | 3000.97 | 412 | 3414.63 | 462 | 3827.86 |
| 13 | 115.24 | 73 | 611.46 | 133 | 1107.25 | 193 | 1603.47 | 253 | 2099.69 | 313 | 2595.91 | 363 | 3009.57 | 413 | 3422.80 | 463 | 3836.46 |
| 14 | 123.41 | 74 | 619.63 | 134 | 1115.85 | 194 | 1612.07 | 254 | 2107.86 | 314 | 2604.08 | 364 | 3017.74 | 414 | 3430.97 | 464 | 3844.63 |
| 15 | 131.58 | 75 | 627.80 | 135 | 1124.02 | 195 | 1620.24 | 255 | 2116.46 | 315 | 2612.25 | 365 | 3025.91 | 415 | 3439.57 | 465 | 3852.80 |
| 16 | 139.75 | 76 | 635.97 | 136 | 1132.19 | 196 | 1628.41 | 256 | 2124.63 | 316 | 2620.85 | 366 | 3034.08 | 416 | 3447.74 | 466 | 3860.97 |
| 17 | 148.35 | 77 | 644.57 | 137 | 1140.36 | 197 | 1636.58 | 257 | 2132.80 | 317 | 2629.02 | 367 | 3042.25 | 417 | 3455.91 | 467 | 3869.57 |
| 18 | 156.52 | 78 | 652.74 | 138 | 1148.96 | 198 | 1644.75 | 258 | 2140.97 | 318 | 2637.19 | 368 | 3050.85 | 418 | 3464.08 | 468 | 3877.74 |
| 19 | 164.69 | 79 | 660.91 | 139 | 1157.13 | 199 | 1653.35 | 259 | 2149.57 | 319 | 2645.36 | 369 | 3059.02 | 419 | 3472.25 | 469 | 3885.91 |
| 20 | 172.86 | 80 | 669.08 | 140 | 1165.30 | 200 | 1661.52 | 260 | 2157.74 | 320 | 2653.96 | 370 | 3067.19 | 420 | 3480.85 | 470 | 3894.08 |
| 21 | 181.46 | 81 | 677.25 | 141 | 1173.47 | 201 | 1669.69 | 261 | 2165.91 | 321 | 2662.13 | 371 | 3075.36 | 421 | 3489.02 | 471 | 3902.25 |
| 22 | 189.63 | 82 | 685.85 | 142 | 1182.07 | 202 | 1677.86 | 262 | 2174.08 | 322 | 2670.30 | 372 | 3083.96 | 422 | 3497.19 | 472 | 3910.85 |
| 23 | 197.80 | 83 | 694.02 | 143 | 1190.24 | 203 | 1686.46 | 263 | 2182.25 | 323 | 2678.47 | 373 | 3092.13 | 423 | 3505.36 | 473 | 3919.02 |
| 24 | 205.97 | 84 | 702.19 | 144 | 1198.41 | 204 | 1694.63 | 264 | 2190.85 | 324 | 2687.07 | 374 | 3100.30 | 424 | 3513.96 | 474 | 3927.19 |
| 25 | 214.57 | 85 | 710.36 | 145 | 1206.58 | 205 | 1702.80 | 265 | 2199.02 | 325 | 2695.24 | 375 | 3108.47 | 425 | 3522.13 | 475 | 3935.36 |
| 26 | 222.74 | 86 | 718.96 | 146 | 1214.75 | 206 | 1710.97 | 266 | 2207.19 | 326 | 2703.41 | 376 | 3117.07 | 426 | 3530.30 | 476 | 3943.96 |
| 27 | 230.91 | 87 | 727.13 | 147 | 1223.35 | 207 | 1719.57 | 267 | 2215.36 | 327 | 2711.58 | 377 | 3125.24 | 427 | 3538.47 | 477 | 3952.13 |
| 28 | 239.08 | 88 | 735.30 | 148 | 1231.52 | 208 | 1727.74 | 268 | 2223.96 | 328 | 2719.75 | 378 | 3133.41 | 428 | 3547.07 | 478 | 3960.30 |
| 29 | 247.25 | 89 | 743.47 | 149 | 1239.69 | 209 | 1735.91 | 269 | 2232.13 | 329 | 2728.35 | 379 | 3141.58 | 429 | 3555.24 | 479 | 3968.47 |
| 30 | 255.85 | 90 | 752.07 | 150 | 1247.86 | 210 | 1744.08 | 270 | 2240.30 | 330 | 2736.52 | 380 | 3149.75 | 430 | 3563.41 | 480 | 3977.07 |
| 31 | 264.02 | 91 | 760.24 | 151 | 1256.46 | 211 | 1752.25 | 271 | 2248.47 | 331 | 2744.69 | 381 | 3158.35 | 431 | 3571.58 | 481 | 3985.24 |
| 32 | 272.19 | 92 | 768.41 | 152 | 1264.63 | 212 | 1760.85 | 272 | 2257.07 | 332 | 2752.86 | 382 | 3166.52 | 432 | 3579.75 | 482 | 3993.41 |
| 33 | 280.36 | 93 | 776.58 | 153 | 1272.80 | 213 | 1769.02 | 273 | 2265.24 | 333 | 2761.46 | 383 | 3174.69 | 433 | 3588.35 | 483 | 4001.58 |
| 34 | 288.96 | 94 | 784.75 | 154 | 1280.97 | 214 | 1777.19 | 274 | 2273.41 | 334 | 2769.63 | 384 | 3182.86 | 434 | 3596.52 | 484 | 4009.75 |
| 35 | 297.13 | 95 | 793.35 | 155 | 1289.57 | 215 | 1785.36 | 275 | 2281.58 | 335 | 2777.80 | 385 | 3191.46 | 435 | 3604.69 | 485 | 4018.35 |
| 36 | 305.30 | 96 | 801.52 | 156 | 1297.74 | 216 | 1793.96 | 276 | 2289.75 | 336 | 2785.97 | 386 | 3199.63 | 436 | 3612.86 | 486 | 4026.52 |
| 37 | 313.47 | 97 | 809.69 | 157 | 1305.91 | 217 | 1802.13 | 277 | 2298.35 | 337 | 2794.57 | 387 | 3207.80 | 437 | 3621.46 | 487 | 4034.69 |
| 38 | 322.07 | 98 | 817.86 | 158 | 1314.08 | 218 | 1810.30 | 278 | 2306.52 | 338 | 2802.74 | 388 | 3215.97 | 438 | 3629.63 | 488 | 4042.86 |
| 39 | 330.24 | 99 | 826.46 | 159 | 1322.25 | 219 | 1818.47 | 279 | 2314.69 | 339 | 2810.91 | 389 | 3224.57 | 439 | 3637.80 | 489 | 4051.46 |
| 40 | 338.41 | 100 | 834.63 | 160 | 1330.85 | 220 | 1827.07 | 280 | 2322.86 | 340 | 2819.08 | 390 | 3232.74 | 440 | 3645.97 | 490 | 4059.63 |
| 41 | 346.58 | 101 | 842.80 | 161 | 1339.02 | 221 | 1835.24 | 281 | 2331.46 | 341 | 2827.25 | 391 | 3240.91 | 441 | 3654.57 | 491 | 4067.80 |
| 42 | 354.75 | 102 | 850.97 | 162 | 1347.19 | 222 | 1843.41 | 282 | 2339.63 | 342 | 2835.85 | 392 | 3249.08 | 442 | 3662.74 | 492 | 4075.97 |
| 43 | 363.35 | 103 | 859.57 | 163 | 1355.36 | 223 | 1851.58 | 283 | 2347.80 | 343 | 2844.02 | 393 | 3257.25 | 443 | 3670.91 | 493 | 4084.57 |
| 44 | 371.52 | 104 | 867.74 | 164 | 1363.96 | 224 | 1859.75 | 284 | 2355.97 | 344 | 2852.19 | 394 | 3265.85 | 444 | 3679.08 | 494 | 4092.74 |
| 45 | 379.69 | 105 | 875.91 | 165 | 1372.13 | 225 | 1868.35 | 285 | 2364.57 | 345 | 2860.36 | 395 | 3274.02 | 445 | 3687.25 | 495 | 4100.91 |
| 46 | 387.86 | 106 | 884.08 | 166 | 1380.30 | 226 | 1876.52 | 286 | 2372.74 | 346 | 2868.96 | 396 | 3282.19 | 446 | 3695.85 | 496 | 4109.08 |
| 47 | 396.46 | 107 | 892.25 | 167 | 1388.47 | 227 | 1884.69 | 287 | 2380.91 | 347 | 2877.13 | 397 | 3290.36 | 447 | 3704.02 | 497 | 4117.25 |
| 48 | 404.63 | 108 | 900.85 | 168 | 1397.07 | 228 | 1892.86 | 288 | 2389.08 | 348 | 2885.30 | 398 | 3298.96 | 448 | 3712.19 | 498 | 4125.85 |
| 49 | 412.80 | 109 | 909.02 | 169 | 1405.24 | 229 | 1901.46 | 289 | 2397.25 | 349 | 2893.47 | 399 | 3307.13 | 449 | 3720.36 | 499 | 4134.02 |
| 50 | 420.97 | 110 | 917.19 | 170 | 1413.41 | 230 | 1909.63 | 290 | 2405.85 | 350 | 2902.07 | 400 | 3315.30 | 450 | 3728.96 | 500 | 4142.19 |
| 51 | 429.57 | 111 | 925.36 | 171 | 1421.58 | 231 | 1917.80 | 291 | 2414.02 | | | | | | | | |
| 52 | 437.74 | 112 | 933.96 | 172 | 1429.75 | 232 | 1925.97 | 292 | 2422.19 | | | | | | | | |
| 53 | 445.91 | 113 | 942.13 | 173 | 1438.35 | 233 | 1934.57 | 293 | 2430.36 | | | | | | | | |
| 54 | 454.08 | 114 | 950.30 | 174 | 1446.52 | 234 | 1942.74 | 294 | 2438.96 | | | | | | | | |
| 55 | 462.25 | 115 | 958.47 | 175 | 1454.69 | 235 | 1950.91 | 295 | 2447.13 | | | | | | | | |
| 56 | 470.85 | 116 | 967.07 | 176 | 1462.86 | 236 | 1959.08 | 296 | 2455.30 | | | | | | | | |
| 57 | 479.02 | 117 | 975.24 | 177 | 1471.46 | 237 | 1967.25 | 297 | 2463.47 | | | | | | | | |
| 58 | 487.19 | 118 | 983.41 | 178 | 1479.63 | 238 | 1975.85 | 298 | 2472.07 | | | | | | | | |
| 59 | 495.36 | 119 | 991.58 | 179 | 1487.80 | 239 | 1984.02 | 299 | 2480.24 | | | | | | | | |
| 60 | 503.96 | 120 | 999.75 | 180 | 1495.97 | 240 | 1992.19 | 300 | 2488.41 | | | | | | | | |

**Code more than 500**

1 Where the code is in the range 501 to **1000** inclusive:

  a. Subtract **500** from the code and use the balance of the code to obtain a pay adjustment figure from the table above.

  b. Add this pay adjustment figure to the figure given in the box alongside to obtain the figure of total pay adjustment to date *  **4134.88**

2 Where the code **exceeds 1000** follow the instructions on **page 3.**

## Tables A - Pay Adjustment Tables                                 Feb 1 to Feb 7  **Week 44**

| Code | Total pay adjustment to date | Code | Total pay adjustment to date | Code | Total pay adjustment to date | Code | Total pay adjustment to date | Code | Total pay adjustment to date | Code | Total pay adjustment to date | Code | Total pay adjustment to date | Code | Total pay adjustment to date | Code | Total pay adjustment to date |
|---|---|---|---|---|---|---|---|---|---|---|---|---|---|---|---|---|---|
| | £ | | £ | | £ | | £ | | £ | | £ | | £ | | £ | | £ |
| 0 | NIL | | | | | | | | | | | | | | | | |
| 1 | 16.28 | 61 | 524.04 | 121 | 1031.80 | 181 | 1539.56 | 241 | 2046.88 | 301 | 2554.64 | 351 | 2977.92 | 401 | 3400.76 | 451 | 3824.04 |
| 2 | 24.64 | 62 | 532.40 | 122 | 1040.16 | 182 | 1547.92 | 242 | 2055.68 | 302 | 2563.00 | 352 | 2986.28 | 402 | 3409.56 | 452 | 3832.40 |
| 3 | 33.00 | 63 | 540.76 | 123 | 1048.52 | 183 | 1556.28 | 243 | 2064.04 | 303 | 2571.80 | 353 | 2994.64 | 403 | 3417.92 | 453 | 3840.76 |
| 4 | 41.80 | 64 | 549.56 | 124 | 1056.88 | 184 | 1564.64 | 244 | 2072.40 | 304 | 2580.16 | 354 | 3003.00 | 404 | 3426.28 | 454 | 3849.56 |
| 5 | 50.16 | 65 | 557.92 | 125 | 1065.68 | 185 | 1573.00 | 245 | 2080.76 | 305 | 2588.52 | 355 | 3011.80 | 405 | 3434.64 | 455 | 3857.92 |
| 6 | 58.52 | 66 | 566.28 | 126 | 1074.04 | 186 | 1581.80 | 246 | 2089.56 | 306 | 2596.88 | 356 | 3020.16 | 406 | 3443.00 | 456 | 3866.28 |
| 7 | 66.88 | 67 | 574.64 | 127 | 1082.40 | 187 | 1590.16 | 247 | 2097.92 | 307 | 2605.68 | 357 | 3028.52 | 407 | 3451.80 | 457 | 3874.64 |
| 8 | 75.68 | 68 | 583.00 | 128 | 1090.76 | 188 | 1598.52 | 248 | 2106.28 | 308 | 2614.04 | 358 | 3036.88 | 408 | 3460.16 | 458 | 3883.00 |
| 9 | 84.04 | 69 | 591.80 | 129 | 1099.56 | 189 | 1606.88 | 249 | 2114.64 | 309 | 2622.40 | 359 | 3045.68 | 409 | 3468.52 | 459 | 3891.80 |
| 10 | 92.40 | 70 | 600.16 | 130 | 1107.92 | 190 | 1615.68 | 250 | 2123.00 | 310 | 2630.76 | 360 | 3054.04 | 410 | 3476.88 | 460 | 3900.16 |
| 11 | 100.76 | 71 | 608.52 | 131 | 1116.28 | 191 | 1624.04 | 251 | 2131.80 | 311 | 2639.56 | 361 | 3062.40 | 411 | 3485.68 | 461 | 3908.52 |
| 12 | 109.56 | 72 | 616.88 | 132 | 1124.64 | 192 | 1632.40 | 252 | 2140.16 | 312 | 2647.92 | 362 | 3070.76 | 412 | 3494.04 | 462 | 3916.88 |
| 13 | 117.92 | 73 | 625.68 | 133 | 1133.00 | 193 | 1640.76 | 253 | 2148.52 | 313 | 2656.28 | 363 | 3079.56 | 413 | 3502.40 | 463 | 3925.68 |
| 14 | 126.28 | 74 | 634.04 | 134 | 1141.80 | 194 | 1649.56 | 254 | 2156.88 | 314 | 2664.64 | 364 | 3087.92 | 414 | 3510.76 | 464 | 3934.04 |
| 15 | 134.64 | 75 | 642.40 | 135 | 1150.16 | 195 | 1657.92 | 255 | 2165.68 | 315 | 2673.00 | 365 | 3096.28 | 415 | 3519.56 | 465 | 3942.40 |
| 16 | 143.00 | 76 | 650.76 | 136 | 1158.52 | 196 | 1666.28 | 256 | 2174.04 | 316 | 2681.80 | 366 | 3104.64 | 416 | 3527.92 | 466 | 3950.76 |
| 17 | 151.80 | 77 | 659.56 | 137 | 1166.88 | 197 | 1674.64 | 257 | 2182.40 | 317 | 2690.16 | 367 | 3113.00 | 417 | 3536.28 | 467 | 3959.56 |
| 18 | 160.16 | 78 | 667.92 | 138 | 1175.68 | 198 | 1683.00 | 258 | 2190.76 | 318 | 2698.52 | 368 | 3121.80 | 418 | 3544.64 | 468 | 3967.92 |
| 19 | 168.52 | 79 | 676.28 | 139 | 1184.04 | 199 | 1691.80 | 259 | 2199.56 | 319 | 2706.88 | 369 | 3130.16 | 419 | 3553.00 | 469 | 3976.28 |
| 20 | 176.88 | 80 | 684.64 | 140 | 1192.40 | 200 | 1700.16 | 260 | 2207.92 | 320 | 2715.68 | 370 | 3138.52 | 420 | 3561.80 | 470 | 3984.64 |
| 21 | 185.68 | 81 | 693.00 | 141 | 1200.76 | 201 | 1708.52 | 261 | 2216.28 | 321 | 2724.04 | 371 | 3146.88 | 421 | 3570.16 | 471 | 3993.00 |
| 22 | 194.04 | 82 | 701.80 | 142 | 1209.56 | 202 | 1716.88 | 262 | 2224.64 | 322 | 2732.40 | 372 | 3155.68 | 422 | 3578.52 | 472 | 4001.80 |
| 23 | 202.40 | 83 | 710.16 | 143 | 1217.92 | 203 | 1725.68 | 263 | 2233.00 | 323 | 2740.76 | 373 | 3164.04 | 423 | 3586.88 | 473 | 4010.16 |
| 24 | 210.76 | 84 | 718.52 | 144 | 1226.28 | 204 | 1734.04 | 264 | 2241.80 | 324 | 2749.56 | 374 | 3172.40 | 424 | 3595.68 | 474 | 4018.52 |
| 25 | 219.56 | 85 | 726.88 | 145 | 1234.64 | 205 | 1742.40 | 265 | 2250.16 | 325 | 2757.92 | 375 | 3180.76 | 425 | 3604.04 | 475 | 4026.88 |
| 26 | 227.92 | 86 | 735.68 | 146 | 1243.00 | 206 | 1750.76 | 266 | 2258.52 | 326 | 2766.28 | 376 | 3189.56 | 426 | 3612.40 | 476 | 4035.68 |
| 27 | 236.28 | 87 | 744.04 | 147 | 1251.80 | 207 | 1759.56 | 267 | 2266.88 | 327 | 2774.64 | 377 | 3197.92 | 427 | 3620.76 | 477 | 4044.04 |
| 28 | 244.64 | 88 | 752.40 | 148 | 1260.16 | 208 | 1767.92 | 268 | 2275.68 | 328 | 2783.00 | 378 | 3206.28 | 428 | 3629.56 | 478 | 4052.40 |
| 29 | 253.00 | 89 | 760.76 | 149 | 1268.52 | 209 | 1776.28 | 269 | 2284.04 | 329 | 2791.80 | 379 | 3214.64 | 429 | 3637.92 | 479 | 4060.76 |
| 30 | 261.80 | 90 | 769.56 | 150 | 1276.88 | 210 | 1784.64 | 270 | 2292.40 | 330 | 2800.16 | 380 | 3223.00 | 430 | 3646.28 | 480 | 4069.56 |
| 31 | 270.16 | 91 | 777.92 | 151 | 1285.68 | 211 | 1793.00 | 271 | 2300.76 | 331 | 2808.52 | 381 | 3231.80 | 431 | 3654.64 | 481 | 4077.92 |
| 32 | 278.52 | 92 | 786.28 | 152 | 1294.04 | 212 | 1801.80 | 272 | 2309.56 | 332 | 2816.88 | 382 | 3240.16 | 432 | 3663.00 | 482 | 4086.28 |
| 33 | 286.88 | 93 | 794.64 | 153 | 1302.40 | 213 | 1810.16 | 273 | 2317.92 | 333 | 2825.68 | 383 | 3248.52 | 433 | 3671.80 | 483 | 4094.64 |
| 34 | 295.68 | 94 | 803.00 | 154 | 1310.76 | 214 | 1818.52 | 274 | 2326.28 | 334 | 2834.04 | 384 | 3256.88 | 434 | 3680.16 | 484 | 4103.00 |
| 35 | 304.04 | 95 | 811.80 | 155 | 1319.56 | 215 | 1826.88 | 275 | 2334.64 | 335 | 2842.40 | 385 | 3265.68 | 435 | 3688.52 | 485 | 4111.80 |
| 36 | 312.40 | 96 | 820.16 | 156 | 1327.92 | 216 | 1835.68 | 276 | 2343.00 | 336 | 2850.76 | 386 | 3274.04 | 436 | 3696.88 | 486 | 4120.16 |
| 37 | 320.76 | 97 | 828.52 | 157 | 1336.28 | 217 | 1844.04 | 277 | 2351.80 | 337 | 2859.56 | 387 | 3282.40 | 437 | 3705.68 | 487 | 4128.52 |
| 38 | 329.56 | 98 | 836.88 | 158 | 1344.64 | 218 | 1852.40 | 278 | 2360.16 | 338 | 2867.92 | 388 | 3290.76 | 438 | 3714.04 | 488 | 4136.88 |
| 39 | 337.92 | 99 | 845.68 | 159 | 1353.00 | 219 | 1860.76 | 279 | 2368.52 | 339 | 2876.28 | 389 | 3299.56 | 439 | 3722.40 | 489 | 4145.68 |
| 40 | 346.28 | 100 | 854.04 | 160 | 1361.80 | 220 | 1869.56 | 280 | 2376.88 | 340 | 2884.64 | 390 | 3307.92 | 440 | 3730.76 | 490 | 4154.04 |
| 41 | 354.64 | 101 | 862.40 | 161 | 1370.16 | 221 | 1877.92 | 281 | 2385.68 | 341 | 2893.00 | 391 | 3316.28 | 441 | 3739.56 | 491 | 4162.40 |
| 42 | 363.00 | 102 | 870.76 | 162 | 1378.52 | 222 | 1886.28 | 282 | 2394.04 | 342 | 2901.80 | 392 | 3324.64 | 442 | 3747.92 | 492 | 4170.76 |
| 43 | 371.80 | 103 | 879.56 | 163 | 1386.88 | 223 | 1894.64 | 283 | 2402.40 | 343 | 2910.16 | 393 | 3333.00 | 443 | 3756.28 | 493 | 4179.56 |
| 44 | 380.16 | 104 | 887.92 | 164 | 1395.68 | 224 | 1903.00 | 284 | 2410.76 | 344 | 2918.52 | 394 | 3341.80 | 444 | 3764.64 | 494 | 4187.92 |
| 45 | 388.52 | 105 | 896.28 | 165 | 1404.04 | 225 | 1911.80 | 285 | 2419.56 | 345 | 2926.88 | 395 | 3350.16 | 445 | 3773.00 | 495 | 4196.28 |
| 46 | 396.88 | 106 | 904.64 | 166 | 1412.40 | 226 | 1920.16 | 286 | 2427.92 | 346 | 2935.68 | 396 | 3358.52 | 446 | 3781.80 | 496 | 4204.64 |
| 47 | 405.68 | 107 | 913.00 | 167 | 1420.76 | 227 | 1928.52 | 287 | 2436.28 | 347 | 2944.04 | 397 | 3366.88 | 447 | 3790.16 | 497 | 4213.00 |
| 48 | 414.04 | 108 | 921.80 | 168 | 1429.56 | 228 | 1936.88 | 288 | 2444.64 | 348 | 2952.40 | 398 | 3375.68 | 448 | 3798.52 | 498 | 4221.80 |
| 49 | 422.40 | 109 | 930.16 | 169 | 1437.92 | 229 | 1945.68 | 289 | 2453.00 | 349 | 2960.76 | 399 | 3384.04 | 449 | 3806.88 | 499 | 4230.16 |
| 50 | 430.76 | 110 | 938.52 | 170 | 1446.28 | 230 | 1954.04 | 290 | 2461.80 | 350 | 2969.56 | 400 | 3392.40 | 450 | 3815.68 | 500 | 4238.52 |
| 51 | 439.56 | 111 | 946.88 | 171 | 1454.64 | 231 | 1962.40 | 291 | 2470.16 | | | | | | | | |
| 52 | 447.92 | 112 | 955.68 | 172 | 1463.00 | 232 | 1970.76 | 292 | 2478.52 | | | | | | | | |
| 53 | 456.28 | 113 | 964.04 | 173 | 1471.80 | 233 | 1979.56 | 293 | 2486.88 | | | | | | | | |
| 54 | 464.64 | 114 | 972.40 | 174 | 1480.16 | 234 | 1987.92 | 294 | 2495.68 | | | | | | | | |
| 55 | 473.00 | 115 | 980.76 | 175 | 1488.52 | 235 | 1996.28 | 295 | 2504.04 | | | | | | | | |
| 56 | 481.80 | 116 | 989.56 | 176 | 1496.88 | 236 | 2004.64 | 296 | 2512.40 | | | | | | | | |
| 57 | 490.16 | 117 | 997.92 | 177 | 1505.68 | 237 | 2013.00 | 297 | 2520.76 | | | | | | | | |
| 58 | 498.52 | 118 | 1006.28 | 178 | 1514.04 | 238 | 2021.80 | 298 | 2529.56 | | | | | | | | |
| 59 | 506.88 | 119 | 1014.64 | 179 | 1522.40 | 239 | 2030.16 | 299 | 2537.92 | | | | | | | | |
| 60 | 515.68 | 120 | 1023.00 | 180 | 1530.76 | 240 | 2038.52 | 300 | 2546.28 | | | | | | | | |

**Code more than 500**

1 Where the code is in the range **501 to 1000** inclusive:

   a. Subtract **500** from the code and use the balance of the code to obtain a pay adjustment figure from the table above.

   b. Add this pay adjustment figure to the figure given in the box alongside to obtain the figure of total pay adjustment to date *   **4231.04**

2 Where the code **exceeds 1000** follow the instructions on **page 3**.

**Week 45**  Feb 8 to Feb 14                                   **Tables A** - Pay Adjustment Table

| Code | Total pay adjustment to date | Code | Total pay adjustment to date | Code | Total pay adjustment to date | Code | Total pay adjustment to date | Code | Total pay adjustment to date | Code | Total pay adjustment to date | Code | Total pay adjustment to date | Code | Total pay adjustment to date | Code | Total pay adjustment to date |
|---|---|---|---|---|---|---|---|---|---|---|---|---|---|---|---|---|---|
| | £ | | £ | | £ | | £ | | £ | | £ | | £ | | £ | | £ |
| 0 | NIL | | | | | | | | | | | | | | | | |
| 1 | 16.65 | 61 | 535.95 | 121 | 1055.25 | 181 | 1574.55 | 241 | 2093.40 | 301 | 2612.70 | 351 | 3045.60 | 401 | 3478.05 | 451 | 3910.95 |
| 2 | 25.20 | 62 | 544.50 | 122 | 1063.80 | 182 | 1583.10 | 242 | 2102.40 | 302 | 2621.25 | 352 | 3054.15 | 402 | 3487.05 | 452 | 3919.50 |
| 3 | 33.75 | 63 | 553.05 | 123 | 1072.35 | 183 | 1591.65 | 243 | 2110.95 | 303 | 2630.25 | 353 | 3062.70 | 403 | 3495.60 | 453 | 3928.05 |
| 4 | 42.75 | 64 | 562.05 | 124 | 1080.90 | 184 | 1600.20 | 244 | 2119.50 | 304 | 2638.80 | 354 | 3071.25 | 404 | 3504.15 | 454 | 3937.05 |
| 5 | 51.30 | 65 | 570.60 | 125 | 1089.90 | 185 | 1608.75 | 245 | 2128.05 | 305 | 2647.35 | 355 | 3080.25 | 405 | 3512.70 | 455 | 3945.60 |
| 6 | 59.85 | 66 | 579.15 | 126 | 1098.45 | 186 | 1617.75 | 246 | 2137.05 | 306 | 2655.90 | 356 | 3088.80 | 406 | 3521.25 | 456 | 3954.15 |
| 7 | 68.40 | 67 | 587.70 | 127 | 1107.00 | 187 | 1626.30 | 247 | 2145.60 | 307 | 2664.90 | 357 | 3097.35 | 407 | 3530.25 | 457 | 3962.70 |
| 8 | 77.40 | 68 | 596.25 | 128 | 1115.55 | 188 | 1634.85 | 248 | 2154.15 | 308 | 2673.45 | 358 | 3105.90 | 408 | 3538.80 | 458 | 3971.25 |
| 9 | 85.95 | 69 | 605.25 | 129 | 1124.55 | 189 | 1643.40 | 249 | 2162.70 | 309 | 2682.00 | 359 | 3114.90 | 409 | 3547.35 | 459 | 3980.25 |
| 10 | 94.50 | 70 | 613.80 | 130 | 1133.10 | 190 | 1652.40 | 250 | 2171.25 | 310 | 2690.55 | 360 | 3123.45 | 410 | 3555.90 | 460 | 3988.80 |
| 11 | 103.05 | 71 | 622.35 | 131 | 1141.65 | 191 | 1660.95 | 251 | 2180.25 | 311 | 2699.55 | 361 | 3132.00 | 411 | 3564.90 | 461 | 3997.35 |
| 12 | 112.05 | 72 | 630.90 | 132 | 1150.20 | 192 | 1669.50 | 252 | 2188.80 | 312 | 2708.10 | 362 | 3140.55 | 412 | 3573.45 | 462 | 4005.90 |
| 13 | 120.60 | 73 | 639.90 | 133 | 1158.75 | 193 | 1678.05 | 253 | 2197.35 | 313 | 2716.65 | 363 | 3149.55 | 413 | 3582.00 | 463 | 4014.90 |
| 14 | 129.15 | 74 | 648.45 | 134 | 1167.75 | 194 | 1687.05 | 254 | 2205.90 | 314 | 2725.20 | 364 | 3158.10 | 414 | 3590.55 | 464 | 4023.45 |
| 15 | 137.70 | 75 | 657.00 | 135 | 1176.30 | 195 | 1695.60 | 255 | 2214.90 | 315 | 2733.75 | 365 | 3166.65 | 415 | 3599.55 | 465 | 4032.00 |
| 16 | 146.25 | 76 | 665.55 | 136 | 1184.85 | 196 | 1704.15 | 256 | 2223.45 | 316 | 2742.75 | 366 | 3175.20 | 416 | 3608.10 | 466 | 4040.55 |
| 17 | 155.25 | 77 | 674.55 | 137 | 1193.40 | 197 | 1712.70 | 257 | 2232.00 | 317 | 2751.30 | 367 | 3183.75 | 417 | 3616.65 | 467 | 4049.55 |
| 18 | 163.80 | 78 | 683.10 | 138 | 1202.40 | 198 | 1721.25 | 258 | 2240.55 | 318 | 2759.85 | 368 | 3192.75 | 418 | 3625.20 | 468 | 4058.10 |
| 19 | 172.35 | 79 | 691.65 | 139 | 1210.95 | 199 | 1730.25 | 259 | 2249.55 | 319 | 2768.40 | 369 | 3201.30 | 419 | 3633.75 | 469 | 4066.65 |
| 20 | 180.90 | 80 | 700.20 | 140 | 1219.50 | 200 | 1738.80 | 260 | 2258.10 | 320 | 2777.40 | 370 | 3209.85 | 420 | 3642.75 | 470 | 4075.20 |
| 21 | 189.90 | 81 | 708.75 | 141 | 1228.05 | 201 | 1747.35 | 261 | 2266.65 | 321 | 2785.95 | 371 | 3218.40 | 421 | 3651.30 | 471 | 4083.75 |
| 22 | 198.45 | 82 | 717.75 | 142 | 1237.05 | 202 | 1755.90 | 262 | 2275.20 | 322 | 2794.50 | 372 | 3227.40 | 422 | 3659.85 | 472 | 4092.75 |
| 23 | 207.00 | 83 | 726.30 | 143 | 1245.60 | 203 | 1764.90 | 263 | 2283.75 | 323 | 2803.05 | 373 | 3235.95 | 423 | 3668.40 | 473 | 4101.30 |
| 24 | 215.55 | 84 | 734.85 | 144 | 1254.15 | 204 | 1773.45 | 264 | 2292.75 | 324 | 2812.05 | 374 | 3244.50 | 424 | 3677.40 | 474 | 4109.85 |
| 25 | 224.55 | 85 | 743.40 | 145 | 1262.70 | 205 | 1782.00 | 265 | 2301.30 | 325 | 2820.60 | 375 | 3253.05 | 425 | 3685.95 | 475 | 4118.40 |
| 26 | 233.10 | 86 | 752.40 | 146 | 1271.25 | 206 | 1790.55 | 266 | 2309.85 | 326 | 2829.15 | 376 | 3262.05 | 426 | 3694.50 | 476 | 4127.40 |
| 27 | 241.65 | 87 | 760.95 | 147 | 1280.25 | 207 | 1799.55 | 267 | 2318.40 | 327 | 2837.70 | 377 | 3270.60 | 427 | 3703.05 | 477 | 4135.95 |
| 28 | 250.20 | 88 | 769.50 | 148 | 1288.80 | 208 | 1808.10 | 268 | 2327.40 | 328 | 2846.25 | 378 | 3279.15 | 428 | 3712.05 | 478 | 4144.50 |
| 29 | 258.75 | 89 | 778.05 | 149 | 1297.35 | 209 | 1816.65 | 269 | 2335.95 | 329 | 2855.25 | 379 | 3287.70 | 429 | 3720.60 | 479 | 4153.05 |
| 30 | 267.75 | 90 | 787.05 | 150 | 1305.90 | 210 | 1825.20 | 270 | 2344.50 | 330 | 2863.80 | 380 | 3296.25 | 430 | 3729.15 | 480 | 4162.05 |
| 31 | 276.30 | 91 | 795.60 | 151 | 1314.90 | 211 | 1833.75 | 271 | 2353.05 | 331 | 2872.35 | 381 | 3305.25 | 431 | 3737.70 | 481 | 4170.60 |
| 32 | 284.85 | 92 | 804.15 | 152 | 1323.45 | 212 | 1842.75 | 272 | 2362.05 | 332 | 2880.90 | 382 | 3313.80 | 432 | 3746.25 | 482 | 4179.15 |
| 33 | 293.40 | 93 | 812.70 | 153 | 1332.00 | 213 | 1851.30 | 273 | 2370.60 | 333 | 2889.90 | 383 | 3322.35 | 433 | 3755.25 | 483 | 4187.70 |
| 34 | 302.40 | 94 | 821.25 | 154 | 1340.55 | 214 | 1859.85 | 274 | 2379.15 | 334 | 2898.45 | 384 | 3330.90 | 434 | 3763.80 | 484 | 4196.25 |
| 35 | 310.95 | 95 | 830.25 | 155 | 1349.55 | 215 | 1868.40 | 275 | 2387.70 | 335 | 2907.00 | 385 | 3339.90 | 435 | 3772.35 | 485 | 4205.25 |
| 36 | 319.50 | 96 | 838.80 | 156 | 1358.10 | 216 | 1877.40 | 276 | 2396.25 | 336 | 2915.55 | 386 | 3348.45 | 436 | 3780.90 | 486 | 4213.80 |
| 37 | 328.05 | 97 | 847.35 | 157 | 1366.65 | 217 | 1885.95 | 277 | 2405.25 | 337 | 2924.55 | 387 | 3357.00 | 437 | 3789.90 | 487 | 4222.35 |
| 38 | 337.05 | 98 | 855.90 | 158 | 1375.20 | 218 | 1894.50 | 278 | 2413.80 | 338 | 2933.10 | 388 | 3365.55 | 438 | 3798.45 | 488 | 4230.90 |
| 39 | 345.60 | 99 | 864.45 | 159 | 1383.75 | 219 | 1903.05 | 279 | 2422.35 | 339 | 2941.65 | 389 | 3374.55 | 439 | 3807.00 | 489 | 4239.90 |
| 40 | 354.15 | 100 | 873.45 | 160 | 1392.75 | 220 | 1912.05 | 280 | 2430.90 | 340 | 2950.20 | 390 | 3383.10 | 440 | 3815.55 | 490 | 4248.45 |
| 41 | 362.70 | 101 | 882.00 | 161 | 1401.30 | 221 | 1920.60 | 281 | 2439.90 | 341 | 2958.75 | 391 | 3391.65 | 441 | 3824.55 | 491 | 4257.00 |
| 42 | 371.25 | 102 | 890.55 | 162 | 1409.85 | 222 | 1929.15 | 282 | 2448.45 | 342 | 2967.75 | 392 | 3400.20 | 442 | 3833.10 | 492 | 4265.55 |
| 43 | 380.25 | 103 | 899.55 | 163 | 1418.40 | 223 | 1937.70 | 283 | 2457.00 | 343 | 2976.30 | 393 | 3408.75 | 443 | 3841.65 | 493 | 4274.55 |
| 44 | 388.80 | 104 | 908.10 | 164 | 1427.40 | 224 | 1946.25 | 284 | 2465.55 | 344 | 2984.85 | 394 | 3417.75 | 444 | 3850.20 | 494 | 4283.10 |
| 45 | 397.35 | 105 | 916.65 | 165 | 1435.95 | 225 | 1955.25 | 285 | 2474.55 | 345 | 2993.40 | 395 | 3426.30 | 445 | 3858.75 | 495 | 4291.65 |
| 46 | 405.90 | 106 | 925.20 | 166 | 1444.50 | 226 | 1963.80 | 286 | 2483.10 | 346 | 3002.40 | 396 | 3434.85 | 446 | 3867.75 | 496 | 4300.20 |
| 47 | 414.90 | 107 | 933.75 | 167 | 1453.05 | 227 | 1972.35 | 287 | 2491.65 | 347 | 3010.95 | 397 | 3443.40 | 447 | 3876.30 | 497 | 4308.75 |
| 48 | 423.45 | 108 | 942.75 | 168 | 1462.05 | 228 | 1980.90 | 288 | 2500.20 | 348 | 3019.50 | 398 | 3452.40 | 448 | 3884.85 | 498 | 4317.75 |
| 49 | 432.00 | 109 | 951.30 | 169 | 1470.60 | 229 | 1989.90 | 289 | 2508.75 | 349 | 3028.05 | 399 | 3460.95 | 449 | 3893.40 | 499 | 4326.30 |
| 50 | 440.55 | 110 | 959.85 | 170 | 1479.15 | 230 | 1998.45 | 290 | 2517.75 | 350 | 3037.05 | 400 | 3469.50 | 450 | 3902.40 | 500 | 4334.85 |
| 51 | 449.55 | 111 | 968.40 | 171 | 1487.70 | 231 | 2007.00 | 291 | 2526.30 | | | | | | |
| 52 | 458.10 | 112 | 977.40 | 172 | 1496.25 | 232 | 2015.55 | 292 | 2534.85 | | | | | | |
| 53 | 466.65 | 113 | 985.95 | 173 | 1505.25 | 233 | 2024.55 | 293 | 2543.40 | | | | | | |
| 54 | 475.20 | 114 | 994.50 | 174 | 1513.80 | 234 | 2033.10 | 294 | 2552.40 | | | | | | |
| 55 | 483.75 | 115 | 1003.05 | 175 | 1522.35 | 235 | 2041.65 | 295 | 2560.95 | | | | | | |
| 56 | 492.75 | 116 | 1012.05 | 176 | 1530.90 | 236 | 2050.20 | 296 | 2569.50 | | | | | | |
| 57 | 501.30 | 117 | 1020.60 | 177 | 1539.90 | 237 | 2058.75 | 297 | 2578.05 | | | | | | |
| 58 | 509.85 | 118 | 1029.15 | 178 | 1548.45 | 238 | 2067.75 | 298 | 2587.05 | | | | | | |
| 59 | 518.40 | 119 | 1037.70 | 179 | 1557.00 | 239 | 2076.30 | 299 | 2595.60 | | | | | | |
| 60 | 527.40 | 120 | 1046.25 | 180 | 1565.55 | 240 | 2084.85 | 300 | 2604.15 | | | | | | |

**Code more than 500**

1  Where the code is in the range **501** to **1000** inclusive:

   a. Subtract **500** from the code and use the balance of the code to obtain a pay adjustment figure from the table above.

   b. Add this pay adjustment figure to the figure given in the box alongside to obtain the figure of total pay adjustment to date *  | **4327.20** |

2  Where the code **exceeds 1000** follow the instructions on **page 3**.

48

## Tables A - Pay Adjustment Tables

**Feb 15 to Feb 21  Week 46**

| Code | Total pay adjustment to date | Code | Total pay adjustment to date | Code | Total pay adjustment to date | Code | Total pay adjustment to date | Code | Total pay adjustment to date | Code | Total pay adjustment to date | Code | Total pay adjustment to date | Code | Total pay adjustment to date | Code | Total pay adjustment to date |
|---|---|---|---|---|---|---|---|---|---|---|---|---|---|---|---|---|---|
| | £ | | £ | | £ | | £ | | £ | | £ | | £ | | £ | | £ |
| 0 | NIL | | | | | | | | | | | | | | | | |
| 1 | 17.02 | 61 | 547.86 | 121 | 1078.70 | 181 | 1609.54 | 241 | 2139.92 | 301 | 2670.76 | 351 | 3113.28 | 401 | 3555.34 | 451 | 3997.86 |
| 2 | 25.76 | 62 | 556.60 | 122 | 1087.44 | 182 | 1618.28 | 242 | 2149.12 | 302 | 2679.50 | 352 | 3122.02 | 402 | 3564.54 | 452 | 4006.60 |
| 3 | 34.50 | 63 | 565.34 | 123 | 1096.18 | 183 | 1627.02 | 243 | 2157.86 | 303 | 2688.70 | 353 | 3130.76 | 403 | 3573.28 | 453 | 4015.34 |
| 4 | 43.70 | 64 | 574.54 | 124 | 1104.92 | 184 | 1635.76 | 244 | 2166.60 | 304 | 2697.44 | 354 | 3139.50 | 404 | 3582.02 | 454 | 4024.54 |
| 5 | 52.44 | 65 | 583.28 | 125 | 1114.12 | 185 | 1644.50 | 245 | 2175.34 | 305 | 2706.18 | 355 | 3148.70 | 405 | 3590.76 | 455 | 4033.28 |
| 6 | 61.18 | 66 | 592.02 | 126 | 1122.86 | 186 | 1653.70 | 246 | 2184.54 | 306 | 2714.92 | 356 | 3157.44 | 406 | 3599.50 | 456 | 4042.02 |
| 7 | 69.92 | 67 | 600.76 | 127 | 1131.60 | 187 | 1662.44 | 247 | 2193.28 | 307 | 2724.12 | 357 | 3166.18 | 407 | 3608.70 | 457 | 4050.76 |
| 8 | 79.12 | 68 | 609.50 | 128 | 1140.34 | 188 | 1671.18 | 248 | 2202.02 | 308 | 2732.86 | 358 | 3174.92 | 408 | 3617.44 | 458 | 4059.50 |
| 9 | 87.86 | 69 | 618.70 | 129 | 1149.54 | 189 | 1679.92 | 249 | 2210.76 | 309 | 2741.60 | 359 | 3184.12 | 409 | 3626.18 | 459 | 4068.70 |
| 10 | 96.60 | 70 | 627.44 | 130 | 1158.28 | 190 | 1689.12 | 250 | 2219.50 | 310 | 2750.34 | 360 | 3192.86 | 410 | 3634.92 | 460 | 4077.44 |
| 11 | 105.34 | 71 | 636.18 | 131 | 1167.02 | 191 | 1697.86 | 251 | 2228.70 | 311 | 2759.54 | 361 | 3201.60 | 411 | 3644.12 | 461 | 4086.18 |
| 12 | 114.54 | 72 | 644.92 | 132 | 1175.76 | 192 | 1706.60 | 252 | 2237.44 | 312 | 2768.28 | 362 | 3210.34 | 412 | 3652.86 | 462 | 4094.92 |
| 13 | 123.28 | 73 | 654.12 | 133 | 1184.50 | 193 | 1715.34 | 253 | 2246.18 | 313 | 2777.02 | 363 | 3219.54 | 413 | 3661.60 | 463 | 4104.12 |
| 14 | 132.02 | 74 | 662.86 | 134 | 1193.70 | 194 | 1724.54 | 254 | 2254.92 | 314 | 2785.76 | 364 | 3228.28 | 414 | 3670.34 | 464 | 4112.86 |
| 15 | 140.76 | 75 | 671.60 | 135 | 1202.44 | 195 | 1733.28 | 255 | 2264.12 | 315 | 2794.50 | 365 | 3237.02 | 415 | 3679.54 | 465 | 4121.60 |
| 16 | 149.50 | 76 | 680.34 | 136 | 1211.18 | 196 | 1742.02 | 256 | 2272.86 | 316 | 2803.70 | 366 | 3245.76 | 416 | 3688.28 | 466 | 4130.34 |
| 17 | 158.70 | 77 | 689.54 | 137 | 1219.92 | 197 | 1750.76 | 257 | 2281.60 | 317 | 2812.44 | 367 | 3254.50 | 417 | 3697.02 | 467 | 4139.54 |
| 18 | 167.44 | 78 | 698.28 | 138 | 1229.12 | 198 | 1759.50 | 258 | 2290.34 | 318 | 2821.18 | 368 | 3263.70 | 418 | 3705.76 | 468 | 4148.28 |
| 19 | 176.18 | 79 | 707.02 | 139 | 1237.86 | 199 | 1768.70 | 259 | 2299.54 | 319 | 2829.92 | 369 | 3272.44 | 419 | 3714.50 | 469 | 4157.02 |
| 20 | 184.92 | 80 | 715.76 | 140 | 1246.60 | 200 | 1777.44 | 260 | 2308.28 | 320 | 2839.12 | 370 | 3281.18 | 420 | 3723.70 | 470 | 4165.76 |
| 21 | 194.12 | 81 | 724.50 | 141 | 1255.34 | 201 | 1786.18 | 261 | 2317.02 | 321 | 2847.86 | 371 | 3289.92 | 421 | 3732.44 | 471 | 4174.50 |
| 22 | 202.86 | 82 | 733.70 | 142 | 1264.54 | 202 | 1794.92 | 262 | 2325.76 | 322 | 2856.60 | 372 | 3299.12 | 422 | 3741.18 | 472 | 4183.70 |
| 23 | 211.60 | 83 | 742.44 | 143 | 1273.28 | 203 | 1804.12 | 263 | 2334.50 | 323 | 2865.34 | 373 | 3307.86 | 423 | 3749.92 | 473 | 4192.44 |
| 24 | 220.34 | 84 | 751.18 | 144 | 1282.02 | 204 | 1812.86 | 264 | 2343.70 | 324 | 2874.54 | 374 | 3316.60 | 424 | 3759.12 | 474 | 4201.18 |
| 25 | 229.54 | 85 | 759.92 | 145 | 1290.76 | 205 | 1821.60 | 265 | 2352.44 | 325 | 2883.28 | 375 | 3325.34 | 425 | 3767.86 | 475 | 4209.92 |
| 26 | 238.28 | 86 | 769.12 | 146 | 1299.50 | 206 | 1830.34 | 266 | 2361.18 | 326 | 2892.02 | 376 | 3334.54 | 426 | 3776.60 | 476 | 4219.12 |
| 27 | 247.02 | 87 | 777.86 | 147 | 1308.70 | 207 | 1839.54 | 267 | 2369.92 | 327 | 2900.76 | 377 | 3343.28 | 427 | 3785.34 | 477 | 4227.86 |
| 28 | 255.76 | 88 | 786.60 | 148 | 1317.44 | 208 | 1848.28 | 268 | 2379.12 | 328 | 2909.50 | 378 | 3352.02 | 428 | 3794.54 | 478 | 4236.60 |
| 29 | 264.50 | 89 | 795.34 | 149 | 1326.18 | 209 | 1857.02 | 269 | 2387.86 | 329 | 2918.70 | 379 | 3360.76 | 429 | 3803.28 | 479 | 4245.34 |
| 30 | 273.70 | 90 | 804.54 | 150 | 1334.92 | 210 | 1865.76 | 270 | 2396.60 | 330 | 2927.44 | 380 | 3369.50 | 430 | 3812.02 | 480 | 4254.54 |
| 31 | 282.44 | 91 | 813.28 | 151 | 1344.12 | 211 | 1874.50 | 271 | 2405.34 | 331 | 2936.18 | 381 | 3378.70 | 431 | 3820.76 | 481 | 4263.28 |
| 32 | 291.18 | 92 | 822.02 | 152 | 1352.86 | 212 | 1883.70 | 272 | 2414.54 | 332 | 2944.92 | 382 | 3387.44 | 432 | 3829.50 | 482 | 4272.02 |
| 33 | 299.92 | 93 | 830.76 | 153 | 1361.60 | 213 | 1892.44 | 273 | 2423.28 | 333 | 2954.12 | 383 | 3396.18 | 433 | 3838.70 | 483 | 4280.76 |
| 34 | 309.12 | 94 | 839.50 | 154 | 1370.34 | 214 | 1901.18 | 274 | 2432.02 | 334 | 2962.86 | 384 | 3404.92 | 434 | 3847.44 | 484 | 4289.50 |
| 35 | 317.86 | 95 | 848.70 | 155 | 1379.54 | 215 | 1909.92 | 275 | 2440.76 | 335 | 2971.60 | 385 | 3414.12 | 435 | 3856.18 | 485 | 4298.70 |
| 36 | 326.60 | 96 | 857.44 | 156 | 1388.28 | 216 | 1919.12 | 276 | 2449.50 | 336 | 2980.34 | 386 | 3422.86 | 436 | 3864.92 | 486 | 4307.44 |
| 37 | 335.34 | 97 | 866.18 | 157 | 1397.02 | 217 | 1927.86 | 277 | 2458.70 | 337 | 2989.54 | 387 | 3431.60 | 437 | 3874.12 | 487 | 4316.18 |
| 38 | 344.54 | 98 | 874.92 | 158 | 1405.76 | 218 | 1936.60 | 278 | 2467.44 | 338 | 2998.28 | 388 | 3440.34 | 438 | 3882.86 | 488 | 4324.92 |
| 39 | 353.28 | 99 | 884.12 | 159 | 1414.50 | 219 | 1945.34 | 279 | 2476.18 | 339 | 3007.02 | 389 | 3449.54 | 439 | 3891.60 | 489 | 4334.12 |
| 40 | 362.02 | 100 | 892.86 | 160 | 1423.70 | 220 | 1954.54 | 280 | 2484.92 | 340 | 3015.76 | 390 | 3458.28 | 440 | 3900.34 | 490 | 4342.86 |
| 41 | 370.76 | 101 | 901.60 | 161 | 1432.44 | 221 | 1963.28 | 281 | 2494.12 | 341 | 3024.50 | 391 | 3467.02 | 441 | 3909.54 | 491 | 4351.60 |
| 42 | 379.50 | 102 | 910.34 | 162 | 1441.18 | 222 | 1972.02 | 282 | 2502.86 | 342 | 3033.70 | 392 | 3475.76 | 442 | 3918.28 | 492 | 4360.34 |
| 43 | 388.70 | 103 | 919.54 | 163 | 1449.92 | 223 | 1980.76 | 283 | 2511.60 | 343 | 3042.44 | 393 | 3484.50 | 443 | 3927.02 | 493 | 4369.54 |
| 44 | 397.44 | 104 | 928.28 | 164 | 1459.12 | 224 | 1989.50 | 284 | 2520.34 | 344 | 3051.18 | 394 | 3493.70 | 444 | 3935.76 | 494 | 4378.28 |
| 45 | 406.18 | 105 | 937.02 | 165 | 1467.86 | 225 | 1998.70 | 285 | 2529.54 | 345 | 3059.92 | 395 | 3502.44 | 445 | 3944.50 | 495 | 4387.02 |
| 46 | 414.92 | 106 | 945.76 | 166 | 1476.60 | 226 | 2007.44 | 286 | 2538.28 | 346 | 3069.12 | 396 | 3511.18 | 446 | 3953.70 | 496 | 4395.76 |
| 47 | 424.12 | 107 | 954.50 | 167 | 1485.34 | 227 | 2016.18 | 287 | 2547.02 | 347 | 3077.86 | 397 | 3519.92 | 447 | 3962.44 | 497 | 4404.50 |
| 48 | 432.86 | 108 | 963.70 | 168 | 1494.54 | 228 | 2024.92 | 288 | 2555.76 | 348 | 3086.60 | 398 | 3529.12 | 448 | 3971.18 | 498 | 4413.70 |
| 49 | 441.60 | 109 | 972.44 | 169 | 1503.28 | 229 | 2034.12 | 289 | 2564.50 | 349 | 3095.34 | 399 | 3537.86 | 449 | 3979.92 | 499 | 4422.44 |
| 50 | 450.34 | 110 | 981.18 | 170 | 1512.02 | 230 | 2042.86 | 290 | 2573.70 | 350 | 3104.54 | 400 | 3546.60 | 450 | 3989.12 | 500 | 4431.18 |
| 51 | 459.54 | 111 | 989.92 | 171 | 1520.76 | 231 | 2051.60 | 291 | 2582.44 | | | | | | |
| 52 | 468.28 | 112 | 999.12 | 172 | 1529.50 | 232 | 2060.34 | 292 | 2591.18 | | | | | | |
| 53 | 477.02 | 113 | 1007.86 | 173 | 1538.70 | 233 | 2069.54 | 293 | 2599.92 | | | | | | |
| 54 | 485.76 | 114 | 1016.60 | 174 | 1547.44 | 234 | 2078.28 | 294 | 2609.12 | | | | | | |
| 55 | 494.50 | 115 | 1025.34 | 175 | 1556.18 | 235 | 2087.02 | 295 | 2617.86 | | | | | | |
| 56 | 503.70 | 116 | 1034.54 | 176 | 1564.92 | 236 | 2095.76 | 296 | 2626.60 | | | | | | |
| 57 | 512.44 | 117 | 1043.28 | 177 | 1574.12 | 237 | 2104.50 | 297 | 2635.34 | | | | | | |
| 58 | 521.18 | 118 | 1052.02 | 178 | 1582.86 | 238 | 2113.70 | 298 | 2644.54 | | | | | | |
| 59 | 529.92 | 119 | 1060.76 | 179 | 1591.60 | 239 | 2122.44 | 299 | 2653.28 | | | | | | |
| 60 | 539.12 | 120 | 1069.50 | 180 | 1600.34 | 240 | 2131.18 | 300 | 2662.02 | | | | | | |

**Code more than 500**

1 Where the code is in the range **501** to **1000** inclusive:

  a. Subtract **500** from the code and use the balance of the code to obtain a pay adjustment figure from the table above.

  b. Add this pay adjustment figure to the figure given in the box alongside to obtain the figure of total pay adjustment to date * | **4423.36** |

2 Where the code **exceeds 1000** follow the instructions on **page 3**.

49

**Week 47**  Feb 22 to Feb 28

**Tables A** - Pay Adjustment Table

| Code | Total pay adjustment to date | Code | Total pay adjustment to date | Code | Total pay adjustment to date | Code | Total pay adjustment to date | Code | Total pay adjustment to date | Code | Total pay adjustment to date | Code | Total pay adjustment to date | Code | Total pay adjustment to date | Code | Total pay adjustment to date |
|---|---|---|---|---|---|---|---|---|---|---|---|---|---|---|---|---|---|
| | £ | | £ | | £ | | £ | | £ | | £ | | £ | | £ | | £ |
| 0 | NIL | 61 | 559.77 | 121 | 1102.15 | 181 | 1644.53 | 241 | 2186.44 | 301 | 2728.82 | 351 | 3180.96 | 401 | 3632.63 | 451 | 4084.77 |
| 1 | 17.39 | 62 | 568.70 | 122 | 1111.08 | 182 | 1653.46 | 242 | 2195.84 | 302 | 2737.75 | 352 | 3189.89 | 402 | 3642.03 | 452 | 4093.70 |
| 2 | 26.32 | 63 | 577.63 | 123 | 1120.01 | 183 | 1662.39 | 243 | 2204.77 | 303 | 2747.15 | 353 | 3198.82 | 403 | 3650.96 | 453 | 4102.63 |
| 3 | 35.25 | 64 | 587.03 | 124 | 1128.94 | 184 | 1671.32 | 244 | 2213.70 | 304 | 2756.08 | 354 | 3207.75 | 404 | 3659.89 | 454 | 4112.03 |
| 4 | 44.65 | 65 | 595.96 | 125 | 1138.34 | 185 | 1680.25 | 245 | 2222.63 | 305 | 2765.01 | 355 | 3217.15 | 405 | 3668.82 | 455 | 4120.96 |
| 5 | 53.58 | | | | | | | | | | | | | | | | |
| 6 | 62.51 | 66 | 604.89 | 126 | 1147.27 | 186 | 1689.65 | 246 | 2232.03 | 306 | 2773.94 | 356 | 3226.08 | 406 | 3677.75 | 456 | 4129.89 |
| 7 | 71.44 | 67 | 613.82 | 127 | 1156.20 | 187 | 1698.58 | 247 | 2240.96 | 307 | 2783.34 | 357 | 3235.01 | 407 | 3687.15 | 457 | 4138.82 |
| 8 | 80.84 | 68 | 622.75 | 128 | 1165.13 | 188 | 1707.51 | 248 | 2249.89 | 308 | 2792.27 | 358 | 3243.94 | 408 | 3696.08 | 458 | 4147.75 |
| 9 | 89.77 | 69 | 632.15 | 129 | 1174.53 | 189 | 1716.44 | 249 | 2258.82 | 309 | 2801.20 | 359 | 3253.34 | 409 | 3705.01 | 459 | 4157.15 |
| 10 | 98.70 | 70 | 641.08 | 130 | 1183.46 | 190 | 1725.84 | 250 | 2267.75 | 310 | 2810.13 | 360 | 3262.27 | 410 | 3713.94 | 460 | 4166.08 |
| 11 | 107.63 | 71 | 650.01 | 131 | 1192.39 | 191 | 1734.77 | 251 | 2277.15 | 311 | 2819.53 | 361 | 3271.20 | 411 | 3723.34 | 461 | 4175.01 |
| 12 | 117.03 | 72 | 658.94 | 132 | 1201.32 | 192 | 1743.70 | 252 | 2286.08 | 312 | 2828.46 | 362 | 3280.13 | 412 | 3732.27 | 462 | 4183.94 |
| 13 | 125.96 | 73 | 668.34 | 133 | 1210.25 | 193 | 1752.63 | 253 | 2295.01 | 313 | 2837.39 | 363 | 3289.53 | 413 | 3741.20 | 463 | 4193.34 |
| 14 | 134.89 | 74 | 677.27 | 134 | 1219.65 | 194 | 1762.03 | 254 | 2303.94 | 314 | 2846.32 | 364 | 3298.46 | 414 | 3750.13 | 464 | 4202.27 |
| 15 | 143.82 | 75 | 686.20 | 135 | 1228.58 | 195 | 1770.96 | 255 | 2313.34 | 315 | 2855.25 | 365 | 3307.39 | 415 | 3759.53 | 465 | 4211.20 |
| 16 | 152.75 | 76 | 695.13 | 136 | 1237.51 | 196 | 1779.89 | 256 | 2322.27 | 316 | 2864.65 | 366 | 3316.32 | 416 | 3768.46 | 466 | 4220.13 |
| 17 | 162.15 | 77 | 704.53 | 137 | 1246.44 | 197 | 1788.82 | 257 | 2331.20 | 317 | 2873.58 | 367 | 3325.25 | 417 | 3777.39 | 467 | 4229.53 |
| 18 | 171.08 | 78 | 713.46 | 138 | 1255.84 | 198 | 1797.75 | 258 | 2340.13 | 318 | 2882.51 | 368 | 3334.65 | 418 | 3786.32 | 468 | 4238.46 |
| 19 | 180.01 | 79 | 722.39 | 139 | 1264.77 | 199 | 1807.15 | 259 | 2349.53 | 319 | 2891.44 | 369 | 3343.58 | 419 | 3795.25 | 469 | 4247.39 |
| 20 | 188.94 | 80 | 731.32 | 140 | 1273.70 | 200 | 1816.08 | 260 | 2358.46 | 320 | 2900.84 | 370 | 3352.51 | 420 | 3804.65 | 470 | 4256.32 |
| 21 | 198.34 | 81 | 740.25 | 141 | 1282.63 | 201 | 1825.01 | 261 | 2367.39 | 321 | 2909.77 | 371 | 3361.44 | 421 | 3813.58 | 471 | 4265.25 |
| 22 | 207.27 | 82 | 749.65 | 142 | 1292.03 | 202 | 1833.94 | 262 | 2376.32 | 322 | 2918.70 | 372 | 3370.84 | 422 | 3822.51 | 472 | 4274.65 |
| 23 | 216.20 | 83 | 758.58 | 143 | 1300.96 | 203 | 1843.34 | 263 | 2385.25 | 323 | 2927.63 | 373 | 3379.77 | 423 | 3831.44 | 473 | 4283.58 |
| 24 | 225.13 | 84 | 767.51 | 144 | 1309.89 | 204 | 1852.27 | 264 | 2394.65 | 324 | 2937.03 | 374 | 3388.70 | 424 | 3840.84 | 474 | 4292.51 |
| 25 | 234.53 | 85 | 776.44 | 145 | 1318.82 | 205 | 1861.20 | 265 | 2403.58 | 325 | 2945.96 | 375 | 3397.63 | 425 | 3849.77 | 475 | 4301.44 |
| 26 | 243.46 | 86 | 785.84 | 146 | 1327.75 | 206 | 1870.13 | 266 | 2412.51 | 326 | 2954.89 | 376 | 3407.03 | 426 | 3858.70 | 476 | 4310.84 |
| 27 | 252.39 | 87 | 794.77 | 147 | 1337.15 | 207 | 1879.53 | 267 | 2421.44 | 327 | 2963.82 | 377 | 3415.96 | 427 | 3867.63 | 477 | 4319.77 |
| 28 | 261.32 | 88 | 803.70 | 148 | 1346.08 | 208 | 1888.46 | 268 | 2430.84 | 328 | 2972.75 | 378 | 3424.89 | 428 | 3877.03 | 478 | 4328.70 |
| 29 | 270.25 | 89 | 812.63 | 149 | 1355.01 | 209 | 1897.39 | 269 | 2439.77 | 329 | 2982.15 | 379 | 3433.82 | 429 | 3885.96 | 479 | 4337.63 |
| 30 | 279.65 | 90 | 822.03 | 150 | 1363.94 | 210 | 1906.32 | 270 | 2448.70 | 330 | 2991.08 | 380 | 3442.75 | 430 | 3894.89 | 480 | 4347.03 |
| 31 | 288.58 | 91 | 830.96 | 151 | 1373.34 | 211 | 1915.25 | 271 | 2457.63 | 331 | 3000.01 | 381 | 3452.15 | 431 | 3903.82 | 481 | 4355.96 |
| 32 | 297.51 | 92 | 839.89 | 152 | 1382.27 | 212 | 1924.65 | 272 | 2467.03 | 332 | 3008.94 | 382 | 3461.08 | 432 | 3912.75 | 482 | 4364.89 |
| 33 | 306.44 | 93 | 848.82 | 153 | 1391.20 | 213 | 1933.58 | 273 | 2475.96 | 333 | 3018.34 | 383 | 3470.01 | 433 | 3922.15 | 483 | 4373.82 |
| 34 | 315.84 | 94 | 857.75 | 154 | 1400.13 | 214 | 1942.51 | 274 | 2484.89 | 334 | 3027.27 | 384 | 3478.94 | 434 | 3931.08 | 484 | 4382.75 |
| 35 | 324.77 | 95 | 867.15 | 155 | 1409.53 | 215 | 1951.44 | 275 | 2493.82 | 335 | 3036.20 | 385 | 3488.34 | 435 | 3940.01 | 485 | 4392.15 |
| 36 | 333.70 | 96 | 876.08 | 156 | 1418.46 | 216 | 1960.84 | 276 | 2502.75 | 336 | 3045.13 | 386 | 3497.27 | 436 | 3948.94 | 486 | 4401.08 |
| 37 | 342.63 | 97 | 885.01 | 157 | 1427.39 | 217 | 1969.77 | 277 | 2512.15 | 337 | 3054.53 | 387 | 3506.20 | 437 | 3958.34 | 487 | 4410.01 |
| 38 | 352.03 | 98 | 893.94 | 158 | 1436.32 | 218 | 1978.70 | 278 | 2521.08 | 338 | 3063.46 | 388 | 3515.13 | 438 | 3967.27 | 488 | 4418.94 |
| 39 | 360.96 | 99 | 903.34 | 159 | 1445.25 | 219 | 1987.63 | 279 | 2530.01 | 339 | 3072.39 | 389 | 3524.53 | 439 | 3976.20 | 489 | 4428.34 |
| 40 | 369.89 | 100 | 912.27 | 160 | 1454.65 | 220 | 1997.03 | 280 | 2538.94 | 340 | 3081.32 | 390 | 3533.46 | 440 | 3985.13 | 490 | 4437.27 |
| 41 | 378.82 | 101 | 921.20 | 161 | 1463.58 | 221 | 2005.96 | 281 | 2548.34 | 341 | 3090.25 | 391 | 3542.39 | 441 | 3994.53 | 491 | 4446.20 |
| 42 | 387.75 | 102 | 930.13 | 162 | 1472.51 | 222 | 2014.89 | 282 | 2557.27 | 342 | 3099.65 | 392 | 3551.32 | 442 | 4003.46 | 492 | 4455.13 |
| 43 | 397.15 | 103 | 939.53 | 163 | 1481.44 | 223 | 2023.82 | 283 | 2566.20 | 343 | 3108.58 | 393 | 3560.25 | 443 | 4012.39 | 493 | 4464.53 |
| 44 | 406.08 | 104 | 948.46 | 164 | 1490.84 | 224 | 2032.75 | 284 | 2575.13 | 344 | 3117.51 | 394 | 3569.65 | 444 | 4021.32 | 494 | 4473.46 |
| 45 | 415.01 | 105 | 957.39 | 165 | 1499.77 | 225 | 2042.15 | 285 | 2584.53 | 345 | 3126.44 | 395 | 3578.58 | 445 | 4030.25 | 495 | 4482.39 |
| 46 | 423.94 | 106 | 966.32 | 166 | 1508.70 | 226 | 2051.08 | 286 | 2593.46 | 346 | 3135.84 | 396 | 3587.51 | 446 | 4039.65 | 496 | 4491.32 |
| 47 | 433.34 | 107 | 975.25 | 167 | 1517.63 | 227 | 2060.01 | 287 | 2602.39 | 347 | 3144.77 | 397 | 3596.44 | 447 | 4048.58 | 497 | 4500.25 |
| 48 | 442.27 | 108 | 984.65 | 168 | 1527.03 | 228 | 2068.94 | 288 | 2611.32 | 348 | 3153.70 | 398 | 3605.84 | 448 | 4057.51 | 498 | 4509.65 |
| 49 | 451.20 | 109 | 993.58 | 169 | 1535.96 | 229 | 2078.34 | 289 | 2620.25 | 349 | 3162.63 | 399 | 3614.77 | 449 | 4066.44 | 499 | 4518.58 |
| 50 | 460.13 | 110 | 1002.51 | 170 | 1544.89 | 230 | 2087.27 | 290 | 2629.65 | 350 | 3172.03 | 400 | 3623.70 | 450 | 4075.84 | 500 | 4527.51 |
| 51 | 469.53 | 111 | 1011.44 | 171 | 1553.82 | 231 | 2096.20 | 291 | 2638.58 | | | | | | | | |
| 52 | 478.46 | 112 | 1020.84 | 172 | 1562.75 | 232 | 2105.13 | 292 | 2647.51 | | | | | | | | |
| 53 | 487.39 | 113 | 1029.77 | 173 | 1572.15 | 233 | 2114.53 | 293 | 2656.44 | | | | | | | | |
| 54 | 496.32 | 114 | 1038.70 | 174 | 1581.08 | 234 | 2123.46 | 294 | 2665.84 | | | | | | | | |
| 55 | 505.25 | 115 | 1047.63 | 175 | 1590.01 | 235 | 2132.39 | 295 | 2674.77 | | | | | | | | |
| 56 | 514.65 | 116 | 1057.03 | 176 | 1598.94 | 236 | 2141.32 | 296 | 2683.70 | | | | | | | | |
| 57 | 523.58 | 117 | 1065.96 | 177 | 1608.34 | 237 | 2150.25 | 297 | 2692.63 | | | | | | | | |
| 58 | 532.51 | 118 | 1074.89 | 178 | 1617.27 | 238 | 2159.65 | 298 | 2702.03 | | | | | | | | |
| 59 | 541.44 | 119 | 1083.82 | 179 | 1626.20 | 239 | 2168.58 | 299 | 2710.96 | | | | | | | | |
| 60 | 550.84 | 120 | 1092.75 | 180 | 1635.13 | 240 | 2177.51 | 300 | 2719.89 | | | | | | | | |

**Code more than 500**

1 Where the code is in the range **501** to **1000** inclusive:

   a. Subtract **500** from the code and use the balance of the code to obtain a pay adjustment figure from the table above.

   b. Add this pay adjustment figure to the figure given in the box alongside to obtain the figure of total pay adjustment to date *  | 4519.52 |

2 Where the code exceeds **1000** follow the instructions on **page 3**.

50

## Tables A - Pay Adjustment Tables

Mar 1 to Mar 7 **Week 48**
(In leap year Feb 29 to Mar 6)

All figures in £. "Total pay adjustment to date" shown alongside each Code.

| Code | Total pay adjustment to date | Code | Total pay adjustment to date | Code | Total pay adjustment to date | Code | Total pay adjustment to date | Code | Total pay adjustment to date | Code | Total pay adjustment to date | Code | Total pay adjustment to date | Code | Total pay adjustment to date | Code | Total pay adjustment to date |
|---|---|---|---|---|---|---|---|---|---|---|---|---|---|---|---|---|---|
| 0 | NIL | 61 | 571.68 | 121 | 1125.60 | 181 | 1679.52 | 241 | 2232.96 | 301 | 2786.88 | 351 | 3248.64 | 401 | 3709.92 | 451 | 4171.68 |
| 1 | 17.76 | 62 | 580.80 | 122 | 1134.72 | 182 | 1688.64 | 242 | 2242.56 | 302 | 2796.00 | 352 | 3257.76 | 402 | 3719.52 | 452 | 4180.80 |
| 2 | 26.88 | 63 | 589.92 | 123 | 1143.84 | 183 | 1697.76 | 243 | 2251.68 | 303 | 2805.60 | 353 | 3266.88 | 403 | 3728.64 | 453 | 4189.92 |
| 3 | 36.00 | 64 | 599.52 | 124 | 1152.96 | 184 | 1706.88 | 244 | 2260.80 | 304 | 2814.72 | 354 | 3276.00 | 404 | 3737.76 | 454 | 4199.52 |
| 4 | 45.60 | 65 | 608.64 | 125 | 1162.56 | 185 | 1716.00 | 245 | 2269.92 | 305 | 2823.84 | 355 | 3285.60 | 405 | 3746.88 | 455 | 4208.64 |
| 5 | 54.72 | | | | | | | | | | | | | | | | |
| 6 | 63.84 | 66 | 617.76 | 126 | 1171.68 | 186 | 1725.60 | 246 | 2279.52 | 306 | 2832.96 | 356 | 3294.72 | 406 | 3756.00 | 456 | 4217.76 |
| 7 | 72.96 | 67 | 626.88 | 127 | 1180.80 | 187 | 1734.72 | 247 | 2288.64 | 307 | 2842.56 | 357 | 3303.84 | 407 | 3765.60 | 457 | 4226.88 |
| 8 | 82.56 | 68 | 636.00 | 128 | 1189.92 | 188 | 1743.84 | 248 | 2297.76 | 308 | 2851.68 | 358 | 3312.96 | 408 | 3774.72 | 458 | 4236.00 |
| 9 | 91.68 | 69 | 645.60 | 129 | 1199.52 | 189 | 1752.96 | 249 | 2306.88 | 309 | 2860.80 | 359 | 3322.56 | 409 | 3783.84 | 459 | 4245.60 |
| 10 | 100.80 | 70 | 654.72 | 130 | 1208.64 | 190 | 1762.56 | 250 | 2316.00 | 310 | 2869.92 | 360 | 3331.68 | 410 | 3792.96 | 460 | 4254.72 |
| 11 | 109.92 | 71 | 663.84 | 131 | 1217.76 | 191 | 1771.68 | 251 | 2325.60 | 311 | 2879.52 | 361 | 3340.80 | 411 | 3802.56 | 461 | 4263.84 |
| 12 | 119.52 | 72 | 672.96 | 132 | 1226.88 | 192 | 1780.80 | 252 | 2334.72 | 312 | 2888.64 | 362 | 3349.92 | 412 | 3811.68 | 462 | 4272.96 |
| 13 | 128.64 | 73 | 682.56 | 133 | 1236.00 | 193 | 1789.92 | 253 | 2343.84 | 313 | 2897.76 | 363 | 3359.52 | 413 | 3820.80 | 463 | 4282.56 |
| 14 | 137.76 | 74 | 691.68 | 134 | 1245.60 | 194 | 1799.52 | 254 | 2352.96 | 314 | 2906.88 | 364 | 3368.64 | 414 | 3829.92 | 464 | 4291.68 |
| 15 | 146.88 | 75 | 700.80 | 135 | 1254.72 | 195 | 1808.64 | 255 | 2362.56 | 315 | 2916.00 | 365 | 3377.76 | 415 | 3839.52 | 465 | 4300.80 |
| 16 | 156.00 | 76 | 709.92 | 136 | 1263.84 | 196 | 1817.76 | 256 | 2371.68 | 316 | 2925.60 | 366 | 3386.88 | 416 | 3848.64 | 466 | 4309.92 |
| 17 | 165.60 | 77 | 719.52 | 137 | 1272.96 | 197 | 1826.88 | 257 | 2380.80 | 317 | 2934.72 | 367 | 3396.00 | 417 | 3857.76 | 467 | 4319.52 |
| 18 | 174.72 | 78 | 728.64 | 138 | 1282.56 | 198 | 1836.00 | 258 | 2389.92 | 318 | 2943.84 | 368 | 3405.60 | 418 | 3866.88 | 468 | 4328.64 |
| 19 | 183.84 | 79 | 737.76 | 139 | 1291.68 | 199 | 1845.60 | 259 | 2399.52 | 319 | 2952.96 | 369 | 3414.72 | 419 | 3876.00 | 469 | 4337.76 |
| 20 | 192.96 | 80 | 746.88 | 140 | 1300.80 | 200 | 1854.72 | 260 | 2408.64 | 320 | 2962.56 | 370 | 3423.84 | 420 | 3885.60 | 470 | 4346.88 |
| 21 | 202.56 | 81 | 756.00 | 141 | 1309.92 | 201 | 1863.84 | 261 | 2417.76 | 321 | 2971.68 | 371 | 3432.96 | 421 | 3894.72 | 471 | 4356.00 |
| 22 | 211.68 | 82 | 765.60 | 142 | 1319.52 | 202 | 1872.96 | 262 | 2426.88 | 322 | 2980.80 | 372 | 3442.56 | 422 | 3903.84 | 472 | 4365.60 |
| 23 | 220.80 | 83 | 774.72 | 143 | 1328.64 | 203 | 1882.56 | 263 | 2436.00 | 323 | 2989.92 | 373 | 3451.68 | 423 | 3912.96 | 473 | 4374.72 |
| 24 | 229.92 | 84 | 783.84 | 144 | 1337.76 | 204 | 1891.68 | 264 | 2445.60 | 324 | 2999.52 | 374 | 3460.80 | 424 | 3922.56 | 474 | 4383.84 |
| 25 | 239.52 | 85 | 792.96 | 145 | 1346.88 | 205 | 1900.80 | 265 | 2454.72 | 325 | 3008.64 | 375 | 3469.92 | 425 | 3931.68 | 475 | 4392.96 |
| 26 | 248.64 | 86 | 802.56 | 146 | 1356.00 | 206 | 1909.92 | 266 | 2463.84 | 326 | 3017.76 | 376 | 3479.52 | 426 | 3940.80 | 476 | 4402.56 |
| 27 | 257.76 | 87 | 811.68 | 147 | 1365.60 | 207 | 1919.52 | 267 | 2472.96 | 327 | 3026.88 | 377 | 3488.64 | 427 | 3949.92 | 477 | 4411.68 |
| 28 | 266.88 | 88 | 820.80 | 148 | 1374.72 | 208 | 1928.64 | 268 | 2482.56 | 328 | 3036.00 | 378 | 3497.76 | 428 | 3959.52 | 478 | 4420.80 |
| 29 | 276.00 | 89 | 829.92 | 149 | 1383.84 | 209 | 1937.76 | 269 | 2491.68 | 329 | 3045.60 | 379 | 3506.88 | 429 | 3968.64 | 479 | 4429.92 |
| 30 | 285.60 | 90 | 839.52 | 150 | 1392.96 | 210 | 1946.88 | 270 | 2500.80 | 330 | 3054.72 | 380 | 3516.00 | 430 | 3977.76 | 480 | 4439.52 |
| 31 | 294.72 | 91 | 848.64 | 151 | 1402.56 | 211 | 1956.00 | 271 | 2509.92 | 331 | 3063.84 | 381 | 3525.60 | 431 | 3986.88 | 481 | 4448.64 |
| 32 | 303.84 | 92 | 857.76 | 152 | 1411.68 | 212 | 1965.60 | 272 | 2519.52 | 332 | 3072.96 | 382 | 3534.72 | 432 | 3996.00 | 482 | 4457.76 |
| 33 | 312.96 | 93 | 866.88 | 153 | 1420.80 | 213 | 1974.72 | 273 | 2528.64 | 333 | 3082.56 | 383 | 3543.84 | 433 | 4005.60 | 483 | 4466.88 |
| 34 | 322.56 | 94 | 876.00 | 154 | 1429.92 | 214 | 1983.84 | 274 | 2537.76 | 334 | 3091.68 | 384 | 3552.96 | 434 | 4014.72 | 484 | 4476.00 |
| 35 | 331.68 | 95 | 885.60 | 155 | 1439.52 | 215 | 1992.96 | 275 | 2546.88 | 335 | 3100.80 | 385 | 3562.56 | 435 | 4023.84 | 485 | 4485.60 |
| 36 | 340.80 | 96 | 894.72 | 156 | 1448.64 | 216 | 2002.56 | 276 | 2556.00 | 336 | 3109.92 | 386 | 3571.68 | 436 | 4032.96 | 486 | 4494.72 |
| 37 | 349.92 | 97 | 903.84 | 157 | 1457.76 | 217 | 2011.68 | 277 | 2565.60 | 337 | 3119.52 | 387 | 3580.80 | 437 | 4042.56 | 487 | 4503.84 |
| 38 | 359.52 | 98 | 912.96 | 158 | 1466.88 | 218 | 2020.80 | 278 | 2574.72 | 338 | 3128.64 | 388 | 3589.92 | 438 | 4051.68 | 488 | 4512.96 |
| 39 | 368.64 | 99 | 922.56 | 159 | 1476.00 | 219 | 2029.92 | 279 | 2583.84 | 339 | 3137.76 | 389 | 3599.52 | 439 | 4060.80 | 489 | 4522.56 |
| 40 | 377.76 | 100 | 931.68 | 160 | 1485.60 | 220 | 2039.52 | 280 | 2592.96 | 340 | 3146.88 | 390 | 3608.64 | 440 | 4069.92 | 490 | 4531.68 |
| 41 | 386.88 | 101 | 940.80 | 161 | 1494.72 | 221 | 2048.64 | 281 | 2602.56 | 341 | 3156.00 | 391 | 3617.76 | 441 | 4079.52 | 491 | 4540.80 |
| 42 | 396.00 | 102 | 949.92 | 162 | 1503.84 | 222 | 2057.76 | 282 | 2611.68 | 342 | 3165.60 | 392 | 3626.88 | 442 | 4088.64 | 492 | 4549.92 |
| 43 | 405.60 | 103 | 959.52 | 163 | 1512.96 | 223 | 2066.88 | 283 | 2620.80 | 343 | 3174.72 | 393 | 3636.00 | 443 | 4097.76 | 493 | 4559.52 |
| 44 | 414.72 | 104 | 968.64 | 164 | 1522.56 | 224 | 2076.00 | 284 | 2629.92 | 344 | 3183.84 | 394 | 3645.60 | 444 | 4106.88 | 494 | 4568.64 |
| 45 | 423.84 | 105 | 977.76 | 165 | 1531.68 | 225 | 2085.60 | 285 | 2639.52 | 345 | 3192.96 | 395 | 3654.72 | 445 | 4116.00 | 495 | 4577.76 |
| 46 | 432.96 | 106 | 986.88 | 166 | 1540.80 | 226 | 2094.72 | 286 | 2648.64 | 346 | 3202.56 | 396 | 3663.84 | 446 | 4125.60 | 496 | 4586.88 |
| 47 | 442.56 | 107 | 996.00 | 167 | 1549.92 | 227 | 2103.84 | 287 | 2657.76 | 347 | 3211.68 | 397 | 3672.96 | 447 | 4134.72 | 497 | 4596.00 |
| 48 | 451.68 | 108 | 1005.60 | 168 | 1559.52 | 228 | 2112.96 | 288 | 2666.88 | 348 | 3220.80 | 398 | 3682.56 | 448 | 4143.84 | 498 | 4605.60 |
| 49 | 460.80 | 109 | 1014.72 | 169 | 1568.64 | 229 | 2122.56 | 289 | 2676.00 | 349 | 3229.92 | 399 | 3691.68 | 449 | 4152.96 | 499 | 4614.72 |
| 50 | 469.92 | 110 | 1023.84 | 170 | 1577.76 | 230 | 2131.68 | 290 | 2685.60 | 350 | 3239.52 | 400 | 3700.80 | 450 | 4162.56 | 500 | 4623.84 |
| 51 | 479.52 | 111 | 1032.96 | 171 | 1586.88 | 231 | 2140.80 | 291 | 2694.72 | | | | | | |
| 52 | 488.64 | 112 | 1042.56 | 172 | 1596.00 | 232 | 2149.92 | 292 | 2703.84 | | | | | | |
| 53 | 497.76 | 113 | 1051.68 | 173 | 1605.60 | 233 | 2159.52 | 293 | 2712.96 | | | | | | |
| 54 | 506.88 | 114 | 1060.80 | 174 | 1614.72 | 234 | 2168.64 | 294 | 2722.56 | | | | | | |
| 55 | 516.00 | 115 | 1069.92 | 175 | 1623.84 | 235 | 2177.76 | 295 | 2731.68 | | | | | | |
| 56 | 525.60 | 116 | 1079.52 | 176 | 1632.96 | 236 | 2186.88 | 296 | 2740.80 | | | | | | |
| 57 | 534.72 | 117 | 1088.64 | 177 | 1642.56 | 237 | 2196.00 | 297 | 2749.92 | | | | | | |
| 58 | 543.84 | 118 | 1097.76 | 178 | 1651.68 | 238 | 2205.60 | 298 | 2759.52 | | | | | | |
| 59 | 552.96 | 119 | 1106.88 | 179 | 1660.80 | 239 | 2214.72 | 299 | 2768.64 | | | | | | |
| 60 | 562.56 | 120 | 1116.00 | 180 | 1669.92 | 240 | 2223.84 | 300 | 2777.76 | | | | | | |

**Code more than 500**

1 Where the code is in the range **501 to 1000** inclusive:

  a. Subtract **500** from the code and use the balance of the code to obtain a pay adjustment figure from the table above.

  b. Add this pay adjustment figure to the figure given in the box alongside to obtain the figure of total pay adjustment to date * **4615.68**

2 Where the code **exceeds 1000** follow the instructions on **page 3**.

**Week 49**  Mar 8 to Mar 14
(In leap year Mar 7 to Mar 13)

**Tables A** - Pay Adjustment Table

| Code | Total pay adjustment to date | Code | Total pay adjustment to date | Code | Total pay adjustment to date | Code | Total pay adjustment to date | Code | Total pay adjustment to date | Code | Total pay adjustment to date | Code | Total pay adjustment to date | Code | Total pay adjustment to date | Code | Total pay adjustment to date |
|---|---|---|---|---|---|---|---|---|---|---|---|---|---|---|---|---|---|
| | £ | | £ | | £ | | £ | | £ | | £ | | £ | | £ | | £ |
| 0 | NIL | | | | | | | | | | | | | | | | |
| 1 | 18.13 | 61 | 583.59 | 121 | 1149.05 | 181 | 1714.51 | 241 | 2279.48 | 301 | 2844.94 | 351 | 3316.32 | 401 | 3787.21 | 451 | 4258.59 |
| 2 | 27.44 | 62 | 592.90 | 122 | 1158.36 | 182 | 1723.82 | 242 | 2289.28 | 302 | 2854.25 | 352 | 3325.63 | 402 | 3797.01 | 452 | 4267.90 |
| 3 | 36.75 | 63 | 602.21 | 123 | 1167.67 | 183 | 1733.13 | 243 | 2298.59 | 303 | 2864.05 | 353 | 3334.94 | 403 | 3806.32 | 453 | 4277.21 |
| 4 | 46.55 | 64 | 612.01 | 124 | 1176.98 | 184 | 1742.44 | 244 | 2307.90 | 304 | 2873.36 | 354 | 3344.25 | 404 | 3815.63 | 454 | 4287.01 |
| 5 | 55.86 | 65 | 621.32 | 125 | 1186.78 | 185 | 1751.75 | 245 | 2317.21 | 305 | 2882.67 | 355 | 3354.05 | 405 | 3824.94 | 455 | 4296.32 |
| 6 | 65.17 | 66 | 630.63 | 126 | 1196.09 | 186 | 1761.55 | 246 | 2327.01 | 306 | 2891.98 | 356 | 3363.36 | 406 | 3834.25 | 456 | 4305.63 |
| 7 | 74.48 | 67 | 639.94 | 127 | 1205.40 | 187 | 1770.86 | 247 | 2336.32 | 307 | 2901.78 | 357 | 3372.67 | 407 | 3844.05 | 457 | 4314.94 |
| 8 | 84.28 | 68 | 649.25 | 128 | 1214.71 | 188 | 1780.17 | 248 | 2345.63 | 308 | 2911.09 | 358 | 3381.98 | 408 | 3853.36 | 458 | 4324.25 |
| 9 | 93.59 | 69 | 659.05 | 129 | 1224.51 | 189 | 1789.48 | 249 | 2354.94 | 309 | 2920.40 | 359 | 3391.78 | 409 | 3862.67 | 459 | 4334.05 |
| 10 | 102.90 | 70 | 668.36 | 130 | 1233.82 | 190 | 1799.28 | 250 | 2364.25 | 310 | 2929.71 | 360 | 3401.09 | 410 | 3871.98 | 460 | 4343.36 |
| 11 | 112.21 | 71 | 677.67 | 131 | 1243.13 | 191 | 1808.59 | 251 | 2374.05 | 311 | 2939.51 | 361 | 3410.40 | 411 | 3881.78 | 461 | 4352.67 |
| 12 | 122.01 | 72 | 686.98 | 132 | 1252.44 | 192 | 1817.90 | 252 | 2383.36 | 312 | 2948.82 | 362 | 3419.71 | 412 | 3891.09 | 462 | 4361.98 |
| 13 | 131.32 | 73 | 696.78 | 133 | 1261.75 | 193 | 1827.21 | 253 | 2392.67 | 313 | 2958.13 | 363 | 3429.51 | 413 | 3900.40 | 463 | 4371.78 |
| 14 | 140.63 | 74 | 706.09 | 134 | 1271.55 | 194 | 1837.01 | 254 | 2401.98 | 314 | 2967.44 | 364 | 3438.82 | 414 | 3909.71 | 464 | 4381.09 |
| 15 | 149.94 | 75 | 715.40 | 135 | 1280.86 | 195 | 1846.32 | 255 | 2411.78 | 315 | 2976.75 | 365 | 3448.13 | 415 | 3919.51 | 465 | 4390.40 |
| 16 | 159.25 | 76 | 724.71 | 136 | 1290.17 | 196 | 1855.63 | 256 | 2421.09 | 316 | 2986.55 | 366 | 3457.44 | 416 | 3928.82 | 466 | 4399.71 |
| 17 | 169.05 | 77 | 734.51 | 137 | 1299.48 | 197 | 1864.94 | 257 | 2430.40 | 317 | 2995.86 | 367 | 3466.75 | 417 | 3938.13 | 467 | 4409.51 |
| 18 | 178.36 | 78 | 743.82 | 138 | 1309.28 | 198 | 1874.25 | 258 | 2439.71 | 318 | 3005.17 | 368 | 3476.55 | 418 | 3947.44 | 468 | 4418.82 |
| 19 | 187.67 | 79 | 753.13 | 139 | 1318.59 | 199 | 1884.05 | 259 | 2449.51 | 319 | 3014.48 | 369 | 3485.86 | 419 | 3956.75 | 469 | 4428.13 |
| 20 | 196.98 | 80 | 762.44 | 140 | 1327.90 | 200 | 1893.36 | 260 | 2458.82 | 320 | 3024.28 | 370 | 3495.17 | 420 | 3966.55 | 470 | 4437.44 |
| 21 | 206.78 | 81 | 771.75 | 141 | 1337.21 | 201 | 1902.67 | 261 | 2468.13 | 321 | 3033.59 | 371 | 3504.48 | 421 | 3975.86 | 471 | 4446.75 |
| 22 | 216.09 | 82 | 781.55 | 142 | 1347.01 | 202 | 1911.98 | 262 | 2477.44 | 322 | 3042.90 | 372 | 3514.28 | 422 | 3985.17 | 472 | 4456.55 |
| 23 | 225.40 | 83 | 790.86 | 143 | 1356.32 | 203 | 1921.78 | 263 | 2486.75 | 323 | 3052.21 | 373 | 3523.59 | 423 | 3994.48 | 473 | 4465.86 |
| 24 | 234.71 | 84 | 800.17 | 144 | 1365.63 | 204 | 1931.09 | 264 | 2496.55 | 324 | 3062.01 | 374 | 3532.90 | 424 | 4004.28 | 474 | 4475.17 |
| 25 | 244.51 | 85 | 809.48 | 145 | 1374.94 | 205 | 1940.40 | 265 | 2505.86 | 325 | 3071.32 | 375 | 3542.21 | 425 | 4013.59 | 475 | 4484.48 |
| 26 | 253.82 | 86 | 819.28 | 146 | 1384.25 | 206 | 1949.71 | 266 | 2515.17 | 326 | 3080.63 | 376 | 3552.01 | 426 | 4022.90 | 476 | 4494.28 |
| 27 | 263.13 | 87 | 828.59 | 147 | 1394.05 | 207 | 1959.51 | 267 | 2524.48 | 327 | 3089.94 | 377 | 3561.32 | 427 | 4032.21 | 477 | 4503.59 |
| 28 | 272.44 | 88 | 837.90 | 148 | 1403.36 | 208 | 1968.82 | 268 | 2534.28 | 328 | 3099.25 | 378 | 3570.63 | 428 | 4042.01 | 478 | 4512.90 |
| 29 | 281.75 | 89 | 847.21 | 149 | 1412.67 | 209 | 1978.13 | 269 | 2543.59 | 329 | 3109.05 | 379 | 3579.94 | 429 | 4051.32 | 479 | 4522.21 |
| 30 | 291.55 | 90 | 857.01 | 150 | 1421.98 | 210 | 1987.44 | 270 | 2552.90 | 330 | 3118.36 | 380 | 3589.25 | 430 | 4060.63 | 480 | 4532.01 |
| 31 | 300.86 | 91 | 866.32 | 151 | 1431.78 | 211 | 1996.75 | 271 | 2562.21 | 331 | 3127.67 | 381 | 3599.05 | 431 | 4069.94 | 481 | 4541.32 |
| 32 | 310.17 | 92 | 875.63 | 152 | 1441.09 | 212 | 2006.55 | 272 | 2572.01 | 332 | 3136.98 | 382 | 3608.36 | 432 | 4079.25 | 482 | 4550.63 |
| 33 | 319.48 | 93 | 884.94 | 153 | 1450.40 | 213 | 2015.86 | 273 | 2581.32 | 333 | 3146.78 | 383 | 3617.67 | 433 | 4089.05 | 483 | 4559.94 |
| 34 | 329.28 | 94 | 894.25 | 154 | 1459.71 | 214 | 2025.17 | 274 | 2590.63 | 334 | 3156.09 | 384 | 3626.98 | 434 | 4098.36 | 484 | 4569.25 |
| 35 | 338.59 | 95 | 904.05 | 155 | 1469.51 | 215 | 2034.48 | 275 | 2599.94 | 335 | 3165.40 | 385 | 3636.78 | 435 | 4107.67 | 485 | 4579.05 |
| 36 | 347.90 | 96 | 913.36 | 156 | 1478.82 | 216 | 2044.28 | 276 | 2609.25 | 336 | 3174.71 | 386 | 3646.09 | 436 | 4116.98 | 486 | 4588.36 |
| 37 | 357.21 | 97 | 922.67 | 157 | 1488.13 | 217 | 2053.59 | 277 | 2619.05 | 337 | 3184.51 | 387 | 3655.40 | 437 | 4126.78 | 487 | 4597.67 |
| 38 | 367.01 | 98 | 931.98 | 158 | 1497.44 | 218 | 2062.90 | 278 | 2628.36 | 338 | 3193.82 | 388 | 3664.71 | 438 | 4136.09 | 488 | 4606.98 |
| 39 | 376.32 | 99 | 941.78 | 159 | 1506.75 | 219 | 2072.21 | 279 | 2637.67 | 339 | 3203.13 | 389 | 3674.51 | 439 | 4145.40 | 489 | 4616.78 |
| 40 | 385.63 | 100 | 951.09 | 160 | 1516.55 | 220 | 2082.01 | 280 | 2646.98 | 340 | 3212.44 | 390 | 3683.82 | 440 | 4154.71 | 490 | 4626.09 |
| 41 | 394.94 | 101 | 960.40 | 161 | 1525.86 | 221 | 2091.32 | 281 | 2656.78 | 341 | 3221.75 | 391 | 3693.13 | 441 | 4164.51 | 491 | 4635.40 |
| 42 | 404.25 | 102 | 969.71 | 162 | 1535.17 | 222 | 2100.63 | 282 | 2666.09 | 342 | 3231.55 | 392 | 3702.44 | 442 | 4173.82 | 492 | 4644.71 |
| 43 | 414.05 | 103 | 979.51 | 163 | 1544.48 | 223 | 2109.94 | 283 | 2675.40 | 343 | 3240.86 | 393 | 3711.75 | 443 | 4183.13 | 493 | 4654.51 |
| 44 | 423.36 | 104 | 988.82 | 164 | 1554.28 | 224 | 2119.25 | 284 | 2684.71 | 344 | 3250.17 | 394 | 3721.55 | 444 | 4192.44 | 494 | 4663.82 |
| 45 | 432.67 | 105 | 998.13 | 165 | 1563.59 | 225 | 2129.05 | 285 | 2694.51 | 345 | 3259.48 | 395 | 3730.86 | 445 | 4201.75 | 495 | 4673.13 |
| 46 | 441.98 | 106 | 1007.44 | 166 | 1572.90 | 226 | 2138.36 | 286 | 2703.82 | 346 | 3269.28 | 396 | 3740.17 | 446 | 4211.55 | 496 | 4682.44 |
| 47 | 451.78 | 107 | 1016.75 | 167 | 1582.21 | 227 | 2147.67 | 287 | 2713.13 | 347 | 3278.59 | 397 | 3749.48 | 447 | 4220.86 | 497 | 4691.75 |
| 48 | 461.09 | 108 | 1026.55 | 168 | 1592.01 | 228 | 2156.98 | 288 | 2722.44 | 348 | 3287.90 | 398 | 3759.28 | 448 | 4230.17 | 498 | 4701.55 |
| 49 | 470.40 | 109 | 1035.86 | 169 | 1601.32 | 229 | 2166.78 | 289 | 2731.75 | 349 | 3297.21 | 399 | 3768.59 | 449 | 4239.48 | 499 | 4710.86 |
| 50 | 479.71 | 110 | 1045.17 | 170 | 1610.63 | 230 | 2176.09 | 290 | 2741.55 | 350 | 3307.01 | 400 | 3777.90 | 450 | 4249.28 | 500 | 4720.17 |
| 51 | 489.51 | 111 | 1054.48 | 171 | 1619.94 | 231 | 2185.40 | 291 | 2750.86 | | | | | | | | |
| 52 | 498.82 | 112 | 1064.28 | 172 | 1629.25 | 232 | 2194.71 | 292 | 2760.17 | | | | | | | | |
| 53 | 508.13 | 113 | 1073.59 | 173 | 1639.05 | 233 | 2204.51 | 293 | 2769.48 | | | | | | | | |
| 54 | 517.44 | 114 | 1082.90 | 174 | 1648.36 | 234 | 2213.82 | 294 | 2779.28 | | | | | | | | |
| 55 | 526.75 | 115 | 1092.21 | 175 | 1657.67 | 235 | 2223.13 | 295 | 2788.59 | | | | | | | | |
| 56 | 536.55 | 116 | 1102.01 | 176 | 1666.98 | 236 | 2232.44 | 296 | 2797.90 | | | | | | | | |
| 57 | 545.86 | 117 | 1111.32 | 177 | 1676.78 | 237 | 2241.75 | 297 | 2807.21 | | | | | | | | |
| 58 | 555.17 | 118 | 1120.63 | 178 | 1686.09 | 238 | 2251.55 | 298 | 2817.01 | | | | | | | | |
| 59 | 564.48 | 119 | 1129.94 | 179 | 1695.40 | 239 | 2260.86 | 299 | 2826.32 | | | | | | | | |
| 60 | 574.28 | 120 | 1139.25 | 180 | 1704.71 | 240 | 2270.17 | 300 | 2835.63 | | | | | | | | |

**Code more than 500**

1 Where the code is in the range 501 to **1000** inclusive:

   a. Subtract **500** from the code and use the balance of the code to obtain a pay adjustment figure from the table above.

   b. Add this pay adjustment figure to the figure given in the box alongside to obtain the figure of total pay adjustment to date *  | 4711.84 |

2 Where the code **exceeds 1000** follow the instructions on **page 3**.

## Tables A - Pay Adjustment Tables

**Mar 15 to Mar 21  Week 50**
(In leap year Mar 14 to Mar 20)

| Code | Total pay adjustment to date | Code | Total pay adjustment to date | Code | Total pay adjustment to date | Code | Total pay adjustment to date | Code | Total pay adjustment to date | Code | Total pay adjustment to date | Code | Total pay adjustment to date | Code | Total pay adjustment to date | Code | Total pay adjustment to date |
|---|---|---|---|---|---|---|---|---|---|---|---|---|---|---|---|---|---|
| | £ | | £ | | £ | | £ | | £ | | £ | | £ | | £ | | £ |
| 0 | NIL | | | | | | | | | | | | | | | | |
| 1 | 18.50 | 61 | 595.50 | 121 | 1172.50 | 181 | 1749.50 | 241 | 2326.00 | 301 | 2903.00 | 351 | 3384.00 | 401 | 3864.50 | 451 | 4345.50 |
| 2 | 28.00 | 62 | 605.00 | 122 | 1182.00 | 182 | 1759.00 | 242 | 2336.00 | 302 | 2912.50 | 352 | 3393.50 | 402 | 3874.50 | 452 | 4355.00 |
| 3 | 37.50 | 63 | 614.50 | 123 | 1191.50 | 183 | 1768.50 | 243 | 2345.50 | 303 | 2922.50 | 353 | 3403.00 | 403 | 3884.00 | 453 | 4364.50 |
| 4 | 47.50 | 64 | 624.50 | 124 | 1201.00 | 184 | 1778.00 | 244 | 2355.00 | 304 | 2932.00 | 354 | 3412.50 | 404 | 3893.50 | 454 | 4374.50 |
| 5 | 57.00 | 65 | 634.00 | 125 | 1211.00 | 185 | 1787.50 | 245 | 2364.50 | 305 | 2941.50 | 355 | 3422.50 | 405 | 3903.00 | 455 | 4384.00 |
| 6 | 66.50 | 66 | 643.50 | 126 | 1220.50 | 186 | 1797.50 | 246 | 2374.50 | 306 | 2951.00 | 356 | 3432.00 | 406 | 3912.50 | 456 | 4393.50 |
| 7 | 76.00 | 67 | 653.00 | 127 | 1230.00 | 187 | 1807.00 | 247 | 2384.00 | 307 | 2961.00 | 357 | 3441.50 | 407 | 3922.50 | 457 | 4403.00 |
| 8 | 86.00 | 68 | 662.50 | 128 | 1239.50 | 188 | 1816.50 | 248 | 2393.50 | 308 | 2970.50 | 358 | 3451.00 | 408 | 3932.00 | 458 | 4412.50 |
| 9 | 95.50 | 69 | 672.50 | 129 | 1249.50 | 189 | 1826.00 | 249 | 2403.00 | 309 | 2980.00 | 359 | 3461.00 | 409 | 3941.50 | 459 | 4422.50 |
| 10 | 105.00 | 70 | 682.00 | 130 | 1259.00 | 190 | 1836.00 | 250 | 2412.50 | 310 | 2989.50 | 360 | 3470.50 | 410 | 3951.00 | 460 | 4432.00 |
| 11 | 114.50 | 71 | 691.50 | 131 | 1268.50 | 191 | 1845.50 | 251 | 2422.50 | 311 | 2999.50 | 361 | 3480.00 | 411 | 3961.00 | 461 | 4441.50 |
| 12 | 124.50 | 72 | 701.00 | 132 | 1278.00 | 192 | 1855.00 | 252 | 2432.00 | 312 | 3009.00 | 362 | 3489.50 | 412 | 3970.50 | 462 | 4451.00 |
| 13 | 134.00 | 73 | 711.00 | 133 | 1287.50 | 193 | 1864.50 | 253 | 2441.50 | 313 | 3018.50 | 363 | 3499.50 | 413 | 3980.00 | 463 | 4461.00 |
| 14 | 143.50 | 74 | 720.50 | 134 | 1297.50 | 194 | 1874.50 | 254 | 2451.00 | 314 | 3028.00 | 364 | 3509.00 | 414 | 3989.50 | 464 | 4470.50 |
| 15 | 153.00 | 75 | 730.00 | 135 | 1307.00 | 195 | 1884.00 | 255 | 2461.00 | 315 | 3037.50 | 365 | 3518.50 | 415 | 3999.50 | 465 | 4480.00 |
| 16 | 162.50 | 76 | 739.50 | 136 | 1316.50 | 196 | 1893.50 | 256 | 2470.50 | 316 | 3047.50 | 366 | 3528.00 | 416 | 4009.00 | 466 | 4489.50 |
| 17 | 172.50 | 77 | 749.50 | 137 | 1326.00 | 197 | 1903.00 | 257 | 2480.00 | 317 | 3057.00 | 367 | 3537.50 | 417 | 4018.50 | 467 | 4499.50 |
| 18 | 182.00 | 78 | 759.00 | 138 | 1336.00 | 198 | 1912.50 | 258 | 2489.50 | 318 | 3066.50 | 368 | 3547.50 | 418 | 4028.00 | 468 | 4509.00 |
| 19 | 191.50 | 79 | 768.50 | 139 | 1345.50 | 199 | 1922.50 | 259 | 2499.50 | 319 | 3076.00 | 369 | 3557.00 | 419 | 4037.50 | 469 | 4518.50 |
| 20 | 201.00 | 80 | 778.00 | 140 | 1355.00 | 200 | 1932.00 | 260 | 2509.00 | 320 | 3086.00 | 370 | 3566.50 | 420 | 4047.50 | 470 | 4528.00 |
| 21 | 211.00 | 81 | 787.50 | 141 | 1364.50 | 201 | 1941.50 | 261 | 2518.50 | 321 | 3095.50 | 371 | 3576.00 | 421 | 4057.00 | 471 | 4537.50 |
| 22 | 220.50 | 82 | 797.50 | 142 | 1374.50 | 202 | 1951.00 | 262 | 2528.00 | 322 | 3105.00 | 372 | 3586.00 | 422 | 4066.50 | 472 | 4547.50 |
| 23 | 230.00 | 83 | 807.00 | 143 | 1384.00 | 203 | 1961.00 | 263 | 2537.50 | 323 | 3114.50 | 373 | 3595.50 | 423 | 4076.00 | 473 | 4557.00 |
| 24 | 239.50 | 84 | 816.50 | 144 | 1393.50 | 204 | 1970.50 | 264 | 2547.50 | 324 | 3124.50 | 374 | 3605.00 | 424 | 4086.00 | 474 | 4566.50 |
| 25 | 249.50 | 85 | 826.00 | 145 | 1403.00 | 205 | 1980.00 | 265 | 2557.00 | 325 | 3134.00 | 375 | 3614.50 | 425 | 4095.50 | 475 | 4576.00 |
| 26 | 259.00 | 86 | 836.00 | 146 | 1412.50 | 206 | 1989.50 | 266 | 2566.50 | 326 | 3143.50 | 376 | 3624.50 | 426 | 4105.00 | 476 | 4586.00 |
| 27 | 268.50 | 87 | 845.50 | 147 | 1422.50 | 207 | 1999.50 | 267 | 2576.00 | 327 | 3153.00 | 377 | 3634.00 | 427 | 4114.50 | 477 | 4595.50 |
| 28 | 278.00 | 88 | 855.00 | 148 | 1432.00 | 208 | 2009.00 | 268 | 2586.00 | 328 | 3162.50 | 378 | 3643.50 | 428 | 4124.50 | 478 | 4605.00 |
| 29 | 287.50 | 89 | 864.50 | 149 | 1441.50 | 209 | 2018.50 | 269 | 2595.50 | 329 | 3172.50 | 379 | 3653.00 | 429 | 4134.00 | 479 | 4614.50 |
| 30 | 297.50 | 90 | 874.50 | 150 | 1451.00 | 210 | 2028.00 | 270 | 2605.00 | 330 | 3182.00 | 380 | 3662.50 | 430 | 4143.50 | 480 | 4624.50 |
| 31 | 307.00 | 91 | 884.00 | 151 | 1461.00 | 211 | 2037.50 | 271 | 2614.50 | 331 | 3191.50 | 381 | 3672.50 | 431 | 4153.00 | 481 | 4634.00 |
| 32 | 316.50 | 92 | 893.50 | 152 | 1470.50 | 212 | 2047.50 | 272 | 2624.50 | 332 | 3201.00 | 382 | 3682.00 | 432 | 4162.50 | 482 | 4643.50 |
| 33 | 326.00 | 93 | 903.00 | 153 | 1480.00 | 213 | 2057.00 | 273 | 2634.00 | 333 | 3211.00 | 383 | 3691.50 | 433 | 4172.50 | 483 | 4653.00 |
| 34 | 336.00 | 94 | 912.50 | 154 | 1489.50 | 214 | 2066.50 | 274 | 2643.50 | 334 | 3220.50 | 384 | 3701.00 | 434 | 4182.00 | 484 | 4662.50 |
| 35 | 345.50 | 95 | 922.50 | 155 | 1499.50 | 215 | 2076.00 | 275 | 2653.00 | 335 | 3230.00 | 385 | 3711.00 | 435 | 4191.50 | 485 | 4672.50 |
| 36 | 355.00 | 96 | 932.00 | 156 | 1509.00 | 216 | 2086.00 | 276 | 2662.50 | 336 | 3239.50 | 386 | 3720.50 | 436 | 4201.00 | 486 | 4682.00 |
| 37 | 364.50 | 97 | 941.50 | 157 | 1518.50 | 217 | 2095.50 | 277 | 2672.50 | 337 | 3249.50 | 387 | 3730.00 | 437 | 4211.00 | 487 | 4691.50 |
| 38 | 374.50 | 98 | 951.00 | 158 | 1528.00 | 218 | 2105.00 | 278 | 2682.00 | 338 | 3259.00 | 388 | 3739.50 | 438 | 4220.50 | 488 | 4701.00 |
| 39 | 384.00 | 99 | 961.00 | 159 | 1537.50 | 219 | 2114.50 | 279 | 2691.50 | 339 | 3268.50 | 389 | 3749.50 | 439 | 4230.00 | 489 | 4711.00 |
| 40 | 393.50 | 100 | 970.50 | 160 | 1547.50 | 220 | 2124.00 | 280 | 2701.00 | 340 | 3278.00 | 390 | 3759.00 | 440 | 4239.50 | 490 | 4720.50 |
| 41 | 403.00 | 101 | 980.00 | 161 | 1557.00 | 221 | 2134.00 | 281 | 2711.00 | 341 | 3287.50 | 391 | 3768.50 | 441 | 4249.50 | 491 | 4730.00 |
| 42 | 412.50 | 102 | 989.50 | 162 | 1566.50 | 222 | 2143.50 | 282 | 2720.50 | 342 | 3297.50 | 392 | 3778.00 | 442 | 4259.00 | 492 | 4739.50 |
| 43 | 422.00 | 103 | 999.50 | 163 | 1576.00 | 223 | 2153.00 | 283 | 2730.00 | 343 | 3307.00 | 393 | 3787.50 | 443 | 4268.50 | 493 | 4749.50 |
| 44 | 432.00 | 104 | 1009.00 | 164 | 1586.00 | 224 | 2162.50 | 284 | 2739.50 | 344 | 3316.50 | 394 | 3797.50 | 444 | 4278.00 | 494 | 4759.00 |
| 45 | 441.50 | 105 | 1018.50 | 165 | 1595.50 | 225 | 2172.50 | 285 | 2749.50 | 345 | 3326.00 | 395 | 3807.00 | 445 | 4287.50 | 495 | 4768.50 |
| 46 | 451.00 | 106 | 1028.00 | 166 | 1605.00 | 226 | 2182.00 | 286 | 2759.00 | 346 | 3336.00 | 396 | 3816.50 | 446 | 4297.50 | 496 | 4778.00 |
| 47 | 461.00 | 107 | 1037.50 | 167 | 1614.50 | 227 | 2191.50 | 287 | 2768.50 | 347 | 3345.50 | 397 | 3826.00 | 447 | 4307.00 | 497 | 4787.50 |
| 48 | 470.50 | 108 | 1047.50 | 168 | 1624.50 | 228 | 2201.00 | 288 | 2778.00 | 348 | 3355.00 | 398 | 3836.00 | 448 | 4316.50 | 498 | 4797.50 |
| 49 | 480.00 | 109 | 1057.00 | 169 | 1634.00 | 229 | 2211.00 | 289 | 2787.50 | 349 | 3364.50 | 399 | 3845.50 | 449 | 4326.00 | 499 | 4807.00 |
| 50 | 489.50 | 110 | 1066.50 | 170 | 1643.50 | 230 | 2220.50 | 290 | 2797.50 | 350 | 3374.50 | 400 | 3855.00 | 450 | 4336.00 | 500 | 4816.50 |
| 51 | 499.50 | 111 | 1076.00 | 171 | 1653.00 | 231 | 2230.00 | 291 | 2807.00 | | | | | | | | |
| 52 | 509.00 | 112 | 1086.00 | 172 | 1662.50 | 232 | 2239.50 | 292 | 2816.50 | | | | | | | | |
| 53 | 518.50 | 113 | 1095.50 | 173 | 1672.50 | 233 | 2249.50 | 293 | 2826.00 | | | | | | | | |
| 54 | 528.00 | 114 | 1105.00 | 174 | 1682.00 | 234 | 2259.00 | 294 | 2836.00 | | | | | | | | |
| 55 | 537.50 | 115 | 1114.50 | 175 | 1691.50 | 235 | 2268.50 | 295 | 2845.50 | | | | | | | | |
| 56 | 547.50 | 116 | 1124.50 | 176 | 1701.00 | 236 | 2278.00 | 296 | 2855.00 | | | | | | | | |
| 57 | 557.00 | 117 | 1134.00 | 177 | 1711.00 | 237 | 2287.50 | 297 | 2864.50 | | | | | | | | |
| 58 | 566.50 | 118 | 1143.50 | 178 | 1720.50 | 238 | 2297.00 | 298 | 2874.50 | | | | | | | | |
| 59 | 576.00 | 119 | 1153.00 | 179 | 1730.00 | 239 | 2307.00 | 299 | 2884.00 | | | | | | | | |
| 60 | 586.00 | 120 | 1162.50 | 180 | 1739.50 | 240 | 2316.50 | 300 | 2893.50 | | | | | | | | |

**Code more than 500**

1 Where the code is in the range **501 to 1000** inclusive:

   a. Subtract **500** from the code and use the balance of the code to obtain a pay adjustment figure from the table above.

   b. Add this pay adjustment figure to the figure given in the box alongside to obtain the figure of total pay adjustment to date *  **4808.00**

2 Where the code **exceeds 1000** follow the instructions on **page 3**.

53

# APPENDIX 4: PAYE TAX TABLES – PAY ADJUSTMENT TABLES

**Week 51**  Mar 22 to Mar 28
(In leap year Mar 21 to Mar 27)

**Tables A** - Pay Adjustment Table

| Code | Total pay adjustment to date | Code | Total pay adjustment to date | Code | Total pay adjustment to date | Code | Total pay adjustment to date | Code | Total pay adjustment to date | Code | Total pay adjustment to date | Code | Total pay adjustment to date | Code | Total pay adjustment to date | Code | Total pay adjustment to date |
|---|---|---|---|---|---|---|---|---|---|---|---|---|---|---|---|---|---|
| | £ | | £ | | £ | | £ | | £ | | £ | | £ | | £ | | £ |
| 0 | NIL | | | | | | | | | | | | | | | | |
| 1 | 18.87 | 61 | 607.41 | 121 | 1195.95 | 181 | 1784.49 | 241 | 2372.52 | 301 | 2961.06 | 351 | 3451.68 | 401 | 3941.79 | 451 | 4432.41 |
| 2 | 28.56 | 62 | 617.10 | 122 | 1205.64 | 182 | 1794.18 | 242 | 2382.72 | 302 | 2970.75 | 352 | 3461.37 | 402 | 3951.99 | 452 | 4442.10 |
| 3 | 38.25 | 63 | 626.79 | 123 | 1215.33 | 183 | 1803.87 | 243 | 2392.41 | 303 | 2980.95 | 353 | 3471.06 | 403 | 3961.68 | 453 | 4451.79 |
| 4 | 48.45 | 64 | 636.99 | 124 | 1225.02 | 184 | 1813.56 | 244 | 2402.10 | 304 | 2990.64 | 354 | 3480.75 | 404 | 3971.37 | 454 | 4461.99 |
| 5 | 58.14 | 65 | 646.68 | 125 | 1235.22 | 185 | 1823.25 | 245 | 2411.79 | 305 | 3000.33 | 355 | 3490.95 | 405 | 3981.06 | 455 | 4471.68 |
| 6 | 67.83 | 66 | 656.37 | 126 | 1244.91 | 186 | 1833.45 | 246 | 2421.99 | 306 | 3010.02 | 356 | 3500.64 | 406 | 3990.75 | 456 | 4481.37 |
| 7 | 77.52 | 67 | 666.06 | 127 | 1254.60 | 187 | 1843.14 | 247 | 2431.68 | 307 | 3020.22 | 357 | 3510.33 | 407 | 4000.95 | 457 | 4491.06 |
| 8 | 87.72 | 68 | 675.75 | 128 | 1264.29 | 188 | 1852.83 | 248 | 2441.37 | 308 | 3029.91 | 358 | 3520.02 | 408 | 4010.64 | 458 | 4500.75 |
| 9 | 97.41 | 69 | 685.95 | 129 | 1274.49 | 189 | 1862.52 | 249 | 2451.06 | 309 | 3039.60 | 359 | 3530.22 | 409 | 4020.33 | 459 | 4510.95 |
| 10 | 107.10 | 70 | 695.64 | 130 | 1284.18 | 190 | 1872.72 | 250 | 2460.75 | 310 | 3049.29 | 360 | 3539.91 | 410 | 4030.02 | 460 | 4520.64 |
| 11 | 116.79 | 71 | 705.33 | 131 | 1293.87 | 191 | 1882.41 | 251 | 2470.95 | 311 | 3059.49 | 361 | 3549.60 | 411 | 4040.22 | 461 | 4530.33 |
| 12 | 126.99 | 72 | 715.02 | 132 | 1303.56 | 192 | 1892.10 | 252 | 2480.64 | 312 | 3069.18 | 362 | 3559.29 | 412 | 4049.91 | 462 | 4540.02 |
| 13 | 136.68 | 73 | 725.22 | 133 | 1313.25 | 193 | 1901.79 | 253 | 2490.33 | 313 | 3078.87 | 363 | 3569.49 | 413 | 4059.60 | 463 | 4550.22 |
| 14 | 146.37 | 74 | 734.91 | 134 | 1323.45 | 194 | 1911.99 | 254 | 2500.02 | 314 | 3088.56 | 364 | 3579.18 | 414 | 4069.29 | 464 | 4559.91 |
| 15 | 156.06 | 75 | 744.60 | 135 | 1333.14 | 195 | 1921.68 | 255 | 2510.22 | 315 | 3098.25 | 365 | 3588.87 | 415 | 4079.49 | 465 | 4569.60 |
| 16 | 165.75 | 76 | 754.29 | 136 | 1342.83 | 196 | 1931.37 | 256 | 2519.91 | 316 | 3108.45 | 366 | 3598.56 | 416 | 4089.18 | 466 | 4579.29 |
| 17 | 175.95 | 77 | 764.49 | 137 | 1352.52 | 197 | 1941.06 | 257 | 2529.60 | 317 | 3118.14 | 367 | 3608.25 | 417 | 4098.87 | 467 | 4589.49 |
| 18 | 185.64 | 78 | 774.18 | 138 | 1362.72 | 198 | 1950.75 | 258 | 2539.29 | 318 | 3127.83 | 368 | 3618.45 | 418 | 4108.56 | 468 | 4599.18 |
| 19 | 195.33 | 79 | 783.87 | 139 | 1372.41 | 199 | 1960.95 | 259 | 2549.49 | 319 | 3137.52 | 369 | 3628.14 | 419 | 4118.25 | 469 | 4608.87 |
| 20 | 205.02 | 80 | 793.56 | 140 | 1382.10 | 200 | 1970.64 | 260 | 2559.18 | 320 | 3147.72 | 370 | 3637.83 | 420 | 4128.45 | 470 | 4618.56 |
| 21 | 215.22 | 81 | 803.25 | 141 | 1391.79 | 201 | 1980.33 | 261 | 2568.87 | 321 | 3157.41 | 371 | 3647.52 | 421 | 4138.14 | 471 | 4628.25 |
| 22 | 224.91 | 82 | 813.45 | 142 | 1401.99 | 202 | 1990.02 | 262 | 2578.56 | 322 | 3167.10 | 372 | 3657.72 | 422 | 4147.83 | 472 | 4638.45 |
| 23 | 234.60 | 83 | 823.14 | 143 | 1411.68 | 203 | 2000.22 | 263 | 2588.25 | 323 | 3176.79 | 373 | 3667.41 | 423 | 4157.52 | 473 | 4648.14 |
| 24 | 244.29 | 84 | 832.83 | 144 | 1421.37 | 204 | 2009.91 | 264 | 2598.45 | 324 | 3186.99 | 374 | 3677.10 | 424 | 4167.72 | 474 | 4657.83 |
| 25 | 254.49 | 85 | 842.52 | 145 | 1431.06 | 205 | 2019.60 | 265 | 2608.14 | 325 | 3196.68 | 375 | 3686.79 | 425 | 4177.41 | 475 | 4667.52 |
| 26 | 264.18 | 86 | 852.72 | 146 | 1440.75 | 206 | 2029.29 | 266 | 2617.83 | 326 | 3206.37 | 376 | 3696.99 | 426 | 4187.10 | 476 | 4677.72 |
| 27 | 273.87 | 87 | 862.41 | 147 | 1450.95 | 207 | 2039.49 | 267 | 2627.52 | 327 | 3216.06 | 377 | 3706.68 | 427 | 4196.79 | 477 | 4687.41 |
| 28 | 283.56 | 88 | 872.10 | 148 | 1460.64 | 208 | 2049.18 | 268 | 2637.72 | 328 | 3225.75 | 378 | 3716.37 | 428 | 4206.99 | 478 | 4697.10 |
| 29 | 293.25 | 89 | 881.79 | 149 | 1470.33 | 209 | 2058.87 | 269 | 2647.41 | 329 | 3235.95 | 379 | 3726.06 | 429 | 4216.68 | 479 | 4706.79 |
| 30 | 303.45 | 90 | 891.99 | 150 | 1480.02 | 210 | 2068.56 | 270 | 2657.10 | 330 | 3245.64 | 380 | 3735.75 | 430 | 4226.37 | 480 | 4716.99 |
| 31 | 313.14 | 91 | 901.68 | 151 | 1490.22 | 211 | 2078.25 | 271 | 2666.79 | 331 | 3255.33 | 381 | 3745.95 | 431 | 4236.06 | 481 | 4726.68 |
| 32 | 322.83 | 92 | 911.37 | 152 | 1499.91 | 212 | 2088.45 | 272 | 2676.99 | 332 | 3265.02 | 382 | 3755.64 | 432 | 4245.75 | 482 | 4736.37 |
| 33 | 332.52 | 93 | 921.06 | 153 | 1509.60 | 213 | 2098.14 | 273 | 2686.68 | 333 | 3275.22 | 383 | 3765.33 | 433 | 4255.95 | 483 | 4746.06 |
| 34 | 342.72 | 94 | 930.75 | 154 | 1519.29 | 214 | 2107.83 | 274 | 2696.37 | 334 | 3284.91 | 384 | 3775.02 | 434 | 4265.64 | 484 | 4755.75 |
| 35 | 352.41 | 95 | 940.95 | 155 | 1529.49 | 215 | 2117.52 | 275 | 2706.06 | 335 | 3294.60 | 385 | 3785.22 | 435 | 4275.33 | 485 | 4765.95 |
| 36 | 362.10 | 96 | 950.64 | 156 | 1539.18 | 216 | 2127.72 | 276 | 2715.75 | 336 | 3304.29 | 386 | 3794.91 | 436 | 4285.02 | 486 | 4775.64 |
| 37 | 371.79 | 97 | 960.33 | 157 | 1548.87 | 217 | 2137.41 | 277 | 2725.95 | 337 | 3314.49 | 387 | 3804.60 | 437 | 4295.22 | 487 | 4785.33 |
| 38 | 381.99 | 98 | 970.02 | 158 | 1558.56 | 218 | 2147.10 | 278 | 2735.64 | 338 | 3324.18 | 388 | 3814.29 | 438 | 4304.91 | 488 | 4795.02 |
| 39 | 391.68 | 99 | 980.22 | 159 | 1568.25 | 219 | 2156.79 | 279 | 2745.33 | 339 | 3333.87 | 389 | 3824.49 | 439 | 4314.60 | 489 | 4805.22 |
| 40 | 401.37 | 100 | 989.91 | 160 | 1578.45 | 220 | 2166.99 | 280 | 2755.02 | 340 | 3343.56 | 390 | 3834.18 | 440 | 4324.29 | 490 | 4814.91 |
| 41 | 411.06 | 101 | 999.60 | 161 | 1588.14 | 221 | 2176.68 | 281 | 2765.22 | 341 | 3353.25 | 391 | 3843.87 | 441 | 4334.49 | 491 | 4824.60 |
| 42 | 420.75 | 102 | 1009.29 | 162 | 1597.83 | 222 | 2186.37 | 282 | 2774.91 | 342 | 3363.45 | 392 | 3853.56 | 442 | 4344.18 | 492 | 4834.29 |
| 43 | 430.95 | 103 | 1019.49 | 163 | 1607.52 | 223 | 2196.06 | 283 | 2784.60 | 343 | 3373.14 | 393 | 3863.25 | 443 | 4353.87 | 493 | 4844.49 |
| 44 | 440.64 | 104 | 1029.18 | 164 | 1617.72 | 224 | 2205.75 | 284 | 2794.29 | 344 | 3382.83 | 394 | 3873.45 | 444 | 4363.56 | 494 | 4854.18 |
| 45 | 450.33 | 105 | 1038.87 | 165 | 1627.41 | 225 | 2215.95 | 285 | 2804.49 | 345 | 3392.52 | 395 | 3883.14 | 445 | 4373.25 | 495 | 4863.87 |
| 46 | 460.02 | 106 | 1048.56 | 166 | 1637.10 | 226 | 2225.64 | 286 | 2814.18 | 346 | 3402.72 | 396 | 3892.83 | 446 | 4383.45 | 496 | 4873.56 |
| 47 | 470.22 | 107 | 1058.25 | 167 | 1646.79 | 227 | 2235.33 | 287 | 2823.87 | 347 | 3412.41 | 397 | 3902.52 | 447 | 4393.14 | 497 | 4883.25 |
| 48 | 479.91 | 108 | 1068.45 | 168 | 1656.99 | 228 | 2245.02 | 288 | 2833.56 | 348 | 3422.10 | 398 | 3912.72 | 448 | 4402.83 | 498 | 4893.45 |
| 49 | 489.60 | 109 | 1078.14 | 169 | 1666.68 | 229 | 2255.22 | 289 | 2843.25 | 349 | 3431.79 | 399 | 3922.41 | 449 | 4412.52 | 499 | 4903.14 |
| 50 | 499.29 | 110 | 1087.83 | 170 | 1676.37 | 230 | 2264.91 | 290 | 2853.45 | 350 | 3441.99 | 400 | 3932.10 | 450 | 4422.72 | 500 | 4912.83 |
| 51 | 509.49 | 111 | 1097.52 | 171 | 1686.06 | 231 | 2274.60 | 291 | 2863.14 | | | | | | | | |
| 52 | 519.18 | 112 | 1107.72 | 172 | 1695.75 | 232 | 2284.29 | 292 | 2872.83 | | | | | | | | |
| 53 | 528.87 | 113 | 1117.41 | 173 | 1705.95 | 233 | 2294.49 | 293 | 2882.52 | | | | | | | | |
| 54 | 538.56 | 114 | 1127.10 | 174 | 1715.64 | 234 | 2304.18 | 294 | 2892.72 | | | | | | | | |
| 55 | 548.25 | 115 | 1136.79 | 175 | 1725.33 | 235 | 2313.87 | 295 | 2902.41 | | | | | | | | |
| 56 | 558.45 | 116 | 1146.99 | 176 | 1735.02 | 236 | 2323.56 | 296 | 2912.10 | | | | | | | | |
| 57 | 568.14 | 117 | 1156.68 | 177 | 1745.22 | 237 | 2333.25 | 297 | 2921.79 | | | | | | | | |
| 58 | 577.83 | 118 | 1166.37 | 178 | 1754.91 | 238 | 2343.45 | 298 | 2931.99 | | | | | | | | |
| 59 | 587.52 | 119 | 1176.06 | 179 | 1764.60 | 239 | 2353.14 | 299 | 2941.68 | | | | | | | | |
| 60 | 597.72 | 120 | 1185.75 | 180 | 1774.29 | 240 | 2362.83 | 300 | 2951.37 | | | | | | | | |

## Code more than 500

1 Where the code is in the range 501 to 1000 inclusive:

   a. Subtract 500 from the code and use the balance of the code to obtain a pay adjustment figure from the table above.

   b. Add this pay adjustment figure to the figure given in the box alongside to obtain the figure of total pay adjustment to date * **4904.16**

2 Where the code exceeds 1000 follow the instructions on page 3.

54

## Tables A - Pay Adjustment Tables

Mar 29 to Apr 4  **Week 52**
(In leap year Mar 28 to Apr 3)

| Code | Total pay adjustment to date £ | Code | Total pay adjustment to date £ | Code | Total pay adjustment to date £ | Code | Total pay adjustment to date £ | Code | Total pay adjustment to date £ | Code | Total pay adjustment to date £ | Code | Total pay adjustment to date £ | Code | Total pay adjustment to date £ | Code | Total pay adjustment to date £ |
|---|---|---|---|---|---|---|---|---|---|---|---|---|---|---|---|---|---|
| 0 | NIL | | | | | | | | | | | | | | | | |
| 1 | 19.24 | 61 | 619.32 | 121 | 1219.40 | 181 | 1819.48 | 241 | 2419.04 | 301 | 3019.12 | 351 | 3519.36 | 401 | 4019.08 | 451 | 4519.32 |
| 2 | 29.12 | 62 | 629.20 | 122 | 1229.28 | 182 | 1829.36 | 242 | 2429.44 | 302 | 3029.00 | 352 | 3529.24 | 402 | 4029.48 | 452 | 4529.20 |
| 3 | 39.00 | 63 | 639.08 | 123 | 1239.16 | 183 | 1839.24 | 243 | 2439.32 | 303 | 3039.40 | 353 | 3539.12 | 403 | 4039.36 | 453 | 4539.08 |
| 4 | 49.40 | 64 | 649.48 | 124 | 1249.04 | 184 | 1849.12 | 244 | 2449.20 | 304 | 3049.28 | 354 | 3549.00 | 404 | 4049.24 | 454 | 4549.48 |
| 5 | 59.28 | 65 | 659.36 | 125 | 1259.44 | 185 | 1859.00 | 245 | 2459.08 | 305 | 3059.16 | 355 | 3559.40 | 405 | 4059.12 | 455 | 4559.36 |
| 6 | 69.16 | 66 | 669.24 | 126 | 1269.32 | 186 | 1869.40 | 246 | 2469.48 | 306 | 3069.04 | 356 | 3569.28 | 406 | 4069.00 | 456 | 4569.24 |
| 7 | 79.04 | 67 | 679.12 | 127 | 1279.20 | 187 | 1879.28 | 247 | 2479.36 | 307 | 3079.44 | 357 | 3579.16 | 407 | 4079.40 | 457 | 4579.12 |
| 8 | 89.44 | 68 | 689.00 | 128 | 1289.08 | 188 | 1889.16 | 248 | 2489.24 | 308 | 3089.32 | 358 | 3589.04 | 408 | 4089.28 | 458 | 4589.00 |
| 9 | 99.32 | 69 | 699.40 | 129 | 1299.48 | 189 | 1899.04 | 249 | 2499.12 | 309 | 3099.20 | 359 | 3599.44 | 409 | 4099.16 | 459 | 4599.40 |
| 10 | 109.20 | 70 | 709.28 | 130 | 1309.36 | 190 | 1909.44 | 250 | 2509.00 | 310 | 3109.08 | 360 | 3609.32 | 410 | 4109.04 | 460 | 4609.28 |
| 11 | 119.08 | 71 | 719.16 | 131 | 1319.24 | 191 | 1919.32 | 251 | 2519.40 | 311 | 3119.48 | 361 | 3619.20 | 411 | 4119.44 | 461 | 4619.16 |
| 12 | 129.48 | 72 | 729.04 | 132 | 1329.12 | 192 | 1929.20 | 252 | 2529.28 | 312 | 3129.36 | 362 | 3629.08 | 412 | 4129.32 | 462 | 4629.04 |
| 13 | 139.36 | 73 | 739.44 | 133 | 1339.00 | 193 | 1939.08 | 253 | 2539.16 | 313 | 3139.24 | 363 | 3639.48 | 413 | 4139.20 | 463 | 4639.44 |
| 14 | 149.24 | 74 | 749.32 | 134 | 1349.40 | 194 | 1949.48 | 254 | 2549.04 | 314 | 3149.12 | 364 | 3649.36 | 414 | 4149.08 | 464 | 4649.32 |
| 15 | 159.12 | 75 | 759.20 | 135 | 1359.28 | 195 | 1959.36 | 255 | 2559.44 | 315 | 3159.00 | 365 | 3659.24 | 415 | 4159.48 | 465 | 4659.20 |
| 16 | 169.00 | 76 | 769.08 | 136 | 1369.16 | 196 | 1969.24 | 256 | 2569.32 | 316 | 3169.40 | 366 | 3669.12 | 416 | 4169.36 | 466 | 4669.08 |
| 17 | 179.40 | 77 | 779.48 | 137 | 1379.04 | 197 | 1979.12 | 257 | 2579.20 | 317 | 3179.28 | 367 | 3679.00 | 417 | 4179.24 | 467 | 4679.48 |
| 18 | 189.28 | 78 | 789.36 | 138 | 1389.44 | 198 | 1989.00 | 258 | 2589.08 | 318 | 3189.16 | 368 | 3689.40 | 418 | 4189.12 | 468 | 4689.36 |
| 19 | 199.16 | 79 | 799.24 | 139 | 1399.32 | 199 | 1999.40 | 259 | 2599.48 | 319 | 3199.04 | 369 | 3699.28 | 419 | 4199.00 | 469 | 4699.24 |
| 20 | 209.04 | 80 | 809.12 | 140 | 1409.20 | 200 | 2009.28 | 260 | 2609.36 | 320 | 3209.44 | 370 | 3709.16 | 420 | 4209.40 | 470 | 4709.12 |
| 21 | 219.44 | 81 | 819.00 | 141 | 1419.08 | 201 | 2019.16 | 261 | 2619.24 | 321 | 3219.32 | 371 | 3719.04 | 421 | 4219.28 | 471 | 4719.00 |
| 22 | 229.32 | 82 | 829.40 | 142 | 1429.48 | 202 | 2029.04 | 262 | 2629.12 | 322 | 3229.20 | 372 | 3729.44 | 422 | 4229.16 | 472 | 4729.40 |
| 23 | 239.20 | 83 | 839.28 | 143 | 1439.36 | 203 | 2039.44 | 263 | 2639.00 | 323 | 3239.08 | 373 | 3739.32 | 423 | 4239.04 | 473 | 4739.28 |
| 24 | 249.08 | 84 | 849.16 | 144 | 1449.24 | 204 | 2049.32 | 264 | 2649.40 | 324 | 3249.48 | 374 | 3749.20 | 424 | 4249.44 | 474 | 4749.16 |
| 25 | 259.48 | 85 | 859.04 | 145 | 1459.12 | 205 | 2059.20 | 265 | 2659.28 | 325 | 3259.36 | 375 | 3759.08 | 425 | 4259.32 | 475 | 4759.04 |
| 26 | 269.36 | 86 | 869.44 | 146 | 1469.00 | 206 | 2069.08 | 266 | 2669.16 | 326 | 3269.24 | 376 | 3769.48 | 426 | 4269.20 | 476 | 4769.44 |
| 27 | 279.24 | 87 | 879.32 | 147 | 1479.40 | 207 | 2079.48 | 267 | 2679.04 | 327 | 3279.12 | 377 | 3779.36 | 427 | 4279.08 | 477 | 4779.32 |
| 28 | 289.12 | 88 | 889.20 | 148 | 1489.28 | 208 | 2089.36 | 268 | 2689.44 | 328 | 3289.00 | 378 | 3789.24 | 428 | 4289.48 | 478 | 4789.20 |
| 29 | 299.00 | 89 | 899.08 | 149 | 1499.16 | 209 | 2099.24 | 269 | 2699.32 | 329 | 3299.40 | 379 | 3799.12 | 429 | 4299.36 | 479 | 4799.08 |
| 30 | 309.40 | 90 | 909.48 | 150 | 1509.04 | 210 | 2109.12 | 270 | 2709.20 | 330 | 3309.28 | 380 | 3809.00 | 430 | 4309.24 | 480 | 4809.48 |
| 31 | 319.28 | 91 | 919.36 | 151 | 1519.44 | 211 | 2119.00 | 271 | 2719.08 | 331 | 3319.16 | 381 | 3819.40 | 431 | 4319.12 | 481 | 4819.36 |
| 32 | 329.16 | 92 | 929.24 | 152 | 1529.32 | 212 | 2129.40 | 272 | 2729.48 | 332 | 3329.04 | 382 | 3829.28 | 432 | 4329.00 | 482 | 4829.24 |
| 33 | 339.04 | 93 | 939.12 | 153 | 1539.20 | 213 | 2139.28 | 273 | 2739.36 | 333 | 3339.44 | 383 | 3839.16 | 433 | 4339.40 | 483 | 4839.12 |
| 34 | 349.44 | 94 | 949.00 | 154 | 1549.08 | 214 | 2149.16 | 274 | 2749.24 | 334 | 3349.32 | 384 | 3849.04 | 434 | 4349.28 | 484 | 4849.00 |
| 35 | 359.32 | 95 | 959.40 | 155 | 1559.48 | 215 | 2159.04 | 275 | 2759.12 | 335 | 3359.20 | 385 | 3859.44 | 435 | 4359.16 | 485 | 4859.40 |
| 36 | 369.20 | 96 | 969.28 | 156 | 1569.36 | 216 | 2169.44 | 276 | 2769.00 | 336 | 3369.08 | 386 | 3869.32 | 436 | 4369.04 | 486 | 4869.28 |
| 37 | 379.08 | 97 | 979.16 | 157 | 1579.24 | 217 | 2179.32 | 277 | 2779.40 | 337 | 3379.48 | 387 | 3879.20 | 437 | 4379.44 | 487 | 4879.16 |
| 38 | 389.48 | 98 | 989.04 | 158 | 1589.12 | 218 | 2189.20 | 278 | 2789.28 | 338 | 3389.36 | 388 | 3889.08 | 438 | 4389.32 | 488 | 4889.04 |
| 39 | 399.36 | 99 | 999.44 | 159 | 1599.00 | 219 | 2199.08 | 279 | 2799.16 | 339 | 3399.24 | 389 | 3899.48 | 439 | 4399.20 | 489 | 4899.44 |
| 40 | 409.24 | 100 | 1009.32 | 160 | 1609.40 | 220 | 2209.48 | 280 | 2809.04 | 340 | 3409.12 | 390 | 3909.36 | 440 | 4409.08 | 490 | 4909.32 |
| 41 | 419.12 | 101 | 1019.20 | 161 | 1619.28 | 221 | 2219.36 | 281 | 2819.44 | 341 | 3419.00 | 391 | 3919.24 | 441 | 4419.48 | 491 | 4919.20 |
| 42 | 429.00 | 102 | 1029.08 | 162 | 1629.16 | 222 | 2229.24 | 282 | 2829.32 | 342 | 3429.40 | 392 | 3929.12 | 442 | 4429.36 | 492 | 4929.08 |
| 43 | 439.40 | 103 | 1039.48 | 163 | 1639.04 | 223 | 2239.12 | 283 | 2839.20 | 343 | 3439.28 | 393 | 3939.00 | 443 | 4439.24 | 493 | 4939.48 |
| 44 | 449.28 | 104 | 1049.36 | 164 | 1649.44 | 224 | 2249.00 | 284 | 2849.08 | 344 | 3449.16 | 394 | 3949.40 | 444 | 4449.12 | 494 | 4949.36 |
| 45 | 459.16 | 105 | 1059.24 | 165 | 1659.32 | 225 | 2259.40 | 285 | 2859.48 | 345 | 3459.04 | 395 | 3959.28 | 445 | 4459.00 | 495 | 4959.24 |
| 46 | 469.04 | 106 | 1069.12 | 166 | 1669.20 | 226 | 2269.28 | 286 | 2869.36 | 346 | 3469.44 | 396 | 3969.16 | 446 | 4469.40 | 496 | 4969.12 |
| 47 | 479.44 | 107 | 1079.00 | 167 | 1679.08 | 227 | 2279.16 | 287 | 2879.24 | 347 | 3479.32 | 397 | 3979.04 | 447 | 4479.28 | 497 | 4979.00 |
| 48 | 489.32 | 108 | 1089.40 | 168 | 1689.48 | 228 | 2289.04 | 288 | 2889.12 | 348 | 3489.20 | 398 | 3989.44 | 448 | 4489.16 | 498 | 4989.40 |
| 49 | 499.20 | 109 | 1099.28 | 169 | 1699.36 | 229 | 2299.44 | 289 | 2899.00 | 349 | 3499.08 | 399 | 3999.32 | 449 | 4499.04 | 499 | 4999.28 |
| 50 | 509.08 | 110 | 1109.16 | 170 | 1709.24 | 230 | 2309.32 | 290 | 2909.40 | 350 | 3509.48 | 400 | 4009.20 | 450 | 4509.44 | 500 | 5009.16 |
| 51 | 519.48 | 111 | 1119.04 | 171 | 1719.12 | 231 | 2319.20 | 291 | 2919.28 | | | | | | | | |
| 52 | 529.36 | 112 | 1129.44 | 172 | 1729.00 | 232 | 2329.08 | 292 | 2929.16 | | | | | | | | |
| 53 | 539.24 | 113 | 1139.32 | 173 | 1739.40 | 233 | 2339.48 | 293 | 2939.04 | | | | | | | | |
| 54 | 549.12 | 114 | 1149.20 | 174 | 1749.28 | 234 | 2349.36 | 294 | 2949.44 | | | | | | | | |
| 55 | 559.00 | 115 | 1159.08 | 175 | 1759.16 | 235 | 2359.24 | 295 | 2959.32 | | | | | | | | |
| 56 | 569.40 | 116 | 1169.48 | 176 | 1769.04 | 236 | 2369.12 | 296 | 2969.20 | | | | | | | | |
| 57 | 579.28 | 117 | 1179.36 | 177 | 1779.44 | 237 | 2379.00 | 297 | 2979.08 | | | | | | | | |
| 58 | 589.16 | 118 | 1189.24 | 178 | 1789.32 | 238 | 2389.40 | 298 | 2989.48 | | | | | | | | |
| 59 | 599.04 | 119 | 1199.12 | 179 | 1799.20 | 239 | 2399.28 | 299 | 2999.36 | | | | | | | | |
| 60 | 609.44 | 120 | 1209.00 | 180 | 1809.08 | 240 | 2409.16 | 300 | 3009.24 | | | | | | | | |

**Code more than 500**

1 Where the code is in the range **501** to **1000** inclusive:

  a. Subtract **500** from the code and use the balance of the code to obtain a pay adjustment figure from the table above.

  b. Add this pay adjustment figure to the figure given in the box alongside to obtain the figure of total pay adjustment to date *   **5000.32**

2 Where the code **exceeds 1000** follow the instructions on **page 3**.

**Weekly, fortnightly or four-weekly pay day on 5 April or, in a leap year, on 4 or 5 April.**

If there are 53 weekly, 27 fortnightly or 14 four-weekly pay
days because the last pay day in the year falls on 5 April
or in a leap year, on 4 or 5 April, follow the appropriate
instructions in the Employer Further Guide to PAYE and NICs
(help book CWG2) – available on line at **www.gov.uk**

56

# Tables A - Pay Adjustment Tables

Apr 6 to May 5 **Month 1**

| Code | Total pay adjustment to date | Code | Total pay adjustment to date | Code | Total pay adjustment to date | Code | Total pay adjustment to date | Code | Total pay adjustment to date | Code | Total pay adjustment to date | Code | Total pay adjustment to date | Code | Total pay adjustment to date | Code | Total pay adjustment to date |
|---|---|---|---|---|---|---|---|---|---|---|---|---|---|---|---|---|---|
| | £ | | £ | | £ | | £ | | £ | | £ | | £ | | £ | | £ |
| 0 | NIL | | | | | | | | | | | | | | | | |
| 1 | 1.59 | 61 | 51.59 | 121 | 101.59 | 181 | 151.59 | 241 | 201.59 | 301 | 251.59 | 351 | 293.25 | 401 | 334.92 | 451 | 376.59 |
| 2 | 2.42 | 62 | 52.42 | 122 | 102.42 | 182 | 152.42 | 242 | 202.42 | 302 | 252.42 | 352 | 294.09 | 402 | 335.75 | 452 | 377.42 |
| 3 | 3.25 | 63 | 53.25 | 123 | 103.25 | 183 | 153.25 | 243 | 203.25 | 303 | 253.25 | 353 | 294.92 | 403 | 336.59 | 453 | 378.25 |
| 4 | 4.09 | 64 | 54.09 | 124 | 104.09 | 184 | 154.09 | 244 | 204.09 | 304 | 254.09 | 354 | 295.75 | 404 | 337.42 | 454 | 379.09 |
| 5 | 4.92 | 65 | 54.92 | 125 | 104.92 | 185 | 154.92 | 245 | 204.92 | 305 | 254.92 | 355 | 296.59 | 405 | 338.25 | 455 | 379.92 |
| 6 | 5.75 | 66 | 55.75 | 126 | 105.75 | 186 | 155.75 | 246 | 205.75 | 306 | 255.75 | 356 | 297.42 | 406 | 339.09 | 456 | 380.75 |
| 7 | 6.59 | 67 | 56.59 | 127 | 106.59 | 187 | 156.59 | 247 | 206.59 | 307 | 256.59 | 357 | 298.25 | 407 | 339.92 | 457 | 381.59 |
| 8 | 7.42 | 68 | 57.42 | 128 | 107.42 | 188 | 157.42 | 248 | 207.42 | 308 | 257.42 | 358 | 299.09 | 408 | 340.75 | 458 | 382.42 |
| 9 | 8.25 | 69 | 58.25 | 129 | 108.25 | 189 | 158.25 | 249 | 208.25 | 309 | 258.25 | 359 | 299.92 | 409 | 341.59 | 459 | 383.25 |
| 10 | 9.09 | 70 | 59.09 | 130 | 109.09 | 190 | 159.09 | 250 | 209.09 | 310 | 259.09 | 360 | 300.75 | 410 | 342.42 | 460 | 384.09 |
| 11 | 9.92 | 71 | 59.92 | 131 | 109.92 | 191 | 159.92 | 251 | 209.92 | 311 | 259.92 | 361 | 301.59 | 411 | 343.25 | 461 | 384.92 |
| 12 | 10.75 | 72 | 60.75 | 132 | 110.75 | 192 | 160.75 | 252 | 210.75 | 312 | 260.75 | 362 | 302.42 | 412 | 344.09 | 462 | 385.75 |
| 13 | 11.59 | 73 | 61.59 | 133 | 111.59 | 193 | 161.59 | 253 | 211.59 | 313 | 261.59 | 363 | 303.25 | 413 | 344.92 | 463 | 386.59 |
| 14 | 12.42 | 74 | 62.42 | 134 | 112.42 | 194 | 162.42 | 254 | 212.42 | 314 | 262.42 | 364 | 304.09 | 414 | 345.75 | 464 | 387.42 |
| 15 | 13.25 | 75 | 63.25 | 135 | 113.25 | 195 | 163.25 | 255 | 213.25 | 315 | 263.25 | 365 | 304.92 | 415 | 346.59 | 465 | 388.25 |
| 16 | 14.09 | 76 | 64.09 | 136 | 114.09 | 196 | 164.09 | 256 | 214.09 | 316 | 264.09 | 366 | 305.75 | 416 | 347.42 | 466 | 389.09 |
| 17 | 14.92 | 77 | 64.92 | 137 | 114.92 | 197 | 164.92 | 257 | 214.92 | 317 | 264.92 | 367 | 306.59 | 417 | 348.25 | 467 | 389.92 |
| 18 | 15.75 | 78 | 65.75 | 138 | 115.75 | 198 | 165.75 | 258 | 215.75 | 318 | 265.75 | 368 | 307.42 | 418 | 349.09 | 468 | 390.75 |
| 19 | 16.59 | 79 | 66.59 | 139 | 116.59 | 199 | 166.59 | 259 | 216.59 | 319 | 266.59 | 369 | 308.25 | 419 | 349.92 | 469 | 391.59 |
| 20 | 17.42 | 80 | 67.42 | 140 | 117.42 | 200 | 167.42 | 260 | 217.42 | 320 | 267.42 | 370 | 309.09 | 420 | 350.75 | 470 | 392.42 |
| 21 | 18.25 | 81 | 68.25 | 141 | 118.25 | 201 | 168.25 | 261 | 218.25 | 321 | 268.25 | 371 | 309.92 | 421 | 351.59 | 471 | 393.25 |
| 22 | 19.09 | 82 | 69.09 | 142 | 119.09 | 202 | 169.09 | 262 | 219.09 | 322 | 269.09 | 372 | 310.75 | 422 | 352.42 | 472 | 394.09 |
| 23 | 19.92 | 83 | 69.92 | 143 | 119.92 | 203 | 169.92 | 263 | 219.92 | 323 | 269.92 | 373 | 311.59 | 423 | 353.25 | 473 | 394.92 |
| 24 | 20.75 | 84 | 70.75 | 144 | 120.75 | 204 | 170.75 | 264 | 220.75 | 324 | 270.75 | 374 | 312.42 | 424 | 354.09 | 474 | 395.75 |
| 25 | 21.59 | 85 | 71.59 | 145 | 121.59 | 205 | 171.59 | 265 | 221.59 | 325 | 271.59 | 375 | 313.25 | 425 | 354.92 | 475 | 396.59 |
| 26 | 22.42 | 86 | 72.42 | 146 | 122.42 | 206 | 172.42 | 266 | 222.42 | 326 | 272.42 | 376 | 314.09 | 426 | 355.75 | 476 | 397.42 |
| 27 | 23.25 | 87 | 73.25 | 147 | 123.25 | 207 | 173.25 | 267 | 223.25 | 327 | 273.25 | 377 | 314.92 | 427 | 356.59 | 477 | 398.25 |
| 28 | 24.09 | 88 | 74.09 | 148 | 124.09 | 208 | 174.09 | 268 | 224.09 | 328 | 274.09 | 378 | 315.75 | 428 | 357.42 | 478 | 399.09 |
| 29 | 24.92 | 89 | 74.92 | 149 | 124.92 | 209 | 174.92 | 269 | 224.92 | 329 | 274.92 | 379 | 316.59 | 429 | 358.25 | 479 | 399.92 |
| 30 | 25.75 | 90 | 75.75 | 150 | 125.75 | 210 | 175.75 | 270 | 225.75 | 330 | 275.75 | 380 | 317.42 | 430 | 359.09 | 480 | 400.75 |
| 31 | 26.59 | 91 | 76.59 | 151 | 126.59 | 211 | 176.59 | 271 | 226.59 | 331 | 276.59 | 381 | 318.25 | 431 | 359.92 | 481 | 401.59 |
| 32 | 27.42 | 92 | 77.42 | 152 | 127.42 | 212 | 177.42 | 272 | 227.42 | 332 | 277.42 | 382 | 319.09 | 432 | 360.75 | 482 | 402.42 |
| 33 | 28.25 | 93 | 78.25 | 153 | 128.25 | 213 | 178.25 | 273 | 228.25 | 333 | 278.25 | 383 | 319.92 | 433 | 361.59 | 483 | 403.25 |
| 34 | 29.09 | 94 | 79.09 | 154 | 129.09 | 214 | 179.09 | 274 | 229.09 | 334 | 279.09 | 384 | 320.75 | 434 | 362.42 | 484 | 404.09 |
| 35 | 29.92 | 95 | 79.92 | 155 | 129.92 | 215 | 179.92 | 275 | 229.92 | 335 | 279.92 | 385 | 321.59 | 435 | 363.25 | 485 | 404.92 |
| 36 | 30.75 | 96 | 80.75 | 156 | 130.75 | 216 | 180.75 | 276 | 230.75 | 336 | 280.75 | 386 | 322.42 | 436 | 364.09 | 486 | 405.75 |
| 37 | 31.59 | 97 | 81.59 | 157 | 131.59 | 217 | 181.59 | 277 | 231.59 | 337 | 281.59 | 387 | 323.25 | 437 | 364.92 | 487 | 406.59 |
| 38 | 32.42 | 98 | 82.42 | 158 | 132.42 | 218 | 182.42 | 278 | 232.42 | 338 | 282.42 | 388 | 324.09 | 438 | 365.75 | 488 | 407.42 |
| 39 | 33.25 | 99 | 83.25 | 159 | 133.25 | 219 | 183.25 | 279 | 233.25 | 339 | 283.25 | 389 | 324.92 | 439 | 366.59 | 489 | 408.25 |
| 40 | 34.09 | 100 | 84.09 | 160 | 134.09 | 220 | 184.09 | 280 | 234.09 | 340 | 284.09 | 390 | 325.75 | 440 | 367.42 | 490 | 409.09 |
| 41 | 34.92 | 101 | 84.92 | 161 | 134.92 | 221 | 184.92 | 281 | 234.92 | 341 | 284.92 | 391 | 326.59 | 441 | 368.25 | 491 | 409.92 |
| 42 | 35.75 | 102 | 85.75 | 162 | 135.75 | 222 | 185.75 | 282 | 235.75 | 342 | 285.75 | 392 | 327.42 | 442 | 369.09 | 492 | 410.75 |
| 43 | 36.59 | 103 | 86.59 | 163 | 136.59 | 223 | 186.59 | 283 | 236.59 | 343 | 286.59 | 393 | 328.25 | 443 | 369.92 | 493 | 411.59 |
| 44 | 37.42 | 104 | 87.42 | 164 | 137.42 | 224 | 187.42 | 284 | 237.42 | 344 | 287.42 | 394 | 329.09 | 444 | 370.75 | 494 | 412.42 |
| 45 | 38.25 | 105 | 88.25 | 165 | 138.25 | 225 | 188.25 | 285 | 238.25 | 345 | 288.25 | 395 | 329.92 | 445 | 371.59 | 495 | 413.25 |
| 46 | 39.09 | 106 | 89.09 | 166 | 139.09 | 226 | 189.09 | 286 | 239.09 | 346 | 289.09 | 396 | 330.75 | 446 | 372.42 | 496 | 414.09 |
| 47 | 39.92 | 107 | 89.92 | 167 | 139.92 | 227 | 189.92 | 287 | 239.92 | 347 | 289.92 | 397 | 331.59 | 447 | 373.25 | 497 | 414.92 |
| 48 | 40.75 | 108 | 90.75 | 168 | 140.75 | 228 | 190.75 | 288 | 240.75 | 348 | 290.75 | 398 | 332.42 | 448 | 374.09 | 498 | 415.75 |
| 49 | 41.59 | 109 | 91.59 | 169 | 141.59 | 229 | 191.59 | 289 | 241.59 | 349 | 291.59 | 399 | 333.25 | 449 | 374.92 | 499 | 416.59 |
| 50 | 42.42 | 110 | 92.42 | 170 | 142.42 | 230 | 192.42 | 290 | 242.42 | 350 | 292.42 | 400 | 334.09 | 450 | 375.75 | 500 | 417.42 |
| 51 | 43.25 | 111 | 93.25 | 171 | 143.25 | 231 | 193.25 | 291 | 243.25 | | | | | | |
| 52 | 44.09 | 112 | 94.09 | 172 | 144.09 | 232 | 194.09 | 292 | 244.09 | | | | | | |
| 53 | 44.92 | 113 | 94.92 | 173 | 144.92 | 233 | 194.92 | 293 | 244.92 | | | | | | |
| 54 | 45.75 | 114 | 95.75 | 174 | 145.75 | 234 | 195.75 | 294 | 245.75 | | | | | | |
| 55 | 46.59 | 115 | 96.59 | 175 | 146.59 | 235 | 196.59 | 295 | 246.59 | | | | | | |
| 56 | 47.42 | 116 | 97.42 | 176 | 147.42 | 236 | 197.42 | 296 | 247.42 | | | | | | |
| 57 | 48.25 | 117 | 98.25 | 177 | 148.25 | 237 | 198.25 | 297 | 248.25 | | | | | | |
| 58 | 49.09 | 118 | 99.09 | 178 | 149.09 | 238 | 199.09 | 298 | 249.09 | | | | | | |
| 59 | 49.92 | 119 | 99.92 | 179 | 149.92 | 239 | 199.92 | 299 | 249.92 | | | | | | |
| 60 | 50.75 | 120 | 100.75 | 180 | 150.75 | 240 | 200.75 | 300 | 250.75 | | | | | | |

**Code more than 500**

1. Where the code is in the range **501** to **1000** inclusive:

   a. Subtract **500** from the code and use the balance of the code to obtain a pay adjustment figure from the table above.

   b. Add this pay adjustment figure to the figure given in the box alongside to obtain the figure of total pay adjustment to date * **416.67**

2. Where the code **exceeds 1000** follow the instructions on **page 3**.

**Month 2**  May 6 to Jun 5 | **Tables A** - Pay Adjustment Tables

| Code | Total pay adjustment to date | Code | Total pay adjustment to date | Code | Total pay adjustment to date | Code | Total pay adjustment to date | Code | Total pay adjustment to date | Code | Total pay adjustment to date | Code | Total pay adjustment to date | Code | Total pay adjustment to date | Code | Total pay adjustment to date |
|---|---|---|---|---|---|---|---|---|---|---|---|---|---|---|---|---|---|
| | £ | | £ | | £ | | £ | | £ | | £ | | £ | | £ | | £ |
| 0 | NIL | | | | | | | | | | | | | | | | |
| 1 | 3.18 | 61 | 103.18 | 121 | 203.18 | 181 | 303.18 | 241 | 403.18 | 301 | 503.18 | 351 | 586.50 | 401 | 669.84 | 451 | 753.18 |
| 2 | 4.84 | 62 | 104.84 | 122 | 204.84 | 182 | 304.84 | 242 | 404.84 | 302 | 504.84 | 352 | 588.18 | 402 | 671.50 | 452 | 754.84 |
| 3 | 6.50 | 63 | 106.50 | 123 | 206.50 | 183 | 306.50 | 243 | 406.50 | 303 | 506.50 | 353 | 589.84 | 403 | 673.18 | 453 | 756.50 |
| 4 | 8.18 | 64 | 108.18 | 124 | 208.18 | 184 | 308.18 | 244 | 408.18 | 304 | 508.18 | 354 | 591.50 | 404 | 674.84 | 454 | 758.18 |
| 5 | 9.84 | 65 | 109.84 | 125 | 209.84 | 185 | 309.84 | 245 | 409.84 | 305 | 509.84 | 355 | 593.18 | 405 | 676.50 | 455 | 759.84 |
| 6 | 11.50 | 66 | 111.50 | 126 | 211.50 | 186 | 311.50 | 246 | 411.50 | 306 | 511.50 | 356 | 594.84 | 406 | 678.18 | 456 | 761.50 |
| 7 | 13.18 | 67 | 113.18 | 127 | 213.18 | 187 | 313.18 | 247 | 413.18 | 307 | 513.18 | 357 | 596.50 | 407 | 679.84 | 457 | 763.18 |
| 8 | 14.84 | 68 | 114.84 | 128 | 214.84 | 188 | 314.84 | 248 | 414.84 | 308 | 514.84 | 358 | 598.18 | 408 | 681.50 | 458 | 764.84 |
| 9 | 16.50 | 69 | 116.50 | 129 | 216.50 | 189 | 316.50 | 249 | 416.50 | 309 | 516.50 | 359 | 599.84 | 409 | 683.18 | 459 | 766.50 |
| 10 | 18.18 | 70 | 118.18 | 130 | 218.18 | 190 | 318.18 | 250 | 418.18 | 310 | 518.18 | 360 | 601.50 | 410 | 684.84 | 460 | 768.18 |
| 11 | 19.84 | 71 | 119.84 | 131 | 219.84 | 191 | 319.84 | 251 | 419.84 | 311 | 519.84 | 361 | 603.18 | 411 | 686.50 | 461 | 769.84 |
| 12 | 21.50 | 72 | 121.50 | 132 | 221.50 | 192 | 321.50 | 252 | 421.50 | 312 | 521.50 | 362 | 604.84 | 412 | 688.18 | 462 | 771.50 |
| 13 | 23.18 | 73 | 123.18 | 133 | 223.18 | 193 | 323.18 | 253 | 423.18 | 313 | 523.18 | 363 | 606.50 | 413 | 689.84 | 463 | 773.18 |
| 14 | 24.84 | 74 | 124.84 | 134 | 224.84 | 194 | 324.84 | 254 | 424.84 | 314 | 524.84 | 364 | 608.18 | 414 | 691.50 | 464 | 774.84 |
| 15 | 26.50 | 75 | 126.50 | 135 | 226.50 | 195 | 326.50 | 255 | 426.50 | 315 | 526.50 | 365 | 609.84 | 415 | 693.18 | 465 | 776.50 |
| 16 | 28.18 | 76 | 128.18 | 136 | 228.18 | 196 | 328.18 | 256 | 428.18 | 316 | 528.18 | 366 | 611.50 | 416 | 694.84 | 466 | 778.18 |
| 17 | 29.84 | 77 | 129.84 | 137 | 229.84 | 197 | 329.84 | 257 | 429.84 | 317 | 529.84 | 367 | 613.18 | 417 | 696.50 | 467 | 779.84 |
| 18 | 31.50 | 78 | 131.50 | 138 | 231.50 | 198 | 331.50 | 258 | 431.50 | 318 | 531.50 | 368 | 614.84 | 418 | 698.18 | 468 | 781.50 |
| 19 | 33.18 | 79 | 133.18 | 139 | 233.18 | 199 | 333.18 | 259 | 433.18 | 319 | 533.18 | 369 | 616.50 | 419 | 699.84 | 469 | 783.18 |
| 20 | 34.84 | 80 | 134.84 | 140 | 234.84 | 200 | 334.84 | 260 | 434.84 | 320 | 534.84 | 370 | 618.18 | 420 | 701.50 | 470 | 784.84 |
| 21 | 36.50 | 81 | 136.50 | 141 | 236.50 | 201 | 336.50 | 261 | 436.50 | 321 | 536.50 | 371 | 619.84 | 421 | 703.18 | 471 | 786.50 |
| 22 | 38.18 | 82 | 138.18 | 142 | 238.18 | 202 | 338.18 | 262 | 438.18 | 322 | 538.18 | 372 | 621.50 | 422 | 704.84 | 472 | 788.18 |
| 23 | 39.84 | 83 | 139.84 | 143 | 239.84 | 203 | 339.84 | 263 | 439.84 | 323 | 539.84 | 373 | 623.18 | 423 | 706.50 | 473 | 789.84 |
| 24 | 41.50 | 84 | 141.50 | 144 | 241.50 | 204 | 341.50 | 264 | 441.50 | 324 | 541.50 | 374 | 624.84 | 424 | 708.18 | 474 | 791.50 |
| 25 | 43.18 | 85 | 143.18 | 145 | 243.18 | 205 | 343.18 | 265 | 443.18 | 325 | 543.18 | 375 | 626.50 | 425 | 709.84 | 475 | 793.18 |
| 26 | 44.84 | 86 | 144.84 | 146 | 244.84 | 206 | 344.84 | 266 | 444.84 | 326 | 544.84 | 376 | 628.18 | 426 | 711.50 | 476 | 794.84 |
| 27 | 46.50 | 87 | 146.50 | 147 | 246.50 | 207 | 346.50 | 267 | 446.50 | 327 | 546.50 | 377 | 629.84 | 427 | 713.18 | 477 | 796.50 |
| 28 | 48.18 | 88 | 148.18 | 148 | 248.18 | 208 | 348.18 | 268 | 448.18 | 328 | 548.18 | 378 | 631.50 | 428 | 714.84 | 478 | 798.18 |
| 29 | 49.84 | 89 | 149.84 | 149 | 249.84 | 209 | 349.84 | 269 | 449.84 | 329 | 549.84 | 379 | 633.18 | 429 | 716.50 | 479 | 799.84 |
| 30 | 51.50 | 90 | 151.50 | 150 | 251.50 | 210 | 351.50 | 270 | 451.50 | 330 | 551.50 | 380 | 634.84 | 430 | 718.18 | 480 | 801.50 |
| 31 | 53.18 | 91 | 153.18 | 151 | 253.18 | 211 | 353.18 | 271 | 453.18 | 331 | 553.18 | 381 | 636.50 | 431 | 719.84 | 481 | 803.18 |
| 32 | 54.84 | 92 | 154.84 | 152 | 254.84 | 212 | 354.84 | 272 | 454.84 | 332 | 554.84 | 382 | 638.18 | 432 | 721.50 | 482 | 804.84 |
| 33 | 56.50 | 93 | 156.50 | 153 | 256.50 | 213 | 356.50 | 273 | 456.50 | 333 | 556.50 | 383 | 639.84 | 433 | 723.18 | 483 | 806.50 |
| 34 | 58.18 | 94 | 158.18 | 154 | 258.18 | 214 | 358.18 | 274 | 458.18 | 334 | 558.18 | 384 | 641.50 | 434 | 724.84 | 484 | 808.18 |
| 35 | 59.84 | 95 | 159.84 | 155 | 259.84 | 215 | 359.84 | 275 | 459.84 | 335 | 559.84 | 385 | 643.18 | 435 | 726.50 | 485 | 809.84 |
| 36 | 61.50 | 96 | 161.50 | 156 | 261.50 | 216 | 361.50 | 276 | 461.50 | 336 | 561.50 | 386 | 644.84 | 436 | 728.18 | 486 | 811.50 |
| 37 | 63.18 | 97 | 163.18 | 157 | 263.18 | 217 | 363.18 | 277 | 463.18 | 337 | 563.18 | 387 | 646.50 | 437 | 729.84 | 487 | 813.18 |
| 38 | 64.84 | 98 | 164.84 | 158 | 264.84 | 218 | 364.84 | 278 | 464.84 | 338 | 564.84 | 388 | 648.18 | 438 | 731.50 | 488 | 814.84 |
| 39 | 66.50 | 99 | 166.50 | 159 | 266.50 | 219 | 366.50 | 279 | 466.50 | 339 | 566.50 | 389 | 649.84 | 439 | 733.18 | 489 | 816.50 |
| 40 | 68.18 | 100 | 168.18 | 160 | 268.18 | 220 | 368.18 | 280 | 468.18 | 340 | 568.18 | 390 | 651.50 | 440 | 734.84 | 490 | 818.18 |
| 41 | 69.84 | 101 | 169.84 | 161 | 269.84 | 221 | 369.84 | 281 | 469.84 | 341 | 569.84 | 391 | 653.18 | 441 | 736.50 | 491 | 819.84 |
| 42 | 71.50 | 102 | 171.50 | 162 | 271.50 | 222 | 371.50 | 282 | 471.50 | 342 | 571.50 | 392 | 654.84 | 442 | 738.18 | 492 | 821.50 |
| 43 | 73.18 | 103 | 173.18 | 163 | 273.18 | 223 | 373.18 | 283 | 473.18 | 343 | 573.18 | 393 | 656.50 | 443 | 739.84 | 493 | 823.18 |
| 44 | 74.84 | 104 | 174.84 | 164 | 274.84 | 224 | 374.84 | 284 | 474.84 | 344 | 574.84 | 394 | 658.18 | 444 | 741.50 | 494 | 824.84 |
| 45 | 76.50 | 105 | 176.50 | 165 | 276.50 | 225 | 376.50 | 285 | 476.50 | 345 | 576.50 | 395 | 659.84 | 445 | 743.18 | 495 | 826.50 |
| 46 | 78.18 | 106 | 178.18 | 166 | 278.18 | 226 | 378.18 | 286 | 478.18 | 346 | 578.18 | 396 | 661.50 | 446 | 744.84 | 496 | 828.18 |
| 47 | 79.84 | 107 | 179.84 | 167 | 279.84 | 227 | 379.84 | 287 | 479.84 | 347 | 579.84 | 397 | 663.18 | 447 | 746.50 | 497 | 829.84 |
| 48 | 81.50 | 108 | 181.50 | 168 | 281.50 | 228 | 381.50 | 288 | 481.50 | 348 | 581.50 | 398 | 664.84 | 448 | 748.18 | 498 | 831.50 |
| 49 | 83.18 | 109 | 183.18 | 169 | 283.18 | 229 | 383.18 | 289 | 483.18 | 349 | 583.18 | 399 | 666.50 | 449 | 749.84 | 499 | 833.18 |
| 50 | 84.84 | 110 | 184.84 | 170 | 284.84 | 230 | 384.84 | 290 | 484.84 | 350 | 584.84 | 400 | 668.18 | 450 | 751.50 | 500 | 834.84 |
| 51 | 86.50 | 111 | 186.50 | 171 | 286.50 | 231 | 386.50 | 291 | 486.50 | | | | | | |
| 52 | 88.18 | 112 | 188.18 | 172 | 288.18 | 232 | 388.18 | 292 | 488.18 | | | | | | |
| 53 | 89.84 | 113 | 189.84 | 173 | 289.84 | 233 | 389.84 | 293 | 489.84 | | | | | | |
| 54 | 91.50 | 114 | 191.50 | 174 | 291.50 | 234 | 391.50 | 294 | 491.50 | | | | | | |
| 55 | 93.18 | 115 | 193.18 | 175 | 293.18 | 235 | 393.18 | 295 | 493.18 | | | | | | |
| 56 | 94.84 | 116 | 194.84 | 176 | 294.84 | 236 | 394.84 | 296 | 494.84 | | | | | | |
| 57 | 96.50 | 117 | 196.50 | 177 | 296.50 | 237 | 396.50 | 297 | 496.50 | | | | | | |
| 58 | 98.18 | 118 | 198.18 | 178 | 298.18 | 238 | 398.18 | 298 | 498.18 | | | | | | |
| 59 | 99.84 | 119 | 199.84 | 179 | 299.84 | 239 | 399.84 | 299 | 499.84 | | | | | | |
| 60 | 101.50 | 120 | 201.50 | 180 | 301.50 | 240 | 401.50 | 300 | 501.50 | | | | | | |

**Code more than 500**

1 Where the code is in the range 501 to 1000 inclusive:

a. Subtract **500** from the code and use the balance of the code to obtain a pay adjustment figure from the table above.

b. Add this pay adjustment figure to the figure given in the box alongside to obtain the figure of total pay adjustment to date * | **833.34**

2 Where the code **exceeds 1000** follow the instructions on **page 3.**

**Tables A** - Pay Adjustment Tables  Jun 6 to Jul 5  **Month 3**

| Code | Total pay adjustment to date | Code | Total pay adjustment to date | Code | Total pay adjustment to date | Code | Total pay adjustment to date | Code | Total pay adjustment to date | Code | Total pay adjustment to date | Code | Total pay adjustment to date | Code | Total pay adjustment to date | Code | Total pay adjustment to date |
|---|---|---|---|---|---|---|---|---|---|---|---|---|---|---|---|---|---|
| | £ | | £ | | £ | | £ | | £ | | £ | | £ | | £ | | £ |
| 0 | NIL | | | | | | | | | | | | | | | | |
| 1 | 4.77 | 61 | 154.77 | 121 | 304.77 | 181 | 454.77 | 241 | 604.77 | 301 | 754.77 | 351 | 879.75 | 401 | 1004.76 | 451 | 1129.77 |
| 2 | 7.26 | 62 | 157.26 | 122 | 307.26 | 182 | 457.26 | 242 | 607.26 | 302 | 757.26 | 352 | 882.27 | 402 | 1007.25 | 452 | 1132.26 |
| 3 | 9.75 | 63 | 159.75 | 123 | 309.75 | 183 | 459.75 | 243 | 609.75 | 303 | 759.75 | 353 | 884.76 | 403 | 1009.77 | 453 | 1134.75 |
| 4 | 12.27 | 64 | 162.27 | 124 | 312.27 | 184 | 462.27 | 244 | 612.27 | 304 | 762.27 | 354 | 887.25 | 404 | 1012.26 | 454 | 1137.27 |
| 5 | 14.76 | 65 | 164.76 | 125 | 314.76 | 185 | 464.76 | 245 | 614.76 | 305 | 764.76 | 355 | 889.77 | 405 | 1014.75 | 455 | 1139.76 |
| 6 | 17.25 | 66 | 167.25 | 126 | 317.25 | 186 | 467.25 | 246 | 617.25 | 306 | 767.25 | 356 | 892.26 | 406 | 1017.27 | 456 | 1142.25 |
| 7 | 19.77 | 67 | 169.77 | 127 | 319.77 | 187 | 469.77 | 247 | 619.77 | 307 | 769.77 | 357 | 894.75 | 407 | 1019.76 | 457 | 1144.77 |
| 8 | 22.26 | 68 | 172.26 | 128 | 322.26 | 188 | 472.26 | 248 | 622.26 | 308 | 772.26 | 358 | 897.27 | 408 | 1022.25 | 458 | 1147.26 |
| 9 | 24.75 | 69 | 174.75 | 129 | 324.75 | 189 | 474.75 | 249 | 624.75 | 309 | 774.75 | 359 | 899.76 | 409 | 1024.77 | 459 | 1149.75 |
| 10 | 27.27 | 70 | 177.27 | 130 | 327.27 | 190 | 477.27 | 250 | 627.27 | 310 | 777.27 | 360 | 902.25 | 410 | 1027.26 | 460 | 1152.27 |
| 11 | 29.76 | 71 | 179.76 | 131 | 329.76 | 191 | 479.76 | 251 | 629.76 | 311 | 779.76 | 361 | 904.77 | 411 | 1029.75 | 461 | 1154.76 |
| 12 | 32.25 | 72 | 182.25 | 132 | 332.25 | 192 | 482.25 | 252 | 632.25 | 312 | 782.25 | 362 | 907.26 | 412 | 1032.27 | 462 | 1157.25 |
| 13 | 34.77 | 73 | 184.77 | 133 | 334.77 | 193 | 484.77 | 253 | 634.77 | 313 | 784.77 | 363 | 909.75 | 413 | 1034.76 | 463 | 1159.77 |
| 14 | 37.26 | 74 | 187.26 | 134 | 337.26 | 194 | 487.26 | 254 | 637.26 | 314 | 787.26 | 364 | 912.27 | 414 | 1037.25 | 464 | 1162.26 |
| 15 | 39.75 | 75 | 189.75 | 135 | 339.75 | 195 | 489.75 | 255 | 639.75 | 315 | 789.75 | 365 | 914.76 | 415 | 1039.77 | 465 | 1164.75 |
| 16 | 42.27 | 76 | 192.27 | 136 | 342.27 | 196 | 492.27 | 256 | 642.27 | 316 | 792.27 | 366 | 917.25 | 416 | 1042.26 | 466 | 1167.27 |
| 17 | 44.76 | 77 | 194.76 | 137 | 344.76 | 197 | 494.76 | 257 | 644.76 | 317 | 794.76 | 367 | 919.77 | 417 | 1044.75 | 467 | 1169.76 |
| 18 | 47.25 | 78 | 197.25 | 138 | 347.25 | 198 | 497.25 | 258 | 647.25 | 318 | 797.25 | 368 | 922.26 | 418 | 1047.27 | 468 | 1172.25 |
| 19 | 49.77 | 79 | 199.77 | 139 | 349.77 | 199 | 499.77 | 259 | 649.77 | 319 | 799.77 | 369 | 924.75 | 419 | 1049.76 | 469 | 1174.77 |
| 20 | 52.26 | 80 | 202.26 | 140 | 352.26 | 200 | 502.26 | 260 | 652.26 | 320 | 802.26 | 370 | 927.27 | 420 | 1052.25 | 470 | 1177.26 |
| 21 | 54.75 | 81 | 204.75 | 141 | 354.75 | 201 | 504.75 | 261 | 654.75 | 321 | 804.75 | 371 | 929.76 | 421 | 1054.77 | 471 | 1179.75 |
| 22 | 57.27 | 82 | 207.27 | 142 | 357.27 | 202 | 507.27 | 262 | 657.27 | 322 | 807.27 | 372 | 932.25 | 422 | 1057.26 | 472 | 1182.27 |
| 23 | 59.76 | 83 | 209.76 | 143 | 359.76 | 203 | 509.76 | 263 | 659.76 | 323 | 809.76 | 373 | 934.77 | 423 | 1059.75 | 473 | 1184.76 |
| 24 | 62.25 | 84 | 212.25 | 144 | 362.25 | 204 | 512.25 | 264 | 662.25 | 324 | 812.25 | 374 | 937.26 | 424 | 1062.27 | 474 | 1187.25 |
| 25 | 64.77 | 85 | 214.77 | 145 | 364.77 | 205 | 514.77 | 265 | 664.77 | 325 | 814.77 | 375 | 939.75 | 425 | 1064.76 | 475 | 1189.77 |
| 26 | 67.26 | 86 | 217.26 | 146 | 367.26 | 206 | 517.26 | 266 | 667.26 | 326 | 817.26 | 376 | 942.27 | 426 | 1067.25 | 476 | 1192.26 |
| 27 | 69.75 | 87 | 219.75 | 147 | 369.75 | 207 | 519.75 | 267 | 669.75 | 327 | 819.75 | 377 | 944.76 | 427 | 1069.77 | 477 | 1194.75 |
| 28 | 72.27 | 88 | 222.27 | 148 | 372.27 | 208 | 522.27 | 268 | 672.27 | 328 | 822.27 | 378 | 947.25 | 428 | 1072.26 | 478 | 1197.27 |
| 29 | 74.76 | 89 | 224.76 | 149 | 374.76 | 209 | 524.76 | 269 | 674.76 | 329 | 824.76 | 379 | 949.77 | 429 | 1074.75 | 479 | 1199.76 |
| 30 | 77.25 | 90 | 227.25 | 150 | 377.25 | 210 | 527.25 | 270 | 677.25 | 330 | 827.25 | 380 | 952.26 | 430 | 1077.27 | 480 | 1202.25 |
| 31 | 79.77 | 91 | 229.77 | 151 | 379.77 | 211 | 529.77 | 271 | 679.77 | 331 | 829.77 | 381 | 954.75 | 431 | 1079.76 | 481 | 1204.77 |
| 32 | 82.26 | 92 | 232.26 | 152 | 382.26 | 212 | 532.26 | 272 | 682.26 | 332 | 832.26 | 382 | 957.27 | 432 | 1082.25 | 482 | 1207.26 |
| 33 | 84.75 | 93 | 234.75 | 153 | 384.75 | 213 | 534.75 | 273 | 684.75 | 333 | 834.75 | 383 | 959.76 | 433 | 1084.77 | 483 | 1209.75 |
| 34 | 87.27 | 94 | 237.27 | 154 | 387.27 | 214 | 537.27 | 274 | 687.27 | 334 | 837.27 | 384 | 962.25 | 434 | 1087.26 | 484 | 1212.27 |
| 35 | 89.76 | 95 | 239.76 | 155 | 389.76 | 215 | 539.76 | 275 | 689.76 | 335 | 839.76 | 385 | 964.77 | 435 | 1089.75 | 485 | 1214.76 |
| 36 | 92.25 | 96 | 242.25 | 156 | 392.25 | 216 | 542.25 | 276 | 692.25 | 336 | 842.25 | 386 | 967.26 | 436 | 1092.27 | 486 | 1217.25 |
| 37 | 94.77 | 97 | 244.77 | 157 | 394.77 | 217 | 544.77 | 277 | 694.77 | 337 | 844.77 | 387 | 969.75 | 437 | 1094.76 | 487 | 1219.77 |
| 38 | 97.26 | 98 | 247.26 | 158 | 397.26 | 218 | 547.26 | 278 | 697.26 | 338 | 847.26 | 388 | 972.27 | 438 | 1097.25 | 488 | 1222.26 |
| 39 | 99.75 | 99 | 249.75 | 159 | 399.75 | 219 | 549.75 | 279 | 699.75 | 339 | 849.75 | 389 | 974.76 | 439 | 1099.77 | 489 | 1224.75 |
| 40 | 102.27 | 100 | 252.27 | 160 | 402.27 | 220 | 552.27 | 280 | 702.27 | 340 | 852.27 | 390 | 977.25 | 440 | 1102.26 | 490 | 1227.27 |
| 41 | 104.76 | 101 | 254.76 | 161 | 404.76 | 221 | 554.76 | 281 | 704.76 | 341 | 854.76 | 391 | 979.77 | 441 | 1104.75 | 491 | 1229.76 |
| 42 | 107.25 | 102 | 257.25 | 162 | 407.25 | 222 | 557.25 | 282 | 707.25 | 342 | 857.25 | 392 | 982.26 | 442 | 1107.27 | 492 | 1232.25 |
| 43 | 109.77 | 103 | 259.77 | 163 | 409.77 | 223 | 559.77 | 283 | 709.77 | 343 | 859.77 | 393 | 984.75 | 443 | 1109.76 | 493 | 1234.77 |
| 44 | 112.26 | 104 | 262.26 | 164 | 412.26 | 224 | 562.26 | 284 | 712.26 | 344 | 862.26 | 394 | 987.27 | 444 | 1112.25 | 494 | 1237.26 |
| 45 | 114.75 | 105 | 264.75 | 165 | 414.75 | 225 | 564.75 | 285 | 714.75 | 345 | 864.75 | 395 | 989.76 | 445 | 1114.77 | 495 | 1239.75 |
| 46 | 117.27 | 106 | 267.27 | 166 | 417.27 | 226 | 567.27 | 286 | 717.27 | 346 | 867.27 | 396 | 992.25 | 446 | 1117.26 | 496 | 1242.27 |
| 47 | 119.76 | 107 | 269.76 | 167 | 419.76 | 227 | 569.76 | 287 | 719.76 | 347 | 869.76 | 397 | 994.77 | 447 | 1119.75 | 497 | 1244.76 |
| 48 | 122.25 | 108 | 272.25 | 168 | 422.25 | 228 | 572.25 | 288 | 722.25 | 348 | 872.25 | 398 | 997.26 | 448 | 1122.27 | 498 | 1247.25 |
| 49 | 124.77 | 109 | 274.77 | 169 | 424.77 | 229 | 574.77 | 289 | 724.77 | 349 | 874.77 | 399 | 999.75 | 449 | 1124.76 | 499 | 1249.77 |
| 50 | 127.26 | 110 | 277.26 | 170 | 427.26 | 230 | 577.26 | 290 | 727.26 | 350 | 877.26 | 400 | 1002.27 | 450 | 1127.25 | 500 | 1252.26 |
| 51 | 129.75 | 111 | 279.75 | 171 | 429.75 | 231 | 579.75 | 291 | 729.75 | | | | | | |
| 52 | 132.27 | 112 | 282.27 | 172 | 432.27 | 232 | 582.27 | 292 | 732.27 | | | | | | |
| 53 | 134.76 | 113 | 284.76 | 173 | 434.76 | 233 | 584.76 | 293 | 734.76 | | | | | | |
| 54 | 137.25 | 114 | 287.25 | 174 | 437.25 | 234 | 587.25 | 294 | 737.25 | | | | | | |
| 55 | 139.77 | 115 | 289.77 | 175 | 439.77 | 235 | 589.77 | 295 | 739.77 | | | | | | |
| 56 | 142.26 | 116 | 292.26 | 176 | 442.26 | 236 | 592.26 | 296 | 742.26 | | | | | | |
| 57 | 144.75 | 117 | 294.75 | 177 | 444.75 | 237 | 594.75 | 297 | 744.75 | | | | | | |
| 58 | 147.27 | 118 | 297.27 | 178 | 447.27 | 238 | 597.27 | 298 | 747.27 | | | | | | |
| 59 | 149.76 | 119 | 299.76 | 179 | 449.76 | 239 | 599.76 | 299 | 749.76 | | | | | | |
| 60 | 152.25 | 120 | 302.25 | 180 | 452.25 | 240 | 602.25 | 300 | 752.25 | | | | | | |

**Code more than 500**

1 Where the code is in the range 501 to **1000** inclusive:

a. Subtract **500** from the code and use the balance of the code to obtain a pay adjustment figure from the table above.

b. Add this pay adjustment figure to the figure given in the box alongside to obtain the figure of total pay adjustment to date * | **1250.01** |

2 Where the code **exceeds 1000** follow the instructions on **page 3**.

## Month 4   Jul 6 to Aug 5

**Tables A** - Pay Adjustment Tables

| Code | Total pay adjustment to date | Code | Total pay adjustment to date | Code | Total pay adjustment to date | Code | Total pay adjustment to date | Code | Total pay adjustment to date | Code | Total pay adjustment to date | Code | Total pay adjustment to date | Code | Total pay adjustment to date | Code | Total pay adjustment to date |
|---|---|---|---|---|---|---|---|---|---|---|---|---|---|---|---|---|---|
| | £ | | £ | | £ | | £ | | £ | | £ | | £ | | £ | | £ |
| 0 | NIL | | | | | | | | | | | | | | | | |
| 1 | 6.36 | 61 | 206.36 | 121 | 406.36 | 181 | 606.36 | 241 | 806.36 | 301 | 1006.36 | 351 | 1173.00 | 401 | 1339.68 | 451 | 1506.36 |
| 2 | 9.68 | 62 | 209.68 | 122 | 409.68 | 182 | 609.68 | 242 | 809.68 | 302 | 1009.68 | 352 | 1176.36 | 402 | 1343.00 | 452 | 1509.68 |
| 3 | 13.00 | 63 | 213.00 | 123 | 413.00 | 183 | 613.00 | 243 | 813.00 | 303 | 1013.00 | 353 | 1179.68 | 403 | 1346.36 | 453 | 1513.00 |
| 4 | 16.36 | 64 | 216.36 | 124 | 416.36 | 184 | 616.36 | 244 | 816.36 | 304 | 1016.36 | 354 | 1183.00 | 404 | 1349.68 | 454 | 1516.36 |
| 5 | 19.68 | 65 | 219.68 | 125 | 419.68 | 185 | 619.68 | 245 | 819.68 | 305 | 1019.68 | 355 | 1186.36 | 405 | 1353.00 | 455 | 1519.68 |
| 6 | 23.00 | 66 | 223.00 | 126 | 423.00 | 186 | 623.00 | 246 | 823.00 | 306 | 1023.00 | 356 | 1189.68 | 406 | 1356.36 | 456 | 1523.00 |
| 7 | 26.36 | 67 | 226.36 | 127 | 426.36 | 187 | 626.36 | 247 | 826.36 | 307 | 1026.36 | 357 | 1193.00 | 407 | 1359.68 | 457 | 1526.36 |
| 8 | 29.68 | 68 | 229.68 | 128 | 429.68 | 188 | 629.68 | 248 | 829.68 | 308 | 1029.68 | 358 | 1196.36 | 408 | 1363.00 | 458 | 1529.68 |
| 9 | 33.00 | 69 | 233.00 | 129 | 433.00 | 189 | 633.00 | 249 | 833.00 | 309 | 1033.00 | 359 | 1199.68 | 409 | 1366.36 | 459 | 1533.00 |
| 10 | 36.36 | 70 | 236.36 | 130 | 436.36 | 190 | 636.36 | 250 | 836.36 | 310 | 1036.36 | 360 | 1203.00 | 410 | 1369.68 | 460 | 1536.36 |
| 11 | 39.68 | 71 | 239.68 | 131 | 439.68 | 191 | 639.68 | 251 | 839.68 | 311 | 1039.68 | 361 | 1206.36 | 411 | 1373.00 | 461 | 1539.68 |
| 12 | 43.00 | 72 | 243.00 | 132 | 443.00 | 192 | 643.00 | 252 | 843.00 | 312 | 1043.00 | 362 | 1209.68 | 412 | 1376.36 | 462 | 1543.00 |
| 13 | 46.36 | 73 | 246.36 | 133 | 446.36 | 193 | 646.36 | 253 | 846.36 | 313 | 1046.36 | 363 | 1213.00 | 413 | 1379.68 | 463 | 1546.36 |
| 14 | 49.68 | 74 | 249.68 | 134 | 449.68 | 194 | 649.68 | 254 | 849.68 | 314 | 1049.68 | 364 | 1216.36 | 414 | 1383.00 | 464 | 1549.68 |
| 15 | 53.00 | 75 | 253.00 | 135 | 453.00 | 195 | 653.00 | 255 | 853.00 | 315 | 1053.00 | 365 | 1219.68 | 415 | 1386.36 | 465 | 1553.00 |
| 16 | 56.36 | 76 | 256.36 | 136 | 456.36 | 196 | 656.36 | 256 | 856.36 | 316 | 1056.36 | 366 | 1223.00 | 416 | 1389.68 | 466 | 1556.36 |
| 17 | 59.68 | 77 | 259.68 | 137 | 459.68 | 197 | 659.68 | 257 | 859.68 | 317 | 1059.68 | 367 | 1226.36 | 417 | 1393.00 | 467 | 1559.68 |
| 18 | 63.00 | 78 | 263.00 | 138 | 463.00 | 198 | 663.00 | 258 | 863.00 | 318 | 1063.00 | 368 | 1229.68 | 418 | 1396.36 | 468 | 1563.00 |
| 19 | 66.36 | 79 | 266.36 | 139 | 466.36 | 199 | 666.36 | 259 | 866.36 | 319 | 1066.36 | 369 | 1233.00 | 419 | 1399.68 | 469 | 1566.36 |
| 20 | 69.68 | 80 | 269.68 | 140 | 469.68 | 200 | 669.68 | 260 | 869.68 | 320 | 1069.68 | 370 | 1236.36 | 420 | 1403.00 | 470 | 1569.68 |
| 21 | 73.00 | 81 | 273.00 | 141 | 473.00 | 201 | 673.00 | 261 | 873.00 | 321 | 1073.00 | 371 | 1239.68 | 421 | 1406.36 | 471 | 1573.00 |
| 22 | 76.36 | 82 | 276.36 | 142 | 476.36 | 202 | 676.36 | 262 | 876.36 | 322 | 1076.36 | 372 | 1243.00 | 422 | 1409.68 | 472 | 1576.36 |
| 23 | 79.68 | 83 | 279.68 | 143 | 479.68 | 203 | 679.68 | 263 | 879.68 | 323 | 1079.68 | 373 | 1246.36 | 423 | 1413.00 | 473 | 1579.68 |
| 24 | 83.00 | 84 | 283.00 | 144 | 483.00 | 204 | 683.00 | 264 | 883.00 | 324 | 1083.00 | 374 | 1249.68 | 424 | 1416.36 | 474 | 1583.00 |
| 25 | 86.36 | 85 | 286.36 | 145 | 486.36 | 205 | 686.36 | 265 | 886.36 | 325 | 1086.36 | 375 | 1253.00 | 425 | 1419.68 | 475 | 1586.36 |
| 26 | 89.68 | 86 | 289.68 | 146 | 489.68 | 206 | 689.68 | 266 | 889.68 | 326 | 1089.68 | 376 | 1256.36 | 426 | 1423.00 | 476 | 1589.68 |
| 27 | 93.00 | 87 | 293.00 | 147 | 493.00 | 207 | 693.00 | 267 | 893.00 | 327 | 1093.00 | 377 | 1259.68 | 427 | 1426.36 | 477 | 1593.00 |
| 28 | 96.36 | 88 | 296.36 | 148 | 496.36 | 208 | 696.36 | 268 | 896.36 | 328 | 1096.36 | 378 | 1263.00 | 428 | 1429.68 | 478 | 1596.36 |
| 29 | 99.68 | 89 | 299.68 | 149 | 499.68 | 209 | 699.68 | 269 | 899.68 | 329 | 1099.68 | 379 | 1266.36 | 429 | 1433.00 | 479 | 1599.68 |
| 30 | 103.00 | 90 | 303.00 | 150 | 503.00 | 210 | 703.00 | 270 | 903.00 | 330 | 1103.00 | 380 | 1269.68 | 430 | 1436.36 | 480 | 1603.00 |
| 31 | 106.36 | 91 | 306.36 | 151 | 506.36 | 211 | 706.36 | 271 | 906.36 | 331 | 1106.36 | 381 | 1273.00 | 431 | 1439.68 | 481 | 1606.36 |
| 32 | 109.68 | 92 | 309.68 | 152 | 509.68 | 212 | 709.68 | 272 | 909.68 | 332 | 1109.68 | 382 | 1276.36 | 432 | 1443.00 | 482 | 1609.68 |
| 33 | 113.00 | 93 | 313.00 | 153 | 513.00 | 213 | 713.00 | 273 | 913.00 | 333 | 1113.00 | 383 | 1279.68 | 433 | 1446.36 | 483 | 1613.00 |
| 34 | 116.36 | 94 | 316.36 | 154 | 516.36 | 214 | 716.36 | 274 | 916.36 | 334 | 1116.36 | 384 | 1283.00 | 434 | 1449.68 | 484 | 1616.36 |
| 35 | 119.68 | 95 | 319.68 | 155 | 519.68 | 215 | 719.68 | 275 | 919.68 | 335 | 1119.68 | 385 | 1286.36 | 435 | 1453.00 | 485 | 1619.68 |
| 36 | 123.00 | 96 | 323.00 | 156 | 523.00 | 216 | 723.00 | 276 | 923.00 | 336 | 1123.00 | 386 | 1289.68 | 436 | 1456.36 | 486 | 1623.00 |
| 37 | 126.36 | 97 | 326.36 | 157 | 526.36 | 217 | 726.36 | 277 | 926.36 | 337 | 1126.36 | 387 | 1293.00 | 437 | 1459.68 | 487 | 1626.36 |
| 38 | 129.68 | 98 | 329.68 | 158 | 529.68 | 218 | 729.68 | 278 | 929.68 | 338 | 1129.68 | 388 | 1296.36 | 438 | 1463.00 | 488 | 1629.68 |
| 39 | 133.00 | 99 | 333.00 | 159 | 533.00 | 219 | 733.00 | 279 | 933.00 | 339 | 1133.00 | 389 | 1299.68 | 439 | 1466.36 | 489 | 1633.00 |
| 40 | 136.36 | 100 | 336.36 | 160 | 536.36 | 220 | 736.36 | 280 | 936.36 | 340 | 1136.36 | 390 | 1303.00 | 440 | 1469.68 | 490 | 1636.36 |
| 41 | 139.68 | 101 | 339.68 | 161 | 539.68 | 221 | 739.68 | 281 | 939.68 | 341 | 1139.68 | 391 | 1306.36 | 441 | 1473.00 | 491 | 1639.68 |
| 42 | 143.00 | 102 | 343.00 | 162 | 543.00 | 222 | 743.00 | 282 | 943.00 | 342 | 1143.00 | 392 | 1309.68 | 442 | 1476.36 | 492 | 1643.00 |
| 43 | 146.36 | 103 | 346.36 | 163 | 546.36 | 223 | 746.36 | 283 | 946.36 | 343 | 1146.36 | 393 | 1313.00 | 443 | 1479.68 | 493 | 1646.36 |
| 44 | 149.68 | 104 | 349.68 | 164 | 549.68 | 224 | 749.68 | 284 | 949.68 | 344 | 1149.68 | 394 | 1316.36 | 444 | 1483.00 | 494 | 1649.68 |
| 45 | 153.00 | 105 | 353.00 | 165 | 553.00 | 225 | 753.00 | 285 | 953.00 | 345 | 1153.00 | 395 | 1319.68 | 445 | 1486.36 | 495 | 1653.00 |
| 46 | 156.36 | 106 | 356.36 | 166 | 556.36 | 226 | 756.36 | 286 | 956.36 | 346 | 1156.36 | 396 | 1323.00 | 446 | 1489.68 | 496 | 1656.36 |
| 47 | 159.68 | 107 | 359.68 | 167 | 559.68 | 227 | 759.68 | 287 | 959.68 | 347 | 1159.68 | 397 | 1326.36 | 447 | 1493.00 | 497 | 1659.68 |
| 48 | 163.00 | 108 | 363.00 | 168 | 563.00 | 228 | 763.00 | 288 | 963.00 | 348 | 1163.00 | 398 | 1329.68 | 448 | 1496.36 | 498 | 1663.00 |
| 49 | 166.36 | 109 | 366.36 | 169 | 566.36 | 229 | 766.36 | 289 | 966.36 | 349 | 1166.36 | 399 | 1333.00 | 449 | 1499.68 | 499 | 1666.36 |
| 50 | 169.68 | 110 | 369.68 | 170 | 569.68 | 230 | 769.68 | 290 | 969.68 | 350 | 1169.68 | 400 | 1336.36 | 450 | 1503.00 | 500 | 1669.68 |
| 51 | 173.00 | 111 | 373.00 | 171 | 573.00 | 231 | 773.00 | 291 | 973.00 | | | | | | | | |
| 52 | 176.36 | 112 | 376.36 | 172 | 576.36 | 232 | 776.36 | 292 | 976.36 | | | | | | | | |
| 53 | 179.68 | 113 | 379.68 | 173 | 579.68 | 233 | 779.68 | 293 | 979.68 | | | | | | | | |
| 54 | 183.00 | 114 | 383.00 | 174 | 583.00 | 234 | 783.00 | 294 | 983.00 | | | | | | | | |
| 55 | 186.36 | 115 | 386.36 | 175 | 586.36 | 235 | 786.36 | 295 | 986.36 | | | | | | | | |
| 56 | 189.68 | 116 | 389.68 | 176 | 589.68 | 236 | 789.68 | 296 | 989.68 | | | | | | | | |
| 57 | 193.00 | 117 | 393.00 | 177 | 593.00 | 237 | 793.00 | 297 | 993.00 | | | | | | | | |
| 58 | 196.36 | 118 | 396.36 | 178 | 596.36 | 238 | 796.36 | 298 | 996.36 | | | | | | | | |
| 59 | 199.68 | 119 | 399.68 | 179 | 599.68 | 239 | 799.68 | 299 | 999.68 | | | | | | | | |
| 60 | 203.00 | 120 | 403.00 | 180 | 603.00 | 240 | 803.00 | 300 | 1003.00 | | | | | | | | |

### Code more than 500

1 Where the code is in the range **501 to 1000** inclusive:

 a. Subtract **500** from the code and use the balance of the code to obtain a pay adjustment figure from the table above.

 b. Add this pay adjustment figure to the figure given in the box alongside to obtain the figure of total pay adjustment to date * | **1666.68**

2 Where the code **exceeds 1000** follow the instructions on **page 3**.

60

## Tables A - Pay Adjustment Tables

Aug 6 to Sep 5 **Month 5**

| Code | Total pay adjustment to date | Code | Total pay adjustment to date | Code | Total pay adjustment to date | Code | Total pay adjustment to date | Code | Total pay adjustment to date | Code | Total pay adjustment to date | Code | Total pay adjustment to date | Code | Total pay adjustment to date | Code | Total pay adjustment to date |
|---|---|---|---|---|---|---|---|---|---|---|---|---|---|---|---|---|---|
| | £ | | £ | | £ | | £ | | £ | | £ | | £ | | £ | | £ |
| 0 | NIL | 61 | 257.95 | 121 | 507.95 | 181 | 757.95 | 241 | 1007.95 | 301 | 1257.95 | 351 | 1466.25 | 401 | 1674.60 | 451 | 1882.95 |
| 1 | 7.95 | 62 | 262.10 | 122 | 512.10 | 182 | 762.10 | 242 | 1012.10 | 302 | 1262.10 | 352 | 1470.45 | 402 | 1678.75 | 452 | 1887.10 |
| 2 | 12.10 | 63 | 266.25 | 123 | 516.25 | 183 | 766.25 | 243 | 1016.25 | 303 | 1266.25 | 353 | 1474.60 | 403 | 1682.95 | 453 | 1891.25 |
| 3 | 16.25 | 64 | 270.45 | 124 | 520.45 | 184 | 770.45 | 244 | 1020.45 | 304 | 1270.45 | 354 | 1478.75 | 404 | 1687.10 | 454 | 1895.45 |
| 4 | 20.45 | 65 | 274.60 | 125 | 524.60 | 185 | 774.60 | 245 | 1024.60 | 305 | 1274.60 | 355 | 1482.95 | 405 | 1691.25 | 455 | 1899.60 |
| 5 | 24.60 | | | | | | | | | | | | | | | | |
| 6 | 28.75 | 66 | 278.75 | 126 | 528.75 | 186 | 778.75 | 246 | 1028.75 | 306 | 1278.75 | 356 | 1487.10 | 406 | 1695.45 | 456 | 1903.75 |
| 7 | 32.95 | 67 | 282.95 | 127 | 532.95 | 187 | 782.95 | 247 | 1032.95 | 307 | 1282.95 | 357 | 1491.25 | 407 | 1699.60 | 457 | 1907.95 |
| 8 | 37.10 | 68 | 287.10 | 128 | 537.10 | 188 | 787.10 | 248 | 1037.10 | 308 | 1287.10 | 358 | 1495.45 | 408 | 1703.75 | 458 | 1912.10 |
| 9 | 41.25 | 69 | 291.25 | 129 | 541.25 | 189 | 791.25 | 249 | 1041.25 | 309 | 1291.25 | 359 | 1499.60 | 409 | 1707.95 | 459 | 1916.25 |
| 10 | 45.45 | 70 | 295.45 | 130 | 545.45 | 190 | 795.45 | 250 | 1045.45 | 310 | 1295.45 | 360 | 1503.75 | 410 | 1712.10 | 460 | 1920.45 |
| 11 | 49.60 | 71 | 299.60 | 131 | 549.60 | 191 | 799.60 | 251 | 1049.60 | 311 | 1299.60 | 361 | 1507.95 | 411 | 1716.25 | 461 | 1924.60 |
| 12 | 53.75 | 72 | 303.75 | 132 | 553.75 | 192 | 803.75 | 252 | 1053.75 | 312 | 1303.75 | 362 | 1512.10 | 412 | 1720.45 | 462 | 1928.75 |
| 13 | 57.95 | 73 | 307.95 | 133 | 557.95 | 193 | 807.95 | 253 | 1057.95 | 313 | 1307.95 | 363 | 1516.25 | 413 | 1724.60 | 463 | 1932.95 |
| 14 | 62.10 | 74 | 312.10 | 134 | 562.10 | 194 | 812.10 | 254 | 1062.10 | 314 | 1312.10 | 364 | 1520.45 | 414 | 1728.75 | 464 | 1937.10 |
| 15 | 66.25 | 75 | 316.25 | 135 | 566.25 | 195 | 816.25 | 255 | 1066.25 | 315 | 1316.25 | 365 | 1524.60 | 415 | 1732.95 | 465 | 1941.25 |
| 16 | 70.45 | 76 | 320.45 | 136 | 570.45 | 196 | 820.45 | 256 | 1070.45 | 316 | 1320.45 | 366 | 1528.75 | 416 | 1737.10 | 466 | 1945.45 |
| 17 | 74.60 | 77 | 324.60 | 137 | 574.60 | 197 | 824.60 | 257 | 1074.60 | 317 | 1324.60 | 367 | 1532.95 | 417 | 1741.25 | 467 | 1949.60 |
| 18 | 78.75 | 78 | 328.75 | 138 | 578.75 | 198 | 828.75 | 258 | 1078.75 | 318 | 1328.75 | 368 | 1537.10 | 418 | 1745.45 | 468 | 1953.75 |
| 19 | 82.95 | 79 | 332.95 | 139 | 582.95 | 199 | 832.95 | 259 | 1082.95 | 319 | 1332.95 | 369 | 1541.25 | 419 | 1749.60 | 469 | 1957.95 |
| 20 | 87.10 | 80 | 337.10 | 140 | 587.10 | 200 | 837.10 | 260 | 1087.10 | 320 | 1337.10 | 370 | 1545.45 | 420 | 1753.75 | 470 | 1962.10 |
| 21 | 91.25 | 81 | 341.25 | 141 | 591.25 | 201 | 841.25 | 261 | 1091.25 | 321 | 1341.25 | 371 | 1549.60 | 421 | 1757.95 | 471 | 1966.25 |
| 22 | 95.45 | 82 | 345.45 | 142 | 595.45 | 202 | 845.45 | 262 | 1095.45 | 322 | 1345.45 | 372 | 1553.75 | 422 | 1762.10 | 472 | 1970.45 |
| 23 | 99.60 | 83 | 349.60 | 143 | 599.60 | 203 | 849.60 | 263 | 1099.60 | 323 | 1349.60 | 373 | 1557.95 | 423 | 1766.25 | 473 | 1974.60 |
| 24 | 103.75 | 84 | 353.75 | 144 | 603.75 | 204 | 853.75 | 264 | 1103.75 | 324 | 1353.75 | 374 | 1562.10 | 424 | 1770.45 | 474 | 1978.75 |
| 25 | 107.95 | 85 | 357.95 | 145 | 607.95 | 205 | 857.95 | 265 | 1107.95 | 325 | 1357.95 | 375 | 1566.25 | 425 | 1774.60 | 475 | 1982.95 |
| 26 | 112.10 | 86 | 362.10 | 146 | 612.10 | 206 | 862.10 | 266 | 1112.10 | 326 | 1362.10 | 376 | 1570.45 | 426 | 1778.75 | 476 | 1987.10 |
| 27 | 116.25 | 87 | 366.25 | 147 | 616.25 | 207 | 866.25 | 267 | 1116.25 | 327 | 1366.25 | 377 | 1574.60 | 427 | 1782.95 | 477 | 1991.25 |
| 28 | 120.45 | 88 | 370.45 | 148 | 620.45 | 208 | 870.45 | 268 | 1120.45 | 328 | 1370.45 | 378 | 1578.75 | 428 | 1787.10 | 478 | 1995.45 |
| 29 | 124.60 | 89 | 374.60 | 149 | 624.60 | 209 | 874.60 | 269 | 1124.60 | 329 | 1374.60 | 379 | 1582.95 | 429 | 1791.25 | 479 | 1999.60 |
| 30 | 128.75 | 90 | 378.75 | 150 | 628.75 | 210 | 878.75 | 270 | 1128.75 | 330 | 1378.75 | 380 | 1587.10 | 430 | 1795.45 | 480 | 2003.75 |
| 31 | 132.95 | 91 | 382.95 | 151 | 632.95 | 211 | 882.95 | 271 | 1132.95 | 331 | 1382.95 | 381 | 1591.25 | 431 | 1799.60 | 481 | 2007.95 |
| 32 | 137.10 | 92 | 387.10 | 152 | 637.10 | 212 | 887.10 | 272 | 1137.10 | 332 | 1387.10 | 382 | 1595.45 | 432 | 1803.75 | 482 | 2012.10 |
| 33 | 141.25 | 93 | 391.25 | 153 | 641.25 | 213 | 891.25 | 273 | 1141.25 | 333 | 1391.25 | 383 | 1599.60 | 433 | 1807.95 | 483 | 2016.25 |
| 34 | 145.45 | 94 | 395.45 | 154 | 645.45 | 214 | 895.45 | 274 | 1145.45 | 334 | 1395.45 | 384 | 1603.75 | 434 | 1812.10 | 484 | 2020.45 |
| 35 | 149.60 | 95 | 399.60 | 155 | 649.60 | 215 | 899.60 | 275 | 1149.60 | 335 | 1399.60 | 385 | 1607.95 | 435 | 1816.25 | 485 | 2024.60 |
| 36 | 153.75 | 96 | 403.75 | 156 | 653.75 | 216 | 903.75 | 276 | 1153.75 | 336 | 1403.75 | 386 | 1612.10 | 436 | 1820.45 | 486 | 2028.75 |
| 37 | 157.95 | 97 | 407.95 | 157 | 657.95 | 217 | 907.95 | 277 | 1157.95 | 337 | 1407.95 | 387 | 1616.25 | 437 | 1824.60 | 487 | 2032.95 |
| 38 | 162.10 | 98 | 412.10 | 158 | 662.10 | 218 | 912.10 | 278 | 1162.10 | 338 | 1412.10 | 388 | 1620.45 | 438 | 1828.75 | 488 | 2037.10 |
| 39 | 166.25 | 99 | 416.25 | 159 | 666.25 | 219 | 916.25 | 279 | 1166.25 | 339 | 1416.25 | 389 | 1624.60 | 439 | 1832.95 | 489 | 2041.25 |
| 40 | 170.45 | 100 | 420.45 | 160 | 670.45 | 220 | 920.45 | 280 | 1170.45 | 340 | 1420.45 | 390 | 1628.75 | 440 | 1837.10 | 490 | 2045.45 |
| 41 | 174.60 | 101 | 424.60 | 161 | 674.60 | 221 | 924.60 | 281 | 1174.60 | 341 | 1424.60 | 391 | 1632.95 | 441 | 1841.25 | 491 | 2049.60 |
| 42 | 178.75 | 102 | 428.75 | 162 | 678.75 | 222 | 928.75 | 282 | 1178.75 | 342 | 1428.75 | 392 | 1637.10 | 442 | 1845.45 | 492 | 2053.75 |
| 43 | 182.95 | 103 | 432.95 | 163 | 682.95 | 223 | 932.95 | 283 | 1182.95 | 343 | 1432.95 | 393 | 1641.25 | 443 | 1849.60 | 493 | 2057.95 |
| 44 | 187.10 | 104 | 437.10 | 164 | 687.10 | 224 | 937.10 | 284 | 1187.10 | 344 | 1437.10 | 394 | 1645.45 | 444 | 1853.75 | 494 | 2062.10 |
| 45 | 191.25 | 105 | 441.25 | 165 | 691.25 | 225 | 941.25 | 285 | 1191.25 | 345 | 1441.25 | 395 | 1649.60 | 445 | 1857.95 | 495 | 2066.25 |
| 46 | 195.45 | 106 | 445.45 | 166 | 695.45 | 226 | 945.45 | 286 | 1195.45 | 346 | 1445.45 | 396 | 1653.75 | 446 | 1862.10 | 496 | 2070.45 |
| 47 | 199.60 | 107 | 449.60 | 167 | 699.60 | 227 | 949.60 | 287 | 1199.60 | 347 | 1449.60 | 397 | 1657.95 | 447 | 1866.25 | 497 | 2074.60 |
| 48 | 203.75 | 108 | 453.75 | 168 | 703.75 | 228 | 953.75 | 288 | 1203.75 | 348 | 1453.75 | 398 | 1662.10 | 448 | 1870.45 | 498 | 2078.75 |
| 49 | 207.95 | 109 | 457.95 | 169 | 707.95 | 229 | 957.95 | 289 | 1207.95 | 349 | 1457.95 | 399 | 1666.25 | 449 | 1874.60 | 499 | 2082.95 |
| 50 | 212.10 | 110 | 462.10 | 170 | 712.10 | 230 | 962.10 | 290 | 1212.10 | 350 | 1462.10 | 400 | 1670.45 | 450 | 1878.75 | 500 | 2087.10 |
| 51 | 216.25 | 111 | 466.25 | 171 | 716.25 | 231 | 966.25 | 291 | 1216.25 | | | | | | | | |
| 52 | 220.45 | 112 | 470.45 | 172 | 720.45 | 232 | 970.45 | 292 | 1220.45 | | | | | | | | |
| 53 | 224.60 | 113 | 474.60 | 173 | 724.60 | 233 | 974.60 | 293 | 1224.60 | | | | | | | | |
| 54 | 228.75 | 114 | 478.75 | 174 | 728.75 | 234 | 978.75 | 294 | 1228.75 | | | | | | | | |
| 55 | 232.95 | 115 | 482.95 | 175 | 732.95 | 235 | 982.95 | 295 | 1232.95 | | | | | | | | |
| 56 | 237.10 | 116 | 487.10 | 176 | 737.10 | 236 | 987.10 | 296 | 1237.10 | | | | | | | | |
| 57 | 241.25 | 117 | 491.25 | 177 | 741.25 | 237 | 991.25 | 297 | 1241.25 | | | | | | | | |
| 58 | 245.45 | 118 | 495.45 | 178 | 745.45 | 238 | 995.45 | 298 | 1245.45 | | | | | | | | |
| 59 | 249.60 | 119 | 499.60 | 179 | 749.60 | 239 | 999.60 | 299 | 1249.60 | | | | | | | | |
| 60 | 253.75 | 120 | 503.75 | 180 | 753.75 | 240 | 1003.75 | 300 | 1253.75 | | | | | | | | |

**Code more than 500**

1 Where the code is in the range **501 to 1000** inclusive:

  a. Subtract **500** from the code and use the balance of the code to obtain a pay adjustment figure from the table above.

  b. Add this pay adjustment figure to the figure given in the box alongside to obtain the figure of total pay adjustment to date * | 2083.35 |

2 Where the code **exceeds 1000** follow the instructions on **page 3**.

**Month 6**  Sept 6 to Oct 5

**Tables A** - Pay Adjustment Tables

| Code | Total pay adjustment to date | Code | Total pay adjustment to date | Code | Total pay adjustment to date | Code | Total pay adjustment to date | Code | Total pay adjustment to date | Code | Total pay adjustment to date | Code | Total pay adjustment to date | Code | Total pay adjustment to date | Code | Total pay adjustment to date |
|---|---|---|---|---|---|---|---|---|---|---|---|---|---|---|---|---|---|
| | £ | | £ | | £ | | £ | | £ | | £ | | £ | | £ | | £ |
| 0 | NIL | | | | | | | | | | | | | | | | |
| 1 | 9.54 | 61 | 309.54 | 121 | 609.54 | 181 | 909.54 | 241 | 1209.54 | 301 | 1509.54 | 351 | 1759.50 | 401 | 2009.52 | 451 | 2259.54 |
| 2 | 14.52 | 62 | 314.52 | 122 | 614.52 | 182 | 914.52 | 242 | 1214.52 | 302 | 1514.52 | 352 | 1764.54 | 402 | 2014.50 | 452 | 2264.52 |
| 3 | 19.50 | 63 | 319.50 | 123 | 619.50 | 183 | 919.50 | 243 | 1219.50 | 303 | 1519.50 | 353 | 1769.52 | 403 | 2019.54 | 453 | 2269.50 |
| 4 | 24.54 | 64 | 324.54 | 124 | 624.54 | 184 | 924.54 | 244 | 1224.54 | 304 | 1524.54 | 354 | 1774.50 | 404 | 2024.52 | 454 | 2274.54 |
| 5 | 29.52 | 65 | 329.52 | 125 | 629.52 | 185 | 929.52 | 245 | 1229.52 | 305 | 1529.52 | 355 | 1779.54 | 405 | 2029.50 | 455 | 2279.52 |
| 6 | 34.50 | 66 | 334.50 | 126 | 634.50 | 186 | 934.50 | 246 | 1234.50 | 306 | 1534.50 | 356 | 1784.52 | 406 | 2034.54 | 456 | 2284.50 |
| 7 | 39.54 | 67 | 339.54 | 127 | 639.54 | 187 | 939.54 | 247 | 1239.54 | 307 | 1539.54 | 357 | 1789.50 | 407 | 2039.52 | 457 | 2289.54 |
| 8 | 44.52 | 68 | 344.52 | 128 | 644.52 | 188 | 944.52 | 248 | 1244.52 | 308 | 1544.52 | 358 | 1794.54 | 408 | 2044.50 | 458 | 2294.52 |
| 9 | 49.50 | 69 | 349.50 | 129 | 649.50 | 189 | 949.50 | 249 | 1249.50 | 309 | 1549.50 | 359 | 1799.52 | 409 | 2049.54 | 459 | 2299.50 |
| 10 | 54.54 | 70 | 354.54 | 130 | 654.54 | 190 | 954.54 | 250 | 1254.54 | 310 | 1554.54 | 360 | 1804.50 | 410 | 2054.52 | 460 | 2304.54 |
| 11 | 59.52 | 71 | 359.52 | 131 | 659.52 | 191 | 959.52 | 251 | 1259.52 | 311 | 1559.52 | 361 | 1809.54 | 411 | 2059.50 | 461 | 2309.52 |
| 12 | 64.50 | 72 | 364.50 | 132 | 664.50 | 192 | 964.50 | 252 | 1264.50 | 312 | 1564.50 | 362 | 1814.52 | 412 | 2064.54 | 462 | 2314.50 |
| 13 | 69.54 | 73 | 369.54 | 133 | 669.54 | 193 | 969.54 | 253 | 1269.54 | 313 | 1569.54 | 363 | 1819.50 | 413 | 2069.52 | 463 | 2319.54 |
| 14 | 74.52 | 74 | 374.52 | 134 | 674.52 | 194 | 974.52 | 254 | 1274.52 | 314 | 1574.52 | 364 | 1824.54 | 414 | 2074.50 | 464 | 2324.52 |
| 15 | 79.50 | 75 | 379.50 | 135 | 679.50 | 195 | 979.50 | 255 | 1279.50 | 315 | 1579.50 | 365 | 1829.52 | 415 | 2079.54 | 465 | 2329.50 |
| 16 | 84.54 | 76 | 384.54 | 136 | 684.54 | 196 | 984.54 | 256 | 1284.54 | 316 | 1584.54 | 366 | 1834.50 | 416 | 2084.52 | 466 | 2334.54 |
| 17 | 89.52 | 77 | 389.52 | 137 | 689.52 | 197 | 989.52 | 257 | 1289.52 | 317 | 1589.52 | 367 | 1839.54 | 417 | 2089.50 | 467 | 2339.52 |
| 18 | 94.50 | 78 | 394.50 | 138 | 694.50 | 198 | 994.50 | 258 | 1294.50 | 318 | 1594.50 | 368 | 1844.52 | 418 | 2094.54 | 468 | 2344.50 |
| 19 | 99.54 | 79 | 399.54 | 139 | 699.54 | 199 | 999.54 | 259 | 1299.54 | 319 | 1599.54 | 369 | 1849.50 | 419 | 2099.52 | 469 | 2349.54 |
| 20 | 104.52 | 80 | 404.52 | 140 | 704.52 | 200 | 1004.52 | 260 | 1304.52 | 320 | 1604.52 | 370 | 1854.50 | 420 | 2104.50 | 470 | 2354.52 |
| 21 | 109.50 | 81 | 409.50 | 141 | 709.50 | 201 | 1009.50 | 261 | 1309.50 | 321 | 1609.50 | 371 | 1859.52 | 421 | 2109.54 | 471 | 2359.50 |
| 22 | 114.54 | 82 | 414.54 | 142 | 714.54 | 202 | 1014.54 | 262 | 1314.54 | 322 | 1614.54 | 372 | 1864.50 | 422 | 2114.52 | 472 | 2364.54 |
| 23 | 119.52 | 83 | 419.52 | 143 | 719.52 | 203 | 1019.52 | 263 | 1319.52 | 323 | 1619.52 | 373 | 1869.54 | 423 | 2119.50 | 473 | 2369.52 |
| 24 | 124.50 | 84 | 424.50 | 144 | 724.50 | 204 | 1024.50 | 264 | 1324.50 | 324 | 1624.50 | 374 | 1874.52 | 424 | 2124.54 | 474 | 2374.50 |
| 25 | 129.54 | 85 | 429.54 | 145 | 729.54 | 205 | 1029.54 | 265 | 1329.54 | 325 | 1629.54 | 375 | 1879.50 | 425 | 2129.52 | 475 | 2379.54 |
| 26 | 134.52 | 86 | 434.52 | 146 | 734.52 | 206 | 1034.52 | 266 | 1334.52 | 326 | 1634.52 | 376 | 1884.54 | 426 | 2134.50 | 476 | 2384.52 |
| 27 | 139.50 | 87 | 439.50 | 147 | 739.50 | 207 | 1039.50 | 267 | 1339.50 | 327 | 1639.50 | 377 | 1889.52 | 427 | 2139.54 | 477 | 2389.50 |
| 28 | 144.54 | 88 | 444.54 | 148 | 744.54 | 208 | 1044.54 | 268 | 1344.54 | 328 | 1644.54 | 378 | 1894.50 | 428 | 2144.52 | 478 | 2394.54 |
| 29 | 149.52 | 89 | 449.52 | 149 | 749.52 | 209 | 1049.52 | 269 | 1349.52 | 329 | 1649.52 | 379 | 1899.54 | 429 | 2149.50 | 479 | 2399.52 |
| 30 | 154.50 | 90 | 454.50 | 150 | 754.50 | 210 | 1054.50 | 270 | 1354.50 | 330 | 1654.50 | 380 | 1904.52 | 430 | 2154.54 | 480 | 2404.50 |
| 31 | 159.54 | 91 | 459.54 | 151 | 759.54 | 211 | 1059.54 | 271 | 1359.54 | 331 | 1659.54 | 381 | 1909.50 | 431 | 2159.52 | 481 | 2409.54 |
| 32 | 164.52 | 92 | 464.52 | 152 | 764.52 | 212 | 1064.52 | 272 | 1364.52 | 332 | 1664.52 | 382 | 1914.54 | 432 | 2164.50 | 482 | 2414.52 |
| 33 | 169.50 | 93 | 469.50 | 153 | 769.50 | 213 | 1069.50 | 273 | 1369.50 | 333 | 1669.50 | 383 | 1919.52 | 433 | 2169.54 | 483 | 2419.50 |
| 34 | 174.54 | 94 | 474.54 | 154 | 774.54 | 214 | 1074.54 | 274 | 1374.54 | 334 | 1674.54 | 384 | 1924.50 | 434 | 2174.52 | 484 | 2424.54 |
| 35 | 179.52 | 95 | 479.52 | 155 | 779.52 | 215 | 1079.52 | 275 | 1379.52 | 335 | 1679.52 | 385 | 1929.54 | 435 | 2179.50 | 485 | 2429.52 |
| 36 | 184.50 | 96 | 484.50 | 156 | 784.50 | 216 | 1084.50 | 276 | 1384.50 | 336 | 1684.50 | 386 | 1934.52 | 436 | 2184.54 | 486 | 2434.50 |
| 37 | 189.54 | 97 | 489.54 | 157 | 789.54 | 217 | 1089.54 | 277 | 1389.54 | 337 | 1689.54 | 387 | 1939.50 | 437 | 2189.52 | 487 | 2439.54 |
| 38 | 194.52 | 98 | 494.52 | 158 | 794.52 | 218 | 1094.52 | 278 | 1394.52 | 338 | 1694.52 | 388 | 1944.54 | 438 | 2194.50 | 488 | 2444.52 |
| 39 | 199.50 | 99 | 499.50 | 159 | 799.50 | 219 | 1099.50 | 279 | 1399.50 | 339 | 1699.50 | 389 | 1949.52 | 439 | 2199.54 | 489 | 2449.50 |
| 40 | 204.54 | 100 | 504.54 | 160 | 804.54 | 220 | 1104.54 | 280 | 1404.54 | 340 | 1704.54 | 390 | 1954.50 | 440 | 2204.52 | 490 | 2454.54 |
| 41 | 209.52 | 101 | 509.52 | 161 | 809.52 | 221 | 1109.52 | 281 | 1409.52 | 341 | 1709.52 | 391 | 1959.54 | 441 | 2209.50 | 491 | 2459.52 |
| 42 | 214.50 | 102 | 514.50 | 162 | 814.50 | 222 | 1114.50 | 282 | 1414.50 | 342 | 1714.50 | 392 | 1964.52 | 442 | 2214.54 | 492 | 2464.50 |
| 43 | 219.54 | 103 | 519.54 | 163 | 819.54 | 223 | 1119.54 | 283 | 1419.54 | 343 | 1719.54 | 393 | 1969.50 | 443 | 2219.52 | 493 | 2469.54 |
| 44 | 224.52 | 104 | 524.52 | 164 | 824.52 | 224 | 1124.52 | 284 | 1424.52 | 344 | 1724.52 | 394 | 1974.54 | 444 | 2224.50 | 494 | 2474.52 |
| 45 | 229.50 | 105 | 529.50 | 165 | 829.50 | 225 | 1129.50 | 285 | 1429.50 | 345 | 1729.50 | 395 | 1979.52 | 445 | 2229.54 | 495 | 2479.50 |
| 46 | 234.54 | 106 | 534.54 | 166 | 834.54 | 226 | 1134.54 | 286 | 1434.54 | 346 | 1734.54 | 396 | 1984.50 | 446 | 2234.52 | 496 | 2484.54 |
| 47 | 239.52 | 107 | 539.52 | 167 | 839.52 | 227 | 1139.52 | 287 | 1439.52 | 347 | 1739.52 | 397 | 1989.54 | 447 | 2239.50 | 497 | 2489.52 |
| 48 | 244.50 | 108 | 544.50 | 168 | 844.50 | 228 | 1144.50 | 288 | 1444.50 | 348 | 1744.50 | 398 | 1994.52 | 448 | 2244.54 | 498 | 2494.50 |
| 49 | 249.54 | 109 | 549.54 | 169 | 849.54 | 229 | 1149.54 | 289 | 1449.54 | 349 | 1749.54 | 399 | 1999.50 | 449 | 2249.52 | 499 | 2499.54 |
| 50 | 254.52 | 110 | 554.52 | 170 | 854.52 | 230 | 1154.52 | 290 | 1454.52 | 350 | 1754.52 | 400 | 2004.54 | 450 | 2254.50 | 500 | 2504.52 |
| 51 | 259.50 | 111 | 559.50 | 171 | 859.50 | 231 | 1159.50 | 291 | 1459.50 | | | | | | |
| 52 | 264.54 | 112 | 564.54 | 172 | 864.54 | 232 | 1164.54 | 292 | 1464.54 | | | | | | |
| 53 | 269.52 | 113 | 569.52 | 173 | 869.52 | 233 | 1169.52 | 293 | 1469.52 | | | | | | |
| 54 | 274.50 | 114 | 574.50 | 174 | 874.50 | 234 | 1174.50 | 294 | 1474.50 | | | | | | |
| 55 | 279.54 | 115 | 579.54 | 175 | 879.54 | 235 | 1179.54 | 295 | 1479.54 | | | | | | |
| 56 | 284.52 | 116 | 584.52 | 176 | 884.52 | 236 | 1184.52 | 296 | 1484.52 | | | | | | |
| 57 | 289.50 | 117 | 589.50 | 177 | 889.50 | 237 | 1189.50 | 297 | 1489.50 | | | | | | |
| 58 | 294.54 | 118 | 594.54 | 178 | 894.54 | 238 | 1194.54 | 298 | 1494.54 | | | | | | |
| 59 | 299.52 | 119 | 599.52 | 179 | 899.52 | 239 | 1199.52 | 299 | 1499.52 | | | | | | |
| 60 | 304.50 | 120 | 604.50 | 180 | 904.50 | 240 | 1204.50 | 300 | 1504.50 | | | | | | |

**Code more than 500**

1. Where the code is in the range 501 to 1000 inclusive:

   a. Subtract **500** from the code and use the balance of the code to obtain a pay adjustment figure from the table above.

   b. Add this pay adjustment figure to the figure given in the box alongside to obtain the figure of total pay adjustment to date *  **2500.02**

2. Where the code **exceeds 1000** follow the instructions on **page 3**.

62

# Tables A - Pay Adjustment Tables

Oct 6 to Nov 5   **Month 7**

| Code | Total pay adjustment to date £ | Code | Total pay adjustment to date £ | Code | Total pay adjustment to date £ | Code | Total pay adjustment to date £ | Code | Total pay adjustment to date £ | Code | Total pay adjustment to date £ | Code | Total pay adjustment to date £ | Code | Total pay adjustment to date £ | Code | Total pay adjustment to date £ |
|---|---|---|---|---|---|---|---|---|---|---|---|---|---|---|---|---|---|
| 0 | NIL | | | | | | | | | | | | | | | | |
| 1 | 11.13 | 61 | 361.13 | 121 | 711.13 | 181 | 1061.13 | 241 | 1411.13 | 301 | 1761.13 | 351 | 2052.75 | 401 | 2344.44 | 451 | 2636.13 |
| 2 | 16.94 | 62 | 366.94 | 122 | 716.94 | 182 | 1066.94 | 242 | 1416.94 | 302 | 1766.94 | 352 | 2058.63 | 402 | 2350.25 | 452 | 2641.94 |
| 3 | 22.75 | 63 | 372.75 | 123 | 722.75 | 183 | 1072.75 | 243 | 1422.75 | 303 | 1772.75 | 353 | 2064.44 | 403 | 2356.13 | 453 | 2647.75 |
| 4 | 28.63 | 64 | 378.63 | 124 | 728.63 | 184 | 1078.63 | 244 | 1428.63 | 304 | 1778.63 | 354 | 2070.25 | 404 | 2361.94 | 454 | 2653.63 |
| 5 | 34.44 | 65 | 384.44 | 125 | 734.44 | 185 | 1084.44 | 245 | 1434.44 | 305 | 1784.44 | 355 | 2076.13 | 405 | 2367.75 | 455 | 2659.44 |
| 6 | 40.25 | 66 | 390.25 | 126 | 740.25 | 186 | 1090.25 | 246 | 1440.25 | 306 | 1790.25 | 356 | 2081.94 | 406 | 2373.63 | 456 | 2665.25 |
| 7 | 46.13 | 67 | 396.13 | 127 | 746.13 | 187 | 1096.13 | 247 | 1446.13 | 307 | 1796.13 | 357 | 2087.75 | 407 | 2379.44 | 457 | 2671.13 |
| 8 | 51.94 | 68 | 401.94 | 128 | 751.94 | 188 | 1101.94 | 248 | 1451.94 | 308 | 1801.94 | 358 | 2093.63 | 408 | 2385.25 | 458 | 2676.94 |
| 9 | 57.75 | 69 | 407.75 | 129 | 757.75 | 189 | 1107.75 | 249 | 1457.75 | 309 | 1807.75 | 359 | 2099.44 | 409 | 2391.13 | 459 | 2682.75 |
| 10 | 63.63 | 70 | 413.63 | 130 | 763.63 | 190 | 1113.63 | 250 | 1463.63 | 310 | 1813.63 | 360 | 2105.25 | 410 | 2396.94 | 460 | 2688.63 |
| 11 | 69.44 | 71 | 419.44 | 131 | 769.44 | 191 | 1119.44 | 251 | 1469.44 | 311 | 1819.44 | 361 | 2111.13 | 411 | 2402.75 | 461 | 2694.44 |
| 12 | 75.25 | 72 | 425.25 | 132 | 775.25 | 192 | 1125.25 | 252 | 1475.25 | 312 | 1825.25 | 362 | 2116.94 | 412 | 2408.63 | 462 | 2700.25 |
| 13 | 81.13 | 73 | 431.13 | 133 | 781.13 | 193 | 1131.13 | 253 | 1481.13 | 313 | 1831.13 | 363 | 2122.75 | 413 | 2414.44 | 463 | 2706.13 |
| 14 | 86.94 | 74 | 436.94 | 134 | 786.94 | 194 | 1136.94 | 254 | 1486.94 | 314 | 1836.94 | 364 | 2128.63 | 414 | 2420.25 | 464 | 2711.94 |
| 15 | 92.75 | 75 | 442.75 | 135 | 792.75 | 195 | 1142.75 | 255 | 1492.75 | 315 | 1842.75 | 365 | 2134.44 | 415 | 2426.13 | 465 | 2717.75 |
| 16 | 98.63 | 76 | 448.63 | 136 | 798.63 | 196 | 1148.63 | 256 | 1498.63 | 316 | 1848.63 | 366 | 2140.25 | 416 | 2431.94 | 466 | 2723.63 |
| 17 | 104.44 | 77 | 454.44 | 137 | 804.44 | 197 | 1154.44 | 257 | 1504.44 | 317 | 1854.44 | 367 | 2146.13 | 417 | 2437.75 | 467 | 2729.44 |
| 18 | 110.25 | 78 | 460.25 | 138 | 810.25 | 198 | 1160.25 | 258 | 1510.25 | 318 | 1860.25 | 368 | 2151.94 | 418 | 2443.63 | 468 | 2735.25 |
| 19 | 116.13 | 79 | 466.13 | 139 | 816.13 | 199 | 1166.13 | 259 | 1516.13 | 319 | 1866.13 | 369 | 2157.75 | 419 | 2449.44 | 469 | 2741.13 |
| 20 | 121.94 | 80 | 471.94 | 140 | 821.94 | 200 | 1171.94 | 260 | 1521.94 | 320 | 1871.94 | 370 | 2163.63 | 420 | 2455.25 | 470 | 2746.94 |
| 21 | 127.75 | 81 | 477.75 | 141 | 827.75 | 201 | 1177.75 | 261 | 1527.75 | 321 | 1877.75 | 371 | 2169.44 | 421 | 2461.13 | 471 | 2752.75 |
| 22 | 133.63 | 82 | 483.63 | 142 | 833.63 | 202 | 1183.63 | 262 | 1533.63 | 322 | 1883.63 | 372 | 2175.25 | 422 | 2466.94 | 472 | 2758.63 |
| 23 | 139.44 | 83 | 489.44 | 143 | 839.44 | 203 | 1189.44 | 263 | 1539.44 | 323 | 1889.44 | 373 | 2181.13 | 423 | 2472.75 | 473 | 2764.44 |
| 24 | 145.25 | 84 | 495.25 | 144 | 845.25 | 204 | 1195.25 | 264 | 1545.25 | 324 | 1895.25 | 374 | 2186.94 | 424 | 2478.63 | 474 | 2770.25 |
| 25 | 151.13 | 85 | 501.13 | 145 | 851.13 | 205 | 1201.13 | 265 | 1551.13 | 325 | 1901.13 | 375 | 2192.75 | 425 | 2484.44 | 475 | 2776.13 |
| 26 | 156.94 | 86 | 506.94 | 146 | 856.94 | 206 | 1206.94 | 266 | 1556.94 | 326 | 1906.94 | 376 | 2198.63 | 426 | 2490.25 | 476 | 2781.94 |
| 27 | 162.75 | 87 | 512.75 | 147 | 862.75 | 207 | 1212.75 | 267 | 1562.75 | 327 | 1912.75 | 377 | 2204.44 | 427 | 2496.13 | 477 | 2787.75 |
| 28 | 168.63 | 88 | 518.63 | 148 | 868.63 | 208 | 1218.63 | 268 | 1568.63 | 328 | 1918.63 | 378 | 2210.25 | 428 | 2501.94 | 478 | 2793.63 |
| 29 | 174.44 | 89 | 524.44 | 149 | 874.44 | 209 | 1224.44 | 269 | 1574.44 | 329 | 1924.44 | 379 | 2216.13 | 429 | 2507.75 | 479 | 2799.44 |
| 30 | 180.25 | 90 | 530.25 | 150 | 880.25 | 210 | 1230.25 | 270 | 1580.25 | 330 | 1930.25 | 380 | 2221.94 | 430 | 2513.63 | 480 | 2805.25 |
| 31 | 186.13 | 91 | 536.13 | 151 | 886.13 | 211 | 1236.13 | 271 | 1586.13 | 331 | 1936.13 | 381 | 2227.75 | 431 | 2519.44 | 481 | 2811.13 |
| 32 | 191.94 | 92 | 541.94 | 152 | 891.94 | 212 | 1241.94 | 272 | 1591.94 | 332 | 1941.94 | 382 | 2233.63 | 432 | 2525.25 | 482 | 2816.94 |
| 33 | 197.75 | 93 | 547.75 | 153 | 897.75 | 213 | 1247.75 | 273 | 1597.75 | 333 | 1947.75 | 383 | 2239.44 | 433 | 2531.13 | 483 | 2822.75 |
| 34 | 203.63 | 94 | 553.63 | 154 | 903.63 | 214 | 1253.63 | 274 | 1603.63 | 334 | 1953.63 | 384 | 2245.25 | 434 | 2536.94 | 484 | 2828.63 |
| 35 | 209.44 | 95 | 559.44 | 155 | 909.44 | 215 | 1259.44 | 275 | 1609.44 | 335 | 1959.44 | 385 | 2251.13 | 435 | 2542.75 | 485 | 2834.44 |
| 36 | 215.25 | 96 | 565.25 | 156 | 915.25 | 216 | 1265.25 | 276 | 1615.25 | 336 | 1965.25 | 386 | 2256.94 | 436 | 2548.63 | 486 | 2840.25 |
| 37 | 221.13 | 97 | 571.13 | 157 | 921.13 | 217 | 1271.13 | 277 | 1621.13 | 337 | 1971.13 | 387 | 2262.75 | 437 | 2554.44 | 487 | 2846.13 |
| 38 | 226.94 | 98 | 576.94 | 158 | 926.94 | 218 | 1276.94 | 278 | 1626.94 | 338 | 1976.94 | 388 | 2268.63 | 438 | 2560.25 | 488 | 2851.94 |
| 39 | 232.75 | 99 | 582.75 | 159 | 932.75 | 219 | 1282.75 | 279 | 1632.75 | 339 | 1982.75 | 389 | 2274.44 | 439 | 2566.13 | 489 | 2857.75 |
| 40 | 238.63 | 100 | 588.63 | 160 | 938.63 | 220 | 1288.63 | 280 | 1638.63 | 340 | 1988.63 | 390 | 2280.25 | 440 | 2571.94 | 490 | 2863.63 |
| 41 | 244.44 | 101 | 594.44 | 161 | 944.44 | 221 | 1294.44 | 281 | 1644.44 | 341 | 1994.44 | 391 | 2286.13 | 441 | 2577.75 | 491 | 2869.44 |
| 42 | 250.25 | 102 | 600.25 | 162 | 950.25 | 222 | 1300.25 | 282 | 1650.25 | 342 | 2000.25 | 392 | 2291.94 | 442 | 2583.63 | 492 | 2875.25 |
| 43 | 256.13 | 103 | 606.13 | 163 | 956.13 | 223 | 1306.13 | 283 | 1656.13 | 343 | 2006.13 | 393 | 2297.75 | 443 | 2589.44 | 493 | 2881.13 |
| 44 | 261.94 | 104 | 611.94 | 164 | 961.94 | 224 | 1311.94 | 284 | 1661.94 | 344 | 2011.94 | 394 | 2303.63 | 444 | 2595.25 | 494 | 2886.94 |
| 45 | 267.75 | 105 | 617.75 | 165 | 967.75 | 225 | 1317.75 | 285 | 1667.75 | 345 | 2017.75 | 395 | 2309.44 | 445 | 2601.13 | 495 | 2892.75 |
| 46 | 273.63 | 106 | 623.63 | 166 | 973.63 | 226 | 1323.63 | 286 | 1673.63 | 346 | 2023.63 | 396 | 2315.25 | 446 | 2606.94 | 496 | 2898.63 |
| 47 | 279.44 | 107 | 629.44 | 167 | 979.44 | 227 | 1329.44 | 287 | 1679.44 | 347 | 2029.44 | 397 | 2321.13 | 447 | 2612.75 | 497 | 2904.44 |
| 48 | 285.25 | 108 | 635.25 | 168 | 985.25 | 228 | 1335.25 | 288 | 1685.25 | 348 | 2035.25 | 398 | 2326.94 | 448 | 2618.63 | 498 | 2910.25 |
| 49 | 291.13 | 109 | 641.13 | 169 | 991.13 | 229 | 1341.13 | 289 | 1691.13 | 349 | 2041.13 | 399 | 2332.75 | 449 | 2624.44 | 499 | 2916.13 |
| 50 | 296.94 | 110 | 646.94 | 170 | 996.94 | 230 | 1346.94 | 290 | 1696.94 | 350 | 2046.94 | 400 | 2338.63 | 450 | 2630.25 | 500 | 2921.94 |
| 51 | 302.75 | 111 | 652.75 | 171 | 1002.75 | 231 | 1352.75 | 291 | 1702.75 | | | | | | | | |
| 52 | 308.63 | 112 | 658.63 | 172 | 1008.63 | 232 | 1358.63 | 292 | 1708.63 | | | | | | | | |
| 53 | 314.44 | 113 | 664.44 | 173 | 1014.44 | 233 | 1364.44 | 293 | 1714.44 | | | | | | | | |
| 54 | 320.25 | 114 | 670.25 | 174 | 1020.25 | 234 | 1370.25 | 294 | 1720.25 | | | | | | | | |
| 55 | 326.13 | 115 | 676.13 | 175 | 1026.13 | 235 | 1376.13 | 295 | 1726.13 | | | | | | | | |
| 56 | 331.94 | 116 | 681.94 | 176 | 1031.94 | 236 | 1381.94 | 296 | 1731.94 | | | | | | | | |
| 57 | 337.75 | 117 | 687.75 | 177 | 1037.75 | 237 | 1387.75 | 297 | 1737.75 | | | | | | | | |
| 58 | 343.63 | 118 | 693.63 | 178 | 1043.63 | 238 | 1393.63 | 298 | 1743.63 | | | | | | | | |
| 59 | 349.44 | 119 | 699.44 | 179 | 1049.44 | 239 | 1399.44 | 299 | 1749.44 | | | | | | | | |
| 60 | 355.25 | 120 | 705.25 | 180 | 1055.25 | 240 | 1405.25 | 300 | 1755.25 | | | | | | | | |

**Code more than 500**

1  Where the code is in the range **501** to **1000** inclusive:

   a. Subtract **500** from the code and use the balance of the code to obtain a pay adjustment figure from the table above.

   b. Add this pay adjustment figure to the figure given in the box alongside to obtain the figure of total pay adjustment to date *   | **2916.69** |

2  Where the code **exceeds 1000** follow the instructions on **page 3**.

**Month 8**  Nov 6 to Dec 5

**Tables A** - Pay Adjustment Tables

| Code | Total pay adjustment to date | Code | Total pay adjustment to date | Code | Total pay adjustment to date | Code | Total pay adjustment to date | Code | Total pay adjustment to date | Code | Total pay adjustment to date | Code | Total pay adjustment to date | Code | Total pay adjustment to date | Code | Total pay adjustment to date |
|---|---|---|---|---|---|---|---|---|---|---|---|---|---|---|---|---|---|
| | £ | | £ | | £ | | £ | | £ | | £ | | £ | | £ | | £ |
| 0 | NIL | | | | | | | | | | | | | | | | |
| 1 | 12.72 | 61 | 412.72 | 121 | 812.72 | 181 | 1212.72 | 241 | 1612.72 | 301 | 2012.72 | 351 | 2346.00 | 401 | 2679.36 | 451 | 3012.72 |
| 2 | 19.36 | 62 | 419.36 | 122 | 819.36 | 182 | 1219.36 | 242 | 1619.36 | 302 | 2019.36 | 352 | 2352.72 | 402 | 2686.00 | 452 | 3019.36 |
| 3 | 26.00 | 63 | 426.00 | 123 | 826.00 | 183 | 1226.00 | 243 | 1626.00 | 303 | 2026.00 | 353 | 2359.36 | 403 | 2692.72 | 453 | 3026.00 |
| 4 | 32.72 | 64 | 432.72 | 124 | 832.72 | 184 | 1232.72 | 244 | 1632.72 | 304 | 2032.72 | 354 | 2366.00 | 404 | 2699.36 | 454 | 3032.72 |
| 5 | 39.36 | 65 | 439.36 | 125 | 839.36 | 185 | 1239.36 | 245 | 1639.36 | 305 | 2039.36 | 355 | 2372.72 | 405 | 2706.00 | 455 | 3039.36 |
| 6 | 46.00 | 66 | 446.00 | 126 | 846.00 | 186 | 1246.00 | 246 | 1646.00 | 306 | 2046.00 | 356 | 2379.36 | 406 | 2712.72 | 456 | 3046.00 |
| 7 | 52.72 | 67 | 452.72 | 127 | 852.72 | 187 | 1252.72 | 247 | 1652.72 | 307 | 2052.72 | 357 | 2386.00 | 407 | 2719.36 | 457 | 3052.72 |
| 8 | 59.36 | 68 | 459.36 | 128 | 859.36 | 188 | 1259.36 | 248 | 1659.36 | 308 | 2059.36 | 358 | 2392.72 | 408 | 2726.00 | 458 | 3059.36 |
| 9 | 66.00 | 69 | 466.00 | 129 | 866.00 | 189 | 1266.00 | 249 | 1666.00 | 309 | 2066.00 | 359 | 2399.36 | 409 | 2732.72 | 459 | 3066.00 |
| 10 | 72.72 | 70 | 472.72 | 130 | 872.72 | 190 | 1272.72 | 250 | 1672.72 | 310 | 2072.72 | 360 | 2406.00 | 410 | 2739.36 | 460 | 3072.72 |
| 11 | 79.36 | 71 | 479.36 | 131 | 879.36 | 191 | 1279.36 | 251 | 1679.36 | 311 | 2079.36 | 361 | 2412.72 | 411 | 2746.00 | 461 | 3079.36 |
| 12 | 86.00 | 72 | 486.00 | 132 | 886.00 | 192 | 1286.00 | 252 | 1686.00 | 312 | 2086.00 | 362 | 2419.36 | 412 | 2752.72 | 462 | 3086.00 |
| 13 | 92.72 | 73 | 492.72 | 133 | 892.72 | 193 | 1292.72 | 253 | 1692.72 | 313 | 2092.72 | 363 | 2426.00 | 413 | 2759.36 | 463 | 3092.72 |
| 14 | 99.36 | 74 | 499.36 | 134 | 899.36 | 194 | 1299.36 | 254 | 1699.36 | 314 | 2099.36 | 364 | 2432.72 | 414 | 2766.00 | 464 | 3099.36 |
| 15 | 106.00 | 75 | 506.00 | 135 | 906.00 | 195 | 1306.00 | 255 | 1706.00 | 315 | 2106.00 | 365 | 2439.36 | 415 | 2772.72 | 465 | 3106.00 |
| 16 | 112.72 | 76 | 512.72 | 136 | 912.72 | 196 | 1312.72 | 256 | 1712.72 | 316 | 2112.72 | 366 | 2446.00 | 416 | 2779.36 | 466 | 3112.72 |
| 17 | 119.36 | 77 | 519.36 | 137 | 919.36 | 197 | 1319.36 | 257 | 1719.36 | 317 | 2119.36 | 367 | 2452.72 | 417 | 2786.00 | 467 | 3119.36 |
| 18 | 126.00 | 78 | 526.00 | 138 | 926.00 | 198 | 1326.00 | 258 | 1726.00 | 318 | 2126.00 | 368 | 2459.36 | 418 | 2792.72 | 468 | 3126.00 |
| 19 | 132.72 | 79 | 532.72 | 139 | 932.72 | 199 | 1332.72 | 259 | 1732.72 | 319 | 2132.72 | 369 | 2466.00 | 419 | 2799.36 | 469 | 3132.72 |
| 20 | 139.36 | 80 | 539.36 | 140 | 939.36 | 200 | 1339.36 | 260 | 1739.36 | 320 | 2139.36 | 370 | 2472.72 | 420 | 2806.00 | 470 | 3139.36 |
| 21 | 146.00 | 81 | 546.00 | 141 | 946.00 | 201 | 1346.00 | 261 | 1746.00 | 321 | 2146.00 | 371 | 2479.36 | 421 | 2812.72 | 471 | 3146.00 |
| 22 | 152.72 | 82 | 552.72 | 142 | 952.72 | 202 | 1352.72 | 262 | 1752.72 | 322 | 2152.72 | 372 | 2486.00 | 422 | 2819.36 | 472 | 3152.72 |
| 23 | 159.36 | 83 | 559.36 | 143 | 959.36 | 203 | 1359.36 | 263 | 1759.36 | 323 | 2159.36 | 373 | 2492.72 | 423 | 2826.00 | 473 | 3159.36 |
| 24 | 166.00 | 84 | 566.00 | 144 | 966.00 | 204 | 1366.00 | 264 | 1766.00 | 324 | 2166.00 | 374 | 2499.36 | 424 | 2832.72 | 474 | 3166.00 |
| 25 | 172.72 | 85 | 572.72 | 145 | 972.72 | 205 | 1372.72 | 265 | 1772.72 | 325 | 2172.72 | 375 | 2506.00 | 425 | 2839.36 | 475 | 3172.72 |
| 26 | 179.36 | 86 | 579.36 | 146 | 979.36 | 206 | 1379.36 | 266 | 1779.36 | 326 | 2179.36 | 376 | 2512.72 | 426 | 2846.00 | 476 | 3179.36 |
| 27 | 186.00 | 87 | 586.00 | 147 | 986.00 | 207 | 1386.00 | 267 | 1786.00 | 327 | 2186.00 | 377 | 2519.36 | 427 | 2852.72 | 477 | 3186.00 |
| 28 | 192.72 | 88 | 592.72 | 148 | 992.72 | 208 | 1392.72 | 268 | 1792.72 | 328 | 2192.72 | 378 | 2526.00 | 428 | 2859.36 | 478 | 3192.72 |
| 29 | 199.36 | 89 | 599.36 | 149 | 999.36 | 209 | 1399.36 | 269 | 1799.36 | 329 | 2199.36 | 379 | 2532.72 | 429 | 2866.00 | 479 | 3199.36 |
| 30 | 206.00 | 90 | 606.00 | 150 | 1006.00 | 210 | 1406.00 | 270 | 1806.00 | 330 | 2206.00 | 380 | 2539.36 | 430 | 2872.72 | 480 | 3206.00 |
| 31 | 212.72 | 91 | 612.72 | 151 | 1012.72 | 211 | 1412.72 | 271 | 1812.72 | 331 | 2212.72 | 381 | 2546.00 | 431 | 2879.36 | 481 | 3212.72 |
| 32 | 219.36 | 92 | 619.36 | 152 | 1019.36 | 212 | 1419.36 | 272 | 1819.36 | 332 | 2219.36 | 382 | 2552.72 | 432 | 2886.00 | 482 | 3219.36 |
| 33 | 226.00 | 93 | 626.00 | 153 | 1026.00 | 213 | 1426.00 | 273 | 1826.00 | 333 | 2226.00 | 383 | 2559.36 | 433 | 2892.72 | 483 | 3226.00 |
| 34 | 232.72 | 94 | 632.72 | 154 | 1032.72 | 214 | 1432.72 | 274 | 1832.72 | 334 | 2232.72 | 384 | 2566.00 | 434 | 2899.36 | 484 | 3232.72 |
| 35 | 239.36 | 95 | 639.36 | 155 | 1039.36 | 215 | 1439.36 | 275 | 1839.36 | 335 | 2239.36 | 385 | 2572.72 | 435 | 2906.00 | 485 | 3239.36 |
| 36 | 246.00 | 96 | 646.00 | 156 | 1046.00 | 216 | 1446.00 | 276 | 1846.00 | 336 | 2246.00 | 386 | 2579.36 | 436 | 2912.72 | 486 | 3246.00 |
| 37 | 252.72 | 97 | 652.72 | 157 | 1052.72 | 217 | 1452.72 | 277 | 1852.72 | 337 | 2252.72 | 387 | 2586.00 | 437 | 2919.36 | 487 | 3252.72 |
| 38 | 259.36 | 98 | 659.36 | 158 | 1059.36 | 218 | 1459.36 | 278 | 1859.36 | 338 | 2259.36 | 388 | 2592.72 | 438 | 2926.00 | 488 | 3259.36 |
| 39 | 266.00 | 99 | 666.00 | 159 | 1066.00 | 219 | 1466.00 | 279 | 1866.00 | 339 | 2266.00 | 389 | 2599.36 | 439 | 2932.72 | 489 | 3266.00 |
| 40 | 272.72 | 100 | 672.72 | 160 | 1072.72 | 220 | 1472.72 | 280 | 1872.72 | 340 | 2272.72 | 390 | 2606.00 | 440 | 2939.36 | 490 | 3272.72 |
| 41 | 279.36 | 101 | 679.36 | 161 | 1079.36 | 221 | 1479.36 | 281 | 1879.36 | 341 | 2279.36 | 391 | 2612.72 | 441 | 2946.00 | 491 | 3279.36 |
| 42 | 286.00 | 102 | 686.00 | 162 | 1086.00 | 222 | 1486.00 | 282 | 1886.00 | 342 | 2286.00 | 392 | 2619.36 | 442 | 2952.72 | 492 | 3286.00 |
| 43 | 292.72 | 103 | 692.72 | 163 | 1092.72 | 223 | 1492.72 | 283 | 1892.72 | 343 | 2292.72 | 393 | 2626.00 | 443 | 2959.36 | 493 | 3292.72 |
| 44 | 299.36 | 104 | 699.36 | 164 | 1099.36 | 224 | 1499.36 | 284 | 1899.36 | 344 | 2299.36 | 394 | 2632.72 | 444 | 2966.00 | 494 | 3299.36 |
| 45 | 306.00 | 105 | 706.00 | 165 | 1106.00 | 225 | 1506.00 | 285 | 1906.00 | 345 | 2306.00 | 395 | 2639.36 | 445 | 2972.72 | 495 | 3306.00 |
| 46 | 312.72 | 106 | 712.72 | 166 | 1112.72 | 226 | 1512.72 | 286 | 1912.72 | 346 | 2312.72 | 396 | 2646.00 | 446 | 2979.36 | 496 | 3312.72 |
| 47 | 319.36 | 107 | 719.36 | 167 | 1119.36 | 227 | 1519.36 | 287 | 1919.36 | 347 | 2319.36 | 397 | 2652.72 | 447 | 2986.00 | 497 | 3319.36 |
| 48 | 326.00 | 108 | 726.00 | 168 | 1126.00 | 228 | 1526.00 | 288 | 1926.00 | 348 | 2326.00 | 398 | 2659.36 | 448 | 2992.72 | 498 | 3326.00 |
| 49 | 332.72 | 109 | 732.72 | 169 | 1132.72 | 229 | 1532.72 | 289 | 1932.72 | 349 | 2332.72 | 399 | 2666.00 | 449 | 2999.36 | 499 | 3332.72 |
| 50 | 339.36 | 110 | 739.36 | 170 | 1139.36 | 230 | 1539.36 | 290 | 1939.36 | 350 | 2339.36 | 400 | 2672.72 | 450 | 3006.00 | 500 | 3339.36 |
| 51 | 346.00 | 111 | 746.00 | 171 | 1146.00 | 231 | 1546.00 | 291 | 1946.00 | | | | | | | | |
| 52 | 352.72 | 112 | 752.72 | 172 | 1152.72 | 232 | 1552.72 | 292 | 1952.72 | | | | | | | | |
| 53 | 359.36 | 113 | 759.36 | 173 | 1159.36 | 233 | 1559.36 | 293 | 1959.36 | | | | | | | | |
| 54 | 366.00 | 114 | 766.00 | 174 | 1166.00 | 234 | 1566.00 | 294 | 1966.00 | | | | | | | | |
| 55 | 372.72 | 115 | 772.72 | 175 | 1172.72 | 235 | 1572.72 | 295 | 1972.72 | | | | | | | | |
| 56 | 379.36 | 116 | 779.36 | 176 | 1179.36 | 236 | 1579.36 | 296 | 1979.36 | | | | | | | | |
| 57 | 386.00 | 117 | 786.00 | 177 | 1186.00 | 237 | 1586.00 | 297 | 1986.00 | | | | | | | | |
| 58 | 392.72 | 118 | 792.72 | 178 | 1192.72 | 238 | 1592.72 | 298 | 1992.72 | | | | | | | | |
| 59 | 399.36 | 119 | 799.36 | 179 | 1199.36 | 239 | 1599.36 | 299 | 1999.36 | | | | | | | | |
| 60 | 406.00 | 120 | 806.00 | 180 | 1206.00 | 240 | 1606.00 | 300 | 2006.00 | | | | | | | | |

**Code more than 500**

1 Where the code is in the range 501 to 1000 inclusive:

  a. Subtract **500** from the code and use the balance of the code to obtain a pay adjustment figure from the table above.

  b. Add this pay adjustment figure to the figure given in the box alongside to obtain the figure of total pay adjustment to date *  | **3333.36** |

2 Where the code **exceeds 1000** follow the instructions on **page 3**.

64

**Tables A** - Pay Adjustment Tables  Dec 6 to Jan 5  **Month 9**

| Code | Total pay adjustment to date | Code | Total pay adjustment to date | Code | Total pay adjustment to date | Code | Total pay adjustment to date | Code | Total pay adjustment to date | Code | Total pay adjustment to date | Code | Total pay adjustment to date | Code | Total pay adjustment to date | Code | Total pay adjustment to date |
|---|---|---|---|---|---|---|---|---|---|---|---|---|---|---|---|---|---|
| | £ | | £ | | £ | | £ | | £ | | £ | | £ | | £ | | £ |
| 0 | NIL | | | | | | | | | | | | | | | | |
| 1 | 14.31 | 61 | 464.31 | 121 | 914.31 | 181 | 1364.31 | 241 | 1814.31 | 301 | 2264.31 | 351 | 2639.25 | 401 | 3014.28 | 451 | 3389.31 |
| 2 | 21.78 | 62 | 471.78 | 122 | 921.78 | 182 | 1371.78 | 242 | 1821.78 | 302 | 2271.78 | 352 | 2646.81 | 402 | 3021.75 | 452 | 3396.78 |
| 3 | 29.25 | 63 | 479.25 | 123 | 929.25 | 183 | 1379.25 | 243 | 1829.25 | 303 | 2279.25 | 353 | 2654.28 | 403 | 3029.31 | 453 | 3404.25 |
| 4 | 36.81 | 64 | 486.81 | 124 | 936.81 | 184 | 1386.81 | 244 | 1836.81 | 304 | 2286.81 | 354 | 2661.75 | 404 | 3036.78 | 454 | 3411.81 |
| 5 | 44.28 | 65 | 494.28 | 125 | 944.28 | 185 | 1394.28 | 245 | 1844.28 | 305 | 2294.28 | 355 | 2669.31 | 405 | 3044.25 | 455 | 3419.28 |
| 6 | 51.75 | 66 | 501.75 | 126 | 951.75 | 186 | 1401.75 | 246 | 1851.75 | 306 | 2301.75 | 356 | 2676.78 | 406 | 3051.81 | 456 | 3426.75 |
| 7 | 59.31 | 67 | 509.31 | 127 | 959.31 | 187 | 1409.31 | 247 | 1859.31 | 307 | 2309.31 | 357 | 2684.25 | 407 | 3059.28 | 457 | 3434.31 |
| 8 | 66.78 | 68 | 516.78 | 128 | 966.78 | 188 | 1416.78 | 248 | 1866.78 | 308 | 2316.78 | 358 | 2691.81 | 408 | 3066.75 | 458 | 3441.78 |
| 9 | 74.25 | 69 | 524.25 | 129 | 974.25 | 189 | 1424.25 | 249 | 1874.25 | 309 | 2324.25 | 359 | 2699.28 | 409 | 3074.31 | 459 | 3449.25 |
| 10 | 81.81 | 70 | 531.81 | 130 | 981.81 | 190 | 1431.81 | 250 | 1881.81 | 310 | 2331.81 | 360 | 2706.75 | 410 | 3081.78 | 460 | 3456.81 |
| 11 | 89.28 | 71 | 539.28 | 131 | 989.28 | 191 | 1439.28 | 251 | 1889.28 | 311 | 2339.28 | 361 | 2714.31 | 411 | 3089.25 | 461 | 3464.28 |
| 12 | 96.75 | 72 | 546.75 | 132 | 996.75 | 192 | 1446.75 | 252 | 1896.75 | 312 | 2346.75 | 362 | 2721.78 | 412 | 3096.81 | 462 | 3471.75 |
| 13 | 104.31 | 73 | 554.31 | 133 | 1004.31 | 193 | 1454.31 | 253 | 1904.31 | 313 | 2354.31 | 363 | 2729.25 | 413 | 3104.28 | 463 | 3479.31 |
| 14 | 111.78 | 74 | 561.78 | 134 | 1011.78 | 194 | 1461.78 | 254 | 1911.78 | 314 | 2361.78 | 364 | 2736.81 | 414 | 3111.75 | 464 | 3486.78 |
| 15 | 119.25 | 75 | 569.25 | 135 | 1019.25 | 195 | 1469.25 | 255 | 1919.25 | 315 | 2369.25 | 365 | 2744.28 | 415 | 3119.31 | 465 | 3494.25 |
| 16 | 126.81 | 76 | 576.81 | 136 | 1026.81 | 196 | 1476.81 | 256 | 1926.81 | 316 | 2376.81 | 366 | 2751.75 | 416 | 3126.78 | 466 | 3501.81 |
| 17 | 134.28 | 77 | 584.28 | 137 | 1034.28 | 197 | 1484.28 | 257 | 1934.28 | 317 | 2384.28 | 367 | 2759.31 | 417 | 3134.25 | 467 | 3509.28 |
| 18 | 141.75 | 78 | 591.75 | 138 | 1041.75 | 198 | 1491.75 | 258 | 1941.75 | 318 | 2391.75 | 368 | 2766.78 | 418 | 3141.81 | 468 | 3516.75 |
| 19 | 149.31 | 79 | 599.31 | 139 | 1049.31 | 199 | 1499.31 | 259 | 1949.31 | 319 | 2399.31 | 369 | 2774.25 | 419 | 3149.28 | 469 | 3524.31 |
| 20 | 156.78 | 80 | 606.78 | 140 | 1056.78 | 200 | 1506.78 | 260 | 1956.78 | 320 | 2406.78 | 370 | 2781.81 | 420 | 3156.75 | 470 | 3531.78 |
| 21 | 164.25 | 81 | 614.25 | 141 | 1064.25 | 201 | 1514.25 | 261 | 1964.25 | 321 | 2414.25 | 371 | 2789.28 | 421 | 3164.31 | 471 | 3539.25 |
| 22 | 171.81 | 82 | 621.81 | 142 | 1071.81 | 202 | 1521.81 | 262 | 1971.81 | 322 | 2421.81 | 372 | 2796.75 | 422 | 3171.78 | 472 | 3546.81 |
| 23 | 179.28 | 83 | 629.28 | 143 | 1079.28 | 203 | 1529.28 | 263 | 1979.28 | 323 | 2429.28 | 373 | 2804.31 | 423 | 3179.25 | 473 | 3554.28 |
| 24 | 186.75 | 84 | 636.75 | 144 | 1086.75 | 204 | 1536.75 | 264 | 1986.75 | 324 | 2436.75 | 374 | 2811.78 | 424 | 3186.81 | 474 | 3561.75 |
| 25 | 194.31 | 85 | 644.31 | 145 | 1094.31 | 205 | 1544.31 | 265 | 1994.31 | 325 | 2444.31 | 375 | 2819.25 | 425 | 3194.28 | 475 | 3569.31 |
| 26 | 201.78 | 86 | 651.78 | 146 | 1101.78 | 206 | 1551.78 | 266 | 2001.78 | 326 | 2451.78 | 376 | 2826.81 | 426 | 3201.75 | 476 | 3576.78 |
| 27 | 209.25 | 87 | 659.25 | 147 | 1109.25 | 207 | 1559.25 | 267 | 2009.25 | 327 | 2459.25 | 377 | 2834.28 | 427 | 3209.31 | 477 | 3584.25 |
| 28 | 216.81 | 88 | 666.81 | 148 | 1116.81 | 208 | 1566.81 | 268 | 2016.81 | 328 | 2466.81 | 378 | 2841.75 | 428 | 3216.78 | 478 | 3591.81 |
| 29 | 224.28 | 89 | 674.28 | 149 | 1124.28 | 209 | 1574.28 | 269 | 2024.28 | 329 | 2474.28 | 379 | 2849.31 | 429 | 3224.25 | 479 | 3599.28 |
| 30 | 231.75 | 90 | 681.75 | 150 | 1131.75 | 210 | 1581.75 | 270 | 2031.75 | 330 | 2481.75 | 380 | 2856.78 | 430 | 3231.81 | 480 | 3606.75 |
| 31 | 239.31 | 91 | 689.31 | 151 | 1139.31 | 211 | 1589.31 | 271 | 2039.31 | 331 | 2489.31 | 381 | 2864.25 | 431 | 3239.28 | 481 | 3614.31 |
| 32 | 246.78 | 92 | 696.78 | 152 | 1146.78 | 212 | 1596.78 | 272 | 2046.78 | 332 | 2496.78 | 382 | 2871.81 | 432 | 3246.75 | 482 | 3621.78 |
| 33 | 254.25 | 93 | 704.25 | 153 | 1154.25 | 213 | 1604.25 | 273 | 2054.25 | 333 | 2504.25 | 383 | 2879.28 | 433 | 3254.31 | 483 | 3629.25 |
| 34 | 261.81 | 94 | 711.81 | 154 | 1161.81 | 214 | 1611.81 | 274 | 2061.81 | 334 | 2511.81 | 384 | 2886.75 | 434 | 3261.78 | 484 | 3636.81 |
| 35 | 269.28 | 95 | 719.28 | 155 | 1169.28 | 215 | 1619.28 | 275 | 2069.28 | 335 | 2519.28 | 385 | 2894.31 | 435 | 3269.25 | 485 | 3644.28 |
| 36 | 276.75 | 96 | 726.75 | 156 | 1176.75 | 216 | 1626.75 | 276 | 2076.75 | 336 | 2526.75 | 386 | 2901.78 | 436 | 3276.81 | 486 | 3651.75 |
| 37 | 284.31 | 97 | 734.31 | 157 | 1184.31 | 217 | 1634.31 | 277 | 2084.31 | 337 | 2534.31 | 387 | 2909.25 | 437 | 3284.28 | 487 | 3659.31 |
| 38 | 291.78 | 98 | 741.78 | 158 | 1191.78 | 218 | 1641.78 | 278 | 2091.78 | 338 | 2541.78 | 388 | 2916.81 | 438 | 3291.75 | 488 | 3666.78 |
| 39 | 299.25 | 99 | 749.25 | 159 | 1199.25 | 219 | 1649.25 | 279 | 2099.25 | 339 | 2549.25 | 389 | 2924.28 | 439 | 3299.31 | 489 | 3674.25 |
| 40 | 306.81 | 100 | 756.81 | 160 | 1206.81 | 220 | 1656.81 | 280 | 2106.81 | 340 | 2556.81 | 390 | 2931.75 | 440 | 3306.78 | 490 | 3681.81 |
| 41 | 314.28 | 101 | 764.28 | 161 | 1214.28 | 221 | 1664.28 | 281 | 2114.28 | 341 | 2564.28 | 391 | 2939.31 | 441 | 3314.25 | 491 | 3689.28 |
| 42 | 321.75 | 102 | 771.75 | 162 | 1221.75 | 222 | 1671.75 | 282 | 2121.75 | 342 | 2571.75 | 392 | 2946.78 | 442 | 3321.81 | 492 | 3696.75 |
| 43 | 329.31 | 103 | 779.31 | 163 | 1229.31 | 223 | 1679.31 | 283 | 2129.31 | 343 | 2579.31 | 393 | 2954.25 | 443 | 3329.28 | 493 | 3704.31 |
| 44 | 336.78 | 104 | 786.78 | 164 | 1236.78 | 224 | 1686.78 | 284 | 2136.78 | 344 | 2586.78 | 394 | 2961.81 | 444 | 3336.75 | 494 | 3711.78 |
| 45 | 344.25 | 105 | 794.25 | 165 | 1244.25 | 225 | 1694.25 | 285 | 2144.25 | 345 | 2594.25 | 395 | 2969.28 | 445 | 3344.31 | 495 | 3719.25 |
| 46 | 351.81 | 106 | 801.81 | 166 | 1251.81 | 226 | 1701.81 | 286 | 2151.81 | 346 | 2601.81 | 396 | 2976.75 | 446 | 3351.78 | 496 | 3726.81 |
| 47 | 359.28 | 107 | 809.28 | 167 | 1259.28 | 227 | 1709.28 | 287 | 2159.28 | 347 | 2609.28 | 397 | 2984.31 | 447 | 3359.25 | 497 | 3734.28 |
| 48 | 366.75 | 108 | 816.75 | 168 | 1266.75 | 228 | 1716.75 | 288 | 2166.75 | 348 | 2616.75 | 398 | 2991.78 | 448 | 3366.81 | 498 | 3741.75 |
| 49 | 374.31 | 109 | 824.31 | 169 | 1274.31 | 229 | 1724.31 | 289 | 2174.31 | 349 | 2624.31 | 399 | 2999.25 | 449 | 3374.28 | 499 | 3749.31 |
| 50 | 381.78 | 110 | 831.78 | 170 | 1281.78 | 230 | 1731.78 | 290 | 2181.78 | 350 | 2631.78 | 400 | 3006.81 | 450 | 3381.75 | 500 | 3756.78 |
| 51 | 389.25 | 111 | 839.25 | 171 | 1289.25 | 231 | 1739.25 | 291 | 2189.25 | | | | | | | | |
| 52 | 396.81 | 112 | 846.81 | 172 | 1296.81 | 232 | 1746.81 | 292 | 2196.81 | | | | | | | | |
| 53 | 404.28 | 113 | 854.28 | 173 | 1304.28 | 233 | 1754.28 | 293 | 2204.28 | | | | | | | | |
| 54 | 411.75 | 114 | 861.75 | 174 | 1311.75 | 234 | 1761.75 | 294 | 2211.75 | | | | | | | | |
| 55 | 419.31 | 115 | 869.31 | 175 | 1319.31 | 235 | 1769.31 | 295 | 2219.31 | | | | | | | | |
| 56 | 426.78 | 116 | 876.78 | 176 | 1326.78 | 236 | 1776.78 | 296 | 2226.78 | | | | | | | | |
| 57 | 434.25 | 117 | 884.25 | 177 | 1334.25 | 237 | 1784.25 | 297 | 2234.25 | | | | | | | | |
| 58 | 441.81 | 118 | 891.81 | 178 | 1341.81 | 238 | 1791.81 | 298 | 2241.81 | | | | | | | | |
| 59 | 449.28 | 119 | 899.28 | 179 | 1349.28 | 239 | 1799.28 | 299 | 2249.28 | | | | | | | | |
| 60 | 456.75 | 120 | 906.75 | 180 | 1356.75 | 240 | 1806.75 | 300 | 2256.75 | | | | | | | | |

**Code more than 500**

1 Where the code is in the range **501** to **1000** inclusive:

a. Subtract **500** from the code and use the balance of the code to obtain a pay adjustment figure from the table above.

b. Add this pay adjustment figure to the figure given in the box alongside to obtain the figure of total pay adjustment to date * 3750.03

2 Where the code **exceeds 1000** follow the instructions on **page 3**.

65

## Month 10  Jan 6 to Feb 5

**Tables A** - Pay Adjustment Tables

| Code | Total pay adjustment to date £ | Code | Total pay adjustment to date £ | Code | Total pay adjustment to date £ | Code | Total pay adjustment to date £ | Code | Total pay adjustment to date £ | Code | Total pay adjustment to date £ | Code | Total pay adjustment to date £ | Code | Total pay adjustment to date £ | Code | Total pay adjustment to date £ |
|---|---|---|---|---|---|---|---|---|---|---|---|---|---|---|---|---|---|
| 0 | NIL | | | | | | | | | | | | | | | | |
| 1 | 15.90 | 61 | 515.90 | 121 | 1015.90 | 181 | 1515.90 | 241 | 2015.90 | 301 | 2515.90 | 351 | 2932.50 | 401 | 3349.20 | 451 | 3765.90 |
| 2 | 24.20 | 62 | 524.20 | 122 | 1024.20 | 182 | 1524.20 | 242 | 2024.20 | 302 | 2524.20 | 352 | 2940.90 | 402 | 3357.50 | 452 | 3774.20 |
| 3 | 32.50 | 63 | 532.50 | 123 | 1032.50 | 183 | 1532.50 | 243 | 2032.50 | 303 | 2532.50 | 353 | 2949.20 | 403 | 3365.90 | 453 | 3782.50 |
| 4 | 40.90 | 64 | 540.90 | 124 | 1040.90 | 184 | 1540.90 | 244 | 2040.90 | 304 | 2540.90 | 354 | 2957.50 | 404 | 3374.20 | 454 | 3790.90 |
| 5 | 49.20 | 65 | 549.20 | 125 | 1049.20 | 185 | 1549.20 | 245 | 2049.20 | 305 | 2549.20 | 355 | 2965.90 | 405 | 3382.50 | 455 | 3799.20 |
| 6 | 57.50 | 66 | 557.50 | 126 | 1057.50 | 186 | 1557.50 | 246 | 2057.50 | 306 | 2557.50 | 356 | 2974.20 | 406 | 3390.90 | 456 | 3807.50 |
| 7 | 65.90 | 67 | 565.90 | 127 | 1065.90 | 187 | 1565.90 | 247 | 2065.90 | 307 | 2565.90 | 357 | 2982.50 | 407 | 3399.20 | 457 | 3815.90 |
| 8 | 74.20 | 68 | 574.20 | 128 | 1074.20 | 188 | 1574.20 | 248 | 2074.20 | 308 | 2574.20 | 358 | 2990.90 | 408 | 3407.50 | 458 | 3824.20 |
| 9 | 82.50 | 69 | 582.50 | 129 | 1082.50 | 189 | 1582.50 | 249 | 2082.50 | 309 | 2582.50 | 359 | 2999.20 | 409 | 3415.90 | 459 | 3832.50 |
| 10 | 90.90 | 70 | 590.90 | 130 | 1090.90 | 190 | 1590.90 | 250 | 2090.90 | 310 | 2590.90 | 360 | 3007.50 | 410 | 3424.20 | 460 | 3840.90 |
| 11 | 99.20 | 71 | 599.20 | 131 | 1099.20 | 191 | 1599.20 | 251 | 2099.20 | 311 | 2599.20 | 361 | 3015.90 | 411 | 3432.50 | 461 | 3849.20 |
| 12 | 107.50 | 72 | 607.50 | 132 | 1107.50 | 192 | 1607.50 | 252 | 2107.50 | 312 | 2607.50 | 362 | 3024.20 | 412 | 3440.90 | 462 | 3857.50 |
| 13 | 115.90 | 73 | 615.90 | 133 | 1115.90 | 193 | 1615.90 | 253 | 2115.90 | 313 | 2615.90 | 363 | 3032.50 | 413 | 3449.20 | 463 | 3865.90 |
| 14 | 124.20 | 74 | 624.20 | 134 | 1124.20 | 194 | 1624.20 | 254 | 2124.20 | 314 | 2624.20 | 364 | 3040.90 | 414 | 3457.50 | 464 | 3874.20 |
| 15 | 132.50 | 75 | 632.50 | 135 | 1132.50 | 195 | 1632.50 | 255 | 2132.50 | 315 | 2632.50 | 365 | 3049.20 | 415 | 3465.90 | 465 | 3882.50 |
| 16 | 140.90 | 76 | 640.90 | 136 | 1140.90 | 196 | 1640.90 | 256 | 2140.90 | 316 | 2640.90 | 366 | 3057.50 | 416 | 3474.20 | 466 | 3890.90 |
| 17 | 149.20 | 77 | 649.20 | 137 | 1149.20 | 197 | 1649.20 | 257 | 2149.20 | 317 | 2649.20 | 367 | 3065.90 | 417 | 3482.50 | 467 | 3899.20 |
| 18 | 157.50 | 78 | 657.50 | 138 | 1157.50 | 198 | 1657.50 | 258 | 2157.50 | 318 | 2657.50 | 368 | 3074.20 | 418 | 3490.90 | 468 | 3907.50 |
| 19 | 165.90 | 79 | 665.90 | 139 | 1165.90 | 199 | 1665.90 | 259 | 2165.90 | 319 | 2665.90 | 369 | 3082.50 | 419 | 3499.20 | 469 | 3915.90 |
| 20 | 174.20 | 80 | 674.20 | 140 | 1174.20 | 200 | 1674.20 | 260 | 2174.20 | 320 | 2674.20 | 370 | 3090.90 | 420 | 3507.50 | 470 | 3924.20 |
| 21 | 182.50 | 81 | 682.50 | 141 | 1182.50 | 201 | 1682.50 | 261 | 2182.50 | 321 | 2682.50 | 371 | 3099.20 | 421 | 3515.90 | 471 | 3932.50 |
| 22 | 190.90 | 82 | 690.90 | 142 | 1190.90 | 202 | 1690.90 | 262 | 2190.90 | 322 | 2690.90 | 372 | 3107.50 | 422 | 3524.20 | 472 | 3940.90 |
| 23 | 199.20 | 83 | 699.20 | 143 | 1199.20 | 203 | 1699.20 | 263 | 2199.20 | 323 | 2699.20 | 373 | 3115.90 | 423 | 3532.50 | 473 | 3949.20 |
| 24 | 207.50 | 84 | 707.50 | 144 | 1207.50 | 204 | 1707.50 | 264 | 2207.50 | 324 | 2707.50 | 374 | 3124.20 | 424 | 3540.90 | 474 | 3957.50 |
| 25 | 215.90 | 85 | 715.90 | 145 | 1215.90 | 205 | 1715.90 | 265 | 2215.90 | 325 | 2715.90 | 375 | 3132.50 | 425 | 3549.20 | 475 | 3965.90 |
| 26 | 224.20 | 86 | 724.20 | 146 | 1224.20 | 206 | 1724.20 | 266 | 2224.20 | 326 | 2724.20 | 376 | 3140.90 | 426 | 3557.50 | 476 | 3974.20 |
| 27 | 232.50 | 87 | 732.50 | 147 | 1232.50 | 207 | 1732.50 | 267 | 2232.50 | 327 | 2732.50 | 377 | 3149.20 | 427 | 3565.90 | 477 | 3982.50 |
| 28 | 240.90 | 88 | 740.90 | 148 | 1240.90 | 208 | 1740.90 | 268 | 2240.90 | 328 | 2740.90 | 378 | 3157.50 | 428 | 3574.20 | 478 | 3990.90 |
| 29 | 249.20 | 89 | 749.20 | 149 | 1249.20 | 209 | 1749.20 | 269 | 2249.20 | 329 | 2749.20 | 379 | 3165.90 | 429 | 3582.50 | 479 | 3999.20 |
| 30 | 257.50 | 90 | 757.50 | 150 | 1257.50 | 210 | 1757.50 | 270 | 2257.50 | 330 | 2757.50 | 380 | 3174.20 | 430 | 3590.90 | 480 | 4007.50 |
| 31 | 265.90 | 91 | 765.90 | 151 | 1265.90 | 211 | 1765.90 | 271 | 2265.90 | 331 | 2765.90 | 381 | 3182.50 | 431 | 3599.20 | 481 | 4015.90 |
| 32 | 274.20 | 92 | 774.20 | 152 | 1274.20 | 212 | 1774.20 | 272 | 2274.20 | 332 | 2774.20 | 382 | 3190.90 | 432 | 3607.50 | 482 | 4024.20 |
| 33 | 282.50 | 93 | 782.50 | 153 | 1282.50 | 213 | 1782.50 | 273 | 2282.50 | 333 | 2782.50 | 383 | 3199.20 | 433 | 3615.90 | 483 | 4032.50 |
| 34 | 290.90 | 94 | 790.90 | 154 | 1290.90 | 214 | 1790.90 | 274 | 2290.90 | 334 | 2790.90 | 384 | 3207.50 | 434 | 3624.20 | 484 | 4040.90 |
| 35 | 299.20 | 95 | 799.20 | 155 | 1299.20 | 215 | 1799.20 | 275 | 2299.20 | 335 | 2799.20 | 385 | 3215.90 | 435 | 3632.50 | 485 | 4049.20 |
| 36 | 307.50 | 96 | 807.50 | 156 | 1307.50 | 216 | 1807.50 | 276 | 2307.50 | 336 | 2807.50 | 386 | 3224.20 | 436 | 3640.90 | 486 | 4057.50 |
| 37 | 315.90 | 97 | 815.90 | 157 | 1315.90 | 217 | 1815.90 | 277 | 2315.90 | 337 | 2815.90 | 387 | 3232.50 | 437 | 3649.20 | 487 | 4065.90 |
| 38 | 324.20 | 98 | 824.20 | 158 | 1324.20 | 218 | 1824.20 | 278 | 2324.20 | 338 | 2824.20 | 388 | 3240.90 | 438 | 3657.50 | 488 | 4074.20 |
| 39 | 332.50 | 99 | 832.50 | 159 | 1332.50 | 219 | 1832.50 | 279 | 2332.50 | 339 | 2832.50 | 389 | 3249.20 | 439 | 3665.90 | 489 | 4082.50 |
| 40 | 340.90 | 100 | 840.90 | 160 | 1340.90 | 220 | 1840.90 | 280 | 2340.90 | 340 | 2840.90 | 390 | 3257.50 | 440 | 3674.20 | 490 | 4090.90 |
| 41 | 349.20 | 101 | 849.20 | 161 | 1349.20 | 221 | 1849.20 | 281 | 2349.20 | 341 | 2849.20 | 391 | 3265.90 | 441 | 3682.50 | 491 | 4099.20 |
| 42 | 357.50 | 102 | 857.50 | 162 | 1357.50 | 222 | 1857.50 | 282 | 2357.50 | 342 | 2857.50 | 392 | 3274.20 | 442 | 3690.90 | 492 | 4107.50 |
| 43 | 365.90 | 103 | 865.90 | 163 | 1365.90 | 223 | 1865.90 | 283 | 2365.90 | 343 | 2865.90 | 393 | 3282.50 | 443 | 3699.20 | 493 | 4115.90 |
| 44 | 374.20 | 104 | 874.20 | 164 | 1374.20 | 224 | 1874.20 | 284 | 2374.20 | 344 | 2874.20 | 394 | 3290.90 | 444 | 3707.50 | 494 | 4124.20 |
| 45 | 382.50 | 105 | 882.50 | 165 | 1382.50 | 225 | 1882.50 | 285 | 2382.50 | 345 | 2882.50 | 395 | 3299.20 | 445 | 3715.90 | 495 | 4132.50 |
| 46 | 390.90 | 106 | 890.90 | 166 | 1390.90 | 226 | 1890.90 | 286 | 2390.90 | 346 | 2890.90 | 396 | 3307.50 | 446 | 3724.20 | 496 | 4140.90 |
| 47 | 399.20 | 107 | 899.20 | 167 | 1399.20 | 227 | 1899.20 | 287 | 2399.20 | 347 | 2899.20 | 397 | 3315.90 | 447 | 3732.50 | 497 | 4149.20 |
| 48 | 407.50 | 108 | 907.50 | 168 | 1407.50 | 228 | 1907.50 | 288 | 2407.50 | 348 | 2907.50 | 398 | 3324.20 | 448 | 3740.90 | 498 | 4157.50 |
| 49 | 415.90 | 109 | 915.90 | 169 | 1415.90 | 229 | 1915.90 | 289 | 2415.90 | 349 | 2915.90 | 399 | 3332.50 | 449 | 3749.20 | 499 | 4165.90 |
| 50 | 424.20 | 110 | 924.20 | 170 | 1424.20 | 230 | 1924.20 | 290 | 2424.20 | 350 | 2924.20 | 400 | 3340.90 | 450 | 3757.50 | 500 | 4174.20 |
| 51 | 432.50 | 111 | 932.50 | 171 | 1432.50 | 231 | 1932.50 | 291 | 2432.50 | | | | | | | | |
| 52 | 440.90 | 112 | 940.90 | 172 | 1440.90 | 232 | 1940.90 | 292 | 2440.90 | | | | | | | | |
| 53 | 449.20 | 113 | 949.20 | 173 | 1449.20 | 233 | 1949.20 | 293 | 2449.20 | | | | | | | | |
| 54 | 457.50 | 114 | 957.50 | 174 | 1457.50 | 234 | 1957.50 | 294 | 2457.50 | | | | | | | | |
| 55 | 465.90 | 115 | 965.90 | 175 | 1465.90 | 235 | 1965.90 | 295 | 2465.90 | | | | | | | | |
| 56 | 474.20 | 116 | 974.20 | 176 | 1474.20 | 236 | 1974.20 | 296 | 2474.20 | | | | | | | | |
| 57 | 482.50 | 117 | 982.50 | 177 | 1482.50 | 237 | 1982.50 | 297 | 2482.50 | | | | | | | | |
| 58 | 490.90 | 118 | 990.90 | 178 | 1490.90 | 238 | 1990.90 | 298 | 2490.90 | | | | | | | | |
| 59 | 499.20 | 119 | 999.20 | 179 | 1499.20 | 239 | 1999.20 | 299 | 2499.20 | | | | | | | | |
| 60 | 507.50 | 120 | 1007.50 | 180 | 1507.50 | 240 | 2007.50 | 300 | 2507.50 | | | | | | | | |

**Code more than 500**

1 Where the code is in the range **501** to **1000** inclusive:

  a. Subtract **500** from the code and use the balance of the code to obtain a pay adjustment figure from the table above.

  b. Add this pay adjustment figure to the figure given in the box alongside to obtain the figure of total pay adjustment to date *  **4166.70**

2 Where the code **exceeds 1000** follow the instructions on **page 3**.

66

## Tables A - Pay Adjustment Tables

Feb 6 to Mar 5 **Month 11**

| Code | Total pay adjustment to date | Code | Total pay adjustment to date | Code | Total pay adjustment to date | Code | Total pay adjustment to date | Code | Total pay adjustment to date | Code | Total pay adjustment to date | Code | Total pay adjustment to date | Code | Total pay adjustment to date | Code | Total pay adjustment to date |
|---|---|---|---|---|---|---|---|---|---|---|---|---|---|---|---|---|---|
| | £ | | £ | | £ | | £ | | £ | | £ | | £ | | £ | | £ |
| 0 | NIL | | | | | | | | | | | | | | | | |
| 1 | 17.49 | 61 | 567.49 | 121 | 1117.49 | 181 | 1667.49 | 241 | 2217.49 | 301 | 2767.49 | 351 | 3225.75 | 401 | 3684.12 | 451 | 4142.49 |
| 2 | 26.62 | 62 | 576.62 | 122 | 1126.62 | 182 | 1676.62 | 242 | 2226.62 | 302 | 2776.62 | 352 | 3234.99 | 402 | 3693.25 | 452 | 4151.62 |
| 3 | 35.75 | 63 | 585.75 | 123 | 1135.75 | 183 | 1685.75 | 243 | 2235.75 | 303 | 2785.75 | 353 | 3244.12 | 403 | 3702.49 | 453 | 4160.75 |
| 4 | 44.99 | 64 | 594.99 | 124 | 1144.99 | 184 | 1694.99 | 244 | 2244.99 | 304 | 2794.99 | 354 | 3253.25 | 404 | 3711.62 | 454 | 4169.99 |
| 5 | 54.12 | 65 | 604.12 | 125 | 1154.12 | 185 | 1704.12 | 245 | 2254.12 | 305 | 2804.12 | 355 | 3262.49 | 405 | 3720.75 | 455 | 4179.12 |
| 6 | 63.25 | 66 | 613.25 | 126 | 1163.25 | 186 | 1713.25 | 246 | 2263.25 | 306 | 2813.25 | 356 | 3271.62 | 406 | 3729.99 | 456 | 4188.25 |
| 7 | 72.49 | 67 | 622.49 | 127 | 1172.49 | 187 | 1722.49 | 247 | 2272.49 | 307 | 2822.49 | 357 | 3280.75 | 407 | 3739.12 | 457 | 4197.49 |
| 8 | 81.62 | 68 | 631.62 | 128 | 1181.62 | 188 | 1731.62 | 248 | 2281.62 | 308 | 2831.62 | 358 | 3289.99 | 408 | 3748.25 | 458 | 4206.62 |
| 9 | 90.75 | 69 | 640.75 | 129 | 1190.75 | 189 | 1740.75 | 249 | 2290.75 | 309 | 2840.75 | 359 | 3299.12 | 409 | 3757.49 | 459 | 4215.75 |
| 10 | 99.99 | 70 | 649.99 | 130 | 1199.99 | 190 | 1749.99 | 250 | 2299.99 | 310 | 2849.99 | 360 | 3308.25 | 410 | 3766.62 | 460 | 4224.99 |
| 11 | 109.12 | 71 | 659.12 | 131 | 1209.12 | 191 | 1759.12 | 251 | 2309.12 | 311 | 2859.12 | 361 | 3317.49 | 411 | 3775.75 | 461 | 4234.12 |
| 12 | 118.25 | 72 | 668.25 | 132 | 1218.25 | 192 | 1768.25 | 252 | 2318.25 | 312 | 2868.25 | 362 | 3326.62 | 412 | 3784.99 | 462 | 4243.25 |
| 13 | 127.49 | 73 | 677.49 | 133 | 1227.49 | 193 | 1777.49 | 253 | 2327.49 | 313 | 2877.49 | 363 | 3335.75 | 413 | 3794.12 | 463 | 4252.49 |
| 14 | 136.62 | 74 | 686.62 | 134 | 1236.62 | 194 | 1786.62 | 254 | 2336.62 | 314 | 2886.62 | 364 | 3344.99 | 414 | 3803.25 | 464 | 4261.62 |
| 15 | 145.75 | 75 | 695.75 | 135 | 1245.75 | 195 | 1795.75 | 255 | 2345.75 | 315 | 2895.75 | 365 | 3354.12 | 415 | 3812.49 | 465 | 4270.75 |
| 16 | 154.99 | 76 | 704.99 | 136 | 1254.99 | 196 | 1804.99 | 256 | 2354.99 | 316 | 2904.99 | 366 | 3363.25 | 416 | 3821.62 | 466 | 4279.99 |
| 17 | 164.12 | 77 | 714.12 | 137 | 1264.12 | 197 | 1814.12 | 257 | 2364.12 | 317 | 2914.12 | 367 | 3372.49 | 417 | 3830.75 | 467 | 4289.12 |
| 18 | 173.25 | 78 | 723.25 | 138 | 1273.25 | 198 | 1823.25 | 258 | 2373.25 | 318 | 2923.25 | 368 | 3381.62 | 418 | 3839.99 | 468 | 4298.25 |
| 19 | 182.49 | 79 | 732.49 | 139 | 1282.49 | 199 | 1832.49 | 259 | 2382.49 | 319 | 2932.49 | 369 | 3390.75 | 419 | 3849.12 | 469 | 4307.49 |
| 20 | 191.62 | 80 | 741.62 | 140 | 1291.62 | 200 | 1841.62 | 260 | 2391.62 | 320 | 2941.62 | 370 | 3399.99 | 420 | 3858.25 | 470 | 4316.62 |
| 21 | 200.75 | 81 | 750.75 | 141 | 1300.75 | 201 | 1850.75 | 261 | 2400.75 | 321 | 2950.75 | 371 | 3409.12 | 421 | 3867.49 | 471 | 4325.75 |
| 22 | 209.99 | 82 | 759.99 | 142 | 1309.99 | 202 | 1859.99 | 262 | 2409.99 | 322 | 2959.99 | 372 | 3418.25 | 422 | 3876.62 | 472 | 4334.99 |
| 23 | 219.12 | 83 | 769.12 | 143 | 1319.12 | 203 | 1869.12 | 263 | 2419.12 | 323 | 2969.12 | 373 | 3427.49 | 423 | 3885.75 | 473 | 4344.12 |
| 24 | 228.25 | 84 | 778.25 | 144 | 1328.25 | 204 | 1878.25 | 264 | 2428.25 | 324 | 2978.25 | 374 | 3436.62 | 424 | 3894.99 | 474 | 4353.25 |
| 25 | 237.49 | 85 | 787.49 | 145 | 1337.49 | 205 | 1887.49 | 265 | 2437.49 | 325 | 2987.49 | 375 | 3445.75 | 425 | 3904.12 | 475 | 4362.49 |
| 26 | 246.62 | 86 | 796.62 | 146 | 1346.62 | 206 | 1896.62 | 266 | 2446.62 | 326 | 2996.62 | 376 | 3454.99 | 426 | 3913.25 | 476 | 4371.62 |
| 27 | 255.75 | 87 | 805.75 | 147 | 1355.75 | 207 | 1905.75 | 267 | 2455.75 | 327 | 3005.75 | 377 | 3464.12 | 427 | 3922.49 | 477 | 4380.75 |
| 28 | 264.99 | 88 | 814.99 | 148 | 1364.99 | 208 | 1914.99 | 268 | 2464.99 | 328 | 3014.99 | 378 | 3473.25 | 428 | 3931.62 | 478 | 4389.99 |
| 29 | 274.12 | 89 | 824.12 | 149 | 1374.12 | 209 | 1924.12 | 269 | 2474.12 | 329 | 3024.12 | 379 | 3482.49 | 429 | 3940.75 | 479 | 4399.12 |
| 30 | 283.25 | 90 | 833.25 | 150 | 1383.25 | 210 | 1933.25 | 270 | 2483.25 | 330 | 3033.25 | 380 | 3491.62 | 430 | 3949.99 | 480 | 4408.25 |
| 31 | 292.49 | 91 | 842.49 | 151 | 1392.49 | 211 | 1942.49 | 271 | 2492.49 | 331 | 3042.49 | 381 | 3500.75 | 431 | 3959.12 | 481 | 4417.49 |
| 32 | 301.62 | 92 | 851.62 | 152 | 1401.62 | 212 | 1951.62 | 272 | 2501.62 | 332 | 3051.62 | 382 | 3509.99 | 432 | 3968.25 | 482 | 4426.62 |
| 33 | 310.75 | 93 | 860.75 | 153 | 1410.75 | 213 | 1960.75 | 273 | 2510.75 | 333 | 3060.75 | 383 | 3519.12 | 433 | 3977.49 | 483 | 4435.75 |
| 34 | 319.99 | 94 | 869.99 | 154 | 1419.99 | 214 | 1969.99 | 274 | 2519.99 | 334 | 3069.99 | 384 | 3528.25 | 434 | 3986.62 | 484 | 4444.99 |
| 35 | 329.12 | 95 | 879.12 | 155 | 1429.12 | 215 | 1979.12 | 275 | 2529.12 | 335 | 3079.12 | 385 | 3537.49 | 435 | 3995.75 | 485 | 4454.12 |
| 36 | 338.25 | 96 | 888.25 | 156 | 1438.25 | 216 | 1988.25 | 276 | 2538.25 | 336 | 3088.25 | 386 | 3546.62 | 436 | 4004.99 | 486 | 4463.25 |
| 37 | 347.49 | 97 | 897.49 | 157 | 1447.49 | 217 | 1997.49 | 277 | 2547.49 | 337 | 3097.49 | 387 | 3555.75 | 437 | 4014.12 | 487 | 4472.49 |
| 38 | 356.62 | 98 | 906.62 | 158 | 1456.62 | 218 | 2006.62 | 278 | 2556.62 | 338 | 3106.62 | 388 | 3564.99 | 438 | 4023.25 | 488 | 4481.62 |
| 39 | 365.75 | 99 | 915.75 | 159 | 1465.75 | 219 | 2015.75 | 279 | 2565.75 | 339 | 3115.75 | 389 | 3574.12 | 439 | 4032.49 | 489 | 4490.75 |
| 40 | 374.99 | 100 | 924.99 | 160 | 1474.99 | 220 | 2024.99 | 280 | 2574.99 | 340 | 3124.99 | 390 | 3583.25 | 440 | 4041.62 | 490 | 4499.99 |
| 41 | 384.12 | 101 | 934.12 | 161 | 1484.12 | 221 | 2034.12 | 281 | 2584.12 | 341 | 3134.12 | 391 | 3592.49 | 441 | 4050.75 | 491 | 4509.12 |
| 42 | 393.25 | 102 | 943.25 | 162 | 1493.25 | 222 | 2043.25 | 282 | 2593.25 | 342 | 3143.25 | 392 | 3601.62 | 442 | 4059.99 | 492 | 4518.25 |
| 43 | 402.49 | 103 | 952.49 | 163 | 1502.49 | 223 | 2052.49 | 283 | 2602.49 | 343 | 3152.49 | 393 | 3610.75 | 443 | 4069.12 | 493 | 4527.49 |
| 44 | 411.62 | 104 | 961.62 | 164 | 1511.62 | 224 | 2061.62 | 284 | 2611.62 | 344 | 3161.62 | 394 | 3619.99 | 444 | 4078.25 | 494 | 4536.62 |
| 45 | 420.75 | 105 | 970.75 | 165 | 1520.75 | 225 | 2070.75 | 285 | 2620.75 | 345 | 3170.75 | 395 | 3629.12 | 445 | 4087.49 | 495 | 4545.75 |
| 46 | 429.99 | 106 | 979.99 | 166 | 1529.99 | 226 | 2079.99 | 286 | 2629.99 | 346 | 3179.99 | 396 | 3638.25 | 446 | 4096.62 | 496 | 4554.99 |
| 47 | 439.12 | 107 | 989.12 | 167 | 1539.12 | 227 | 2089.12 | 287 | 2639.12 | 347 | 3189.12 | 397 | 3647.49 | 447 | 4105.75 | 497 | 4564.12 |
| 48 | 448.25 | 108 | 998.25 | 168 | 1548.25 | 228 | 2098.25 | 288 | 2648.25 | 348 | 3198.25 | 398 | 3656.62 | 448 | 4114.99 | 498 | 4573.25 |
| 49 | 457.49 | 109 | 1007.49 | 169 | 1557.49 | 229 | 2107.49 | 289 | 2657.49 | 349 | 3207.49 | 399 | 3665.75 | 449 | 4124.12 | 499 | 4582.49 |
| 50 | 466.62 | 110 | 1016.62 | 170 | 1566.62 | 230 | 2116.62 | 290 | 2666.62 | 350 | 3216.62 | 400 | 3674.99 | 450 | 4133.25 | 500 | 4591.62 |
| 51 | 475.75 | 111 | 1025.75 | 171 | 1575.75 | 231 | 2125.75 | 291 | 2675.75 | | | | | | | | |
| 52 | 484.99 | 112 | 1034.99 | 172 | 1584.99 | 232 | 2134.99 | 292 | 2684.99 | | | | | | | | |
| 53 | 494.12 | 113 | 1044.12 | 173 | 1594.12 | 233 | 2144.12 | 293 | 2694.12 | | | | | | | | |
| 54 | 503.25 | 114 | 1053.25 | 174 | 1603.25 | 234 | 2153.25 | 294 | 2703.25 | | | | | | | | |
| 55 | 512.49 | 115 | 1062.49 | 175 | 1612.49 | 235 | 2162.49 | 295 | 2712.49 | | | | | | | | |
| 56 | 521.62 | 116 | 1071.62 | 176 | 1621.62 | 236 | 2171.62 | 296 | 2721.62 | | | | | | | | |
| 57 | 530.75 | 117 | 1080.75 | 177 | 1630.75 | 237 | 2180.75 | 297 | 2730.75 | | | | | | | | |
| 58 | 539.99 | 118 | 1089.99 | 178 | 1639.99 | 238 | 2189.99 | 298 | 2739.99 | | | | | | | | |
| 59 | 549.12 | 119 | 1099.12 | 179 | 1649.12 | 239 | 2199.12 | 299 | 2749.12 | | | | | | | | |
| 60 | 558.25 | 120 | 1108.25 | 180 | 1658.25 | 240 | 2208.25 | 300 | 2758.25 | | | | | | | | |

**Code more than 500**

1 Where the code is in the range **501 to 1000** inclusive:

a. Subtract **500** from the code and use the balance of the code to obtain a pay adjustment figure from the table above.

b. Add this pay adjustment figure to the figure given in the box alongside to obtain the figure of total pay adjustment to date * **4583.37**

2 Where the code **exceeds 1000** follow the instructions on **page 3**.

67

## Month 12  Mar 6 to Apr 5

### Tables A - Pay Adjustment Tables

| Code | Total pay adjustment to date | Code | Total pay adjustment to date | Code | Total pay adjustment to date | Code | Total pay adjustment to date | Code | Total pay adjustment to date | Code | Total pay adjustment to date | Code | Total pay adjustment to date | Code | Total pay adjustment to date | Code | Total pay adjustment to date |
|---|---|---|---|---|---|---|---|---|---|---|---|---|---|---|---|---|---|
| | £ | | £ | | £ | | £ | | £ | | £ | | £ | | £ | | £ |
| 0 | NIL | | | | | | | | | | | | | | | | |
| 1 | 19.08 | 61 | 619.08 | 121 | 1219.08 | 181 | 1819.08 | 241 | 2419.08 | 301 | 3019.08 | 351 | 3519.00 | 401 | 4019.04 | 451 | 4519.08 |
| 2 | 29.04 | 62 | 629.04 | 122 | 1229.04 | 182 | 1829.04 | 242 | 2429.04 | 302 | 3029.04 | 352 | 3529.08 | 402 | 4029.00 | 452 | 4529.04 |
| 3 | 39.00 | 63 | 639.00 | 123 | 1239.00 | 183 | 1839.00 | 243 | 2439.00 | 303 | 3039.00 | 353 | 3539.04 | 403 | 4039.08 | 453 | 4539.00 |
| 4 | 49.08 | 64 | 649.08 | 124 | 1249.08 | 184 | 1849.08 | 244 | 2449.08 | 304 | 3049.08 | 354 | 3549.00 | 404 | 4049.04 | 454 | 4549.08 |
| 5 | 59.04 | 65 | 659.04 | 125 | 1259.04 | 185 | 1859.04 | 245 | 2459.04 | 305 | 3059.04 | 355 | 3559.08 | 405 | 4059.04 | 455 | 4559.04 |
| 6 | 69.00 | 66 | 669.00 | 126 | 1269.00 | 186 | 1869.00 | 246 | 2469.00 | 306 | 3069.00 | 356 | 3569.04 | 406 | 4069.08 | 456 | 4569.00 |
| 7 | 79.08 | 67 | 679.08 | 127 | 1279.08 | 187 | 1879.08 | 247 | 2479.08 | 307 | 3079.08 | 357 | 3579.00 | 407 | 4079.04 | 457 | 4579.08 |
| 8 | 89.04 | 68 | 689.04 | 128 | 1289.04 | 188 | 1889.04 | 248 | 2489.04 | 308 | 3089.04 | 358 | 3589.08 | 408 | 4089.00 | 458 | 4589.04 |
| 9 | 99.00 | 69 | 699.00 | 129 | 1299.00 | 189 | 1899.00 | 249 | 2499.00 | 309 | 3099.00 | 359 | 3599.04 | 409 | 4099.08 | 459 | 4599.00 |
| 10 | 109.08 | 70 | 709.08 | 130 | 1309.08 | 190 | 1909.08 | 250 | 2509.08 | 310 | 3109.08 | 360 | 3609.00 | 410 | 4109.04 | 460 | 4609.08 |
| 11 | 119.04 | 71 | 719.04 | 131 | 1319.04 | 191 | 1919.04 | 251 | 2519.04 | 311 | 3119.04 | 361 | 3619.08 | 411 | 4119.00 | 461 | 4619.04 |
| 12 | 129.00 | 72 | 729.00 | 132 | 1329.00 | 192 | 1929.00 | 252 | 2529.00 | 312 | 3129.00 | 362 | 3629.04 | 412 | 4129.08 | 462 | 4629.00 |
| 13 | 139.08 | 73 | 739.08 | 133 | 1339.08 | 193 | 1939.08 | 253 | 2539.08 | 313 | 3139.08 | 363 | 3639.00 | 413 | 4139.04 | 463 | 4639.08 |
| 14 | 149.04 | 74 | 749.04 | 134 | 1349.04 | 194 | 1949.04 | 254 | 2549.04 | 314 | 3149.04 | 364 | 3649.08 | 414 | 4149.00 | 464 | 4649.04 |
| 15 | 159.00 | 75 | 759.00 | 135 | 1359.00 | 195 | 1959.00 | 255 | 2559.00 | 315 | 3159.00 | 365 | 3659.04 | 415 | 4159.08 | 465 | 4659.00 |
| 16 | 169.08 | 76 | 769.08 | 136 | 1369.08 | 196 | 1969.08 | 256 | 2569.08 | 316 | 3169.08 | 366 | 3669.00 | 416 | 4169.04 | 466 | 4669.08 |
| 17 | 179.04 | 77 | 779.04 | 137 | 1379.04 | 197 | 1979.04 | 257 | 2579.04 | 317 | 3179.04 | 367 | 3679.08 | 417 | 4179.00 | 467 | 4679.04 |
| 18 | 189.00 | 78 | 789.00 | 138 | 1389.00 | 198 | 1989.00 | 258 | 2589.00 | 318 | 3189.00 | 368 | 3689.04 | 418 | 4189.08 | 468 | 4689.00 |
| 19 | 199.08 | 79 | 799.08 | 139 | 1399.08 | 199 | 1999.08 | 259 | 2599.08 | 319 | 3199.08 | 369 | 3699.00 | 419 | 4199.04 | 469 | 4699.08 |
| 20 | 209.04 | 80 | 809.04 | 140 | 1409.04 | 200 | 2009.04 | 260 | 2609.04 | 320 | 3209.04 | 370 | 3709.08 | 420 | 4209.00 | 470 | 4709.04 |
| 21 | 219.00 | 81 | 819.00 | 141 | 1419.00 | 201 | 2019.00 | 261 | 2619.00 | 321 | 3219.00 | 371 | 3719.04 | 421 | 4219.08 | 471 | 4719.00 |
| 22 | 229.08 | 82 | 829.08 | 142 | 1429.08 | 202 | 2029.08 | 262 | 2629.08 | 322 | 3229.08 | 372 | 3729.00 | 422 | 4229.04 | 472 | 4729.08 |
| 23 | 239.04 | 83 | 839.04 | 143 | 1439.04 | 203 | 2039.04 | 263 | 2639.04 | 323 | 3239.04 | 373 | 3739.08 | 423 | 4239.00 | 473 | 4739.04 |
| 24 | 249.00 | 84 | 849.00 | 144 | 1449.00 | 204 | 2049.00 | 264 | 2649.00 | 324 | 3249.00 | 374 | 3749.04 | 424 | 4249.08 | 474 | 4749.00 |
| 25 | 259.08 | 85 | 859.08 | 145 | 1459.08 | 205 | 2059.08 | 265 | 2659.08 | 325 | 3259.08 | 375 | 3759.00 | 425 | 4259.04 | 475 | 4759.08 |
| 26 | 269.04 | 86 | 869.04 | 146 | 1469.04 | 206 | 2069.04 | 266 | 2669.04 | 326 | 3269.04 | 376 | 3769.08 | 426 | 4269.00 | 476 | 4769.04 |
| 27 | 279.00 | 87 | 879.00 | 147 | 1479.00 | 207 | 2079.00 | 267 | 2679.00 | 327 | 3279.00 | 377 | 3779.04 | 427 | 4279.08 | 477 | 4779.00 |
| 28 | 289.08 | 88 | 889.08 | 148 | 1489.08 | 208 | 2089.08 | 268 | 2689.08 | 328 | 3289.08 | 378 | 3789.00 | 428 | 4289.04 | 478 | 4789.08 |
| 29 | 299.04 | 89 | 899.04 | 149 | 1499.04 | 209 | 2099.04 | 269 | 2699.04 | 329 | 3299.04 | 379 | 3799.08 | 429 | 4299.00 | 479 | 4799.04 |
| 30 | 309.00 | 90 | 909.00 | 150 | 1509.00 | 210 | 2109.00 | 270 | 2709.00 | 330 | 3309.00 | 380 | 3809.04 | 430 | 4309.08 | 480 | 4809.00 |
| 31 | 319.08 | 91 | 919.08 | 151 | 1519.08 | 211 | 2119.08 | 271 | 2719.08 | 331 | 3319.08 | 381 | 3819.00 | 431 | 4319.04 | 481 | 4819.08 |
| 32 | 329.04 | 92 | 929.04 | 152 | 1529.04 | 212 | 2129.04 | 272 | 2729.04 | 332 | 3329.04 | 382 | 3829.08 | 432 | 4329.00 | 482 | 4829.04 |
| 33 | 339.00 | 93 | 939.00 | 153 | 1539.00 | 213 | 2139.00 | 273 | 2739.00 | 333 | 3339.00 | 383 | 3839.04 | 433 | 4339.08 | 483 | 4839.00 |
| 34 | 349.08 | 94 | 949.08 | 154 | 1549.08 | 214 | 2149.08 | 274 | 2749.08 | 334 | 3349.08 | 384 | 3849.00 | 434 | 4349.04 | 484 | 4849.08 |
| 35 | 359.04 | 95 | 959.04 | 155 | 1559.04 | 215 | 2159.04 | 275 | 2759.04 | 335 | 3359.04 | 385 | 3859.08 | 435 | 4359.04 | 485 | 4859.04 |
| 36 | 369.00 | 96 | 969.00 | 156 | 1569.00 | 216 | 2169.00 | 276 | 2769.00 | 336 | 3369.00 | 386 | 3869.04 | 436 | 4369.08 | 486 | 4869.00 |
| 37 | 379.08 | 97 | 979.08 | 157 | 1579.08 | 217 | 2179.08 | 277 | 2779.08 | 337 | 3379.08 | 387 | 3879.00 | 437 | 4379.04 | 487 | 4879.08 |
| 38 | 389.04 | 98 | 989.04 | 158 | 1589.04 | 218 | 2189.04 | 278 | 2789.04 | 338 | 3389.04 | 388 | 3889.08 | 438 | 4389.00 | 488 | 4889.04 |
| 39 | 399.00 | 99 | 999.00 | 159 | 1599.00 | 219 | 2199.00 | 279 | 2799.00 | 339 | 3399.00 | 389 | 3899.04 | 439 | 4399.08 | 489 | 4899.00 |
| 40 | 409.08 | 100 | 1009.08 | 160 | 1609.08 | 220 | 2209.08 | 280 | 2809.08 | 340 | 3409.08 | 390 | 3909.00 | 440 | 4409.04 | 490 | 4909.08 |
| 41 | 419.04 | 101 | 1019.04 | 161 | 1619.04 | 221 | 2219.04 | 281 | 2819.04 | 341 | 3419.04 | 391 | 3919.08 | 441 | 4419.00 | 491 | 4919.04 |
| 42 | 429.00 | 102 | 1029.00 | 162 | 1629.00 | 222 | 2229.00 | 282 | 2829.00 | 342 | 3429.00 | 392 | 3929.04 | 442 | 4429.08 | 492 | 4929.00 |
| 43 | 439.08 | 103 | 1039.08 | 163 | 1639.08 | 223 | 2239.08 | 283 | 2839.08 | 343 | 3439.08 | 393 | 3939.00 | 443 | 4439.04 | 493 | 4939.08 |
| 44 | 449.04 | 104 | 1049.04 | 164 | 1649.04 | 224 | 2249.04 | 284 | 2849.04 | 344 | 3449.04 | 394 | 3949.08 | 444 | 4449.00 | 494 | 4949.04 |
| 45 | 459.00 | 105 | 1059.00 | 165 | 1659.00 | 225 | 2259.00 | 285 | 2859.00 | 345 | 3459.00 | 395 | 3959.04 | 445 | 4459.08 | 495 | 4959.00 |
| 46 | 469.08 | 106 | 1069.08 | 166 | 1669.08 | 226 | 2269.08 | 286 | 2869.08 | 346 | 3469.08 | 396 | 3969.00 | 446 | 4469.04 | 496 | 4969.08 |
| 47 | 479.04 | 107 | 1079.04 | 167 | 1679.04 | 227 | 2279.04 | 287 | 2879.04 | 347 | 3479.04 | 397 | 3979.08 | 447 | 4479.00 | 497 | 4979.04 |
| 48 | 489.00 | 108 | 1089.00 | 168 | 1689.00 | 228 | 2289.00 | 288 | 2889.00 | 348 | 3489.00 | 398 | 3989.04 | 448 | 4489.08 | 498 | 4989.00 |
| 49 | 499.08 | 109 | 1099.08 | 169 | 1699.08 | 229 | 2299.08 | 289 | 2899.08 | 349 | 3499.08 | 399 | 3999.04 | 449 | 4499.04 | 499 | 4999.08 |
| 50 | 509.04 | 110 | 1109.04 | 170 | 1709.04 | 230 | 2309.04 | 290 | 2909.04 | 350 | 3509.04 | 400 | 4009.08 | 450 | 4509.04 | 500 | 5009.04 |
| 51 | 519.00 | 111 | 1119.00 | 171 | 1719.00 | 231 | 2319.00 | 291 | 2919.00 | | | | | | |
| 52 | 529.08 | 112 | 1129.08 | 172 | 1729.08 | 232 | 2329.08 | 292 | 2929.08 | | | | | | |
| 53 | 539.04 | 113 | 1139.04 | 173 | 1739.04 | 233 | 2339.04 | 293 | 2939.04 | | | | | | |
| 54 | 549.00 | 114 | 1149.00 | 174 | 1749.00 | 234 | 2349.00 | 294 | 2949.00 | | | | | | |
| 55 | 559.08 | 115 | 1159.08 | 175 | 1759.08 | 235 | 2359.08 | 295 | 2959.08 | | | | | | |
| 56 | 569.04 | 116 | 1169.04 | 176 | 1769.04 | 236 | 2369.04 | 296 | 2969.04 | | | | | | |
| 57 | 579.00 | 117 | 1179.00 | 177 | 1779.00 | 237 | 2379.00 | 297 | 2979.00 | | | | | | |
| 58 | 589.08 | 118 | 1189.08 | 178 | 1789.08 | 238 | 2389.08 | 298 | 2989.08 | | | | | | |
| 59 | 599.04 | 119 | 1199.04 | 179 | 1799.04 | 239 | 2399.04 | 299 | 2999.04 | | | | | | |
| 60 | 609.00 | 120 | 1209.00 | 180 | 1809.00 | 240 | 2409.00 | 300 | 3009.00 | | | | | | |

**Code more than 500**

1 Where the code is in the range **501** to **1000** inclusive:

a. Subtract **500** from the code and use the balance of the code to obtain a pay adjustment figure from the table above.

b. Add this pay adjustment figure to the figure given in the box alongside to obtain the figure of total pay adjustment to date *  **5000.04**

2 Where the code **exceeds 1000** follow the instructions on **page 3**.

68

Tables B to D (April 2020)

**HM Revenue & Customs**

# Taxable Pay Tables
# Manual Method

These tables are intended for the very small number of employers who are exempt from the requirement to file Real Time Information online.

If you're an employer operating PAYE in real time you're no longer able to run your payroll manually and you do not need to use these manual tables. Instead you should be using software that is capable of filing payroll information online. Find out more at www.gov.uk/payroll-software

Keep using Tables A 1993 issue – Pay Adjustment Tables.

Use pages:
- 4, 6, 7, 8, 10 and 11 for monthly paid employees – English and Northern Irish rates
- 4, 6, 7, 9, 10 and 11 for weekly paid employees – English and Northern Irish rates
- 12, 14, 15, 16, 19, 20, 21 and 22 for monthly paid employees – Scottish rates
- 12, 14, 17, 18, 19, 20, 21 and 22 for weekly paid employees – Scottish rates
- 23, 25, 26, 27, 29 and 30 for monthly paid employees – Welsh rates
- 23, 25, 26, 28, 29 and 30 for weekly paid employees – Welsh rates

Use from 6 April 2020

## How to use these tables

These tables are aimed at the small number of employers who have an agreed exemption from online filing and who'll be operating a manual payroll. Employers exempt from filing payroll information online may find it easier to run their own payroll software or HMRC's Basic PAYE Tools and file their payroll information in real time. For more information, go to www.gov.uk/payroll-software

If you use these tables please make sure that you have disposed of your previous tax tables.

---

### How to use a tax code

For **code BR** always multiply the whole pay by 0.20 (20%) to find the tax deduction at the English and Northern Irish basic rate.

For **code D0** always multiply the whole pay by 0.40 (40%) to find the tax deduction at the English and Northern Irish higher rate.

For **code D1** always multiply the whole pay by 0.45 (45%) to find the tax deduction at the English and Northern Irish additional rate.

For **code SBR** always multiply the whole pay by 0.20 (20%) to find the tax deduction at the Scottish basic rate.

For **code SD0** always multiply the whole pay by 0.21 (21%) to find the tax deduction at the Scottish intermediate rate.

For **code SD1** always multiply the whole pay by 0.41 (41%) to find the tax deduction at the Scottish higher rate.

For **code SD2** always multiply the whole pay by 0.46 (46%) to find the tax deduction at the Scottish top rate.

For **code CBR** always multiply the whole pay by 0.20 (20%) to find the tax deduction at the Welsh basic rate.

For **code CD0** always multiply the whole pay by 0.40 (40%) to find the tax deduction at the Welsh higher rate.

For **code CD1** always multiply the whole pay by 0.45 (45%) to find the tax deduction at the Welsh additional rate.

For **all other codes** follow the guidance in the rest of this booklet.

For **week 1/month 1 codes** always use the first line, against '1', in the column headed Week/Month.

---

## Taxable pay

Throughout these tables, 'taxable pay' means any amount of pay after you have used the Pay Adjustment Tables, Tables A and entered the amount in column 5 of the RT11. To use Tables A you need to know the:

- employee's tax code
- tax week/month number covering the date of payment – see the charts on page 3

Using the employee's date of payment to identify the tax week or the month, use Table A for the appropriate week or month to establish taxable pay. Round down taxable pay to the nearest pound.

### Example of how to establish 'taxable pay' using the Pay Adjustment Tables, Tables A

---

**Example 1 – all codes including prefixes S and C except BR, SBR, CBR and prefix D, SD and CD codes**

Employee's code is **431L, S431L or C431L**

The pay month is in **Month 4**

| | |
|---|---|
| **Pay in the month is** | £925.00 |
| Plus **previous pay to date** | £2,475.00 |
| **Total pay to date** | £3,400.00 |
| Minus Pay Adjustment Tables A figure at Month 4 | £1,439.68 |
| **Total taxable pay to date** | £1,960.32 |
| Rounded down to the nearest pound | £1,960 |

This is the taxable pay to be used in the calculations using these tax tables.

---

**Example 2 – only codes BR, SBR or CBR**

Employee's code is **BR, SBR or CBR**

The pay month is in **Month 4**

| | |
|---|---|
| **Pay in the month is** | £800.00 |
| Plus **previous pay to date** | £2,400.00 |
| **Total pay to date** | £3,200.00 |

You do not need to use the Pay Adjustment Tables A for codes BR, SBR and CBR.

So tax is due on the whole of the pay for this month.

| | |
|---|---|
| **Total taxable pay to date** | £3,200.00 |
| Rounded down to the nearest pound | £3,200 |

For each code take the RT11 column 5 figure, for example, £3,200, and either:

- use Table B on pages 6 and 7 for code BR
- use Scottish Table D1 on page 19 for code SBR
- use Welsh Table B on pages 25 and 26 for code CBR

Or

- multiply by 0.20 (20%)
  £3,200 x 0.20 = £640.00

---

2

## Details of annual tax rates

| | | | |
|---|---|---|---|
| English and Northern Irish basic rate | 20% | on taxable income | £1 to £37,500 |
| English and Northern Irish higher rate | 40% | on taxable income | £37,501 to £150,000 |
| English and Northern Irish additional rate | 45% | on taxable income | £150,001 and above |
| Scottish starter rate | 19% | on taxable income | £1 to £2,085 |
| Scottish basic rate | 20% | on taxable income | £2,086 to £12,658 |
| Scottish intermediate rate | 21% | on taxable income | £12,659 to £30,930 |
| Scottish higher rate | 41% | on taxable income | £30,931 to £150,000 |
| Scottish top rate | 46% | on taxable income | £150,001 and above |
| Welsh basic rate | 20% | on taxable income | £1 to £37,500 |
| Welsh higher rate | 40% | on taxable income | £37,501 to £150,000 |
| Welsh additional rate | 45% | on taxable income | £150,001 and above |

> PAYE tax rates and thresholds are effective from 6 April 2020. Following recent Scottish Parliamentary approval, 2019 to 2020 rates will remain operative until 10 May 2020, which will then be superseded by the rates shown here.

## Maximum deduction

You should not deduct more than 50% of your employees pay in tax. If after calculating the tax the amount to be deducted is more than 50% of pay then you should contact the dedicated helpline for advice.

## Monthly chart to work out which month number to use

This is the same as the RT11 month number.

### Monthly chart

| Period | Month number | Period | Month number |
|---|---|---|---|
| 6 April to 5 May | 1 | 6 October to 5 November | 7 |
| 6 May to 5 June | 2 | 6 November to 5 December | 8 |
| 6 June to 5 July | 3 | 6 December to 5 January | 9 |
| 6 July to 5 August | 4 | 6 January to 5 February | 10 |
| 6 August to 5 September | 5 | 6 February to 5 March | 11 |
| 6 September to 5 October | 6 | 6 March to 5 April | 12 |

## Weekly chart to work out which week number to use

This is the same as the RT11 week number.

### Weekly chart

| Period | Week number | Period | Week number | Period | Week number | Period | Week number |
|---|---|---|---|---|---|---|---|
| 6 Apr to 12 Apr | 1 | 6 Jul to 12 Jul | 14 | 5 Oct to 11 Oct | 27 | 4 Jan to 10 Jan | 40 |
| 13 Apr to 19 Apr | 2 | 13 Jul to 19 Jul | 15 | 12 Oct to 18 Oct | 28 | 11 Jan to 17 Jan | 41 |
| 20 Apr to 26 Apr | 3 | 20 Jul to 26 Jul | 16 | 19 Oct to 25 Oct | 29 | 18 Jan to 24 Jan | 42 |
| 27 Apr to 3 May | 4 | 27 Jul to 2 Aug | 17 | 26 Oct to 1 Nov | 30 | 25 Jan to 31 Jan | 43 |
| 4 May to 10 May | 5 | 3 Aug to 9 Aug | 18 | 2 Nov to 8 Nov | 31 | 1 Feb to 7 Feb | 44 |
| 11 May to 17 May | 6 | 10 Aug to 16 Aug | 19 | 9 Nov to 15 Nov | 32 | 8 Feb to 14 Feb | 45 |
| 18 May to 24 May | 7 | 17 Aug to 23 Aug | 20 | 16 Nov to 22 Nov | 33 | 15 Feb to 21 Feb | 46 |
| 25 May to 31 May | 8 | 24 Aug to 30 Aug | 21 | 23 Nov to 29 Nov | 34 | 22 Feb to 28 Feb | 47 |
| 1 Jun to 7 Jun | 9 | 31 Aug to 6 Sep | 22 | 30 Nov to 6 Dec | 35 | 1 Mar to 7 Mar | 48 |
| 8 Jun to 14 Jun | 10 | 7 Sep to 13 Sep | 23 | 7 Dec to 13 Dec | 36 | 8 Mar to 14 Mar | 49 |
| 15 Jun to 21 Jun | 11 | 14 Sep to 20 Sep | 24 | 14 Dec to 20 Dec | 37 | 15 Mar to 21 Mar | 50 |
| 22 Jun to 28 Jun | 12 | 21 Sep to 27 Sep | 25 | 21 Dec to 27 Dec | 38 | 22 Mar to 28 Mar | 51 |
| 29 Jun to 5 Jul | 13 | 28 Sep to 4 Oct | 26 | 28 Dec to 3 Jan | 39 | 29 Mar to 4 Apr | 52 |
| | | | | | | 5 April (use the week 1 table) | 53 |

3

# English and Northern Irish rate

## English and Northern Irish monthly paid

If you do your payroll on a monthly basis use this table.

| Month | Column 1 | Month | Column 1 | Month | Column 1 |
|-------|----------|-------|----------|-------|----------|
| 1 | 3125 | 5 | 15625 | 9 | 28125 |
| 2 | 6250 | 6 | 18750 | 10 | 31250 |
| 3 | 9375 | 7 | 21875 | 11 | 34375 |
| 4 | 12500 | 8 | 25000 | 12 | 37500 |

Work out which week the pay is for – there's a chart on page 3.

Pick the month you need from the Month column in the table. Look at the figure in Column 1.

Is your employee's total taxable pay to date less than or equal to the figure in Column 1?
If so, use English and Northern Irish Table B on pages 6 and 7.

If your employee's total taxable pay to date is more than the amount in Column 1,
use English and Northern Irish Tables C and D on pages 8, 10 and 11.

## English and Northern Irish weekly paid

If you do your payroll on a weekly basis use this table.

| Week | Column 1 | Week | Column 1 | Week | Column 1 |
|------|----------|------|----------|------|----------|
| 1 | 722 | 21 | 15145 | 41 | 29568 |
| 2 | 1443 | 22 | 15866 | 42 | 30289 |
| 3 | 2164 | 23 | 16587 | 43 | 31010 |
| 4 | 2885 | 24 | 17308 | 44 | 31731 |
| 5 | 3606 | 25 | 18029 | 45 | 32452 |
| 6 | 4327 | 26 | 18750 | 46 | 33174 |
| 7 | 5049 | 27 | 19472 | 47 | 33895 |
| 8 | 5770 | 28 | 20193 | 48 | 34616 |
| 9 | 6491 | 29 | 20914 | 49 | 35337 |
| 10 | 7212 | 30 | 21635 | 50 | 36058 |
| 11 | 7933 | 31 | 22356 | 51 | 36779 |
| 12 | 8654 | 32 | 23077 | 52 | 37500 |
| 13 | 9375 | 33 | 23799 | | |
| 14 | 10097 | 34 | 24520 | | |
| 15 | 10818 | 35 | 25241 | | |
| 16 | 11539 | 36 | 25962 | | |
| 17 | 12260 | 37 | 26683 | | |
| 18 | 12981 | 38 | 27404 | | |
| 19 | 13702 | 39 | 28125 | | |
| 20 | 14424 | 40 | 28847 | | |

Work out which week the pay is for – there's a chart on page 3.

Pick the week you need from the Week column in the table. Look at the figure in Column 1.

Is your employee's total taxable pay to date less than or equal to the figure in Column 1?
If so, use English and Northern Irish Table B on pages 6 and 7.

If your employee's total taxable pay to date is more than the amount in Column 1,
use English and Northern Irish Tables C and D on pages 9, 10 and 11.

4

## How to use English and Northern Irish Table B – weekly paid

### Example 3 – all codes except BR and D prefix codes

Employee's code is **431L**
The pay week is in **Week 11**

| | |
|---|---|
| **Pay in the week is** | £203.00 |
| Plus **previous pay to date** | £1,827.00 |
| **Total pay to date** | £2,030.00 |
| Minus Pay Adjustment Tables A figure at Week 11 code 431L | £913.66 |
| **Total taxable pay to date** | £1,116.34 |
| Rounded down to the nearest pound | £1,116 |

You'll already have used Pay Adjustment Tables A and completed your RT11 up to and including Column 5.

First use Table B on pages 6 and 7 for the nearest round figure below £1,116, it's £1,100.

Then use Table B on pages 6 and 7 for the remainder of £1,116, it's £16.

| Total taxable pay to date | Total tax due to date | Total taxable pay to date | Total tax due to date |
|---|---|---|---|
| 800 | 160.00 | 14 | 2.80 |
| 900 | 180.00 | 15 | 3.00 |
| 1000 | 200.00 | 16 | 3.20 |
| 1100 | 220.00 | 17 | 3.40 |
| 1200 | 240.00 | 18 | 3.60 |
| 1300 | 260.00 | 19 | 3.80 |
| 1400 | 280.00 | 20 | 4.00 |
| 1500 | 300.00 | 21 | 4.20 |
| 1600 | 320.00 | 22 | 4.40 |

| | |
|---|---|
| Tax due on £1,100 from Table B | **£220.00** |
| Plus tax due on £16 from Table B | **£3.20** |
| **Total tax due** | **£223.20** |

### Example 4 – code BR only

Employee's code is **BR**
The pay week is in **Week 11**

| | |
|---|---|
| **Pay in the week is** | £140.00 |
| Plus **previous pay to date** | £1,360.00 |
| **Total pay to date** | £1,500.00 |

You do not need to use the Pay Adjustment Tables A for code BR.

Therefore, tax is due on the whole of the pay for this month.

| | |
|---|---|
| **Total taxable pay to date** | £1,500.00 |
| Rounded down to the nearest pound | £1,500 |

Take the RT11 Column 5 figure, for example, £1,500 and either:
• use Table B on pages 6 and 7
• multiply by 0.20 (20%)
  £1,500 x 0.20 = £300.00

| Total taxable pay to date | Total tax due to date |
|---|---|
| 1200 | 240.00 |
| 1300 | 260.00 |
| 1400 | 280.00 |
| 1500 | 300.00 |
| 1600 | 320.00 |
| 1700 | 340.00 |
| 1800 | 360.00 |
| 1900 | 380.00 |
| 2000 | 400.00 |

5

## Table B – English and Northern Irish basic rate (tax at 20%)

Pages 2, 4 and 5 tell you when to use this table.

### Table B – Tax at 20%

**Tax due on taxable pay from £1 to £15,000**

| Total taxable pay to date | Total tax due to date | Total taxable pay to date | Total tax due to date | Total taxable pay to date | Total tax due to date | Total taxable pay to date | Total tax due to date | Total taxable pay to date | Total tax due to date |
|---|---|---|---|---|---|---|---|---|---|
| 1 | 0.20 | 51 | 10.20 | 100 | 20.00 | 5100 | 1020.00 | 10100 | 2020.00 |
| 2 | 0.40 | 52 | 10.40 | 200 | 40.00 | 5200 | 1040.00 | 10200 | 2040.00 |
| 3 | 0.60 | 53 | 10.60 | 300 | 60.00 | 5300 | 1060.00 | 10300 | 2060.00 |
| 4 | 0.80 | 54 | 10.80 | 400 | 80.00 | 5400 | 1080.00 | 10400 | 2080.00 |
| 5 | 1.00 | 55 | 11.00 | 500 | 100.00 | 5500 | 1100.00 | 10500 | 2100.00 |
| 6 | 1.20 | 56 | 11.20 | 600 | 120.00 | 5600 | 1120.00 | 10600 | 2120.00 |
| 7 | 1.40 | 57 | 11.40 | 700 | 140.00 | 5700 | 1140.00 | 10700 | 2140.00 |
| 8 | 1.60 | 58 | 11.60 | 800 | 160.00 | 5800 | 1160.00 | 10800 | 2160.00 |
| 9 | 1.80 | 59 | 11.80 | 900 | 180.00 | 5900 | 1180.00 | 10900 | 2180.00 |
| 10 | 2.00 | 60 | 12.00 | 1000 | 200.00 | 6000 | 1200.00 | 11000 | 2200.00 |
| 11 | 2.20 | 61 | 12.20 | 1100 | 220.00 | 6100 | 1220.00 | 11100 | 2220.00 |
| 12 | 2.40 | 62 | 12.40 | 1200 | 240.00 | 6200 | 1240.00 | 11200 | 2240.00 |
| 13 | 2.60 | 63 | 12.60 | 1300 | 260.00 | 6300 | 1260.00 | 11300 | 2260.00 |
| 14 | 2.80 | 64 | 12.80 | 1400 | 280.00 | 6400 | 1280.00 | 11400 | 2280.00 |
| 15 | 3.00 | 65 | 13.00 | 1500 | 300.00 | 6500 | 1300.00 | 11500 | 2300.00 |
| 16 | 3.20 | 66 | 13.20 | 1600 | 320.00 | 6600 | 1320.00 | 11600 | 2320.00 |
| 17 | 3.40 | 67 | 13.40 | 1700 | 340.00 | 6700 | 1340.00 | 11700 | 2340.00 |
| 18 | 3.60 | 68 | 13.60 | 1800 | 360.00 | 6800 | 1360.00 | 11800 | 2360.00 |
| 19 | 3.80 | 69 | 13.80 | 1900 | 380.00 | 6900 | 1380.00 | 11900 | 2380.00 |
| 20 | 4.00 | 70 | 14.00 | 2000 | 400.00 | 7000 | 1400.00 | 12000 | 2400.00 |
| 21 | 4.20 | 71 | 14.20 | 2100 | 420.00 | 7100 | 1420.00 | 12100 | 2420.00 |
| 22 | 4.40 | 72 | 14.40 | 2200 | 440.00 | 7200 | 1440.00 | 12200 | 2440.00 |
| 23 | 4.60 | 73 | 14.60 | 2300 | 460.00 | 7300 | 1460.00 | 12300 | 2460.00 |
| 24 | 4.80 | 74 | 14.80 | 2400 | 480.00 | 7400 | 1480.00 | 12400 | 2480.00 |
| 25 | 5.00 | 75 | 15.00 | 2500 | 500.00 | 7500 | 1500.00 | 12500 | 2500.00 |
| 26 | 5.20 | 76 | 15.20 | 2600 | 520.00 | 7600 | 1520.00 | 12600 | 2520.00 |
| 27 | 5.40 | 77 | 15.40 | 2700 | 540.00 | 7700 | 1540.00 | 12700 | 2540.00 |
| 28 | 5.60 | 78 | 15.60 | 2800 | 560.00 | 7800 | 1560.00 | 12800 | 2560.00 |
| 29 | 5.80 | 79 | 15.80 | 2900 | 580.00 | 7900 | 1580.00 | 12900 | 2580.00 |
| 30 | 6.00 | 80 | 16.00 | 3000 | 600.00 | 8000 | 1600.00 | 13000 | 2600.00 |
| 31 | 6.20 | 81 | 16.20 | 3100 | 620.00 | 8100 | 1620.00 | 13100 | 2620.00 |
| 32 | 6.40 | 82 | 16.40 | 3200 | 640.00 | 8200 | 1640.00 | 13200 | 2640.00 |
| 33 | 6.60 | 83 | 16.60 | 3300 | 660.00 | 8300 | 1660.00 | 13300 | 2660.00 |
| 34 | 6.80 | 84 | 16.80 | 3400 | 680.00 | 8400 | 1680.00 | 13400 | 2680.00 |
| 35 | 7.00 | 85 | 17.00 | 3500 | 700.00 | 8500 | 1700.00 | 13500 | 2700.00 |
| 36 | 7.20 | 86 | 17.20 | 3600 | 720.00 | 8600 | 1720.00 | 13600 | 2720.00 |
| 37 | 7.40 | 87 | 17.40 | 3700 | 740.00 | 8700 | 1740.00 | 13700 | 2740.00 |
| 38 | 7.60 | 88 | 17.60 | 3800 | 760.00 | 8800 | 1760.00 | 13800 | 2760.00 |
| 39 | 7.80 | 89 | 17.80 | 3900 | 780.00 | 8900 | 1780.00 | 13900 | 2780.00 |
| 40 | 8.00 | 90 | 18.00 | 4000 | 800.00 | 9000 | 1800.00 | 14000 | 2800.00 |
| 41 | 8.20 | 91 | 18.20 | 4100 | 820.00 | 9100 | 1820.00 | 14100 | 2820.00 |
| 42 | 8.40 | 92 | 18.40 | 4200 | 840.00 | 9200 | 1840.00 | 14200 | 2840.00 |
| 43 | 8.60 | 93 | 18.60 | 4300 | 860.00 | 9300 | 1860.00 | 14300 | 2860.00 |
| 44 | 8.80 | 94 | 18.80 | 4400 | 880.00 | 9400 | 1880.00 | 14400 | 2880.00 |
| 45 | 9.00 | 95 | 19.00 | 4500 | 900.00 | 9500 | 1900.00 | 14500 | 2900.00 |
| 46 | 9.20 | 96 | 19.20 | 4600 | 920.00 | 9600 | 1920.00 | 14600 | 2920.00 |
| 47 | 9.40 | 97 | 19.40 | 4700 | 940.00 | 9700 | 1940.00 | 14700 | 2940.00 |
| 48 | 9.60 | 98 | 19.60 | 4800 | 960.00 | 9800 | 1960.00 | 14800 | 2960.00 |
| 49 | 9.80 | 99 | 19.80 | 4900 | 980.00 | 9900 | 1980.00 | 14900 | 2980.00 |
| 50 | 10.00 | | | 5000 | 1000.00 | 10000 | 2000.00 | 15000 | 3000.00 |

6

## Table B – English and Northern Irish basic rate (tax at 20%) continued

Pages 2, 4 and 5 tell you when to use this table.

### Table B – Tax at 20%
#### Tax due on taxable pay from £15,100 to £37,500

| Total taxable pay to date | Total tax due to date | Total taxable pay to date | Total tax due to date | Total taxable pay to date | Total tax due to date | Total taxable pay to date | Total tax due to date | Total taxable pay to date | Total tax due to date |
|---|---|---|---|---|---|---|---|---|---|
| 15100 | 3020.00 | 20100 | 4020.00 | 25100 | 5020.00 | 30100 | 6020.00 | 35100 | 7020.00 |
| 15200 | 3040.00 | 20200 | 4040.00 | 25200 | 5040.00 | 30200 | 6040.00 | 35200 | 7040.00 |
| 15300 | 3060.00 | 20300 | 4060.00 | 25300 | 5060.00 | 30300 | 6060.00 | 35300 | 7060.00 |
| 15400 | 3080.00 | 20400 | 4080.00 | 25400 | 5080.00 | 30400 | 6080.00 | 35400 | 7080.00 |
| 15500 | 3100.00 | 20500 | 4100.00 | 25500 | 5100.00 | 30500 | 6100.00 | 35500 | 7100.00 |
| 15600 | 3120.00 | 20600 | 4120.00 | 25600 | 5120.00 | 30600 | 6120.00 | 35600 | 7120.00 |
| 15700 | 3140.00 | 20700 | 4140.00 | 25700 | 5140.00 | 30700 | 6140.00 | 35700 | 7140.00 |
| 15800 | 3160.00 | 20800 | 4160.00 | 25800 | 5160.00 | 30800 | 6160.00 | 35800 | 7160.00 |
| 15900 | 3180.00 | 20900 | 4180.00 | 25900 | 5180.00 | 30900 | 6180.00 | 35900 | 7180.00 |
| 16000 | 3200.00 | 21000 | 4200.00 | 26000 | 5200.00 | 31000 | 6200.00 | 36000 | 7200.00 |
| 16100 | 3220.00 | 21100 | 4220.00 | 26100 | 5220.00 | 31100 | 6220.00 | 36100 | 7220.00 |
| 16200 | 3240.00 | 21200 | 4240.00 | 26200 | 5240.00 | 31200 | 6240.00 | 36200 | 7240.00 |
| 16300 | 3260.00 | 21300 | 4260.00 | 26300 | 5260.00 | 31300 | 6260.00 | 36300 | 7260.00 |
| 16400 | 3280.00 | 21400 | 4280.00 | 26400 | 5280.00 | 31400 | 6280.00 | 36400 | 7280.00 |
| 16500 | 3300.00 | 21500 | 4300.00 | 26500 | 5300.00 | 31500 | 6300.00 | 36500 | 7300.00 |
| 16600 | 3320.00 | 21600 | 4320.00 | 26600 | 5320.00 | 31600 | 6320.00 | 36600 | 7320.00 |
| 16700 | 3340.00 | 21700 | 4340.00 | 26700 | 5340.00 | 31700 | 6340.00 | 36700 | 7340.00 |
| 16800 | 3360.00 | 21800 | 4360.00 | 26800 | 5360.00 | 31800 | 6360.00 | 36800 | 7360.00 |
| 16900 | 3380.00 | 21900 | 4380.00 | 26900 | 5380.00 | 31900 | 6380.00 | 36900 | 7380.00 |
| 17000 | 3400.00 | 22000 | 4400.00 | 27000 | 5400.00 | 32000 | 6400.00 | 37000 | 7400.00 |
| 17100 | 3420.00 | 22100 | 4420.00 | 27100 | 5420.00 | 32100 | 6420.00 | 37100 | 7420.00 |
| 17200 | 3440.00 | 22200 | 4440.00 | 27200 | 5440.00 | 32200 | 6440.00 | 37200 | 7440.00 |
| 17300 | 3460.00 | 22300 | 4460.00 | 27300 | 5460.00 | 32300 | 6460.00 | 37300 | 7460.00 |
| 17400 | 3480.00 | 22400 | 4480.00 | 27400 | 5480.00 | 32400 | 6480.00 | 37400 | 7480.00 |
| 17500 | 3500.00 | 22500 | 4500.00 | 27500 | 5500.00 | 32500 | 6500.00 | 37500 | 7500.00 |
| 17600 | 3520.00 | 22600 | 4520.00 | 27600 | 5520.00 | 32600 | 6520.00 | | |
| 17700 | 3540.00 | 22700 | 4540.00 | 27700 | 5540.00 | 32700 | 6540.00 | | |
| 17800 | 3560.00 | 22800 | 4560.00 | 27800 | 5560.00 | 32800 | 6560.00 | | |
| 17900 | 3580.00 | 22900 | 4580.00 | 27900 | 5580.00 | 32900 | 6580.00 | Where the exact | |
| 18000 | 3600.00 | 23000 | 4600.00 | 28000 | 5600.00 | 33000 | 6600.00 | amount of taxable | |
| 18100 | 3620.00 | 23100 | 4620.00 | 28100 | 5620.00 | 33100 | 6620.00 | pay is not shown add | |
| 18200 | 3640.00 | 23200 | 4640.00 | 28200 | 5640.00 | 33200 | 6640.00 | together the figures | |
| 18300 | 3660.00 | 23300 | 4660.00 | 28300 | 5660.00 | 33300 | 6660.00 | for 2 (or more) | |
| 18400 | 3680.00 | 23400 | 4680.00 | 28400 | 5680.00 | 33400 | 6680.00 | entries that make up | |
| 18500 | 3700.00 | 23500 | 4700.00 | 28500 | 5700.00 | 33500 | 6700.00 | the amount of | |
| 18600 | 3720.00 | 23600 | 4720.00 | 28600 | 5720.00 | 33600 | 6720.00 | taxable pay to the | |
| 18700 | 3740.00 | 23700 | 4740.00 | 28700 | 5740.00 | 33700 | 6740.00 | nearest £1 below. | |
| 18800 | 3760.00 | 23800 | 4760.00 | 28800 | 5760.00 | 33800 | 6760.00 | | |
| 18900 | 3780.00 | 23900 | 4780.00 | 28900 | 5780.00 | 33900 | 6780.00 | | |
| 19000 | 3800.00 | 24000 | 4800.00 | 29000 | 5800.00 | 34000 | 6800.00 | | |
| 19100 | 3820.00 | 24100 | 4820.00 | 29100 | 5820.00 | 34100 | 6820.00 | | |
| 19200 | 3840.00 | 24200 | 4840.00 | 29200 | 5840.00 | 34200 | 6840.00 | | |
| 19300 | 3860.00 | 24300 | 4860.00 | 29300 | 5860.00 | 34300 | 6860.00 | | |
| 19400 | 3880.00 | 24400 | 4880.00 | 29400 | 5880.00 | 34400 | 6880.00 | | |
| 19500 | 3900.00 | 24500 | 4900.00 | 29500 | 5900.00 | 34500 | 6900.00 | | |
| 19600 | 3920.00 | 24600 | 4920.00 | 29600 | 5920.00 | 34600 | 6920.00 | | |
| 19700 | 3940.00 | 24700 | 4940.00 | 29700 | 5940.00 | 34700 | 6940.00 | | |
| 19800 | 3960.00 | 24800 | 4960.00 | 29800 | 5960.00 | 34800 | 6960.00 | | |
| 19900 | 3980.00 | 24900 | 4980.00 | 29900 | 5980.00 | 34900 | 6980.00 | | |
| 20000 | 4000.00 | 25000 | 5000.00 | 30000 | 6000.00 | 35000 | 7000.00 | | |

7

## Tables C

### How to use Tables C1 and C2 – English and Northern Irish monthly paid

You'll already have used Pay Adjustment Tables A and completed your RT11 up to and including Column 5.

| Example 5 – Table C1 | |
| --- | --- |
| Example payment is for **Month 4** | |
| Taxable pay to date from RT11 column 5 | **£20,233.00** |
| Find tax due at **higher rate** – 40% | |
| **Taxable pay** | **£20,233.00** |
| Minus taxable pay Column 1 | **£12,500.00** |
| **Taxable pay at 40%** | **£7,733.00** |

| Example 6 – Table C2 | |
| --- | --- |
| Example payment is for **Month 4** | |
| Taxable pay to date from RT11 Column 5 | **£57,500.00** |
| Find tax due at **additional rate** – 45% | |
| **Taxable pay** | **£57,500.00** |
| Minus taxable pay Column 4 | **£50,000.00** |
| **Taxable pay at 45%** | **£7,500.00** |

First use Table D1 on page 10 for the nearest round figure below £7,733.00, it's £7,700.

Then use Table D1 on page 10 for the remainder of £7,700, it's £33.

Use Table D2 on page 11 to find tax due on £7,500.

| Taxable pay | Tax |
| --- | --- |
| £ | £ |
| 7400 | 2960.00 |
| 7500 | 3000.00 |
| 7600 | 3040.00 |
| 7700 | 3080.00 |
| 7800 | 3120.00 |
| 7900 | 3160.00 |
| 8000 | 3200.00 |

| Taxable Pay | Tax |
| --- | --- |
| £ | £ |
| 29 | 11.60 |
| 30 | 12.00 |
| 31 | 12.40 |
| 32 | 12.80 |
| 33 | 13.20 |
| 34 | 13.60 |
| 35 | 14.00 |

| Taxable pay | Tax |
| --- | --- |
| £ | £ |
| 7300 | 3285.00 |
| 7400 | 3330.00 |
| 7500 | 3375.00 |
| 7600 | 3420.00 |
| 7700 | 3465.00 |
| 7800 | 3510.00 |
| 7900 | 3555.00 |

| Higher rate tax due on £7,700 from Table D1 | **£3,080.00** |
| --- | --- |
| Plus tax due on £33 from Table D1 | **£13.20** |
| | **£3,093.20** |
| Add figure from Table C1 Column 3 for **Month 4** | **£2,500.00** |
| **Total tax due** | **£5,593.20** |

| Additional rate tax due on £7,500 from Table D2 | **£3,375.00** |
| --- | --- |
| Add figure from Table C2 Column 5 for **Month 4** | **£17,500.00** |
| **Total tax due** | **£20,875.00** |

### Tables C – English and Northern Irish monthly paid

Page 4 tells you when to use these tables.

| | Table C1 | | | | Table C2 | | |
| --- | --- | --- | --- | --- | --- | --- | --- |
| | **Employee paid at monthly rates** | | | | **Employee paid at monthly rates** | | |
| Month | Column 1 If total taxable pay to date exceeds £ | Column 2 And total taxable pay to date does not exceed £ | Column 3 Total tax due to date on pay in Column 1 £ | Is the total taxable pay to date more than the amount in Column 1 and does not exceed the amount in Column 2? If Yes, add to the figure in Column 3 the tax at 40% (as shown in Table D1 – higher rate (tax at 40%) on page 10) on the amount by which the total taxable pay to date exceeds the figure in Column 1. If No, and the total taxable pay to date exceeds the figure in Column 2, use Table C2. | Column 4 If total taxable pay to date exceeds £ | Column 5 Total tax due to date on pay in Column 4 £ | If total taxable pay to date exceeds the figure in Column 4. Add to the figure in Column 5 the tax at 45% (as shown in Table D2 – additional rate (tax at 45%) on page 11) on the amount by which the total taxable pay to date exceeds the figure in Column 4. |
| 1 | 3125 | 12500 | 625.00 | | 12500 | 4375.00 | |
| 2 | 6250 | 25000 | 1250.00 | | 25000 | 8750.00 | |
| 3 | 9375 | 37500 | 1875.00 | | 37500 | 13125.00 | |
| 4 | 12500 | 50000 | 2500.00 | | 50000 | 17500.00 | |
| 5 | 15625 | 62500 | 3125.00 | | 62500 | 21875.00 | |
| 6 | 18750 | 75000 | 3750.00 | | 75000 | 26250.00 | |
| 7 | 21875 | 87500 | 4375.00 | | 87500 | 30625.00 | |
| 8 | 25000 | 100000 | 5000.00 | | 100000 | 35000.00 | |
| 9 | 28125 | 112500 | 5625.00 | | 112500 | 39375.00 | |
| 10 | 31250 | 125000 | 6250.00 | | 125000 | 43750.00 | |
| 11 | 34375 | 137500 | 6875.00 | | 137500 | 48125.00 | |
| 12 | 37500 | 150000 | 7500.00 | | 150000 | 52500.00 | |

8

# Tables C – English and Northern Irish weekly paid

Page 4 tells you when to use these tables.

## Table C1

### Employee paid at weekly rates

| Week | Column 1 If total taxable pay to date exceeds £ | Column 2 And total taxable pay to date does not exceed £ | Column 3 Total tax due to date on pay in Column 1 £ |
|---|---|---|---|
| 1 | 722 | 2885 | 144.56 |
| 2 | 1443 | 5770 | 288.73 |
| 3 | 2164 | 8654 | 432.90 |
| 4 | 2885 | 11539 | 577.07 |
| 5 | 3606 | 14424 | 721.24 |
| 6 | 4327 | 17308 | 865.41 |
| 7 | 5049 | 20193 | 1009.98 |
| 8 | 5770 | 23077 | 1154.15 |
| 9 | 6491 | 25962 | 1298.32 |
| 10 | 7212 | 28847 | 1442.49 |
| 11 | 7933 | 31731 | 1586.66 |
| 12 | 8654 | 34616 | 1730.83 |
| 13 | 9375 | 37500 | 1875.00 |
| 14 | 10097 | 40385 | 2019.56 |
| 15 | 10818 | 43270 | 2163.73 |
| 16 | 11539 | 46154 | 2307.90 |
| 17 | 12260 | 49039 | 2452.07 |
| 18 | 12981 | 51924 | 2596.24 |
| 19 | 13702 | 54808 | 2740.41 |
| 20 | 14424 | 57693 | 2884.98 |
| 21 | 15145 | 60577 | 3029.15 |
| 22 | 15866 | 63462 | 3173.32 |
| 23 | 16587 | 66347 | 3317.49 |
| 24 | 17308 | 69231 | 3461.66 |
| 25 | 18029 | 72116 | 3605.83 |
| 26 | 18750 | 75000 | 3750.00 |
| 27 | 19472 | 77885 | 3894.56 |
| 28 | 20193 | 80770 | 4038.73 |
| 29 | 20914 | 83654 | 4182.90 |
| 30 | 21635 | 86539 | 4327.07 |
| 31 | 22356 | 89424 | 4471.24 |
| 32 | 23077 | 92308 | 4615.41 |
| 33 | 23799 | 95193 | 4759.98 |
| 34 | 24520 | 98077 | 4904.15 |
| 35 | 25241 | 100962 | 5048.32 |
| 36 | 25962 | 103847 | 5192.49 |
| 37 | 26683 | 106731 | 5336.66 |
| 38 | 27404 | 109616 | 5480.83 |
| 39 | 28125 | 112500 | 5625.00 |
| 40 | 28847 | 115385 | 5769.56 |
| 41 | 29568 | 118270 | 5913.73 |
| 42 | 30289 | 121154 | 6057.90 |
| 43 | 31010 | 124039 | 6202.07 |
| 44 | 31731 | 126924 | 6346.24 |
| 45 | 32452 | 129808 | 6490.41 |
| 46 | 33174 | 132693 | 6634.98 |
| 47 | 33895 | 135577 | 6779.15 |
| 48 | 34616 | 138462 | 6923.32 |
| 49 | 35337 | 141347 | 7067.49 |
| 50 | 36058 | 144231 | 7211.66 |
| 51 | 36779 | 147116 | 7355.83 |
| 52 | 37500 | 150000 | 7500.00 |

Is the total taxable pay to date more than the amount in Column 1 and does not exceed the amount in Column 2?

If Yes, add to the figure in Column 3 the tax at 40% (as shown in Table D1 – higher rate (tax at 40%) on page 10) on the amount by which the total taxable pay to date exceeds the figure in Column 1.

If No, and the total taxable pay to date exceeds the figure in Column 2 use Table C2.

## Table C2

### Employee paid at weekly rates

| Column 4 If total taxable pay to date exceeds £ | Column 5 Total tax due to date on pay in Column 4 £ |
|---|---|
| 2885 | 1009.78 |
| 5770 | 2019.57 |
| 8654 | 3028.91 |
| 11539 | 4038.70 |
| 14424 | 5048.49 |
| 17308 | 6057.83 |
| 20193 | 7067.61 |
| 23077 | 8076.95 |
| 25962 | 9086.74 |
| 28847 | 10096.53 |
| 31731 | 11105.87 |
| 34616 | 12115.66 |
| 37500 | 13125.00 |
| 40385 | 14134.78 |
| 43270 | 15144.57 |
| 46154 | 16153.91 |
| 49039 | 17163.70 |
| 51924 | 18173.49 |
| 54808 | 19182.83 |
| 57693 | 20192.61 |
| 60577 | 21201.95 |
| 63462 | 22211.74 |
| 66347 | 23221.53 |
| 69231 | 24230.87 |
| 72116 | 25240.66 |
| 75000 | 26250.00 |
| 77885 | 27259.78 |
| 80770 | 28269.57 |
| 83654 | 29278.91 |
| 86539 | 30288.70 |
| 89424 | 31298.49 |
| 92308 | 32307.83 |
| 95193 | 33317.61 |
| 98077 | 34326.95 |
| 100962 | 35336.74 |
| 103847 | 36346.53 |
| 106731 | 37355.87 |
| 109616 | 38365.66 |
| 112500 | 39375.00 |
| 115385 | 40384.78 |
| 118270 | 41394.57 |
| 121154 | 42403.91 |
| 124039 | 43413.70 |
| 126924 | 44423.49 |
| 129808 | 45432.83 |
| 132693 | 46442.61 |
| 135577 | 47451.95 |
| 138462 | 48461.74 |
| 141347 | 49471.53 |
| 144231 | 50480.87 |
| 147116 | 51490.66 |
| 150000 | 52500.00 |

If total taxable pay to date exceeds the figure in Column 4. Add to the figure in Column 5 the tax at 45% (as shown in Table D2 – additional rate (tax at 45%) on page 11) on the amount by which the total taxable pay to date exceeds the figure in Column 4.

9

## Table D1 – English and Northern Irish higher rate (tax at 40%)

Also to be used for tax code D0. Pages 4, 8 and 9 tell you when to use this table.

| Taxable pay £ | Tax £ | Taxable pay £ | Tax £ | Taxable pay £ | Tax £ | Taxable pay £ | Tax £ | |
|---|---|---|---|---|---|---|---|---|
| | | | | | | | | **Table D1 – Tax at 40%** |
| 1 | 0.40 | 51 | 20.40 | 100 | 40.00 | 5100 | 2040.00 | Where the exact amount of taxable pay is not shown, add together the figures for 2 (or more) entries to make up the amount of taxable pay to the nearest £1 below. |
| 2 | 0.80 | 52 | 20.80 | 200 | 80.00 | 5200 | 2080.00 | |
| 3 | 1.20 | 53 | 21.20 | 300 | 120.00 | 5300 | 2120.00 | |
| 4 | 1.60 | 54 | 21.60 | 400 | 160.00 | 5400 | 2160.00 | |
| 5 | 2.00 | 55 | 22.00 | 500 | 200.00 | 5500 | 2200.00 | |
| 6 | 2.40 | 56 | 22.40 | 600 | 240.00 | 5600 | 2240.00 | |
| 7 | 2.80 | 57 | 22.80 | 700 | 280.00 | 5700 | 2280.00 | |
| 8 | 3.20 | 58 | 23.20 | 800 | 320.00 | 5800 | 2320.00 | |
| 9 | 3.60 | 59 | 23.60 | 900 | 360.00 | 5900 | 2360.00 | |
| 10 | 4.00 | 60 | 24.00 | 1000 | 400.00 | 6000 | 2400.00 | |
| 11 | 4.40 | 61 | 24.40 | 1100 | 440.00 | 6100 | 2440.00 | |
| 12 | 4.80 | 62 | 24.80 | 1200 | 480.00 | 6200 | 2480.00 | |
| 13 | 5.20 | 63 | 25.20 | 1300 | 520.00 | 6300 | 2520.00 | |
| 14 | 5.60 | 64 | 25.60 | 1400 | 560.00 | 6400 | 2560.00 | |
| 15 | 6.00 | 65 | 26.00 | 1500 | 600.00 | 6500 | 2600.00 | |
| 16 | 6.40 | 66 | 26.40 | 1600 | 640.00 | 6600 | 2640.00 | |
| 17 | 6.80 | 67 | 26.80 | 1700 | 680.00 | 6700 | 2680.00 | |
| 18 | 7.20 | 68 | 27.20 | 1800 | 720.00 | 6800 | 2720.00 | |
| 19 | 7.60 | 69 | 27.60 | 1900 | 760.00 | 6900 | 2760.00 | |
| 20 | 8.00 | 70 | 28.00 | 2000 | 800.00 | 7000 | 2800.00 | |
| 21 | 8.40 | 71 | 28.40 | 2100 | 840.00 | 7100 | 2840.00 | |
| 22 | 8.80 | 72 | 28.80 | 2200 | 880.00 | 7200 | 2880.00 | |
| 23 | 9.20 | 73 | 29.20 | 2300 | 920.00 | 7300 | 2920.00 | |
| 24 | 9.60 | 74 | 29.60 | 2400 | 960.00 | 7400 | 2960.00 | |
| 25 | 10.00 | 75 | 30.00 | 2500 | 1000.00 | 7500 | 3000.00 | |
| 26 | 10.40 | 76 | 30.40 | 2600 | 1040.00 | 7600 | 3040.00 | |
| 27 | 10.80 | 77 | 30.80 | 2700 | 1080.00 | 7700 | 3080.00 | |
| 28 | 11.20 | 78 | 31.20 | 2800 | 1120.00 | 7800 | 3120.00 | |
| 29 | 11.60 | 79 | 31.60 | 2900 | 1160.00 | 7900 | 3160.00 | |
| 30 | 12.00 | 80 | 32.00 | 3000 | 1200.00 | 8000 | 3200.00 | |
| 31 | 12.40 | 81 | 32.40 | 3100 | 1240.00 | 8100 | 3240.00 | |
| 32 | 12.80 | 82 | 32.80 | 3200 | 1280.00 | 8200 | 3280.00 | |
| 33 | 13.20 | 83 | 33.20 | 3300 | 1320.00 | 8300 | 3320.00 | |
| 34 | 13.60 | 84 | 33.60 | 3400 | 1360.00 | 8400 | 3360.00 | |
| 35 | 14.00 | 85 | 34.00 | 3500 | 1400.00 | 8500 | 3400.00 | |
| 36 | 14.40 | 86 | 34.40 | 3600 | 1440.00 | 8600 | 3440.00 | |
| 37 | 14.80 | 87 | 34.80 | 3700 | 1480.00 | 8700 | 3480.00 | |
| 38 | 15.20 | 88 | 35.20 | 3800 | 1520.00 | 8800 | 3520.00 | |
| 39 | 15.60 | 89 | 35.60 | 3900 | 1560.00 | 8900 | 3560.00 | |
| 40 | 16.00 | 90 | 36.00 | 4000 | 1600.00 | 9000 | 3600.00 | |
| 41 | 16.40 | 91 | 36.40 | 4100 | 1640.00 | 9100 | 3640.00 | |
| 42 | 16.80 | 92 | 36.80 | 4200 | 1680.00 | 9200 | 3680.00 | |
| 43 | 17.20 | 93 | 37.20 | 4300 | 1720.00 | 9300 | 3720.00 | |
| 44 | 17.60 | 94 | 37.60 | 4400 | 1760.00 | 9400 | 3760.00 | |
| 45 | 18.00 | 95 | 38.00 | 4500 | 1800.00 | 9500 | 3800.00 | |
| 46 | 18.40 | 96 | 38.40 | 4600 | 1840.00 | 9600 | 3840.00 | |
| 47 | 18.80 | 97 | 38.80 | 4700 | 1880.00 | 9700 | 3880.00 | |
| 48 | 19.20 | 98 | 39.20 | 4800 | 1920.00 | 9800 | 3920.00 | |
| 49 | 19.60 | 99 | 39.60 | 4900 | 1960.00 | 9900 | 3960.00 | |
| 50 | 20.00 | | | 5000 | 2000.00 | 10000 | 4000.00 | |
| | | | | | | 20000 | 8000.00 | |
| | | | | | | 30000 | 12000.00 | |
| | | | | | | 40000 | 16000.00 | |
| | | | | | | 50000 | 20000.00 | |
| | | | | | | 60000 | 24000.00 | |
| | | | | | | 70000 | 28000.00 | |
| | | | | | | 80000 | 32000.00 | |
| | | | | | | 90000 | 36000.00 | |
| | | | | | | 100000 | 40000.00 | |

10

## Table D2 – English and Northern Irish additional rate (tax at 45%)

Also to be used for tax code D1. Pages 8 and 9 tell you when to use this table.

### Table D2 – Tax at 45%

| Taxable pay £ | Tax £ | Taxable pay £ | Tax £ | Taxable pay £ | Tax £ | Taxable pay £ | Tax £ | |
|---|---|---|---|---|---|---|---|---|
| 1 | 0.45 | 51 | 22.95 | 100 | 45.00 | 6000 | 2700.00 | Where the exact amount of taxable |
| 2 | 0.90 | 52 | 23.40 | 200 | 90.00 | 6100 | 2745.00 | pay is not shown, add together the |
| 3 | 1.35 | 53 | 23.85 | 300 | 135.00 | 6200 | 2790.00 | figures for 2 (or |
| 4 | 1.80 | 54 | 24.30 | 400 | 180.00 | 6300 | 2835.00 | more) entries to |
| 5 | 2.25 | 55 | 24.75 | 500 | 225.00 | 6400 | 2880.00 | make up the amount of taxable |
| 6 | 2.70 | 56 | 25.20 | 600 | 270.00 | 6500 | 2925.00 | pay to the nearest |
| 7 | 3.15 | 57 | 25.65 | 700 | 315.00 | 6600 | 2970.00 | £1 below. |
| 8 | 3.60 | 58 | 26.10 | 800 | 360.00 | 6700 | 3015.00 | |
| 9 | 4.05 | 59 | 26.55 | 900 | 405.00 | 6800 | 3060.00 | |
| 10 | 4.50 | 60 | 27.00 | 1000 | 450.00 | 6900 | 3105.00 | |
| 11 | 4.95 | 61 | 27.45 | 1100 | 495.00 | 7000 | 3150.00 | |
| 12 | 5.40 | 62 | 27.90 | 1200 | 540.00 | 7100 | 3195.00 | |
| 13 | 5.85 | 63 | 28.35 | 1300 | 585.00 | 7200 | 3240.00 | |
| 14 | 6.30 | 64 | 28.80 | 1400 | 630.00 | 7300 | 3285.00 | |
| 15 | 6.75 | 65 | 29.25 | 1500 | 675.00 | 7400 | 3330.00 | |
| 16 | 7.20 | 66 | 29.70 | 1600 | 720.00 | 7500 | 3375.00 | |
| 17 | 7.65 | 67 | 30.15 | 1700 | 765.00 | 7600 | 3420.00 | |
| 18 | 8.10 | 68 | 30.60 | 1800 | 810.00 | 7700 | 3465.00 | |
| 19 | 8.55 | 69 | 31.05 | 1900 | 855.00 | 7800 | 3510.00 | |
| 20 | 9.00 | 70 | 31.50 | 2000 | 900.00 | 7900 | 3555.00 | |
| 21 | 9.45 | 71 | 31.95 | 2100 | 945.00 | 8000 | 3600.00 | |
| 22 | 9.90 | 72 | 32.40 | 2200 | 990.00 | 8100 | 3645.00 | |
| 23 | 10.35 | 73 | 32.85 | 2300 | 1035.00 | 8200 | 3690.00 | |
| 24 | 10.80 | 74 | 33.30 | 2400 | 1080.00 | 8300 | 3735.00 | |
| 25 | 11.25 | 75 | 33.75 | 2500 | 1125.00 | 8400 | 3780.00 | |
| 26 | 11.70 | 76 | 34.20 | 2600 | 1170.00 | 8500 | 3825.00 | |
| 27 | 12.15 | 77 | 34.65 | 2700 | 1215.00 | 8600 | 3870.00 | |
| 28 | 12.60 | 78 | 35.10 | 2800 | 1260.00 | 8700 | 3915.00 | |
| 29 | 13.05 | 79 | 35.55 | 2900 | 1305.00 | 8800 | 3960.00 | |
| 30 | 13.50 | 80 | 36.00 | 3000 | 1350.00 | 8900 | 4005.00 | |
| 31 | 13.95 | 81 | 36.45 | 3100 | 1395.00 | 9000 | 4050.00 | |
| 32 | 14.40 | 82 | 36.90 | 3200 | 1440.00 | 9100 | 4095.00 | |
| 33 | 14.85 | 83 | 37.35 | 3300 | 1485.00 | 9200 | 4140.00 | |
| 34 | 15.30 | 84 | 37.80 | 3400 | 1530.00 | 9300 | 4185.00 | |
| 35 | 15.75 | 85 | 38.25 | 3500 | 1575.00 | 9400 | 4230.00 | |
| 36 | 16.20 | 86 | 38.70 | 3600 | 1620.00 | 9500 | 4275.00 | |
| 37 | 16.65 | 87 | 39.15 | 3700 | 1665.00 | 9600 | 4320.00 | |
| 38 | 17.10 | 88 | 39.60 | 3800 | 1710.00 | 9700 | 4365.00 | |
| 39 | 17.55 | 89 | 40.05 | 3900 | 1755.00 | 9800 | 4410.00 | |
| 40 | 18.00 | 90 | 40.50 | 4000 | 1800.00 | 9900 | 4455.00 | |
| 41 | 18.45 | 91 | 40.95 | 4100 | 1845.00 | 10000 | 4500.00 | |
| 42 | 18.90 | 92 | 41.40 | 4200 | 1890.00 | 20000 | 9000.00 | |
| 43 | 19.35 | 93 | 41.85 | 4300 | 1935.00 | 30000 | 13500.00 | |
| 44 | 19.80 | 94 | 42.30 | 4400 | 1980.00 | 40000 | 18000.00 | |
| 45 | 20.25 | 95 | 42.75 | 4500 | 2025.00 | 50000 | 22500.00 | |
| 46 | 20.70 | 96 | 43.20 | 4600 | 2070.00 | 60000 | 27000.00 | |
| 47 | 21.15 | 97 | 43.65 | 4700 | 2115.00 | 70000 | 31500.00 | |
| 48 | 21.60 | 98 | 44.10 | 4800 | 2160.00 | 80000 | 36000.00 | |
| 49 | 22.05 | 99 | 44.55 | 4900 | 2205.00 | 90000 | 40500.00 | |
| 50 | 22.50 | | | 5000 | 2250.00 | 100000 | 45000.00 | |
| | | | | 5100 | 2295.00 | 200000 | 90000.00 | |
| | | | | 5200 | 2340.00 | 300000 | 135000.00 | |
| | | | | 5300 | 2385.00 | 400000 | 180000.00 | |
| | | | | 5400 | 2430.00 | 500000 | 225000.00 | |
| | | | | 5500 | 2475.00 | 600000 | 270000.00 | |
| | | | | 5600 | 2520.00 | 700000 | 315000.00 | |
| | | | | 5700 | 2565.00 | 800000 | 360000.00 | |
| | | | | 5800 | 2610.00 | 900000 | 405000.00 | |
| | | | | 5900 | 2655.00 | 1000000 | 450000.00 | |

11

## Scottish rate

### Scottish monthly paid

If you do your payroll on a monthly basis use this table.

| Month | Column 1 | Month | Column 1 | Month | Column 1 |
|-------|----------|-------|----------|-------|----------|
| 1 | 174 | 5 | 869 | 9 | 1564 |
| 2 | 348 | 6 | 1043 | 10 | 1738 |
| 3 | 522 | 7 | 1217 | 11 | 1912 |
| 4 | 695 | 8 | 1390 | 12 | 2085 |

Work out which month the pay is for - there's a chart on page 3.

Pick the month you need from the Month column in the table. Look at the figure in Column 1.

Is your employee's total taxable pay to date less than or equal to the figure in Column 1? If so, use Scottish Table B on page 14.

If your employee's total taxable pay to date is more than the amount in Column 1, use Scottish Tables C and D on pages 15, 16, 19, 20, 21 and 22.

### Scottish weekly paid

If you do your payroll on a weekly basis use this table.

| Week | Column 1 | Week | Column 1 | Week | Column 1 |
|------|----------|------|----------|------|----------|
| 1 | 41 | 21 | 843 | 41 | 1644 |
| 2 | 81 | 22 | 883 | 42 | 1685 |
| 3 | 121 | 23 | 923 | 43 | 1725 |
| 4 | 161 | 24 | 963 | 44 | 1765 |
| 5 | 201 | 25 | 1003 | 45 | 1805 |
| 6 | 241 | 26 | 1043 | 46 | 1845 |
| 7 | 281 | 27 | 1083 | 47 | 1885 |
| 8 | 321 | 28 | 1123 | 48 | 1925 |
| 9 | 361 | 29 | 1163 | 49 | 1965 |
| 10 | 401 | 30 | 1203 | 50 | 2005 |
| 11 | 442 | 31 | 1243 | 51 | 2045 |
| 12 | 482 | 32 | 1284 | 52 | 2085 |
| 13 | 522 | 33 | 1324 | | |
| 14 | 562 | 34 | 1364 | | |
| 15 | 602 | 35 | 1404 | | |
| 16 | 642 | 36 | 1444 | | |
| 17 | 682 | 37 | 1484 | | |
| 18 | 722 | 38 | 1524 | | |
| 19 | 762 | 39 | 1564 | | |
| 20 | 802 | 40 | 1604 | | |

Work out which week the pay is for - there's a chart on page 3.

Pick the week you need from the Week column in the table. Look at the figure in Column 1.

Is your employee's total taxable pay to date less than or equal to the figure in Column 1? If so, use Scottish Table B on page 14.

If your employee's total taxable pay to date is more than the amount in Column 1, use Scottish Tables C and D on pages 17, 18, 19, 20, 21 and 22.

12

## How to use Scottish Table B – weekly paid

**Example 7 – all prefix S codes except SBR and SD prefix codes**

Employee's code is **S431L**
The pay week is in **Week 18**

| | |
|---|---|
| **Pay in the week is** | £85.00 |
| Plus **previous pay to date** | £1,527.00 |
| **Total pay to date** | £1,612.00 |
| Minus Pay Adjustment Tables A figure at Week 18 code S431L | £1495.08 |
| **Total taxable pay to date** | £116.92 |
| Rounded down to the nearest pound | £116 |

You'll already have used Pay Adjustment Tables A and completed your RT11 up to and including Column 5.

First use Table B on page 14 for the nearest round figure below £116, it's £100.

Then use Table B on page 14 for the remainder of £116, it's £16.

| Total taxable pay to date | Total tax due to date | Total taxable pay to date | Total tax due to date |
|---|---|---|---|
| 100 | 19.00 | 11 | 2.09 |
| 200 | 38.00 | 12 | 2.28 |
| 300 | 57.00 | 13 | 2.47 |
| 400 | 76.00 | 14 | 2.66 |
| 500 | 95.00 | 15 | 2.85 |
| 600 | 114.00 | 16 | 3.04 |
| 700 | 133.00 | 17 | 3.23 |
| 800 | 152.00 | 18 | 3.42 |
| 900 | 171.00 | 19 | 3.61 |
| 1000 | 190.00 | 20 | 3.80 |

| | |
|---|---|
| Tax due on £100 from Table B | **£19.00** |
| Plus tax due on £16 from Table B | **£3.04** |
| **Total tax due** | **£22.04** |

13

## Table B – Scottish starter rate (tax at 19%)

Pages 12 and 13 tell you when to use this table.

### Table B – Tax at 19%

#### Tax due on taxable pay from £1 to £2,085

| Total taxable pay to date | Total tax due to date | Total taxable pay to date | Total tax due to date | Total taxable pay to date | Total tax due to date |
|---|---|---|---|---|---|
| 1 | 0.19 | 51 | 9.69 | 200 | 38.00 |
| 2 | 0.38 | 52 | 9.88 | 300 | 57.00 |
| 3 | 0.57 | 53 | 10.07 | 400 | 76.00 |
| 4 | 0.76 | 54 | 10.26 | 500 | 95.00 |
| 5 | 0.95 | 55 | 10.45 | 600 | 114.00 |
| 6 | 1.14 | 56 | 10.64 | 700 | 133.00 |
| 7 | 1.33 | 57 | 10.83 | 800 | 152.00 |
| 8 | 1.52 | 58 | 11.02 | 900 | 171.00 |
| 9 | 1.71 | 59 | 11.21 | 1000 | 190.00 |
| 10 | 1.90 | 60 | 11.40 | 1100 | 209.00 |
| 11 | 2.09 | 61 | 11.59 | 1200 | 228.00 |
| 12 | 2.28 | 62 | 11.78 | 1300 | 247.00 |
| 13 | 2.47 | 63 | 11.97 | 1400 | 266.00 |
| 14 | 2.66 | 64 | 12.16 | 1500 | 285.00 |
| 15 | 2.85 | 65 | 12.35 | 1600 | 304.00 |
| 16 | 3.04 | 66 | 12.54 | 1700 | 323.00 |
| 17 | 3.23 | 67 | 12.73 | 1800 | 342.00 |
| 18 | 3.42 | 68 | 12.92 | 1900 | 361.00 |
| 19 | 3.61 | 69 | 13.11 | 2000 | 380.00 |
| 20 | 3.80 | 70 | 13.30 | 2085 | 396.15 |
| 21 | 3.99 | 71 | 13.49 | | |
| 22 | 4.18 | 72 | 13.68 | | |
| 23 | 4.37 | 73 | 13.87 | | |
| 24 | 4.56 | 74 | 14.06 | | |
| 25 | 4.75 | 75 | 14.25 | | |
| 26 | 4.94 | 76 | 14.44 | | |
| 27 | 5.13 | 77 | 14.63 | | |
| 28 | 5.32 | 78 | 14.82 | | |
| 29 | 5.51 | 79 | 15.01 | | |
| 30 | 5.70 | 80 | 15.20 | | |
| 31 | 5.89 | 81 | 15.39 | | |
| 32 | 6.08 | 82 | 15.58 | | |
| 33 | 6.27 | 83 | 15.77 | | |
| 34 | 6.46 | 84 | 15.96 | | |
| 35 | 6.65 | 85 | 16.15 | | |
| 36 | 6.84 | 86 | 16.34 | | |
| 37 | 7.03 | 87 | 16.53 | | |
| 38 | 7.22 | 88 | 16.72 | | |
| 39 | 7.41 | 89 | 16.91 | | |
| 40 | 7.60 | 90 | 17.10 | | |
| 41 | 7.79 | 91 | 17.29 | | |
| 42 | 7.98 | 92 | 17.48 | | |
| 43 | 8.17 | 93 | 17.67 | | |
| 44 | 8.36 | 94 | 17.86 | | |
| 45 | 8.55 | 95 | 18.05 | | |
| 46 | 8.74 | 96 | 18.24 | | |
| 47 | 8.93 | 97 | 18.43 | | |
| 48 | 9.12 | 98 | 18.62 | | |
| 49 | 9.31 | 99 | 18.81 | | |
| 50 | 9.50 | 100 | 19.00 | | |

Where the exact amount of taxable pay is not shown add together the figures for 2 (or more) entries that make up the amount of taxable pay to the nearest £1 below.

# Tables C

## How to use Tables C – Scottish monthly paid

You'll already have used Pay Adjustment Tables A and completed your RT11 up to and including Column 5.

| **Example 8 – Table C1** | |
| --- | --- |
| Example payment is for **Month 4** | |
| Taxable pay to date from RT11 Column 5 | **£3,505.00** |
| Find tax due at **basic rate** – 20% | |
| **Taxable pay** | **£3,505.00** |
| Minus taxable pay Column 1 | **£695.00** |
| **Taxable pay at 20%** | **£2,810.00** |

| **Example 9 – Table C4** | |
| --- | --- |
| Example payment is for **Month 4** | |
| Taxable pay to date from RT11 Column 5 | **£57,500.00** |
| Find tax due at **top rate** – 46% | |
| **Taxable pay** | **£57,500.00** |
| Minus taxable pay Column 10 | **£50,000.00** |
| **Taxable pay at 46%** | **£7,500.00** |

First use Table D1 on page 19 for the nearest round figure below £2,810.00, it's £2,800.

Then use Table D1 on page 19 for the remainder of £2,810, it's £10.

Use Table D4 on page 22 to find tax due on £7,500.

| Taxable pay | Tax |
| --- | --- |
| £ | £ |
| 2600 | 520.00 |
| 2700 | 540.00 |
| 2800 | 560.00 |
| 2900 | 580.00 |
| 3000 | 600.00 |
| 3100 | 620.00 |

| Taxable pay | Tax |
| --- | --- |
| £ | £ |
| 6 | 1.20 |
| 7 | 1.40 |
| 8 | 1.60 |
| 9 | 1.80 |
| 10 | 2.00 |
| 11 | 2.20 |
| 12 | 2.40 |

| Taxable pay | Tax |
| --- | --- |
| £ | £ |
| 7100 | 3266.00 |
| 7200 | 3312.00 |
| 7300 | 3358.00 |
| 7400 | 3404.00 |
| 7500 | 3450.00 |
| 7600 | 3496.00 |
| 7700 | 3542.00 |

| | |
| --- | --- |
| Basic rate tax due on £2,800 from Table D1 | **£560.00** |
| Plus tax due on £10 from Table D1 | **£2.00** |
| | **£562.00** |
| Add figure from Table C1 Column 3 for **Month 4** | **£132.05** |
| **Total tax due** | **£694.05** |

| | |
| --- | --- |
| Top rate tax due on £7,500 from Table D4 | **£3,450.00** |
| Add figure from Table C4 Column 11 for **Month 4** | **£18,388.85** |
| **Total tax due** | **£21,838.85** |

## Tables C – Scottish monthly paid

Page 12 tells you when to use these tables.

### Table C1

**Employee paid at monthly rates**

| Month | Column 1 If total taxable pay to date exceeds | Column 2 And total taxable pay to date does not exceed | Column 3 Total tax due to date on pay in Column 1 | Month | Column 1 If total taxable pay to date exceeds | Column 2 And total taxable pay to date does not exceed | Column 3 Total tax due to date on pay in Column 1 | Is the total taxable pay to date more than the amount in Column 1 and does not exceed the amount in Column 2? |
| --- | --- | --- | --- | --- | --- | --- | --- | --- |
| | £ | £ | £ | | £ | £ | £ | If Yes, add to the figure in Column 3 the tax at 20% (as shown in Table D1 – basic rate tax at 20%) on page 19) on the amount by which the total taxable pay to date exceeds the figure in Column 1. |
| 1 | 174 | 1055 | 33.06 | 7 | 1217 | 7384 | 231.23 | |
| 2 | 348 | 2110 | 66.12 | 8 | 1390 | 8439 | 264.10 | |
| 3 | 522 | 3165 | 99.18 | 9 | 1564 | 9494 | 297.16 | If No, and the total taxable pay to date exceeds the figure in Column 2, use Table C2. |
| 4 | 695 | 4220 | 132.05 | 10 | 1738 | 10549 | 330.22 | |
| 5 | 869 | 5275 | 165.11 | 11 | 1912 | 11604 | 363.28 | |
| 6 | 1043 | 6329 | 198.17 | 12 | 2085 | 12658 | 396.15 | |

15

## Tables C – Scottish monthly paid continued

Pages 12 and 15 tell you when to use these tables.

### Table C2

#### Employee paid at monthly rates

| Month | Column 4 If total taxable pay to date exceeds £ | Column 5 And total taxable pay to date does not exceed £ | Column 6 Total tax due to date on pay in Column 4 £ | Month | Column 4 If total taxable pay to date exceeds £ | Column 5 And total taxable pay to date does not exceed £ | Column 6 Total tax due to date on pay in Column 4 £ |
|---|---|---|---|---|---|---|---|
| 1 | 1055 | 2578 | 209.26 | 7 | 7384 | 18043 | 1464.63 |
| 2 | 2110 | 5155 | 418.52 | 8 | 8439 | 20620 | 1673.90 |
| 3 | 3165 | 7733 | 627.79 | 9 | 9494 | 23198 | 1883.16 |
| 4 | 4220 | 10310 | 837.05 | 10 | 10549 | 25775 | 2092.43 |
| 5 | 5275 | 12888 | 1046.32 | 11 | 11604 | 28353 | 2301.69 |
| 6 | 6329 | 15465 | 1255.37 | 12 | 12658 | 30930 | 2510.75 |

Is the total taxable pay to date more than the amount in Column 4 and does not exceed the amount in Column 5?

If Yes, add to the figure in Column 6 the tax at 21% (as shown in Table D2 – intermediate rate (tax at 21%) on page 20) on the amount by which the total taxable pay to date exceeds the figure in Column 4.

If No, and the total taxable pay to date exceeds the figure in Column 5, use Table C3.

### Table C3

#### Employee paid at monthly rates

| Month | Column 7 If total taxable pay to date exceeds £ | Column 8 And total taxable pay to date does not exceed £ | Column 9 Total tax due to date on pay in Column 7 £ | Month | Column 7 If total taxable pay to date exceeds £ | Column 8 And total taxable pay to date does not exceed £ | Column 9 Total tax due to date on pay in Column 7 £ |
|---|---|---|---|---|---|---|---|
| 1 | 2578 | 12500 | 529.09 | 7 | 18043 | 87500 | 3703.12 |
| 2 | 5155 | 25000 | 1057.97 | 8 | 20620 | 100000 | 4231.91 |
| 3 | 7733 | 37500 | 1587.17 | 9 | 23198 | 112500 | 4761.10 |
| 4 | 10310 | 50000 | 2115.95 | 10 | 25775 | 125000 | 5289.89 |
| 5 | 12888 | 62500 | 2645.15 | 11 | 28353 | 137500 | 5819.08 |
| 6 | 15465 | 75000 | 3173.93 | 12 | 30930 | 150000 | 6347.87 |

Is the total taxable pay to date more than the amount in Column 7 and does not exceed the amount in Column 8?

If Yes, add to the figure in Column 9 the tax at 41% (as shown in Table D3 – higher rate (tax at 41%) on page 21) on the amount by which the total taxable pay to date exceeds the figure in Column 7.

If No, and the total taxable pay to date exceeds the figure in Column 8, use Table C4.

### Table C4

#### Employee paid at monthly rates

| Month | Column 10 If total taxable pay to date exceeds £ | Column 11 Total tax due to date on pay in Column 10 £ | Month | Column 10 If total taxable pay to date exceeds £ | Column 11 Total tax due to date on pay in Column 10 £ |
|---|---|---|---|---|---|
| 1 | 12500 | 4597.11 | 7 | 87500 | 32180.49 |
| 2 | 25000 | 9194.42 | 8 | 100000 | 36777.71 |
| 3 | 37500 | 13791.64 | 9 | 112500 | 41374.92 |
| 4 | 50000 | 18388.85 | 10 | 125000 | 45972.14 |
| 5 | 62500 | 22986.07 | 11 | 137500 | 50569.35 |
| 6 | 75000 | 27583.28 | 12 | 150000 | 55166.57 |

If total taxable pay to date exceeds the figure in Column 10. Add to the figure in Column 11 the tax at 46% (as shown in Table D4 – top rate (tax at 46%) on page 22) on the amount by which the total taxable pay to date exceeds the figure in Column 10.

16

# Tables C – Scottish weekly paid

Page 12 tells you when to use these tables.

## Table C1

### Employee paid at weekly rates

| Week | Column 1 If total taxable pay to date exceeds £ | Column 2 And total taxable pay to date does not exceed £ | Column 3 Total tax due to date on pay in Column 1 £ |
|---|---|---|---|
| 1 | 41 | 244 | 7.79 |
| 2 | 81 | 487 | 15.39 |
| 3 | 121 | 731 | 22.99 |
| 4 | 161 | 974 | 30.59 |
| 5 | 201 | 1218 | 38.19 |
| 6 | 241 | 1461 | 45.79 |
| 7 | 281 | 1704 | 53.39 |
| 8 | 321 | 1948 | 60.99 |
| 9 | 361 | 2191 | 68.59 |
| 10 | 401 | 2435 | 76.19 |
| 11 | 442 | 2678 | 83.98 |
| 12 | 482 | 2922 | 91.58 |
| 13 | 522 | 3165 | 99.18 |
| 14 | 562 | 3408 | 106.78 |
| 15 | 602 | 3652 | 114.38 |
| 16 | 642 | 3895 | 121.98 |
| 17 | 682 | 4139 | 129.58 |
| 18 | 722 | 4382 | 137.18 |
| 19 | 762 | 4626 | 144.78 |
| 20 | 802 | 4869 | 152.38 |
| 21 | 843 | 5112 | 160.18 |
| 22 | 883 | 5356 | 167.77 |
| 23 | 923 | 5599 | 175.37 |
| 24 | 963 | 5843 | 182.97 |
| 25 | 1003 | 6086 | 190.57 |
| 26 | 1043 | 6329 | 198.17 |
| 27 | 1083 | 6573 | 205.77 |
| 28 | 1123 | 6816 | 213.37 |
| 29 | 1163 | 7060 | 220.97 |
| 30 | 1203 | 7303 | 228.57 |
| 31 | 1243 | 7547 | 236.17 |
| 32 | 1284 | 7790 | 243.96 |
| 33 | 1324 | 8033 | 251.56 |
| 34 | 1364 | 8277 | 259.16 |
| 35 | 1404 | 8520 | 266.76 |
| 36 | 1444 | 8764 | 274.36 |
| 37 | 1484 | 9007 | 281.96 |
| 38 | 1524 | 9251 | 289.56 |
| 39 | 1564 | 9494 | 297.16 |
| 40 | 1604 | 9737 | 304.76 |
| 41 | 1644 | 9981 | 312.36 |
| 42 | 1685 | 10224 | 320.16 |
| 43 | 1725 | 10468 | 327.75 |
| 44 | 1765 | 10711 | 335.35 |
| 45 | 1805 | 10955 | 342.95 |
| 46 | 1845 | 11198 | 350.55 |
| 47 | 1885 | 11441 | 358.15 |
| 48 | 1925 | 11685 | 365.75 |
| 49 | 1965 | 11928 | 373.35 |
| 50 | 2005 | 12172 | 380.95 |
| 51 | 2045 | 12415 | 388.55 |
| 52 | 2085 | 12658 | 396.15 |

Is the total taxable pay to date more than the amount in Column 1 and does not exceed the amount in Column 2?

If Yes, add to the figure in Column 3 the tax at 20% (as shown in Table D1 – basic rate (tax at 20%) on page 19) on the amount by which the total taxable pay to date exceeds the figure in Column 1.

If No, and the total taxable pay to date exceeds the figure in Column 2 use Table C2.

## Table C2

### Employee paid at weekly rates

| Week | Column 4 If total taxable pay to date exceeds £ | Column 5 And total taxable pay to date does not exceed £ | Column 6 Total tax due to date on pay in Column 4 £ |
|---|---|---|---|
| 1 | 244 | 595 | 48.40 |
| 2 | 487 | 1190 | 96.60 |
| 3 | 731 | 1785 | 145.00 |
| 4 | 974 | 2380 | 193.19 |
| 5 | 1218 | 2975 | 241.60 |
| 6 | 1461 | 3569 | 289.79 |
| 7 | 1704 | 4164 | 337.99 |
| 8 | 1948 | 4759 | 386.39 |
| 9 | 2191 | 5354 | 434.59 |
| 10 | 2435 | 5949 | 482.99 |
| 11 | 2678 | 6543 | 531.19 |
| 12 | 2922 | 7138 | 579.59 |
| 13 | 3165 | 7733 | 627.79 |
| 14 | 3408 | 8328 | 675.98 |
| 15 | 3652 | 8923 | 724.39 |
| 16 | 3895 | 9517 | 772.58 |
| 17 | 4139 | 10112 | 820.99 |
| 18 | 4382 | 10707 | 869.18 |
| 19 | 4626 | 11302 | 917.59 |
| 20 | 4869 | 11897 | 965.78 |
| 21 | 5112 | 12491 | 1013.98 |
| 22 | 5356 | 13086 | 1062.38 |
| 23 | 5599 | 13681 | 1110.58 |
| 24 | 5843 | 14276 | 1158.98 |
| 25 | 6086 | 14871 | 1207.18 |
| 26 | 6329 | 15465 | 1255.37 |
| 27 | 6573 | 16060 | 1303.78 |
| 28 | 6816 | 16655 | 1351.97 |
| 29 | 7060 | 17250 | 1400.37 |
| 30 | 7303 | 17845 | 1448.57 |
| 31 | 7547 | 18440 | 1496.97 |
| 32 | 7790 | 19034 | 1545.17 |
| 33 | 8033 | 19629 | 1593.36 |
| 34 | 8277 | 20224 | 1641.77 |
| 35 | 8520 | 20819 | 1689.96 |
| 36 | 8764 | 21414 | 1738.37 |
| 37 | 9007 | 22008 | 1786.56 |
| 38 | 9251 | 22603 | 1834.97 |
| 39 | 9494 | 23198 | 1883.16 |
| 40 | 9737 | 23793 | 1931.36 |
| 41 | 9981 | 24388 | 1979.76 |
| 42 | 10224 | 24982 | 2027.96 |
| 43 | 10468 | 25577 | 2076.36 |
| 44 | 10711 | 26172 | 2124.56 |
| 45 | 10955 | 26767 | 2172.96 |
| 46 | 11198 | 27362 | 2221.16 |
| 47 | 11441 | 27956 | 2269.35 |
| 48 | 11685 | 28551 | 2317.76 |
| 49 | 11928 | 29146 | 2365.95 |
| 50 | 12172 | 29741 | 2414.36 |
| 51 | 12415 | 30336 | 2462.55 |
| 52 | 12658 | 30930 | 2510.75 |

Is the total taxable pay to date more than the amount in Column 4 and does not exceed the amount in Column 5?

If Yes, add to the figure in Column 6 the tax at 21% (as shown in Table D2 – intermediate rate (tax at 21%) on page 20) on the amount by which the total taxable pay to date exceeds the figure in Column 4.

If No, and the total taxable pay to date exceeds the figure in Column 5 use Table C3.

17

## Tables C – Scottish weekly paid continued

Pages 12 and 17 tell you when to use these tables.

### Table C3
#### Employee paid at weekly rates

| Week | Column 7 If total taxable pay to date exceeds £ | Column 8 And total taxable pay to date does not exceed £ | Column 9 Total tax due to date on pay in Column 7 £ |
|---|---|---|---|
| 1 | 595 | 2885 | 122.15 |
| 2 | 1190 | 5770 | 244.30 |
| 3 | 1785 | 8654 | 366.46 |
| 4 | 2380 | 11539 | 488.61 |
| 5 | 2975 | 14424 | 610.76 |
| 6 | 3569 | 17308 | 732.51 |
| 7 | 4164 | 20193 | 854.66 |
| 8 | 4759 | 23077 | 976.81 |
| 9 | 5354 | 25962 | 1098.96 |
| 10 | 5949 | 28847 | 1221.12 |
| 11 | 6543 | 31731 | 1342.86 |
| 12 | 7138 | 34616 | 1465.01 |
| 13 | 7733 | 37500 | 1587.17 |
| 14 | 8328 | 40385 | 1709.32 |
| 15 | 8923 | 43270 | 1831.47 |
| 16 | 9517 | 46154 | 1953.22 |
| 17 | 10112 | 49039 | 2075.37 |
| 18 | 10707 | 51924 | 2197.52 |
| 19 | 11302 | 54808 | 2319.68 |
| 20 | 11897 | 57693 | 2441.83 |
| 21 | 12491 | 60577 | 2563.57 |
| 22 | 13086 | 63462 | 2685.73 |
| 23 | 13681 | 66347 | 2807.88 |
| 24 | 14276 | 69231 | 2930.03 |
| 25 | 14871 | 72116 | 3052.19 |
| 26 | 15465 | 75000 | 3173.93 |
| 27 | 16060 | 77885 | 3296.08 |
| 28 | 16655 | 80770 | 3418.24 |
| 29 | 17250 | 83654 | 3540.39 |
| 30 | 17845 | 86539 | 3662.54 |
| 31 | 18440 | 89424 | 3784.70 |
| 32 | 19034 | 92308 | 3906.44 |
| 33 | 19629 | 95193 | 4028.59 |
| 34 | 20224 | 98077 | 4150.75 |
| 35 | 20819 | 100962 | 4272.90 |
| 36 | 21414 | 103847 | 4395.05 |
| 37 | 22008 | 106731 | 4516.80 |
| 38 | 22603 | 109616 | 4638.95 |
| 39 | 23198 | 112500 | 4761.10 |
| 40 | 23793 | 115385 | 4883.26 |
| 41 | 24388 | 118270 | 5005.41 |
| 42 | 24982 | 121154 | 5127.15 |
| 43 | 25577 | 124039 | 5249.31 |
| 44 | 26172 | 126924 | 5371.46 |
| 45 | 26767 | 129808 | 5493.61 |
| 46 | 27362 | 132693 | 5615.77 |
| 47 | 27956 | 135577 | 5737.51 |
| 48 | 28551 | 138462 | 5859.66 |
| 49 | 29146 | 141347 | 5981.82 |
| 50 | 29741 | 144231 | 6103.97 |
| 51 | 30336 | 147116 | 6226.12 |
| 52 | 30930 | 150000 | 6347.87 |

Is the total taxable pay to date more than the amount in Column 7 and does not exceed the amount in Column 8?

If Yes, add to the figure in Column 9 the tax at 41% (as shown in Table D3 – higher rate (tax at 41%) on page 21 on the amount by which the total taxable pay to date exceeds the figure in Column 7.

If No, and the total taxable pay to date exceeds the figure in Column 8 use Table C4.

### Table C4
#### Employee paid at weekly rates

| Week | Column 10 If total taxable pay to date exceeds £ | Column 11 Total tax due to date on pay in Column 10 £ |
|---|---|---|
| 1 | 2885 | 1061.07 |
| 2 | 5770 | 2122.14 |
| 3 | 8654 | 3182.75 |
| 4 | 11539 | 4243.83 |
| 5 | 14424 | 5304.90 |
| 6 | 17308 | 6365.51 |
| 7 | 20193 | 7426.58 |
| 8 | 23077 | 8487.20 |
| 9 | 25962 | 9548.27 |
| 10 | 28847 | 10609.34 |
| 11 | 31731 | 11669.95 |
| 12 | 34616 | 12731.03 |
| 13 | 37500 | 13791.64 |
| 14 | 40385 | 14852.71 |
| 15 | 43270 | 15913.78 |
| 16 | 46154 | 16974.40 |
| 17 | 49039 | 18035.47 |
| 18 | 51924 | 19096.54 |
| 19 | 54808 | 20157.15 |
| 20 | 57693 | 21218.23 |
| 21 | 60577 | 22278.84 |
| 22 | 63462 | 23339.91 |
| 23 | 66347 | 24400.98 |
| 24 | 69231 | 25461.60 |
| 25 | 72116 | 26522.67 |
| 26 | 75000 | 27583.28 |
| 27 | 77885 | 28644.35 |
| 28 | 80770 | 29705.43 |
| 29 | 83654 | 30766.04 |
| 30 | 86539 | 31827.11 |
| 31 | 89424 | 32888.18 |
| 32 | 92308 | 33948.80 |
| 33 | 95193 | 35009.87 |
| 34 | 98077 | 36070.48 |
| 35 | 100962 | 37131.55 |
| 36 | 103847 | 38192.63 |
| 37 | 106731 | 39253.24 |
| 38 | 109616 | 40314.31 |
| 39 | 112500 | 41374.92 |
| 40 | 115385 | 42436.00 |
| 41 | 118270 | 43497.07 |
| 42 | 121154 | 44557.68 |
| 43 | 124039 | 45618.75 |
| 44 | 126924 | 46679.83 |
| 45 | 129808 | 47740.44 |
| 46 | 132693 | 48801.51 |
| 47 | 135577 | 49862.12 |
| 48 | 138462 | 50923.20 |
| 49 | 141347 | 51984.27 |
| 50 | 144231 | 53044.88 |
| 51 | 147116 | 54105.95 |
| 52 | 150000 | 55166.57 |

If total taxable pay to date exceeds the figure in Column 10. Add to the figure in Column 11 the tax at 46% (as shown in Table D4 – top rate (tax at 46%) on page 22) on the amount by which the total taxable pay to date exceeds the figure in Column 10.

18

## Table D1 – Scottish basic rate (tax at 20%)

Also to be used for tax code SBR. Pages 2 and 12 tell you when to use this table.

### Table D1 – Tax at 20%

| Taxable pay £ | Tax £ | Taxable pay £ | Tax £ | Taxable pay £ | Tax £ | Taxable pay £ | Tax £ | |
|---|---|---|---|---|---|---|---|---|
| 1 | 0.20 | 51 | 10.20 | 100 | 20.00 | 5100 | 1020.00 | Where the exact |
| 2 | 0.40 | 52 | 10.40 | 200 | 40.00 | 5200 | 1040.00 | amount of taxable |
| 3 | 0.60 | 53 | 10.60 | 300 | 60.00 | 5300 | 1060.00 | pay is not shown, |
| 4 | 0.80 | 54 | 10.80 | 400 | 80.00 | 5400 | 1080.00 | add together the |
| 5 | 1.00 | 55 | 11.00 | 500 | 100.00 | 5500 | 1100.00 | figures for 2 (or |
| 6 | 1.20 | 56 | 11.20 | 600 | 120.00 | 5600 | 1120.00 | more) entries to |
| 7 | 1.40 | 57 | 11.40 | 700 | 140.00 | 5700 | 1140.00 | make up the |
| 8 | 1.60 | 58 | 11.60 | 800 | 160.00 | 5800 | 1160.00 | amount of taxable |
| 9 | 1.80 | 59 | 11.80 | 900 | 180.00 | 5900 | 1180.00 | pay to the nearest |
| 10 | 2.00 | 60 | 12.00 | 1000 | 200.00 | 6000 | 1200.00 | £1 below. |
| 11 | 2.20 | 61 | 12.20 | 1100 | 220.00 | 6100 | 1220.00 | |
| 12 | 2.40 | 62 | 12.40 | 1200 | 240.00 | 6200 | 1240.00 | |
| 13 | 2.60 | 63 | 12.60 | 1300 | 260.00 | 6300 | 1260.00 | |
| 14 | 2.80 | 64 | 12.80 | 1400 | 280.00 | 6400 | 1280.00 | |
| 15 | 3.00 | 65 | 13.00 | 1500 | 300.00 | 6500 | 1300.00 | |
| 16 | 3.20 | 66 | 13.20 | 1600 | 320.00 | 6600 | 1320.00 | |
| 17 | 3.40 | 67 | 13.40 | 1700 | 340.00 | 6700 | 1340.00 | |
| 18 | 3.60 | 68 | 13.60 | 1800 | 360.00 | 6800 | 1360.00 | |
| 19 | 3.80 | 69 | 13.80 | 1900 | 380.00 | 6900 | 1380.00 | |
| 20 | 4.00 | 70 | 14.00 | 2000 | 400.00 | 7000 | 1400.00 | |
| 21 | 4.20 | 71 | 14.20 | 2100 | 420.00 | 7100 | 1420.00 | |
| 22 | 4.40 | 72 | 14.40 | 2200 | 440.00 | 7200 | 1440.00 | |
| 23 | 4.60 | 73 | 14.60 | 2300 | 460.00 | 7300 | 1460.00 | |
| 24 | 4.80 | 74 | 14.80 | 2400 | 480.00 | 7400 | 1480.00 | |
| 25 | 5.00 | 75 | 15.00 | 2500 | 500.00 | 7500 | 1500.00 | |
| 26 | 5.20 | 76 | 15.20 | 2600 | 520.00 | 7600 | 1520.00 | |
| 27 | 5.40 | 77 | 15.40 | 2700 | 540.00 | 7700 | 1540.00 | |
| 28 | 5.60 | 78 | 15.60 | 2800 | 560.00 | 7800 | 1560.00 | |
| 29 | 5.80 | 79 | 15.80 | 2900 | 580.00 | 7900 | 1580.00 | |
| 30 | 6.00 | 80 | 16.00 | 3000 | 600.00 | 8000 | 1600.00 | |
| 31 | 6.20 | 81 | 16.20 | 3100 | 620.00 | 8100 | 1620.00 | |
| 32 | 6.40 | 82 | 16.40 | 3200 | 640.00 | 8200 | 1640.00 | |
| 33 | 6.60 | 83 | 16.60 | 3300 | 660.00 | 8300 | 1660.00 | |
| 34 | 6.80 | 84 | 16.80 | 3400 | 680.00 | 8400 | 1680.00 | |
| 35 | 7.00 | 85 | 17.00 | 3500 | 700.00 | 8500 | 1700.00 | |
| 36 | 7.20 | 86 | 17.20 | 3600 | 720.00 | 8600 | 1720.00 | |
| 37 | 7.40 | 87 | 17.40 | 3700 | 740.00 | 8700 | 1740.00 | |
| 38 | 7.60 | 88 | 17.60 | 3800 | 760.00 | 8800 | 1760.00 | |
| 39 | 7.80 | 89 | 17.80 | 3900 | 780.00 | 8900 | 1780.00 | |
| 40 | 8.00 | 90 | 18.00 | 4000 | 800.00 | 9000 | 1800.00 | |
| 41 | 8.20 | 91 | 18.20 | 4100 | 820.00 | 9100 | 1820.00 | |
| 42 | 8.40 | 92 | 18.40 | 4200 | 840.00 | 9200 | 1840.00 | |
| 43 | 8.60 | 93 | 18.60 | 4300 | 860.00 | 9300 | 1860.00 | |
| 44 | 8.80 | 94 | 18.80 | 4400 | 880.00 | 9400 | 1880.00 | |
| 45 | 9.00 | 95 | 19.00 | 4500 | 900.00 | 9500 | 1900.00 | |
| 46 | 9.20 | 96 | 19.20 | 4600 | 920.00 | 9600 | 1920.00 | |
| 47 | 9.40 | 97 | 19.40 | 4700 | 940.00 | 9700 | 1940.00 | |
| 48 | 9.60 | 98 | 19.60 | 4800 | 960.00 | 9800 | 1960.00 | |
| 49 | 9.80 | 99 | 19.80 | 4900 | 980.00 | 9900 | 1980.00 | |
| 50 | 10.00 | | | 5000 | 1000.00 | 10000 | 2000.00 | |
| | | | | | | 20000 | 4000.00 | |
| | | | | | | 30000 | 6000.00 | |
| | | | | | | 40000 | 8000.00 | |
| | | | | | | 50000 | 10000.00 | |
| | | | | | | 60000 | 12000.00 | |
| | | | | | | 70000 | 14000.00 | |
| | | | | | | 80000 | 16000.00 | |
| | | | | | | 90000 | 18000.00 | |
| | | | | | | 100000 | 20000.00 | |

19

# Table D2 – Scottish intermediate rate (tax at 21%)

Also to be used for tax code SD0. Pages 16 and 17 tell you when to use this table.

## Table D2 – Tax at 21%

| Taxable pay £ | Tax £ | Taxable pay £ | Tax £ | Taxable pay £ | Tax £ | Taxable pay £ | Tax £ | |
|---|---|---|---|---|---|---|---|---|
| 1 | 0.21 | 51 | 10.71 | 100 | 21.00 | 5100 | 1071.00 | Where the exact |
| 2 | 0.42 | 52 | 10.92 | 200 | 42.00 | 5200 | 1092.00 | amount of taxable |
| 3 | 0.63 | 53 | 11.13 | 300 | 63.00 | 5300 | 1113.00 | pay is not shown, |
| 4 | 0.84 | 54 | 11.34 | 400 | 84.00 | 5400 | 1134.00 | add together the |
| 5 | 1.05 | 55 | 11.55 | 500 | 105.00 | 5500 | 1155.00 | figures for 2 (or |
| 6 | 1.26 | 56 | 11.76 | 600 | 126.00 | 5600 | 1176.00 | more) entries to |
| 7 | 1.47 | 57 | 11.97 | 700 | 147.00 | 5700 | 1197.00 | make up the |
| 8 | 1.68 | 58 | 12.18 | 800 | 168.00 | 5800 | 1218.00 | amount of taxable |
| 9 | 1.89 | 59 | 12.39 | 900 | 189.00 | 5900 | 1239.00 | pay to the nearest |
| 10 | 2.10 | 60 | 12.60 | 1000 | 210.00 | 6000 | 1260.00 | £1 below. |
| 11 | 2.31 | 61 | 12.81 | 1100 | 231.00 | 6100 | 1281.00 | |
| 12 | 2.52 | 62 | 13.02 | 1200 | 252.00 | 6200 | 1302.00 | |
| 13 | 2.73 | 63 | 13.23 | 1300 | 273.00 | 6300 | 1323.00 | |
| 14 | 2.94 | 64 | 13.44 | 1400 | 294.00 | 6400 | 1344.00 | |
| 15 | 3.15 | 65 | 13.65 | 1500 | 315.00 | 6500 | 1365.00 | |
| 16 | 3.36 | 66 | 13.86 | 1600 | 336.00 | 6600 | 1386.00 | |
| 17 | 3.57 | 67 | 14.07 | 1700 | 357.00 | 6700 | 1407.00 | |
| 18 | 3.78 | 68 | 14.28 | 1800 | 378.00 | 6800 | 1428.00 | |
| 19 | 3.99 | 69 | 14.49 | 1900 | 399.00 | 6900 | 1449.00 | |
| 20 | 4.20 | 70 | 14.70 | 2000 | 420.00 | 7000 | 1470.00 | |
| 21 | 4.41 | 71 | 14.91 | 2100 | 441.00 | 7100 | 1491.00 | |
| 22 | 4.62 | 72 | 15.12 | 2200 | 462.00 | 7200 | 1512.00 | |
| 23 | 4.83 | 73 | 15.33 | 2300 | 483.00 | 7300 | 1533.00 | |
| 24 | 5.04 | 74 | 15.54 | 2400 | 504.00 | 7400 | 1554.00 | |
| 25 | 5.25 | 75 | 15.75 | 2500 | 525.00 | 7500 | 1575.00 | |
| 26 | 5.46 | 76 | 15.96 | 2600 | 546.00 | 7600 | 1596.00 | |
| 27 | 5.67 | 77 | 16.17 | 2700 | 567.00 | 7700 | 1617.00 | |
| 28 | 5.88 | 78 | 16.38 | 2800 | 588.00 | 7800 | 1638.00 | |
| 29 | 6.09 | 79 | 16.59 | 2900 | 609.00 | 7900 | 1659.00 | |
| 30 | 6.30 | 80 | 16.80 | 3000 | 630.00 | 8000 | 1680.00 | |
| 31 | 6.51 | 81 | 17.01 | 3100 | 651.00 | 8100 | 1701.00 | |
| 32 | 6.72 | 82 | 17.22 | 3200 | 672.00 | 8200 | 1722.00 | |
| 33 | 6.93 | 83 | 17.43 | 3300 | 693.00 | 8300 | 1743.00 | |
| 34 | 7.14 | 84 | 17.64 | 3400 | 714.00 | 8400 | 1764.00 | |
| 35 | 7.35 | 85 | 17.85 | 3500 | 735.00 | 8500 | 1785.00 | |
| 36 | 7.56 | 86 | 18.06 | 3600 | 756.00 | 8600 | 1806.00 | |
| 37 | 7.77 | 87 | 18.27 | 3700 | 777.00 | 8700 | 1827.00 | |
| 38 | 7.98 | 88 | 18.48 | 3800 | 798.00 | 8800 | 1848.00 | |
| 39 | 8.19 | 89 | 18.69 | 3900 | 819.00 | 8900 | 1869.00 | |
| 40 | 8.40 | 90 | 18.90 | 4000 | 840.00 | 9000 | 1890.00 | |
| 41 | 8.61 | 91 | 19.11 | 4100 | 861.00 | 9100 | 1911.00 | |
| 42 | 8.82 | 92 | 19.32 | 4200 | 882.00 | 9200 | 1932.00 | |
| 43 | 9.03 | 93 | 19.53 | 4300 | 903.00 | 9300 | 1953.00 | |
| 44 | 9.24 | 94 | 19.74 | 4400 | 924.00 | 9400 | 1974.00 | |
| 45 | 9.45 | 95 | 19.95 | 4500 | 945.00 | 9500 | 1995.00 | |
| 46 | 9.66 | 96 | 20.16 | 4600 | 966.00 | 9600 | 2016.00 | |
| 47 | 9.87 | 97 | 20.37 | 4700 | 987.00 | 9700 | 2037.00 | |
| 48 | 10.08 | 98 | 20.58 | 4800 | 1008.00 | 9800 | 2058.00 | |
| 49 | 10.29 | 99 | 20.79 | 4900 | 1029.00 | 9900 | 2079.00 | |
| 50 | 10.50 | | | 5000 | 1050.00 | 10000 | 2100.00 | |
| | | | | | | 20000 | 4200.00 | |
| | | | | | | 30000 | 6300.00 | |
| | | | | | | 40000 | 8400.00 | |
| | | | | | | 50000 | 10500.00 | |
| | | | | | | 60000 | 12600.00 | |
| | | | | | | 70000 | 14700.00 | |
| | | | | | | 80000 | 16800.00 | |
| | | | | | | 90000 | 18900.00 | |
| | | | | | | 100000 | 21000.00 | |

20

# Table D3 – Scottish higher rate (tax at 41%)

Also to be used for tax code SD1. Pages 16 and 18 tell you when to use this table.

## Table D3 – Tax at 41%

| Taxable pay £ | Tax £ | Taxable pay £ | Tax £ | Taxable pay £ | Tax £ | Taxable pay £ | Tax £ |
|---|---|---|---|---|---|---|---|
| 1 | 0.41 | 51 | 20.91 | 100 | 41.00 | 5100 | 2091.00 |
| 2 | 0.82 | 52 | 21.32 | 200 | 82.00 | 5200 | 2132.00 |
| 3 | 1.23 | 53 | 21.73 | 300 | 123.00 | 5300 | 2173.00 |
| 4 | 1.64 | 54 | 22.14 | 400 | 164.00 | 5400 | 2214.00 |
| 5 | 2.05 | 55 | 22.55 | 500 | 205.00 | 5500 | 2255.00 |
| 6 | 2.46 | 56 | 22.96 | 600 | 246.00 | 5600 | 2296.00 |
| 7 | 2.87 | 57 | 23.37 | 700 | 287.00 | 5700 | 2337.00 |
| 8 | 3.28 | 58 | 23.78 | 800 | 328.00 | 5800 | 2378.00 |
| 9 | 3.69 | 59 | 24.19 | 900 | 369.00 | 5900 | 2419.00 |
| 10 | 4.10 | 60 | 24.60 | 1000 | 410.00 | 6000 | 2460.00 |
| 11 | 4.51 | 61 | 25.01 | 1100 | 451.00 | 6100 | 2501.00 |
| 12 | 4.92 | 62 | 25.42 | 1200 | 492.00 | 6200 | 2542.00 |
| 13 | 5.33 | 63 | 25.83 | 1300 | 533.00 | 6300 | 2583.00 |
| 14 | 5.74 | 64 | 26.24 | 1400 | 574.00 | 6400 | 2624.00 |
| 15 | 6.15 | 65 | 26.65 | 1500 | 615.00 | 6500 | 2665.00 |
| 16 | 6.56 | 66 | 27.06 | 1600 | 656.00 | 6600 | 2706.00 |
| 17 | 6.97 | 67 | 27.47 | 1700 | 697.00 | 6700 | 2747.00 |
| 18 | 7.38 | 68 | 27.88 | 1800 | 738.00 | 6800 | 2788.00 |
| 19 | 7.79 | 69 | 28.29 | 1900 | 779.00 | 6900 | 2829.00 |
| 20 | 8.20 | 70 | 28.70 | 2000 | 820.00 | 7000 | 2870.00 |
| 21 | 8.61 | 71 | 29.11 | 2100 | 861.00 | 7100 | 2911.00 |
| 22 | 9.02 | 72 | 29.52 | 2200 | 902.00 | 7200 | 2952.00 |
| 23 | 9.43 | 73 | 29.93 | 2300 | 943.00 | 7300 | 2993.00 |
| 24 | 9.84 | 74 | 30.34 | 2400 | 984.00 | 7400 | 3034.00 |
| 25 | 10.25 | 75 | 30.75 | 2500 | 1025.00 | 7500 | 3075.00 |
| 26 | 10.66 | 76 | 31.16 | 2600 | 1066.00 | 7600 | 3116.00 |
| 27 | 11.07 | 77 | 31.57 | 2700 | 1107.00 | 7700 | 3157.00 |
| 28 | 11.48 | 78 | 31.98 | 2800 | 1148.00 | 7800 | 3198.00 |
| 29 | 11.89 | 79 | 32.39 | 2900 | 1189.00 | 7900 | 3239.00 |
| 30 | 12.30 | 80 | 32.80 | 3000 | 1230.00 | 8000 | 3280.00 |
| 31 | 12.71 | 81 | 33.21 | 3100 | 1271.00 | 8100 | 3321.00 |
| 32 | 13.12 | 82 | 33.62 | 3200 | 1312.00 | 8200 | 3362.00 |
| 33 | 13.53 | 83 | 34.03 | 3300 | 1353.00 | 8300 | 3403.00 |
| 34 | 13.94 | 84 | 34.44 | 3400 | 1394.00 | 8400 | 3444.00 |
| 35 | 14.35 | 85 | 34.85 | 3500 | 1435.00 | 8500 | 3485.00 |
| 36 | 14.76 | 86 | 35.26 | 3600 | 1476.00 | 8600 | 3526.00 |
| 37 | 15.17 | 87 | 35.67 | 3700 | 1517.00 | 8700 | 3567.00 |
| 38 | 15.58 | 88 | 36.08 | 3800 | 1558.00 | 8800 | 3608.00 |
| 39 | 15.99 | 89 | 36.49 | 3900 | 1599.00 | 8900 | 3649.00 |
| 40 | 16.40 | 90 | 36.90 | 4000 | 1640.00 | 9000 | 3690.00 |
| 41 | 16.81 | 91 | 37.31 | 4100 | 1681.00 | 9100 | 3731.00 |
| 42 | 17.22 | 92 | 37.72 | 4200 | 1722.00 | 9200 | 3772.00 |
| 43 | 17.63 | 93 | 38.13 | 4300 | 1763.00 | 9300 | 3813.00 |
| 44 | 18.04 | 94 | 38.54 | 4400 | 1804.00 | 9400 | 3854.00 |
| 45 | 18.45 | 95 | 38.95 | 4500 | 1845.00 | 9500 | 3895.00 |
| 46 | 18.86 | 96 | 39.36 | 4600 | 1886.00 | 9600 | 3936.00 |
| 47 | 19.27 | 97 | 39.77 | 4700 | 1927.00 | 9700 | 3977.00 |
| 48 | 19.68 | 98 | 40.18 | 4800 | 1968.00 | 9800 | 4018.00 |
| 49 | 20.09 | 99 | 40.59 | 4900 | 2009.00 | 9900 | 4059.00 |
| 50 | 20.50 | | | 5000 | 2050.00 | 10000 | 4100.00 |
| | | | | | | 20000 | 8200.00 |
| | | | | | | 30000 | 12300.00 |
| | | | | | | 40000 | 16400.00 |
| | | | | | | 50000 | 20500.00 |
| | | | | | | 60000 | 24600.00 |
| | | | | | | 70000 | 28700.00 |
| | | | | | | 80000 | 32800.00 |
| | | | | | | 90000 | 36900.00 |
| | | | | | | 100000 | 41000.00 |

Where the exact amount of taxable pay is not shown, add together the figures for 2 (or more) entries to make up the amount of taxable pay to the nearest £1 below.

21

## Table D4 – Scottish top rate (tax at 46%)

Also to be used for tax code SD2. Pages 16 and 18 tell you when to use this table.

### Table D4 – Tax at 46%

| Taxable pay £ | Tax £ | Taxable pay £ | Tax £ | Taxable pay £ | Tax £ | Taxable pay £ | Tax £ |
|---|---|---|---|---|---|---|---|
| 1 | 0.46 | 51 | 23.46 | 100 | 46.00 | 6000 | 2760.00 |
| 2 | 0.92 | 52 | 23.92 | 200 | 92.00 | 6100 | 2806.00 |
| 3 | 1.38 | 53 | 24.38 | 300 | 138.00 | 6200 | 2852.00 |
| 4 | 1.84 | 54 | 24.84 | 400 | 184.00 | 6300 | 2898.00 |
| 5 | 2.30 | 55 | 25.30 | 500 | 230.00 | 6400 | 2944.00 |
| 6 | 2.76 | 56 | 25.76 | 600 | 276.00 | 6500 | 2990.00 |
| 7 | 3.22 | 57 | 26.22 | 700 | 322.00 | 6600 | 3036.00 |
| 8 | 3.68 | 58 | 26.68 | 800 | 368.00 | 6700 | 3082.00 |
| 9 | 4.14 | 59 | 27.14 | 900 | 414.00 | 6800 | 3128.00 |
| 10 | 4.60 | 60 | 27.60 | 1000 | 460.00 | 6900 | 3174.00 |
| 11 | 5.06 | 61 | 28.06 | 1100 | 506.00 | 7000 | 3220.00 |
| 12 | 5.52 | 62 | 28.52 | 1200 | 552.00 | 7100 | 3266.00 |
| 13 | 5.98 | 63 | 28.98 | 1300 | 598.00 | 7200 | 3312.00 |
| 14 | 6.44 | 64 | 29.44 | 1400 | 644.00 | 7300 | 3358.00 |
| 15 | 6.90 | 65 | 29.90 | 1500 | 690.00 | 7400 | 3404.00 |
| 16 | 7.36 | 66 | 30.36 | 1600 | 736.00 | 7500 | 3450.00 |
| 17 | 7.82 | 67 | 30.82 | 1700 | 782.00 | 7600 | 3496.00 |
| 18 | 8.28 | 68 | 31.28 | 1800 | 828.00 | 7700 | 3542.00 |
| 19 | 8.74 | 69 | 31.74 | 1900 | 874.00 | 7800 | 3588.00 |
| 20 | 9.20 | 70 | 32.20 | 2000 | 920.00 | 7900 | 3634.00 |
| 21 | 9.66 | 71 | 32.66 | 2100 | 966.00 | 8000 | 3680.00 |
| 22 | 10.12 | 72 | 33.12 | 2200 | 1012.00 | 8100 | 3726.00 |
| 23 | 10.58 | 73 | 33.58 | 2300 | 1058.00 | 8200 | 3772.00 |
| 24 | 11.04 | 74 | 34.04 | 2400 | 1104.00 | 8300 | 3818.00 |
| 25 | 11.50 | 75 | 34.50 | 2500 | 1150.00 | 8400 | 3864.00 |
| 26 | 11.96 | 76 | 34.96 | 2600 | 1196.00 | 8500 | 3910.00 |
| 27 | 12.42 | 77 | 35.42 | 2700 | 1242.00 | 8600 | 3956.00 |
| 28 | 12.88 | 78 | 35.88 | 2800 | 1288.00 | 8700 | 4002.00 |
| 29 | 13.34 | 79 | 36.34 | 2900 | 1334.00 | 8800 | 4048.00 |
| 30 | 13.80 | 80 | 36.80 | 3000 | 1380.00 | 8900 | 4094.00 |
| 31 | 14.26 | 81 | 37.26 | 3100 | 1426.00 | 9000 | 4140.00 |
| 32 | 14.72 | 82 | 37.72 | 3200 | 1472.00 | 9100 | 4186.00 |
| 33 | 15.18 | 83 | 38.18 | 3300 | 1518.00 | 9200 | 4232.00 |
| 34 | 15.64 | 84 | 38.64 | 3400 | 1564.00 | 9300 | 4278.00 |
| 35 | 16.10 | 85 | 39.10 | 3500 | 1610.00 | 9400 | 4324.00 |
| 36 | 16.56 | 86 | 39.56 | 3600 | 1656.00 | 9500 | 4370.00 |
| 37 | 17.02 | 87 | 40.02 | 3700 | 1702.00 | 9600 | 4416.00 |
| 38 | 17.48 | 88 | 40.48 | 3800 | 1748.00 | 9700 | 4462.00 |
| 39 | 17.94 | 89 | 40.94 | 3900 | 1794.00 | 9800 | 4508.00 |
| 40 | 18.40 | 90 | 41.40 | 4000 | 1840.00 | 9900 | 4554.00 |
| 41 | 18.86 | 91 | 41.86 | 4100 | 1886.00 | 10000 | 4600.00 |
| 42 | 19.32 | 92 | 42.32 | 4200 | 1932.00 | 20000 | 9200.00 |
| 43 | 19.78 | 93 | 42.78 | 4300 | 1978.00 | 30000 | 13800.00 |
| 44 | 20.24 | 94 | 43.24 | 4400 | 2024.00 | 40000 | 18400.00 |
| 45 | 20.70 | 95 | 43.70 | 4500 | 2070.00 | 50000 | 23000.00 |
| 46 | 21.16 | 96 | 44.16 | 4600 | 2116.00 | 60000 | 27600.00 |
| 47 | 21.62 | 97 | 44.62 | 4700 | 2162.00 | 70000 | 32200.00 |
| 48 | 22.08 | 98 | 45.08 | 4800 | 2208.00 | 80000 | 36800.00 |
| 49 | 22.54 | 99 | 45.54 | 4900 | 2254.00 | 90000 | 41400.00 |
| 50 | 23.00 | | | 5000 | 2300.00 | 100000 | 46000.00 |
| | | | | 5100 | 2346.00 | 200000 | 92000.00 |
| | | | | 5200 | 2392.00 | 300000 | 138000.00 |
| | | | | 5300 | 2438.00 | 400000 | 184000.00 |
| | | | | 5400 | 2484.00 | 500000 | 230000.00 |
| | | | | 5500 | 2530.00 | 600000 | 276000.00 |
| | | | | 5600 | 2576.00 | 700000 | 322000.00 |
| | | | | 5700 | 2622.00 | 800000 | 368000.00 |
| | | | | 5800 | 2668.00 | 900000 | 414000.00 |
| | | | | 5900 | 2714.00 | 1000000 | 460000.00 |

Where the exact amount of taxable pay is not shown, add together the figures for 2 (or more) entries to make up the amount of taxable pay to the nearest £1 below.

22

# Welsh rate

## Welsh monthly paid

If you do your payroll on a monthly basis use this table.

| Month | Column 1 | Month | Column 1 | Month | Column 1 | |
|---|---|---|---|---|---|---|
| 1 | 3125 | 5 | 15625 | 9 | 28125 | Work out which month the pay is for - there's a chart on page 3. |
| 2 | 6250 | 6 | 18750 | 10 | 31250 | Pick the month you need from the Month column in the table. Look at the figure in Column 1. |
| 3 | 9375 | 7 | 21875 | 11 | 34375 | |
| 4 | 12500 | 8 | 25000 | 12 | 37500 | |

Is your employee's total taxable pay to date less than or equal to the figure in Column 1?
If so, use Welsh Table B on pages 25 and 26.

If your employee's total taxable pay to date is more than the amount in Column 1,
use Welsh Tables C and D on pages 27, 29 and 30.

## Welsh weekly paid

If you do your payroll on a weekly basis use this table.

| Week | Column 1 | Week | Column 1 | Week | Column 1 | |
|---|---|---|---|---|---|---|
| 1 | 722 | 21 | 15145 | 41 | 29568 | Work out which week the pay is for - there's a chart on page 3. |
| 2 | 1443 | 22 | 15866 | 42 | 30289 | Pick the week you need from the Week column in the table. Look at the figure in Column 1. |
| 3 | 2164 | 23 | 16587 | 43 | 31010 | |
| 4 | 2885 | 24 | 17308 | 44 | 31731 | |
| 5 | 3606 | 25 | 18029 | 45 | 32452 | |
| 6 | 4327 | 26 | 18750 | 46 | 33174 | |
| 7 | 5049 | 27 | 19472 | 47 | 33895 | |
| 8 | 5770 | 28 | 20193 | 48 | 34616 | |
| 9 | 6491 | 29 | 20914 | 49 | 35337 | |
| 10 | 7212 | 30 | 21635 | 50 | 36058 | |
| 11 | 7933 | 31 | 22356 | 51 | 36779 | |
| 12 | 8654 | 32 | 23077 | 52 | 37500 | |
| 13 | 9375 | 33 | 23799 | | | |
| 14 | 10097 | 34 | 24520 | | | |
| 15 | 10818 | 35 | 25241 | | | |
| 16 | 11539 | 36 | 25962 | | | |
| 17 | 12260 | 37 | 26683 | | | |
| 18 | 12981 | 38 | 27404 | | | |
| 19 | 13702 | 39 | 28125 | | | |
| 20 | 14424 | 40 | 28847 | | | |

Is your employee's total taxable pay to date less than or equal to the figure in Column 1?
If so, use Welsh Table B on pages 25 and 26.

If your employee's total taxable pay to date is more than the amount in Column 1,
use Welsh Tables C and D on pages 28, 29 and 30.

## How to use Welsh Table B – weekly paid

**Example 10 – all prefix C codes except CBR and CD prefix codes**

Employee's code is **C431L**

The pay week is in **Week 11**

| | |
|---|---|
| **Pay in the week is** | £203.00 |
| Plus **previous pay to date** | £1,827.00 |
| **Total pay to date** | £2,030.00 |
| Minus Pay Adjustment Tables A figure at Week 11 code C431L | £913.66 |
| **Total taxable pay to date** | £1,116.34 |
| Rounded down to the nearest pound | £1,116 |

You'll already have used Pay Adjustment Tables A and completed your RT11 up to and including Column 5.

First use Table B on pages 25 and 26 for the nearest round figure below £1,116, it's £1,100.

Then use Table B on pages 25 and 26 for the remainder of £1,116, it's £16.

| Total taxable pay to date | Total tax due to date | | Total taxable pay to date | Total tax due to date |
|---|---|---|---|---|
| 800 | 160.00 | | 14 | 2.80 |
| 900 | 180.00 | | 15 | 3.00 |
| 1000 | 200.00 | | 16 | 3.20 |
| 1100 | 220.00 | | 17 | 3.40 |
| 1200 | 240.00 | | 18 | 3.60 |
| 1300 | 260.00 | | 19 | 3.80 |
| 1400 | 280.00 | | 20 | 4.00 |
| 1500 | 300.00 | | 21 | 4.20 |
| 1600 | 320.00 | | 22 | 4.40 |

| | |
|---|---|
| Tax due on £1,100 from Table B | £220.00 |
| Plus tax due on £16 from Table B | £3.20 |
| **Total tax due** | **£223.20** |

**Example 11 – code CBR only**

Employee's code is **CBR**

The pay week is in **Week 11**

| | |
|---|---|
| **Pay in the week is** | £140.00 |
| Plus **previous pay to date** | £1,360.00 |
| **Total pay to date** | £1,500.00 |

You do not need to use the Pay Adjustment Tables A for code CBR.

Therefore, tax is due on the whole of the pay for this month.

| | |
|---|---|
| **Total taxable pay to date** | **£1,500.00** |
| Rounded down to the nearest pound | **£1,500** |

Take the RT11 Column 5 figure, for example, £1,500 and either:
- use Table B on pages 25 and 26
- multiply by 0.20 (20%)
  £1,500 x 0.20 = £300.00

| Total taxable pay to date | Total tax due to date |
|---|---|
| 1200 | 240.00 |
| 1300 | 260.00 |
| 1400 | 280.00 |
| 1500 | 300.00 |
| 1600 | 320.00 |
| 1700 | 340.00 |
| 1800 | 360.00 |
| 1900 | 380.00 |
| 2000 | 400.00 |

24

## Table B – Welsh basic rate (tax at 20%)

Pages 2, 23 and 24 tell you when to use this table.

### Table B – Tax at 20%

#### Tax due on taxable pay from £1 to £15,000

| Total taxable pay to date | Total tax due to date | Total taxable pay to date | Total tax due to date | Total taxable pay to date | Total tax due to date | Total taxable pay to date | Total tax due to date | Total taxable pay to date | Total tax due to date |
|---|---|---|---|---|---|---|---|---|---|
| 1 | 0.20 | 51 | 10.20 | 100 | 20.00 | 5100 | 1020.00 | 10100 | 2020.00 |
| 2 | 0.40 | 52 | 10.40 | 200 | 40.00 | 5200 | 1040.00 | 10200 | 2040.00 |
| 3 | 0.60 | 53 | 10.60 | 300 | 60.00 | 5300 | 1060.00 | 10300 | 2060.00 |
| 4 | 0.80 | 54 | 10.80 | 400 | 80.00 | 5400 | 1080.00 | 10400 | 2080.00 |
| 5 | 1.00 | 55 | 11.00 | 500 | 100.00 | 5500 | 1100.00 | 10500 | 2100.00 |
| 6 | 1.20 | 56 | 11.20 | 600 | 120.00 | 5600 | 1120.00 | 10600 | 2120.00 |
| 7 | 1.40 | 57 | 11.40 | 700 | 140.00 | 5700 | 1140.00 | 10700 | 2140.00 |
| 8 | 1.60 | 58 | 11.60 | 800 | 160.00 | 5800 | 1160.00 | 10800 | 2160.00 |
| 9 | 1.80 | 59 | 11.80 | 900 | 180.00 | 5900 | 1180.00 | 10900 | 2180.00 |
| 10 | 2.00 | 60 | 12.00 | 1000 | 200.00 | 6000 | 1200.00 | 11000 | 2200.00 |
| 11 | 2.20 | 61 | 12.20 | 1100 | 220.00 | 6100 | 1220.00 | 11100 | 2220.00 |
| 12 | 2.40 | 62 | 12.40 | 1200 | 240.00 | 6200 | 1240.00 | 11200 | 2240.00 |
| 13 | 2.60 | 63 | 12.60 | 1300 | 260.00 | 6300 | 1260.00 | 11300 | 2260.00 |
| 14 | 2.80 | 64 | 12.80 | 1400 | 280.00 | 6400 | 1280.00 | 11400 | 2280.00 |
| 15 | 3.00 | 65 | 13.00 | 1500 | 300.00 | 6500 | 1300.00 | 11500 | 2300.00 |
| 16 | 3.20 | 66 | 13.20 | 1600 | 320.00 | 6600 | 1320.00 | 11600 | 2320.00 |
| 17 | 3.40 | 67 | 13.40 | 1700 | 340.00 | 6700 | 1340.00 | 11700 | 2340.00 |
| 18 | 3.60 | 68 | 13.60 | 1800 | 360.00 | 6800 | 1360.00 | 11800 | 2360.00 |
| 19 | 3.80 | 69 | 13.80 | 1900 | 380.00 | 6900 | 1380.00 | 11900 | 2380.00 |
| 20 | 4.00 | 70 | 14.00 | 2000 | 400.00 | 7000 | 1400.00 | 12000 | 2400.00 |
| 21 | 4.20 | 71 | 14.20 | 2100 | 420.00 | 7100 | 1420.00 | 12100 | 2420.00 |
| 22 | 4.40 | 72 | 14.40 | 2200 | 440.00 | 7200 | 1440.00 | 12200 | 2440.00 |
| 23 | 4.60 | 73 | 14.60 | 2300 | 460.00 | 7300 | 1460.00 | 12300 | 2460.00 |
| 24 | 4.80 | 74 | 14.80 | 2400 | 480.00 | 7400 | 1480.00 | 12400 | 2480.00 |
| 25 | 5.00 | 75 | 15.00 | 2500 | 500.00 | 7500 | 1500.00 | 12500 | 2500.00 |
| 26 | 5.20 | 76 | 15.20 | 2600 | 520.00 | 7600 | 1520.00 | 12600 | 2520.00 |
| 27 | 5.40 | 77 | 15.40 | 2700 | 540.00 | 7700 | 1540.00 | 12700 | 2540.00 |
| 28 | 5.60 | 78 | 15.60 | 2800 | 560.00 | 7800 | 1560.00 | 12800 | 2560.00 |
| 29 | 5.80 | 79 | 15.80 | 2900 | 580.00 | 7900 | 1580.00 | 12900 | 2580.00 |
| 30 | 6.00 | 80 | 16.00 | 3000 | 600.00 | 8000 | 1600.00 | 13000 | 2600.00 |
| 31 | 6.20 | 81 | 16.20 | 3100 | 620.00 | 8100 | 1620.00 | 13100 | 2620.00 |
| 32 | 6.40 | 82 | 16.40 | 3200 | 640.00 | 8200 | 1640.00 | 13200 | 2640.00 |
| 33 | 6.60 | 83 | 16.60 | 3300 | 660.00 | 8300 | 1660.00 | 13300 | 2660.00 |
| 34 | 6.80 | 84 | 16.80 | 3400 | 680.00 | 8400 | 1680.00 | 13400 | 2680.00 |
| 35 | 7.00 | 85 | 17.00 | 3500 | 700.00 | 8500 | 1700.00 | 13500 | 2700.00 |
| 36 | 7.20 | 86 | 17.20 | 3600 | 720.00 | 8600 | 1720.00 | 13600 | 2720.00 |
| 37 | 7.40 | 87 | 17.40 | 3700 | 740.00 | 8700 | 1740.00 | 13700 | 2740.00 |
| 38 | 7.60 | 88 | 17.60 | 3800 | 760.00 | 8800 | 1760.00 | 13800 | 2760.00 |
| 39 | 7.80 | 89 | 17.80 | 3900 | 780.00 | 8900 | 1780.00 | 13900 | 2780.00 |
| 40 | 8.00 | 90 | 18.00 | 4000 | 800.00 | 9000 | 1800.00 | 14000 | 2800.00 |
| 41 | 8.20 | 91 | 18.20 | 4100 | 820.00 | 9100 | 1820.00 | 14100 | 2820.00 |
| 42 | 8.40 | 92 | 18.40 | 4200 | 840.00 | 9200 | 1840.00 | 14200 | 2840.00 |
| 43 | 8.60 | 93 | 18.60 | 4300 | 860.00 | 9300 | 1860.00 | 14300 | 2860.00 |
| 44 | 8.80 | 94 | 18.80 | 4400 | 880.00 | 9400 | 1880.00 | 14400 | 2880.00 |
| 45 | 9.00 | 95 | 19.00 | 4500 | 900.00 | 9500 | 1900.00 | 14500 | 2900.00 |
| 46 | 9.20 | 96 | 19.20 | 4600 | 920.00 | 9600 | 1920.00 | 14600 | 2920.00 |
| 47 | 9.40 | 97 | 19.40 | 4700 | 940.00 | 9700 | 1940.00 | 14700 | 2940.00 |
| 48 | 9.60 | 98 | 19.60 | 4800 | 960.00 | 9800 | 1960.00 | 14800 | 2960.00 |
| 49 | 9.80 | 99 | 19.80 | 4900 | 980.00 | 9900 | 1980.00 | 14900 | 2980.00 |
| 50 | 10.00 | | | 5000 | 1000.00 | 10000 | 2000.00 | 15000 | 3000.00 |

25

## Table B – Welsh basic rate (tax at 20%) continued

Pages 2, 23 and 24 tell you when to use this table.

### Table B – Tax at 20%
#### Tax due on taxable pay from £15,100 to £37,500

| Total taxable pay to date | Total tax due to date | Total taxable pay to date | Total tax due to date | Total taxable pay to date | Total tax due to date | Total taxable pay to date | Total tax due to date | Total taxable pay to date | Total tax due to date |
|---|---|---|---|---|---|---|---|---|---|
| 15100 | 3020.00 | 20100 | 4020.00 | 25100 | 5020.00 | 30100 | 6020.00 | 35100 | 7020.00 |
| 15200 | 3040.00 | 20200 | 4040.00 | 25200 | 5040.00 | 30200 | 6040.00 | 35200 | 7040.00 |
| 15300 | 3060.00 | 20300 | 4060.00 | 25300 | 5060.00 | 30300 | 6060.00 | 35300 | 7060.00 |
| 15400 | 3080.00 | 20400 | 4080.00 | 25400 | 5080.00 | 30400 | 6080.00 | 35400 | 7080.00 |
| 15500 | 3100.00 | 20500 | 4100.00 | 25500 | 5100.00 | 30500 | 6100.00 | 35500 | 7100.00 |
| 15600 | 3120.00 | 20600 | 4120.00 | 25600 | 5120.00 | 30600 | 6120.00 | 35600 | 7120.00 |
| 15700 | 3140.00 | 20700 | 4140.00 | 25700 | 5140.00 | 30700 | 6140.00 | 35700 | 7140.00 |
| 15800 | 3160.00 | 20800 | 4160.00 | 25800 | 5160.00 | 30800 | 6160.00 | 35800 | 7160.00 |
| 15900 | 3180.00 | 20900 | 4180.00 | 25900 | 5180.00 | 30900 | 6180.00 | 35900 | 7180.00 |
| 16000 | 3200.00 | 21000 | 4200.00 | 26000 | 5200.00 | 31000 | 6200.00 | 36000 | 7200.00 |
| 16100 | 3220.00 | 21100 | 4220.00 | 26100 | 5220.00 | 31100 | 6220.00 | 36100 | 7220.00 |
| 16200 | 3240.00 | 21200 | 4240.00 | 26200 | 5240.00 | 31200 | 6240.00 | 36200 | 7240.00 |
| 16300 | 3260.00 | 21300 | 4260.00 | 26300 | 5260.00 | 31300 | 6260.00 | 36300 | 7260.00 |
| 16400 | 3280.00 | 21400 | 4280.00 | 26400 | 5280.00 | 31400 | 6280.00 | 36400 | 7280.00 |
| 16500 | 3300.00 | 21500 | 4300.00 | 26500 | 5300.00 | 31500 | 6300.00 | 36500 | 7300.00 |
| 16600 | 3320.00 | 21600 | 4320.00 | 26600 | 5320.00 | 31600 | 6320.00 | 36600 | 7320.00 |
| 16700 | 3340.00 | 21700 | 4340.00 | 26700 | 5340.00 | 31700 | 6340.00 | 36700 | 7340.00 |
| 16800 | 3360.00 | 21800 | 4360.00 | 26800 | 5360.00 | 31800 | 6360.00 | 36800 | 7360.00 |
| 16900 | 3380.00 | 21900 | 4380.00 | 26900 | 5380.00 | 31900 | 6380.00 | 36900 | 7380.00 |
| 17000 | 3400.00 | 22000 | 4400.00 | 27000 | 5400.00 | 32000 | 6400.00 | 37000 | 7400.00 |
| 17100 | 3420.00 | 22100 | 4420.00 | 27100 | 5420.00 | 32100 | 6420.00 | 37100 | 7420.00 |
| 17200 | 3440.00 | 22200 | 4440.00 | 27200 | 5440.00 | 32200 | 6440.00 | 37200 | 7440.00 |
| 17300 | 3460.00 | 22300 | 4460.00 | 27300 | 5460.00 | 32300 | 6460.00 | 37300 | 7460.00 |
| 17400 | 3480.00 | 22400 | 4480.00 | 27400 | 5480.00 | 32400 | 6480.00 | 37400 | 7480.00 |
| 17500 | 3500.00 | 22500 | 4500.00 | 27500 | 5500.00 | 32500 | 6500.00 | 37500 | 7500.00 |
| 17600 | 3520.00 | 22600 | 4520.00 | 27600 | 5520.00 | 32600 | 6520.00 | | |
| 17700 | 3540.00 | 22700 | 4540.00 | 27700 | 5540.00 | 32700 | 6540.00 | | |
| 17800 | 3560.00 | 22800 | 4560.00 | 27800 | 5560.00 | 32800 | 6560.00 | | |
| 17900 | 3580.00 | 22900 | 4580.00 | 27900 | 5580.00 | 32900 | 6580.00 | | |
| 18000 | 3600.00 | 23000 | 4600.00 | 28000 | 5600.00 | 33000 | 6600.00 | | |
| 18100 | 3620.00 | 23100 | 4620.00 | 28100 | 5620.00 | 33100 | 6620.00 | | |
| 18200 | 3640.00 | 23200 | 4640.00 | 28200 | 5640.00 | 33200 | 6640.00 | | |
| 18300 | 3660.00 | 23300 | 4660.00 | 28300 | 5660.00 | 33300 | 6660.00 | | |
| 18400 | 3680.00 | 23400 | 4680.00 | 28400 | 5680.00 | 33400 | 6680.00 | | |
| 18500 | 3700.00 | 23500 | 4700.00 | 28500 | 5700.00 | 33500 | 6700.00 | | |
| 18600 | 3720.00 | 23600 | 4720.00 | 28600 | 5720.00 | 33600 | 6720.00 | | |
| 18700 | 3740.00 | 23700 | 4740.00 | 28700 | 5740.00 | 33700 | 6740.00 | | |
| 18800 | 3760.00 | 23800 | 4760.00 | 28800 | 5760.00 | 33800 | 6760.00 | | |
| 18900 | 3780.00 | 23900 | 4780.00 | 28900 | 5780.00 | 33900 | 6780.00 | | |
| 19000 | 3800.00 | 24000 | 4800.00 | 29000 | 5800.00 | 34000 | 6800.00 | | |
| 19100 | 3820.00 | 24100 | 4820.00 | 29100 | 5820.00 | 34100 | 6820.00 | | |
| 19200 | 3840.00 | 24200 | 4840.00 | 29200 | 5840.00 | 34200 | 6840.00 | | |
| 19300 | 3860.00 | 24300 | 4860.00 | 29300 | 5860.00 | 34300 | 6860.00 | | |
| 19400 | 3880.00 | 24400 | 4880.00 | 29400 | 5880.00 | 34400 | 6880.00 | | |
| 19500 | 3900.00 | 24500 | 4900.00 | 29500 | 5900.00 | 34500 | 6900.00 | | |
| 19600 | 3920.00 | 24600 | 4920.00 | 29600 | 5920.00 | 34600 | 6920.00 | | |
| 19700 | 3940.00 | 24700 | 4940.00 | 29700 | 5940.00 | 34700 | 6940.00 | | |
| 19800 | 3960.00 | 24800 | 4960.00 | 29800 | 5960.00 | 34800 | 6960.00 | | |
| 19900 | 3980.00 | 24900 | 4980.00 | 29900 | 5980.00 | 34900 | 6980.00 | | |
| 20000 | 4000.00 | 25000 | 5000.00 | 30000 | 6000.00 | 35000 | 7000.00 | | |

Where the exact amount of taxable pay is not shown add together the figures for 2 (or more) entries that make up the amount of taxable pay to the nearest £1 below.

26

# Tables C

## How to use Tables C – Welsh monthly paid

You'll already have used Pay Adjustment Tables A and completed your RT11 up to and including Column 5.

| Example 12 – Table C1 | |
|---|---|
| Example payment is for **Month 4** | |
| Taxable pay to date from RT11 column 5 | £20,233.00 |
| Find tax due at **higher rate** – 40% | |
| Taxable pay | £20,233.00 |
| Minus taxable pay Column 1 | £12,500.00 |
| Taxable pay at 40% | £7,733.00 |

| Example 13 – Table C2 | |
|---|---|
| Example payment is for **Month 4** | |
| Taxable pay to date from RT11 Column 5 | £57,500.00 |
| Find tax due at **additional rate** – 45% | |
| Taxable pay | £57,500.00 |
| Minus taxable pay Column 4 | £50,000.00 |
| Taxable pay at 45% | £7,500.00 |

First use Table D1 on page 29 for the nearest round figure below £7,733.00, it's £7,700.

Then use Table D1 on page 29 for the remainder of £7,700, it's £33.

Use Table D2 on page 30 to find tax due on £7,500.

| Taxable pay £ | Tax £ |
|---|---|
| 7400 | 2960.00 |
| 7500 | 3000.00 |
| 7600 | 3040.00 |
| 7700 | 3080.00 |
| 7800 | 3120.00 |
| 7900 | 3160.00 |
| 8000 | 3200.00 |

| Taxable Pay £ | Tax £ |
|---|---|
| 29 | 11.60 |
| 30 | 12.00 |
| 31 | 12.40 |
| 32 | 12.80 |
| 33 | 13.20 |
| 34 | 13.60 |
| 35 | 14.00 |

| Taxable pay £ | Tax £ |
|---|---|
| 7300 | 3285.00 |
| 7400 | 3330.00 |
| 7500 | 3375.00 |
| 7600 | 3420.00 |
| 7700 | 3465.00 |
| 7800 | 3510.00 |
| 7900 | 3555.00 |

| | |
|---|---|
| Higher rate tax due on £7,700 from Table D1 | £3,080.00 |
| Plus tax due on £33 from Table D1 | £13.20 |
| | £3,093.20 |
| Add figure from Table C1 Column 3 for **Month 4** | £2,500.00 |
| **Total tax due** | **£5,593.20** |

| | |
|---|---|
| Additional rate tax due on £7,500 from Table D2 | £3,375.00 |
| Add figure from Table C2 Column 5 for **Month 4** | £17,500.00 |
| **Total tax due** | **£20,875.00** |

## Tables C – Welsh monthly paid

Page 23 tells you when to use these tables.

### Table C1
#### Employee paid at monthly rates

| Month | Column 1 If total taxable pay to date exceeds £ | Column 2 And total taxable pay to date does not exceed £ | Column 3 Total tax due to date on pay in Column 1 £ |
|---|---|---|---|
| 1 | 3125 | 12500 | 625.00 |
| 2 | 6250 | 25000 | 1250.00 |
| 3 | 9375 | 37500 | 1875.00 |
| 4 | 12500 | 50000 | 2500.00 |
| 5 | 15625 | 62500 | 3125.00 |
| 6 | 18750 | 75000 | 3750.00 |
| 7 | 21875 | 87500 | 4375.00 |
| 8 | 25000 | 100000 | 5000.00 |
| 9 | 28125 | 112500 | 5625.00 |
| 10 | 31250 | 125000 | 6250.00 |
| 11 | 34375 | 137500 | 6875.00 |
| 12 | 37500 | 150000 | 7500.00 |

Is the total taxable pay to date more than the amount in Column 1 and does not exceed the amount in Column 2?

If Yes, add to the figure in Column 3 the tax at 40% (as shown in Table D1 – higher rate (tax at 40%) on page 29) on the amount by which the total taxable pay to date exceeds the figure in Column 1.

If No, and the total taxable pay to date exceeds the figure in Column 2, use Table C2.

### Table C2
#### Employee paid at monthly rates

| Column 4 If total taxable pay to date exceeds £ | Column 5 Total tax due to date on pay in Column 4 £ |
|---|---|
| 12500 | 4375.00 |
| 25000 | 8750.00 |
| 37500 | 13125.00 |
| 50000 | 17500.00 |
| 62500 | 21875.00 |
| 75000 | 26250.00 |
| 87500 | 30625.00 |
| 100000 | 35000.00 |
| 112500 | 39375.00 |
| 125000 | 43750.00 |
| 137500 | 48125.00 |
| 150000 | 52500.00 |

If total taxable pay to date exceeds the figure in Column 4. Add to the figure in Column 5 the tax at 45% (as shown in Table D2 – additional rate (tax at 45%) on page 30) on the amount by which the total taxable pay to date exceeds the figure in Column 4.

27

## Tables C – Welsh weekly paid

Page 23 tells you when to use these tables.

### Table C1

**Employee paid at weekly rates**

| Week | Column 1 If total taxable pay to date exceeds £ | Column 2 And total taxable pay to date does not exceed £ | Column 3 Total tax due to date on pay in Column 1 £ |
|---|---|---|---|
| 1 | 722 | 2885 | 144.56 |
| 2 | 1443 | 5770 | 288.73 |
| 3 | 2164 | 8654 | 432.90 |
| 4 | 2885 | 11539 | 577.07 |
| 5 | 3606 | 14424 | 721.24 |
| 6 | 4327 | 17308 | 865.41 |
| 7 | 5049 | 20193 | 1009.98 |
| 8 | 5770 | 23077 | 1154.15 |
| 9 | 6491 | 25962 | 1298.32 |
| 10 | 7212 | 28847 | 1442.49 |
| 11 | 7933 | 31731 | 1586.66 |
| 12 | 8654 | 34616 | 1730.83 |
| 13 | 9375 | 37500 | 1875.00 |
| 14 | 10097 | 40385 | 2019.56 |
| 15 | 10818 | 43270 | 2163.73 |
| 16 | 11539 | 46154 | 2307.90 |
| 17 | 12260 | 49039 | 2452.07 |
| 18 | 12981 | 51924 | 2596.24 |
| 19 | 13702 | 54808 | 2740.41 |
| 20 | 14424 | 57693 | 2884.98 |
| 21 | 15145 | 60577 | 3029.15 |
| 22 | 15866 | 63462 | 3173.32 |
| 23 | 16587 | 66347 | 3317.49 |
| 24 | 17308 | 69231 | 3461.66 |
| 25 | 18029 | 72116 | 3605.83 |
| 26 | 18750 | 75000 | 3750.00 |
| 27 | 19472 | 77885 | 3894.56 |
| 28 | 20193 | 80770 | 4038.73 |
| 29 | 20914 | 83654 | 4182.90 |
| 30 | 21635 | 86539 | 4327.07 |
| 31 | 22356 | 89424 | 4471.24 |
| 32 | 23077 | 92308 | 4615.41 |
| 33 | 23799 | 95193 | 4759.98 |
| 34 | 24520 | 98077 | 4904.15 |
| 35 | 25241 | 100962 | 5048.32 |
| 36 | 25962 | 103847 | 5192.49 |
| 37 | 26683 | 106731 | 5336.66 |
| 38 | 27404 | 109616 | 5480.83 |
| 39 | 28125 | 112500 | 5625.00 |
| 40 | 28847 | 115385 | 5769.56 |
| 41 | 29568 | 118270 | 5913.73 |
| 42 | 30289 | 121154 | 6057.90 |
| 43 | 31010 | 124039 | 6202.07 |
| 44 | 31731 | 126924 | 6346.24 |
| 45 | 32452 | 129808 | 6490.41 |
| 46 | 33174 | 132693 | 6634.98 |
| 47 | 33895 | 135577 | 6779.15 |
| 48 | 34616 | 138462 | 6923.32 |
| 49 | 35337 | 141347 | 7067.49 |
| 50 | 36058 | 144231 | 7211.66 |
| 51 | 36779 | 147116 | 7355.83 |
| 52 | 37500 | 150000 | 7500.00 |

Is the total taxable pay to date more than the amount in Column 1 and does not exceed the amount in Column 2?

If Yes, add to the figure in Column 3 the tax at 40% (as shown in Table D1 – higher rate (tax at 40%) on page 29) on the amount by which the total taxable pay to date exceeds the figure in Column 1.

If No, and the total taxable pay to date exceeds the figure in Column 2 use Table C2.

### Table C2

**Employee paid at weekly rates**

| Column 4 If total taxable pay to date exceeds £ | Column 5 Total tax due to date on pay in Column 4 £ |
|---|---|
| 2885 | 1009.78 |
| 5770 | 2019.57 |
| 8654 | 3028.91 |
| 11539 | 4038.70 |
| 14424 | 5048.49 |
| 17308 | 6057.83 |
| 20193 | 7067.61 |
| 23077 | 8076.95 |
| 25962 | 9086.74 |
| 28847 | 10096.53 |
| 31731 | 11105.87 |
| 34616 | 12115.66 |
| 37500 | 13125.00 |
| 40385 | 14134.78 |
| 43270 | 15144.57 |
| 46154 | 16153.91 |
| 49039 | 17163.70 |
| 51924 | 18173.49 |
| 54808 | 19182.83 |
| 57693 | 20192.61 |
| 60577 | 21201.95 |
| 63462 | 22211.74 |
| 66347 | 23221.53 |
| 69231 | 24230.87 |
| 72116 | 25240.66 |
| 75000 | 26250.00 |
| 77885 | 27259.78 |
| 80770 | 28269.57 |
| 83654 | 29278.91 |
| 86539 | 30288.70 |
| 89424 | 31298.49 |
| 92308 | 32307.83 |
| 95193 | 33317.61 |
| 98077 | 34326.95 |
| 100962 | 35336.74 |
| 103847 | 36346.53 |
| 106731 | 37355.87 |
| 109616 | 38365.66 |
| 112500 | 39375.00 |
| 115385 | 40384.78 |
| 118270 | 41394.57 |
| 121154 | 42403.91 |
| 124039 | 43413.70 |
| 126924 | 44423.49 |
| 129808 | 45432.83 |
| 132693 | 46442.61 |
| 135577 | 47451.95 |
| 138462 | 48461.74 |
| 141347 | 49471.53 |
| 144231 | 50480.87 |
| 147116 | 51490.66 |
| 150000 | 52500.00 |

If total taxable pay to date exceeds the figure in Column 4.

Add to the figure in Column 5 the tax at 45% (as shown in Table D2 – additional rate (tax at 45%) on page 30) on the amount by which the total taxable pay to date exceeds the figure in Column 4.

28

## Table D1 – Welsh higher rate (tax at 40%)

Also to be used for tax code CD0. Pages 23, 27 and 28 tell you when to use this table.

### Table D1 – Tax at 40%

| Taxable pay £ | Tax £ | Taxable pay £ | Tax £ | Taxable pay £ | Tax £ | Taxable pay £ | Tax £ | |
|---|---|---|---|---|---|---|---|---|
| 1 | 0.40 | 51 | 20.40 | 100 | 40.00 | 5100 | 2040.00 | Where the exact amount of taxable pay is not shown, add together the figures for 2 (or more) entries to make up the amount of taxable pay to the nearest £1 below. |
| 2 | 0.80 | 52 | 20.80 | 200 | 80.00 | 5200 | 2080.00 | |
| 3 | 1.20 | 53 | 21.20 | 300 | 120.00 | 5300 | 2120.00 | |
| 4 | 1.60 | 54 | 21.60 | 400 | 160.00 | 5400 | 2160.00 | |
| 5 | 2.00 | 55 | 22.00 | 500 | 200.00 | 5500 | 2200.00 | |
| 6 | 2.40 | 56 | 22.40 | 600 | 240.00 | 5600 | 2240.00 | |
| 7 | 2.80 | 57 | 22.80 | 700 | 280.00 | 5700 | 2280.00 | |
| 8 | 3.20 | 58 | 23.20 | 800 | 320.00 | 5800 | 2320.00 | |
| 9 | 3.60 | 59 | 23.60 | 900 | 360.00 | 5900 | 2360.00 | |
| 10 | 4.00 | 60 | 24.00 | 1000 | 400.00 | 6000 | 2400.00 | |
| 11 | 4.40 | 61 | 24.40 | 1100 | 440.00 | 6100 | 2440.00 | |
| 12 | 4.80 | 62 | 24.80 | 1200 | 480.00 | 6200 | 2480.00 | |
| 13 | 5.20 | 63 | 25.20 | 1300 | 520.00 | 6300 | 2520.00 | |
| 14 | 5.60 | 64 | 25.60 | 1400 | 560.00 | 6400 | 2560.00 | |
| 15 | 6.00 | 65 | 26.00 | 1500 | 600.00 | 6500 | 2600.00 | |
| 16 | 6.40 | 66 | 26.40 | 1600 | 640.00 | 6600 | 2640.00 | |
| 17 | 6.80 | 67 | 26.80 | 1700 | 680.00 | 6700 | 2680.00 | |
| 18 | 7.20 | 68 | 27.20 | 1800 | 720.00 | 6800 | 2720.00 | |
| 19 | 7.60 | 69 | 27.60 | 1900 | 760.00 | 6900 | 2760.00 | |
| 20 | 8.00 | 70 | 28.00 | 2000 | 800.00 | 7000 | 2800.00 | |
| 21 | 8.40 | 71 | 28.40 | 2100 | 840.00 | 7100 | 2840.00 | |
| 22 | 8.80 | 72 | 28.80 | 2200 | 880.00 | 7200 | 2880.00 | |
| 23 | 9.20 | 73 | 29.20 | 2300 | 920.00 | 7300 | 2920.00 | |
| 24 | 9.60 | 74 | 29.60 | 2400 | 960.00 | 7400 | 2960.00 | |
| 25 | 10.00 | 75 | 30.00 | 2500 | 1000.00 | 7500 | 3000.00 | |
| 26 | 10.40 | 76 | 30.40 | 2600 | 1040.00 | 7600 | 3040.00 | |
| 27 | 10.80 | 77 | 30.80 | 2700 | 1080.00 | 7700 | 3080.00 | |
| 28 | 11.20 | 78 | 31.20 | 2800 | 1120.00 | 7800 | 3120.00 | |
| 29 | 11.60 | 79 | 31.60 | 2900 | 1160.00 | 7900 | 3160.00 | |
| 30 | 12.00 | 80 | 32.00 | 3000 | 1200.00 | 8000 | 3200.00 | |
| 31 | 12.40 | 81 | 32.40 | 3100 | 1240.00 | 8100 | 3240.00 | |
| 32 | 12.80 | 82 | 32.80 | 3200 | 1280.00 | 8200 | 3280.00 | |
| 33 | 13.20 | 83 | 33.20 | 3300 | 1320.00 | 8300 | 3320.00 | |
| 34 | 13.60 | 84 | 33.60 | 3400 | 1360.00 | 8400 | 3360.00 | |
| 35 | 14.00 | 85 | 34.00 | 3500 | 1400.00 | 8500 | 3400.00 | |
| 36 | 14.40 | 86 | 34.40 | 3600 | 1440.00 | 8600 | 3440.00 | |
| 37 | 14.80 | 87 | 34.80 | 3700 | 1480.00 | 8700 | 3480.00 | |
| 38 | 15.20 | 88 | 35.20 | 3800 | 1520.00 | 8800 | 3520.00 | |
| 39 | 15.60 | 89 | 35.60 | 3900 | 1560.00 | 8900 | 3560.00 | |
| 40 | 16.00 | 90 | 36.00 | 4000 | 1600.00 | 9000 | 3600.00 | |
| 41 | 16.40 | 91 | 36.40 | 4100 | 1640.00 | 9100 | 3640.00 | |
| 42 | 16.80 | 92 | 36.80 | 4200 | 1680.00 | 9200 | 3680.00 | |
| 43 | 17.20 | 93 | 37.20 | 4300 | 1720.00 | 9300 | 3720.00 | |
| 44 | 17.60 | 94 | 37.60 | 4400 | 1760.00 | 9400 | 3760.00 | |
| 45 | 18.00 | 95 | 38.00 | 4500 | 1800.00 | 9500 | 3800.00 | |
| 46 | 18.40 | 96 | 38.40 | 4600 | 1840.00 | 9600 | 3840.00 | |
| 47 | 18.80 | 97 | 38.80 | 4700 | 1880.00 | 9700 | 3880.00 | |
| 48 | 19.20 | 98 | 39.20 | 4800 | 1920.00 | 9800 | 3920.00 | |
| 49 | 19.60 | 99 | 39.60 | 4900 | 1960.00 | 9900 | 3960.00 | |
| 50 | 20.00 | | | 5000 | 2000.00 | 10000 | 4000.00 | |
| | | | | | | 20000 | 8000.00 | |
| | | | | | | 30000 | 12000.00 | |
| | | | | | | 40000 | 16000.00 | |
| | | | | | | 50000 | 20000.00 | |
| | | | | | | 60000 | 24000.00 | |
| | | | | | | 70000 | 28000.00 | |
| | | | | | | 80000 | 32000.00 | |
| | | | | | | 90000 | 36000.00 | |
| | | | | | | 100000 | 40000.00 | |

29

## Table D2 – Welsh additional rate (tax at 45%)

Also to be used for tax code CD1. Pages 27 and 28 tell you when to use this table.

### Table D2 – Tax at 45%

| Taxable pay £ | Tax £ | Taxable pay £ | Tax £ | Taxable pay £ | Tax £ | Taxable pay £ | Tax £ | |
|---|---|---|---|---|---|---|---|---|
| 1 | 0.45 | 51 | 22.95 | 100 | 45.00 | 6000 | 2700.00 | Where the exact amount of taxable pay is not shown, add together the figures for 2 (or more) entries to make up the amount of taxable pay to the nearest £1 below. |
| 2 | 0.90 | 52 | 23.40 | 200 | 90.00 | 6100 | 2745.00 | |
| 3 | 1.35 | 53 | 23.85 | 300 | 135.00 | 6200 | 2790.00 | |
| 4 | 1.80 | 54 | 24.30 | 400 | 180.00 | 6300 | 2835.00 | |
| 5 | 2.25 | 55 | 24.75 | 500 | 225.00 | 6400 | 2880.00 | |
| 6 | 2.70 | 56 | 25.20 | 600 | 270.00 | 6500 | 2925.00 | |
| 7 | 3.15 | 57 | 25.65 | 700 | 315.00 | 6600 | 2970.00 | |
| 8 | 3.60 | 58 | 26.10 | 800 | 360.00 | 6700 | 3015.00 | |
| 9 | 4.05 | 59 | 26.55 | 900 | 405.00 | 6800 | 3060.00 | |
| 10 | 4.50 | 60 | 27.00 | 1000 | 450.00 | 6900 | 3105.00 | |
| 11 | 4.95 | 61 | 27.45 | 1100 | 495.00 | 7000 | 3150.00 | |
| 12 | 5.40 | 62 | 27.90 | 1200 | 540.00 | 7100 | 3195.00 | |
| 13 | 5.85 | 63 | 28.35 | 1300 | 585.00 | 7200 | 3240.00 | |
| 14 | 6.30 | 64 | 28.80 | 1400 | 630.00 | 7300 | 3285.00 | |
| 15 | 6.75 | 65 | 29.25 | 1500 | 675.00 | 7400 | 3330.00 | |
| 16 | 7.20 | 66 | 29.70 | 1600 | 720.00 | 7500 | 3375.00 | |
| 17 | 7.65 | 67 | 30.15 | 1700 | 765.00 | 7600 | 3420.00 | |
| 18 | 8.10 | 68 | 30.60 | 1800 | 810.00 | 7700 | 3465.00 | |
| 19 | 8.55 | 69 | 31.05 | 1900 | 855.00 | 7800 | 3510.00 | |
| 20 | 9.00 | 70 | 31.50 | 2000 | 900.00 | 7900 | 3555.00 | |
| 21 | 9.45 | 71 | 31.95 | 2100 | 945.00 | 8000 | 3600.00 | |
| 22 | 9.90 | 72 | 32.40 | 2200 | 990.00 | 8100 | 3645.00 | |
| 23 | 10.35 | 73 | 32.85 | 2300 | 1035.00 | 8200 | 3690.00 | |
| 24 | 10.80 | 74 | 33.30 | 2400 | 1080.00 | 8300 | 3735.00 | |
| 25 | 11.25 | 75 | 33.75 | 2500 | 1125.00 | 8400 | 3780.00 | |
| 26 | 11.70 | 76 | 34.20 | 2600 | 1170.00 | 8500 | 3825.00 | |
| 27 | 12.15 | 77 | 34.65 | 2700 | 1215.00 | 8600 | 3870.00 | |
| 28 | 12.60 | 78 | 35.10 | 2800 | 1260.00 | 8700 | 3915.00 | |
| 29 | 13.05 | 79 | 35.55 | 2900 | 1305.00 | 8800 | 3960.00 | |
| 30 | 13.50 | 80 | 36.00 | 3000 | 1350.00 | 8900 | 4005.00 | |
| 31 | 13.95 | 81 | 36.45 | 3100 | 1395.00 | 9000 | 4050.00 | |
| 32 | 14.40 | 82 | 36.90 | 3200 | 1440.00 | 9100 | 4095.00 | |
| 33 | 14.85 | 83 | 37.35 | 3300 | 1485.00 | 9200 | 4140.00 | |
| 34 | 15.30 | 84 | 37.80 | 3400 | 1530.00 | 9300 | 4185.00 | |
| 35 | 15.75 | 85 | 38.25 | 3500 | 1575.00 | 9400 | 4230.00 | |
| 36 | 16.20 | 86 | 38.70 | 3600 | 1620.00 | 9500 | 4275.00 | |
| 37 | 16.65 | 87 | 39.15 | 3700 | 1665.00 | 9600 | 4320.00 | |
| 38 | 17.10 | 88 | 39.60 | 3800 | 1710.00 | 9700 | 4365.00 | |
| 39 | 17.55 | 89 | 40.05 | 3900 | 1755.00 | 9800 | 4410.00 | |
| 40 | 18.00 | 90 | 40.50 | 4000 | 1800.00 | 9900 | 4455.00 | |
| 41 | 18.45 | 91 | 40.95 | 4100 | 1845.00 | 10000 | 4500.00 | |
| 42 | 18.90 | 92 | 41.40 | 4200 | 1890.00 | 20000 | 9000.00 | |
| 43 | 19.35 | 93 | 41.85 | 4300 | 1935.00 | 30000 | 13500.00 | |
| 44 | 19.80 | 94 | 42.30 | 4400 | 1980.00 | 40000 | 18000.00 | |
| 45 | 20.25 | 95 | 42.75 | 4500 | 2025.00 | 50000 | 22500.00 | |
| 46 | 20.70 | 96 | 43.20 | 4600 | 2070.00 | 60000 | 27000.00 | |
| 47 | 21.15 | 97 | 43.65 | 4700 | 2115.00 | 70000 | 31500.00 | |
| 48 | 21.60 | 98 | 44.10 | 4800 | 2160.00 | 80000 | 36000.00 | |
| 49 | 22.05 | 99 | 44.55 | 4900 | 2205.00 | 90000 | 40500.00 | |
| 50 | 22.50 | | | 5000 | 2250.00 | 100000 | 45000.00 | |
| | | | | 5100 | 2295.00 | 200000 | 90000.00 | |
| | | | | 5200 | 2340.00 | 300000 | 135000.00 | |
| | | | | 5300 | 2385.00 | 400000 | 180000.00 | |
| | | | | 5400 | 2430.00 | 500000 | 225000.00 | |
| | | | | 5500 | 2475.00 | 600000 | 270000.00 | |
| | | | | 5600 | 2520.00 | 700000 | 315000.00 | |
| | | | | 5700 | 2565.00 | 800000 | 360000.00 | |
| | | | | 5800 | 2610.00 | 900000 | 405000.00 | |
| | | | | 5900 | 2655.00 | 1000000 | 450000.00 | |

30

NOTES

NOTES

NOTES

NOTES

# DON'T JUST *DO PAYROLL*...

# #**BE**PAYROLL

JOIN THE CIPP FOR ALL THE **SUPPORT, KNOWLEDGE** AND **RESOURCES** YOU NEED TO HELP YOU EXCEL IN YOUR PAYROLL CAREER.

JOIN THE CIPP TODAY AT **CIPP.ORG.UK/JOIN**

the **chartered institute** of **payroll professionals**

*leading the profession*